Leader, Zachary.

The life of Kingsley
Amis.

$39.95

DATE		

The Life of Kingsley Amis

The Life of Kingsley Amis

Zachary Leader

PANTHEON BOOKS
NEW YORK

Library of Congress Cataloging-in-Publication Data

Leader, Zachary.
The life of Kingsley Amis / Zachary Leader.
p. cm.
Includes bibliographical references and index.
ISBN 978-0-375-42498-4
1. Amis, Kingsley.   2. Novelists, English—20th century—Biography.
3. Critics—Great Britain—Biography.   I. Title.
PR6001.M6Z77 2007
828'.91409–dc22   2006035012
[B]

www.pantheonbooks.com

Printed in the United States of America

First United States Edition

2 4 6 8 9 7 5 3 1

To my Mother and the memory of my Father

Contents

Illustrations

All illustrations marked * are courtesy of Lady Kilmarnock.

SECTION ONE

1 Amis family wedding photograph*; 2 W.R. Amis with Cannon Street Football Club (*Carrow Works Magazine*, Vol. XIV:2, January 1921, by kind permission of Unilever from an original in Unilever Archives); 3 KA, aged nine*; 4 KA's childhood home, 7 Ena Road, Norbury (Drawing by George Murray); 5 F.R. Dale, Headmaster, City of London School (by kind permission of the Headmaster, City of London School); 6 Rev. C.J. Ellingham, Classics Master, CLS (by kind permission of the Headmaster, City of London School); 7 CLS boys at Marlborough College during the Second World War, 1940 (by kind permission of the Headmaster, City of London School); 8 The Great Ice Storm of January 1940 (*Marlborough College Natural History Society Report*, by kind permission of the Master, Marlborough College); 9 KA, c. twelve years old (British Library Reproductions © The British Library Board); 10 Philip Larkin and fellow undergraduates, St John's College, Oxford, Summer 1942 (courtesy of the Philip Larkin Estate, Society of Authors); 11 KA and fellow undergraduates, St John's College, Oxford, Summer 1942 (courtesy of the Philip Larkin Estate, Society of Authors); 12 Lieutenant KA and fellow officers, 1945*; 13 KA's batman, Bert Wootton, c. 1945 (courtesy of the Kingsley Amis Literary Estate);

14 St John's College Humanitarian Society, 1947 (courtesy of Sir Mervyn Brown); 15 Hilly at seventeen, 1946*; 16 KA, Hilly and her sister Margaret 'Miggy' Partington (née Bardwell), 1948*; 17 KA, Hilly and Mandy, their dog, 1949*; 18 Leonard Bardwell ('Daddy B'), c. 1935–39 (by kind permission of the East Surrey Morris Men website: www.esmm.org.uk); 19 KA at Abbey Timbers, 1946 (courtesy of the Philip Larkin Estate, Society of Authors); 20 Margery and Leonard Bardwell, Abbey Timbers, c. 1948–50 (courtesy of Margaret Righton, née Bardwell); 21 William Bardwell, Hilly's older brother (courtesy of Margaret Righton); 22 Bruce Montgomery, 1958 (courtesy of the Philip Larkin Estate, Society of Authors); 23 Philip Larkin, 1962 (courtesy of the Philip Larkin Estate, Society of Authors); 24 John Wain, 1958 (© Mark Gerson/National Portrait Gallery, London); 25 KA's students at Swansea, Geoffrey Nicholson, David Rees and Clive Gammon (published in *Dawn*, 1952, the official publication of the Students' Union Council, University College, Swansea (LF1215D18)); 26 KA in staff-student *Hamlet*, 1953 (The Bodleian Library, University of Oxford, MS Eng. c. 6050, fol.65); 27 KA, Swansea, 1958 (© Slim Aarons/Getty Images)

SECTION TWO

28 KA, 1955 (John Deakin/Vogue ©The Condé Naste Publications Ltd.); 29 KA and Hilly with Philip, Sally and Martin, 1955 (Daniel Farson/Hulton Archive/Getty Images); 30 University College of Swansea, 1952 (Image from *Swansea University College Brochure* by kind permission of University College, Swansea); 31 Anthony Powell, Philip Larkin, KA and Hilly, 1958 (courtesy of the Philip Larkin Estate, Society of Authors); 32 Journalists at the bar at Rules, c. 1960 (photograph by Ormond Gigli); 33 KA, 1957 (National Portrait Gallery © Diane Fernald, the Estate of Rollie McKenna); 34 Robert Conquest, 1963 (courtesy of the Philip Larkin Estate, Society of Authors); 35 KA, Hilly and Jean McAndrew in Princeton, New Jersey, 1959*; 36 Martin, Sally and Philip Amis, Princeton, 1958*; 37 KA, Hilly and Aunt Gladys, Washington, DC, 1958*; 38 W.R. Amis, Princeton, 1959*; 39 Sally, Princeton, 1958 *; 40 Life at Madingley Road, Cambridge, by Elisabeth Rukeyser, 1963 (© Elisabeth Rukeyser); 41 Hilly, Sally, George and Pat Gale and Timothy Houghton, Swansea, c. 1960–61*; 42 KA and Robert

Graves, pushing car, Deya, Majorca, 1962 (courtesy of William Graves); **43** KA at wedding reception of Elisabeth and William Rukeyser, 1963 (courtesy of Elisabeth and William Rukeyser); **44** KA with Robert Graves, Deya, 1962 (courtesy of William Graves); **45** KA and Hilly, Swansea, *c.*1960 (King Collection/Retna); **46** KA, Yugoslavia, 1963*

SECTION THREE

47 KA and Elizabeth Jane Howard at their wedding reception, the offices of Jonathan Cape, 29 June 1965 (*Daily Sketch*/photograph by Don Price); **48** KA and EJH at 108 Maida Vale, c. 1967 (© Giselle Freund/Nina Beskow); **49** EJH, 1975 (© Jerry Bauer); **50** KA outside Lemmons, 1970 (© Mark Gerson); **51** KA and EJH, Sanderson advertisement, Lemmons, 1973 (by kind permission of Arthur Sanderson and Sons); **52** EJH, Colin Howard and Sargy Mann at Lemmons, 1969 (courtesy of Elizabeth Jane Howard); **53** Amis in Greece, Summer 1969 (courtesy of Elizabeth Jane Howard); **54** KA and EJH with Keeleys and friends, Greece, summer 1969 (courtesy of Elizabeth Jane Howard); **55** EJH with Dolly Burns, Jamaica, 1966 (courtesy of Elizabeth Jane Howard); **56** KA with Czech guide, 1966 (courtesy of Elizabeth Jane Howard); **57** KA at Vanderbilt, 1967 (courtesy of Vanderbilt University Special Collections and University Archive); **58** Sally Amis, 1973*; **59** Martin Amis, 1973 (cover of *The Rachel Papers*); **60** Philip Amis, *c.*1980*; **61** Colin Howard, 1970 (courtesy of Elizabeth Jane Howard); **62** Jaime Boyd and Hilly, 1984*; **63** Alastair Boyd, 1992 (courtesy of Alastair Boyd); **64** KA at his 70th birthday party, with Martin Amis, Mavis Nicholson and Paul Fussell, 16 April 1992*; **65** Philip Larkin in Brynmor Jones Library, University of Hull, 1981 (photograph © Christopher Barker, courtesy of the Philip Larkin Estate, Society of Authors); **66** KA at pub in Wales, with Michael and Virginia Rush and Stuart Thomas, 1994 (courtesy of Michael and Virginia Rush); **67** The Queen's, Regents Park Road, 1990 (photograph by Jaime Boyd)*; **68** KA at home, 194 Regents Park Road, 1990 (© Martin Black); **69** The Coffee Room, Garrick Club, painting by Julian Barrow, 1989 (Garrick Club/The Art Archive); **70, 71** KA in Laugharne, Wales, August 1995 (courtesy of Michael and Virginia Rush); **72** KA leaving Swansea, with Eric

Jacobs in the background, August 1995 (courtesy of Michael and Virginia Rush).

INTEGRATED ILLUSTRATIONS

Letter from KA to Philip Larkin, 27 January 1950 (The Bodleian Library, Oxford); Letter from Hilly to KA, 12 May 1965 (Henry E. Huntington Library, San Marino, California); Page from guestbook of Virginia and Michael Rush, 31 August 1995, Swansea (courtesy of Michael and Virginia Rush).

Introduction

Kingsley Amis was not only the finest British comic novelist of the second half of the twentieth century but a dominant force in the writing of the age: at the heart of the pre-eminent poetical grouping of the period, the Movement, and complexly implicated in its various schemes of self-promotion; the earliest of redbrick novelists and Angry Young Men (a connection Amis consistently denied, but one he also cultivated, as his correspondence suggests); the most prominent literary figure among political, cultural and social polemicists, for elite and popular audiences alike. That he was also a compelling person, a man of alarming appetites and energies, the funniest man most people had ever met, or the cleverest, or the rudest, helped to make him a celebrity, everywhere quoted in newspapers and periodicals. Nor was his life dull, as he claimed the lives of most writers were. Deprivation may have been to his friend Philip Larkin what daffodils were to Wordsworth, but Amis wanted no part of it. Though prolific – the author of twenty-five published novels,[1] seven books of poetry (including pamphlets), eleven works of non-fiction (excluding pamphlets), seventeen edited volumes, several dozen short stories, nine television and radio plays, over 1,300 pieces of uncollected journalism, and almost two thousand letters – his life away from the desk was full of incident, shaped by and shaping powerful trends and forces.

Amis's views on literary biography and autobiography were slippery. In a review of a life of Robert Graves he praises the biographer for reminding readers that 'whatever a poem may be, it is not just a text on a page but also a part of somebody's life'.[2] Yet such reminders diminish the work: 'poems are peculiarly vulnerable to the kind of reductive, deuniversalising, anecdote-hatching process the biographer cannot help subjecting them to'.[3] Attempts to read his own writing biographically Amis mostly met with scorn, yet he defends his *Memoirs* (1991), which focus on others rather than himself, partly on the grounds that 'I have already written an account of myself in twenty or more volumes, most of them called novels.' In the next sentence, this assertion is turned on its head and then partly righted: 'Novels they fully are, too, and those who know both them and me will also know that they are firmly unautobiographical, but at the same time every word of them inevitably says something about the kind of person I am.'[4] In 'Real and Made-up People', an article published in 1973 in the *Times Literary Supplement*, Amis asserts that drawing from life never works: 'the closer the likeness to the real interesting person, the less interesting he will be in the novel'. Yet he also says that 'all my heroes start from me and in a sense stay with me, even when there are a half a dozen of them occupying the same book'[5] – even when he gives them qualities and capacities he does not possess. Andrew Davies, who adapted Amis's *The Old Devils* for television, once heard him say that 'a good source of material and a salutary exercise was to take an aspect of his own character he wasn't particularly proud of, push it to the limit (in fictional form, of course) and see what happened'.[6] 'By projecting himself into an entity that is part of himself and yet not himself,' Amis writes in 'Real and Made-up People,' the author 'may be able to see more clearly, and judge more harshly, his own weaknesses and follies; and, since he must know that no failings are unique, he may be helped to acquire tolerance for them in others'.[7]

Less laudable motives also play a part in Amis's mixing of real and made-up people. Revenge, for example. In 1970, aged forty-eight, Amis met a right-wing businessman, later a Tory MP, named Harold Soref, who tried to persuade him to write a favourable article about South Africa's political system.[8] Soref, an acquaintance of Amis's friend John Braine, invited them both to lunch at the Reform Club. Amis protested that he knew nothing of South Africa apart from what he read in the papers, but his host was undeterred. 'I shouldn't really have gone,' Amis was later to write, 'but I am an inveterate luncher, curiosity called as ever, and I had made it clear that I was committed to nothing but to listen.' At the lunch, Amis and Braine were hurried into the dining room after a single drink, a grave sin in Amis's book. When Amis chose items not on the set menu (nothing fancy, perhaps liver and bacon) Soref tried to block him. He was also 'shy on the booze'. 'Right, my lad, I thought, it may take a year, it may take five, but you'll be getting it back for this.' It took a year. A version of Soref appears in *Girl, 20* (1971), disguised as Harold Meers, the editor of a newspaper; Amis appears 'split into a famous musician, Roy Vandervane, and a journalist friend of his called Douglas'. Here they are at table; Douglas has taken Harold's lead and ordered from the cheaper set menu:

Roy was finding it more difficult to come to a decision, frowning and cocking his head . . . Finally he said.

'Tomato salad . . . yes. Then . . . I think duckling and orange sauce. And a green salad.'

'Three tomato salads.' Harold made an emendation on the pad. 'Duckling and . . . Where do you see that?'

'Over here,' said Roy with some force, hitting his finger at the à la carte section of the menu.

'Oh. Oh, over there. Duckling,' said Harold, in the tone, abruptly assumed, of a fanatical vegetarian. He made no move to write.

Roy swept his hand across his front as if cutting off a final chord. 'Could I change my mind?'

'By all means.'

'I'd like a whole lobster, please, cold, and stuffed with, uh, a portion of caviare. And a green salad, as I said.'

'All I'm thinking of is the time. It wouldn't be lined up like, uh, for instance, the steak and kidney pie.'

'They'll be lined up separately, the lobster and the caviare, and there's no need for the chaps in the kitchen to do the actual stuffing. Get the doings brought to me and I'll stuff it myself.'

Harold gave up at that point.[9]

This is how the life finds its way into the writing, disguised, displaced, complicatedly reconfigured. 'Someone complained that I put a "real" restaurant in it,' Amis once said, about a review of his last published novel, *The Biographer's Moustache* (1995), 'but once it's in the novel, even if it's a real place, it isn't real any more. Not quite.'[10] At times in the pages that follow, particularly those dealing with the early years, I shall draw on Amis's fiction and poetry to speculate about the life, but there are dangers in such speculation. In two of his novels, *The Riverside Villas Murder* (1973) and *You Can't Do Both* (1994), Amis offers what look like thinly disguised portraits of his childhood and youth. When asked by his friend and biographer Eric Jacobs how much real life there was in them he conceded in general that they were 'pretty accurate', while making the qualification that they remained novels. In real life, for example, Amis's father insisted that he leave the bathroom door unlocked when he took a bath. In *The Riverside Villas Murder*, so, too, does the fourteen-year-old hero's father, who resembles Amis's father in other respects. But Amis's father never invaded the bathroom to see what he was up to, as does the father in the novel.[11]

With non-fictional evidence there are also problems. In the *Memoirs*, the impulse to entertain can override truth. In a draft of the chapter Amis wrote about his friend Robert Conquest, the poet and historian, he tells a story about a drunken party Conquest attended in the 1950s. With what Amis calls 'exemplary persistence and rashness', Conquest persuaded an attractive girl at the party to accompany him upstairs. When they had finished in the bedroom, he chivalrously sent the girl downstairs by herself, so as not to risk damaging her reputation, and then shimmied down 'a convenient drainpipe', later re-entering the house by the front door, 'having ostensibly, or even perhaps actually, gone to the pub to buy some cigarettes'. After several more drinks, Conquest approached another attractive girl and began chatting her up. In mid-proposition, she slapped him in the face, 'a real tooth-loosener'. It was the same girl, the one he'd been to bed with an hour earlier.

Conquest enjoyed this story but told Amis it had nothing to do with him. So Amis stuck it in the chapter about the writer Philip Toynbee, 'whom it fits down to the ground, especially since he's dead'.[12] The story appears in the *Memoirs* on page 185 with an asterisked footnote reading: 'Bob Conquest heard this story too, but his recollection of it differs slightly from mine.' When the *Memoirs* were published, a number of people about whom Amis writes accused him of misrepresentation or fabrication.[13] Others, eyewitnesses, thought his accounts of people and places fair and accurate, especially those describing serious misconduct. With the *Memoirs*, then, as with biographical speculations drawn from the fiction, one must be careful. So, too, with verbal testimony, in particular when drawn from interviews in newspapers and periodicals. Towards the end of his life much of what Amis said to journalists was said for effect or fun or to cause trouble. According to Jacobs, in his obituary of Amis in the *Guardian*, 'he believed that, when at the typewriter, absolute integrity should prevail.

But when a writer came to sell himself and his wares in the market-place, more or less anything went. He made mischief on his own behalf and in doing so did some mischief to his reputation.'[14] When talking to people he respected or loved he could also say things he knew weren't true. When Jacobs's biography came out in 1995, it caused considerable upset in the Amis household, partly because it contained unflattering descriptions of Amis's father-in-law, Leonard Bardwell, quoted from letters to Philip Larkin. Bardwell was the father of Amis's first wife, Hilly. She was angry with Amis both for what he had written and for giving Jacobs permission to quote it. When she complained to their son Martin, he asked his father if he'd read Jacobs's biography before it was published. Amis said he hadn't. 'You could have saved yourself a lot of trouble if you had,' Martin told him; to which Amis replied: 'Yes, but then I'd have to have *read* it, wouldn't I?' But he had read it. The biography's claim was that it drew on first-hand testimony from its subject, who was able to check its speculations in person and in draft.[15] Among Amis's papers in the Huntington Library in San Marino, California, is a typed draft of Jacobs's biography, with Amis's handwritten corrections and comments, most of which Jacobs incorporated in the published book. Though not all the pages are anno-tated, and it is possible that Amis skipped bits or read cursorily, the evidence suggests that what he told Martin wasn't true. What he would not have read, however, at least not in the draft, were the offending quotations about Leonard Bardwell, which don't appear there; Jacobs was only later given access to Amis's letters to Larkin. It is just possible that when Amis told Martin that he hadn't read the book, he meant the version that incorporates the quotations.

These quotations need also to be considered carefully, like all evidence from the letters, especially those to Larkin. Amis's letters to Larkin distort the life in several ways. To begin with, they create the impression of a man who will say anything, about himself and others. The two friends egged each other on in the correspondence and recognised ensuing exaggerations. 'I must say here, by the way, how much funnier than RGP is our conception of old Rodge,' writes Amis in a letter of 20 August 1948, of a common friend from Oxford, later a relation. 'Not that it's a "wrong conception," it's just much funnier, that's all.' Amis makes a similar point in defence of the passages about Hilly's father. 'She couldn't see that when he was writing to Larkin he was making a joke out of her father,' Jacobs reports Amis as saying, 'not a serious assault.'[16] Comparable jokes occur in the Amis/Conquest correspondence. Conquest several times remarks on the dangers of confusing the writer, whether of letters or novels, with the man. 'Marriage bloody good,' he informs Amis in a letter of 7 October 1980, 'though no one reading passages in The Egyptologists, Peach Key, The Tit Man etc. written at other periods would expect the author ever to utter such sentiments.'[17] Anthony Powell also stresses the dangers of taking statements from the writing, especially from private letters, at face value. In a journal entry of 6 June 1987, he quotes a particularly harsh reference Larkin makes about Amis in a letter to Conquest: 'The only reason I hope I predecease him, is that I'd find it next to impossible to say anything nice about him at his memorial service.'[18] Powell comments: 'The essence of this kind of savage remark (with others) is probably acceptable within a circle of three old friends as satire that will be understood, but rather different when offered to the general public including malicious journalists out of context.'[19]

Six themes shape this biography: the formative influence of Amis's early upbringing, which he himself identified as a key to his personality and to many of the most pressing concerns of his fiction and poetry; the aggression which is so marked a feature of his character and writings; his astonishing energy (to his son Martin he was 'a great engine of comedy'); his sense of writing as craft or profession; his hostility to distinctions between high culture and low and concomitant attraction to popular forms; and his lifelong obsession with egotism, selfishness, inconsiderateness, qualities he acutely anatomises and censures in his writing even as they threaten to overwhelm him in life. The biography shows what it was like to meet Amis and to be him. It makes a case for the breadth and depth of his writing and it tells the story of how and why he did what he did, both as a writer and as a man. This last objective involves discussion of Amis's working methods, in the case of *Lucky Jim*, for example, carefully unravelling the complex story of the novel's several drafts and the controversial role Larkin played in its genesis. Amis sought both popular and literary acclaim; how he attained them tells us much about the man himself but also about the literary world (of publishers, agents, editors, critics) he had to negotiate. For the most part the narrative proceeds chronologically, without authorial intrusions or imagined conversations between biographer and subject. The tidying tendencies of biography are often deplored by literary theorists and academics, but Amis's life is not easily tidied, even when told chronologically. Though the focus throughout is on Amis himself he is presented in the light of a detailed historical context; where relevant, I relate his writings not only to those of contemporaries but to those of writers in his tradition, either as defined by himself or others. But one can't include everything. 'Really, universally, relations stop nowhere,' Henry James wrote, 'and the exquisite problem of the artist is eternally but to draw, by a geometry of his own, the circle in which they shall happily *appear* to do so.'[20] This is a problem for the biographer as well, even one embarked on a full-scale life.

In Amis's case, there is ample room for such a life. Eric Jacobs's *Kingsley Amis: A Biography* (1995), which he wrote while Amis was still alive, is thin on significant aspects of its subject's life and work, notably his education, his literary influences, his poetry, his relations with his children, several important friendships, his promiscuity and his neuroses. It also offers only a brief account of the literary and cultural world Amis entered into in the early 1950s and helped to shape in succeeding decades. Jacobs's closeness to his subject is at times a weakness as well as a strength; he is not uncritical, but his criticisms are mostly those Amis himself has voiced, in his fiction and elsewhere, and his manner recalls the Amis of the *Memoirs*. One feels throughout the inevitably constraining presence of the book's subject. Richard Bradford's *Lucky Him: The Life of Kingsley Amis* (2001) offers almost no new biographical information but attends very closely to autobiographical intimations in the fiction. It is less a life of the writer than an interpretation of that life through the writings. Martin Amis's portrait of his father in *Experience* (2000) is openly partial, in several respects; for all its clear-sightedness it is in no sense a full-scale life. My edition of Amis's *Letters* (2000) offers a life of sorts, but its picture of the man is distorted by gaps in the correspondence (no letters to parents, almost none to his first wife or his children). The preponderance and power of the letters to Philip Larkin also distort. Larkin was central to Amis's life and art, but his centrality is magnified in the correspondence and potentially misleading. Moreover, the ebb and flow of the friendship is only partially documented and explained in the *Letters*. They do not tell us why the two friends grew apart in the 1960s, nor do they make clear the role literary envy played in their relationship.

How the themes of the biography interweave, in the work as well as the life, is suggested in *You Can't Do Both*, described in its blurb as 'strongly autobiographical'. In the novel's first chapter, the reader is offered a description of the effect jazz has on its hero, Robin Davies, who is fourteen, like Peter Furneaux, the hero of *The Riverside Villas Murder*. A friend puts a Louis Armstrong record on:

Something quite fast and very raucous and subversive. At an early point one of the trumpet men produced a ferocious, clearly intentional discord that made Robin draw in his breath and also acted on him as a tremendous encouragement, as if thousands of good chaps were telling him they understood exactly how he felt about life and that he was right and would win.[21]

This moment is characteristic of its author in several respects, beginning with its conjunction of aesthetic pleasure and attack. Aggression was for Amis only in part a product of outrage or indignation – at assorted slights, pretension, stupidity, bloody-mindedness. Often it appears in the most innocuous of contexts, as in the humour he extracts from awkward physical movements. In *Take a Girl Like You* (1960), a character runs up to bowl: 'Dick paced out his run and came tottering and skipping up to the wicket and bowled as if throwing a bomb while being shot at.'[22] Earlier in the novel a character sneezes: 'he shifted his shoulders around like someone having things thrown at him from different positions, rocking much more than before in the rocking-chair and making a string of short tearing screeching noises'.[23] Explaining what it was like to be Kingsley Amis partly means explaining how he came to see and depict the world in this way, as suffused with violence, anger, threat.

You Can't Do Both takes its title from two parallel episodes of restriction: in the first, early on, Robin's father stops him from having tea with a friend, on the grounds that the family has made a previous engagement for the evening. Even though he'll be back from tea by 6.30 and the evening engagement isn't until eight, Robin's father insists: 'I'm sorry old boy. You can't do both. I'm sorry.'[24] In an episode at the end of the novel, Robin, now an adult, is presented with an ultimatum by his wife:

If I ever stop being sure you're not trying to get away with something then I'm off for good with Margaret and Tilly, all right? You can have the three of us, or you can have everyone else. Not both.[25]

The adult Robin is a womaniser and his behaviour is implicitly linked, here and throughout the novel, to his upbringing. The pleasure jazz affords Robin is also linked, in several ways, to this upbringing, in particular to his isolation in the family setting. Robin is, in effect, an only child, as was Amis himself, and as a consequence not only subject to excessive parental monitoring but, as Amis has written of his own childhood behaviour, 'overready to defend his interests'.[26] Robin's father, like Amis's father, became a parent comparatively late in life, and was less flexible and resilient than a younger parent might be. He was also officiously protective, invariably distrusting or disapproving even the most unobjectionable of potential companions (that he loves his son, in the bluff, undemonstrative manner of his age and class, and enjoys his company, the novel also scrupulously records). It is significant that part of the pleasure jazz affords Robin, in addition to its raucous exuberance and aggression (that 'ferocious discord'), is that it seems to connect him to 'thousands of good chaps'. Amis, the most clubbable of men, wouldn't (also couldn't) live alone. Though his habitual stance was oppositional, he craved companionship throughout his life; though fiercely independent of fashion as a writer, he deplored writing as mere expression or experiment, consistently attending to the audience and its needs. The family background, these instances suggest, helps to explain Amis's compulsion not only to attack but to lose himself in pleasure and comradeship. It makes sense to start at home.

I

Family

Kingsley William Amis was born on 16 April 1922, in a nursing home on the edge of Clapham Common in South London. The family he was born into was lower middle class and suburban. The name 'Kingsley' comes from his mother's cousin (whose twin sister was named 'Queenie'); 'William' was Amis's father's name. Kingsley was a large baby and born when his mother was thirty-one, seven years into marriage. That the birth was difficult may have accounted, according to family lore, for the absence not only of further children but of further marital relations.[1] Amis's parents were devoted to each other, but it was openly understood, at least in later years, that his father had sought sexual companionship outside the marriage. In his *Memoirs* (1991), Amis is circumspect, and uncertain, about his father's activities in this sphere: 'Apart from the fact of my own existence, no sort of detail of his sexual life ever reached me until very late on. I have often been tempted to think that it was never a very active one, but experience teaches that nothing is likely to fall more wildly astray than this sort of judgment, even as regards contemporaries whom one knows intimately.' As for discussing sexual topics with his mother, Amis recalls a 'fierce (and absurdly visible) shake of the head' at the mention in his presence of 'somebody's honeymoon or some such depravity'.[2] He was probably fourteen at the time.

It is his father's attitudes to sex, though, which Amis singles out for censure. His prime concern was masturbation, the subject of 'a short course of harangues' in which Amis senior laid out 'in some detail' the dangers of self-abuse, how it 'thinned the blood and the victim eventually fell into helpless insanity'. About all other aspects of sex his father remained silent. If the harangues were 'silly and perhaps worse', the silence was 'wrong'; less because it left the son uninstructed, though this Amis regrets, than because it denied him an 'all clear' or 'formal permit'. Later in life Amis made sure he delivered such a permit to his own sons, not only through a short talk when they were 'I suppose, seven and six years old',[3] but ten or so years later, after they'd been sexually launched. In the summer of 1965, he took both boys to lunch in Soho, then bought them, in the younger son's words, 'a *gross* of condoms: 144'.[4] Though Amis avoids explicit sex scenes in his fiction, his frankness about sex in real life was habitual, and often, as here, celebratory, 'full of fun' (an Amis catch-phrase). But at other times it could be aggressive, powered by retaliatory or reactive relish against just the sort of parental prudery recalled in the *Memoirs*. 'A man's sexual aim,' we are told by Roger Micheldene in *One Fat Englishman* (1963), is 'to convert a creature who is cool, dry, calm, articulate, independent, purposeful into a creature that is the opposite of these; to demonstrate to an animal which is pretending not to be an animal that it is an animal.'[5]

The home into which Amis was born was a small, semi-detached villa, 16 Buckingham Gardens, the first of three houses the family would occupy in Norbury, London SW16, a ward of the borough of Croydon. Norbury, the adult Amis remarked, lacked identity. It was less distinguished even than neighbouring Streatham. 'At least Streatham had been a country town in the eighteenth century, where Dr. Johnson would drive out to see Mrs. Thrale for tea.'[6] Norbury was hardly a town at all. 'Half the parts south of the river,' comments Stanley Duke, of *Stanley and the Women* (1984), also born in SW16, 'were never proper places at all, just collections of assorted buildings filling up gaps and named after railway stations and bus garages.'[7] Norbury gained its name in 1878, when the railway arrived. 'The stretch between Streatham and Croydon was too long so they planted a station in between and called it after the only named building in the area, a house called Norbury Manor',[8] described in the *Memoirs* as 'somebody's not-all-that-nearby country house'.[9] The first, perhaps only, literary reference to Norbury pre-Amis,[10] occurs in a Sherlock Holmes story, 'The Yellow Face' (1894). Holmes and Watson arrive from London by train, exit the High Road, and soon find themselves in 'a narrow lane, deeply rutted, with hedges on either side'. They have come to meet a client, Grant Munro, a hop merchant with 'a nice eighty-pound-a-year villa in Norbury . . . very countrified, considering that it is so close to town'.[11] Almost fifty years later, when both Amis and Peter Furneaux, the hero of *The Riverside Villas Murder*, were fourteen, and the population of Norbury was nearing 10,000, this sense of the nearness of the country persists. 'They reached Norbury', we are told in *The Riverside Villas Murder*, 'where the trams ended and the buildings began to thin out. After a left fork at Thornton Heath Pond, fields appeared.'[12]

Fields, like other aspects of nature, figure infrequently in Amis's memories of childhood. There was Pollards Hill, where, like Peter, he used to fly model aeroplanes, and where the view was green as far as the eye could see. Behind the house at Buckingham Gardens, and beyond its garden, ran a river of sorts, the Graveney, sluggish and ditch-like in places, but always known as 'The Brook'. It is unlikely to have flowed along young Amis's dreams, let alone composed his thoughts to infant softness, as the Derwent did for Wordsworth as a child, but it makes at least one appearance in his fiction. In *The Riverside Villas Murder*, it runs under the High Road and past the Tennis Club, as in real life. Peter can see it from a circular window on the landing at the top of the stairs. Though 'too small for any real boats . . . having it there, being able to walk along its banks, was marvellous, especially in the hour before dusk'.[13]

Such evocations are rare. Amis's upbringing included few 'blinding theologies of flowers and fruit',[14] to quote his friend Philip Larkin, another child of the suburbs. The Norbury land-marks that predominate in Amis's interviews and recollections are non-rural: the Gaumont Cinema (tickets ninepence), the Streatham Astoria (where he saw John Gielgud play Hamlet, probably in 1935), the Carlotta Tea Rooms, the Tennis Club, the Ice Rink, the Norbury Library, and row after row of cheap suburban houses: dwarf Tudor, pebbledash ('where you put up cement and literally hurl gravel at it').[15] Each of the three Norbury houses Amis and his parents lived in conformed to post-1918 suburban type: sitting room, dining room and kitchen downstairs; three bedrooms (one a box room), bath and toilet upstairs; attic for storage. The rooms were small, the internal walls thin, the outsides of the houses covered in poor-quality stucco. The second house the family lived in, at 7 Ena Road, was marginally more spacious than the first, and had a large oak tree in the garden; the third, at 53 Gilpin Road, marginally more spacious than the second. All were within walking distance of each other, and none further than a ten-minute walk from Norbury station.[16]

From the time he was twelve and old enough to attend the City of London School, Amis walked to Norbury station with his father every morning, five days a week. Had CLS held classes on Saturdays, when his father worked a half-day, it would have been six. His father's City office was near the school and he insisted that his son stay by his side throughout their journey, rather than join up with friends.[17] In the *Memoirs*, Amis presents his father as controlling in general, but also for reasons of class and economy. His father's father, Joseph James Amis (called Pater or Dadda), had been a prosperous glass merchant, lived in state in a large house called Barchester in Purley, and sent all three of his sons to CLS as fee-paying pupils (though he sent none to university: out of 'meanness', the grandson suspects). Amis's father was acutely conscious of having come down in the world: 'The family had slipped a rung,' Amis told one interviewer. 'I suppose they were frightened of toppling into the working class'.[18]

Financial anxieties also restricted Amis's youth. When father and son quarrelled about use of the wireless, though musical taste was at issue, money was involved, too. Amis's father was tired after work and wanted quiet; but the house was small and 'the partition walls were not especially thick, and most sounds went through them'. Such fights 'might have been solved in a different kind of household and house and neighbourhood'.[19] In *You Can't Do Both*, Robin Davies's father always unplugs the wireless when he's not using it. Though 'not the man to go as far as forbidding the use of the wireless when he was not there . . . neither was he the man to allow this to happen whenever any Tom, Dick or Harry took it in his head to try it'.[20] The father's behaviour in this instance is not just controlling, it is also mean and careful, conjuring up a grey world of limited resources, a world Peter Furneaux's father also inhabits. When Captain Furneaux is attacked at home, the intruder cannot be identified because the hallway light has been switched off: 'unlike many of us I have to watch the pennies and electricity costs the earth these days'.[21] When the father lays a fire, the result is invariably 'small, neither catching nor quite going out for hours on end, and rich in smoke'.[22]

Peter's father is an unprospering estate agent with a small office in Norbury. Robin's father holds down 'a safe office job in London'.[23]

Kingsley's father was a clerk in the London office of the mustard manufacturer J. and J. Colman, at 108 Cannon Street, Blackfriars. He was born on 27 July 1888 (according to his birth certificate and company records, though Amis's *Memoirs* make him a year younger), joined the firm in October 1913, aged twenty-five, and stayed until his retirement in the mid-1950s (previously, he had worked at Elder's and Fyffe's, the banana importers, also as a clerk). His starting salary at Colman's, as a junior clerk in the Foreign Section, was £110 per annum. Two years later, just before he went into the army, it was £135. Shortly after he returned from the war ('tending airships in Scotland', a Royal Naval Air Service posting which, given the alternatives, Amis rightly calls 'cushy'),[24] he took up a new position in the Export Insurance Department, and his salary more than doubled. Then his career seems to have stalled. From 1920 until his retirement his salary went up in very modest and not always yearly increments. In 1922, the year his son was born, it was £390; in 1934, when Amis entered the City of London School, it was £420, a rise of just £30 in twelve years. Six years later, when Amis entered Oxford as an Exhibitioner, his father was earning £470. On such a salary the family could not afford to run a car, pay more than a year's school fees ('gambling successfully that I would get a scholarship in the year that followed'),[25] or go on holiday abroad.

'It is a sad fate to be the child of the urban or suburban middle-classes,' Amis has written. 'As a first or a fourth *are* the only dignified kinds of degree to get, so one's upbringing must be conducted either in several establishments with several bathrooms or in one with none, if it is to distil any glamour potential.'[26] Or any sympathy. Though the privations of Amis's early upbringing may well have played some part in the greedy or gobbling nature of his pursuit of pleasure in later years, they ought not to be exaggerated. There are worse fates than never rising above a senior clerk's pay: getting fired, for instance, a not unheard of occurrence in the Depression years of the 1930s, and one Amis knew his father feared. Nor was Amis senior's work simple drudgery. Although he was a clerk, he had a secretary and some executive responsibilities. He was required to learn Spanish to deal with South American customers to whom the company sold its Savora brand, a blander mustard than the English variety. At one point he was even offered the chance to be Colman's representative in South America, a clear promotion, but his wife refused to go. He was never offered promotion again.[27]

William Amis played an active role in the office culture at 108 Cannon Street. The name W.R. Amis figures several times in the company's magazine, in reports of the annual Colman Cricket Cup match between employees of the London and Norwich offices. There's also a two-page article, signed 'W.R. Amis, Hon. Secretary', about the founding of the Cannon Street Football Club, an effort that 'presented many difficulties at the outset'. After detailing these difficulties, Amis senior mentions that the team has won three of its first four matches, 'a most auspicious beginning'. Yet results were not what mattered: 'The great feature of the Club so far being the truly sporting spirit in which the matches have been played, that *esprit de corps* which is fostered by any kind of game or recreation, and which helps so much to solve the difficulties encountered in the more serious occupations in life.'[28] When Colman's merged with Reckitt's (makers of Brasso and Dettol) in 1938, the Cannon Street office closed and most of its functions were transferred to Norwich. Any staff who remained were moved to a smaller office in Bedford Square: 'father was left behind in the Bedford Square office. But he loved the City and talked endlessly about it.'[29]

Though Amis's father considered himself a failure and not much valued by 'the horrible mustard people' (his son's description),[30] he was not a bitter man. Acquaintances found him 'immensely good humoured' (this from a woman who also reports that he 'wasn't above a nudge in the ribs, a pinch on the bottom'),[31] pleasant, kindly, civilised and polite. In appearance he was neat and dapper, stockily built, with broad shoulders, of medium height, and nattily dressed 'in one of his grey or brown lounge suits'.[32] He had a dark, handsome face, with 'a nice big nose' that made him look Jewish (according to his son, though this is hard to see from surviving photographs).[33] Keen on sport throughout his life, he played tennis 'vigorously well into middle age' and 'actively captained the local [cricket] side into his sixties'.[34] He played the piano, had a good singing voice, and at social gatherings was much given to elaborate jokes and imitations. Both Amis's parents 'were always on the lookout for a quirk' (among neighbours, shopkeepers, friends from the Tennis Club) and would 'never repeat a conversation without imitating the voice, doing the actions'.[35] Amis's first cousin, John (son of James Amis, William's younger brother), later a well-known singer and music broadcaster, remembers 'Uncle Bill' as 'a very funny man, giving near blasphemous imitations of King George's Christmas Day speech that shocked Grandpa' (partly because they involved much spitting and coughing). John's sister Joan also remembers him as funny, 'dressing up in weird clothes for my benefit when I was a small child. He once appeared with a pair of men's pants over his head. With one arm in one of its long legs, he immediately became an elephant!'[36]

Amis's memories of his father's humour are not always as positive or approving. Although his father had 'a talent for physical clowning and mimicry that made him, on his day, one of the funniest men I have known', he also had 'a rowdy, babyish streak in him which caused him, when perfectly sober, to pretend to be a foreigner or deaf in trains and pubs'. This quality Amis believes he also saw in his father's father, 'a jokey, excitable, silly little man', who delivered his comic stories 'typically without any preamble, to trap you into thinking you were hearing about some real event'.[37] The father's humorous routines could often fall horribly flat, as is suggested in *You Can't Do Both*, when Robin brings home a girlfriend from Oxford, the girl he will eventually marry.

On his entrance, Mr. Davies put on what was for him a tremendous show of cordiality and welcome . . . It led without interval into one of the sustained bouts of clowning he went in for a couple of times a year and would describe afterwards without detectable penitence as a case of letting his sense of humour get the better of him. On this occasion he performed a not very well observed take-off of a gallant Continental gentleman, bowing low, making as if to kiss Nancy's hand, loudly delivering a flowery speech of welcome in a generic foreign accent at a speed that precluded interruption. Every few seconds he pretended to trip over his own feet. For what in theory was a comic turn it was a remarkably effective means of disconcerting someone meeting him for the first time.[38]

Everyone in the room is embarrassed by this performance, including its performer, who immediately apologises. As Robin's mother puts it: 'I just never know when my husband's going to start playing the fool in his own inimitable fashion . . . What a way to greet a poor girl in a strange house.'[39]

Far from being 'inimitable', the father's humour reveals him as a familiar type. V.S. Pritchett, a writer with whom Amis is sometimes compared,[40] and one who came from a comparable class background, has written of his own father that he 'must have been very shy, for in public he had somehow to make himself into a person visible to all. In restaurants he was a mixture of the obsequious and the bumptious; he would speak to the manager in a very pretentious way.' William Amis, according to his eldest grandson, Philip, was no easier in such settings: 'he used to boss waiters around, he was embarrassing about it'. The characters in Pritchett's fiction behave with similar awkwardness. In seeking to escape what they feel to be the limitations and failures of their outer existence or class position, they live out their lives as performances, theatrically expanding their personalities.[41] Amis provides an example of such behaviour in *You Can't Do Both*. Robin's father is like Amis's father, described by Amis as 'not one for letting things slide. He thought you had to interfere with things'.[42] When he suspects that Nancy and his son have been indulging in 'improper' conduct while alone in the house, he interrogates the young couple, discovers the truth of his suspicions (through Nancy's blushes), and 'with great reluctance' asks her to pack her bag and leave the family home immediately. At this date, Nancy is not quite eighteen. In the midst of his interrogation, 'all at once, Robin saw his father half-consciously enjoying his sense of being chairman of a small committee, and felt his hatred, which had subsided a good deal in the last minute, flare up again satisfactorily'.[43] The closing adverb here is telling, suggesting as it does that Robin has inherited the self-dramatising gene. Also noteworthy is the way the father's performance overrides outer realities or considerations, such as Nancy's feelings.[44]

That the insecurity of William Amis's class position, with its consequent self-inflation, helps to explain him, is a view taken by his younger grandson, Martin, in a passage from *Experience*. The passage begins with a quotation from the *Memoirs*:

'As I came to sense the image in which my father was trying to mould my character and future . . . I began to resist him, and we quarrelled violently at least every week or two for years.' And I can see it, I can hear it, like a bad marriage, Gramps, who wielded so little power in the external world, attempting by mere iteration to impose his will.[45]

The adult Amis could barely disguise his irritation and boredom in the face of such 'iteration', especially when combined with bumptious playfulness. Here he is, in a letter of 24 May 1958, complaining to Larkin about 'the continuous presence of my male relative':

Why doesn't he go away for good? Failing that, why can't he go away for a very long time and then go away again almost as soon as he has come back? I can't pass him anything or he says *Danke*. I can't let him pass me anything or he says Excuse Fungus. I can't look for anything (an exercise frequently required in this establishment) or he says *Qu'est-ce que tu cherches?* When my friends call (as one or two of them are still continuing to do for the moment) he *talks to them*. When Hilly and Mavis and Mary Morgan were having a girls' chat he *sat with them* for 2 *hrs*. He doesn't like old people, you see. He likes young people. You will agreee peee[46] it's a fallacy that old people are interested in the concerns of young people. They don't want to hear what the young say. They want to make the young hear what they say. More of a triumph to bore a young person, who has more alternatives to being so bored than an old person.

The rigidity of Amis's father had religious as well as class origins. William Amis, according to his son, 'regarded himself as a rebel in a mild way'. He had suffered, he said, from 'a very inflexible kind of Christian upbringing' and from the fierce quarrels with his parents that this upbringing engendered.[47] Though he and his wife were raised as strict Baptists, by the time they were married 'they had abandoned nearly all religious observances'.[48] In an interview following the publication of *You Can't Do Both*, Amis admitted: 'I had the same sort of religious upbringing or lack of it as my hero has, or hasn't.'[49] That is, his parents, too, defied their parents over religion, moved from Chapel to Church of England, never much went to church, never invoked church doctrine or dogma, never even sent their son to Sunday School. In Amis's upbringing, 'God never came into the conversation. God was never actually referred to or appealed to, and there was no question of displeasing God by my actions or trying to please him.'[50] Yet 'all the Christian morality that went with the doctrine . . . stayed in place: the conscientiousness, the patience, the frugality . . . Matthew Arnold would have worried less about the survival of Christian ethics in an age without literal faith if he could have had a few chats with the old man.'[51]

This element of moral strictness in their grandfather's make-up is also remembered by the Amis grandchildren. How he 'keenly and inventively and rather sternly' played with them, how he once reduced Martin 'to a tantrum of misery when he found himself maintaining that it was "natural" to have "more feeling as a grandfather" for

the first-born son'. Martin, the second-born son, adored his grandfather and burst into tears at this declaration. The grandfather 'tried
to soften it but he wouldn't unsay it; he wouldn't bend to the severity
of my distress'. The grandson wonders at 'the fantastic obduracy of
the man', how he 'wouldn't tell a salutary white lie to calm a sobbing,
squealing, supplicating child'.[52] But a note of sympathy for the grandfather is also sounded. As the phrase 'found himself maintaining'
implies, he was at least uncomfortable with what he was saying.[53]

    Amis himself admitted that he had inherited his father's obduracy.
In *Experience*, Martin Amis quotes the closing stanzas of his father's
elegy, 'In Memoriam W.R.A.', subtitled 'ob. April 18th, 1963'. These
stanzas detail the later, more distant relations between father and
son (in which the son mostly ignored, or tried to ignore, the father),
as opposed to the combative and intimate relations of the Norbury
years, the years of Amis's adolescence:

> The on-and-on of your talk
> My gradually formal response
> That I could never defend
> But never would soften enough,
>   Leading to silence,
>   And separate ways.
>
> Forgive me if I have
>   To see it as it happened:
> Even your pride and your love
> Have taken this time to become
> Clear, to arouse my love.
> I'm sorry you had to die
>   To make me sorry
>   You're not here now.

'Forgive me if I have / To see it as it happened.' The son is as unable
to temporise as the father (just as he will later be unable to temporise
when commenting, for example, on his son's fiction). 'I had acquired
from somewhere a very liberal helping of adolescent intellectual arrogance, while inheriting in full measure my father's obstinacy.'[54]

    'In Memoriam W.R.A.' takes as its starting point an imagined moment
of fellowship between father and son, a moment occasioned by:

A *Cricket Match*, between
The *Gentlemen of Cambridge*
And the *Hanover Club*, to be played
By the *Antient Laws* of the *Game*

. . .

In *Antient Costume*
For a *Good Cause*.

This match actually took place, some months after his father's death, and Amis played in it, captaining one of the sides. It is referred to in correspondence, and in a draft version of the poem its location in Cambridge (Jesus Common) and sponsor (the National Playing Fields Association) are specified. Amis imagines his father laughing with him at his appearance at the crease: 'With a bat like an over-grown spoon . . . in my ruffles and tights'. When Amis makes an early declaration he imagines his father's approving eye, 'Half shut with laughter / (And pride and love)'. Then he imagines the two of them 'over pints, / Part of a chatting circle'. In Amis's reverie, the father asks the son if he recalls a childhood dream of playing cricket professionally, and how 'I fixed up a coach, but you said / You were working too hard for exams?' (the father tried to get the son a trial with Surrey as well, which also didn't work out). At this point the poem darkens into the final stanzas, with their awkward truths ('Forgive me if I have to . . .'). But awkward truths are present from the start: in the ludicrousness of the figure the son cuts, in the amused acceptance of this ludicrousness on both their parts, in what this acceptance implies about loss and limitation. The elegy is loving but clear-sighted, gently evoking both the father's dreams for himself and his son, and, implicitly, the consequences of such dreams, the comic types they produce, as figured in Amis at the crease.

The complexity of Amis's feelings about his father can be gathered from 'Pater and Old Chap', a 1957 *Observer* article about Warwick Deeping's novel, *Sorrell and Son* (1925). This novel has been much derided by academic critics, but it was a huge commercial success in its day, and Amis ponders its best-selling ingredients. He begins with its initial situation: 'Sorrell is an unemployed ex-officer, is divorced, has a young son to bring up.' Its plot is then summarised: 'the father rises via hotel porter to hotel manager with a directorship, the son becomes a promising surgeon'. The relationship between father and son, though, is the ingredient that matters: 'a rapturous wish-fulfilling dream of perfect filial love lies at the core of the book, involving absolute rejection of the mother and absolute devotion to the father, and hinting at a disturbance in the author of dimensions normally reserved for figures of pan-European stature'.[55]

No such disturbance shaped Amis, but in both his fictional and non-fictional evocations of childhood it is the father who dominates. In *The Riverside Villas Murder*, the mother is simply away. In *You Can't Do Both*, the parental death that is recounted in detail is the father's. The final meeting between father and son is among the most affecting scenes in the book, in any Amis book, and has several Deeping-like touches. 'How are you, Dad?' asks Robin as he enters his father's room in the nursing home. 'All the better for seeing you, old chap.' When the father attempts to apologise, the son won't hear of it:

'Dad, there's nothing to forgive.'
His father's face and voice took on some of their old faintly theatrical sternness when he said, 'Oh yes there is, Robin, as you well know.'
'In that case I do forgive you. For not sending me to Sunday school and for everything else.'
'Thank you for saying that, old chap.'[56]

'The ideal, though by no means the only possible, reader of *Sorrell and Son*,' Amis writes, 'is a middle-aged white-collar worker in the industrial suburbs who feels menaced by a falling real income, a decline in status and the emergence into power and affluence of uncouth persons who sneer at what he feels and stands for.'[57] William Amis fits this description neatly, and his politics seem to have been pretty much those of the novel and its 'ideal' reader. In the *Memoirs*, Amis identifies his father as 'an ex-Liberal of the Lloyd George denomination who went Tory after the Great War and for years was active in his constituency and in the local Ratepayers' Association'.[58] What he does not identify are the specific terms in which the father expressed his politics. These are on display in *Sorrell and Son*, and were already unacceptable in 1963. Though an ideal reader of 1963 'would find no difficulty in agreeing that "the wrong people have got the money" nowadays . . . he would probably be chary of endorsing the view that working people "exuded a perfume of stale sweat"'.[59] William Amis, the evidence suggests, would not, and

though his son distances himself from such views, he also recognises their appeal:

The social antagonisms of a considerable stratum are dramatized in these
pages; the more rabidly inclined, indeed, are likely to derive a guilty excitement akin to that engendered by pornography. Kindred prejudices, some
dated, some still rampant, are accommodated. There is a persistent thread
of anti-Americanism; there is continual deprecation of the 'highbrow' and
'clever'; 'sex is nature' and like eating your dinner, but by a deft synthesis
it also includes 'the mystery of woman'; Freud and all that needn't be taken
seriously, we aren't abnormal – 'the abnormality could be looked for on
the Continent'; people with money and fame, like film stars, are unhappy
and want to be like you and me.[60]

Amis has called his father 'the most English human being I have
ever known',[61] and there is a sense ('you tell us what sense,' Amis
would say at this point) in which his Deeping-like prejudices have
an 'English' or historical as well as a class origin. There were
Wemmicks and Micawbers before the loss of Empire (Micawber is
thought to have resembled Dickens's father), but the type comes into
its own in an age of decline and retrenchment. The self-inflating
tendencies of men like William Amis and Sawdon Pritchett (father
of V.S.) might partly be reactions against intimations of national as
well as personal limitation and loss. This is the impression created
by 'A Journey – There and Back', an 11,000-word account of a trip
Amis's father made to the United States in 1957, shortly after 'the
tragic loss of my wife and my retirement from business almost
synchronized'. This trip was not his idea: 'a visit abroad would never
have occurred to me'. It was urged on him 'by my many friends',
and enthusiastically seconded by his sister, Gladys, who lived in
Washington, DC, and whom he hadn't seen in twenty years. There
is some evidence that Amis Senior wanted the memoir published,
and that his son did not. Amis showed the essay to his friend Esmond
Cleary, an economics lecturer at the University College of Swansea,
who liked William Amis and shared his passion for cricket; after
reading it, Cleary sought to return it to Amis, but the offer was
declined: 'Leaving it with me was a useful way of resisting, for the
moment, paternal pressure.' It would be best for all concerned,
Cleary was led to believe, if the memoir simply disappeared.

It is not hard to see why Amis wanted the memoir to disappear.

It begins with his father's anxieties about status or recognition. 'All was hurry and bustle and everyone seemed to be too concerned with his own business even to notice me.' He walks into the ship's dining room, which is filled with 'pleasant and friendly' Americans, and 'suddenly a fear came over me that they might ask me whether I had been to the States before, and in due time sure enough they did. "No" was my whispered reply "this is my first trip on a Liner", feeling as small as the smallest worm, and just as ignorant.' Soon such anxieties recede and he becomes the life of the party. New friends induce him not only to join them in horse-racing and bingo games but 'to dress up as an American tourist for the Fancy Dress Parade'. When his ship arrives in New York, the anxieties return. At the railway station, no one helps him. It took an hour before he found a man 'who consented to give us his attention'.

This man's race is not specified, but one can guess it from the passage that follows, which introduces the Washington portion of his trip:

Before singing the praises of Washington as a City, I must refer to my very first impression of its' [sic] inhabitants. I was amazed downtown to observe the proportion of black over white. The infestation seems to me to be about ten to one; this, of course, is not the case, but what struck me most forcibly was their arrogance and pushfulness and lack of regard for the whites – it must be seen to be believed. The worst of it is, the whites seem to bear this without a murmur, but I am sure this is merely outward show and they are really seething inside, as I am. I felt as though I had been pitchforked into a nigger colony – I'm sorry, I shouldn't have used the word 'nigger', it could lead to serious trouble if I was to be heard using it in public – this is true, not fiction.[62]

Later in the memoir he complains that the courts are too frightened to prosecute blacks 'for fear of being accused of discrimination'. This is true even in cases of rape and murder, 'in which the blacks seem to specialize'.[63] But the complaint he begins with, the one that strikes him 'most forcibly' and makes him 'seethe', is that of black presumption: 'their arrogance and pushfulness and lack of regard for the whites'. In a 1957 review of Richard Hoggart's *The Uses of Literacy*, Amis contrasts working-class and middle-class fears. Middle-class fears revolve around questions of status and decorum; compared with the fears of the working class, they 'show up as neurotic, unreal and self-regarding'.[64] Blacks are to be deplored in William Amis's essay because they are literally as well as figuratively pushy: 'barging past you in buses and streetcars or pushing in front of you in queues with never a "by your leave"'.[65] They don't know their place.

Knowing your place was a problem for William Amis as well, which may account for his vehemence on the subject. Soon after his arrival in Washington, he discovers that the Queen is to visit: 'I had an idea I might be able to cadge an invitation to one of the Functions to be held at the British Embassy, so I called there and signed the Visitors' Book, and was told there that my best plan was to write to the Social Secretary. This I did, but owing, no doubt, to my having no claim to fame or to my social standing not being sufficiently high, I had to be content with a very polite and charming refusal.' On the voyage back to England he pays for a first-class cabin and reports that 'the company are making a fuss of me. On top of this I had an invitation to have cocktails with the Purser.' He mingles with the officers: 'What a fine looking man the Captain is, tall, iron-grey, well-built, genial and immaculate – just the sort of chap you feel you could trust in an emergency.' As for the other officers, they're 'all good-looking perfectly groomed and with a distinct flavour of R.N. about them'. Those from the lower orders are also admirable. Three hundred Royal Canadian Air Force Personnel and their families are on board: 'a nice bunch of blokes . . . their conduct was exemplary'. Here is heaven on earth, a paradise in which those below don't push and those above invite you for cocktails.[66]

Young Amis's upbringing was restricted as much by his mother's anxieties as by his father's. Rosa Annie Lucas Amis (who preferred to be called Peggy, since her given names derived from two maiden aunts who had died of drink) was born in 1890, the daughter of Jemima Sweetland and George Lucas, a tailor's assistant in the Brixton Hill branch of Izaac Walton's, a chain of gentleman's outfitters. Not very remarkably, her aim as a parent, like her husband's, was to make her son 'the sort of chap you feel you could trust', while also treating him as a species of native, or native sympathiser. When Amis listened to jazz on the wireless, it 'put my father in mind, or so he said, of a lot of savages dancing round a pot of human remains' (a remark prompted by Duke Ellington's *Black, Brown and Beige* suite, 'something about as far from primitivism as jazz had then got').[67] Though a softer and more sympathetic parent than her husband, Peggy Amis shared his views and was comparably controlling in her sphere. 'Mother did everything for me,' Amis recalled in an interview.

It was rather like being the colonial State of a more powerful nation. Just as in Uganda in the old days, you were guaranteed protection but didn't get much say in policy. When I came home from school, there were always four slices of Hovis,[68] thick with marmalade, already cut in half for me. If she could have eaten them for me, she would have done![69]

Once Amis was prevented from going on a school trip by his mother because he had a spot on his face: 'No,' she declared, 'I'm not risking you there.'[70] On another occasion, while an undergraduate at Oxford, Amis and a group of friends had been invited to work on a farm, but his parents would neither let him go nor explain their refusal. As Amis remembers it, his mother 'chucked a fainting fit'. Then his father said: 'See what you've done?' 'Monstrously unfair,' is how he later characterised their behaviour.[71]

It was over food that his mother's anxieties and controlling impulses took their most extreme forms. Her two great fears for young Kingsley were undernourishment and irregularity (though in *You Can't Do Both* it is the father who asks: 'Have you done your bigs this morning, Robin?').[72] Amis was thin and small when young, and though the doctor had pronounced him well nourished, his mother was not reassured, complaining that she could see his breastbone. As late as age twelve or thirteen,

[s]he tried to beef me up with stuff like Parrish's Chemical Food, a fearful reddish liquid which was supposed to turn your teeth black unless you bypassed them by sucking it through a straw. More directly, she would sit opposite me at the dinner-table pushing forkful after forkful into my mouth, not an ideal way of encouraging the appetite – for solids, that is. Here again I feel I can spot a contributory cause of later developments.[73]

In his fiction, Amis offers a glimpse of the mostly bland, unobjectionable food being pushed into his mouth. 'What's in store for us?' asks Mr Davies as the family sits down to lunch in *You Can't Do Both*. 'Just a bit of ham and salad,' Mrs Davies answers. 'Very suitable for the time of year, my love,' Mr Davies replies.[74] Peter's mother in *The Riverside Villas Murder* serves 'liver and bacon and cold apple pie' for supper. Later in the novel, father and son are served a lunch of 'boiled cod and parsley sauce', while for dessert 'both got some tinned mandarin oranges down'. At tea, Peter is offered a digestive biscuit: 'he could never decide whether they revolted him more than they bored him or the other way on'.[75] 'Ever since my mother stopped forcing me to eat it,' announces Jim Dixon in *Lucky Jim*, 'rhubarb and I have been conducting a relationship that can swing between love and hatred.'[76] Even in the face of a sumptuous tea in *The Riverside Villas Murder*, laid on by the omniscient detective, Colonel Manton, Peter pauses. The Colonel knows why: 'I quite realize you may not be able to dispose of everything absolutely down to the last crumb, but you're not to mind that. I'm an only child like you, and my mother spent most of her time giving me frightful drubbings for not getting through a side of beef at every meal.'[77]

Later in childhood, at an age even his mother found 'too old for force-feeding', Amis was subjected to 'mere verbal encouragement'. Eventually, a weird ritual developed 'whereby after some minutes I would say plaintively, "Mum, would you sort it for me?" And she would divide the unconsumed portion into what I was allowed to leave and what I *must* eat. Oh dear. The thought of it makes me quail even now, and no waiter can hope for my friendship if he draws attention to my less-than-empty plate.'[78] The almost uniform dismay with which food, plain English as well as fancy foreign, is greeted in Amis's novels is striking. From *Lucky Jim* onwards, eating is either an ordeal or a bore: 'He darted back to the sideboard, picked up a slippery fried egg and slid it into his mouth whole . . . Chewing violently, he doubled up a piece of bacon and crammed it between his teeth.' (In later passages the bacon Jim is offered is described as 'vermilion'.) Almost chief among the many things Jim objects to about Professor Welch's son Michel is that he spends the day 'stuffing himself with filthy foreign food of his own preparation, in particular, Dixon gathered, spaghetti and dishes cooked in olive oil . . . fit punishment for one so devoted to coagulated flour and water and peasants' butter-substitute, washed down, no doubt, by "real" coffee, of high viscosity'.[79] In *Take a Girl Like You*, Martha Thompson puts a plate of fish and potatoes in front of Jenny Bunn: 'The fish was probably haddock, with a horny, pimply skin. There were a lot of potatoes, and some unexpected colours to be seen among them here and there. They were steaming briskly. So was the fish.' Jenny copes with this meal by 'sucking at a few mouthfuls of fish as if they were toffees, until they were small enough to swallow. She looked down at her plate. On it was a lot of fish, haddock actually, almost as much as had been there when she began. In fact – although this could not be right – there seemed to be slightly more.'[80] These are representative instances, and the list could be extended right through to Amis's last novel. It is dumbfounding that he became a restaurant critic at the end of his life.

Amis's mother's main realm was the kitchen, and *she* wasn't undernourished. Philip Amis's sole memory of his paternal grandmother is of 'something fat in the kitchen'. Martin Amis's memories are only marginally more specific: 'a dark presence, richly embroidered, aromatic, calorific'.[81] Peggy Amis died in 1957, which accounts for the sparsity of these memories; her body was found in her bedroom, felled by a single stroke that rendered her, as Amis wrote to Larkin, 'dead before she hit the floor' (the exact words used to describe Mrs Davies's death in *You Can't Do Both*).[82] Amis remembers her as timid, gentle, nervous, yet also 'a great jam-making, cricket-tea-preparing figure'.[83] She had auburn hair, a fine complexion, and in the single early photograph I have seen, looks neither fat nor 'calorific'. In the *Memoirs*, Amis calls her 'by common consent an attractive woman'.[84] Mavis Nicholson, a pupil and friend of Amis's from Swansea, later a journalist and television personality, remembers her as 'pretty, dark, short . . . witty'. To John Amis, 'Auntie Rosie always smelt of face-powder and spoke in impetuous gusts, laughing immoderately with a curious hissing sound' (perhaps because of a weak heart, or the cigarettes she smoked, or both).[85] To Hilly, Amis's first wife, she was 'rather good fun', 'always prepared to help out in the kitchen'. But she could also be 'very judgmental' ('You should have the nappies on the line by now . . .') and was often bewildered by the chaotic domestic life of her son and his family.

Furnishings were Peggy Amis's responsibility as well as food, and like the food they were bland, unremarkable. Hilly remembers the interior of the Amis family home (in Berkhamsted by this stage) as both comfortable and pin-neat, with lots of chintz, bunny-rabbit ornaments, porcelain figurines. 'There was nothing of value at all in the house, I would say. But *they* valued the house, they thought it was lovely.' Whether Amis's lifelong indifference to his surroundings was innate or a product of an early environment like this, is impossible to tell. Occasionally in his fiction he pronounces on specific items of interior decoration, as in the 'awful pretend-velvet curtains and gold-bordered pelmet' found in the Davies' parlour in *You Can't Do Both*. But the look of things like sofas and chairs is mostly ignored or only very generally and instrumentally evoked.[86] In *The Riverside Villas Murder* we learn almost nothing about the interior of the Furneaux household, in a novel lovingly littered with period detail (gleaned both from memory and from a month's back numbers of *The Times*, *Punch* and the *Radio Times*), from Turban cigarettes, to 'Geraldo and His Gaucho Tango Orchestra' (performers Peter's father suspects of being 'no nearer South America than Golders Green or Stepney'),[87] to Anzora hair oil.

Peggy Amis may have been timid and nervous outside her circle, but within it she was thought of as 'good fun', 'jolly', 'fond of a giggle, a fag, a gin and tonic'.[88] Nor was she incapable of standing up for herself or making enemies. She did not, for example, get on with her sister-in-law, John Amis's mother, and the feeling was mutual. 'She had committed the unforgivable sin of pipping mother to the post in the maternal stakes,' cousin John explains, 'Kingsley being born just a few weeks before I was.'[89] Within John Amis's family 'Auntie Rosie' was thought of as 'impulsive and a bit flighty', 'not terribly trustworthy' (for no reason he can remember). This is not an impression others seem to have shared. Even in those passages in the *Memoirs* in which Amis recalls his mother's mysterious male admirers, or explains her rivalrous feelings towards her younger sister, Dora, there is no sense of her as unreliable or out of line. The admirers never laid a finger on her, Amis is 'quite sure';[90] his grandmother had shown favouritism to the younger Dora, and Dora was understandably resented. The only time Amis presents his mother's behaviour as the least bit unconventional is when she stands up to his father and future parents-in-law directly: a rare and heroic occurrence, occasioned by their threats of excommunication and boycott when Hilly's pregnancy before marriage is discovered. In *You Can't Do Both*, Robin's mother takes a comparable stand over Nancy's pregnancy. But she also mediates between father and son in less dramatic ways, even abetting minor deceptions. On Saturday mornings, while the father is at work, she leaves Robin alone, 'letting it be thought he had spent the time with her or in her charge'. She is also much given to sympathetic looks, squeezes of the hand, outings and chats. Though Robin is 'not the sort of boy to admit to loving his mother', the 'surge of liking' he feels for her at such moments sounds like love.[91]

Like her husband, Peggy Amis had a good singing voice, and her 'attractive mezzo-soprano' was often heard at the musical evenings Amis remembers as an important ingredient of his parents' social life. This social life was not without variety: dinner-dances, Tennis Club and constituency Conservative Association parties and events, invitations from neighbours, family parties and visits (Barchester, where William Amis's parents lived, was half an hour away by bus, Lowth Road in Camberwell, where Peggy's parents and Aunt Dora lived, two bus rides away). John Amis recalls a family party in 1927, probably at Barchester, when cousin Robert and Aunt Gladys were visiting from America. The three over-excited five-year-old cousins, Kingsley, Robert and John, were seated on a sofa, and one was sick all over it. Neither John nor Robert can remember which of the cousins was the culprit. Robert's sole memory of family parties is of the terrifying appearance of his grandparents: 'like something from Transylvania. I'd never seen anything like it in my life.' In the *Memoirs* Amis describes similar feelings of fear and revulsion, as does cousin John in his memoirs.

Parties at home mostly involved neighbours. Indoor evening hospitality took the form of bridge rolls filled with cress or fish paste. Most drinking took place in the pub, yet the house was not without drink: his mother kept a small bottle of gin, 'and there was Empire burgundy – *Keystone*'. When Amis went to France in 1945 and was offered decent wine for the first time he refused it, 'thinking, you see, of the Keystone'.[92] As for visits to neighbours, Amis remembers several. The man next door, at 9 Ena Road, promised to open his bottle of champagne on the day he became a senior manager at Liberty's. As Amis recalls, 'the day came and *we* didn't see any of the champagne'.[93] This neighbour subsequently moved to more affluent Purley, where Amis and his family would visit him. After the visit, he would drive the family back only as far as the bus stop, never to Norbury itself, a journey of some ten extra minutes. Among other neighbours, Amis lists 'Billy Mingo, Mrs. Apps, the Coatses, and Mrs. Nurser, who had no husband, which I found so interesting'.[94] The Coatses were Catholic, which worried Amis (especially when their son Dennis showed him a picture of a sacred bleeding heart). Mrs Nurser sounds as if she may have been the seed for dangerous Mrs Trevelyan in *The Riverside Villas Murder*; Billy Mingo for Bobby

Bailey, from the poem of the same name, although Amis told Eric Jacobs that he had borrowed the name from 'a small-time pimp in Swansea'.[95]

'Bobby Bailey' offers a verse equivalent of the scenes between Peter and his friend Reg in *The Riverside Villas Murder*. In poem and novel the pleasures of childhood are depicted as both innocent and transgressive. The poem is set some time before 1935, when Amis was not quite in his teens.

> Norbury Avenue. And there's Bobby Bailey's –
>   Flagged pathway, tall front door;
> What super fun to just turn up, and find him
>   Sprawled on the playroom floor.
>
> Toppling West Kents, Carabineers, 5th Lancers
>   With a mad marble-barrage,
> Doling out Woodbines, Tizer and eclairs in
>   The loft above the garage,
>
> Or mouthing *Shitface!* at his sister Janet,
>   Vision so rarely seen,
> Slightly moustached, contemptuous, fine-featured,
>   Full-breasted, and sixteen.

What is celebrated here is the freedom to 'just turn up', 'sprawl', 'topple', as well as to smoke, curse, binge on sugary treats, and evade adult surveillance. 'They're very nice, your parents,' Philip Larkin once said to Amis, 'but they never leave you alone, do they?'[96] Here are two corroborating instances from the correspondence with Larkin: 'You must be mad to think I can come to London on the 30th,' Amis writes on 22 December 1951: 'Of course I'd like to come and resent not being able to, but don't you realise dear man that my progenitrix and her husband will be here then, and Oh Pud stay and see the New Year in with us and Oh Pud we don't often see you and Oh Pud we shan't be here much longer, quite apart from the fact that Hilly wouldn't stand being left alone with them, nor would it make me easy in my mind if she were.' 'Pud', here, a family nickname, comes from 'puddies' or fingers, which Amis's mother was always telling him to wash before meals. A similar maternal plea for total attention is sarcastically recounted in a letter of 9 February 1948: 'Next week-end Hilary and I are going to Berkhamsted. My mother wants us to arrive there on the Friday evening and stay until the Monday morning, so that we can have the maximum time there. There won't be much to do, of course, but the four of us will be quite happy, I expect, on our own, in the family circle.' Such (to Amis) pointless sociability, his sense of being fussed over, smothered (at twenty-six as at twelve), may account in part both for a lifelong desire to let loose in violent reaction, and for the projection of repressed violence on to the world. In *Lucky Jim* the reader is offered ample explanation for the hero's aggressive imaginings. Among other things, Jim Dixon is on probation at his job, subject to the whims of an idiot boss, somehow unable to extricate himself from the terrible Margaret. When he dreams of pushing a bead up Margaret's nose, or beating the boss around the head and shoulders with a bottle until he explains why he gave his sons French names, the novel itself offers all the explanation the reader needs. But the impulse to write about a man who feels as Jim feels, and the ability to do so from the inside, derive partly from Amis's own family background.

In Amis's accounts of this background in interviews and conversation a single moment of parental neglect or inattention is said to have played a formative and disabling role in later life. From childhood onwards Amis suffered from night terrors and screaming fits. When asked about these (by Hilly, and by Eric Jacobs) he attributed them to a wrong answer he gave his father when he was 'eight, nine or ten'. The parents had been invited out for the evening and the father had asked: 'Do you need a babysitter?' Amis's reply was 'No', but 'I should have said "I think I should have one."' When left alone that night he remembers having 'the feeling that someone was going to climb in the window and murder me'.[97] From this moment on, Amis claims, he was frightened of the dark, of being alone, of being shut up, as in a lift – or an aeroplane, ten being the age of his first and only aeroplane flight, 'a five-bob flip' in a D.H. Dragon Rapide at Croydon Aerodrome, then London's main airport. In his account of this flight, in Jacobs's biography, it is the sense of the ground not being where it should be that terrified Amis; when describing it in correspondence, he also associates the flight with feelings of claustrophobia, of being cut off from help, denied exit. In *The Folks That Live on the Hill* (1990), the Amis-like hero, Harry Caldecott, describes a comparably upsetting and formative experience, again at ten. Young

Harry is reading about soldiers at the front, comes across a passage which describes their existence as 'ninety nine per cent boredom and one per cent fear', and recognises 'straight away that that was a kind of description of his own life. At school, though he had not really known it at the time, he had tried to cover up the fear part by being the silly one, but this had stopped being any good by the time he was about twenty.'[98]

The Folks That Live on the Hill is concerned at moments with the question of genetic inheritance. Harry's ex-wife's niece, Fiona, is an alcoholic. It has been suggested to Fiona that she looks just like a great-aunt who was also an alcoholic. One of Harry's several good deeds in the novel is to discover the untruth of this sugges-tion and communicate it to Fiona. *The Folks That Live on the Hill* appeared in 1990, the year before Amis's *Memoirs* were published. In Chapter 1 of the *Memoirs*, entitled 'Family', the question of genetic inheritance is raised implicitly not only through Peggy Amis's superstitious refusal to be known by her given names, but through Amis's extended or set-piece accounts of his maternal Aunt Dora and his paternal Uncle Leslie. These accounts are also cautionary tales and help to explain Amis's sometimes ruthless treatment of his parents, from the early years of his marriage right through to his father's death in 1963.

Aunt Dora was 'the star of Lowth Road, my knockout rela-tive'. She was some five years younger than Amis's mother, and though always nice to her nephew, made him wary, in part because 'uneasiness radiated from her',[99] in part because of the 'envy and resentment' she inspired in his mother. Dora's peculiarities were those of an obsessive-compulsive: she was forever picking up dirt and debris from the floor, oblivious to whatever else was going on or being said at the time; she also had a phobia about matches, which she never thought satisfactorily extinguished. She would pick dead matches out of ashtrays, whisk them off to the kitchen, and drown them under the tap. This odd behaviour, Amis wrote, 'did little to alleviate the fears of madness which have worried me from time to time throughout my life'[100] – and which appear in unexpected moments in the *Memoirs*, as in the several para-graphs Amis devotes to the claim that masturbation leads to insanity ('Having raised the question I thought it might be worth doing a little digging into the matter . . .')[101] or his offhand remark that the Denmark Hill chapel where his grandfather played the organ was near the site of what is today 'the celebrated and capacious Maudsley mental hospital'.[102]

But eccentric behaviour was only part of Dora's story, and of what made that story so vivid for Amis. Dora had been briefly married but soon returned to live in Lowth Road (according to Amis's father, because her mother had sabotaged the marriage by spreading false rumours about the fidelity of Dora's husband). Dora then spent much of her life looking after her mother (whom Amis hated, in part because of her treatment of her husband, the one grandparent he liked). When Dora's neurotic symptoms grew more pronounced, she was placed in an institution. Here she 'flourished', becoming a valuable assistant in its kitchen and canteen. One day news was conveyed to her of her mother's death and 'from that moment all her neurotic symptoms disappeared forever'. This sudden cure Amis calls 'one of those events you can do little with except be mightily struck by it'. Dora was released from the institution as a patient but stayed on to work in and help manage its kitchen. Eventually she was offered a top catering job in a large London teaching hospital, but on the point of taking it, died – 'all too cruelly soon after achieving her freedom'.[103]

The story of Uncle Leslie, a paternal uncle, also involves 'abnormality' and the baleful influence of parents. Leslie was the youngest of Joseph James and Julia Spinks Amis's three sons and the only one never to marry. He was also the only son to go into the family glass business (John's father, James Preston Amis, worked for Seligman Brothers, a City bank). When Dadda or Pater died, at over seventy, the business he had built was already in decline, partly on account of competition from large chain stores such as Woolworths. Leslie presided over its demise, while simultaneously caring for his aged mother, described by Amis as 'a large dreadful hairy-faced creature who lived to be nearly ninety and whom I loathed and feared'. Barchester was sold and mother and son set up house together a little further south of Purley, in Warlingham. In the *Memoirs* Amis describes Uncle Leslie's life as follows:

His routine took him every weekday evening from the commuter station to the pub opposite, where he would tank up sufficiently to face Mater's company till her bedtime. After supper on lighter evenings he drove her to the same or another pub. Unwilling or unable to get out of the car, she would be fetched glasses of port, though whether he used to climb back aboard to drink beside her or returned to the pub for some sort of company I have never tried to discover.[104]

Leslie was a serious drinker, even more so than Dadda, whose breath always smelt of whisky. He also once told Amis's father that he fancied men. But when Mater finally died, Leslie closed down what was left of the business, went on a world cruise, and, as John Amis's father put it to cousin Robert, 'got *sexy* . . . went quite *sexy*, you see'. When Amis's father felt his son was old enough to hear him speak freely about such matters, he confirmed this account. 'With much amusement and fragments of envy and admiration', the father revealed that, 'according to report, Leslie had fucked every female in sight'. But Leslie, too, died soon after his 'release' or 'cure'. Thus both portraits make the same implicit point, about the dangerous influence of parental constraint. Nor was this a point that Amis only came to late in life, while at work on the *Memoirs*. The portrait of Uncle Leslie begins: 'As I grew to adolescence I was able to picture his horrible life.'[105] In other words, Amis first pictured Leslie's life at precisely the period when he and his father 'violently quarrelled at least every week or two for years'.[106] When Amis resists parental wishes and constraints – or constraints of any sort – he is driven mostly by love of pleasure. Nice things *are* nicer than nasty things, as he often insisted. But in addition to depriving one of nice things, constraints such as those parents apply may also have been associated by Amis with much more serious deprivations, as in these instances: of sanity, sexual normality, life itself. That there is an element of fear beneath Amis's appetite for freedom and pleasure may help to account for the violence with which they are pursued.

2

Reading and Writing

Amis started writing at a very early age. When Philip Larkin told an interviewer that he himself had begun writing 'at puberty, like everyone else', Amis was astonished. 'He left it until puberty? I'd been writing for years by puberty.' It was Amis's mother who got him started: 'I can remember at seven or eight saying to my mother that I had nothing to do and she suggested that I write something, not because she wanted to encourage me to be a writer but just so I might amuse myself.' On rainy afternoons, when bookless or bored with reading, Amis not only wrote stories but produced little comics, tracing drawings in newspaper advertisements and making up tales to go with them. He also wrote poems, based on those he'd read at school or in books he'd been given by his parents.[1] 'I wanted to be a writer,' he told Eric Jacobs, 'before I knew what that was.'[2] That he did not know what a writer was reflects the world he was born into, 'as unconcerned with literature as most lower-middle-class children must have been in the South London of the years that followed the First World War'. In the Norbury of Amis's youth, 'I would as soon have expected to fall in with a Hottentot as with a writer.'[3]

Yet his home was not without books. Amis describes his mother as an 'inveterate' reader,[4] though not literary. Her tastes in fiction ran to 'good trash'.[5] In the *Memoirs* Amis names Norah C. James and Ann Bridge as authors his mother favoured.[6] In a letter to Larkin of 25 September 1946, he passes along 'a little service' his mother would like Larkin to perform for her: 'She doesn't know the names of enough men and ladies who put down words for people to read, and this hampers her at Boot's[7] because they always give her the wrong ones and she doesn't find 8 [out] till she gets them home. Could you therefore . . . suggest a few names?' Amis lists Hilda Lewis, Philip Gibbs, Ethel Mannin, 'W.S. Maugham ("as long as he isn't too near the bone")', Margaret Lane, Gilbert and Pamela Frankau and Daphne du Maurier as novelists his mother likes, and Naomi Jacob and Ruby Ayres as novelists she doesn't like. 'In other words she likes writers who pretend to write well rather than those who don't bother to pretend.'

Writers who don't bother to pretend sometimes produce what G.K. Chesterton calls 'good bad books', a phrase George Orwell used as the title for a 1945 essay on contemporary middlebrow reading habits. *Uncle Tom's Cabin* is a 'good bad' book, as is Rider Haggard's *She* or the Sherlock Holmes stories.[8] Books of this sort would find a staunch supporter in the adult Amis. His mother's favourites belonged in a different category, one identified in an earlier Orwell essay, 'Bookshop Memories' (1936). In this essay Orwell partly recounts his experiences working in a lending library of the sort Amis's mother frequented: 'the usual "twopenny no-deposit" library of five or six hundred volumes, all fiction'. The most frequently borrowed books from the library Orwell worked in were not by Priestley, Hemingway, Walpole or Wodehouse, but by Ethel M. Dell, followed by Warwick Deeping. Authors like Ethel M. Dell produced 'the average novel – the ordinary, good-bad, Galsworthy-and-water stuff which is the norm of the English novel'. 'Good-bad' novels had literary pretensions, unlike 'good bad books'. Their readers, Orwell claims, were exclusively female; males read 'either the novels it is possible to respect or detective novels'.[9]

In the *Memoirs*, Amis lists the writers his father read as R. Austin Freeman, Francis Grierson and John Rhode, detective novelists 'from the middle part of the spectrum'. Though this list is 'not exhaustive', it still 'seemed and seems to me woefully short, especially for somebody by nature neither stupid nor incurious'.[10] Though not as censorious of his son's reading as of his music – reading at least made no noise – Amis's father still viewed it with suspicion. Why, the son imagines the father thinking, 'ruin my eyes over a book when I could have been out in the fresh air (working off the impulse to masturbate)'.[11] To Amis's father, not reading was a matter of manners as well as health: 'reading in public was deemed rude, while reading in private was anti-social'.[12]

Among Amis's wider family only his maternal grandfather, George Lucas, was interested in literature. He was also, as has been said, the only grandparent Amis liked. Grandfather Lucas bought and read books of verse as well as fiction, including the collected works of all the major English poets. Part of a room in his little house in Lowth Road in Camberwell was lined with these books. Amis remembers his grandfather reading aloud from *The Prelude* and other favourites, while 'Gran' made mocking faces and gestures, a habit 'which helped to make me hate her very much'.[13] Grandfather Lucas died when his grandson was only 'seven or eight', round about the time the grandson began writing. Amis hoped to inherit part of his grandfather's library but Gran only allowed him five volumes, insisting that he write 'from his grandfather's collection' on the flyleaf of each. He chose Coleridge, Byron, Shelley, Wordsworth and Keats, and still possessed the Coleridge at the time of his death in 1995.

Amis could remember only one other figure from his Norbury youth who was the least bit literary. This was his mother's admirer 'Uncle' Tommy, a family friend who would bribe young Kingsley with a Mars bar whenever he showed up unexpectedly (and without his elderly wife) at the Amis home. Uncle Tommy subscribed to *John o' London's Weekly*, a literary magazine 'of the Jack-Squire-Jack-Priestley persuasion', and had what seemed to Amis a lot of books, including one or two 'in the Tauchnitz edition, a Continental imprint specialising in stuff considered too dirty by British publishers'. *Lady Chatterley's Lover*, young Kingsley quickly ascertained, was not among them, but 'a then almost equally illustrious monument of supposed filth, Aldous Huxley's *Point Counter Point*, was – in two volumes'. On a later occasion, the Huxley novel provided Amis with 'perhaps the greatest literary disappointment I have ever suffered'. Having secured an entire afternoon free from parental interruption, he settled down with the novel for what 'I confidently foresaw as a banquet of obscenity, only to realise after not very long that the stuff was about as arousing as the *Magnet*, a number of which I hope I had the sagacity to hold in reserve.'[14]

The influence of the *Magnet*, a boys' magazine, if not of *Point Counter Point*, is clear from the earliest of Amis's writings that survive. These were assignments for his English master, Mr Ashley, written when Amis was eleven and twelve and in his last year at Norbury College, a small fee-paying primary school. Norbury College, founded in 1903, occupied a large double-fronted house near Pollards Hill South, just along the London Road from Amis's first school, St Hilda's. St Hilda's, though a girls' school, took boys in the lower forms. Amis stayed there very briefly, made no friends, but fell in love with the befringed and 'improbably elegant' Miss Barr, who took English. 'It is here, perhaps,' he jokes in the *Memoirs*, 'that we can date my first devotion to the glories of our literature.' At Norbury College, his first English teacher, Mr Waller, was less alluring, though most boys approved his preference for reading stories rather than parsing or sentence analysis. The sorts of stories Mr Waller liked 'were about the Great War ("I've copped it in the back, sir") or lethal espionage in Eastern Europe ("For God's sake shoot me and have done with it"). But I could get all that at home' – that is, in boys' books and magazines. What made Amis's next English teacher, Mr Ashley, stand out, was his youth, his 'direct eye', and the fact that he cared about poetry, 'including what was then fairly modern poetry (the Georgians)'.[15]

Despite the presence of Mr Ashley, and the appointment of T.A. Briggs, the long-time art master, as headmaster in 1932, Norbury College was neither particularly arty nor intellectual. It started off as an ordinary preparatory school and became a proper secondary school only in 1925, after examination by the Board of Education. The headmaster before Briggs was R.G.P. Howie, who in 1925 renamed the school Norbury College, a title with aspirations. Mr Howie was a Tory councillor and became a family friend of the Amises. William Amis would have approved his emphasis on exercise and fitness (the school had good playing fields at Pollards Hill) and on producing 'all rounders', defined in a 1932 article about the school as 'those who are good both at work and games'. Every summer term the school awarded a silver cup, inscribed with the motto '*Mens sana in corpore sano*', to the best all-rounder, with half the points coming from schoolwork and half from sport. There were also prizes for work alone (among them a copy of *The Zoo and Aquarium Book* inscribed 'FIRST PRIZE, Awarded to K.W. Amis, Form 4A, Norbury College, 1932'), and much was made of the school's successes at open examinations, but Norbury College was no forcing house. 'The old idea of driving is gone,' Briggs told the local newspaper. 'We try to make them feel we are going along the same line they are going.'[16] In the *Memoirs* and elsewhere, Amis remembers the school fondly. Though not much good at games or handicrafts (incompetent even when devotedly gluing together

$^1/_{72}$ scale models of the S.E.5a, Fokker Triplane and Camel aero-planes from wood-and-wire construction sets), 'in everything else I was fine'.[17] It was at Norbury College that he learned to like school, both in class and on the playground. He even fell in love again, this time with the headmaster's daughter, 'a gay girl who had a fringe [as had Miss Barr] and liked Gracie Fields and Henry Hall'.[18]

Amis's writings at Norbury College survive in a single notebook and consist of poems, a précis of a passage from Herodotus, a précis in dialogue form of a scene from *The Merchant of Venice*, and stories, mostly on set topics.[19] That so many assignments take the form of stories is likely to have been a matter of choice. When asked to write on 'Faith', for example, Amis chose to dramatise the tale of Damon and Pythias, whose faithful friendship reforms the brutal tyrant of Sicily (Dionysius of Syracuse in the classical legend). As is the case with almost all the assignments in the notebook, this one is written in the clearest of hands, contains no spelling mistakes or grammatical errors, receives a high mark (nineteen out of twenty), but is still clearly the work of an eleven-year-old, or a young twelve-year-old. When Pythias's father is killed by the tyrant, his son reacts indignantly: 'At this Pythias went to the capital, and told the ruler exactly what he thought of him.' Other endearing moments betray writerly ambition, as in the line, '"Hands up," he emitted', taken from an untitled story in epistolary form, introduced by a familiar romance or adventure story preamble: 'These letters were found in a dug-out near Mons. How they got there is unknown. It is known, however, that Johnson was killed in action in 1918, and Miles died from his wounds after the War.'

Other stories begin no less melodramatically: 'As the dawn broke over the desolate world, a hunting horn rang out'; 'Above the sand-dunes there rose the towers of a city, gleaming white in the pitiless sun'; 'From out of the impenetrable blackness of the autumn night came a stage-coach, headed by two splendid jet-black horses.' This last opening comes from an early assignment in the notebook enti-tled 'Norbury and District 17th Century', an unpromising topic, one would have thought, for an adventure-mad eleven-year-old. Yet Amis produces a masked highwayman ('"Stand and deliver," said the figure in a deep voice'), sinister atmospherics ('a lightning-flash stabbed the heavy clouds'), even a daredevil escape. The story ends: '"Croydon," he gasped. "We are saved."' It is sometimes said that in later years we revert to the tastes and prejudices of youth. Towards the end of his life, Amis told his son Martin, the only books he could read were the sort that began: 'A shot rang out' or 'A scream rent the air' (or, the son added, contained sentences like: 'Later that night he took her again').

Only a very few assignments attempt humour. 'Manners Makyth Man' earned twenty out of twenty from Mr Ashley, but the vigour of its initial comedy, partly mocking pretension or presumption, soon gives way to something more conventional:

There came a deafening tattoo on the front door knocker, and Mrs. Chuggins put her sewing on the pseudo-Jacobean chair, and rose to her feet. Crossing the imitation Turkish carpet, she came to the bogus oak door, and opened it. She went out, to return a few seconds later with something faintly resembling a boy. Its collar was awry, its hair was an impenetrable jungle, its face was dirty, its stockings were down, its coat was torn. 'Ho! 'arold you are dirtee.' Thus Mrs. Chuggins, standing with her hands on her hips, and gazing none too proudly at her son. 'What 'ave you been doin'?' 'Stopping a little boy from bein' licked,' piped the small apparition. 'That was *fine* of you, 'arold,' said Mrs. Chuggins, 'and who was the little boy?' 'Me,' fluted the vision.

A second comic story, 'A Boy', earns a rare low mark from Mr Ashley, but has its moments of subversive energy. The titular 'Boy', another cheeky chappy like ''arold', is messy, with matted hair, worn shoes and a satchel spilling books. He is joyous, because it is the last day of term, his happiness 'undimmed' by a school report described as 'like nothing on earth'. In other words, unlike his creator, whose school reports were invariably excellent, 'He was not a good boy, this boy.' The story concludes with the boy's return home, and catches something of his anarchic spirit, perhaps because Amis wrote it at the end of his own school year, after the presumably fraught business of earning a place, but not a scholarship, at City of London School. In the *Memoirs*, Amis describes himself in late 1934, only a few months after this story was written, as 'an undersized, law-abiding, timid person'.[20] Here is the ending of the story:

He came to his house, flung his books through the window, yelled: 'See you at 'ar-parse eight, mum. My report's on the winder-sill,' fell over the step, stumbled, recovered, dashed to the gate, vaulted it, and rushed off to join his friends, yelling, and screaming.

In the *Memoirs* Amis recalls only two of his compositions from primary school. The first was a 99-line blank-verse poem about the miracle of Santa Sophia at Constantinople, a set topic if ever there was one. It is dated 28 February 1934, so Amis wrote it when he was eleven. Mr Ashley gave it twenty out of twenty and pronounced it the best in the form, untroubled by its matter-of-factness and see-saw rhythms, clear from the opening lines:

> 'Twas in the days of Constantine the Great;
> That on a hill in fair Byzantium,
> The monarch, strong but vain, did plan to build
> In sight of all mankind, a stately church.

Behind such a poem it is hard to detect influence, but influence was already at work. It was Mr Ashley who introduced Amis to the poetry of Alfred Noyes, for example, author of 'The Highwayman', a poem Amis included in *The Amis Anthology* (1988), his 'personal choice of English verse'. As Amis writes in the notes to the *Anthology*, 'we tend to be most responsive to the poems we meet in our adolescence, and in my case, given the natural time-lag, those belonging to the period 1900–1920 would be likely to be over-represented among them'.[21]

By adolescence, here, Amis means early adolescence, even pre-adolescence; at least that is what is suggested by an anecdote concerning another *Anthology* selection, '1887', A.E. Housman's 'splendidly positive' poem commemorating Queen Victoria's Golden Jubilee. Amis first encountered this poem in his second year at the City of London School, when he was thirteen or fourteen. Already, he confesses, 'I suspected it of being ironical, so alien had anything and everything Victorian become at that stage . . . [I]t was years before I stopped being nervously on the alert for pomposities in "In Memoriam" and complacency in the works of Browning, apologising for Arnold's literariness and keeping altogether clear of Kipling and Newbolt (and, incidentally, trying to admire Hopkins).'[22] In the *Anthology*, the adult Amis deplores this schoolboy modishness, defiantly reinstating childhood favourites. Elsewhere, writing in 1985, he challenges readers 'to see if they can claim to be quite unmoved by "The Highwayman" and not stirred at any point by Charles Kingsley's "Ode to the North-East Wind," whose "jingoism" and fascist references to fox-hunting they are to do their best to overlook'.²³ He even finds room in the *Anthology* for four poems by Sir Henry Newbolt ('Play up! play up! and play the game!'), including 'He Fell Among Thieves', which, for all its 'large bits of class and empire', he calls, again in 1985, 'one of the greatest poems of the last hundred years'.²⁴ These judgements are provocations, but they are not only provocations. Though the adult Amis's poetical tastes were narrow, fair-minded readers of the *Anthology*, especially those weaned on modernist precepts, are likely to be grateful to Amis for introducing them to the poems he read in primary school, not least 'He Fell Among Thieves' and 'The Highwayman'.

The other Norbury College composition Amis mentions in the *Memoirs* was his 'first published work', a story of some 300 words (the length of most of the notebook stories) entitled 'The Sacred Rhino of Uganda'. This story appeared in the school magazine, no copy of which has been traced, and seems not to have been a set assignment. Amis describes Mr Ashley as having been 'properly sarcastic' about it, in particular about its 'taut impressionistic prose' ('He clutches at his side . . . pitches forward . . . unconscious').²⁵ Mr Ashley, like Amis himself, evidently had more patience for cliché, especially hard-boiled cliché; no sarcastic comment accompanies the sentence, 'He met me with the business end of a newish automatic', for example, from the epistolary story. As for the plot of 'The Sacred Rhino,' it concerns a certain 'Captain Hartly [*sic*]', who shoots the rhino, is set upon by 'native worshippers', and somehow escapes, Amis can't remember how. What Amis can remember is the story's first sentence: '"We must set out as soon as possible," said Captain Hartly to his son, Mark.' Opening a story with dialogue would nowadays be associated with Graham Greene, he comments, 'but people who'd read *Magnet* and the *Wizard* knew all about that'.²⁶

Magnet and the *Wizard*, and a host of other boys' magazines – *Gem, Chums, Rover, Modern Boy, Hotspur* – were at the centre both of Amis's early reading and of his writing. The 'tripe' Peter Furneaux is accused of poring over by his father at the beginning of *The Riverside Villas Murder* is an adventure story in the *Wizard*. Later in the novel Peter empties the contents of his school attaché-case on to the bed. In addition to his homework books there are 'copies of *The War of the Worlds* and *Carry on, Jeeves* from the form library, and that day's *Wizard*'.²⁷ A similar mix is found in the reading material Robin Davies, also fourteen, brings with him on a visit to relatives in Wales in *You Can't Do Both*: 'On a plain blue bedspread he laid out one by one *Just William*, *The Island of Dr. Moreau*, Durrell on algebra, *British Battleships*, a bound volume of *Chums* and, with a low growl of resignation, Bury's *History of Rome*.' Magazines like *Wizard* and *Chums* contained both school stories and adventure stories, following a pattern established by the older weeklies, *Magnet* and *Gem*, started just before 1910. The adventure stories were mostly set in exotic locales – the Wild West, the frozen north, the deserts of Arabia (the setting of one of Amis's stories for Mr Ashley); the school stories were set in fictional public schools (Greyfriars in *Magnet*, St Jim's in *Gem*). The main characters in the school stories were mostly fourth-formers, aged fourteen and fifteen; each story was between 15,000 and 20,000 words, complete in itself, though often connected to the previous week's story. The magazines were read by boys of all classes, but according to George Orwell, in his celebrated essay, 'Boys' Weeklies', written in 1939, they held a special appeal for pupils at non-ancient and cheaper private day and boarding-schools. Orwell himself worked briefly at one such school (while Amis attended another, CLS) and reported that 'not only did all the boys read the *Gem* and *Magnet*, but they were still taking them fairly seriously when they were fifteen or even sixteen. These boys were the sons of shopkeepers, office employees and small business or professional men.'[28]

The fantasies fed by the weeklies are recalled by Amis in a 1965 article on 'Childhood Heroes'. Amis's hero is the air ace 'Biggles', the creation of Captain W.E. Johns. 'Biggles' is Captain James Bigglesworth of the Royal Flying Corps, and many of his adventures appeared in the *Modern Boy* before transfer to hard cover. In recounting the appeal of Biggles, Amis offers glimpses of how his reading shaped his interior life while at primary school:

When I was ten or eleven, I was one of the leading imaginary fighter pilots of my era. My daytime addictions at that time were Russian cigarettes out of the machine at Thornton Heath Pond, bawdy conversation in the stable-like cloakrooms of Norbury College, the *Modern Boy*, bike rides and liquorice. But every night for what seemed like years I was in the thick of it in the bullet-torn smoke-filled skies above Arras or Bethune, lying on my side in bed with my legs lifted and extended in a posture supposed to be like that of a pilot's in the cut-away diagram of a Camel aeroplane I had seen in *Chums*.[29]

Part of the appeal Biggles had for Amis, who was small for his age, was his 'undistinguished physique'. Amis and his schoolmates also appreciated what he called the 'negative virtues' of the Biggles stories: 'no impossible feats and no heroics, no irrelevant scene-painting, no messages about character or England, no girls'. This is not to say that accuracy about air battles, or realism in general, was what Amis was after, even when reading aviation magazines such as the *Aeroplane*, the twenty-fifth birthday number of which Peter reads in *The Riverside Villas Murder*. 'What drew me to the Camel's engine was not an interest in machinery,' the adult Amis recalls, 'but an interest in what I would now call "romance"'. That Biggles was not superhuman licensed the romance: 'With his opportunities one might be able to do nearly as well.' Biggles was 'a knight of the air . . . at least as real as any other kind of knight I have read about'. Only when disbelief was suspended, though, could 'the central image of these adventures, the air battle between fighter aeroplanes . . . do its work unimpeded'. Whether this work survived twelve-year-old Amis's unhappy experiences at Croydon Aerodrome with the Dragon Rapide, he does not say. In the Biggles article, he rather underplays how much they frightened him, and says nothing at all about their impact on his fantasies: 'I didn't enjoy any of it, especially not the banking. Biggles wasn't there and I couldn't get to him inside my head.'

Fourteen-year-old Robin Davies shares eleven-year-old Amis's tastes in such stories. As he and his fellow pupils file out of assembly, Robin reflects on how different they are from the boys in the stories he likes:

These fictional boys either behaved like men of forty or carried on like comic lunatics or were wasters, scapegraces, bounders. Such characters smoked Turkish cigarettes, drank brandy and soda, ate duck and green peas, played poker for money and betted on the horses when they were not balancing pails of water over the door of the masters' common-room or setting fire to the Head's trousers on Speech Day. Sometimes they stole. Robin enjoyed such stories as he enjoyed tales of pirates or the Wild West, and had little time for stuff about licking the House cricket XI into shape, outwitting rotters and slackers, etc. But he was very well pleased with his own real school and tended to follow its rules and customs instinctively.[30]

In 'Boys' Weeklies' Orwell puts the case for the formative influence of childhood reading: 'It is probable that many people who could consider themselves extremely sophisticated and "advanced" are actually carrying through life an imaginative background which they acquired in childhood from (for instance) Sapper and Ian Hay. If that is so, the boys' twopenny weeklies are of the deepest importance.'[31] Amis would agree. Where he did not agree, calling Orwell's essay 'entertaining but characteristically fatuous',[32] was in its claims that the weeklies offered 'a perfectly deliberate incitement to wealth fantasy' and 'pumped into [their readers] the conviction that the major problems of our time do not exist, that there is nothing wrong with *laissez-faire* capitalism, that foreigners are unimportant comics and that the British Empire is a sort of charity-concern which will last for ever'.[33] To young Amis it was not snobbery, or primarily snobbery, that made the public school settings of these stories appealing: 'The attraction of the Greyfriars – St. Jim's kind of life, with its Eton suits, bizarre slang, prize cups, elaborate raggings, teas around the study fire, breakings of bounds, dormitory feasts and so on, was that it was remote, more than half-way to fantasy, and yet intelligible to any schoolboy.'[34] As for moral uplift or political indoctrination, 'I suspect that children's fiction pleases its intended readers best when they sense that their elders would find it utterly beneath their notice.'[35] Nor are children always passive or uncritical readers. The characters Amis liked, we recall, were not the ones he was supposed to like: not clean-living Harry Wharton of Greyfriars, but Loder of St Jim's, 'the rotter of the sixth'. Loder was the sort of boy who made fun of team spirit and football; his prototype was Flashman, the archetypal villain and bully from *Tom Brown's Schooldays* (1857), a character brilliantly reanimated as an adult by George MacDonald Fraser, a great favourite of Amis's in later years.

What Amis the adult reader owed most to his 'non-literary' upbringing was a habit of quick and independent judgement. 'For my friends and me,' he writes of his early reading, 'the written word had the same status as films, records, cricket, the wireless, aeroplanes: irresistibly attractive, to be swallowed whole and unthinkingly.' This is certainly the way Peter Furneaux reads. While he waits to be interviewed by Colonel Manton, Peter browses through a John Dickson Carr novel Manton has recommended. He only browses because 'it would be awful to get all caught up in the story and then not be able to follow it through'. But he does get caught up, over a passage about the differences between real-life and fictional murders: 'Bloody good, said Peter to himself, reading on.'[36] Peter's reaction is immediate and 'unthinking'. Amis not only judged like this when young, but valued such judgements throughout his life, as he explains in the 1974 essay 'Louis Armstrong and Tea at Grandma's'. This essay begins by describing his reading habits when he was Peter's age:

I never much considered the idea that certain kinds of written word might be somehow better than others until I was about fourteen, by which time one has done a very large part of one's literary growing-up (as of other kinds of growing-up). To be sure, there was English, there was *The Golden Treasury*, there was Shakespeare, but, as with everything else, that kind of stuff was either instantly like Louis Armstrong and Don Bradman (*Hamlet*) or instantly like museums and tea at Grandma's (*The Merchant of Venice*).

Immediacy of impact was always an important literary value for Amis, and he sought it out in writing from all periods. Even after teaching English at university for fourteen years, he was still able to declare that 'a book that I have to work at, to get into, to read another book about first, etc., is not the book for me. I will not make allowances: what do I care if they liked it that way then because there was no television.'[37] This bold confession isn't quite as philistine as it sounds. Amis is not saying that only books 'for him' have merit. *Jude the Obscure* has merit, 'is a great book, one of the greatest works of art of its splendid century. But its lack of immediacy, however indispensable to the attainment of all its other effects, is still a lack.'[38] Nor is the quality of immediacy incompatible with complexity: 'even the most complex pieces have immediacy too: Donne's *Songs and Sonets*, *Paradise Lost*. Donne I find myself in the end unable to care for very heartily; *Paradise Lost* is the greatest poem in our language, and the most difficult, and, without being the most attractive, nevertheless undiminishably attractive.'[39] Many would agree with this assessment of *Paradise Lost*, though how one comes to terms with the poem's difficulty, or takes the full measure of its attractiveness, without having to work at it, read other books (*The Iliad*, for example), or 'get into' its unconventional syntax, Amis does not say.[40]

Amis taught at universities from 1949 to 1963, a time when Practical Criticism was at its height, but his relative indifference as a reader or critic to questions of context, or his unwillingness to let such questions hobble judgement, was a childhood inheritance. In a letter of 29 February 1984 to Robert Conquest, Amis discusses literary value judgements in terms that recall Peter Furneaux's reactions as a reader, rather than the precepts of I.A. Richards. His target is a review by Blake Morrison, a writer elsewhere described as 'remarkably unpissy considering he's a youngster':[41] 'The trouble with chaps like that is they have no taste – I don't mean bad taste, just the mental organ that makes you say This is bloody good and This is piss is simply missing, and they have to orientate themselves by things like "importance" and "seriousness" and "depth" and "originality" and "consensus" (=trend).' Amis had little time for such orientating: 'I cannot much care if Swinburne influenced a lot of people, or if he was like Turner, or if Ruskin thought he was good. I am left, at the end, clutching almost the same handful of poems as the one I grabbed in youth.'[42] Amis's attitude to judgement or value, like his attitude to context, also had a childhood origin. When F.R. Leavis, the most influential literary academic in Britain in the 1950s, describes 'the common pursuit of true judgement', a phrase from T.S. Eliot, as 'how the critic should see his business and what it should be for him', or insists that the critic's 'perceptions and judgements are his, or they are nothing',[43] he is expressing views long held by Amis, and attributed by him to the sort of background this chapter has been tracing.

The nature and importance of childhood reading are considered by Amis in a 1974 essay on Chesterton's *The Man Who Was Thursday* (1908), which he calls 'the first grown-up novel I remember reading outside school'.[44] Amis first read *The Man Who Was Thursday* in 1935, when he was thirteen, having come to it through the Father Brown stories. When Chesterton died a year later, his was 'the first total stranger's death that meant anything to me personally'. Amis calls the novel 'a boy's book as well as a grown-up's book, along with *Hamlet* and *The Mill on the Floss*, and not along with *King Lear* and *Middlemarch*'. What he means by this distinction he finds hard to explain, except to say that 'a boy either gobbles a book up or throws it away,' and that adolescents categorise books 'as terrific or tripe'.[45] The opening of *The Man Who Was Thursday* is terrific: it 'caught me by the scruff of the neck', 'I was not merely hooked, I was bowled over.' Yet nothing especially exciting happens in the first few pages: two poets argue about art and anarchism in a suburban garden. This garden is ordinary enough, as are the quaint redbrick houses that surround it, but a strange sunset, one that seems, surreally, 'full of feathers and of feathers that almost brushed the face', suffuses the atmosphere, mingling with the glow from big Chinese lanterns hanging 'like some fierce and monstrous fruit' in the 'dwarfish' trees.[46]

When he first read *The Man Who Was Thursday*, thirteen-year-old Amis only partly understood the argument between the two poets in the opening pages. He knew he was 'for' art but had no very clear idea of what anarchism was, suspecting that it might be 'a sinister and alluring fantasy' invented by Chesterton himself. He did not, of course, do anything to corroborate or disprove this suspicion. 'I may have noticed indifferently that the book was first published in 1908.' So much for context. When the adult Amis rereads *Thursday* (he claims to have read it fifty times),[47] he knows what anarchism is and what is of value – also what is of its age – in the novel's account of anarchism: 'Chesterton foretold the shape of some of our present discontents.' Yet 'all in all, I rather envy the younger self of mine who thought that the bad men in *Thursday* were anarchists, or bomb-throwers, or political assassins, chiefly because they had to be somebody'.[48] He also writes wistfully of his adolescent reaction to the gathering facetiousness of the novel, which as an adult he finds irritating: 'as a lad I thought the fault was in me – a sadly dated reaction – or was reading too fast to notice'.[49] It is over the novel's improbabilities or impossibilities, though, that 'boy Amis and man Amis differ most sharply'. When the Council of Anarchists, whose members are named after the days of the week, breakfasts on an open-air balcony in Leicester Square just before a February snowstorm, and two days later it is hot at seven in the morning in the countryside near Calais, 'a juvenile defence works best: the open-air breakfast is fun, and the snowstorm is exciting, and every schoolboy knows (what grown-ups have forgotten) that France is much hotter than England'.[50]

Here and elsewhere in Amis's criticism, he champions a kind of experience that he feels is undervalued by the literary world. Though his accounts of adolescent reading are partly a lament for inevitable loss, they also point to qualities he believes to be perfectly compatible with more adult pleasures. These qualities he will systematically set about rehabilitating or reinventing in the middle years of his career as a novelist, but he valued them throughout his life. As he told an interviewer in 1974, speaking of the contemporary literary scene:

[T]he child and the adolescent parts of the reader of serious fiction aren't being catered to, as they were catered to by serious writers a hundred or more years ago. Dickens, for example, got a lot of child and adolescent into his books. I don't mean just his characters, though that's important, too, or his way of looking at things, but as covering the kind of appeal he made: trying to horrify you, trying to thrill you, trying to make you feel afraid, trying to divert you even at the most superficial level. One of the reasons why he's better than most of the people around is that the high-brow novel hasn't emerged yet. It *all* went in. So this really is a split which took place long ago. The action novel, the thriller, the ghost story, science fiction, the western, the stories of espionage and private eyes and all that kind of thing: all separate little streams. And then there's another stream which is the serious novel where the writer is sort of letting the side down a bit, if he includes something from the other streams.[51]

Only very briefly, in early adolescence, did Amis entertain 'high-brow' notions of seriousness. His musical cousin John remembers being floored by Amis's sophistication as a fourteen-year-old. John, who lived in West Norwood, made the occasional impromptu weekend or holiday visit to cousin Kingsley in Norbury, a trek of some three or four miles across Streatham Common. These visits were infrequent partly because the cousins' mothers did not get on, partly because of the trek (which is probably why Amis himself was never willing or permitted to reciprocate). The two cousins used to play records together in Amis's room, and once when John told Kingsley that he had been doing a little musical composition, Kingsley offered him some prose poems to set to music, 'in the style of Rimbaud'.[52]

From Alfred Noyes at twelve to Rimbaud at fourteen is a change that can be attributed to Amis's new school. In a 1978 essay on Kipling, Amis explains how he was influenced by literary fashion at CLS. It wasn't until the late 1960s that Amis really read Kipling. Until then most of what he knew he had picked up in his primary school years: a handful of poems from anthologies; the Jungle Books, 'which were likely to be pressed on one by uncles and such'; and *Stalky and Co.* (1899), Kipling's school story ('a school story by a famous writer. I thought: certain to be good. I was disappointed: though the word hadn't yet acquired that sense, I couldn't "identify" with any of the three lads'). As for exposure to Kipling at City of London, 'in those days living authors were seldom as much as mentioned in the class-room, but they were constantly discussed informally, at any rate at my school, by both masters and boys'. Kipling did not figure in these discussions, certainly not approvingly. He was considered 'vulgar, a writer of journalism and doggerel, a "word-smith"; so they said, but obviously what they meant was that he stood for England and the Empire, and that was embarrassing or worse; even as a schoolboy one could feel that'.[53] In the six and a half years he was at CLS Amis came across a bit more of Kipling's writing, 'largely I suppose in anthologies'. He admits to having been thrilled and frightened by 'those two strange and terrible stories, "The Mark of the Beast" and "At the End of the Passage",' and also to have read more of the poetry, including 'Danny Deever', which he calls 'about the most harrowing poem in the language'. The power of the poetry he sensed from the start, 'but I didn't do what I should have done and did do with other poets I first came to in anthologies and go in search of the *collected* poems: it must have been that old anti-imperialist prejudice still working away somewhere'.[54]

In *You Can't Do Both* Amis provides a fictional example of how such shifts in taste originate. When Robin and his parents visit their neighbours, the Carpenters, Robin meets their son, Jeremy, who is down from Cambridge for the weekend. Robin is invited to visit Jeremy's room and inspect his books and records (this is the scene in which the trumpeter's 'ferocious discord' is sounded, on a Louis Armstrong record). Jeremy has books by Aldous Huxley and D.H. Lawrence on his shelves, which gives Robin 'a little surge of excitement',[55] a lesser version of the charge the Armstrong record will produce. Jeremy offers to lend Robin some books: not the Lawrence, of course, his parents would not approve ('they've never read a word he's written but they know it's all filth'),[56] but some books of poetry, including a volume containing Auden's poem 'Get there if you can' (from *Poems*, his first collection, published in 1930), with its, to Robin, mysterious references to the hounding of 'Lawrence, Blake and Homer Lane'. Some months later, when they meet in Wales, Jeremy asks Robin what he's been reading. Robin answers by telling him about his schoolwork, but the older boy interrupts, mockingly: 'Good for you, young 'un, said Harry Wharton gruffly. What about those books I lent you, did you bring any of those?'[57] It is time, Jeremy is implying (not without calculation), for Robin to put aside childish things, by which he means not so much schoolwork as the *Magnet*, where Harry Wharton has his adventures and protects 'young 'uns' (a relevant theme in this context). A fourteen-year-old like Robin, at a school like Robin's, will still be reading *Magnet*, but now he'll be reading Auden as well. And Rimbaud, too.

3

City of London

Amis owed a great deal to the education he received at the City of London School, intellectually, socially and morally, a debt he handsomely acknowledged. The school opened in 1837, though it claims a more ancient origin. In 1442 a town clerk named John Carpenter, who had been MP for the City and a power in City politics (an executor of the will of Dick Whittington, Lord Mayor and London benefactor), bequeathed properties to the City 'to maintain . . . in perpetuity, four boys born within the City of London, who shall be called *Carpenter's Children*'.[1] These properties grew in value over the next four hundred years and when the school was founded by an Act of Parliament in 1834, the income they generated helped to provide its funding. The impetus for the creation of the School was a wider educational movement of the early 1830s, one which saw the establishment of schools by University College (1830) and King's College (1831), themselves only recently established (both are now part of the University of London, founded in 1836). All three schools served a growing middle-class demand for modern, non-denominational London day schools: modern in the sense that they offered instruction in other subjects as well as classics, non-denominational in that they placed no religious restrictions on entry, though boys were given religious instruction, with readings from the Authorized Version of the Bible and the Book of Common Prayer at assembly. This entry policy applied even to King's College School, though King's College itself had been founded as a direct Church of England response to non-sectarian University College. Many of the boys who attended the

City of London School in 1837 were from Dissenting or non-Anglican families, including Roman Catholic families, though few if any boys from Jewish families attended the school before 1840.[2] An early bene-factor, Sir David Salomons, the first Jew to be elected Sheriff of the City, founded the Salomons Scholarship at CLS in 1845 to commem-orate 'the removal of those disabilities which formerly attached to the Jewish subjects of this realm'.[3] The writer John Gross, who attended the school some years after Amis, remembers passing the bust of Salomons every morning on his way to assembly, at which, after announcements, Jews, Roman Catholics and other non-Anglicans would be absented from prayers.

Most of the boys who attended the school in the 1830s were the sons of City freemen or householders and lived within walking distance of its initial premises in Milk Street, near the Guildhall. One hundred years later, when Amis attended the school, as had his father and paternal uncles, boys came from farther afield, though in class terms the parent body was broadly similar. In 1922, the year Amis was born, 37 per cent of pupils had fathers who were clerks or commercial agents, as was Amis's father; 33 per cent had fathers who were wholesale or retail tradesmen, like Amis's grand-fathers; and 22 per cent had fathers who worked in the professions. In 1837, school fees were £8 per annum, roughly half those at the schools of University College and King's College. In 1934 fees were comparably modest: just £30 per term, £90 per annum. That Amis's father had difficulty meeting these fees (from a salary of £420 in 1934) did not make him unusual: in 1932, the fees of as many as 154 CLS boys were in arrears. The salaries of the teachers were often higher than those of the parents, as were their social back-grounds. In 1936 only one master at the School earned less than £400 (in addition to being able to educate his children free at CLS Boys or Girls), and the top salary was £830, for the senior master in charge of modern languages.[4]

The school's ties to the City were as obvious in 1934 as in 1837. CLS was governed by the City corporation, which set up commit-tees to oversee its finances and hiring policies. The Lord Mayor presented the prizes on speech day and doffed his cap to the school as he processed by it in the annual Lord Mayor's Show (accompanied by a contingent of CLS Officer Training Corps cadets, including Amis himself one year). The school badge and motto (*Domine dirige nos*) were the City badge and motto. Gross remembers being taught

Chaucer by Amis's favourite teacher, the Reverend C.J. Ellingham: 'When he took us through the *Prologue* to *The Canterbury Tales*, he was admirable at bringing the *pilgrims* to life. When he couldn't quite resist scoffing at the five guildsmen in the *Prologue*, with their prosperous City careers and their ambitious wives ("It is full fair to be yclept 'Madame'"), you wondered if he might not be working off a few subversive feelings about the school's Mansion House and Guildhall connections.'[5] In Amis's time at CLS there were more scholarship boys, mostly from London and Middlesex County Council primary schools, than there had been in his father's time. 'My fellows, I saw dimly, were drawn from a wide spectrum,' Amis recalls: 'accents varied from ones that discomforted me to ones that made me feel superior.'[6] Though the school counted a prime minister, Herbert Asquith (at CLS from 1864 to 1870), among Old Citizens, the preponderance of boys, Asquith included, came from the classes it was founded to serve: the middle and lower middle classes.

In 1934 CLS was located in what Amis describes as a 'rather oppressively dignified' brick and Portland stone building with 'lots of corridors and a vast agoraphobic playground'.[7] This building stands on the north bank of the Thames, just west of Blackfriars Bridge, on the Victoria Embankment. It is now the headquarters of the J.P. Morgan Bank, the present school having moved in 1984 to new premises on the Embankment, to the east of Blackfriars Bridge. Pevsner describes the older building's Renaissance style as 'amazingly unscholastic', but it was purpose-built in 1883, chosen in a competition from among fifty-three designs.[8] To get to it from Blackfriars station involved a walk of a hundred yards: up the station steps, past the prefect on cap duty (boys not wearing school caps were punished), past the white bulk of the Unilever building ('the imposing offices of a firm of industrial chemists', in *You Can't Do Both*),[9] to a side entrance on John Carpenter Street. Only in the sixth form were boys permitted to enter the school by the front steps leading on to the Embankment. Amis and his father caught the 8.05 train from Norbury and the journey took about an hour. Classes were over at 3.30, and unless he was staying on for games, which involved 'a horrible dog-leg journey'[10] from the school's playing fields in Grove Park to the parental home, or had OTC, which all boys joined at fourteen and which drilled at Wellington Barracks, or was attending some society or other (Music Society, School Society, League of Nations Union), Amis would be home at 4.30.[11]

When Amis entered the school, boys could opt for one of three 'sides' or areas of specialisation: Classical (Greek and Latin), Modern (French, German, Spanish, with some Latin) or Science (physics, chemistry, biology). Amis was on the Classical side, the fashionable side at the school, also the surest path to an Oxbridge scholarship or exhibition (in part because there were more scholarships and exhibitions in classics than in other subjects). In the *Memoirs* Amis writes that his father wanted him to have 'a more successful version'[12] of his own career: that is, to work in the City, but to make more money and to be socially more secure. Other boys from modest backgrounds, particularly Jewish boys (some 15 per cent of all pupils, Amis estimates), never considered going to university, unless they were planning to enter one of the professions. These boys often took languages on the Modern side, as did Denis Norden, an exact contemporary of Amis's at CLS, later a writer and broadcaster. Norden, whose father made bridal dresses, entered CLS on a scholarship. When his father's business prospered, the scholarship was relinquished. Then the business went bust. Norden's decision to enter CLS on the Modern side was influenced by his father, who had been at the Grocers' School, several cuts below CLS. His father was impressed that boys on the Modern side could take Spanish. In the 1930s, as Amis's father could attest from his experiences with 'the horrible mustard people', South America was considered the coming place, the market of the future. So Norden took Spanish, plus French and Latin (the only class he shared with Amis). Amis remembered him as glamorous and brilliant: 'The school intellectual. If I'd been asked to name a boy who might be a great writer or professor, I'd have mentioned Norden.'[13] Norden, though, saw himself as merely flash: the boys who were truly brilliant were mostly on the Classics side. This was the school's view as well, despite its pioneering role in the teaching of mathematics, science, modern languages and English literature. 'Until after the First War,' writes the school historian, A.E. Douglas Smith, 'the Classical Side were almost officially recognized as the aristocrats of the School and the School Captain was automatically a classic.'[14]

Part of what kept this tradition alive in Amis's day was the influence of the headmaster, F.R. Dale, 'the very model of a traditionalist', according to John Gross, 'if tradition is allowed to include tolerance, good sense and a considerable capacity for innovation'.[15] Dale came to the school in 1929 at forty-six, having previously been headmaster of Plymouth College (1920–29) and sixth form classics master at Leeds Grammar School (1906–16). He was educated at Oundle and Trinity College, Cambridge, where he was a major scholar and took a double first in the Classical Tripos. An officer in the Royal Welch Fusiliers, the regiment of Siegfried Sassoon, David Jones, and the Robert Graves of *Goodbye to All That*, he rose rapidly to the rank of Major, won both the DSO and the MC, for gallantry on the Western Front, and served as the company commander of a specialist sniper detachment. Dale was a distinguished scholar as well as a war hero: president of the London branch of the Classical Association, authority on Greek pronunciation, author of learned articles on the *Odes* of Horace. He was also good at games, impressing the boys by playing cricket with them at Grove Park. In other words, he was precisely the sort of figure a classical education was meant to produce: the English 'all-rounder'. 'While the Public Schools retain their quality,' he declared in a speech in 1942 defending the study of classics, 'there will always be some production of hand-made scholars, who begin with Latin verbs and Greek particles and end with some understanding of permanent values in human life and civilisation, because they have seen something of oratory and history, poetry and philosophy at its earliest and best. Such men are needed and valued, and not in the learned professions only.'[16]

F.R. Dale was 'worshipped' by the boys, but he was also taciturn, austere and forbidding. 'He listened well,' recalled C.E. Bond, who taught modern languages at the school, 'but could cut short any irrelevant loquacity with brutal finality.'[17] Gross remembers him as 'tall, lean and erect, with white hair, a dark moustache and a yellowish complexion, and he looked as hard as a walnut'.[18] Amis held him 'in terrified veneration'.[19] Norden thought he 'looked more like a headmaster than any headmaster who ever lived'. Peter Baldwin, a classicist a year below Amis (later Sir Peter, Permanent Secretary at the Department of Transport), attributed Dale's withdrawn manner to the war: 'four years in the trenches: you wouldn't forget that, would you?' To boys raised on stories of military bravery – by Kipling, Henty, John Buchan, Percy F. Westerman, and in the twopenny weeklies – he was a familiar heroic type. As a scholar, as Amis puts it in the *Memoirs*, he was also heroic: 'To hear him read Greek verse, observing tonic accent, metrical ictus and the run of the meaning all at once, was to be given a distant view of some ideal beauty as well as to marvel at a virtuoso . . . He was human, too. If ever a kind of man vanished for good, his did.'[20] And he was beloved by his staff. He behaved with them like a colleague rather than a boss; he left them alone to get on with their work; he staunchly supported them in disputes and campaigned on their behalf over pay. In his own teaching (mostly in the fourth and sixth forms) he was strict, but he was not without jokes and games, including what Gross describes as 'a rich repertory of insults and exhortations to jolly us along ("Village idiot! Doesn't know the way to the Spotted Cow")'.[21] Amis was good at imitating Dale, both his exhortations ('Get it right, not wrong. Black, not white. Cat, not dog') and reprimands ('Some boys,' began a much-requested mock-address, 'have been cycling on the Chapel roof').[22] When Norden won a school essay competition in the fifth form, he selected *The Collected Stories of Guy de Maupassant* as his prize book, a rather racy choice. Dale passed it to him 'with a slight lift of the eyebrow'.

Like all boys at CLS, Amis learned at least some science or English in each year prior to the sixth form. In his first few years he would have had something like three classes a week in English in comparison to nine in Latin and Greek. In the fifth form, at fifteen or sixteen, boys sat School Certificate examinations, the precursors of O Levels. Amis took eight such examinations (five were needed to attain the certificate), in Greek, Latin, English, scripture, history, French, elementary mathematics and additional mathematics. He achieved a pass with credit in all subjects. The classicists at CLS were somewhat superior about School Certificate, which had only been created in 1917 and was originally intended for grammar school pupils. It had to be passed, as two years later Higher School Certificate examinations, precursors of A Levels, had to be passed, but the examinations that mattered, the truly testing examinations, were for Oxbridge entrance and scholarship. Amis claimed to have passed his scripture paper for School Certificate almost by accident. He had done very little studying. On the morning of the examination he happened to read through some notes on the authorship of the Epistle of James. When just this topic appeared as a question on the examination paper he answered it and passed. In later years, Amis would deplore falling educational standards. A glance through the School Certificate examination papers for 1937 suggests why. All candidates for the scripture paper, for example, had to spend a third of their time translating passages from the Greek Testament

(Amis's answer to the question on the authorship of the St James Epistle accounted for only a sixth of his mark). On the English General Paper students were asked to answer questions on four of eight texts: 'Il Penseroso', *In Memoriam, Rewards and Fairies, She Stoops to Conquer, The Pilgrim's Progress, The Rape of the Lock, The Winter's Tale* and *Utopia*. In the English Books Paper the books in question were *Paradise Lost*, Goldsmith's *Selected Essays*, Wordsworth's poetry, and Carlyle's *The Hero as Poet, The Hero as Man of Letters*.

Almost the first of Dale's reforms when he arrived at CLS was to institute streaming, considered a progressive move in 1929. By 1934, all students, whether Classical, Modern or Science, were divided into A and B streams. Amis was in the Classical A stream, which meant that in the third form he studied Greek as well as Latin. B-stream boys on the Classical side stuck with Latin throughout. In addition to language and literature classes in Greek and Latin, Amis studied Greek history in the fourth form and Roman history in the fifth. In *You Can't Do Both*, he offers a glimpse of what he and his fellow pupils felt about these subjects and of what the work itself was like. According to Robin Davies, a pupil in C4A, Roman history was 'generally considered to be far worse than Greek, all about Corn Laws'.[23] Hence the sigh with which he unpacks Bury's *History of Rome* at the start of his summer holiday in Wales. The fifth-former from whom he had bought the book 'was going into the Maths Sixth and had taken his last look at [it] with ominous relief'.[24] As for Greek history, it was taught by 'Mr. Oakley' (the name of a real-life classics master at CLS, famed for his spooner-isms, as in 'A scoop of boy trouts').[25] In the novel's opening pages, after a lesson in which Robin learns all about 'the fateful night battle on the plateau of Epipolae',[26] Mr Oakley departs the class-room (the boys stay put) and Mr Pearson enters, for Latin unseen, a lesson in which boys 'went up to him in turn at his desk to have their last week's efforts briefly gone over; the rest of the time they translated one of his selections from the much-hated book they used for this purpose.' Robin, who will become a classics don at Oxford, is good at such lessons, as was Amis: his mark for the previous week's unseen is 'beta-alpha,' not bad for 'a rather tough week'. The present assignment, 'an almost insultingly easy couple of paragraphs of Caesar',[27] he finishes ten minutes early. For home-work that night Robin has a passage of *The Aeneid* to construe.

Weekend homework is finished by Saturday teatime, leaving only 'his *Alcestis* vocabulary to swot up in the train on Monday morning'.[28] At the end of the year Robin and the other boys in C4A will revise for, sit, and be marked on examinations 'of local importance only; School Certificate would not come until next year; even so, Robin performed well as usual, even at Scripture'.[29]

The classical fifth was a noteworthy year for Amis not merely because of School Certificate but because he would be taught by the Reverend C.J. Ellingham, the most remarkable of a remarkable group of classics masters at the school, including Oakley, Dale, J.B. Marsh ('Boggy', naturally) and P.J. Copping, 'who once captivated us all by replying with incomparable, table-turning deftness to a disingenuous question from Rigden about castration: "I don't know whether any of you have ever been to a horse-fair," the answer led off.'[30] Ellingham had come to CLS in 1924, aged thirty-two, from Dulwich College, where, from 1921, he had been an assistant master. While at Dulwich he also served as a deacon, then a priest, in Southwark. He was educated at Merchant Taylors' School and St John's College, Oxford, where he studied classics and theology and won several prizes, including the Craven Prize. He was a Navy signaller during the First World War and, when CLS was evacuated to Marlborough in 1939, drilled the boys in semaphore, Morse and other aspects of signalling, early instruction which may have encouraged Amis to join the Royal Corps of Signals in 1942. Amis describes him as 'tall, stooped, grey haired, with a terrifying glance'.[31] Leonard Richenberg, a friend from the same form, remembers Amis calling Ellingham 'the grim scribe', but also recalls Ellingham as 'very ready to laugh . . . [he] would relax completely when amused'.[32] Like Dale, he was charismatic. Or as Amis puts it: 'I suppose one has to use some crappy word like magnetism. You kept your eyes on him.'[33]

Ellingham had energy as well as magnetism. 'He wouldn't have liked me saying it,' Amis admits, 'but he was a muscular Christian, no shrinking violet.'[34] In the school magazines of the period, his activities are reported everywhere: chairing debates and societies, delivering talks, speeches, sermons, judging prize competitions, supervising games and giving dramatic readings. 'I overworked him,' Dale confessed in a 1957 speech at Ellingham's retirement, 'not only as yoke-fellow to H.C. Oakley in the Latin and Greek of CVI and CVA, but also as master in charge of the school's English . . . He was always, too, a working parson in the Church of England. His work as School Chaplain, too little used in London, flowered in Marlborough.'³⁵ Ellingham's capacity for work was remarked upon by Marsh, who taught Amis Greek in C3A. Marsh remembered how in summer terms Ellingham would be out at Grove Park every Wednesday and Saturday bowling endlessly for boys who wanted batting practice. In winter terms he supervised junior rugger: 'in which, by skilled refereeing, he stirred his panting teams to a final score such as 33 points to 31, leaving them only too eager for the next match in the following week'.³⁶

Ellingham took streaming to heart, dividing C5A into greyhounds and duds (or 'tortoises', according to another master, C.N. Vokins).³⁷ 'Well I suppose we'd better do this bit of Latin,' Amis remembers him saying. 'Let's start with the duds – Wainwright, you begin. Now White. Right, that's enough of the duds, let's have a few greyhounds – Amis?' These orders were issued jokingly: 'The duds weren't a bit upset,' Amis insisted. 'After all, he praised them generously. It was all entirely good-humoured and benevolent.'³⁸ To Dale, Ellingham was at his best with weaker boys: 'I remember Acton [a science master] saying to me that Adlam could get a chair-leg through the School certificate. Mr. Ellingham likewise had a remarkable understanding of the comparative duffer and he spared no pains to make him less so.' Marsh, too, commented on Ellingham's ability to interest less gifted pupils: 'I remember a Greek unseen which he wrote for the 5A describing in hilarious terms a rugger match between the Colts and Masters. All the names were translated syllable by syllable into Greek, so that the fascination of discovering the incidents was increased by the amusement of translating the names.'³⁹ It was characteristic of Ellingham to value rugby in part because 'the clumsy boy can make something of it. For soccer you must be adroit.'

On the occasion of his retirement, Ellingham wrote an article in which he confessed to having 'done some silly things' early in his career: 'I was dismayed at the low standard in classics reached by many of Classical Upper VI. I expected too many potential scholarship winners. When I learned that though we gain our share of scholarships, our real claim of honour is that we help to make men who are kindly and tolerant and unassuming and straight, I worried less about the howlers.'⁴⁰ Yet expectations remained high in Ellingham's classes. He thought duds as well as greyhounds could pass School Certificate, at least that portion he prepared them for, in one year rather than the standard two, using the time saved for lessons in general culture. He brought a gramophone into class and played classical records to the boys. He taught them about painting from a National Gallery catalogue. These lessons and the English classes he taught had a profound effect on Amis. 'He was passionate about art and poetry,' Amis recalled. 'I mean half the things I know now about art and music, I learnt then, from him.'[41] Though Amis gained important enthusiasms from Ellingham, he also discovered that 'certain avocations and interests were not for me: I had no graphic gift of any kind, the theatre was boring (though the cinema was not), you could keep Dadaism and all that, architecture ought to be comprehensively done away with'.[42]

It was as a teacher of literature and composition that Ellingham mattered most to Amis. Like Dale, Ellingham was famed for quoting long passages of poetry he had learned by heart, a talent Amis himself acquired. Marsh remembers coming across a statue by Munnings while out on a walk with Ellingham and others. On its plinth was carved the line: 'He has outsoared the shadow of our night.' Ellingham laconically identified the quote ('Shelley: Adonais'), then quoted the other eight lines of the stanza. When his friends expressed astonishment (*Adonais* is fifty-five stanzas long), Ellingham replied: 'Well, I always liked that poem.'[43] Ellingham's example was reinforced by school policy and teaching methods. Dale, for example, insisted that the boys choose Shakespeare for school plays, since memorisation ensured 'that it would remain with them for life'.[44] Eric Rogers, a year below Amis, remembers having to memorise a passage in *The Aeneid* on his first day in Classics 4A. Seventy years later he could still recite it from memory. When Martin Amis became a writer, he and his father often talked late into the night about literature and other matters. The son would marvel at the father's memory: '"My God. He knows *all English poetry*." Ten lines here, twenty lines there, of Shakespeare, Milton, Marvell, Rochester, Pope, Gray, Keats, Wordsworth, Byron, Tennyson, Christina Rossetti, Housman, Owen, Kipling, Auden, Graves, and of course Larkin.'[45]

Ellingham shared something of Dale's literary tastes as well as his teaching methods. Marsh remembers Dale praising the vernacular passages in *The Waste Land*: Eliot 'gave the language of the woman in the pub without putting a word wrong'.[46] According to Rogers, Dale read the poem beautifully, then threw the book down and denounced it as 'bloody pessimistic trash'. Ellingham had comparably mixed feelings about modernist writers. Though he admired *The Waste Land*, he had little time for Pound, partly because of what he identified as inaccuracies and illiteracies in Pound's 'adaptations' from the Latin. Ellingham gave Amis an offprint of an article he had written about these adaptations, which Amis found 'most readable'.[47] It was Marsh who introduced Amis to the very latest writers. In the fourth form, he lent Amis copies of Auden and MacNeice, 'but I made nothing of them at that time, 1936–37'.[48] In the same year, in January 1937, Ellingham read a paper to the School Society on 'The Decline of the Novel', in which he argued that 'writers today have a morbid and pessimistic bias, that they cannot conceive sympathetic heroes and that hardly any are capable of executing a psychological treatment of real characters'.[49] This paper may have been a response to a paper delivered to the School Society in October 1936 on James Joyce's *Ulysses*, a remarkable choice for discussion in a school. The *Ulysses* paper was delivered by a sixth-former, P.M. Fraser, later a Fellow of All Souls, at an evening session of the society restricted to its 'senior section'. In an account of this session, the school magazine describes Joyce as the 'most unorthodox in style and subject of British writers', and the session's large audience as 'attracted by the inimitable Joyce or the inimitable Fraser, who had grown his hair long for the occasion . . . The discussion was very spirited.'[50]

The discussion after Ellingham's talk was also spirited and the audience almost as large, including 'a number who had imbibed his teaching and come up for more'.[51] Ellingham's position on the modern novel was conservative, but open to debate; the School Society was a forum for such debate. Though Amis called him 'the man who actually taught me most', he was never an Ellingham clone or creature. In December 1939, despite several years' exposure to Ellingham's tastes, Amis published a prose poem in the school magazine, the sort he had wanted cousin John to set to music. The poem's appearance, Amis writes in the *Memoirs*, 'drew Ellingham's proper contempt'.[52] Amis took a while to come round to Ellingham's literary preferences, and some he never accepted (T.E. Lawrence, for example), but a taste for strong opinion openly argued they shared from the start. When in February 1940 a recently appointed English teacher, Mr Sharp, read a paper to the School Society on G.K. Chesterton, the school magazine reported that his ranking of 'The March of the Black Mountain' over 'Lepanto' occasioned controversy: 'Mr Ellingham, who was in the chair, disagreed and proceeded to read "Lepanto" for the sake of those who were unacquainted with it. There followed some heated argument, which had to be cut short as it was getting late.'[53] Amis suggests the likely nature of the argument in a note to 'Lepanto' in *The Amis Anthology*: 'This poem will never be tolerated, let alone enjoyed, by a progressive intelligentsia to whom there can be no such thing as a just feat of arms . . . [Yet] anyone susceptible to poetry is likely to feel at some time for some time that "Lepanto" is a very great poem.'[54]

The view of poetry implicit in this note may also owe something to Ellingham. The fact that one can disagree with a poem's ideas or politics and still admire it was brought home to Amis most forcefully by Ellingham's championing of A.E. Housman. Ellingham was 'a very unequivocal Christian' yet Housman was his favourite poet, and Housman was an atheist: 'so I saw for ever that a poem is not a statement and the poet "affirmeth nothing"'.[55] Ellingham on Housman may also have reinforced young Amis's Louis Armstrong/ Tea at Grandma's distinction, as well as the related distinction between books 'for him' and great books. In May 1940 Ellingham read a paper to the School Society the gist of which was 'that though he did not think Housman was the greatest English poet he was his favourite, because he suited his temperament'.[56] This summary Amis himself probably wrote (it was unsigned, but Amis was an active member of the society and one of the school magazine's editors). Later, Amis, too, declared Housman his favorite poet: 'I came to share Mr. Ellingham's preference and eventually retain it even in face of Larkin's work.'[57] That Housman should suit Ellingham's temperament caused Amis to ponder the nature of his teacher's belief, his attraction to works that voiced 'rebellion against the divine will'.[58] The memory of Ellingham may also have played some part in Amis's unwillingness to condemn believers, even in his most militantly or outspokenly atheistical works. James Churchill, in *The Anti-Death League* (1966), says that 'only those with no sense of right or wrong'[59] can believe in God, but this is not what the novel says, for all the vehemence of its protests against evil, suffering, death and God. 'You atheist?' Yevtushenko, the Russian poet, asked Amis in 1962. 'Well yes, but it's more that I hate him.'[60] Yet in the 1987 essay, 'Godforsaken', Amis describes himself as an 'unwilling unbeliever', one who accedes to the principle 'that human beings without faith are the poorer for it in every part of their lives'.[61] Ellingham's example, both as a believer and as a believer attracted to powerful expressions of doubt, may lie behind such views.

A sense of Ellingham the man comes through most clearly in his book on English composition, *Essay Writing: Bad and Good* (1935). Amis reread the book in 1986 and was struck again by 'just how much has stayed in my memory, and how much it has influenced me'.[62] The book was intended for pupils from 13 to 16 years of age, and often refers to School Certificate and other examinations its readers will face. It is divided into two parts: 'Style', with chapters on 'Conciseness', 'Vigour', 'Beauty', 'The Sentence' and 'The Paragraph'; and 'The Essay', with chapters on 'The Essay in Making', 'The Descriptive Essay', 'The Expository Essay', 'The Argumentative Essay', 'The Critical Essay' and 'The Imaginative Essay'. The book's method is direct and practical. Its examples are drawn from the writing of the boys themselves and the sort of writing boys read. The tone or register of the book is informal, sympathetic, yet never ingratiating – like the man himself, apparently. 'Ellingham didn't force intimacy on one,' Amis remembers, 'but he would always listen and was always warm and friendly towards us.'[63]

Here is Ellingham on 'vigour', a quality hard to pin down. He begins by anticipating common misconceptions: 'Vigorous English is not merely to be used when you are excited or angry. Any English which does its work well, and shows exactly what the writer means, is vigorous. Feeble writing leaves the reader to do all the work.'[64] The examples that follow show how well Ellingham understood schoolboys, including the ungifted or merely dutiful:

Do not try to bluff the reader. It is your work to describe, and if your words are inadequate, no verbal device will make the reader do your work for you. If you are describing a sunset, and feel that 'the sunset was beautiful' is not enough, it is bluff to write 'the sunset was amazingly beautiful.' You have not avoided the duty of describing the sunset. You have only made your task harder, for now you must show that it was amazing as well as beautiful.[65]

The same brisk manner is used when commenting on examples from more confident pupils, including jokey ones:

A boy wrote of the saxophone 'invented by Saxe, presumably a half-wit, for no man in his right mind would have invented such a woe-begone instrument.' We will allow him to call Saxe a half-wit, and his invention a woe-begone instrument; but he need not have taken such pains to point out the obvious. 'A woe-begone instrument, invented by Saxe, presumably a half-wit,' pays the reader the compliment of assuming that he can follow the thought.[66]

As this passage suggests, Ellingham was both tolerant and demanding with cheeky pupils (the sort Amis may have been by the time he reached C5A), a doubleness found in his sensible advice on slang: 'if you decide to use slang, never apologise for it with quotation marks. You cannot have it both ways.'[67] Ellingham's own wit is everywhere apparent in the book. Here is another cautionary sample sentence, the sort Amis might have produced for Mr Ashley, his prep-school master, again from the 'vigour' chapter: 'The dewdrops on the grass sparkled with a thousand times the lustre of diamonds on the neck of some dusky beauty.' Ellingham comments: 'It is unlikely.' In Part II, in the chapter on 'The Essay in Making', he discusses introductions. The chapter begins: 'I have seen it laid down in books that an essay must have an introduction. I do not agree.'[68] There follow subsections on the several ways of avoiding dullness recommended in such books, beginning with 'The Anecdote'. Ellingham has little time for the anecdote: 'A dutiful young writer trying to achieve an anecdote is a pitiful sight.' Here is the example he offers: 'While sitting in a tram the other day, I overheard one working man say to another, "Have you paid your Trade Union subscription yet, Bill?" This at once brings up the question of Trade Unions.'[69] Gross remembers a legend that Ellingham had once written across some boy's school report: 'Bottom – needs kicking.'

For reasons Amis would approve and eventually make his own, Ellingham chooses 'The School Story' as a sample topic in the chapter on 'The Critical Essay'. The chapter begins with 'three necessary cautions', the first of which is

Be scrupulously honest. A good book for you is the book which you enjoy, not the book which you imagine the reader will expect you to enjoy. If you try to cheat, you will soon be found out. You cannot vamp up enthusiasm for the 'sublime masterpieces of English literature' if you read or enjoy nothing but Edgar Wallace or Angela Brazil. If it is a crime to enjoy Edgar Wallace, which I deny, do not be a furtive criminal. If he really wrote rubbish you may find it out from an analysis of your reasons for liking him.[70]

In the third caution the reader is introduced to the sample essay topic, as if in the course of conversation: 'Never lose sight of the actual books which you have read. If I had to write an essay on School Stories, I would start by writing on a piece of paper [he then lists twelve school stories, beginning with Farrar's *Eric*, ending with Wodehouse's *Mike*, and including Kipling's *Stalky and Co.* and Hughes's *Tom Brown*] which are all different. I think some of them good and some of them bad. But I would try not to lose sight of any of them.'[71] The choice of such a topic might at first seem like what Amis would later call 'arse-creeping the young', in that the schoolboy reader is invited to approach material with which he is familiar, but he is unlikely to have thought about it analytically or systematically. Much of the rest of the chapter is devoted to constructing an essay on the question: 'How then do you decide what a good school story is?' First, though, Ellingham offers a piece of advice that reveals his knowledge of the genre and its limitations:

There is a type of school story, usually sold for threepence, in which the French master is a German spy, and the Science master an American gangster fleeing from justice; and the bully is hand in glove with dope smugglers, and the nervous new boy is the unrecognised heir to a fortune, and is rescued from kidnappers by the head prefect in a racing aeroplane; and the headmaster is mistaken for the hero by some skylarking louts in the Lower Fifth, who drop a pot of tar over his head; and so on.

If you feel this is bad because it is improbable, you have a start for your analysis.[72]

In the course of structuring the essay into sections on plot, character and language, Ellingham insists upon reasons, discrimination, seeks to 'improve opinion into knowledge', in Samuel Johnson's phrase (this identification Ellingham would cut, along with the inverted commas, both of which he thought bad manners when quoting well-known authors). Even in works of child fantasy it is possible 'to distinguish between the exaggerations of artistry, of caricature, of propaganda, and of mere clumsiness. To my mind the good boy Redwood in *Tom, Dick, and Harry* is credible; the good boy Arthur in *Tom Brown* is just possible; and the good boy Russell in

Eric is wholly inconceivable; or the incredible Stalky is a little irritating; while the equally incredible Psmith in *Mike* can be swallowed whole.'[73] Later on he warns against defensive reserve or superiority: 'Do not be ashamed of admiring . . . [C]riticisms of poetry by boys, at any rate, seldom err on the generous side.' Less confident boys are warned against assuming 'that the poem must be good if it is there to be criticised'.[74] In advice like this, one senses Ellingham's shrewdness, common sense and goodwill.

Like all boys at City of London, excepting 'a despised minority of pacifists and other freaks',[75] Amis was drafted into the Officer Training Corps at fourteen. The OTC met twice a week, on Mondays and Thursdays, and its activities mostly consisted of drills and marching, though Amis also mentions trips to a rifle range (where he became 'a First-Class shot'),[76] field days, and a two-week summer camp. On OTC days boys came to school in military uniform. One of the reasons Amis initially chose the mounted section of OTC, in which boys took weekly riding lessons from a Colonel Lawrence, was that he liked wearing breeches instead of trousers and got to tie his puttees in a special way.[77] Amis rose to the rank of Sergeant and took his duties seriously, even looking through a book on 'section leadership' in the cavalry, a War Office publication which a fellow student had discovered in a bookshop near the Temple. In the *Memoirs* he declares that 'for quite some time I thought that if I failed to become a writer I would go into the army. (Even in later years, at least up to 1980 when I published my novel *Russian Hide-and-Seek*, the military life continued to cast something of a spell).'[78] But not the mounted military life. As Amis told Jacobs, he 'hated being on a horse when it cantered'.[79] Before the school was evacuated to Marlborough in 1939 he had switched from the mounted section to the signals section, encouraging his friend Cyril Metliss to do so as well.

That Ellingham had been a signaller may have had something to do with this switch, but adolescent embarrassment and laziness also played their parts. Denis Norden remembers treading on a man's foot on the underground on his way home from OTC. 'Watch it, mate,' he was told, 'or I'll report you to the Sergeant Major, and he'll tell your Mum.' Gross recalls how OTC 'blighted Sunday evenings, which had to be given over to blancoing and polishing'. Like Norden, Metliss 'felt pathetic' wearing his OTC uniform on the tube. 'Why don't you join the signals,' Amis suggested in 1939;

'we only have to dress up once a month as opposed to once a week.'[80] Yet even after he settled in the sixth form and began to gain some small reputation for flamboyance and anti-establishment views, the OTC retained important attractions for Amis. Norden found marching 'very satisying and pleasurable; Sergeant-Major made you feel the delights of uniformity, which had never occurred to me.' Amis associated pleasure with comradeship, 'thousands of good chaps'. Part of the appeal of tales of soldierly heroism, he told Jacobs, was that 'as an only child, being a soldier implied membership of an organisation in which "imaginary comrades were shadow brothers"'.[81] It was a tradition in the OTC for older boys to carry the rifles of younger, smaller boys on longer marches; Peter Baldwin remembers Amis doing this.

Events on the Continent lent OTC a different kind of attraction or importance. Amis describes his understanding of these events as limited, though what he heard of them at CLS was likely to counter what he heard of them from home. In September 1937, soon after Amis entered the sixth form, the School Parliament was disbanded (though it revived again in 1940), because, as Peter Baldwin puts it, 'everyone was in the opposition. They were all Labour to a man.' Amis only became interested in politics later in the sixth form. Before that he attended a few meetings of the CLS branch of the League of Nations Union, but mostly because they were also attended by CLS girls, whose school was nearby. In *You Can't Do Both*, Robin Davies ties himself into knots at one such meeting, because of the presence of girls. 'While he pretended to consider where to sit, Robin asked himself what he had expected. That all the girls in the place should rush at him, tearing off their clothes as they came? Regretfully no. Such things took place only in America.' When Robin returns to the present, 'sanity and boredom' are restored: 'There really was going to be a talk on the rise to power of the National Socialist government in Germany.'

This talk is attended by schoolmasters, schoolmistresses and other adults, as well as boys and girls, and delivered by an unnamed famous writer just back from Berlin.

The famous writer stood up and very soon was talking of Munich and von Papen, Brownshirts and Ludendorff, Reichstag and Hindenburg. Robin, who had joined in the applause for something to do, knew almost nothing of Adolf Hitler and his Nazis except that they were giving the

German Communists a bad time, which was obviously much to be welcomed. Hence he was mildly surprised to gather, from what the famous writer was saying, that it was more complicated than that and that the Communists had a case, to do with some election on 5th March 1933 [the German general election]. As well as being mildly surprising, this was mildly irritating. If the famous writer had been about fifty years younger, Robin might have dismissed such obvious perversity as only to be expected of a woman.[82]

The year is 1936 or 1937. In real life the speaker might have been introduced by Denis Norden, branch secretary, eventually overall secretary of the public schools section of the League, or by Mr Oakley, both of whom were listed as officers of the branch in reports of its meetings in the school magazines of the period. Among other political events reported in the magazines were a debate of 4 February 1937 on the 'total abolition of the House of Lords', a motion passed by nine votes to five and supported by 'Liberals, Socialists, Communists and the most amiable Fascist we have yet met'. On 12 March there was a talk on 'The Materialist Conception of History', described in the school magazine as a discussion of 'the dry pages of Marx and Engels'. On 22 June, 'absolute pacifism' was discussed, under the joint auspices of the School Society and the League of Nations Union. At such meetings, the views Amis is likely to have brought to school from home, views such as those hinted at in Robin's reactions to the speech of the famous writer, would have been quickly countered. The school prided itself on its tolerance: 'Scholarships and reasonable fees prevent our school from becoming a nursery for one layer of society,' declares an editorial of March 1937. 'From Mile End to Kensington boys come to be taught, and the voices of Capitalism, Communism and Fascism are given a free utterance and an equal hearing.' 'Free utterance', certainly, but 'equal hearing'? 'There was a general feeling that you were left of centre rather than right of centre,' Metliss recalls. 'You didn't come from rich backgrounds and you didn't come from established backgrounds.' As Amis moved progressively leftward in the sixth form he was hardly alone, even when he identified himself as a Communist in 1941, in the school's reconvened Parliament. Although there were no Communist cells or reading groups in CLS, anti-Fascist sentiment at the school had been strong well before Munich. Meanwhile, the likelihood of war and the vulnerability of the school in its location on the Embankment were becoming increasingly clear. By the time Amis entered his second year of the sixth form in 1938, plans for the school's evacuation to the country were already in hand.

4

CLS at Marlborough

On 26 September 1938, at the height of the Sudetenland Crisis, F.R. Dale wrote to the parents of boys in both the Junior and Senior Schools asking whether they would withdraw their sons from CLS if it relocated to the country, a move that would entail only 'reasonable' extra cost. At this point the new location had not been finalised, though negotiations had begun for the purchase of three large houses in Denbighshire, North Wales. When the Munich Agreement removed the immediate threat of war, a few days after Dale sent his letter, negotiations for the Welsh properties were suspended. In London, however, the school had already begun preparations to defend itself against aerial bombardment. Amis's 'vast agoraphobic playground', recently diminished by a newly constructed building, 'was reduced almost to a vanishing point',[1] according to the school magazine, by vast heaps of sand unloaded for protection against attack.

In the next few months, Dale sought alternatives to the North Wales scheme, and by late autumn had reached an agreement with the Master of Marlborough College, George Turner, that in the event of war the school would move to Wiltshire and share the college's facilities. On 20 March 1939, notices were sent to all CLS parents about the agreement and about plans for the move. Dale was lucky to have pulled this deal off: almost as soon as it was confirmed, the government requisitioned the buildings of Cheltenham College, which immediately but unsuccessfully sought a similar arrangement. What Dale and Turner agreed was that CLS would have access to all college classrooms, playing fields and other facilities, including the dining hall, but that CLS boys and masters would be billeted in town. CLS would pay Marlborough £2,000 a year for heat, light and maintenance; it would provide extra cooks for the dining room, at the cost of another £2,000; and a third £2,000 would be set aside for the relief of parents unable to meet boarding fees. These fees were calculated at 22s. 6d. a week for billeting and 15 shillings for food. Presumably Amis's father paid them. He had paid no tuition fees for his son since 1935, when Amis was awarded a Corporation scholarship.

Marlborough, a town of some 4,000 inhabitants in 1939, is located eighty miles west of London, on the road to Bath. The college itself was founded in 1843, six years after CLS, and was originally intended to provide inexpensive boarding education for the sons of Anglican parsons. By 1939 it had become a highly regarded public school (John Betjeman, Louis MacNeice and Anthony Blunt were old boys) and there is some evidence that both boys and masters looked down on their CLS counterparts. This was certainly Amis's impression. He thought the Marlborough boys 'outrageously stand-offish'[2] and says he had almost no contact with them during his five terms in Wiltshire. This absence of contact, however, was at least partly a product of the complicated arrangements necessitated by cohabitation. The two schools shared almost nothing except premises, and those during the day only. When Marlborough boys used the classrooms, CLS boys were in the dining hall or on the playing fields, and vice versa. There were no mixed classes or afternoon activities, with the exception of occasional discussions about rules between the two school captains, the loan of some CLS juniors to the College Choir (Marlborough had no junior school and lacked treble voices) and the occasional squash or other sporting competition. 'We saw very little of them really,' one boy recounted, 'except at half-past twelve when we were waiting to enter their classrooms.'[3] As Dale rather delicately puts it, 'the two schools slightly disturbed one another's intellectual concentration; each school thought the other had rather untidy ways in classrooms; some College rules, which we obeyed, were hard to remember. The Marlborough boys were always most courteous and tolerant.'[4]

Something of the attitude of the college to the school is suggested by a letter its Master, Turner, wrote to the Mayor of Marlborough supporting the plan to billet CLS boys and masters in town: 'From the point of view of the town, I think that there may be a good deal to be said for such an arrangement. The City of London School Boys are decently brought up and trained in some degree of responsibility. They would be much less inconvenient lodgers than, for instance, a large number of small children from the poorest districts of London.'⁵ CLS owed a good deal to Turner; his successor as Master, F.M. Heywood, was initially somewhat less accommodating. However, in his complaints about stand-offishness, it is perfectly possible that Dale was being truthful as well as diplomatic in his description of the Marlborough boys as 'courteous and tolerant'. Schoolboys are clannish, and their masters can be, too. Anyone who has been to a post-match tea at an English public school (indeed, at any school) will recall how little mixing there is between teams.

The move to Marlborough, when finally it came, had been carefully choreographed and rehearsed, but in the event the school arrived at Savernake, the nearest station, two hours ahead of schedule.⁶ A second train full of mothers and babies arrived, instead of the primary school children local evacuation officers had expected. Later an unplanned wave of soldiers appeared, in search of billets. Many of the billets designated for CLS boys were still occupied by holiday-makers, soldiers and women working for the Ministry of Health. Amis was among one hundred or so boys who spent their first nights in Wiltshire in temporary accommodation, first in the college gymnasium, then in a barn, on cots. The job of arranging billets had been entrusted by Dale to Ellingham and the deputy head of school, C.G. Nobbs. Between them they had found accommodation for 700 boys and forty masters, with no billets further than a twenty-five-minute walk from college. Ellingham considered his work for CLS during the war years the high point of his career: 'For me Marlborough was the climax. After it my school life drifted more or less calmly to its close.'⁷

Amis was billeted in a small workman's cottage at Number 1 Bath Road. This was where Ellingham and his wife, Edna, were billeted, along with four other boys: Richenberg, the School Captain, Saul Rose, another classics sixth-former, Horwich, an economics sixth-former, and a boy named Lacey, a mathematician. Though only minutes from the college, the cottage at Bath Road was located on a watermeadow and very cold and damp. It had been empty for some months before CLS took it over and had neither hot water nor electricity. The only heating was supplied by the sitting-room fireplace and a kitchen stove. Baths were taken in a portable tub in the kitchen, with water heated on the stove. There was an earth closet in the back garden which had to be cleared regularly. The bedroom Amis shared with Richenberg was tiny, six feet by seven, with room only for truckle beds. On one memorable occasion it was so cold that the urine in their chamberpot froze.[8]

The boys spent little time in the cottage. The first class of the day for CLS pupils was at eight and no boy was allowed to return to his billet until after tea, or to leave college later than 7.30, though boys over fourteen could be out until eight.[9] It was forbidden to visit other billets without permission. Billet hostesses were not asked to provide more than a hot drink, morning and evening. Smoking was forbidden at all times, a rule comparatively easy to circumvent on the way to and from billets. The trek back to billets in winter darkness was remembered by one boy as 'a dim procession of dusky figures groping their way through the blackout helped only by luminous discs attached to their lapels or small torches in their hands'.[10] Lights went out for all boys at ten. Amis's memories of evenings at the cottage were of the Ellinghams and their charges crowded round the sitting-room fire, the boys finishing their homework.[11] He also describes the conversations he had in the cottage with Ellingham, Richenberg and Rose as affording 'an optimistic preview of the university'.[12]

Richenberg and Amis had been friends and desk-mates since the third form and were stars of the Classical side. But both came to question the utility of a Classical education. Richenberg was good at maths and wanted to become a mathematician; Amis wanted to be a writer and was keen on studying English. In the end, only Amis made the switch. At Oxford, Richenberg read PPE at Corpus Christi, was awarded a double First, took a B.Litt. in economics, and became an economics don at Jesus College, though only for a year. He then moved to the Treasury as an economic adviser and eventually went into business, where he made and lost a great deal of money. He and Amis remained friends even after a misunderstanding over Amis's novel *I Want It Now* (1968), in the first chapter of which a party is held at the home of a rich, celebrity-seeking couple named Reichenberg. Len Dowsett, Richenberg's successor as School Captain, remembers him as brilliant, on one occasion playing and winning three simultaneous games of chess while blindfolded.[13] Norden describes him as 'dazzling, the one we thought would leave a mark'. Saul Rose, Amis's other close friend in the cottage, also went on to

Oxford, where he read classics at New College and stayed on after the war, becoming Fellow and bursar.

Both Richenberg and Rose were Jewish. That Amis's closest friends at CLS were Jews, in a school in which, at the time, only 15 per cent of boys were Jewish, might be considered noteworthy; at CLS itself, Baldwin claims, 'it would not have been remarked upon at all'. Amis mentions a single instance of anti-Semitism in the *Memoirs*: a scene in which the OTC Regimental Sergeant-Major, 'a man in his forties, I suppose, who had presumably been a long serving warrant officer or NCO' (also a 'wildly flaunting homosexual') upbraided Richenberg in public for 'something appalling like having an epaulette-button undone'. The RSM pointedly asked Richenberg his name and his religion, questions to which he clearly knew the answers. 'I suppose there is no such thing as an audible hush or silent intake of breath,' Amis recalls, 'but it was as if every Gentile in hearing turned white.'[14] Norden and Metliss remember one other instance: a fight, Metliss dates it 1936–37, involving CLS boys who were Jewish and CLS boys who were supporters of the British Union of Fascists. The Fascist boys came to school one day wearing black shirts, clothing subsequently banned by Dale. Norden remembers that they attacked him as much for being Secretary of the League of Nations Union, thus a 'milksop' or 'commie', as for being Jewish.

In *You Can't Do Both*, Robin's friend and desk-mate, Embleton, is Jewish ('What a shemozzle,' he is made to say at one point).[15] Robin admits to having 'always been slightly afraid of Embleton when they were at school', Embleton being both clever and clear-sighted about Robin's failings, in particular about that piece of him 'that says it's all right to go after something you want if you really want it'[16] (seventeen-year-old Nancy, for example). As far as I am aware, neither Richenberg nor Amis ever recalled comparable tensions in their friendship, though Richenberg did speak of Amis's self-consciousness about his feelings, his inability to trust expressions of affection. Though there was 'a great affinity' between the room-mates, Amis suffered from 'a difficulty over his own emotions'.[17] Amis mentions no such difficulty, but he does recall a sense of having been caught out and disapproved of, though by Ellingham not Richenberg:

I have sometimes suspected that Mr. Ellingham did not greatly care for me. He saw through my affectations, found unconvincing my excuse for not playing games much . . . considered, probably rightly, that I pulled less than my weight in the primitive cottage half a dozen of us were to share when the school was evacuated to Wiltshire in 1939. But he knew I was clever, thought I might be some good some day and helped in more ways than he knew about.[18]

These suspicions were not unfounded. As another master, C.N. Vokins, recalled to Eric Jacobs,[19] Amis did not cope well with the 'unforeseen strains' of life at Marlborough: 'He resented the extra restraint that had to be imposed if the two schools were to live in harmony. Above all, he resented being in billets.' For two years in London Amis had enjoyed the privileges of a sixth-former: not just using the school's Embankment entrance, but being able to go off to lunch at the Lyons tea-shop near Blackfriars Bridge, or to visit nearby record- and bookshops (with his daily pocket money of 1s. 3d., Amis told an interviewer, he could purchase two cheese rolls for lunch, reserving the rest for the purchase of classical records).[20] These freedoms were likely to have been especially prized by Amis, given his controlling parents. At home, all Amis's domestic needs were still taken care of by his mother, who literally spoon-fed him. Some part of his reluctance to help with billet chores may have derived from such spoon-feeding. When it came to 'clearing' the earth closet and keeping it clean, Vokins reports, presumably repeating what he heard from the Ellinghams, 'Amis seldom did his stint when his turn came round.' Vokins had observed Amis's impatience with curbs and restrictions well before the move to Marlborough. 'He was a plague to the master of . . . form C4A, who often complained bitterly in the Common Room of Amis's behaviour.' Vokins thinks Amis may have been goaded into bad behaviour by the master's 'rather pompous manner', but sheer intellectual frustration also played a part: 'He was very conscious of his ability and resented any constraints that prevented him from proving it.' When Ellingham taught him in the fifth form, quickly identifying him as greyhound not dud, he 'soon had him in hand and opened his eyes to the meaning of scholarship'. Ellingham and Oakley 'stretched him to his limit'.

Yet Amis was hardly a rebel, hardly even a character, at least until the move to Marlborough. Norden, who left school before the move, remembers him as 'undistinctive,' 'amiable', a term Amis himself uses in the *Memoirs*: 'To be accepted you had only to be amiable;

to be liked you needed pre-eminently to be able to raise a laugh occasionally.'[21] That Amis had no trouble raising laughs was clear early on, to masters and boys. Marsh, who taught him in C3A, remembered a story Amis wrote for him describing a train journey from Cannon Street to the school playing grounds at Grove Park, an imitation of Chaucer's Prologue. 'It was so good that I kept it' (it has not survived).[22] George Blunden (later Sir George, Deputy Governor of the Bank of England) recalls a five-minute play Amis wrote in which the only words spoken were 'more toast', delivered 'with every conceivable emotion and emphasis' by a cast of six. Amis reserved for himself the star part, that of a disgruntled waiter.[23] In these and other activities, Amis was remembered as 'full of fun' as well as funny, easy to get on with, a joiner. Until the move to Marlborough, he largely avoided games; when forced to take up rugby after the move, he found he liked it. Though 'unskilled', according to Amis's friend Peter Baldwin, he was the sort of boy who 'got stuck in the scrum', 'bonded in the team'. In 1940, according to the Easter 1941 issue of the school magazine, he was awarded 2nd XV Colours; for three matches he even played for the 1st XV. He participated in House rugby, cricket, tennis and athletics. According to Jacobs, Amis's time at Marlborough was 'the most physically energetic of Kingsley's life'.[24] In this period, he was also Captain of his House, an editor of the school magazine, secretary of the Musical Society, and on the committees of the Dramatic and School Societies. He earned his Certificate 'A' from Junior Training Corps or JTC (successor to OTC), at the rank of Sergeant and with the designation '1st Class Shot'.

In his last year at CLS, in September 1940, Amis was made a prefect. This honour he treated, again in Baldwin's words, 'as a bit of a joke'. Metliss recalls him as 'part of all the establishment procedures (prefect etc.), while cocking a snook at them at the same time'. Later in life, Amis contrasted his behaviour at CLS with that of more anarchic boys. In the *Memoirs*, he recalls a boy named Wybrow, very like the wild boys in the stories he wrote for Mr Ashley at Norbury College. Wybrow is the boy Amis says he remembers 'most vividly' among his contemporaries at CLS:

Wybrow, that great rampager and iconoclast, loping through the corridors with one hand ready to dart out in assault, the other clutched inward for defence, his whole being permanently gathered for the delivery of a jeering guffaw, his ravaged face and elbowing, shoving demeanour an advertise-ment of instinctive revolt . . . Whenever I remember Wybrow I am saddened at the thought of all that pulsating violence going to waste in commerce or trade, instead of enlivening the cultural pages of a Sunday newspaper. I suppose I envied him his air of being completely his own man.[25]

Wybrow left CLS before the move to Marlborough, which Amis regrets: 'I would give a lot to be able to see, in retrospect, the figure of Wybrow ranging contumeliously across the front court of the college, kicking a Marlborough prefect's rolled umbrella out of his hand or jostling an important parent at the gate.'[26]

The intelligence and sensitivity with which the school dealt with Amis in his sixth-form years helped to shape him socially as well as intellectually. It also played a part in forming his attitudes to in-stitutions. That Ellingham sensed Amis's attraction to a Wybrow-like subversiveness and aggression may have had something to do with his billeting him at Number 1 Bath Road. Ellingham knew how to handle Amis, who respected him, though he also, as Amis suggests, thought he had intellectual potential;[27] he may have wanted to keep an eye on him as he prepared for entrance examinations to Oxford and Cambridge. According to Richenberg's successor as School Captain, Len Dowsett, Dale may have been thinking along similar lines when he made Amis a prefect. In 1940, at the end of the summer term, Richenberg, the School Captain, recommended that Amis be made a prefect in the next term, in September. This recommenda-tion, Dowsett remembers, encountered fierce opposition from 'Crusader types' whom Amis set out to shock: 'He used to pretend to the Crusaders that he was a raving homosexual – often by speaking in glowing sexual terms about one of the younger boys in front of these types.' Richenberg's recommendation of Amis was rejected. When Dowsett returned to school after the summer vacation, he was astonished, therefore, to hear Dale read out Amis's name on the list of prefects.[28] By making Amis a prefect, Dale may have hoped not only to give him a greater sense of responsibility but to counter the priggishness of other prefects, a move of a piece with the intelligent tolerance Dale encouraged throughout the school.[29]

Richenberg was convinced that Amis was merely playing at being homosexual, and Richenberg shared a room with Amis for a year. But Richenberg also felt that the wartime transformation of CLS from day to boarding-school encouraged both homosexual crushes and jokes about such crushes, a view Cyril Metliss, a year below Amis, echoed. Metliss was fourteen when he met Amis. He had come to the school at eight and was 'a true cockney', having been born in his father's pub in Smithfield. Metliss was on the Modern not the Classical side and like a number of Jewish boys at CLS never considered going on to university. He and Amis became close because of their love of classical music. 'He led me,' Metliss remembers, 'but I wasn't far behind.' Metliss also loved poetry, about which Amis knew much more than he did. When the school moved to Marlborough, Metliss was unhappy; his billet, unlike Amis's, was far from college and 'I got fed up.' He left CLS after only a term in Wiltshire, studied accountancy, was articled at sixteen, went into business, and eventually became chief accountant at British Land, the huge property company. Until he went into the navy in 1941 Metliss kept in touch with Amis. 'I'd meet him in Marlborough on a weekend and we'd walk along Marlborough's High Street, singing, humming Mozart all the way down. We were very close.' He and Amis also got together during the holidays. 'He would come and visit me when we were in the pub in Newman Street,' Metliss recalls. Amis was eighteen, so his parents were forced to loosen the reins a bit. He and Metliss would sit in the pub lounge while Metliss's mother served in the bar. Amis would have a glass of bitter ('he liked his glass of beer, even then') and after an hour or so they'd go off to the proms, at nearby Queen's Hall, standing with other promenaders for a shilling.

That same summer of 1940 the Amises moved from Norbury to Berkhamsted in Hertfordshire. Norbury was near the flight path of German bombers, which frightened Amis's mother, though the town was to suffer little damage. Metliss visited Amis in Berkhamsted: 'It was very romantic, in the sense that we'd go up to a nearby hill under a tree and we'd have books of verse and we'd read them. He'd say: "You must read this." We'd just sit and read alone.' On one of Metliss's visits back to Marlborough Amis told him: 'If you hadn't left I would have tried to have a relationship with you. It's too late now, though.' Metliss believes that if Amis really had contemplated some sort of sexual relationship, it was unlikely to have involved more than mutual masturbation, a practice innocently indulged by Peter Furneaux and his friend Reg in *The Riverside Villas Murder*. 'He was interested in girls but there were no girls,' is how Metliss describes Amis's situation at Marlborough (it was also his own). Or as Amis puts it in *The Riverside Villas Murder*: 'what Peter did with his friends was regarded by them all, in a ready consensus, as quite okay (as well as very enjoyable) because they only did it because they could not get girls yet and until they could get girls.'[30]

Amis's feelings for Metliss were deeper than Peter's for Reg, at least as Metliss recalls them.[31] In his poem 'An Ever-Fixed Mark', from *A Look Round the Estate* (1967), later reprinted (rather broad-mindedly on the editor's part) in *The Penguin Book of Homosexual Verse* (1982), Amis distinguishes between two sorts of schoolboy homosexuality. One sort is practised by 'Buck':

> Years ago at a private school
> Run on traditional lines,
> One fellow used to perform
> Prodigious feats in the dorm;
> His quite undevious designs
> Found many a willing tool.

> On the rugger field, in the gym,
> Buck marked down at his leisure
> The likeliest bits of stuff;
> The notion, familiar enough,
> Of 'using somebody for pleasure'
> Seemed handy and harmless to him.

A quite different example is offered by 'Ralph':

> But another chap was above
> The diversions of such a lout;
> Seven years in the place
> With the kid he followed about:
> What interested Ralph was love.

> He did the whole thing in style –
> Letters three times a week,
> Sonnet-sequences, Sunday walks;
> Then, during one of their talks,
> The youngster caressed his cheek,
> And that made it all worth while.

Amis's intended 'relationship' with Metliss sounds more Ralph-like than Buck-like, though Buck-like tendencies figured prominently in his later relations with women. A more interesting fictional parallel is provided in *You Can't Do Both*, a novel begun shortly after Metliss re-established contact with Amis in the early 1990s. The two friends had lost touch after Metliss went into the navy, and when Metliss decided to arrange a meeting, after seeing Amis interviewed on television, they hadn't communicated in over fifty years. After an initial trial, of a sort Amis often employed in later years to weed out bores (Metliss saw through it immediately), the friendship resumed, with regular lunches and much discussion of music and old times. Amis's pocket diaries for this period intersperse entries such as '1.0 C. Metliss on me but he books' with '203 days of novel (142)', a progress report on *You Can't Do Both*. By the time of this second entry (that is, before he had reached page 142 in his draft), Amis had written the scene in *You Can't Do Both* in which Cambridge undergraduate Jeremy Carpenter follows fourteen-year-old Robin Davies to Wales, invites Robin out to lunch, fills him with Château-Latour 1924, takes him for a ride in his sports car and then for a stroll on 'the top of a slope above a gentle valley'.[32] Robin and Jeremy sit down on the grass for a rest. Jeremy makes the most tentative of passes at Robin, is rebuffed, and Robin falls asleep. When Robin wakes they discuss the poetry Jeremy has earlier lent him.

'If you're writing fiction,' Amis once told Andrew Davies, 'it's too tame, and maybe too painful, to try to recreate what did happen. But you can be faithful to the emotion, while you're inventing incidents.'[33] In the scene between Robin and Jeremy, the emotions Amis is being faithful to are those both of seducer, or would-be seducer, and seduced, or near-seduced. At lunch Jeremy entertains Robin with stories of Cambridge: 'He turned out to be a wonderful mimic.'[34] He makes the dons sound like senile idiots, as in Amis's much-admired impersonation of Lord David Cecil: 'I want you all to wemembah . . .' He makes funny faces, including 'a killing upper-class-moron face with a lot of blinking and as many as possible of the lower teeth showing'.[35] He assumes the lead when discussing poetry, music, culture in general. And he reveals that there's a piece of himself 'that says it's all right to go after something you want if you really want it',[36] even if that something is fourteen, like Robin (or seventeen, like Nancy). Jeremy and the autobiographical Robin, in other words, have their similarities. It is clear from extant photographs that Amis would also be familiar with the emotions of the seducer's object, the near-seduced. Fourteen-year-old Amis's looks, like Peter's in *The Riverside Villas Murder*, 'were of the sort that had two or three times led strange men, encountered on the train to or from school or while waiting for it, to take an undue interest in him'.[37] He was slim and handsome, with straight blond hair brushed diagonally across his forehead, fair skin, a clear complexion, and regular features. Among the most delicate or masterly scenes in *The Riverside Villas Murder* are those between Peter and the homosexual detective, Colonel Manton, where in the end both behave impeccably. The important challenge to Peter's innocence in the novel, one that makes clear Amis's complex feelings about the heedless pursuit of what 'you really want', comes from a woman.

Amis's romantic impulses at Marlborough – romantic in several senses – were fed by the Wiltshire setting. 'The rural attractions were tremendous, imparting a kind of zest to adolescent melancholy, and for many years my every attempt to visualize a generic country scene would call up some memory of Marlborough.'[38] In 'He Curses His Insensibility', a prose poem published in the December 1939 issue of the school magazine, young Amis's angst-ridden speaker (half Byron, half Shelley, wholly adolescent) is as insensible to nature as to love. The 'poem' (perhaps his most embarrassing schoolboy effort) ends: 'Shadows, trees, sky: this is the holier trinity. But its divine power fails to transfigure a reluctant heart, and in vain the wind of love fans the cheek of the libertine.' *And a jolly good thing, too*, the mature Amis might say; does say, in effect, perhaps with this very poem in mind ('wind of love' has overtones of Wordsworth or Shelley), in the last stanza of 'Ode to the East-North-East-by-East Wind', from *A Case of Samples* (1956):

> Well now, since blowing things apart's your scheme,
>   The crying child your metaphor,
> Poetic egotists make you their theme,
>   Finding in you their hatred for
> A world that will not mirror their desire.
> Silly yourself, you flatter and inspire
>   Some of the silliest of us.
>   And is that worth the fuss?

To an adolescent it is, especially an adolescent from the suburbs newly exposed to the beauties of nature. All four of the poems Amis published in the school magazine, the only poems we have from him for these years, are Romantic in sentiment. The best of them, 'Prometheus', was published in July 1939, before the move to Marlborough. It is Shelleyan and Byronic not only in subject matter but in manner (Byronic in the manner of *Childe Harold* rather than *Don Juan*, or of Byron's own 'Prometheus'), with echoes also of Keats and Coleridge. That the speaker's excesses ('I alone / Untouched') are those of a character from myth provides a saving distance, one abetted by formal features: correct, unobtrusive couplets, a flatness or straightforwardness of statement. The poem is adolescent but also impersonal, almost an exercise. Since it is the best of the lot, as well as representative and short, I quote it in its entirety:

> First came forgetfulness. Then the shapes whirled
> Darting their ghastly tongues at me, and curled
> In colours, violet, golden, smoky red;
> At last they merged, and all were one instead:
> A steady, glossy crimson, and it burned
> Unwinkingly, implacably. Then turned
> The circle, and I broke through to the air.
> I saw the lurking moon above, and there
> Were the stark trees alone, and there the hill
> Silent beneath the sky. But then a chill
> Passed through me, for the scene, and the deep dome
> The sky – all was this crimson monochrome;
> I was it all, and it was I. There came
> Drums in my ears, my face scorched at the flame
> Leaping about me in the midst, and higher
> It sprang, until the world was one vast fire,
> A roaring holocaust, and I alone
> Untouched, stood gazing as if turned to stone.
> For in that furnace was eternity,
> And God threw back its doors that night, for me.

This is an improvement on Amis's first school magazine poem, 'Prelude', published in Easter 1939 and described in the *Memoirs* as 'a kind of suburbanite's *Waste Land* tizzied up with bits of Wilde'.[39] Excepting the odd inversion or poeticism ('Then turned / The circle', 'There came / The drums'), 'Prometheus' is comparatively cringe-free.[40] Not so 'He Reads Immortality in the Eyes of a Virgin', published in July 1940.

Here sexual longing is expressed in the most elevated metaphysical terms. The poem ends:

> Be sure now, my soul, that this is the moment for
>   which you pine,
> This the split second which you have ever desired to fashion
> Into eternity; treasure this when all else has no worth;
> This is your one happiness before death; this is the
>   hour of your birth

When Amis calls his CLS poems 'of appalling pretentiousnesss and affectation', lines like these come to mind. For hints of the writer Amis would become, we have only lost or irrecoverable sources: the *Canterbury Tales* parody, the 'more toast' playlet, the impersonations and impressions. According to Philip Larkin, writing of Amis in 1941: 'No one who knew Kingsley at that time would deny that what chiefly distinguished him was this genius for imaginative mimicry.'[41]

There were three weeks of fine weather in September 1939, nearly three weeks for the CLS boys to get used to their new surroundings before classes began on the 19th, and even the notoriously sedentary Amis seems to have spent some part of them exploring the surrounding countryside. The college itself, its buildings and grounds, also had its attractions, among them the 'dear diligent indolence' (Keats) of summer afternoons spent lying on the terrace slope just below the 1st XI cricket pitch while the college or the school played a match. The attractions of winter were more strenuous, though no less beautiful, especially those of the first winter, which was freakishly cold. The temperature fell below 20° Fahrenheit and there was an ice storm, recalled in an editorial in the March 1940 issue of the school magazine (these editorials were unsigned, though usually written by the School Captain, in this case, Richenberg, aided by his co-editors, K.W. Amis and J. Reid): 'We have seen every twig on every tree encased in its own translucent jacket of ice, sometimes inches thick, and twenty-foot boughs have come crashing to the ground, snapped like matchsticks beneath the weight of the accumulated ice. A somewhat Netherlandish touch was added to the picture when boys began to skate to school.'[42] Fifty years later Amis himself recalled this storm, in the poem he appended to his *Memoirs* and titled 'Instead of an Epilogue'. The poem is dedicated 'To H' (in manuscript, 'To Hilly, my love') and the second of its three sections or stanzas reads in part:

> In 1940 when I was eighteen
> In Marlborough, going out one winter's morning
> To walk to school, I saw that every twig,
> Every leaf in the vicar's privet hedge
> And every stalk and stem was covered in
> A thin layer of ice as clear as glass
> Because the rain had frozen as it landed.
> The sun shone and the trees and shrubs shone back
> Like pale flames with orange and green sparkles.

The Marlborough winters had their comical as well as poetical moments. The college itself was little warmer than Amis's cottage. In the cellar of the Old Music School several CLS boys were discovered warming themselves round a Tortoise stove into which they were systematically feeding Marlborough's early historical records. The boys didn't just skate to school, they skated in school, playing games of ice hockey on the frozen swimming pool, to the fury of college authorities.[43] They also skated down the town's broad, sloping High Street, across and along which ropes were strung to prevent pedestrians breaking their legs and necks. This High Street, with its Elizabethan penthouse and handsome Town Hall, provided the CLS boys with their few town amusements: the Polly tea rooms, the Merlin café, Knapton's, Duck's, where, as far as wartime shortages allowed, boys could fill up on toast and jam, Bath and sticky buns, crumpets, muffins, lardy cakes. The one cinema in Marlborough was off limits to CLS boys, though, and relations with town inhabitants were infrequent and distant, as with the boys from the college. The town was preoccupied, distracted: by the sudden appearance of all sorts of military vehicles, including tanks parked in a lane off the High Street, by the coming and going of men and women in uniform, some soon to depart for France, by shortages of food staples and petrol for non-essential vehicles, by the constant drone of aircraft from nearby training fields, by thoughts of invasion, bombardment, casualty and loss. The boys shared these thoughts, listening intently to their radios for news of the outside world, of London in particular.

As has been suggested, once at Marlborough Amis became more politically engaged, moving steadily to the left. His name figures prominently in accounts of the school's reconvened Parliament (because he wrote them, according to Jacobs),[44] though this prominence sometimes seems less a product of conviction than of the desire to cut a dash. The manner of the accounts is lightly ironical, only just cocking a snook. In the Easter 1941 issue of the school magazine, the last Amis would co-edit, the account begins by straightforwardly describing as 'convincing and sincere' Peter Baldwin's speech for the Opposition attacking 'the fundamental philosophy of capitalism'. Baldwin is followed by a pro-government speaker who mounts an impassioned defence of Polish valour, 'on which', Amis notes, 'nobody had cast the smallest imputation'. When Government supporters curtail Opposition supporters, several of the latter withdraw in protest, including one, H.G. Williams Ashman, described in the *Memoirs* as the CLS boy who taught Amis most 'about upper-middle-class life',[45] who tried to sing 'The Red Flag' in the Lobby. Then Amis himself makes an appearance: 'The Deputy Leader of the Opposition now arose to attack the bill on every conceivable ground, laying stress on its Fascist tendencies.'[46] In his report on a later session, Amis is more openly self-mocking: 'The only Communist member (K.W. Amis) rose and fiercely attacked the Government with a speech of which three-quarters was unacknowledged quotation from Lenin.'[47]

Amis's comic gift is only sometimes served by these schoolboy contexts. In School Society debates he can sound merely facetious, as when debating such motions as 'women should not wear trousers' (proposed by Horwich, opposed by Richenberg) or 'the invention of printing was a bad thing' (proposed by Amis), or 'it is better to wash behind the ears than brush the hair' (proposed by Amis, opposed by Horwich) or 'black is white' (opposed by Amis).[48] His cultural interests at this time, the time of prose poems and adolescent angst, were as highbrow as they would ever be. Jazz and other forms of popular music took second place to an interest in classical music, including what some thought of as advanced or avant-garde classical music. As secretary of the Musical Society, Amis had a strong say in which records were played and discussed at meetings. The school magazine for March 1940 lists works by Mozart, Beethoven, Brahms and Dvořák but ends with Vaughan Williams's Fourth Symphony and William Walton's Viola Concerto. As the anonymous author of the report explains (it is Amis, one suspects, speaking of himself with familiar irony): 'The artistic conscience of the committee insisted upon the inclusion of these last two works in the face of the vigorous protests which greeted both their announcement and their performance.'[49]

In addition to a 'Gramophone Section', the Musical Society had an 'Appreciation Section', which consisted of Sunday afternoon classes on music history and elementary score-reading. These classes were held by the music master, Mr Taylor, and provided Amis with what little knowledge he possessed of the technical aspects of music. (Why Amis's father, himself a competent pianist, never insisted his son learn to play a musical instrument, when he ordered him around about everything else, frequently puzzled his son.) In addition to attending Mr Taylor's classes, Amis joined the School Choir, and just about learned to sight-read.[50] He loved singing in four-part harmony, describing it as 'the apex, still unrivalled in my experience, of non-sensual pleasures'.[51] Among the first works analysed in Mr Taylor's appreciation classes were Tchaikovsky's Pathétique and Brahms's First Symphony. According to Jacobs, Taylor explained the Brahms so well 'that it remained the piece of its kind Kingsley understood best for the rest of his life'.[52] As for Tchaikovsky, Amis singles him out for special praise in 'Rondo for My Funeral' (1973), an essay describing his tastes in classical music. Unlike the Amis of 1939, the Amis of 1973 had little time for modern composers; Tchaikovsky is 'the solitary post-classical figure I swallow whole'. He also makes a familiar distinction in the essay between 'favourite' and 'great' composers:

Mozart is for me the greatest composer, greatest artist. Tchaikovsky is my favourite composer. He idolized Mozart, and by no coincidence: both, in whatever different ways, have the capacity to administer sharp jolts to the emotional solar plexus while ostensibly being nothing more than gay, airy, pretty. Yes, Tchaikovsky bears down much harder at other times; his music has a palpable design on me; he wants me to participate in his forebodings, his passions, his bouts of wild energy, his despairs, and I do, wholeheartedly.[53]

This sounds very like Amis on the pleasures of genre fiction, pleasures he also associates with childhood or adolescent experience ('trying to horrify you, trying to thrill you, trying to make you afraid'). His more 'wholehearted' participation in the musical equivalent of such pleasures 'is the priceless recompense of my amateur status'.[54] Amis the novelist cannot help but notice when Chesterton is inconsistent about the seasons in *The Man Who Was Thursday*; comparable musical failings pass him by completely. When a musician friend tells him that Bach's 'bass line left something to be desired', Amis replies, 'it will never, I think, leave much to be desired by me',[55] since he can never tell for sure 'when a work takes a wrong or unfortunate turn'.[56] Hence in part the strength of music's appeal. 'Since starting to find it in my early teens,' Amis declares, 'music has given me more pleasure, and more intense pleasure, than any other art.' Literature takes second place, while 'any sort of visual thing, from a cameo to a cathedral, comes just about nowhere at all.' He goes further: 'only a world without love strikes me as instantly and decisively more terrible than one without music. Yes, friendship would beat music too, but not instantly.'[57]

Mr Taylor's music appreciation classes were one of a number of extra activities arranged by CLS masters during Amis's time at Marlborough. The boys had to be kept busy; when not working or playing outdoor games they were often bored. As the editors of the December 1939 issue of the school magazine explain:

We have been taken from the hobbies and recreations of our homes, the cinema has been closed to us, and at first many of us were hard put to it to find something to do. Many used their legs or their cycles to explore Savernake Forest or the Wiltshire Downs, or the Valley of the Kennet, but some are too urbanised to find much pleasure in moving from place to place, except in a car. So leisure for them meant either harassing their landladies, or drifting up and down the High Street, which no doubt is one of the most attractive High Streets in England, but cannot interest for ever.[58]

Though the CLS masters were unused to twenty-four-hour responsibilities, they quickly adjusted, and in Amis's memory, 'none . . . showed signs of the appalling extra burden of work, replete with boredom and irritation, they must have had to shoulder'.[59] In addition to making games compulsory, they opened sixth-form societies and clubs to fourth- and fifth-formers; they set up a school cinema in the science block, with Saturday afternoon screenings mainly of old British films; they supervised extra play readings (in which Amis often figured, taking lead roles in Auden and Isherwood's *The Ascent of F6* and Chesterton's *Magic*) and extra debates; new clubs and societies were devised, including woodwork, metalwork, photography, model railways and aeroplanes, Monopoly and other games. The presence of the wives of some of the masters also helped boys unused to being away from home, and not only younger boys. According to J.B. Marsh, Ellingham's wife, Edna, had to comfort eighteen-year-old Amis on several occasions when he woke in the middle of the night with screaming fits. Though Amis never mentioned these fits to Marsh, he later told him how much he had admired Mrs Ellingham and how 'he had used her as a model for some of his female characters'.[60] Richenberg remembered nothing of such episodes, but he left CLS before Amis; they may have occurred only in the two following terms, when Amis was approaching the Oxford scholarship examination, as well as succeeding uncertainties and fears, including those of war. It was not until late August 1940, for example, that the long-feared blitz began, first in London, then in the provinces.

One of the many extra duties Ellingham took on at Marlborough was coaching Amis for his Oxbridge examinations, particularly for the General Paper.[61] It was Ellingham, Amis suspected, who had smoothed the way for his transfer from Classics to English in 1938, his second year in the sixth form. This transfer obliged CLS to hire a master equipped to prepare him for examinations in English to scholarship level. Amis was the sole boy from CLS to petition to take such examinations, partly, one suspects, because there were comparatively few scholarships in English at Oxbridge; as Amis remembers it (perhaps mistaking a total number for the number available to any one applicant in any one year), two at Oxford and two at Cambridge. The two Oxford colleges Amis names are St John's and Christ Church; the only Cambridge college he names is St Catherine's, which means Selwyn was the other, since in 1940 candidates for Cambridge scholarships applied to one of several groupings of colleges and Selwyn was the only other college in St Catherine's grouping to offer scholarships in English. The specialist English master CLS hired to tutor Amis was good at rugby, Richenberg remembers, but less good, certainly less good than Ellingham, at preparing students for examination.

By late 1940, though, Amis was a well-practised examinee. After taking Higher School Certificates in Group I (Classics) in 1938, he took Group II (Modern Studies) in 1939, sitting papers in Latin and English, and subsidiary papers in Greek and French. In his third sixth-form year, the first at Marlborough, he took Group II again, this time in Greek and English, with Latin as a subsidiary subject. He also took the scholarship examination in English at St Catherine's

College, Cambridge, earlier in the year, in March 1940, unsuccessfully. Amis passed all his School or Higher School Certificate examination papers with credit, but in none was he awarded a distinction (unlike Philip Larkin, who passed both English and history with distinctions in 1940). Taking Higher School Certificates in English a second time was good preparation for a second go at a scholarship. To begin with, it meant that he had to prepare double the range of works or authors in certain areas: for example, six Shakespeare plays, not three, or two period papers not one. The period papers Amis could choose from give a sense of the rigour of the curriculum: '1564–1616' (with questions on *The Faerie Queene*, Book I, *Dr Faustus*, Bacon's *Essays*, Wyatt, Surrey and Sidney, Renaissance drama and prose fiction), '1616–1700' (Clarendon, *The Pilgrim's Progress*, Pepys, the hated Dryden, the Authorized version of the Bible), '1700–1790' (Addison, Steele, Pope, Gay, Swift, Goldsmith, Gray, Johnson, Collins, Cowper), '1790–1832' (a comparable range) and '1832–1880' (ditto). In his last year at CLS, after three successive years of Higher Certificate examinations, and a failed first scholarship examination at Cambridge, Amis received intensive individual tuition in English in preparation for a second scholarship examination at Oxford. This punishing schedule of examinations and extra tutorials helps to explain not only how he finally won his Exhibition ('a sort of cut-price scholarship')[62] to St John's College, Oxford, but how he arrived there both so well read and so weary of reading, at least of reading for examination.

In later years, as I have suggested, Amis made clear his debt to the City of London School, and not just his academic debt. 'After heaven knows how much special provision, extra work, and breaking precedent for me at CLS, my foolhardy wishes were accommodated,' he wrote of the switch to English: 'I cannot in this space explain what I owe to the school for letting me, against its better judgement, have my way, but it is large.'[63] At a special dinner held in 1985 to commemorate the work of CLS masters during the Marlborough years, Amis spoke of their skill and selflessness. Vokins recalls how all the masters who were present were moved by Amis's praise. In the *Memoirs*, at the end of the chapter titled 'Schools', Amis quotes the concluding paragraph of his essay 'City Ways' (1958). This paragraph stresses the qualities he most valued at CLS, qualities he often found in short supply outside school, at home in particular:

'Life at a large day-school in a large city,' I once wrote, 'embodies a freedom which I should guess to be unique, a freedom based on heterogeneity. Where there is no [social] orthodoxy there can be no conformity and no intolerance. This was certainly true of the City of London School. I have never in my life known a community where factions of any kind were less in evidence, where differences in class, upbringing, income group and religion counted for so little. In particular although perhaps fifteen per cent of the boys were Jewish, not a single instance of even the mildest anti-semitism [with the exception noted earlier] came to my attention in the seven years I was a pupil there. The academic teaching was of a standard not easily to be surpassed, but more important still was that lesson about how to regard one's fellows, a lesson not delivered but enacted. Thanks indeed for that.'[64]

5

Wartime Oxford

Amis went up to Oxford in late April 1941. He arrived 'in impeccably proletarian style, being driven over from my parents' house in Berkhamsted by the family butcher in his battered Morris, and approaching the wrong way up Plough Lane'. When Amis and the butcher finally reached St John's, he was assigned 'a nasty little pair of rooms in the top corner of the front quad', a fate he attributes to having come from 'a comparatively lowly school'.[1] He may be right in this attribution, but St John's had few pupils from the more exclusive public schools, unlike, say, Balliol, another 'grammar school' college, which, according to Amis's near-contemporary, Roy Jenkins, nonetheless 'had a sizable contingent of Etonians', including 'a leavening of peers'.[2] In Philip Larkin's first novel, *Jill* (1946), set in wartime Oxford and written shortly after Larkin left St John's, the terrified hero, John Kemp, has a room-mate, Christopher Warner, who was at school 'at Lamprey, you know'. Kemp has never heard of Lamprey, but later learns that its 'exact social status' was 'less high than [he] had imagined'.[3] According to Alan Ross, who arrived at the college in the same year as Amis, St John's may not have been 'one of the more fashionable of Oxford colleges, but it [was] one of the most agreeable, modest in scale and without pretensions. Few of its undergraduate members had much money.'[4]

That Amis arrived at Oxford in April was a direct result of the war. Male undergraduates in the humanities were allowed to defer call-up for at least a year; at most they were allowed a grace period of four terms. But some parents and school advisers feared the government might change its mind about the grace period, as it did about the call-up age, which changed twice during Amis's four wartime terms at St John's. In order to ensure a period at the university, more and more sixth-formers with places sought entrance before the end of the year, and Oxford allowed them to matriculate at the beginning of Hilary term (January to March) or Trinity term (April to June) as well as Michaelmas term (October to December). To obtain the maximum four-term grace period, Amis had to promise the Vice-Chancellor of the university that he would be willing to become a schoolmaster after graduation. This promise was only partly strategic; Amis admired his masters at CLS and considered schoolteaching as good a way as any to support himself while writing. Auden, after all, had taught in a school after university.

The war had other effects on Oxford. Many humanities courses were shortened, as was Amis's Part I English course. Teaching and undergraduate residence sometimes ran on into the vacations; the line between term and vacation began to blur for everyone, not just the idle. Though the city was never bombed, despite the importance of Cowley for munitions and the threatened targeting of cultural centres in the 'Baedeker' raids of 1942, 'there were frequent false alarms, and German bombers could be heard throbbing their way through the night skies to the midlands and the north'.[5] A university fire brigade was formed, enlisting dons, students and scouts; students (Larkin, for one) took on war work, such as nightly fire-watching duties; huge water tanks were placed in college quads, and mullioned windows were taped and curtained for blackout. At St John's, a third of the buildings were requisitioned by the section of the Ministry of Food responsible for the white fish and potato ration (the college's wartime nickname was Fish and Chips); the student population dwindled (there were no more than sixty undergraduates overall at St John's); and most young dons disappeared, as Larkin puts it, 'to the forces or the ministries or whatever'.[6]

The social life of the undergraduates was affected in several ways. With new arrivals every term, distinctions of seniority weakened; so did college stereotypes (aesthete and hearty, for example). As virtually no good news arrived from any battle front during Amis's four wartime terms at Oxford, careerism faded. In Larkin's words, 'effort expended on one's post-war prospects could hardly seem anything but a ludicrous waste of time'. 'Brideshead' high living largely disappeared, a relief to scholarship and grammar school types for whom, again in Larkin's words, 'a lack of *douceur* was balanced by a lack of *bêtises*'.[7] College feasts and other festivities were suspended. Petrol rationing meant nobody ran a car. There were no expensively decorated rooms; most undergraduates doubled up, few were rich, and luxurious furnishings were in any event in short supply. Amis's 'set' consisted of 'a sitting room about big enough to throw a party for six, and a bedroom with a bed, a cupboard and a wash-stand in it'.[8] Because of coal shortages only a single fire per staircase was permitted each day, so Amis and the other undergraduates on staircase three often worked, entertained and listened to music together in the same room. There were no lavish supper or drinks parties, though getting drunk was common. According to Larkin, 'everyone paid the same fees (in our case, 12s. a day) and ate the same meals'.[9] The character of these meals can be judged from Amis's contributions to the St John's College Kitchen and JCR Suggestions Books, which range from simple denunciation ('When I have potatoes in their jackets at home the jackets are worth eating. Here jacket and potato are fucking awful. What is wanted is not necessarily *no* potatoes-in-jackets, but *better* potatoes in jackets') to mock-mathematical demonstration, as in the following post-war complaint about cheese, accompanied by a swarm of seconding signatures:

Sir, We should like to bring this cheese business forward again. A month's cheese ration, I am told, measures 6" x 3" x 1" = 18 ins.[3] ∴ a week's cheese ration consists of 18 ÷ 4 = 4½ ins.[3] Therefore cheese ration for 1 meal = 2¼ ins.[3] Waiving the ¼ in.[3], we should have a piece of cheese measuring 2" x 1" x 1", TWICE A WEEK. If Peedel [Seedel?] wants to make his bloody macaroni things, let him make them WITHOUT cheese and let us have our cheese ration *ourselves*.

We don't think other members appreciated what a fucking hell of a lot of cheese they were missing. Now they do, perhaps we shall get some more support for this. Yrs. K.W. Amis.[10]

As for meals out of college, Amis mentions 'the Chinese', also known as the Stowaway ('two courses, meat and veg *and* a sweet for 1s.10d'),[11] and the British Restaurant. The latter, a wartime and post-war institution, had branches in Gloucester Green and St Aldate's, in the Town Hall. It was run by the government, customers sat at trestle tables, the food was simple and served at cost price

(1s. 3d. for shepherd's pie or sausage and mash and rice pudding). Otherwise students in search of a cake or a hot drink might frequent the Cadena in Broad Street or Fuller's or Elliston and Cavell in the Cornmarket, good places for meeting girls. In the second of Larkin's undergraduate 'schoolgirl' novels, *Michaelmas Term at St Bride's,* as Marie mounts 'the carpeted steps of Elliston and Cavell to drink coffee' she sees her friend Margaret sitting alone, coolly composed, 'while the clouds of smoke and conversation billowed around her. Sometimes an undergraduate would approach, fingering his tie, and ask, "Is anyone sitting here?" Margaret's "I hope not," like three drops of water from an icicle, sent him scuttling incontinently away.'[12] When real-life Margarets were enticed into male undergraduates' rooms, it was mostly coffee they were offered. 'So thirty years on, when the cake-queues / And coffees have gone by the board,' begins the final stanza of Larkin's 'Poem about Oxford', composed in 1970 and subtitled 'for Monica'.

Drinking, for undergraduates, mostly took place in pubs, despite the best efforts of the proctors, but also in college, where beer from the buttery could be taken to one's rooms. The pubs Amis frequented included the Lamb and Flag, right next door to St John's; the Eagle and Child, known as the Bird and Baby, just across the road; and the Victoria Arms in Walton Street, also nearby, which had a room with a battered piano. Hotel bars such as the Randolph were considered a trifle grand for Amis's wartime circle. Everyone drank beer. Few could afford spirits or drank much wine (the college allowed undergraduates to purchase a single bottle of wine a term from the buttery). According to Amis's friend Mervyn Brown, another scholarship boy (later Sir Mervyn, ambassador to Madagascar, among other places), it was not unusual to drink six pints in an evening. Amis drank no more than anyone else, Brown remembers, a view corroborated by other contemporaries. He did, however, succeed in getting drunk almost as soon as he arrived. Richenberg, Rose and other CLS friends welcomed him to Oxford with a sherry party at Balliol. He had never drunk sherry before, consumed 'not much more than half a bottle', emerged into the fresh air of Broad Street to find 'everything was luminous with wonder', somehow managed the hundred yards back to his rooms, and was soon after visited by two young men from the Oxford University Conservative Association. 'One of them,' Amis recalls, 'perhaps noting the chamber-pot I was holding on my lap, added, "but perhaps we had better return at a more convenient time".'[13]

None of the dozen or so CLS 'men' who welcomed Amis to Oxford were at St John's. But shortly after he arrived, on 5 May, Amis met a St John's student he knew: Norman Iles, with whom he had shared digs in Cambridge a year previously, when they were both there in vain pursuit of the same scholarship in English. Iles quickly established himself at the centre of Amis's circle of friends at St John's. According to Larkin, he had spotted Amis's name posted on a list of new arrivals, pronouncing him 'the hell of a good man'. When Larkin asked in what way he was good, Iles replied: 'He shoots guns.'

I did not understand this until later in the afternoon when we were crossing the dusty first quadrangle a fair-haired young man came down staircase three and paused on the bottom step. Norman instantly pointed his right hand at him in the semblance of a pistol and uttered a short coughing bark to signify a shot – a shot not as in reality, but as it would sound from a worn sound-track on Saturday afternoon in the ninepennies.

The young man's reaction was immediate. Clutching his chest in a rictus of agony, he threw one arm up against the archway and began slowly crumpling downwards, fingers scoring the stonework. Just as he was about to collapse on the piled-up laundry . . . he righted himself and trotted over to us. 'I've been working on this,' he said, as soon as introductions were completed. 'Listen. This is when you're firing in a ravine.'

We listened.

'And this when you're firing in a ravine and the bullet ricochets off a rock.'

We listened again. Norman's appreciative laughter skirled freely: I stood silent. For the first time I felt myself in the presence of a talent greater than my own.[14]

What Amis remembered of the meeting was Larkin's offering him a cigarette, 'the equivalent those days of a glass of rare malt whisky',[15] and doubly rare, he would learn, coming from Larkin. 'Philip was careful,' recalled Noel Hughes, a friend from school and St John's. 'It was hard work getting a drink out of him.'[16] In later years, Amis would describe Larkin as 'mean', while also insisting that he would always stand his round.[17]

Iles played a key role in the early friendship between Amis and

Larkin, the most important of Amis's life. Iles, like Larkin, had come up to St John's the previous October to read English; he was Larkin's tutorial partner (teaching, like accommodation, was doubled up in wartime). Iles was 'lower class rather than bourgeoisie', as he put it to Larkin, 'a comparison', Larkin adds, 'which, in his way of thinking at least, gives him victory immediately'.[18] Brought up by a single mother, he was educated at Bristol Grammar School. By the time he got to Oxford, Iles had had enough of study. Amis describes him as 'a kind of ideal bad undergraduate, cutting lectures, not delivering essays, doing what he could to undermine the academic outlook'.[19] According to Larkin, 'he had little use for self- or any other kind of discipline', for reasons with which Larkin fully sympathised. 'I don't wonder you're sick of all printed matter after the education you've had,' he wrote to Iles on 17 April 1941, two weeks before Amis arrived at St John's. 'Secondary education as embodied in the School cert. is Evil Incarnate . . . A headmaster whose sole aim was to train children to carry 200lb. packs on their heads would be universally called a dangerous maniac. Yet that's all that people like old Moore or whoever your head was were doing. The *sods*!'

Iles's reaction against authority reached well beyond the academic study of English. Amis remembers him as 'large, large-faced, out of condition, with an air of half-serious hostility to the world in general, to any received idea'.[20] Larkin describes him as 'impatient and contemptuous . . . Any action or even word implying respect for qualities such as punctuality, prudence, thrift or respectability called forth a snarling roar like that of a Metro Goldwyn Mayer lion and an accusation of bourgeoisisme; ostentatious courtesy produced a falsetto celestial effect; ostentatious sensibility the recommendation to "write a poem about it".'[21] For Amis, Iles's 'underlying attraction was that of the cynic or nihilist who gives others a guilty pleasure by going much further than they would have dared to go on their own'[22] – in real life at least, as opposed to on paper. Iles had a comparable attraction for Larkin. 'I have no recollection of ever hearing Philip admit to having enjoyed, or again to be ready to tolerate, any author or book he studied, with the possible exception of Shakespeare,'[23] wrote Amis of the undergraduate Larkin. It was Iles, the grammar-school rebel, who encouraged such attitudes.[24] In addition, he was an ideal bad college man, 'stealing coal or "borrowing" jam (severely rationed) and other consumables out of neighbours' rooms'.[25] Though Iles was later to defend such behaviour as 'symbolic' ('it was a breaking of the law, it was boasting, it was a feeling of liberation. Thank God we never got caught'),²⁶ his 'borrowings' from Larkin, together with other impositions, eventually drove them apart, as Amis and Larkin grew closer.²⁷

It was Iles, not Amis, to whom Larkin seems to have written during the first two term breaks after Amis arrived.²⁸ As Larkin says in his 1975 introduction to *Jill*, while he, Amis and others 'were undergoing a process of adjustment, Norman's rejection of his new environment was total: as time went on, it tended to cut him off'.²⁹ Most of Iles's energies at Oxford went into organising pub crawls, skiving, and elaborating private jokes and fantasies. Amis found it 'interesting, even startling,' that he managed not only to pass his required examinations but to qualify for officer training.³⁰ It was Iles, with Larkin, who invented the 'Yorkshire scholar' on the way to and from tutorials. 'We had a particular hate for the man who was like us but did not revolt,' explains Iles, 'who went on working; who flitted silently from his rooms to the library and back again . . . He was the man who knows the ropes and stays inside them.'³¹ In the introduction to *Jill*, Larkin preserves some of the scholar's sayings: '"Had tea wi' t' Dean on Sunday – I showed him I'd been reading his book." "Never lose a chance to make a good impression." "What play have you written about?" "*King Lear*. You see, I've DONE *King Lear*." "Ay." "Ay."'³² In *Jill* proper, he appears as Whitbread, the one who informs John Kemp of the 'exact social status' of Lamprey College. In *Hurry on Down* (1953), by John Wain, another St John's man, he appears as Hutchins, 'an unpleasantly dogged and humourless young man' who lectures the hero, Charles Lumley, on exam preparation ('I go over each little plot of the subject carefully. Preliminary survey, then a closer reading, and then, three months later, revision').³³ He also makes an appearance as an oenophile ('You well up on the Barossas, friend?') in Amis's short story 'The 2003 Claret' (1958).³⁴ Larkin suspected that the character gave Iles 'more emotional release than myself . . . but I was sufficiently acquainted with the climate of the scholarship year to enjoy keeping the game going'.³⁵

This acquaintance Larkin gained at King Henry VIII Grammar School in Coventry, which he entered as a preparatory school pupil at eight. In the 1930s, King Henry VIII Grammar School was a day school much like CLS: academically rigorous (all its masters had to

have first-class degrees from Oxbridge), literary, of ancient foundation, with pupils mostly drawn from middle-class, professional families, though with a growing number of scholarship boys.[36] It differed
from CLS in one important respect: its headmaster, A.C.C. Burton,
was unloved by both masters and boys. Larkin called him 'the resident thug'.[37] It was Burton who suggested to Larkin's father that
his son forgo the scholarship year and apply directly to St John's,
with which King Henry VIII had long-established ties, including
several closed scholarships. Given the uncertainties of war, and the
fact that he could afford it, the father agreed. Larkin passed the
entrance examinations in March 1940, knew he'd been admitted a
month later, took Higher School Certificate at the end of the academic
year, and entered St John's in October as a fee-paying 'commoner'.
Though he never experienced the direct pressures of the scholarship
year, he saw them close up. Moreover, unlike Amis, his resentment
of 'Secondary education as embodied in the School cert.' was largely
untempered by affection or respect for those who taught him or for
the school itself.

Though Larkin was shy, unathletic, gawky and a stammerer, the
boys admired him, as Andrew Motion, Larkin's biographer, puts it,
'for the sarcastic rhymes he composed about the teachers, and for his
skill in not taking the rap'.[38] 'Something about him compelled respect,'
James Sutton, his closest friend at school, remembers: 'He was no softy
and he had presence.'[39] In the sixth form he became almost as active
a joiner as Amis was at Marlborough: debating and taking part in
play-readings (despite the stammer), writing for the school newspaper,
cutting a figure. 'Term by term,' writes Motion, he 'took on the bright
colours he associated not only with painters but with the Romantic
and *fin de siècle* writers he had begun to read.'[40] Students at King
Henry VIII did not have to wear uniforms to school, and Larkin was
remembered for his yellow knitted gloves, green jacket, bright red tie.
When Amis first met him at St John's, a typical Larkin outfit consisted
of 'tweed jacket, wine-coloured trousers, check shirt, bow tie . . . in my
suburban way I considered it was flashy of him to go on like that'.[41]
There was also flash or posturing in Larkin's brief flirtation with school
politics, on the right rather than the left. With two friends he formed
what Motion calls 'a facetious anti-Marxist trinity, supporting Franco's
cause in the Spanish Civil War'.[42] Another of his close friends at school,
a boy named Colin Gunner, was the class rebel, full of energy, jokes
and disrespect, distrusted both by school authorities and by Larkin's

father.[43] 'Larkin relished this bad influence,' writes Motion, 'since Gunner kept him "in fits" and encouraged the feeling that to be seriously interested in something didn't necessarily involve being pompous about it. It was a role in Larkin's life which would eventually be played by a far more famous contemporary.' Larkin described him as 'a kind of pre-Kingsley'.[44]

Larkin's friend James Sutton was in some ways Gunner's antitype. Sutton was unselfconsciously passionate about art and ideas, with ambitions to be a painter (he, too, would go on to Oxford, to study at the Slade School of Art, recently evacuated from London).[45] The letters Larkin wrote to Sutton in the 1940s were different from those he wrote to Gunner, Amis and, to some extent, Iles; they were less exclusively jokey, playful and harsh. Sutton initially sparked Larkin's interest in jazz, which Larkin fanned into obsession. But the jazz rant of the letters to Sutton was interspersed with serious, approving and detailed references to writers, D.H. Lawrence and W.H. Auden in particular;[46] the letters Larkin wrote to Amis in the early 1940s were more reticent about literary enthusiasms, certainly about enthusiasm for Lawrence.

Lawrence's influence over Larkin in his undergraduate years is clear. 'I am reading Lawrence daily (like the Bible) with great devotion,' he writes to Iles on 23 July 1941. 'To me, Lawrence is what Shakespeare was to Keats and all the other buggers,' he writes to Sutton a year later, on 6 July 1942. Earlier, on 20 March 1942, again to Sutton, he announces he's been reading *Sons and Lovers* and feels 'ready to die. If Lawrence had been killed after writing that book he'd still be England's greatest novelist.' Part of what appealed to Larkin about Lawrence is what appeals to all adolescents about him, and about Blake, too: his championing of instinct, appetite, excess. 'As Lawrence . . . said,' Larkin writes to Iles, on 23 July 1941: '"The reason the English Middle Classes chew every mouthful 30 times is that a bite any bigger than a pea would cause stoppage in their narrow guts," (or words to that effect). Which I approve.' Larkin was also drawn to the messianic strain in Lawrence. 'As L. says,' he writes to Sutton in the letter of 6 July 1942, 'life is a question of what you thrill to. But there has been a change in English psyche. The wind is blowing "in a new direction of time," and I feel that you and I, who will be if anyone the new artists, are onto it. I am not confident about this, nor am I prepared to argue about it, but it seems likely to me.'

Larkin and Sutton shared a Laurentian sense of mission and election, and Motion sees Sutton as playing a key role in encouraging Larkin to write, by which he means 'to connect his solitary "dream world" with the world at large'.[47] Gunner also encouraged Larkin to write, but in a quite different way. 'Together we got to work on reality,' Larkin recalls of the private jokes and schemes he and Gunner elaborated, 'and imposed fantasy after fantasy upon our dreary day-school life, until not only had I no time for anything else but I hardly believed anything else existed . . . Essentially they were fantasies of revenge upon our schoolmasters, mixed with fantasies of brutality too good-natured and free of sexual flavouring to be called sadistic, but at the same time of suspiciously illiberal tendencies.'[48] Larkin's novel *Jill* both tells the story of and grows out of such writing. The imaginary sister John Kemp invents, in defence against an alternately drab and intimidating wartime Oxford, is said to be at school at Willow Gables, the fictional setting of *Trouble at Willow Gables*, the first of Larkin's affectionate pastiches of girls' school novels, with their passionate crushes, hopeless embarrassments, quarrels between chums and innocent voyeurism, written while he was meant to be studying for examinations. Originally, *Trouble at Willow Gables* was private fantasy, the sort of thing he and Gunner, later he and Amis, worked on together; it was intended only for a few close friends. *Jill* is partly about the needs such fantasies feed as well as the dangers they pose. Like Larkin at KHS, John Kemp is so engrossed in fantasy that eventually he has 'no time for anything else' and 'hardly believed anything else existed'.[49] When *Jill* came out in 1946, Amis recognised Kemp's outer life, but found his inner one 'dreamy, romantic, sensitive, the work of someone I had never met before, invisible Philip. I found them hard, if not impossible, to reconcile.'[50] Amis's Larkin was 'to outward view an almost aggressively normal undergraduate of the non-highbrow, non-sherry-sipping sort . . . wholly gregarious'.[51] Later in the friendship Larkin would give Amis more access to the 'invisible Philip', but his initial reticence or wariness never wholly disappeared.

Partly this wariness can be traced to Larkin's relations with his father. Sydney Larkin, OBE, FRSS, FSAA, FIMTA, came from roughly the same class and commercial background as Amis's father, but he was a very different man. To begin with, he was successful: a powerful and respected local official, City Treasurer of Coventry for over twenty years. Then there was his personality. Though as controlling as William Amis, he was much more fearsome: quick-tempered, imperious, cutting and dismissive, contemptuous of women in general, and of his wife and daughter in particular. Politically he was further to the right than Amis's father. An admirer of Hitler and the efficiencies of the German state, he attended several of the Nuremberg rallies in the 1930s and as late as 1939 displayed Nazi regalia both at home and in his office.[52] Yet Larkin's father was a cultured man: in addition to being sharp-witted he was sophisticated and adventurous in his tastes, especially his literary tastes. It was the father who introduced the son to Lawrence. A final difference between the two fathers concerns the way they treated their sons: unlike William Amis, Sydney Larkin had both the means and the inclination to indulge Philip. When Larkin first discovered jazz, his father bought him a drum kit. Larkin admired his father, but he also feared and hated him, an ambivalence that helped both to draw him to Amis, as a sort of antidote, and to keep him at a distance.[53]

This distance derived also from Larkin's devotion to Lawrence and his followers, about whom Amis is unlikely to have been as enthusiastic, or as convincingly enthusiastic. In Amis's first term at Oxford, John Layard gave a series of informal lectures that Larkin attended. Whether Amis attended them as well isn't clear, though he alludes indirectly to Layard in his fiction. Layard had studied modern languages and then psychiatry at Cambridge, under both W.H.R. Rivers and Homer Lane, the very Homer Lane mentioned in the Auden poem Jeremy gives Robin in *You Can't Do Both*. Layard had met and had a brief affair with Auden in Berlin in 1926 and Auden drew on his theories of human psychology in his poems. As he declares in *Letter to Lord Byron* (1936), with Byronic matter-of-factness: 'I met a chap called Layard and he fed / New doctrines into my receptive head.' These doctrines derived not only from Homer Lane but from Lawrence's anti-Freudian *Fantasia of the Unconscious* (1922), the first page of which warns the reader 'straight off that I stick to the solar plexus'. At their core is the belief that to deny impulse or instinct is to violate the inner law of one's nature, and that the result will be physical as well as mental disease. This belief Larkin endorses in his correspondence with Sutton and Iles. In Amis's pungent summary: 'Philip rather fell for Layard – all that piss about the liar's quinsy.'[54]

Larkin was also taken with Layard's view of women, the subject of his closing lecture, 'a damn fine talk'. This talk Larkin summarises in a letter to Sutton of 16 June 1941: 'The solution as he saw it was that women should be the priestesses of the unconscious and help men to regain all the vision they have lost . . . What women must do is – as they are in the unconscious, rubbing shoulders with all these archetypes and symbols that man so needs – is bring them up and give them to man. How this is to be done, he didn't really know.'[55]

Amis was unsure how long Larkin remained under Layard's spell. Motion thinks that 'all the signs are that for a while Layard occupied Larkin greatly, and left a mark which was never entirely eradicated'.[56] Perhaps, but within two years of the letter to Sutton, Larkin was amusing his Oxford friends Bruce Montgomery and Diana Gollancz with readings from *Michaelmas Term at St Bride's*, the sequel to *Trouble at Willow Gables*, in which Layard's ideas are mangled and mocked. After meeting her icy friend Margaret in Elliston and Cavell, his heroine Marie attends 'a most interesting talk; it was all about some islands in the South Seas. Manakula, or somewhere' (in 1942 Layard published *Stone Men of Malekula*, an account of the inhabitants of an island in the New Hebrides). The talk is given by 'John Barnyard' and Marie becomes 'a keen convert'.[57] She writes down her dreams in an attempt to psychoanalyse herself (Larkin did this, too), lectures Margaret on 'my masculine principle – my animus',[58] misquotes Blake, sees archetypes everywhere, and decides to 'cure' her sister Philippa of her obsession with belts (symbols of 'that stage of our development when we were worms'), with disastrous results. Marie is endearingly clueless, gets everything wrong, and though Layard is not precisely responsible for her misconstructions, at the very least they call into question his view of women as 'priestesses of the unconscious'.

What Amis thought of Layard, Lawrence and Lane in the early 1940s – his later hostility is clear – is suggested in *You Can't Do Both*, not only in the scenes involving Jeremy and Robin but in those set in Oxford in which Robin loses his virginity. After Jeremy's attempted seduction of Robin falls flat, Robin asks him to explain the lines in 'Get there if you can' about Lawrence, Blake and Homer Lane. Jeremy thinks Lane 'the most interesting of the three' and summarises his ideas as follows: 'Stop hating and fearing your desires. If you feel bad, depressed and bored and so on, all that means is that your desires are putting pressure on you to go and do what you really want to do, instead of what you think you *ought* to do. If you follow that principle, even if it seems bizarre or shocking of you to, then it'll be like recovering from an illness, you'll feel well and start to be happy.'[59] This advice Jeremy himself follows when he leaves Cambridge, with unfortunate results. The fragile state Robin finds him in later in the novel is the product of prejudice, to be sure, both legal and social, but also, perhaps, of bad faith. In his case, Jeremy admits to Robin, 'all that sacredness-of-desire stuff was just queer propaganda'.[60]

You Can't Do Both sees 'the autonomy of the will . . . Homer Lane and all that'[61] as a contributing factor to Robin's selfishness, but only as a contributing factor. Nancy puts the truth to Robin at the novel's end: 'I remember you said, when Tilly was just a baby, you said Lawrence's motto was just It's all right when I do it, without realising, I mean you didn't realise it was your motto too. That stuff you read didn't *condition* you, you chose it because it was what you wanted to hear.'[62] Among the incidents in the Oxford section of the novel which support Nancy's view is the episode in which Robin first sleeps with a woman. In his second year as an undergraduate, a female friend from the Classical Society, Patsy Cartland, confides in him that any advances he might make to her friend Barbara Bates 'would be well received'.[63] When Barbara subsequently makes clear her willingness to sleep with Robin, she lends him 'Vanderdecken's *Happier Love* (1937, printed in Holland)',[64] a sex manual, though not a real one (Amis borrowed the author's name from *The Flying Dutchman*). It does not help. At their first encounter in bed, Robin loses his virginity (just), but is awkward, self-conscious, and not especially attentive to Barbara. Afterwards, he initiates a brief exchange about the Vanderdecken book:

'Sorry, I suppose I was working myself up to saying I think, I was wondering if the Vanderdecken approach was necessarily the right one, scientific or trying to be when the whole thing is supposed to be to do with instinct and the unconscious mind and feeling rather than thinking and . . . all that.'

'And D.H. Lawrence. I know. The trouble with that is that no amount of instinct and feeling and the rest of that will make a man understand that for instance a woman has a different sexual and psychological make-up from a man. That's a fact that has to be learnt like the exports of Finland have to be learnt.'[65]

By their next meeting Robin has rejected Vanderdecken totally, calling him a 'pietistic Netherlander'. Instead he prepares for Barbara's arrival in the manner of Norman Iles: not only stealing coal to make a healthy fire for his room but 'plundering the jam reserves of Cornish, the snivelling Christian biologist who inhabited the set of rooms under his'.[66] As soon as Barbara arrives, Robin kisses her 'with some fervour', gives her no time to sit down, hauls her into his bedroom, and is on top of her almost immediately. As Amis the narrator puts it: 'Vanderdecken's first objection to what followed might well have been that it followed rather soon, though he would have found it hard to fault Robin's performance in point of enthusiasm and evident enjoyment.'[67] Later on, with some remorse, Robin describes the encounter as 'a near-rape which [Barbara] tried to make the best of but refused to lie about'.[68]

Amis lost his virginity, he told Jacobs, in circumstances much like those of Robin Davies. Amis joined the Oxford University Labour Club soon after he arrived at St John's. In his second year at Oxford a female club member confided to him that another girl, a mutual acquaintance, would be willing to sleep with him if he asked her. Amis may have been timid about flying or riding horses, but he was bold in his approach to women.[69] When the Labour Club girl informed Amis that she would, indeed, sleep with him, she gave him, he told Jacobs, 'an improving book to read first, a manual with a title along the lines of "Happy Marriage" and an author with a Dutch-sounding name, both now forgotten'.[70] The only other thing Amis told Jacobs about this episode, or that Jacobs printed about it, was that he was too shy to go by himself to the chemist's to purchase condoms, so asked his friend George Blunden to accompany him. Blunden agreed, later calling his part in the story his one 'enormous' contribution to English letters.

In both real-life and fictional versions there is something odd about the behaviour of the woman, as well as Amis/Robin, in this story. In *You Can't Do Both* Robin suspects that Barbara was herself a virgin when she went to bed with him and 'had used Patsy in a little stratagem (not a very brilliant one but good enough to fool him)'.[71] But what is Barbara's motive? The novel offers no suggestion that she is in love with Robin or even much fancies him, though he is meant to be fanciable (the undergraduate Amis was slim and handsome). There are women who set about losing their virginity in as calculated a way as this, but they were probably rarer in 1942 than they are today. That they were likely to be less rare, though, among female members of the Oxford University Labour Club, especially the Labour Club of 1942, than among their counterparts in, say, the Classical Association, Amis and others were convinced, for several reasons. To begin with, left-wing girls were meant to be sexually as well as politically anti-bourgeois. When Iris Murdoch arrived at Somerville in 1938 she chose to sit at what was known in the college as the 'wild' table in the dining hall, the table primarily of Labour Club and Communist Party members, of girls with bohemian hairstyles and clothing and a reputation for frequent changes of partner.[72] Then there was the nature of the Labour Club itself. The Oxford University Labour Club Amis joined in the spring of 1941 had recently suffered a convulsion. In April of the previous year, it had been split apart by a breakaway group of more moderate leftists, founded by Roy Jenkins and Tony Crosland (both future Labour ministers) and Leo Pliatsky (a prefect at CLS a year or so above Amis; later Sir Leo and a Treasury Office mandarin). This new group took the somewhat cumbersome title of the Oxford University Democratic Socialist Club and quickly attracted over 400 members (out of a university population not much bigger than 3,500). According to Jenkins, its initial treasurer (Crosland was its first chairman, Jenkins replacing him a year later), these figures 'well-outdistanced' those of the old club, 'which became a bunkered rump'.[73]

The cause of the split was the dominance of Communist members in the Labour Club executive. When Jenkins was elected to the executive in December 1939 he was one of only three members not following the party line, the main tenets of which were support for the Nazi–Soviet pact, support for the Soviet invasion of Finland, and opposition to war with Germany. Having to toe this line had already done considerable damage to club membership and recruitment. It was one thing to be a Communist or to support the Communist line when that line supported an anti-Fascist popular front; quite another when it involved alliances with Nazis. According to Denis Healey, who joined the club in October 1936, becoming a Communist the following summer, in the months just before the Nazi–Soviet pact of August 1939, a third of undergraduates at the university were Labour Club members, and of these, 'about two hundred were members of the Communist Party'.[74] 'For the young in those days,' Healey writes, 'politics was a world of simple choices. The enemy was Hitler with his concentration camps. The objective was to prevent a war by standing up to Hitler. Only the Communist

Party seemed unambiguously against Hitler.'[75] These are almost exactly the words Cyril Metliss uses to describe his own reasons for joining the Young Communist League in December 1939, right after he'd left CLS, though while he was still in contact with Amis. 'If you were anti-fascist in the 1930s you became a Communist, because they were the only people fighting fascism. And I grew up in an environment in which, as a Jew, you were automatically anti-fascist.'

Those who remained in the Communist Party (CP), and the party-dominated Labour Club 'rump', rationalised the Nazi–Soviet pact and the attack on Finland as, in Healey's words, 'a reaction to the failure of Britain and France to build a common front against Hitler'. The willingness to accept this rationalisation owed something to party conditioning. According to Philip Toynbee, an undergraduate at Christ Church earlier in the 1930s, and an open recruiter for the CP (he claimed to have recruited nearly fifty new members in a single term),[76] for all the compassion and idealism of many individual members, the student branch of the Oxford Communist Party 'practised dishonesty almost as a principle'. This dishonesty took the form of disguising motives and affiliations and infiltrating rival or establishment organisations and institutions, including non-political ones like churches. According to Peter Conradi, Iris Murdoch's biographer, party members were to be found in 'all of the committees of the League of Nations Union, the Liberal Club, the Student Christian Movement'. Moreover, 'two of the five Conservative Club committee, and two even of the ten British Union of Fascists', were secret or 'closed' Communists.[77] Party members were encouraged to value loyalty, ruthlessness, ends over means. 'The Party was, of course, indelicate, authoritarian and possessive,' Toynbee writes. 'Its effectiveness depended on a crudity of judgement which began with political bluntness and extended to a blunt insensitivity about love affairs and all other human relations. There was a "line" for love; there was almost a line for friendship.'[78]

I am not suggesting that the Labour Club girl to whom Amis lost his virginity was 'recruiting'. By his second year at Oxford Amis was already a member both of the Labour Club and of the Communist Party. Only that the odd manner in which she, like her fictional counterpart in *You Can't Do Both*, set about bedding him (also, perhaps, her lending of the sex manual) may owe something to the view of personal relations Toynbee describes, an instrumental view, one often thought inimical to the purposes of art. In my edition of Amis's correspondence, a book of some 1,200 pages, there are only two items in which Martin Amis claims he cannot recognise his father. These are the first two letters in the book, both written to a fellow under-graduate Amis was trying to prevent from abandoning the Party. Martin describes these letters as 'humourlessly chivvying', their tone 'earnest, elderly, "soppy-stern" . . . alien'.[79] Here is a sample from the first one, written on 5 November 1941: 'Now, really, you know, this won't do at all, leaving the Party like that. Tut, tut, John. I am seri-ously displeased with you . . . So rejoin the Party right away. Not the YCL [Young Communist League] – that is only a bleeding kinder-garten, or, an excuse for getting to know lascivious young ladies – as if that needed an excuse anyway.' A later passage in the same letter is more subtly manipulative, notwithstanding hinted doubts and concessions: 'Your reference to the wangling of Party members onto committees, is, as you justly remark, a commonplace to the initiated, among whom, however, it is technically known as "the selection of the best and most representative candidate by free discus-sion before the votes are actually cast." This bears an interesting (though superficial) resemblance to elections in the Soviet Union.'

The undergraduate Amis is writing to here, John Lloyd, came up to Corpus Christi in the same term as Amis came up to St John's and met him in a study group on 'Colonialism' organised by the student branch of the Oxford Communist Party. 'I became his "contact" as it was called, and he eventually persuaded me to join the Communist Party. At first I disagreed with their "line" on the war . . . However, when Russia was attacked by Nazi Germany the C.P. changed its line to one of ardent support for the war. I believe I joined just before or after the Soviet Union was attacked'[80] – that is, just before or after 22 June 1941. According to George Blunden, in the summer or Trinity term of 1941 Amis asked him to accom-pany him to three Communist Party meetings (Amis was not yet a member and didn't want to go alone). Blunden was bored, put off by the Marxist jargon, and did not join up. Amis, however, did. It is possible, then, that Amis only became a member after the Party had changed its line on the war. Martin Amis has little time for such mitigation. In *Koba the Dread* (2002) he lists all the abuses and outrages his father would have had to have ignored when he joined the Party in June 1941, as well as the public protests (which led to indignant Soviet denials), and concludes with a quotation from Robert Conquest's *The Great Terror*: 'There was no reasonable excuse for believing the Stalinist story. The excuses which can be advanced are irrational.'[81]

John Lloyd left the Communist Party because 'my father would have been horrified'; Amis seems to have joined it for the same reason, 'in a boring, old-fashioned, textbook way'.[82] Looking back on his decision, and on how it affected his life as an undergraduate, Amis stresses non-political motives and factors:

Belonging was at least cheap and it involved girls, not very nice-looking ones, though, most of them, but it also meant reading, or trying to read, Marx, Lenin and Plekhanov (aargh), going to 'study groups' and meetings, *speaking* at meetings, on balance a poor return for having, in this most banal of ways, rebelled against my father (these words too probably deserve their inverted commas).[83]

In the event, his father's reaction was unsatisfying: 'you'll grow out of it'.[84] That his father was not the only person Amis sought to upset or impress by becoming a Communist may partly explain his status as an 'open' member of the Party (of 200 student members in the year or so before Amis joined, thirty were 'open', including Denis Healey and Iris Murdoch).[85] Among the fixed items in every issue of the CLS school magazine was an 'Oxford Letter' (there was also a 'Cambridge Letter') detailing the activities of 'Old Citizens'. The letter in the December 1941 issue begins by announcing that 'This term all Oxford O.C.'s are tinged with some shade of red from scarlet pink-wards, because [Saul] Rose has become Secretary of the Labour Club.' It then announces that 'Amis is very red and very musical. He combines both accomplishments neatly by leading the Labour Club choir. His favourite colour for clothes is still green, but this may only be a concession to bourgeois feeling.'[86] The reference here is to a visit Amis made to Marlborough College in green corduroy trousers, then associated with agricultural workers. Wearing such trousers was seen as swanking, and he was debagged, or at least that is what is suggested by an obituary notice in the 1996 CLS *Gazette*, the Old Citizens' magazine, in which the trousers were remembered as 'looking more decorative hanging from a lamp post in the court'.[87]

In a later Oxford Letter (April 1942), which it is possible Amis himself wrote, his rise in the Labour Club is recorded. He now edits the Club *Bulletin* and 'sells Left Wing literature to the proletariat.

No doubt he gets it free. His spirit of comradeship induces him to play before soldiers the gramophone records for which he conceived so strong an attachment at School.' These activities were part of Amis's new duties as Labour Club cultural secretary. Rose, meanwhile, had become club chairman, a burden eased by 'his predecessor in that office, who reappears at weekends to give him the benefit of her own experience'. This predecessor was Iris Murdoch, who had handed the post of cultural secretary over to Amis when she became chairman. It was Murdoch who officially initiated Amis into the Party: 'When I went along to be inducted,' he told the journalist Graham Turner, 'it was rather like being taken to the priest and asked if you'd got a vocation, and the person who signed me up was Iris Murdoch. She's a great pal now but then I found her absolutely terrifying.'[88]

In the last Oxford Letter to contain reports from Amis's wartime terms, he is described as 'still a very active member of the Communist Party, though his political prejudices do not debar him from recognising the personal charm of at least one member of the peerage'.[89] The identity of this person remains a mystery. The only girl Amis names whom he pursued in wartime Oxford ('slightly but unavailingly') was Chitra Rudingerova, half-Jewish, Czech, from Badminton ('Chitra' is the name of the eponymous heroine of a play by Tagore, the Bengali poet). Rudingerova was reading history at St Hilda's and on the committee of the CP. She made an impression on Larkin as well. He found her 'decidedly attractive' but also described her as 'a full-time Party girl. She was known to interrupt kisses to say "Remember the Party comes first." In a drunken fit of bravado I asked her to tea and she came. We ate toast and marmalade, and she told me I was decadent. Nothing else happened.'[90]

The reaction of Amis's circle to his politics was mixed. Though he sought to recruit friends to the Party, and stuck tenaciously to the party line, he neither badgered nor nagged. When Mervyn Brown resisted his attempts to recruit him to the Labour Club, Amis backed off. As the second passage from the letter to John Lloyd suggests, he could poke fun at party or left-wing dishonesties. Among the impersonations that quickly earned him his reputation at Oxford as a mimic of genius, one capable of immediately demonstrating, in Larkin's words, 'that something was horrible or boring or absurd', was that of 'the local comrade': 'Eesa poincher see . . . assa poincher see'.[91] When Iris Murdoch was culture secretary of the Labour Club she organised worthy meetings on Ireland and working-class Oxford history; when Amis replaced her he played jazz records and printed Larkin's 'morbid and unhealthy' poems (a phrase the committee used of 'Disintegration', published in the *Bulletin* in February 1942).[92] 'I was an open [CP member],' Amis told an interviewer, 'because obviously they weren't going to entrust me with any difficult or confidential task.'[93] Those who knew Amis from non-political settings or contexts often found it hard to take his politics seriously: he was too keen on fun. Sometimes, it seemed to Larkin, Amis 'suffered the familiar humorist's fate of being unable to get anyone to take him seriously at all'.[94] Yet in argument he was unyielding: Edward du Cann, a fellow undergraduate at St John's, later a Conservative minister, thought he had 'political steel';[95] 'in his contentious mood,' writes Larkin, 'he could be (intentionally) very irritating, especially to those who thought party politics should be suspended until the war was over.'[96] Though partly motivated by a desire to shock or swim against the stream, such a motive was not incompatible with idealism. Looking back in 1961 to his politics twenty years earlier he said: 'I got to the right age at the right time to feel the pull of the good, brave cause, the attractions of warning England of dangers insufficiently visible to the majority, the established, the reactionary, the complacent, the old.'[97] The old especially. On this same occasion Amis admitted that his youthful idealism was coloured by 'fears and aggressions', the sort, presumably, fathers, among others, inspire. Or as his Princeton friend Russell Fraser put it, 'quarreling with his elders got his juices flowing . . . When the old man died, others took his place.'[98]

Jazz was for Amis part of this quarrel, but only part. That 'older people were against it then' he describes as an 'added recommendation'. Amis's interest in jazz began while at school, as we have seen. It was not until he reached Oxford, however, that he realised that most of what he had been listening to over the radio was not strictly jazz at all, but dance music, 'suspect because "commercial"'.[99] Larkin explains about dance bands: 'Their leaders were national celebrities, and had regular time on the radio: 5:15 to 6:00 in the afternoon, for instance, and half-past ten to midnight . . . about every sixth piece they made a "hot" number, in which the one or two men who could play jazz would be heard. The classic "hot" number was "Tiger Rag."'[100] Larkin found these hot numbers 'so exciting that I would listen to hours of dance music in order to catch them when they came, in this way unconsciously learning many now-forgotten lyrics'.[101] When Peter Furneaux accompanies his parents to the Tennis Club dance in *The Riverside Villas Murder* his heart sinks when he discovers that the band, Bert Soper's Rhythm Boys, consists only of a pianist, a drummer, a violinist and a clarinet player: 'there was no sign of a trumpet, which ruled out the prospect of any hot numbers worth the name. And there was equally nothing in the way of a guitar or piano-accordion which meant no tangoes.'[102] Later in the novel Peter and Reg play 'Moonlight Kisses', a tango by Troise and his Mandoliers, a band they had seen at the local Gaumont. The music is described in a way which calls to mind Robin's description of Jeremy Carpenter's Louis Armstrong record, quoted in the Introduction (it 'made Robin draw in his breath and acted on him as a tremendous encouragement'): 'Almost at once, an accordion played a fast ascending run that put Peter in mind of a bird taking flight and made him want to shiver.'[103] In 1961, in the first of Amis's two appearances on *Desert Island Discs*, record number one was 'Moonlight Kisses'. 'Troise and his Mandoliers,' he told Roy Plomley, 'meant a lot to us, me and my pals, I suppose around the age of eleven and twelve and so on. And we all trooped down to see them when they appeared at the Streatham Astoria at a stage show.'

Amis loved speed and raucousness in jazz, from the hot numbers of radio dance bands onwards. This consistency of taste is clear from an interview in June 1989 in *Jazz Express* in which he was asked to pick his five favourite jazz records and explain why he liked them. Number one, 'Bucking with Buck', featured Wild Bill Davison 'at his most outrageous. It's got that screaming quality that I like so much.' In number two, 'Dream Man' by Fats Waller, 'what's particularly good is the daintiness of Bill Coleman's trumpet, contrasted with the brutal, forceful style of Waller'. Number three, 'Tuxedo Junction', is especially prized for 'just one moment where [Red Allen] loses his temper and squeals for a couple of bars' (Amis then offered what the interviewer called 'a spirited re-enactment'). Number four, 'Running Wild', 'starts off at boiling point with no elaborate preparations of any sort. Bechet solos for three choruses in his fast, loud, strident style which I prefer.' Finally, 'It's Right Here for You', with Pee Wee Russell, is praised for solos that seem at first to consist 'chiefly of horrible out-of-tune noises . . . then you realise the noises actually fit the melodic line'.[104] The emphasis in this last quotation is characteristic: the emergence of the melodic line matters less for itself than as a licence for exhilarating effects, those 'horrible out of tune noises'.

When Amis met Larkin he immediately recognised and deferred to Larkin's greater knowledge about jazz. Even Mervyn Brown, a talented saxophonist and the only one in their circle who could read music, acknowledged that Larkin knew more about jazz than he did, at least in an historical and discographic sense. Larkin had a good record collection, which played a key role in bringing him together with Amis. 'I was a fan,' Amis recalls of Larkin and their respective jazz backgrounds, 'but not such a one as I became under his tutelage. I had a few records, but I had started when I was twelve, then like a bloody idiot sold them. Then started again. So when I went up to Oxford I had a few by Louis Armstrong, Fats Waller, Artie Shaw, and I had a rather good gramophone . . . Philip would often come to my room for the gramophone, and took me in hand and introduced me to all these people I'd never heard of.'[105] Chief among them were Billy Banks and his Rhythmmakers: 'I was particularly struck by what we called the Banks sides, twelve of them cut in 1932 by a small band that included the trumpeter Henry Allen, the clarinettist and tenor saxophonist Pee Wee Russell and, on four of the twelve, Fats Waller . . . Banks himself was the singer, a sort of counter-tenor.'[106] James Silvester, a fellow jazz fan and friend of Amis's from St John's, has suggested that part of the appeal of these sides (as opposed to others with the same personnel or some of the same personnel) was their use of guitar *and* banjo to push the rhythm along. This is especially true of the Banks side Amis names, in the second of his appearances on *Desert Island Discs*, as the favourite of his eight choices: 'Running Wild', described in *Jazz Express* as starting 'at boiling point'.[107] Amis was obsessed with this record while at Oxford: 'Trumpet and clarinet wove magic flourishes and arabesques between the lines'; 'To catch an earful was to enter a world of as yet uncharted, un-written-about romance, innocent, almost naive.' It was Larkin who provided him with his only access to it: 'Philip had a copy, I had none and could not get one: the record was deleted, out of print.'[108]

Jazz revealed a range of affinities between the two friends. Part of its appeal to Larkin, for example, was that 'this was something we had found for ourselves, that wasn't taught at school (what a prerequisite that is for nearly everything worthwhile)'.[109] Though Amis was less negative about school than Larkin, he, too, associated jazz with non-school pleasures: 'one more indisputably good thing along with films, cricket, science fiction, the wireless and all that'.[110] Jazz also brought with it a more general sense of connectedness or solidarity: to Amis, it suggested approval from 'thousands of good chaps'; to Larkin, according to Motion, 'it was the means by which his stammering shyness could be set aside; it was his most enjoyable way of feeling part of a community'.[111] What Larkin looked for in jazz was what Amis looked for: immediacy of impact, strong feeling. In reply to the critic and music broadcaster Steve Race, Larkin explained his resistance to Charlie Parker and his followers – in effect, to jazz modernism – in an article published in 1984, a year before his death. Part of this resistance, he admitted, derived from his limitations as a musician; more important was the value he placed on emotional directness, a criterion he explains in terms almost identical to those employed by Amis in 'Louis Armstrong and Tea at Grandma's':

What I don't believe about art is that it should require special knowledge or special training on the part of its consumers. Art is enjoyment, first on the part of the writer, painter or musician, and then, by communication, on the part of the reader and looker and listener. But the second enjoyment has to come out of the first, not out of the conscious learning of technical theory.

You have to give the audience something to hold on to, right from the start, and this is just what I have never found in those by-now-venerable ancestors Parker, Davis and Monk.[112]

Larkin also had theories about the role of race in the music he loved: 'What got me was the rhythm. That simple trick of the suspended beat, that had made the slaves shuffle in Congo Square on Saturday nights, was something that never palled.'[113] In 1940, while in his last year at King Henry VIII School, he wrote a 'little essay' which connected this rhythm both to slavery and to the unconscious: 'Nobody sees that the stridency of jazz is the most important thing about it, for it symbolizes the importance and urgency of its problem. The modern unconscious has chosen to symbolize its predicament of subjection through the music of a subject people; its predicament of imprisonment through the unvarying monotony of the 4/4 Rhythm; its panic at the predicament through the arresting texture of the jazz tone. Jazz is the new art of the unconscious, and is therefore improvised, for it cannot call upon consciousness to express its own divorce from consciousness.'[114] Nothing like this is to be found in the many passages about jazz in Larkin's correspondence with Amis. This is partly because Larkin knew Amis didn't go in much for this kind of theorising, in any cultural field, partly because Amis seems early on to have distrusted excessive claims made on behalf of the unconscious (though he invoked them when it served his purposes). Larkin may also have realised the racial insult or slight implicit in such claims, at least in respect to jazz. Chief among what he would later call 'the subtler aspects of the colour problem' is 'the resentment felt by Negro musicians at the idea that jazz is "natural" to them, and that they therefore deserve no great applause for playing it'.[115] The two friends stuck mostly to exuberant praise, minute discriminations and scatological abuse. As Larkin explains in the Introduction to *Jill*: 'I suppose we devoted to some hundred records that early anatomizing passion normally reserved for the more established arts. "It's the *abject entreaty* of that second phrase . . ." "What she's actually singing is *ick-sart-mean* . . ." . . . "Isn't it marvellous the way Bechet . . ." "Isn't it marvellous the way the trumpet . . ." "Isn't it marvellous the way Russell . . ."' Russell, here, is Pee Wee Russell, saxophonist and clarinettist, '*mutatis mutandis*, our Swinburne and our Byron. We bought every record he played on that we could find, and – literally – dreamed about other items on the American Commodore label.'[116]

The quality of attack or aggression Amis valued in jazz was accompanied by another feature he and Larkin especially associated with Russell and the white Chicagoans (Eddie Condon, Muggsy Spanier, Frank Teschemacher, Mezz Mezzrow, Dave Tough, Joe Sullivan, among others): self-consciousness. According to Larkin, writing to Sutton on 16 September 1941:

the Chicagoans are the only gang that play jazz as white people should. Nichols' parlour-tricks are merely intellectual & Bix's 'beauty' is escapist. No white man can play negro music without a 'lowering' of himself. The Chicagoans are conscious of this, and their jazz is cynical and sardonic. They don't go for the negro's childlike beauty, but they go for his rhythm. Chicago style is jazz sarcasm . . . I should say the Chicagoans are more intelligent, more 'artists' than Nichols or Bix . . . they are conscious of a certain self-contempt. And they are ecstatically thrilled by the rhythm – but not as a negro is, with his whole body, but with their nerves. And their playing is nervous and tense and dirty – exemplified by Mezzrow, the dope-taker, or Tough, the gin-drinker.

The Chicagoans combined the power of the unconscious with irony. They could be ecstatic, thrilled, lost in the rhythm, yet knowing. To someone like the undergraduate Amis, who was both politically committed *and* funny, including about the failings and realities of the politically committed, the Chicagoans offered a model. So, too, for Larkin, for whom artistic success – the publication of *Jill* – required the integration of internal and external worlds, worlds carefully segregated in much of his daily life in wartime Oxford, certainly in his early relations with Amis. The Chicagoans were also valued for their sheer wildness, seen in part as a product of their whiteness. As Larkin wrote to Amis, on 7 January 1946, 'in my opinion negroes are . . . not neurotic enough to work up feverish excitement . . . [Henry] Allen is one of the few neurotic negroes and therefore I like him.'[117]

The immediate community jazz helped bring the two friends into contact with centred on St John's and consisted of like-minded under-graduates – beer-drinking, record-playing, happy to mock authority, although with little wish to challenge it openly. 'On a typical evening,' writes one of their number, James Willcox, 'towards the end of dinner, someone – Iles, perhaps, or KWA – would say to his neigh-bour at table – P.L. or Nick Russel: "Coming to the Bird and Baby?" Others of the group, seeing two or three kindred spirits moving off, would drift to join them. After drinking a good deal of beer we would go back to the College and to somebody's rooms to listen to jazz, played loudly and discussed loudly. Others, distracted by the noise, might come to join the party.'[118] If the pub they went to before returning to college had a piano, Larkin might play it, in Amis's words, 'with some proficiency in an unemphatic style'; if no outsiders were present, Amis might 'sing, or rather bawl, a series of lyrics culled from records'.[119] Larkin also remembers parties that began right after hall, with bottles of beer bought from the buttery and taken up to someone's rooms.

These parties were frequently held in Larkin's set: 'then would come messages. "The Dean says less noise, Sir" – and so forth. There were two confrontations that didn't do my reputation any good or anybody else's for that matter.' In addition to Amis, Larkin, Iles, and Willcox himself, the gatherings might include Nick Russel, David

Williams, Mervyn Brown, Philip Brown, Hilary Morris, Edward du Cann, David West and Graham Parkes, all St John's undergraduates. In due course, the circle spread beyond St John's to include Larkin's friends Frank Dixon from Magdalen and Dick Kidner from Christ Church. According to Larkin, Nick Russel, Amis and others, at some point a group of core members sought to formalise the gatherings, calling themselves 'The Seven', a name that appears also in one of Larkin's unfinished and untitled undergraduate stories.[120] But the beer and the general rowdiness soon saw off attempts at seriousness, even the unaffected, blokish seriousness which seems to have been the closest the group came to having a defining feature or ethos. Motion believes the group 'anticipated the principles which were more coherently described by The Movement in the 1950s'.[121]

The word 'blokish' may mislead. The name 'The Seven' referred to a specific group of undergraduates: Iles, Larkin, Amis, Philip Brown, Hilary Morris, Nick Russel and David Williams.[122] But it may also have been homage of sorts to W.H. Auden and his circle. Auden's fame in the 1930s owed much to the intellectual glamour of the 'Auden Group' or 'Gang', including Christopher Isherwood, Stephen Spender, Cecil Day-Lewis, Edward Upward and others. This group was an extension of Auden's circles at school and at Oxford. As Edward Mendelson puts it: 'At Oxford, like many young writers before or since, Auden made plans to conquer the literary world with the help of chosen allies.'[123] But it was not just literary fame Auden was after; his aims were also for mankind, often expressed in his early poetry in terms of a restoration of lost unity: between self and other, subject and object, conscious and unconscious, individual and society. 'Only in a group of very moderate size, probably not larger than twelve, is it possible for the individual under normal circumstances to lose himself,' he wrote in an essay of 1934.[124] This faith in the saving properties of the group Auden took over in part from his friend Gerald Heard, in *The Social Substance of Religion* (1931). For Heard: 'In the like-minded group, numbering about a dozen, the individual can experience complete release. His whole nature is not only purged: it is evolved to higher capacity and higher manifestation.'[125] The group is 'the essential first step' towards 'the salvation of civilization'.[126] Something of this spirit animated 'The Seven', as is suggested by the group's motto, 'SUMUS', burnt by poker over a fireplace in one of Iles's rooms. This inaugurating 'ceremony' took place in 1940 at a drinking party; under the motto the participants also burnt their initials. As Iles explains, in a memoir entitled 'Our Group', published in the December 1999/January 2000 issue of the *London Magazine*:

'We are' is an answer to 'You are not.' It was an answer to the Dean of the College, to academic learning, to our homes and parents, to the rules of society, and to the war itself. All these cried. 'You are not.' 'We are,' we replied.

In addition, it meant this. We are ourselves, whole, and will grow whole. We are greater than learning, intellect, logic, convention and desire to get on in life. It had the idea of ourselves as natural forces, growing as a flower does – or as a tree.[127]

The undergraduates who call themselves 'The Seven' in Larkin's story affect a camp and flirtatious manner. They are described in ways that recall Isherwood's account of his circles at Repton and Cambridge in *Lions and Shadows* (1938) ('Let me earnestly advise you to *buy* "Lions and Shadows",' Larkin writes to Amis in October 1943: 'He is exactly like we are, and the story of his life at Cambridge and elsewhere is magnificent').[128] When members of the Seven meet in Larkin's story they embrace and call each other 'My Angel', in 'satirical tones of passion'. The main character, Peter, is an obviously autobiographical figure; Peter's closest friend, Edwin, is a thinly disguised Iles. Most of the homosexual banter in the story takes place between Peter and Edwin, who speculate on the appeal of two other members of the group, Philip, a medical student, and Robin, Philip's friend. In the course of the story Peter describes his regard for what is 'most important' and 'human' about his male friends as 'jokingly and half-ashamedly concealed under a cloak of homosexuality . . . a badge of unconventionality against the rest of the college'. His aim in cultivating this image is to produce 'shocked envy'.[129] Amis, we know, sought to shock in comparable ways at Marlborough. Though he was determinedly heterosexual at Oxford, within the St John's circle he seems also to have boasted of schoolboy crushes and conquests. Larkin had almost nothing to do with women in his first two years at Oxford, partly because he was shy and less conventionally attractive than Amis, partly because his sexuality seems to have been a more complicated matter than Amis's, certainly judging by early writings such as the 'schoolgirl' novels. His first letters to Amis, after Amis left Oxford for the army, contain several references to the attractiveness of male undergraduates and other young men; sometimes these references occur just after he has commented on Amis's adventures with young women, as if keeping up, or are immediately followed by jokey disclaimers, as in a letter of 20 August 1942: 'Might I remind you that the greatest artists and philosophers did not enjoy the benefits of heterosexuality. If I were not too lazy, I would get up a few references for you. (NB This is *not* serious – do you catch the note of hysteria.)' When Amis himself makes the occasional homosexual reference, it seems almost a gesture of friendship or solidarity.

The Amis character in Larkin's story is called Geoffrey and it is hard to know what to make of him and of Peter's reaction to him. Perhaps in revision Larkin would have toned down its harshnesses or clarified its ambiguities. This story is set at the beginning of Amis/Geoffrey's second year at Oxford, when he and Larkin/Peter had only known each other for a term and were not yet close. We first encounter Geoffrey in hall: 'Peter surveyed the group happily. At his suggestion it had formally been named "The Seven," although with Robin, who had only recently become known to them, they numbered eight. Besides Edwin, Philip and himself, the three senior members who were now in their fourth term, there were Alec, John, Idris and Geoffrey. Peter imagined that with the possible exception of Geoffrey, the rest did not feel anything towards the society except a mild team-spirit.' After supper, the group lingers in hall:

Often conversations were started that had to be continued in rooms over coffee; but the Seven nearly always sat until eight o'clock, smoking and talking . . . If there was nothing to talk about, Geoffrey would give an imitation of one or other of the Senior Training Corps Sergeants, or one of the dons. Peter despised Geoffrey ultimately, but had a liking for him because he flattered him and could make him laugh. He had a gift for mimicry of a very high order: any peculiarity he could caricature and use as a nucleus for a fantastic monologue, that, always the same, passed into the repertory of the group's humour, and from which isolated phrases might become commonly used. Peter admired this talent, but for an indefinable quality Geoffrey possessed – perhaps that of being too honest, too open, too generous, and ready to consider others while being himself inferior – he assumed an attitude of scorn for him. There was something about Geoffrey's whole carriage that made him impossible to take seriously: the very obtuse angles of the head and body, and of the body and legs gave a subtle humour to his walk and bearing that aroused in Peter amused contempt. He had fair hair and had lived in London. Apart from being an ardent Communist, he had a love of classical music and occasionally wrote poems, which he showed to Peter. But none of these spiritual qualities were treated with the least respect by Peter, Philip or Edwin, all of whom continually reminded him of his revelations made about his school life, given in one of his moods of sincere and honest confession. Peter had a notion that he felt nothing deeply and occasionally [the following word is illegible] with Edwin who had introduced him a term before into the group. They had met a year before as schoolboys, taking scholarships at Cambridge.

Throughout his life, Larkin was capable of this kind of harshness in reference to Amis, even when they were closest. His comments about Amis in letters to friends, particularly women friends, could be cruelly dismissive.[130] In an autobiographical essay he wrote in 1943 about his years at Oxford, Larkin repeats the most intriguing aspect of the above criticism, though by now it is much less harshly expressed. Kingsley 'had an amazing sense of humour and a capacity for open confession that was a trifle startling'.[131] Whether Larkin objected to such confessions because he felt they were too easy, a product of Amis's 'feeling nothing deeply', or because they embarrassed him, or because he envied Amis his confidence or naturalness, is impossible to tell.

The camp behaviour cultivated by some members of the St John's circle is unlikely to have shocked the college authorities; certainly not Amis's moral tutor, who wanted to sleep with him, Amis suggests.[132] But it shocked others. In 1944, while stationed in Belgium, Amis and a fellow officer, E. Frank Coles, collaborated on an autobiographical novel entitled 'Who Else Is Rank'. The novel was never finished and exists only in portions, but a survey of chapters completed and projected and a list of characters and aliases make clear the time span it intends to cover: it traces the experiences of the two narrators, Francis Archer (Amis) and Stephen Lewis (Coles), from their first meeting in November 1943, at Headington Hill Hall in Oxford, headquarters of Second Army Signals, to Archer/Amis's demobilisation and return to Britain in August 1945. This closeness to real-life events and characters (Francis is several times mistakenly referred to in the manuscript as 'Kingsley' or 'Bill', the name he used in the army) helps to account for its weaknesses as a novel, its lack of shape or dramatic tension in particular.[133] 'Is WEIR printable?' asks Larkin on 9 July 1945, 'and has it a plot?' The answer to both questions, at least to judge by the surviving manuscript, is no. Half the chapters were to be written by Amis and half by Coles, though the two authors went over each other's work and commented on it. That Archer is, indeed, Amis is suggested also in correspondence, as when Amis warns Coles on 12 July 1945 that 'if you do put in something on what I look like I insist on seeing it first'. When Francis and Stephen meet in the second chapter, written by Coles, Francis is described as '⅔ bachelor of arts at the university of Oxford' (which is not quite right for Amis), 'a slight fair young man', 'awkward like a colt not a clown', and voluble ('Archer covered the whole field of jazz, homosexuality, Middle English letters at Oxford without pausing and had hummed two whole movements of the Jupiter and was beginning the third'). In the following chapter, entitled 'The Party', Francis takes Stephen back to old college, 'St. James', to meet his friends. He and Stephen have themselves only just met. When they reach the college they head for the rooms of Archer's particular friend, 'Bruno Coleman' (the 'schoolgirl' novels were written under the pseudonym Brunette Coleman):

We entered a doorway and climbed some steep wooden stairs, the sound of somebody practising the clarinet mixing with the blare of a gramophone. We went up to the room where the gramophone was coming from, and Archer knocked. Several voices roared 'Come in.' We went in. The room was in semi-darkness and smelt strongly of beer and more faintly of vomit. A tall young man in purple corduroys was dancing round the room in time to the music which was very loud. He stopped and stared at us. Two figures on the sofa raised incurious heads. Two others by a sideboard paused in the act of pouring beer into glasses. The gramophone shouted in the silence. They all said; 'Christ, it's Francis.' The man in the coloured trousers came forward and his mouth curved into an uncertain smile. He was as pale as Archer and wore thick horn-rimmed glasses and an orange bow-tie that did not rob him of a certain naturalness. 'Hallo, Francis,' he said quite quietly and normality was restored, but he did not shake hands.

Later in the passage Stephen notices two figures sitting on a sofa, one with his arm around the other. Bruno spots them and says to the one doing the embracing: 'Oh don't mind us . . . carry on if he wants you to.' The embracer is indignant, or mock-indignant: 'You bastard, Bruno . . . why don't you start on Francis?' More sexual banter follows, then the talk switches to jazz and Auden. Francis, meanwhile, gets very drunk, ignores Stephen, and Stephen falls into conversation with the other undergraduate on the sofa, Maurice Hiller. Hiller asks:

'Have you known Archer long?' 'A very short time indeed; exactly six hours.' 'What do you think of him?' 'He is intelligent, childish and vicious; a common enough combination. But he is interesting . . . Am I right about him?' 'Oh Christ you're right enough so far . . . especially the vicious part.'

Then Francis reappears: 'He flung his arm round Hiller's neck and laid his face against his own. "I haven't half missed you, Maurice. Have you missed me," he crooned. Hiller struggled to reply and gave me an alarmed glance, but he made no attempt to free himself from Francis's embrace.' As Francis drags Hiller away to converse on a sofa Stephen describes him as 'flushed and repulsive'. Stephen decides to leave and as the chapter ends is confronted by the college porter. 'No consideration they haven't got,' the porter complains, after 'a burst of drunken inane laughter from upstairs'. Stephen is older than Francis and married and as he turns into the High, he feels anger and then self-pity for being 'held responsible for what I had endured for three hours'. In other words, he is shocked; Archer and friends have succeeded in creating an impression that recalls Larkin on Russell and the white Chicagoans. Stephen depicts the undergraduates as would-be Byrons and Swinburnes, debauched, sarcastic, 'nervous and tense and dirty'.

One other moment in 'The Party' is worth considering in this context. Stephen crosses over to Bruno's bookcases and takes down a volume entitled *Chaucer: The Man and His Work*. Its pages are covered in annotations:

At first I read both the text and the pencilled comments in the margin; soon I found I was reading only the comments and my sympathy which did not amount to approval was wholly with the commentator. A long and flowery metaphor paralleling the richness of medieval literature with a gorgeously appointed palace had been carefully converted into a description of a combined brothel and lavatory. Similarly a paean on the greatness of the Poet was transformed into an account of a sex life of spectacular irregularity. It was continually suggested that Chaucer's favour at court was due to other things than his literary merit.

This subversive attitude is one Amis and Larkin took towards almost everything they were required to read for their English degree. Amis's wartime terms involved a heavy concentration on Old and Middle English texts. The approaches taken to these texts by his tutors and lecturers were textual and philological, or largely textual and philological. 'All Old English and nearly all Middle English works produced hatred and weariness in nearly everybody who studied them,' Amis recalls. 'The former carried the redoubled impediment of having Tolkien, incoherent and often inaudible, lecturing on it.'[134] (Tolkien, he wrote elsewhere, 'spoke unclearly and slurred the important words, and then he'd write them on the blackboard but keep standing between them and us, then wipe them off before he turned around.')[135] Amis liked his English tutor at St John's, Gavin Bone, son of the First World War artist, Muirhead Bone. A specialist in Anglo-Saxon poetry, Bone was 'a very nice, very tolerant man'.[136] Larkin rather regretted how badly he and Iles treated him in tutorials, especially after learning that he was ill with cancer (he would die in 1942). Bone seems to have detected little literary promise in Larkin, about whom he was reported to have delivered what Larkin called 'the highest academic compliment I received as an undergraduate': 'Mr. Larkin can see a point, if it is explained to him.'[137] There is no record of what Bone thought of Amis. Motion and others have suggested that Bone's stress, in his posthumously published *Anglo-Saxon Poetry: An Essay with Specimen Translations in Verse* (1943),[138] and presumably in his teaching as well, on the importance of the native word stock, and on 'Englishness' in general, may have influenced Amis and Larkin. When Jacobs repeated this suggestion in a draft of his biography ('It is possible that something of his distinctive attitudes rubbed off on Amis'), Amis wrote in the margin: 'but extremely unlikely'.[139] The suggestion was dropped in the finished manuscript.

It was not just the content of their English course that Amis and Larkin objected to; they also balked at having to toe a line about what they read. 'I can just about stand learning the filthy lingo it's written in,' wrote Larkin to Amis about Old English poetry (elsewhere referred to as 'ape's bumfodder'). 'What gets me down is being expected to *admire* the bloody stuff.'[140] Larkin makes a similar point about the syllabus in its entirety (it stopped with the Romantics). As he writes in a letter of 18 October 1942 to Amis, by now in training at Catterick in Yorkshire: 'You have to learn two things about each poet – the "wrong" attitude and the "right" attitude. For instance, the "wrong" attitude to Dryden is that he is a boring clod with no idea of poetry, and the right one is that he is a "consummate stylist" with subtle, brilliant *masculine*, etcetera etcetera. Irrespective of what *you personally feel* about Dryden these two attitudes must be *learnt*, so that you can refute one and bolster up the other. It just makes me *crap*.'[141] Amis thought such resentment widespread: 'Whatever one made of it in private, most people at Oxford, not just Philip, treated literature in this sense as a pure commodity, a matter for evasion and fraud, confidence trickery to filch a degree.'[142] Amis himself recalled preparing for examinations by reducing the whole of English literature to 'two sides of a postcard'. The idea was to regurgitate the line. For example, he told Jacobs, there were only three things one needed to know about Pope: his social eye, the merits of his couplets and his proto-Romanticism.[143]

In defiance of examination pressure – private defiance, character-istically – Amis and Larkin resorted to parody and mockery, both of canonical texts and of their scholarly champions. This defiance involved not only subversive annotation and mimicry but collabo-rative efforts of a sort Larkin had enjoyed with Gunner and Iles. Larkin remembers a Chaucer parody, 'The Bursar's Tale';[144] Amis remembers a series of 'obscene and soft-porn fairy stories' he and Larkin wrote together in his second year: 'The Queen Who Dreamed', 'The Tale of the Jolly Prince and the Distempered Ghost', which features a flatulant medieval spirit whose farts sounded 'like the breaking of an apple branch under the weight of good fruit'.[145] There was also much 'horse-pissing', a form of 'denigration-by-obscene-accretion' involving the epithet 'horse-piss'. 'Surely you hated liter-ature more than I did,' Larkin protested in a letter to Amis of 16 January 1981: 'How about "I have gathered up six slender basket-fuls OF HORSEPISS"?[146] "I hop alwey behinde" TRYING TO BUGGER HIM EH.' After Amis went off to the army and began corresponding with Larkin, the parodies and insults grew more elab-orate, inventive and scabrous. Even the Romantics, who continued to influence the poetry of Larkin as of Amis, came in for abuse. The poetry of Oxford contemporaries, especially those who had published, was predictably savaged. 'Kingsley and I used to read other people's poems,' Larkin remembers, 'and seriously planned getting a rubber stamp made – or rather two rubber stamps made, one for each of us – reading "What does this mean?" and "What makes you think I care?"'[147]

Larkin took the lead in literary matters as in jazz.[148] 'I saw at once that Philip had been much more concerned here than I had been,' Amis writes. 'He quickened my interest in or even introduced me to the work of Auden (above all), Isherwood, Betjeman, Anthony Powell, Montherlant (a lonely foreigner) and Henry Green, to *The Rock Pool* (Connolly), *At-Swim-Two-Birds* (Flann O'Brien) and *The Senior Commoner* (Julian Hall).'[149] Some of the works and authors listed here Amis was put on to by Larkin after Amis had gone off to the army; some were themselves introduced to Larkin by Bruce Montgomery, also of St John's, whom he only became close to after Amis left, and who would not figure significantly in Amis's life until after the war. But there was no question that Larkin knew more about modern writing than Amis, thanks in large measure to Sydney Larkin. As for the two friends' own writing, here, too, Larkin was more advanced: to begin with, he had been published. In November 1940, shortly after coming up to Oxford, one of his poems, 'Ultimatum', appeared in the *Listener*, the literary pages of which were edited by J.R. Ackerley. By Amis's arrival, in April 1941, Larkin had already published several of the nearly dozen poems that would appear in magazines during his three years as an undergraduate. In a letter to Motion, Amis described Larkin when first they met as seeming 'always the senior partner' in spite of his shyness, as 'the stronger personality, always much better read, with his views very firmly fixed. I was always full of ridiculous, foolish, very young man's ideas. But he seemed to have grown up.'[150]

Amis wrote very little in his wartime terms at Oxford, but he seems still to have wanted to be a writer, a poet in particular. In the autobiographical essay, Larkin remembers him as 'a member of the C.P. and . . . consequently only interested in literature as a sideline. His bookcase was crammed with unreadable books' (presumably, 'Marx, Lenin, Plekhanov'). At one point in 'The Party' Stephen asks Hiller if Fran writes poems: 'Oh I expect so; most of us do.' But Hiller hasn't seen any. Amis's fame in college and beyond, such as it was, derived from his humour, especially his impersonations and set pieces. Larkin told him he 'lived in a world of the most perfectly refined pure humour'.[151] 'He could rescue our spirits from the blackest pit,' Noel Hughes recalls.[152] 'He was mostly a name to me as a mimic and creator of amazingly realistic sound effects,' writes Alan Ross.[153] Larkin points to a photograph taken on a sunny lawn in the summer of 1942, just before Amis was to go off to the army in July. It depicts most of the wartime St John's circle and reminds Larkin 'how much of our daily exchanges were informed by Kingsley's pantomimes'. Here is Larkin's description:

In the foreground crouches Kingsley himself, his face contorted to a hideous mask and holding an invisible dagger: 'Japanese soldier,' my note says, but I have forgotten why. Edward du Cann is withdrawing the safety pin from an invisible hand-grenade with his teeth (*In the Rear of the Enemy*, one of Kingsley's Russian documentaries); Norman and David Williams are doing the 'first today' routine, Wally Widdowson has a curiously stiff thumbs-in-belt stance ('Russian officer' – was this part of *In the Rear of the Enemy?*), and David West ('Roumanian officer') is attempting to represent a contemporary saying that every Roumanian private had a Roumanian officer's lipstick in his knapsack. The rest are engaged in the eternal gang warfare.[154]

Amis in the photograph is like the anarchic hero of 'A Boy', his Norbury College story: mischievous, undaunted by a school report 'like nothing on earth'. Though neat in dress, he was in other ways messy, careless as well as carefree: 'His room, which grew to be our centre, was gradually made chaotic: records, papers, teacups and plates, books borrowed and not returned – all were thrown about the room in astonishing confusion. Nor would his fire ever burn. Nor would his cupboard shut.' At the end of four terms devoted to politics, drinking, the pursuit of young women, elaborate mockery of the English syllabus, of lecturers, of the conventional view, Amis was awarded a second in Part I of his examinations. Presumably he had sat the examinations by the time the photograph was taken. He would not yet have known his results. What he knew was that he was going off to war. From the photograph one cannot tell. 'I was fundamentally – like the rest of my friends – uninterested in the war,' wrote Larkin in the 1943 autobiographical essay.[155] To Nick Russel, recalling Oxford at this period, the war was 'about as actual as newsreel pictures'.[156] Denis Healey recounts the story of Balliol's annual dinner on St Catherine's night in 1939, at which Arnold Toynbee told the assembled undergraduates that their fate was to be broken on the wheel like her: 'we were irritated rather than alarmed'.[157] 'He was not a good boy, this boy,' the Norbury College story tells us of its hero. Wartime Oxford, for all its privations and stringencies, gave Amis the chance to be such a boy and he jumped at it.

6

The War

Amis served in the army a little over three years: two in England, on training and manoeuvres, one on the Continent, in France, Belgium, Holland and Germany, as part of the Second Army Signals Corps, attached first to Main Headquarters then to Rear Head-quarters. In July 1942 Amis reported to Catterick Camp in Yorkshire for basic training. Unlike many of his Oxford contemporaries ('I used to think it was most'),[1] he had been certified A1, 'not even A(x)1 Psychopathic', the 'enviable distinction' of a composer friend (not his composer friend Bruce Montgomery, who, like Larkin, was declared unfit for less enviable reasons, Montgomery for congenital deformity of the feet, Larkin for poor eyesight). At Oxford Amis had been required to join the Senior Training Corps or STC (he would have been called up into the ranks immediately had he refused). This involved signals training as well as uniformed drilling one and a half days a week, something he enjoyed and was good at, thanks to his years in OTC. STC offered other satisfactions: 'hearing Sergeant-Major Reid, a Scots guardsman who, by believable repute, had killed fifteen Germans at Dunkirk with his bayonet, bawl at Lord This of Magdalen and the Hon. That of Christ Church'.[2] Because of OTC and STC, Amis's basic training at Catterick was abbreviated, lasting only two months, which 'handicapped me to the end in my own understanding of the army'.[3] It was immediately followed by a posting of twenty-six weeks to a Royal Signals unit for officer-cadets, 152 OCTU, also at Catterick.

Amis joined the Signals for several reasons: because he had the requisite maths ('they got me into the Signals in the first place');[4] 'because it contained a better class of chap' (and meant a smooth path to commission, given his prior training);[5] and because he was less likely to get killed there than in other service branches ('We're always in the back,' a friend from Oxford, Norman Manning, assured him, 'we don't go further forward than Brigade').[6] According to 'I Spy Strangers' (1962), one of three Amis stories drawing on his wartime experiences, this last motive helped to shape the training regimen at 152 OCTU and elsewhere. Because his superiors possessed 'the inferiority feelings common to all technical troops', they not only cultivated a 'heavily martial persona', but inflicted many irrelevant combat exercises on their charges:

All present could very well remember the cross-country runs, the musketry competitions, the three-day infantry tactics schemes with smoke-bombs and a real barrage, the twelve-mile route marches in respirators which had seemed in retrospect to show such a curious power of inverted prophecy when the unit finally completed its role in the European theatre of war without having had to walk a step or fire a shot.[7]

Signals training exercises took place not only at Catterick but at several postings in southern England. In March 1943 Amis went first to Southern Command Signals in West Farnham near Salisbury; then to High Wycombe in Buckinghamshire; then to Bisley Camp in Surrey; then to Headington Hill Hall in Oxford (a large estate subsequently owned by Robert Maxwell); back to Catterick for an advanced wireless course; back to Headington Hill; back to High Wycombe; and finally, in May 1944, to Tunbridge Wells in Kent, Amis's last UK posting. The purpose of a number of the exercises at these locations, especially those in Amis's last seven months in England, from November 1943 to his landing at Normandy on 30 June (over three weeks after D-Day, on 6 June), was to learn to set up and dismantle communications systems as rapidly as possible. Some exercises had codenames: Eagle, Mara, Goldbraid, Blank; the instructions for Operation Overlord, the invasion itself, were labelled 'Top Secret', recalling Operation Apollo in *The Anti-Death League* (1966), a novel set at an unnamed army base in the English countryside.

When Amis landed in Normandy, he did so as part of a 'large and lavishly equipped' Second Army Main Headquarters signals unit. Crossing the Channel was already routine to the Americans who manned Amis's landing craft; he rolled ashore on a jeep 'through an inch or two of water'.[8] Neither then nor later did Amis face direct enemy fire. In Normandy there was heavy air activity at night, though this was more a matter of noise than of danger. Shortly after Amis's arrival, during the battle for Caen, a Mosquito aircraft broke in two, falling to earth on either side of a caravan containing the chief signals officer, Brigadier R.H.R. Steward. On another occasion, an artillery shell spattered fragments lightly on Amis's tent. In their progress through France he was often 'close enough to see the terrible litter of German dead'.[9] Around Falaise, the bodies had fallen 'so recently that there had been no time even to bulldoze some to the roadside'. The bodies of dead horses 'seemed almost more pitiful, rigid in the shafts with their upper lips drawn above their teeth as if in continuing pain. The dead cows smelt worse.'[10] Amis was twenty-two when he landed at Normandy and this was his first trip abroad.

Amis's job in the Signals, he told Jacobs, was like that of a post-master in a post office, 'with the difference that most of his customers were officers senior to him who gave him a bad time when things went wrong'.[11] There were three branches of Headquarters in the Second Army, each with a corresponding detachment of signals officers and men: Tactical Headquarters, where Lieutenant-General Dempsey, overall commander of the Second Army, conducted operations, Main Headquarters and Rear Headquarters. Though figures fluctuated, some fifty signals officers in total were attached to these three branches, commanding about a thousand men. Lieutenant K.W. Amis was attached first to Main Headquarters, then Rear Headquarters, never to the smaller Tactical Headquarters. He and his fellow signals officers sent and received messages to and from three directions: upwards, mostly to 21st Army Group, commanded by General Montgomery; downwards, to Second Army's own corps and divisions; and sideways, to allied officers or to officers from other service branches, especially 83 Group of the RAF. Messages could be transmitted through line communications, wireless and dispatch rider, although for Amis 'in practice, many hours of duty were spent answering telephone calls from the staff or staffs around one'. These calls were mostly 'inquiries made in a chiding spirit at best', which made them unpleasant, though 'nothing at all in comparison to being shot at'.[12] After 8 November 1944, Amis moved from Main Headquarters to a 'tele op' section in Rear Headquarters. This section consisted of fourteen officers and forty or so men, including keyboard operaters, clerks and technical support staff. The section was manned round the clock, in three eight-hour shifts. When on duty, Amis ran the office, aiming to ensure the speedy and efficient flow of traffic. His job description was that of assistant signalmaster, a subaltern's position; his boss, the signalmaster, was a captain.

In the draft of 'Who Else Is Rank' there is a single sheet entitled 'A Necessary Piece of Groundwork – The Signal Office'. Only a paragraph long, it describes a typical temporary office (Amis drew on this paragraph for the army chapter of his *Memoirs*). Archer is the narrator:

My desk is near the rear wall of the signal office and from it I can see nearly everything that is going on . . . At the other end of the room there are two six-foot tables end to end; these are called the counter. When people come into the room with messages they give them to one or other of the clerks who are facing them. I watch the industrious backs of the clerks: on the left Cpl Green emptying a large tray full of traffic received from the other formations; on the right Cpl Latimore and Smailes push traffic out to the ccts. Between them and me, also with his back to me, sgt. Prester leans forward over his table and bellows into a telephone. On my left sgt. Lee sits at a table and makes up packets of messages for the DR runs; on my right cpl. Marvin faces enormous racks of expired traffic, noting on a sheet the time of clearance. Tennyson, the locations clerk, is almost completely hidden by a wooden palisade on which he hangs a huge file stiffened with metal, like an old bible, which is supposed to show where every unit in the army lives. Just this side of the counter is a window leading to the teleprinter vehicle which is backed against it in the school yard. Operators clatter up and down the boxes which form steps to it. From inside it comes the rattle of the teleprinters and an almost continuous sound of swearing.

It was this sort of office that Amis and his fellow signals officers and men set up and dismantled eighteen times in the course of the Second Army's year-long advance, mostly from one small town or village or field to another.[13] In the first few months, through September, Main Headquarters moved quickly, sometimes as frequently as every two days. The constant movement 'went well with Normandy tummy (acute diarrhoea and fever), heavy continuous rain and arriving after dark in a field you had not seen in the light and where no latrines had been dug, but it still beat being killed'.[14] In a chapter of 'Who Else Is Rank' entitled 'You Are Going to Dingden W2395', Amis gives an account of such a move. Rear Army Headquarters is in Germany, in the process of relocating. Eighty per cent of the unit has gone off with a recce party, leaving Archer and a 'tiny minority' to 'pack and load the stores, to herd and cage the looted cattle and poultry, to dig out the quite inadequate 3-tonners and to hitch on behind these the smart but always defective civilian cars, to marshal on a road never fit for anything more than farm carts'. When Archer finally gets his men and vehicles into place in the convoy, and the remnants of the unit move out, they come to a T-junction: 'Sandy swung to the right, McIntyre to the left, and the truck in front of me stalled. There was no help for it: "Where's the bloody map, Waller?" . . . While I studied the map, those trucks I had had behind me in the centre stream, having decided my jeep was giving trouble, had overtaken me and turned some to the right and some to the left.' When at last his men are reunited and arrive at their proper location, Archer is informed by his superior officer that the building designated as a signals office is a barn full of straw. 'If you are to be ready in time you'll have to make a start tonight,' he is told: 'the only other place is the farm house and I want that for the mess.' Archer then walks into the mess, which he immediately recognises as 'the ideal sig-office layout', a conclusion he stifles as he passes through three large and luxuriously appointed rooms, the third and most luxurious of which his superior has commandeered for personal use.

Frank Coles, co-author of 'Who Else Is Rank', offers a thinly fictionalised portrait of Amis as officer in a chapter entitled 'Francis in Sackcloth'.[15] Amis 'quite liked F in Sckclth', he wrote to Coles on 12 July 1945, but thought it too short: 'Look at the lovely long one I did about you!' He also, as mentioned in the previous chapter, suggests that Coles add something about the way he looks, while insisting 'on seeing it first'. Coles/Stephen begins by detailing Francis's inadequacies and vulnerabilities:

Francis was not at his best in the army. His virtues were of a kind that could not possibly win approval there and a military environment seemed to exaggerate his faults many times over. He was easily discountenanced which argued inefficiency, he too readily told the truth and was therefore considered irresponsible, he was honest in his opinions and this made him conceited, he unguardedly made intelligent contributions to the desultory conversations in the mess and was accused of posing, he was polite and considerate to his inferiors and was therefore unable to exercise command. He looked, above all in uniform, little more than a boy and was made to feel that this disqualified him from making any positive contribution to the life and work of the unit . . . For some years before the army claimed him Francis must have been accustomed to intelligent companions and he was slow not to recognise but to adjust himself to the change. He never learned that the unforgivable thing was to lose face.

Amis corroborates much of this portrait in his own contributions to 'Who Else Is Rank' and to some extent in his later army stories and the *Memoirs*. On matters of appearance he fully concurs: 'I looked a goon and a bleeding civvy in uniform.'[16] (Larkin thought he looked 'completely false, like an advert in Austin Reed's'.)[17] In manner, too, he admits to being unsoldierly. In the Introduction to *Jill*, Larkin claims that within an hour of his commission Amis was reprimanded by a major for having his hands in his pockets.[18] This is a trifle exaggerated: the incident took place in Oxford in June 1943, some months after Amis's commission; as Amis recounts it in the *Memoirs*, he, Larkin and some chums (Larkin names them in a letter of 5 June) were on their way to a pub and as they passed a Military Police office, 'with immense bravado, I stuck my hands into my trouser pockets'. Within seconds a red-capped corporal appeared, Amis was summoned to speak to a deputy provost marshal, a young major, and cautioned in front of his smirking friends: 'I must reprimand you for your sloppy and unsoldierly behaviour just now and advise you strongly not to repeat it.'[19] In 'Court of Inquiry' (1956), a story which draws on Amis's army experiences, Archer, making a first appearance in print, entered a room 'and probably did his best to salute the Court smartly. The effort forced you to notice how badly he did it.'[20] If Amis's unsoldierly manner was partly willed, his messiness seems to have been congenital. When Lewis first visits Archer's tent in 'What's Cooking', the second chapter of 'Who Else Is Rank', the first thing he notices is his bed: 'It did not appear to have been made for some time and was covered with an assortment of irrelevant objects: the top of a fountain pen, a letter beginning Darling Fran in a very rounded feminine handwriting, a copy of Thomas's The Map of Love with a smear across one of the pages, a comb flecked with dandruff, a battledress blouse with no buttons or badge, a bootlace, a dirty towel clammily adhering to a piece of palmolive soap . . . I looked up to find Archer's eyes on mine. He looked down with a blush.'

Young Amis's propensity to blush cannot have helped him as an officer. It certainly doesn't help Archer in 'Court of Inquiry', which is based on a real-life incident. The court in question is of dubious authority ('a complete farce . . . just a bit of sabre-rattling')[21] and the 'charge' Archer faces is a minor one, a mere pretext, though in defending himself against it, the narrator tells us, he 'was shaking a good deal and throwing his hands about. When he paused, blushing violently, I glanced at the other members of the court.' The narrator, a sympathetic captain, suspects that Archer's main tormentor, Major Raleigh, 'enjoy[ed] humiliating Archer for looking young and unsure of himself'. In another army story, 'I Spy Strangers' (1962), set just after the war's conclusion, when the troops need diverting, Archer presides over a mock Parliament for enlisted men. Archer is the Speaker and at his first cry of 'Order, order' is described as 'blushing slightly'.[22] Later, at the scene of a drunken brawl involving senior officers, instead of helping or taking matters in hand, 'he spent the time quailing under the major's stare'.[23]

Archer's offence in 'Court of Inquiry' was to leave a charging-engine behind during a move (this was Amis's offence, too: 'I was the unfortunate Lieutenant Archer who was given a bad time by his company commander').[24] The charging-engine was obsolete and surplus to requirements; had it worked, which it hadn't 'in living memory',[25] it would have taken 'about a fortnight to charge half a dozen batteries'.[26] But it was Archer's responsibility and as he frankly admitted to the inquiry: 'I just forgot.'[27] The point of the story, the point also of Amis's account to Jacobs of the incident upon which it was based, is not just the major's petty vindictiveness but its intent and effect: the production of 'a shameless lickspittle willing to go along with almost anything his superiors tell him'.[28] Yet the story also makes clear that losing the charging-engine was not Archer's first offence. On a previous long road trip he had abandoned a trailer with a puncture (as opposed to repairing it on the spot, presumably), first taking the precaution to remove all its wheels so it wouldn't be stolen. When he returned for it, it had been stolen. On an earlier move, he forgot a telephone-exchange vehicle, though it was later recovered. This last offence was mostly the fault of a dipsomaniacal sergeant, though Archer refused to blame him. 'Couldn't run the section without him,' he confesses, with what the narrator calls 'his habitual lost look'. 'I'm not competent,' he explains. 'He knows how to handle the blokes, you see.'[29] The Archer of 'Court of Inquiry' is like the Archer of 'Francis in Sackcloth': easily discountenanced, unguarded, oblivious or indifferent to questions of face.

How efficient Amis was as an officer is hard to tell. In 'Francis in Sackcloth', Coles describes Archer as 'not especially efficient', adding that 'he certainly did not display unbounded energy or a willingness to do other people's work'. In 'Court of Inquiry' the sympathetic narrator describes Archer as 'no less incompetent, or no more incompetent, than most of us, though with Raleigh, the Adjutant and Captain Rowney (the second-in-command of the Company) taking turns to dispute this with him, his chronic lack of confidence was hardly surprising'.[30] As for technical competence, though good enough in mathematics to be commissioned in the first place, Amis was no boffin. The advanced wireless course he took at Catterick 'included the first trials of a line-of-sight telegraphy (unsuccessful) and of the ancestor of the telex machine (successful) and qualified me to operate a radio link with Moscow if need be. I passed out with a Q2, equivalent to a Third in a degree course and . . . never touched a wireless set again.'[31] Though in his poetry and fiction about the war Amis shows respect for technical prowess, in an undated letter to Larkin (it is missing its opening pages) he describes the boredom the course inspired, as when looking uncomprehendingly at 'huge valves with glowing filaments, enormous dynamos whirring round, gigantic meters with needles as big as toothbrushes', or listening to an engineer 'pathetically trying to explain the working of electrical machinery. I should have liked to connect the engineer between two terminals, switch the juice on and let him take a packet, ole boy.'[32] This description is accompanied by a request that Larkin send back a letter Amis has shown him from a Captain York (the name given the bullying Adjutant in 'Who Else Is Rank'): 'We may need it for evidence that we're entitled to our 2nd pips.'[33]

Amis was kept away, or kept himself away, from everyday as well as advanced equipment and machinery. Jeeps were a particular bugbear, the subject of a whole chapter in 'Who Else Is Rank'. Several years after the war Larkin read the 'Rank' material and claimed to like it and find it funny. In a letter of 9 February 1948, Amis reminded him that 'not all of what Archer writes in the 1st

person was written by me, and similarly for Lewis', adding that
'there are some things there that I wouldn't willingly let die (me and
jeeps, for example, which I did, of course)'. Amis learned to drive
in the army but after his experiences with jeeps rarely drove again.
'Frowning with concentration, he would steer the little vehicle round
the roads and tracks of the camp,' he writes of Archer, 'holding the
steering wheel delicately in his hands as if it were an antique.'
Changing gear was all but beyond Archer: 'as he ground the gears,
his face would contract with physical distaste'. If anything was discovered to have gone wrong with the jeep, 'it was nearly always after
Francis had had it out. He was scared of driving at night and often
forced himself to do so. He never actually had a smash but at least
half the officers in the unit declared after a night trip with Francis
that they would never go with him again. After one evening when
forgetting what gear he was in, he had nearly torn out the gear box,
missed a tank transporter by less than a foot and had been grazed
and knocked broadside across the road by a three-tonner.' Archer's
batman, Waller ('Where's the bloody map, Waller?'), rarely permitted
him use of the jeep after this incident.[34] In 'My Enemy's Enemy'
(1955), the earliest of the army stories, Thurston, the Amis character, is only permitted to drive the jeep when accompanied by his
batman.[35] In several chapters of 'Who Else Is Rank', Archer has to
beg fellow officers for lifts into town.

   In 'Release', a poem dedicated to Frank Coles and first published
in *Bright November* (1947), his first collection, Amis describes how
the army had changed him and what he hoped for now that he was
'no longer cramped / In someone else's clothes, not my colour'.
Although the poem makes no mention of shaky hands or blushes,
the psychological toll taken by incidents of the sort described in the
stories and the unfinished novel is clear:

> What have they given me?
> A catalogue of fears: of the telephone,
> Of entering a crowded room by myself,
> Of loud voices calling me to interview,
> Of typewritten notes, of arriving late at night

'They' in this passage are Amis's superior officers and, as earlier
lines suggest, their damaging legacy was moral as well as psychological. On parting from his unit, Amis writes, 'I was kind / And

shook their hand, forgetting to remember . . . / The hostile advice, the shameful, flattering speech.' In addition to fears and phobias, young Amis sees the army as having fostered deception of self as well as others, as the phrase 'forgetting to remember' may suggest. What Amis has in mind is not just the self-abasement of 'shameful, flattering speech', but its subsequent denial or rationalisation. In 'Court of Inquiry', as the blushing Archer throws his hands about, openly admitting to 'negligence and inefficiency', he turns to Major Raleigh: 'Archer seemed to be trembling. He said: "What makes me so ashamed is that I've let the Company down. Completely. And I don't see what I can do about it . . . It's no use saying I'm sorry, I know that."' At this point the narrator notices that Raleigh, too, is blushing, no longer enjoying himself.

Still holding his gaze, Archer burst out: 'I'm so sorry to have let you down personally, Major Raleigh. That's what gets me, failing in my duty by you, sir. When you've always been so decent to me about everything, and backed me up, and . . . and encouraged me.'
 This last, at any rate, was a flagrant lie. Had it not been, Archer would not have been where he was now.[36]

'Court of Inquiry' is made tricky and intriguing by the narrator's inability to tell how much of Archer's self-abasement is an act. Archer is let off with an embarrassed reprimand and when the narrator visits him in his section office, to apologise for having participated in the inquiry, the lieutenant is inattentive, only rousing himself 'to take a cigarette off me' and to wonder again at the 'irrelevance' (according to the major) of the fact that the charging engine was useless, obsolescent, surplus to requirements. Archer then calls his behaviour at the hearing an act: 'You didn't need to tell me that the thing had no standing. But I had to pretend that I thought it had, don't you see? – and behave like a hysterical schoolgirl.' The narrator wonders about this explanation: 'Archer was a good mimic . . . but it was perhaps questionable whether any amount of ordinary acting talent could have produced the blushes I had seen. On the other hand, I had no way of knowing how deeply he had thrown himself into the part.' Archer goes on to say that standing up for his rights against Raleigh would only have made matters worse: 'As it was I think I even made him feel he'd gone too far. The crack about him always backing me up was rich, I thought.'[37]

The hearing Amis himself was subjected to in 1945, he told Jacobs, was like that described in 'Court of Inquiry'. Major Raleigh, who appears also in 'Who Else Is Rank', was based on Amis's superior officer ('Metcalf' in the alias list), a comparable bully. When in 1991 an interviewer from the *Sunday Times* asked Amis which person he'd disliked or despised most over the years, Amis was silent for a moment, then replied: '"Oh, some people in the army." Officers? "Yes." For what reason? "For bullying. For the overuse of power and using it outside its proper place."'[38] What relation Archer's behaviour in court had to Amis's behaviour in real life is impossible to tell, but the intensity of this reply is suggestive. In the story, as in 'Release', the army itself is mostly held responsible. At the end, 'Archer no longer looked lost. Nor did he look particularly young. It was true, I thought, that the Army would lick anyone into shape. You could even say that it made a man of you.'[39] But 'Court of Inquiry' also suggests that Archer succumbs too quickly and abjectly to the major's pressure, out of fear.[40] At school, Amis thought of himself as timid, admiring those who were bold and wild, while leaning on more mature types;[41] at university, although much given to violent denunciation in private, he played by the rules in public. Though scathing about the examination system, he would never have openly defied or derided it by deliberately failing his course, as Christopher Isherwood claims he did at Cambridge. No doubt class considerations played a part in Amis's greater timidity, but so did greater timidity.

In 'My Enemy's Enemy' the theme of moral cowardice and the corrupting effect of the army, or of certain army types, is again central, although in this case the Amis-figure, Captain Tom Thurston, is older than Archer or Amis, married and a womaniser (more like the story's author than his wartime self). Thurston runs a signals office and kowtows to superiors, or is forced to kowtow to superiors. When Brigadier the Lord Fawcett, 'the largest and sharpest thorn in the side of the entire Signals unit',[42] demands a special dispatch rider to drive a hundred miles to Brussels to drop off his soiled laundry, Thurston complies. Fawcett is based on Colonel the Lord Glenarthur, described in the *Memoirs* as 'the biggest shit on the entire staff'.[43] In the *Memoirs*, Amis is clear about having to acquiesce in Glenarthur's demands. He tried 'more than once to get the Signals brigadier to do something about Lord Glenarthur and his SDRs [Special Dispatch Riders], but the Staff are the Staff'.[44] In

'My Enemy's Enemy', Fawcett's request necessitates not only the dispatch of one rider but the disturbance of another, 'who might have been driving all day . . . [and was now] condemned at best to a night either on the Signals Office floor or on a run half across Belgium in the small hours with a genuine message of some kind'.[45] Lieutenant Dalessio, a technical officer, has overheard Thurston's exchange with Fawcett: '"You're letting him have one, are you?" If asked his opinion of Thurston, he would have described him as a plausible bastard. His acquiescence in such matters as this, Dalessio would have added, was bloody typical.'[46]

A similar charge is implicitly levelled against Archer in 'I Spy Strangers', set in July 1945, a week or so before the results of the British general election. When Major Raleigh tries to punish a left-wing sergeant who has offended him, he is prevented from doing so not by Archer, who shares the sergeant's politics and has 'personal reasons'[47] for hating Raleigh (as we know from 'Court of Inquiry', which precedes 'I Spy Strangers' in the 1962 collection in which it first appears), but by Sergeant Doll, whose speeches at the mock Parliament reveal him to be a Fascist as well as a rabid anti-Communist. The left-wing sergeant, Hargreaves, is heedless and half hysterical in denouncing the government, and he is neither as bright nor as well informed as Doll (whose speeches are impressive, like late or right-wing Amis at his most powerful). Hargreaves's motives for speaking out contrast with Archer's reserve: 'The temptation to play safe was strong. But he must resist it. He could not have it said that he had covered up his real programme with comfortable platitude. That was what They had always done.'[48] As Speaker, a position that seems to have come to him from the men (to whom, we are told, he was unfailingly polite), Archer is meant to be neutral, though he allows 'a half-buried sympathy'[49] to enter his tone when addressing Hargreaves. Like the plausible Thurston, he mostly keeps quiet.

Class anxieties play a crucial role in these writings about the army, as in Amis's own wartime experiences, complicating political and personal loyalties. In 'Francis in Sackcloth' Coles attributes part of Archer's difficulties with his superiors to his not being a gentleman, or what they think of as a gentleman: 'From a young man straight from Oxford certain things were expected such as good manners, at any rate to superiors and equals on occasion, a willingness to vouchsafe the origins of words suspected of coming from the Latin or the Greek, an indifference to politics and a lack of displayed interest in sex.' Not only did Archer fail to meet any of these expectations but his friend and fellow officer Patsy Kerry ('Mayo' in the alias list), also straight from Oxford, did, and Archer suffered in comparison: 'Francis it was felt was a person who was not a gentleman but who had become an officer.' Yet, as Coles points out, of the officers in Second Army Signals, 'the nearest approach we had to a real gentleman would probably have chilled a cavalry mess with horror'. Amis openly admits that the class background of his superiors played its part in his inability or unwillingness to behave in ways they would approve. For the most part, he wrote in the *Memoirs*, his senior officers

seemed to share a low level of general culture. There were men who had been Post Office engineers or warrant officers in the Regular Army; I could see the point of them all right. There were some odds and sods like me who knew a bit of maths or physics. And there were, perhaps the majority, what a character in another short story of mine called, rather harshly perhaps, 'a bunch of ignorant jumped-up so-called bloody gentlemen from the Territorial Army', bank managers, local solicitors, estate agents, Rotary Club types.[50]

When Archer sees Lewis in the officers' mess in 'What's Cooking', the latter is reading *Bouvard et Pécuchet*, the perfect book for such surroundings. 'What a bunch they all were,' declares Thurston in 'My Enemy's Enemy': 'most of the higher-ranking ones had been lower-ranking officers in the Territorial Army during the Thirties . . . The war had given them responsibility and quick promotion, and their continued enjoyment of such privileges rested not on their own abilities but on those of people who had arrived in the unit by a different route' – from engineering work with the Post Office, like Dalessio, or from the ranks. As a consequence they were insecure about their authority and obsessed with appearances. Amis never knew for certain what his commanding officer, Lieutenant-Colonel G.F.H. Walker, 'a large self-assertive fellow', did in civilian life, 'but it cannot have been anything involving specialised knowledge, perhaps some form of civil administration or shopkeeping'.[51] Like the Colonel in 'My Enemy's Enemy', all Walker cared for was the way things looked: there were 'many stories of the Colonel's spell as a company commander in England. Three weeks running he had presented his weekly prize of £1 for the smartest vehicle to the driver of an obsolete wireless-truck immobilised for lack of spare parts.'[52]

Major Raleigh is the epitome of the Territorial Army type. He, too, is an appearances man: in 'Court of Inquiry' he strides through camp 'carrying a short leather-covered cane and a pair of string-and-leather gloves'.[53] Raleigh is the source of two of Professor Welch's most memorable traits in *Lucky Jim*: the way he drives ('Raleigh's car pulled up suddenly, as it always did when Raleigh himself was driving') and the store he sets on being called Professor ('None of us ever omitted the "sir",' says Archer of Raleigh. 'I don't think there was another field officer in the British army who attached so much importance to not having a Sir left out').[54] As Raleigh hurries Archer into his office, he pauses briefly 'to exhort a driver, supine under the differential of a three-tonner, to get his hair cut'.[55] Here and elsewhere, Raleigh, the Adjutant and others of their ilk recall the dapper William Amis: in social and professional background, in the manner in which they exercise authority, in not leaving well enough alone, in their philistinism and propensity for play-acting or self-dramatising (which is partly why Amis calls them 'jumped-up'). 'I wouldn't go all the way with you there, old boy,' is the way Raleigh talks, like Sorrell.[56] Also like Sorrell are Raleigh's politics, his sense, in 'I Spy Strangers', that as a Labour victory approaches, 'something monstrous and indefinable was growing in strength, something hostile to his accent and taste in clothes and modest directorship and ambitions for his sons and redbrick house in Purley with its back-garden tennis-court'.[57] Major Raleigh is a man full of fantasies and daydreams. 'In the weeks since the war ended,' we learn in 'I Spy Strangers', 'he had been possessed and tormented by dreams of triumph, renown or at least advancement. One of these . . . disguised as an unuttered joke, involved the removal with ignominy of the C.O. . . . "Where's Raleigh? Get hold of Raleigh. There's only one man for this job and that's Dick Raleigh."'[58] Later he dreams of titles: 'Lieut.-Col. R.W. Raleigh, R. Sigs' sounds authentic to him, as does 'Winkworth (West) Conservative Association – *Chairman*: Colonel Richard W. Raleigh.'[59]

Culture is as much a flashpoint for Raleigh and Archer as for Amis Senior and Junior. 'Come on Fran,' Raleigh pushes, 'let's have one of your famous intellectual justifications: what is it that makes Strav [Stravinsky] better than this sort of thing?' (that is, better than the *Warsaw Concerto*, which in real life Amis denounced to his adjutant as 'worthless commercialism', earning a snap inspection the following week).[60] Raleigh's fictional question occurs in Chapter 11 of 'Who Else Is Rank' (the chapter is untitled) and is followed by an assertion that 'the sort of people who say they like that sort of thing – I hope you won't take this the wrong way Fran – are usually youngsters who have to be up-to-date; they think it's clever to profess a liking for something new and unusual, no matter what it is.' This sounds like Captain Furneaux in *The Riverside Villas Murder* or Robin's father in *You Can't Do Both*, which is to say, it sounds like William Amis. In 'I Spy Strangers'[61] Raleigh recommends R.C. Sherriff's *Journey's End* to Archer (that it has an heroic character in it named Raleigh is unmentioned in the story): 'Really gets the spirit of the trenches, the feel of what it was like.'[61] Raleigh wants the unit to perform the play but Archer tells him 'it's been out of print for years', though copies may be available from the British Drama League. This uncharacteristic bit of obtruded symbolism reappears at the story's conclusion. Labour's landslide victory has been announced and thanks to Sergeant Doll both Hargreaves and Archer have escaped Raleigh's vindictive plotting. Raleigh has not been promoted. As he sits at an almost empty table, his eye just misses 'a letter from the British Drama League saying that *Journey's End* was not available'.[62]

Archer welcomes the new world Raleigh fears. Sergeant Doll has been talking about England, which sets Archer thinking:

'England.' Not your England, Archer said to himself, not the petrol-flogging C.Q.M.S.'s England, not the major's England or Cleaver's England or the Adjutant's or the Colonel's or Jack Rowney's or Tom Thurston's, but to a certain extent Hargreaves's England and absolutely my England, full of girls and drinks and jazz and books and decent houses and decent jobs and being your own boss.'[63]

It is this England that Amis tries to hold on to in his wartime correspondence with Larkin (judging by the little of it that survives). 'On Archer's table lay a letter he had been writing to a friend of his at Oxford,' we learn in 'I Spy Strangers'; 'one who, like most of his contemporaries, was medically unfit for military service . . . The letter was full of detailed assertions of hatred and misery, unsolicited news about what Archer's two girlfriends in England had been writing to him, and inquiries about issues of jazz records.'[64] The bit about girl-friends recalls Larkin's unease with Amis's openness, and was the sort of thing that made Amis's army acquaintances uneasy as well. In the first chapter of 'Who Else Is Rank', Archer's fellow officers are bothered not only by the fact that he plays no games, takes less exercise than anyone in the company ('though when he could not avoid it he showed agility') and writes poetry on a typewriter in the Signals Office, but by his open and unembarrassed two-timing of girlfriends, the freedom of his talk of homosexual friends at Oxford and his habit of referring to heterosexual intercourse 'much as the rest spoke of football, eating or drinking'. This openness was tempera-mental but may also have been political, as much an attempt to create 'my England' as the undeviating politeness Archer showed to his men or his willingness to defend left-wing positions against right-wing superiors.

During Amis's wartime years he had several sexual flings as well as his first serious love affair. The affair was with a married woman, Elisabeth Anne Simpson, whom he met in August 1943 while on the advanced wireless course in Yorkshire. Larkin writes to Amis on 20 August that Elisabeth 'sounds delightful, honest she does. I know she isn't really.' This is the earliest reference to her in the correspondence. The story of their first meeting, in the King's Arms pub in Richmond, near Catterick, is recounted in a chapter of 'Who Else Is Rank' entitled 'Rhapsody' (or so Jacobs implies in his biog-raphy, in pages unchallenged by Amis). 'Elisabeth Russell' or 'Betty' is described by Archer as 'quite good looking', with long dark brown hair, 'rather peculiar eyes a long way apart', a turned-up nose, and 'a big mouth, with little teeth like a child's'. Though she doesn't say much on this first meeting, she has 'a very attractive husky sort of voice'.

On the walk home from the pub Elisabeth lets Archer put his arm around her, but does not let him kiss her. Archer cautiously asks about her husband and she answers reluctantly. She gives him her number and makes him promise to call, looking 'very hard' into his eyes. Eventually they meet again, in Darlington, where she lives. This time 'she didn't shrink from me at all, but kissed me very hard, harder than I'd been kissing her'. At a later meeting, at Catterick station, there is more kissing and some awkward petting. '"You mustn't do that," she said. I felt like crying; "But I like you very

much" I said. "You wouldn't have done that if you really liked me."'
Now Elisabeth tells Archer about her husband: how they'd known
each other since childhood; how his parents and hers were friends
and encouraged them to get married; how they were married at
eighteen, when he was on leave from Dunkirk (making Elisabeth
twenty-one, the same age as Archer and Amis); how they thought
they were in love, though she subsequently discovered that he had
been seeing another woman in Manchester, had slept with her before
the marriage, and was still seeing her; and how she (Elisabeth, that
is) had a child with him, also named Elisabeth. Despite the child,
she tells Archer, 'He means nothing to me now.'

Soon Archer falls for Elisabeth: 'I began to realise that this attachment had developed along other lines than I had intended.' He
decides he must tell her how he feels: 'I love you. I want you. But
I've no idea for how long; probably not for always.' Elisabeth listens
solemnly and replies that she feels the same: 'but I am not sure
about the third part . . . I think it may quite possibly be for always.'
Some time after Archer's wireless course finishes (in October, like
Amis's) there is a tearful departure scene at Darlington station: 'It
had all felt rather like the end of the world and I was very tired
and soon fell asleep. I didn't wake up until the train drew in to
King's X.'

In October, at Catterick, Amis began writing poems about Elisabeth.
The first of these, 'For Elisabeth's Birthday', appeared in *Bright
November*, itself dedicated to her. Like most of his wartime poems
(twenty-two survive in fair copy, with appended date and place of
composition), it is obscure, in the manner of early Auden, whose poetical influence Amis later said 'helped, but also hindered, by suggesting
that riddles were okay'.[65] Tensions in the relationship are hinted at:
there is frustration and anger on his part, timidity on hers: 'So on
your birthday I make these diagnoses / Dried with the flames of anger,
and my wish / Is for the renewal of the charges of love.' Later in
October, in 'Introduction to Elisabeth Anne', there are again intimations of anger, a quarrel, disappointment, but there is also hope. 'The
accepted fiction from a husky voice' (presumably Elisabeth's, as in
'Who Else Is Rank') leads to guarded optimism: 'Waking the busy
heart to gradual hoping / But not knowing'. Presumably the heart in
question is Amis's, though the precise nature of 'the accepted fiction'
is anyone's guess. 'When the heart is busy to know,' the poem opens,
'the portents / Become indispensable, and the fable / Is resorted to'

(early Amis, like early Auden, is littered with unhelpful definite articles: 'the fable', 'the accepted fiction', 'the busy heart', 'the portents').
Again, what seems to be alluded to is Amis's uncertainty about the
affair, his sense that he may be deluding himself about it.

When the course at Catterick finished in October, Amis was given
leave, the first part of which he seems to have spent with Elisabeth
in Yorkshire. By 6 November he was with his parents in Berkhamsted,
where he would stay until his leave ended on the 19th. Amis's hopes
for the first part of his leave, and a portion of the uncertainty and
disappointment he expresses in the Elisabeth poems, may be alluded
to at the end of the chapter entitled 'Schemes' in 'Who Else Is Rank'.
'I've just heard from Betty,' Archer writes to Lewis, who is on
manoeuvres. 'She says she won't sleep with me if all I want is to
sleep with her. I don't understand these women. It seems impossibly
difficult to explain the simplest things; this is probably only an
excuse not to sleep with me when I go up to see her. The trouble
with her is she's so confoundedly respectable.'[66] This complaint
Archer will voice again in later chapters.

Elisabeth almost certainly slept with Amis during the first part of
his leave. While Amis was at Berkhamsted his father learned of the
relationship, through what in the *Memoirs* Amis calls 'a series of
implausibilities and coincidences unacceptable in any kind of fiction
or drama, reflecting moreover no kind of discredit on my father'.[67]
What happened is spelled out in the Jacobs biography, in an account
Amis himself must have provided: 'One evening his father ran out
of cigarettes and went rummaging for supplies in Kingsley's overcoat pocket. There he found what he was looking for, a packet of
Player's, or so he thought. But when he opened the packet he discovered not cigarettes but French letters. Kingsley had left himself with
a surplus, having over-estimated his needs.'[68] After a characteristically forthright quizzing on the father's part, the truth of Elisabeth's
marital status was revealed. In Amis's words from the *Memoirs*, 'as
well as really shocking him this put him in a fix'.[69] To begin with,
what punishment could the father exact? Amis was now being paid
by the army so there was no question of withholding his allowance
(his father had continued to handle Amis's finances at Oxford, doling
out his scholarship money in instalments). He was on leave and his
mother was anxious to be with him, so to banish him was impossible. The father's recourse was to write a letter:

a paragraphed 500-worder with all the commas and much else in place . . . I am heartily glad not to have that letter by me now. I had let him down, he said, and here and there he made me feel I had. (Remember that this was 1943 and I was twenty-one.) More painful was his self-reproach at not having seen to it that my morality had been trained to resist such temptation. 'I'd ask you to give her up,' he said, 'if I thought you'd take the slightest notice,' which daunted me. Then he managed a snobbish insinuation about her and I immediately felt better.[70]

When Amis writes to Larkin on 6 November begging him to come down to Berkhamsted for a visit, he may be alluding indirectly to tensions over Elisabeth: 'you can surely come over here for *two* or *three* days. Please try. It is very nasty here on one's own. My parents would be very glad to have you, if you see what I mean. I think they regard you as a "stabilizing influence" on me ("Does Philip care for girls much?" "Well, not an awful lot; he likes them, though." Silent registration of approval.)' It is clear from the letter that Amis was unrepentant about the affair. What neither the letter nor the *Memoirs* reveal is how furious he was with his father. According to Hilly Amis, the episode had a lasting effect: 'He never forgave his father for all that stuff with Elisabeth.'

That Elisabeth never knew of the confrontation between Amis and his father is suggested in 'Ecstasy', the second of the three chapters of 'Who Else Is Rank' to deal with the affair. Elisabeth asks Archer what his father thinks of her, and he answers: 'I think he thinks you're a designing woman.' The 'Ecstasy' chapter describes the first part of another leave Amis took, in March 1945, when he was stationed in Belgium with Second Army Rear Headquarters.[71] Only one poem about Elisabeth survives from the period between the two leaves: 'Elisabeth Anne's Intermezzo' ('Elisabeth's Intermesso' in *Bright November*), finished on 17 June at Bisley, Surrey. The subject of this poem is the difficulty of parting and of prolonged separation: 'Neither of us could find how to be true: / From her the coward's silences; from me / The indignation found too weak to try'; as a consequence, 'The agonising love became the mere' (that is, diminished in intensity), though this may not be what the poem's conclusion suggests: 'Heart's injury will not forget us so. / In dreams your distant face weeps and says No.'

When the two lovers meet again in 'Ecstasy', it is not clear at first how much of their feeling for each other has survived the 'intermesso'.

The chapter opens with Archer on a train to York. He is to meet Elisabeth at the station and the two of them are to go on to Leeds, where they'll spend two nights in a hotel. When they can't find a room in Leeds, they end up in a hotel in York. Archer is very nervous as the train pulls into York station, having convinced himself that Elisabeth won't be there. When he finally sees her, 'I felt my heart plunge and the blood rush to my face, and I realised to my annoyance that I was shaking.' He had not seen Elisabeth in over a year and she looked 'more attractive than I had ever seen her before'. At the hotel she is confident, composed, unembarrassed. 'I never felt less ashamed of anything in my life,' she tells Archer as she steps forward into his arms. Archer's response is revealing: 'I felt no longer a spectator at my own reactions; for the first time I was lost in another person and none of me could stand aside.' This confession is like the concluding lines of 'Letter to Elisabeth', one of only six poems from *Bright November* to be included in Amis's *Collected Poems: 1944–1979*. It is not among the poems that survive in draft, though the concluding lines provide a clue to its date:

> At last, love, love has taught me to speak straight,
> To make my body walk without a strut;
> Dearest, on our first anniversary
> Nothing exists now that can go awry.
> The eyes that looked good-bye will look at love
> As from this sleep we know ourselves alive.

If the anniversary referred to here is that of their first meeting or lovemaking, then the poem was probably written *circa* August or November 1944. Amis is celebrating a loss of self-consciousness he equates with maturity: no more irony or duplicity, no more posing; perhaps, one is tempted to add, no more blushing, embarrassment being as much an index of self-consciousness as irony.

After they make love, Archer asks Elisabeth about her husband. He is to return home soon and has asked Elisabeth to have him back. 'I am going to do that, Francis,' she tells him. 'After being here with you, I know what I want to do, but there's no way that I can see that I can do it. You said you wanted to marry me once, but honestly darling, it's impossible, isn't it . . . I've got to have him back: Elisabeth will be going to school in a year or so, and she'll be needing a hundred and one things.' Archer accepts her decision:

'I don't like anything about it, but I can't see any other way out.' Later, when Elisabeth asks if he's been faithful to her during their separation, he admits he hasn't, partly defending himself by referring to a long period in which she did not write (the 'coward's silences' of 'Elisabeth's Intermesso'): 'I thought I'd lost you.' Here and throughout the chapter professions of intense feeling alternate with defeated realism. Though he claims to be 'no longer a spectator at my own reactions', 'lost in another person . . . [so that] none of me could stand aside', the evidence is mixed. Soon after they make love Archer lies in bed watching Elisabeth wash: 'You're going to remember the way she does that, I thought. I knew I shouldn't forget either the way she brushed her hair, how her eyebrows lifted as she cleaned her teeth, how she took off her stockings.'

These words were written by Amis within months, perhaps weeks, of the real-life scenes that sparked them. In a letter of 1985, Frank Coles recalls VE Day, 8 May 1945: 'I was at Lüneburg [in Germany], but not in Monty's tent receiving the Nazi surrender. I was in the Countess's bedroom in Schellenberg hammering out the first draft of "Who Else Is Rank" with Bill Amis. The beginning of his literary career and the end of mine. Under the bed were five dozen bottles of Moselle and beside it was a beautifully bound set of the first collected edition of M. Voltaire's work.' In 'The End of the War', the novel's account of this moment, Archer reminds Lewis: 'Don't forget we're ranking tonight' (that is, working together on 'Who Else Is Rank'). Lewis insists that they work 'at the schloss' (that is, in his room at Schellenberg Castle, once the Countess's). Working practices like these raise questions about the intensity of Amis's feelings for Elisabeth. It is striking how soon after the affair their intimacies became material for fiction, and collaborative fiction at that. One thinks of Larkin's unease, or that of his fictional *alter ego*, Peter, with the intimate disclosures of Geoffrey (Amis), and Peter's suspicion that Geoffrey's openness signals lack of depth.

Questions of feeling and decorum recur in 'The Escape', the third chapter to deal with the affair with Elisabeth. 'The Escape' is not included in the 'survey of work complete and incomplete' (with its list of aliases) that accompanies the manuscript of 'Who Else Is Rank', as the events it is based on occurred after 12 June 1945, the date on the survey. It was probably written less than a year later, in the summer of 1946, as a letter to Larkin of 8 July 1946 suggests. Amis writes of having just reread 'Ecstasy' ('the account I wrote of me and Elisabeth going away together'), and pronounces it 'DEVOID OF MERIT OF ANY KIND'. Undaunted, he decides to write an account 'ab8 being taken out of a brown suit and bei[ng] put into an ordinary one'[72] (that is, about being demobbed). This account, 'The Escape', is subtitled 'from an unfinished novel', a phrase bracketed and added in pencil just below the title. The year's separation between 'The Escape' and the earlier chapters may explain the change of Elisabeth's surname from Russell to Cauldwell (a slip, presumably), though the carefully handwritten substitutions of 'Hamberton' for 'York' in the typescript are puzzling. The setting is an unnamed holding unit a short drive from York/Hamberton. Archer is to be demobbed in two days. Amis was demobbed in Yorkshire in September 1945, at Thirsk, not far from Darlington and Catterick. After turning in his uniform Archer telephones Elisabeth at her office (her husband has by now returned from the war); she no longer works there and he makes no effort to contact her at home. He visits the hotel they stayed at six months earlier and finds it unchanged, even recognising the thin, pale, lascivious-looking waitress Elisabeth had pointed out to him in 'Ecstasy'. The emptiness Archer feels in these scenes is of a piece with the emotions inspired by the brusque, indifferent treatment he receives at Thirsk. Personal feelings and emotions are woven into a larger mood of post-war deflation or anticlimax, the mood 'The Escape' means to evoke.

Amis's other relations with women while in the army involved ATS (Auxiliary Territorial Service) girls, nurses, Belgian and French girls. In addition, he may have continued a relationship, what sort is unclear, with a girl from Oxford, Elizabeth Gregson, with whom he was corresponding (Amis refers to her several times in his letters to Larkin).[73] Chief among the ATS girls was May, also met at Catterick. 'What a pity May is called May,' Larkin writes to Amis on 25 August, five days after commenting on Elisabeth: 'that is one of the names I simply cannot stand . . . But I am sure she is "shy as the squirrel," and looks perfectly delightful; dressed as an "A.T.S.," as you illogically put it.' Amis 'did not let things go too far' with May, he told Jacobs,[74] but his letters refer to her almost as frequently as they do to Elisabeth, judging by Larkin's responses to them, and at one point he even says May wants to marry him.[75] 'You must be jolly careful not to let them tangle, ole boy,' Larkin writes to Amis on 12 October: 'Betty sounds a real Tartar.'[76] As for non-Catterick flings, Jacobs mentions only an unnamed South African girl with whom Amis had a liaison in a caravan in High Wycombe (she was 'borrowed' from Thomas Balogh, the Hungarian refugee and economist, later an adviser to Harold Wilson).[77] On the Continent Amis had several adventures. In Brussels he got very drunk and in the same evening slept first with a prostitute and then with a waitress, contracting scabies. This episode raised 'the insoluble question' of whether he got the scabies from the prostitute or the waitress, and if from the former whether he'd given it to the latter ('I hoped not'). As for the visit to the prostitute: 'what I had in theory gone there for in the first place – that occurred satisfactorily. It was preceded by a longish solo dance round the room with one leg in and one out of my trousers, which made the tart laugh a lot.'[78]

Some time in 1944 – dating is difficult for 1944, since only one Amis letter survives for the year – Amis met a girl called Gail, though 'her real name was Gabrielle', samples of whose correspondence ('Gail-storms' or 'Gabrielliana') he sent to Larkin on 25 November. Gail/Gabrielle was 'of the educated classes: she talks with a more refined accent than I do and has obviously had a quasi-public-school education'. Though the daughter of a parson and much concerned to preserve her virginity, she was shockingly frank about sex. Her last letter, Amis told Larkin, 'contains some absolute jewels of middle-class morality at *the same time* as being the most shameless yet'. She tells Amis: 'I am the type for a home and children not for a mistress.' Then she tells him: 'My cunt is small . . . my clitoris is warm and soft . . . In spite of all I have said I still want you to make love to me. I want to stroke your cock and feel your hands on my cunt and feel our naked bodies pressed together.' As Amis tells Larkin: 'I quite agree; I don't believe it either.'

In July 1944 in Tierceville, in France, Amis writes a poem about Gabrielle, 'Gabrielle's Birthday' ('When foreign sand obscures the body's eye' in *Bright November*), in which she is depicted as eager 'to know the heart of sin without the sin'. What Amis emphasises is the innocence of her sexuality: she is 'Venus burning in a virgin star', 'a green girl loving the sun', its 'hand-like beams prising her dress awry'. Like other poems Amis wrote in the early 1940s, 'Gabrielle's Birthday' champions naturalness and instinct. In 'For of No Sentement I This Endite', one of only two surviving poems he wrote while a wartime undergraduate (its date is February 1942), Amis attacks an unnamed academic or academic type, 'feeling's

Antichrist / (Not seldom by the flesh enticed)', the sort of man who asks, presumably in superior tones, if there's 'Anything new in what you say?' and prefers 'many books / On which he cerebrally looks' to the view outside his window.

That Amis too could be cerebral and superior in his role as apostle of sex and instinct is suggested in several chapters of 'Who Else Is Rank'. Here is an exchange between Archer and a French girl he meets in May 1945 outside Lüneburg, from 'Le Lac des cygnes':

I tried to kiss her but she moved her head away. 'No please do not try to do that.' 'Why not? Don't you like me?' 'Yes of course; I like you but I do not like you to do that.' 'I can't see why not.' – 'But Francis it is wrong . . . Tell me – would you like your sister to do that?' – 'It's entirely her own affair what she does.' – 'I am sorry: would you say it again?' – 'My sister can do as she pleases; it is not for me to interfere.' – 'Ah, you do not take my meaning.' – 'Never mind; I shan't try again.'

A similarly lofty tone can be detected in another exchange about sex in the chapter entitled 'Jeeps'. Archer is talking to his fellow officer Patsy Kerry, the sort of Oxford man his superiors approve. Patsy wants to borrow Archer's jeep to go to town that evening:

'Don't tell me it's a girl, Patsy.' He was amused and Patsy became nettled, as he had expected he would. 'Of course it's a girl; why the hell shouldn't it be? What's funny in that for Christ's sake?' 'What's she like?' 'Very nice.' 'Does she like you?' 'I think so.' 'Have you slept with her?' 'No I don't [–]' Patsy was flushed and emphatic. 'Don't be childish,' F said, rudely; 'Of course you want to if you like her.' 'I tell you I don't,' he replied with real anger.

Later, after Francis agrees to lend Patsy the jeep: '"There's just one stipulation I make." "What's that?" "That you tell me about this woman when you get back." "Why should I?" "Because I want to know."'

The desire to irritate and annoy animated Amis all his life. 'It was as though his only pleasure was derived from being outrageously provoking,' writes Lewis of Archer. In many instances, such as these involving Archer, his aim was in part connected to a conscious plan or programme (one remembers how provoking he could be at Oxford when defending the party line). After a hectoring exchange with a nurse he fancies, in the untitled story Amis wrote while stationed at Bruges, Archer wonders 'why didn't he stop these foolhardy, callous, adolescent experiments?' Amis's openness about sex, his parading of rational attitudes, derived in part from his reading. In the army he had begun to read, or read seriously, some of the writers most talked about at Oxford, Auden in particular. Among the books Amis bought while on manoeuvres in southern England (carefully noting date and place of purchase) were Auden's *Poems* (1930), which contains 'Get there if you can' (from the 1933 edition onwards), *The Orators* (1932), *Another Time* (1940) and Auden and Isherwood's *The Dog Beneath the Skin* (1935).[79] Auden's influence on Amis's poetry was in some respects short-lived. By 9 March 1949 Amis was complaining to Larkin about 'that crazy Awdon type': 'I'm just not interested in all that guff about man fucking himself up.' The sort of thing Amis had in mind is suggested by a question posed in the opening prose poem of *The Orators*: 'What do you think about England, this country of ours where no one is well?' To answer this question, here and elsewhere in Auden's early poems, 'the symptoms have to be diagnosed, named, brought into the open, made to weep and confess'.[80] These words are Stephen Spender's and they apply also to what Archer is doing when he pushes Patsy about sex. There is something 'adolescent' (Archer's word) about his truth-telling and hyper-rationality as there is about similar qualities in early Auden. As Spender puts it: 'There is a flaw of feeling in his early work. He is intellectually over- and emotionally underdeveloped. Hence the schoolboyish ruthlessness.'[81]

During Amis's army years, revolutionary fervour gives way, or gives way more frequently than at Oxford, to dreams of personal pleasure and autonomy. Like Archer's ideal England in 'I Spy Strangers', Amis's is now only 'to a certain extent' like that of Hargreaves, the Marxist sympathiser. Archer wants 'decent houses and decent jobs and being your own boss' but only after 'girls and drinks and jazz and books'.[82] Life in the army, 'which clears the mind wonderfully',[83] explained why, not only because its pleasures and liberties were in short supply, but because it showed Amis that the qualities required of revolution were as well. 'Communism and socialism were, after all, about more than ideas,' Amis told Jacobs. 'They were about ideals too, requiring some degree of self-sacrifice and altruism for their fulfilment. Amis had seen little of that in the army.'[84] Yet, as has been suggested, it would be wrong to see Amis's waning radicalism as motivated wholly by unserious or apolitical impulses. Not being straight and open about sex, Auden, among others, would claim, was partly what was wrong with England, what made it a place 'where no one was well'; a healthy society could be worked towards in several ways. This seems to have been the message Amis took from Auden and Isherwood's *The Dog Beneath the Skin*, briefly discussed in *Socialism and the Intellectuals* (1957). Though he calls it 'a comparatively straightforward political play', its 'actual political content, even the anti-fascist content, is very small. It is jostled by a whole lot of other interests, in which the desire to shock the *bourgeoisie* was important. And that *bourgeoisie* which Auden and his friends were so interested in ridiculing and denouncing was the *bourgeoisie* of Flaubert [one recalls Stephen Lewis reading *Bouvard et Pécuchet* in the officers' mess at Headington] rather than that of Marx.'[85]

Though Amis's army poems rarely pronounce on 'England', the Auden vocabulary of symptom, illness, repression, diagnosis and cure is everywhere apparent – as it seems also to have been in the poems he wrote in wartime Oxford, judging not only from 'For of No Sentiment I This Endite' but from 'Complaint', dated October 1941, with its command to 'Let not a dead clockmaker's hand / Compress the spring that must expand.' 'Repeating the daily formula this analysis I make,' declares the speaker, only half ironically, in 'Poème Sérieuse', written in April 1944 at High Wycombe. This speaker is 'caught on society's contracting leash'. In 'For Signalman Caulfield', 'the accused' (he is unnamed) who once 'acquiesced' (about what is not specified), now, in the manner of Archer or Homer Lane or Auden, 'went by what he thought his soul advised / Raised an untopical issue and refused / To recognise the claims of decency'. 'You're going to lose,' cries Sergeant Hargreaves in the mock Parliament in 'I Spy Strangers'. 'You're on the side of death. History'll get you. Auden warned you but you never listened.'[86] Later Archer tells him: 'I thought that bit about Auden came in very well.'[87]
    The Auden influence can be detected in the style and tone of the wartime poems as well as in their content. As Clive James suggests, Auden is heard not only in individual lines – 'Still flows your northern river like a pulse ('Letter to Elisabeth'), 'Meanwhile the radiation sprang from the tentative rod' ('Radar'), 'Our closeness was an exponential term' ('Elisabeth's Intermesso') – but in whole stanzas, which

requires of the imitator 'a high degree of technical ability'.[88] The sample stanza James offers is from 'Belgian Winter', which, coincidentally, Paul Fussell singles out as the only early Amis poem in which 'Auden's influence has been tamed by a sense of life rather than literature.'[89]

> But there are people here, unable to understand,
> Randy for cigarettes, moving hands too
> Jerky to move in love; their women matrons, their daughters
> Fanatically guarded or whores with lovely teeth;
> Their sons come from somewhere else, fair of skin;
> The children have thick white socks and an English laugh,
> Bearers of flowers, quiet and pointlessly clean,
> Showing their parents up, not easily amused.

'Belgian Winter' is less obscure than Amis's other early poems, described by Fussell as 'university stuff aimed not at the general reader but at clever friends and colleagues who were wild for Auden, Eliot, and Donne'.[90] Yet James is right to call the stanza he quotes Audenesque: in its symptom-collecting; its *de haut en bas* detachment; its startling detail (the children 'pointlessly clean'). James singles out 'the way Auden made the *prosaic* sound poetic',[91] as the quality of his verse most likely to have attracted Amis, and the one with lasting influence; it is achieved here in the mixing of idioms or registers, the juxtaposition of 'randy for cigarettes' with genteel locutions like 'bearers of flowers' and 'fair of skin'.

Among the best of the wartime poems are 'Poem for Captain D' and 'Radar', both written at Catterick towards the end of the advanced wireless course (in September and October 1943 respectively). The poems stand out not only for their relative clarity but for the mostly admiring attitudes they take towards their subjects. Though 'hatred and misery' figure prominently in Amis's accounts of army life both in the letters to Larkin and in his poems and stories, for the most part he respected what in the *Memoirs* he calls 'the technical side, the apparatus that ran the line and radio systems on which the entire role of the unit depended'. Accordingly, he also respected the men who organised this apparatus, in particular the 'small ungregarious ex-PO major who, with his junior technicians, saw to it that the Second Army Signals actually carried out the job it had been designed for'.[92] Presumably this man was the model for

Major Rylands in 'My Enemy's Enemy', about whom Major Raleigh complains. Major Rylands was also ex-PO and Raleigh thinks of him as 'the root of all the trouble', by which he means the laxness and indiscipline of subalterns like Lieutenant Dalessio, who 'isn't interested in anything but his bloody circuit diagrams and test frames and what-have-you'.[93] Captain D. ('Captain Peter Davies', according to the poem's title in *Bright November*) seems to share with Major Rylands and Dalessio a wholehearted absorption in his work, as the first three stanzas of Amis's poem suggest:

> Years ago now you dismissed your toys
> and started to play with the wireless set
> and earlier far than most little boys
> you marked down the stations you wanted to get.
>
> You soldered connections on the 'fridge
> and stood on a chair to repair the light
> the house wiring you learned with a Wheatstone Bridge
> filled the car batteries with electrolyte.
>
> And now you teach the formulae of
> the force indispensable to living
> you have found a term that equates with love
> and thrown out of circuit the vague misgiving.

Though Captain D's teaching counters 'the vague misgiving' (its nature is unspecified) the same cannot quite be said of the power and mystery of radar, celebrated in the poem of the same name. The poem mimics scientific or technical mastery through its own formal command, another Auden trademark:

> Kolster and Dunmore made a remarkable valve
> Which would bind forever the sense of the plunging wave
> Riddling the grid they gazed at a colander
> Bending like a bough to and fro in the created heat.

Later the poem will call into question the purposes to which radar has been put (this is *its* 'vague misgiving'): making of 'the innocent scientist / A living directing-horn for the ears of war'. But such questioning is hardly what the poem is about.[94] In subsequent stanzas radar is associated with such words as 'throttled', 'pushing', 'sprang', 'dragged' (in revision Amis adds 'crammed' and 'smote'). Radar shapes waves into a shifting ('bending') colander-like grid, as a poem shapes words into metrical patterns, stanzas, networks of imagery and allusion. Amis's wartime admiration for Auden as craftsman can be connected with his admiration for Captain D and others on 'the technical side'.

In late May 1945, several weeks after VE Day, Amis's Signals section was run down and eventually disbanded. He himself was sent to an RHU [Reinforcement Holding Unit] in Minden in Westphalia, where along with several hundred other officers he sat around waiting to discover his fate. The weather was hot and sweaty and the atmosphere poisonous. Coles describes it in his portion of a chapter of 'Who Else Is Rank' entitled 'The Parting':

Francis seemed dazed all this time and uncomprehending. The rest of the officers were drunk for long periods, or spent their days scheming to get preferment or at worst a comfortable job after the disbandment. A mushroom underground movement sprang up . . . which clumsily conspired to give at any rate the favoured members of the unit further employment in Europe . . .⁹⁵ At night there were parties when fortified with champagne and spirits you had to demonstrate obsequiousness and servility to senior officers while in return they covered you with a saliva of false affection and gratitude.

Archer 'couldn't endure this' and eventually snapped. Late one night, after a party, he and his fellow officers find themselves listening to the Colonel as he praises the unit. Archer is invited to say a few words, introduced by the Colonel in terms that anticipate, and may have been the germ of, the mock Parliament in 'I Spy Strangers': 'silence for Lieutenant Archer, member for Enger, and former member for Headington, Southampton, Bayeux, Amiens, Horst, Dingden and all the rest'. The speech that follows reminds us that the Archer of 'Who Else Is Rank', like his creator, still had something of Hargreaves in him in 1945. It also warns against simple biographical readings. In 'I Spy Strangers', Amis contrasts Archer's caution and self-interest with Hargreaves's passion and tactlessness. In 'Who Else Is Rank' both sets of qualities are associated with Archer. Amis is under no obligation to make the two Archers consistent; his purposes in the story are different from those of the novel, which is partly documentary (as Amis writes to Coles on 12 July 1944: 'Fran's angle on Parting isn't bad – it's what happened too'). In the novel, Archer responds to the Colonel as would Hargreaves: he agrees about the success of the unit but attributes it solely to the men: 'we must see to it after we're demobilised that these common men, from whom we're separated only by a traditional barrier – we're no more than common men ourselves – benefit from the work that has been done, and if the system won't let that happen, well, we shall have to change the system'. The Colonel objects and accuses Archer of talking a 'load of balls'. The war was won not by any single class but by 'team work' (a value much praised by William Amis), 'comradeship, the mutual confidence, the old helping hand'. Moreover, Archer has brought politics into the mess, a taboo. Infuriated, Archer storms out, insisting that politics 'come in everywhere'.

On 11 August 1945, after the move to Minden, Amis wrote a letter to his batman, Bert Wootton ('Waller' in 'Who Else Is Rank'), who had stayed behind in Bruges after the disbanding of the section:

My dear Wootton,

I was very sorry to leave here without saying good-bye to you in person, but I've a feeling that the War Office wouldn't have let me wait till your return. So it's got to be like this. I should like to thank you most gratefully for looking after me so well during my stay with the section. And I valued you not merely as a batman (though you were all right at that) but as a person whom I felt I had come to know. I may see you 'out there' – *if* either of us go, or perhaps as I rather hope in civvy life, though not in the Sigs Memorial Club. Meanwhile, thanks again for everything, and I should like to hear from you: I shall be writing to the section from time to time. The marks are a very inadequate return for your services but they are all I have to give.

All the best, Bert: I hope we meet again.

Yours sincerely,
K.W. Amis

This affectionate and unpatronising letter goes some way towards qualifying the picture Amis and Coles present of Archer/Amis in 'Who Else Is Rank'. Here Amis sounds self-possessed, unselfconscious, an officer of the best sort. The sardonic reference to the 'Sigs

Memorial Club' is natural and unpresuming, worth recalling when reading 'A Reunion', the long poem Amis wrote in 1976 about a gathering of signals officers from his unit. This poem was inspired by a real-life reunion attended by Amis in 1975, held not in 'the Sigs Memorial Club' but in 'one of those assembly room places off the Edgware Road'.[96] What is striking about 'A Reunion', written when Amis was fifty-four, is the way it singles out for praise the very qualities the Colonel values in 'Who Else Is Rank':

> So, when one of us had his leave stopped,
> Was awarded a dose of the clap
> Or an extra guard, or was dropped
> Up to his ears in the crap,
> Or felt plain bloody browned off,
> He never got left on his own:
> The others had muscle enough
> To see that he soldiered on.

These acts of comradeship (Amis calls them 'Small kinds and degrees of love') involve both officers and enlisted men, though not equally. In the biography, Jacobs says they were 'more likely to be found among the lower ranks than the officers',[97] which squares with a letter Amis wrote to Larkin on 15 January 1977. This letter responds to Larkin's praise of 'A Reunion' and his reference to Amis's 'love-hate relation with Her Majesty's Forces': 'About the Ormy . . . I loved, well, liked a lot of the blokes and one or two of the officers, and hated some of the blokes, most of the officers and being on duty. Right?'

Earlier in the poem the differences between youthful and mature perceptions are raised, in a manner which recalls several moments from Amis's wartime fiction. The speaker, 'Bill', asks if anyone has run into 'Nicholls':

> A privilege granted to few
> Is meeting a pratt on the scale
> Of Nicholls: by common consent
> A nitwit not fit to shift shit;
> Whether more of a bastard or cunt,
> Views varied, one has to admit.

Ex-Major Sandy MacClure announces that he and Nicholls 'met now and then for a jar'. Bill and the others are shocked; Bill even remembers Sandy swearing 'back then / They could come and take you away / If you ever drank with him for fun.' Sandy is unperturbed:

> 'Oh yes?' said MacClure. 'Well, you know
> How it is – you exaggerate. And
> It was all a long time ago;
> Now we're older, we understand
> Other blokes, or some of us do.
> One thing about Nicholls, Bill,
> He always stuck up for you,
> And you needed a spot of goodwill.'

The passage recalls important themes in Amis's wartime fiction and poetry and in his subsequent writings about the war: his youthful extremity, the animosity it provoked, the good-heartedness and sense of fairness of some fellow officers and men, the vindictiveness of others. The tone of the poem as a whole is far removed from that of the awkward young officer Amis depicts himself as having been, a difference which is partly what the poem is about. But it is not far removed from the tone of the letter to Wootton. Whether Amis was capable of writing such a letter before the war or in his early years in the army is uncertain. That he could do so on the eve of his return to civvy life ought to be remembered.

What ought also to be remembered, and has been rather under-represented in this chapter, as in the wartime writings upon which it is largely based, is Amis's continuing capacity to amuse, even at his most irritating. If Stephen was quick to catch out Francis's 'least suggestion of exhibitionism, false modesty, assumed righteousness or revolutionary fervour, deliberate childishness or femininity, or any of the subtler forms of hypocrisy',[98] Francis's speciality was teasing Stephen out of his dignity, principally by treating him 'like a ridiculous small boy'. On such occasions he would 'fuss round him, strike his hand, coo at him in baby-language, stare inanely into his eyes'. In addition to achieving their desired effect (of both annoying Stephen and catching him out) these comic goadings revealed to Francis a truth he had only half realised about his friend: that 'parallel with his sometimes flaunted maturity, his authoritativeness, his masculinity in behaviour, in instincts, in talk, his refusal to be stampeded into a conclusion or an emotion, there was a very childish impatience, an intolerance, a lack of logic – in a word, an adolescent quality about him'. On the evidence of 'Who Else Is Rank', Coles soon came to appreciate the intelligence and perceptiveness that underlay Amis's humour. What made the humour compelling, however, was its energy and life: 'there was no meal that was not duller if Francis was not on duty, no incident that was not livelier if Francis had not witnessed it too; no topic except shop that you could discuss unless Francis was present. Francis kept open a narrow channel along which we could sometimes escape from it all.' Archer's vision of an England awash with 'girls and booze and jazz and books' was in part a reaction against the narrowness of this channel. It was also, Amis told an interviewer, 'very much how I felt. And when I voted Labour by proxy in 1945, this is what I had in mind. I didn't expect the government to bring me girls, but I did share in the general feeling of optimism and liberty abroad at the time.'[99] He was twenty-three and would test this feeling back at Oxford. 'The barrier to the days ahead is down,' he writes in 'Release', dedicated to Frank Coles, 'and the young girls approach.'

7

Post-war Oxford

Amis's hopes of an early return to civilian life rested on a Class B release. On 10 September 1945 he wrote to Larkin that his chances of getting one were 'about . . . even'. The purpose of the release, described in the *Memoirs* as 'a wise government measure', was 'to get scholarship boys and other talented fellows like me back at top speed into civilian life and the tasks of peace'.[1] In 'I Spy Strangers', Archer escapes Major Raleigh through a Class B release. Sergeant Doll has seen 'a letter from the head of his college in Oxford, the Master I think he called himself. It said they were arranging his release from the Army and reckoned he'd be out in good time to go into the college when the term begins, which I gather is about the 10th of October'.[2] Such letters relieved their recipients of dangerous as well as irksome duties. Without one, Amis was convinced, he would have been shipped to the Far East, where, though the war was over, 'plenty of disagreeable things remained to be done, in the course of which one might have got shot by Communists or just died of some tropical disease, as had befallen one of my college mates'. This mate was Michael MacNaughton-Smith, the only undergraduate in Amis's immediate St John's circle not to have survived army service.

The Oxford Amis returned to was an Oxford without Larkin. After gaining his First in English in June 1943, Larkin spent six months at home with his parents in Warwick writing and reluctantly applying for and failing to find jobs. Eventually, in December 1943, he was appointed Librarian, Wellington, Shropshire, employed by Wellington Urban District Council. Here he was to stay for almost three years, until September 1946, when he was appointed Assistant Librarian, University College of Leicester, a post he held for four years. It was in this post-war period, from late 1945 onwards, that the Amis–Larkin friendship blossomed. Though their correspondence had begun in wartime, it wasn't until now that it could be supplemented by frequent visits: by Larkin to Oxford or Berkhamsted, where Amis's parents lived, or to Harwell, where Hilary Bardwell's parents lived; by Amis to Wellington, later Leicester, or to Warwick, where Larkin's parents lived. There were also several meetings in London, as well as a trip to Dublin. During the war there were periods when the two friends wrote weekly; now there were periods when they wrote every few days.[3]

Only two dozen or so letters by Larkin to Amis survive from the period 1945–47, none from 1944 survive, and none from April 1947 onwards (until June 1967, a gap of twenty years). Larkin was much better at saving Amis's correspondence than Amis was at saving Larkin's, and the 200 or so surviving Amis letters from post-war Oxford contain some of his funniest and most memorable writing. The letters are meant to entertain as well as inform and are often written with fanatical ingenuity. They are also astonishingly frank. Larkin may have 'despised' Amis at first for his openness, but he soon came not only to relish but to emulate it. As Amis writes on 19 June 1946, in terms that apply as much to their correspondence as to their private conversation:

I enjoy talking to you more than to anybody else because I never feel I am giving myself away and so can admit to shady, dishonest, crawling, cowardly, brutal, unjust, arrogant, snobbish, lecherous, perverted and generally shameful feelings that I don't want anyone else to know about; but most of all because I am always on the verge of violent laughter when talking to you and because you are savagely uninterested in all the things I am uninterested in.

Five days later Amis again describes what he values in the friendship, and by implication the correspondence: 'I have a feeling that what we have to say to each other is more or less inexhaustible – by which I mean that we DON'T feel (a) as one feels with women so often that once one has worked through what has happened to each since the last meeting there will be little left to say; nor (b) as

one feels with other friends . . . that one has been through everything once and all ones conversation is a re-working of former
themes.'

As the friendship progresses, it becomes more hermetic or exclusive as well as intimate, as does the correspondence. 'I find that
when I meet somebody nice and intelligent (which happens RARELY)
I become annoyed because even though they *are* nice and intelligent, there is so much *to teach them,* and it's TOO MUCH TROUBLE
to teach them thigns that we don't have to teach each other.' This
is from a letter of 25 September 1946. A year later, on 5 September
1947, Amis returns to the theme: 'I talked in the pub the other night
to a young chap and his young lady about things like Russia and
women. I reflected to myself that they were quite nice people, and
then I imagined how I would view them in company with you, viz.
as BORING CRAPS. And then it came to me as a nasty reflection
that they were *much nicer* than the average young chap and young
lady, and that nearly all the people I should meet in this crazy life
would be far more *boring* and *crappy,* which made me feel sad and
frightened incidentally old boy.' This fear we shall return to. What
matters here is the extreme closeness of the relationship, almost like
that of lovers, Amis elsewhere suggests. 'You're not to take this the
wrong way, old boy,' he writes to Larkin on 22 April 1947, 'but I
am still conscious of how intensely I enjoyed beng in those houses
of drink in your presence, as intense (tho' not the same) as if I were
with "some girl." '4 Elsewhere in the correspondence confessions like
this are quickly followed by the mock-endearment 'dalling'. Before
Larkin's first visit to Amis and his family in Berkhamsted he fusses
about train times: 'please go on trying to find out how I get to you,'
he writes to Amis on 14 December 1945, 'and how I get back again,
an' all that, I know you will, you are so sweet, your Loving wife,
Doris.'5

The intimacy and exclusiveness of the friendship accounts for the
difficulty of many passages in the letters, a product of numerous
private jokes, allusions, obscure abbreviations, associational leaps
and word games. Most books, records, poems and songs, for example,
are referred to by the first and last words of their titles, as in 'Mr.
Train' for *Mr Norris Changes Trains.* Some are identified by the
first letters, or first few letters, of their first and last words, as in
'GB' for *Goodbye to Berlin,* or 'Appara' for *Appointment in Samarra.*
Often the writing proceeds associationally: 'I love the *persistent*

mis-spelling of authors' names,' declares Amis in a letter of 25 May 1947, 'it's amazing how it lowers the tome wainsh the tone. Talking of Wainsh . . .'[6]

Misspellings – 'beng', 'sam', 'dalling', 'thign' – are of several sorts. Some derive from simple typos, as in 'teh' for 'the', or 'thiknign' for 'thinking' (which to Larkin 'sounds really extraordinary – a character in Ibsen? Pastor Thiknign?');[7] others are laboriously crafted, as in 'methsleevs' for 'themselves', or 'darts B.A.' for 'bastards'. On 11 August 1945, before a visit to the dentist, Amis admits to being terrified: 'I TSLIL EFEL EKIL PENG YMFELS HTIW RFITHG EERVY EMIT I OG.'[8] Then there are phonetic spellings, often parodies of the sort of prim, suburban pronunciation mocked in the fiction, as in Chapter 4 of *Lucky Jim* where Margaret comments on Christine after their first meeting: 'Pity she's so refained, though.' Among the most frequent of the phonetic spellings in the letters of the 1940s are 'ab8' for 'about' and 'hay' for 'how', which parody the Oxfordshire English of college servants like the dreaded St John's porter Henry Payne. The intent of the misspellings is often subversive. 'Seriously though', for obvious reasons, is treated with special violence: when not typed upside down and backwards (an astonishing visual joke), it becomes 'Esoursyl htuohg'. After such ingenious manglings the appearance of the correct spelling becomes an event, as in a letter of 22 June 1947 when Amis places it in the middle of an otherwise blank page.

Amis's letters to Larkin are an important – in some cases the sole – source of this chapter's account of his experiences and feelings in post-war Oxford, and their limitations as evidence need recalling. The two friends exaggerated their flaws, fears and hatreds in their correspondence. In a letter of 29 December 1945, Amis called Larkin's correspondence 'the above-water visible part of a vast, sunken continent of self-nourished, fantastically amusing malice'.[9] In real life, as opposed to on paper, or at least in real life when not alone with Amis, Larkin could appear shy, withdrawn, reserved. Though often drily cutting, he was rarely as ferocious or subversive in person as in the correspondence. Amis in person was noisier, more outspoken than Larkin, but more amiable than the Amis of the letters – which is not to say that the Amis of the letters has no amiable moments.

Amis's main concerns in the letters of the immediate post-war period are those he identified in 'I Spy Strangers': 'girls and booze and jazz and books'. He also spends much time denouncing bores, narrow-mindedness, egotism, conventions (especially about sex), poverty, bad sounds, bad words and bad lines. Pursuit of girls seems to have begun immediately. Though ostensibly pining for Elisabeth, by 11 December 1945 he was advising Larkin to chuck his girl-friend 'the way I got rid of June'.[10] All we know of June from the letters is that he got rid of her because of the appearance of Gill (Gillian Williams), an art student at the Slade. Amis met Gill (some-times Jill) through Mervyn Brown, with whom he lived on the same staircase in St John's. Brown was almost as interested in girls as Amis and was wooing a friend of Gill's from the Slade, a girl named Cynthia. Larkin was avid for details about Gill: 'Is she nice to talk to, or does she like bad words and bad sounds and bad lines? . . . Are you going to write to her during the vacation? Yes, you are.'[11] Amis answers the next day: 'She is very nice to talk to. Her voice and what she says are of a perfect harmony with her appearance, which is child-like, piteous without being soft (you know what I mean), and – to me at any rate, *and to you* – irresistibly attractive without knowing it.' As for liking bad words and bad sounds and bad lines: 'She is the sort of person in whom the existence of tastes or thoughtthinking [is] . . . *astronomically* irrelevant'[12] – at least until Amis tires of her coyness. 'Our whole relationship has been compounded of lust and worship and exasperation on my side,' Amis writes to Larkin on 31 January, 'and *just bloody cretinism* on hers . . . she won't let me kiss her or anything.'[13] On 12 March he repeats to Larkin her valediction in a letter to Graham Parkes, also on Amis's staircase, to whom she seems to have transferred her affec-tions: 'Yours Gillian (I think!).' Less than a week later Amis tells Larkin that 'Graham and I have made up "Jill's Blues" of which the last verse is: My man's gone down to the river Lord / baby he's standing on the brink / Who's the woman made him do it Lord? it's me I think.'

By March 1946 Amis was in hot pursuit of another pretty young art student, this one from the Ruskin College of Art. One morning in January or early February, Hilary Bardwell, known as Hilly, and two girlfriends, also Ruskin students, were drinking coffee in Elliston and Cavell's. As Hilly explains in 'Why I Married Lucky Jim', an article published in the *Daily Mail* on 14 April 1958, 'during the coffee break most of the girls would rush down to the cloakroom, do themselves up, and then trip along to Elliston's or Kemp's for their coffee'. That morning a friend of Hilly's told her that several male undergraduates were interested in meeting her. Notes were passed, a common flirty practice. One of the undergraduates was reading chemistry, a second was reading PPE and the third, Amis, was reading English. It was the chemist, the dark one, Hilly fancied ('I like dark chaps'), but the prospect of chatting to him about chemistry put her off. 'I was most interested in the English Literature one because of the subject.' Though Amis was commonly thought attractive, Hilly was not initially taken with his looks. At the time he had what she called 'a pretty ruthless haircut'. There was also the matter of his teeth, which were 'all over the place and yellow and snarly'. In addition, his clothes were terrible: 'and being only seventeen I had very set ideas on what attractive young men should wear'. His jacket was a hairy, ginger-coloured tweed (it was part of a suit, though not, he told Jacobs, his demob suit, as Hilly suspected), worn with a pair of policeman's trousers, or what looked like policeman's trousers. 'He didn't have any money, you see, and he also had no idea about clothes. None of us had any money but he *really* picked the worst.' As Hilly recalls in the newspaper article: 'I found myself wondering if perhaps chemistry should have been the choice after all. One could always read up on the subject.'

Yet Amis was lively. When he came over to Hilly's table he dominated the group: 'he was the one who made everyone laugh . . . and that was attractive'. It also turned out that 'we had a whole lot of things in common, which was wonderful for me'. The most important of these things was jazz. Hilly's eldest brother, Bill, was a musician and had a serious collection of jazz records: 'so I knew all about the Billie Holidays and stuff, and not many girls did then'. That Hilly herself had records, as well as access to her brother's collection, was a plus in Amis's eyes, especially as some of the brother's records were out of catalogue and unobtainable. 'By the end of our third date,' she writes, 'I was minus Hoagy Carmichael's *Georgia on My Mind* and had in replacement a dull but workable bicycle lamp.' 'I wasn't fooled by any of that,' she later recalled of Amis's proposed record swaps and deals. In 'Why I Married Lucky Jim' she jokes of having made a mental note 'that I must marry this man: in order to get my brother's property back in the family'.[14]

At first, Hilly wasn't sure about Amis. 'Half of him appealed to me greatly – the funny, laughing, chatty, poetry-writing side of him.' She was also impressed by how intelligent and knowledgeable he was: 'I knew from the start that this man would teach me a lot.'[15]

What did not appeal, in addition to the ginger suit, was his peevishness and impatience: 'endless complaints about what seemed to me harmless things like apparently ordinary, nice people coming through the swing-door at Elliston's restaurant. He'd start muttering, "Look at those fools, look at that idiot of a man," and so on. If doors got stuck, or he was held up by some elderly person getting off a bus, or the wind blew his hair all over the place, he would snarl and grimace in the most irritating fashion.' Hilly also worried about having enough to say to Amis. One day, when his ill humour was particularly irritating, she determined to avoid meeting him again and put off any definite arrangements. In the newspaper article she describes what happened next:

After I had not seen him for a few days he suddenly burst in on me just as I was trying to draw one of the Greek stone chaps in the Ashmolean Museum, and demanded a statement as to whether I was giving him up for good – or would I please come out with him again?

Actually, it was just before this episode that I had the misfortune to look into one of those nasty three-winged mirrors. I saw to my horror what a curious nose I had.

I remember going all hot with despair and thinking how extraordinary it was that I'd managed to get a chap interested in me at all, and how I must be crazy to care about ginger clothes and any other slight imperfection of Kingsley.

So, of course, I leapt at my second chance.

To celebrate resumed relations they went off to tea at Fuller's, a slightly more romantic venue than the one Hilly thinks Amis probably took her to on their first date: Lyon's Corner House, for tomatoes on toast. Amis's appearance had improved since the first date: his hair had grown out and when he took off his 'rather nice army mackintosh' she was struck by a 'stunning' green polo-neck sweater, at which she stared so hard 'that I forgot all about the policeman's trousers'. After Fuller's they went to several pubs and 'with me talking as much as Kingsley, we walked back to my digs arm in arm. Just down an alley called Friar's Entry we had our first kiss – and very nice it was too.'

Amis refers only sparsely to these episodes in his letters to Larkin. Hilly makes her first appearance in the surviving correspondence in a letter of 21 February 1946 (in the *Memoirs* Amis wrongly says they met in May): 'Hilary, so far from being 22, is 17, younger than Jill, and hence not nearly so depraved as I had hoped.' Four days later he reports more encouragingly: not only has she said 'I can't stand Ellington after about 1930', but she 'brought some of her records in the other day. One of them was "Georgia on My Mind," by Hoagland ("Hoagy") Carmichael. That's right. On HMV magenta label. B6133. With Ellington's mystery song on the back. No, I don't mind that. Yes, she has sold it to me. For 7/6 (the price of a front and rear cycle lamp). Yes, I am glad I've got it. No, I don't suppose you are. Yes, she has got some others, nearly all cut-out and collector's items.'

On the sexual front, signs were also encouraging. Amis reports the following 'pattern conversations':

'After that I worked at some kennels with some dreadful women, two of them. They were lesbians. (Me; "Did they lezz with each other or with other people?" – geuss Who I maent eh you old Bugar I know my sort) With each other and with the dogs too. It was rather sordid.'

'Sex, sex, sex, nothing but sex all day long.'

Amis comments: 'She is seventeen. I like that.'[16] On 7 March, he reports other things he approves: 'Hilary is coming on nicely. She does really like jazz. Her breasts are concave on top. And she likes me.'[17] Five days later he announces that she 'is having her portrait painted in the nude. That's right. No, not by me. She said, did I think she was right to agree to having it done? I said, Yes, I thought she was. I'm sorry to have to tell you this, but it's a man who's doing the painting.' In this letter, Amis also voices worries: 'the quasi-Ruth implications of this business are coming out and I want to push them back again but can't quite see how I am going to do that, you see'.

'Ruth,' here, is Larkin's girlfriend in Shropshire, Ruth Bowman, later, briefly, his fiancée. Larkin met Ruth in the Wellington library in the autumn of 1943, when she was sixteen and he was twenty-one. The 'quasi-Ruth implications' of Amis's relationship with Hilly may refer to his uneasiness about Hilly's age and innocence, or about leading her on, or about her wanting greater commitment or attention from him. In the letter of 7 March Amis confesses to feeling 'a little low'.[18] He has agreed to take Hilly to a dance at the Randolph

Hotel. She has bought a new evening dress. It will cost him 12s. 6d. to get into the dance 'and I don't really want to go, very much, at all. But you will know why I am going.' By March Hilly's reservations about Amis had disappeared: 'In love with him? Yes, absolutely dippy about him, and I went on getting dippier and dippier.'[19] When term finished at Oxford, Amis stayed on an extra week until Hilly finished her term at the Ruskin. When she saw him off at the railway station, she found herself 'quite bowled over by the feeling of sadness at seeing his big head disappear out of sight as the train moved out of the station, with two whole weeks to get through before term started again'.[20]

Amis sent Larkin a further report on Hilly on 18 March, just before leaving Oxford: 'pattern conversation with H: "Haven't you ever slept with a woman?" "Yes." "Good, good; yes yeah,"' which elicits Amis's comment: 'She was saying "yes yeah" *before* she heard me say it.' Amis has lent her *Goodbye to Berlin*, which she liked. On 24 March, writing from Berkhamsted, he tells Larkin: 'she keeps showing that she would be interested in things to do with notes and words and celluloid . . . whether I were there or not, which I must say I rather like'. As for sex, in the next sentence he adds: 'And I think she will, too, if you see what I mean. (You do).' In extracts such as these, Amis presents Hilly in part as a figure of fantasy. Early in February he and Larkin had begun writing a soft-porn story entitled 'I Would Do Anything for You,' a sort of Willow Gables spin-off. Its principal characters are 'Jennifer and Marsha, two art students in Oxford'. They spend much of their time 'playing old jazz records out of curiosity, and painting each other'. The plot involves various lesbian crushes and seductions, including 'a furious struggle with Mady in pajamas' (Mady, another art student, is described as 'rich, reckless, promiscuous, athletic'). The story itself has not survived, only a synopsis and a set of brief character sketches. Marsha, aged seventeen, looks like Hilly: '5' 6". Small bones, sturdy. Golden bronze hair. Tawny eyes, slightly slanting. High cheek-bones'. When Amis writes to Larkin he sometimes adopts the persona of a young girl like Marsha. At such moments, the style, childish hand and misspelt words recall similar features in Hilly's letters from the 1940s, extracts from which Amis sends Larkin on 29 March: '" . . . vaguely trying to solve the problem of existence, we had tea at lions . . ." " . . . thank you so much for the Fats record . . ." " . . . 'The Map of Love' . . ."[21] " . . . went up on the downs on my pony befor breakfast . . ."' Amis's comment on these extracts is: 'Yes yes yes yes yes yes yes yes yes.'

Though 'absolutely dippy' about Amis, Hilly was not blind to his faults. It was obvious that Amis was attracted to her, 'but I could tell that he would also go for almost anyone'. As for romance: 'He loved to be in a crowd of friends. He didn't like heavy stuff. Didn't want to have long silent walks with a girl unless it ended with one thing, you know. That was the point of doing any of that.' She remembers his behaviour as 'brilliantly selfish'. Yet she also recalls him as vulnerable. She had to walk him home at night after dates, 'because of the frights. I understood that completely. Right: he's frightened. You can't help being frightened.' She says all Amis's friends at Oxford knew he couldn't go home by himself at night, but Mervyn Brown didn't know, nor did his jazz friends, John Postgate and James Silvester, nor Leonard Richenberg. Amis's fears did not lower him in Hilly's estimation; he was matter-of-fact about them, and she was too. As she later declared: 'I had a great understanding of people's fears.'

Like her older sister, Margaret, and her three older brothers, Bill, Brian and Mick, Hilly was educated at Bedales, a progressive boarding-school in Steep, near Petersfield in Hampshire. Hilly was eight in 1936 when she entered Dunhurst, the junior school at Bedales, and it was her experiences there that helped her to understand people's fears. During the first two years she was badly bullied by a girl named Barbara, who made her steal, 'which was not on my agenda', and say stupid things in assembly: 'I was terrified of her. Really terrified.' By 1937, when the bullying was at its height, Margaret, who was three years older, was already in the senior school, as was Mick, who was five years older (Bill and Brian were long gone, being thirteen and ten years older respectively). Margaret has no memory of Barbara. Though Hilly complained to her parents about the bullying, they thought she was exaggerating or fantasising; none of her siblings had complained in this way. Hilly was also having trouble with her schoolwork, which was again unlike her siblings, all of whom had done well in school, 'with nice reports and so on'. She simply took no interest in lessons and would not or could not apply herself.

When the war broke out in 1939, the Bardwell parents worried about Bedales' proximity to Portsmouth, an obvious target for enemy bombing. Hilly and Margaret were removed to Dr Williams's School for Young Ladies in North Wales, a school the family had learned of while vacationing in the area; Mick was sent to a boarding-school in Staffordshire. Both girls hated their new school and Hilly was soon in trouble: 'I was wild. There was no question about it . . . I was just the sort of child I'd be worried about my children associating with.' Eventually Hilly ran away and was asked to leave; she had been there two terms. Margaret left, too. Both girls then returned to Bedales, bombing fears having receded. The bullying Barbara was still there but she left Hilly alone: 'The spell was broken.' Yet Hilly continued to do no work. 'I wasn't interested. I was mad about animals. Horse-riding and stuff like that. I spent most of my time in the school farm.' In *You Can't Do Both* Nancy describes a comparable school history. After telling Robin she was 'absolutely hopeless' as a student, Robin says she was probably just badly and boringly taught:

'Oh, not me, I was bored all right, but that was because I couldn't follow what they were saying after about the first sentence. I just wasn't up to it, you see. The word must have got round eventually among the teachers, because after a bit they all stopped including me in the lesson and just let me sit at the back and keep quiet and read and draw. My mother taught me to read when I was quite little, but I've never learned how to count properly. If you asked me to write down, well, er, ten thousand in figures I'd be stuck. I know it's a one with noughts after it, but I'm not sure how many noughts.'[22]

Margaret thinks Hilly was dyslexic. 'She never did learn to spell. She didn't learn to read or write till she was about thirteen. Things like that – reading and writing – just didn't come into her life at all.' Several times Margaret was taken aside by teachers and asked: 'Can't you do anything about Hilly? She just spends all her time feeding her rabbits and doesn't take part in the school at all.' Bedales may have been a progressive school, but it was no Summerhill. Students were meant to work and to pass their examinations. Hilly did neither. 'I must have been a very worrying awful child,' she remembers; 'my parents were in despair.' After one last 'stupid report, a true report' (it read 'She is unteachable'), Hilly ran away again and was again asked to leave. She was fourteen. Her parents managed to find her a place at the Beltane School in Wiltshire, a more 'free and easy' progressive school than Bedales, according to Margaret. Here she remembers spending 'another jolly year, I thought'. She did no work, but had 'a great time with friends ... sneaking out to the farm again ... catching wild horses and riding them'. She stayed at the Beltane for a year only. 'She was asked to leave every school she went to,' Margaret says. 'People didn't understand dyslexia in those days.'

Hilly claims she was perfectly happy at school, once the bullying stopped and as long as she was not made to work. But she sucked her thumb into early adolescence ('Very secretly towards the end, mind you,' Nancy quickly adds, after confessing her own thumb-sucking), was sometimes withdrawn and depressed and lacked confidence. After the Beltane School she worked in several jobs: as a trainee kennel-maid in a set of kennels in Bracknell, Berkshire (presided over by the lesbians she was to tell Amis about); as a helper in several wartime day nurseries, first in Palmers Green, where her parents lived at the time, then in Harwell, near Didcot, in Oxfordshire, where they moved after her father's retirement; and as a stable-girl, both in Wales and in the New Forest in Hampshire. The New Forest job, caring for beautiful Arab horses, she loved, but after six months the stables went bust. Then Hilly decided to go to art school. 'All along I did well at art ... I knew I was not brilliant but I was competent.' In addition to art classes in school she had taken weekly private lessons in London and was able to compile a portfolio of pictures. She applied to the Ruskin, was accepted and her parents agreed to pay her tuition. Like all the Bardwell children she was also given an allowance of £3 a week, which she used for food and digs. At first she would go home to Harwell at weekends, a journey of an hour or so by bus, but she soon made friends among the Ruskin girls ('a lot of us were seventeen') and, being good-looking, began to attract male attention. Though she valued her independence, she stayed in close touch with her family: 'I'd always ring up. I became more of a dutiful daughter, but at a distance.'

As at Bedales, Hilly soon encountered problems with her work. 'I remember someone saying: "You never stick to anything, do you? I don't think you could finish making a rabbit cage."' Her problems as an art student began with drawing. One of her instructors, the painter Barnett Freedman, told her she couldn't draw and that she would never get anywhere as an artist unless she could. 'I took this really to heart,' she remembers. 'I really tried.' Soon, though, she concluded that he was right, and at the end of the year, 'I easily switched to doing something else.' When Amis met her in January 1946 she was supplementing her allowance by working as Ruskin's 'head model', which he wrongly thought meant 'best model' rather than 'model of heads', a mistake which no doubt contributed to his hopes of her being depraved. In fact, though she liked men, 'liked to get on with them and so on' and 'had had the odd kiss or so', in sexual terms she was almost as innocent as she looked: 'I wasn't that interested, really.' In other respects, she had plenty of experience, certainly for a girl of seventeen. She had lived away from her parents for long periods, had withstood disapproval and censure from school and other authorities, had broken rules, run away. Though unassertive in manner, neither truculent nor outwardly rebellious, she could be stubborn, wilful and wild.

This is not quite how Amis remembers her when writing about the time of their first meeting. In 1991, in the third and last stanza of 'Instead of an Epilogue', the touching poem 'To H.' that closes his *Memoirs*, Amis offers a portrait of Hilly at seventeen:

> In '46 when I was twenty-four
> I met someone harmless, someone defenceless,
> But till then whole, unadapted within;
> Awkward, gentle, healthy, straight-backed,
> Who spoke to say something, laughed when amused;
> If things went wrong, feared she might be at fault,
> Whose eye I could have met for ever then,
> Oh yes, and who was also beautiful.

In the manuscript version of the stanza from which these lines come, entitled 'To Hilly My Love', Amis had originally written 'sturdy in hands and feet' rather than 'healthy, straight-backed'. The effect of this minor alteration is to make the finished poem's Hilly slightly less substantial or 'sturdy' a figure than she is in draft, perhaps also than she was in real life. It is doubtless true that at seventeen she was awkward, gentle, harmless and in some ways defenceless, but she could also be strong, brave, even reckless. She had a robust appetite as well. In 'Why I Married Lucky Jim', Hilly writes of her relief at discovering that she could eat as much as she liked in front of Amis: 'He always says: "I love to see you eat – go on, eat some more."'

That she wasn't frightened of Amis, of his cleverness, energy and aggression, is also worth noting. When Ruth Bowman first met Amis he alarmed her. (Hilly was not alarmed when she first met Larkin.) In early January 1946 Larkin came down to London to meet with R.A. Caton of the Fortune Press, which was to publish *Jill*. While Larkin saw Caton, Amis was to meet Ruth, who was studying English at King's College, London. Then Larkin would join them and Amis would take him off to Berkhamsted, where Larkin would meet and stay with the Amis family for the first time. These arrangements necessitated much fussing about train times, which Amis found tiresome. When he asked who exactly benefited from the meeting with Ruth, Larkin replied, in a letter of 8 January: 'YOU benefit insofar as you meet Ruth and therefore have an item of information about me which no one else bar Bruce [Montgomery] has. RUTH benefits insofar as she sees me and sees you: she has had a surfeit of you over the last three months and now wants very much to see what you are like.'[23]

Ruth was nervous about the visit: 'Philip had extolled his friend so warmly that I felt apprehensive about his arrival.' Unlike Hilly, she was immediately struck by Amis's attractiveness: 'He had good, clearly defined features and beautiful wavy hair of which I came to realise he was enormously proud. Kingsley and his comb were never far apart. This handsome appearance and his air of confidence greatly impressed me.' Soon she was also impressed by 'his great talent for mimicry, his ability to make whatever he described vividly alive and his huge sense of the ridiculous'. Though subsequent meetings 'were always amusing and enjoyable at least outwardly, I never felt quite at ease with Kingsley. He was *so* clever, *so* witty that he made me feel inadequate (easily done in those days) and I suspected that he viewed me with a cynical and not entirely friendly eye. I feared his influence over Philip.' That Hilly felt few such fears about either Amis or Larkin can be explained in several ways: Larkin seems to have been less jealous of others intruding on the friendship than was Amis (though this impression may derive partly from the absence of Larkin letters from the period); Larkin took to Hilly from the start; his brilliance was quieter, less outwardly intimidating than Amis's ('it took a bit longer for Philip to blossom,' Hilly remembers, 'he'd need a few drinks and so on'); Amis's attraction to Hilly was stronger, or more single-minded, than Larkin's to Ruth. But it is also possible that Hilly was simply surer of herself than Ruth, that she was, indeed, the sort of person 'who spoke to say something, laughed when amused'. Before her first meeting with Larkin, she knew that 'if I didn't like him it would be very bad. But there was no problem with that. I thought he was wonderful. He made Kingsley happy.'

As Amis's relationship with Hilly progressed so, too, did his campaign to get her into bed. 'We have been arguing for the past week about sleeping in the same bed with each other,' he writes to Larkin on 13 May. 'First she said no, and I said she would have to say yes, then she said yes, and I said I had forced her into it and what she meant was no, then she said no, and I feel hurt and angry and disappointed and am trying to make her say yes, and there for the moment the matter rests . . . If only one could be ruthless about these things!' Amis's irritation at this point leads him to disparage women in general. At Larkin's suggestion, he has been reading *Les Jeunes Filles*, the novel sequence by Henri de Montherlant (Larkin had been put on to Montherlant by Bruce Montgomery, who was reading modern languages at St John's). To Larkin, writing in 1979, the four novels that make up the sequence, all written in the 1930s, constitute an attempt 'to blow at least the capital letters off Women, Love and Marriage'.[24] The titular girls or 'jeunes filles' torment Montherlant's hero, Pierre Costals, a successful young novelist. Costals mounts 'a colossal barrage against women', and throughout the sequence, 'daily quotations for a Misogynist's Calendar appear on every page'. Yet Costals is 'not the monster he claims'; he has moments of generosity, affection and sympathy towards women. When eventually he allows himself to become engaged, as Larkin puts it, 'his procrastination is literally "self" preservation, an inability to immolate himself to his own generosity'.[25] Larkin calls *Les Jeunes Filles* 'a satire on women that is also an exposure of men'.[26] For Amis, in the letter of 13 May, Montherlant's feelings 'are our feelings', by which he means not only feelings that might end up on a Misogynist's Calendar but ambivalences, the sort that lead him to argue Hilly first into and then out of bed, then to be angry with himself for having done so. 'Women appear to me as basically dull, but as basically pathetic too,' he writes, in full Montherlant mode, 'and while this makes us annoyed, it still doesn't allow us to say rude things to them, about them. It is one's very indifference to their feelings that turns one's anger into pity a-bim a-bom a-bem-bammy-bum.' Nine days later he reports to Larkin: 'Hilly has yielded.'

By this point Amis has been introduced to Hilly's family. In the letter of 13 May he writes of visiting Abbey Timbers, the Bardwell home on the outskirts of Harwell, with Hilly and Christopher Tosswill, a friend from Queen's College, Oxford. They are given tea by Hilly's father, 'an extraordinary old man like a music-loving lavatory attendant' (Martin Amis's comment on this description is: 'sorry, Mum, but the writer in me knows a bullseye when he sees one').[27] This is Amis's first reference to Leonard Sidney Bardwell, a man who, by everyone else's account, was perfectly pleasant and amiable, if a little eccentric. He was sixty when Amis met him and only recently retired from a career in the Ministry of Agriculture. The eldest of five sons, he had been brought up in Hammersmith and Chester and educated at Latymer Upper School in Hammersmith, where he had a scholarship, and at the King's School, Chester. His father was a master builder who died in 1899, at the age of forty. In 1900, when Leonard was fourteen, to ease the burden of raising five boys by herself, his mother agreed to allow him to move to Chester to live in the family of her wealthy brother, William Clark. Here he was reunited with his first cousin Margery, an only child, whom he had met five years earlier and who would eventually become his wife and Hilly's mother.

William Clark made his fortune in trade. He was born in Shoreditch, left school at fourteen and moved to Chester at sixteen, where he was employed as assistant to the owner of Bradley's, a small firm selling working men's clothing. By twenty-five he was a partner in the firm, now greatly expanded, with branches throughout the North of England. It was William Clark's hope that his nephew would eventually take over the business. At sixteen Leonard was removed from school and apprenticed first in the Lancaster branch of Bradley's, then in branches in Millom and Runcorn. As events soon proved, he had neither an interest in nor an aptitude for business. In 'In My Younger Days', a family history written by Hilly's mother, she expresses astonishment that her father failed to recognise his nephew's 'undoubted intellectual gifts'.[28] Had Leonard been allowed to stay in school, 'he would almost certainly have won a scholarship and subsequently taken up some academic career. But I have to remind myself of the then prevailing tradition that a business should at all costs be kept within the family.'[29] For someone from her father's strict Nonconformist background, moreover, a background Margery was to reject, there was something frivolous about going off to university. Earning a living came first.

Though it took him a while, William Clark eventually accepted that his nephew was not cut out for trade. Leonard returned to London, took an examination to qualify for a junior clerkship in the Civil Service, studied at night for a more demanding Civil Service examination, passed it, and eventually ended up in the Ministry of Agriculture, where he stayed for over thirty years. Among his concerns at the Ministry was the regulation of the export of animals. In 1914, after patiently outlasting his uncle's reservations (mostly having to do with the marriage of first cousins), Leonard married Margery and the young couple, twenty-six and twenty-eight respectively, settled in a pleasant semi-detached house between Kingston and Wimbledon. Hilly and her elder brothers and sister were brought up in Kingston-upon-Thames, in a second, more substantial house, Coombe Hill. Margery was already a wealthy woman, having inherited a fortune from her uncle, Anthony Bradley (William Clark had cannily married the boss's sister), a sleeping partner in the firm. Most of this fortune was held in trust for her children, should any appear, but the 'very considerable'[30] interest generated by her uncle's investments was made available to her from twenty-one onwards. Yet she and Leonard lived modestly: 'such things as furs and jewellery had no appeal to me'.[31] She even insisted that when her father died his fortune should go to charity; she and her family had more than enough money already. When she herself died, half her money went to Cancer Relief.

Leonard Bardwell stuck with his job at the Ministry of Agriculture, but he was never very interested in it. What he was interested in was everything else, particularly everything of a cultural or folk cultural nature. He played the piano and the concertina, sang and was a keen dancer and follower of Cecil Sharp, founder of the English Folk Dance Society and English Folk Song Society. He liked all forms of dance but Morris dancing was his special love; Margaret remembers that he danced a jig every May morning in Oxford. He was also an impressive linguist, specialising in what Martin Amis calls 'languages of limited utility': in addition to Welsh, Swedish and Romansch (heard only in the Swiss canton of Grisons), he seems to have known 'Romany *and* the tongue of the tinkers'.[32] He was a bibliophile, collecting first editions of books and the earliest issues of newspapers and periodicals. He loved camping and walking, preferred the country to the city, was keen on local geography and Ordnance Survey maps. All this knowledge he was eager to impart.

None of it was likely to be of interest to Amis. Then there was his manner of dress. He wore a beret. He carried a rucksack ('How fearfully unerring that is as a badge,' Amis complained to Larkin). After Amis and Hilly were married and living in Swansea, the Bardwells came to visit. 'He goes around in a blue shirt, with his braces in full view, trying to disgrace me,' complained Amis.[33]

There are lots of these complaints in the letters Amis wrote to Larkin in the 1940s. There are also lots of complaints about Amis's own father, and his mother, and Hilly's mother, and just about everybody else he meets. But 'Daddy B' (Amis's own father was 'Daddy A') becomes a monster of comic egotism in the correspondence, the obvious and acknowledged prototype of Professor Welch in *Lucky Jim*, as well as the source of Amis's funniest writing in the 1940s. Here is his second appearance in the correspondence (after the lavatory-attendant crack), in a letter of 15 July 1946, preceded by a description of two of Hilly's brothers, one of them Bill, whose Hoagy Carmichael record Amis now possessed. Larkin had recently met Hilly, when he visited Oxford in mid-June:

Hilary is very nice, as you will agree (she dreamed you were kissing her the other night), and I am enjoying very much being with her. But her family, who put in sporadic, *unneeded* visits are nasty. She has two brothers,[34] who are EXCREMENTALLY EVIL. One has *sandals* and *saffron* trousers, and No Socks, and a *green* shirt, and plays the *recorder* (yes) and likes Tudor music, and has a BAD wife and a BAD voice which says BAD words. I don't like the other one. He came across the lawn to meet me, his hand outstretched and an indefensible smile on his face. Hilary said 'This is Kingsley.' – 'Why, hullo, Peter,' he said to me very cordially. 'I'm not Peter,' I said. Then I became aware he was talking to a dog behind me. (The dog smells of corpses). 'No, I know that' he said: 'I was talking to the dog.' 'I see,' I said. And the father does folk dancing (polk dancing? pock dancing? fock dancing?).[35]

Larkin's response, on 17 July, is that 'Hilary's family sounds an awful price to pay for Hilary.' He also seconds Amis's distrust of the folksy, the arty, the bohemian, admitting that 'I am getting to the stage when I HATE anybody who does anything UNUSUAL at ALL.'[36] But elsewhere he eggs Amis on about Daddy B, sensing a rich comic vein. Here are two more outraged passages. In the first, written on 25 August 1948, Amis has recently returned from a weekend in Harwell:

He kept telling me, all the time I was staying at Abbey Timbers, all about his linguistic travels in one of the larger and more sparsely populated cantons of the Swiss Confederation. Now, I don't want to know about that: why didn't he take that into account . . . Another time he helped me to more curry and put it all over the handles of my knife and fork. Another time I passed him the sauce bottle, which was nearly empty, upside down, so that he wouldn't have to shake the sauce down anew. He just sat and watched while I held it, so that I had to wait until enough sauce had come out for him to signify that he had all he needed.

A year later, in a letter to Larkin of 14 September 1949, Amis reports another mealtime incident:

The only event in my stay worth reporting was when at breakfast this morning I noticed there were no cups on the table and announced my discovery in a low murmur; Daddy B sprang up and went into the kitchen, and I felt some remorse at letting him go instead of me, until he returned with a sole cup, which having filled with tea, milk and sugar, he raised wordlessly to his lips, afterwards continuing his meal. I learn he has no sense of smell, and now make a point of farting silently in his presence.

Martin Amis believes that it was Daddy B's innocence that provoked his father's 'ornate resentment': 'the Bardwells were so innocent. I could tell they were innocent when I was *six*.'[37] But as the above examples suggest, other qualities, though perhaps related ones, were involved, including self-absorption, an easy and unearned sense of entitlement (or so it seemed to Amis), inconsiderateness. After a particularly vituperative passage about Daddy B in a letter of 12 July 1949, Amis draws a striking comparison:

You will laugh at what I have written, I expect; but to me it gives an analogous feeling, except that it is personal, to reading a speech by Churchill; something contentedly stupid that you can't alter. I shall swing for the old cockchafer unless I put him in a book, *recognisably*, so that he will feel *hurt* and *bewildered* at being so *hated*.

Which is what Amis did, of course, with *Lucky Jim*, though Daddy B apparently never recognised himself in Professor Welch. The comparison with Churchill, or a Churchill speech, suggests that the feelings Daddy B aroused in Amis were related to those that swept

Labour into power in 1945: resentment that the wrong people were in charge, had the money, had to be listened to and treated with respect. These feelings were fed by Amis's experiences in the army but they fit a familiar pattern, that of his father's view of things, though the specific objects of his father's resentment were different.

If the Bardwells and Harwell provide a key ingredient of *Lucky Jim*, Berkhamsted and Daddy A inspire the novel that precedes it, 'The Legacy'. This was Amis's first finished book-length fiction, conceived in the winter of 1945–46, begun in the summer of 1947, completed in the summer of 1948, much revised and rejected in the next two and a half years and never published. Its hero is 'Kingsley Amis', described by his creator as 'a young man like myself only nastier'.[38] The setting is contemporary. Twenty-four-year-old Kingsley,[39] newly returned from the war, has been left a legacy of £30,000 by his recently deceased father, Lionel. By the terms of the will, he only gets the money if he marries before his twenty-fifth birthday (a girl approved of by his elder brother, Sidney, the executor of the estate) and enters the family firm and works there for the rest of his life. The nature of this firm is unspecified, though its offices are near Cannon Street, site of William Amis's office, and samples of its goods, wrapped in tissue paper, line a cupboard, as the domestic glassware sold by Amis's grandfather's firm might have done in his office.[40] If Kingsley fails to meet the terms of the will, the money goes to 'The League of the New Tabernacle', an evangelical society 'founded in 1935 by a retired golf champion'.[41] The first of the terms, Kingsley thinks, poses no problem, since he has recently become engaged to Jane Taylor, barely nineteen, a girl he met two years previously when stationed in Hamberton in Yorkshire (where Elisabeth comes from in 'The Escape'). Jane is pretty and sensible and works as a clerk in a bank. Kingsley wants to be a writer and has just had a book of poems accepted 'by a small London firm' (the thinly disguised Fortune Press, whose proprietor, R.A. Caton, also thinly disguised, makes his first appearance here in an Amis novel).[42] Though he has no interest in joining the family firm, Kingsley is perfectly prepared to pretend he does, if doing so will secure the legacy. Elder brother Sidney, seven years his senior, sets the plot in motion: he vetoes Jane.

The action takes place mostly in Whitstead, a version of Berkhamsted. The milieu is that of Amis's parents, at its uppermost

Above: Left to right, KA's grandparents (Joseph James and Julia Spinks Amis) and parents (William Robert and Rosa Annie Lucas Amis), at the wedding of 'Uncle Pres and Auntie Poppy' (Mr and Mrs James Preston Amis), Denmark Hill, 20 June 1914. Uncle Leslie is at top right; Aunt Gladys at bottom, third from left.

Above: W.R. Amis (far left), with the Cannon Street Football Club, employees of the London office of the mustard manufacturer J. and J. Colman, 1921.

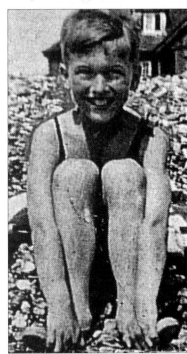

Above: KA, aged nine.

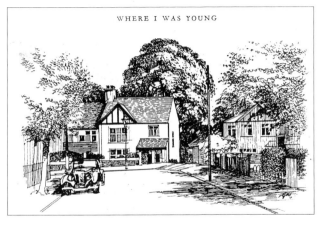

Left: 7 Ena Road, Norbury, London SW16, the second of KA's childhood homes.

Left: F.R. Dale, Headmaster, City of London School, 1929–50.

Right: Rev. C.J. Ellingham, Classics master, CLS, 1929–57, 'the man who actually taught me most'.

Below: CLS boys at Marlborough College, 1940.

Left: KA, *c*. twelve years old.

Right: The Great Ice Storm, Marlborough, 1940: 'And every stalk and stem was covered in / A thin layer of ice as clear as glass' ('Instead of an Epilogue', *Memoirs*).

Above: In the gardens of St John's College, Oxford, summer 1942. Left to right: David West, Dai Williams, Mervyn Brown, Philip Larkin, Hilary Morris, Norman Iles, J.B. Widdowson, Philip Brown.

Below: 'In the Rear of the Enemy' (see Chapter 5), enacted in the gardens of St John's College, summer 1942. KA kneeling front and centre; standing, left to right: Mervyn Brown, J.B. Widdowson, Edward du Cann, Michael MacNaughton-Smith, Nick Russel, Philip Brown, Dai Williams, Norman Iles, Graham Parkes, David West.

Right: Lüneburg Heath, the day the Germans surrendered, 7 May 1945. Lieutenant K.W. Amis (second from left, middle row), E. Frank Coles, co-author of 'Who Else Is Rank', on his right.

Left: Bert Wootton, KA's batman (second from right), somewhere in north-west Europe, *c.* 1945.

Right: St John's College Humanitarian Society, including post-war undergraduates and college staff, 1947. Middle row: Nick Russel (second from left), Edward du Cann (third from left), KA (fifth from left), Mervyn Brown (second from right) and Graham Parkes (far right).

Above: Hilly at seventeen, 1946.

Right: Hilly, KA and Margaret
('Miggy') Partington (née Bardwell),
Marriner's Cottage, Eynsham,
Oxfordshire, 1948.

Left: KA and Hilly,
pregnant with
Martin, at
Marriner's Cottage,
with Mandy, the
dog, 1949.

Above: Leonard Bardwell ('Daddy B'), far right, playing the concertina, with fellow East Surrey Morris Men, *c.* 1936-39.

Right: KA at Abbey Timbers, 1946.

Above: Bill Bardwell (b. 1915), Hilly's older brother, a Bertrand prototype.

Right: Margery and Leonard Bardwell ('Mummy B and Daddy B').

Above: Bruce Montgomery, 1958.

Right: Philip Larkin, 1962.

Below: John Wain, 1958.

Above: KA's students, left to right, Geoff Nicholson, David Rees, Clive Gammon, University College of Swansea, 1952.

Above: KA as Osric, kneeling in front, in staff-student *Hamlet*, 1953. Esmond Clearey, standing, far right.

Left: KA in Swansea, 1958.

edges: the Golf Club, the saloon bar, the Conservative Association. Sidney is its presiding spirit: part William Amis, part Major Raleigh, but more formidable. In India during the war, Sidney won a string of decorations, including an OBE. After 'toying with the idea of an Army career',[43] he returns to civilian life as a retired major (Kingsley returns as a lieutenant, with a Class B release). Before demobilisation, Sidney strides around District Headquarters like Major Raleigh, swinging his walking stick, upbraiding soldiers for their appearance ('I'm opposed to that chap's moustache on moral grounds').[44] Like William Amis, he bullies waiters and has a penchant for funny foreign accents. Like them both, he has local political ambitions (he is running for a seat on the council in the forthcoming municipal elections). His idiom is part officers' mess, part *Sorrell and Son*: Kingsley is 'Kingers', 'old chap', 'old man'; an acquaintance of dubious character is 'one of nature's four-letter men'.[45] Kingsley finds Sidney frightening as well as commanding and has 'never been able to tell when he's serious'. Though he rates him 'well above the average for honesty and truthfulness', when it comes to tolerance, 'I can't really tell.'[46] In 1951 Amis's Oxford friend James Michie arranged for him to receive a two-page report on 'The Legacy' from a reader for Collins, Doreen Marston, the mother of Adrian Marston, another Oxford friend. In it she describes Sidney, aptly, as 'a first class "faux-bonhomme"'.[47]

Sidney's grounds for rejecting Jane are social:

'It's a matter of class, old boy, pure and simple; no, let me explain just what I mean. I've got as little time for class distinction as you have, in the ordinary way; it's nothing to me what sort of grandparents type A may have had, or where type B went to school; but unfortunately it's not such a simple matter as it seems. We can condemn the fact that there are these distinctions, but at the same time they are a fact and can't be got away from. We can't change the world overnight, old boy, however much we may want to. Now Jane's father was a grocer; she's none the worse for that; plenty of fine blokes I've known have started from a darned sight less; but again, we aren't deciding on people's moral character, we're trying to find you a wife. Jane comes from a, I won't say a lower, but a different, a totally different kind of background or social sphere or what-have-you. That's established, is it? I'm not asking you to agree with me, but do you follow me so far?'[48]

He does, but he holds his tongue, as 'argument would, I knew, mean reiteration prolonged beyond endurance'.[49] '"You'll just have to find yourself someone else, old boy," said Sidney gently.'[50] At this point, Kingsley resolves 'to defeat Sidney, to establish for good my divergence from him and his allies' (including both individuals and institutions, such as the Golf Club, the council, the Cross Keys, an upmarket hotel restaurant where Sidney's friends often meet). When he declares: 'I love Jane',[51] Sidney's reaction is immediate and harsh:

He turned like a man who is called an abusive name in the street: 'Love; what the hell are you talking about? You read too much, that's your trouble. Pick someone for your wife who comes from the same sort of family as yours and who you get on with and have fun with; but leave love out of that, there's a dear good sensible fellow. You run off and get somebody like Stephanie[52] for your wife; she's the sort for you, not an ignorant little tart like Jane who's good at bedroom games and gets you to call it love to save her conscience.'[53]

Sidney's crudeness here recalls William Amis's letter after discovering his son's affair with Elisabeth. The letter made Amis feel guilty, until his father 'managed a snobbish insinuation about her'.[54] It also recalls Hilly's claim that Amis 'never forgave his father for all that stuff with Elisabeth, his first love'. That the novel grew out of this episode, as well as out of a more general dissatisfaction with his parents and their world, is clear from Amis's letters. 'I don't know why it is, but being at home has got much worse than it ever was before,' Amis writes to Larkin on 15 December 1945: 'I think in my book there will have to be a lot about being at home and not liking it.' If 'my book' here is 'The Legacy', it is the novel's first mention in the correspondence. The second may occur in a letter of 1 July 1946, just after a visit with Larkin: 'The things I enjoyed most about the week-end were the discussions about my brother and the film imitations.' Presumably this brother is 'Sidney', who makes his unannounced début in the correspondence in a letter of 20 July:

I am gong to the man who TAKES ALL YOUR TEETH AWAY next week. I don't want to do that, really, very much, you see, hardly at all, awfully, really. It is going to HURT, but much WORSE than that he is gong to TAKE A LOT OF TEETH AWAY, so that young ladies will dislike my face

AND NOT WANT TO LET ME GET ON TOP OF THEM. 'Can't see what you're bellyaching about, old chap,' said Sidney, opening 'Country Life'; 'dentists these days aren't what they used to be like, you know. Anyway, for goodness' sake try to face up to facts. It's got to be done some day, so why not now? Going to the dentist never worries *me*. That reminds me: I want to cut the hedge. Seen the shears, old boy?' he asked, clenching his fists and moving his crooked elbows in and out at his sides.[55]

Whether at this point Sidney was simply a fantasy figure Amis and Larkin were concocting, as they and Norman Iles concocted the Yorkshire Scholar, or a character in a projected novel, is unclear. It is also unclear ten days later, when Amis wonders, in a letter to Larkin: 'don't you think Sidney spends a lot of his time explaining *things you know about* to you? "Auden – that's WH Auden, the poet, old boy – a sine qua non – something you can't do without, old boy[56] – HMV, the gramophone wallahs, old boy."' It is not until 21 September 1946 that we can be sure of Sidney's relation to 'my book', in the first letter to use the book's title:

Did I tell you I had worked out the plot of The Legacy? One tghing I have just decided is the kidnapping part. Max Anders (Basic English) and Donald Dougal (anarchic Scot) and I confront Sidney with a letter carrying evidence of an intrigue between him and a married woman. Either he signs (1) a document accepting my girl as a fitting wife (2) a business contract drawn up by us, or we publish the letter. He doesn't sign, because he doesn't agree with it, and thinks the whole thing is a joke, we don't mean it, we're tight, after all old boy I've known you for a good many years now: I'm damned certain you wouldn't pull a dirty trick like that on your own brother: *that's not your style* at all. And he broke into some laughing. Give him back the letter, I said. Do you like that? I do.[57]

Larkin calls this plot (which Amis doesn't in the end use) 'really effective and rather horrible'.[58] The horribleness, I believe, refers less to the kidnapping than to Kingsley's calm capitulation ('Give him back the letter, I said') and Sidney's acuity. Sidney is a monster (in an interview in 1990 Amis called him 'a sort of Mr Hyde'),[59] but he is not wrong about his brother: Kingsley really is the sort of person Sidney thinks he is. Though Kingsley is the novel's narrator and we are meant to sympathise with his predicament, it is clear to us much sooner than it is to him not only that he values the money from the legacy more than he does Jane but that he belongs in the Whitstead world. After Sidney's veto, Kingsley moves out of the large, comfortable family house he, Sidney and their sister Mary have been living in, and finds rooms in a local boarding-house. This boarding-house and its inhabitants are terrible: grim, frayed, depressing. Kingsley is betting on Sidney's capitulation, hoping he can outstay him, for he knows that Sidney loves him and is pained by the separation. But the bleak character of his new life, the life he finds himself in as soon as he rejects Sidney's world, overwhelms him:

A picture of myself aged sixty, without money or family or friends, flared up in my mind like a firework set-piece; tawdry, ridiculous and terrifying, it advertised the supremacy of loneliness among all known evils. I decided, as I decided once as a child after seeing in a forbidden medical book the photograph of a leper's face, that I must devote all my waking hours to the systematic avoidance of such a horror . . . For the moment at least it could not touch me; I was moving out of its field of force, the world of McClintoch [a fellow boarder, originally 'Donald Dougal'], of the public bar we had visited together, of the bath-room at the boarding-house with soap and hair in the plug-hole, of the long curving street with the election posters at the end and the windows in every house shut and fastened; the world I had decided I must explore. Stephanie knew nothing of it and while I was with her it would not exist for me. Perhaps this was why I now felt I would rather see her than any other person, a feeling that would have seemed unlikely to me at any previous time.[60]

It is fear of loneliness that drives Kingsley back to the Whitstead world. Amis himself knew this fear and how it could override moral considerations. But other less excusable or involuntary motives contribute to Kingsley's capitulation. '"The most notice-able characteristic of Kingsley Amis in his domestic life,"' Sidney tells Jane, in mock-clinical tones, '"is his extreme and incorrigible laziness . . . He was accustomed from his earliest years to having everything done for him and always tried to carry this principle into adult life."'[61] The prospect of being poor and having to fend for himself does not appeal to Kingsley. In a letter of 29 September 1948, Amis laid out for Larkin the factors influencing Kingsley's behaviour:

What I meant the theme or central problem to be was not the coin, but mesmerism by S (plus a bit of that brotherly buggery you refer to, all unconscious) as a symbol or concentrated expression or most convenient version or what have you of the attraction S's way of life has for K despite his theories of the good life . . . [T]hat's why Stephanie is featured and why the political angle comes in and why it's necessary to try to show that it's not just Sidney as a person, though K. may think it is from time to time.[62]

In the end, Amis's censure of his hero is made explicit by the novel's oddest and most admirable character, Kingsley's friend Maximilien De Jong ('Max Anders' in the plot summary of 21 September 1946). Max is a foreigner who makes his living as a translator, which is a joke, since his English is so peculiar, often ridiculous. When Max realises that Kingsley is drifting away from commitment to Jane, he turns on him: 'You think that because you have written down some men on a list inside your head as nasty you will never be on that list yourself; that is a wrong, stupid and smelly word.'[63] It is not enough, Max insists, to know bad behaviour when one sees it, to criticise, patronise and sneer; one must behave well oneself. This is a key theme throughout Amis's writing, and one with clear autobiographical implications. Few writers have written as perceptively about bad behaviour as Amis or been as consistently accused of it. How, then, does the writing relate to the life? Is it a way of understanding it, or excusing it, or apologising for it? 'The Legacy' is characteristic of Amis's later writing in another important respect. Though Amis consistently disparaged the novel and was pleased it was never published, while at work on it he often liked what he had written. 'I feel rather conceited about that bequest thing,' he writes to Larkin on 3 September 1948: 'it seems to me flaringly funny, even when it's supposed to be serious. The hero is *such* an ANUS, with his piddling little cogitations and triumphs, his turdy-faced superiorities, his indecipherable gestures of distaste.'[64] 'Kingsley,' in other words, is Amis's first hero as shit, a more representative protagonist than Jim Dixon, who is merely, in some ways, unheroic.

Max De Jong's odd way of speaking grows directly out of Amis's post-war correspondence, being related to the 'Basic English' styles he and Larkin delighted in. 'Basic English' was designed in the 1920s by the linguistic psychologist C.K. Ogden both as a first step in the teaching of English and as an auxiliary language. It consisted of a selection of 850 simple words from which it was thought any feeling, perception or idea could be generated. The result was often funny, to Amis and Larkin certainly: 'I find that our basic english styles have diverged somewhat,' writes Amis to Larkin on 11 December 1945. 'My vein now is of long intentionally cumbrous and periphrastic sentences . . . ". . . I am knowing about of what I am speaking about . . ." ". . . Dryden didn't know about that of what that he was talking about about Chaucer . . ."'[65] The comic appeal of Basic English is partly explained by Anthony Powell, in a remark Amis quoted in a radio talk entitled 'The Comic Muse': 'that any piece of human behaviour will seem absurd if described precisely enough'.[66] In the same talk Amis cites examples from Flann O'Brien's *At Swim-Two-Birds*, several times mentioned approvingly in the Amis-Larkin letters of the period: 'The three of us were occupied in putting glasses of stout into the interior of our bodies and expressing by fine disputation the resulting sense of physical and mental well-being'; 'Rousseau, a member of the French nation'. Max says similar things: 'I have long eaten my breakfast meal',[67] 'I wish for everything to be in your lives that is good',[68] 'Do not decide it in your mind at now.'[69] While at work on 'The Legacy', Amis's prose was so saturated with Basic English locutions, or mock–Basic English locutions, that they seep into the narrative proper. Some are caught in revision, as when 'in the chair opposite the one I was occupying' becomes 'opposite mine' or 'in the direction of' becomes 'at'.[70]

Max is a character different in kind from the others in the novel. His peculiar way of talking is broader and more mannered even than Sidney's and is one of several signs that 'The Legacy' has modernist or experimental aspirations, is partly an attempt to tease and subvert realist expectations. Calling the hero 'Kingsley Amis' is another of these signs, as is the novel's penchant for pointlessly detailed observation. In the pub, McClintoch orders drinks from 'a very tall man with grey hair and horn-rimmed spectacles with thick ear-pieces who was obviously the landlord. The latter put a broad hand on the handle of the beer-engine and the beer rushed into our glasses.'[71] In Mrs Marston's report on 'The Legacy', passages like these are criticised and Amis is offered advice about them as if he were unaware of their effect: 'Too much detail makes for dullness . . . You will be surprised at how easy it is to shift people about without telling the reader that you are doing so. You need seldom describe them going upstairs, shutting doors, hanging up their coats, etc.' But Amis wants too much detail (though he doesn't want to bore readers); he wants an effect like the one Flaubert achieves with *Bouvard et Pécuchet*, in which the dullness, pointlessness and absurdity of the bourgeois world is evoked in the depicting as well as the things depicted. This is the manner also of the book which Amis says was a direct model for 'The Legacy', Julian Hall's *The Senior Commoner* (1932), which in the *Memoirs* Amis calls 'a wonderful marsh-light of a novel whose influence in 1946 or so helped to render ['The Legacy'] unpublishable.'[72] It was Larkin who put Amis on to *The Senior Commoner*, having written *Jill* 'under [its] influence', and Amis read it in April 1947, three months before he began writing his novel. In a 1967 interview Larkin describes the novel: 'It was an account of life at Eton, written immediately after the man left Eton. It was extremely dry, extremely mature, a collection of little linked scenes – mostly dialogue – involving everybody from the headmaster and vice-provost down to the boys. What was remarkable about it was the deliberate use of irrelevant detail in setting a scene. I showed it Kingsley, and he was equally amused by it – parts of it were very funny.'[73]

Mrs Marston's report was by no means the novel's first rejection. Another post-war Oxford acquaintance, Kenneth Tynan, newly down from Magdalen, arranged for Amis to have lunch in London with Mark Longman, the publisher. Amis brought along the first three chapters of 'The Legacy'. On 9 March 1949, Amis reported to Larkin that 'Longmans sent the Legacy back, of course, saying it was "altogether too slight." That's true in its way, I suppose, but there are plenty of other things to its discredit I would have said before that.' Several months later, on 9 May, Amis reports that Gollancz had also turned it down (it had been sent there via Bruce Montgomery, a friend of Diana Gollancz, the publisher's daughter and a student at the Slade). Victor Gollancz's rejection note read simply: 'I don't think THE LEGACY quite comes off.' It was next sent to a publishing friend of Nick Russel's, also at Collins.[74] Again it was rejected. On 25 May, after a long silence, A.P. Watt, the agent, agreed to take it on and sent it everywhere. A little over a year later, on 30 July 1950, Amis reports to Larkin that he's had a note from Watt saying 'he can't understand why nobody will publish the thing' (as Amis later recalled, it 'was rejected by, I think, fourteen publishers before my agent gave up the struggle').[75] Amis admitted the novel's failings, but attributed the rejections to its experimental character. This, at least, is what he suggests when objecting to Mrs Marston's criticisms, in the letter of 8 January 1951:

I think Mrs M is QUITE RIGHT in about half of what she says, but the rest of the time she's missing the point isn't she? I don't say she'd like it if she saw it but she's missing the point isn't she? I mean detail's the point isn't it? Now if she can't *see* that (I'M NOT ASKING HER TO LIKE IT) what chance have I got old boy? They want you to write novels like other novels don't they? I don't want to do that.

Later in life, long after Amis had become staunchly anti-experimental, he described 'The Legacy' as 'full of affectation, full of modernistic tricks, full of all the kinds of shock tactics that very soon afterwards I despised completely'.[76] Yet the novel has its virtues: it can be funny in just the way the author intends; the moral issues it raises are subtly dramatised; its depictions of the Berkhamsted milieu are well worth stealing from for *Take a Girl Like You*; and the relationship between the two brothers is psychologically complex and of real, if implicit or displaced, autobiographical interest.

Like the fictional Kingsley, the real-life one published his first book of poems in the immediate post-war years. 'Why don't you get your words together and send them to the Fortune Press?' Larkin wrote to Amis on 12 December 1945: 'they'd publish them'.[77] Larkin himself had published his first volume, *The North Ship*, with the press in July, and would publish *Jill* there in October 1946. His connection with the firm was established in late 1944, when he was asked to submit poems for its anthology *Poetry from Oxford in Wartime*, edited by William Bell and published in February 1945. Getting one's work accepted at the Fortune Press was not difficult – what was difficult was dealing with its notorious proprietor, R.A. (Reginald Ashley) Caton. Caton earned his living through property as well as publishing, and at the time of his death owned ninety-one houses in his home town of Brighton. In 1924 at the age of twenty-five he founded the Fortune and Merriman Press, later the Fortune Press, which specialised in such soft-porn titles as *Bachelor's Hall*, *Boys in Their Ruin* and *Chastisement across the Ages*. He also published a number of distinguished poets, including Dylan Thomas, Roy Fuller, C. Day-Lewis and Larkin, and several influential anthologies, among them the first gathering of 'The New Apocalypse' poets in 1940. From 1930 to 1970 he published over 600 titles.

Amis and Larkin were not alone in complaining about Caton. As anyone who did business with him soon discovered, he was dilatory, inefficient, mean, secretive and double-dealing. Like many of Caton's authors, Amis was obliged to help finance publication: he had to purchase fifty copies at discount (at a cost of £10), which his mother helped to sell to friends in Berkhamsted. But it was Caton's procrastination that drove his authors to distraction. 'THAT SOD CATON *still* hasn't replied to my letter,' writes Amis in a typical complaint of 2 December 1946. When, after months of silence, proofs finally arrived, in May 1947, they included none of the six new poems Amis had sent him in December, though they did include the single poem he wanted excised. Accompanying the proofs, Amis writes to Larkin on 25 May, was 'a request that they be sent back the next day'.[78] 'He has robbed me of the last remaining particle of pleasure at seng my book in proof after *inconceivable* delays,' Amis wrote on 5 May. When the book was published in September, Amis paid Caton a visit at his London offices. This visit, he reports to Larkin on 12 September, afforded 'so much material that I can only put down a little of what happened'. After retailing a variety of Caton's complaints and wheedlings, Amis tells of an incident involving the telephone: 'During our interview a girl rang up and he made me take the call ("tell 'em Mr. Caton's gone out for a few minutes"). The girl was foreign and beside herself with passion at having vainly tried to get him for a week. This I endeavoured to suggest to him, but he converted it into an instance of what he had to put up with from people.' When the subject of Amis's future arose, he reports, 'having once told him I was leaving Oxford last June to get him to hurry my book I was instantly caught up in a wind-tunnel of improvised deceit – about which he was censorious and watchful'.

Bright November contains thirty-one poems, the majority of them written in wartime. Though Amis thought its title 'CORNY' and too much like 'Jaybee Priestley', he chose it over its rival, 'Silence finding' ('which I can't even bear to *say* now'), because 'it isn't a quotation, it isn't one of the patterns we hate, and it's reasonably cheerful'.[79] Caton priced the book at six shillings and sent out no review copies; Amis himself had to do so. It received only two notices, an admiring paragraph in the *Berkhamsted Gazette*, arranged by a friend, and a puff from Larkin in *Mandrake*, an Oxford literary periodical.[80] Amis described the Berkhamsted notice to Larkin in a letter of 29 September as combining 'the companionable elementariness of a scholl arghsh school magazine with the lowbrow jauntiness of John o' London's: "We feel sure that many ex-service men will echo the sentiments expressed in 'Release' . . ."'[81] In Oxford, where Amis had begun to make a name for himself in poetry circles (publishing poems in *Cherwell* and *Mandrake*), the book made more of a splash. As he reports to Larkin on 19 October: 'The Isis says the appearance of my buck is the literary event of the tum, which is nice of them. They add "Unlike most clever boys, he is fair, English, clean-shaven, and makes musical noises."'[82] Looking back on the volume, in a 1988 article entitled 'Publishers Be Damned', Amis located it 'somewhere in the middle-to-upper drivel category'. The 'incredibly varied defects' of its constituent poems explained the absence of reviews. The only thing the poems shared 'was a cheap modernity or modernism, a trendiness or tricksiness based on hasty reading of Auden and other, more merely fashionable figures'.[83]

Auden's influence on Amis's early poems has already been noted. William Empson's influence, neither 'merely' fashionable nor short-lived, was second only to Auden's. On 17 September, Amis responded to a detailed commentary on *Bright November* from Larkin. After thanking his friend for his 'approval of what you approve of' he took mild issue with him about questions of indebtedness: 'I don't think the ones you think are Ordenish are all that Ordenish, but I agree on the Empsonian ones and am surprised you didn't pick out IV[84] as another one; it was written under E's direct influence.' In the same 1974 interview in which Amis characterised Auden's influence as mixed, he praised Empson more straightforwardly: 'He showed that strict forms were all right. Not only all right, but a great help. And that rhyming was all right.'[85] 'Elisabeth's Intermesso' is Empsonian not only because it is difficult ('It is not for nothing that Empson's favourite poet is Donne,' Amis elsewhere writes),[86] but because of its form. It consists of six three-line stanzas, the first and third lines of which rhyme, and a closing couplet; each line is of ten syllables, heavily end-stopped. Empson was especially associated with three-line stanzaic forms, including *terza rima* and villanelle. When, for example, Robert Conquest called Amis's poems 'Empsonic', Amis agreed but vowed, as he put it in a letter of 16 April 1954, 'not to write another poem in 10-syllable lines, 3-line stanzas, for another ten years'.

Empson was important to Amis as a critic as well as a poet. In a review of *Argufying* (1987), a late collection of Empson's essays, Amis recalls how influential 'the Master (W.E.)', as he's called in the letter to Conquest, was in the 1940s:

In Oxford during the Second World War, a great many people seemed to be reading two works of criticism: *The Allegory of Love* by C.S. Lewis and *Seven Types of Ambiguity* by William Empson. Of the two, the drawback to the Lewis was that you had to read a lot of other books, medieval ones and such, to get much out of it, and Lewis himself was unglamorously teaching and examining in the Oxford English school. Empson was younger (by eight years), not a don in that sense, hardly more than an undergraduate, a Cambridge man, an expert on psychology and new stuff like that – a pioneer – we would probably have called him 'exciting' if that usage had been around then. And his book had the great merit of being sufficient in itself with no rotten old romances and epics to wade through.[87]

'I was in as deep as any,' Amis confesses of his early attraction to Empson. He even stole the Oxford Union's copy of *Seven Types*, 'as the cognoscenti called it' (that it was out of print at the time 'I suppose both aggravates and extenuates the offence').[88] Empson's influence was if anything more pervasive after the war than during it, both in the wider university and at St John's itself. When Al Alvarez came up to Corpus Christi, Oxford, in 1949, he thought of Empson as 'the incarnation of brilliance'.[89] Alvarez founded the Critical Society, a student discussion group which immediately became 'the hottest ticket in town';[90] that Empson was its first speaker was fitting, since it 'had been founded in his honour'.[91]

At St John's, the 'Empsonic' was also in favour. When Gavin Bone died he was eventually replaced as Fellow in English by J.B. Leishman, who had been an undergraduate at St John's before going on to teach at the University College of Southampton. In 1934 Leishman published *The Metaphysical Poets: Donne, Herbert, Vaughan, Traherne* and when Amis was taught by him, from 1945 to 1947, he was at work on a book on Donne, published in 1951 under the title *The Monarch of Wit*. Leishman was a Germanist as well as an authority on seventeenth-century poetry. Since the 1930s he had been collaborating with Stephen Spender on a translation of Rilke's *Duino Elegies*. This collaboration had been arranged by Leonard Woolf of the Hogarth Press and was not a happy one. Spender complained that Leishman was 'a grim Germanic character of total seriousness – the sort of man who could exhaust a subject like a Hoover taking dust out of a carpet'. Leishman complained bitterly of Spender's dilatoriness.[92] In the *Memoirs*, Amis calls Leishman 'a man of great sweetness and extraordinariness'. Though he did not always share Leishman's opinions, he seems to have admired his intellectual toughness and taste not only for poetic difficulty but for the mixing of idioms, as much properties of Donne, who combined love poetry with metaphysics, as of Empson, whose poetry and criticism were both collo-quial and arcane. Though the topic of Rilke 'luckily never came up',[93] Amis was aware of, even paid lip service to, Leishman's European or high-brow tastes. On 18 January 1946, while complaining to Larkin of having to write an essay on Langland, he announces that: 'I've discovered the way to my tutor's heart – he likes all those shags like Pickarso . . . and Klee . . . so I say things like "blue period" and "delicate colour sense" instead of things like "Saga-like" and "piling-on images".'

As this quote suggests, the war had done little to moderate Amis's cynicism about academic study. Once again, he had very little to say in favour of any author on the English syllabus. In a letter to Larkin of 18 March 1946, he writes of an impending college exam-ination on that 'fine old relic of Anglo-Saxon culture; that remark-able survival of that civilization from which our own, in however indirect a fashion, is derived; I refer of course to the anonymous, crass, purblind, infantile, *featureless* HEAP OF GANGRENED ELEPHANT'S SPUTUM, "Barewolf"'. Two months later he com-poses a poem entitled 'Beowulf', a revised version of which appears in *Bright November*. Its last stanza reads:

> Someone has told us this man was a hero.
> But what have we to learn in following
> His tedious journey to his ancestors
> (An instance of Old English harking back)?

On 23 August 1947, in response to a letter praising the study of Anglo-Saxon at Oxford, in the periodical *Time and Tide*, Amis wrote an anonymous reply (his first published letter) arguing that the subject was 'void of appeal' to many undergraduates and only on the syllabus because it was easy to mark. As for Anglo-Saxon literature: 'the prose is admitted even by initiates to be stumbling and graceless; the verse is shackled by continual repetition of idea'. The heroic content of the verse, moreover, is barbarous:

The warriors and broken-down retainers who strut bawling across its pages repel by their childish fits of self-glorification and self-pity; exploits stated but not shown to be glorious are shown but not stated to derive from self-interest dressed up as duty and lust for renown masquerading as nobility, the whole interleaved with natural descriptions in which every poetic opportunity is missed and moral maxims of an indescribable triteness.

Medieval literature is almost as bad. Though Leishman 'pronounced himself "very pleased" with my essay on the levels of Cah warrggh Chaucer's fart', this was because Amis hid what he really thought. As he writes to Larkin on 15 May 1946: 'If I say, that I am of the opinion, that the levels, of his art, anywhere, are all, of the same level, as the level, of the big pipe, that takes away, the waste matter, from a public lavatory . . . then, I am sure, the man, who teaches me, will, be quite sure, that I am, trying to be funny, and will not, like it, at all, THE SODDING OLD *FOOL*.' A year later Amis has a new antipathy, worse even than Chaucer (though still not as bad as *Beowulf*): Dryden. On 26 March 1947 he suggests to Larkin a new scale for assessing literary merit: 'I think "one dryden" ought to be a sort of unit of hate for a writer – only D. achieves 1.00, elsewhere the figure is always less than one, eg, –

Johnson .5 dryden	Jonson .85 dryden	
Keats .5 "	Shelley .85 "	
Milton .9 "	Chaucer .9 "	
	(i.e. 'tends to' 1 dryd.)	

Ironically, when Amis sat his Schools in December 1947 (as at CLS, he had been allowed extra time, a term in this case, though why is unclear), among the papers he did best on were those covering the early periods. Larkin sent him a good luck letter to arrive on the morning of his first examination. Four days after he'd finished, in a letter of 6 December, Amis wrote to thank him, describing the exams as 'not much better or worse than I expected'. Amis's preparation relied heavily on anticipating questions, 'an enormous gamble',[94] and giving the examiners exactly what they wanted. 'I have never written anything finer in its way,' he recalled in the *Memoirs*, 'than my answer to the question "Why is *The Battle of Maldon*[95] made much of?", a positive firework-display of hypocrisy and exaggeration.'[96] At the time, though, as he confessed to Larkin, all he felt certain of was that 'I wrote a good answer praising the works of Mr. Pope which I expect they liked.' When he was not called in for a post-examination viva, he feared his chances of gaining a First were remote. On 19 December, he wrote remorsefully to Larkin: 'I feel I have ruined my career by beng two lasy inm fsz in months gone buy.' When his results finally arrived, he was shocked: he'd got a First. On 27 December, he wrote to Larkin to explain: 'I got β++ for Old Eng and B10 (1700–1830), αβ for Spenser and Milton (Christ!) and α for Chaucer (*Jesus!*) and B9 (1400–1700): "well, Mr Amis, in view of those details we'd better look upon you as *our mediaevalist*, eh, mm?"'[97]

Amis's success in Schools meant that he could stay at Oxford as a research student and would not have to find a job as a teacher, a prospect that had begun to fill him with dread in the months leading up to the examinations. The previous June he had gone to the University of Oxford Department of Education to fill in a form about teaching. As he told Larkin on 16 June: 'When I came to the part that said "Games and other interests" I put my fountain-pen down on my writing table, and thought to myself for a little while; then I picked up my fountain-pen again and dipped the nib into the ink-bottle, and wrote down on the paper: "CRICKET RUGBY FOOTBALL SQUASH DRAMATICS MUSICAL APPRECIATION DEBATES." After that I felt *much sadder*, as if I had been writing to a girl to tell her I couldn't see her any more, and *much more frightened*, as if I were an ambassador at a peace conference breaking his government's orders.' Pursuing a B.Litt. in English might be boring, but it wasn't frightening. In a letter to Larkin of 22 June, the prospect of teaching chilled:

Your evocations of the life of a young Vsher were very exact and made me feel like a man in a cage, unable to get out, particularly the bursts of ringing laughter that would penetrate into the corridors and make the headmaster put his head inside the door: 'what's all this noise here?' 'I'm sorry, sir, we were just –' 'Oh Amis, I didn't see you. Will you come out and have a word with me in the passage a minute? All of you get on with your work . . . Now, Amis, this is the third time you've . . .' '. . . very sorry . . . inexperienced . . . doing my best . . . won't happen again . . . socks up . . . too much for you . . . not really what the school expects . . . young . . . don't want to have to . . .' OH GOD SAVE ME FROM THY WRATH OH GOD SAVE[98]

Amis was candid with Larkin about his fears, and funny, too. On 16 June 1947, he confessed that he felt 'very depressed this evening. I feel sometimes a slight excess of sexual energy without object, not even towards masturbation, and not even – I think – towards very young girls. I feel as if I am on the threshold of some new and fearsome perversion that is going to burst into my conscious mind with the force of a mastodon's fart. Do you ever feel like that? Because if you *do*, it won't make me feel better when I feel like that, but it will make me feel less afraid when I don't feel like that and am thinking of the times when I do feel like that.' Later in the summer, on 25 July, he faced the prospect of being on his own while his parents were on holiday, 'which I *shan't* like, because being alone at *nights* makes me feel *frightened*'. He somehow managed a whole week by himself, though housekeeping defeated him ('My mother seems to have been very good at PREVENTING THE PLACE STINKING; *I'm not*. You've no idea how bad is the smell given off by bad meat').[99] Amis's fearfulness made him sympathetic to the fears of others. In the letter of 27 December, the examination results letter, Amis tried to reassure Larkin, whose father was ill with what would prove to be terminal cancer. Throughout his life, whenever he sought to comfort or condole, Amis invariably struck the right note. Here he also made clear what he thought was the difference between Larkin's anxieties and his own:

I was very sorry to hear that your father isn't well; I can imagine that it worries and depresses you. I hope it won't be long before they know how to deal with whatever he's got. I was also sorry to hear about your worrying, but I don't think it very likely that you really are suffering from an anxiety neurosis: you don't strike me as at all a hysterical person and from what I know of these things they are marked by periodical outbursts of hysteria led up to by *increasing* and *unaccountable* anxiety. But I know that whatever your trouble is called it remains a trouble. I don't like hearing about your depression, and though I don't expect the reflection is of much value I'd say that it is the product of what is happening around you as much as what's happening inside you, which at least might make you think that there's nothing wrong with your brain.

Around the time he was writing these words, shortly after receiving his examination results, Amis paid a visit 'to the loony bin at Littlemore', a psychiatric hospital in Oxford.[100] He went to consult a doctor about panic attacks and unaccountable fears. This doctor, a psychiatrist named Armstrong, Amis 'trusted on sight, perhaps because he really was a trustworthy man, perhaps because he was the first member of his profession I had encountered'. What the psychiatrist said to Amis was: 'While I can't tell you that you'll never go mad any more than I can say you'll never break a leg, you show no sign of it at the moment.' Apparently, this was what Amis needed to hear, for he 'stayed cured for ten years', excepting 'a few momentary lurches on dark nights'.[101] Amis does not identify the sources of his panic attacks, but they were as likely to have been set off by what was 'happening around' him as 'happening inside' him. To begin with, there were examination pressures and fears about the future. At Marlborough, at a time of comparable pressures, he had woken at night screaming and had to be comforted by Mrs Ellingham. At the end of 1947, however, there were pressures of another sort. In the letter he wrote to Larkin on 6 December, after passages on smoking, new jazz releases, how he felt he'd done in his exams, and a planned collaboration with Bruce Montgomery (to write the libretto for an opera), Amis matter-of-factly announced: 'Hilly and I are making a man at the moment which is worrying me rather, but not as much as it might because we have assembled a lot of chemicals which are inimical to the continued retention of the fertilised ovum.' These chemicals, Hilly remembers, never in fact materialised, and by the time he visited Dr Armstrong, after receiving his Schools results, the options facing Amis and Hilly were alarming.

Amis and Hilly had been a couple for over eighteen months, since at least May 1946, when she first 'yielded'. They went regularly to OU Jazz Club evenings 'and even danced'; they went punting and 'had all the fun of being brassily cheated at St. Giles's fair'; Hilly impressed Amis 'by being rejected as not readily hypnotisable at a so-called hypnotist's stage show, and in a different way by washing her hair and her smalls in the Randolph and, much to my trepidation, in the bath-house at St John's'.[102] There were further visits to Abbey Timbers; Hilly came to stay with Amis and his parents at Berkhamsted, once for a week; during term time they sneaked off on weekend coach trips to London, staying at inexpensive hotels; in the summer of 1946 they even went on a two-and-a-half-week holiday together to France, doing almost no sightseeing, sleeping in a room of their own in the hôtel du Cheval de Bronze at Remiremont in the Vosges (where Amis was terrified the proprietor would throw them out for immorality). Christopher Tosswill was along on the France holiday, though his girlfriend pulled out at the last moment, much to Hilly's dismay. Tosswill eventually got on Amis's nerves; as Amis complained to Larkin, in a letter of 15 September, 'he is PRAID OF THINGS ABOUT HIMSELF: "Everybody knows I'm unapproachable after a long journey *until I've been fed.*"' There were also moments of tension with Hilly, who was left alone while the two men worked on their studies. 'There was little life in the village,' she recalls, and Amis and Tosswill 'really did work very hard'. She read the whole of *War and Peace* during the holiday but missed female company in particular. Amis complained to Larkin of her demands while in France, though by the end of the holiday everything was all right between them.

Amis was not exactly faithful to Hilly during this period. In December 1946 he wrote to his first love, Elisabeth Simpson, asking if she'd be interested in seeing him, and she wrote back yes (though nothing seems to have come of the exchange).[103] He fantasised about a schoolgirl he and Hilly had seen in a Lyon's tea-shop and came close to asking her out. In January 1947, at Berkhamsted, he went to a dance and saw an attractive girl with a thin, sullen face, black eyes and hair and 'noticeable' breasts ('When I stared at her,' he reported to Larkin, 'she looked back disinterestedly, half-closing her eyes. She was TWELVE YEARS OLD TWELVE YEARS OLD TWELV').[104] In June a girl named Noel, not otherwise mentioned in the correspondence, turned up in Oxford 'and I saw her and removed a lot of her clothing in Xt ch meadows, but I didn't shag her because I decided it would spoil thigns with Hilly . . . I think I am a very nice man to behave like that under extreme provocation. The next day I had a letter from EAS [Elisabeth] as a kind of reward from destiny.'[105] Later in the summer, in Berkhamsted, he had several dates with a local girl named Helen, a figure in some ways like Stephanie, the Whitstead girl Sidney approves of in 'The Legacy'. On 1 September, while Hilly was on vacation with her parents, Amis told Larkin that Helen had written to him from Cornwall, where she was on holiday, informing him that 'she'll be back AFTER HILLY GETS BACK'. When his parents visited the parents of another girl he'd been seeing in Berkhamsted, named Daphne, 'Daphne said well if he's not serious about this Hilary we can go straight ahead with fixing him up with Helen.' He also learned that Helen's parents 'have got even more money than I suspected and that Helen is "keen"

I LIKE HEARING THAT but I feel myself to have got into something that I shall not enjoy getting 8 of.'[106]

When Amis returned to Oxford in October 1947, he and Hilly were closer than ever, at least geographically. For the second year running he was in digs in St John's Street (in his first year back, in 1945–46, he had lived in a handsome set of rooms in New Quad, only recently evacuated by the white fish and potato administrators). He was now at number 55 St John's Street (rather than number 19) and Hilly's digs were at number 57. Amis was working flat out for Schools (*'nine hours a day sitting on my arse in my lodgings reading smelly books'*),[107] while Hilly had, as she wrote to Larkin on 29 October, 'another *nasty* job, they call it being a "Home Help" but I won't bore you with the details'. Amis's examinations began on 27 November and had finished by the time Hilly told him she was pregnant. On 20 December he learned that he'd got his First. The plan now was to return to their respective families for the Christmas holidays and then visit a specialist in London, 'the nasty man'. As Amis informed Larkin on the 27th, this man 'is going to give [Hilly] an injection of a substance derived from the interior of a cow, which we hope will cease her Mary Shelley activities. The man lives in Park Lane, W.1, and going there will make me very frightened, and paying the bill afterwards will fill me with a variety of emotions; but if the injection doesn't work, then Hilly will have to submit to a surgical operation, costing £100.' Later in the same letter, Amis told Larkin that he was planning to visit Abbey Timbers for the New Year, returning to Berkhamsted by 3 January, 'when I shall be going to a jolly party in the house of some neighbours, at which I hope to meet a pretty young widowed lady whom I have noticed in the neighbourhood'. It is hard not to see Amis's tone in this letter, his jokey detachment, as a trifle callous.

Amis did not write again to Larkin until 12 January. He had 'a lot on my mind; more on it than I have ever had on it in the whole of my life before'. What follows is an extraordinary account, a sort of short story, many details of which he would later incorporate in *You Can't Do Both*. He and Hilly travelled to London on a Tuesday to see 'the nasty man', who said he couldn't help but that he knew someone who could, though it would cost them 100 guineas. In other words, Hilly would need an operation, which would have to be scheduled right away. Frank Coles, with whom they were staying Tuesday night, agreed to put Hilly up while she recovered. The next day they travelled to Mitcham to see if they could borrow 100 guineas from Christopher Tosswill ('before you read any further,' Amis tells Larkin, 'you would probably like to be assured that I'm not trying to borrow 100 gns or any other sum from you'). Christopher was willing to lend the money but said it would take him a week to get it out of the Post Office. Amis and Hilly then spent Wednesday night in Kingston, at Hilly's ninety-two-year-old grandmother's house. Here Amis called Nick Russel to see if he could borrow 100 guineas from him, but his money, too, was tied up in the Post Office. Amis then rang up his father in Berkhamsted for the number of an old schoolfriend, Keith Lightfoot, 'who is rich and on military duty in the city of Paris'. Lightfoot eventually agreed to wire the money, 'after a lot of joking on his side'. Thursday was spent trying to arrange appointments with 'the nasty man', who had not yet given them the name and address of his friend, the doctor who would operate on Hilly. Thursday night was spent at the flat of Gillian Williams ('it's me, I think'), near the BBC. The doctor who would perform the operation could not see them until Friday at five, so they spent the next day walking around the city in the rain, then at the movies, then in a tea-shop, 'for most of the time next to a deformed man with a curious disc-shaped growth on his neck, who shook all the time'.

When they met the doctor at 5 p.m. on Friday it turned out he was from Central Europe 'and very agreeable and reassuring, looking like a successful and respected American film director'. Amis reproduces his accent in the letter. He claimed the operation, which was scheduled for Monday, was simple, would take only two hours, and that Hilly could go home straightaway. Then Hilly returned to Abbey Timbers for the weekend, and Amis stayed in London and had a long talk with a friend of Coles, 'a real doctor' named Hugh Price.

He said that, contrary to what I had earlier been led to believe, the operation would be a very serious matter, that there was perhaps 1 chance in 20 that Hilly would have a haemorrhage afterwards and die of it, that there was a much greater chance that she would be rendered permanently sterile, and a greater chance still that being deprived of her child would make her (a) bitter and (b) bitter towards me. He summed up his view of the measures proposed by the Central European doctor as 'sheer butchery,' and added that he was aware, by reason of his experience as an Assistant

Medical Officer of Health for his Borough, of the existence of a band of Central Europeans in the particular area and of their part in other illegal acts like murder and blackmail.

The next morning Amis met again with the Central European doctor and insisted that Hilly be admitted to a nursing home after the operation for at least a week. Reluctantly, angrily as well, the doctor rang up a friend of his and booked Hilly into a room in a Central European hotel in London, where he would attend to her after the operation for three days. After a second discussion with Hugh Price, Amis decided that these arrangements were also inadequate:

So I then thought that, since I had been intending to marry Hilly at some point anyway, no time could be better than the present; that it would be intolerable if, through my miserable scruples, anything nasty were to happen to Hilly; that even with the great nuisance of having a child, the upset and responsibility of 'starting a new home,' and the unwelcome constraint on my freedom, these were better than such a disaster as might happen, better too than losing Hilly eventually even if no actual disaster happened. I went down to Abbey Timbers and told Hilly all this and, as I had expected, she agreed that it would be best to get married. I rang up the Central European doctor and told him we wouldn't be coming. I told my parents what had happened and they now accept the position. If by any chance I've failed to evoke in you what it felt like to be me between last Tuesday and Saturday, let me add that I felt as if I had committed an outrage on a schoolgirl and then murdered her, leaving my identity card near the body, and as if I were in a dentist's chair with a dentist about to take all my teeth out without anaesthetic, a measure that might postpone my capture for a few days. I'm very glad I don't feel like that any more.

As regards the impending marriage, it's hard not to look upon it as a *faute de mieux*, though this feeling is decreasing slightly. I don't want a filthy baby, but Hilly is so overjoyed by the prospect that it seems unkind not to allow it, and since I'm determined to keep Hilly and she would never be happy for any length of time without a baby, having one sooner or later seems inevitable. Since I enjoy living with Hilly better than I enjoy living anywhere else, it's difficult to believe that I shan't enjoy living with her all the time, especially since it'll mean in addition that I shall be able to do as I like, eat the food I like, and stop worrying about not being able to ejaculate when I want to. As against this I shall have to 'find somewhere to live,' and eventually spend money on a *pram* and *furniture*, and have to nurse the baby, but I can foresee myself not minding these things as much as I have minded other things in my life, and this time I shall be getting things in return. Also, Hilly has £3 a week of her own *for life*,[108] which makes me feel happier. I should be glad to have your unprejudiced opinion on this situation. I don't want you to think (anymore than I want to think) that it will mean our association had become less intimate. You know of course what Hilly's opinion of you is (you bastard). I imagine we shall be living in Oxford for some time yet. I'd like to see you very soon.

Though Amis says here that he 'had been intending to marry Hilly at some point', it is impossible to tell what would have happened had she not got pregnant. He was fonder of Hilly than of any other girl, was keen to be with her and knew they were thought of as a couple – by her parents, his parents, by friends in Oxford and Berkhamsted. Bruce Montgomery kept telling him he should marry her, which irritated him.[109] When Roger Partington ('old Rodge'), his future brother-in-law, 'told Mrs. Bardwell he "wasn't happy" about the relationship between Hilly and me',[110] he took offence ('The BUMFACED CHEEK'). But he might easily have let things drift, wanting both Hilly and 'everyone else'. There is no evidence that he wished to be married at this time or was ready to be a husband and father. 'The great thing about Hilly,' he writes to Larkin on 22 August 1947, 'is that when I don't want to talk to her, she doesn't mind; or at least she doesn't complain, which is the sam thing for our sort',[111] a disquieting remark, even granting the confessional bravado and posturing so frequent in the correspondence with Larkin. 'However fond I am of a young lady I like to do things away from her occasionally,' he tells Larkin on 1 April 1946, counselling him about Ruth: 'which is only the same sort of thing as playing other records than Spider Crawl when Sp. C. is still one's favourite record.'

Hilly's attitude to the pregnancy was clear and simple. She loved Amis and wanted to marry him and to have his baby: 'When I fell in love I fell in love, that was very much it.' But if Amis did not want the baby she was prepared to abort it. She put no direct or spoken pressure on him. Still, Amis knew full well what she wanted: 'As I had expected, she agreed that it would be best to get married.' Two days after the long letter Amis wrote Larkin on 14 January, Hilly also wrote: 'I expect Kingsley has written by now telling you all the amazing things that have happened. I still feel very dazed,

I'm very happy and flattered and I can't help feeling pleased about the troublesome baby – if a little alarmed.' 'Flattered', here, is the word that touches; the admission that she 'can't help feeling pleased' and the gently ironic description of the baby as 'troublesome', both of which could be said to make light of trouble while indulging the Kingsley view, are more collected or composed. A similar composure underlies Hilly's description of more immediate difficulties: 'I'm going to have some very nasty moments soon when I tell my mother and father that I'll have to get married soon *because* a baby's turning up in July, but not half so bad as it would have been having it cut out by a slimy Pole.'

Part of Hilly's difficulty in facing her parents was admitting that she'd deceived them. Her mother had allowed her to go to France with Amis and Christopher Tosswill because 'she trusted me'. It had reassured her that there would be 'another chap there and [that] his girlfriend was supposed to be along', but their presence was not what mattered. 'She was horrified, indeed, when I obviously had broken the rules and had gone to bed with him and so on.' After Bedales, Hilly's sister Margaret led what she described as 'quite a wild life' as a student at the Architectural Association in London, but she never slept with anyone, partly because 'I was conscious of not wanting to do anything to upset my parents.' It was not that she found her parents frightening; on the contrary, she did not want to upset them because 'they were very mild people . . . I mean, they were much too nice, my parents'. When Hilly delivered her news, the Bardwells felt betrayed as well as shocked, and refused to attend the wedding, as did Amis's father. At this moment, Amis's mother, an otherwise 'gentle creature', took matters in hand. As Amis explains in the *Memoirs*, she 'told my father not to be such a fool with his threats of excommunication and persuaded my future parents-in-law not to boycott the ceremony as they had been intending'.[112]

Once they came round, the Bardwells insisted that the marriage take place as soon as possible: on Wednesday, 21 January 1948, in the Register Office of the Oxford Town Hall. All four parents were present. As Hilly recalls:

My mother and father and I travelled grimly up by bus from Harwell. Kingsley met us straight from his digs with his parents and grimly they stood there while a rather drunk chap married us. And then we went to the Randolph Hotel and had coffee and I think my mother had made a cream cake. We had no new clothes; there was no question of being able to. And then Kingsley went back to his digs. His parents got the bus back to Berkhamsted and I got in the bus back to Harwell with my parents. And that was it.

The only guest at the wedding seems to have been Nick Russel, who, according to Amis, in a letter to Larkin of 25 January, 'laughed at the back while a Hitchcock fat character with bursting eyes and lips like wizened Paris sausages . . . said the words over us'. That evening Nick treated the newlyweds to dinner at the George. The ceremony itself, as Amis describes it, was no ceremony at all: 'We only had two sentences each to repeat . . . and then there was nothing to do but signing and paying money'. Between coffee at the Randolph and dinner at the George, Amis wrote a letter to the Secretary of Faculties at Oxford 'for admission as Probationer Student to the B.Litt. course in English Language and Literature'. Here, then, was his future: research student, husband, father.

8

Newly Married: Oxford and Eynsham

Within days of the marriage Amis and Hilly had found a place to live. On 26 January 1948 they moved into what Amis described to Larkin as a very expensive flat at 14 Norham Road in Summertown, North Oxford.[1] This flat consisted of one large all-purpose room with a kitchen opening from it, plus bath and loo. In the *Memoirs* Amis remembers both place and period as 'sunny and spacious'.[2] The Bardwells helped out the newlyweds with crockery, cutlery, pots and pans, a carpet sweeper, bed linen 'and between two and three hundred pounds'. 'As far as I can see,' Amis reported to Larkin, 'we shan't be short of money.' Between them they would have a combined income of 'about £550 this year, apart from a little bit of capital'. Soon after they moved in, a third resident was added to the household: 'a small, dapper but dignified ginger cat called Winkie', an 'implacable' hunter, of moths in particular.[3] Hilly remembers the early months of the marriage as 'lovely': Amis was deeply engaged in his studies, preparing for first-year B.Litt. examinations; Larkin came to stay, sleeping in the flat's other twin bed, next to which Hilly would neatly arrange his slippers. She took great pleasure in cooking things Amis liked: 'I enjoyed that. I enjoyed playing house.' She also recalls, as does Amis in the *Memoirs*, the pleasure she took in beating him at halma, a card game her grandmother had taught her: 'I was outrageously chuffed, thinking there's one thing I can do better than him.' Though Amis still stared at women in the street, ostentatiously complaining when a bus obscured his view (a provocation Hilly 'felt I shouldn't rise to'), there was not at this time 'much fooling around'.

'I am starting to think that I shall find marriage more *convenient* than single life,' wrote Amis to Larkin on 25 January. 'I hope I shall be going on thinking it in a month's time.'

By the evidence of the letters, Amis's hope was realised, though he still found plenty to complain about. The drawbacks of marriage, he was to explain, involved other people, principally one's parents. On 9 February Amis inaugurated a series of pastiche letters to Larkin. What is striking about these letters is the initial absence of typos, misspellings, exclamation marks, underlinings, capitals or profanities. Here is the opening of the 9 February letter, part of which was quoted in Chapter 1:

My Dear Philip,

It was very nice to get your letter, and I intended to reply to it more quickly than I am, but of course, as you will allow, marriage has its ties as well as its freedoms, and some how I am not writing until now. On Friday my parents were here, and were delighted by the bright and cheerful appearance of our little den, and the obviously smooth-running and contented look of our small ménage! . . . Yesterday too Hilary and I went and had lunch at Abbey Timbers with her parents and my parents. We each had half a glass of wine with our lunch, so you can imagine that it was a real family party! Then in the afternoon I talked to my mother and my mother-in-law and played that game with the glass and the alphabet round the table, and then Hilary and I came back last night too late for me to go to the film society. But so I said when the Bardwells asked me, I didn't feel all that set on going: it would probably not have been much of a programme . . . Next week-end Hilary and I are going to Berkhamsted. My mother wants us to arrive there on the Friday evening and stay until the Monday morning, so that we can have the maximum time there. There won't be much to do, of course, but the four of us will be quite happy, I expect, on our own, in the family circle. You can see how busy we've been: I must say I shall be FUCKING GLAD when Hilly is too BLOWN OUT with a child CONCEIVED 8 OF WEDLOCK for us to go near either of our parents. The trouble with marriage, my dear little fellow, is not that you are too much on your own with your wife, but that you are too much alone with your mother-in-law, and your father, and your father-in-law, and your mother, and your mother's friends, and your father-in-law's friends, and your father's friends, and your mother-in-law's friends . . . I forgot to tell you that *to-morrow* morning my wife and I are having a cup of coffee to drink in Elliston and Cavell's *with a friend of my mother-in-law's.*

In the same letter, Amis asked Larkin to tell him more about a lecturer's job in English at Leicester; he had yet to see an advertisement for it. At this point, Amis was in the last year of his Exhibition ('rather impudently stretched to four years')[4] and was scanning the pages of the *Times Educational Supplement* for university positions (the *Higher* did not yet exist). By taking a B.Litt. he hoped to better his chances of getting such a job, though the degree, he soon discovered, involved 'quite a lot of genuine work',[5] including attendance at a course of lectures 'put in on the Oxford principle of fending prospective candidates off by the prospect of intrinsic boredom combined with entire practical uselessness'.[6] In May he would be examined on the material which formed the first part of the course, including the history of English studies, taught by the 'narcotic' David Nichol Smith. When Larkin teased Amis about his work for the B.Litt., Amis was indignant: 'What do you mean to say, playing at research? Did you ever work in Duke Humfrey [in the Bodleian], with the spectacle cases of dons clicking round you like twigs snapping under the feet of wild beasts.'[7] At his viva for the examination, Amis reported to Larkin, Nichol Smith commented on his answer to a question on English studies as a field: '"you seemed rather to like it, didn't you?" I replied in the affirmative.' In the same letter to Larkin, on 11 May, Amis mentions Lord David Cecil, the younger son of the fourth marquess of Salisbury, the man who would be assigned to supervise the 40,000-word thesis that was to make up the second part of the course: 'Had I seen Cecil when I came to see you? He is a very silly man.'[8] Ten days later he again writes to Larkin: 'Tell Monica[9] that Cecil in the flesh strikes me as a *silly, unhelpful, posturing oaf.*'[10]

In Amis's *Memoirs*, Cecil's unhelpfulness is memorably recalled. According to the Instructions to Candidates for the B.Litt. it was the supervisor's job to contact supervisees and to meet with them at least twice a term. By the middle of his second term Amis had heard nothing from Cecil, so he went round to New College one weekday morning to find him. Here is his reconstruction of an exchange with a New College porter: '"You're looking for *who*, Sir?" he asked, as if I had inquired about the Shah of Persia. When he was sure he had heard me correctly he summoned a nearby colleague and pointed me out to him as a curiosity. "Look, here's a young gentleman looking for Lord David Cecil!" Then, turning back to me and chuckling intermittently, he went on, "Oh no, sir.

Lord David? Oh, you'd have to get up very early in the morning to get hold of him. Oh dear, oh dear. Lord David in college, well I never."'[11] By 28 May Amis still hadn't met with Cecil, though by now probably by design: 'I'm hating starting my thesis,' he wrote to Larkin, 'gong again to the Bodleian, reading silly and useless pamphlets, starting new note books, looking through bibliographies. I hope to change from Cess-hole to Bateson soon.' The letter ends: 'Getting down to it now eh Amis bum.'

Bateson, here, is F.W. Bateson, Fellow of English at Corpus Christi College, described in the *Memoirs* as 'youngish . . . as dons went'.[12] Amis described Cecil, in contrast, in the letter of 11 May to Larkin, as having 'a good many years on his back'.[13] But Cecil was a year younger than Bateson, having been born in 1902. That he seemed older may have derived in part from his professional standing; in the very year he and Amis were busy avoiding each other, 1948, he was appointed Goldsmith's Professor of English at Oxford. Bateson was only a lecturer and his standing in the English Faculty was that of an outsider of sorts, though one well versed in current trends in English studies. He was also 'a bit leftie in a sort of Bevanish way'.[14] (Among other things, he had written a volume for Gollancz's Left Book Club entitled *Towards a Socialist Agriculture*). While 'for much of male Oxford, especially undergraduate male Oxford, Lord David was a bit of a joke, one with a touch of lower-middle-class resentment lurking in it',[15] Bateson's manner and appearance, for all his learning, were, according to Al Alvarez, his student in 1949, more down-to-earth, like those of a farmer.[16] In Amis's words, he 'looked bucolic and donnish in about equal measure, which was right for one who had been, perhaps still was, agricultural correspondent of the then *New Statesman and Nation*'.[17] Amis was adept at mimicking Cecil's extraordinary voice and lecturing style, an imitation he appropriated from John Wain but soon made his own, complete with hand gestures and darting, swooning movements of the head: 'Laze . . . laze and gentlemen, when we say a man looks like a poet . . . dough mean . . . looks like Chauthah . . . dough mean . . . looks like Dvyden . . . dough mean . . . looks like *Theckthpyum* [or something else barely recognisable as "Shakespeare"] . . . Mean looks like Shelley [pronounced "Thellem" or thereabouts]. Matthew Arnold [then prestissimo] called Shelley beautiful ineffectual angel Matthew Arnold had face [rallentando] like a *horth*. But my subject this morning is not the poet Shelley. Jane . . . Austen . . .'[18]

When Amis passed his B.Litt. examinations in early May, he had little idea what to choose as a thesis topic, 'except that I had a fondness for the Pre-Raphaelites'. The topic he and Bateson eventually 'cobbled up'[19] combined this fondness with Bateson's interest in the sorts of questions raised by Q.D. Leavis's influential *Fiction and the Reading Public* (1932), questions of audience and of the relation of literary institutions (publishers, editors, booksellers, bookclubs, periodicals, etc.) to literary production. Amis had bought Leavis's book soon after his return to Oxford in early 1946 and described it to Larkin, in a letter of 25 February, as 'sodding good'. At first the title of his thesis was 'Decline of the Audience for Poetry from 1850–Present Day',[20] a mammoth topic eventually narrowed to 'English Non-Dramatic Poetry, 1850–1900, and the Victorian Reading Public'. When Amis outlined the aims of the thesis, in a first proposal of March 1949, the English Faculty Board rejected it, in a letter of 17 March, on the unhelpful grounds 'that the subject proposed was not one that could be profitably studied for the degree'.[21] A second proposal was then submitted by Amis on 2 May and accepted, perhaps because it specified the means by which the topic would be investigated: through letters and memoirs, both of poets and their admirers, but also through reviews, advertisements, expository articles, public lectures and statistics of sales, library circulation and publication in magazines and anthologies. In the first proposal Amis suggested that his thesis would bear out the contention that there was an 'ideal process of poetry's diffusion', one that moved from the poet's 'inner public' to a circle of 'intermediate followers' to an 'outer, general public', and that whenever this process was in some way abrogated or abbreviated, 'the effect on the poet's work and on the prestige of poetry [was] likely to be marked and deleterious'.

Amis's proposed thesis had recognisable literary critical and theoretical affiliations. The Oxford English Faculty of 1949, according to Alvarez, could be broadly divided into three factions: the philologists, whose interests were confined to Anglo-Saxon and early medieval writing; the textual scholars, who produced definitive editions, often of 'very minor' poets; and the 'appreciative' critics, such as Cecil, 'who preferred not to sully their sensibilities with argument or detail'.[22] Outside Oxford ('everywhere except Oxford', is how Alvarez puts it), a fourth faction was in vogue, that of a more rigorous and analytic criticism, one associated with I.A.

Richards, Empson and the Leavises at Cambridge, and with the so-called New Critics in the United States (Cleanth Brooks, Robert Penn Warren, John Crowe Ransom and others). Bateson sought to combine the analytic rigour of these critics with the learning of textual and other scholars. Though an admirer of *Scrutiny*, the periodical founded by the Leavises, Bateson quarrelled publicly in the 1930s with what he described as F. R. Leavis's 'insistence on reading everything written in English as though it was written yesterday'.[23] Instead, he called for 'a discipline of contextual reading', one that infused 'social issues, in the widest sense of the term, into purely literary criticism'.[24] Hence the title of his last published book: *The Scholar Critic*.

Bateson's ambitions for English study marked him as an outsider not only in the Oxford English Faculty but in core Leavisite and New Critical circles. He was too much the critic for the scholars, too analytic for the 'appreciators' (as 'engaged' as any of the Leavisites who sniped at Cecil in *Scrutiny*), and too much the scholar for the 'Scrutineers'. His pupils, though, found him both learned and approachable, qualities also attributed to Amis as a tutor. According to Alvarez, Bateson would listen to weekly tutorial essays 'with great concentration, puffing his pipe and making little squeaking noises when provoked, then he told you the vital facts you had missed, the sources, the references, the textual variants – he had them all at his fingertips. And he would argue . . . he paid you the compliment of arguing with you seriously.'[25] That Amis seems to have shared Bateson's interest in the role of historical and social factors in literary production, or was willing to feign such an interest for the purposes of the thesis, may seem surprising, given his later professed indifference, quoted in Chapter 2, to context, as well as his stress on the primacy of clear and forceful judgement. But Bateson was humanly acceptable, as well as clever and learned – and from an Oxford perspective modern. Though in the wider world Bateson was thought of as challenging key aspects of the Leavisite or New Critical approach, in Oxford he was thought of as challenging establishment figures such as Cecil and Nichol Smith. Bateson himself saw his approach from an Oxford perspective, as allied with new trends. When in 1951 he launched the periodical *Essays in Criticism*, printing an attack on Keats's 'self-indulgence' by Amis in its second number, his declared aim was 'to provide Oxford with a journal that might perform a complementary function in that university to the one performed so brilliantly by *Scrutiny* in Cambridge'.[26]

For Bateson to become Amis's supervisor Amis had to fill in a form and get Cecil to sign it, a mere formality, Bateson assured him, though one that 'involved finding him'.[27] This Amis managed by accident, spotting Cecil outside Blackwell's bookshop and stammering out his request. Cecil, Amis recalls in the *Memoirs*, 'offered me no help at all as I explained what I wanted'.[28] Later in Cecil's rooms, 'the actual business, the finding then the filling-in of the actual form, went off with surprising ease; he probably had a desk-compartment with a coded label meaning FORMS FOR FUCKING FOOLS WHO ARE FED UP WITH ME JUST POCKETING MY FEE AND WANT A SERIOUS SUPERVISOR'.[29] What Amis wrote on the form, dated 19 October 1948, was: 'I ask the favour of changing my B.Litt. supervisor to Mr. F.W. Bateson, suggesting that a subject as socio-logical and diffused as the above might more profitably be approached under the guidance of a bibliographical specialist', which Bateson partly was. Amis later came to doubt that Cecil was as unconcerned about the switch as he seemed at the time, or that he was placated by Amis's explanation, given the subsequent fate of the finished thesis. Cecil's relations with Bateson may not have been easy, as suggested by Amis's recollection, in a 1986 interview, of Bateson's initial response when he approached him about the switch: 'This can't go on, come to me instead of fooling around with that aristocratic lazybones.'[30]

In addition to his work on the B.Litt. and 'The Legacy', begun the previous summer, Amis was occupied in 1948 with the first of several musical collaborations with Bruce Montgomery, whom he only got to know properly after the war. Montgomery, the son of a civil servant in the India Office, was educated at Merchant Taylors' School (like Ellingham) and came from a middle-class background similar to Larkin's, though the impression he created among his fellow undergraduates was altogether more exotic. He took up a place at St John's two terms before Amis, who first laid eyes on him shortly after arriving in Oxford in spring 1941, perhaps even on his first morning in college. Montgomery was on his way to the St John's bath-house dressed in a silk dressing-gown 'in some non-primary shade', walking in a manner both 'eccentric and mincing' (as Amis would later discover, because his feet were congenitally deformed, the condition that kept him out of the army) and with 'an indefinable and daunting air of maturity'.[31] 'Here was an *under-graduate*,' Amis thought, 'the real thing.' In later, full-dress sightings, Montgomery 'inclined to a fancy waist-coated, suede-shoed style with cigarette-holders and rings'. But Montgomery's appearance was only part of what made him daunting. He was an accomplished musician, an organ scholar (both college organist and choirmaster). He conducted the University Choir and the orchestra of the University Musicians' Club, once in a performance of Constant Lambert's *The Rio Grande*, which he re-scored himself, and in which Amis sang. He kept a grand piano in his rooms in college and provided piano accompaniment for the University Ballet Club, sometimes with Donald Swann, and twice for visiting members of the Ballet Rambert. He composed the music for several university theatre productions and for his own plays. He painted: a framed water-colour of his school was displayed prominently in his rooms, among other works. He had written a book, 'Romanticism and the World Crisis', subtitled 'An Essay on the Culture and Politics of the XXth Century', a work of some 160 pages attributing the rise of Fascism to Romanticism. This work was much indebted not only to Wyndham Lewis but to a host of intimidatingly foreign luminaries (he was a good linguist, reading modern languages at Oxford): Henri de Montherlant, Charles Maurras, Julien Benda, Hermann Keyserling. Charles Williams, poet, novelist, theological writer, publisher and 'Inkling', offered to help him find an agent. Williams also introduced Montgomery to C.S. Lewis and J.R.R. Tolkien. Montgomery's girlfriend, the up-and-coming actress Muriel Pavlow, was impressive, too. She would visit him in Oxford when not touring with a play or filming, and was thought to be his lover (Amis told Montgomery's biographer, David Whittle, that Montgomery hoped at one point to marry Pavlow). The setting of Montgomery's social life also distinguished him from most undergraduates: instead of drinking beer in pubs, he drank spirits in the bar at the Randolph Hotel.

Amis was not the only undergraduate at St John's to think Montgomery out of his league. To Alan Ross, his tutorial partner, 'there was no doubt . . . who, of us all, appeared the most sophisticated, best-read, widely connected and gifted'. Though only a year older than Amis and Ross, Montgomery seemed 'light years ahead in experience'.[32] Larkin agreed: 'it hardly occurred to me that he was an undergraduate, not in the same sense that I was'. Once he got to know him, however, in just about his last term at Oxford, Larkin discovered 'unsuspected depths of frivolity, and we were soon spending most of our time together swaying about with laughter on bar-stools'.[33] It was Montgomery who introduced Larkin not only to Montherlant but to H.L. Mencken, John Dickson Carr, Flann O'Brien, Baudelaire and Théophile Gautier, whose *Mademoiselle de Maupin*, with its openly bisexual heroine, influenced the Willow Gables stories. Larkin in turn introduced Montgomery's enthusiasms to Amis. In the Introduction to *Jill*, Larkin credits Montgomery with having contributed 'a curious creative stimulus' to the period 1943–46. It was Montgomery and his friend Diana Gollancz, the publisher's daughter, to whom Larkin read each new instalment of his Willow Gables stories, composed in the midst of studying for finals. For the next three years, Larkin 'wrote continuously as never before or since', producing *Jill* in a year, many of the poems that would appear in *The North Ship* and a second novel, *A Girl in Winter*, finished in 1945, though not published until 1947. 'Possibly,' Larkin writes in the Introduction to *Jill*, Montgomery's 'brisk intellectual Epicureanism was just the catalyst I needed'.[34] As he put it in the autobiographical essay he wrote in 1943, at the end of the summer, 'Bruce's irresponsibility and self-confidence were exactly what I needed at the time and our friendship flared up like a flame in oxygen.'[35]

Though Amis had met Montgomery in 1941–42, when singing in college and university choirs, he, too, only really got to know him in 1943, when stationed at Headington and on subsequent leaves. By the time Amis returned to Oxford after the war Montgomery had already established himself not only as a composer and musician, earning enough money from film scores to enter 'the world of success you read about in the papers, there with the first gin-and-tonics and Jaguars',[36] but as a writer of crime fiction, under the pseudonym Edmund Crispin (in the letters, 'Crippen', 'Crips', 'Crip' and 'Creep-in'). The first of the Crispin novels, *The Case of the Gilded Fly* (1944), was written while Montgomery was still an undergraduate, and published by Gollancz (according to Larkin it was written in ten days in the Easter vac).[37] Though not always to Amis's taste, the Crispin novels betray opinions and attitudes he would approve. To begin with, the villains in the early novels are arrogant artists or artist-types (like Bertrand in *Lucky Jim*): the villain of *The Case of the Gilded Fly*, a dramatist, leads the hero, the detective

Gervase Fen (based on Montgomery's tutor at St John's, W.R. Moore), to conclude that 'the artistic temperament is too often only an alibi for a lack of responsibility'; the villain of *Holy Disorders* (1945), the second Crispin novel, is called 'affected, arty, with no soul, no morals'. In the third novel, *The Moving Toyshop* (1946), Fen amuses himself by devising lists of 'Unreadable Books' and 'Detestable Characters', recalling, for example, Amis's list of 'Twelve Bad Men', from a letter to Larkin of 29 April 1946 (it begins: '1. The Author of Beowulf (capt.)'), or his literary 'personnels' (modelled on jazz personnels), as in 'Big Ben Jonson and his Tribesmen', from a letter to Larkin of 30 January 1947. Amis would also have found Montgomery's musical tastes congenial; to his composing tutor, Thomas Armstrong, then organist at Christ Church, Montgomery 'seemed pretty conservative . . . too anxious to produce something well-written, approachable and performable to be very experimental'.[38] At first, Montgomery's visits from London stirred mixed feelings in Amis. Though 'the gentlest of souls',[39] full of jokes and generous with drinks, Montgomery was doing too well, and his past closeness to Larkin was unsettling: 'I like Bruce very much, really,' Amis writes to Larkin on 1 July 1946, 'I envy him his assurance, but he's much too successful for me. Whenever I am with him I feel simultaneously superior and inferior to him.'

Amis's uneasiness with Montgomery would largely disappear once he'd had some success himself, and every time he saw him he liked him more. He was also pleased to be working on the opera with Montgomery, provisionally titled 'To Move the Passions'. In the letter to Larkin of 6 December in which he announced Hilly's pregnancy he described the opera's plot: 'It is all about two eighteenth century dramatists collaborating on a masque to be performed before the King.'[40] But the opera was never completed. In a letter to Larkin of 24 April 1948, Amis announced that 'Bruce has composed about 15 minutes of TMTP.' These fifteen minutes, he subsequently discovered, were cannibalised 'for a film score that had been running late'.[41] Amis and Montgomery were still hoping to return to the opera as late as January 1950,[42] but they never did, in part because other collaborations intervened. All that survives of 'TMTP' is a second draft of the first act libretto,[43] in which the central characters, John Lambert, a middle-aged dramatist, and Nathaniel Phillipson, his younger rival, are introduced. Their dialogue consists almost entirely of insults, in the manner of the *agon* or slanging match between

Aeschylus and Euripides in Aristophanes' *The Frogs*. The younger Phillipson, the more fashionable figure, is a follower of the rules, and his entry is heralded by a chorus of critics praising nature, decorum and formal regularity, in the tradition of Boileau or Pope (their views 'derived from the course on Augustan literary theory I was giving in my lectures at Swansea at the time').[44] Lambert disdains rules. The two playwrights so despise each other that they defy the King's request – until the entry of Lambert's eighteen-year-old ward, Emilia, who is innocent but wise. Phillipson takes one look at Emilia and is smitten; Lambert already loves her. Presumably the rest of the opera would have mixed amatory and aesthetic rivalry. As for Amis's libretto, it is lively and technically adept, written in imitation of what Amis calls Wilfred Owen's 'consonantal rhyme or chime', by which, presumably, he means Owen's 'pararhymes', imperfect or half-rhymes such as, to pick at random from the libretto, 'rare' / 'here', 'reminds' / 'commands', 'crowd' / 'road'. The only thematic interest in the libretto is its association of youth with decorum or restraint and age with Romantic excess, an alignment soon to be associated with Movement writing in general. Though in the finished work, 'virtue and middle age were to triumph' (according to Amis's recollection in the *Memoirs*),[45] this is not the impression left by the fragment, where there is little to choose between the two composers.

After finishing Act I of the libretto in June 1948,[46] Amis busied himself typing out 'The Legacy' (for the last time, he hoped) and contemplating a work of potboiling criticism, one quite independent of the B.Litt. thesis. Through Leishman he had been put in touch with a professor of English at the University of Tucumán in Argentina, Jack Rush, who commissioned him to write a book on Graham Greene for 1,500 Argentinian dollars (£75 7s. 6d., as estimated by his father). This book was to be part of a series of critical studies of English writers. Its recommended length was 120 pages (some 40,000–50,000 words, Amis guessed). Though Rush gave no delivery date, Amis thought it reasonable to suggest late October as the earliest possible deadline. His plan, he wrote to Larkin, who was contemplating a similar volume on D.H. Lawrence, was to make the book 'elementary in parts, tell them the plots of each grgr book & so on, with a chapter on grgr's life and present job etc., and give a last chapter of critical a praise ment'.[47] In October Amis wrote to Greene himself about the book, though their letters do not survive ('his letter was very nice,' Amis reported to Larkin on 27 October: '"Naturally,

I am very complimented . . . I wd be glad to meet you . . ."").[48] Though Amis finished the book, it has not survived (it seems never to have been printed, the manuscript was never returned, Amis was never paid). The actual writing gave him little pleasure. By 18 November he was complaining to Larkin of turning 'into the kind of critic into whose arse my foot yearns to sink: full of those Scrutiny clichés like "directly offered" and "insufficient indication of an intention" and "new alignment of important forces"'.[49] By 23 January 1949 it was 'nearly 7/8 done';[50] by 20 March he learned from his friend John Wain, another Tucumán recruit, that 'the Argentinos can't pay us any money'. In April a letter from Tucumán confirmed this gloomy news, though Rush said the press would go ahead with printing the work if, Amis told Larkin, 'I agree. I agree.'[51]

Amis's revenge on Rush and Tucumán was to turn R.A. Caton (of the Fortune Press, already a character, if unnamed, in 'The Legacy') into L.S. (for 'Lazy Sod') Caton in *Lucky Jim*, Chair of History of Commerce at the University of Tucumán. It is to Caton's 'new historical review with an international bias, or something'[52] that Dixon sends 'The Economic Influence of the Developments in Shipbuilding Techniques, 1450 to 1485', the article on which his hopes of retaining his job depend. Dixon considers the title of the article perfect, 'in that it crystallizes [its] niggling mindlessness, its funereal parade of yawn-enforcing facts, the pseudo-light it threw upon non-problems . . . "In considering this strangely neglected topic," it began. This what neglected topic? This strangely what topic? This strangely neglected what? His thinking all this without having defiled and set fire to the typescript only made him appear to himself as more of a hypocrite and fool.' Once he has submitted the article, months go by and Dixon hears nothing. Then he discovers that Caton has translated it into Italian and printed it under his own name in 'the journal of some Italian historical society'.[53]

In addition to Montgomery, the most important of the new friends Amis made in post-war Oxford were John Wain, James Michie and Kenneth Tynan. Wain, the son of a prosperous dentist from Stoke-on-Trent, was educated at Newcastle-under-Lyme High School. Like Larkin, he was a fee-paying pupil both at school and at university (also like Larkin, he was exempted from military service because of poor eyesight).[54] Unremarkable at school, he blossomed at Oxford, arriving at St John's in January 1943, by which time Amis had gone off to war and Larkin was studying for finals. Wain's literary heroes were Orwell, Samuel Johnson and J.B. Priestley, plain-speaking, unaffected men of good sense and judgement. C.S. Lewis, his tutor (Leishman had not yet taken over from Bone, who died in 1942), became a mentor and Wain turned himself into 'a miniature Lewis . . . a quick-fire debater'.[55] Though Amis had his doubts about Wain's plain-man persona (eyeing his tweed hat and walking stick with the sort of suspicion he normally reserved for facial hair), he admired his savvy and shared a number of his enthusiasms, in particular for jazz and for Larkin's writing. It was Larkin, Wain implies, who brought them together in the first place. As he puts it in his memoir, *Sprightly Running* (1962), 'we were both, so to speak, swimming in the thin fluid that solidified only when Philip Larkin arrived'. Here and elsewhere in his autobiography, Wain presents Larkin as the dominant figure in a 'nebulous' Oxford literary scene. Larkin paved the way and was, according to Wain, 'already regarded as a Flaubertian saint of letters'.[56]

In 1946, aged twenty-one, Wain was awarded a First in English and immediately elected to a junior research fellowship at St John's. 'Why are you shong your teeth in that way,' Amis wrote to Larkin after informing him of Wain's success, 'and screwing up your eyes, and bending forward, and crying 8 as if in pain?'[57] A year later, Wain was also appointed to a lectureship in English at Reading University, while retaining the fellowship at St John's. Here he became friendly with another young English lecturer, Frank Kermode. Wain's success helped to kindle Amis's own academic ambitions when he returned from the war, 'inciting me to go for my First, pointing me towards a provincial college lectureship and away from the suburban schoolmaster's job I had vaguely envisaged'.[58] Wain also inspired the life Amis sought for himself as a postgraduate, combining academic work (a study of early nineteenth-century literary criticism, in Wain's case) with the writing of poetry and novels. Wain had been a fixture on the Oxford poetry scene since 1945, when as a second-year undergraduate he and Arthur Boyars launched the literary magazine *Mandrake* (Boyars would later include four Amis poems in *Oxford Poetry (1948)*, which he edited with Barry Harmer). *Mandrake* not only published writing by Amis, Larkin, Tynan and its editors, but by established London poets, including C. Day-Lewis. Moreover, it ensured that the writing Wain and Boyars approved of was favourably received, as when Amis was commissioned to review Larkin's second novel, *A Girl in Winter*, or Larkin to review *Bright November*. If

Wain helped to launch Amis as a poet, Amis helped to launch Wain as a novelist. Though Wain's first novel, *Hurry on Down*, was published in late 1953, some months before *Lucky Jim*, he would later claim that he began it in part because Amis seemed to be having so much fun writing 'The Legacy'. More generally, Amis credited Wain with encouraging him 'to be some sort of proper writer instead of the dabbler I had largely been',[59] by which he may have meant not just a disciplined writer but a professional one, with an eye to the sorts of market and other realities he was investigating in his thesis.

Wain was a generous friend to Amis in the immediate post-war years, sending him pupils to tutor from St John's and alerting him to various job openings and fellowships. Though Amis sometimes found his literary opinions predictable or pious, Wain could be 'funny on subjects outside the syllabus of English'.[60] Like Montgomery, he helped Amis to keep abreast of modern writing, recommending Angus Wilson, whose fiction Amis came to like, and 'a man named Nabokov, who wrote a book called the real life of Sebastian Knight',[61] whose fiction he came not just to dislike but to deplore (these names Amis passed along to Larkin in a letter of 23 April 1949). Wain also sought to include Amis in his circle of young English dons and students, including Kermode at Reading, and Robson and Alvarez at Oxford. Later, Wain's connections would help not only to publish Amis's second collection of poems, *A Frame of Mind*, and to launch *Lucky Jim*, but to publicise other Movement writers, as well as the Movement itself. After Amis left Oxford for Swansea, he visited Wain at Reading. This visit, he wrote to Larkin, was 'very frightening': 'I don't say most of the people I met weren't craps of a sort, but they knew a lot about Eng Lit, especially about recent developments in the crit of that lit. I felt not only provincial, which I don't mind, but dull, which I do.'[62] It was only later, in the mid-1950s, that Wain's unshakeable sense of entitlement ('he was shamelessly vain,' Alvarez remembers, 'Steineresque in his vanity, though better read') began to grate.

Though Wain helped to keep Amis in touch with the Oxford poetry scene, his influence on Amis's actual poems or poetical practice was minimal. He sounded all the right notes when talking of poetry. The aim of *Mandrake*, he wrote in its fourth number (Winter 1946), was to 'oppose sham and cant . . . by quietly fostering honest workmanship'. However, his own early verse, eventually collected in *Mixed Feelings* (1951), was too indebted to Empson for Amis's taste;[63] he even wrote a poem entitled 'Eighth Type of Ambiguity'. Amis thought Wain's attachment to three-line stanza forms and ten-syllable metres ('Why doesn't old John get out of that tears a reamer thing?')[64] contributed to 'diffuseness and slackness',[65] the principal weaknesses of his poems. He was much more enthusiastic about the poetry of an even younger Oxford figure, James Michie (b. 1927), an undergraduate at Trinity whom he got to know in 1948. Amis and Michie used to meet weekly outside the Radcliffe Camera to dissect each other's poems. Michie's effect on Amis in 1948 was something like Montgomery's effect on Larkin in the three preceding years:

During what cannot have been more than five or six weeks I produced about the same number of poems . . . about half my average yearly output over my poetry-writing life. James produced about as many. Nothing like it has happened to me before or since. I wish I knew what was at work. It was not competition, more mutual example.[66]

What Amis and Michie 'instantly and tacitly' agreed to aim for was 'clarity', hardly a strong point of *Bright November*. This aim Michie attained, Amis thought, even in poems on ominously 'poetical' subjects. 'An instance of how good he is,' he reported to Larkin in a letter of 18 November 1948, 'is that he can allude to pan, or pry, eh, puss?[67] Or bay tow vhen or the garden of eden in his poems, or even call poems after them, without me minding at all when I've read them.'[68] For a while, Amis thought Michie's talent not only 'more promising' than his own, but as promising as Larkin's.[69]

Amis and Michie laid out their poetical allegiances in the Foreword to *Oxford Poetry (1949)*, which they edited in succession to Boyars and Harmer. How they became editors is described in the *Memoirs*, in an account confirmed by Michie. *Oxford Poetry* was published by Basil Blackwell and at Amis's suggestion they simply went to Blackwell's bookshop and asked to be made co-editors of the 1949 volume. When questioned about their qualifications, they answered: 'We're poets, aren't we?' This response worked, 'chiefly because neither of the men we spoke to could think of a reason for turning us down'.[70] Then they set about contacting potential contributors. John Bayley, eventually Warton Professor of English at Oxford (some years after marrying Iris Murdoch), remembers Amis coming round to his undergraduate rooms in New College in 1948 soliciting contributions: 'Since he was already quite famous in university circles I knew who he was although we had never met.' Bayley was impressed by Amis's clothes, in particular a brown tweed jacket and cherry-red polo sweater, which he wore 'without giving the impression of having taken any thought about them' (probably because he hadn't, though at this time he often wore brightly coloured ties and sweaters). Amis was 'friendly and polite in a pleasant unselfconscious way: he seemed natural. Indeed, he was natural, and I think this natural Amis stayed with him all his life alongside the other one', by which Bayley means the late 'fantasy persona which grew to be so life-like'.[71] Bayley's point can also be applied to Amis's persona in the letters, the one that figures so prominently here. The Amis of the letters is natural all right, in the sense of uninhibited, but he is rarely natural in the sense Bayley means (that is, easy, amiable, unselfconscious), a sense others remarked upon and one readers can easily lose sight of, in part because the letters crowd it out, in part because it issues less frequently in anecdote.

Bayley contributed three poems to *Oxford Poetry (1949)* (under the name Oliver Bayley) and like other poems in the volume their debt to Auden is clear. In the Foreword, Amis and Michie are quite open about Auden's presiding influence. It was hardly surprising that the poems submitted to them by Oxford students were derivative; what was surprising was how many of them imitated Alfred Noyes or G. Rostrevor Hamilton (author of 'A Cross in Flanders') rather than Auden or MacNeice:

The typical furniture of the mass of the poems was not, as we soon came to wish it would be, the telegraph-pole and the rifle, but the amethyst and the syrup; the typical subject not the rehearsed response, but the beautified rapture; the typical rhyme not of 'lackey' and 'lucky', but of 'bliss' and 'kiss.'[72]

The editors' preference for hardness, coolness and specificity helps to explain a subsequent kicking delivered to Dylan Thomas. What marks the poems they have chosen, Amis and Michie declare, is in part 'an anxiety to enforce meaning locally as well as in the whole', an anxiety they trace to Auden. 'If this is a correct view, it is bound to increase one's respect for Auden, at any rate for the early Auden, just as the few poems traceable to Dylan Thomas, none of which are printed here, seem to indicate that his work, whatever its intrinsic merits, is a harmful influence.'[73]

The third noteworthy friend Amis made in post-war Oxford was Kenneth Tynan, who came up to Magdalen in the term when Amis returned to St John's, and who would later become the most influential theatre critic of the age. Tynan's milieu was closer to that of Montgomery than to Wain's or Michie's. Theatrical in several senses, he was a fixture at the bars of the Randolph Hotel and the Oxford Playhouse. 'The mere sight of his velvet suits, damask shirts, etc.,' writes Amis in the *Memoirs*, 'even perhaps the sound of his voice, was enough to suggest that, as Philip Larkin wrote of this period, "all that was starting up again."'[74] Tynan makes his first appearance in Amis's correspondence in a letter of 24 October 1946, where Amis describes him to Larkin as 'a HOMOSEXUAL BUGGER and doesn't mind the sang so'. Later Amis calls him 'that crazy womanish fellow' and praises him as a mimic.[75] Tynan shared Amis's dislike of Edith Sitwell and delighted Amis by uncovering an instance of critical dishonesty in a Sitwell essay on Shakespeare.[76] He also, as we've seen, put Amis in touch with Mark Longman, in a failed attempt to get 'The Legacy' published. It was Tynan's sex life, though, that fascinated Amis, and that he knew would fascinate Larkin. Tynan told Amis 'that he is a say dissed, that he has a young lady who is a mass o' kissed, that when they have fun she dresses up as a SKOOLGERL and he as an *Vsher*, and that there is no violent whipping (violence, he says, is a degradation of sadism), only work with a cane, a gym-show and a hairbrush. He offered to give me an exhibition if I was interested. I said I was.'[77] Whether this exhibition ever took place is unknown, though when Amis and Hilly had a party in November 1948, Amis tried to lure Larkin down to Oxford with the news that 'that womanish character will be here, with his cruel charmer'.[78]

The Amises could have a party because they'd moved. In June 1948 they rented a cottage in Eynsham, a village twenty minutes from Oxford on the Witney road, a distance of some six miles. Marriner's Cottage had three bedrooms: 'one for my wife and myself, one for the baybay, and one for our friends. There are two beds in the last-named, so if any of our friends wishes to bring his young lady with him, that can be easily arranged.'[79] The other thing Amis liked about Marriner's Cottage was that it would cost no more than the flat in Norham Road. Though Winkie came along, Hilly was 'already drawing up lists of breeds of dog, in order to select a satisfactory one for howling while I sleep, whining while I work and barking while I play the gramophone'. Soon after they moved in, he wrote to Larkin, Nick Russel spent three nights in the spare room quite comfortably; a dog had been found (an Alsatian, 'Hilly's protegee, called Mandy'); and the village pub, right next door, 'where nobody ever comes in',[80] was discovered to have a piano in it, as well as a real parrot.[81] The cottage was pretty, with a trellised front door, a stone-flagged passage 'from front to rear', a walled garden, rambling roses, hollyhocks, a walnut tree 'and the best gooseberries I have ever tasted'. Some evenings, 'encouraged by a saucer of milk, a hedgeghog came visiting'. There was a fishmonger 'strong on sprats', a stone bridge over the river, a good bus service to Oxford, and a village green big enough to hold a fair. On one occasion, 'a very pregnant Hilly got stuck in the whirligig upside down'.[82] As term ended and the baby approached, Amis busied himself with literary projects. On 23 July, he reported to Larkin that 'It is a race now between Sally [the baby], the leg. and Grgr. Sally's the one to put your money on.'[83]

Amis's feelings about 'Sally' were complex and have to be read through the distorting filter of the letters to Larkin, which were not only shockingly frank but meant primarily to entertain. In the long letter describing the decision to call off the abortion, Amis declared, 'I don't want a filthy baby.' Yet he also foresaw 'not minding' having to nurse it and spend money on a 'pram' and 'furniture', at least not as much 'as I have minded other things in my life'. In March, he and Hilly went to stay with Hilly's sister, Margaret, known as Miggy. Margaret had married Roger Partington, a chemist from St John's ('old Rodge' in Amis's letter to Larkin of 30 August 1948) and they lived in the country with their infant daughter. At the time of the visit Roger was away in Paris. 'I won't say any more about my niece,' Amis wrote to Larkin, 'because it'll depress me too much. She is very small and looks like the American actor who played Veronica Lake's father in "I married a witch." She has two cries: a soft, pitiful sobbing, and, arising out of it, a sudden hard bubbling screech, which produces, in a smaller way, the effect of a dentist's drill which has been buzzing ordinarily in a soft portion of a tooth and then skids abruptly on to a piece that is hard, reverberant and very painful.' During this visit, naturally enough, there was 'a lot of talk about cot-blankets and things . . . by which I am affected much as you might expect a condemned man to react to an overheard proposal to whitewash the interior of the execution-shed'.[84]

A week later, the sheer brutishness of infant behaviour, or rather its '*single-minded intensity*', 'angers' Amis. 'As if they feared that by omitting to yell filthily for a second or two, they might be deprived of a drop of milk.'[85] Hilly, meanwhile, has grown enormous. In a letter of 4 April, Amis signs off with a greeting from her: 'Mountainous sends her love.' On 23 July, as Hilly's due date looms, so, too, do adult responsibilities. These Amis violently rebuffs, as in the following passage of imagined dialogue: 'On Monday I go to the hospital to have the cysts cut out of my ears.[86] This fills me with agonizing fears; oh don't be such a baby, if I *were* a baby, which I'm NOT, I'd SHIT all over you.'[87] Then there are encroaching parents and in-laws. After a long Whitsun weekend at Abbey Timbers, Amis announces to Larkin: 'I think I could make a large sum of money by hiring myself out as a *listener to bores*: I am better at being told things I do not want to know than anybody else, except you.'[88] Yet when Hilly is brought to hospital on 10 August, Amis moves to Abbey Timbers, where he will stay until she is released after the baby's birth. When the due date passes Hilly is anxious and uncomfortable. 'I feel really sorry for her in this weather,' Amis tells Larkin, while also reporting his wish that 'slender young ladies with taut bodies and hard brutal faces would not keep riding their fortunate bicycles past my lonely little wo shfsh window'.[89] The delayed birth, he reports on 13 August, is nerve-racking: 'It is all "rather a strain," but it would be rather less of a strain if I weren't under the strain of continually proving to my mother-in-law that it is all rather a strain.'

When 'Sally' finally arrives, at 8.45 in the morning of 15 August 1948, she turns out to be 'Philip William Nicol'. That evening Amis writes to Larkin with the news, and though he begins with a mini-tirade against Mummy B, quickly dismisses his annoyance as 'querulousness beside what Hilly must have suffered'. His description of the baby is sweet as well as funny:

My little son has very fair hair and a conical head (it will not stay conical, they said), and a face like that of an ageing railway porter who is beginning to realise his untidiness has meant that he'll never get that ticket collector's job he's been after for twenty years. His weight, they said, would be about eight pounds. I don't know what this business is supposed to make you feel; I seem just the same as before. Hilly is very happy and glad, as I am, to have something to name after you.

Five days later, Hilly and the baby are still in hospital and his parents have come up from Berkhamsted, to join forces with the Bardwells: 'I really must be careful not to get to hate my son because of the interest people take in him; I had my parents here and had to talk to them and the B's about him for hours.'⁹⁰ On 25 August, the day after Hilly and the baby's release from hospital, Amis writes about Philip's first night at home. He woke twice, at 2.35 and 5.30:

Despite this, and despite watching him take the breast yesterday afternoon, during which he shat thin mustard pickle on to Hilly's apron and then pissed over the arm of the chair, I feel much more kindly towards him than I thought I should . . . [H]e seems an inoffensive and almost apologetic little boy, with a face only about half as ugly as I had expected. I haven't seen him when he's just been, or is being, sick yet, of course.

What the letters to Larkin give little sense of is how anxious Amis grew in the months surrounding the baby's birth, though his complaints of boils and cysts might suggest psychological as well as physical distress. It was in this period that he visited Dr Armstrong at the 'loony bin at Littlemore'. On one occasion, at least, his anxieties could not be hidden. John Postgate, son of the writer, broadcaster and food expert, Raymond, and a physics research student at Balliol, remembers meeting Amis in the street in Oxford in the period just before Philip was born. Postgate, a jazz friend, was not yet especially close to Amis, though they often met at the Oxford University Rhythm Club, where Postgate played trumpet for the Bandits, the university jazz band. Amis was in a terrible state, 'massively anxious'. Postgate remembers talking with him about his anxieties and about how strange it was that he was so distraught: 'I said, "Come and have tea. We'll hear some records."' At Postgate's lodgings Amis was given tea and toast (with 'six different varieties of jams', Postgate remembers). They listened to records and Amis calmed down. Postgate was accustomed to friends having nervous crises, but had never thought of Amis as an anxious person. It was the prospect of the coming baby that frightened him: 'he was suffering from the *couvade*'.

After Philip's birth, his godfather and namesake came to visit, accompanied by Ruth Bowman, whom Amis had first met briefly in London in 1946. 'I'm looking forward to seeing your vglie Mugge,' Amis wrote to Larkin on 14 September. 'Dew realise it'll be the longest time we shall have had together since 1942? Dalling?'[91] Hilly, too, was keen to see Larkin. While still in hospital she wrote to tell him how glad she was that Sally was a boy and could be named Philip: 'I only hope he'll live up to the name, but I'm afraid if you saw him now you'd do the "you're nasty" business at him . . . I'm so looking forward to your visit.' Hilly also looked forward to having another woman at Marriner's Cottage. Though she loved the cottage, and Miggy and the Partingtons weren't far away, she often felt isolated and overburdened in Eynsham. 'There were long days alone with a baby, and everything was done by hand.' When Larkin and Ruth arrived, Ruth's first impression of the Amises was that 'they seemed very happy together'.[92] But she also disapproved of what she called Kingsley's 'detached view of marriage and father-hood'. Amis and Larkin spent most of the visit closeted together 'playing jazz records, drinking and having a thoroughly and exclusively masculine good time'. Ruth liked and admired Hilly but felt sorry for her. She seemed 'permanently tired out', yet 'accepted her new life placidly enough, and put me to shame with her even temper and unfailing good humour'. Only once did Ruth see Hilly angry. On a fine afternoon she and Hilly set out to walk to Witney, leaving the baby in Amis's care. The sleeping infant was put in his pram in the garden and Amis was instructed to bring him in immediately if the weather turned. In the middle of the walk there was a sudden, heavy thunderstorm and Hilly, worried, insisted that they return home straight away. On opening the front door the two women were hit by the sound of jazz at full volume, 'but of pram and baby there were no sign. Poor Hilly dashed outside to find a very wet baby lying in sodden blankets. Kingsley was mildly surprised at his wife's rage. He assured her that he had no knowledge of rain.'

Amis is unlikely to have missed Ruth's disapproval. Over the course of the visit he seems to have said something about her to Larkin that he not only regretted but feared might put the friendship at risk. Larkin and Ruth had been engaged since May and Amis did not approve. 'Do you wish that I should congratulate you upon its account?'[93] is how he responded to the news in a letter of 28 May. At this comment, Larkin seems not to have taken offence.

What exactly Amis said during the visit is unknown (Hilly has no memory of the episode), but it led to a quick and worried apology, both at the end of the visit and in an immediately subsequent letter of 26 September:

My dear Philip,

   I want to catch the 5.0 post with this and say again, however inadequately, that I really do repent of saying what I said to you when and how I said it. It strikes me that I have acted as a very coarse and unlovely person would act: with some people (old R*dge for instance) I wouldn't mind doing that, but with Hilly you are the person I least want to hurt, and having done so I am really very sorry. I should hate to think, as I said, that this will make any difference between us, dalling . . .

   You needn't worry that I'll say or write anything to Ruth about any of this . . .

   Shoot my mouth off bum,

   Kingsley

Larkin's response to this letter left Amis 'relieved and pleased'. Ruth had not overheard the offending remarks, and Amis felt he could write to her, 'funnily and reassuringly, telling her what is true, that she can come here again if she wants to'.[94] The episode is noteworthy because it makes clear how much Larkin's friendship meant to Amis at this period in his life, and how selfish he could be about it. It is not so much that he did not want Larkin to have girlfriends, more that he didn't want his meetings with him to be intruded upon; he may also have behaved 'coarsely', or more coarsely than usual, because of the pressures surrounding the arrival of the new baby.

   These pressures were relieved by a week-long visit Amis paid to Larkin at his mother's house in Warwick and then at Leicester, soon after Larkin and Ruth's stay at Eynsham. During Larkin's father's illness that winter (he died on 26 March), Amis repeatedly offered to come up either to Leicester or to Warwick; after the father's death, he and Hilly invited Larkin to stay in almost every letter. The visit Amis finally made, in the week of 7–14 October, was restorative in several senses: the unpleasantness over Ruth was further smoothed, Amis and Larkin's mother seem to have got on well (he subsequently sent her a parcel of 'goodies' as well as a thank-you note), and the two friends had plenty of time for walks and pub crawls. As always on such visits, Amis came away feeling smarter, stronger, funnier and determined 'to work harder and write much more'. Back at Marriner's Cottage on 15 October he reported to Larkin: 'I am doing Grgr with greater speed and I hope attention, I have written down ideas for three poems, I have bought a handy little notebook – sorry, note-book – to keep always in my clothing, I have bought a large and expensive book with ruled lines in which I have begun a journal.'[95]

During the Leicester part of the visit, Amis stayed with Larkin in his digs on Dixon Drive, a name he would remember, in 'a house smelling of liniment, with a landlady who resembled a battered old squirrel and a dough-faced physicist co-lodger'. On Saturday morning Larkin had to go into college and Amis accompanied him. They stopped for coffee in the university common room and Amis 'looked round a couple of times and said to myself, "Christ, some-body ought to do something with this." Not that it was awful – well, only a bit; it was strange and sort of *developed*, a whole mode of existence no one had got on to from outside, like the SS in 1940, say. I would do something with it.'[96] This episode has been cited as the moment *Lucky Jim* was born, but it was not the first time Amis had thought of using the academic scene at Leicester, or some fictional equivalent, as the setting for a new novel. On 20 August, before the visit, he announced: 'You know when I've finished the legacy I'm going to start a comic novel, featuring Monica [Jones, a lecturer in English, with whom Larkin was romantically involved] and Molly and Collins and young Collins . . .'[97] and old Rodge and his wife – it would be a marvellous welter of dr stx derisive hatred.'[98] Two weeks after the visit, in a letter of 2 November, Amis had already discerned what would become an important strand of the novel's plot, Jim's difficulties with Margaret. In his most recent letter Larkin had recounted an awkward moment with Monica: 'I laughed like bogray over the Moniker bizness; if yo' aren't very care-filled yo'll find yo-self back in the renning. The relationship wd dateless go well into my leicester novel.'[99] As this comment suggests, the new novel started off being about Larkin. 'For a short time, I was to tell his story,' Amis admits in the *Memoirs*, though 'as it turned out, Dixon resembles Larkin not in the smallest parti-cular, not even in place of origin.'[100]

In November 1948 the Amises held a party, which despite pleas from Hilly as well as Amis, Larkin did not attend. In the *Memoirs*,

Amis recalls the party as a huge success, 'as close as I ever got to glittering, at Oxford or anywhere else'.[101] Ken Tynan came, with a contingent of suitably exotic theatrical types, including the cruel masochist. The poetry people came: Arthur Boyars, Barry Harmer, James Michie (with a blonde girlfriend whose racy poems he and Amis printed pseudonymously in *Oxford Poetry (1949)*, so as not to outrage her parents). Bruce Montgomery came, bringing several friends at very short notice (for which he made amends by helping to clean up when someone vomited). There were Randolph Bar comics and wits, university musicians and jazz fans, old St John's chums, 'groupies' from the Playhouse, the Experimental Theatre Club and the *Cherwell*. Miraculously, the neighbours did not complain and there was relatively little damage. The party was merely noisy and drunken, with 'a little fornication'.[102] That none of this fornication involved Amis may partly account for the rather down-beat report of the evening Larkin received, in a letter of 5 December. Though all went 'technically well', Amis 'didn't enjoy myself much, partly because the girl I particularly wanted to come, because she is very beautiful in a slightly negroid way, didn't come, and another girl who did come was shaygged by 2 men during the evning, but I wasn't either of them'.[103]

Amis's interest in shagging other girls than Hilly had abated slightly in the months leading up to Philip's birth, but by the time of the party was back to full strength. By December, moreover, Hilly was pregnant again. This time 'Sally' turned out to be 'Martin Louis', another 'slip-up' (to use Hilly's phrase), though now there was no question of abortion. These were hard months for Hilly, who was still only twenty. She was often alone in Eynsham and 'felt very low there'. The single friend she made in the village was a working-class Irishwoman named Anastasia who had six children and whose husband beat her. 'She picked me up, basically. She used to come round and insist upon doing some housework, without me paying her or anything. She brought half the kids with her. That was a relief.' Amis was often away, ostensibly in the Bodleian, and not good at hiding his extra-marital flings and ambitions. Hilly found notes in his jacket pockets. He left the larger of the two notebooks he'd purchased after his visit to Leicester, a journal of sorts, lying about the cottage and Hilly read it. She was bored and couldn't stop herself. It contained explicit references not only to other women but to how he hadn't wanted a child. There was a detailed description of a pass he made at Hilly's best friend, which she resisted at first but finally succumbed to. There were pornographic passages. There were also passages about Hilly, including tender and tormented passages. 'Why is Hilly crying as if her heart would break? I can't bear to hear somebody break her heart like this.'[104]

Hilly never told Amis she'd read the journal and never said anything to the best friend, but she half suspected Amis knew. 'He'd leave it around with private written on it,' she recalled; 'he quite liked torturing me in a funny way.' Though there were many good times at Marriner's Cottage, and Hilly never doubted Amis's fondness for her, his philandering weakened the marriage from the start. In these early years, she remembers, 'I went very quiet and that was the only sort of way I could handle it.' She tried to tell herself that Amis's other girls meant nothing to him, that he never took them seriously. She saw other husbands behaving as he did, though 'none so successfully . . . because he was so attractive'. But his strayings hurt and 'I wasn't old enough or sensible enough or wise enough to handle them better.' They also undermined her confidence, eventually leading to her own affairs. 'However satisfactory your sex life is with your husband, if he constantly goes off you're bound to feel a bit inadequate.'

In addition to going quiet, turning a blind eye, refusing to be provoked, and focusing on Amis's obvious affection for her, Hilly worked at being one of the boys, a man's woman. At Oxford and Eynsham, and at first at Swansea, she had no interest in other men, but she was an affectionate and open person, good-looking, without pretension or side and instantly liked by everyone, as she has been all her life. Her letters to Larkin, always a favourite, are playful and flirtatious in a bucking-up fashion, one Amis himself sometimes adopted with his friend. Here she is trying to get Larkin to come to the party: 'I do hope my husband has expressed to you enough how you must come to our party and get drunk and be *my* boy at it, and listen to all the good records. And if you really must stay at the Randolph you must, but how I would like it much better if you could stay with us . . . I'm very much looking forward to seeing you again, and wear that white sweater. Lots of love, Hilly.' Larkin's affection for Hilly, whom he called 'the most beautiful woman I have ever seen without being in the least pretty', adding, parenthetically, 'I am sure you know what I mean, and I hope she will too', was comparably flirtatious and jokey. 'He always pinched my bottom,' Hilly recalls. 'They all did – absolutely above board.' When

Larkin, a keen amateur photographer, asked Amis if he thought Hilly would pose for nude photographs, Amis put his 'dirty-picture proposal' to her and obtained 'a modified assent': 'She is prepared to do corset-and-black-stocking or holding-up-a-towel stuff, and bare bosom stuff ("there'll be jackafuck they'll be bigger when I'm feeding the new baby") but is a bit hesitant about being quite undraped, "though I'll probably get bolder when I start").'[105]

Being a good sport was not always easy, especially as the family expanded. On 30 December 1949, Hilly wrote to Larkin in full ironic-permissive mode: 'I think we shall like it here [they had recently moved to Swansea] . . . Poor Kingsley will miss his lovely Oxford mistresses, but alas I had no masters to miss, but I shall see what I can do among the Welsh – Welsh parsons may be rather nice.'[106] Several years later, in a letter of 5 August 1952, written shortly after turning twenty-four, she tells Larkin about what Amis calls 'a mild lesbian business she had the other evening'. These words come from the letter Amis was writing Larkin at the same time, in which he calls Hilly's letter 'a consolation prize' for his own lack of gossip. The relevant passage from Hilly's letter begins: 'You would have liked to have been here the other evening', and recounts, quite sexily, how she received a lesbian pass. The anecdote is a little gift to Larkin. It is followed, however, by a passage concerning Bruce Montgomery, almost as great a favourite of Hilly's as Larkin (also Martin's godfather), and this passage makes clear how difficult it was for her to maintain the masculine Amis–Larkin view:

I was sorry to hear from K that Bruce thought I'd snubbed him, I had no intention of doing it, only I'd rather lost the [k]nack of enjoying casual leg feelings by Billy's [Amis's] friends. How ever much I like them, it leaves me wondering what to do next when all they want I'm sure is a friendly leg feel back, I shall have to try something though. Having children rather buggers up a lot of things like that – you see things are totally nice for me now and I don't want anything else to happen, the children take all my spare energy up, and I'm sure if every one else was married and had children they'd feel the same. It's just that I'm one groove ahead or behind and I can't slip into the way of being easy like I was about leg feeling and so on, it's such a pity, but there it is.

In addition to tensions at home, the new family had worries about money and Amis's career prospects. It took Amis almost two years to find an academic job, beginning with the February 1948 enquiry to Larkin about a lectureship in Leicester. On 4 April he told Larkin he'd applied for a job at Liverpool, 'starting at £425 pa'; he reckoned his chances 'as abt 3 in 10'.[107] On 22 June he wrote that 'they don't want me at Bedford. I am rather sick abt. it'.[108] On 20 March 1949, the same day Wain informed him that 'the Argentinos can't pay us any money', he reported: 'No news from Durham: there won't be.'[109] On 25 May, he described himself as 'all lapped in thesis bum and job application bum', adding 'I haven't got King's one . . . and feel deep rest.'[110] On 9 June 1949 he announced: 'I have an interview for that cunt-only place in London on Tuesday,[111] which makes me nervous already. But glad too. I hope I get it; it's about the last chance I shall get.' It wasn't. On 19 July he reported 'trying for jobs in Manchester and Prague lordy lordy'. On 25 August Martin was born (Amis described him to Larkin as having 'one of the most protesting faces I ever saw')[112] and in the letter announcing his birth, Amis added 'it looks as if my Prague job might come off'. It didn't. On 6 September, Hilly and Martin came back from hospital; that week Amis was to be interviewed at Bristol. 'I hope,' he wrote, 'that I get a bloody *job* before long, or I'll be on the breadline, wacker'.[113] On 20 September he still hadn't heard from Bristol, the lease at Marriner's Cottage was almost up, another place to live had not been found (partly because of the job situation) and the family was planning to move to Abbey Timbers 'indefinitely, though not, I hope, for very long'.

As the date for leaving Eynsham approached, Amis developed trench mouth, 'with minor streptococcal variants and suspected diphtheria'.[114] Hilly and Anastasia were left to pack up most of the cottage by themselves ('I was glad to miss it in a way, but felt sorry for H').[115] On the day of the move, a Monday, a wire arrived from Swansea, inviting Amis to an interview on Friday. On Wednesday (he was too weak to do anything on Monday and Tuesday) Amis wired back saying he was ill and could he come for interview the following Tuesday? On Thursday Swansea wired back saying they had to make their decision on Saturday, 'in other words,' Amis wrote to Larkin that same day, 'fack you Jack'. Amis then wired back saying he'd be there on Friday (that is, the next day). Swansea was in a tight spot, which was the reason for the rush: a member of the English Department, Bernard Blackstone, a senior lecturer, had been appointed Professor of English at the University of Istanbul; classes were about to begin and a replacement was needed immediately. In the *Memoirs*, Amis attributes the department's predicament to national character: 'the Welsh as a whole being even lazier than the English, they had all gone off on their long vacations before getting round to filling the post'.[116]

The journey to Swansea occasioned more anxiety for Amis than the interview itself. The doctor who was treating him at Abbey Timbers, 'who I must admit is a good doctor . . . a friend of the fambly too', insisted that he not travel without an escort. As Amis reported to Larkin in a letter of 6 October:

There's quite a nice funny clever little man named Burden at New C. [New College] who's been on one or 2 interviews with me; if he's going to this one, good enough; but if not – then *guess who***!!ffffx*??!* yes, YOU'VE HIT IT (a big hand, folks) ITS DADDY BEEEEEE!!!!! . . . He *would* enjoy the trip so! To his beloved Wales!! Won't it be *marvellous* if Kingsley gets the job!!! Professor Dai ap Faeces is there, who wrote the first really scholarly Welch grammar, I'll get it and show you . . . So handy for the National Scheissbedsodd, too.

In the end, Amis was spared Daddy B, though whether Burden accompanied him is not clear. Amis described his competitors for the job in a subsequent letter of 17 October 1949, addressed from his new lodgings in Swansea after he had taken up his duties. There had been four other candidates, three of whom he was glad to have defeated (which suggests that the fourth was Burden): 'Evans, a big, very short man with tonsured fair hair, a convoluted tobacco-pipe and a face like an old Rugby football converted, by a tyro hand, into the semblance of a red pumpkin; a nameless cadaver with castellated teeth who talked in baying cockney of his qualifications; and a Manchester man, his face sored but not shaven by shaving, who talked with his mouth almost shut'. Amis may well have been a poor interviewee: with a First from Oxford, a B.Litt. in the works, a book of poems published, and the backing, presumably, of Bateson and Leishman, it is odd that he had received no offers; the Swansea job really was the last of the year, and no great plum. Those who have seen or heard Amis in interviews or discussions on radio or television will know that he rarely seemed comfortable in live formats. 'I personally can't argue or discuss, let alone be funny, in circumstances of the least formality,' he wrote to a BBC Talks producer in

1957, 'however loosened up with preliminary chaff and alcohol.'[117] As a lecturer, he needed a text (from which he could then safely depart); as a broadcaster, he needed a script. Without one, he could seem, and be, defensive, hostile, costive as well as caustic. The last-minute nature of the Swansea interview, or his weakened health, or both, may have allowed him to relax. If his account of the other candidates was at least partly fair, he would not have been intimidated by the competition.

Immediately after the interview Amis returned to Abbey Timbers where, he drily informed Larkin, 'I was able to pick up stacks of useful information on Wales and the Welsh from Daddy B, who . . . wouldn't rest till he had given me as complete a picture of the set-up as his means allowed'.[118] On his last day in Oxford, instead of 'a melancholy communion with all I know and love so well . . . I said goodbye to all the people I didn't want to say g-b to and hardly any I did.' Then he, Hilly and Martin took a bus to Berkhamsted, to see his parents and Philip, who had been staying with them while Hilly supervised the move from Eynsham. Amis was pleased to see Philip, who 'was walking and looks very pretty and good-humoured. When you take a thing from him, he doesn't cry: "thanks indeed for that"'. At the end of the weekend in Berkhamsted, on 16 October 1949, Amis set off to Swansea to begin his new life. The journey was the 'finale to over a week of travel-erethism . . . 8½ hours from door to door'. It had been arranged by his father, who allowed fifteen minutes between arrival in London by Green Line coach and departure to Swansea by train. In the event, Amis reached the train thirty seconds before it pulled away, pouring sweat after a frantic, suitcase-laden sprint. The coach driver, he wrote to Larkin, 'was new, looking wonderingly about him at all the strange buildings and cars, his foot rising from the accelerator in alarm whenever a vehicle approached him', the first of a catalogue of comic frustrations punctuating the journey, and one which would find its way into *Lucky Jim* (when Dixon, desperate to catch Christine at the station, finds himself with a bus driver who pauses 'for learners to practise reversing across his path', then continues so slowly that toddlers 'retrieve toys from under his just-revolving wheels').[119] The next morning ('this morning') he met his colleagues and some students and was '"shown round" the library and the main university building and the old arts building and the new arts building and the seminar rooms and the room reserved for research students and members of staff and the new hall and the old refectory and the new refectory and the science block'.

Amis wrote to Hilly daily from Swansea, but the letters do not survive.[120] What he did not do, so busy was he with classes and lectures and tutorials and meeting people and being invited for drinks and coffees and teas, was find a place for his family to live. Hilly was grateful for the letters ('That was very sweet of him') but she was stuck in Abbey Timbers with the children and her parents, who were exhausted and exhausting, worn out with childcare and worry about the state of her marriage ('Oh God, was he going to ditch her?' is what she suspected they were thinking). To give them some peace she and the children went to Berkhamsted for an extended visit, which was equally exhausting. Hilly liked her mother-in-law, but on this occasion 'Mummy A' was bossy and censorious. As the weeks went by and there was still no summons from Amis, everyone grew tense. Though the letters kept coming, and were full of reassurances about missing Hilly and the family (perfectly genuine reassurances, judging by the letters to Larkin),[121] Amis simply couldn't find a suitable house or flat. He claimed he was looking: 'I need all the time I can get for *house-hunting*,' he complained to Larkin, 'and thinking about house-hunting.'[122] But in Hilly's words, 'he didn't have a clue how to find a place . . . He was totally impractical.' Finally, in mid-November, Mummy B volunteered to take Philip so that Hilly herself, with infant Martin, could travel to Swansea and join the search. She found a place in three days. Amis was delighted: 'My good-wife and little baybay son came down here last week,' he wrote to Larkin on 22 November, 'and we enjoyed ourselves very much. We also found a flat, into which we shall be moving on 16th December.'[123] Mission accomplished, Hilly returned to Abbey Timbers with Martin, rented a van, packed it with their possessions, and on the 19th she, Amis and the two children moved into a ground-floor flat at 82 Vivian Road in Swansea, 'in an ill-built house, rather too small and with no room to put anything'.[124] Four days later, amidst a blizzard of complaints, Amis reported to Larkin: 'I am really very happy here.'

9

Swansea

Amis was hired by the University College of Swansea as an assistant lecturer in English at a salary of £300. In the *Memoirs* he estimates that this salary, plus child allowances of £50, was 'about £4,200 at today's values', whereas a contemporary assistant lecturer, that is, one who started work in 1991, the year the *Memoirs* were published, would be paid £12,000 (roughly half what a beginning lecturer would be paid in 2005).[1] Even in 1949, £300 was a small salary, nor would it be much improved in subsequent years, when increased by annual £50 raises. In his first few years at Swansea, before Hilly received a legacy from her mother's estate, Amis often complained to Larkin about how poor he was; he also, on several occasions, asked Larkin for small loans. To make ends meet he had eventually to take on extra teaching at the WEA (Workers' Educational Association) and mark the Welsh equivalent of Higher School Certificate examination papers. In the summer of 1950 he and a colleague in the English Department at Swansea, David Sims, marked all 800 scripts (of an average length of sixteen pages) for one of the English papers, a task that took them about two weeks, working from nine to fourteen hours a day, and paid them £55 each. For a period, also in 1950, Hilly went out to work five nights a week washing up at the café in the Tivoli Cinema in Mumbles, a district west of the university along Swansea Bay, once a small fishing village.

From January to May 1950, to save money and gain space, the family shared a house with Sims's girlfriend, Margaret Ashbury Vakil (later Aeron-Thomas) and her young daughter. On weekends,

Sims also lived with them, staying away during the week for 'public-relations' sake',[2] since Margaret had recently divorced. A social worker (her job was to visit children at risk), Margaret Vakil was paid slightly less than Amis: £27 per month. She remembers Hilly asking her boss at the café if she could take home bones and scraps of food for her dog (a fictitious one, Mandy had been left behind at Abbey Timbers), though in fact she used them to make 'gorgeous' pea soup,[3] enough to feed the household for a fortnight ('I only took scraps from the best tables,' Hilly recalled in a newspaper profile, adding that she 'occasionally took a packet of sausages, too').[4] Amis would babysit and Hilly would arrive home, with her bag of leftovers, to find him 'waiting at the table with a knife and fork. We were perfectly happy, we saw the funny side of it.' In an essay entitled 'My First Job',[5] Amis recalls that he and his Swansea friends were obsessed with smoking, an index of 'how meagre our outlets were, how few our escapes from grim reality'. In addition to being unable to get drunk oftener than once a week (on beer or cider, the latter at eightpence in the public bar or ninepence in the private, a source of contention),[6] Amis could afford just ten cigarettes a day, a hardship he survived by biting his nails and mixing tobacco with herbal-smoking mixture, 'horrible muck but cheap'. Sims preferred smoking what were known as 'nips', cigarettes made out of the tobacco from discarded butt-ends. 'Once, not meeting my eye, David confessed to me he had re-rolled and smoked all the nips left at the end of the day in the Common Room ashtrays.'[7]

Amis liked his work. The department he joined was small, congenial and relaxed. In addition to Professor W.D. Thomas, his boss, there were three other members of staff: Isabel Westcott, BA (Bristol), B.Litt. (Oxon), a churchy, middle-aged spinster 'of sweetness and natural propriety'[8] whose nominal specialism was the novel and who helped Thomas run the department; J.O. ('Jo') Bartley, MA (Belfast), an Ulsterman who had been a professor of English in India but now was only a lecturer, and who was interested in drama; and Sims, BA (Oxon), the only member of the department of Amis's age, a linguist and Old English specialist. According to the *Report of the Council of the University College of Swansea* for 1948–49, which lists the research activities of all departments, not one of these new colleagues had published anything in the year before Amis arrived – not so much as an article or review – nor, Bartley excepted, would any of them ever publish a book. Bartley was commended in the

Report for giving 'valuable assistance to the Dramatic Society and to the Little Theatre', Miss Westcott for playing an active part 'in the social and religious life of the community' and for being 'indefatigable in the interests of the students', Sims for being promoted from assistant lecturer to lecturer, and Thomas for college administration, external examining and extramural tutoring. Amis described Thomas to Larkin in a letter of 29 October as 'a smiling, smoking, light-suited man of about 58, who doesn't drive me hard'. The teaching he assigned Amis, his newest and lowliest member of staff, was tailored to Amis's interests: 'The Professor doesn't want me to do what I don't want to do,' he wrote to Larkin on 22 November: 'So I don't do, no nor never shall, any old words. I begin with the Elizabethans. Your predictions about doing the Clerk's Tale . . . were, I am glad to say, inaccurate.'[9]

As a beginning teacher, Amis had to prepare all his lectures from scratch, but his actual teaching schedule was not especially heavy. According to the *Report of the Council*, the University College of Swansea had a total of 1,002 full-time students in 1948–49, the year before Amis was hired, of whom 471 were in the Faculty of Arts and 207 took English courses, though only twenty-four students took the two-year Part II Honours programme in English.[10] Amis's initial teaching schedule was lighter than that of his colleagues: 'I have 5 hrs. work a week at the college, and about another 12 preparing stuff,' he told Larkin. There were essays and assignments to mark throughout the year but degree classification depended on three-hour written papers at the end of years one and three. There was no grade inflation, certainly by today's standards. In 1949 only four students in the whole of the Faculty of Arts had been awarded Firsts, none in English. Department meetings were amiable, conducted in a fug of smoke: 'Everyone smoked and Professor Thomas was generous with his cigarettes,' remembers Sam Dawson, who came to Swansea as an assistant lecturer two years after Amis. Most administrative tasks were handled by Thomas, aided by Miss Westcott, the departmental dogsbody and a stickler for detail. Thomas exploited Miss Westcott but also put up with her. When Jo Bartley described him as 'mothered' by her, Thomas corrected him by quietly muttering 'smothered'.[11] Still, as Amis recalls in the *Memoirs*, everyone went out of their way not to offend her, a mark of the good feeling in the department: 'The ease with which one avoided swearing in front of her, the readiness with which expressions like "Goodness gracious!" sprang to one's lips in her presence, was a perpetual wonder.'[12]

Amis's initial lecturing duties were outlined to Larkin in the letter of 29 October: 'I am lecturing on Renaissance Currents of Thought, Victorian Currents of Thought, and Poetry. For the first I read out my Lewis notes, for the second my thesis notes, for the third I say what I think; it doesn't really matter what I say.' Though Amis always lectured from a text or extensive notes, he frequently looked up from them, often to add sardonic comments or jokes. He was conscientious about not missing classes and handing back written work, though he rarely revised his lectures.[13] Mavis Nicholson (Mainwaring then) remembers his walking into the lecture hall for the first time. He was wearing a belted camel-hair coat with the collar turned up and she turned to a girlfriend and said: 'Here comes talent.' He specialised in outrageous judgements and assertions, which shocked and thrilled his students. Nicholson recalls one lecture that began: 'We don't like Keats, *you know*' ('you know', always pronounced sardonically, was an Amis catch-phrase, like 'full of fun', and quickly taken up by the students). Clive Gammon, part of the group that formed round Amis, later a journalist at Time-Life, the *Sunday Times* and Beaverbrook's *Express*, remembers him reciting a little poem in class:

> Wordsworth wrote 'The Prelude'
> And that was all right.
> But it was a prelude
> To a lot of shite.

The effect of such irreverence was to jerk Amis's students out of what Nicholson called their 'schoolgirl clichés' about literature. Though Amis rarely answered questions after lectures, in tutorials and outside class he was open and unpatronising when discussing writers and writing. 'To our confusion,' Gammon says, 'he took us seriously, as equals, listened to our naïve notions, once in a while deferred to our callow opinions and taught us not to blindly follow received opinion . . . [W]hen you'd get an essay back from him, it would be covered with thoughtful, useful, unwounding comments.'[14]

Part of Amis's appeal to his students at Swansea was what they saw as his glamour. Though only a few years older than some of the students he taught and from the same sort of class and economic background as many of them, he had arrived with a First from Oxford, had served in Normandy, had a beautiful wife, who was also sweet and friendly, and was himself handsome, like 'a junior lead in one of those tennis-anyone comedies still popular at the time'.[15] Mavis Nicholson likened the Amises to Scott and Zelda Fitzgerald. To Gammon, Amis's sudden appearance in Swansea in 1949 was 'as if a brilliantly-hued tropical bird had come winging into our still blitz-battered town'. Then there were Amis's flash friends. When Bruce Montgomery came to visit, he, Amis and Gammon went drinking. At closing time Amis offered to call a cab. Montgomery gently corrected him: 'No Kingsley. We pay a man to call us a cab.' Yet as the students knew, the Amises had almost as little money as they did, at least until the arrival of Hilly's legacy. John Morgan, later a journalist and broadcaster (at the *New Statesman* and *Panorama*, the television current affairs programme), was a student of Amis's and a good friend. At the leaving party the Amises hosted for him after he'd finished his course, Morgan arrived with a tin of rabbit stolen from his grandmother in Morristown: 'those were hard times . . . we felt the Amises were short'.[16] Gammon remembers helping Amis load Martin's pram with empty beer flagons to return to the Uplands Hotel, so he could get the deposit money back. 'Ah empties,' Amis later recalled, 'my only form of saving at the time.' In addition to Morgan, Gammon and Mavis Nicholson, the other students in Amis's circle in his first few years at Swansea were Geoff Nicholson, who would also become a journalist, at the *Observer* and elsewhere, and was already Mavis's boyfriend, Mary Madden, who would marry John Morgan, and David Rees, who would become literary editor of the *Spectator*. These students babysat for the Amises, attended their parties, drank with Amis and other faculty friends at the Bryn-y-Mor pub and the Uplands Hotel and met him for coffee on Saturday mornings at the Grand Hotel, opposite Swansea's High Street station, before moving on to beer as midday approached.

It is no surprise that the female students in the circle were attractive. 'I had a tut. the other day on the poems of T. Wyat,' wrote Amis to Larkin in the letter of 29 October: 'a girl with a very well filled sweater giggled silently for fifty minutes. "Laughter is the first sign of sexual attraction"' (a quotation from Isherwood's *Lions and Shadows*, said by 'Weston' or Auden). Mavis

Nicholson would agree ('It's sexy to laugh a lot'), describing Amis at Swansea as 'very lecherous', 'more promiscuous than anybody we'd ever met'. Amis more or less made a pass at all attractive females, students and wives included, yet in a manner that seems rarely to have offended and did not involve force or false promises or threat. David Sims, a bachelor until 1952, was similarly rakish, but his approach to women was different. According to Jean Cleary, a young research assistant at the time, not yet married to Esmond Cleary, a lecturer in Economics, 'Kingsley liked women . . . He talked to women, whereas David didn't.' After the Clearys married, Amis made a pass at Jean ('I think he preferred his girls to be married, on the whole'), which she rejected: 'But he was very easy about it – if you said no, or push off, he wasn't bothered.' When Cleary heard of the pass, he was not upset. To explain why, he tells a story involving Jo Bartley, 'a great groper'. Bartley was much liked by his colleagues and a good teacher, but he was also a drunk. Cleary remembers him at an Amis party crawling out of the room on his hands and knees in pursuit of Hilly. 'He's going after her,' he warned Amis, who replied: 'Oh, she's very strong.' Jean Cleary cites the war as an explanation for the prevailing tolerance and licence. Many of the students and lecturers in 1949 were ex-servicemen and unlikely to be satisfied 'with a little hand-holding'.

Within the English Faculty, Sims was Amis's closest friend. He and Amis, and later Dawson, shared an office in the Arts building, while Bartley and Isabel Westcott also shared an office. Only Professor Thomas (always 'W.D.') had an office of his own. Sims was intellectually impressive, 'a very distinguished and original mind', according to Dawson, a view seconded by Cleary. He was short, balding, quick to laugh, a bit shy or withdrawn, yet a very good actor (Laertes in the 1953 college production of *Hamlet* in which Amis played Osric). 'We were both interested in literature,' writes Amis in the *Memoirs*, 'a rarity then as now, and also in commoner pursuits',[17] a reference, perhaps, to their womanising. With Amis, Cleary recalls, Sims was often intellectually dominant, though overshadowed in other respects. Glanmor Williams, a history lecturer at Swansea, later Sir Glanmor, an historian of Wales and long-time Professor and Head of Department, suspects Amis had a harmful effect on Sims's academic career (a suspicion later held about Amis's effect on junior faculty at Princeton): 'Not so much because his world was too wild but because he had a habit of poking fun at people who were taking academic life seriously.' Williams mentions 'two or three people I can think of who were themselves very serious academics, and who were very friendly with Amis and in his particular group at one time, but they dropped out because they realised that Amis was far too inclined to make fun of people' – that is, people of influence as well as people who took research seriously. Amis was no respecter of rank, had no 'bump of reverence', to use Dawson's phrase, which was fine as long as Thomas was head of department. Thomas was amiable, urbane, kindly. Though, as Williams puts it, 'obviously lazy as far as research went', he was good with his staff, sure enough of himself not to need much flattery or stand on his dignity. At his death in 1954, Amis called him 'a lazy fucker, but a very decent chap, which seems remarkable in a professor'.[18] His formidable wife, Edith, was trickier, very much the professor's wife. 'You don't have a very good opinion of those who are set in authority over you,' she once observed to Amis. He didn't.

Chief among those in authority over Amis at Swansea was the college Principal, J.S. Fulton, later Sir John, then Lord Fulton. Swansea was founded in 1920, as the fourth of the original constituent colleges of the University of Wales, itself founded in 1893 (the other colleges were Aberystwyth, Cardiff and Bangor).[19] He was an ambitious man who would leave Swansea in 1961 to become the first Vice-Chancellor of the University of Sussex; after leaving Sussex, in 1967, he went on to chair both a Royal Commission on the Civil Service and the British Council. Form was important to him: he was keen that lecturers wear gowns; he once objected to professors and lecturers appearing together on the same radio programme, which he likened to mixing officers and men.[20] Academics often disparage administrators, as administrators disparage academics, but there was a strong sense among Amis's circle that Fulton's values were phoney. Though a socialist, he sent his sons to Eton. His initiatives were perceived as splashy and modish. He introduced an interdisciplinary lecture and tutorial course for first-year students ('putting some polish on these miners' children', is how Cleary described its aims). The tutorials were in small groups which tutors were encouraged to meet informally, over tea or coffee ('On Friday I am giving a little coffee party for six of the students,' Amis reported to Larkin in a letter of 6 February: 'I am inviting the one I want to bugger and the two I want to fuck.')[21] Though the tutors for the course were drawn exclusively from college staff (on what Cleary calls a 'voluntary/compulsory' basis, a typical Fulton arrangement), the lectures were delivered by external as well as internal speakers; Isaiah Berlin came from Oxford to speak on Marxism, for example. Amis was asked to deliver one of these lectures soon after he arrived, before *Lucky Jim* made him famous, a mark, perhaps, of the favour in which he was held by Fulton, who played a part in his hiring. Glanmor Williams, another lecturer in the series, recalls Fulton telling him to watch out for Amis: 'I remember Fulton saying to me: "Oh, we've got a very great catch, you know. This young man, Kingsley Amis, who's just come, he's very, very good, he's highly recommended by people in Oxford . . . He's already a good poet, you know, and they think he's going to be quite a novelist."' Yet Amis had little time for Fulton (in the *Memoirs* he calls him 'an Oxford–Balliol–Lindsay–sociological–philistine'),[22] particularly after the appointment of Thomas's successor in 1954. Fulton was instrumental in this appointment, which Amis bitterly opposed. Moreover, after he left Swansea, Fulton became an increasingly prominent spokesman for the expansion of higher education, which Amis also opposed.

The college Fulton presided over in 1949 had few buildings of distinction; in fact, few buildings at all. There was Singleton House, a Regency Gothic mansion, once called Singleton Abbey, set off from what Amis describes in the *Memoirs* as 'a straggle of sheds rather like those of Norbury College (these were full of scientists), some one-storey lecture rooms and a couple of grander or larger but not horrible structures'.[23] One of these not horrible structures was the Arts building, opened in 1925. Here each arts department had its own room (the inhabitants of the English room, Cleary remembers, were 'always laughing'), plus shared offices. If the buildings were unprepossessing, the grounds weren't. The college was set in a corner of rolling, coastal parkland, 'facing the great sweep of Swansea Bay and forming – then – the most attractive university setting I have ever seen'.[24] This setting was both a pleasure in itself and partial compensation for the town proper, as well as its industrial surrounds. The approach to Swansea by train badly shook Amis when he arrived for interview. In 1949, according to Gammon, 'unreconstructed Landore, an industrial wasteland just outside town . . . looked as if it had been carpet bombed, then camouflaged in acid green and toxic yellow and used as headquarters by invading aliens'.[25] The town centre, heavily bombed during the war, is evoked by Amis in *The Evans Country*, a sequence of six poems first published in 1962, then expanded to eleven poems in 1967 in *A Look Round the Estate: Poems 1957–67*. The sequence traces the amorous adventures of a character named Dai Evans, who lives in 'Aberdarcy', a thinly disguised Swansea, the setting also of Amis's second novel, *That Uncertain Feeling* (1955). Dai's seedy affairs and liaisons play out against a backdrop of urban ugliness. Here is the first stanza of the opening poem, 'Aberdarcy: the Main Square':

> By the new Boots, a tool-chest with flagpoles
> Glued on, and flanges, and a dirty great
> Baronial doorway, and things like portholes,
> Evans met Mrs Rhys on their first date.

The poem's penultimate stanza draws the connection between Dai's seedy endeavours and 'redeveloped' Swansea most directly:

> The journal of some bunch of architects
> Named this the worst town centre they could find;
> But how disparage what so well reflects
> Permanent tendencies of heart and mind?

These tendencies were as apparent to Amis in his earliest years at Swansea as in 1962, but viewed less bitterly. Though his descriptions of the urban landscape of Aberdarcy in *That Uncertain Feeling* are unidealised, there is marginally more sympathy for the place and its inhabitants than there is in *The Evans Country*. Here is what John Lewis, the librarian hero of the novel, likes about the pub he always visits after work:

For me, its virtue lay in its position, at the corner of the square which formed the turning-round point for the Cwmhyfryd bus-route. Seeing a bus pass the windows from left to right gave nice time to drink up, stroll outside and catch it as it completed its tour past the chain stores, the Hubert Barrington Huws Art Gallery and Concert Rooms and the seven mass-produced high-class tailoring establishments, and finally moved from right to left up to the queue-shelter in front of the Electricity Showrooms. The convenience of this quite outweighed the slight disadvantage afforded by visual and aural contact with the pub's other patrons . . . You might get, it was true, an occasional grocer or butcher in his Yacht Club blazer and lavender trousers, a publican or two in subfusc accompanied by an ignorant doctor or two in sportive checks, the odd golfing-jacketed cinema-manager, café-owner or fish-shop proprietor, and you might even hear a couple of such people lamenting the fact that there wasn't the money about these days before ordering two double *cordon bleu* brandies and forty cigarettes, but there was often something strangely inspiriting, even uplifting, in the sight of such well-equipped pursuit of the good life. And if it all made you think that these chaps represented the new privileged classes in 'our society,' you could console yourself with the thought that there was a lot to be said for them compared with the old privileged classes.[26]

In *The Evans Country* closeness to Dai Evans and his world is mostly lowering. In *That Uncertain Feeling* John Lewis's world is viewed as Philip Larkin views Hull in 'The Large Cool Store', a poem from *The Whitsun Weddings* (1964). Larkin's poem, written in 1961 after a visit to Hull's Marks and Spencer, contrasts its 'Modes For Night' ('Lemon, sapphire, moss-green, rose / Bri-Nylon Baby-Dolls and Shorties') with more mundane clothing ('Knitwear, Summer Casuals, Hose / In browns and greys, maroon and navy'), the sort that 'Conjures the weekday world of those / Who leave at dawn low terraced houses / Timed for factory, yard and site'. That such customers also crave 'Modes For Night' shows

> How separate and unearthly love is,
> Or women are, or what they do,
> Or in our young unreal wishes
> Seem to be: synthetic, new,
> And natureless in ecstasies.

Here, as in *That Uncertain Feeling*, the 'permanent tendencies of heart and mind' revealed to Amis and Larkin by their respective provincial towns, breed sympathetic identification as well as dismay, with the places themselves as well as their inhabitants. From the start, the view Amis took of Swansea was mixed, only partly removed and superior. It was like William Cooper's view of Leicester in *Scenes from Provincial Life*, published earlier in the year. In a letter to Larkin of 11 October 1950, Amis described the effect

Cooper's novel had on him: 'the attitude it carries is a powerful antidote against depression in a place like this, I find. For some days I felt detached and observant and contented, in a way that I think is better than the Isherwood way, because it's less self-regarding and disingenuous . . . it's a detachment that doesn't preclude participation, much more whole-hearted than the Isherwood "I" was capable of.'[27] It is the Cooper attitude, or something like it, that underlies Amis's depictions of Swansea in his early fiction and poetry. To Dylan Thomas, whom *That Uncertain Feeling* mocks, Swansea is an 'ugly, lovely town'; Amis would concur, even when describing its most beautiful features, the views it affords of the bay and the sea:

I passed a fried-fish shop where, I saw with approval, there was going to be frying to-night, then, at the corner by the Y.M.C.A., crossed over and turned off. This brought me a view of the sea. It looked like an almost perfect sheet of yellowish rock running from the line of roof-tops hiding the beach to the docks over on the right, to the power-station at Tai-mawr, and, beyond the estuary, to the blast furnace at the Abertwit strip-mill, a fat red cylinder rising, so it seemed at this distance, from the surface of the water.[28]

A tour of the places Amis lived in Swansea, including those he lived in after becoming successful, is no treat or outing: they all look either mean or nondescript, certainly from the perspective of his later life in London. Amis lived in digs until Hilly and the boys arrived, first at 134 St Helen's Road, in a house belonging to 'a nice Irish couple and their little son', a week later in a nearby house at 20 St Helen's Crescent, 'with a different Irishman',[29] an eccentric Latinist at the university named Willie Smyth who would provide Amis with a starting point for *Take a Girl Like You* ('how to get a girl for Willie' was to be the novel's plot).[30] Willie was 'pedantic, pernickety, letting nothing inaccurate or of uncertain meaning go by – not an aphrodisiac quality'.[31] He was also garrulous. His great passions were radio receivers, which he made and refined, Latin, and public transport. Digs in provincial towns figure memorably in Amis's early fiction (the 'Willie' character in *Take a Girl Like You*, Graham McClintoch, shares digs with the novel's hero) and are drawn from real-life experiences. The digs at St Helen's Crescent, in addition to 'looking on to the green that surrounds the vile concrete Guildhall with its tall unimposing clock-tower',[32] were spectacularly inconvenient: the bath and toilet could only be reached through Amis's bedroom, 'a common Welsh arrangement';[33] the light to the sitting room was located in the hall, round the corner, and one could never find it, since the light in the hall was always switched off. If Amis left the sitting room for half an hour his deaf landlady scooped the fire out of the grate and shovelled it into the grate in her own room. The meals she served were at inconvenient hours and usually not hot.[34] Willie was no oil painting and his 'always startling unspectacled face'[35] was the first thing Amis saw each morning, as he passed through Amis's bedroom on the way to the bath.

Amis spent six weeks at St Helen's Crescent. The flat Hilly found for the family at 82 Vivian Road, in the Sketty district, just north-west of the university and a little further from the town centre, had its own inconveniences. Though located on the ground floor, there were fourteen steps from the street to the front door, 'and most of the time', Amis wrote to Larkin on 23 December, 'I am carrying a pram or a baby up or down them'. In place of 'deaf-landlady bum and bad-food bum and celibacy-bum' he now suffered 'bottle-mixing bum and coal-cellar bum and up-early bum'. Though he had an area of sorts to work in, the flat was small, the children noisy and the nappy pail full. 'Hilly has a great deal to do, and I feel impelled to help her with some of it.' A week after this declaration, in a New Year's Day letter to Larkin, Amis paints a typical morning scene: it is raining, a little boy is crying, and 'about me in the air moves smoothly a bland smell of human piss. On the fireguard a child's night-gear steadily scorches' (a mini-parody or horse-pissing of Coleridge's 'Frost at Midnight'). When, later in January, the family moved with Margaret Vakil and her daughter into a 'whole house',[36] at 11 Haslemere Road, also in Sketty, life was easier for Hilly and Amis, given the halving of domestic tasks as well as rent. But the house was also noisier, not just because it had three small children in it as opposed to two, but because Margaret herself was noisy. 'Margaret who is a big girl is bounding elfinly on to David's lap,' Amis reported to Larkin on 27 January, 'and you compress your lips, as she says "Kingsley looks quite disgusted with us"'. This same letter ends with a virtuoso list of domestic 'bums':

```
      I'll meet you in Oxford if you'll lend me
the money. Ah, go and wash your mouth out.

          Go and get the coal in        )
          Go and get Martin             )
          Put the kettle on             )
          Help me in with the pram      )
          Help Margaret wash up         )
          I haven't seen it             )
          Change Philip for me          )
          Get your own breakfast, dear  )
          Make the tea                  )
          Do me a jam sandwich          )     BBUUGHMMMM
          Make Martin's feed for me     )
          Where did you put it?         )
          There's someone at the door   )
          Philip had it, I think        )
          Empty the pails               )
          Take the dustbin to the front )
          Look for it if it isn't there )
          The hall light's gone again   )
          The fire's going out          )
```

Kingsley

*Hilly sends her love
and thanks for the card.* [37]

The promise of release from at least some of these bums arrived in late February in the person of a cleaning lady, Betty, arranged by Margaret from her social work. Betty was a prostitute whose husband, a Norwegian sailor, beat her. She first appeared at Haslemere Road in the midst of a coffee party/tutorial Amis had arranged for his students. She had just been robbed and was shaken, and asked to be allowed to spend the night. She was, Amis reported to Larkin in a letter of 18 February, 'quite good-looking, but very dirty, and smelt a little, so when she offered me an evening out, with all drinks paid for and a shag at the end gratis, I declined, and persisted in my refusal even when she offered to pay our coal-bill in addition, a matter of some £2–15, out of her earnings. But I still think it was one of the nicest compliments I've ever had paid me.' Amis was to use Betty, and Margaret as well, as starting points for characters in the story 'Moral Fibre' (1958), set in Aberdarcy, with John Lewis, the librarian, as protagonist. The fictional Betty's offer to Lewis is also declined.

The whole episode left Amis feeling 'pleased that the woman I am living with is my wife, and at present I have no intention of deserting her, nor have I ever beaten her up'. Immediately after recounting the incident, in the same paragraph, Amis reported to Larkin, again, perhaps, with 'Frost at Midnight' in mind, that 'a gust from the Irish sea suddenly beat against the house, so that it seemed to stagger like a ship in a gale. A coal clattered on to the hearth. I noticed a patch of damp sprawled in one corner of the ceiling.'[38]

In late March or early April 1950 Larkin paid his first visit to the Amises at Swansea, 'one of the most successful we have ever engineered'.[39] In May, the family parted amicably with Margaret and her daughter and moved to the first of two flats in the Mumbles Road, at number 644, amidst the cafés, restaurants and pubs along Swansea Bay. Mavis Nicholson remembers these flats as chaotic, as does Hilly. But Hilly liked the liveliness of Mumbles Road and had several female friends in the area. Amis's thoughts, at this time, turned to Oxford. Larkin had read Amis some new poems during his stay and these, Amis told him, together with an advertisement he saw for a research fellowship at Balliol, inspired 'Four Poems about Oxford'. The second of these poems, he wrote to Larkin, 'owes something to your debat'[40] (perhaps 'Round the Point / debat inedit / nineteen-fifty', the title Larkin gives to the first of two little Shavian playlets James Booth published in his edition of Larkin's early fictions).[41] It is worth quoting as an index of Amis's mood after six months in Swansea:

2.

Better to grit your teeth, and get away;
One runs to seed so here, I always say.

I never say that.

One must, though it's not easy at the start,
Enter the modern world, and play one's part.

I had to get a job, if that's what you mean.

After the Army, Oxford's rather trifling;
When you came back, didn't you find it stifling?

Since you ask me, no; I thought where I'd been was
more trifling. And stifling too, if you must use the word.

Three years of boredom's quite enough for me.
You must find life much fuller now you're free.

Fuller of what?

Amis's answer would be work (in addition to teaching, he was
finishing up his B.Litt. thesis and not much enjoying it, working 'on
average 8 hrs. a day, including week-ends'),[42] domestic chores and
money worries. Oxford, in contrast, seemed full of good things, as
in the fourth poem:

4.

Here is a list of things I have understood.

i.   There are only two sorts of things, bad and good.

ii.   When he gets the good, a man ought to be glad.

iii.   When he gets the bad, a man ought to be sad.

iv.   Some of the good are joking, smoking, soaking,
        And (if you will permit the expression) poking.

v.   In a bad place these are absent, or even banned.

vi.   In a good place they are frequent, or ready to hand.

vii.   And I want as much of them as I can stand.

Oxford may have looked 'a good place' in April, but it would
not look so for long. In a letter of 12 May Amis wrote to Larkin
that he had at last finished his B.Litt. thesis and had gone to
Oxford to check some references, to talk to Bateson and Leishman
about the fellowship at Balliol, and to meet old friends, including
old mistresses.[43] He reported all sorts of complications and splits
among the friends and feared he might have offended Nick Russel,

who discovered he had been there and had not looked him up (Russel was distraught over a woman and Amis 'decided I didn't want any of that, thank you very much'). Amis also reported that the first number of *Essays in Criticism* was due out in January and that Bateson had encouraged him (and through him, Larkin) to contribute: 'I shall probably re-do my Meredith chapter for it . . . Then I am going to attack C.S. Lewis, and perhaps Laud David. I shall enjoy doing them, shan't I?' On his return from Oxford Amis was at last free, until late June, to 'get on with my own stuff. I am thinking of a squib sequence, to be called *The lives of the English poets*. And there is my opera [with Montgomery], and my novel.⁴⁴ I feel quite happy about my writing: except that nobody will publish it, of course.'⁴⁵ By early July Amis was marking Higher School Cert. papers; when he'd finished, he immediately began preparing an extramural summer school course. 'I have been shorter of money than I can ever remember,' he wrote to Larkin on 30 July. 'The children eat a lot of food now, and to live in this house costs a lot of money. In the last week of each month, half a pint of beer is an unwarrantable extravagance and I have to allow for things like 2d phone-calls and stamps for letters. There isn't much to smoke most of the time, either.' In addition, he had not got the job at Balliol.

In September Amis and Hilly, with Martin, spent a weekend in Oxford, leaving Philip with the Bardwells at Abbey Timbers. They also visited James Michie in London. Larkin came down to Oxford and among other things he and Amis discussed Amis's novel, already 10,000 words long. Meanwhile, Amis had been tinkering with his thesis and was having problems getting it typed; he did not submit it to the English Faculty until October. As a consequence of this tinkering he was behind in preparing lectures for the new term.⁴⁶ By 11 October 1950, the family had moved to the second of the flats on Mumbles Road, at number 382, 'a nicer house', though with a less civil landlady. The letter Amis wrote Larkin on this day reported a tragedy: 'Margaret's little child died of tubercular meningitis a week or so ago.'⁴⁷ 'It was all very traumatic,' Hilly recalled; yet Amis wrote unfeelingly to Larkin about the child's death. He was fractious and in low spirits at the time, worn down by work, money worries and a stream of rejections: for his poetry, for his unpublished novel 'The Legacy', for the fellowship. On 28 October he reported to Larkin that he had written an attack on Keats for Bateson[48] ('Why don't you chaps start liking something for a change?'),[49] also that he was getting 'a trifle implicated with a lady student'. On 12 November 'the only big news' he had to report was that Hilly had broken a prized Eddie Condon record, 'which has made me more fed up with being married than anything that has ever happened to me . . . [W]hy did she have to *choose* that record to break of my whole collection? I am still sore about this, though it happened over a week ago.'[50] Later in the same letter, reporting on a visit from an Oxford friend, Peter Oldham, he recounts how Hilly 'spewed 5 pints of cider over the pub-floor; fairly unobtrusively, but a bad time was had by all'. Hilly's resulting hangover meant Amis had to do the children and the chores the next day, 'with a more minor hangover BUT WITH A HANGOVER'. This incident and the broken record, plus 'a certain amount of peevishness on both sides for the last couple of weeks . . . has reduced our relations to the lowest point I can remember. I feel fed up rather than concerned about it. I can't work here very satisfactorily, either: there is no room where I can be alone & poetry can never be written. All the same, Hilly's growing disinclination to stay here (or at least be contented here) arouses only irritation and foreboding in me. There is talk of clearing a bedroom for me: that would help everything a lot. I am getting a little more involved with that lady student.'

Four days later, on 16 November, Amis went up to Oxford to defend his B.Litt. thesis. The senior examiner chosen by the Faculty Board for the viva was Professor Lord David Cecil, the supervisor Amis had dropped for Bateson. The second examiner was J.B. Bamborough, a recently appointed junior Fellow in English at Cecil's college. Amis's account of the viva in a letter to Larkin of 27 November was brief and ominous. The letter ended: 'Of what value would you say your thesis* would be to a critic of nineteenth-century bum.' Below, the asterisked note read: 'I went to Oxford for one night recently and was viva'd on this, not very comfortably, by Prof. Lrd. D. Cecil & another. They thought I hadn't borne out my main contention. O Lor'. Haven't heard yet.' He would hear soon enough. On 17 December he wrote to Larkin: 'They've turned my thesis down, the direct descendants of sexual perverts. No explanation yet, if ever: I may have to sweat semen re-doing it.' Then Bateson wrote, explaining that 'though he was very indignant about it and thought I had been unfairly treated, it wouldn't be much use rewriting my thesis'. Amis received Bateson's letter the same day he received a form from the War Office, 'the one they will use to see whether they want to call me up for training for their filthy war [in Korea]'. 'Oh Christ, the number of people who will ask me about and commiserate with me for the rejection of my thesis,' Amis continued.[51] 'My tongue nearly seized up telling about 350 people what the bloddy thesis was about and when I was putting it in, who my filthy examiners were, etc. SONS OF SODS SHOULD BE SODDED.'

For an Oxford B.Litt. thesis in English (as opposed to the rarer and more demanding D.Phil.) to be failed was unusual. The weeding-out process for the B.Litt. mostly took place in the first or examined part of the course. When Amis was hired by Swansea it was simply assumed his thesis would pass. That it did not was an embarrassment, though no threat to his job. The reasons for the failure are stated in a written report to the English Faculty Board signed by Cecil and Bamborough. The report is a paragraph long:

Mr. Amis's thesis[52] is a study of the relation between author and audience as exemplified in the careers of a selected number of Victorian poets. He seeks to discover in each case the nature of the particular audience and also the effect of its taste on the authors [*sic*] work. From the information he also tries to establish in general propositions the whole question of author and reader. Mr. Amis is keenly interested in his subject and has done some genuine work on it. But he cannot be said to have illuminated it. The information he has been able to gather about the audience is too scattered and indeterminate to afford a solid basis for generalisations; nor are such general propositions as he does hazard, always supported by his facts. Indeed with an honesty that does him credit, he admits this. It must be said that Mr. Amis is not always accurate in detail and that he sometimes expresses himself in terms so loose as to be misleading. In viva he did produce some new evidence in support of one or two of his points. Otherwise he did not strengthen his position, as he was curiously reluctant to commit himself. In these circumstances we do not feel justified in granting him the degree.

'I dare say it was not a very good thesis,' admits Amis in the *Memoirs*, but that was not, he suggests, why it failed. 'I suspected then and still think very likely, I had been caught in a spot of academic crossfire.'[53] 'We blamed it all on Cecil, of course,' Hilly recalls, and there were grounds for doing so. In addition to Amis's rejection of Cecil for Bateson, a sort of rival of Cecil's, there was the sociological as opposed to appreciative character of the thesis itself, and Cecil's behaviour at the viva, at least as recounted by Amis:

I had opened my introduction [to the thesis] by outlining what I took to be the normal or average process whereby a poet's work reaches the public . . . To save having to say 'usually' or 'often' or 'in some cases' or 'perhaps' and all those all the time I had prefixed to this statement some formula like 'Let me now outline this supposedly normal process. A Poet writes in the first place for his close friends.' Lord David read that much aloud and then snapped as if personally offended, 'Do you mean *alwith*?'

'No, sir,' I said, 'and in fact if you go on to the next sentence you'll see that I specifically say I don't mean always and propose to take note of cases where it doesn't apply.'

'*Oh*,' he said, if anything more affronted than ever, as if I had somehow concealed this information from him until that very moment.

If I had not failed my degree before entering the room, which is quite possible, I certainly had by then, and without having gone on to say what I felt, which was something like, 'and if you were less fucking conceited and lazy you might have been able to notice that for yourself.' As a final point of interest, I noticed that, with old-world discourtesy, the chairman of the examination board had not bothered to rub out the pencilled marginalia he had made on the top copy. The only intelligible word appearing there was ALWAYS embellished with exclamation-marks and question-marks. There were more question-marks and assorted squiggles on the rest of the Introduction (a short section) and I think a few more on some closely following pages. Nothing further.[54]

Amis's account of the introduction to his thesis is broadly accurate. In the first paragraph the claims he makes for his main argument are carefully qualified: 'Its greatest merit is that it is convenient and clear, and though it may not win assent at first glance, most of the evidence assembled has tended to show that it is, within limits, valid. Where it has proved unsatisfactory, the evidence that renders it so has not been withheld . . . It is not claimed that anything approaching a formula or dogma has been attained.'[55] Amis then lays out the theory itself, in the second paragraph:

A poet writes his poetry originally for a small circle of intimate friends, keeping before him as he writes their probable response, and afterwards soliciting their opinion. This small group, having helped to shape the poetry (they are not necessarily poets themselves, but are persons of literary inclination), use their personal influence to recommend it to a larger circle. This second group, formed partly, in the period under discussion, as a result of publication by the poet, provides a band of followers who owe allegiance primarily to him rather than to other poets. Members of this following use the means open to them to carry the poet's work to general readers of poetry. A poet thus has a threefold audience, and for convenience' sake its three constituents have been labelled the inner, intermediate and outer audiences. The process is taken to be the norm. When the norm is not followed, by an omission of one of the three stages, by an overhasty or delayed transition from one to another, or by reason of the poet's ceasing to write for his inner audience, his work, as well as his fame, will suffer.[56]

Though Amis describes Cecil's reason for rejecting the thesis – that its argument is unqualified (*'alwith?'*) and thus impossible to defend – as unfair, it could be argued that it failed precisely because it forwards its claims too tentatively, too diffidently, and because it so conscientiously records exceptions.[57] Amis's manner in the thesis is casual, unexercised, as it seems to have been in the viva, where, according to the examiners, 'he was curiously reluctant to commit himself'.[58] The thesis ends with a chapter on Robert Browning, whose relation to his audience is in some ways the hardest to reconcile with Amis's theories. Its concluding section begins by alluding to the first sentence of the thesis as a whole: 'Like all other artistic endeavours, the writing of poetry is a social act, a communication between one man and another.'[59] In the case of Browning, however,

communication was not an aim; it was a by-product, however valuable, of his true aim: to satisfy himself by what he wrote. Most of his readers would agree that if there is anything unsatisfactory in Browning's method it is its periodic breakdowns in communication, a tendency, if a handy piece of jargon may be used, to private statement. This is more than the ancient charge of 'obscurity' in modern dress, because it implies a reason for such failures. It is mentioned, not with the absurd intention of suggesting that Browning should or could have written by a different method, but merely to propound an explanation of the difficulties inherent in the method that was used. Those to whom these difficulties are trivial ought, perhaps, to be grateful that Browning's private income allowed him to publish at his own expense for twenty years or more, and to refuse (c.1886) the offer of £400 for a single poem to be printed in a Boston magazine.[60]

These are the final words of the thesis, excluding appendices and bibliography. It is not hard to see how they might irritate: by offering no general conclusions, that is, to the thesis as a whole; by ending with an exceptional case and on a minor note (with the anecdote about the magazine); by implying that Browning's 'obscurity' is a failing, while not actually saying so. The ending is of a piece with the thesis as a whole in its semi-detached air, its refusal to make claims or clinch arguments. In the *Memoirs*, Amis identifies one of the 'failures' of the thesis (presumably realised after the viva, since it is not mentioned in the examiners' report), as not presenting himself 'as an indefatigable, endlessly curious and imaginative researcher. For instance, having joyfully come across an American scholar's book on the literary career of Swinburne,[61] which gave me every fact I needed, I came totally clean about him and it, instead of cunningly offering the results as those of patient, widespread personal digging.'[62] This refusal to dress up is seen also in the way the thesis proceeds: dutifully, mechanically, from D.G. Rossetti to Meredith to Christina Rossetti, William Morris, James Thomson, Swinburne, Hopkins, Wilde (and other poets of the decadence), Edward Fitzgerald and Browning. In each chapter (there are eleven, spread over 144 pages), Amis gathers bits of biographical and bibliographical evidence and in the same order: first for inner, then for intermediate, then for outer audiences. There is no pretence of completeness or urgency; the thesis is undisguisedly a job of work.

Amis claims to have 'turned up some interesting material – interesting to me, at least' in the thesis, specifically 'about D.G. Rossetti and his unexpected insistence on entertainment as an essential ingredient of poetry'.[63] This insistence is seen as part of Rossetti's overall attitude towards the audience. 'If such an attitude includes what must sometimes seem an excessive tendency to self-advertisement,' Amis wrote in the thesis, 'it is also, on a larger view, a desirable and healthy attitude'[64] – words which recall Amis's own lifelong willingness to publicise his work, to sit for interviews and profiles or answer journalists' queries, if not always patiently. Though written reluctantly or with the left hand, Amis's thesis uncovered literary precedents for his own practice as a writer. He undertook the thesis because he needed a job and thought a B.Litt. would improve his chances of getting one he would not hate. In the process, while collecting evidence for the saving properties of the audience, he may well have found encouragement for his conviction that writing could and should be both popular and serious.

The question of why the thesis failed remains. For all its flaws and weaknesses, it is well written, intelligent in its treatment of the evidence it presents, and, as the examiners admit in their report, the product of 'some genuine work'. Amis clearly did himself no favours in the viva (he was never good in such settings), but it is hard not to suspect bias as a factor in his failure; or not to imagine the same thesis passing if submitted by another pupil, one who hadn't snubbed the chief examiner while aligning himself with a supervisor from a rival camp. J.B. Bamborough will have none of this: 'I'm sure the failure was a disappointment to him, and it isn't surprising that he constructed a kind of mythology to account for it and to comfort himself . . . Cecil seems to play the major villainous part. But the examination was conducted in the usual way: we both read the thesis independently before meeting to compare notes. We were in complete agreement, and there is no question that Cecil overbore my judgement or persuaded me to subscribe to a view which I did not genuinely hold. (I was certainly not biased against Amis; I hardly knew him and had only met him tangentially.) We may both have been mistaken in our judgement, but we arrived at it honestly . . . [T]he truth is straightforward if dull: Amis ploughed because his work was not up to scratch.'[65]

Amidst the gloom of thesis bum and no-money bum, Mummy B.'s estate offered a well-timed ray of hope. Hilly was to receive a legacy of £5,000 and the Amises could buy a decent house, among other things. 'I wish the money would come,' Amis wrote to Larkin in a letter of 8 January 1951, 'then I could silence them with suits, tongue-tie them with ties, dumbfound them with drinks I have drunk' (in the event, he told Jacobs, he contented himself with an elaborate metal cigarette-roller, 'more to symbolise his new well-being than to actually use').[66] Hilly, too, saw the money in part as a way of getting back at others or the world, writing to Larkin four days later: 'The stupid term has started & I am having a lovely time looking round houses and being snooty about them. We haven't got the money yet but it should be here in the middle of next month – I hope. Mummy is going to lend me the money if we see a house we want before the money arrives.'[67] Two weeks later they had found one: at 24 The Grove, a three-storey terraced house in the Uplands district of Swansea near where they'd lived in Sketty (also near Dylan Thomas's birthplace at Cwmdonkin Drive). The house cost £2,200: 'I took Mummy B's cheque for £2,400 down to my bank and paid it in,' Amis wrote to Larkin on 26 January, 'I liked paying that cheque in.'[68] Once they had taken possession of the house, Amis and Hilly ran through it 'yelling and hooting and growling as they celebrated their new space and freedom'.[69] With the remainder of the £5,000 they bought a car, a washing machine, a fridge and new furniture (*'from Heal's'*).[70] Mavis Nicholson had never seen such luxury, or such imaginative interior decoration. Hilly painted the rooms of the house in bright, bold colours. She bought scrub-topped tables ('We hadn't seen them before'). She put a big school clock on the wall in the kitchen (no one in Swansea had seen that either). None of these touches mattered to Amis. What mattered was that it was now possible for him to have a room of his own in which to write, a tiny, untidy study at the end of a long corridor, facing a wall from the house next door and a steeply sloped back garden. He was twenty-eight years old, a junior lecturer in an obscure provincial university. His first novel had been turned down everywhere. His thesis had been failed. Poverty had worn his nerves and his marriage. 'When I get my nice new typewriter and a room to myself I shall start writing *Dixon & Xtine*,'[71] he told Larkin, in the same letter that announced both Bateson's advice not to resubmit the thesis and Mrs Marston's wounding reader's report on 'The Legacy'. He would begin by revising what he had, the letter continued, addressing all the criticisms made against 'The Legacy': 'cutting out a lot of redundancy, inserting stacks of conflict, strengthening my female characterisation, grammaticising my writing, and whacking away with the old funniness'. The result, *Lucky Jim*, would be hailed as the finest comic novel of the post-war period. Amis's life would be utterly transformed.

10

Making *Lucky Jim*

As money worries receded, Amis began to be anxious about the Korean War and the 'filthy bomb-drunk Yanks'. 'They're not getting me,' he wrote to Larkin on 26 January 1951. 'I'm not gong. A list of non-cooperators is being got up in the college here.'[1] On 12 March he apologised to Larkin for a long silence, but 'I have been soiling-with-excrement my undergarments in case I should be called for this filthy Z reserve thing. This would have entailed a lot of nasty business with appeals and tribunals and what-would-you-do-if-you-saw-a-North-Korean-defiling-your-marriage-partner and possibly civil or even military detention. However, it now seems clear that they have missed me, *this year*.'[2] A lesser worry involved Professor Thomas, who had to report on Amis's character, industry, trustworthiness, etc., to the council. Amis was afraid Thomas would say something about the 'lady student' he had become involved with, the one about whom he'd written to Larkin. This fear proved groundless, though instead Thomas told Amis, according to Amis's letter of 26 January, 'that he had been rather concerned about the way I seemed to do rather more denigration in my lectures than he thought was helpful. He had seen some of the answers to the Browning questions last year, and thought that I had been rather unfair to him.' Amis told Thomas he'd guard against this tendency, but thought the criticism unwarranted: 'if they want me to praise these sods, why do they only give me *filthy Jane Austen, stupid bloody snorting Browning, shrieking Dickens, et.al.*, to lecture on?'

Amis's best students understood comments like these: 'The joke

was that he knew and we knew that all of this was tongue-in-cheek,'
recalls Clive Gammon. But it wasn't all tongue-in-cheek. Amis did
write admiringly of Austen, Browning and Dickens. Austen 'set out
bravely to correct conventional notions of the desirable and
virtuous',[3] Browning invented 'a poetic language that makes most
of his work instantly recognisable, lively, compressed, colloquial and
yet like no speech that was ever spoken',[4] Dickens's 'abounding
vigour' rendered most objections 'irrelevant'.[5] But he deplored or
was irritated by aspects of their writing as well: Austen's 'habit of
censoriousness where there ought to be indulgence, and indulgence
where there ought to be censure' 'corrupts' *Mansfield Park*;[6]
Browning 'knew a lot, but was sometimes too aware of it',[7] in addition to being needlessly obscure; Dickens's 'ubiquitous, obsessive
repetition, the inability to leave anything, good or bad, alone – what
Saintsbury called "that damnable iteration"',[8] produces 'cumulative
effects of great power' but can also 'fill the reader with exasperated
ennui'. Such assertions are cogently as well as robustly argued and
exemplified. That Amis loved saying outrageous things, loved denigration, especially in his early years, and habitually expressed his
opinions forcefully sometimes leaves one with the impression that
he didn't like anything. This impression is particularly strong in the
letters to Larkin. But the letters also make clear his preferences,
which are often instrumental; like those of many writers, they serve
or further his own writing. In a letter to Larkin of 9 December
1952, Amis reported that he had gathered together all his 'vital
books' (not the same as 'best books') on a single shelf of the bookcase in his study.

It [the list] consists (if you care) of volumes of poetry by W.H. Auden,
John Betjeman, Lawrence Durrell, piss [because out of alphabetical sequence]
John Donne, Andrew Marvell, Alfred Baron Tennyson, William
Wordsworth, W.B. Yeats and piss Robert Graves; works of fiction by John
Dickson Carr, Cyril Connolly, Graham Greene, Julian Hall, Christopher
Isherwood, James Joyce, Henri de Montherlant, Flann O'Brien, Anthony
Powell; and works of general interest by Cyril Connolly, William Empson
(add piss William Empson to the list of poetry), Graham Greene, Arthur
Hutchings (*A companion to Mozart's pianoforte concertos*), piss Robert
Graves, Q.D. Leavis, W. Somerset Maugham and Stephen Potter (NOT
FARCKIN GAMESMANSHIT ETC but *The muse in chains*). *The north
ship*[9] will be added if I ever get hold of another copy, *Jill* and *A girl in*

winter when I get them back from loan. Piss Alexander Pope should be added to the poetry. And piss Eddie Condon to the general-interest. There are only three volumes I feel really bad about not having on that shelf: *Old lights for new chancels*,[10] unreturned by some forgotten criminal; *Living*,[11] and *Poems*, by George Herbert.

In addition to work on his lectures and on 'Dixon and Christine', Amis was much occupied in the early months of 1951 with a second opera collaboration with Bruce Montgomery. This collaboration, for a one-act chamber opera, derived from a commission by the Arts Council and promised both recognition and pay. At first, the opera was to have five singing parts, then four. By 8 January the number of parts had been reduced by the Arts Council to three and Bruce was '"Half-inclined to cry off" Jaysusmaryanjoseph I'm not; it's all I've got left for the moment,' Amis wrote to Larkin, apart from '*filthy Dombey and son* for the first year people'.[12] The basic premise of the libretto had been 'fudged up' by Amis and Montgomery in January. The setting is Amberley Hall, Sir Thomas Beaumont's country house, which his wife professes to hate but uses for assignations with her youthful lover, Frederick Oldham.[13] When Sir Thomas unexpectedly appears, Phyllis hides Frederick behind a screen, though he's anxious to be discovered and thus free of her, 'a neat twist on the screen formula'.[14] Frederick, an intellectual and 'one of the richest men in society', is a standard-issue Restoration rake, like Rochester or a hero in Congreve or Wycherley:

> A hunter now of love, rough-riding
> Full tilt across a neighbour's holding,
> Like any hunter, checked by nothing
>   Until the prey is caught,
> I rode love down, and, the chase ended,
> Dry-mouthed with hunger, lay and feasted,
> Then, surfeited, sat up and wondered
>   Where was the truth I sought.[15]

The opera ends, after several witty reversals, with all three characters happily resolved to live in the country, another twist, given the conventions of Restoration comedy.[16]

After several maddening delays,[17] Montgomery finally finished setting Amis's words. In the end, only a section of the opera was

performed, on 30 March 1952, as part of a radio programme entitled 'Apollo in the West', on the BBC's West of England Home
Service. The section lasted about fifteen minutes and Amis received
a performance fee of 13 shillings per minute.[18]

Hilly's legacy and the new house meant that the Amises now had
means and space to entertain. Even when poor, Amis was, in John
Morgan's words, 'a dazzling reckless host'.[19] Now he became a more
frequent one. By March the Amis social circle had expanded beyond
the English Department. Amis met two philosophers he particularly
liked: Peter Winch (he also liked Winch's wife, Erica) and Roy Holland,
a Mozart-lover 'whose chief thing is being nice'. He met Esmond
Cleary, 'a young gap-toothed economist' with a liking for jazz and a
girlfriend (Jean, soon to be his wife) 'who tries to stop him drinking'.[20]
Through the Clearys, or along with the Clearys, he met Eddie Cooney,
described to Larkin in a letter of 12 March as 'a dark social scientist
whose talent is for being funny and who is having a mild affair with
Hilly (don't tell her I told you so)';[21] Cooney would eventually marry
Clive Gammon's sister, Barbara, one of several students Amis was
pursuing at the time. Margaret Vakil, meanwhile, had thrown over
David Sims and taken up with the *crachach*, a pejorative Welsh term
for the local bourgeoisie, what Hilly called 'the dentist and solicitor
crowd'. Margaret introduced the Amises to several boring boyfriends
from this crowd, including 'a fearful Tory solicitor' who once took
Amis fishing.[22] In the summer of 1951, in addition to expanding their
social circle, the Amises had a number of visitors from Oxford and
elsewhere. 'The house keeps filling with self-invited craps,' Amis
complained to Larkin on 15 July: 'honestly, old boy, without a word
of a lie three pages of Dixon and I'm licked for the day' (though he
adds that he's now up to page 94 'and make myself laugh a bit more
often than formerly'). At the time of this letter, a thirteen-year-old boy
and a ten-year-old boy were staying with the Amises, plus their three
rabbits (to go with Hilly's two, in addition to her dog and cat).
Simultaneously, the house was overrun with builders and decorators:
'Craps continually pore in to fix the curtains and fit the curtains and
lay the lino and instal the immersion heater and put doors on the
airing cupboard and paint the surrounds and varnish the surrounds
and paint the wall and seal-up the sewer pipe and re-lay the garden
steps and put up the shelves and altogether they are continually pouring
in and stopping me from working.'

With money and a bigger house came regular domestic help. Hilly found a daily named Eva Garcia, a sturdy Welshwoman of Celt–Iberian stock, born the same year as Amis. Eva quickly became a fixture in the family and remained so for the next ten years, until the Amises left Swansea for Cambridge in 1961. She was married to Joe Garcia, a steel-rigger, also of Celt–Iberian stock, described by Martin Amis as 'a kind, cubiform, semiliterate, longsuffering grafter who was actually *taller* sitting down than standing up'.[23] Eva was famously imperturbable, picking her way through the house the morning after wild parties, methodically cleaning and tidying, unbothered by mess and bottles and drunken, sleeping partygoers. Philip Amis remembers the house 'smelling like a pub' in the mornings after parties; the parties themselves he describes as 'big, jazzy, with lots of people getting very drunk, shouting, dancing; it sounded like they were having a wonderful time'. He and Martin would sit on the stairs listening intently 'and hoping someone would come up and give us 2/6 or something'.

None of the wildness at 24 The Grove offended Eva. Her son Michael, ten in 1951, sometimes accompanied her when she went to work at the Amises'; he remembers neither complaints nor censoriousness. At the end of the workday Hilly would drive Eva, or Eva and Michael, or Eva and Michael's younger sister, Hilary, back to their home in the Maryhill district of Swansea. Cars were a rarity in Maryhill and Michael remembers both the stir their appearance caused and Hilly's habit of driving straight over roundabouts. To Martin, Eva was 'great and terrible' – great when 'belting out a song as she made my tea, and elegantly swivelling on the slab of her orthopaedic boot', terrible when suffering from migraine or dilating on the miseries of others, a favourite, revivifying topic. 'Once, down on the Mumbles Road,' Martin recalls, 'the family encountered a traffic jam caused by a serious accident. In the car there was a murmur of anxiety that Sally [Martin's sister, then two or three] might see something frightening. Finally we approached the crossroads, and there on the verge was a twitching, blood-bespattered figure half-covered by an old overcoat. We seemed to be safely past when Eva propped Sally up on the back seat and said, "Look at him, Sall. *Writhing in agony* he is."'[24]

In addition to the room of his own at 24 The Grove, Amis's writing was helped in this period by several visits to and from Larkin, always a creative tonic. In September 1950 Larkin had left Leicester to take up a post as Sub-Librarian at Queen's University, Belfast. Amis came to visit him for a few days in mid-April 1951 and then travelled with him to Dublin for a brief holiday (Hilly could not go because of the children). On the eve of the visit, Amis announced he would arrive 'full of fine wit and money[25] and journals and money and news and money', though when it occurred to him that the trip to Dublin might involve a customs inspection, he thought better of the journals.[26] The holiday was judged a success by Amis and was followed in August by Larkin's first visit to 24 The Grove. Less than three months later, Amis announced in a letter to Larkin: 'I've finished Dixon now . . . I've finished the first go-through and have put it aside in the hope of forgetting it a bit until such time as I can judge it a leetle more objectively.'[27] On 2 December, he apologised for not having written earlier, blaming college work, domestic chores, Hilly having been poorly with 'colds and things', and an article he was trying to finish for Bateson before the Christmas break (to leave the holidays free for revision of the novel). 'Don't hate me honey for not writing,' the letter concluded. 'Glad your life is on the up-and-up. You couldn't say that about mine, d'you see, because it wouldn't be true, d'you see.' On 22 December he wrote again to say that he'd finished the Bateson article but had postponed the 'Dixon' revisions until after the holidays.

In London at the beginning of the New Year Amis and Larkin had another brief meeting.[28] 'Its insufficient duration seemed more than usually obtrusive,' Amis complained on 7 January: 'God, to think of seeing you regularly at coffee, of having you to tea . . .[29] Things like that don't happen do they.'[30] Larkin had not yet read 'Dixon and Christine' through, though he'd read a preliminary draft of the first few chapters and Amis had provided him with a detailed synopsis of the plot. During the April 1951 visit, they had discussed the novel's characters and structure and Amis had incorporated a number of Larkin's suggestions. On 18 January 1952, Amis wrote to thank Larkin for 'your remarks on Dixon' and to defend it, perhaps against a slight: 'I feel myself that there's much more going on in it than in the legsy,[31] and you might agree if you read it through AS MUCH HAPPENS AS IN EITHER OF YOUR BOOLDY THINGS.[32] And boy gets girl too, you sam.[33] And there's a bit of sub-pornography in it.'[34]

Soon after he wrote these words, Amis was again overwhelmed

by money worries. His openness with Larkin at this point in their friendship is worth remarking upon. The letters he writes in the years just prior to the publication of *Lucky Jim* give the impression of a man who is wholly trusting and frank with his friend. The many private jokes, allusions, obscure abbreviations – 'you sam', 'legsy' – that litter their pages are partly tokens or assertions of friendship. At the same time, serious matters are frequently treated as jokes, or also as jokes. On 7 February, for example, Amis wrote to cancel a planned visit to Belfast: 'you see, Hilly's money is all spent now, and Income Tax man wants me to give him £8 to spend, and the electricity man wants me to give him £10 to spend, and what with one thing and another . . . I don't see myself spending circa £10 on coming to Belfast, much as I shd. like to come there.'[35] On 27 February, the thought of his thirtieth birthday filled Amis with 'impotent horror'. He could see nothing to look forward to:

What am I doing here? Or anywhere, for that matter. If only someone would *take me up*, or even *show a bit of interest*. If only someone would publish some books of mine, I could write some; as it is, I hardly get near writing any at all. I'm too frightened to send *Dixon* on the rounds. And other things? That old winged boa-constrictor, sex, still has me in his coils, and is flying around with me looking for a good shit-marsh to drop me into . . . Still a lecturer at 45 CHRIST Senior Lecturer at Durham at 45 CHRIST Lecturer at OKKKKKERRRRRRRHRHRHRHRGHGHGHGHGHGHRGHRGHRGH RIEEEEEEEEEEEEESSSSSSSSST You know the sort of thing that's going to happen to me? With my teeth even worse than they are (I have had gingivitis for some time) dressing in camel-hair waistcoat and bow-ties, I shall be laughing and talking loudly in the pubs at lunch-time, a one for the girls, imagining I am impressing the young men by my keen com bom *contempraneity*, passing myself off as a grand chap, referring to my successful friends, 'Oh yes, Bruce and I were very thick at one time; dropped his old friends, of course, when he made Covent Garden,' 'Nonsense now, my dear young lady, have another of the same; after all, I'm here to see you don't come to any harm, eh boys?' All this of course will be taking place in one of the smaller and poorer provincial cities.

Several weeks after this letter, Amis gathered his courage together and sent the manuscript of 'Dixon and Christine' to Michael Joseph. He was pretty broke ('I rarely spend money now, except on razor-blades and herbal smoking mixture').[36] His weekly teaching load was now nine hours, not five. A recent visit to John Wain at Reading University, as we have seen, had made him feel both provincial and dull, since everyone there seemed to know much more about literature and criticism than he did.[37] Though Bateson had published his poems and articles in *Essays in Criticism*, he was not optimistic about the job market, which he described as 'pretty tight'.[38] In a letter of 19 April to Larkin Amis declared himself too broke to attend a party in London to celebrate the publication of the first PEN anthology, *New Poems 1952*, edited by Clifford Dyment, Roy Fuller and Montagu Summers, which contained his poem 'Masters' as well as three poems by Robert Conquest and three by D.J. Enright, though none by Larkin (in the event, he would find the money to attend). Then Daddy B came to stay. 'As the train drew in,' Amis reported to Larkin, on 19 May, 'I began swearing in a whisper and very fast, like a man about to go to a concert who pisses as much as he can beforehand, even though he may not want to at the time . . . I sang softly that Beethoven concerto jingle, over and over again,[39] my heart lifting as more and more passengers came into view without any sign of him . . . Whenever his face was turned away from mine, I screwed my own into a dazzle-pattern of hatred and fury. I can now see what makes fathers fling their children out of the house with a few bob at the age of sixteen: mine ran up to him with cries of delighted welcome.'

Some six weeks after Amis had submitted the manuscript of 'Dixon and Christine' to Michael Joseph, he still hadn't heard a word and began to fear they'd lost the manuscript. They hadn't. On 18 June he reported to Larkin that the novel had been turned down and was 'now being rejected I suppose by a pal of John Wain's, though this time for slightly different reasons no doubt' ('not having alive or exciting enough characters', it turned out).[40] The real trouble with 'Dixon and Christine', Amis told Larkin in the same letter, was that 'it isn't "sensitive" enough to make up for its lack of concern with matters of importance like religion and the sense of guilt and our predicament as Europeans'. At this low point, Amis suffered a second rejection. When an English job at Queen's University, Belfast finally materialised, Amis applied, was interviewed in late June, and didn't get it. The visit, however, was no mere nadir ('dinar' or 'drain' in the letters); it also marked the beginning of a reversal in Amis's fortunes, one that would lift him out of obscurity for the rest of his life. Amis arrived in Belfast with a copy of the rejected manuscript of 'Dixon' and Larkin at last read it through, offering detailed criticisms. These criticisms were to form the basis of a new and thorough revision, one Amis found so exciting that in subsequent letters his failure to get the Queen's job barely figures.[41]

Key to the revision was Larkin's suggestion that 'D[ixon] should sod up the romantic business actively.'[42] In the draft rejected by Michael Joseph and others Amis had presented Jim's eventual triumph over his rivals as a matter of pure contingency, so that readers would feel 'that if chaps in the shit climbed out of the shit, it's by good luck, not by their own efforts – I tried to make that one of the morals'. This moral might be true and worth pointing, but it was not, Larkin seems to have argued, very interesting. What was needed instead, in Amis's paraphrase, was a 'monstrous offensive by Dixon against the others'. Amis outlined several forms this offensive might take, requesting that Larkin 'please do *ponder* these suggestions'. The letter in which he made this request, written on 24 July 1952, was the first of several in which he referred to the revision as a joint effort: 'We should be able to fudge up something good between us.'

A partial typescript of 'Dixon and Christine' (twenty-four of its 230 pages are missing) survives and makes clear that the basic ingredients of *Lucky Jim* were already in place. These were summarised by Amis in note form in the essay 'Real and Made-up People': 'University shags. Provincial. Probably keen on culture. Crappy culture. Fellow who doesn't fit in. Seems anti-culture. Non-U. Non-Oxbridge. Beer. Girls. Can't say what he really thinks. Boss trouble. Given chores. Disasters. Boring boss (a) so boring girl (b). Nice girl comes but someone else's property.'[43]

The differences between 'Dixon' and *Lucky Jim* are of several sorts, beginning with names. Most strikingly, Jim is 'Julian' in the 'Dixon' typescript (the only Jim in 'Dixon' is James Michie, the intimidatingly well prepared ex-service student named after Amis's Oxford friend, fellow poet and co-editor).[44] Welch, cumbersomely, is merely a senior lecturer, not the professor; Dixon cultivates him because he has influence with the professor, whose name is Scarfe ('Ned's the hand behind the throne,' a friend tells him, 'the Polonius of your outfit').[45] In 'Dixon', Gore-Urquhart is an art critic not a business magnate, never appears in person and is unrelated to Christine; his function is to pronounce on Bertrand's paintings, which he does to devastating effect.[46]

In 'Dixon and Christine' the question of Dixon's retaining his job barely figures. It is mentioned in the opening chapter as an explanation for his cultivating Welch and then disappears for long stretches. Even when he recalls that he is on probation as a lecturer, or when Professor Scarfe upbraids him, Dixon expresses little anxiety: from the beginning he's been pondering an alternative career in London, in advertising. More prominent are his difficulties with 'Veronica Beale', the Margaret character, framed initially as a matter of getting her into bed.[47] Christine appears in the novel's first chapter (she does not appear until Chapter 4 in *Lucky Jim*) and much is made of her courting by Julian and their falling in love, in long, joke-free conversations about their feelings. She is already endowed with the vivifying particulars that make her more than just a male fantasy-figure (as when her body is said to feel 'rounded, and rather bulky'[48] in Dixon's arms or her hair to smell of 'well-brushed hair').[49] Bertrand, like his father and Veronica, is less horrible in 'Dixon' than in *Lucky Jim*, is capable of self-doubt and remorse, and is even chivalrous at the end. In several scenes, the story is told from his point of view. When Gore-Urquhart dismisses his paintings we're meant to feel sorry for him. His decision at the end of the novel to go off to Paris to learn to draw (Hilly gave up painting because she was told she couldn't draw) is presented as brave rather than delusional.

When Larkin suggested to Amis that he needed to 'sod up the romantic business actively', what he seems to have meant was that the novel needed to be more like a romance, with proper dragons and witches. Bertrand, his parents and Veronica had to be more straightforwardly monstrous as well as comical. In addition to simplifying the blocking figures, Amis had also to tell the story exclusively from the hero's point of view. As he was later to explain, *Lucky Jim* conforms to mythic patterns of comedy and romance, offering 'a young man at odds with his surroundings, and trying to make his way, and suffering comic misfortunes, and getting the girl – it can't fail, really.' Larkin's suggestions were attempts to throw these patterns into relief. He called for the number of characters to be thinned; he suggested a climactic confrontation or unmasking: the disastrous lecture (a scene Amis thought would be 'awfully difficult to do' but which produced the novel's famous comic set piece, the drunken 'Merrie England' lecture).[50] Larkin recalled his advice as: 'cut this, cut that, let's have more of the other. I remember I said Let's have more "faces" – you know, his Edith Sitwell face and so on.

The wonderful thing was that Kingsley could "do" all those faces himself – "Sex Life in Ancient Rome" and so on.'[51]

Amis accepted most of Larkin's points immediately. As he wrote on 24 July, his first task was 'making the job business much more important, as you suggested: so Dixon begins by planning a minor revenge on Bertrand as representative of the hated Welches as a compensation for all the shit-eating with Bertrand's father'.[52] He also embraced a number of Larkin's more detailed suggestions, at one point asking 'How many Dixon faces do you think there ought to be? I mean a lot, 10 or so, or just 3 or 4?'[53] On 5 August he wrote asking Larkin's opinion on a list of proposed additions and alterations, including excising a lengthy passage describing Dixon's Yorkshire upbringing (in *Lucky Jim* Dixon comes from Lancashire); expanding the arty weekend at the Welches' (it would draw on such Abbey Timbers weekends as that of Whitsun 1949, in which Amis experienced 'all the usual kicks, an account of a blind fiddler, over eighty he is, at Adderbury, a meritless short story shown to me by mummy b, a talentless and flavourless sonatina played me, gratu-itously, by Wm');[54] and turning Gore-Urquhart into 'a friend of Christine's boss in London, one of the family, or even her uncle'.[55] On 21 August 1952 Amis apologised to Larkin for answering so promptly, 'but I wanted to tear away at D & C while the excite-ment generated by your letter was fresh'.[56] He was writing from Abbey Timbers, where Daddy B 'has been telling me all about Switzerland: notably that the Swiss are very fine watchmakers (yes, really they are) . . . Fine Welch material, that'. Amis's determination to make the revised Welch, now a professor, both more prominent and more maddening, like Daddy B in the letters, was fed by subse-quent encounters. 'He was here recently,' Amis wrote to Larkin on 6 November: 'As a matter of fact, it was his visit that made me get on with [the revision] at last.' On New Year's Eve the rest of the Bardwell family supplied material, Hilly's musician brother William (Wm) especially: '"I don't like musical instruments to look like pieces of furniture,"' Amis reported him as saying. 'Now, why doesn't he like that? There's no actual *danger of confusion*, is there? And he was also continually agitating and fulminating about his filthy French food, "not being able to eat this unless it had that with it" . . . I got in one good blow about not liking the tubular flour-and-water food beloved of indigent peasants (though I wasn't able to put it as well as that, naturally. I don't think he noticed, anyway), but was robbed of the chance of getting in the companion about peasants' butter-substitute. But there's a place for both in *Dixon* (p.150 now).'

On 8 September 1952, just before beginning the final revision, Amis had written to Larkin laying out his plans for a number of aspects of the novel they had discussed. A paragraph each was devoted to 'the library', 'the lecture', 'the job', 'Bertrand's pass', 'Medievalism' – in Christopher Hitchens's phrase, 'eventual core ingredients' of the new version.[57] Amis also asked Larkin 'to skim quickly through the typescript, making marginal indications of anything that displeases you? ("Bad style," "Damp squib," bad bits of dialogue and so on, to prevent me using them again).' Ten days later he sent Larkin 'a summarized complete synopsis for final checking', a carbon of which, he assured him, he had kept. This synopsis was *Lucky Jim* entire, the whole plot worked out, integrating new strands such as the failed 'special subject' intrigue, the successful 'threatening letter' intrigue (against Johns, Dixon's creepy co-lodger), the 'series of arty debacles' that make up the arty weekend at the Welches', and the how and why of Gore-Urquhart's rescuing Dixon at the end. The letter concluded with Amis asking Larkin to return the annotated manuscript by registered post, as he was anxious to make a start.

Most of Larkin's comments on style Amis pronounced 'just, especially the ticks', but some he resisted. Larkin thought Amis was wrong to have female characters swear even mildly (as in 'God' or 'Christ') or use such words as 'sex', 'buggery' or 'sod'. 'People don't talk like that, especially ladies'; 'Ladies don't talk about sex'; 'People of Mrs. W's generation would surely say "emotional matters" or "affairs of the heart"' (rather than "sex matters").'[58] On 4 October, in the course of commenting on a trip Larkin took to the Lake District with Monica Jones, his lecturer friend from Leicester, Amis commented: 'Sorry to hear your trip was disappointing "from the sex point of view," as Mrs. Welch *would* say (she's *modern*, don't you see).'[59] As for taking the Lord's name in vain: 'You exaggerate (though I'm prepared to admit I exaggerate the other way) about ladies saying Christ. Casting about among my female acquaintance here I can think of six women *in as many seconds* who are accustomed to invoking that Entity.' Others of Larkin's marginal comments warn against overwritten or artifical dialogue, as in '*terribly* unnatural' or 'This speech might come from a stage play TOO BAD to be produced' or simply 'Horrible smell of arse' (subsequently 'HS

of A') or 'GRUESOME AROMA OF B' (presumably 'BUM').[60] A
third species of annotation concerned pacing, as in 'not going quickly
enough or revealing enough' (of a conversation about Bing Crosby),
'too detailed for their purpose' (of similar conversations), 'a bit long-
winded', 'a bit drawn out', 'another of those conversations'. The
best of these annotations reads: 'This speech makes me *twist about*
with boredom', a comment that made Amis laugh 'like a nadir' (that
is, drain).[61]

Armed with Larkin's comments, suggestions and marginal annotations, Amis embarked on the final revision of 'Dixon' in late October,
finishing a little over five months later, on 30 March 1953. On
3 March he wrote listing the new bits he thought Larkin would especially like: 'the madrigal-singing, the Welsh tune ('you *bloody* old
fool'), the phone-interview with Dixon as the reporter, the Johns
letter, Bill Atkinson, Welch and the revolving door, the Principal, and
the faces. I think that there's less HS of A in the Christine scenes,
and I'm pretty sure that there are none of those Bing-Crosby conversations you rightly condemned in the previous version. May I say
again how helpful those comments in the margin of the old MS were?
I've called it *Lucky Jim* now[62] to emphasise the luck theme – epigraph
Oh, lucky Jim, How I envy him *bis*. Bertrand is as *a la* Tosswill as
you could stand now, I hope. I am afraid you are very much the
ideal reader of the thing and chaps like you don't grow on trees,
course not.'

Amis's work on the revision – a remarkable transformation in so
short a time and almost wholly improving – was sped by a sudden
stroke of Dixon-like good fortune. In the potted biographies at the
end of the PEN *New Poems 1952* anthology Amis had mentioned
that he was 'Working on a novel set in a provincial university.'
Hilary Rubinstein, who had known Amis slightly at Oxford, and
who now worked at Gollancz, saw the note and wrote to him on
28 November asking if he might see the novel when it was finished.
Amis wrote back on 8 December saying yes. It 'would never make
an author's or publisher's fortune, but I think it is quite funny; that,
at any rate, is its aim'. He was at work on the final draft 'and should
be able to get it to you in February or March'. By 16 March Amis
had typed just over half of the revised version and by the 30th the
job was done. 'I have just this moment finished my last task on that
Dickson thing,' he wrote to Larkin, 'so that it is all ready to send
to a lot of men who don't know a good thing when they see one,

and by way of celebration am letting you hear the good news at once . . . It comes to 349 pages of quarto, which is about 87,000 words, which is a lot.' There was no time to show Larkin the fully revised and freshly typed manuscript, but Amis had little heart for further tinkering: 'no, or almost no, bugger is going to make me do anything to it ever again'. Nevertheless, it wasn't until 15 April, a day before his thirty-first birthday, that Amis sent it off to Gollancz.

On the birthday itself Amis received confirmation of a second stroke of good fortune. John Wain had recently been appointed producer of a BBC Third Programme series entitled *First Reading*, which was meant to replace John Lehmann's book series *New Soundings*. Lehmann's series had run from 9 January 1952 until 11 March 1953, and a recurring theme of its editorial introductions was the damaging effect, like 'bud blast', current conditions, including post-war privation and the nuclear threat, had on new writers; the writers Lehmann took pride in having promoted were mostly older and already had reputations (Edith Sitwell, George Barker, Vernon Watkins), though he also broadcast poems by younger writers, including Wain.[63] The purpose of *First Reading*, Wain later explained, was 'to move a few of the established reputations gently to one side and allow new people their turn'.[64] Hence his decision to broadcast an extract from *Lucky Jim* in the first programme, though the novel had yet to secure a publisher let alone a date of publication. On the morning of his birthday Amis received a letter from the BBC informing him that a fifteen-minute excerpt of *Lucky Jim* (about 2,000 words) would be broadcast on 26 April. On 16 April he immediately wrote to Rubinstein: 'Since I still believe (in the face of much contrary evidence) that acceptance by the BBC is a recommendation rather than the reverse, I pass this information along in the hope that someone at your end shares my belief.' The extract Wain chose was the bed-burning scene, in which Dixon wakes up in his room at the Welches', still drunk from the previous night, to discover that he's burnt a jagged hole in his bedding, then sets about trying to disguise and hide it, with disastrous results. The scene is one of the funniest in the novel yet Wain chose it for polemical as well as entertainment purposes, as an example of the sort of writing the programme approved. The new writers, he declared at the beginning of the broadcast, 'are suspicious of anything that suggests sprawling or lack of discipline'; though 'keenly aware of belonging to a tradition', that tradition looked beyond 'the last thirty years' and put 'more recent discoveries . . . into perspective'.[65] That these introductory remarks were immediately followed by the *Lucky Jim* excerpt suggested that the novel was, among other things, tough-minded, new, important. In London, Harry Hoff (William Cooper) heard the programme and called to his wife: 'Come and listen to this. Somebody's been reading *Scenes from Provincial Life*.'[66] Two days later Amis received an acceptance letter from Gollancz and on 5 May he wrote to Larkin with the news: 'Good, isn't it? It will be dedicated to you.'

The process of turning 'Dixon and Christine' into *Lucky Jim* was not without its tensions, chiefly those involving the rival claims of art and friendship, art and love. How Amis and Larkin balanced these claims sheds light on their relationship. Larkin helped Amis because Amis was his friend but also because he believed in his talent: 'My general conviction was that Kingsley was quite the funniest writer I had ever met in letters and so on – and I wanted everyone else to think so too.'[67] Larkin not only lent his time and judgement to the revision of 'Dixon and Christine' but seems not to have protested when Amis drew important plot strands from his friend's life, even when these were likely to cause embarrassment. Dixon resembles Larkin in aspects of his relationship with Margaret, a character based on Monica Jones, whose full name was Margaret Monica Beale Jones. It was at Larkin's insistence that Veronica Beale's name in the first version was switched to Margaret Peel. Amis at first wanted it changed to Margaret Jones, but Larkin understandably objected. Larkin seems not to have objected, however, when Amis borrowed Monica's gestures and aspects of her appearance in creating Veronica. Monica, Larkin wrote to his friend Judy Egerton, 'dresses rather specially'.[68] As Andrew Motion puts it, she went in for 'film-star-academic's glasses,[69] and . . . brightly coloured, handmade, unconventional clothes'[70] (black sweaters and brilliantly patterned dirndl dresses, eccentric blouses, fishnet stockings). Amis, of course, was suspicious of all unconventionality in dress, which he saw as affectation (at his first appearance, Bertrand is described as wearing 'a lemon-yellow sports coat, all three buttons of which were fastened, and displaying a large beard which came down further on one side than on the other, half-hiding a vine-patterned tie').[71] In *Lucky Jim* Amis dresses Margaret in a Monica-like 'arty get-up of multi-coloured shirt, skirt with fringed hem and pocket, low-heeled shoes, and wooden beads',[72] an ensemble Jim (always 'James' to her) finds marginally less objectionable than 'the green Paisley frock in combination with the low-heeled quasi-velvet shoes'.[73]

Margaret's affectations, including her laugh like 'the tinkle of tiny silver bells'[74] ('How close we seem to be tonight, James,' she whispers in the pub. 'All the barriers are down at last, aren't they?') make Dixon want to do things like 'give an inarticulate shout and run out of the bar'.[75] The extent to which Monica was like this is open to question, though Larkin once asked Amis: 'you weren't actually there taking notes [of our conversation] were you?'[76] To Amis, recalling her to Motion, there was 'a sort of adhesive thing' about Monica Jones, 'not quite predatory, but still . . . ,'[77] a comment that applies also to Margaret. Margaret is neurotic and unsuitable but Jim cannot extricate himself from their 'relationship' (in quotation marks because he can never quite figure out how or when it started). 'He'd been drawn into the Margaret business by a combination of virtues he hadn't known he possessed: politeness, friendly interest, ordinary concern, a good-natured willingness to be imposed upon, a desire for unequivocal friendship. Then suddenly he'd become a man who was "going round" with Margaret.'[78]

Larkin also had difficulties extricating himself from unsuitable women, unsuitable in Amis's eyes certainly: not just from Monica but from Ruth Bowman. This difficulty Amis mostly saw as weakness or cowardice, but he also saw its connection to decency. 'If Jim is such a slime,' he asked an interviewer, 'why doesn't he tell Margaret to leave, as he could do?' This is a question Anthony Powell ponders in his *Journals*,[79] wondering at the obsolete or Wodehousian character of Jim's attacks of chivalry. To Amis, in the interview, such attacks are motivated by 'responsible concern' ('Bertrand would have no trouble at all getting rid of Margaret'),[80] which is also Christine's view. Jim has been accusing himself and Christine of cowardice:

I'm sticking to Margaret because I haven't got the guts to turn her loose and let her look after herself, so I do that instead of doing what I want to do, because I'm afraid to. It's just a sort of stodgy, stingy caution that's the matter with us; you can't even call it looking after number one.[81]

Jim's account of his behaviour here recalls the ultimately craven and conformist 'Kingsley' in 'The Legacy', though 'stingy' (with emotions as with money) suggests Larkin. Here is how Christine makes the opposing case, the case for responsible concern:

Don't you ever think people do things because they want to do them, because they want to do what's for the best? I don't see how it helps to call doing the right thing caution and lack of guts. Doing what you know you've got to do's horrible sometimes, but that doesn't mean to say it isn't worth doing.[82]

Like all Larkin's girlfriends, Monica was rightly wary of Amis, on the grounds that he was likely to see any romantic attachment of Larkin's as a threat, and any girlfriend as inadequate. She had other reasons for disapproving of Amis; as she told Motion, 'Kingsley wasn't just making faces all the time, he was actually trying them on. He didn't know who he was.'[83] Amis carefully excludes from Margaret's character the intelligence, wit and acuity that helped to draw Larkin to Monica. But his denigration of Monica may also have been inspired by more generous impulses. Amis thought his friend deserved more out of life than he was getting, not just more recognition as a writer but more pleasure, more 'nice things', better things, too. Monica may not have been as bad as Margaret, but Amis thought of her as more trouble than she was worth ('Why do you go around with her such a lot?' he asked in the letter about the Lake District trip),[84] which seems sometimes to have been Larkin's view as well – despite the fact that he was simultaneously writing disparagingly to Monica about Amis.[85] Amis's letters frequently urge Larkin to look elsewhere, to be braver or less reticent with women. Like Larkin, Amis found Winifred Arnott, Larkin's librarian colleague, attractive ('You can tell her I thought she was fine if you like')[86] and encouraged him to pursue her: 'How did the AWA[87] party go off? I'm all agog to hear. You'r a fool if you let that one go by. *What does it matter* if she repels you, I mean repulses you? What ders it *matter*? Nothing venture, nothing AWAWWOOO LEGGO MY P . . .';[88] 'You are mad, you know. I *told* you the bloody woman was interested in you. I think you can take the following things about what she said in her letter as established (H. agrees with me): "It's a sexual reference directed straight at you"';[89] 'Have another go, Jack; don't be put off by this I-thought-we-knew-each-other-better-than-that stuff. Grab her in private next time';[90] 'Pull yourself together about AWA. You think you don't like her because you are afraid of her, see. That's all it is. Plunge your hand into her bosom why don't you.'

That Larkin didn't drop or rebuke Amis over Winifred or over his 'cutting at' Monica in 'Dixon' (the phrase is Amis's to Larkin)[91] is telling. Several years after the publication of *Lucky Jim*, on 24 September 1956, Amis wrote to Larkin after a 'sodding good day' reading over their correspondence. The only passages in the Larkin letters to disquiet Amis were about 'missruth and veronica beale': 'hope you didn't tell those poor girls the awful wounding things you told me'. In the depiction of Margaret, Motion has written, 'the parallels indicate that Larkin must have been astonishingly rude and indiscreet about Monica to allow Amis to suppose he could use this diluted version. Alternatively, they suggest that Amis must have been extraordinarily thick-skinned to think he could create these resemblances and expect his friendship with Larkin to survive.'[92] But Amis had judged his friend correctly. Had Larkin really been upset with the depiction of Margaret he could have protested, as he protested about the character's name; nothing in Amis's side of the correspondence, the only side that survives, suggests that he did. The sole surviving expression of upset over the depiction occurs in one of Larkin's annotations to the 'Dixon' manuscript. Veronica and Dixon are having an argument, in the presence of Bertrand and Christine, about the abysmal level of culture in Hamberton, which Dixon attributes to lack of money and opportunity, a view Veronica derides:

'Oh, spare us the socialism, Julian, for God's sake,' Veronica said with the special grin she reserved to accompany this kind of remark. It showed a very large number of her teeth, one canine slightly flecked with lipstick.

'You don't have to be a socialist to see that,' Dixon said mildly.

'I shouldn't have thought so, either,' Christine murmured, sitting up even straighter in her chair.

Veronica inclined her head farcically. 'I bow down before the protagonists of the welfare state.'

'Ah, enlightenment at last,' Dixon said.

'If the welfare state embodies enlightenment I'm a Dutchman.'

'For a Hollander you talk the English blooding good.'[93]

Next to this passage Larkin wrote: 'This makes me TERRIBLY ANGRY,' and beside its final lines: 'Cut, is my vote.' The source of Larkin's anger is unspecified: he may be objecting to Veronica's

Monica-like grin at the beginning; or the passage's caricature of her (or his own?) right-wing views; or Amis's use of some real-life argument, perhaps recounted by Larkin, perhaps involving Amis himself, on one of his visits to Leicester. Whatever the source of Larkin's upset, the argument disappears in *Lucky Jim*, to be replaced by a related argument Bertrand and Jim have about rich and poor ('If one man's got ten buns and another's got two...');[94] it is Bertrand's and Mrs Welch's rather than Margaret's politics Amis satirises in *Lucky Jim*, though Margaret is said to sing in the local Conservative Club choir.

When Larkin met Monica Jones in autumn 1946, he entered into what Motion has called 'the most important relationship of his life'.[95] From the start, though, his feelings about her, like his feelings about all his women, were ambivalent, particularly in the period 1949–53, when Amis was revising 'Dixon'. This ambivalence played a part in the difficulties Larkin was having with his own fiction in this period and doubtless coloured his feelings about Amis and 'Dixon'. Larkin had published two novels before Amis began work on 'Dixon and Christine', but he would not publish a third. He would not finish a third. Amis started his writing career wishing to be a poet, and became a novelist who had written poems; Larkin started his writing career wishing to be a novelist, and became a poet who had written novels. While Amis was soliciting advice from Larkin, Larkin was abandoning his attempt to write a third novel, portions of which Amis had read. In February 1949, after Amis had begun writing 'Dixon', Larkin began work on a fourth novel, one he seems never to have shown Amis or even told him about. This novel, like 'Dixon', was set in a provincial university town, recognisably Leicester, and had a Monica-like central character, Augusta Bax. Larkin wrote 233 pages of a first draft before abandoning it in December 1949. On 6 July 1953 he wrote to his friend Patsy Strang explaining why he abandoned the novel and was unlikely to take it up again: 'I *can't* write this book: if it is to be written at all it should be largely an attack on Monica, & I *can't* do that, not while we are on friendly terms.'[96]

What survives of the novel are forty or so pages of notes, in Larkin's fiction workbook, plus four fragments or chapters of a revised version, amounting to some seventy-five printed pages (the original 233-page draft has not survived). The revised version, according to its editor, James Booth, was written some time after November 1953 (the last few pages of notes in the fiction workbook are titled 'Further considerations 1953'). Larkin only returned to the novel, then, after 'Dixon' had become *Lucky Jim* and been accepted by Gollancz. Larkin's novel, judging by the notes and the revised fragments, would have differed from Amis's in several respects: it would have been darker, its comedy more muted and intermittent, its central characters more complex, its ending bittersweet at best. According to Larkin's workbook for the novel, Augusta's development or growth was to be its thematic centre: 'Through the course of the action the emphasis in her character shifts from self sufficiency & conceit to an appalled liking for the company of others & a wish to be absorbed in them.' In the surviving fragments, Augusta's affectations and fantasies are especially prominent and her appearance and obsession with clothes 'very close' (Booth's words) to those of Monica herself, as Monica acknowledged when she read the manuscript for the first time in 1999.[97] Augusta is presented as smart, accomplished, cruelly witty but also sad and comical in her self-construction: 'her ideal,' reads one of the early notes, 'is a complete cauterizing of emotion & she plays at being her own grandmother, very county & true blue & practical'.[98] When battered by a series of disappointments, she gives in to the need for companionship, a decision or release about which both she and Larkin have mixed feelings: 'Don't lose sight of her final situation,' Larkin reminds himself in a note, 'of outwardly despising what she clings to.' Presumably the reader was meant to leave the novel uncertain whether the need for others is cowardly ('clinging') or brave (overcoming an upbringing which left her 'unable to get along with others because she was never taught how'). This uncertainty may reflect, among other things, Larkin's own mixed feelings about Monica, feelings Amis may have drawn on when giving Dixon a conscience about Margaret, or when allowing himself to make Margaret insufferable.

One final point of connection between 'Dixon and Christine' and Larkin's unfinished novel is worth noting. Augusta is not wholly friendless. She feels affection for her head of department, himself a pretty waspish character, also fussy and old-maidish. In the revised fragments, the head is up for a professorship, being only 'Lecturer-in-Charge'. If he gets it, 'his life, he felt, would be a success: if not, a failure'.[99] His chances, however, are slim in the extreme, partly because he hasn't written much, especially not recently, partly because he has long been feuding with the Principal, a man named Welsh (who wants his staff to wear gowns, as did Fulton at Swansea). The name Welsh does not appear in the notes and it is possible that Larkin borrowed it from 'Dixon'. He may even have borrowed the theme of a lecturer depending for a job on a boss he hates from Dixon's depending on Professor Welsh. In later years Larkin would sometimes grumble about not being properly credited for the amount of help he gave Amis with *Lucky Jim*. He once told Maeve Brennan, another girlfriend who viewed Amis warily, that Amis had 'stolen' *Lucky Jim* from him. He cannot, though, as has been suggested recently, have meant this seriously.[100] Even if there was evidence, which there isn't, that Amis knew the 'Augusta Bax' novel, or knew of it, and that he borrowed elements from it, he would have been doing so directly under Larkin's eye, and for very different fictional purposes. Larkin may have envied Amis's success with *Lucky Jim* and may even have been inhibited as a novelist by that success – at precisely the time he was coming into his own as a poet, it should be added – but he was not inhibited because Amis had somehow stolen or used up his material.

The help Larkin gave Amis with *Lucky Jim* was crucial to its success, as Amis fulsomely acknowledged, both in public and in private. From the first, Larkin had been instrumental in Amis's development as a writer. As Amis wrote to him in a letter of 27 August 1950, had Larkin not encouraged him as a poet, 'I'm inclined to think I shdn't have tried much more when the war and EAS packed in.' As for fiction, 'The Legacy' 'only got written in response to your suggestions, & without *The leg* there would have been no further prose-words'. But there were other debts: 'Also, dear man, I have to thank you for *stopping me from being a shit* and *encouraging me to be funny* in the right way and *getting me interested in modern po*: (all this in various intangible ways) . . . I felt I had to get this said some time, and hope it hasn't embarrassed you.' Amis had written some 10,000 words of 'Dixon and Christine' when Larkin received this letter. Though Amis may have been indelicate or unfeeling in his treatment of Monica in 'Dixon', this is not an accusation one could make about his treatment of Larkin. In the letter of 5 May 1953 announcing Gollancz's acceptance of *Lucky Jim*, Amis asks about Winifred Arnott. He is 'glad to hear the AWA business has taken a turn for the better' and again encourages Larkin to 'Climb down off that fence.' In an earlier letter he had encouraged Larkin not to despair about his fiction: 'For God's sake keep up on your story. If I can keep on at mine, you can keep on at yours.'[101] Here he replies to the news that Larkin has returned to what he called his 'Leicester novel': 'Glad about your novel, though I've forgotten (if I ever knew) what "the Leicester one" was going to be.'[102] There is no reason to disbelieve him.

Fame and Friendship

Amis was lucky to be published by Gollancz. Among the firm's other authors were George Orwell, Ivy Compton-Burnett, Elizabeth Bowen, Dorothy L. Sayers, Edith Sitwell, Daphne du Maurier, Ford Madox Ford and A.J. Cronin. In addition, it published the monthly titles of the Left Book Club, a creation, in 1936, of its founder and governing director, Victor Gollancz. Rubinstein, Gollancz's nephew, had an eye for talent; his other discovery in 1953 was Nadine Gordimer. Though Rubinstein admired Amis's novel – something Amis suspected Gollancz did not, at least not initially[1] – and was struck straight away by what he called 'its original, underivative humour', he had no inkling of its coming fame: 'It would be lovely if I could say that I recognised a book that was going to set the tone for a decade, but I didn't.' Rubinstein reported some disquiet in the firm about the novel's title, which was thought 'faintly novel-ettish', though Amis's proposed alternative, the original 'Dixon and Christine', elicited little enthusiasm. Rubinstein also doubted, until he got to know Amis, that Jim Dixon would have drunk ten pints of beer at one sitting.[2]

Rubinstein quickly set about securing puffs or supporting quotes for the novel, a common practice at Gollancz, which was known for hard-sell promotion. Gollancz books mostly came in distinctive yellow dust jackets, often emblazoned with excerpted comments from reviewers, or in the case of first-time novelists, pre-reviewers, and eye-catching superlatives ('Sensational', 'Spell-binding') in contrasting inks and typefaces. Amis was uneasy about such hype.

When he finally saw the blurb for *Lucky Jim*, he told Larkin, he was relieved, 'knowing what VG can be like, fearing something like: "Compared by eminent critics to Henry James, Tacitus, Leopardi, Schubert, Carter Dickson and Caravaggio, Kingsley Amis's uproarious, side-splitting, tear-jerking, cock-standing," etc.'[3] When *That Uncertain Feeling*, his second novel, was published by Gollancz in 1955, Amis was especially flattered by 'the omission of blurb and of *Jim* reviewers' quotes. I take that as a gesture of confidence by VG Ltd and it is duly appreciated.'[4] With *Lucky Jim*, necessarily, he was less fastidious. When Rubinstein wrote on 16 June 1953 to say that C.P. Snow had produced 'a really first rate quote' for the novel, Amis was, he wrote back the next day, 'very glad'. Snow had taken over from Charles Morgan in 1948 as lead book critic for the *Sunday Times* and his fortnightly reviews often called for a return to traditional fictional forms and virtues, attacking modernist experiment. Snow's quote read: 'LUCKY JIM is humorous, self-mocking, hopeful and endearing. For promise and achievement combined, it is the best first novel I have read in the last two years.' Four days later, Rubinstein informed Amis that he had secured a second puff: from John Lehmann, the man John Wain had replaced on the radio, early champion, as editor of the periodical *New Writing*, of Auden, Isherwood, Spender and V.S. Pritchett. Lehmann was still a figure of influence in literary circles, in part as prospective editor of the revived *London Magazine*, which published its first number early in 1954. Amis had met him at the PEN party for *New Poems 1952*, the party he was almost too poor to attend, describing him at the time, in a letter to Larkin of 6 June 1952, as 'false and smiling'. Though Amis agreed with Rubinstein that Lehmann's puff was a bit condescending, 'that doesn't matter – the long-haired boys ought to queue up for anything recommended by Mr. New-Writing-New-Soundings'.[5]

Rubinstein also sent copies of *Lucky Jim* to Harry Hoff (William Cooper), a friend of Snow's, who had already been struck by the *First Reading* excerpt in April; to the literary editor of the London *Evening Standard*, Eric Hiscock, who was considering it for the newspaper's 'Book of the Month' selection (a process that helped to delay its publication until January);[6] to J.D. Scott, literary editor of the *Spectator*, who would play a key role in the promotion of Amis's career in several ways; to Anthony Powell, literary editor of *Punch* and a novelist Amis admired; and to *Vogue*, 'always on the look-out for brilliant new writers'.[7] The possibility of publicity in *Vogue* tickled Amis. Siriol Hugh-Jones, the magazine's enthusiastic features editor, loved the novel (while also finding it '*quite* terrifying') and planned to run a short article about it in the November issue, together with an author's photograph. Amis presented himself at the *Vogue* offices on 16 September to be photographed and was then taken off to lunch with Rubinstein and Miss Hugh-Jones, whom he described to Larkin as 'very passionate in agreeing with you'.[8] The resulting photograph in the magazine made him look like a matinée idol.

Amis's advance for *Lucky Jim* was £100, payable upon date of publication, though he managed to secure an early £25 instalment with a begging letter of 20 July. A month later Gollancz succeeded in selling the American rights to Doubleday for an advance of $2,500, and after the November publication date was put back, Amis again begged an advance on the advance: 'about half of the full amount (a good bit over £300?),' as he wrote to Rubinstein on 26 November, 'would just do us nicely, equip the baby with nappies and buy me a couple of drinks and a shirt as well'. After his lunch with Rubinstein and Miss Hugh-Jones, Amis went drinking with John Wain, where he learned ('ho ho') that the combined English and American advances for *Lucky Jim* were nearly twice those Wain had received for his own first novel, *Hurry on Down*, which would be published in August. Wain convinced Amis that he needed an agent and on 17 July 1953 Amis wrote to Rubinstein to say he was now a client of Curtis Brown. He would stay with the agency until 1965, represented by Graham Watson in London and Alan Collins in New York.

Amis was not unknown to J.D. Scott and the *Spectator* when Rubinstein sent them an advance copy of *Lucky Jim* in July 1953. In addition to the *First Reading* broadcast in April, Scott would have known of him through Anthony Hartley, in effect the magazine's poetry editor. Hartley's first review for the *Spectator* appeared on 10 July 1953 and praised Amis's and Wain's contributions to *New Poems 1953*. Hartley had been friendly with Wain and 'vaguely'[9] knew Amis and Larkin at Oxford, where he had read English at Exeter College. In May he had written to Amis offering to 'place' some of his poems for him, presumably at the *Spectator* (though he had connections at other publishing venues).[10] Amis duly sent his poems to Hartley and on 31 July 1953 'Revenge', a poem about innocence, violence and dream, appeared in the magazine. 'Did you see my poem in the Spectator?'[11] Amis wrote to Larkin on 3 August. 'Not a very good one, and I seem to recall you thinking so too, but by me and in the Spectator.' (It was never reprinted.) Amis several times encouraged Larkin to send his poems to Hartley, describing him in the same letter of 3 August as 'one of the Wain entourage so I'm sure he knows about you'. Soon Amis, Larkin and Wain became regular contributors to the magazine's books pages, Amis and Wain eventually as lead reviewers. Soon, also, Hartley and 'the Spectator lot'[12] became frequent London drinking companions.

If, as seems likely, it was Wain who put Hartley on to Amis, the good turn was wholly typical. In addition to featuring *Lucky Jim* on the initial *First Reading* broadcast, Wain arranged for a small booklet of Amis's poems to be published by the University of Reading School of Fine Art. This booklet, *A Frame of Mind* (1953), would be the second in a series of limited editions organised by Professor J.A. Betts of the Fine Art Department, who relied on Wain, a colleague from the English Department, for advice about which young poets to choose. Wain's *Mixed Feelings* (1951) was the first booklet in the series. The association with Wain brought notoriety as well as notice. The polemical tone of the initial *First Reading* broadcast was sounded in subsequent programmes, even amplified, and provoked a reaction among critics, one that would eventually lose Wain his job (he was replaced by Ludovic Kennedy on 24 September 1953, at the end of a six-week contract). Hugh Massingham, radio reviewer for the *New Statesman*, thought the programmes 'deplorable' and mocked Wain's editorial agenda, complaining in an article of 18 July that 'there was something faintly ridiculous in treating young men, whom some of us have never heard of, with the solemnity that should be reserved for Mr. Eliot or Mr. Empson'. The extract from *Lucky Jim* was singled out for censure ('on the strength of two sentences!' Amis complained to Rubinstein).[13] In the following issue, that of 25 July, Massingham returned to the attack, regretting the loss of Lehmann's *New Soundings* and concluding that Wain's series would only convince listeners (as many as 100,000 by some estimates)[14] 'that modern writing is a bore'. This issue also contained responses to Massingham's initial attack, in the form of letters from Wain and G.S. Fraser, 'perhaps the principal poetry reviewer in London',[15] and himself a contributor to the series (though not exactly youthful, having been born in 1915). Fraser had recently published an anthology of new writing entitled *Springtime*, among whose fifty contributors were Amis, Wain, Larkin, Elizabeth Jennings, Donald Davie and Thom Gunn, all soon to be labelled Movement writers. In the introduction to *Springtime* Fraser called them 'Empsonians' and 'Academics', and in his letter to the *New Statesman* he defended Wain's identification of them as leaders of a new and important literary generation, if not quite 'a new Elizabethan era' (the newspaper cliché Wain employed, alluding to the recent coronation, in the third *First Reading* programme):

They [the writers of the new generation] are most typically (Mr. Corke, Mr. Davie, Mr. Alvarez, Mr. Wain himself) young dons, and often young dons in provincial universities. The centre, moreover, of their intellectual universe lies not in London, but in Oxford or Cambridge. In that sense, *we* perhaps look provincial to them. They discuss passionately not what Mr. Toynbee said about Mr. Connolly but what Dr. Leavis said about Mr. Bateson. They think metropolitan urbanity rather hollow and metropolitan smartness rather vulgar. Perhaps, in fact, their attitude towards us is a little like that of D.H. Lawrence towards Bloomsbury.[16]

The *New Statesman* controversy over the *First Reading* programmes played an important part in promoting the sense of new factions and alignments in the literary scene. In Larkin's words, the programmes 'got attacked in a very convenient way, and consequently we became lumped together'.[17] There were subsequent letters from John Lehmann (deploring provincialism) and Fraser again (defending it, by citing George Eliot, Bunyan and Thomas Hardy), with V.S. Pritchett summing up judiciously, on 3 October.[18] Other periodicals joined in. On 16 October in *Truth* George Scott wrote an article entitled 'The Challenges that Face Mr Lehmann and Mr Spender', in which he detected among his contemporaries 'a profound feeling that amounts almost to knowledge that a literary renaissance *is* about to take place, or is taking place now, in Britain'. This renaissance, Scott claimed, looked as if it might be ignored by the newest and most promising literary periodicals, *Encounter*, edited by Spender and Irving Kristol, the first number of which had just appeared, and Lehmann's *London Magazine*, which would not be launched until February. Spender promptly replied in the next issue of *Truth*, that of 23 October, asking Scott to name some of the authors he had in mind, which Scott did in the issue of 30 October. Wain was in Switzerland at the time, recovering from TB, and Amis wrote to him on 6 November, commenting on Scott's list:

George Scott, as you may have seen or heard, gave the boys a write-up in a reply to Spender's reply to his attack on *Encounter*. In a list of 28 white hopes of English letters were featured you, of course, me, of course, Al [Alvarez], Philip L, Mairie [MacInnes], Wallace [Robson] (why him?), Don Davie, Lizzie Jennings, Gunn, George F[raser], and on the debit side Arthur [Boyars], James Firkup [Kirkup], Hilary Corke. It was a full page in *Truth*, of all rags. Love-a-prick Kennedy [Wain's radio replacement] is as bad as you might expect: one can't be more devastating than that. I suppose you get the NS there; if not, Salter ballocked him in this week's, said he was as 'infuriating' as you, but in a different way . . . *Encounter* has been mauled on every side. It's a pity you're away; with you as general, the boys could move right into control. It occurs to me to try an old gag – more for my amusement than yours, I imagine:

JACK WAIN AND THE PROVINCIAL ALL-STARS
Wain (tpt, voc) directing Phil Larkin (clt), 'King' Amis (tmb), Don Davie (alto), Al Alvarez (pno), Tommy Gunn (gtr), George 'Pops' Fraser (bs), Wally Robson (ds).

> Drop me off at Reading/Up the country
> Lay your racket/Things ain't what they used to be
> It's the talk of the town/ How'm I doing hey hey

This was the tone Amis adopted throughout the early manoeuvring and media-jockeying that got the Movement its name. Though he mocked the publicity game, he was willing to play it, partly for reasons of literary principle. As he reminded Wain in the same letter (Wain was threatening to publish no poetry for five years): 'every inch of newsprint we can cover means less for K.R. [Kathleen Raine] and her pals; that's the way to look at it'. Amis openly admitted that he was also motivated by simple egotism: 'I want to get my name in the paper, too.' A third motive, though, almost as strong as those of principle and personal publicity, was a lifelong attraction to groups, gangs, circles, cliques, clubs, clubs within clubs, cabals, collaborations. Wholly typical was Amis's obvious delight at delivering a 'small piece of good news' to Larkin in a letter of 29 June 1953: 'Bateson is printing "Fiction and the Reading Public"[19] in the October issue along with my Beowulf and a thing by Donald Davie . . .'[20] Won't it be nice to be together, dalling, in *E in C*? The Oct. issue will also contain my shelling of Rodgers,[21] so order a copy for all your N.I. [Northern Ireland] litty friends.' Also typical was a scheme Amis seems to have suggested to the Fantasy Press. This press, located in Swinford, near Eynsham, outside Oxford, had been founded in 1952 by Oscar Mellor and produced small selections of poems (six or so per poet) mainly by Oxford and Cambridge undergraduates. The first of its pamphlets was by Elizabeth Jennings; later it published pamphlets by Thom Gunn, Donald Davie, Larkin, Amis and John Holloway – in other words, 'the boys'. 'Shall I try to arrange a quadripartite volume,' Amis asked Larkin on 28 April 1954: '(you, me, D. Davie, Wain) with the Fantasy Press?' Larkin thought not, though several months later Amis tried again: 'Look old man: may I ask you to reconsider your ideas (which I fully, or let's say reasonably well, understand) on not appearing in a Fantasy foursome or sixsome? The names provisionally put forward by this Mellor man are now you, me, John Wain, Davie, Thom Gunn, Donald Hall. The last two are in favour, I gather, also John. Don't know about Davie yet.'

This scheme, which came to nothing, originated several months after the initial critical and commercial success of *Lucky Jim*, as well as the more limited but favourable reception of both *A Frame of Mind* and Amis's individual Fantasy pamphlet. By April 1954, as we shall see, Amis's name was widespread in literary circles. Though 'the boys' had not yet become 'the Movement', a name that would not be applied to them until October, a group identity was forming, one Amis was happy at first to promote. He liked bringing together good chaps (as in Robin Davies's 'thousands of good chaps'); he also, sporadically, liked plotting and scheming. His efforts on behalf of the boys fed a larger, habitual sociability, one that sometimes seemed as important as work. 'My trouble is knowing too many people, too many sods,' he wrote to Larkin on 27 November 1953. 'I feel I need social get-togethers simultaneously with being a Dixonian boredom-detector.'[22] In this respect, he was quite different not only from Larkin but from Wain, for whom literary politics were more a matter of ends than of means. For Amis, means were also ends in literary politics.

Only once, after the Movement got its name, was Amis able to convince Larkin to join him in print in a collaborative poetical effort.

The resulting scheme was thoroughly subversive: a series of eight parodies of Movement poets entitled 'All Aboard the Gravy Train: Or Movements among the Younger Poets', which they hoped to publish under the pseudonym 'Ron Cain.' Amis tried to place the parodies (of Davie, Conquest, Enright, Gunn, Jennings, Wain and the authors themselves) first with Spender at *Encounter*, then with Lehmann at the *London Magazine*. The only copy of the parodies to survive was included in a letter Amis wrote to Larkin on 27 December 1956; the first reference to them occurred in a letter two months earlier, on 24 September: 'I send you All aboard the gravy train . . . It would be nice to get the whole thing off to Spender soon. The only alteration to the text I've made is to put "guessed" for "thought" in wild ones . . .[23] I must say the poems still strike me as good and bloody funny. Hope we can make some money out of them.'[24]

　Money, however, certainly the sort they'd make from the parodies, was less important to Amis on this occasion than mischief, a desire, as he puts it in the letter of 24 September, to 'set the old sods by the ear'. The identity of these old sods is uncertain. Presumably they are anti-Movement critics like David Wright, whose views Larkin disparaged in a letter to Conquest of 5 December 1956:

God what puking riff-raff turned up to root for Wright. I felt inclined to produce a little Dobsonish verse:

> To +++++ ++++++ and others
> Why don't you have a go,
> If you're so bloody clever?
> Why don't you have a go
> At *In Homage to Poe*,
> *Death of Pan*, or whatever?
> Why don't you have a go,
> If you're so bloody clever?

It is also possible, certainly by 1956, that the 'old sods' are Movement supporters rather than detractors, Cadmus-like polemicists who could be lured into disparaging the parodies as tin-eared. When Lehmann and Spender declined to publish the parodies Amis suggested that Larkin send them to his friend George Hartley of the Marvell Press, editor also of the periodical *Listen*: 'We shouldn't get any money from them, but it's a way of getting them into print, and there's always the chance old Fraser will pontificate maladroitly about them and lay himself open.'[25] From the first, Larkin had been suspicious of Movement lobbying. As he wrote to Patsy Strang on 9 October 1954: 'People like Anthony Hartley and G.S. Fraser are very stupidly crying us all up these days: take my word for it, people will get very sick of us (or *them*; that is, Wain, Gunn, Davie, Amis).' Larkin's them/us distinction here is thoroughly Amisian (Amis's exclusion notwithstanding): 'A bloody shame we can't tell them who we'd be rid of if we could,' Amis writes to Larkin on 28 September 1956, apropos of various writers promoting the Movement: 'All except you and me, dalling.'[26] In the end, neither Spender nor Lehmann accepted the parodies, either because they simply did not think much of them, or because the *Spectator* had published a parody the previous year,[27] or because, given prior real or perceived hostility, they wished to avoid the impression either of piling it on or missing the boat (or train). It is also possible that Spender and Lehmann wished to withdraw, if only temporarily (they were editors, after all), from infighting of any sort.[28]

The figure who was closest to Amis in his attitudes to literary politics and collaboration, and who took a comparable pleasure in occasional bouts of mischief and manoeuvring, was Robert Conquest, whom he first met at the PEN party in the spring of 1952. Conquest, soon to be Amis's closest friend after Larkin, was slightly senior to Amis, having been born in 1917. His father was from an old Virginia family and in the American Ambulance Corps with the French Army during the First World War (for which he was awarded the Croix de Guerre at Verdun); his mother was English. Born in Great Malvern in Worcestershire, he was brought up in England and France (he didn't visit the United States until his early thirties, and though he had an American passport until joining the British Army in 1939 and thought of himself as Anglo-American or Anglo-Virginian, culturally he was British). Though there had been money on his father's side of the family, much of it was lost in the Great Depression and as a child Conquest, his sisters, Charmian and Lutie, and his parents lived in a succession of houses and villas rented over the years, some more modest than others (though the family always had 'a cook, a nanny, etc.').[29] He went to school in Malvern, then to Winchester (the fees for which were partly paid by relatives), spent a year at the University of Grenoble (a sort of gap year which also involved travel in Europe, including Bulgaria, home of a friend he had made in Paris), then went to Magdalen College, Oxford, where he read PPE as an Exhibitioner.

Conquest is often cited as influencing Amis's politics. This influence he mostly denies or underplays. Like Amis, he joined the Communist Party as an open member in his first year at Oxford, where he was an undergraduate from 1936 to 1939. This was the CP of Denis Healey and Philip Toynbee and Conquest stayed in it as an open member for eighteen months at most (while also a member of the Carlton Club). He claims never to have been an especially committed party member, a view others have doubted:[30] 'I had girl trouble and it took up too much time.' He also thought a number of his comrades 'bloody fools'. 'When you have a party that is headed by Philip Toynbee,' he told an interviewer in 2003, 'it's not very serious.'[31] He did not turn against Communism completely, however, until he was posted to Bulgaria during the war: 'If you'd been there in 1944–45 you became anti-Communist in a shot . . . They were dreadful and got worse and worse.'

The fact that Conquest enlisted in the Oxfordshire and Buckinghamshire Light Infantry when war broke out underlined his opposition to the Party's neutralist line. He became an intelligence officer for a month or two in 1943 and then won a posting to the School of Slavonic Studies in London to learn Bulgarian. Halfway through this posting he was sent to the Balkans, where he did 'a bit of fighting and patrolling in partisan territory'. In 1944 he was appointed liaison officer to the Bulgarian forces fighting under the Soviets and when the war ended he stayed on in the Balkans as press attaché to the British Legation in Sofia. This was his first civilian job and he stuck with it until 1948, watching the Soviets impose totalitarian rule on the Bulgarians, to whom they had promised democracy. His return to London was not without difficulties, in part because, though already married, he was involved with a young woman, Tatiana Mihailova, whom he helped to escape to Britain. Without this help, she would probably have been 'purged' by the new regime. Tatiana was 'strikingly attractive' (the phrase is Amis's),[32] and once back in London, Conquest divorced his first wife and married her. He also went to work for the Foreign Office, in the newly formed Information Research Department, which had been set up by Attlee's government. The aim of this department, a smaller equivalent of the Political Warfare Executive, was to counter the lies and evasions of Soviet apologists. As Conquest put it in a 1989 article in the *TLS*: 'The struggle to combat the intensive Stalinist propaganda effort was left until 1948 to the Orwells and Koestlers. But Britain's Labour leaders had taken a decision to fight back at home and abroad. At the time, many of us, including myself, were strongly for Labour and its Bevanite left wing – which took the hard anti-Stalinist line until some years later.'

Conquest claims that his work at the IRD, like his subsequent work as an independent historian, was motivated less by ideology than by simple inquisitiveness: 'everything was semi-secret but you could deduce what was going on, the struggles in Moscow and so on. My first book was just finding out what was happening. What is this? Why don't we know this?' When Conquest left the IRD in 1956 to take up a two-year research appointment at the London School of Economics, he did so partly to write a book about Soviet politics: 'I could not get anyone [at the IRD] interested in the obscurer but not (I thought) impenetrable intrigues and manoeuvres within the Kremlin, which constituted all there was of Soviet politics. Strange, for you might have thought this would have been of importance to diplomacy.' The resulting book, *Power and Politics in the U.S.S.R.* (1960), the first of twenty-one books (to date) Conquest has published on Soviet history, politics and international affairs, was 'overwhelmingly a matter of factual investigation and deduction, with very little on the human rights and terror side', though he admits the Soviet leaders don't come out of it particularly well. But even in *The Great Terror* (1968), the work that made him famous, it is the mustering and ordering of evidence, the cool and precise instancing of atrocities, that makes the book so powerful.

When Conquest and Amis became friends in the 1950s, he was no right-wing ideologue or extremist, nor, he would argue, have such labels ever fitted him. Until the rise of Mrs Thatcher in the mid-1970s, he voted Labour. Though passionately anti-Heath in the Conservative leadership struggle of 1975, he thought of his opposition as coming from the left. There is little evidence from the correspondence with Amis of Conquest pushing a political line; it is Amis not Conquest who raises political issues. Amis was further left than Conquest in the mid-1950s, or more conventionally left, which produced what Amis called the occasional 'mild conflict', but he was no supporter of the Soviet Union and readily admitted the truth of Conquest's formulation that 'Generally speaking, everybody is reactionary on subjects they know about.' In the *Memoirs* he recalls Conquest pointing out to him that 'while very "progressive" on the subject of colonialism and other matters I was ignorant of, I was a sound reactionary about education, of which I had some knowledge and experience'.[33] For the most part, though, political questions rarely figured in the early years of the friendship. Amis remembered hearing very little about Conquest's work at the Foreign Office or about his subsequent career as an independent historian and Sovietologist.

The initial points of contact between the two friends were poetry and 'fun'. At the 1952 PEN party, where they first met, Conquest recited to Amis the whole of *Mexican Pete*, a poem he and a school and Oxford friend, John Blakeway, had written in 1939, 'a very long sequel' to the bawdy *Eskimo Nell*. In Conquest's sequel, Pete, the poem's hero, sets out to avenge his erstwhile colleague 'Deadeye Dick', the hero of *Eskimo Nell*, who had suffered, in Amis's paraphrase, a 'total rout and sexual humiliation'.[34] Pete's triumph is partly attributable to what he has learned in 'Bangelstein's College of Sexual Knowledge', where 'It won't be a neuter you'll get as a tutor, but our oldest, randiest priest, / Who knows every appliance of sexual science and the mystic smut of the East' (etc.). In addition to poetry, bawdy parties, literary collaboration and pretty women, Conquest liked drink, though he was never in Amis's league in this respect. After the recitation, he, Amis and Tatiana spent a couple more hours at the PEN party 'laughing continuously and getting very drunk on Dry Martinis'. What Conquest remembers about the evening is how quickly he and Amis hit it off and how neither of them was much interested in meeting the most famous people in the room (supposedly the aim of all young men, according to Stephen Spender).[35] Amis's account of his journey home recalls the aftermath of an earlier epochal or inaugurating moment, his first sherry party at Oxford. He had to get to Abbey Timbers, where he and Hilly were spending the night. The nearest station was Didcot:

[M]y memories of what happened after I left the PEN comprise walking down or up the King's Road, which was incandescent with magic, sitting in a train trying and failing to read the first page of a detective novel I had read the whole of more than once before, and waking with a start to see a sign saying DIDCOT *decelerating* past the window, while two black men opposite stared at me in wonder and concern.[36]

Conquest was and is a brilliant writer of light or comic verse, especially limericks and other 'obscene and disruptive forms'.[37] In the *Memoirs* Amis quotes a number of these limericks, including the following favourite of Philip Larkin's, which Larkin called a 'sure sign of genius – I knew it by heart after one reading':[38]

All the World's a Stage

Seven ages: first puking and mewling;
Then very pissed off with one's schooling;
Then fucks; and then fights;
Then judging chaps' rights;
Then sitting in slippers; then drooling.

Sometimes Amis and Conquest collaborated on limericks. 'Need it be added,' Conquest has written of Amis's part in such collaborations, 'that this sort of activity is the purest, if not the highest creation? No considerations of money or publication apply. It is truly art for its own sake, taking up time which might otherwise have gone into the "next novel." But it may also be thought of as the expression of that superfluity of energy on which a main body of work must subsist.'[39] Perhaps the best-known Amis–Conquest limerick concerns the novelist and critic Brigid Brophy, who had been snide about Amis in a book review:

The first man to fuck Brigid Brophy
Was awarded the Krafft-Ebing Trophy,
Plus 10,000 quid
Which, for what the chap did,
Will be widely denounced as a low fee.

When Larkin sent Conquest an inscribed copy of *High Windows* it read: 'For Bob Il Miglior Fabbro (or whatever it was) – at least over 5 lines.' Amis describes the qualities that made Conquest so good at light verse as 'careful and conscious craftsmanship, the delight in overcoming self-imposed difficulties without apparent effort, gracefully, [and, quoting Anthony Powell,] "a capacity for taking enormous pains in relation to any enterprise at hand"'.[40]

These qualities figure both in Conquest's 'serious' poems and in his historical researches. The second also figures not only in his periodic efforts to defend and promote the new poets (in the letters pages of newspapers and magazines and in anthologies), but in the various games, private and practical jokes and schemings he and Amis delighted in: the invention of characters named 'Tupper', for example, as in 'Emeritus Professor "Stuffy" Tupper and his wife Poppy', an admittedly crude joke ('but harmless') originated by Amis and Larkin and then fantastically elaborated by Conquest, who 'went away and produced a whole enormous family of Tuppers, including Whirly (the helicopter pioneer) and Bangy and Bashy (the wrestling twins)';[41] a suggestive gallery of professions and identities (worked on by Amis as well), 'starting with coke-soaker, kirk-sacker, cox-hooker et al., to add to the series that included far-kin households (the familial arrangements of an Amazonian tribe who abhor any form of intercourse with close relatives, but strike up lasting attachments to cousins and such)' and firkin hassles (over metric and other measuring disputes); and fiendish practical jokes, as when, in June 1956, Amis received an official-looking envelope addressed to 'Lieut. K.W. Amis, R. Signals, Class "B" Reserve Call-up (Malaya)' or, two years later, when Larkin, a devoted fan of girlie magazines, received, as Amis recounts it, 'a letter on government paper, as from the Vice Squad, Scotland Yard . . . the heading, "Regina v. Art Studies Ltd." Proceedings were being taken in the matter of the above, said the writer, under the Obscene Publications Act 1921, also Regina v. Abse (1952) and Regina v. Logue (1957).' Larkin's attendance as a witness 'might be required'.[42] Larkin spent a terrified afternoon at his solicitor's office before realising the letter was a joke. When the solicitor presented him with a bill for £10, he sent it on to Conquest in a letter of 15 March 1958. The letter begins:

You sodding fool. I hope you get a laugh out of the enclosed, wch arrived (at my request) this morning. It isn't a cod; i.e. *somebody's got to pay it.* You can guess whom I have in mind. Why can't you play your japes on David Wright or Christopher Logue or some bastard who wd benefit from a cold sweat or two? Instead of plaguing yr. old pals.

Conquest was uncontrite – Larkin's solicitor should have seen through the joke right away, the Act and the cases were fictitious – but he paid up and Larkin soon forgave him.

Though Conquest had not yet published a book when Amis met him, his poems had appeared in anthologies and regularly in the

Listener (since 1947) and the *New Statesman* (since 1950) and he had won a PEN prize for a long war poem. In 1951 he was also awarded a Festival of Britain poetry prize, along with D.J. Enright, the first of the new writers to become a friend. He was well enough connected in London poetry circles to be asked to co-edit the second PEN anthology, *Poems 1953*, with Michael Hamburger and Howard Sergeant, for which he solicited a contribution from Amis ('Wrong Words'). (When one of Conquest's poems was criticised in October 1952 in the *Listener* Amis wrote in to defend it and to ridicule the attacker.)[43] *Poems 1953* also included contributions from Conquest himself, Enright and Elizabeth Jennings, and in its introduction they and Amis were grouped together, as in Fraser's *Springtime*. Conquest quite liked the poems Amis published in the early 1950s, but he also thought them dry, too much under Empson's influence, a fault they shared with Wain's and Alvarez's poems (Amis's later poetry he valued very highly, in part because it had 'loosened up'). In a draft of his introduction to a second anthology, *New Lines* (1956), which came to be seen as a sort of Movement manifesto, Conquest had originally included an attack on just this quality of dryness, identifying it, ironically, as a 'Movement' fault.

As Amis began coming more frequently to London, to promote *Lucky Jim* or for journalistic or other purposes (lunch with Harry Hoff, Anthony Powell, J.D. Scott, PEN-like literary parties, dinner with the Gollanczes) he and Conquest became fast friends. Soon, on London visits, Amis, or Amis and Hilly, were invited to stay for a night or two in a spare room in the Conquests' small house in Hampstead. Other writers to whom this hospitality was extended included Enright and his wife, Madeleine, Davie, Wain and Larkin, though the Amises stayed 'quite frequently'.[44] Like Amis, Conquest was a generous host and naturally gregarious, but he may also have been seeking distraction from domestic problems; Tatiana was diagnosed with schizophrenia in 1956 and they separated for a time in the middle of the year, though they soon got back together (remaining so until 1958). They divorced in 1962, on what Conquest calls 'goodish terms'.[45] During the resulting periods of Conquest's 'bachelordom in practice',[46] when he was no longer living in the Hampstead house, Amis would sometimes ask to borrow his flat for assignations. On one such occasion Conquest rigged a tape-recorder to the light switch so that when Amis turned it on he heard the words 'Lucky sod', an allusion to Amis's poem 'Nothing to Fear', which begins: 'All fixed: early arrival at the flat / Lent by a friend, whose note says *Lucky sod*.' Conquest several times visited the Amises in Swansea in the mid-1950s; on one occasion he was invited to 'bring wife or Ann Other', a play on the cricket usage A.N. Other (when, unknown to Amis, the name of Conquest's girlfriend *was* Ann). When Hilly, of whom Conquest was very fond, got wind of his facilitating role in Amis's adulteries, he told her: 'I had no choice. I was just fulfilling my duties in the men's union.' Her visible reaction was understanding: 'She didn't show an ounce of resentment.'

When Hartley reviewed Conquest's PEN anthology in July 1953 in the *Spectator*, he took a *First Reading* line, deploring the religiosity, emotionalism and obscurity (that is, non-Empsonian obscurity) of the old guard, the poets of the Forties.[47] The review was part of an overt campaign to identify the *Spectator* with new writers. Partly this campaign was a matter of standards – Hartley was a committed Empsonian – though circulation was also a consideration. In addition, Hartley shared Amis and Conquest's sense of fun. Philip Oakes, another of the young writers he championed, recalls how Hartley 'made no attempt to hide his glee when a malicious paragraph in the *Spectator* irritated some venerable elder. And when we met now and then for a drink he would hint at great plans afoot to create further embarrassment and upset.'[48]

The Hartley review that mattered most to Amis's early reputation was 'Critic between the Lines', which appeared in the *Spectator* on 8 January 1954, three weeks before the publication of *Lucky Jim*. It contrasted two recently published collections of poems, Edith Sitwell's *Gardeners and Astronomers* and Richard Eberhart's *Undercliff*, to illustrate 'the present divided state of poetry'. For Hartley the first of the two main camps into which contemporary poetry was divided 'stems from the early Eliot, passes through the poets of the Thirties (especially Auden and Empson) and ends with our young academic poets, the University Wits (Kingsley Amis and Donald Davie, for example). The second begins with bits of Yeats, bits of Pound and a good deal of outside help from French Symbolists and Rilke. It takes in Dylan Thomas and *The New Apocalypse* to end in what might be called our Neo-Symbolists (Kathleen Raine and others).' The excesses of the University Wits were said to be exemplified in Eberhart's poems, which 'often fall into the bathos of bare statement'; the excesses of the Neo-Symbolists were exemplified by Sitwell, whose verse 'illustrates the consequences of letting imagery rip'.

Sitwell was on a visit to Los Angeles when this review appeared but managed to get a reply in the *Spectator* on 22 January. She accused Hartley of failing to notice that the imagery he complained of as extravagant was in fact adapted from one of John Donne's Sermons: 'Would it not have been wiser for your reviewer, before being quite so impertinent, to have read more widely?' Later in her letter Dame Edith declared: 'I shall, no doubt, be told that little Mr. Tomkins (or whatever his name may be), this week's new great poet, does not incorporate in his work phrases from the past, giving them a twist, and importing new meaning. That is so. But more than one great poet does.' Amis then entered the fray: 'Watch out for my letter, signed "Little Mr. Tomkins," in this coming number,' he wrote to tell Larkin on the 26th: 'Have you read the Sitwell stuff in the current one? Filthy *underbred plebeian guttersnipe*, eh?' Amis's letter appeared in the issue of 29 January, the week *Lucky Jim* was published. It began: 'As last week's great new poet, I was very glad to see that letter from Doctor Sitwell telling Mr. Anthony Hartley that it's okay for great poets to copy bits out of dead writers.' It ended by referring to lines Hartley had most objected to ('Where the wine like peridots and beryls / rises in the budding fig branches'): 'Personally I think the sap of a tree is more like Double Diamond than peridots and beryls. It just shows how we great poets differ.'

Amis's Tomkins letter was not the only one elicited by Hartley's review. On the same date both Wain and Elizabeth Jennings wrote in to defend it, in particular its concluding call for a compromise between the two camps. Among the responses in the next week's issue, that of 5 February, was a second pseudonymous letter, not by Amis, signed 'PERIDOT AND BERYL', which wondered if 'all Dr Sitwell's poetry, as well as the bits in which our names are given, [are] bits copied from dead writers?' On the 19th, Sitwell herself replied, again from California, declaring that 'the same wearisome person' must have written the two pseudonymous letters: 'Both letters have the same theme song and are sung in the same distinguished style.' She concluded on a conciliatory note, however, one rich in unintended irony: 'Mr. Hartley and I have at least one thing in common. I gather he admires the work of Mr. Kingsley Amis. I have not, as yet, read Mr. Amis's poetry, but I have read his most remarkable, most distinguished first novel *Lucky Jim* with enthusiastic admiration.'

Sitwell was one of Gollancz's authors and he had sent her a copy of the novel. Hartley and J.D. Scott at the *Spectator* were delighted: here was just the sort of publicity they craved, with more in the offing; Amis was delighted, too, but he was also embarrassed, especially as Dame Edith had written to him personally to praise *Lucky Jim*. These developments he described in a mock cable to Rubinstein on the 15th:

FLASH – EDITH SITWELL WRITES FROM SUNSET BOULEVARD TO THANK AUTHOR FOR LUCKY JIM STOP HAS READ IT TWICE IN TEN DAYS STOP QUOTE BORN WRITER STOP BRILLIANT STOP I DO NOT REMEMBER WHEN I HAVE READ A MORE VITAL AND VITALISING FIRST WORK IN PROSE STOP UNQUOTE AND MORE IN SAME STRAIN INCLUDING INVITATION TO LUNCH WHEN SHE NEXT IN LONDON STOP SENSATIONAL DEVELOPMENTS WILL FEATURE IN CORRESPONDENCE COLUMNS S P E C T A T O R THIS WEEK STOP ORDER YOUR COPY NOW STOP WILL BE GREAT FOR PUBLICITY BUT EMBARRASSING FOR SELF STOP FOR GODS REPEAT GODS SAKE KEEP ALL THIS QUIET STOP YOU WILL SEE WHY WHEN S P E C T A T O R APPEARS BT SWANSEA DTO 160945 BT IMMEDIATE GPS 118 AR AR KKKK

Amis and the *Spectator* had differing views on how best to respond to Sitwell's public letter. Amis wanted to 'make decent amends to old ES for being Little Mr. Tomkins', he told Larkin, since she'd praised him 'both privately and publicly'. Hartley and Scott, with whom, he also told Larkin, he'd been conferring by telephone from Swansea (a status indicator, like announcing 'got myself an accountant now, you sam')[49] wanted him to 'laugh it off' rather than apologise. But he didn't want to laugh it off, and not only because Sitwell had praised him: 'Feel I shall put my foot in it, get branded as mean sod, bloody fool,' he complained to Larkin. Then, with genuine exasperation: 'Fuck them; why won't they let me be humble?'

In the end Amis produced a letter that satisfied all parties. It concluded: 'A writer at the outset of his career can rarely hope for such generous praise as that contained in the last paragraph of Dr. Sitwell's letter. I am sincerely grateful to her. At the same time I feel I should point out that I myself am "Little Mr. Tomkins." Yours faithfully, Kingsley Amis.' In private, he wrote more 'humbly'. Sitwell responded generously; when she returned to London the Amises were duly invited to lunch, an account of which Amis offered Larkin in a letter of 8 July: 'Had a corking fine lunch with my pal the Dame,' is how the account begins. Among the other guests were 'a man called Mister John Pope-Hennessy and an other man called Mister James Pope-Hennessy: as fine and select a brace of turds as you could hope to find anywhere'.[50]

By 15 February, the date of Amis's cod-telegram to Rubinstein, *Lucky Jim* had been out for three weeks, had sold 7,500 copies, and was already in its fifth impression ('quite modest impressions', Rubinstein admitted, 'not of the Daphne du Maurier class yet, I am afraid – but pretty nice all the same').[51] Reviews of the novel, of which there were a gratifying number, were almost uniformly positive. Gollancz had been right to favour January publication; as fewer books were published then, reviews were easier to come by. Anthony Powell in *Punch* called Amis 'the first promising young novelist who has turned up for a long time';[52] John Betjeman in the *Daily Telegraph* called *Lucky Jim* the funniest novel he had read since *Decline and Fall*;[53] *The Times* found it 'genuinely comic'; the *Spectator*, unsurprisingly, thought it 'very funny'.[54] Only the review in the *Sunday Times* by the novelist Julian Maclaren-Ross (the model for 'X. Trapnel' in Powell's *Dance to the Music of Time*) took the Massingham line, calling Dixon an 'ignorant buffoon' and accusing Amis of confusing 'farce with comedy, schoolboy grubbiness with wit'.[55] Typically, Amis reported to Larkin, the *Sunday Times* review was the only one Daddy B had seen (until he came across the review in 'the *News Chron*, the only other unfavourable one').[56] Amis's own parents' reaction, he reported in a letter of 15 March to his cousin John Amis, was 'to the very word' what John had predicted: 'morbid and sordid ran their refrain, though tremendously good as well of course'.

It was Larkin's reaction that mattered most. 'Nice of you to be saying all those nice things about the results of my spare-time literary activity,' Amis wrote to him on 23 January: 'Glad above all that *Jim* is satisfactorily funny. I want it to be other things as well, but if it can only be one thing then that's the one I'd have picked.' Though people praise books for all sorts of reasons, that Larkin was genuine in his enthusiasm for *Lucky Jim* is suggested by a letter Montgomery wrote to him on 13 February: 'You were quite right . . . *Lucky Jim* is a wonderful book, and what interests me about it is that it's not *only* stupendously funny, it's a great many other things as well – an unexpectedly rich and many-sided job . . . God, how I laughed. Queer, isn't it, to think that a friend of ours should have written such superb stuff. Talk about entertaining angels unawares.' John Wain's reaction was also enthusiastic: 'I have never read such a consistently *enjoyable* book,' he wrote to tell Amis just after publication; it 'made me, time after time, stop reading to scream with laughter'.[57]

Now began the days when, as Amis put it, 'the postman became a welcome visitor'.[58] A cheque for £388 arrived from Doubleday, the remainder of the American advance, or most of it. Victor and Ruth Gollancz wrote to invite the Amises to London for a party. Two more cheques arrived from Gollancz and 'a great feeling of *bonhomie* swept through me as I took them out of their envelopes'.[59] Amis and Hilly bought new clothes, then a television, then a three-speed turntable for the gramophone (later they bought a car, the green Morris Minor Michael Garcia remembers Hilly driving straight over roundabouts). Rubinstein wrote informing Amis about enquiries over film rights. In April the Boulting Brothers took out an option on *Lucky Jim* for £200 (which meant Amis would get £2,000 if the film was made). Amis reported to Larkin that Hitchcock was considering directing it. The BBC began writing with requests to appear on various arts programmes. Amis appeared in a panel on poetry at Oxford, with C.S. Lewis, among others. Anthony Powell invited him to review for *Punch*. His photograph appeared in *Vogue* (the matinée idol one, delayed to coincide with publication) and *Tribune*. Fan mail began arriving: the critic and anthropologist Geoffrey Gorer, whom he'd never met, wrote to say that it had been 'a number of years since I have so enjoyed and admired a first novel';[60] Ken Tynan wrote in similarly complimentary terms. No letters had yet arrived from 'cultural nymphs', he complained to Larkin, though he had received one 'from a boy at school I wanted to bugger; too late now'.[61] On 29 March he told Larkin that he'd heard from Elisabeth Simpson, his wartime love: 'The familiar writing still had power to make me pant and tremble slightly. The text was very short beginning "Dear Bill" and ending "Sincerely, Betty Simpson" and consisting largely of the sentence "May I congratulate you on the publication of your first novel – I think perhaps I may."'[62] 'If I'm a writer,' Amis had complained to Larkin on 9 December, with publication still weeks away, 'why don't rich hostesses cultivate me? Why don't people write to me asking me to write things for them, commissioning film-scripts etc.? Why am I not competed for by

Christ by beautiful, imroal soal oral oral intercourse – moral girls? Who does me this, ha?'[63] Less than three weeks before publication Amis wrote to Larkin again: 'What I want, cully, is a chance to decide, *from personal experience*, that a life of cocktail parties, cars, week-ending at rich houses, wine, night-clubs and jazz won't bring happiness. I want to *prove* that money isn't everything, to *learn* that pleasure cloys.'[64] He was to get his chance.

12

Uncertain Feelings

On 25 January, publication day, Amis took Hilly out to dinner at the Bush pub and restaurant in Swansea. When he ordered a bottle of Veuve Clicquot the waiter asked: 'Can you afford it, boy?' He could. The celebration was only in part for *Lucky Jim*. A week earlier Hilly had given birth to Sally Myfanwy Amis, their third child,[1] born on 19 January at 2.05 a.m. at home, with the assistance of a midwife. 'When I started having Sally,' Hilly remembers, 'it was at night and we hadn't got a telephone.' Amis had to go to a callbox to contact the midwife, but it was dark and he was frightened: 'When he was anxious,' Hilly explains, 'he'd go for Martin because Martin was the calmest of the three.' So Amis went to the boys' bedroom and picked up Martin, who was four, and took him, huddled up in a blanket, to the callbox: 'Martin was asleep and unaware at the time. Philip would have been more startled at being woken up in the night. Martin was far more relaxed.' Just before the baby appeared, the midwife sent Amis downstairs to boil a kettle of water. When he returned, he recalled to Larkin,

H. was breathing gas and air pretty fast and a pink fuzzy head had begun to appear. I went quickly downstairs and read a page of *Lucky Jim* with great attention. After 2–3 minutes there was the sound of a baby crying. That was that; H. is very fit, apple-cheeked as ever, and very pleased with herself for producing a girl. So am I. The baby is quite hefty and looks no worse than might be expected. Rather better, really. I hope she has a lovely childhood and has a lovely time at school and makes a lot of lovely chums and brings them home. A girl ought to think she can bring her friends in and introduce them to her parents.

This passage, with its joke vision of Sally's 'lovely childhood', inspired Larkin's poem 'Born Yesterday' (its other inspiration was Yeats's 'A Prayer for My Daughter'), subtitled 'for Sally Amis' and dated 20 January 1954:

> Tightly-folded bud,
> I have wished you something
> None of the others would:
> Not the usual stuff
> About being beautiful,
> Or running off a spring
> Of innocence and love –
> They will all wish you that,
> And should it prove possible,
> Well, you're a lucky girl.
>
> But if it shouldn't, then
> May you be ordinary;
> Have, like other women,
> An average of talents:
> Not ugly, not good-looking,
> Nothing uncustomary
> To pull you off your balance,
> That, unworkable itself,
> Stops all the rest from working.
> In fact, may you be dull –
> If that is what a skilled,
> Vigilant, flexible,
> Unemphasised, enthralled
> Catching of happiness is called.

Amis received his copy of 'Born Yesterday' on 23 January and wrote back immediately: 'Sodding good and touching was the poem, moving me a good deal as poem and as friendship-assertion. I think it's about the nicest thing anyone could do for any new-born child.' Hilly wrote as well, on the 26th, calling it 'the most beautiful personal poem I've ever read'. She would 'put it in my special box of letters

& things, to keep for her. It's the nicest possible thing you could have done.' The poem was later printed in Larkin's collection *The Less Deceived*, aptly, given the way it wishes 'something / None of the others would: / Not the usual stuff'.

In addition to praise and thanks for 'Born Yesterday', Hilly's letter to Larkin shared something of Amis's excitement at this period. As she later recalled of their good fortune: 'I was thrilled, absolutely overjoyed. I couldn't *believe* it was happening.' The letter also makes clear a touching personal motive for the pleasure publication brought: 'this month has been so full of good things happening that I'm still in a daze, it's such a lovely relief to me to think that in spite of marrying and having got kids Kingsley has managed to write "Lucky Jim" – I always had a fear that I might have buggered it up for him one way & another' ('one way & another' is a characteristic Hilly locution, like 'the world was my lobster').

That Amis at times felt trapped by domestic life is clear from *That Uncertain Feeling*, the novel he was at work on when Sally was born. In the letters, domestic complication is treated almost exclusively as an occasion for comedy, as when he writes to Rubinstein that 'as far as I can make out only three of the kids who rush yelling in and out while I'm working belong to me. Though of course one can never be absolutely sure' – a remark to which we shall return.[2] Though they were no longer living in a flat on the Mumbles Road amid squalling babies and soaking nappies ('just like in *That Uncertain Feeling*', Hilly told an interviewer in 1958) domestic life was still crowded and disorderly, especially in the period when Hilly was heavily pregnant and another family, that of their friend Tom Brennan, came to live with them for 'a month or two'. Brennan had arrived in Swansea just after the war to direct the Social Survey of South-West Wales (1949–53) and to head the college's Research Department for Social and Economic Sciences. His number two on the project was Eddie Cooney, with whom Hilly had had a brief affair. The Amises took the Brennan family in when funding ran out for Brennan's post and his unit was disbanded. During their stay, Amis wrote to Larkin on 7 October 1953, there were 'five children about instead of just the two. The man, Tom Brennan is a Yorkshireman of about 35 . . . [H]e talks away the material for half a novel every evening. His wife, of course, is Tecky [her maiden name was 'Teck'], which is all very well. His second son, Mark, I should like to saw slowly to pieces, jeering at him all the time . . . Life is all right really, but I sometimes wish my wife had had her baby, so that her tummy wouldn't be sticking out the way it does.'³ In a letter of 15 December, Amis again joked about what must have been a pretty chaotic domestic set-up. He told of an episode involving a crowded bathroom. Desperate to get to the loo, Amis flung open the door to discover 'my wife [eight months pregnant] and my younger son in the bath and my elder son about to climb into it. Not much of a sight for a man trying to get a lobster out of his arse, hey? Still, I had them out of there pretty blunt, I mind telling you.'⁴

When Amis announced to Larkin, in an earlier letter of 9 June 1953, that 'Sally' was on the way – Martin was also 'Sally' before his birth – he professed himself unbothered, 'except in so far as it may diminish the amount of what they call French dinner-wine drunk by me'. This air of easy unconcern recalls a letter written several weeks earlier, on 26 May: 'No, my wife's boy-friend [not Cooney] isn't anyone you know. He has very nearly stopped being it now. They don't seem to last long with Hilly. By the way, keep your old mouth buttoned about this if you will; not that it really matters, I suppose.' A resigned tone can also be heard beneath the humour with which Amis discusses his own extra-marital flings, as in the remark, quoted in the previous chapter, about 'that old winged boa-constrictor, sex . . . looking for a good shit-marsh to drop me into'.⁵ Amis had no illusions about the trouble succumbing to his desires would cause him, but this was no guarantee of wisdom or restraint. In a letter of 27 November, for example, he informs Larkin he has sex all figured out:

The only reason I like girls is that I want to fuck them, which is adolescent, cheap, irresponsible, not worth doing, a waste of time, not much fun anyway really, a needless distraction from my real vocation, destructive of any real power of understanding women which as a novelist HOOHOO should be important to me, contemptible, something I shouldn't be at my age and as a married man, liable to make me a laughing-stock, narrowing, impracticable, destructive of real sexual pleasure in the end, something originating in my upbringing, neurotic. All I have to do now is stop wanting to fuck girls and I shall have the thing licked.

As in many instances in the correspondence with Larkin, the joke is elaborately worked, but it describes a serious problem for Amis, as for John Lewis, the hero of *That Uncertain Feeling*. It also describes a serious problem for Amis's wife, as for John Lewis's wife, though Hilly, a real not a made-up person, was both more vulnerable and bolder than Jean Lewis, who only pretends to be involved in an affair which Lewis, for his own complicated reasons, half welcomes. Hilly may have been almost as domestically burdened as Jean in *That Uncertain Feeling* – the Amises' Swansea friends instantly identified Jean's situation as Hilly's – but she was also prepared, at moments, to follow Amis's lead, not just in drinking and flirting, but in sexual promiscuity and experimentation, taking lovers, sleeping with friends or the partners of friends, engaging in various couplings, including, at least once, a threesome.

Out of one of these couplings grew Amis and Hilly's belief, firm though never corroborated by tests, that Sally was not Amis's child. This belief, based on Sally's looks, was shared with close friends, and, remarkably, known by Martin and Philip in their early adolescence, though Sally herself never knew or suspected anything, nor, according to Hilly at least, did she or Amis ever say anything to the supposed father, who remained a friend. Neither Hilly nor the boys themselves can remember how the boys found out; Philip always assumed he'd heard it from his mother, though Hilly remembers being shocked when he turned to her and asked, after the man had left the house, 'What's Sal's Dad doing here?' How Hilly could be so certain about 'Sal's Dad' is suggested by an eerily analogous certainty recounted in *Experience*, her son's memoir, when an adult Martin showed her a picture of the two-year-old daughter he suspected, rightly as it would turn out, he had fathered with a married woman at the time separated from her husband:

—What do you think, Mum? I said, as she snatched the photograph from my hand.
— . . . *Definitely.*
—What should I do?
—Nothing. Don't do anything, dear.

Amis himself treated Sally as his own child and never expressed the slightest doubt about her identity as his daughter in his correspondence, even in the letters to his most intimate friends, even when, in later years, they recounted the calamities of Sally's adult life. Only in retrospect can one make anything of the phrase quoted above, from the letter of 8 May 1955, that when it comes to a child's parentage 'of course one can never be absolutely sure'. Sally was an alcoholic who, in effect, drank herself to death at the age of forty-six, the sort of alcoholic who needs frequently to be rescued and rehabilitated, who drops out of sight only to turn up in hospital or a police station. The anxiety and energy expended upon such a person by those who love and care for her can fray and infuriate; that no member of the family, including her brothers in their adolescence, ever said anything to her about her 'father' is remarkable, a tribute both to them and to her, to her vulnerability and absence of malice. Only once, late in life, when he and Sally were at their closest, did Amis comment publicly on her situation, in a thinly disguised fictional portrait, one that alludes in a coded fashion both to Sally's supposed parentage and to its effect on his feelings for her.

Beneath its easy manner, *The Folks That Live on the Hill* (1990) is a teasing and risky novel. Its hero, Harry Caldecote, lives in the same street in Primrose Hill (Regents Park Road) as Amis lived in for the last ten years of his life. Out of his front window he can see a wine store named Potandum; out of Amis's front window he could see a wine store named Bibendum. His local pub, just up the road, is the King's; Amis's local pub, just up the road, was the Queen's. During the working week Harry lunches at his club, the Irving, along the road from the Garrick, where Amis lunched most weekdays. There are other such parallels and when in his biography Jacobs described Amis's life in Regents Park Road as 'in its mood as well as much of its detail very like the circumstances of Harry Caldecote',[6] Amis did not demur (as he did elsewhere in the margins of a draft copy of the biography Jacobs gave him to vet). When Anthony Powell read the novel he was immediately struck by the chances, autobiographical rather than artistic, Amis took.[7] Powell had in mind the depiction of Harry's brother, Freddie, whom he thought was modelled on Amis's friend and neighbour in Primrose Hill, the biographer and historian Peter Quennell. This depiction is not exactly flattering, though it is nothing like as unflattering as that of Freddie's domineering wife, Désirée, whom others in Amis's circle identified as modelled on Quennell's wife, Marilyn (Harry had been at Oxford with Désirée, as Amis had been with Marilyn). That *The Folks That Live on the Hill* was dedicated to Peter Quennell, Powell recorded in his journal, 'at once aroused thought that this might be to alleviate Quennell's own appearance in the novel. Perhaps an unworthy suspicion.'8 Another Primrose Hill neighbour of Amis's, though not part of his circle, Selina Hastings, reported to Powell an incident in the local hairdresser's, which he recorded in a subsequent journal entry: 'Marilyn Quennell brought in Peter (almost hand-cuffed to her), saying "Will you cut its [*sic*] hair. Get rid of those whiskers and those disgusting hairs in the nostrils." She then left. Peter settled in chair, attended by new, somewhat unpolished assis-tant, who said: "Allo, Peter, 'aven't seen you for some time. 'Ow've you been?" No reply. "Seen anything of Kingsley lately?" No reply. "You write books too, don't you?" No reply. "What are they about?" "I'd rather have my hair cut without conversation."'9

Powell is not suggesting that Freddie is Peter or Désirée is Marilyn, only that Amis has drawn them close enough to the Quennells to risk causing offence. Often in the later novels, Amis seemed to enjoy causing offence, as he did in real life. More remarkable than the portraits of Freddie and Désirée, though, is the portrait of Fiona Carr-Stewart or Fi, an alcoholic whose life is as close to Sally's at the time the novel was written as Harry's was to Amis's. Presumably Amis thought she'd never read it, a calculation he seems to have got right. Fiona lives in a council flat near Primrose Hill, as did Sally. She has an unsuitable Irish boyfriend, as did Sally. In periods of sobriety, she tries to help people out with errands and shopping, as did Sally. The novel is full of unsentimental sympathy for Fi's situation. When asked why she drinks she replies: '"Well, one answer is I start feeling too frightened not to. The other is just I don't know." "What are you frightened of?" "The only answer is that I really don't know."'10 The degrees of Fiona's unhappiness are care-fully observed: 'at this stage she only felt miserable and ashamed and no use to anyone instead of absolutely awful'.11 Though pathetic, Fiona is not all innocent suffering: 'she kept her head down in further pretended humility while she waited to be let out';12 'if Fiona had been drunk she could have coped with this [a woman's intrusive enquiries], nipped it in the bud, had a wonderful time in fact, bashed the slag if it came to it'.13

Fiona is Harry's ex-wife's niece but much is made in the novel of how he treats her like a daughter. Like Amis at the time of writing, Harry is single, after two failed marriages, and outwardly seems free of responsibility, except for what Désirée calls 'that wretched dipso-maniac creature he has to keep pulling out of doss-houses'. As

Freddie says, though, Fi is 'no actual legal concern of his, as you frequently remind him'.[14] Earlier in the novel there is a reference to the question of inherited characteristics. Harry considers the idea that Fi's alcoholism is genetic, passed down from some distant relative she shares with her Great-Aunt Annie, who died of a liver complaint (cirrhosis, Fi suspects). Fi has seen a photograph of Great-Aunt Annie that looks just like her, but Harry discovers another photograph that looks quite different: 'You see? Not you . . . Not your lineage, not your branch of the family, not somebody who inherited something along with you, not your blood, not your stock. So you're not hemmed in by your ancestry. You can step out of it. It isn't you after all.'[15] The issue of Fi's 'stock' plays in Harry's mind and it is hard not to see it as growing out of comparable questions about Sally's stock. 'What you put into fiction isn't the things that happen to you,' Amis has written, 'it's [what] the things that happen to you make you think up.'[16] In Fi's case, Harry knows, a mistaken notion of lineage sometimes makes her feel doomed; there is no evidence that Sally felt comparably doomed by her inheritance. It seems likely that Harry's protective feelings towards Fi resembled Amis's for Sally. 'In the last years of his life,' Martin Amis has written, '[my father] told me that in his most defenceless insomnias he tended to worry about Sally and what it would be like for her when he was dead: the loss of general support, the loss of purpose, of *raison*.'[17] Whether Amis was secretly, if only very slightly, pleased with himself, with the 'disinterested' nature of his worry, as is Harry, is impossible to say. Amis presents Harry as 'a recognisably Fieldingesque good man', in the words of the critic Robert Bell, 'not only decent but actively benevolent';[18] an element of wish-fulfilment is at work in the novel. But Amis is also unflinching about both the severity of Fiona's problems and the possibility that someone could or should have done something more about them; an element of self-punishment is also present. 'Whoever it was let this happen,' says the aged neighbour she often helps, 'whoever brought her up so called, that's who I'd like to get my hands on.'[19]

That Uncertain Feeling was published a year and a half after *Lucky Jim* and played a crucial role not only in establishing Amis as the best-known and most controversial of new writers but in giving these writers an identity. It also offers a glimpse of something very like the non-academic side of the Amises' social circle in Swansea.

The plot of the new novel occurred to Amis while he was still at work on *Lucky Jim*; an eight-page, single-spaced synopsis and analysis of characters has survived, dated September 1952. The first reference to the novel in the letters, however, does not surface until around the time Gollancz accepted *Lucky Jim*. 'What do you do when you've run out of backgrounds?' Amis asked Larkin on 26 May 1953. 'I've done Berkhamsted and carledge life, I won't do Oxford, the Ormy is more or less out of the question . . . which leaves only bourgeois life in Swansea, and that's really too boring to do.' By 3 August, he had begun writing, though as he complained to Larkin, 'everything that has happened in it so far is boring'.[20] Two weeks later he was progressing slowly but steadily, he reported to Rubinstein.[21] By the end of the summer progress was more rapid: he hoped to get 'about ½'[22] done before term started and on 6 November informed Rubinstein that he had reached page 154. Then he hit a snag. On 29 December he wrote to Larkin that the novel was 'turning out *disastrously short*; only 65,000 this draft, which will mean filthy descriptive padding I suppose and probably a scene "written in," a sure ticket for beng borng'.[23]

Amis began a second draft of *That Uncertain Feeling* in the New Year. As he told Rubinstein on 17 January 1954: 'This is the final draft and as before is progressing swiftly.[24] I thought I could do it in one draft, but it seems I am a two-draft man and must just accept the fact. I hesitate to give you a date, but some time in March, if things go well.' In fact, he would not produce the manuscript until February 1955, almost a year later than expected. Partly the delay was a matter of how busy he had become. As soon as *Lucky Jim* was published, Clive Gammon remembers, 'he had to write down in a book that he'd see you on Thursday'. Much of what occupied him was journalism. In early February Amis was appointed fiction reviewer for the *Spectator*, which meant producing a round-up review every two or three weeks. In the eleven months remaining in 1954 he reviewed seventy-five novels for the magazine, often covering three or four novels per review. Amis was daunted at first: 'Reading other men's reviews I'm dismayingly struck by how clever they are and how much they know; mine'll be a 4th form effort: This book is quite good, I enjoyed reading it. It is about a man who gets caught up in bum.' His fears proved groundless. When a press-cutting agency sent Anthony Powell a short extract from Amis's first *Spectator* review, a comparison of books by Wodehouse and Thurber, because it contained a well-disposed remark about him, Powell, who had no idea who 'Kingsley Amis' was, thought 'the style seemed so assured that I suspect[ed] a *nom de guerre* masking an experienced contributor, possibily even a vehicle for several persons to write anonymously'.[25] Soon, as Paul Fussell puts it, 'other critics and commentators were imitating the no-nonsense, can-the-bullshit tone'. Fussell also credits Amis with 'bringing to non-academic criticism a refreshing focus on literature itself as the subject of interest – rather than on literature as an auxiliary to politics, ideology or manners'.[26] To Karl Miller, who edited the books pages of the *Spectator* at the end of the 1950s, the literary criticism of the post-war period was 'as judicial, as fault-findingly ambitious, and as youthfully and generationally vengeful, as any there has ever been',[27] and Amis was at its heart: 'To the older literati he was his jokes and sneers and funny faces, a low and vulgar fellow – which helped to endear him to readers of his own age. To his friends he seemed gifted, abrasive, condignly abusive, enjoyable, engrossing. He was the glamorous beauty of his circle. For me, as the receiver of his typescripts, he was the complete contributor: punctuation-perfect, presentation-perfect, no chink for subbing to climb in and vent itself.'[28]

That Amis found it hard to teach a full load, read and review several novels a fortnight, sleep with every woman he fancied, drink as many drinks as he could, go to all the parties he could, and finish *That Uncertain Feeling* is understandable. Hence, his impatience with longer novels: Saul Bellow might have his virtues, Amis grudgingly admitted in an omnibus review of 21 May 1954, but *The Adventures of Augie March* 'claims our attention for two and a half times the number of words usually offered';[29] Doris Lessing might be an author 'of obvious intelligence' but *A Proper Marriage*, reviewed on 8 October 1954, is 'pumped up into a piece of stodge as long as two novels . . . Even the author of *The Bostonians* . . . might have been expected to get a situation or two under way in 150,000 words.'[30] Amis's impatience in his fiction reviews with anything that retards narrative often connects to a distrust of modernist or experimental writing, but not always. He was caustic about Bellow ('behind [the hero] is Mr. Bellow, right in there pitching with his gaiety and good humour, his fizzing dialogue, his vitality') because *Augie March* was one of four novels he had to read and review in a fortnight, though effortfulness was a complaint he made in less pressured contexts about Bellow's prose.

Being too busy was only part of the reason Amis had difficulty finishing *That Uncertain Feeling*. Fear of failure also played its part. On Boxing Day in 1954, writing in the *Sunday Times*, C.P. Snow called *Lucky Jim* 'one of the three or four greatest critical and popular [fictional] successes of the last twenty years', a comment he was later to qualify by saying he meant among first novels.[31] Even with this qualification, such a comment might inhibit. A month earlier, in the Christmas Books number of the *Spectator*, Amis himself briskly stoked expectations, in the form of 'a few disconnected observations about the hundred and fifty or so novels I have read, or started to read, in the course of the year'. These novels Amis divided into two categories: 'the run-of-the-mill novel, often by a woman author' and 'the more ambitious effort, usually by a man'. Each had its distinctive strengths and weaknesses: 'To the first sort of novelist one wants to say "Do something harder"; to the second "Do something properly."' Presumably *That Uncertain Feeling* would show how to do both. Then there was Amis's prominence in the controversy surrounding 'the Movement', which had at last got its name, thanks to J.D. Scott's anonymous literary leader, 'In the Movement', published in the *Spectator* on 1 October 1954. Scott's article drew heavily on earlier controversy, particularly that generated by Hartley in a *Spectator* article of 27 August, 'Poets of the 1950s'; by an anonymous *TLS* Commentary piece of 24 September, 'Everyman's Poetry', which named Amis as well (and which he rightly guessed had been written by G.S. Fraser); and by Wain's *First Reading* programmes and subsequent controversy. By the time Scott's leader appeared giving the Movement its name, Amis was probably its best-known member. The most influential passage in the leader, much-quoted in later years, certainly fitted him more accurately than it did others of the writers Scott listed.[32] The Movement writers, Scott claimed, were 'bored by the despair of the Forties, not much interested in suffering, and extremely impatient of poetic sensibility, especially poetic sensibility about "the writer and society." So it's goodbye to all those sad little discussions about "how the writer ought to live," and it's goodbye to the Little Magazine and "experimental writing." The Movement, as well as being anti-phoney, is anti-wet; sceptical, robust, ironic, prepared to be as comfortable as possible.'

Such labelling could have an unhelpful effect on young writers, a point made by Evelyn Waugh in a letter responding to Scott's leader, published on 8 October: 'Please let the young people of today get on with their work alone and be treated to the courtesy of individual attention. They are the less, not the more, interesting if they are treated as a "Movement."' Whether Waugh's sympathy extended to Amis is unlikely. According to Anthony Powell, with whom Amis was soon friendly, Waugh had 'a kind of obsession with Amis', whom he persistently referred to as 'Ames' or 'Little Kingsley'.[33] This obsession Powell may well have told Amis about; at their first meeting, in March 1954, they discussed Waugh and presumably continued to do so at subsequent meetings. Partly it derived from the impression that Amis was being positioned as a young pretender, author of 'the funniest novel since *Decline and Fall*'; partly it derived from his role as Movement standard-bearer. Inevitably, *That Uncertain Feeling* would be greeted, by old guard and new, not just as a novel but as a 'Movement' novel. Hence Amis's gathering impatience with Movement campaigning. 'What a load of bullshit all that was in the *Spr* about the new movt. etc.,' he wrote to Larkin on 18 October. 'Useful up to a point, but the point is nearly here, I feel; someone should tell old GSF to pipe down a little before people think he's buggering all our arses – I'm thinking of the TLS leader now, not the Spr thing.'

That all the attention Amis was receiving in 1954 played some part in delaying his progress on *That Uncertain Feeling* is suggested by several passages in the letters. 'I feel in a sense "they can't stop me now",' Amis wrote to Larkin only two weeks after publication of *Lucky Jim*, in the full flush of initial good notices and sales, 'except when I take up my novel and feel how easy it will be to stop myself'.[34] 'I've been feeling so frightened about *TUF* going badly, and then so pleased about it seeming to go well,' he wrote Larkin on 18 October, and in an addendum, written on 1 November: 'For a long time I was trying not to face the feeling that I'd defiled my couch, irremediably.' Gollancz, he knew, was eager to begin advertising the novel. On 1 October Amis had written to Rubinstein apologising in advance for not being able to submit the manuscript by the end of the month, as promised, and urging him 'not to worry and to continue your exemplary patience'. What finally did the trick, he wrote to Rubinstein on 18 October, was seeing the novel announced in the *New Statesman*. By 13 November, he wrote to Larkin, in response to Larkin's question, he had 'done one draft of all of it, six different drafts of the first part of it (yes, really) and have at the time of writing done a final draft up to p.123. Hope to finish it by Christmas YAHAHAGH.' When the book was finally published and well received, Amis wrote to tell Victor Gollancz how pleased he was: 'I really was beginning to have kittens about it, in fact had been having mild ones for some time, and this was probably why the MS turned up on your desk some time after dead-line. Every time I went through it there seemed to be more wrong with it.'[35]

One other factor may have weighed on Amis as he worked over *That Uncertain Feeling*. Though Larkin had provided him with details about libraries and librarians (John Lewis, the novel's hero, is a librarian) he had little else to do with the new novel, certainly in comparison with the help he provided for *Lucky Jim*. Larkin had found it hard to deal with the success of *Lucky Jim*. That Amis suspected as much is suggested by the 'you sams' and 'herk herms' that litter his accounts of fancy parties, literary celebrities, new cars and accountants. 'Had a good time in London recently,' he wrote Larkin on 20 December 1954, 'spot of the Widow and a few mouth-fuls of caviare with my pals the Tynans, lunch with VG, lunch with deputy ed. of Evening Standard, etc. All that kind of thing, you know.' After a year of such reports, protective ironies notwith-standing, Larkin was mildly fed up, as in a letter to Monica Jones of January 1955, about a recent 'glimpse of the rich life of the Amis household': 'It's not his *success* I mind so much as his immunity from worry and hard work, though I mind his success as well.'[36] Such comments were tailored to Monica, who disliked Amis, and were partly meant to please (as she probably knew, since Larkin continued to see the Amises, visiting them in Swansea and else-where).[37] But they also expressed something of what Larkin felt.

When Amis became aware of a rumour that Larkin had 'written' *Lucky Jim* is uncertain, but shortly after *That Uncertain Feeling* was published he made reference to it, in a letter to Larkin of 15 September 1955.[38] In this letter Amis thanked Larkin for praising the novel and commented on some criticisms Larkin had made. He then alluded to the rumour:

Don't know why you want to take that attitude about what you call your 'own contribution.' Only the Q. and A. bit and the gambit bit, wasn't it? Plus a few library stories, of course. We writers have got to take our mate-rial where we find it, you know. And if you won't use the grand stuff that falls into your lap you can't blame someone whoooo-ooh-noooh.

Incidentally, that JBW fantasy about the rumour about you writing my books is probably based on your having idly mentioned that a few *Jim* cracks were your doing (I'm not forgetting that more than a few cracks was your doing). Then he tells it back to you, as it were, in typically exaggerated form.

Without Larkin's side of the correspondence it is difficult to tell what is being described here. Presumably Larkin himself had made reference to the rumour, or suggested it was being spread by Wain. Amis does not sound particularly perturbed and the passage ends on a characteristic note of encouragement about Larkin's own fictional efforts: 'Before we leave this general Topick, I think you ought to turn your journal into a novel, editing it nacherly, and not preserving the journal form. It would be bloody funny, and not too much trouble. Think it over, boy. Finally, I am most relieved and happy that you liked *TUF* as a whole. You're the one whose opinion counts, as you know.'

What is suggested here is that Amis was 'relieved and happy' that Larkin liked the new novel in part because this novel was so exclusively Amis's own. For whatever reason – increased confidence, overwork, which always slowed his correspondence, a growing sense of distance on Larkin's part, pride – Amis had kept Larkin uninformed about *That Uncertain Feeling*. He was right to do so, as a second letter Larkin wrote to Monica Jones suggests, this one written in February 1955, shortly after the manuscript was finally submitted. The second letter is partly joking: 'oh please God, make them return it, with a suggestion that he "rewrites certain passages." Nothing would delight me more. And I refuse to believe that he can write a book on his own – or at least a good book.' If Amis at times shared this belief, for all his confidence, or sensed that Larkin held it, it may have delayed the book's progress. In either case, he was reluctant to consult him.

Aside from its painstaking revision, the most striking feature of the genesis of *That Uncertain Feeling* was how much of it Amis had worked out in the 1952 synopsis. John Lewis, the finished novel's hero, is very close in character and background to the hero Amis described in the synopsis. That hero, David Harry, was born in 1926, as was Lewis, making him twenty-six in the novel's present, the same age as Dixon in *Lucky Jim*. David's father, like John's father, held a minor administrative post in a colliery, was English-speaking, not particularly interested in religion and averagely active in Labour politics. His mother, to quote the synopsis, was 'from N. Wales, based on Mrs. Larkin. Perhaps father dead, David has problem of accommodating mother. ?One sister gone away to marry.' In the finished novel, the mother and sister, drawn as they are from Larkin's family, disappear; the father alone figures, and only at the end. Amis is very particular about David's class and educational background and he is vigilant about stereotypes. He warns himself to 'avoid cliché of making parents too fanatically keen on David's advancement through education. D is the very good but not quite first-rate scholar. Grammar School, Swansea; scholarship to College, failed for Oxford. First in History.' After college, David takes an education diploma, hates the 'prac' part of his training, fails to get a job as a journalist and ends up as a librarian.

In addition to sketching out the main lines of David Harry's character, Amis's synopsis also offers an account of his marriage, though in this case there is a significant discrepancy between initial conception and finished work. In the synopsis, Jean Harry is said to have been born in 1931, which made her fifteen when David met and seduced her. The closeness of David's marriage to Amis's is clear: 'she his mistress throughout Coll, the affair falling off when marriage takes place, he already unfaithful once. His seduction of her at that age a perpetual cause of reproach by Jean to D, tho' perh. revealed lateish, and of secret self-reproach by D. They get married at all because (1) D's genuine affection for J; this never lost sight of (2) afraid of hurting J (3) Prof Ross [Jean's father], and D's mother, and all D's and J's friends, are expecting it.' These are pretty much the circumstances of Amis's own marriage, minus Hilly's pregnancy. The state of the marriage in the novel's present, as described in the synopsis, recalls Amis's marriage in the early Swansea years. In the synopsis Amis calls the marriage 'not exaggeratedly unhappy', then lists the 'destructive factors' threatening it, including David's several adulteries, his laziness and 'occasional irritation' (originally 'moodiness and depression'), and Jean's hardness, based, David later learns, 'on a refusal to play for sympathy and an incapacity to give love when she feels that its basis in him is absent, consists only of forms to make life pleasant'. This assessment by Jean of what David feels about her 'is 50% too pessimistic', Amis adds. Jean's hardness also derives from how little money the couple have and the demanding business of raising small children, 'tho' D intermittently supports her here'. Jean is only happy, the synopsis states, when she detects 'real love' in David's actions: 'most of the time she's violently but secretly unhappy, but the children console her some of the time. Always a slim girl, she is becoming painfully thin, and so less attractive. Not a highly-sexed person.'

What happened to Amis in a similar situation we know: he wrote *Lucky Jim*, which helped with the money part, though it did nothing to free him from what the synopsis calls 'sexual obsessions', the sort that drop men in shit-marshes. John Lewis, in the finished novel, is in David's and Amis's position (prior to *Lucky Jim*, that is) but the business of Jean's age has been dropped; only a few muted allusions suggest that one of John Lewis's sexual obsessions is with very young girls. When the prospect of a promotion in the library arises in *That Uncertain Feeling*, it promises to ease the hero's money worries. Then Amis introduces a woman who not only corrupts the promotion process, what the synopsis calls 'the jobbery' (her husband has influence), but perfectly fits the more conventional of David's sexual fantasies. This woman, Elizabeth Gruffydd Thomas (Gruffyd Williams in the finished novel), is two years older than David, buxom, highly sexed, 'ready for D semi-consciously', and of a higher social class, that of the English-speaking Welsh bourgeoisie or *crachach*.[39] David is attracted to Elizabeth, the synopsis says, for 'straight sex, plus talkative and affectionate manner; [it is] only later that the social advantages become important'.

Amis is anxious in the synopsis to complicate everyone's motives and characters. David must be shown to have virtues as well as vices: 'Play up his anxiety for J, determination to keep away from E.' When David sees Elizabeth in the Mermaid Bar, after steering clear of her, he is filled with horror: 'what's the use of trying if my luck lets me down like this?' David must be shown to be considerate to staff and readers in the library. He has a theory 'that you ought to do good actions even when you know your motives are bad'. The novel must include 'everything that will establish him as a man *trying to be good*, and trying to be a good husband, good librarian, good friend etc. too' (the novel's original title was to be 'The Moral Man'). At the same time, David is often not a good man. In a note about Chapter 8, Amis reminds himself to show Elizabeth 'having [a] twinge of conscience, especially about J[ean], but overcoming it soon: suggestion that really D no better than her except in that he's more of a worrying type'. As part of his attempt to be good, David 'tries to drive out of his head the feeling that there is something creditable in being sexually disturbed', by which Amis here mostly means highly sexed, a cocksman, though he may also be referring to a darker element, as suggested in a note that reads: 'Shame continually just below surface for statutory rape of J.' This element of violation all but vanishes in the finished novel, unlike Elizabeth's soft-pornographic appeal, which Amis explains in the synopsis: 'E fits him because she pictorially voluptuous, because she lustful in manner etc, because she got plenty of money, because she'll be willing, and (in the sense that there'll be places and times) able, to play his game with him.' That Elizabeth fits David's fantasies, however, does not prevent Amis from equipping her with needs of her own; she takes up with David 'partly thro real kindness, partly to get a lover, partly (unconsciously) to ruin him and his marriage'. As with all the characters, even the odious Welsh windbag Capel Probert (Gareth Probert in the finished novel), an attempt is made to see her from the inside. 'There must be no malice seen by the author anywhere,' Amis reminds himself; 'special care needed with Probert.'

This last injunction, like the refusal to involve Larkin, is part of Amis's determination to 'do something harder' as well as 'properly' in *That Uncertain Feeling*. Though sex will be a central preoccupation in the new novel, the synopsis suggests, he must 'resist the interpretation that all these people bouncing away at every chance they get'. The novel will be funny about sex but it will also be dark about it, and analytic, full of what the synopsis calls 'sexual theorising', the sort to be found in Amis's later novels. Though critics and reviewers made much of Lewis's connection to Jim Dixon, of similarities, or supposed similarities, in their class outlooks and attitudes to culture, he seems closer to Patrick Standish of *Take a Girl Like You*, Amis's fourth novel, not only in his views on women and sex but in his bouts of panic and anxiety. The major difference between Lewis and just about any other Amis protagonist is that he doesn't drink. In the synopsis, Amis ends with three notes to himself: on sex, money and drink. 'Nobody is going to be a drinker,' he declares, 'not even Probert. Imply that D's attitude to it too adolescent and self-dramatising. Even E only drinks to conform.' Given the effortless comedy Amis could extract from descriptions of drink and drunkenness, this injunction, too, looks like an attempt at something harder.

I3

'Fun'

That Amis thought there was a 'disturbed' element in his own sexual make-up at the time he was at work on *That Uncertain Feeling* is clear from personal reminiscence, from the correspondence and from the poetry he wrote while composing and revising the novel. For a while the Amises had a beach hut on Langland Bay, just along from Swansea Bay, and in a letter of 3 August 1953, Amis wrote to Larkin about a recent episode involving a family outing there:

On Saturday on the beach I saw the most beautiful person I have ever seen in the whole of my life. She was blonde and fair-skinned, with a face of great sweetness and placidity; she was about fourteen; she was tall; she had long childish legs and a small childish bottom; she had a light refined voice; she had a friend called Wendy; she walked with a slow pliant step; she had enormous breasts. I'm not telling you this just to torture you, though I can tell you I was tortured. I had my eye on her for about 15 seconds at a range of 4 or 5 yards; at the end of that time I had a considerable horn, no mean achievement when sitting on a crowded beach surrounded by family and friends and wearing wet bathing trunks. When this had departed, a feeling of great fear took its place, the old narrowly-escaped-being-run-over-in-the-street one, with trembling and disturbed breathing. Finally a feeling of great happiness and release from tension which took some hours to disperse. I found myself reflecting that youth and physical beauty are two very exciting things, and very important things, and how they can make you sad sometimes somehow, and somehow happy sometimes too.[1]

Though there is no evidence that Amis ever acted on his feelings for girls as young as fourteen, some element of his attraction to the more petite or innocent-looking of his female students may have been related to it, as was his initial attraction to Hilly. Amis was perfectly open with his colleagues about the female students he pursued, though this hardly marked him as unique; David Sims was comparably frank and busy. Glanmor Williams, Amis's historian colleague, did not approve of lecturers sleeping with students and once told him so, precipitating a brief row. What shocked Williams, though, was something Amis said on another occasion, when he pointed to a very pretty student and complained that 'she looks at me as though she's saying *I want to fuck you* and *she's* not supposed to say that, *I'm* supposed to say that.' For a time, Amis fancied the girl who played Ophelia in the staff-student production of *Hamlet*, just the role to feed fantasies about young girls. In a letter of 28 September 1953 he recounted to Larkin what happened between them at the cast party: 'This followed your prediction to an uncanny degree as regards forcing my hand into etc., but devil the thing else, or devil anything very much else, was I able to do, beyond holding her head while she was being sick, feeling romantic walking along the Mumbles Road with her, and trying not to wince at some of the awful things she was saying.'[2]

The appeal of the more mature Elizabeth in *That Uncertain Feeling* leads Lewis to ponder the pornographic. At a moment of maximum tension and distress between himself and Jean, Lewis spots a photograph in a pile of old newspapers in the kitchen: 'it was curvesome Marietta DuForgue vacationing at Las Palmas, now rather creased and stained with tea. Marietta DuForgue and her curvesome colleagues had had a bad effect on me. Or was she only a less harmful or correspondingly less exciting, version of Elizabeth?'[3] Throughout his life, though more stridently towards the end of it, when goaded by and goading feminists, Amis defended his interest in such photographs, including somewhat more explicit ones.[4] In an April 1993 *Spectator* review of Andrew Motion's biography of Larkin, Amis accused Motion of affecting 'pious horror' at Larkin's taste for 'dirty pics', which he called 'porn only by courtesy'. The review ends: 'If he has never leered, or even looked, at a photograph of a naked female, he is some kind of freak. If he has, he is no worse than a medium-sized hypocrite.'

The sort of porn that appealed to John Lewis, as to his creator, ought not to be confused with the sort Martin Amis, for example, has written about, even the sort, or some of the sort, Larkin leered at. The effectiveness of Amis's put-down of Motion is weakened by the range of Larkin's tastes, not all of which were as tame or conventional as Amis's. Though Larkin's champions like to see him as more sensitive, less crude, than Amis, with respect to matters sexual,[5] the evidence is mixed. A birthday telegram from Amis in 1956 begins: 'Greetings Larkin. Merry Birthday. Stop. Eager for 18th. Stop. Bring Bizarre. Stop. I will judge whether it is for my sort. Stop.' Why Larkin suspected *Bizarre* (a sex magazine, presumably) would not be for Amis's sort is suggested by an Amis letter of 1950: 'I found the drawings horrible, and the letterpress spoke piercingly to me of my normality. I did quite like the schoolgirl bits, but this punishment idea doesn't appeal to me, any more than all this stuff about old women and heavy make-up and shoes and corsets. I like long hair. I even like make-up sometimes. But no more than I like bread and butter and marmite. I must say I view the disappearance of the pornographic in favour of the "faddist" . . . with some regret.'

Conquest was closer to Amis than Larkin in this respect. His attitude to the bizarre is suggested in two limericks about sex with animals. 'FZS' in the first stands for 'Fellow of the Zoological Society' and 'PZS' in the second for 'President of the Zoological Society.'

> I was thrilled when I went to the zoo
> They allowed me to roger the gnu
> And a young FZS
> Remarked to me 'Yes
> It's a privilege granted to few.'

The second limerick ends with a line Amis worked on with Conquest:

> There was plenty of good-natured chaff
> When I went back to fuck the giraffe
> And the old PZS
> Could hardly suppress
> A dry professorial laugh.

For Amis and Conquest, as for most Amis heroes, sexual fantasy means straightforward heterosexual fantasy. In the early years of their friendship in the 1950s, when Amis was working on *That*

Uncertain Feeling and visiting London often, he and Conquest used to lunch regularly in Soho. After these lunches they would drop by a few 'adult' book and magazine shops. On one such occasion, Thom Gunn, a fellow Movement poet and Conquest contributor, was invited along. 'Very decent of him to come,' Conquest remembers Amis commenting (Gunn was gay). 'We took it for granted he wouldn't mind,' Conquest recalled, with the teasing confidence that characterises his several poems and essays in defence of porn. Where Amis differed from Conquest was in his refusal to defend soft porn on high cultural grounds. For Conquest, the relation of ideal female beauty, whether conceived of by *Playboy* or Praxiteles, to real-life women is complementary rather than antagonistic.[6] For Amis, pursuit of the ideal is just a licence to indulge, as in his poem 'A Dream of Fair Women', published in *A Case of Samples: Poems 1946–1956* (1956), and written in late 1952 or early 1953.[7] The poet imagines himself surrounded by 'a squadron of draped nudes':

> Each girl presses on me her share of what
> Makes up the barn-door target of desire:
>   And I am a crack shot.
>
> Speech fails them, amorous, but each one's look
> Endorsed in other ways, begs me to sign
>   Her body's autograph-book;
> 'Me first, Kingsley; I'm cleverest' each declares.
> But no gourmet races downstairs to dine,
>   Nor will I race upstairs.

What sort of men dream like this? the poet asks, a question John Lewis ponders in *That Uncertain Feeling*. The poem's answer is those who find 'Love's ordinary distances too great', who 'See no arrival that can compensate / For boredom on the way'. Such men, like the poem's 'Kingsley', 'seek / The halls of theoretical delight, / The women of that ever-fresh terrain, / The night after tonight'. The ideal, in other words, is delusory, distracting, destructive, something for the 'really weak' rather than a spur, though its pursuit may also be hard-wired into the male psyche. For Conquest, in contrast, ideals of female beauty can be stepping-stones, as in the concluding lines of his poem 'Literature in Soho', about visiting an adult bookshop:

> . . . Those who don't like icons of
>   Women, for all their talk of 'love'
>   Don't like women much either.
>
> Relying for their sustenance instead
>   On vague creatures in their head,
>   Simpering, sopping wet . . .
>
> —Beyond word's fantasy, or vision's pose,
>   Through sex and the feminine one knows
>   Oneself. Then others. And then love.[8]

Amis could be serious about porn, but not in this way. When he described men looking at women, either on stage or in magazines, the result was for the most part comic. In *Take a Girl Like You*, the idea for which he had begun working on soon after finishing *That Uncertain Feeling*, he describes a strip show, focusing on how silly it is, and how male timidity makes it even sillier. Patrick Standish, very drunk, is taken by his suave friend Julian to a club in Soho:

The curtains were pulled aside and it was all right . . . For a minute or two he was happy in an unreflecting, undifferentiating way; then his spirits began to fall, taking their first and biggest knock when he noticed that none of the dozen or so girls could properly be said to be naked at all – wherever he looked there was spangle and sequin and jolly little cone and ever so cunning triangle or in some cases what did triangle's job just as well mind you but was actually star or Chinese lantern or dirty great question mark . . . And why were they all so tall, too tall for their width, as if they had been on the rack, and too tall for women anyway, and rushing to and fro like that as in an octuple game of squash, and singing . . . and grinning and popping their eyes . . .[9]

Later, as Patrick gets even drunker, the girls appear dressed as fish:

Patrick did his best to stare . . . determined to get his, or Julian's, money's worth, but his view was so frequently impeded by girls with lobster-claw gloves, girls with sea-horse hats, girls with sword-fish masks, that he soon just let them welter reasonlessly before him, like a Sioux at Twickenham.[10]

Take a Girl Like You develops themes, episodes and details from *That Uncertain Feeling*. The strippers here recall the description of full-figured Marietta Duforgue 'wearing a curious yachting costume consisting mainly of a peaked cap, a pair of seaman's boots, and a small, inefficient-looking telescope'.[11] Julian provides an explanation for this sort of costuming, one that recalls darker aspects of male desire, the sort that figure prominently in *Take a Girl Like You* and are alluded to in the synopsis of *That Uncertain Feeling*, with its talk of statutory rape.

What a lot of people get out of this sort of caper is a reassurance thing: you know, we saw the lot and there they all were prancing about and we didn't feel a flicker, must be pretty normal kinds of chaps, mustn't we? . . . Of course, it wouldn't be the thing for most of our fellow members and guests if there actually were some real nudity here. They want a demonstration of how clean and straightforward and entertaining and part-of-a-spending-spree and good-fun-for-all-concerned sex really is, not all those peculiar old other things they're liable to suspect it may possibly be when they read the *News of the World*, or pass a girls' school at playtime, or cut across the common last thing at night.[12]

In *That Uncertain Feeling* John Lewis does not pass a girls' school at playtime or cut across a common at night, but early in the novel he passes some tennis courts and stops to watch two girls playing. One of these girls, modelled on the longest-lasting and most gamine of Amis's student conquests, catches his attention: 'She had short shorts and well-shaped hips, and was bounding about very prettily, or so it seemed to me.' While Lewis watches, musing generally on the attractiveness of attractive women, the girl approaches: '[she] turned and came to retrieve a ball, leaning forward directly in front of me to gather it. I wished she hadn't; the result was something that a member of the Watch Committee and myself would concur in liking not to see, though from different motives, one might hope.'[13]
Lewis knows he should not be lingering at the tennis courts, but knowing makes no difference when sex has him in its coils. His subsequent guilt leads only to comic rationalisation, further coils. Here he is returning home to Jean from a meeting with Elizabeth: 'Feeling a tremendous rakehell, and not liking myself much for it, and feeling rather a good chap for not liking myself much for it, and not liking myself at all for feeling rather a good chap, I got indoors, vigorously

rubbing lipstick off my mouth with a handkerchief.'[14] In *Take a Girl Like You*, Patrick voices a comparably knowing and ineffectual regression: 'I'm sorry. I know I'm a bastard but I'm trying not to be . . . But I'm not trying to get credit with you by saying I know I'm a bastard. Nor by saying I'm not trying to get credit. Nor by saying I'm not trying to by saying . . . trying . . . you know what I mean. Nor by saying that. Nor by saying that.'[15]

Jean Lewis soon loses patience with apologies like these. 'But what can I do,' John shamefacedly asks her, 'All I can do is tell you . . .':

'And when you've told me you'll feel all right about it until the next time, and then we have this again? That's what you want, isn't it?' She threw the things into the basin and turned and faced me. 'Now listen to me. Perhaps you think I don't know you. I do, though. I know the look when you start fancying a woman . . .'

'Jean, I can understand . . .'

'Great one for understanding you are, aren't you? "Oh yes, I understand how you feel, I understand you're feeling a bit cheesed just at the moment, so let me cheer you up . . ."'

'Isn't there anything I can do?'[16]

There is: he can stop sleeping with other women; which is to say, there isn't, because he can't.

Men who do not control themselves sexually are not always jokes, or only jokes, in Amis's writing. Patrick Standish takes Jenny Bunn's virginity in what is, in effect, an act of rape (the sort Amis had originally envisioned in David Harry's past). Other protagonists are presented as weak, tawdry, dog-like, in the manner of Dai Evans in *The Evans Country*, the lower-middle-class pornography-fancier and serial seducer who lives in Aberdarcy, the setting also of *That Uncertain Feeling*. That Amis possessed Dai-like propensities in this period of his life, for all his charm, literary celebrity and good looks, is amply testified to in the letters and reminiscences. Just as Dai enjoys 'a fearsome thrash with Mrs. No-holds-barred / (Whose husband's in his surgery till 7)', so Amis was exercised by 'the rugby-fancier's wife', a woman who showed him a fixture list of the Swansea and District Rugby Football Club, pointing out all the home matches her husband would attend. 'Her meaning beng,' Amis reported to Larkin, in a letter of 24 September 1956, 'then you CAN SLIP IN AND SLIP IT IN BACH. The Fixture card seems to go like this A

(away) HHHHHAHHHHHAHHHHHHAHHHHHHHHHAHH-
HHHHHHHHHHHHHHHHHHHHHHHHHHH . . . Oh what a
sodding fool I am. Oh what am I gong to *do*.'

Larkin made a poem out of these 'difficulties', or out of what
they made him feel about difficulties of his own. 'Letter to a Friend
about Girls', the idea for which seems to have come to Larkin in
1957,[17] was finished in December 1959. It makes clear the compet-
itiveness, the intermingling of envy and superiority, in his feelings
towards Amis in the 1950s. Larkin envied Amis's worldly success,
which partly meant his success as a novelist, yet as a poet he felt
himself Amis's superior, since verse *per se* was superior to fiction
and his verse superior to Amis's, views Amis shared. As for the
comparison of love-lives, while Larkin envied Amis's more glamorous girls and successful conquests, the weight and depth of feeling
evoked by his own failed encounters with 'a different gauge of girl'
suggest a dimension of experience superior to Amis's. It is by no
means clear from the poem's closing quotation, for example, which
friend is Hamlet and which Horatio:

'Letter to a Friend about Girls'

After comparing lives with you for years
I see how I've been losing: all the while
I've met a different gauge of girl from yours.
Grant that, and all the rest makes sense as well:
My mortification at your pushovers,
Your mystification at my fecklessness –
Everything proves we play in separate leagues.
Before, I couldn't credit your intrigues
Because I thought all girls the same, but yes,
You bag real birds, though they're from alien covers.

Now I believe your staggering skirmishes
In train, tutorial and telephone booth,
The wife whose husband watched away matches
While she behaved so badly in a bath,
And all the rest who beckon from that world
Described on Sundays only, where to want
Is straightaway to be wanted, seek to find,
And no one gets upset or seems to mind

At what you say to them, or what you don't:
A world where all the nonsense is annulled,

And beauty is accepted slang for yes.
But equally, haven't you noticed mine?
They have their world, not much compared with yours,
But where they work, and age, and put off men
By being unattractive, or too shy,
Or having morals – anyhow, none give in:
Some of them go quite rigid with disgust
At anything but marriage: that's all lust
And so not worth considering; they begin
Fetching your hat, so that you have to lie

Till everything's confused: you mine away
For months, both of you, till the collapse comes
Into remorse, tears, and wondering why
You ever start such boring barren games
– But there, don't mind my *saeva indignatio*:
I'm happier now I've got things clear, although
It's strange we never meet each other's sort:
There should be equal chances, I'd've thought.
Must finish now. One day perhaps I'll know
What makes you be so lucky in your ratio.

One of those 'more things,' could it be? *Horatio*.

When Larkin first told Amis the premiss of 'Letter to a Friend about Girls', Amis thought it 'an absolutely fucking marvellous idea', in part because he instantly saw it as a potential collaboration, a species of 'fun', like a joint poem or limerick. In late 1957, Amis was a successful novelist and critic. As a poet, however, he was blocked (relatively speaking, *A Case of Samples: Poems 1946–1956* appeared in 1956). 'Can't "seem" to write verse these days,' he complained to Larkin on 9 November, which was 'one reason why I want you to send me some of your letter to a friend: I reckon it might easily stir me to a reply, not a polemical one of course, but a further discussion of some of the points you raise . . . I think some sort of joint, or alternating, effort of this kind might be bumper fun. Or isn't that in tune with your original conception? What do you say?' Amis's openness here was characteristic, though as the finished poem suggests, unlikely to appeal. In the same letter he was quick to play down his role as cocksman, though in incriminatingly Dai-like terms: 'don't get me wrong (though I suppose it needn't be "me" in the poem); what I mean is I am no Don J at all, really, I merely work a pennyworth of fucking in with an intolerable deal of wire-pulling, horn-having, would-you-like-to-see-me-in-my-play-suit-Anna-darling mythologizing and looking at, or wishing I had the chance of looking at, pics for fans of the fuller figure'.

It didn't look a pennyworth to others. The rugby-fancier's wife, from the Swansea *crachach*, recalled parties at the Amises' in which every woman present was invited by the host to visit his greenhouse in the garden; they all knew what the invitation meant. Al Alvarez tells a similar tale, recalling a weekend stay, also some time in the mid-1950s: 'During a long, drunken Saturday evening, Kingsley disappeared into the garden with each of the women in the party. While they were gone the rest of us sat around trying to make conversation and pretending not to be embarrassed. Half an hour later our host and whichever lucky lady had gone with him sauntered back in, smoothing their clothes and hair but not quite able to conceal the wild furtive triumph in their eyes.'[18] Amis was not the only male at such gatherings to misbehave. James Bartley, his colleague in English, who on a previously cited occasion was seen crawling upstairs on his hands and knees in pursuit of Hilly, once decided to take his shirt off at a party, 'ostensibly for greater coolness', Amis reported to Larkin, though 'actually I think to display the grey rug on his chest to the young ladies. Hilly, for a lark you know, ripped his flies open, expecting him to grab his trousers before they fell. He didn't, nor had Hilly remembered his frequent boast of wearing no underclothes, the filthy bugger. So there he was, naked to the knees, and a nastier sight. He held it for half a minute or so, gazing round. The party broke up soon after. I got to bed 3.45.'[19] As these anecdotes suggest, the women in the Amis circle were themselves bold, wild. In a letter of 27 December 1956, Amis described a publisher friend of his 'falling over a dinner-wagon and breaking a lot of crockery on the occasion (he told me afterwards) of having his balls suddenly seized during an embrace with the rugby-enthusiast's wife'.[20]

The impression such episodes made on Larkin was that Amis inhabited a world in which 'no one gets upset or seems to mind / At what you say to them, or what you don't: / A world where all the nonsense is annulled.' Larkin chose to take Amis's more blokish or jokey accounts of his world at face value; but, of course, there was another side to these accounts. Alvarez's anecdote about Amis's disappearances into the garden includes a description of his behaviour the following morning:

Kingsley's way of apologizing, over breakfast the next morning, was to launch into a long rigamarole about his fear of death. He was turning it on, of course, indulging himself for our benefit, although what he was saying sounded genuine enough. But he was also missing the point: being an interesting writer with interesting neurotic preoccupations doesn't mean never having to say you're sorry.

What got to me most about the whole performance was that everyone was miserable – the women who went outside with Kingsley as much as those who were left behind, even Kingsley himself – but nobody said a word. Whatever our reasons – embarrassment, shyness, humiliation, misplaced good manners – we went on behaving as though nothing unusual were happening. And that is what the Movement poets do when they write: they pretend that all's well with the world provided they keep their backs turned on what they really feel.[21]

Alvarez may accurately have described the aftermath of Amis's behaviour on Saturday night but it is hard to accept his more general description of Amis as turning his back on what he really feels. Consider John Lewis, who not only shares a number of Amis's fears and phobias but is also subject to panic attacks. Lewis has always been terrified of going out alone at night, but when it looks, after Jean's furious, tearful rejection, as though his philandering has wrecked their marriage, he flees the house and runs blindly through the night streets:

I felt as if something had happened which had made me feel very frightened, and that I must do something which would make me feel even more frightened if I was ever to get rid of the first frightening thing . . . I looked to the end of the street, to where it curved up and sideways; no, nobody there at all . . . After I'd run to the end of the long street I stopped for a moment and looked back. There was still nobody there. On each side of the street were the houses, all looking exactly the same under the irregularly-spaced streetlights. Although a window or two was illuminated I couldn't believe there were people in the houses either. I wondered what would happen if I went and knocked on one of the doors. If anybody answered I'd say: 'Does Mr. Rigby live here?' just as I used to plan to do when I was a child and hurrying home from Cubs on Wednesday nights in the winter. If I got frightened, I used to say to myself, I'd knock on the nearest door and ask for Mr. Rigby . . . I came to another corner . . . That was the way to the sea, and I knew now that that was the way I'd wanted to go all the time, even when I turned uphill. This would be down, of course, and would make me less out of breath, but I might be able to make up for that by going as fast as I could, dangerously fast, and so leave myself no attention to spare from the task of not falling over.[22]

For later Amis heroes, as for Amis himself, drink performed this fear-obliterating function; then drink itself became a problem. At the time of *That Uncertain Feeling*, the same was true of women and sex, as in the poem 'Nothing to Fear', written in the late 1950s or early 1960s, though not published until the 1967 collection *A Look Round the Estate*. The poem, quoted earlier, describes an assignation at a flat 'lent by a friend, whose note says *Lucky sod*' (Conquest's message in his practical joke).[23] The speaker awaits the arrival of his mistress and though everything is set ('Drinks on the tray; the cover-story pat / And quite uncheckable') he suddenly experiences 'a slight trembling, / Dry mouth, quick pulse-rate, sweaty hands, / As though she were the first'. She is not, of course, nor do the speaker's panic symptoms derive from impatience, or fear of failure, or fear of the burning power of beauty ('I'm asbestos, see?'). The poem concludes:

> It's a dead coincidence
> That sitting here, a bag of glands
> Tuned up to concert pitch, I seem to sense
> A different style of caller at my back,
> As cold as ice, but just as set on me.

This is hardly the response of a man pretending all's right with the world. But even when Movement types do adopt such a posture it is often for comic effect. Robert Conquest, a man who simply 'wakes up happy' (according to his wife), is briskly empirical about the sorts of feelings expressed in 'Nothing to Fear'. Here he is in a letter to Larkin of 8 October 1960:

Your points on K are interesting. Note also his new line that screwing is a way of forgetting about dying. Negative thinking there, eh? And allowing ten fucks a week at twenty minutes each, it leaves an awful lot of time for seeing the skull beneath the skin, lifeless creatures underground, etc. It's something we all have to get used to, what? Curtis Brown won't handle that for us.

Amis could be comparably robust about death and its palliatives; but only sometimes. Nor was the act itself all that mattered in his 'new line'; fantasising about the act, and about beautiful women, also played its part. When in *That Uncertain Feeling* John Lewis asks his famous questions about women's breasts – 'Why did I like women's breasts so much? I was clear why I liked them, thanks, but why did I like them *so much*?'[24] – he points to what Amis saw at this time as a real problem in his life. The question is jokey but Amis is hardly, as Alvarez claims, avoiding his feelings. The passage that comes closest to answering Lewis's questions is from *Take a Girl Like You*, Amis's most considered meditation on the compulsive nature of his fantasising and womanising. Patrick Standish is suddenly overwhelmed by fearful sensations:

While he was picturing this, his heart vibrated in the way it had recently started to do and he had the familiar, but never at other times imaginable, feeling of being outside himself, as if his brain had suddenly frozen, become a fixed camera, while his body continued to breathe and walk and turn its head about in a simulcrum of attention. Terror made him catch his breath; pins and needles surged in his fingers . . . Just nerves he said to himself. Nothing to do with dying . . . Perhaps a little bit to do with going mad. That would be unusual, because he was pretty sound these days on the bonkers question. Meditations on the old last end were giving him a good deal more trouble. Well thinking about sex as much as possible was the only way to lick that.[25]

14

Abroad

In March 1955 Amis won the Somerset Maugham Award for *Lucky Jim*, the terms of which required that he spend not less than three months on travel or residence abroad. The award is administered by the Society of Authors and was worth £400; Martin Amis won it for *his* first novel, *The Rachel Papers* (1973). Amis's mixed reactions to winning are voiced in a letter to Larkin of 28 March 1955: 'don't tell Hilly, who I shall be taking with me, but the whole prospect fills me with alarm and depression. If it weren't for her, and the fact that it would look too eccentric to turn it down... Ah, soul. What a sodding *waste of time* it'll all be. *A great honour, though, of course.*' Amis's immediate thought about the literary use to which he would put his time abroad was to write a long short story about Dixon's experiences on the 'Continong'. The sorts of experiences he had in mind were elaborated in the same letter to Larkin: 'being punched by a taxi-driver outside the Gare St. Lazare, spewing under the Sacré Coeur... pursued by Bertrand down the Boul, Miche.' To Rubinstein, who had wired him the news, he wrote in thanks and to ask: 'By the way, who were the judges? Victor Gollancz, Ruth Gollancz and Hilary Rubinstein?'[1]

After considering several locations, the Amises settled on Portugal as the place for their residence abroad. The whole family would go, departing on 23 June and returning on 27 September, to fit into Amis's university summer vacation. Accommodation had been found for them, through Maggie Ashbury Vakil, now Aeron-Thomas. Maggie had married John Aeron-Thomas, a wealthy industrialist and owner of the *Newport Argus*, and it was through Aeron-Thomas's father that the Amises were fixed up. They were to stay as 'paying guests with an English business type about a dozen miles from Lisbon near the sea'.[2] This business type, J.G. ('Billy') Barley, was employed as a translator in the offices of a Portuguese firm run by a family named Pinto Basto, friends of Aeron-Thomas Senior. Barley grew up in Portugal and had Portuguese nationality, but his father was English. He had a portrait of the Queen on the wall and drank his tea from a Coronation mug. In a letter to Larkin of 10 July, Amis described him as 'very amiable in a childish way, which is a heap better than some mature ways'. His wife, who was pure Portuguese, he described as 'an amiable half-wit'. It was their house, however, which the Amises objected to, being 'very small, SMALLER THAN WE WERE LED TO BELIEVE'.[3] Like the Amises, the Barleys had three children, two boys and a girl. Each family had two bedrooms, one for the boys and one for the parents and daughter. In the daytime the Barleys' bedroom was converted into what was meant to be the Amises' private sitting room. There was also a dining room, a kitchen, a hallway in which the maid slept and a single bathroom-with-lavatory. All the rooms were small, several of them created by Barley in the previous month by building new interior walls. The entire floor-space of the house (there was only one floor) was roughly that of a badminton court. It was impossible to get away from the children. Amis and Hilly's bedroom 'has Sally in it for about 16 hours out of 24'.[4] All the chairs were hard (Amis claimed he hadn't sat in an easy chair since he'd left the boat), the lavatory smelt, the maid was inefficient, there were flies everywhere ('fucking all the time. Any moment a pair of buzzing bodies, quite out of control, will fall down on your arm or your lunch')[5] and Mrs Barley proved incapable of providing any meals eighteen-month-old Sally could eat, as well as any meals on time. 'You will need no convincing,' Amis wrote to Larkin on 28 July, 'that to have Hilly carrying a yelling Sally about for an hour before each meal (an activity broekn foekn broken by short periods when I decided that holding a yelling Sally myself might be preferable to watching a distressed Hilly holding a yelling Sally) was hell'.

After about a month the Amises found more suitable accommodation in the Algarve, in the south of Portugal, though to avoid a row and recriminations Amis was forced to pay Barley an extra month's bed-and-board in compensation for leaving early, plus a further £40 (at what Amis later discovered was an unfavourable rate of exchange) for expenses incurred in altering the house. The move was made possible by an eccentric Irishman named Harold Tyrell, 'a Belfast Prod by origin',[6] to whom they were introduced by visiting friends from Swansea. Tyrell had a 'mountain chalet' in Monchique, not far from Lagos and about fifteen miles from the beach at Praia da Roche, and offered to lend it to the Amises free of charge. It would not be available until mid-August (when Tyrell's sister would vacate it, to return to Belfast) but Tyrell knew of a cheap *pensão* the Amises could stay in in the meantime. The rooms in this *pensão*, Amis reported to Larkin, were larger and cheaper than those at the Barleys', the board was '*slightly* better', it had a lounge with an easy chair in it, and the bathroom 'smells only of soap'.[7] The mountain chalet was also better than the Barley house, though it still offered Amis plenty to complain about (being in Portugal, which is to say, abroad). Towards the end of their stay in the chalet Amis offered the Clearys a summary of its attractions, after listing 'a sort of basic kit' of what the traveller to Portugal needs:

(1) a DDT spray with a half-gallon storage-tank (2) a placard saying in Portuguese WHAT THE FUCKING HELL ARE YOU STARING AT? (3) a crate of detective novels (4) a jar of pills which promote constipation (5) a solicitor as travelling companion . . . Between us and the coast is a lot of hill with trees growing on it. They are of various kinds, I understand. Down the road a mile or so is Monchique, where the villagers assemble to give us a barrage of stares every time we turn up there. My haircut there was the occasion of a kind of primitive festival. The garden of this bungalow is small but wild; it contains a miniature forest where a doomed and very noisy pig roams. We're going to eat it on Monday. Also in the garden is a centrifugal pump, which I pump a lot. A toad, at least two lizards, some savage wasps, some bloodsucking wasps, some bloodsucking flies, many more ordinary flies and some gigantic humming moths share the garden with the pig, and half a dozen dogs have got into the habit of dropping in too, sometimes penetrating, without formal invitation, into the kitchen.[8]

Amis intended letters like these, most of them to Larkin, to serve as a journal to be mined for 'Dixon on the Continong'. He was already planning scenes, based on real-life episodes: 'One of the things that will happen to Dixon when he comes to Portugal on behalf of Gore-Urquhart is a ride on the back of a motorbike after dark, in a high wind, part of the way through very fast traffic in Estoril, with a Portuguese in front *practising his English*';[9] another thing that would happen to him was that he would meet the real Kingsley Amis.[10] Tyrell and his Goanese wife, Amis quickly decided, would figure in the story as well (as, indeed, they do in *I Like It Here* (1958), the work it became, a novel not about Dixon but about Garnet Bowen, a hero like him, also like his creator). Tyrell's bizarre impromptu floor-shows in the lounge of the *pensão* and the local café included such items as an imitation of 'four different people reciting *The Charge of the Light Brigade* ("by Charles Longfellow")'.[11] His wife, who 'talks all the time', had a memorable accent: '"Hurrawllnd,"' she cries to her husband, spotting Amis's empty glass, 'ornder another of thawz mwontles (bottles) off vine. The rad.'

Amis's public complaints about abroad predated the trip to Portugal and were mostly directed at those who romanticise or overvalue foreign places and cultures, both high and low.[12] In *Lucky Jim* there is Dixon's irritation at Welch's wearing a beret, giving his sons French names, putting on a play by Jean Anouilh ('Why couldn't they have chosen an English play?').[13] Amis explains the source of such irritation in 'Is the Travel Book Dead?', a book review that appeared in the *Spectator* on 17 June 1955, six days before the Amises departed for Lisbon. The review attacks Laurie Lee's *A Rose for Winter*, about Andalusia, and Peter Mayne's *The Narrow Smile*, about the Pathan tribesmen of the Afghan–Pakistan border. Lee is censured for his 'rightly unfashionable' prose style, which Amis thinks representative of its type, being full of 'empty and indecent poeticism' (hence the wilfully prosaic nature of his own descriptions, as in 'Between us and the sea is a lot of hill, with trees growing on it. They are of various kinds, I understand'). Lee and Mayne are both criticised for romanticising primitive places (while anathematising 'the exhausted sterilities of Western civilisation'), a form of escapism and *nostalgie de la boue*. Mayne's book, the better of the two, is attacked for its formal deficiencies; it is a travelogue, which 'means that the encounters he describes are for the most part indecisive, and the factual thread upon which he strings them is inadequate to bear their weight'. Both authors would have done better to put their observations about foreign places and peoples into a novel, as did Forster in *A Passage to India*, as would Amis in *I Like It Here*.

Amis's travel anxiety – an underlying factor in his lifelong antipathy to abroad – increased as the date of departure neared. The business of 'GETTING FIXED UP'[14] (passports, money, typhoid injections, travel and lodging arrangements) terrified as well as bored him. He began to develop neurotic symptoms. 'Why do my legs keep aching in the way that they do?' he asked Larkin on 10 June, two weeks before departure. 'They feel as if I have rheumatism all the time.' The trip down the Estoril coast to Monchique, recounted to Larkin in a letter of 22 August, involved 'an above-par dose of doubt, horror and despair'. During a long wait for the ferry at Tagus, Amis faced 'a lot of wondering about where to pay, and when, and how much'. 'Being abroad seems compounded of the dull and the frightening (trying to find your way in Lisbon, for example),' he wrote to Larkin on 10 July. There were other personal motives for disliking abroad. Despite his brilliance as a mimic and his success with Latin and Greek at school, Amis was no linguist (and like Garnet Bowen had a 'fear of making a fool of himself').[15] Though wary of outsiders, among friends Amis was often the centre of attention; not being able to communicate when abroad bothered him more than it would less social or gregarious types. 'I think abroad is fine as long as you don't expect much from it,' he wrote to Larkin on 22 August. 'If you don't like anybody very much you might as well be abroad as anywhere else I suppose, but if you like to choose your friends, your company, your entertainment etc. you will be better off at home.' As for making new friends, this was near-impossible: 'because they're foreign and don't understand what you're saying and you're not here long enough, and WHY THE HELL SHOULD YOU make friends with the locals, when it's so difficult'.[16]

These sentiments were partly tailored to Larkin's prejudices ('Not that you need any convincing,' one litany ends).[17] They also related to what Garnet Bowen, speaking of himself, calls a 'long history of lower-middle-class envy directed against the upper-middle-class traveller'.[18] In the immediate post-war period the government imposed a £50 currency restriction on UK residents, to discourage foreign travel; when Amis and his fellow Movement writers complained about abroad, Anthony Hartley has suggested, they were making 'a sort of mythical virtue out of necessity, pretending that Birmingham is as interesting a place to inhabit as Berlin, or that the amenities of Manchester compare with those of Milan'.[19] For Larkin, 'nothing, like something, happens anywhere' ('I Remember, I Remember'); similarly, for John Holloway, in a 1957 article entitled 'A Writer's Prospect', 'nothing is likely to be gained by packing off hastily to Rapallo, the Isles of Greece, or any other hot favourite'. Writers who think otherwise are hopeless romantics, the sort who, in Larkin's 'Poetry of Departures', indulge escapist fantasies: 'swagger the nut-strewn roads / Crouch in the fo'c'sle, / Stubbly with goodness'. Movement writers are less deceived. In a letter to Conquest of 31 July, Amis made explicit the connection between travel and romantic indulgence. After returning to 'this [Laurie] Lee business', he mentions another negative review he has just written for the *Spectator*, of a book of Dylan Thomas's posthumous stories and essays: 'I think the 2 classes (a) chaps who think abroad is mystically fine (b) chaps who think L.L. and D.T. are "true poets" overlap quite a lot in practice.'[20] Amis's best-known linking of the two classes occurs in D.J. Enright's *Poets of the 1950s* (1955), the book that some people think of as the first Movement anthology. In his brief prose preface to its selection of his poems, he declares: 'nobody wants any more poems about philosophers or paintings or novelists or art galleries or mythology or foreign cities'. Donald Davie, in verses addressed to Amis and paraphrasing his view, calls such poems 'the privileged classes' shorthand'.[21] When Enright received the draft of Amis's preface, he wrote back in mock protest from Japan, where he was living when *Poets of the 1950s* was first published: 'it put paid to me, since practically everything I was writing at the time concerned Japanese cities'. Amis answered that it was perfectly OK to write poems about foreign parts 'if one lived in them'.[22]

I Like It Here, 'by common consent my worst novel', is singled out by Amis as the one work in which, 'out of laziness or sagging imag-ination', he tried 'to put real people on paper'.[23] So Barley becomes Oates, Harold Tyrell becomes Harry Bannion, his adopted son, Afilhado (Portuguese for adopted), remains Afilhado, the toddler Sally becomes the toddler Sandra, and so forth. As a result, the very faults Amis hoped to avoid by turning his experiences of Portugal into a novel rather than a travelogue become faults of the novel. As one reviewer, Samuel Hynes, later a friend, put it, 'through these random events move random characters . . . who appear and disap-pear without apparent necessity'. To G.S. Fraser, writing in the *New*

Statesman, I Like It Here is 'less a novel than a series of farcical incidents loosely tied to a travel narrative'.[24] Amis himself comments on the temptations of verisimilitude in Chapter 5 of the novel. Bowen is a jobbing reviewer and literary journalist, also an aspiring playwright. A central character in the play he is working on, or meant to be working on, 'Teach Him a Lesson', is his hated mother-in-law: 'the details of Mrs. Knowles's behaviour were so finely discriminated that to change anything in the interests of camouflage would bring about a fatal dilution'.[25]

Though Bowen has little of Amis's aptitude or application as a writer, he shares a number of his beliefs and attitudes, including not only his view of abroad ('I like it here, you see')[26] but his sense that those who take a contrary view are likely to favour writing he disapproves of or finds boring. This sense Bowen arrives at courtesy of a creaky and contrived literary mystery Amis folds into his account of the exasperations of foreign travel (the latter drawn largely from the letters to Larkin). It is Bowen's publishing friend, Bennie Hyman (whose boss, 'old Weinstein', suggests Gollancz), who sets the mystery plot in motion. Bowen has been offered a lot of money by an American magazine to write 'a new kind of travel article', the sort 'he had pretended to think desirable'.[27] The offer was too opulent to turn down. When Hyman hears of Bowen's commission, he offers him a second one. Hyman has been sent a copy of what purports to be the latest novel by one of his firm's authors, the secretive and long-silent Wulfstan Strether, for many years resident in Portugal, previously in Spain. Strether, Hyman thinks, is 'the one indisputably major talent to have arisen since the death of Conrad'.[28] But is the novel genuine? Strether's editor at the firm is recently deceased, had never met him, and seems to have destroyed all relevant files. None of the other editors has seen or met him. In the letter accompanying the new novel, Strether, if he is Strether, declares it will be his last (its title is 'One Word More'), that he is abandoning secrecy and reclusiveness, and that he hopes to come to London soon. Hyman wants Bowen to visit him in Portugal and determine whether he is who he says he is, not 'a disappointed writer who wants to make fools of the literary world'.[29] 'Just the thing for you this, isn't it?' Hyman declares. 'You and your sham-detecting lark . . . A sort of test in a way.'[30]

When Bowen meets Strether (for it is Strether, he eventually establishes), he proves to be an impressive-looking man of about sixty whose way of speaking 'recalled Charles Morgan rather than anything Downing College [Leavis's college] would approve – though the distinction was admittedly a fine one'.[31] Without embarrassment, the novelist gestures towards his bookshelves, which contain 'copies of all my published works, alongside those of Jane Austen, of George Eliot, of Hardy, Conrad and James, Flaubert and Proust, of the great Russians'.[32] Amis offers the reader a passage from 'One Word More', a marvellous parody of late James (like the passage from Probert's play 'The Martyr' in *That Uncertain Feeling*, a parody of Dylan Thomas).[33] It is two pages long and concerns the novel's chief characters, Frescobaldi and Yelisaveta. The novelist's own name prepares us for these even more perfect ones: 'Strether' comes from James's *The Ambassadors* (in the *Memoirs* Amis claims that the only work of James he has read 'to its conclusion' is *The Aspern Papers*, a possible source here)[34] and 'Wulfstan' is the name of the most boring of Anglo-Saxon writers, hence of all English writers, author of such homilies as *Sermo Lupi ad Anglos* ('Address to the English').[35] Unsurprisingly, neither Strether's manner nor his 'tradition' is to Bowen's taste. 'While amiable enough', Strether is 'a terrible old crap'.[36] As for his writing, Bowen objects to it 'on grounds of clarity, common sense, emotional decency and general morality';[37] but then, as he says earlier, 'I never seem to get on with great novelists.'[38] When the two men visit Henry Fielding's tomb, something Amis himself did while in Portugal, Bowen is anxious to avoid Strether's 'English Men of Letters series eloquence'. Bowen says he admires Fielding 'very much'.[39] Strether says he does, too. But that's not all he says. It is surely not right, he continues smoothly, to claim

that the utterances of comedy, whatever their purity or power, can move us as we are moved by the authentic voice of tragedy. That alone can speak to us of the loneliness and the dignity of man. And this, my friend, means that much as I reverence this assured master of the picaresque I am unable to consider him my equal. In the field of the novel he is indeed the colossus of the eighteenth century, but I cannot feel posterity will place him beside . . . will care to place him beside the colossus of the twentieth.

When Bowen realises Strether is referring to himself here, his pretend coughing fit only just disguises 'a monosyllable of demented laughter'.[40] For Bowen, Fielding is 'the only non-contemporary novelist who could be read with unaffected and wholehearted interest, the only one who never had to be apologised for or excused on the grounds of changing taste'. What appeals to him about Fielding's world is its moral clarity, a simplification, perhaps, 'but that hardly mattered beside a moral seriousness that could be made apparent without the aid of evangelical puffing and blowing'.[41] This moral seriousness *I Like It Here* aims to emulate by showing how Bowen changes over time. The initial mild contempt he shows for Strether softens into protectiveness, as in a scene in the novel's penultimate chapter when the older man's false teeth have been half-knocked out of his mouth and Bowen gently tends to him.[42] Similarly, in the final chapter Bowen realises that 'the most important thing' about his wife,[43] 'the biggest point there could be about anybody,'[44] is her integrity.

I Like It Here, in John McDermott's words, is the 'most bookish' of Amis's novels, 'densely strewn' with the names of writers, 'fifty named figures in all'.[45] Bowen's identification with Fielding and the tradition of 'amiable humorists' consciously defies literary fashion, both academic and journalistic, just as the depiction of Strether mocks both Leavis's 'Great Tradition', as the books on his shelf suggest, and 'mandarin' or 'English Men of Letters' types like Somerset Maugham, Charles Morgan and Cyril Connolly. In *The Great Tradition*, Leavis declares that 'life isn't long enough to permit of one's giving much time to Fielding'.[46] As for Maugham, Amis's distance from his benefactor is politely registered. When Afilhado recounts the story of a mutiny at sea, 'a powerful, useless thrill ran through Bowen. Here was a story for someone, but not, unfortunately, for him. Only a rather worse or much older writer than himself could tackle it satisfactorily. W. Somerset Maugham (on grounds of age, not lack of merit) was the kind of chap.'[47]

Amis admired Fielding but had a more complicated and qualified attitude to him than Bowen. In a letter to Larkin of 10 July 1955, he calls Larkin 'the recipient of My Portuguese Journal,' an allusion to Fielding's *Journal of a Voyage to Lisbon* (1755), which Fielding himself, in the Preface, calls 'a novel without a plot'. There are few other allusions to Fielding in the correspondence and his name never once appears in the 1,200 pages of the selected *Letters*; nor does he figure much in Amis's criticism, unlike, say, Waugh, Isherwood, Powell, Dickens and Austen. Robert Bell, one of Amis's most perceptive critics, calls Fielding the novelist he 'praised most often and most highly';[48] presumably he means in the fiction. Bell lists a number of traits and values the two writers shared, including pugnaciousness, 'manly' camaraderie or clubbability, the mixing of high intellect with low cultural tastes, clarity and straightforwardness of style, meticulous craftsmanship, an eye for 'human folly, our appetitive passions and self-exonerations', a love of farce and parody, especially of 'figures of pretence and fatuity', a sometimes sentimental or simplified prizing of common sense and ordinary decencies ('candor, kindness, magnanimity, charity and generosity of spirit') and a distrust of 'sublime possibility or extraordinary capacity'.[49]

But Amis is also unlike Fielding, as well as implicitly critical of his influence. *I Like It Here* is not the only Amis novel to discuss Fielding which uses attitudes to him as a way of revealing character. Fielding is also discussed in *Difficulties with Girls* (1988), a sequel to *Take a Girl Like You*, set seven years after the original, in 1967. In the midst of an argument about Patrick Standish's continuing infidelities, Jenny Standish (née Bunn) takes a copy of *Tom Jones* from the bookshelf. This copy contains Patrick's annotations and Jenny points to an underlined passage concerning what Fielding calls Tom's 'gallant' behaviour 'to all women in general': 'Though he did not always act rightly, yet he never did otherwise without feeling and suffering for it.' 'So that's all right, isn't it, Patrick?' comments Jenny, in the manner of her earlier self in *Take a Girl Like You* or of Jean Lewis in *That Uncertain Feeling*. 'What am I to do?' asks an abject Patrick, a response familiar from earlier exposed philanderers. Jenny's answer is 'Well, for a start you could try reading some different books.'[50] For Jenny, at least, Fielding is a figure whose moral generosity Patrick has used to excuse or facilitate bad behaviour, the heedless pursuit of 'what you really want'; Fielding is to the Patrick of *Difficulties with Girls* as D.H. Lawrence was to the undergraduate Robin Davies or his would-be seducer Jeremy Carpenter in *You Can't Do Both*.

Tom Jones was not the book Jenny was looking for when she approached the bookshelf. What she was looking for was an omnibus edition of the stories of Somerset Maugham. As she says to Patrick,

'you're sure to remember how he's always talking about love, how a fellow loved a woman for twenty years and never breathed a word, and another woman who was always loyal to her husband and a model wife to him even though she was in love with his best friend all the time – you know. All about people not doing things they very much wanted to do because they thought they had an obligation to someone else. And going on not doing what they wanted for years on end, not just a couple of weeks. Perhaps none of it counts really because he was queer, you told me, or perhaps it was just one of those literary conventions we used to hear about in the sixth form. Love without going to bed. What an idea.'[51]

If Jenny presents Maugham in a better light than Fielding, it is worth recalling that she has always had quaint, romantic notions of love, virginity, fidelity, notions as out of date in Patrick's eyes as Maugham is in Bowen's, out of date even in Jenny's eyes, having 'a thin, sort of last-year's feel to them'.[52] Part of Amis approves the passing of these notions, but part of him does not; and it is this part that marks his distance from Fielding as surely as it does from the whole 'great-writer period', which includes the period of Strether, 'say roughly between *Roderick Hudson* and about 1930, death of Lawrence and the next bunch all just starting off – Greene, Waugh, Isherwood, Powell. Or perhaps 1939'.[53]

The fact that Maugham himself was an enthusiastic supporter of Fielding and of *Tom Jones* ought to be borne in mind when thinking of Strether as Maugham-like, particularly as Amis probably knew of this enthusiasm when at work on *I Like It Here*. Had Patrick Standish read Maugham's *Ten Novels and Their Authors*, published in the same year as *Lucky Jim*, he would have found several passages in the chapter on 'Henry Fielding and *Tom Jones*' to annotate. Here is Maugham on Fielding's Amis-like love of fun:

He was fond of the bottle and he liked women. When people speak of virtue, it is generally sex they have in mind, but chastity is only a small part of virtue, and perhaps not the chief one. Fielding had strong passions, and he had no hesitation in yielding to them. He was capable of loving tenderly. Now love, not affection, which is a different thing, is rooted in sex, but there can be sexual desire without love. It is only hypocrisy or ignorance that denies it. Sexual desire is an animal instinct, and there is nothing more shameful in it than in thirst or hunger, and no more reason not to satisfy it.[54]

Like Bowen, Maugham feels 'there is something contemporary'[55] about Fielding; he also carefully distances himself from Strether-like 'Great Tradition' types, the sort of people 'who cannot read *Tom Jones* . . . I am thinking of those who would not demur if you classed them as members of the intelligentsia, of those who read and re-read *Pride and Prejudice* with delight, *Middlemarch* with self-complacency, and *The Golden Bowl* with reverence.'[56] The recipient of the Somerset Maugham Award for 1954 is likely to have known this passage; the literary type or prejudice it identifies is at the heart of *I Like It Here*.

After seven years together, the same number of years Hilly had been married to Amis in 1956, the Jenny Standish of *Difficulties with Girls* is depicted as worn down by Patrick's infidelities, as Amis's infidelities had worn down Hilly. Garnet Bowen's wife Barbara, in contrast, is brimming with energy. But then, Bowen's roving eye notwithstanding, her marriage is not only a good deal more secure than Jenny's or Jean Lewis's or Hilly Amis's, but grows more so over the course of the novel. In addition to her integrity, the qualities Bowen admires in Barbara are her vivacity and naturalness. 'You could tell a lot from the fact that when she waved her hand to people, as she was always doing, she waved it from the shoulder instead of the wrist, and that when she stirred a pan on the stove she waggled her bottom to the same rhythm.'[57] Her letters betray a similar exuberance:

The kids are all being very good and send their love, David and Mark have some questions about God to ask you when you get back ! ! ! Good boy about not playing Benny Himon's game about Strether. I'm sure you're doing the right thing. Look after yourself, podge, sometimes I want you so much I feel I could break in two. I love your ears. Love, love, love you.

        yum yum yum yum yum
          Barbie
x (bitey one)   X (open mouth one)[58]

Though Barbara can get him down, Bowen will never pain her by telling her how. 'What made that certain were things like the closing phrases and interjections of her letter. No part of his nature could resist them or put reservations on what they stood for.'[59] As for 'that old winged boa-constrictor, sex', to Bowen's amazement, 'going to bed with all that slender brunette beauty continued to be both emotionally edifying and unbeatable fun – as if the *Iliad* or some other gruelling cultural monument had turned out to be a good read as well as a masterpiece'.[60]

*   *   *

Amis did not begin work on *I Like It Here* until his return to Swansea in late September. In Portugal his time was spent on reviews, on the epistolary 'journal' to Larkin and others, on trips to the beach with Hilly and the family (Hilly did all the driving on these trips and Amis sat in the front seat with Sally on his lap, peeing on him). What kept him going amidst the flies and the foreigners were cheap Portuguese wine and *medronha*, a local liqueur, and good news from home. The first bit of good news, relayed to Larkin on 28 July, was that *Lucky Jim* 'is to be filmed *and* broadcast'. In a 30 July instalment of the same letter, after describing Barley's grasping ways, Amis told Larkin that he was at the 'synopsis' stage for the new novel: 'Provisional title *Pay Up and Look Pleasnat* (you know).' In late August Rubinstein reported on the reception of *That Uncertain Feeling*, published on the 22nd: sales were good, reviews largely positive. 'My neurotic forebodings about the book have proved to be unjustified,' Amis wrote back to him on 2 September. 'I really think the reviewers have been most generous.' Soon after Amis's return to Swansea, Gollancz agreed to publish a book of his poems,[61] a mark of how keen they were to keep him on side. Ten months then passed in which Amis did no work on the novel. He was back teaching and swamped with journalistic and other commitments. It was not until 19 July 1956 that he wrote to Larkin asking him to 'bring the letters I wrote to you from Portugal. I want to get some of that stuff written down before I forget all about it.'[62] By August he had begun writing *I Like It Here* and a year later he had finished, though Gollancz, to his intense irritation, postponed publication until January 1958.[63]

During the period Amis was at work on *I Like It Here*, or meant to be at work on it, his marriage came close to collapse. Hilly had fallen in love and was threatening to leave him. The man she fell for was Henry Fairlie, political columnist on the *Spectator* and coiner of the phrase 'the establishment' (though A.J.P. Taylor also claimed paternity). By all accounts, including those of ex-lovers and cuckolded partners, Fairlie was a man of great charm. He was also, like almost everyone else in the journalistic circles in which he moved – circles the Amises were introduced to through Hartley and Scott at the *Spectator* – a serious drinker. 'Henry was a very good lover,' reported a former girlfriend, 'if you managed to get hold of him in the morning.'[64] Fairlie's reputation as a political commentator was at its height when the Amises met him, especially among fellow commentators. 'For a time in the Fifties,' recalls Paul Johnson, 'he was probably the most influential political journalist in the country.' Alan Watkins, who was to succeed Fairlie at the *Spectator*, remembers asking himself: 'Who would you rather be? Would you rather be Mr. Justice Devlin (even then the most glamorous judge, though he had yet to be elevated to the Court of Appeal and, briefly, the House of Lords)? Or would you rather be Henry Fairlie. And I answered it: Well, I would rather be Mr. Henry Fairlie.'[65]

Fairlie was spectacularly irresponsible. Not just an adulterer and frequently drunk, but, as Watkins puts it, 'often a beggar man, even (it must be said) on occasion a thief'.[66] Peregrine Worsthorne, in his memoirs, calls him 'a Grub Street genius', but also describes how his selfishness often left his wife and children 'without the price of a pair of shoes or, far worse, the wherewithal to pay the children's school fees'.[67] Yet few could resist Fairlie's charm, which began with what the critic and journalist Philip Hope-Wallace called his 'delinquent ploughboy grin'. Mavis Nicholson remembers Hilly, when most besotted, mooning about the house singing: 'He's a tramp, but I love him.' Catherine Dove (later Freeman), pretty, lively, just down from Oxford and with a traineeship at the BBC, was introduced to Amis and Fairlie by Brian Inglis of the *Spectator* (Inglis was to become the paper's editor in 1959). She remembers drinking with the *Spectator* crowd in a pub near the paper's offices at 99 Gower Street (it moved to 56 Doughty Street in 1975). 'Henry was a shocking fellow,' is how she decribes Fairlie, 'but we [the other women in the circle] all knew him . . . he made a dead set for us.' Amis she recalls as 'a young man about town, very much in the pub, very flirtatious, very cheerful'. The difference between the two was that Fairlie, of whom she was very fond, was 'a joke figure . . . an *absurd* adulterer. I don't think he *ever* spent the night alone. He made everyone laugh. He was like a great big baby.' Kingsley, on the other hand, 'struck me as very much in control of himself, not likely to make a fool of himself, nor indeed be caught out very much'. He was also, she thought, 'the best-looking man in the group'.

Fairlie first enters Amis's correspondence in a letter to Conquest of 17 April 1956: 'Bloody funny all that Fairlie conversation. You did damn well, I thought: cool and funny and on the point. I hate these all-or-nothing thinkers: "the meaning of marriage is X" – without seeing that it can be Y & Z, & A & B & C, and even P & Q too, even though it may well *be* X for some chaps.'[68] But Amis also enjoyed

Fairlie's company and soon the Fairlies were visitors to Swansea. 'Old H.F. is getting on fine here,' Amis wrote to Conquest on 20 June: 'he spent 40 minutes the other evening rebuking me for swearing and telling jokes about madmen.' On 28 September, Fairlie was mentioned again, in a letter to Conquest recounting Amis's failed attempts to seduce Marigold Hunt (later to become Mrs Paul Johnson): 'she insisted on El Vino's, so that she could meet her boyfriend AH SOUL and John Raymond joined us after approximately fifty seconds' tete a tete, so we didn't get much done, except drink . . . Dazed and dejected journey back to Swansea the next day, to find Henry there. Tells me Pic Post have offered him £2500 p.a. to work for them; says he will . . . Anyway, it means he will pay me back the £6 he owes me.'[69] What Henry was doing in Swansea was left unspoken in the letter, though it was no secret. Several months earlier, on 19 June, Bruce Montgomery wrote to Larkin that he had seen the Amises in London: Kingsley had put on a bit of weight while Hilly 'has thinned down a lot, and makes sheep's eyes at Henry Fairlie'.[70] The Clearys remember dropping Amis at the station to catch the London train just as Fairlie was arriving to visit Hilly. Esmond Cleary describes Fairlie as 'totally unreliable'[71] but also clever and knowledgeable; he was particularly impressed by Fairlie's prediction of the Suez adventure.

'Hilly adored Henry Fairlie,' recalls Mavis Nicholson, and she did so partly because Fairlie was romantic in his treatment of the women he pursued. Tom Pocock, naval correspondent on *The Times*, met Fairlie in 1953 and remembers his courting of several women. He went after an attractive woman's pages editor with great bunches of red roses, sent every day to her office. Flowers also figure in the less successful pursuit of Janet Fraser, the very young and pretty secretary of Sir William Haley, editor of *The Times*. 'Henry staged a great wooing,' Pocock says of this campaign, 'but then he treated all his girlfriends magnificently, took them out to the best Charlotte Street restaurants.' As Fraser told Pocock, after one such dinner Fairlie rode back with her in a taxi to her basement flat in Chelsea. There they sat drinking coffee until one in the morning, when she said 'Henry, you're going now.' Fairlie asked if he could sleep on the couch, but she insisted he go; she knew he had friends in London who would put him up (at the time the Fairlies lived in Brighton). When she got up the next morning very early, about seven, she opened her front door into the basement area to discover it filled with cut flowers, in the middle of which Fairlie had placed a complete set of the morning papers (he knew she loved newspapers). Fairlie had walked from her flat in Chelsea to King's Cross, the only place you could get all the morning's papers at that hour, then caught a taxi to Covent Garden market, filled the taxi with armfuls of cut flowers, then rode with it to Chelsea and unloaded the lot, before walking to the Turkish Baths in Jermyn Street, where he stayed until he arrived for work at *The Times* the next day. This extravagance did not get the secretary into bed, though it endeared him to her, as similar behaviour endeared him to other women he wooed, even those who thought him absurd. The suspicion of something bogus about the anecdote owes more to Fairlie's behaviour than to its recounting. Yet such behaviour was never wholly or quite an act; Fairlie mostly did fall for the women he sought to bed, was no ordinary cad or bounder. When he made a play for Siriol Hugh-Jones, Amis's champion at *Vogue*, she was amused, but told him at the outset that she had recently been diagnosed with a serious cancer. According to Pocock, who introduced them, and Hugh-Jones's daughter, Fairlie became her lover and stayed loyal to her to the end, visiting her in hospital until the day she died. It is easy to see why Hilly succumbed to Fairlie: though always sure of Amis's fondness for her, she was neglected in small ways as well as large ones, taken for granted as well as betrayed, which is partly what drove her to affairs in the first place.

That Fairlie was as much in love with Hilly, or thought he was, as she was with him was soon brought sharply home to Amis. In a letter to Larkin of 22 October 1956 Amis explained how he learned of the seriousness of the affair. His explanation comes after a paragraph of literary gossip:

Actually the light or bantering tone of the above is a poor index of how I feel this evening. On Friday a verbal statement was made to me by my wife by which I was given to understand that, far from just having an affair with old Henry Fairlie, she is in love with him and he with her. The topic of divorce from the married state was next raised, and no decision reached. It will be reached in the course of the next few months, so that the amorous pair can decide whether they are victims of an 'infatuation,' or of 'something more important.' I think – but I find it hard to work out what I think – that my marriage has about one chance in four of surviving till next summer.

The letter goes on to talk about the children, whom Amis does not want taken away from him, about the cessation of 'marital rights' while a decision is awaited, about Fairlie (who 'though a most charming lad, is a rather emotional and unreliable one . . . not quite the kind of chap one wants to see *in loco parentis* to one's kids') and about the difference between 'having one's wife fucked' and 'having her taken away from you, plus your children'. Towards the end of the letter, after enjoining Larkin, the only friend he has told, to silence, Amis comes back to the topic: 'I can't imagine how it will all turn out. Dividing the records, selling the house, storing the furniture and all that, it seems inconceivable. Reckon I shall resign here and go to London or somewhere when the time comes.' The letter ends: 'Amis asked for the Court's discretion in respect to his bum, Kingsley.'

Amis had one other piece of serious and alarming news for Larkin. Sally, aged two years and nine months, had had an accident, a fall from a table in the garden; she landed on her head and fractured her skull.[72] The fall led to 'vomiting, convulsions, coma, 999, ambulance, casualty ward and the rest of the caper. After about 3 hours it was established that she was not going to die, and it is very likely that her brain is undamaged.' The doctors would not know for certain about this latter proposition until the following day. When the following day came, they reported no damage, though Sally was to be kept under observation for several weeks. Hilly stayed with her in hospital. Amis relayed these developments coolly to Larkin, but was in a state. The Clearys remember Martin and Philip ringing their doorbell on the day of the accident and asking them to 'come stay with us and my Dad', which they did. It was the first time they had seen for themselves how anxious Amis could become when frightened or stressed, though they had guessed as much from *That Uncertain Feeling*.

About two weeks after Sally's accident, Fairlie wrote to Amis asking for a meeting. Amis refused to see him, explaining why in a remarkable letter, dated 1 November 1956, which makes clear not only how much he valued his family, and disapproved of Fairlie, but what he thought more generally about marriage and adultery.

Dear Henry,

No, we are not going to meet if I can avoid it, because I should not enjoy it and because there is no need for it. There is no need for it because, in the first place, I am not interested in knowing just how keen a man is on taking the most valuable thing I own (my family) away from me because he wants a part of it (my wife), and even if you wanted Hilly twenty times more than I do, that would not make me any more inclined to let her go. So I don't want to know how you feel about this business. And there is nothing more to tell you about how I feel than you must already have guessed. And when you talk of us explaining to each other what the situation means to each of us, what you mean is that you want a chance of showing how much more you care than I do. You would be, and are, wasting your time.

I haven't the slightest doubt that you and Hilly are in love with each other. But it remains true that you are having an affair, and the situation of an affair – absence, partings, reunions, letters, phone-calls, guilt, grief – sharpens and heightens such feelings of love until people are prepared to act foolishly and cruelly upon them. This will be agonising for them, but not as agonising as it is for those who are suffering instead of merely inflicting cruelty, and if they are already selfish and ruthless by nature, as I think you are, they will be less agonised still. – I do not mean that these are by any means the only things in your nature, or that you have a monopoly of them, but they are stronger in you than in most people I know, as I observed before I knew anything of the Hilly business (I didn't at all dislike you for these things then, just made sure I gave you no opportunity to exercise them at my expense. At least that is what I thought I was making sure of.) You are also excitable to the point of instability (more than most of us), and so when Hilly tells me that you are prepared to leave not only Lisette but Simon and Charlotte too in order to go to Hilly, I take this as an indication of the depth of your love, yes, but far more as a sign of the irresponsibility and greed of which you are capable. A second marriage, founded on the unhappiness (in varying degrees) of seven other people, must take its stand, much more than a first marriage on love, sexual, romantic, exclusive, continuous love. The moment that love suffers the slightest blemish (such as a first marriage could survive without difficulty) the marriage needs the utmost patience, resolution, calm, self-restraint etc. – qualities rather less noticeable in you than in others. Am I lacking in charity? Well, what do you expect? And what is all this about emotional blackmail? Do try to see some difference between feeling bad about trying to take Hilly away from me and me feeling bad about having Hilly and my children taken away from me. You and she have each got someone who wants you. You should welcome the notion of an endurance test because of this.

Write again only if urgent: reading yours & writing this have been no fun.
   Kingsley.

One evening in the following week Amis 'offered Hilly her freedom'. This was at 8 p.m. By 3 a.m. the next morning, he reported to Larkin on 4 November, 'the successive application of tears and pork sword had brought hubby right back into the picture again'. There then followed a period in which Amis felt 'a little resentful' towards Hilly, not on account of the affair, he claimed, but on 'extra-amatory grounds': 'her laziness, her continuous peevishness with the children, her utter lack of any interest in anything whatsoever'. The harshness of this characterisation, as of the 'pork sword' reference, sounds also in his impatience with her reaction to a further development, one which he had thought would work in his favour. Fairlie, whose financial affairs, in the words of his obituary in *The Times*, 'were always but slenderly under his control',[73] had been arrested for failing to appear before the bankruptcy courts and was made to spend a night in Brixton prison:

You'd imagine that the irresponsibility of which that kind of thing is evidence would tend on the whole to cool the amatory flame in his mistress, or at least not to feed it. Ah, but you'd be wrong. Makes him more of a wild, wayward, own-worst-enemy, feckless victim of persecution from those who are older, less gay, less handsome and attractive (they are all jealous of him, you see), more stodgily literal-minded about things like money and promises than he. The only thing I can't quite accept about Henry is that he isn't an Irishman.[74]

The letter conveying this news ends: 'It isn't that I dislike you, but Henry is much more of a bum, Kingsley.'

On 20 November 1956, in advance of a projected visit to Hull, where Larkin had been appointed University Librarian in March of the previous year, Amis informed his friend that 'my marriage now has the odds heavily on my side' (elsewhere in the letter he reminded Larkin about staying 'in your flat not elsewhere, hunh? You know my little phobia about this'). On 6 December he was able to announce that 'I have more or less got my wife back (no Henry for 6 months; resumption of marital relations; much increased cordiality between the partners to

the matrimonial arrangement in question) for the time being, and
that is sodding good-oh.' In addition, Sally was 'fine, thank you, not
a moment's anxiety since she left hospital'. Three months later, on
19 February 1957, Amis was reporting that 'after a mild setback'
relations with Hilly were 'much better now than for a long time
before even the Henry business began. Old Harry F. is bug erred
now, I confidently say.' Partly, Amis's confidence came from the fact
that Fairlie had gone incommunicado, refusing to answer Hilly's
letters, in the manner of his treatment of creditors or bankruptcy
courts. As far as Amis could see, the marriage had survived: 'I know
I've said this sort of thing before, but this time I can't see things
going wrong at this end. Must keep my hands off the cute-ease,
though. There's one here who – but I mustn't go into that.'

Amis's projected visit to Larkin never took place. At the last minute,
on 22 November 1956, he sent a telegram cancelling, followed by
a brief letter of explanation. He did not come, he told Larkin, because
he would have been miserable company, not solely on account of
the Fairlie business or the Sally business, but because 'my young
lady whom I was very attached to (not the rugby enthusiast's wife)
has just decided to give me up'. This young lady was Mavis
Nicholson, since 1952 the wife of Geoff Nicholson, Amis's friend
and former student. Mavis and Geoff were close to both Amises.
Though not the first of Hilly's friends to sleep with Amis, she was
the first Hilly did not turn against or sour on as a consequence, in
part because she had grown used to Amis's philandering, in part
because of her own adulteries, in part because, as Hilly puts it,
'somehow she was never a threat, we were all in love with Mavis'.
Amis's affair with Mavis began some time after the acceptance of
Lucky Jim, during a period of frequent visits to London. Mavis and
Geoff lived in a flat in the Cut in Waterloo where they often put
up Amis, or Amis and Hilly. Several times in London, Amis invited
her to stand in for Hilly as guest or partner at some social event
when Hilly was stuck in Swansea with the kids, or was seeing Henry
Fairlie. When the Boulting Brothers, after numerous complications,
finally began filming *Lucky Jim*, in the autumn of 1956, Amis was
invited to watch rehearsals and shooting. On one occasion, when
Hilly could not come, Amis took Mavis in her place. She remembers the two of them having breakfast at Claridge's with film people,
then being driven in a chauffeured Rolls-Royce to the studios. It

was a freezing morning and the chauffeur tucked a blanket round their legs for the drive to Elstree. She and Amis were thrilled and a trifle intimidated by the glamour of the occasion. 'You're being worshipped,' she said to him. 'You're going to be really big.'[75]

Mavis agonised over the affair with Amis. In late November 1956 she broke it off, but by December it was back on again. In the same letter (of 6 December) in which Amis announced that 'I have more or less got my wife back', he also stated that 'As a consequence (though I can quite see how you can't quite see how this can be so) I have got my girl-friend back too. And that, as well, is very nice (indeed to fook). So, in response to your kind inquiry, yes, my love-life is quite near an even keel at the moment.' When Larkin wrote to tell Amis that he was planning a visit to London in February, he suggested that Amis come up for it, to join him at an Eddie Condon concert. Amis replied on 2 January approving the concert plan ('yes of course cully, I'm game'), adding that 'g-f [girlfriend] may want to come when she gets wind of it. So may her hubby, but he's a very decent chap. You'll like him.' As the visit approached, Amis wrote to Larkin to suggest that they 'both stay with my girl and her hubby – no awkwardness, never fear. Have fixed it with my girl.'[76] The visit was a great success: Amis pronounced Larkin 'on cracking form . . . more cheerful than I'd seen you for some time' and reported that 'Mavis thought you were very attractive . . . She is a dear little thing, that one.'[77]

The affair with Mavis was different from most of Amis's other affairs; it was as much an expression of affection as desire. Only in the 1960s, when Amis supported the Vietnam War and Geoff and Mavis opposed it, were relations between them strained. Mavis was flirtatious and up for fun. She and Hilly took delight in teasing Amis, which he loved. She was a good mimic and could imitate his odd, penguin-like walk perfectly, a performance he often requested. Amis could be flauntingly boorish, belching and farting during meals or to punctuate tunes, and the two women would round on him in mock-fury, or partly mock-fury: 'Do you know how unappealing this is?' they would cry. 'You think you're attractive at all costs. But you're not.' More soberly, Amis would quiz them about female habits and feelings, how certain sorts of women would react in certain circumstances. Their answers would sometimes find their way into the novels, as would snatches of their letters or character-istic turns of phrase or gestures. While the relative health of the

Bowen marriage in *I Like It Here* may derive from the restored good relations and 'increased cordiality' of Amis and Hilly post-Fairlie, Barbara Bowen's attractions, like aspects of her appearance, derive from both Hilly and Mavis.

In September 1956, just before Hilly broke the news to Amis of the seriousness of her feelings for Fairlie, the Amises and the Nicholsons had gone on holiday together, along with the Nicholsons' friend, Tom Griffiths, an engineer, also from Swansea. They spent almost two weeks in Pramousquier, near Cavalière, on the southern tip of the French Riviera. Writing to Larkin on 9 September, soon after arriving, Amis complained bitterly about the journey from London and the Frenchness of the French, but also admitted 'it would be wrong to pretend I'm not enjoying myself'.[78] In the course of the holiday, the two couples and Griffiths amused themselves by constructing an elaborate and slightly creepy fantasy: the three men pretended they were the women's children: Geoff was Mavis's child, Kingsley was Hilly's child and Tom was the child of their imaginary sister, who'd gone off to Australia. Kingsley pretended to have a temper tantrum when Geoff got too much attention; Hilly and Mavis got to treat their husbands as literal as well as figurative babies. 'Is Kingsley getting too red, darling?' Mavis would ask Hilly. Mavis remembers the fantasy as funny and clever (funny enough for Amis to write down, though it has been lost), alternately defusing and heightening erotic tensions between the two couples. The holiday was enough of a success for Amis to agree to go abroad again the following summer, this time to Bordeaux.[79] In the right circumstances, with the right people, abroad could be perfectly tolerable, even enjoyable, though getting there, and the thought of getting there, always induced boredom and anxiety. In the next two decades Amis frequently went on holiday outside Britain, both in Europe and further afield; he even, on several occasions, lived abroad for extended periods and twice seriously considered more permanent moves. Though never a Maugham-like Strether, he was no Garnet Bowen either.

15

Widening Horizons

By the mid-1950s the Amises' social life had widened both within Swansea and outside it. It was James 'Jo' Bartley who introduced them to the hard-drinking *crachach* crowd from which Elizabeth Gruffydd Williams and her friends in *That Uncertain Feeling* were partly drawn. Amis found this crowd more sympathetic and congenial than John Lewis found its fictional equivalent; from it came several lifelong friends. Chief among these friends were Stuart Thomas, a solicitor, and his wife Eve.[1] Stuart Thomas, eight years older than Amis, was educated at Swansea Grammar School and the University of Wales, Aberystwyth. After a war spent in Burma and India, he entered his father's firm of solicitors, D.O. Thomas and Co., a large general practice. He was a friend of Dylan Thomas, with whom he'd been at school, and became a trustee of his Literary Estate in 1953, the year Dylan died. It was through him that Amis would also become a trustee of the estate. Stuart Thomas was a man who provoked strong feelings. Though warm, loyal and considerate to his friends, to outsiders or those he took against he could present a very different face. Clive Gammon describes him as 'one of the most unpleasant men I've ever met: rude, notoriously malevolent, sardonic . . . a kind of goblin'. The literary academic Ralph Maud, a scholar and editor of Dylan Thomas's poetry, remembers being summoned into Thomas's offices in Swansea. Thomas was seated at his desk and took his time before looking up from his work. There was no place for anyone else to sit. Late in his life Amis routinely spent three weeks in August and September, when the

Garrick Club shut, staying with the Thomases in Swansea. Every weekday he and Stuart would go off for drinks at the Bristol Channel Yacht Club, until Stuart was asked to leave the club, after over forty years' membership, on the grounds of what one fellow member, a friend, called 'general horribleness'. It was thought Stuart's unwelcoming presence at the bar put off younger and prospective members. This same friend remembers Stuart staring out of the window of the club as Sir Michael Llewellyn, the Lord-Lieutenant of West Glamorgan, approached, resplendent in an elaborate brass-buttoned blazer: 'Who's this fucking fireman,' Stuart muttered.[2]

Eve Thomas (née Davies) was in some ways as formidable as her husband, or as Elizabeth Gruffydd Williams or the women of *The Old Devils* (1986).[3] She was smart, lively, independent, very funny and salty, extremely attractive, a good drinker and a good smoker. She lived to be almost ninety. The Thomases met the Amises through Bartley, probably by way of Eve's friend Gwenllian Hancock, whose father had been Professor of History at Swansea. Gwenllian married the Principal of the local art college and she and her husband became friendly with the man who later succeeded her father as Professor of History, David Quinn, who had known Jo and Elsa Bartley in Northern Ireland. The Bartleys fitted into the 'dentist and solicitor' crowd because they were older and more sophisticated than Amis's other university colleagues, at least according to Eve Thomas. They both drank 'like mad' and Elsa was 'very good looking', with an Eton crop; Gwenllian was also good-looking, as well as a drinker (she died of cirrhosis of the liver). There was a 'restless', 'impatient' quality about social life in this crowd, which Eve Thomas attributed to the war. 'We sought the company of people we enjoyed,' Eve remembered; 'we were very sociable,' recalled Rona Williamson (née Thomas), whose father was headmaster of a local grammar school (not Swansea Grammar), and whose brother went out with Stuart Thomas's sister.[4] Rona, also attractive and exuberant, remembers picnics on the Gower with the Amises, including one when Amis brought a thermos of martinis to the beach. The women in the circle were described by her as 'glamorous', 'racy'; several thought themselves depicted in *That Uncertain Feeling*. When the wife of the Welsh composer Daniel Jones was suggested as a possible model for a character in the novel, she was indignant, not because the character had been unfaithful but because she'd slept with a dentist.

The Amises were welcomed into the Thomas set because they

were themselves glamorous, hard-partying, witty and lively. They also had the money for it, though Eve Thomas was at pains to stress that few of her friends had much money at the time; they were all starting out in their careers and had young families to support. It was also a plus in this circle that the Amises were English not Welsh. Then there was Amis's literary celebrity: 'Kingsley was really considered kind of a star,' Hilly remembers. 'We were accepted as Dylan Thomas had been, and we, of course, were not so much trouble as Caitlin and Dylan had been.' The Amises soon learned to keep academic and bourgeois circles 'pretty separate', though 'they all sort of vaguely knew each other'. Esmond Cleary remembers a newly arrived colleague at Swansea recounting what a *crachach* acquaintance had said about socialising with academics: 'We don't mix with people from the university. They have second-hand prams and their children pick things up from the floor.' Younger academics, in particular, were looked down upon; as Glanmor Williams puts it: 'too poverty stricken, not flash enough.' The only members of the English Department Eve Thomas knew were the Bartleys and the Amises.

John Lewis's attitudes in *That Uncertain Feeling* to the sort of circle the Amises began moving in after the publication of *Lucky Jim* had an impact on Amis's reputation as a literary rebel. Lewis begins the novel 'as a sworn foe of the *bourgeoisie*, and especially the Aberdarcy *bourgeoisie*, and especially the anglicised Aberdarcy *bourgeoisie*'.[5] He feels 'embarrassed defensiveness'[6] when introduced to *crachach* types, with reason. Elizabeth's friend Paul Whetstone, for example, greets him with 'the glance of a great conductor introduced to a dancing xylophonist'.[7] But Lewis thinks times are changing. Though he notes a new-minted quality to Elizabeth's air of authority, he concludes that it 'didn't matter, did it, now it was no longer true, thank God, that it took three generations to make a gentleman?'[8] Eventually, Lewis's anti-bourgeois prejudices soften, as he imagines the prejudices of Elizabeth's crowd do towards him: 'They might not be very bright and they did perhaps fit into my old category of upper-class, but it was getting rather late in the day to bother with things like categories. There weren't so many amiable and light-hearted people about that one could afford to turn sour or sociological on them when they turned up.'[9] In the end, Lewis's self-interested faith in progress, driven mostly by lust for Elizabeth, gives way to a no less self-interested reversion to class solidarity: in the last chapter he chucks the rigged promotion and leaves Aberdarcy for the town of his birth, Fforestfawr (Dai Evans's home town as well, in *The Evans Country*), an ending many found improbable, damagingly so, in part because Fforestfawr is largely defined through Lewis's father, a figure of perfect goodness. This father performs a function in *That Uncertain Feeling* like that of Gore-Urquhart in *Lucky Jim*, but *Lucky Jim* is a different sort of novel, one whose improbabilities are licensed by comic or romance convention; to Bruce Montgomery, writing to Larkin on 6 November 1955, 'the final chapter was preposterous . . . like something bound in by mistake from some completely different work'. In later years Amis explained Lewis's retreat to Fforestfawr in terms that recall the complications of the synopsis: 'What is at work is partly scruples, but not enough alone to make him act in a scrupulous way. What is also at work then is an attack of sexual panic. Despite his views of himself – which are partly ironical, as a striding, sneering Don Juan – when he finds himself behaving like that he realizes he hasn't got what it takes; he's afraid of being really involved with Mrs. Gruffydd Williams, and he's afraid of what this will do to his marriage. It's very largely a selfish fear which he then dresses up partly with scruples.'[10] As for Fforestfawr as 'working-class-Arcadia', this is a view, he told Larkin, 'some chaps (not necessarily you) have over-emphasised'.[11]

The reviews *That Uncertain Feeling* received were, as Rubinstein wrote to tell Amis in Portugal, largely positive, but their focus on class, often exposing the reviewer's snobbery, obscured the complexity of Amis's character drawing. To the reviewer in the *Evening News* Lewis was simply 'an outrageous little bounder'. Elizabeth Bowen, writing in *Tatler*, pronounced the Aberdarcy gentry 'staggeringly common'.[12] Julian Maclaren-Ross, in the *Listener*, could not believe that Lewis Senior, a 'proletarian parent', could be addicted to the Ximenes crossword in the *Observer*. Harry Ritchie makes a good point about the retrospective effect such comments had on the reputation of *Lucky Jim*. Though Jim Dixon was, like Lewis, 'something of a lower-class social misfit . . . the novel's university setting meant that critics had assumed [his] plights were caused by problems peculiar to the closed world of academia. Conveniently, Dixon's university was redbrick, so *Lucky Jim* could be categorized under the two headings for the Movement – "academic" and "provincial." In *That Uncertain Feeling* the social background was more orthodox and reviewers were now more confident that Amis was a novelist of class-based comedy'¹³ – as he had been in *Lucky Jim*.

What bound John Lewis, Jim Dixon, Garnet Bowen and their creator together in the eyes of many reviewers was not just their class, variously associated with scholarships, the welfare state and the 1944 Butler Education Act, but their mocking attitudes to high culture, their lack of what Sam Dawson, talking of Amis, called 'the bump of reverence'. In the December 1955 issue of *Encounter* Evelyn Waugh described Amis and his fellow Movement writers as products of 'L'Ecole de Butler', though the Butler Act was in fact too late for any of them. 'A new wave of philistinism', Waugh prophesied, would issue from 'these grim young people coming off the assembly lines in their hundreds every year and finding employment as critics, even as poets and novelists'. Waugh's line was seconded by Spender in a June 1956 editorial in *Encounter* entitled 'This New England'. Spender thought 'the more concentrated ugliness of nineteenth-century slums' only marginally worse than the uniformity of today's 'spreading grey of suburbs': 'Everywhere the price paid for diffused facilities is sacrifice of quality.' The most memorable of these attacks occurred on 25 December 1955 in the 'Books of the Year' pages of the *Sunday Times*. It was launched by Somerset Maugham himself, who had just got round to reading *Lucky Jim*, which he called 'a remarkable novel', though one of 'ominous significance'. Maugham's sense of the novel's social impact was astute, though he misread it on several levels, from specifics of plot and character to overall intent (he was right, however, about Amis's attitude to university expansion):

I am told that today rather more than 60 per cent of the men who go to the universities go on a Government grant. This is a new class that has entered upon the scene. It is the white-collar proletariat. Mr. Kingsley Amis is so talented, his observation is so keen, that you cannot fail to be convinced that the young men he so brilliantly describes truly represent the class with which his novel is concerned.

They do not go to the university to acquire culture, but to get a job, and when they have got one, scamp it. They have no manners, and are woefully unable to deal with any social predicament. Their idea of a celebration is to go to a public house and drink six beers. They are mean, malicious and envious. They will write anonymous letters to harass a fellow undergraduate and listen in to a telephone conversation that is no business of theirs. Charity, kindness, generosity, are qualities which they hold in contempt. They are scum. They will in due course leave the university. Some will doubtless sink back, perhaps with relief, into the modest class from which they emerged; some will take to drink, some to crime and go to prison. Others will become schoolmasters and form the young, or journalists and mould public opinion. A few will go into Parliament, become Cabinet Ministers and rule the country. I look upon myself as fortunate that I will not live to see it.

Maugham's exempting of Amis from censure, his treating him as mere observer, was uncharacteristic of critics hostile to the new class, especially to its supposed philistinism. Jim Dixon's 'Filthy Mozart' was simply assumed to express Amis's taste, though Amis adored Mozart. But such identifications were not always wrong. When John Lewis daydreams 'the ideal interview, which would secure the ideal candidate in the minimum time', he moves from a series of imagined exchanges about library duties (this is the material Amis got from Larkin) to ones about culture:

Q. Have you any other interests?
A. *Welsh History, Welsh manners and customs, Welsh Rugby football, Dylan Thomas, Welsh amateur drama, Welsh arts and culture.*
Q. Have you heard of T.S. Eliot?
A. *Yes.*
Q. Are you interested in films, drinking, American novels, women's breasts, jazz, science fiction?
A. *Give me a good play any day, I like a quiet pint or two at the Club on a Sunday after chapel, I read Mark Twain at school, my wife is a school-teacher, I'd sooner hear a nice choir, I don't seem to get much time for recreational reading.*[14]

John Lewis's real preferences are Amis's, as many readers would have recognised: the pointedly unexpanded 'Yes' in answer to the question about T.S. Eliot suggests Movement hostility; women's breasts and drinking suggest the novels themselves; a preference for American and genre fiction over foreign and modernist fiction is everywhere apparent in Amis's *Spectator* reviews, which allude to Fitzgerald, Dickson Carr and popular science fiction writers rather than Proust, Kafka or Virginia Woolf. When *I Like It Here* was published the charges of philistinism and provincialism were well established; at times the parading of Bowen's cultural prejudices seems designed to provoke them. 'One of the jobs performed by this novel,' suggests John McDermott, 'is the guying by parody and comic exaggeration of the reviewers' version of Amis's fiction.'[15] In later years, Amis was much given to such guying; it was also one of the motives behind the 'Ron Cain' parodies (discussed in Chapter 11), written at the same time. Still, Bowen's views are often Amis's, as are Lewis's and Dixon's.

The view of Amis as exemplar as well as chronicler of the new class led to his association with a second literary grouping, that of the Angry Young Men. When John Osborne's *Look Back in Anger* opened at the Royal Court in May 1956, Kenneth Tynan began his review of it in the *Observer* by citing the Maugham attack on Amis. The review begins: '"They are scum," was Mr. Maugham's famous verdict on the class of State-aided university students to which Kingsley Amis's *Lucky Jim* belongs; and since Mr. Maugham seldom says anything controversial or uncertain of wide acceptance, his opinion must clearly be that of many. Those who share it had better stay well away from John Osborne's *Look Back in Anger*, which is all scum and a mile wide.' The review ends by calling *Look Back in Anger* 'the best young play of its decade'. The *New Statesman* reviewer thought the play's subject 'the seamy side of the Kingsley Amis world'. The reviewer in the *Financial Times* called Jimmy Porter 'unlucky Jim', the title also of a review in *Time and Tide*.[16] On 12 July 1956, in the first of two articles in the *Daily Mail*, the young freelance journalist Dan Farson, as key a figure in the creation of the Angry Young Men as Hartley and Scott were in the creation of the Movement, declared that 'the postwar generation has suddenly arrived', listing Amis first among the four 'remarkable young men' who were its leaders (the other three were Osborne, Colin Wilson, author of *The Outsider*, published at the end of May, and Michael Hastings, an eighteen-year-old tailor whose first play, *Don't Destroy Me*, would open on 25 July). On 26 July the label 'Angry Young Men' first appeared in print, in an article in the *Daily Express* by John Barber headlined TODAY'S ANGRY YOUNG MEN AND HOW THEY DIFFER FROM SHAW. Previously, over a drink with Osborne, George Fearon, a press officer at the Royal Court Theatre, had told him 'I suppose you're really – an angry young man',[17] a comment Osborne repeated on television. But it was not until the Barber article that the description was extended to other writers. These writers were the same four singled out by Farson (John Braine, the only 'Angry' Amis became friendly with, would not be included until a year later, with the publication of *Room at the Top*). Amis was called 'the sort of man who likes billiards, bars and progressive jazz clubs' and whose heroes 'prefer beer and blondes to brains', a description which recalls V.S. Pritchett's review of *That Uncertain Feeling* in the *New Statesman* on 20 August 1955. This review, published under the pseudonym 'Richard Lister', described Amis as 'brashly, vulgarly, aggressively un-sensitive', 'a literary Teddy boy'. As for the world inhabited by Amis's characters, it is 'the world that has succeeded the posh . . . the world of the Welfare State in all its crudity'.

Amis had little time for the Angry Young Man label. He disliked the theatre (part of what's wrong with Garnet Bowen's writing is that it's for the theatre), had not seen *Look Back in Anger*, was 'surprised and unflattered'[18] when Farson described it to him as 'an Amis sort of play' and never commented on *Don't Destroy Me*, no doubt because he never saw it.[19] Amis's *Spectator* review on 15 June 1956 of *The Outsider* (published by Gollancz, which clearly had its finger on the pulse) made his antipathy to the qualities attributed to the Angry Young Men unmistakable. The 'most untenable and annoying' of these qualities was a supposed 'larger share, if not a monopoly, of depth and honesty and sensitivity and intensity and acuity and insight and courage and adulthood – especially that'. For Amis, adulthood was just what outsider types lacked: 'Few people who can read and write could have failed to be wandering outlaws of their own dark minds in their youth's summer, say about the age of sixteen. And it is a persona many of us revert to in our more shamelessly adolescent moments.' The outsider's isolation, a product in part of his superiority, was another quality unlikely to impress Amis, the most social of men: 'He has no strong affections, and his lack of ordinary warmth makes him divide the human race into himself on one side, plus the odd hero-figure or two, and "the mob" on the other.' Then there was the related immodesty of the outsider's cosmic perspective, his privileged awakening 'to the chaos of existence, to the unreality of what the literal-minded take to be reality. He does not accept the conditions of human life, and finds release from its prison only in moments of terror and ecstasy' – or anger. Such irrationalism or emotionalism Amis opposed, 'feeling as I do that one is better off with too much reason than with none at all'. Amis ended the review on a note of modesty, irony and humour, characteristic Movement rather than Angry Young Man or outsider qualities. While prepared to admit that the outlook Wilson describes was unlikely to be eradicated by 'a course of P.T. and cross-country running, or a good dose of salts', there might be 'curative properties in . . . ordering up another bottle, attending a jam session, or getting introduced to a young lady'.[20]

After the appearance of Amis's review Wilson initiated a correspondence with him. 'Had an incredible letter from Capitaine C. Wilson of the Légion Etrangère,' Amis announced to Conquest on 20 June 1956. 'I give him two years before paranoia closes over his head.' In his initial letter of 15 June, Wilson declared as complete a lack of sympathy for Amis's work as Amis had for his, though he also admitted he had not yet read any of Amis's books (he persuaded his girlfriend to do so, and she reported back to him), shuddered at Amis's 'anti-culture' line, and vowed to knock him off his pedestal in order to establish 'a lot of things I want to establish – vital things for the course of modern history'. Amis wrote a draft reply, dated 19 June, in a tone of studied calm: 'Dear Mr W., Please try not to be too upset by my review: I know how galling these things can be, but after the excellent press your book has had, I shouldn't have thought you had any real need to worry. After all, if your work is any good it'll make its way in spite of anything that weekend reviewers like myself say about it. Yours sincerely.'[21] On 21 June Wilson wrote again, claiming he had not really been upset by Amis's review and apologising to him for any rudeness in his previous letter, which he attributed to an article he was working on for the *Sunday Times*, an attack on logical positivism ('your review came as a last straw after losing my temper with A.J. Ayer's blatherings'). Losing one's temper, of course, was no bad thing in Wilson's view: 'all this attacking is a necessary corollary to my next book, which is on the vital need for a new religion if our civilisation is to be saved'. In a later letter, on the 29th, Wilson tried to arrange a meeting with Amis in Cardiff (Wilson was visiting North Devon with Dan Farson, who may have concocted the idea of a get-together, as he did of get-togethers between other Angries) but Amis put him off. He also put him off in London, though eventually they had several meetings. At one of these, in 1957 (perhaps in Swansea, where Wilson once visited), Wilson offered Amis a bottle of whisky which, given Wilson's interest in murder,[22] Amis was too frightened to drink. It stayed on Amis's shelf until 'an intrepid psychiatrist pal guzzled it with no ill-effects, or none but the usual'.[23]

Farson was not the only figure eager to bring the Angry Young Men together. In 1957 the publisher Tom Maschler, later to become Amis's publisher, invited several supposed Angries (aside from Amis, Osborne and Wilson among the original four, these included Kenneth Tynan, Lindsay Anderson, Bill Hopkins, Stuart Holroyd, John Wain and Doris Lessing, a lone female Angry) to explain their views in a book entitled *Declaration*. Amis refused to participate, partly because he had already, in January, published *Socialism and the Intellectuals*, which several contributors to *Declaration* disparage, partly for reasons Maschler quotes in the book's introduction: 'I hate all this pharasaical twittering about the "state of our civilisation," and I suspect anyone who wants to buttonhole me about my "role in society." This book is likely to prove a valuable addition to the cult of the Solemn Young Man.'[24] Privately, Amis was especially scornful of Wain's contribution to the book: 'Christ, what about this *Declaration* thing,' he complained to Larkin, in a letter of 15 October 1957. 'He's [Wain's] not an angry young man, you sam, so he gets together with them all to say he isn't. Ho hum, ho hum. Well with you as the Auden and me as the Isherwood *de nos jours*, "our society" is dong not so bad, but with ole JBW as the Stephen Spender I reckon it's being given short weight, hey?'

Amis's hostility to Wain had been growing since the publication of *Lucky Jim*. Wain played a crucial role in Amis's rise to fame and was generous in promoting his work. But as Amis's career prospered, Wain's fell off. Wain's manner, his arrogance and self-importance, began to grate on Amis, as on others. To Al Alvarez, who was inspired by Wain at Oxford and adopted by him 'as his bright young protégé',[25] being Wain's friend 'was a tricky business'. He was 'a man without much modesty who sincerely believed he was a great genius and would tolerate no one he couldn't patronize'.[26] Alvarez believes Amis turned on Wain after a slighting comment from him just before *Lucky Jim* was published. Even after Amis was hugely successful 'and Wain was scraping a living, a fairly pathetic figure in terms of worldly success', Amis's underlying sense of injury persisted. In the *Memoirs* Amis tells several stories which suggest why, beginning with the one alluded to by

Alvarez. In the summer of 1953, when both *Lucky Jim* and *Hurry on Down* were in press, Amis told Wain that his advance was £100: "'Oh. I'm getting two hundred and fifty for mine." He leaned forward. "You see – mine isn't Joe Soap's first novel."'[27] A second story Amis tells, from some five years later, opens with Wain asking 'Are you working on anything at the moment?'

This way of putting the matter suggests fast and economically that the one questioned is a mere part-timer, dashing off a rondeau or epigram should the spirit move him, otherwise selling antique furniture or sitting on his bum. 'Yes,' I said.

'Oh. What is it?'

Could it have been a monograph on the fauna of Kentucky? 'A novel,' I said with restraint, not adding 'actually' or 'called *Fuck You*.'

John gave me a sly, old-pals' wink. 'Make it a good one this time, eh?'[28]

Amis admired *Hurry on Down* but came to resent its coupling with *Lucky Jim*, in part because he thought it distorted and diminished his novel's character and reputation. This coupling began even before the novels were published; if *Lucky Jim* had appeared in November 1953, as originally scheduled, John Raymond would have discussed them together on the radio, he told Hilary Rubinstein.[29] It also persisted: as late as 24 January 1958 Amis was complaining, in a letter to the *TLS*, about the way its reviewer noted 'certain alleged parallels between features of Mr. Wain's work and features of my own, observing in deadpan fashion that in each case Mr. Wain got in first'. Amis's complaints were understandable not only because of the mostly pointless or strained nature of the parallels adduced and the way they obscured important distinctions in theme, tone, situation and style, but because they suggested an equivalence in merit.

The main points of comparison between the two novels – the legitimate points – concern their heroes. Charles Lumley, Wain's hero, can be related to Jim Dixon in several ways, particularly in his preoccupation with jobs and earning a living, a preoccupation shared by Joe Lampton in *Room at the Top* as well as Jimmy Porter, though Jimmy is not much employed. This connection Amis explained in a 1975 interview with Dale Salwak, quoting an unnamed 'someone' who claimed 'that the weakness of the English novel of the twentieth century up to the time he was talking about (could be 1939) was that nothing happened until after 6:00 pm or on Saturday and Sunday'.[30] *Lucky Jim* and *Hurry on Down*, in contrast, were 'to a large extent about people at work'.[31] Amis suggested another similarity between the two novels, as well as a crucial difference, in a letter to Wain of 6 November 1953 praising *Hurry on Down*: 'It is very funny in parts and does succeed above all in getting across a grotesque and twisted view of life (which is what I try to do, though it's not the same view – this I think is where we're similar).'

The difference Amis alludes to in this passage derives largely from Lumley's disconnection from society, which has an outsider quality to it. The Angry Young Man label fits him in a way it hardly fits Dixon, for all Dixon's frustration and irritation. Lumley has outlaw pretensions, comes from a higher social class than Dixon, went to 'the University' (that is, Oxbridge) not university. His disaffection is wilful, existential, recalling Amis's comments in the Wilson review on the outsider's bourgeois origins, his suspicion that 'the incidence of Outsiderism among builders' foremen or bookies' runners must be low'.[32] Lumley wants out of the social system, which is different from what Dixon wants; Dixon merely wants out of academe, or at least that part of academe ruled over by Professor Welch. Lumley is obsessed with, because he feels imprisoned by, his class; Dixon rarely mentions class. Lumley is physically brave as well as violent, neither of which Dixon is.[33] Lumley feels superior to those he meets, which is not quite what Dixon feels about the people in his world. Lumley is a sneerer, Dixon is not.

By the summer of 1957, when Amis was finishing *I Like It Here*, *Lucky Jim* had become, in J.D. Scott's words, 'a book so much discussed and argued about and hated and admired that few people seem to remember any longer what it's about'.[34] Yet Amis frequently described what it was about, in defiantly literary rather than social or political terms. Jim gets Christine at the end because he's the hero of a comedy or comedy-romance and because, as the novel tells us, 'for once in his life he resolved to bet on his luck',[35] which is to say, to trust in comic providence. Comedy in this sense, like romance, is on the side of the young and of nature. Jim's desire for Christine is 'as natural to him, as unimportant and unobjectionable, as reaching out to take a large ripe peach from a fruit dish'.[36] As Amis wrote to Harry Ritchie, in reply to Ritchie's queries about the novel's connection to the Angry Young Men and related phenomena,

I had no social (class, etc.) intentions at all: what class are the Welches? As for politics, of course Bertrand is a Conservative (the buns conversation) because Dixon hates him. Of course Margaret sings in the Conservative choir. As for culture, of course he hates Mozart; I must have said already that him hating Castelnuovo-Tedesco wouldn't be any good. Because of course Welch loves Mozart. Same with the madrigals, etc. None of these things, Mozart, madrigals, Bertrand's kind of painting, were particularly fashionable or unfashionable, they were just things I happened to know about that D would hate. As regards the provincialness and so on, after thinking it over I would put it like this. The decision to set it in the North, and make the hero non-bourgeois and put in a lot about his job was taken in the same spirit as a detective-story writer of that period deciding he would rather not set it in a pleasant Sussex village and not have the baronet murdered in his library at the Towers. A literary decision in that it had to do with the structure, characterisation etc. of that book, but not literary in the sense that would make it a shot in a campaign or a unit in a literary offensive against mandarinism or anything else. Nothing programmatic or manifesto-ish about it.[37]

In the case of *That Uncertain Feeling*, where class details figure explicitly, social or political readings were inevitable, throwing out of focus or obscuring the novel's ethical concerns. As Amis wrote to Philip Oakes on 17 September 1955 from Portugal: 'The book is supposed to be about morals or morality, or our modern version of these. The marriage and to a lesser extent the job business are offered as typical forms in which moral issues present themselves today.' With *Lucky Jim*, cultural rather than class details predominate. Yet Amis knew full well that cultural details have class implications, just as he knew that in giving Dixon the background he gave him, he was producing a new kind of hero, despite fitting him into a traditional comic plot. When in a benign mood, or convinced of the literary bona fides of the enquirer, Amis would admit as much, as in the following letter of 6 January 1958 to the American academic, William Van O'Connor:

Dixon is supposed to be the son of a clerk, an office worker (like myself) . . . [T]here are certainly many like him in that they are the first generation in their families to have received a university education, they have won their way up by scholarships all through, they are not the conventional Oxford – Cambridge academic types, they don't embrace the manners, customs and pastimes of that type (sherry, learned discussion, tea-parties with the Principal's wife, chamber concerts) but stick to their own, to the ones their non-academic contemporaries share (beer, arguments in pubs, amorous behaviour at – and outside – dances, jazz). Dixon has seen, throughout his life, power and position going to people who (he suspects) are less notable for their ability than their smooth manners, their accents, the influence they or their fathers can wield. The money thing is less important; Dixon is hard-up himself, and is a bit suspicious of the rich, but is far more of Oxford-accented 'culture.' If he were closely questioned about this, he would probably admit in the end that culture is real and important and ought not to be made the property of a sort of exclusive club which you can only enter if you come from the right school – culture ought to be available to everyone who can use it; but such an avowal would be very untypical of him and you would probably have to get him very drunk first.

It is tempting to think of Amis as drunk, or at least intoxicated, when he wrote *Socialism and the Intellectuals*, though on fame not alcohol. The thirteen-page pamphlet, published by the Fabian Society in January 1957, is just the sort of 'pharisaical twittering' about 'the state of our civilisation' and my 'role in society' Amis complained of to Maschler when refusing to contribute to *Declaration*, a point Maschler noted in his introduction.[38] The underlying theme of the pamphlet had been anticipated by an article Amis wrote for the *Spectator* on 2 December 1955, 'Mind We Don't Quarrel', which described his participation in a protest in Swansea against capital punishment. The occasion of the protest was a visit to the Swansea Guildhall by the Home Secretary, Gwilym Lloyd George. When Amis arrived there were only four protesters present: three women, two of whom were Jean Cleary and Hilly, and a baby, Sally. Eventually a handful of students arrived, several philosophers from the university, a novelist, a journalist and his wife, an historian's wife and eight actors from the local repertory company. A banner was unfurled reading HANGING IS SHAMEFUL, with Amis holding one end and Jean Cleary the other, the newspapers took photos, the Chief Inspector warned the demonstrators to keep out of the road ('Else we shall quarrel. Mind we don't quarrel'), the official party passed by and stared, except for the Home Secretary, whose expression and movements were governed by 'a kind of dedicated detachment'. Then everyone went home. The article ends on a note of deflated solidarity:

Well, there it was. We got our little puff in the press, national as well as provincial, even though they reported us at half our real strength – hardly a necessary tactic . . . I wonder how generally true it is that distinguished support for political or social measures tends to come from the professions, the middle-class intelligentsia and the young. Is it just that these are three groups with the leisure to get up petitions, organise meetings and attend demonstrations on weekday afternoons? I hope it is. Anyway, I shall always be glad that we had all taken the trouble to turn out and not minded looking faintly ludicrous and ineffectual. That was a small price to pay, in my own case, for wasting the time and arousing the annoyance of the Chief Inspector, and even – if it's not too fantastic a hope – giving the Home Secretary a small passing twinge.

Socialism and the Intellectuals begins with the admission that its author is not especially well informed about politics. This admission his friends in Swansea would second. The Clearys claim that the only newspaper they ever saw Amis read was a tabloid (though not all tabloids in the 1950s were unrespectable). A paragraph of biography then follows: parents, schooling, 'the callow Marxist phase that seemed almost compulsory in Oxford', disillusion with communism during army service, 'which clears the mind wonderfully', a first Labour vote, by proxy, in 1945, then subsequent Labour votes 'in all three general elections since, as well as in all local elections'. The paragraph ends with the prediction that he will continue to vote Labour 'to the end of my days, however depraved the Labour candidate may be and however virtuous his opponent'.[39] As for current political involvement: at elections he puts a Labour poster in the front window and loans his car to the local party, but he does not canvass (Hilly did the canvassing and was generally regarded as the more convinced socialist, according to David Quinn, Professor of History at Swansea),[40] nor has he become a member of the Labour Party or of any other political organisation except the Association of University Teachers, 'one of the smallest trade unions, if that is the right term, in the country'.[41] The rest of the pamphlet attempts to explain why.

Amis's field of reference is quickly narrowed. The middle-class intelligentsia he is most interested in does not include intellectuals associated with universities, on the grounds that such intellectuals have 'a settled job which, however tenuously, does bring them into contact with reality'.[42] His concern is rather with 'self-employed' intellectuals, both literary and artistic, the sort who appear regularly in the broadsheet and periodical press.[43] In the 1930s, these intellectuals were politically radical; they have now turned to the right. What marks their politics is a naïve romanticism, 'an irrational capacity to become inflamed by interests and causes that are not one's own, that are outside oneself'.[44] Hence the appeal of Marxism, which is also attractive because it 'involves violence'. Amis swipes at Auden (by way of Orwell, himself 'a romantic like the rest'),[45] when he says that for radical intellectuals it soon 'becomes natural to write airily about political murders and read about them in appreciation'. If this account of the radical intellectual 'sounds hostile or bad-tempered, I had better say at once that I see myself as a sufferer from political romanticism just as much as the next man'[46] – though presumably not as much as the intellectuals he has just been criticising.

Today, however, there is nothing for the politically inclined intellectual, the Thirties-style radical, to be romantic about: 'no Spain, no fascism, no mass unemployment'.[47] With Russia a lost cause – definitively, since Hungary – all that is left are what Amis calls non-political causes, 'or ones that are not in the first place political: the colour bar, horror-comics, juvenile delinquency, abolition of capital punishment, the reform of the laws relating to divorce and homosexuality'. These are unlikely to generate protests any more energetic than the one he described in the *Spectator* article. As for protests over Cyprus, then struggling for independence, as a Labour Party sociologist of Amis's acquaintance told him, 'nobody turns up'.[48] The invasions of Suez and Hungary occurred just three weeks before Amis began writing *Socialism and the Intellectuals*, but they, too, look unpromising: 'If the crises settle down quickly, as at the moment they show signs of doing, they will soon slip the minds of most people, intellectuals and non-intellectuals alike.'[49] Though he does not mention it, Amis joined at least one anti-Suez protest in November 1956, marching along Mumbles Road to the university. He was at the head of the column and at one point, or so he told Jacobs, was berated by an old lady who tore the placard from his chest and chased him down a side-street, though he soon rejoined the march.[50] He also, though only briefly, attended a local Labour Party meeting on Suez, 'breaking a habit of nearly fifteen years' standing'.[51] The boring nature of the political rhetoric at the meeting soon drove him away and he has since relapsed into inactivity, merely 'chatting about politics with my friends'.[52] As for equality, a key tenet of Socialist policy, the more the Labour Party presses for it the more uncomfortable the self-employed intellectual becomes, since his or her position has always been one of privilege (private education, Oxbridge). Wages are now so high, Amis imagines such intellectuals complaining, 'that some of them are actually better off than we are ourselves. We never contemplated *that*.'[53] Amis says nothing of his own position here, though in his letters to Larkin in this period he several times grouses about taxes.[54]

The pamphlet's conclusion is that the present political apathy of the intelligentsia is nothing to grieve over, not just because intellectuals are more likely to be wrong on any given issue than 'the ordinary Labour party or trade union man'[55] but because 'the best and most trustworthy political motive is self-interest'. Amis then admits that he shares the 'widespread suspicion of the professional espouser of causes, the do-gooder, the archetypal social worker who knows better than I do what is good for me'.[56] The liberal sentiments which end the pamphlet are as limp as those which end the *Spectator* article. Amis's only motive for political activism, he admits, is 'a sense of guilt. And this is not enough. How agreeable it must be to have a respectable motive for being politically active.'[57]

Socialism and the Intellectuals began life as a talk Amis gave to 'a weekend school'[58] held by the Fabians the previous Easter. The talk's chief aim was 'to draw as many hear-hears as possible' and in this it succeeded. The pamphlet, he admits in its first paragraph, is a 'tarted–up version' of the talk; its faults, he seems to be implying, are those of showiness, superficiality. Many of its arguments are 'likely to be wearisomely familiar' and its only claim is 'that someone like me is advancing them'.[59] Why someone like Amis is worth listening to about politics is suggested in the first sentence of a review of the pamphlet by J.W. Lambert in the *Sunday Times*, on 6 January 1957: 'Whether he likes it or not, Mr. Kingsley Amis is widely regarded as the spokesman of the post-war generations.' Later in the review Lambert calls him 'one of the liveliest and most talented men in England'. When Arnold Kettle reviewed the pamphlet in the *Daily Worker* on 12 February he declared that 'Kingsley Amis is as much a part of the world of 1957 as television, rock 'n' roll and the FA cup.'

What exactly Amis himself meant by the phrase 'someone like me' is hard to determine. After exempting the academic intellectual from scrutiny at the pamphlet's opening, he takes the Thirties writers, Spender, Auden and Day-Lewis, as prime examples of the self-employed intelligentsia. Since he mocks both their earlier left politics and their current rightward turn, and since he himself is employed by a university, presumably we are to think of him as apart from them, as we do later when he declares that 'some of my best friends are intellectuals'. But when he talks of the personal dimension of Thirties radicalism, its origin in rebellion against parents, he has himself in mind as well. By the end of the pamphlet the distinction between Amis the commentator and the sorts of intellectuals he discusses has become confused.[60] This confusion may reflect changes in Amis's professional and personal life – his widening social circles in London and Swansea, the increasing celebrity of his work as poet, novelist and literary journalist.

Amis's university friends, acquaintances and superiors were aware of his changed status and circumstances, also of his changing views. David Quinn has described Amis's claim in *Socialism and the Intellectuals* that he would always vote Labour as 'ingenuous'. By 1956, the members of Amis's 'pub circle', Quinn recalled, though 'brilliantly amusing', were 'all, or almost all, extremely right-wing Tories – especially Stuart Thomas . . . and J.O. Bartley . . . [,] Daniel Jones, the composer, and, I suspect, the brilliant raconteur, Wynford Vaughan-Thomas . . . so that he was absorbing through the skin almost a rightward attitude'.[61] Quinn also cites Amis's contacts among right-wing journalists associated with the *Spectator* as an important source of this attitude. Amis's love of Fleet Street, with its jammed pubs, political gossip and correspondents just back from exotic assignments, persisted throughout his life. According to Elizabeth Jane Howard, his second wife, it was not politics *per se* that interested him; what interested him was the company of male political journalists.[62] These journalists were mostly on the right, as Quinn suggests, but by no means in the same way or exclusively. Chief among them were Fairlie and George Gale, briefly labour correspondent of the *Manchester Guardian*, later a writer and editor at the *Daily Express* and *Spectator*. Both were Tories. Their friend John Raymond, another key figure in the circle, was assistant literary editor of the *Daily Telegraph*, and a socialist. Fairlie and Raymond had been leader-writers on *The Times* along with Peregrine Worsthorne, who still worked there. Worsthorne, a Tory, was also part of the group, along with his friend Paul Johnson, on the left in the 1950s, who was a frequent visitor from Paris, where he worked on the French magazine *Réalités* and wrote articles on France for the *New Statesman* (in 1955 Johnson returned to England permanently to work for the *New Statesman*). Among more peripheral or later Fleet Street acquaintances were the literary editors Terence Kilmartin, at the *Observer*, and Karl Miller, at the *Spectator*, John Davenport, lead fiction reviewer for the *Observer*, and Derek Marks, political correspondent for the *Daily Express*. In addition to their intelligence, high spirits and success in their fields, these men mostly came from congenial or unthreatening class backgrounds (the exception was Worsthorne); like Amis himself, they were uncowed, uncowing, unchippy.

Amis was not alone among his new journalistic acquaintances in valuing literary skills as well as personal qualities – charm, cleverness, humour, sociability – above political allegiance. 'He was responsive to anyone he thought could write a good sentence,' is how Clive James explained Amis's friendships both with those on the right in the 1950s, when he was on the left, and those on the left in the 1970s, when he was on the right. At the outbreak of the Suez Crisis, when Paul Johnson produced a book denouncing the Anglo-French-Israeli invasion, his friend Peregrine Worsthorne immediately savaged it 'at leader-page length' in the *Daily Telegraph*, 'much to Paul's delight since the resulting furore enormously helped the book's sales which in turn helped to improve his finances'.[63] The friendship was never in danger. 'People here never allow party politics to enter personal life,' Johnson claims, exempting only 'the very hard-left fringe'. Nor was the periodical press consistently ideological or *parti pris*. In 1959 the *Spectator* voted Labour.[64] In Worsthorne's words, 'these were the years of Butskellism, when both Labour and Conservative parties vied with each other to occupy the middle ground – ideology did not seem to matter'.[65]

The depth and seriousness of the political conservatism of some of Amis's new acquaintances, notably Fairlie, Gale and Worsthorne, is sometimes asserted, not least by the figures themselves. Worsthorne and Gale had been at Peterhouse, Cambridge, where they were influenced by the philosopher Michael Oakeshott. In his memoirs, Worsthorne describes Fairlie's Toryism as Burkean, grounded in an almost mystical notion of the sacredness of the English constitution. Gale is described by Amis in the *Memoirs* as a thinker of comparable weight. Though 'a sterling pub-man and foe of bullshit', Gale's journalistic career 'has never given his talents of clear, unflinching thought the outlet they deserve'. Gale laboured for over twenty years on a large work of political philosophy, but never finished it. 'For Christ's sake, George,' writes Amis in the *Memoirs*, '*get it done*. We need it.'[66] It is hard to see this last phrase ('We need it') as anything but 'friendship-assertion', since Amis was even less interested in, or knowledgeable about, political philosophy than he was in or about politics itself. The sort of conservative he became – was already becoming in the mid-1950s – was the Conquest sort, as resistant to right-wing as to left-wing ideology. In 1984, when at his most reactionary, Amis was asked by Blake Morrison if he was interested in 'people like Roger Scruton': 'a look of horror came over his face . . . "*No*, I'm a Thatcherite, all right, but I don't want what I and a lot of people vaguely feel to be turned into an ideology. If I say I'm against the NHS, for instance, I don't want this to be an issue of freedom versus responsibility. It's the pragmatic money-men who interest me, not the philosophers. Mrs. Thatcher I associate with enterprise and hard work – hardly 'ideas'."'[67]

There were several connections between Amis's Fleet Street friends and his Swansea friends. Geoff Nicholson and another ex-student, John Morgan, were both employed as journalists in London, though at the time they moved in less exalted circles than Fairlie and Gale. George Gale's wife Pat had family in Swansea, and the Gales frequently visited the Amises when down to see Pat's mother and sisters. The Gales and the Stuart Thomases got on well, though the Clearys remember the Gales, Pat in particular, as 'weird' (they got on better with other Amis visitors, the Anthony Powells, Bruce Montgomery, Larkin). Pat Gale was beautiful, dramatic and wildly bohemian. Her sisters were beautiful, too. One was a finalist in the Swansea heat of the 1956 Mazda Queen of Light competition, which Amis, through a girlfriend of Bob Conquest's, was asked to judge, much to his delight. In the *Memoirs* Amis says he believes he first met George Gale in 1955, probably at a party at the *Spectator*. The Gales and the Amises first got together in Swansea that Christmas and subsequently spent several brief holidays at Dylan Thomas's boathouse in Laugharne, which Stuart Thomas, in charge of the Thomas estate, let them borrow. George Gale, 'George G. Ale' in

Private Eye, was as prodigious a drinker as Stuart Thomas, and comparably gruff and forbidding in manner, though he could also be kindly, as could Thomas. A further similarity between the two men was the irregularity of their marriages. Stuart Thomas's marriage was only outwardly conventional. In many ways he and Eve led separate social lives and sometimes their friends wondered what kept them together. After discussing several instances of Stuart's bad behaviour, I once asked Eve Thomas why he was so rude. 'How should I know,' she answered. 'Ask his mother.' The irregularity of the Gale marriage derived in part from their shared volatility. Worsthorne writes of a dinner he and his wife were to have at the Gales' home in Staines, after a picnic with the Fairlies. It was the first time the two couples had met: 'After drinking for hours, George growled something about sending out for fish and chips.' Worsthorne protested. 'Why don't you like fucking fish and chips?' Gale roared, accusing Worsthorne of snobbery 'and much else'. Pat Gale then took Worsthorne's side, 'screaming at George to mind his fucking manners'.[68] While the Gales raged on, Henry Fairlie slipped out to the pub with Worsthorne's wife, Claudie. Later that night at about eleven they all had a hideous meal at 'a local eating joint', then returned to the Gales' for bed: 'What the sleeping arrangements were I cannot remember,' writes Worsthorne, 'possibly because I don't want to remember.'[69]

Amis's frequent trips to London took their toll, as he several times lamented in the press as well as in correspondence. They almost always involved getting drunk. Bruce Montgomery reports several meetings, for lunch and dinner, in which Amis passed out from drink.[70] On 25 June 1956 Amis wrote to Larkin that on one such meeting he and Montgomery ran into John Dickson Carr, a great Amis hero. Amis had drunk so much he could remember nothing about the meeting except that Carr 'seemed a very decent little chap and very pleased to hear I knew and liked his books'. After one particularly jolly and extended lunch in June 1956, Amis was hit by a car while crossing the street in front of the London Press Exchange. He was hardly sober but he was also on the pedestrian crossing. 'Wasn't run over,' he corrects Larkin, in a letter of 16 July 1957, 'was knocked dane. Can't remember anything: concussion bum . . . seeing double all the shaggin time.' Amis was to meet the Nicholsons that night at six. At 5.30 they received a call from the Charing Cross Hospital about his accident. He was all right, but

Above: KA in *Vogue*, 1955.

Above: KA and Hilly with Philip, Sally and Martin, at 24 The Grove, Swansea, 1955.

Left: University College of Swansea, 1952.

Right: Anthony Powell, Hilly, KA and Philip Larkin, 1958.

Left: Journalists at the bar at Rules, in Covent Garden: Henry Fairlie (second from left), John Raymond (third from left), Tom Pocock (far right).

Below left: Robert Conquest, 1963.

Below right: KA, 1957.

Above: Hilly, Jean McAndrew and KA, Princeton, New Jersey, 1959.

Below: Martin, Sally and Philip, Princeton, 1958.

Above: Aunt Gladys, KA
and Hilly, Washington,
D.C., 1958.

Right: W.R. Amis
('Daddy A'),
271 Edgerstoune Road,
Princeton, 1959.

Above: Sally, 271 Edgerstoune Road,
Princeton, 1958.
Below: Hilly, Sally and Nancy, Hilly's dog,
with Pat and George Gale and Timothy
Houghton, Swansea, *c.* 1960.

Above: A surreal vision of life at
9 Madingley Road, Cambridge,
by Lis Rukeyser. See Chapter 18.

Above: KA and Robert Graves pushing car, Deya, Majorca, 1962.

Left: KA and Robert Graves, Deya, 1962.

Right: KA, best man at the wedding of Elisabeth and William Rukeyser, Eltham, 1963.

Left: Marital harmony, Swansea, *c.* 1960.

Below: KA on the beach in Yugoslavia, lipstick graffiti by Hilly, 1963.

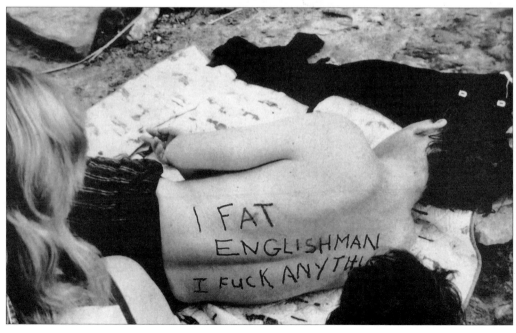

I FAT ENGLISHMAN I FUCK ANYTH

heavily sedated and bandaged, with a patch over one eye. Would the Nicholsons come round to pick him up? This they did, returning him to their flat, summoning their doctor to look him over, and putting him to bed in his vest and underpants, as it was a hot summer's evening. At this point what sounds like a much-rehearsed anecdote followed, though Mavis Nicholson swears it was true. The next morning a passing neighbour stopped by for a chat. He had recently embarked on an MA in Contemporary English Literature and his favourite author, he told Nicholson, was Kingsley Amis. At that minute the door opened and Amis stumbled into the room in his underpants, bandaged like the Invisible Man. 'Mavis. Where am I?' he asked. 'Don't worry,' she answered, 'you're with us.' Amis then turned to the neighbour: 'Who are you?' The neighbour told him his name. Then Mavis turned to the neighbour and said: 'This is Kingsley Amis.'[71]

It was not just drink that made the London visits exhausting; Amis drank in Swansea as well. It was the pace, the seamless progress from lunch to drinks to more drinks to dinner out. Sometimes trips to London were combined with trips to Oxford or Abbey Timbers, which made them more wearing. On 14 March 1954 Amis described one such trip in late February, from Swansea to Abbey Timbers, to Oxford, to London, to Oxford again, where Amis was to participate in a poetry brains trust (the other participants were C.S. Lewis, G.S. Fraser, James Kirkup and Herbert Palmer). Hilly and Bruce Montgomery accompanied him for parts of the trip, which involved dinners with the Bardwells, at All Souls and with Oxford friends, then a day in London commencing with drinks with 'the *Spectator* lot', a 'tremendous lunch' at Montgomery's club, the IMA (International Musicians' Association), called by Amis 'the most drunken institution in the world',[72] more drinks with Tony Hartley and J.D. Scott, then dinner and drinks with Ken Tynan and his wife, by which time Amis 'was so pissed I could hardly speak'. The next day there were pre-lunch drinks with P.H. Newby, a novelist and BBC Talks producer, then lunch and drinks with Anthony Powell, then drinks with Montgomery at the IMA. Montgomery decided to accompany the Amises back to Oxford. They drank in the railway carriage, then drank at the Randolph Hotel until forty minutes after the time Amis was due to meet his fellow brains-trusters for sherry. Dinner was at the Café de Paris ('I had a sole apparently encased in hessian'). At the brains trust itself Amis was 'sullen, jerky and facetious by turns'.

In September 1957, after several years of such jaunts, Amis wrote a humorous article in the *Daily Express* entitled 'Why You Won't Sell Me the Bright Lights: No – Not Even Now I've Hit the Jackpot'.[73] In it he recommends London 'as a means of shortening your life-span', unbeatable for 'richer food, stronger drink, later nights, and more of whatever else you fancy'. In Swansea, in contrast, life is 'quiet, orderly'. 'Admittedly, being a lecturer involves lecturing', but otherwise Amis liked his life as a provincial don, liked his colleagues, liked the 'local life' (in London there would be none, 'except with milkmen and tobacconists'), liked the routine. 'When not engaged with academic matters,' he explains, 'I pursue my spare-time literary activities, do my stuff as husband and father and regale myself with my friends.' In London, if you are literary, you spend all your time with literary types and end up 'with nothing worthwhile to write about and no chance to write about it'. As for work versus fun, 'inevitably you reach a stage when not working becomes more horrible than working'.

This picture of Amis's life in Swansea is more than a little rose-tinted, even excepting problems with Hilly. Life at the university was not without its tensions, inevitable given Amis's increasing celebrity. Well before *Lucky Jim* was published, he began worrying about how it would be received by his colleagues. 'I don't know whether your firm makes a practice of putting in the "all-characters-are-fictitious" formula at the front of their books,' he wrote to Rubinstein on 6 May 1953. 'If so it might make my life smoother if something were appended to it in my case.' On 21 June Amis confessed to Larkin: 'I am terrified now of the probable local effect of the thing . . . I keep finding more and more bits that might be taken as referring to people here.'[74] That the university described in the novel had only 'a couple of points in its physical set-up in common with Leicester (to lead people away from Swansea), e.g. the cemetery opposite', would not matter; it was still possible, Amis recognised, 'that some of the men may hate me here for ridiculing aspects of college life in general.'[75]

Amis's professor, W.D. Thomas, would not be one of them. In the same letter to Larkin in which Amis decribed his Oxford–London–Oxford jaunt he also reported that 'my smiling, smoking man in the light suit is no more, as you will have heard. I feel very sorry about this.' Thomas died of a thrombosis at sixty-four, shortly after retire-ment. 'Everyone seems to miss him greatly and I can understand it.'

A month before Thomas died, James Kinsley was appointed to succeed him, coming to Swansea from a lectureship at Aberystwyth. Kinsley was neither Amis's nor the department's choice. Only two applicants had been interviewed for the job, the other being John Holloway, a poet and critic subsequently identified with the Movement. Here is how Amis described the two candidates in a letter to Larkin of 19 January 1954:

One was a man 34 this year, author of 2 books, one technical-philosophical, one critical, of one or two articles, of several poems in such places as the Kenyon Review, The New Statesman, and so on. The other was a man 32, Scotsman, author of an article suggesting why the secnond farx 2nd edition of Warton's Essay on Pope didn't appear until 26 years after the 1st, and editor-designate of the Dryden Oxford text. When I add that the first man impressed most of those concerned as pleasant and intelligent, the 2nd as ugly and pompous, you will have no difficulty in guessing which one got the job. Yes, that's right. The 1st one was John Holloway, the 2nd one Kinsley (a cross between me and the compiler of that report you've been reading? No), who, in addition to the facts adduced, was hated by everyone at Aberystwyth, smokes a pipe and is a Scottish Methodist lay-preacher.

Amis thought Kinsley got the job because the Principal of Swansea, John Fulton, was not only a fellow Scot but a fellow Balliol man: 'The dirty log-rolling bastard. Doesn't matter to *him*, see, who directs teaching and research in the English Dept. I feel as I've I'd swive bride as if I'd *lost something valuable*; that Holloway man might have been really good to have here. Filthy twisting, *mistaken* bastard.' Fulton was an ambitious man and saw Kinsley as a way to smarten up the English Department after the unpunishing Thomas regime, in particular to enhance what today would be called its research profile. Kinsley was a big man, very strong physically, with an aloof, gruff manner.[76] He developed an immediate antipathy to Amis, no doubt because Amis was neither frightened of him nor much concerned to hide his own dislike. Amis soon discovered that Kinsley had asked the professor of pure mathematics, Rowland 'Tug' Wilson, at the time the senior professor at the university, how one went about sacking someone; it was clear to Wilson that Kinsley had Amis in mind. Wilson explained to Kinsley that it was almost impossible to sack a lecturer in Amis's position, that it had happened only once in his experience, in the 1920s, and that the person in question was insane.[77]

The measuring rod Kinsley used in his battle not only with Amis but with what he mostly saw as the other slackers in the department was scholarly publication. What scholarly articles had Amis published? What monographs? On 10 April 1956, Amis wrote to Larkin that Kinsley was 'trying to get me held at the efficiency bar – on grounds of inefficiency, oddly enough'. Were he to succeed, Amis's salary would stop at £900; otherwise, it would rise to £1,100, at annual £50 increments.[78] The decision to hold a lecturer at the efficiency bar was made by the head of department. The grounds for doing so were inadequate teaching, administration and, most importantly, research. Amis was OK on the teaching front, or so he thought. For all his trips to London, he was scrupulous about not missing lectures and about marking papers; he was also well regarded as a lecturer, certainly in the early years. Yet rumours persisted about absences from class, a measure of his growing celebrity and ubiquity in the periodical press and on radio.[79] In 1954 he appeared in the media – as reviewer, essayist, poet, short-story writer, correspondent – thirty-four times, while also publishing *Lucky Jim* and the poetry pamphlet *Kingsley Amis: No. 22, The Fantasy Poets*. In 1955, the year *That Uncertain Feeling* was published, he appeared forty times. In 1956, when Kinsley sought to stop him at the efficiency bar, he appeared forty-one times, in addition to publishing *A Case of Samples: Poems 1946–1956*, appearing in the Enright and Conquest Movement anthologies and editing *Oscar Wilde: Poems and Essays*. None of these appearances or publications counted as far as Kinsley was concerned: they were not scholarship. Amis had almost no academic publications (the possible exceptions were several brief pieces in *Essays in Criticism*, one drawn from the failed B.Litt)[80] and did no administration. It did not matter to Kinsley that for over a year now Amis had been writing 'literary' review-essays for the *Spectator* (on Byron, Lawrence, Austen, Dickens and so forth) as well as fiction round-ups; it did not matter that he was being asked to lecture on literary topics at Oxford and Cambridge (where he outraged the Leavisites by breezily denouncing Henry James 'as a turgid windy and pretentious old arsehole')[81] as well as on the Third Programme.

Amis took pains over his literary pieces: 'I now have to do as much research as would do for a Ph.D. every fortnight; an expert on Peacock this week, an expert on Swift or Arnold (I haven't decided yet) in a fortnight's time. Cripes it's worse than lecturing.'[82] Though not scholarship, these pieces were certainly criticism, and influential criticism at that. Not everyone will agree when Paul Fussell calls Amis 'the first intelligent British critic to bring his wide command of literature, as well as his wit, to the task of seriously opposing the critical orthodoxy of Modernism', but when Fussell defends Amis against the charge that he was only a reviewer, he makes the telling point that T.S. Eliot's 'The Metaphysical Poets', 'which powerfully influenced the taste of a generation', began life as a review.[83] Amis's attacks in the *Spectator* on the anti-democratic character of, for example, Lawrence's criticism, all 'egomania, fatuity, and gimcrack theorizing . . . bitterness and censoriousness, too', or on the self-importance of 'the Jameses, the Woolfs, the Lawrences' ('To be spared all that for the time being, even if it means forgoing some real talent, is not total disaster'), are meant to provoke, but they are also perceptive and well instanced; they point to something really there.[84]

When Kinsley arrived in Swansea he devoted all his energies and all his spare time to editing Dryden, Amis's least favourite poet. Editing was research. According to Glanmor Williams, Kinsley was a tremendously hard worker, very dour, with little sense of humour: 'He believed that people in his department, or indeed any English department, should put their noses to the grindstone.' To Amis, Kinsley was a bore and a bully; to Kinsley, Amis was unserious, like his colleagues. None of these colleagues, though, irritated Kinsley as Amis did or were as subversive of his authority. Not only did Amis do no scholarly work, he denigrated those who did, and in print. In 'The Scholar as Critic', a lead *Spectator* review of W.P. Ker's *On Modern Literature: Lectures and Addresses* (4 November 1955), Amis describes Ker as 'an old-fashioned scholar', one whose faults as a critic are 'typically those of the academic'. Chief among these faults 'is the tendency to use learning as a way of wriggling away from the issue, to liken Burns to Boethius or suggest a difference between Jane Austen and Ben Jonson. Then there is the practice of using literature as the jumping-off ground into something else.' Also typical is Ker's lack of 'verbal dexterity: his resources when menaced with the obligation of textual comment were either to quote fifty or sixty lines or to observe that great poems are miraculous'. These views would have dismayed Kinsley, as would the depiction of professors in *Lucky Jim*. At academic conferences he resented having to field questions about Amis's novel ('Did people really behave like Jim in the Swansea English Department? Were senior academics like Neddy Welch really employed by his university?').[85] Then there was Amis's own 'verbal dexterity', at department meetings and functions. 'Kingsley had a devastating tongue, he really could be quite unkind,' Williams remembers. 'I say that even though I had great admiration for his intellectual abilities, because he was a very clever man, very clever and very quick . . . and he didn't give a damn – I mean he didn't give a damn for Kinsley's position as professor.'

When Kinsley went after Amis, Amis took his case directly to Fulton. Though Fulton had been instrumental in hiring Kinsley, he sided with Amis. This was a crucial moment in Amis's career at Swansea, for it made clear that he could almost do as he wanted in future. 'Fulton was very much on Amis's side over the period,' Williams recalled; 'he *liked* the idea of having a very well-known and gifted novelist and poet on our staff' (at a time when such figures rarely lectured in university English departments). Once Kinsley realised Amis had Fulton's backing, he made efforts to get on with him. By 25 June 1956 Amis was complaining to Larkin that 'my prof is nice to me now, having realised how deeply he has plunged his foot in by trying to be nasty to me. The bad thing now is that one of his ways of being nice to me is to "put things my way," arranging for me to do a review for R.E.S. [Review of English Studies] NO MUNNEEEEE and lecturing to objurgatory miners at Bridgend NOT ENUFFF MUNNEEEEE.'[86] An offshoot of the confrontation with Kinsley was that relations with Bartley suffered. For a while Amis thought Bartley was 'siding with my bog prog prof just a little over this dispute. I still feel irritated about that.' As for subsequent relations with Kinsley, though Amis was outwardly civil, his real feelings were obvious, to Kinsley as to others.

In April 1956, the same month Kinsley tried to hold Amis at the efficiency bar, the Amis family moved house from 24 The Grove to 53 Glanmor Road. The new house was also in the Uplands district, about a quarter of a mile from the old one, higher up the hill and 'infinitely more palatial'. Instead of selling the house at 24 The Grove, they let Eva Garcia and her family live there for a peppercorn rent. The chief attraction of the new house as far as Amis was concerned was that it gave him a study 'as big as a real room'.[87] It was at Glanmor Road that the Amises had what their academic and *crachach* friends remember as their most riotous parties, often attended by guests from London and elsewhere. The household, in Martin Amis's words, was 'definitely bohemian by lower-middle-class standards. I'd find my mother with her feet on the table smoking cigarettes and playing jazz, and that shocked even me.' Once, on the morning after an all-night party, Pat Gale opened the front door to one of Martin's friends; her appearance was so strange (she resembled Morticia in the Addams family) that Martin had to explain it away by saying she'd gone to a fancy dress party as a beatnik. As for relations between his parents, Martin remembers feeling 'consternated' when things grew rocky; he recalls sitting on the stairs listening to a terrific row and then 'next morning, father coming up with a breakfast tray, dodging the missiles being thrown at him'.[88] But he also remembers much physical affection between his parents.

Philip's memories are more painful, probably because he was a bit older and more aware of what was going on. They begin with a sense of being abandoned. The parents were frequently away, sometimes for long periods. 'They did go away a lot,' Mavis admits. 'It became very exciting for them. They became famous and rich.' When Eva and Joe took over 24 The Grove, Philip claims, 'we spent whole summers living at their house'. Eva was 'like a mum, really', the three Amis children 'would have regular meals and watch telly with the family, go to sleep in their beds with them', the boys with Michael, Sally with Michael's sister, Hilary. 'It was bloody awful,' Philip remembers. 'I hated it. But we were forced to do it because Hilly and Kingsley were having such a wild time.' It was Sally 'who had a really terrible time'. At one point, for reasons Philip cannot remember, she 'ended up living opposite Eva and Joe with an entirely new family'. The Garcias were 'very sweet people', according to Philip, but they were crude, with manners the children were not used to. There was swearing in the Amis household, but nothing like the swearing at the Garcias'. Joe had 'a heart of gold' but his appearance was alarming: he was thickly muscled, he'd come home from work 'filthy', sometimes drunk, his false teeth 'all over the place'. Eva had a heart of gold, too, 'but she had a temper on her'. Their friends from Maryhill were 'grim-looking', their friends' children 'horrible'. 'It was like a century ago the way these people lived, incredibly primitive.'

Amis and Hilly were not, at this time, responsible parents. They were too distracted – by 'fun', work, marital discord. To Philip, Amis was 'a distant figure', sometimes imperious; 'he could put on a very mean look and shout very loudly. It was terrifying.' To Martin, he was 'always in his study'. Once, when Martin had been caught stealing money and cigarettes from his mother's purse (this was at 24 The Grove, so he was not yet eight), 'my mother told me to present myself at my father's study, to be hit'. After the spanking, Martin later learned, his father wept, 'as he always did when he hit us'.[89] Though scary and cutting when angered, Amis was no disciplinarian; in Martin's words, he was 'a pretty pathetic chastiser of his children'. In *Experience*, Martin recounts an episode in which, provoked beyond endurance, Amis 'eventually took a hairbrush to us, but so limply that we giggled about it for a whole hour after he went downstairs'.[90] Amis cried after this episode as well, which made Martin feel guilty. Hilly remembers Amis as interested in and entertained by the children – this is obvious from *I Like It Here* – 'as long as they didn't get in his way'. He was not the sort of father who 'withheld praise or anything like that'. He was also determined not to stop them from doing all sorts of things his parents had stopped him from doing – just as his parents had been determined not to force religion upon him as it had been forced upon them.

Hilly was a loving mother and fiercely protective when the children were threatened. When Martin was beaten up by older boys, 'immediately she lashed up the three big dogs: Nancy, certainly, and Flossie? And Bessie? With anxious adoration I watched her go down the hill, like Charlton Heston or Steve Reeves wielding the reins of the chariot . . . She returned half an hour later, still furious and still unavenged.'[91] But Martin recounts episodes of criminal permissiveness. 'I let him do *everything*,' Hilly once told Martin, speaking of Martin's stepbrother, Jaime, who also adores her, 'I let *you* do everything.' This remark was uttered in Spain, at a picnic Martin recalls: 'I was a childless twenty-eight, standing with my arms outspread under one tree or another in case Jaime, then four or five, fell out of it. My mother looked up from her sandwich, and flicked a hand backwards through the air. – I let him do *everything*, I let *you* do everything.' 'We spent all-day and all-night car journeys on the roof rack of the Morris 1000, the three of us, in all weathers, slithering in and out while my mother frowned into the windscreen.'[92] The two boys were allowed to canoe alone from Swansea Bay to Pembroke Bay, 'a distance of several miles west along the (notoriously and, in that direction, increasingly unpredictable) Welsh coast',[93] a near-disastrous folly that made the front pages of the *Swansea Evening Post*. The children were allowed to smoke a cigarette at Christmas; when he was nine, Martin was given a pack of cigarettes at Christmas. Martin remembers his childhood as 'idyllic',[94] but then he was 'an equable little boy, easily the "easiest" of the Amises'.[95]

The lack of structure or order in the household was much remarked upon by the Amises' friends, even those who were charmed by their bohemian ways. 'Yes, know what you mean about the Amises,' Bruce Montgomery wrote to Larkin on 17 January 1956: 'their modus vivendi strikes me as altogether slightly strange – in the sense of alien, incomprehensible. Now that I've stayed with them twice, I shall take with me, on the next occasion, (a) an ashtray, (b) a wastepaper basket, (c) an alarm clock, (d) a goblin teasmade, (e) an electric torch, (f) clotheshangers, (g) two extra pillows, and (h) a bedside lamp; also, now I come to think of it, extra towels, a private bathroom and a variety of spiked, bullet-proof armour for domestic animals; oh, and earplugs for the radiogram ... *That* sounds thoroughly unkind, too, when they're always so affable and keen for one to be there; it's just that asking for any of these things would be to burden their consciences and their understandings more than could reasonably be borne. And of course I'm immensely fond of them both.'[96] The writer Theo Richmond remembers sitting down on a sofa in the living room at Glanmor Road on the arm of which rested a half-eaten tin of baked beans with a knife sticking out of it. 'There was no attempt to organise anything, like meals or bedtimes,' Marigold Johnson says. 'They were very wild,' her husband Paul adds. 'Hilly was a genuine bohemian, whereas Kingsley was an only child' – by which Johnson meant, in this context, unsuited to looking out for, or bothering about, other people's needs.

In March 1957, while Sally Amis was in Berkhamsted being taken care of by her grandparents, Rosa ('Peggy') Amis had a stroke and was 'dead before she hit the floor'.[97] The circumstances of the death were particularly upsetting, for William Amis had just gone off to work and Sally was left alone all day with her grandmother's body. When Amis's father returned home he discovered his wife lying dead on the bedroom floor, her face smeared with the lipstick Sally had removed from her purse and clumsily tried to apply to her lips. Sally was three years old and the effect of the death was traumatic: 'when she got back to Swansea family friends noticed how anxious the experience had made her. If she saw her father asleep, friends noticed, she would try to prise his eyes open for fear that he, too, had died.'[98] There is only a single brief mention of his mother's death in Amis's correspondence of the period. On 27 March he wrote to thank his friend Derek Gardner 'for all you did in practical and moral aid', and to report that his father was 'picking up extraordinarily well'.[99] Hilly remembers Amis as shocked by his mother's death but showing little emotion. In the *Memoirs* Amis calls her 'the first of the appallingly long line of figures in my life whom I have come to value altogether more highly, to appreciate the uniqueness of, now they are gone'.[100]

16

Princeton

Amis only began to gain the attention of American readers with the publication of *That Uncertain Feeling* in 1956, the date of the US edition. *Lucky Jim* had been bought by Doubleday in August 1953 for an advance of $2,500, almost nine times the advance Amis received from Gollancz. A month later Amis met his American editor, Pyke Johnson, 'a sort of humble Lloyd Nolan', at Doubleday's London office.[1] Amis liked Johnson, who impressed him with his knowledge of jazz and promised to look into sending him records 'as part of my royalties'. However, five months later, on 24 February 1954, Amis received 'rather a gloomy letter from Doubledays – good reviews, poor sales'.[2] His reaction was characteristic: 'What do I care . . . with 7/8 of $2500 in the bag.' Amis felt flush, could afford all the drink and visits to London he wanted, and America was far away. It didn't matter that the market in America meant big or bigger money. Elizabeth Jane Howard has written that 'Kingsley's complete indifference to money, and his natural and chronic generosity, meant that he preferred not to consider finances.'[3] As his income rose, he made no investments, bought no stocks or shares, had no building society accounts, showed no desire to accumulate property, goods or works of art. Everything he earned he spent, on himself and his family, thoughout his life. His attitude to literary celebrity was similarly relaxed. Though hardly indifferent to questions of fame and reputation, he was only concerned with his standing in Britain, a view that may have owed something to fiction publishing in the 1950s, less transatlantic than it is now, or than it would soon become (in the 1970s, for example, when Martin Amis was at a similar stage in his career). When Doubleday turned down *That Uncertain Feeling*, Amis was unfussed: 'I can't say I blame them,' he confessed in January 1956 to an American admirer; sales of *Lucky Jim* had 'failed to top 2000'.[4]

The firm that took Amis over from Doubleday was Harcourt Brace. His editor there was J.H. McCallum, who was to play a key role in Amis's life in the next few years. *That Uncertain Feeling* was published on 23 February and a month later McCallum sent Amis the first batch of American reviews, 'the most important of which by far is the one by Edmund Wilson in the March 24th *New Yorker* . . . very much a Good Thing'. Wilson's review began: '"After Evelyn Waugh, what?" this reviewer asked six years ago. The answer was Angus Wilson. Mr. Wilson is still doing well . . . But what is to be the next phase in England, and how will it be written about? The answer, already, is Kingsley Amis.' Amis is the answer because he gives voice to a new class. In Wilson and Waugh, 'the old orientations have been partly lost. In the work of Kingsley Amis, we see everything from the point of view of such baseless unoriented new people.' The effect of Amis's fiction 'on the higher levels of British journalism', Wilson informs his American audience, has been 'curious to watch'; Amis's novels 'have become the subject of controversy, on which people sometimes fiercely take sides'. Maugham on *Lucky Jim* is quoted as a prime example.

Wilson had his reservations about *That Uncertain Feeling*: 'all the characters are more or less unpleasant' and since the narrator is the hero, 'we are never allowed to escape from the squalors of his personality'. At the same time, Amis knows 'exactly what he is doing'; the characterisation is 'psychologically sound'. Though Elizabeth Gruffydd-Williams and her crowd are 'horrible', 'it is part of the satiric humour that these people should represent for Lewis the glamour of the privileged classes'. At the end of the review Wilson compares Amis's characters with those of Anthony Powell, 'also rather unattractive, though presented with better manners'. Amis's characters interest Wilson more: 'uncertain and perplexed though they are, they still have something to build, to win'.

The Wilson review was 'very much a Good Thing' because it was ultimately favourable, presented Amis as 'the next phase' and was written by America's most respected man of letters. Among Wilson's admirers was the poet and critic R.P. Blackmur, Professor of English at Princeton, director both of the Creative Writing program and of the Christian Gauss Seminars in Criticism. There were three sets of Gauss Seminars per year, each consisting of six weekly lectures followed by an hour's discussion. Blackmur picked the lecturers, in consultation with a board, and was always on the lookout for lecturers who could also teach creative writing (partly to staff the Creative Writing program, partly to supplement the Gauss stipends).[5] It was Blackmur who invited Amis to Princeton for the academic year 1958–59. In the previous year, W.H. Auden had been a Gauss lecturer and earlier lecturers included Randall Jarrell, Delmore Schwartz, Erich Auerbach, Paul Tillich, V.S. Pritchett, Leon Edel and Edmund Wilson. Wilson's seminars in 1952 eventually became *Patriotic Gore: Studies in the Literature of the American Civil War* (1962). Attendance at the Gauss Seminars was by invitation only, also determined by Blackmur, and the audience was small and select. Among attendees were Robert Oppenheimer, of the Manhattan Project, John Berryman, a Blackmur protégé, Irving Howe, Dwight Macdonald (along with 'almost every member of the *Partisan Review* crowd')[6] and Mary McCarthy, Wilson's ex-wife, usually with her friend, Hannah Arendt. It is unlikely, given his acquaintance with Wilson and McCarthy, that Blackmur would have missed Wilson's Amis review. If he did, his editor at Harcourt Brace, J.H. McCallum, would have drawn it to his attention.

McCallum became Blackmur's editor the same year he became Amis's American editor. Amis first met McCallum in London in October 1957, after publication of the American edition of *A Case of Samples*. At this meeting McCallum seems to have floated the idea of Amis spending a year at Princeton.[7] Amis first mentions the idea in a letter of 9 November, a response to a McCallum letter of 31 October which promised 'to get to work at once' on arranging the visit: 'I would adore to go to Princeton, which as you know is very highly thought of over here – a friend of mine at the College in Swansea [Esmond Cleary] had a year there, 1948 I think, and is most enthusiastic about it. And Blackmur, of course, is a great hero of everybody's. I and all my family are in a state of most tremendous premature excitement, telling each other to keep our fingers crossed. I can sum it up by saying yes, we are interested. And you can quote me.' McCallum forwarded this letter to Blackmur on the 13th, 'for I feel in this instance you are your own best salesman'.

The letter did the trick. By 18 February 1958, after thanking

McCallum for sending a couple of positive reviews of *I Like It Here* ('most encouraging, especially after the mainly hostile press the book has received over here'), Amis announced that 'I have everything lined up at this end . . . I haven't yet asked officially for leave, but the college authorities know of my intentions and approve (so they should, by God).' His only worry concerned the size of the family he would be bringing over: 'wife, 3 children and father. I shall quite understand if Princeton can't "up the stipend" on their account, and am prepared to live quietly with occasional orgies financed by my New York publisher.' As for transportation costs, Amis had already been in touch with 'the Fulbright people' about a travelling grant, presumably at McCallum's or Blackmur's suggestion.

Amis was keen to go to America. He had survived the Portugal stay. Twice he'd gone on holiday in France and enjoyed himself. In mid-April 1958 he undertook a two-week lecture tour of Denmark, accompanied by Hilly and the boys (Sally stayed with the Garcias). 'An almost painless journey,' is how his diary of the tour opens: 'Doubt, horror and despair only raising their heads intermittently and for short periods.' It was not until the tour's last day, 19 April, that travel anxieties recurred, a product of 'apprehension at thought of embarkation'. How Amis dealt with this apprehension is recorded in the diary: 'fight it, adduce sensible consolations, curse myself as I will.' After 'a good lunch with abundant snaps' (as well as talk of 'England and its inferiority to Denmark, a subject discreditably easy to fall into'), he felt fine. The diary concludes aboard ship: 'Marital rites on the top bunk enliven the evening. Asleep easier than on voyage out.'

As long as he did not have to fly, Amis could make the journey to the United States. Once there he would have a job ('enforced idleness was always to be one of his principal objections to going abroad')[8] and there would be no problems with language. As for his feelings about America and Americans, these were never as negative as the later writings and interviews sometimes suggest (as in *Jake's Thing*, published in 1978, in which the hero reflects that 'everything horrible or foolish was worse if it was also American. Modern architect – modern American architect. Woman who never stops talking – American woman who never stops talking. Zany comedian – zany American comedian. Convert to Buddhism . . .').[9] In the *Memoirs*, written in 1990, Amis says that he knew instantly upon arrival in New York that 'this was my second country and always would be'.[10] America was the land of jazz, science fiction, the movies. It also helped to shape his writing. Its influence on his criticism, with its habitual focus on the work itself (a tenet of the New Critics), its demotic idiom or register (Fussell's 'can-the-bull-shit tone') and its allusions to American rather than European, especially French, writing and culture, has already been noted; it is acknowledged in the description of Blackmur, a New Critical pioneer, as 'a great hero of everybody's' (though flattery or calculation may also figure here). The importance of America to Amis's fiction was stressed by Wilson. In *That Uncertain Feeling*, Wilson writes in the *New Yorker* review, 'American influence plays a conspicuous role', though not always happily. 'The author has evidently been reading a good deal of American fiction, and the tone of his hero owes something to this, as well as the conversation of the other characters. They are full of American wisecracks and of wisecracks picked up from the movies.'

The excitement of the Amis family at the prospect of a year in America was unsurprising. Hilly was a fan of American popular culture. For Martin and Philip, aged ten and nine, America was the land of comic books, cartoons, Westerns. The boys planned for the trip by devising American names for themselves: 'Mine was Marty. Adapting one of his middle names Philip had come up with Nick, Junior.' The retired Daddy A, who came to live with the Amises in Swansea after his wife's death, was also pleased at the prospect of the year. He had been bored in Swansea: 'although he had often visited us there with my mother, he knew virtually nobody of his own generation,'[11] according to Amis. Only recently returned from a trip to see his sister Gladys in Washington, DC, he could play the seasoned transatlantic traveller and offer advice. Amis had applied for and seemed to have secured a Fulbright Travelling Grant to cover transportation costs to America. When difficulties arose over the grant, Amis wrote to Larkin on 30 July, 'my father . . . made himself very useful with suggestions, as you might guess'.

The appointment Blackmur offered Amis was as Lecturer and Resident Fellow in Creative Writing at Princeton for the academic year September 1958 to June 1959. He was invited to give the Gauss Seminars for February–March. He would receive $8,000 altogether: a $5,000 salary from the English Department, supplemented by $2,000 from the Humanities Council at Princeton, and a $1,000 travel allowance charged to the Gauss Seminar account. The $8,000 total, roughly twice his Swansea salary, was the occasion of much grousing from Larkin and Conquest. 'Did you see Kingsley blowing off his mouth to a representative of the Sunday Dispatch last Sunday?' Larkin asked Conquest, in a letter of 18 October 1958. 'Sounded on velvet over there . . . 7000 dollars plus $1000 travelling stint for a few lectures over 8 months. Brughughhughugh.' As it turned out, $8,000 was not enough; Blackmur was obliged to come up with extra money, or find ways for Amis to come up with extra money. Part of the problem, Blackmur wrote to McCallum on 1 August 1958, was that 'because of his own dillydallying, we were compelled to take for him a very pleasant but very expensive house – to the tune of three thousand dollars'. Blackmur therefore asked McCallum 'to try to dig up a few monies for Amis'. He himself set about arranging lectures at other universities. A reading was booked for 13 October at the Library of Congress in Washington, DC, at a fee so high that in writing to the Director of its Poetry Office, Roy P. Basler, Amis professed to feel 'a little horrified about accepting so much money for doing so little'.[12] Blackmur's friend Cleanth Brooks, another New Critic, arranged a lecture for Amis at Yale ('In this instance,' Brooks wrote, 'we shall clearly be doing ourselves and our students the favour').[13] Other lectures were arranged by Harry Levin at Harvard, Irving Howe at Brandeis, Samuel Hynes at Swarthmore, Richard Richman at the Institute of Contemporary Arts, Washington, DC (where Amis met Walter Lippmann), and by contacts at Johns Hopkins, Smith, Rutgers, Vassar, the University of Chicago, the University of Illinois at Champaign-Urbana and Andover School. The usual fee for such lectures was $300 plus travel expenses.[14]

The Amises were to sail to New York on the *Queen Elizabeth* on 4 September and in the weeks prior to departure Amis was plagued with arrangements. There were endless forms to fill out and a medical examination for the Fulbright. At the American consul's office in Cardiff, he was asked if he had ever been a member of the Communist Party. 'I didn't hear that properly,' replied the consul after his answer, 'but if you had said yes, it would be more difficult.'[15] At one stage the Fulbright looked to have fallen through[16] and the cultural attaché at the US Embassy in London was unable to intervene. The berths obtained on the *Queen Elizabeth* distributed the family 'in far-flung corners in different holds' (though 'a wan smile briefly lit my features on finding that my father is sharing a cabin with three strangers').[17]

Amis developed anxiety symptoms. The medical examination included tests for heart rate, both standing and after exercise. The latter test upset Amis and in subsequent weeks, he wrote to Larkin, 'the old ticker has been . . . hopping and fluttering as I lie in bed. Oh well. It'll either turn out to be an intermittent contractile irregularity occurring in 40% of sedentary males and of no connexion with any known malfunction, or else a rare systolic disorder of the ventricles with fatal termination except in cases of successful surgery (noticeable improvement in 60% of recovering cases). Just one or the other.'[18] 'I feel rather panicky about the Yank trip,' Amis confessed to Larkin in a later letter: 'afraid of taxi drivers whose fathers and brothers were shot by the British in 1916 was it and so on. Much afraid of not being able to teach Creadive Wriding properly, or indeed at all. Not at all afraid of liking it so much over there I feel I must stay. Much more afraid of hating it so much over there I feel I must come back by about Bonfire Night. More afraid still of finding I haven't got any money.'[19] On the eve of departure a tumour was discovered in Sally's leg. It proved benign but she and Hilly had to delay their passage while Sally recovered from an operation to remove it. Amis, Philip, Martin and Daddy A would make the journey by themselves; Hilly and Sally would follow several weeks later. Though there had been a series of goodbyes in London, Robert Conquest travelled down to Swansea for the weekend to see the Amis men off. In a letter to Larkin of 10 September he described the visit and tried to imagine how Amis would manage 'with Pa, two boys, ships, curtains, New York? Oh dear, there's a real bold buccaneering type.'

In the *Memoirs* Amis says nothing of the voyage itself, though he does describe his first impressions of New York and New Jersey: 'the marvellously foreign-looking building-fronts of that area, recalling to me Italy or Spain' (though he had not been to either), then 'the wondrous multi-coloured lights of the New Jersey Turnpike, at that time utterly unparalleled at home'.[20] When they reached Princeton, some fifty miles south, they were taken straight to the house Blackmur had rented for them, at 271 Edgerstoune Road.[21] This house belonged to the liberal journalist Murray Kempton, who wrote about politics for the *New York Post* and other New York papers. Kempton and his family were spending a year in Italy – Kempton had a Fulbright – and Blackmur or another acquaintance from the Gauss board suggested that the Amises rent their house. On 14 August Blackmur wrote to Amis to describe the house. He had just paid it a visit, 'and in spite of the huge rent, which I assure you is much less than the Kemptons could have got from different tenants, I rather think the space and ease of it will make it worth while for you, and if your wife is like other women I know, she will probably rejoice in the gadgets. These last I shall go out and attempt to master in their initial stages before you get here.'

Hilly loved the house: 'I thought it was brilliant.' Amis, who never bothered much about his surroundings, was less effusive. The house was located on a quiet, semi-rural street two and a half miles from the Princeton campus. All the houses on the lower part of Edgerstoune Road, including the Kemptons', were post-war. Number 271 was built in 1949, one of four identical 'ranch style' houses on the same lower stretch ('Is a ranch-style house built from the proceeds of bull?' Larkin asked Conquest).[22] Amis describes the house in a notebook in which he also records his first impressions of American manners and locutions. 'Ranch-type', it begins, means 'not split-level'. The living room gets most attention, with its floor-to-ceiling windows at the back, peaked ceiling with cross-beams and flagged fireplace. Its chairs – one of the few features of interior design to matter to Amis – are 'canvas skin on iron frame, hard on back of thighs, reducing circulation'. Despite the room's many windows and lamps (Amis counts fourteen bulbs) it is 'still hard to read' in it. In the *Memoirs*, Amis describes the look of the neighbourhood as 'posh-rural . . . with a great deal in the way of lawn, few flowers, no fences, and a patch of woodland at the back where deer would sometimes wander'.[23] In the notebook he says the woodland makes the house seem 'quite cut off'. The most noticeable feature of the landscape are the trees ('get gen on trees,' the notebook advises). A small river runs at the end of the road. The driveways leading up to the road are marked by 'wagon wheels with rim embedded, bearing wooden plate with name: or effigy of e.g. miniature negro'. Blue jays and cardinals sound in the woods, as does a gasoline saw 'like a motorbike in difficulties'.

According to John McAndrew, three doors down, fifty-five children lived on the lower stretch of Edgerstoune Road in 1958. The Amis children were in paradise. There were five McAndrew daughters, ranging in age from sixteen to four. 'We could have gangs by age category,' recalls Megan McAndrew, who was in Martin's class. The neighbourhood was safe and 'the parents didn't really think they had to know where you were at all times'. Shortly after the female Amises arrived, Hilly took Sally in a stroller on long walks through the neighbourhood and down by the river. The other mothers were quick to introduce themselves and soon parents as well as children became friends. In Amis's words, 'Edgerstoune Road was alive with neighbours helping with the children, finding plumbers, schools, maids, mechanics, cars, talking about Europe, which they were all constantly visiting, protesting Anglophilia, inviting one to cocktails and to brunch.'[24] Many of the men in the neighbourhood commuted to Manhattan daily, which took about an hour. It was a neighbourhood of young professionals: advertising executives, lawyers, journalists, salesmen and academics. The town attorney lived next door to the Amises and was the neighbourhood grouch, scaring off children and complaining about noise. When a baseball sailed on to his property from the Kempton front lawn, narrowly missing his wife, he muttered about 'a law case I'd have loved to have'.[25]

John and Jean McAndrew were the most important of the neighbourhood friends the Amises made in their year at Princeton. John McAndrew was forty-six in 1958, ten years older than Amis. He came from a working-class family in Youngstown, Ohio, trained as a lawyer, but after the war went into sales and advertising. 'Work in advertising is seasonal, like coal mining,' Jean McAndrew explained. 'When the company you work for loses a big account, they cut back their work force, and you're out of a job, and he was unemployed part of the year that we came to know the Amises so well, and so there was quite a lot of free time to play.' John McAndrew liked to play. He was tall, good-looking and gregarious. 'He could be charming,' remembers Mina Kempton, Murray's wife, 'very generous and always available'. He was also a big drinker, by some accounts an alcoholic, and his marriage was rocky. His wife Jean, who came from a relatively wealthy family and went to Vassar, had married John in 1941. Both McAndrews were impressed by people from the university and by writers. In Mina Kempton's words, the Amises were 'a big deal for them . . . they were besotted'. The two men became friends, as did their wives, and before the year was out Amis and Jean had an affair, as did Hilly and John, a more serious one, almost as serious for Hilly as the Henry Fairlie affair had been. 'The family mythology is that my father was very much in love with Hilly and talking about leaving and following her to London,' Megan recalls. Yet the two couples remained friends, as the Amises managed to remain friends with other couples with whom they were comparably involved at Princeton, the wildest period of their marriage.

*   *   *

R.P. Blackmur, Amis's 'boss' at Princeton, made his name in the 1920s and 1930s as the author of definitive early assessments of Pound, Eliot, Yeats, Wallace Stevens and Marianne Moore, poets whose difficulty was matched by the difficulty of his own poems. In 'Olympus',[26] a verse tribute to Blackmur, John Berryman writes of the 'sublime assurance' and 'comprehensive air of majesty' of his criticism, qualities combined with a prose style variously described by other admirers as 'oblique', 'gnomic', 'cramped and literal'.[27] Alvarez thought the style of Blackmur's later criticism, mostly on the European novel, derived from the notoriously obscure prefaces of Henry James, no great advertisement in Amis's eyes. Yet Blackmur and Amis had a good deal in common. Blackmur was distrustful of Romantic ideology, thought philosophy and theology 'a grosser type of response to experience than literature',[28] and had little time for the inflated claims of scholarship, at least when forwarded by Princeton equivalents of James Kinsley, Amis's professor and head of department at Swansea. A professor himself, and formidably learned, Blackmur remained an outsider in the Princeton English Department, partly by choice, partly because his colleagues envied his literary celebrity, partly because he had no Ph.D. In fact, he had no university degree at all, did not even have a high-school diploma. After a dispute with one of his teachers, he dropped out of Cambridge High and Latin School, in Cambridge, Massachusetts, a decision supported by his family, and eventually got a job working at the Mandrake Bookshop near Harvard. Here he seems to have spent most of his time reading. He sat in on courses at Harvard unofficially but never enrolled in one, then began writing poetry and publishing criticism in the Cambridge quarterly *Hound and Horn*, which he would eventually help to edit, and the Chicago monthly *Poetry*. When Allen Tate brought him to Princeton in 1940 as an associate in the Creative Arts Program, he had published a well-received volume of poems and two volumes of essays, the distillation of almost twenty years of freelance writing. His association with the English Department began in 1946, as Resident Fellow in Creative Writing. In 1951 he was made a tenured full professor, though unusually for professors of English of his day he was never offered a chair.

Blackmur's circle at Princeton was drawn from the ranks of younger, mostly untenured faculty, often those who thought of themselves as writers as well as academics, from luminaries of the Institute of Advanced Study, where he had spent years during the war (along with Bertrand Russell and Niels Bohr), from Gauss seminarians and lecturers in creative writing, and from a semi-permanent constituent of the Gauss audience, writers and intellectuals from New York as well as Princeton and Rutgers, for whom the seminars were a sort of 'social center'.[29] As a teacher Blackmur treated the students who interested him 'as though they were as intelligent as he was when both he and they knew all too well that they weren't',[30] a pedagogic strategy Amis used as well, also a form of courtesy. When Amis met him in 1958, Blackmur was fifty-four years old, white-haired, professorial, tweedy. In political terms, he thought of himself as a 'Tory Anarchist'; in personal terms, he was, in Alvarez's phrase, 'implacably private'. Blackmur and Alvarez 'talked endlessly' and Blackmur was god-father to Alvarez's son, Luke, yet Alvarez never once heard him mention his parents or ex-wife and 'when the sweet-tempered woman who was with him for years finally moved out he never mentioned her either'.[31] Blackmur's talk was mostly about literature and books and he sometimes pontificated,[32] but he could also be funny and gossipy. In addition, Amis soon discovered, he was a great drinker and luncher. In the *Memoirs*, Amis calls him a 'shifter of enough bourbon for two quite thirsty men, and smoker of enough Luckies (was it?) for several of any sort, and great teller of tales'. Once a week Blackmur had lunch with Robert Oppenheimer at Lahiere's, a French restaurant and Princeton institution (it figures, minimally disguised, in J.D. Salinger's 1955 story, 'Franny'). Amis and Blackmur also lunched there weekly, Amis invariably ordering 'a dozen large clams and . . . two small bottles of Foreign Guinness, a lunch fit for a king'.[33] Blackmur was a generous host at the parties he held at his home after each Gauss lecture. His friend and junior colleague Edmund ('Mike') Keeley, at the time an untenured faculty member and recently published novelist, has described these parties as punishing, 'the weak at heart at moments overwhelmed by the bourbon or the relentlessly elevated dialogue or the host's loquacious good humour'.[34] Alvarez remembers Blackmur at such parties 'dispensing whiskey in tumblers big enough to wash your hands in'.[35]

At one of their lunches Blackmur raised the question of what Amis would be lecturing on in his Gauss Seminars. Amis had not yet given the matter much thought, though before leaving Swansea he took care to pack his lectures and notes on eighteenth-century literary criticism,[36] imagining he might draw on them for Gauss purposes. Blackmur, however, had a suggestion. He had heard, perhaps through McCallum, that Amis was a science fiction fan and had 'one of the finest collections of science fiction in private hands'.[37] Why not give his Gauss Seminars on science fiction? This suggestion appealed to Amis. By 26 October he had agreed to take the suggestion up, writing urgently to Robert Conquest, a fellow fan, for help: 'If ever Amis did anything to win your support, vouchsafe it now. Honestly, if you can send me any griff, or any names of anything that might contain griff, any good stories, but especially stuff *about* s-f, let me know, eh? I'm particularly weak on the early days . . . If you imagine yourself addressing a learned (i.e. academic, not learned s-f wise) audience on this topic I'm sure you'll come up with something.' Amis took a large suitcase to Brentano's bookstore in New York, filled it with SF paperbacks and magazines, and set about the task of planning and writing the lectures that would become *New Maps of Hell: A Survey of Science Fiction* (1960), 'the first such if not the very first academic notice the stuff had received'.[38] The lectures were to begin in February, which meant he had almost four months to prepare them.

In addition, that is, to teaching 'Creadive Wriding', a task that proved surprisingly enjoyable. Amis's teaching obligations consisted of a dozen or so hour-long weekly or fortnightly conferences with individual students. At these conferences Amis would comment on a piece of the student's writing and offer suggestions. He also had to teach a weekly 'precept', a Princeton term for seminar, in which six or eight students would gather to discuss assigned stories from a single large anthology (one of the stories in the anthology was 'The Aspern Papers', 'surely a dangerous model, especially for Americans').[39] Amis wasn't keen on teaching the precepts, but he liked the conferences. These took place in his office in the main Firestone Library, a blockish building with what the notebook calls a 'barley-sugar tower – by order of alumni'. Amis's office, at the end of a corridor, lay 'between *Philately* and *Woodrow Wilson Collection*' and offered a view 'of much greenery as well as many a structure' (the vagueness is a characteristic joke). Here Amis spent his working day, writing as well as teaching, though until mid-March most of his time was devoted to the Gauss Seminars.

Amis's students had to be interviewed before they were admitted to Creative Writing, a task he shared with Mike Keeley, who helped

Blackmur to administer the programme as well as teach it. Keeley had been told by Leslie Fiedler, one of Amis's predecessors, that Amis was 'just like *Lucky Jim*'. Once he'd read *Lucky Jim*, he was keen to meet its author. When Amis arrived at his office, Keeley explained what his teaching duties would be, then the two of them began conducting interviews. By the time they'd finished, they were 'great friends', so much so that Amis felt able to confide in Keeley a delicate personal problem. His wife would be arriving in a few days and he needed to purchase 'what you call rubbers'. Would Keeley show him where he could do so? More importantly, would he accompany him? Amis had made the same request of George Blunden at Oxford. Though brazen as a lover, in public places he was often timid. Once the mission was accomplished, 'off we went to have a drink'. Amis's openness immediately appealed to Keeley, as did his startling opinions about literature. 'He was brilliantly nasty about the writers I loved,' Keeley remembers; 'the outrageousness of his opinions drew me', partly because as prospective scholars 'we weren't trained to do that. We were trained to be careful in what we said.'

The students Amis encountered at Princeton, and his experiences teaching creative writing, are described in an *Observer* article of 30 November 1958 entitled 'The Creation of Literature'.[40] The first student he describes is 'a charming round-faced New Yorker currently engaged in creating a musical comedy about university football'. At their first session Amis asked him who his favourite writers were, 'not Melville or James or Faulkner, I made it clear, but his *favourite* writers'. The student's answer was 'Red Smith', a featured sports writer on the *Herald Tribune* (Smith once described a pitcher as so fast 'he could throw a lamb-chop past a wolf'). Though the student also liked Shaw, Salinger and Ray Bradbury, the last two 'popular choices among the class as a whole', what impressed Amis was the ease with which he named Smith. 'Like many of his contemporaries,' Amis wrote of the student, 'he behaves and talks with a wholly non-arrogant assurance that is less common, I fancy, among British undergraduates.' This student was probably Frank Deford, who became a sportswriter, novelist and broadcaster, and whose undergraduate writing was impressive enough for Amis to recommend him to Curtis Brown, something he also did for another student, Ed Hirsch, described in the *Memoirs* as 'clever enough to cause me the occasional twinge of uneasiness'.[41]

Blackmur was pleased with Amis's teaching. Julian Moynahan, another young writer and untenured assistant professor, overheard him calling Amis a 'honey' of a teacher, rare praise.[42] Though Creative Writing gave Amis 'a lot of pleasure and taught me a lot about America and about literature',[43] he also had reservations about it. These began with the programme's academic setting, 'the presence just around the corner of all that great writing: Melville on the shelves, James in the syllabus, Faulkner still fresh in mind from the instructor's latest interpretation'. Amis was 'bowled over' by the amount of talent he encountered at Princeton,[44] but at times he was also dismayed by the deforming or inhibiting weight of precedent and context, as when one student, 'a natural writer if ever such could be detected at the age of nineteen', asked him whether he was 'putting enough style in', or another, the only poet he taught, defended an incomprehensible phrase on the grounds that 'I just don't take much account of the reader. Anything he gets out of my poems is all right with me.' Behind this last comment Amis sensed 'the foggy notion that if you turn out to be any good someone or other will write a book about you explaining what you meant'. As he warned in the *Observer* article, 'we pickle a rod for our own backs when we are patient with the obscurity of the great'. Amis also expressed doubts about the influence of New Criticism,

whereby every syllable of the work under discussion is relentlessly probed for its symbolical or cross-referential value. In the seminars which I conduct, discussions will rage for ten minutes on such questions as the significance of the two shades of yellow in the clothes worn by the wife and husband in Lawrence's 'Two Blue Birds,' or the possible Homeric overtones of the name Helen in Hemingway's 'The Snows of Kilimanjaro.' I almost got to the point of asking [the Deford student] why the heroic quarterback is called Ace: is it an emblem of isolation (the single pip), or is it a token of ambivalence (Ace counting high or low)? Poor Ace would be loaded with both if he appeared in the works of Marcus Denker, where Sartre seems, as we go to press, to be vanquishing Salinger.

The Creative Writing students Amis grew closest to at Princeton were William Rukeyser and Mark Rose, both in their second year, and Timothy Houghton, a year ahead. Rukeyser became a financial journalist, eventually editing *Fortune* and *Money* magazines. His memories of Amis as a teacher 'are entirely positive', but it was as a friend that he meant most. 'Kingsley once mentioned to me the great freemasonry of people between twenty and forty,' Rukeyser recalls. 'He welcomed me and my cohort into the grown-up world.' Rose, who became an English professor at Yale and then at the University of California, Santa Barbara, remembers Amis as 'charismatic, constantly poking holes in anything that was overblown'. Befriending the young was for Amis 'part of the aggressive anti-pomposity'; to find oneself befriended, 'immensely seductive'. Rose was 'a Jewish kid from Bayonne, New Jersey' (Rukeyser was also Jewish, from New Rochelle, New York) and seeing the world through Amis's eyes 'was very useful to me . . . helped me to navigate Princeton in the 1950s'. Princeton was stuffy as well as intimidating, which made the Amis view 'wildly refreshing and a great deal of fun'. Only later did Rose come to see Amis's influence as limiting. After Amis returned to Swansea, Blackmur invited Rose to study with him, but he never took the offer up, mostly because Blackmur was reputed to be incomprehensible and after a year with Amis 'anything incomprehensible was not going to be for me'. As Rose grew to admire Blackmur's criticism, its difficulty notwithstanding, he realised Amis was 'a closer off as well as an opener up'. This was a fact about Amis Keeley also came to realise, partly through Amis's refusal to read Faulkner, Keeley's great hero (as well as the inspiration of his first novel, which Amis also refused to read). Keeley recalls a game played at parties at Princeton which involved confessing to things one had never done and gaining points if others had done them: 'Kingsley'd never done almost anything. He'd never read *War and Peace*, or tried to. He'd never been to Penn Station. He'd never been to the top of the Empire State building. He always won.' Timothy Houghton, the third of the students Amis was close to at Princeton, came from a rural rather than a suburban background. Although on campus he lived extravagantly, or seemed to, affecting a countrified gentility, in reality he came from a New England family of modest means. Rose remembers him as 'slight, somewhat ironic, a sweet kid'; Rukeyser as 'very serious about writing'. All three students followed Amis to Britain after they graduated from Princeton. 'They lived with us, practically,' Hilly recalls, 'on and off, for months on end.' Rukeyser went to Cambridge, ostensibly to do research in English. Rose went to Oxford, where he took his English studies more seriously. Houghton went directly to Swansea to write, eventually taking up residence with the Amises in Glanmor Road.

Amis's arrival in Princeton was heralded in the local and student press. *Lucky Jim* was described as 'the most widely discussed British novel of the decade', its author 'the center of a storm of controversy across the Atlantic'.[45] After three weeks of publicity, the *Daily Princetonian* ran an article that began: 'Mr Amis has by now been so thoroughly interviewed, described and labelled that some brief description of his work becomes almost a necessity.' In November, thanks to the Angry Young Man label, he was invited to participate in a debate at Hunter College in New York on the question 'Is There a Beat Generation?' The other participants in the debate were Jack Kerouac, Ashley Montagu, an English anthropologist 'of a popularising sort' (author of *Man: His First Two Million Years*, among other books), and James Wechsler, editor of the *New York Post* and author of *Revolt on the Campus*. The debate was immediately hijacked by Kerouac, who spoke first and overran his allotted ten minutes by another fifty. His talk was boring and incoherent, invoking such ancestral Beats as 'Popeye, Laurel and Hardy and Humphrey Bogart'.[46] According to the *Village Voice*, in an account reprinted in the *Daily Princetonian*, when Kerouac finished speaking, he disrupted those who followed by dashing on and off stage, trying to drag Allen Ginsberg up to speak, and general clowning. Wechsler looked 'angry if not young', Montagu looked on the verge of sleep, as well as 'just the way the Ladies League thinks a professor should look', and Amis looked bewildered, 'perplexed by the mad audience, but in a friendly way trying to understand the madness'. In the diary she kept in her first few months at Princeton, Hilly records Kerouac's antics ('balancing things on his head and making faces') and the audience's impatience ('Stay out, you ———,' someone shouted as Kerouac walked off stage during Montagu's speech). Amis, she records with wifely pride, took 'exactly ten mins having raised quite a few laughs and got a good round of applause'. In the *Memoirs*, Amis wonders 'why on earth had I gone there, one who had been trying to get away from the Angry Young Men?' Answer: 'The usual mixture of curiosity and vanity.'[47]

Amis's celebrity at Princeton meant lots of invitations. There were academic friends, principally among the younger faculty, including Mike Keeley and his wife Mary, Julian and Liz Moynahan, Russell and Phil Fraser, Charles Davis and his wife Gene (Davis was the first black faculty member at Princeton), and later, through Gauss connections, Paul Fussell, at Rutgers, and his wife Betty. Then there were neighbourhood friends, introduced through the McAndrews, and wealthier friends acquired through Amis's literary connections. Chief among this latter category was Amis's agent, Alan Collins, who lived in state in nearby Hopewell, New Jersey, in a house George Washington once slept in, which now boasted a swimming pool, a tennis court and a bowling lane. Mike Keeley once bowled there with Elizabeth Bowen, another Collins client. Amis and Bowen 'took to each other at once', bonding poolside through large bourbons on the rocks ('she was a good little drinker').[48] Another literary friend, Sandy Richardson, Keeley's editor at Doubleday (Thomas Pynchon's first editor), also had a place in Hopewell. Richardson had serious jazz connections and he and his wife took the Amises to New York jazz clubs; they also gave them a going-away party in their garden at which several Amis heroes performed live, including the black trumpeter Rex Stewart, the clarinettist Buster Bailey, the trombonist J.C. Higginbotham (whose hand Amis shook 'with more reverence than that of W.H. Auden on a different occasion'),[49] and another trumpeter named Joe Thomas. Though Amis was somewhat disappointed at the performances, he liked Bailey's 'enthusiastic tomming (tomming is or was the buttering-up of whites by a black) – "Ain't he the most, Kingsley!" he would bawl as other musicians finished their solos.'[50] Among other acquaintances in this sphere were the novelist Caroline Gordon, ex-wife of Allen Tate, and her daughter and son-in-law, Nancy and Percy Wood. The Woods liked to entertain. Percy Wood was a psychiatrist who made a lot of money running a residential care centre for wealthy patients with psychological problems. The parties at the Woods' were especially lavish. So, too, were the parties given by a wealthy businessman, Donald Mackie, and his wife, Fleury, a couple who, according to Fussell, 'had almost no intellectual interests at all, but they had very good cocktails'. Amis was invited to their parties because he was in the news: 'He was just a passing celebrity. He could have been a film star.' Soon the Amises were asked out more nights than even they could manage. 'Everybody was after him, in one way or another,' Keeley remembers, 'and he was after everybody, in one way or another.'

He was also after everybody in New York. In the *Memoirs* Amis pays tribute to the city in typically trenchant style. Though he spent only a few nights there, he visited often enough while at Princeton 'to convince me that anyone who makes a business of hating it or being superior to it, and there were plenty then, home-grown and foreign, is a creep, and that anyone who walks up Fifth Avenue (say) on a sunny morning without feeling his spirits lift is an asshole'.[51] Amis's trips to New York included lunches with McCallum and visits to Harcourt Brace and Curtis Brown. Before departing for America, Amis had let Graham Watson, his London agent, know that he was worried about money. Edith Haggard of Curtis Brown's New York office duly solicited commissions from magazines. Meetings and deals were set up with *Harper's*, *Town*, *Gentleman's Quarterly*, *Atlantic*. Meetings were also set up with and through Cindy Degner, who handled drama for Curtis Brown. An option for a stage adaptation of *Lucky Jim* had been taken out by New York producers; writers were being scouted; an article would be planted in the *New York Times*. Though the project eventually fell through, it was still very much alive while Amis was at Princeton.

At the end of October, Amis wrote to Anthony and Violet Powell describing his visits to New York in terms that made them sound as jammed and life-shortening as his visits to London:

[M]y first day there was the English tourist doing the place in 12 hours, and included a conversation with a publisher (6'3", son of Middle West miner, Montenegrin ancestry),[52] lunch with queer Broadway producer, party at magazine office (martinis at 4 p.m. – oogh ergh), dinner in Greenwich Village (mainly palate-eroding cheese), intellectual party (during which I heard one bearded man ask another if he really understood what artistic integrity was – honest, now), jazz session with a lot of conscientious inter-racial camaraderie, and finally slumber in Auden's bed – all right, all right, WHA is in Rome. Plucking down a copy of Crabbe's poems in the flat (which belongs to Auden) I saw on the flyleaf 'To Wystan. We must love one another AND die. Cyril.' Didn't look at any others for fear of anti-climax.[53]

Amis's host for that evening was Gene Lichtenstein, deputy literary editor at *Esquire*. In the *Memoirs*, Amis says the party was held to celebrate the magazine's twenty-first birthday, but the magazine was founded in 1933, so the birthday was the twenty-fifth. He also writes that he had a story in the birthday issue, but the only story he published in *Esquire* while in America was 'Moral Fibre', published in March 1959. *Esquire* gave lots of parties, and Amis seems to have conflated the party he mentions in the letter to the Powells with the birthday party. In any event, at one of these parties he met Norman Mailer, 'who was not stabbing anyone at the time', as well as the cartoonist Jules Feiffer, 'who left my side at once when I turned my head to utter a short phrase to a third party'.[54] Lichtenstein was subletting Auden's apartment on St Mark's Place in October 1958 and remembers the evening Amis reported to the Powells: the jazz club he took Amis to after dinner was the Five Spot, just across from Auden's apartment: 'Amis was pretty much drunk and missed his last train to Princeton, to my consternation, so I said stay overnight.'[55]

Lichtenstein remembers meeting Amis and Hilly at a party in London in 1959 and inviting Amis to visit him in New York. 'It would be great if you could write for us,' he said. 'Come up from Princeton for lunch and we'll work something out.' What *Esquire* worked out, after buying 'Moral Fibre', was that Amis should review films for the magazine, replacing Dwight Macdonald, a writer associated with the magazines *Partisan Review* and *Politics*. Coincidentally, Macdonald was delivering the first set of Gauss Seminars for the academic year and Amis went to them, or some of them: 'That old idiot Dwight Macdonald has been giving a seminar on mass culture,' he wrote Conquest on 26 October, 'ah stuff that.' Yet Amis was impressed that Macdonald 'had clearly done some work on his lectures'.[56] The title of the column Amis took over from Macdonald was 'The Art of the Film' and his brief was to review 'foreign' (i.e., non-American) films only. He accepted the job because it was well paid – as he reported to Conquest, who passed the news on to Larkin, 'Payment works out at 2/6 a word', almost three times what English periodicals paid[57] – also because *Esquire* was highly regarded. Rust Hills, its literary editor and Lichtenstein's boss, published stories and articles by Norman Mailer, Saul Bellow, John Cheever and other major figures; Dorothy Parker was the magazine's book reviewer.

Amis complained about the films he had to see for *Esquire* ('fucking phoney foreign films' was his invariable response to the mention of any non-American movie, Rose recalls) and Lichtenstein thought his reviews strained (he also thought Dorothy Parker's reviews strained). But they got him into New York once a week and, as with almost everything he wrote, have their funny and perceptive moments. Unexpected ones, too. For Amis, the visual always takes second place, even in films. *The Mistress*, a Japanese film reviewed in his first column, in the issue of January 1959, courts the epithet 'exquisite' but 'there is often rather a long time between one exquisite moment and the next: this is the art cinema all right'. The film's look or design is mostly what accounts for its appeal and Amis dutifully and sensitively attends to it: 'the fragile little houses that make everything look like a stage set, the bridges over streams, the willows and water lilies. All *japonaiserie*, if you like, but good *japonaiserie*. Beyond this there are some fine uses of black and white: the shifting light playing on the heroine's face as rain cascades down the window-pane, lovely shots of her picking her way daintily through a splashing downpour.' There are also unexpected moments in what Amis writes about Brigitte Bardot, in addition to expected ones. In a July review of *Love Is My Profession*, based on a Simenon story, he describes the Bardot appeal:

That incredible face, with its little-sausage lips turned outward ever so slightly by her ever-so-slightly protruding teeth (hence the permanently incipient pout) is not the sort one can admit getting tired of without undergoing all kinds of suspicions, affected imperturbability being the least of these. And the same applies, with redoubled force, to any dissatisfaction with her non-facial aspects. But I do feel that, after all due weight has been given to her union of childishness and sexiness and the inflammatory potentiality of this, there is something unsexy and even enervating about her as well . . . One finds oneself, after twenty minutes or so, watching the actors and actresses instead. Symbol or not, there are limits to the appeal of a pin-up in motion.

Enjoyable in a more familiar fashion are Amis's objections to Satyajit Ray's *Aparajito*, about a poor family in India. After an opening sequence establishing the protagonists' 'remarkably uneventful' lives, 'about forty minutes pass, enlivened by such events as the small boy's visit to the man upstairs to borrow matches', an episode rendered 'in such toiling, conscientious detail that I wondered once or twice whether we might not be in for some strong drama after all'. Though the film's length and scenic variety give it an air of inclusiveness, 'in fact it leaves out a great deal: sex, money, community, leisure, the seasons. Only a highbrow of really apostolic ferocity could continuously enjoy *Aparajito*' (in the *Memoirs* he calls it 'the most boring film I have ever seen in my life').[58] Other foreign films and filmmakers are more noisily objectionable. Reporting in April on the American première of *He Who Must Die*, an adaptation of a Nikos Kazantzakis novel, Amis recounts turning up at the Beekman Theater to discover that the screening is to be preceded by a speech from Kazantzakis's translator, all about the film's 'fullness of spirit and sincerity of vision', as well as the 'fundamental questions from which modern artists shy away'. Amis comments: 'All this talk about "courage" which fills the air whenever anybody these days undertakes to be pretentious – is it really so intrepid to bite off more than one can chew?' Amis always loved the movies, but the movies he loved were American. He also delighted in flaunting his lowbrow tastes. *Beverly Hills Cop*, he told Christopher Hitchens, was 'a flawless masterpiece'.

About a month after the Amises arrived in Princeton the whole family, children and Daddy A included, travelled to Washington, DC, where Amis was to give a reading at the Library of Congress and a lecture at the Institute of Contemporary Art. They would stay with Aunt Gladys and her second husband, Virgil I. Case. Amis had not seen Aunt Gladys, to whom as a boy he used to write letters and send poems and stories, in over twenty years, since her last visit to England. Uncle Virgil he had never seen at all. He immediately took to them both. Though their house on S Street was small and without much in the way of drink or tasteful furnishings, 'they had their sun-porch and the rumpus-room and plenty of parties, and in a beat-up-Chevvy, hamburger-joint kind of way they showed us something very American: what a good time non-well-off people could have'.[59] Uncle Virg turned out to be 'a flamboyant grey-haired figure in overalls and a baseball cap . . . tattooed from head to foot', an improbable husband for Aunt Gladys, an admirable, hard-working woman who never lost the anxieties and pretensions of her upbringing, according to Robert Foster, her son. Amis implicitly confirms Robert's view when he explains how Uncle Virg and Daddy A got on: 'After all, Uncle Virg was used to the English.'[60] Though Amis never got his wish of seeing Uncle Virg and Dadda (Amis's grandfather) together, almost as good was Uncle Virg and Walter Lippmann. This meeting took place at a party at the Institute of Contemporary Arts: 'To my uneasiness, and also without the emergence of any clear idea of how they had done it, my father and Uncle Virg attached themselves to the party.' Uncle Virg approached the great foreign policy sage, remembered by Amis as large, gloomy and mostly uncommunicative, and asked him a question about

'Shanghai Shek', making the Taiwanese ruler 'sound like somebody on a level with, say, Texas Dan'. The question brought Lippmann alive. He talked 'for an hour or so about it without stopping much'.[61]

Amis's reading at the Library of Congress was for its Archive of Recorded Poetry and Literature, begun in 1943 by Allen Tate, at the time consultant in poetry to the library. Amis put some thought and effort into preparing the reading, which was held on 13 October, writing to the Poetry Office with the estimated lengths of individual poems and prose extracts and confessing that he found the task of selection difficult, 'there being much to bear in mind regarding completeness, contrast etc.'[62] All the poems he read came from *A Case of Samples*, which gathers together the poems from the Reading University and Fantasy pamphlets, plus a few additional poems. He also read three prose extracts, one from each of the novels.[63] The poems were grouped to show the range of his verse, an important feature to him. 'Every poem is an attempt at solving a completely new problem,' he had written in his statement of purpose in Enright's *Poets of the 1950s* (1955), adding that he was drawn to verse forms 'I haven't used before, or at any rate until recently'.[64] Hence, in part, the title *A Case of Samples*. Only six poems from *Bright November* appeared in Amis's *Collected Poems* (when required to list his publications for Princeton he left out *Bright November*),[65] though all but one of the poems in *A Case of Samples* were included, and mostly in the same order. The omission was 'A Poet's Epitaph', an attack on Dylan Thomas: 'They call you "drunk with words"; but when we drink / And fetch it up, we sluice it down the sink. / You should have stuck to spewing beer, not ink.'

W.S. Merwin reviewed *A Case of Samples* in the *New York Times* and identified its contents as of three kinds: 'poems of generalized intellectual statement, dense with wit of the sort inevitably called metaphysical'; a second sort of serious poem, 'ironic or elegiac, or both; describing, or telling stories, both very well'; and 'the overtly funny pieces', which 'owe as much to Auden and Betjeman as they do to Empson' and are for the most part 'enviable: hard, delightful and as funny on the third reading as on the first'.[66] The opening three poems Amis read at the Library of Congress belong to Merwin's second grouping. Amis's pencilled note for 'Masters' (in a copy in the Huntington Library which contains introductory notes for most of the poems he read in Washington) identifies it as 'anthology piece

– generalizn on military men, empire builders'. As the opening stanza makes clear, the poem is about control, a central concern of the volume as a whole, as of other Movement volumes:

> That horse whose rider fears to jump will fall,
> Riflemen miss if orders sound unsure;
> They only are secure who seem secure;
>   Who lose their voice lose all.

Fearfulness motivates and underlies the military man's air of mastery (as it does the poet's). Even when the poem calls for release in the concluding stanzas, formal control is maintained. This control, Movement types would argue, gives the poem its power:

> The eyes that will not look, the twitching cheek,
> The hands that sketch what mouth would fear to own,
> Only these make us known, and we are known
>   Only as we are weak:

> By yielding mastery the will is freed,
> For it is by surrender that we live,
> And we are taken if we wish to give,
>   And needed if we need.

W.S. Merwin thought Amis's poems were sometimes 'sentimental in a peculiar slangy, brittle way', and this is true of 'A Bookshop Idyll' ('Something Nasty in the Bookshop' in the Reading pamphlet), another poem about control and release. The introductory note to it in the Huntington copy reads 'Bad po more afectg than it shd be: mawkishness > cleverness littiness.' The 'bad po' in question is the sort chosen and written by women: 'love po.' Again, what the poem admires is something beyond control, beyond 'cleverness littiness'. The risk it runs is 'mawkishness', sentimentality. This risk Amis acknowledged in the Enright anthology, conceding that for 'the newer poets, including myself, . . . the strict forms seem to give some of them the idea that they can be as sentimental and trite as they please, provided they do it in *terza rima*'. Here are the final stanzas of 'A Bookshop Idyll':

> Should poets bicycle-pump the human heart
>   Or squash it flat?

> Man's love is of man's life a thing apart;
>   Girls aren't like that.
>
> We men have got love well weighed up; our stuff
>   Can get by without it.
> Women don't seem to think that's good enough;
>   They write about it,
>
> And the awful way their poems lay them open
>   Just doesn't strike them.
> Women are really much nicer than men:
>   No wonder we like them.
>
> Deciding this, we can forget those times
>   We sat up half the night
> Chockfull of love, crammed with bright thoughts,
>   names, rhymes,
>   And couldn't write.

When in 1986 the feminist academic Jan Montefiore wrote to Amis asking for permission to quote 'A Bookshop Idyll' in a monograph she had written on feminism and poetry, she included the reading that would accompany it. Amis wrote back granting permission but taking issue with the reading: 'I really don't suggest (nor is it my opinion) that the love-poem is a quintessentially female mode; I was trying to make a more general point to the effect that women are less inhibited about expressing their feelings than men are, at any rate in our society. And though I'm pleased you think the poem good-natured, surely the people it patronises are not women but men, who cut a pretty sorry figure in the last verse.'[67]

Amis read 'A Bookshop Idyll' just after an extract from *Lucky Jim*. The second of the novel extracts he read was the episode in Chapter 10 of *That Uncertain Feeling* in which Lewis adopts a disguise to evade John Gruffyd-Williams. The episode is broad farce and Amis may have chosen it in conscious defiance of Edmund Wilson, whose *New Yorker* review singled it out as 'weak', 'clumsily implausible'. As if in contrast, Amis then read a group of five distinctly 'serious' poems, all in different ways about poetry, even when poetry is never mentioned. 'On Staying Still', for example, is ostensibly about a broken boat lying halfway up the beach on Swansea Bay. Donald

Davie once lamented the absence 'of outward and non-human things apprehended crisply for their own sakes' in Movement poetry.[68] He has a point with Amis, as Amis wittily admitted in 'Here Is Where', also from *A Case of Samples*. This is how 'Here Is Where' begins:

> Here, where the ragged water
> Is twilled and spun over
> Pebbles backed like beetles,
> Bright as beer-bottles,
> Bits of it like snow beaten,
> Or milk boiling in saucepan . . .
>
> Going well so far, eh?

This is how the poem ends:

> The country, to townies,
> Is hardly more than nice,
> A window-box, pretty
> When the afternoon's empty;
> When a visitor waits,
> The window shuts.

One of the remarkable things about 'Here Is Where' is how good the opening lines are; the similes all work, help to describe things seen or there. Amis can, if required, 'apprehend crisply' the outward and the non-human; it is simply that he refuses to do so 'for their own sakes'. As he says in a middle stanza. 'Why drag in / All that water and Stone?' In 'On Staying Still', they are dragged in to make a point about poetry. Amis begins by describing the boat's hull:

> Black in every light,
> But swathed with sand that glows
> From ginger to chocolate
> Then ginger-dust. The seas
> Soak it for no reason
> Each tide-rise, finding it
> Dried by the sun for no
> Reason, or already wet

> With rain before they are near
> To strike poses of passion:
> Bravery of blind colour,
> Noble gesture of spray,
> And eloquence of loud noise
> That shake not a single spar.

The poetical implications of the contrast between the boat's stillness and the sea's violent motion emerge through the terms Amis uses in describing the tide-rise: 'poses', 'Bravery', 'gesture', 'eloquence'. The pencilled note in the Huntington copy reads: 'Real experience – broodg shows po here unspectacular virtue or mere avoidance of showy self-regarding energy.' The 'po' Amis admires, figured in the boat, is real, understated, unrhetorical, unlike the sea's 'eloquence of loud noise'. In its showiness and 'self-regard' the sea's energy is like that of the wind in Amis's 'Ode to the East-North-East-by-East Wind', also from *A Case of Samples*, though not read in Washington. In the second stanza of the 'Ode', the wind round Mount Everest is said to 'blow / Gigantic bits of rock about, for no / Reason', while in the third stanza Amis applauds the way old map-makers depict it 'with an infant's cheeks that swell / So that they shut your puffy eyes; / No need for you to care or notice where / You kick and writhe and scream in wincing air.' The Huntington note to the 'Ode' reads: 'atak on conv. Rism [Romanticism] – Shelley[;] also hatred of wind: not just symbol.' The anti-Romantic bias of 'On Staying Still' is evident in its quiet close, where the view of nature that prevails emphasises renewal and rebirth, as in *Lucky Jim* or Shakespearean romance:

> The hulk's only use
> Is as mark for pebble-thrower
> Or shade for small anemone,
> But that is not nothing;
> And staying still is more,
> When all else is moving
> To no end, whether
> Or not choice is free
> Good that decay recalls
> (By being slow and steady)
> Blossom, fruitful change

> Of tree to coal, not any
> Changeless tidal fury.

The themes of 'On Staying Still' are taken up more explicitly in 'Against Romanticism', the last of the poems in its grouping (hence Robert Conquest's decision to include it in the polemical *New Lines* anthology, together with the even more explicit 'A Poet's Epitaph'). These are its opening lines:

> A traveller who walks a temperate zone
> – Woods devoid of beasts, roads that please the foot –
> Finds that its decent surface grows too thin:
>   Something unperceived fumbles at his nerves.
> To please an ingrown taste for anarchy
>   Torrid images circle in the wood,
> And sweat for recognition up the road
>   Cramming close the air with their bookish cries.

The cries from the images 'in the wood' and 'up the road' are 'bookish' because they come from literature or fantasy, not life. The poet disapproves of them but also implies that their appearance is inevitable: eventually the traveller grows tired of decent surfaces (metre, for instance); the taste for anarchy that causes 'something unperceived' to fumble at his nerves is 'ingrown'. At its most considered, in poems like this, Amis's opposition to the Romantic is corrective, an attempt to restore a balance. The poem has no illusions about putting an end to Romantic impulses, to prophecy, idealism or rage; it is a counterweight to, not a negation of, the tendencies against which it kicks.

This is the position also of 'Romance', the poem that ended the reading.[69] Amis's note to 'Romance' reads: 'Can't throw out Rism all the way even when it explained.' The poem presents the image of 'a youngster in the lonely night' listening to 'the sound of saxophones'. These saxophones come from what is for him 'Adulthood's high romantic citadel, / The Tudor Ballroom of the Grand Hotel'. Through his window the youngster sees the 'long skirts and fair heads' of the revellers in the hotel, 'an image nothing could dispel' and one the poem contrasts with older, more conventional Romantic images. Behind both old and new images, though, lies a common ('ingrown'?) impulse:

Those other dreams, those freedoms lost their charm,
Those twilight lakes reflecting pine or palm,
Those skies were meanly large and wrongly calm.

What then but weakness turns the heart again
Out in that lonely night beyond the pane
With images and truths of wind and rain.

The propensity to dream, the Romantic propensity, may be 'weakness' but it is ineradicable. This is the message of the other two poems from the final grouping, 'A Dream of Fair Women' and 'A Song of Experience' (from which *A Case of Samples* takes its name). In 'A Song of Experience', a narrative poem, we are presented with another traveller, discovered having a drink in a pub: 'We asked him over when the talk turned hearty / And let him tell of women he had known.' These women came in 'all colours, white and black and coffee'. Some were easily seduced, others took more effort, all benefited from his touch, none detained him:

The inaccessible he laid a hand on,
    The heated he refreshed, the cold he warmed.
What Blake presaged, what Lawrence took a stand on,
    What Yeats locked up in fable, he performed.

And so he knew, where we can only fumble,
    Wildly in daydreams, vulgarly in art;
Miles past the point where all illusions crumble
    He found the female and the human heart.

In this discovery, 'Nausicaa and Circe were the same.' Experience, 'that living element', brought truth, the core of a mystery. Yet the poem ends with the traveller draining his drink, paying up and leaving by himself:

I saw him, brisk in May, in Juliet's weather,
    Hitch up the trousers of his long-tailed suit,
Polish his windscreen with a chamois-leather,
    And stow his case of samples in the boot.

In 'A Dream of Fair Women', as we have seen, the poem's 'Kingsley' is forever seeking 'The halls of theoretical delight, / The women of that ever-fresh terrain, / The night after tonight'. Pursuit of the ideal, the poem suggests, is delusory, destructive, distracting, something for 'the really weak'. The salesman of 'A Song of Experience' has no such delusions about ideal women. But is he more appealing? Is he not the prototype of Dai Evans of *The Evans Country*? Who would want to be him, for all his conquests? By titling *A Case of Samples* as he does, identifying himself with the busy, solitary salesman, Amis hints at the limitations as well as the strengths of the values his poems put forward. The poem's clear-sightedness matches that of his pursuit of pleasure in real life.

This pursuit would not reach its height until the spring, after the Gauss Seminars had been delivered, though plenty of opportunities for fun remained. A sampling of entries from Hilly's diary for October and November 1958 gives a sense of what domestic and social life was like for the Amises early in their year at Princeton. When Halloween at last arrived, everyone had a fine time, adults included. The children went trick-or-treating and 'even the man next door who hates children gave them some nuts'. There was a party for the adults, with masks and costumes (Blackmur wore a goblin mask 'with giant plastic ears and nose', several women dressed as sexy witches). The party had plenty of dancing 'which I always enjoy' and 'lots to drink'; it didn't end until 2 a.m. The next day, a Saturday, everyone went their separate ways: Amis was taken to a Princeton football game and a pre-game party, Philip went to Boy Scouts, Daddy A took Martin to the movies, Sally played 'with Tommy Green up the road' and Hilly pottered about the house, preparing a drinks party for later in the afternoon ('none of them leave till 7.30'). After the party, Hilly and Amis went off to dinner with the Keeleys at the home of David Dodge, the travel and mystery writer, after which there were more drinks and party games. The evening ended at 2.30 a.m. and Sunday was spent recuperating. On Monday Hilly and Amis went to New York to have lunch 'with John Mcleary . . . he's K's agent from Harquit' (the mistakes here are indicative; Hilly did not keep up with the details of Amis's professional life), saw 'a very boring Danish film', met 'the chaps from Esquire for pre dinner drinks', then 'a rather horrid Chinese meal', then coffee at Gene Lichtenstein's flat. Just past midnight they caught the train home and were in bed by 1.45 a.m. The next day, 4 November, there were invitations to attend election night parties ('most of our friends seem to be Democrats'), which they declined; they also declined invitations for Wednesday, 5 November, as Thursday was the night of the 'Beat Generation' debate. At the weekend there were more parties, including 'a barn dance at a millionaire's place in a village called Hopewell about 8 miles away'.

Several entries discuss the progress and activities of the children.[70] Philip is happy at his Princeton school: 'it's good to see him mixing so well and making friends so easily' (according to the McAndrew girls, Philip was the charismatic one, very good-looking);[71] Sally 'is fine now with sitters – and rather looks forward to holding forth without anyone to cramp her style';[72] Martin's teacher ('very young and pretty') pronounces him 'above average in everything'. 'He really is a child born under a lucky star,' Hilly writes, 'not an unhappy moment does he ever seem to have and yet he is not cocky or over pleased with himself – now I come to think of it he has never given me a bad moment all his life.'[73] Hilly read an article in an English newspaper which claimed that the Amis children now watched television three hours a day, and she indignantly denies this in the diary: 'they never see it for more than an hour and very often don't have it on at all – Scrabble is their great craze and riding their bikes.'[74] The Scrabble craze was nurtured by Daddy A, who helped with babysitting and entertaining the children. Daddy A was almost as sociable a man as his son, but only sometimes included in the Amises' invitations. R.W.B. Lewis, the Edith Wharton scholar, and his wife Nancy, liked and felt sorry for 'Bill', and often invited him over; he is remembered as a peripheral figure by the Amises' other Princeton friends and acquaintances. On 14 November, Hilly records that he has gone to Washington to visit Aunt Gladys for a few days: 'it's very nice to be on our own for a bit – although the kids miss him and he really is very good – it's just that the poor chap is there *all the time* – this affects K more than me – I'm afraid one day there will be such a book written around this subject.'[75]

By mid-November Amis was well into preparations for the Gauss Seminars. In addition to soliciting 'griff' from Conquest and reading through his suitcase of SF paperbacks, he devised a questionnaire which he sent, on headed Gauss stationery and with the help of a secretary provided by Princeton, to twenty prominent SF authors, among them John Wyndham, Isaac Asimov, Ray Bradbury and

Arthur C. Clarke. He also sent questionnaires to editors of the most important SF magazines, who were asked about the nature and size of the audience for science fiction, the medium's increasing popularity among intellectuals, the role of the scientific element in the genre, its function (aside from entertainment), how it had evolved, and its relation to SF on radio, television and film. Most authors and editors responded, flattered by or approving the academic attention. Bradbury ended his questionnaire: 'God speed on your six seminars, and let me know what sort of reception you get, will you? I think it's wonderful you're doing this work, and am naturally prejudiced and hopeful of the effects you will produce.'[76] Some weeks before the first seminar, to be held on 5 February 1959, Amis sent out a science fiction reading list to Gauss invitees. The list contained a dozen titles, including four anthologies of stories and novels by well-known figures such as Isaac Asimov (*I, Robot*) and Arthur C. Clarke (*Earthlight*). It began, however, with works by relatively obscure or specialist practitioners: *A Case of Conscience* by James Blish, *The Demolished Man* by Alfred Bester and *The Space Merchants* by Frederik Pohl and C.M. Kornbluth. These were the titles to which Amis referred most frequently in the seminars, at greatest length, and, in the case of *The Space Merchants*, with most respect (Frederik Pohl, he declared, was 'the most consistently able writer science fiction, in the modern sense, has yet produced').[77] The reading list also recommended 'any recent issue' of *Astounding Science Fiction*, *Galaxy Science Fiction* or the *Magazine of Fantasy and Science Fiction*.

The seminars were held on the second floor of the Firestone Library on Thursdays at 8.30 p.m. It was expected, Blackmur wrote on 21 January, 'that those who accept our invitation will participate in the discussion, and will sustain their attendance throughout the series'. Amis had some experience of Gauss Seminar discussion, from his attendance not only at Dwight Macdonald's seminars but at those given in January by the art critic Clement Greenberg. Keeley describes a typical exchange at one of the discussions attended by Amis. The questioner was Hannah Arendt:

One remembers, for example, the extremely distinguished lady author often down from New York who was given to posing questions, in a heavy German accent, that might begin as follows: 'I have only one question to ask our eminent speaker. It is in three parts. The first part has to do with – how shall I put it delicately? – the basic confusion, not to say essential contradiction, obvious in the speaker's clearly absurd proposition that . . .'; and perhaps ten minutes later the speaker might be allowed to say: 'If I understand you correctly, and that I can hardly be expected to believe, let me attempt to approach the third part of your question first, because, having lost the drift of much of the other two parts, it would surely not be fruitful . . . ,' to which Kingsley Amis, in town to await his own 'Gauss' on science fiction later in the year, might be heard to mumble: 'Just like bloody Oxford.'[78]

Amis was unlikely to be fazed by such questions. In an October 1959 essay on 'The Delights of Literary Lecturing', in the American magazine *Harper's*, he makes reference to 'those well-tested life-belts – asking for a 250-word question to be repeated, answering it with a monosyllable, breaking into uncontrollable laughter, etc.'[79]

Amis began his first seminar, entitled 'Definitions and Ancestry', by drawing parallels between science fiction and jazz: both (in the words of *New Maps of Hell*, the minimally revised printed version of the seminars, the source also of subsequent quotes) are 'addictions' and thus most likely to be contracted 'in adolescence or not at all'; both emerged at roughly the same time, 'in the second or third decade of the century,' and 'underwent rapid internal change around 1940'; both are 'characteristically American products' with 'a noticeably radical tinge', though in the case of jazz, 'whose material is perforce non-political, radicalism of some sort often appears in the attitudes of those connected with it'; and both have 'in the last dozen years begun to attract the attention of the cultural diagnostician',[80] a portent, perhaps also a cause, of decline. Amis then offered a one-sentence definition of the genre:

Science fiction is that class of prose narrative treating of a situation that could not arise in the world we know, but which is hypothesised on the basis of some innovation in science or technology, or pseudo-science or pseudo-technology, whether human or extra-terrestrial.[81]

As Amis admits, this is the sort of definition that demands footnotes, but at its core is the issue of plausibility. Hypothesised innovations such as the 'space-warp' or 'hyper-drive' (a mechanism for getting around Einstein and travelling to the farthest part of our galaxy or other galaxies) are, or may be, implausible, but what matters 'is that they are offered as plausible and that efforts are made to conceal their implausibility'.[82] The importance of the issue of plausibility to Amis is that it helps to differentiate science fiction, of which he approves, from fantasy, of which he disapproves: 'in practice the arbitrary and whimsical development of nearly every story of fantasy soon puts it beyond recovery'.[83] When Amis was commissioned to edit the *New Oxford Book of Light Verse* (1978), the successor to Auden's 1938 anthology, he made a similar objection to nonsense verse. Amis quotes 'Old Mother Hubbard': 'She went to the alehouse / To get him some beer; / But when she came back / The dog sat in a chair.' He comments: 'What would Mother Hubbard or the poet have had the dog do? What of it that he sat in a chair instead? I dare say he did sit in a chair. A little of "Old Mother Hubbard," and there are fourteen stanzas of it in the received version, goes a long way with me. Like many nursery rhymes, it is whimsical, or nonsense in the derogatory meaning of the word.'[84]

The rest of the first seminar, an uneffortful trot through the early days of SF, was itself cribbed from a trot, L. Sprague de Camp's *Science Fiction Handbook* (1953), sent to Amis by Brian Aldiss, after urgent appeal.[85] The second seminar, delivered on 12 February, was 'Modern Science-Fiction: Its Nature, Place and Scope'. In this seminar Amis dated the present era as beginning 'quite suddenly around 1940', with the rapid expansion of SF magazines and the appearance of a number of new writers, 'among them many of the best-known names of today'. Now, at last, the genre could claim 'some degree of literacy'.[86] This remark was typical: Amis made no claims for the literary value of most science fiction.[87] The genre interested and entertained him, but he wrote of it with detachment, in the manner in which he had written of the relations between Victorian poets and their audiences in his failed Oxford B.Litt. When considering the question of why the modern age of science fiction began when it did, or at all, his answer was: 'I am not sure.'[88] All he could suggest about the sudden influx of new and better writers in 1940 was that, unlike their predecessors, 'they grew up with the medium already in existence. More simply, few things are much good to begin with, and the inferiority of early Elizabethan drama is not what makes Shakespeare's appearance remarkable.'[89] As an interpreter, he was comparably reticent or conservative. 'I should not like to discourage the use of these methods,' he wrote of interpretations based on Freudian symbolism, 'and I am only being autobiographical if I say that what a man thought he was saying is often more interesting than what he might really have been saying.'[90]

At the end of the second seminar Amis raised the question of the function of science fiction. 'Its most important use,' he declared, 'is a means of dramatising social inquiry, as providing a fictional mode in which culture can be isolated and judged.'[91] In the three subsequent seminars he divided or 'mapped' the field according to areas enquired into: unconscious wishes, hopes and fears (19 February); gender stereotypes, colonialism, deviancy and conformity (5 March); and technological and commercial developments (12 March). These seminars, the meat of the series, contained readings of individual stories and novels, often involving much wry plot summary and exposition. Common tropes or motifs were identified,[92] as well as common attitudes or prejudices,[93] and comparisons were drawn with other forms of popular fiction: 'that insensate denial of rationality which is notoriously to be found in much 'tec and thriller writing', Amis pointed out, plays little part in science fiction, an absence he approved, since 'whatever may be said of too little reason as a choice of evils in our private life, in the public domain we ought always to choose too much'.[94]

At the heart of science fiction's appeal to Amis is its closeness to his earliest reading. His descriptions of science fiction magazines, for example, make them sound like boys' weeklies. The SF story types and attitudes he identifies recall those of boys' fiction. There is the 'space opera', where 'Mars takes the place of Arizona with a few physical alterations . . . and Indians turn up in the revised form of what are technically known as bug-eyed-monsters, a phrase frequently abbreviated to BEMs.'[95] There are tales of space exploration, in which the beings encountered, and their treatment, recall similar scenes in H. Rider Haggard.[96] Sex plays almost no part at all, an absence the adult Amis deplores.[97] Character drawing is rudimentary. As in boys' adventure stories, 'it must be shown quickly that the familiar categories of human behaviour persist in an unfamiliar environment, and the book's whole tenor would be set awry by the kind of specifying, distinguishing, questioning form of characterisation to which general fiction has accustomed us'.[98]

That the pleasures of science fiction are partly those of early reading is a point Amis made most clearly at the end of the fifth seminar, entitled 'Utopias and Social Criticism – 2'. The utopian sub-genre is praised not only for attracting 'some of the best minds in the field', but for performing 'a valuable introductory service for those who blench at the sight of a BEM'.[99] *The Space Merchants*, by Frederik Pohl and C.M. Kornbluth, 'which has many claims to being the best science-fiction novel so far',[100] is praised for its admonitory satire – of worrying economic trends, the growth of industrial and commercial power, the advertising profession – yet for all its humour and insight, something is missing, at least for an 'addict' like Amis, the sort who craves 'fearful menace of the old-fashioned type, lethal instead of merely undesirable, and originating on Mars, not Madison Avenue'. Mention of addiction returns us to the first seminar, where Amis discussed the relation of science fiction to jazz, and of both to adolescence:

[J]ust as some listeners will find that the Modern Jazz Quartet surpasses Louis Armstrong's Hot Five in everything but immediacy, so certain kinds of readers will respond to a really gutty cosmic disaster in a way that no utopias, however inventive and witty, can quite match. Often, I think that part – and I mean part – of the attraction of science fiction lies in the fact that it provides a field which, while not actually repugnant to sense and decency, allows us to doff that mental and moral best behaviour with which we feel we have to treat George Eliot and James and Faulkner, and frolic like badly brought-up children among the mobile jellyfishes and unstable atomic piles.[101]

In the final seminar Amis discussed the genre's prospects and laid down what he thought should be its aims. These aims included attracting a wider and more sophisticated readership ('I myself fully appreciate the destructive force of an unflattering notion of one's fellow-readers whenever I pick up Jane Austen or D.H. Lawrence'),[102] kicking out the cranks who have given the genre a bad name (John Campbell, L. Ron Hubbard, A.E. van Vogt) and welcoming a much-needed 'invasion from above' (the sort William Golding's fiction might be thought to herald). He then concluded, a trifle grandiloquently, that science fiction offered the best, in some cases the only, way of looking beyond 'the attempted solution of problems already evident to the attempted formulation of problems not yet distinguishable', and that if it continued on its present path, it would not only secure its own future but 'make some contribution to the security of our own',[103] a prognosis that recalls comparable professions of faith at the end of *Socialism and the Intellectuals* and the *Spectator* article 'Mind We Don't Quarrel'.

Amis stuck closely to his scripts when delivering the seminars but was not noticeably nervous, nor did he appear nervous during the discussion sessions. Hilly thinks some part of his confidence derived from how well he had been treated at Princeton: 'They made him feel very important . . . He'd never had so much adoration.' Mark Rose vaguely recalls a hostile exchange between Amis and the philosopher Hilary Putnam at one seminar, but otherwise remembers the discussions as 'less lively' than anticipated. Blackmur had been bold to suggest science fiction as a topic for a Gauss audience, but the talks themselves generated little controversy. As Keeley suggests, this was because Amis was the only person present who knew anything about the subject. Rose, who helped Amis by loaning him reference books, and was himself to become an authority on science fiction (as well as on Shakespeare), admired the lectures, though the book they became 'hasn't been significant for lo these twenty years'.[104] Among New York publishers word of mouth was positive and spread quickly; Amis and his agents had trouble keeping rival magazine editors and publishers at bay. When the American edition of *New Maps of Hell* came out, it was well reviewed. British publication was delayed largely because Victor Gollancz was disinclined to publish something 'so eccentric and ticklish'[105] directly after the poor reception of *I Like It Here*. When it did come out, though, in 1961, notices were good. On 24 February William Golding wrote an approving review in the *Spectator*, calling the book 'scholarly and at the same time an amusing parody of the scholar's method'. More importantly, when Hilary Rubinstein realised that most of the authors discussed in the book had never been published in Britain, he set about acquiring and publishing them for Gollancz. Soon the firm had the most influential and lucrative science fiction list in Britain.

Two days after his final seminar on 19 March, Amis and Hilly set off by train for Illinois, where he would deliver a lecture entitled 'The Angry Young Men and After' to university audiences at Chicago and Champaign-Urbana (his other staple lecture was 'Problems of a Comic Novelist'). It was at Champaign-Urbana that Amis claimed to have experienced a moment of miraculous transformation. On the afternoon of his lecture, after a single drink at lunchtime, 'I reached a state of dazzling euphoria, as has happened to me only three or four other times in my life, and never since.'

At the lecture itself, and the party afterwards, 'I was at the apex of my form.' As the party finished, Amis overheard one faculty wife ask another, '"How much do you think there is in national characteristics? Have you ever met a *reserved* Englishman?"'[106]

Amis's high spirits continued back in Princeton. Spring arrived, and with it the barbecue and the picnic. In her memoir, *My Kitchen Wars* (1999), Betty Fussell includes a chapter about Princeton in the 1950s entitled 'Hot Grills'. In it she distinguishes between 'the respectables of the Princeton English Department' and the young academics who circled around Blackmur. For the young academics, 'picnics in the wild were rebellion against the white-glove tea parties given by graying deans and their mousy wives . . . Picnics were also a rebellion against the four-walled kitchen lives of most of us faculty wives.'[107] The Princeton of the Amises' year was 'an outpost of Cheever territory':

you could drink your way across town from party to party in one long moveable feast. While the women tended the grill, the men tended the thermoses of iced martinis and wrestled with the corkscrews . . . Drinking was men's work, and the men went at it manfully. The women drank too, of course, and not just to keep up with the men. Drinking was vital to our picnics, loosening tongues and lips and hearts and kidneys . . . the unspoken rule was that you could do things on a picnic that you couldn't or wouldn't do in a parlor.[108]

These things were mostly sexual: 'being horny was the reason for our picnics, drink merely the excuse'. Like the women in Amis's circles in Britain, those in Betty Fussell's world thought of themselves as making up for lost time: 'we had learned during wartime, first the hot and then the cold one, to seize the day . . . We wanted to gather all the rosebuds we could find, *now*.'[109] Despite this readiness, however, when the Amises arrived, 'few were prepared. Kingsley cut a swath a mile wide through the faculty wives.' As a couple, the Amises 'inspired a whole year of husband- and wife-swapping'.[110] Amis made passes at every attractive woman he saw, regardless of marital status. He propositioned Betty Fussell while she stood in the bathroom washing out a nappy. He made a pass at Mary Keeley, at Gene Davis, at Liz Moynahan, at Jan Richardson, at Phil Fraser, all married to friends. 'It was compulsive,' remembers Keeley, but 'if you said no it was all right . . . he wouldn't press it with people who would have a problem, but otherwise he never gave up'. 'You had to look to your wife,' Russell Fraser remembers. 'What he said to me when I bristled at him was "Nothing personal, Old Man," and in a very extraordinary way that must have been so.' A number of the passes led to affairs, several of them serious. 'There was no scandal left in who had slept with Kingsley,' Betty Fussell writes. 'Who hadn't?'[III]

In *One Fat Englishman* (1963), the novel Amis set in 'Budweiser', a thinly fictionalised Princeton (all the colleges in the novel are named after beers), there are several outdoor parties. Roger Micheldene, the most repellent of Amis's fictional heroes, is taken on a picnic *à deux* with Mollie Atkins, the wife of Strode Atkins, a drunken Anglophile. '"Do you come here often?" Roger asked as, with a thick belt of trees and bushes between them and the road, they came to a small clearing and spread the blanket on top of fallen leaves and thin grass.'[112] Roger, a visiting Englishman, doesn't drive and it is Mollie who has brought him to this trysting place. As they talk, Mollie unpacks the picnic hamper: 'Next to her as she sat on the blanket there now lay a bottle of gin, a bottle of dry vermouth, a wooden ice-bucket with a copper lid, a slender glass jug, a glass stirring rod and two glasses.'[113] Later in the novel, in bed with another woman, Helene Bang, Roger is asked 'What is it about women that makes you want them?' and responds with the previously quoted remark about aiming 'to demonstrate to an animal which is pretending not to be an animal that it is an animal'. Before he answers, Helene cautions him: 'And please, no biology lesson.' Here is his answer in full:

'Well, I think it's most frightfully obscure, really' . . . Whether or not his motives about women were obscure, he did not think they were. A man's sexual aim he had often said to himself, is to convert a creature who is cool, dry, calm, articulate, independent, purposeful into a creature that is the opposite of these: to demonstrate to an animal which is pretending not to be an animal that it is an animal. But it seemed a good moment to be quiet about all that. 'What would you say?' he asked after a short pause. 'A way of getting to know someone better than you can in any other way? That sort of thing?'[114]

Roger expects Helene to miss his wicked irony. But for Amis wicked irony was part of his sexual appeal, as was his shocking frankness.

Betty Fussell only got to know Amis towards the end of his visit and never met Hilly, but she had known of their reputations: 'I tried to imagine resisting Kingsley's irresistible combination of comedy and sex, as he single-mindedly put one in the service of the other, and I longed to put it to the test. Laughter is the most powerful seduction of all, and for these English, America, with her straitlaced Puritans, was one big laugh-in. They would as soon fuck as say the word; they seemed to have no verbal or sexual inhibitions at all.'[115]

'We had a wild year,' Hilly concedes, 'no question about it, but it seemed sort of containable', partly because they and everyone else knew they'd be returning to Swansea. At first Hilly had trouble keeping up with all the revelling. Amis, of course, had remarkable stamina, even in an age and milieu of heavy drinkers (a writerly milieu, in which Faulkner, Fitzgerald and Hemingway were heroes): 'physically,' recalls Russell Fraser, 'he must have been a very tough sort of guy. He could drink a lot and stay up all night and I was tempted to follow him and I wasn't nearly tough enough.' Neither was Hilly. As her diary for October and November records, she several times fell asleep while post-prandial arguments and party games roared on. 'You can't possibly start drinking at teatime,' she would say to herself. But on weekends drinking began 'anytime', usually with 'huge bloody marys'. As early evening approached, with more parties to follow, Amis and friends 'were almost legless'. 'So after that I thought I must join in. That's the answer. But, of course, I always had to keep an eye on the kids.' Soon the Amises 'got to know everyone' and 'everyone zoomed in on Kingsley, thought we were good fun'. Spring and summer 'roller-coastered', parties were bigger, with 'everyone set on having a good time'. Several of the couples in the Amis circle, or circles, had rocky marriages, 'and people do go a bit mad at that time'. Keeley recalls a party at night at Alan Collins's estate at which, at Hilly's suggestion, most of the guests took their clothes off and jumped into the pool. When Collins turned the pool lights on, inadvertently, he claimed, Hilly 'was furious'; the mood had been spoiled. 'For once I'm having fun and you want me to stop and go with that bloody Blackmur,' is what Keeley remembers her saying. Hilly liked Blackmur, thought him 'very sweet, very nice', but academic or intellectual discourse, the sort that dominated Blackmur's parties, bored her (in this she was like Blackmur's wife, a painter, who left him because 'I just couldn't stand the talk, talk,

talk').[116] A version of this party appears in Chapter 12 of *One Fat Englishman*.

Hilly remembers the year at Princeton as 'wonderful', though it had its bad moments. One evening, alone with the children, she received an anonymous phone call from a woman: 'You realise your husband's screwing every dame in Princeton?' 'Everyone but you, evidently,' she replied. Then 'I sort of put the phone down and had a big drink.' What the woman said was 'probably true', but Hilly 'was in no position to point a finger'. Pretty, charming, open, unpretentious and wild, she attracted lots of attention; John McAndrew was not her only lover. At the same time, life at home, domestic life, was also good: the children were thriving, she and Amis 'were getting on very well'. Philip Amis's memories of Princeton were also positive: 'I loved America. Had a great time.' That his mother and father 'were partying really hard' and sometimes had 'huge rows' was nothing new. Philip remembers Hilly falling in love with John McAndrew, but 'by then, I suppose, we were used to it, that was sort of normal carrying on. We were used to that disappointment one feels when − "Oh, so it's all right to do that, that's okay then."' Philip remembers John McAndrew at one point 'keeping his distance' and has no idea what his father felt about the affair. But then his father was 'going to bed with anything that moved'. Philip was ten at the time. Martin, a year younger, says nothing of these matters in *Experience*, though he does recount an unsettling episode during one of his parents' parties. It is almost his sole mention of the Princeton period in the memoir.

I was lying in bed on a bright summer evening . . . My parents were giving one of their parties, and I could hear it, like a baritone schoolyard, several walls away. Sometimes at these events my brother and I served as paid waiters: $3 each, on one famous occasion. But it was apparently too late for me to be up, though the room felt full of day and I seemed a great distance from sleep. It was 1959 and I was nearly ten − and fully Americanised, for now: accent, crewcut, racing bike with whitewall tyres and electric horn . . .

The door opened and a dapper middle-aged man smiled and confidently entered, followed by a woman in a grey silk blouse beneath a black jacket, dark-haired, handsome, even distinguished, with artistic bones. At the sight of me her face 'lit up': it is the what-have-we-here? expression of the adult who lacks all talent with children (under more normal circumstances they

approach on tiptoe and address you in an idiocy-imputing singsong).
Throughout she remained by the open door, one hand holding a cocktail
glass, the other flat on her breastbone. The man came towards the bed
and sat down on the foot of it. After some general inquiries he introduced
the notion that he was a doctor and that it would be a good thing if he
examined me. Grateful for the diversion, I slipped readily out of my pyjamas.

Now, looking back, I wonder how many children came before and after
me, and I wonder how far it went. In my case it went as far as what is
usually called 'fondling,' but the word is blasphemously inapt.[117]

What is recalled most vividly here is the image of the attractive, collu-
sive woman, one hand flat on her breastbone, no protector at all.

'I realised you couldn't possibly carry on like that,' Hilly recalls of
life at Princeton, 'without having a terrible fall and causing an awful
lot of misery to a lot of people.' Hence, in part, the decision to
return to Swansea. Amis had been offered another two years at
Princeton but turned them down. The ostensible reason was the children's education, though, as Amis puts it in the *Memoirs*, 'in fact
they would probably have done as well in America'. Another factor
was how little work – fiction and poetry, that is – he managed to
get done in America: 'When we sailed I had seven pages of my
current novel and four poems to show for the whole of my nine-
or ten-month stay.' Both Amises had a sense of home and missed
it, and Hilly also missed her family. 'I muttered to myself about
being thirty-seven,' Amis writes, 'just too old to set about becoming
an American, which was what was really at stake. But I soon realised
we had simply left too many friends behind, too much of everything, and wanted to get home.'[118]

Early in July, only a week or so before their departure, Hilly and
Amis took a weekend trip with Jean and John McAndrew to Martha's
Vineyard, stopping along the way at the Newport Jazz Festival. At
the last minute the Amises' babysitter pulled out and the two couples
decided that the elder McAndrew daughters, Linda, seventeen, and
Karen, fifteen, could take care of the other children themselves, all
six of them, including five-year-old Sally and four-year-old Maura.
Soon after the parents left on their trip, the children devised a game
involving Hilly's Volkswagen Beetle.[119] They rolled it out of the
garage to the top of the gently sloping driveway and with one child
steering and another perched on the bonnet rolled it back down

again. When it came to Martin's turn to steer the car he couldn't find the brake pedal and in a panic turned the wheel to the right, so that the car went over a flower bed, then headed towards the house. Twelve-year-old Shelagh, riding on the bonnet, stuck her foot out to stop the car and put it through the dining-room window. Miraculously, neither she nor anyone else was badly hurt and the window was replaced. While the children were devising these games, their parents were approaching Newport. On the way, they saw a fried clam joint and pulled over. Here Kingsley announced: 'Oh good, I want more than my share before anyone else has had any,' a line that became a catch-phrase in the McAndrew family and was to appear in *Take a Girl Like You*, uttered by Patrick Standish.[120]

Once back in Princeton, the Amises had little time to pack and to say their goodbyes. They had booked passage on the *Liberté*, a ship of the French Line. Some time during the journey, both Amises wrote to the McAndrews. This is how Amis's portion of the letter ends:

I feel now I never made the long speech of thanks to you that you certainly merited, the two of you: and this is not at all because I find it difficult to say what is in my mind or any of that tack: as you know, I find it *notoriously* easy. So it must just have been that you kept making me too stoned to do so much as ask for a match. But you do know, I hope, that you did more than all the others did between them to make our stay such paralysing, coronary-inducing fun. Thanks 1,000,000.

See you soon, eh? Must go and grab a drink before the band starts up in the bar. There are 2 guys in it who play the clarinet *in French*.

Love to all,

Kingsley.

As it turned out, the Amises would never see John McAndrew again. He died suddenly of an aneurysm on 19 September 1962, though after his death Jean stayed in touch with Hilly and several times came to visit. The Amises had turned the McAndrews' life upside down. 'It was completely a lost year in my parents' lives,' Megan told me. 'They had this great failure of rectitude. They all shed inhibitions for a year and everybody encouraged everybody else to do it.' Though Megan suspects her father had had adventures before the Amises, her mother had not; marrying John McAndrew had been her moment of wildness. That she went to bed with Amis, without any illusions that the relationship would last, 'was part of the whole chaos of that year'. Others who came into contact with the Amises also fell under their spell, though in different ways. The younger faculty in Blackmur's circle drank heavily at the time and were, in Keeley's words, 'on the make to some degree' (he means sexually). When Amis and Hilly arrived they encouraged these tendencies. Amis was 'always available . . . always quietly being funny and quietly on the make'. As Mary Keeley puts it, 'he inspired people to co-operate'. Yet nobody's marriage or career was destroyed by the Amises, or destroyed exclusively by the Amises. Among those I interviewed there were few bitter or remorseful memories.[121] Still, it was a dangerous as well as an exhilarating time. 'I couldn't see how it could possibly go on at that pitch,' Hilly remembers thinking, 'and I couldn't see it slowing down really.'

17

Patrick and Dai

The first thing Amis had to do when he returned to Swansea was to explain to Philip Larkin why he hadn't written him a single letter while at Princeton. Hilly beat him to the punch, in an undated letter at the end of July that sounds as if it was written late at night, under the influence of drink: 'don't tell the bugger I said, but I could *kill* him for not writing to you while we were in U.S.A. The fucking bastard bloody well deserves to be shot & all I can say & why I should go on doing this I can't think, is that he feels very badly about it (he really does) and is about to write you *now*.' The day before Amis's letter arrived Larkin wrote to Conquest, on 1 August, to report the Hilly letter: 'nothing from KWA. Perhaps someone has bitten his hands off.' Amis's silences were a familiar complaint in the Larkin/Conquest correspondence for 1959 (the only letter Conquest received from Amis while Amis was at Princeton was the request for help with the Gauss Seminars). On 16 December Larkin reported to Conquest: 'Had a letter from K today, much to my amazement – thought he must want something, but no.' On 2 March 1960, after another period of not hearing from Amis, Conquest 'fell back on the theory that his hand had withered away.' On 1 June Larkin wrote to Conquest: 'No sign of Kingsley. I sometimes wonder if I shall ever see him again. See him, Christ! – even hear from him again, eh?' In a letter of 24 June to Larkin, Conquest came up with a new explanation for Amis's silences: 'Clitoris-Fiddler's Cramp, that's what it is.'

Amis's own explanation, in a letter to Larkin of 30 July 1959, was, he admitted, no excuse: 'I don't see how I can apologise for such a thing, exactly, but I can plead that I wrote no more than four personal letters the whole time I was away, in every case to people who had written several times to me (no imputation, o' boy), that I left many an important, i.e. financially-concerned, non-private letter unwritten, that for the first half of my time there I was boozing and working harder than I have ever done since the Army, and that for the second half I was boozing and fucking harder than at any time at all. On the second count I found myself at it practically full-time.' Amis's continued silence, or relative silence, in the months after his return was partly explained by a determination to make up for lost writing time. As he explained to the Powells, in a letter of 4 June 1960, the first letter he had written to them not only since the return from Princeton but since October 1958, 'It seems getting on for inconceivable that we've been back in the Motherland all this time without getting to see you. Actually we've been bogged down by this and that: penury, for one thing, which is connected with another thing, my having to finish the novel I started in 1955[1] or bust – the connection is via the fact that writing the novel meant I had to stop doing all that criticising in the papers that used to bring me in so much money.'

The return to Swansea was difficult for both Amises. 'We felt very flat,' Hilly remembers, 'all our friends seemed very sober. We used to think: "God, what are we doing tonight? Nothing".' 'In many ways I like being back,' Amis explained to Larkin in the letter of 30 July 1959, 'and to find that life is a little duller in Swansea than in Princeton need occasion no surprise.' Yet soon the Motherland's 'main bores' were converging on him 'at a huge rate, as if on purpose to show it in a bad light'. There was also the question of absent lovers. Amis had left Princeton in the midst of several romantic entanglements, though none as serious as Hilly's affair with John McAndrew. In her initial letter to Larkin, Hilly confessed she was pining: 'I'm in love with a filthy Yank, he's a Catholic with 5 girls & is 47 yrs. Oh well (secret).' Amis did not go in much for pining, embarking instead on new affairs. By December his amorous adventures had so 'ramified' that Hilly was ready to leave him. She had found letters from a new girlfriend. Amis's carelessness about such letters had got him into trouble before and would do so again. On this occasion, as he wrote to Larkin on 15 December, Hilly was furious and 'initiated the most strenuous and painful row we have ever had. I am to give all that up, it appears, with an exemption clause covering my Yank girl when she turns up over here in the summer.' Amis reluctantly agreed to Hilly's ultimatum: 'Trouble is it's so hard to give all that up, habit of years and all that, and such bloody good fun too. Especially just after finding the most splendid busty redhead in an ideal location. But being walked out on by H. (and kids), the sure-fire consequence of any further discovery, is a rather unwelcome prospect too. You can't have it both ways, you see. Got to make up your mind which you want and stick to it. What are you trying to do, anyway? Prove something to yourself?' The letter ends: 'You don't care about me or the children; all you want is to stick your cock up some woman's bum, K.'

The complications and tensions of the Amis marriage were common knowledge to their friends. Karl Miller, at the time literary editor of the *Spectator*, and his wife, Jane, had been weekend guests at Glanmor Road when Hilly initiated the row over the letters. Amis wrote to Miller on 17 December apologising for the scene: 'I might say the tiny spot of discord you witnessed, after swelling to unprecedented proportions, has now more or less totally eased off.' Yet Larkin and Conquest were still speculating about the Amis marriage in March: Conquest had 'heard some vague stuff in London' about a break-up. 'Are they actually separating?' he asked Larkin on 2 March. 'And why? It'll be a bit of a blow to him, as he depends on her (it seems to me) a good deal. What's he done to offend her? Screwed her mother? (But do tell me the position, in case I drop a brick).' Later in the month, in a letter to Larkin of 27 March, Conquest speculated more generally about the marriage: 'What Hilly *really* minds, I always think, is K's unromantic attitude to her – "You *are* looking sweet and marvellous" is better than "What about a screw, old tart," I always feel.' That Amis himself was aware of Hilly's feelings or needs, while also ignoring them, was clear from *Take a Girl Like You*, which he was at work on throughout this period. 'He isn't ever going to turn up, Jenny,' Amis has Patrick declare, 'that bloke with the honour and the bunches of flowers *and* the attraction.'[2]

Mark Rose, Amis's student at Princeton, met up with Amis and Hilly in London in September 1960, at the end of a tour of the Continent. In a short story Rose wrote about the Amises on his return to Princeton, he provides a thinly fictionalised portrait of their marriage at the time. The story was published in 1961 in the *Nassau Literary*

Magazine, the Princeton review, under the title 'Harold Be Thy Name'.[3] Amis thought Rose had promise as a writer: he and Conquest included one of his stories in *Spectrum III* (1963), the third of five annual science fiction anthologies they edited for Gollancz.[4] Rose makes few claims for 'Harold Be Thy Name', which, like the science fiction story, he wrote as an undergraduate; its value ('such as it is') lies in its 'typical Amisisms of the time'.[5] Harold is the Amis character. He is forty, has twinkly blue eyes, is generous with money and drinks, and is very funny, a quality mostly asserted rather than shown. The narrator, Lew Eakin, a young American, calls him 'the apostle of laughter'.[6] Lew, recently graduated from university, arrives in London in September, at the end of a tour of the Continent. 'All summer he had looked forward to his stay with Harold in London,' the narrator tells us; 'he had mentioned his visit to almost everybody he met.'

Lew is taken out to dinner by Harold and Myra, where they are joined by Isadore and Ethel Mertz, friends from New York. Harold helped to pay their fare over and found Isadore a job. He and Ethel are having an affair. At the restaurant there is much drinking, as there will be when the party moves on to a Soho jazz club. Harold presides at the head of the table, beaming, joking, winking, imitating the accents of other diners, pawing Ethel. Myra is described as 'blonde, with a long, full figure that was decidedly attractive'. Rose remembers Julian Moynahan, who taught him as a freshman at Princeton, asking him what he thought of his wife, Liz, a vivacious, attractive woman, the 'Yank girl' Hilly would exempt when she showed up in the summer of 1960. 'I know what you think of her,' Moynahan said before Rose could reply, 'you think of her as just on the edge of sexual availability.' In 'Harold Be Thy Name', this is what Lew thinks of Myra. At the jazz club, as at the restaurant, Harold and Ethel flirt openly, Myra gets very drunk, kisses Lew on the lips and insists upon dancing with him (Harold and Isadore won't dance). After Harold suddenly departs with Ethel, Isadore, 'with desparate hilarity', explains how 'he walked right out of here with her, respectable and cheeky as anything. He almost always takes Ethel. It's perfectly all right with her. She worships him.' Earlier, Lew had been upset when he heard Harold had left with Ethel. 'Don't look so shocked,' Myra had scolded him. 'There's no reason to be shocked. He'll be home when we get there.' Lew is baffled that Harold has 'been so thoughtless about hurting Myra. Didn't Harold care about Myra?'

When Myra and Lew arrive back at the house, they find Harold huddled on the front stoop, jolly, still drunk, unwilling to confront the babysitter: '*I* can't face her. We're three hours late, you know.' After Myra puts Harold to bed, she offers Lew a cup of tea. Lew, himself drunk, asks 'permission to be ridiculous for a moment' and explains to her how much Harold means to him, how he has changed his life, bringing 'the Good News that things are funny and the person who takes them seriously is a fool'. But Lew also explains that Harold has forgotten the code that says 'Thou shalt not give pain.' 'Don't be an ass,' Myra responds. 'Nothing is that simple.' 'You see,' Lew answers smiling, 'just then I committed the great sin. I took something seriously.' Calling Lew 'wonderfully foolish', Myra leans over and kisses him. He feels her tongue, which both embarrasses and excites him. '"There!" she said, blushing. "Now get off to bed. Go on!"'

The next morning Lew makes an awkward and unwelcome pass at Myra. He has misread the kiss and hurt her feelings. Harold shambles into the room, 'his face florid and smiling, dressed in tweeds. With his considerable belly and uncontrollable hair he looked rather like a younger brother of Falstaff.'[7] Lew watches Harold kiss Myra and suddenly realises 'he loves her, actually loves her'. That night, at a party at the house, Ethel Mertz is back on Harold's lap. Isadore, drunk again, takes a swing at him: '"Isadore, put your glasses on," Harold said in a kind, coaxing voice. "Have a drink and you'll feel better."' When Mertz wanders off, Harold says: 'Sorry I hurt the poor chap's feelings. Wouldn't want to hurt him for all the world.' By now Lew is drunk, too, and insists Harold choose between Ethel and Myra, to which Harold responds, 'You're drunk, old man.' When Lew persists, Harold gently tells him, 'This is none of your business.' Lew feels Harold's arm on his shoulder, the room veers dangerously, and Harold says, 'Old Lew. Old silly old drunken sod.' Lew sees 'love streaming from Harold's face' and looks back at him with love. 'How could he ever have been so mean as to ask Harold to make a choice?'

Lew is young and out of his depth, but his inability to figure Harold out, resist his appeal, or get him to explain himself, recalls comparable difficulties encountered by Amis's more experienced friends. Though obviously fond of Hilly, Amis was often oblivious or indifferent to her feelings, in print as in person. In May 1960, he published five new poems in *Encounter*. In one of these poems,

'Sight Unseen', the speaker openly delights in ogling girls on the street, lamenting lost opportunities. From Oxford onwards, as we have seen, Amis always, in Hilly's words, 'made such a big job of "Ah! That bus has got in the way of that one,"' as in 'Sight Unseen', where 'This happens every bloody day: / They about-turn, they duck / Into their car and drive away, / They hide behind a truck.' 'I felt I shouldn't rise to it,' was Hilly's reaction. In 'Nothing to Fear', discussed earlier, the speaker details his preparations for an assignation and suffers a panic attack. Only the most obtuse or critically purist of Amis's readers, certainly not anyone who knew him, would fail to connect these speakers with their author, especially as Amis makes no attempt to disguise them as characters, as in other poems. Part of the appeal of such poems is their autobiographical daring or unembarrassability. But what of Hilly, as Lew might put it? Hilly did not always read Amis's poems but she read the novels. Sometimes Amis would test passages out on her to see if they worked, and she'd invariably praise them. 'It's hard enough for them to be doing it and I didn't feel confident enough in myself to say this is wrong.' Besides, 'they always did seem to work'. Her reaction to *Take a Girl Like You* was complex. She admired the novel but told Amis 'I think Patrick's an absolute shit' ('I often felt like saying "And you're an absolute shit yourself"'). As Hilly recalls it, Amis would defend himself by claiming 'this [character] is really so and so, and that person would also be a bit of a shit'. The mix of hurt, anger, affection and loyalty Hilly felt towards Amis at this time is suggested in a letter she wrote to Jean and Esmond Cleary, who were away on exchange at the University of Puerto Rico.[8] This letter, undated but written some time in the summer of 1960, reports on family and friends, comments on the Clearys' news ('glad your infant has got over her troubles and is full of fun') and advises them to ring the McAndrews if ever they're in New Jersey. 'You've missed bugger all this year,' Hilly tells them in the first paragraph, 'flat boredom from month to month, a few hysterical parties – great big ballings out – me getting drunk and calling K a "fucking bastard who can only think of fucking etc." – in *front* of Andrew Brown, Daddy A, and Sam [Dawson]! Oh well.'[9] Towards the end of the letter she reports that 'K. has finished his long novel, and sent it in – called 'Take a Girl Like You' no one's said they've liked it so far, which is nasty – I think it's very good.'

* * *

Though Amis cut back on his journalism in order to finish *Take a Girl Like You* he wrote several articles of note in the year after the return from Princeton. On 2 October 1959 he published a short piece in the *Spectator* explaining how he would vote in the upcoming elections. Swansea West, his constituency, was a marginal Labour seat and he was a marginal Labour voter. He opposed the Tories out of a 'natural aversion to the spectacle of any Conservative success', an inability to forget 'the grubby bravado of their Suez venture' and distaste for 'their neurotic anti-Americanism (so important a factor in the motivation of Suez)'. He also disliked what he saw as their narrow self-interest: 'Conservatism never had an idea at all, except to hold on to its wallet.' The Labour Party was not much better, but at least it 'had an idea in its head once . . . now almost forgotten'. What Amis disliked about Labour, which he called 'sinister as well as fatuous and revolting', was its condescension: 'I reckon it has a slightly higher proportion than the Tory Party of smooth persons who know what is good for me better than I do.' The level of political sophistication behind what Amis called his 'anti-Tory, not pro-Labour' vote was summed up by Conquest in a letter to Larkin of 8 November: 'In spite of all the Fabian pamphlet common-sense stuff . . . he's still got a lot of East Lynne romantic myth about Tory villains twisting their moustaches and foreclosing mortgages – and about Suez and Nyasaland as well. Not that I didn't want a change myself.' Conquest thought Amis 'ought to attend to his correspondence instead of farting around polling stations'.

Shortly after the Tory victory Amis published an essay in the periodical *New World Writing* entitled 'You That Love England; or Limey Stay Home'. The essay revisits his reasons for returning to Swansea. It begins with thoughts of Macmillan and the election, then recalls the distaste with which he invariably encountered upper-class Englishmen when he was in America, especially those 'with theatrical (etc.) tendencies': 'the definitive hostility I felt towards them, such as I never felt towards even the most formidable-looking American, taught me something about the extent to which class-consciousness still hangs on in the British psyche, or at least in my own' (a prominent theme in *One Fat Englishman*).[10] Amis also reflects on the differences between British and American intellectual life. It is often urged by 'Europeanised Americans' that 'American literary life is narrowed by its isolation from other forms of activitiy, and that the English writer is in far closer contact with the adjacent worlds of journalism, politics and (whether or not he works in a university) education: any success at all enables him to meet anybody he likes'. Amis would agree, but does not see the English writer's situation as preferable. After his experiences in the United States, 'I am strongly drawn to an environment in which the editorship of an important review, for example, does not make one a sovereign figure, and in which the anti-conformist or anti-cocktail-party writer is to some degree a natural phenomenon instead of what he cannot help being in England, a deliberate eccentric or high-and-dry regionalist.'[11]

When Amis wrote these words he was in Swansea not London, 'writing my novel like an absolute Trojan'.[12] Had he stayed in the States, he speculates in the article, he'd have tired of New York parties after a year or two, and in order to write would have ended up in a hut in Vermont: 'and since I already occupy a hut of sorts in Swansea in preference to a flat in London, coming to America might not have all that much point'.[13] With the mention of writing, a new and more complex motive for Amis's decision to return to England surfaces, one that connects to remarks in the *Memoirs* and correspondence about England as 'home':

A writer who changes his country takes his future in his hands. W.H. Auden and Christopher Isherwood, those hero-figures of my late adolescence, cut their own artistic throats when they moved to America in 1939 – not, as I now see, because of anything sinister in American life, but because they severed their connections with the themes that had given their work its quality; in Auden's case the English neurotic and rural England, in Isherwood's the English neurotic and urban Europe.[14]

The importance of home to a writer reappears in the most interesting literary article Amis wrote in the immediate post-Princeton period, his attack on Vladimir Nabokov's *Lolita* in a review of 6 November 1959 in the *Spectator*.[15] It also plays a part in Amis's gathering suspicion of all American writing, not just modernist American writing. *Lolita*, Amis declares, is both 'bad as a work of art' and 'morally bad – though certainly not obscene or pornographic'. What makes it bad as art is its obtrusive style. For Amis, 'style, personal style, a distinguished style, usually turns out in practice to mean a high idiosyncratic noise level in the writing, with plenty of rumble and wow from imagery, syntax and diction'. The sort of people who value style in this sense are 'people of oldster age group or literary training', those with a 'hankering for "experiment"', who level 'snorting accusations of literary gracelessness' against younger novelists (himself, for instance).[16] Their counterparts in the world of ideas yearn 'for uplift, or rich man's Billy Graham, which masquerades as reasoned antipathy to modern British philosophy'.[17] Amis quotes several passages from *Lolita* and then comments that 'no extract . . . could do justice to the sustained din of pun, allusion, neologism, alliteration, *cynghanedd*, apostrophe, parenthesis, rhetorical question, French, Latin, "anent," "perchance," "would fain," "for the nonce" – here is style and no mistake'. As for the argument that it is Humbert's style not Nabokov's to which he is objecting – that style here is 'characterisation' – 'what of Nabokov's last novel, *Pnin*, which is not written in the first person and sounds the same?'[18]

The English of *Lolita* is 'émigré's euphuism', which Amis sees as 'a natural consequence of Nabokov's having had to abandon his natural idiom'. As Nabokov himself puts it, he was forced to give up his 'untrammelled, rich and infinitely docile Russian tongue for a second-rate brand of English, devoid of any of those apparatuses – the baffling mirror, the black velvet backdrop, the implied associations and traditions – which the native illusionist, fractails flying, can magically use to transcend the heritage in his own way.' Here is Nabokov's problem, and the problem with Nabokov, enacted 'with characteristic tricksy indirection'. The émigré's only recourse is 'the laborious confection of equivalent apparatuses in the adoptive language: the whole farrago of imagery, archaism, etc., which cannot strike even the most finely tuned foreign ear as it strikes that of the native speaker'.[19] That Nabokov was a better writer before he went to America is suggested to Amis by a story of 1948 entitled 'Colette', in which 'the germ of *Lolita* is clearly discernible' (though Amis fails to mention that early or Russian Nabokov, 'fractails flying', is hardly untricksy). His tragedy 'has been his separation from Europe, the source of his natural subject-matter as well as his natural language'.[20]

To the extent that American writing is émigré writing it is subject to strictures of this sort. But then all American writing is émigré writing. In 'Sacred Cows', an undated essay published in 1990 in *The Amis Collection*, Amis imagines what would have happened had the early American Congress which voted that English should be the national language chosen Cree or some other Native American tongue instead:

one of the more probable results would be that they would now have what at present, after a great deal of conscious effort, they show no signs of ever producing – a distinctively American literature. Instead, they offer a vast number of books in English that in some ways resemble what I shall have to call British literature and in other ways don't. Those other ways are likewise non-American, whether they spring from other European cultures like German or French (the latter by direct borrowing) or from non-national cultures: Jewish, Negro. No coherent tradition could emerge from all that, and without a tradition any writer is adrift, nervously self-assertive, an individualist lost in a crowd of individualists.[21]

Before he went to America Amis had already cast a disapproving eye over what might be called the 'nervously self-assertive' tendencies of Saul Bellow's fiction (always 'right in there pitching with his gaiety and good humour, his fizzy dialogue, his vitality'). Now he had a theory to explain their origins and what he objected to about them. What is wrong with Bellow is what is wrong with Nabokov, Amis argues in 'Sacred Cows': 'neither . . . writes English. Nabokov, in a way peculiar to foreigners, never stops showing off his mastery of the language; his books are jewels a hundred thousand words long. Bellow is a Ukrainian-Canadian, I believe. It is painful to watch him trying to pick his way between the unidiomatic on the one hand and the affected on the other.'[22] Amis's son Martin would later declare Nabokov and Bellow his literary fathers, once jokingly informing a Californian audience, 'The project is to become an American novelist.'[23] Exactly, his father would have complained, which is why in part he objected to the son's fiction, was unable or unwilling to read it. To the extent that the son had made himself a 'stylist', all rumble and wow and individualism, he had become an American novelist.

There is a point here, but it is taken to ridiculous ends, as in Shaw's dismissal of *Hamlet* or Tolstoy's of *Lear*. It is perfectly possible to admire the writing of both Amises or of Faulkner as well as Waugh. Amis's theory is instrumental: it helps him to identify and forward his own needs and strengths as an author. It recalls Byron's class-based objections to the cockney Keats, another 'nervously self-assertive' writer, busily loading every rift with ore. Amis didn't like Keats either.[24] Later in his life, Amis objected to American literature in ways that made him sound bigoted as well as limited in his tastes. 'Been having to look at some mod Yank po recently and by Christ it stinks,' Amis wrote to Larkin on 15 February

1982. 'John CIARDI Howard NEMEROV J.V. CUNNINGHAM X.J. KENNEDY What's the matter with them? Why can't they talk sense and be natural? Why do they have to go on in a special way all the time? Of course they're all foreigners, aren't they? All right while they were called Longfellow and Dickinson and Whitman. Not *much* FUCKING GOOD, mind you, but all right. But then they started being called Sandburg and Schwartz. See?' That Amis thought WASP or nineteenth-century American writers 'not much fucking good' in the same way as non-WASP or twentieth-century writers is suggested by his remarks on Melville in 'Sacred Cows'. What is wrong with *Moby-Dick* is that it 'shows the author's will at work in places where it has no business to be: the style *shall* be individual, the scope *shall* be universal, the whole thing *shall* be profound, a masterpiece.' It is dismaying, however, that Amis thinks things got worse when American writers 'started being called Sandburg and Schwartz' (he may have thought Sandburg Jewish), though the remark was said in 1982, it is worth remembering, in a private letter to Larkin. In 1959 Amis was creating Jenny Bunn's dad, suspiciously revolving Patrick's surname: 'He muttered "Schtundish" to himself whenever Patrick was mentioned . . . it was one of his ways, and happened with almost every new boy-friend: there had been Veelricht and Ullingheim and Lighlunt and Yohanstein and no doubt there would have been Tawmpzohn too if Dick was single.'[25]

Take a Girl Like You marks a new stage in Amis's fiction. Though extremely funny, it is also more challenging than its predecessors, as aggressive to the reader as to its characters. In the late 1950s, Amis seemed intent on pushing his life and work right up to the edge. Nowhere is this aggressive impulse clearer than in the scene where Patrick takes Jenny's virginity while she is drunk, an act he would be prosecuted for today. The scene so upset the sympathetic John McCallum that he was moved to protest. In a letter of 29 July 1960 McCallum wrote to Amis reporting his reactions to the novel, as well as those of other in-house readers. After registering overall enthusiasm and declaring that this was Amis's best book yet, McCallum listed four objections, the last being to Patrick's seduction of Jenny, which 'turned my stomach just a bit'. To begin with, was it necessary for Patrick to succumb to Sheila Torkington, the headmaster's daughter, on the afternoon of the day he hoped to seduce Jenny, immediately afterwards discovering that Sheila was pregnant (a related objection was that Amis had made Sheila 'physically repellent to the reader'). The episode with Sheila was 'more depressing than comic'; was it 'truly essential to the plot'? Milder objections were raised to the Ormerod–Edgerstoune business, which was thought too vague and offhandedly dismissed at the end, and to the scene involving Miss Sinclair, John Whittaker and Whittaker's father, also at the end, which was thought forced, arbitrary and dependent upon characters long absent from the narrative.

Harcourt Brace was planning to offset the Gollancz edition for American publication. By the time Amis received McCallum's relayed objections the Gollancz edition was in press and it was too late to make changes. Amis reported the situation to McCallum on 24 August, but 'out of interest' briefly addressed his points. Only the Ormerod–Edgerstoune episode he admitted as a weakness, though a minor one. The remoteness of the episode with Miss Sinclair and the Whittakers he defended on the grounds that it illustrated 'how unexpectedly and deviously these things can happen: you can err through pure inadvertence'. As for Patrick's succumbing to Sheila, the objection McCallum listed first, it '*is* depressing, and is meant to be. I wanted some pretty dark places in the comedy, and this is one.' Ditto the seduction of Jenny: 'See point 1. The drunkenness is a dramatisation of the "unfairness" Jenny complains about in sexual relations.' Amis wants the reader to be shocked by Patrick's behaviour. We are to react to him, Christopher Ricks has suggested, as Samuel Johnson said Richardson wished us to react to Lovelace: 'It was in the power of Richardson alone to teach us at once esteem and detestation; to make virtuous resentment overpower all the benevolence which wit, elegance and courage excite, and to lose at last the hero in the villain.'[26]

In an interview in 1975 Amis called Patrick 'the most unpleasant person I've written about'.[27] At one point, driving through the rain, Patrick is described as 'lucky enough to send the greater part of a puddle over a sod in ragged clothes who was doing his level best to blow his nose into the gutter'. Elsewhere it is said of him that 'trying not to be a bad man took up far more energy than he could, or was prepared to, spare from trying not to be a nasty man, a far more pressing task'.[28] To some reviewers, Patrick's nastiness was matched by that of the novel itself. The *TLS* reviewer, writing on 9 September, called it 'a very nasty book . . . the worst novel ever written by a man who can write as well as Mr Amis'. John Coleman, in the *Spectator*, commented on the novel's 'dark note, harsh, accurate and repeatedly struck'.[29] Amis's staunchest academic defenders also stress the novel's darkness and harshness. To David Lodge the seduction of Jenny 'in all its furtive squalor, misery and remorse, is brilliantly done – so brilliantly that it alienates Patrick from the reader'.[30] 'The fantasies of hostility and aggression present in even the earliest novels,' John McDermott writes, 'were rendered acceptable by their comic excesses. But from this point onward they become more frequent . . . and more unpleasant.'[31] Yet for many they can also be exhilarating and funny. Karl Miller points to the essay 'What Became of Jane Austen?' in which Amis's 'well-founded objections' to *Mansfield Park* are followed by praise for Austen's 'invigorating coldness', what Miller calls 'a coldness sometimes indistinguishable from hostility', one that 'has you seeing an affinity between Austen and Amis'.[32] Amis's hostility, however, means to wound as well as invigorate, to turn the stomach just a bit.

The hostility is directed at the reader as well as the novel's characters, a result of Amis's decision to tell almost half the story from Patrick's point of view, to put us on his side. Like Lovelace in *Clarissa*, Patrick has attractive qualities, including a conscience. That he succumbs to Sheila leaves him feeling 'more ashamed and humiliated than he had ever felt in his life'.[33] When Sheila tells him Horace Charlton has got her pregnant he immediately gives her the money for an abortion. His fears of death and panic attacks evoke sympathy. Like the speaker in Amis's poem 'Romance', he once loitered at his window and 'could still feel a twinge of that uncomplicated and ignorant melancholy'.[34] He is capable both of self-awareness ('I'm not a very nice sort of chap, I'm afraid')[35] and remorse, putting his head in his hands in a way 'that was no mere piece of stage business'.[36] As Jenny says, commenting on this gesture: 'Oh yes, I'm sure it can't be much fun for you to be like you are. You're far from being a pig in a lot of things and so you're bound to get hurt yourself now and then.'[37] More complicatedly, we are told that 'he hoped if he ever saw himself as a bastard, instead of just seeing himself as seeing himself as a bastard, he would be drunk or in bed with a woman at the time'.[38] Patrick is like Jenny's cheeky pupil Michael Primrose, aged ten, who 'would be a terrible one for the women when he grew up . . . being not only lively and able to show he was wicked, but also simply incapable of noticing opposition'.[39] Early

in the novel Patrick explains to Jenny what goes through his mind
when he's after something, as when he first tried to seduce her:

God, it's as if I was tight – you know, I haven't got the car so I want to
be driven home, and that chap's got a car, hasn't he? So he'll drive me
home, won't he? He happens to live in the other direction, but that doesn't
matter, does it? because he won't mind, will he? Because he's got to do it,
hasn't he? And if he says he doesn't want to, then it's *You bloody drive
me home, Jack, and like it, because I want it, see?* Oh Christ. Terrifying.⁴⁰

The desire to wound in *Take a Girl Like You* is found also in *The
Evans Country*, conceived at roughly the same time, though not
published until 1962.⁴¹ In 'Aberdarcy: The Main Square', the first
poem in the sequence, Dai Evans's tawdry intrigues with Mrs Rhys
('the time they slunk / Back from that lousy weekend in Porthcawl')
are played out against a tawdry urban backdrop. Here are the poem's
last two stanzas (the first was quoted earlier, in Chapter 9):

> The journal of some bunch of architects
> Named this the worst town centre they could find;
> But how disparage what so well reflects
> Permanent tendencies of heart and mind?
>
> All love demands a witness: something 'there'
> Which it yet makes part of itself. These two
> Might find Carlton House Terrace, St. Mark's Square,
> A bit on the grand side. What about you?

This challenge to the reader – are you so much grander? So much
better? – is sounded again at the very end of the sequence in 'Aberdarcy:
The Chaucer Road', where Dai returns home after 'A fearsome thrash
with Mrs. No-holds-barred', greets his wife Megan, eyes his supper,
then settles down in front of the telly ('Don't think I'll bother with
the club tonight,' a line Larkin especially prized). The last stanza reads:

> Nice bit of haddock with poached egg, Dundee cake,
> Buckets of tea, then a light ale or two,
> And 'Gunsmoke,' 'Danger Man,' the Late Night Movie –
> Who's doing better, then? What about you?

Dai Evans makes his first appearance in Amis's writings in a letter to Larkin of 15 December 1959. 'My own "writing" is going all right,' he reports to Larkin, 'but I keep not being able to do anything on my novel, turning our shour out brief not-to-be-printed porno-graphic interludes – Jenny caught her by the back hair and pulled viciously downward. Anna cried out; Jenny sniggered and thrust her c—.' As for poetry, 'the Muse visits me but seldom'. Recently, however, Amis has composed something worth a look. Would Larkin 'tell me if the following quatrain is a) all right b) a complete poem or does it need more?'

> Hearing how tourists, dazed with reverence,
> Look through sun-glasses at the Parthenon,
> I thought of that cold night outside the Gents
> When Dai touched Gwyneth up with his gloves on.

Larkin probably approved, since the quatrain was one of the five poems Amis published in *Encounter* in May 1960, where it was titled 'Terrible Beauty' (in the Evans sequence it is 'Aldport (Mystery Tour)'). It is 'nasty' in the way *Take a Girl Like You* is nasty: 'When Dai touched Gwyneth up with his gloves on' means to turn the stomach just a bit. The feelings it evokes also unsettle, in the way Patrick's seduction of Jenny unsettles; the reader is made to feel complicit in the bad behaviour of both heroes, recalling the initial challenge of 'Aberdarcy: The Main Square': 'What about you?' John McDermott writes well about the trap Amis sets the reader in *The Evans Country*: 'The ironist's fork forces the reader to choose between a "yes" that would acknowledge the squalidness of his own amours and the "no" that sounds superior, unfeeling and, possibly, hypo-critical.'[42] Amis's aim, here and throughout the sequence, like his aim in *Take a Girl Like You*, is as aggressive as Roger Micheldene's explanation of what makes him want women.

Patrick's Dai-like propensities are especially disturbing because they are directed at Jenny Bunn. *Take a Girl Like You* contains not only 'the most unpleasant person I've written about' but a heroine 'quite opposite to what Patrick could ever possibly be like, a good character who comes to grief and who has faults that one cannot get moral about'. Jenny's instincts are 'wholly good', she is 'generous, has great humility, too much'. Though naïve, she also 'sees things for what they are, would never be wrong about a person even though she might be taken in by some things about them'.⁴³ This description, also from the 1975 interview, recalls the poetic 'Epilogue' to 'H.', that is, Hilly, in Amis's *Memoirs*, which describes her, when Amis first met and pursued her, as 'whole, unadapted within; / Awkward, gentle, healthy, straight-backed, / Who spoke to say something, laughed when amused; / If things went wrong, feared she might be at fault.' Amis's friends immediately recognised the resemblance between Jenny and Hilly (though they also recognised aspects of Mavis and Davina Gammon, Clive Gammon's wife). Larkin thought Jenny's character inconsistently depicted, he told Conquest, in a letter of 7 October 1960, 'perhaps because she said so many things that sounded like Hilly'.⁴⁴ Some readers have found Jenny impossibly good, as much a figure of male fantasy as Patrick's porn dream-girls (described in *Difficulties with Girls*, the sequel to *Take a Girl Like You*, as 'wise, compassionate, silent and with enormous breasts'). As Anthony Powell puts it, by way of explaining his dislike of Jenny in a journal entry of 4 October 1988, the year the sequel was published: 'Were I a feminist I should find Kingsley's sentimentalities far more insulting than his acerbic estimations of female behaviour.'⁴⁵ Though natural instinct is invariably amoral and animalistic with Amis's heroes, in the women these heroes fall for, marry and betray it is usually serious and admirable, a sign of health, unselfishness, unanxious self-possession. Here is how Jenny goes to sleep, a description that appears twice in *Take a Girl Like You*: 'Jenny turned over on her side and slowly let her feet push down the bed, put her hand under the pillow and spread the fingers as she always did. She relaxed. She was asleep.'⁴⁶

That Jenny is both generous and shrewd as well as natural is seen in the wonderful things she notices and says. Like Hilly, she is very keen on animals (the books on her bookshelves when 'not called things like *God's Little Acre* or *The Robe*, were called things like *First Steps with Figures* or *Claws, Paws and Hooves*').⁴⁷ In a chapter written from her point of view (there are sixteen of these, as opposed to eleven for Patrick) she describes the chickens Dick Thompson keeps as 'moving about as if they were very excited about something but knew how to keep it under control . . . They seemed to be expecting her and at the same time inquisitive about who she was'⁴⁸ (a passage which recalls the 'affected curiosity' with which the squirrels in *One Fat Englishman* glance about, or William Boot's hotel room in the early pages of Waugh's *Scoop*, decorated in magenta and gamboge, 'colours which – it had been demonstrated by experiments on poultry and mice – conduce to a mood of dignified gaiety').[49] Jenny's observations about men, a number of them gleaned by Amis from close interrogation of Hilly and Mavis, are comparably acute and funny. Here she is on Patrick's kisses: 'He kissed her again, but it was quite different: calm and gentle and without him having to shove his teeth against hers to show how keen he was. It was really much nicer like this, if only they knew. All that tongue work was very overrated and, when you came to think about it, rather rude as well.'[50] 'Rude' is a big word with Hilly. 'So . . . *rude*' was her response to Eric Jacobs's article about Amis's last days, which he sought to publish within a week of the writer's death. 'She always got a lot of mileage out of this word,' Martin Amis writes in *Experience*: 'She meant: so abrupt, so rough, so coarse.'[51] I once asked Hilly if she'd read my edition of Amis's correspondence: 'No dear,' she replied, 'I think it's rude to read other people's letters.' But she also sent me what letters she had, including the ferocious letter to Henry Fairlie.

What Jenny wants, she tells Patrick, is to 'find one chap and stick to him right from the start. See, I'm just not cut out for – going to bed with people.'[52] Despite the life she and Amis led in the 1950s and early 1960s, this is also Hilly's view of what she herself had wanted, one shared by most of the people who knew her well. It is hard not to attribute some part of the violence or aggression of *Take a Girl Like You* to self-disgust on Amis's part, not only for his Patrick-like behaviour, but for what this behaviour had done to Hilly: hurting her, turning her from her nature. At the same time, Amis does nothing to soften or counter Patrick's view that Jenny's traditional pieties are silly as well as outdated (a view easier to maintain when the piety in question is virginity rather than fidelity). The modern generation might be '*money mad*, or *pleasure mad*, or *only interested in what they could get out of life*',[53] but Amis puts these words into Mr Bunn's mouth, and Mr Bunn is mostly a joke figure, always on about 'chaps with beards and silk scarves marching to and fro with their banners and petitions and I don't know what all and showing off' and women 'in those tight slacks and not bothering with soap and water'[54] (he gets Dick Thompson to buy his round, however, which is a point in his favour). The presence of Julian Ormerod also supports the Patrick view. Amis has described Julian as 'all that Patrick ought to be and isn't, because though immoral sexually, let's say (many people would disapprove of the way he conducts his life), Julian actually knows what one should do and what one can do and what one should not do. And it's Julian who denounces Patrick for his behaviour.' Julian and Jenny 'are in a sense my two favourite types. One is the person who is naïve and shrewd . . . The other admirable person is like Julian, entirely his own man, not preyed upon by anxieties, guilts, doubts, but nevertheless, in fact, is sufficiently so that he can afford to behave morally. I mean by that, he would never have treated Jenny as Patrick did because he'd just have decided he had to leave her.'[55] Larkin thought Julian's characterisation 'leant heavily on the Conquest *persona*', though Conquest sees little resemblance.[56] One thing that connects them is their sense of humour, especially when confronted with the least whiff of theory. 'You know, all this women business often strikes me as being a power thing really,' reflects Patrick, immediately after hooting his horn 'to make an attractive back turn round'. 'Lot in that, of course,' Julian replies. 'Though I can't help thinking that sex is pretty firmly tied up with it somewhere or other.'[57] Conquest is a difficult figure to pigeon-hole, as entirely his own man as a man could be. But he has a personal background and a career as a writer and historian. Julian's background and occupation are shadowy in the extreme, which calls into question his plausibility as a mediating figure between Patrick's trendy amorality (Bernard Bergonzi, Malcolm Bradbury and others see him as heralding the Swinging Sixties)[58] and Jenny's old-fashioned principles. When Ann Thwaite wrote to Amis to defend Jenny against those who thought her both impossibly good or sensible and thinly drawn, she was less certain of Julian. On 30 November 1960 Amis wrote back to say how glad he was she'd liked the novel, 'particularly that you thought the Jenny parts came off all right – which was the one thing I was really scared about. I might have gone so horribly and irretrievably wrong there. I know what you mean about Julian, of course, but would say as a sort of half-excuse that his implausibility was part of his character, and of his role. But that's pretty fine-spun, I know.'

Amis's anxieties about Jenny's characterisation played a part in the elaborate and protracted genesis of *Take a Girl Like You*. Amis started work on the novel in 1955, then put it aside in 1956 to write *I Like It Here*, then took it up again. 'I was very nervous because it was going to be a new departure for me; I even made about twelve drafts of the first chapter.'[59] These drafts do not survive but eighty pages of notes do, some forty-seven numbered in a notebook begun in Portugal, followed by a further thirty-three unnumbered pages.[60] Several factors made the new novel so demanding: its length (it is Amis's longest novel), the dual narrative points of view, one of them female, a much larger and more closely observed cast of secondary characters, the darkness and severity of the comedy. As Amis told Salwak in a 1975 interview: 'I was saying, to put it very crudely, I hope they'll go on laughing, but this time they won't be able to escape the notion that I'm saying something serious. I don't mean profound or earnest, but something serious.'[61]

The first pages of the Portugal notebook, now at the Harry Ransom Center in Texas, are devoted to character, with sections on Dick Thompson, Graham McClintoch (the Willie Smyth character, getting a girl for whom was the novel's starting point, Amis told the Clearys), Anna (Jenny's fellow lodger at the Thompsons'), Jenny herself, Patrick, then a Julian character (Oliver Harris in the notes).[62] Under the headings for each of these characters Amis enters telling details or snatches of dialogue. Dick Thompson smokes 'with that awful lustful enjoyment as if only he really understood cigarettes'.[63] Graham McClintoch 'dresses like a man twice his age'[64] and speaks pedantically, which leads Amis to add 'watch Ieuan Jenkins'[65] (that is, watch out not to make him too like John Lewis's pedantic colleague Ieuan Jenkins in *That Uncertain Feeling*). The first notes about Jenny make her sound like Mavis: 'Is small (5'1" – insists on the 1") . . . Has very quick movements, but steady gaze.'[66] Elsewhere he calls her 'Disneyish, like a young animal'[67] (like 'a small deer in *Bambi*' in the finished novel).[68] The first set of notes for Jenny and Patrick come after those for the secondary characters, as if Amis were building the novel from the periphery. The opening entry for Patrick is atypically analytic or summarising: 'NB Above all must be initially sympathetic. Must be made *emotionally* "drink all, eat, pay nowt" – his favourite accusation against Thompson in the literal sphere. He is mean from point of view of feeling: must have what he wants but never pays for it . . . Likeable, humorous, dangerous. Sympathetic for 1st half.'[69] Patrick is thus conceived from the start as drawing readers in, setting them up.

In addition to notes on characters, there are notes grouped under the headings 'General', 'Threads' and 'Possible Scenes'. A page is devoted to 'Candidates for twelve bad men', which refers to a mock cricket team Patrick draws up, in the manner of Amis and Larkin's mock jazz personnels (the finished list has Dick as captain, Selwyn Lloyd as wicket-keeper, John Coltrane at number four, Milton at five and Beethoven as twelfth man). Other pages contain a 'Chart of sexual alignments and pursuits' and lists of scenes and groupings of scenes. Some of the notes under the heading 'General' are jokes or games, equivalents of the unprintable pornographic episodes Amis mentions to Larkin: one such note matches the novel's cast of characters with those in *Hamlet*, e.g. Jenny with Ophelia, Graham with Polonius (or Horatio), Anna with the Player Queen, Ormerod with Fortinbras; another entry experiments with naughty acronyms, a Conquest speciality, as in 'Fellow's obviously a member of the Cambridge University New Testament Society', crossed out in the notebook and replaced with 'Shropshire and Hertfordshire Imperial Training School' (in the finished novel, Julian says of the proprietor of the local hotel restaurant, 'I rather tend to associate him with the Shropshire and Hertfordshire Infantry Training School').[70] In the notebook's later, unnumbered pages Amis begins to think about plot, as in the headings 'Sequence One: Arrival' and 'Sequence Two: Jam Session'. The 'Arrival' sequence lists five numbered scenes, beginning '1. Conversation between J and D; J's pov. D laughs like rook. V. amiable to her. Impresses on her need for economy. Tea in 10 mins. Geyser. 10.1' (where '10.1' refers to those pages of the notebook which describe the geyser and Dick's laugh). Especially striking is another late page on which Amis lists the novel's first twenty scenes, next to each of which he adds a 'P' or a 'J' (under the heading 'pov') and then letters to denote which characters figure prominently (they are in capitals) and which peripherally (lower case). Here and throughout the notes Amis's focus is on character and structure. Almost nothing is said about the novel's setting (modelled on Berkhamsted, the Whitstead of 'The Legacy', though as Amis reassured Rubinstein, 'I think I've satisfactorily confused the issue by pointing pretty clearly to Beaconsfield as well as Berkhamsted').[71] There are snatches of dialogue but no reflections on style. The novel's themes are rarely and only very indirectly mentioned, as in the note: 'All J's ideas, good and bad, are disproved by the end. She can realise this if carefully done.' No reference is made to literary or other models (*Hamlet* excepted). Several critics have pointed to connections between *Take a Girl Like You* and *Clarissa*, but neither Richardson nor any other novelist is referred to in the notes.

Amis has called *Take a Girl Like You* his favourite novel. The letters suggest he was unworried by its mixed critical reception. Sales helped here: within two months of publication over 20,000 copies had been sold, along with film and serialisation rights, the latter purchased by *Women's Mirror* (which must have amused Amis, since Jenny is said to have picked up her sentimental notions of married life from *Woman's Domain*).[72] After mentioning the hostile *TLS* review to the Powells in a letter of 27 September 1960, Amis quoted Liberace: 'I cried all the way to the bank.'[73] Almost as soon as the novel was finished Amis took on more journalism and began visiting London regularly. Some novelists are exhausted after finishing their novels, especially long and difficult ones. Amis was energised. He was now reviewing fiction fortnightly for the *Observer*, as well as writing its monthly science fiction column.[74] On 2 November, after a weekend in 'Kingfish Bay' (i.e., Swansea), Conquest reported to Larkin that Amis was 'finishing a set of S.F. stories'[75] and would soon begin work on 'the Egyptological book' (a novel he and Conquest were working on together). On a subsequent weekend Amis came to London and Conquest reported 'fantastic racket at the Gales, denunciations rows booze etc. (scenes too)'.[76] Later in the month Amis agreed to give evidence at the trial of *Lady Chatterley's Lover*, despite antipathy to Lawrence. On the day he was due to testify, he failed to appear: 'I left Swansea just in time to miss your letter,' he wrote in apology to Michael Rubinstein, Hilary Rubinstein's elder brother, acting on behalf of Penguin Books, 'and got back six hours or so after I should have been available in court.'[77] According to Conquest, writing to Larkin on 2 November 1960, Amis failed to appear 'because he was at the time participating in an adulterous rendezvous. Pity he didn't just make it, breathing heavily, smeared with lipstick and fly-buttons mostly undone, to testify that Lady C was a sacred monogamous work.' On 13 January, Conquest wrote again to Larkin to tell him about a new flat he'd rented in London. It had a spare room and Larkin was invited to stay whenever he wanted. Of course, Amis would probably be there with one of his girlfriends, 'but we could pretend to be mutes, couldn't we? Trusty blind eunuchs, I mean. Who are they? Oh they're quite safe darling: Mustafa, say something to the lady. Glubashlubaslubablubla-mammum. You see, dear?'

Amis's high spirits after the completion of *Take a Girl Like You* made him keen to travel. In early September he and Hilly made a second trip to Denmark, this time to a writer's conference in

Copenhagen. Iris Murdoch and John Bayley were there and Bayley remembers Amis reading brilliantly from one of his novels. He also remembers a lunch at which Amis ordered smoked salmon and scrambled eggs as both a first and second course, because he liked them so much. On their return to London, Amis and Hilly took Sandy and Jan Richardson, visiting from Princeton, to a nightclub. Amis gave Larkin an account of the club in a letter of 24 September 1960:

You know, night clubs is a thing I've decided I don't want any of, at all, ever. When we returned from Denmark we took the Richardsons to another, slightly less bad (but not less expensive) one, where the cabaret led off with the introduction of a pretty girl with just about the gig frig biggest tits I've ever seen on the hoof – 42, 44, christ knows, I wouldn't. After she'd faced the audience and bowed, an action that nearly caused me to send our table flying over my shoulder, she brought out a PIANO ACCORDEON and played it enthusiastically (and rather skilfully) for ten minutes or so, and that was the last we saw of the tits. God. Anything else. Banjo. Ukelele. Harmonica. Basset-horn. Viola da gamba (especially that). But a fucking *piano accordeon*. I mean, like seeing Betty Grable taking part in a sack race. Or Anita Ekberg in a crinoline.

Princeton visitors like the Richardsons fired the Amises with thoughts of a return to the States. For all his talk of the dangers of leaving home, Amis had come to share Hilly's boredom with Swansea, expressed both in letters and directly to friends.[78] There was also a specific literary reason for him to return. As he explained in a letter of 23 November 1960 to Cindy Degner at Curtis Brown: 'I have a novel about the U.S. to write[79] which I can't write until I've seen the bloody place again. For an extended period.' By 2 December, Perry Knowlton, also of Curtis Brown, had written to Wallace Stegner about a visiting post for Amis at Stanford, as well as to contacts at Williams College in Massachusetts and San Francisco State University. On 16 December, Degner informed Amis of an intriguing offer from *Playboy*: would Amis be interested in becoming its fiction editor and overseeing its reviews columns? The magazine would pay handsomely and Degner was sure Amis could also pick up some teaching at the University of Chicago.

The dangers of changing one's country, of losing touch with one's themes and subjects, were now forgotten. The danger now was cultural nationalism, as suggested in Amis's response of 24 September 1960 to a questionnaire Larkin sent him on behalf of the Standing Conference of National and University Libraries (SCONUL). Larkin was to give a talk to SCONUL on the preservation of British literary manuscripts and Amis was one of twenty 'leading British writers' (including T.S. Eliot, E.M. Forster and Graham Greene) whose opinions he solicited. Amis's opinion is unlikely to have pleased Larkin: 'I will sell any of my manuscripts to the highest bidder, assuming such bidder to be of reputable standing, and I have no feeling one way or another about such bidder's country of origin. It seems to me no more incongruous that the Tate Gallery should have a large collection of Monets (say) than that Buffalo University should have a collection of Robert Graves manuscripts (say). I view with unconcern the drift of British manuscripts to America, where our language is spoken and our literature studied.'

Whether Amis ever seriously considered the *Playboy* offer (Conquest and Larkin would have had a field day had they known of it) is unclear. That he actively sought an extended stay, even a '(semi)-permanent job', in America, is not.[80] By December, however, a dramatically different possibility had entered the picture, one initially planted and nurtured by Pat and George Gale. As Amis explained to John McCallum: 'Swansea, dear good old place that it is, was getting me and Hilly into such a state of hypnotised boredom that we felt we must break out or die – and breaking out meant, for both of us, coming to the U.S.A. more or less indefinitely. Only one thing restrained me from sending you a distress signal, the possibility that I might swing a job in Cambridge (Eng., not Mass.). Well, this rather remote chance (as it looked at first) has now come off: the rubber-stamping has yet to be completed, but for all intents and purposes I am fixed with a fellowship to Peterhouse.' McCallum was to put his exertions as 'chief immigration officer' on hold. Amis declared that he and Hilly were 'very thrilled, of course' with the Peterhouse offer and expected to enjoy themselves 'for a time anyway'.[81] But they were also sorry not to be coming immediately to the States. As Amis later wrote to Alan Collins, his American agent, 'we feel it'd be only fair to give Cambridge a whirl before doing anything drastic about leaving England'.[82] In other words, mixed feelings about the Cambridge move were present from the start, as was a residual sadness about leaving Swansea – 'dear good old place that it is'.

18

Cambridge

In 1958 William Stone, 'the Squire of Piccadilly', died at the age of 101. Stone, the first scholar of the College in Natural Sciences and a Peterhouse benefactor, had managed to gain control of over half the sets in Albany in Piccadilly, a block of exclusive bachelors' chambers converted from the Duke of York's house in 1803, and at his death left them to the college, together with so much money that its holdings were increased by some 160 per cent. Peterhouse is both the oldest and smallest college in Cambridge. Small colleges, it was thought, could not be expected to cover all subjects taught at the university and English was among the subjects not covered at Peterhouse. With the sudden access to the Stone money, however, the college was able to finance not only a new residential building, the William Stone building (1964), but to consider filling gaps in its fellowship. English was an obvious gap, given its popularity and the fame of the Cambridge English Faculty. Several Peterhouse undergraduates had switched to English as soon as they came up, obliging the college to farm them out to external supervisors, an unsatisfactory arrangement. As E.J. Kenney, tutor and college lecturer in classics, pointed out, whether Peterhouse approved or not, there would be increasing pressure to read English at the college.

Size was not the only reason Peterhouse had been reluctant to appoint a fellow in English. The college's great strength among arts subjects was history. No fewer than four professors in the Cambridge History Faculty were at Peterhouse the year Amis was appointed: Herbert Butterfield, the Master, famed for *The Whig Interpretation of History* (1931), a short and powerful attack on 'progressivist' accounts of English history (in which parliamentary democracy is seen to evolve through a continuous process of improvement); Michael Postan, an economic historian; Denis Brogan, a United States historian; and David Knowles, a medieval historian. There were also two college lecturers in history: Denis Mack Smith, whose field was modern Italian history, and Brian Wormald, the Senior Tutor, a specialist in sixteenth- and seventeenth-century English history. In addition to history, the college was strong in engineering and the sciences, particularly molecular biology. Both the historians and the scientists at Peterhouse tended to look down on English, but the college's three tutors, Wormald, Kenney and D.B.C. Taylor, a lecturer in mechanical sciences, were in agreement that the time had come to bow to popular demand. One way to do so, while preserving the snooty Peterhouse view, was to appoint a practising writer rather than a conventional academic, or an academic who was also a practising writer. Wormald knew just the man: Kingsley Amis.

Wormald knew Amis through George and Pat Gale. George had read history at Peterhouse, where he was taught by Wormald, awarded firsts in both parts of the Tripos, and briefly contemplated an academic career, studying for a period at Göttingen University in Germany before joining the Manchester *Guardian* in 1951 as a leader-writer and reporter on labour affairs. Gale maintained close ties with Wormald, Butterfield and several other fellows of the college. Wormald adored Pat Gale, whose dark good looks and theatrical manner had a special appeal for certain donnish types (including the political philosopher Michael Oakeshott, a key influence on Peterhouse history, also the lover of Wormald's wife, Rosemary). 'She always had admirers,' Hilly remembers of Pat Gale, 'and she always went for the dons.' When the Amises moved to Cambridge, Pat introduced Hilly to several of these dons ('including my next husband to be') and for a while Hilly was 'quite into the intellectual scene'. 'They amused me,' she recalls. 'They were killing old things, rather sweet, and they loved to be with Pat and me. They thought Christmas had come.' According to the historian and political theorist Maurice Cowling, who would become Pat's second husband, it was Pat who persuaded Wormald to push Amis for the Peterhouse job. The Gales were keen that the Amises move closer to London, or Staines, where they lived. It was Pat who invited

Wormald along for a weekend with the Amises and others at Dylan Thomas's boathouse in Laugharne in what was then Pembrokeshire. The Amises and the Gales spent several weekends together at Laugharne, thanks to Stuart Thomas, executor of the Dylan Thomas estate. Cowling remembers Wormald driving down from Cambridge on a red motorcycle.

Brian Wormald spent almost seventy years at Peterhouse. He read history there as an undergraduate, was appointed a Fellow in 1938, and had been a senior tutor since 1952. He was an ordained deacon and served as chaplain as well as Dean of the college. In his memoirs, Peregrine Worsthorne recounts his first vision of Wormald, presiding over the scholarship examinations Worsthorne took in Peterhouse Hall in 1942. In addition to a monocle, Wormald wore 'highly polished silver buckle pumps, an Anglican-type soutane with crimson facings which matched his crimson socks and an anguished expression which only the deepest kind of spiritual doubts could possibly justify'.[1] These doubts led Wormald into the Catholic Church; the anguished looks, however, extended beyond spiritual matters to questions of historical interpretation. 'Supervision by angst,' was how one former pupil described Wormald's teaching technique;[2] according to an obituary in *The Times*, 'his method, if it can be called a method, involved pauses, silences and a great deal of cigarette smoke'.[3] Wormald published a study of Clarendon in 1951 and did not publish another book until 1993, when during a period of illness a long-marinated study of Bacon was 'liberated' from him by his publishers.[4] Despite his eccentricity and lack of productivity he had the confidence of Butterfield, who relied on his tutors. Though Wormald's advice as senior tutor was not always followed by the Fellows, on this occasion, especially as it was seconded by Kenney, Taylor and the Master, it carried the day without much debate.

Cowling, who came to Peterhouse from Jesus College in 1963, just after Amis left, believes it unlikely that many Peterhouse Fellows would have read Amis's fiction, even *Lucky Jim*. Kenney thinks a number 'didn't really know who he was or what he was noted for'. The only significant opposition his proposed election encountered, Cowling himself probably engendered. He never liked Amis and advised David Knowles 'not to touch him with a barge pole'. Amis's possible selection as a Fellow had been under informal discussion for over a year when Butterfield, somewhat unusually, asked each Fellow at a Governing Body meeting to comment on the proposed appointment. Knowles confessed to 'being a little disappointed in Mr. Amis. Indeed, if I hadn't known who he was, I shouldn't have known who he was, so to say'.[5] Knowles also didn't like what he'd heard about Amis from colleagues outside the college (Cowling, presumably). After a list of Amis's publications had been requested, Knowles read *Lucky Jim* and was not impressed, but then he was a medieval historian, teetotal and a Benedictine monk. Professor Postan, the economic historian, also read *Lucky Jim* and couldn't understand what was so funny about the article on the development of shipbuilding techniques 1450–85: 'Fellow had a perfectly good topic.'[6] Not everyone in the college was so unworldly: Butterfield and Brogan were astute, witty and mischievous observers of the contemporary scene and knew exactly what they were doing by appointing Amis as opposed to a more conventional academic; Denis Mack Smith and Leslie Orgel, a Fellow in Natural Sciences, spoke warmly in favour of *Lucky Jim*, arguing that it was an important novel as well as a good one, inaugurating a new genre in fiction.[7] Once informal approval had been reached by the Fellows, Amis was invited to dine in Hall. As Kenney puts it: 'You have a look at the man. You dine him and have a look at him.' There was no formal interview, a boon for Amis given his unease in such settings. At no point was the English Faculty consulted. On 27 February 1961, Minute 48 of the College Order Book recorded an offer to Amis of a college lectureship in English with ten years' seniority as well as an official fellowship. The moneys attached to these posts amounted to some £2,000 per annum, in addition to free accommodation and a free domus meal per day. According to Richard Skaer, a zoologist elected in the same year as Amis, 'it is clear that Kingsley was given favourable treatment'.[8] Without such treatment, suggests John Beer, Amis's successor as Fellow in English, he would have been offered less money than he was getting at Swansea.[9]

But not less prestige. As Eric Jacobs puts it: 'by the beginning of the 1960s Amis had made progress on all fronts except one, that of his own profession of university teacher ... A mere lecturer is what he still was, earning the scale rate for his job as he had done since 1949. He had not climbed even a single rung on the career ladder to senior lecturer, let alone shimmied up as far as reader or professor.'[10] Amis was happy enough in Swansea, had good friends there, both within and outside the university, had the protection of the Principal, whose influence he otherwise deplored, and could mostly teach what he wanted. But the English Department was small, narrow in its interests and influence, and presided over by a man he neither liked nor respected. After the excitements of Blackmur and other critical high flyers at Princeton, Swansea seemed intellectually dead. Cambridge, in contrast, was 'a whole flight of steps up the academic hierarchy from Swansea . . . and it had Dr. F.R. Leavis at it'.[11] Though Cambridge was a bastion of privilege, the year at Princeton had given privilege an acceptable face, perhaps because it was foreign, unthreatening. As Amis also admits in the *Memoirs*, the Cambridge job represented 'the hope of a kind of displaced return to Oxford, an echo of the romantic view of it which intervening time had enhanced'.[12]

In 'No More Parades', an essay Amis wrote for *Encounter* after he left Cambridge, he recalled his initial thoughts about accepting the Peterhouse offer. 'I told myself that things like the passage of time and a couple of Labour governments would have put paid to the class business and also have seen off the old dons. Cambridge, moreover, was not Oxford: to my contemporaries it had always seemed mysteriously more "go-ahead" than the other place.'[13] He was not wrong about 'the class business', at least in respect of the dons. But 'go-ahead' was hardly the term he would apply to the place intellectually. What Amis was looking for at Cambridge was 'an experience primarily concerned with the things of the mind, the study of literature in particular'.[14] Donald Davie, a Fellow of Caius, informed him, almost immediately, that this expectation was 'naïve', 'He pumped me about what it was like to teach English at Cambridge, and I was eloquently jaundiced about it,' Davie recalls in his memoirs, 'only to have to back-pedal lamely and unconvincingly, when he revealed that that very day he had accepted an invitation from Peterhouse to move there.'[15]

Part of Amis's disappointment with Cambridge derived from the fact that his was a college not a faculty appointment. In Oxford, a college appointment normally carries with it full participation in the faculty, including lecturing, examining and a generous salary. Not in Cambridge, where college fellows without faculty appointments can be made to feel like second-class citizens. Moreover, Amis's appointment was seen by some faculty members, Leavis for one, as an intentional slight, not only because the faculty had not been consulted, but because of what some saw as Peterhouse's high-handed treatment of the man who had for several years been looking after the college's few students in English. This man, Leo Salingar, received a curt note from the college informing him that his services as a supervisor would no longer be needed. Salingar had influential supporters in the faculty and at the time of Amis's appointment was himself in search of a fellowship (he would get one at Trinity College the next year, where he taught me). An able, dedicated teacher and a respected scholar, though almost as unproductive as Wormald, he was no great wit. Cambridge, though, in Amis's words, was 'the least damaging place in England in which not to be found funny'.[16] That Peterhouse positively valued Amis's wit made it exceptional, while also suggesting an underlying scepticism about English as an academic discipline. As the engineering don, Chris Calladine, elected a Fellow the year before Amis, recalls, 'the selling point was that for *English* it was better to have a successful practitioner than a "dry scholar"'.[17]

It was the behaviour of Peterhouse as much as the writing itself that provoked Leavis into describing him as a pornographer. Leavis's jibe was uttered at an English faculty meeting at which it was suggested that Peterhouse be consulted about a problem concerning car parking: 'Peterhouse can't expect to be taken seriously about anything now that it's given a fellowship to a *pornographer*,' Leavis announced, a remark to which Davie and John Holloway immediately objected.[18] Leavis had already referred dismissively in print to Amis's writing,[19] but his hostility may have been exacerbated by a lecture Amis gave at Cambridge shortly before the Peterhouse offer. This lecture, if not actually delivered to the Doughty Club, the undergraduate literary society of Downing, Leavis's college, was attended by several of his acolytes. As soon as Amis finished speaking, one of them stood up to denounce him: 'What you seem to be implying . . .' Halfway through the ensuing denunciation, Amis lapsed into 'that smug, smiling, nodding thing, where you know exactly what you're going to say'. His grinning reply was: 'Yes, that more or less sums up my position.'[20]

Even had Amis been offered a faculty post, his intellectual expectations were unlikely to have been met. What seemed to him to interest the literature dons at Cambridge was literary politics not literature, or, more precisely, literary politics at Cambridge. 'What I got was talk about intra-Faculty discord and personal quarrels, syllabus changes and retentions, the proportion of Firsts to other classes, the attendance at old so-and-so's lectures – inevitably, no doubt, but discussed far more exclusively than I remembered from my provincial days, when a not necessarily very profound remark about Traherne or Tennyson would come up now and then.'[21] Those English dons Amis got to know, he never warmed to. Davie would join him occasionally for lunchtime sessions at Miller's wine bar in King's Parade, but their relations had 'always been slightly constrained'. In his memoirs, Davie claimed that 'there's no British writer among my contemporaries whom I have admired more, and the consciousness of this is a little embarrassing to both of us'.[22] In *his* memoirs, Amis's sole mention of Davie at Cambridge was of 'his accusing me, accurately enough, of thinking him square (though I thought and think him better things besides).'[23] George Watson, of St John's, the man who had taken over Amis's teaching at Swansea while he was in Princeton, also admired him and soon invited him to dinner in Hall (where his colleagues 'were abashed not to find a lumpish oaf who threw things and broke things but a well-suited figure interested in vintage wines and the musical compositions of lesser members of the Bach family').[24] Watson's year at Swansea had been enlivened by stories of Amis and his influence. 'I keep pretty quiet about my madrigals,' one colleague confessed to him. Then there was the story of Amis's appearance on a lecture platform in a new suit: 'When a student whistled in mock-admiration he made a full turn before his audience and said brightly "Like it?"'[25] In Cambridge, though, Watson found Amis 'over-reverent of what scholars did. I remember him consulting me then on what can only have been an unrealistically erudite study of literary utopias, mostly forgotten works of the nineteenth century, and cannot regret he did not do it.'[26] Amis does not mention Watson in the *Memoirs*, but he does mention George Steiner, whom he'd known of at Princeton, and who had also come to Cambridge in 1961, as a founding fellow of Churchill College. Steiner amused Amis but was hardly a kindred spirit. To begin with, Amis thought him stingy with drink (though nowhere near as stingy as his Churchill colleague Andrew Sinclair). Then there was his 'unspoken claim to pantophany – speaker's knowledge of every (major) language', a trait Amis both distrusted and thought of as American (it was shared by Ezra Pound, for example).[27] That Amis's contacts with English dons were rare left him with a sense of 'injured merit', even though those he did have were unstimulating. As he concludes in the *Encounter* article, 'perhaps I felt I got less than was my due as a man of letters',[28] an understandable reaction given his celebrity in the wider world.

As partial compensation, Amis's relations with the scientists and historians of Peterhouse were perfectly pleasant and amiable. In *Encounter* he called the college 'an oasis of good nature and common sense'.[29] He liked Butterfield and Brogan in particular, especially after hearing the latter assert 'to me and others that there were fifty states in the United States and he had fucked in forty-six of them'.[30] The Fellows were all keen to get to know Amis – his arrival had been heralded in the press, as at Princeton – and found him lively and entertaining, with 'lots of funny stories, some unprintable'.[31] Calladine remembers Amis asking a scientist at dinner what sorts of noises computers made, then imitating a range of possibilities (he was writing a television play at the time and there was a scene with a computer in it). Another Fellow, Stavros Papastavrou, a classicist, was asked what the modern Greek word for 'underpants' was, which Amis thought he might use as the name of a Greek island in one of his novels. Amis's great and lasting contribution to Peterhouse social life, though, was his altering the custom of Fellows filing into Hall for dinner in order of seniority. 'Kingsley, very sensibly, changed all that,' recalls Richard Skaer: 'He simply went in and sat with the person to whom he was speaking before the bell for dinner was sounded.'[32] The custom was never revived.

This was not Amis's only eyebrow-raising moment. At the end of Governing Body meetings Fellows were exhorted to keep all minutes and confidential papers safely hidden. After the first meeting, Amis strode across the Combination Room and threw his into the fire: 'another novelty for us,' Calladine comments.[33] What little Amis said at meetings was modest and good-humoured, though on one occasion, recounted in the *Memoirs*, he raised a fuss. In the course of a small admissions committee meeting, committee members were asked to choose between two applicants with similar test scores, one from a state school, one from a public school. When it was suggested that, as they were otherwise equal, the applicant from the state school should be awarded the place, Amis objected: 'As I think the only non-public schoolboy present, I don't see why a chap's having been to one should actually be held against him.' This objection was met with 'remorseful consternation' and resulted in a second look at the applicants' records, though neither Amis nor Kenney, also on the committee, could remember which applicant finally got the place.[34] The 'remorseful' nature of the committee's consternation suggests that Amis's objection reflected the Peterhouse ethos. Though in 1961 Peterhouse was by no means the breeding ground of Conservatism with a capital C that it would later become, its approach to history could be thought of as conservative in tendency or effect.[35] At the heart of this approach was a sceptical attitude to liberal pieties, a determination to make progressive liberalism doubtful about itself, one shared even by those who would identify themselves as liberal, such as Denis Brogan. Amis was familiar with this determination from Gale and other Fleet Street acquaintances, also from Conquest. As liberalism and radicalism gathered strength in the 1960s, especially in universities, the oppositional streak in Amis's character, the one that had led him to the left in the 1940s and 1950s, responded to the Peterhouse view.

Amis's teaching responsibilities at Peterhouse were not on the surface particularly arduous. In his first year, he was responsible for six Part I students, plus another three who had switched to English in previous years. These students he would meet for weekly supervisions in a first-floor room that formed a bridge between one end of the Old Court and the Chapel. 'Modest and elegant' inside, according to one first-year student, Roger Deakin, from the outside the room looked 'like something in Venice'.[36] In the *Memoirs*, Amis calls it 'a covered bridge between two main buildings'. A later office he describes as 'a place like a suburban drawing-room in an apartment-house down Trumpington Street'.[37] With the exception of a remark about King's College chapel at dusk – 'cold and lonely, a setting more appropriate to an unhappy love affair than to the bustling exchange of ideas'[38] – these are Amis's only comments, in the *Memoirs* and elsewhere, on the buildings of Cambridge, one of the chief joys, or compensations, of living there; as for the gardens and backs, about these he says nothing at all. Amis's preferred teaching site, according to his students, was the Little Rose pub, right across from the college.[39] Several students mention adjourning there to finish or continue supervisions. Deakin was surprised when Amis announced, in the middle of his first supervision, that it was half-past ten and time for a glass of Madeira.

Deakin remembers Amis's teaching fondly, praising its perfect blend of formality and informality. 'He treated us with great respect and a refreshing directness.' Though he addressed students as 'Mr Deakin' or 'Mr Handford', he also invited them to lunch or for a drink. Deakin recalls an early supervision on Milton's 'Lycidas', in which he misunderstood the word 'winds' in the lines 'We drove afield, and both together heard / What time the gray-fly winds her sultry horn.' Amis invited Deakin to read the lines aloud and 'sure enough, I mispronounced "winds" to rhyme with "finds"'. Deakin describes Amis as having 'hawkish, hooded' eyes and 'a sudden, sharp piercing glance', but on this occasion he behaved 'gently', merely asking: 'How exactly would you wind a horn?' Another first-year student, Richard Eyre, later Sir Richard, Director of the National Theatre, remembers being taught Shakespeare by Amis. Eyre produced an essay on *Twelfth Night* full of the opinions of 'Spurgeon, Wilson Knight, Dover Wilson' and Amis 'gently, but courteously' cast it aside. '"But what do you think of this play?" he would ask. "Do you think it's any good? . . . I mean as a play. It says it's a comedy. Fine. But does it have any decent jokes?"' Eyre calls these questions 'good teaching, or, closely allied, good direction'. Though 'shocking' they were also 'healthy', especially for 'a young and impressionable man ripe to become a fundamentalist in matters of literary taste'. Eyre knew perfectly well that Amis's irreverence was calculated, but he 'never patronised me and always encouraged me'.[40]

Most of the students who were taught by Amis at Cambridge shared Eyre's view, but there were exceptions. Jeremy Taylor, taking Part I of the Tripos at the end of Amis's first year, found him 'dismissive and uninterested'.[41] Amis was Director of Studies as well as Fellow in English and it was his responsibility to make sure that the Peterhouse students were properly entered and prepared for both parts of the Tripos examination as well as Prelims. On at least two occasions he set the wrong texts and on a third he entered a student for a forbidden combination of papers. Only by going cap in hand to the University Senate and persuading it to pass a special statute, was Amis able to save the degree of the student in this last case.[42]

Eyre, 'a callow eighteen-year-old', was thrilled to drink with Amis and the *Observer* critic John Davenport at Miller's wine bar, gossiping about the literary world. 'Grown-up drinking, as well as poetry, featured strongly in our education with Amis,' Deakin recalls. Derek Frampton, who arrived in Peterhouse to read English in 1961, remembers meeting Brian Aldiss and Gerald Kaufman at a drinks party at the Amis house, where students 'were made to feel the centre of attention'.[43] Michael Frohnsdorff describes similar parties where 'we mixed with academic and literary friends almost on an equal footing'. Frampton also remembers Hilly organising morning drinks parties in the college gardens. Amis liked socialising with undergraduates and thought it the right thing to do: 'All the young men I asked said the chief thing wrong with the place was this lack of contact.'[44] But not all the students were helped by his tolerant attitude towards drinking. Perhaps the most able of his students, the son of a London publican, who wrote brilliant, iconoclastic essays and dressed all in black, was often drunk and once walked straight into the River Cam in winter and was lucky to be rescued. Amis was dining at a feast in Hall when he was summoned by the undergraduate's irate landlady, who was intent on evicting him. Another student, a heavy drinker and seriously unstable, failed his exams, attempted suicide and dropped out. Amis, it was thought, did not do enough to help these students; some Fellows considered him, if not exactly a bad influence, 'not as good as he might be with fragile students'.[45]

Amis's reaction in the *Memoirs* to such accusations is unflustered. The publican's son he calls 'no fool academically and a drunk'. He remembers him apologising profusely about the River Cam business 'while holding a glass of something', a scene which took place in Amis's house: 'The thing was that, without much noticing, he had become a sort of friend of the family as well as being a periodic bloody nuisance and quite an interesting fellow to teach.'[46] That this student had problems was not Amis's fault: 'nothing of the discredit for [his] walk into the Cam can be fairly claimed by me. He was the sort of young man who does that sort of thing anyway.' As for the other undergraduate, Amis recalls his arriving one day for supervision, sitting in total silence, then 'throwing himself at my feet, kissing the toe of one of my shoes and murmuring brokenly, "Help me."' The student was on a bender, a periodic occurrence. Amis claims that he eventually learned to cope with him 'after a fashion. But it was a pest and somehow not right.' Towards the end of Amis's second year at Cambridge, when he was deeply involved in the affair with Elizabeth Jane Howard and relations with Hilly were at their nadir, he missed or had sometimes to reschedule supervisions and was not always available for consultation. There were occasional murmurings about negligence but also about his socialising with students. The nearest Amis came to acknowledging any uneasiness about this was an admission in the *Memoirs* that 'there could be something faintly, now and then not so faintly, disreputable about the kind of open house Hilly and I kept in Madingley Road'.[47]

The house in Madingley Road took a while to find. Amis was offered and accepted his post at Peterhouse in February 1961. On

17 May Bob Conquest wrote to Larkin that Amis 'has publicly advertised, in some paper, his failure to get a house in Cuntab so far. Perhaps hoping some sucker for literature will offer him one free.' No such sucker had appeared by the end of the academic year. On 11 July Larkin wrote to Conquest to say that he was sorry to hear that 'Kingers is ropey.' Any number of reasons might be adduced to explain Amis's state: the prospect of leaving Swansea, the prospect of the move itself, problems with women (Liz Moynahan's return to Princeton was imminent); 'comes of brooding over hanging, maybe,' was Larkin's suggestion, a reference to Amis's participation in April in a rally at the Albert Hall against capital punishment. Later in August, still without a house in Cambridge, the whole family went on holiday to Sitges, where Amis wrote to Larkin on the 14th commenting on his first bullfight, described as unbeatable 'for child-ishness, brutality and *boredom*'. The move from Swansea seems to have taken place shortly before 22 September, the date on which Amis wrote to the poet Vernon Watkins apologising for having to leave without saying goodbye and informing him that some books he'd borrowed could be collected from Stuart Thomas. This letter was written from the Mill House, West Wratting, a village twelve miles east of Cambridge in the Haverhill direction. Though the Amises had, at last, found a suitable house in Cambridge, they could not get into it for several months. The cottage they rented in the interim, on the outskirts of the village and set some distance from the road, was large, warm, comfortable, pretty and only yards from a picturesque windmill. They were there three and a half months, much of it spent by Hilly driving to and from Cambridge, for both Amis and Martin, who was now a pupil at the Cambridgeshire High School for Boys (Philip was boarding at the Friends' School in Saffron Walden and Sally attended a local private school). Hilly remembers these months as particularly difficult for the children: 'another upheaval . . . losing their friends . . . starting again'.

The house at 9 Madingley Road, almost directly across from Churchill College, was big (it had eight bedrooms) and, in Amis's phrase, 'posh'. Hilly thought it both 'handsome' and 'character-less', while also believing it was haunted, or at least that Sally's room was haunted: 'It had a funny smell once a month. Evidently awful things had happened there . . . there was a killing there or a suicide.' The house has since been demolished, though all the houses around it, comparably substantial brick villas, remain standing. The feature of the house most frequently remarked upon was its garden, the best part of an acre, Rukeyser, his old Princeton student, estimates. This garden backed on to playing fields, had elm trees, rose bushes, an extensive shrubbery, a greenhouse and a shed large enough to house a donkey named Debbie. Frohnsdorff describes a Sunday afternoon drinks party in the garden to which he took his girlfriend from London. At some point he lost sight of her in the shrubbery and was alarmed when he heard her screaming – with delight: 'she was with the children who were leading the donkey which she had been induced to ride.' Martin Amis remembers that 'it was no big thing . . . to watch my mother and our family friend Theo Richmond, both of them exhausted by laughter, riding through one of the sitting-rooms on Debbie, our pet donkey, who, every morning, would stick her head through the kitchen window and neigh along with Radio Caroline.'[48] This kitchen, where a fair bit of living took place, was large enough, Frohnsdorff remembers, to have C.P.E. Bach's 'Magnificat' playing at one end and a jazz record at the other. Frohnsdorff and his girlfriend arrived for the Sunday party to discover Amis holding court there, entertaining everyone with the Ximenes crossword (Rukeyser also remembers Amis holding court in the kitchen, imitating 'The man with the shoe fetish', a favorite routine from his 'Krafft-Ebing Suite'). Eventually, 'a number of figures in various states of undress dreamily wandered through, without introduction. It seemed they were staying that weekend, as usual.' Then the party adjourned to the patio with drinks and bottles.

One of the figures likely to have wandered into the kitchen was Amis's Princeton student Mark Rose, who drove over from Oxford most weekends in a little Morris 1000 and, forty years later, reckons 'I could still probably do the drive in my sleep.' Rose, too, remembers Debbie in the living room, and also recalls Hilly's two German shepherds, Rose and Sidney, named after his parents. The feature of the house that most impressed Mark Rose, who had already experienced an English winter, was its downstairs central heating. The behaviour at Madingley Road might be bohemian, but 'the appurtenances of living were, for Brits at that time, very middle-class, very comfortable'. Russell Fraser, over from Princeton in the summer of 1962, was also struck by how comfortable the house was, how well the Amises lived. It was at this time that Fraser realised that Amis was becoming 'more and more the grand figure'. Hilly, in contrast, remained unchanged, immune to the temptations of fame and fortune. For her the house was mostly 'quite a handful to look after'. Lis Garnett, later to become Lis Rukeyser, noticed how little furniture there was in 9 Madingley Road. The furniture from 53 Glanmor Road, a much smaller house, was scattered thinly about the new house: Hilly was too busy or distracted or disaffected to buy more, while Amis was always oblivious to such matters, as long as he had some comfortable chairs.

In order to help her with the house and the children, Hilly employed Nickie, a single mother, aged about thirty. Recently separated from her husband, she was very posh, attractive, and had a highly disturbed young son. Rumour had it that she had been homeless before she moved in with the Amises, also that she and her son had lived for some weeks in a public lavatory. 'By today's standards I'm sure she would be diagnosed as mentally ill,' Rukeyser believes. Among other peculiarities, she was convinced she had the powers of a witch. In his *Memoirs*, Amis refers to her as 'the au pair', while Philip describes her as 'a sort of posh slave'. 'She just made life easy for Hilly,' Philip explains; 'they were helping each other, both going through a rough patch together.' Martin's memories are less benign: he thought Nickie had rather an easy time of it, running the Amises' social life, giving parties for them rather than helping Hilly much with humdrum tasks and errands. Nickie had what Amis describes as 'a steady middle-aged admirer . . . universally known and addressed as Bummer (Scott)',[49] but she was generous with her favours: she slept with Rukeyser, Rukeyser's future brother-in-law, several Peterhouse students, 'the big man himself', in Rukeyser's phrase, and Philip, aged fourteen. In the *Memoirs*, Amis alludes offhandedly to her effect on the students: 'No doubt their chief reason for dropping in was to catch some of the pearls of wisdom I might be letting fall, though the attractiveness of our au pair conceivably came into it.'[50] Bummer Scott was an older man, in his sixties or early seventies, very large, often dressed in safari or military clothing. He drove a battered Land Rover and spoke beautiful English. Amis once told Rukeyser that 'if you want to know how the English language ought ideally to be spoken just listen to Bummer'. Bummer was often drunk and, as Amis puts it, 'noteworthy, too, for having an accident with his car on his way home after every visit to us without exception'.[51]

The Gales and their children were also frequent visitors to Madingley Road, when the Amises weren't visiting the Gales. Between the two households there was what Rose describes as 'a sort of floating party'. The Gales' house in Staines was actually half of a house, a grand one. Theirs was the half with the ballroom. As Amis puts it, George 'had a longing, curious in such a pub-man and sterling foe of bullshit, for baronial grandeur'.[52] Mark Rose remembers the Staines house as 'theatrical' (as well as a bit decrepit), well suited to Pat and George, both self-dramatising types; he found the Amis household 'orderly compared to the Gale household'. 'It was very wild and, I suppose, dissolute,' according to Peregrine Worsthorne, 'there were fights and so on.' The Gales, too, had an accommodating au pair, Ronnie. '*Everybody* had slept with her,' Rose remembers. One morning, after a party at which Rose ended up in bed with the au pair, he stumbled downstairs and George said amiably: 'Got a bit of Ronnie, didn't you?' This was Amis's attitude at Madingley Road.[53]

On weekend mornings at Madingley Road, there'd be a trip to the Merton Arms, the Amises' local,[54] sometimes before breakfast. Amis had a fling of some sort with a barmaid, Hilly told Mark Rose, a sixteen-year-old, and one night the barmaid stood outside 9 Madingley Road, calling up to the window for 'Billy', the name Amis used in the army and Hilly sometimes used as an endearment. The girl, Hilly told Rose, was 'like a cat in heat'; she had no idea who 'Billy' was. This was a rare disclosure from Hilly; she almost never talked to Rose about her marriage and when she did was ironic and funny about it. The person she confided in was Pat. When the house was full, Hilly and Pat would disappear for long walks with the dogs. Pat liked tension and intrigue and when it didn't exist would create it. Philip Amis describes her as 'very tricky, but great'. Pat could be fierce and frequently got on Amis's nerves: 'My father and she would fight. They would shout at each other.' But Amis admired her lack of pretension. Rose tells of one time when Pat's tooth, a false one in the front, fell out and she carried on unfazed. 'It was damaging to her beauty and I remember Kingsley saying to me "That's really impressive."'

During the Amises' two years at Cambridge Philip was at boarding-school and relieved to be away from domestic upheavals. When he came back for holidays, Madingley Road 'seemed the same as Swansea, lots of parties'. The guests at these parties remember Philip as awkward, embarrassed by the goings-on in the house, a nice boy but not an easy one. Rukeyser describes him as 'very fragile, compared to Martin'. Martin, at thirteen, was more engaged with adults, steadier, and less sensitive, 'more of a regular kid'. Frampton talked with Martin about the Campaign for Nuclear Disarmament and provided him with material to read. Martin liked talking to his father's students and friends and never seemed disturbed by the household's unconventional comings and goings: 'The house on Madingley Road differed from every other don's house in the city: students could be found in it, regularly. They stayed the night. They drove the car. They read or dozed in the garden. They made some of my meals. I enjoyed their presence.'[55] As for eight-year-old Sally, Lis Rukeyser remembers her flitting about the house, 'flying around in circles', often in costume. Frampton says she was fond of dramatic entrances. She once approached him on tiptoes, arms outstretched, announcing 'I'm going to be a ballerina. What are you going to be?' Frampton thought she might have been watching *The Philadelphia Story*, but couldn't be sure. To Rose, Sally was 'a very pretty little waif-like kid, very protected'.

Waif-like kids figure in several stories from the Amises' years at Cambridge. One of these stories, perhaps apocryphal but current at the time, concerns the Gale children.[56] As at Madingley Road, there were always strangers wandering around the Gales' house in Staines. One such stranger, a male guest still drunk from the previous night's party, got up very early in the morning to pee, then stumbled into the kitchen for something to eat. There he encountered one of the Gale children, perhaps eight, standing in front of the refrigerator. After asking the child if he was all right and learning that he was hungry, the man offered to cook him an egg. 'What's an egg?' the child replied. When Lis Rukeyser first stayed at Madingley Road in 1962, she was eighteen, a student of sculpture at Goldsmiths College in London. She had come to visit her brother, who spent a lot of time with the Amises. It was he who introduced Lis to Bill Rukeyser, whom she was to marry the next year, with Amis as best man. On a subsequent visit, Lis painted a picture of the Madingley Road scene, a surreal vision dominated by naked, mostly featureless figures, a menacing black panther, empty bottles, an overturned glass, opened tins of food, one of baked beans which somebody's hand empties on to a plate, and a constellation of disembodied faces. Chief among these faces is Pat Gale's, framed by straight black hair. Around and below her are four other faces, at least three of children (the Gales had four sons). The background is composed of black-and-white stripes and checkerboard squares, distorted in the manner of a painting by di Chirico. Lis meant the painting to convey something of the disorienting, and alarming, atmosphere of Madingley Road, at least to a girl of eighteen. The faces of the children in the painting are hard to read – watching, intent, unsmiling.

Yet there was much laughter at Madingley Road. Looking back on his friendship with Amis, Rukeyser is clear-sighted. Amis liked him, enjoyed his company, treated him as an equal, was very generous and helpful to him, and in their late-night drinking sessions taught him 'many important things, none of which I could remember in the morning'. But the friendship remained on the surface. Once when Rukeyser's brother, Louis,[57] was about to visit from the States, Amis asked Rukeyser: 'Is he like you?' As Rukeyser considered the question, Amis cut in: 'Is he like you? Does he drink? Is he jolly?' This was the level at which Amis interacted with most of his friends. 'You were not going to unburden yourself of your innermost feelings,' Rukeyser recalls, 'that wasn't the way it went. Once you accepted this rather heavy price, he gave excellent value.' The pub sessions, long lunches, hilarious breakfasts, wild parties, jokes, imitations and routines 'were the most entertaining of the twentieth century'. Amis tells several very funny stories about parties at Madingley Road, including one in which Anthony Powell dances with the wife of the Cambridge poet Burns Singer, 'a very black black girl with an unreconstructed Mississippi accent who was a fully qualified psychiatrist, or perhaps psychologist, with a practice in London and an intense and vocal interest in her subject'.[58] Perhaps the best of the stories, though, if not the likeliest, concerns Powell's 'often hugely drunk' friend John Davenport, who lived at Duxford, below Trumpington:

I never saw John Davenport dance, but we did have him to the house, on one occasion to have dinner (and get pissed) and stay the night, reasoning cogently that Duxford was too far from Cambridge for him to put us on his list of those who might be advantageously dropped in on in future. During the evening he popped out to the outside lavatory, adjusting his hair, tie, etc., in the mirror formed by the window of an adjacent hut. Unknown to him, the hut contained the family's pet donkey, Debbie by name, who looked inquisitively out at him. Hilly thought she heard a faint scream as John presumably took Debbie's face for a reflection of his own.

He rushed back indoors asking wildly what had happened to his face, and had to be shown Debbie directly before he could be calmed.[59]

Thursdays were Amis's days to visit London, where he lunched with Conquest and other friends, appeared on radio programmes and conducted affairs. On 2 October 1961, after the return of the Moynahans to Princeton, Conquest wrote to Larkin that Amis was 'in fine form, and entering a new sex life . . . He explains that he needs a new girl to take his mind off the one that's just gone.' On the 13th Conquest wrote again, and Amis added a paragraph of his own: 'I'm up in Town sponging on Bob, or at least that's what I had in mind. Unfortunately the young lady had an attack of conscience or something like that at the last minute.' As for his initial impressions of Cambridge: 'I'm not sure I shall be able to take Cantab, actually. Like Oxford only full of shits you don't know instead of shits you do.' On 12 December Conquest wrote to tell Larkin about the way Amis's girlfriends left his flat littered with earrings, compacts, etc., 'which my girls then take offence at'. On 11 January he reported: 'a visit from KWA yesterday has left everyone a little ragged'. In addition to carousing in London and Cambridge almost as punishingly as he had in New York and Princeton, Amis was working flat out. Though his contact time as a lecturer at Peterhouse amounted to only nine hours a week, the syllabus for the Tripos obliged him to prepare a number of new subjects and authors: 'It had not occurred to me before that Aristotle was an English moralist or that a knowledge of later foreigners and other-worlders was necessary to an understanding of the English drama.'[60] Amis was also under pressure from his publisher. In order to purchase 9 Madingley Road, he had been obliged to solicit what his agent, Graham Watson, called a 'huge loan' from Gollancz, an advance of £5,000 for two books: a volume of stories (*My Enemy's Enemy*) to be delivered in the summer of 1962, and a novel (*One Fat Englishman*) to be delivered in the summer of 1963.[61] Early in 1962, Hilly wrote to Mike and Mary Keeley apologising for Amis's silences and explaining their plans for the coming summer. Amis was exhausted from overwork, which is why he hadn't written. Though he needed a holiday 'more than any bugger I've met for a long time', they would not be coming to the States that summer, as vaguely planned. Hilly was pregnant and by the summer would be unable to travel. The baby was due in early September, which means it was conceived the December before. As for Amis coming by himself, 'you know how it is . . . he doesn't like the idea of travelling alone (no fun)'. Hilly's letter was undated but addressed from Madingley Road, which the Amises moved into in early January 1962. The letter is the only printed reference I have found to the pregnancy. Shortly after Hilly wrote it, she had an abortion, at Amis's insistence.

It is in *One Fat Englishman* that one glimpses something of the toll Amis's relentless pursuit of 'fun' was taking, mostly on himself as opposed to others (in *Take a Girl Like You*, in contrast, Jenny's inner life is looked at as closely as Patrick's). Roger Micheldene, the novel's rebarbative hero, is an English publisher visiting Budweiser College (a thinly disguised Princeton)[62] ostensibly in pursuit of new authors. Roger is forty years old, Amis's age at the time he was working on the novel, weighs sixteen stone and is in reality in pursuit of Helene Bang, wife of the amiable Danish philologist Ernst Bang, a visiting professor at Budweiser. Roger is a cartoon-like character, but the novel he presides over is cartoon-like, a thinly textured comic satire, more like early Waugh than *Take a Girl Like You*. 'Of the seven deadly sins,' we learn in its first chapter, 'Roger considered himself qualified in gluttony, sloth and lust but distinguished in anger.'[63] This anger he bestows indiscriminately: 'It was his habit . . . to blaze away at any human target that might move across his sights, as many a London waiter, hotel servant and telephone operator could have testified.'[64] Russell Fraser tells a story of having lunch with Amis at the Garden House Hotel in Cambridge in 1962. Amis arrived in an open-necked shirt, to sniffy looks from 'the stuffy patrons and stuffier waiters'. The sommelier showed him the wine list, 'murmuring a benediction in French. "I'll have the Graves," Kingsley told him, pronounced to rhyme with "waves." Lifting his glass, he sniffed, tasted, and spat the wine on the table. "Very good," he said.'[65] In *One Fat Englishman*, Roger calls a waiter over after ordering an expensive cigar. 'Staring woundingly into the waiter's eyes', he crushes out the cigar after only a few puffs: 'in the ensuing hush . . . without any rancour', he explains to the waiter that the wrapper had been cracked, the head imperfect. The violence of Roger's gesture, together with the management's distressed and rejected offer 'of any other cigar he fancied', makes him feel good: 'As he talked he had felt great waves of power flooding in towards him.'[66] Later, when warned that he's about to say something he'll be sorry for, he replies: 'those are the only things I really enjoy saying'.[67] In lovemaking, he prefers his partner to be silent: 'What this vocal accompaniment did was to distract him from that total absorption in his own sensations which he required from what he was now doing.'[68] Amis makes only perfunctory efforts to illustrate Roger's gluttony and sloth, but they are communicated indirectly, through his lust, which is both greedy and lazy, impatient of the other person's needs and feelings.

Roger, like Patrick, knows how horrible he is. As Amis puts it, 'being a bastard and realizing it is a kind of cross he bears'.[69] When Helene, whom he seems actually to love, proves evasive in conversation, 'a part of Roger – one of which the rest of him on the whole disapproved – wanted to step forward and give [her] a medium-weight slap across the chops'.[70] Roger is a lapsed Catholic and on the rare occasions when he addresses God in prayer he does so in a bullying, bartering fashion. It is God's fault that he's angry all the time, for surrounding him with bastards and bloody fools. If, though, God will help him out with Helene, 'I'll take her away and marry her, or else I'll stop seeing her. Either way I shan't be going on like this, which I agree is very bad.'[71] It is Helene who asks Roger, 'What is it about women that makes you want them?'[72] But she asks other questions as well: 'What's the matter with you, Roger?', 'Why are you always like this?', 'What makes you behave this way?', 'Why are you so awful?'[73]

Roger offers several answers. The first involves his father and social class. 'I think a frightful lot of it's tied up with being a snob, you know. Very angst-producing business, being a snob. No time to relax and take things easy. You have to be on duty all the time, as it were.'[74] Roger traces his snobbery to his father, who went to Charterhouse and Magdalen College, Oxford, but was the son of a man in trade. 'No little sod ever had it easier,' he says of his father. 'He didn't make the money. It was his father who'd done that. Magnificent old boy. Screwed a quarter of a million quid out of the peasantry in twenty years by flogging them bloody awful crockery and glass ware as he called it. Learned to drink claret and fish salmon and ride to hounds and adored it.'[75] Roger's father never did anything in his life because 'doing anything was what the lower classes did'. He wouldn't have pictures in his house – his father bought Courbets and Delacroixs – 'because parvenus do that'. He wouldn't marry a débutante because 'night-club owners and toy-balloon manufacturers do that'. So he squandered his father's fortune, leaving Roger to inherit only his flaws: social insecurity, selfishness, spite. There was no Charterhouse for Roger: 'Berkhamsted was good enough for me, he thought.' Roger admits that this explanation goes only so far, but then 'I've got to blame someone for what I'm like, haven't I?'[76]

Roger's snobbery functions as an antidote to his observations about America. That the Americans he encounters barely notice or are merely amused by his snubs and snooty put-downs, makes him splutter. Christopher Ricks thinks the aggression in *One Fat Englishman* is Swiftian: 'it is less a novel than a trap' (that is, for the reader); 'few books have been written quite so insinuatingly about, and to elicit prejudice'.[77] But it is Roger, not the reader, Amis means to torment, from his opening humiliation by the poolside (where he swelters in his tweeds, too fat to expose himself in a bathing suit) to the final discovery aboard the ship back to England that he will be cabined with the drunken Strode Atkins, like Tony Last stuck in the Amazon at the end of Waugh's *A Handful of Dust*, McDermott's astute parallel.[78] Roger, as David Lodge has argued, is 'full of self-hatred'. Amis was not Roger – wasn't yet fat, was never a social snob, adored America (certainly at the time the novel was being written) – but he had Roger-like tendencies. That self-hatred was one of these tendencies his treatment of Roger suggests (the circularity of the argument notwithstanding). One way of understanding what was about to happen in Amis's life is to see him at a sort of dead end, the sort to which Roger is brought at the novel's conclusion.

Roger's dead end is no mere matter of snobbery. He is in despair, a condition implicit in his excesses but also explicitly diagnosed. This diagnosis Amis puts in the mouth of the college priest, Father Colgate, whom Roger initially dismisses as a 'dog-collared buffoon'.[79] Father Colgate claims he can 'detect infallibly the signs of a soul at variance with God. You, my son, are very gravely disturbed. You are in acute spiritual pain – the infallible sign of a soul at variance with God.' He also says: 'A man does not act like a child unless his soul is hurting him. Your soul is hurting you, Mr Micheldene.'[80] That Roger acts like a child is obvious. He acts like a baby. As Helene puts it, just after they've made love: 'Why do you want to do this so much? . . . I didn't mean with me personally, I meant with everybody. That's who you really want, isn't it? Everybody?'[81] Roger wants to swallow the world, like an infant raging for the breast, an analogy that might have sent this book sailing across the room had he or Amis been able to read it. Neither had much time for what Roger calls 'that Oedipus piffle',[82] let alone 'pre-Oedipal piffle'. But Roger's rage, aggression and greed are like those attributed by psychoanalytic theorists to preverbal infancy. The aetiology and sequencing these theorists ascribe to such rage, aggression and greed may be bizarre and unpersuasive, but the conviction that they are ultimately fuelled by the fear of death strikes a chord. To the shrinks, this fear is a product of the infant's projection of its destructive feelings on to the world, feelings which can persist beyond infancy. Amis's adult fear of death, like Roger's, he explains as a matter of simple observation: death is an objective fact, like unmerited suffering; there is reason to be fearful and if God exists, He is to be hated.[83] In the novels that follow, Amis focuses on this fear and its causes with a new directness, taking emotional as well as formal risks. In his life, too, he seeks out new paths, as if the old ones, Roger's ones, were leading inexorably to Roger's end.

19

Waking Beauty

At this point Robert Graves makes an entrance. Amis had been in contact with Graves in 1954, when on 2 October he wrote a teasing letter about an article Graves had published in *Punch* on 8 September. In this article, entitled 'Varro's Four Hundred and Ninety Books', Graves complains of successful authors 'who somehow manage to reduce output to ten words a day (which means a novel of average length every two years)'. Amis leapt gleefully on these figures, pointing out 'that ten words a day for two years will only give you a 7,300-word novel, which is a good deal under average length even these days'. The letter ended: 'Must stop now and write my word for the day. I plan to bring out a *conte* every 20 years.' Graves could take a joke and wrote a friendly postcard back. In *Experience* Martin Amis recounts a similarly tolerant response, in 1968, to teasing in person. When told to treat the seventy-three-year-old Graves 'as if he's a god', Martin's cheeky friend Rob initiated the following exchange. The setting was Deya, a dramatic hillside village in Majorca. The poet and his youthful, unannounced visitors had only just met:

The five of us looked out on the rocky acres – spurs and tors, terraces, arthritic olive trees. Then Rob said to Robert,
   — Make that mountain open up.
   — What?
   — Turn it into a volcano.
   — What?

— Go on. You can do it. Make that cloud go away.
— Oh, you're—
— Summon a tidal wave.
— You little—
— Make the moon come out.
— Ooh, you—
— Make the—
And Robert got hold of Rob and roughly tickled him.[1]

Graves's unoffended postcard to Amis elicited a generous fan letter, written on 25 October. After cautioning the great man 'not to take that "movement" stuff in the *Spectator* too seriously', Amis declared that 'for my money you're the best poet now writing in English . . . all my friends agree on how good you are'. He also claimed Graves as an influence on his own poems: 'Reading you has done such poems as I've written a power of good.' Graves's influence on Amis's poetry was obvious. When Larkin described Amis in 1964 as an 'utterly original' poet, he added the qualification, 'when he's being himself, not when he's Robert Graves'.[2]

The appeal of Graves's poems to Amis and 'all my friends', by which in 1954 he is likely to have meant Larkin, Conquest and Wain, is not difficult to understand. In his love poems, Graves combines intense feeling, both erotic and romantic, with a cool, dry, sardonic manner; in his early war poems, he is similarly passionate and controlled. From the 1950s onwards Graves had set his face against modernist tendencies, a rejection which Movement polemicists applauded. In the preface to *New Lines 2* (1963) Conquest used Graves to suggest that modernist innovations were beginning to look like 'peripheral additions to the main tradition of English poetry'; in the same year, in the introduction to his *Anthology of Modern Poetry*, Wain cited Graves to support the view that modernism was now 'old-fashioned', a position also argued by D.J. Enright in 1960, in an article entitled 'Robert Graves and the Decline of Modernism'. Blake Morrison, from whom these instances have been culled, stresses another factor in Graves's appeal to Amis and his friends: the debunking, unmasking impulse that shapes his poems, one which occupies 'a large, indeed an unduly large, place in Movement poetry'. Being less deceived was a Movement ideal; by Morrison's calculation, 'over half the poems in Amis's *A Case of Samples*, for example, make it their duty to expose the gap between a purported and an actual truth, and a good many of these are indebted to Graves'.³

Amis's high opinion of Graves continued throughout his life. In the *Memoirs*, he describes the effect Graves's poetry had on him in terms that recall the effect Hardy had on Larkin: 'that of encouraging you to write a poem yourself'.⁴ In *The Amis Anthology* (1988), his 'personal choice of English verse', Graves is represented by twelve poems, the same number as Larkin and one fewer than Housman, who has more poems in the volume than anyone else, but the selection contains no poems about 'all that Muse and Moon and Goddess and White Goddess stuff'.⁵ From the first, in Oxford after the war, Amis and his fellow admirers sought out the 'disenchanted' rather than the 'enchanted' Graves. For them, Graves's mysticism was detachable from the poems that mattered, partially listed by Amis in the *Memoirs* as 'Recalling War', 'The Cuirassiers of the Frontier', 'Love in Barrenness'.⁶ More surprising omissions from Amis's selection are the icy 'Counting the Beats', singled out by Larkin as a sign of the poet's 'continual readiness to try for new effects'⁷ and the much-anthologised 'Down, Wanton, Down!' in which desire is chided in terms that recall the Amis of the 1950s:

> Down, wanton, down! Have you no shame
> That at the whisper of Love's name,
> Or Beauty's, presto! Up you raise
> Your angry head and stand at gaze?
>
> Poor bombard-captain, sworn to reach
> The ravelin and effect a breach –
> Indifferent what you storm or why,
> So be that in the breach you die!
>
> Love may be blind, but Love at least
> Knows what is man and what mere beast;
> . . .

On 17 December 1961, soon after settling in Cambridge, Amis chose Graves's *More Poems, 1961* as one of his *Observer* 'Books of the Year', describing his poetry as 'helplessly original', the sort that 'never gets near taking into account anyone else's, past or present'. Yet formally Graves was a traditionalist. 'Make new metres by all means,' he advised Wilfred Owen in 1917, 'but one must observe the rules where they are laid down by custom of centuries.'[8] Like Amis, Graves was trained in the classics; he, too, revered Housman, their St John's predecessor. Graves also deplored poetical obscurity, carefully distinguishing it from controlled doubleness or equivocacy, a virtue he forwards in his Shakespearean criticism, identified by Empson as the inspiration for *Seven Types of Ambiguity*.[9] When young poets came to Graves for advice, according to Miranda Seymour, one of his biographers, 'they found an honest critic with a nose for nonsense. Gentle on minor defects of rhyme or metre, he was blunt about the need for absolute clarity.'[10]

After their exchange of letters in 1954 there seems to have been no further contact between Amis and Graves until the summer of 1962. In May of that year Amis received a commission from Robert M. Wool, editor of *Show* magazine, an American periodical, to write a profile of Graves. This commission came through Cindy Degner of the New York office of Curtis Brown and the fee offered was $800 plus travel expenses. Amis accepted the commission partly because the fee was generous enough to allow him to bring the whole family to Deya – the visit would be a holiday as well as an assignment – and partly because he admired and was intrigued by Graves. 'What did he think he was doing,' Amis asks in the *Memoirs*, recalling his thoughts in 1962, 'stuck away in Majorca like that since 1929 and the age of thirty-four (with ten years' involuntary absence from 1936 to 1946)? To have made a permanent departure from England was a most unusual step in those days for a healthy heterosexual not wanted for fraud.'[11]

In June 1962 Graves travelled to Oxford to deliver the Creweian Oration, one of his duties as Professor of Poetry at Oxford (a post to which he had been elected in 1961, for five years). Amis and Hilly arranged to meet him for lunch, that same day dropping in on Mark Rose. The Amises and Graves hit it off immediately and though Graves was usually reluctant to be 'profiled' by journalists and no great champion of younger writers (at least those in print), he pronounced Amis 'one of the few non-phoneys', someone it would be fun to have around.[12] An August visit was arranged and on 10 July, after Graves had returned home, Amis wrote with specific travel plans. He, Hilly and the children would be arriving at Palma, the island's capital, on 12 August and leaving nine days later, on the 21st. Graves was the only person they knew in Majorca. Could he recommend a place to stay? Graves himself lived on the eastern edge of Deya in a house he had designed and built in the local style, with rough-hewn limestone slabs and a tiled roof. He also owned an old house in the centre of the village, at the top of a hill next to the church. This house, La Posada, was 'handsome but decrepit',[13] with an outdoor privy shared with the Graveses' donkey, Isabella. The Amises would be right at home.

Hilly remembers Graves as 'great fun and a very good one for Kingsley to look up to for a change, because he was very distinguished and wild at the same time'. To thirteen-year-old Martin, sullen, self-conscious and 'tubby', Graves seemed the archetypal 'warrior-poet', tall, angular, with a 'thousand-mile stare' and a 'loose-limbed physicality': 'I remember him scaling the rocks that leaned up from the sandless shore[14] – and bounding over them as he came back the other way and leapt flailing into the water.'[15] Hilly's most vivid image of this first visit to Deya is of Amis puffing to keep up with Graves in their daily walks, usually down and up the wooded ravine that led to the beach, a twenty-minute hike. Amis and Graves would work in the mornings and swim or walk in the afternoons, the often unshaven Graves attired in shorts, low socks, a white, short-sleeved shirt and a broad-brimmed Majorcan hat, a rare 'bardic touch', as Amis puts it in the *Memoirs*. 'His often mentioned air of authority was clearly evident but with it went an open, friendly air less noted. His conversation turned out to be humorous, inquisitive, warm and surprisingly down-to-earth.'[16]

Graves and his wife Beryl had three sons (William, 22, Juan, 18, and Tomas, 9) and a daughter (Lucia, 19), all in residence that August. To Hilly, the sons were almost as 'marvellous-looking, amazing' as their father. The daughter was also good-looking, judging by the Irving Penn photograph accompanying Amis's *Show* article. What the sons remember of the Amises was their car, a rented Volkswagen station wagon, rolling off the paved drive into a ditch, a mishap experienced by other visitors, including Alan Sillitoe.[17] The two families, plus Karl Gay (né Goldschmidt), Graves's secretary-cum-assistant, pitched in to get the car back on to the drive. Juan, a budding musician and photographer, also recalls a drunken evening in which Amis sang blues, 'not at all badly'. William, recently returned from studying in the States, remembers Amis as impressed by how cheap the liquor was in Deya and by Robert's discipline as a writer. There was something to be said for a life without students, high table feasts, hectic parties, even a telephone, though this was not to say that Graves was a recluse who lacked a social life. He worked all day and held court in the evenings, 'innocently basking in admiration' from family and friends, including any number of 'hangers-on, droppers-in',[18] 'artists' and 'musicians' of a sort Deya has always attracted. Graves first came to Deya at the end of the 1920s with the American poet Laura Riding, his collaborator and first 'Muse'. The village had been recommended to Riding by Gertrude Stein and Alice B. Toklas.

Amis was surprisingly attracted to Graves's way of life on Deya. He was even tolerant of the Graves circle. What impressed him most was the eight-foot row of books – novels, volumes of poetry, essays, criticism, biographies, books for children – above the poet's desk, all written by Graves himself. Since coming to Cambridge less than a year earlier, Amis had been working flat out, but on journalism, teaching and a collection of stories (sent to Gollancz on 19 June, on schedule). He had written almost no verse and very little of his novel, *One Fat Englishman*. In the *Show* article he contrasts Graves's writerly existence with one very like his own: 'Graves is just not available for the television appearances, the publishers' cocktail parties and writing of book reviews for the popular press, the giving of one's views on anything from artificial insemination to Zoroastrianism which, for many people, constitute the major part of the literary life, and the more enjoyable part, too.'[19] Amis also contrasts Graves's social life with his own. By the summer of 1962, Amis's social life, including his romantic life, had grown almost as frenetic as it had been at Princeton, which is to say, almost as distracting and exhausting. For Graves, the 'centre of existence' was his desk, where he wrote in undisturbed comfort (had Amis come in winter he might well have revised this opinion). Though the Graves circle was small, its entertainments were free of the formalities and affectations Amis found increasingly restricting and irritating in Cambridge. On the night the Amises arrived from Palma, Graves greeted their slowly approaching car by wandering into the beam of its headlights: though they were two hours late, he had simply guessed they were due, walked up to the main road and found them. Then he hoisted Sally on to his shoulders and led the way to an outdoor party, illuminated by candles and 'the most brilliant moonlight imaginable'.[20] The Amises were introduced to the Graves family and friends, helped to say good-night to a troupe of local musicians, and were soon plied with what Amis describes in the *Show* article as pizza, hot dogs and local red wine. What was left of the party continued well into the night, with folk songs, guitar playing and easy talk. It was the perfect welcome.

Amis suspected that Graves's jaundiced views of his fellow poets derived from a dislike of competition, which 'may have played its part in his decision to leave England'. It was obvious that Graves 'liked, if not to dominate, at least to be top man'.[21] Amis had no fear of competition, at least at this point in his life, but he, too, had top-man tendencies. It is a measure of how attractive he found Graves and his life that he felt a desire not only to live like him but 'perhaps even . . . to be one of his court'.[22] In the months that followed the August visit, a plan evolved for Amis to resign his fellowship at Peterhouse and for the family to spend a year in Majorca, not in Deya but in Soller, a bigger town, further north along the coast road. They would move at the end of the academic year. 'I was all for it,' Hilly recalls, though in retrospect she thinks 'I must have been mad thinking he would stick it.' She now sees the move as a sign of the coming dissolution of their marriage: 'We were both on the verge of what happened, really, without fully coming to terms with it. We thought another change might . . .' What? Bring them together? Block out old habits and hurts? 'It was silly thinking, really.'[23]

But the visit to Deya was energising. Soon after returning to Cambridge, Amis wrote to Graves, on 4 September, to tell him, 'I've been fired by your example to attempt an 8 a.m. start to the writing day. Difficult, though. Bloody things like seeing bank managers, rescuing neurotics (Christ, what sort of slack do they think *I* have?) etc. keep getting in the way.' Nevertheless he had produced a new poem (for the 'Evans' sequence) and 'another dozen are queuing up'. Also heartening was the imminent arrival of Bill Rukeyser, nominally to write a dissertation on D.H. Lawrence. Rukeyser's supervisor, Graham Hough, was a Fellow in English at Christ's. 'One piquant feature of the situation,' Amis had written to Rukeyser on 20 June, was 'that Hough hates me ("Fellow like that shouldn't be here," was his reported comment), and so, I suppose can't have known of your connection with me when he accepted you'. Just before term began the news of John McAndrew's death reached the Amises. Eve and Stuart Thomas were staying at Madingley Road at the time and Eve remembers Stuart and a distraught Amis waking her – the two men had been up drinking – to announce that 'something terrible has happened. Hilly's lover has just died in Princeton.' After cabling Jean McAndrew with his and Hilly's love and an invitation to 'COME OVER IMMEDIATELY WITH KIDS' Amis sat down on 26 September to write a letter of commiseration, reiterating the invitation and calling John McAndrew 'one of my closest and dearest friends'. A week later he and Hilly set off for Cheltenham, where he was to take part in the town's annual Literary Festival. Amis had been written to in July by the festival organiser, Elizabeth Jane Howard, who professed herself delighted to hear that he would be coming and bringing his wife.

In fact, Jane Howard was anything but delighted. Not because she disliked Amis or his wife, but because he had been invited without her knowledge. The invitation had come from the recently launched *Sunday Telegraph*, which had agreed to offer £1,500 to sponsor a panel at the festival, a coup for Jane, as previously the festival had attracted little sponsorship. The topic chosen for the panel by the paper's editor, Donald McLachlan, who would act as its chair, was 'Sex in Literature'. The speakers Jane had recruited were the French novelist Romain Gary, an ex-lover, and the American novelists Joseph Heller and Carson McCullers. When Jane discovered that the *Sunday Telegraph* had also invited Amis, she was furious: four speakers were too many for a panel; Amis was an 'Angry Young Man' and 'would think the whole thing was silly';[24] as festival director, it was her job to pick speakers, or at least to be consulted about them. Her protests were fruitless: Amis could not be disinvited; if she insisted, it was implied, sponsorship would be withdrawn. Jane appealed to Peregrine Worsthorne, her cousin and the *Sunday Telegraph*'s deputy editor; he, too, argued that the paper could not go back on its word.

In 1962 the Cheltenham Literary Festival was neither as big nor as well known as it is today. It had almost no money, and lukewarm support from the local community. Jane played an important role in the development of the festival and worked for eight months to raise its profile, for a director's fee of £300 plus expenses. She was innovative, well organised, full of energy and well connected. When the Arts Council appointed her, in February 1961, she was thirty-seven years old, the author of three successful novels: *The Beautiful Visit* (1950), which won the John Llewellyn Rhys Prize, *The Long View* (1956), a Book Society Choice, and *The Sea Change*

(1959), described by Amis's friend John Davenport in the *Observer* as 'a triumph'. These books had established her as a serious novelist with commercial appeal, a description that fitted Amis as well. In addition, she was known to the wider public through frequent appearances on radio and television, as an interviewer and critic. Charming, funny and extremely good-looking, with high cheekbones, waist-length blonde hair and long, shapely legs, Jane was handsome in her beauty and could also be imperious and haughty, often, she now explains, out of shyness. When she and Amis met at Cheltenham – they had met previously in passing, in television studios in London and once also when she was with Kenneth Tynan – she was on her second unhappy marriage, with a string of affairs behind her, mostly with married men, including the writers Laurie Lee, Arthur Koestler and Cecil Day-Lewis as well as Tynan and Romain Gary. As her memoirs make clear, in part because of how much attention they devote to it, romantic love had always been for Jane 'the most important thing in the world',[25] 'the most desirable, the most important of human emotions'.[26] Yet she had long thought of herself as 'incapable of sustaining, inspiring or receiving it'.[27] She attributes this sense of inadequacy to her mother, from whom she never got 'what I wanted – the kind of uncritical affection that transcends everyday mishaps, arguments or wrong-doing on my part. Now, I think she made efforts to love me, but she couldn't do anything without criticism, and I suspect she experienced it herself from *her* mother.'[28] For all her beauty, talent and accomplishments, Jane often felt insecure and inadequate and was much given to self-pity.

Jane's background was upper middle class and prosperous. The family money came from a timber business, Howard Brothers, founded after the First World War by her paternal grandfather, Alexander Howard, jokingly nicknamed 'the Brig', because he'd never been in the army. Jane and her two younger brothers, Robin and Colin, grew up in a house in Lansdowne Road in Holland Park, near the home of their maternal grandparents, Sir Arthur Somervell, a composer and music educationalist, and his wife, Edith, a woman of wide culture who spoiled Jane 'with a magnificent carelessness that I thoroughly appreciated'.[29] Jane's mother, Katherine, trained as a dancer and spent just over a year with Diaghilev's Ballets Russes in Paris and Rome. It was in Rome that she met David Howard, Jane's father. When they decided to marry, the Brig insisted that Katherine give up dancing; upper-middle-class wives, like lower-middle-class wives, were not meant to work or have careers, certainly not as dancers. So Katherine gave up dancing, a decision she came bitterly to regret, and 'took to middle-class married life with more money than she'd ever had before, servants, a house to keep'.³⁰ Her new life also included family holidays and weekends in East Sussex, first at the Brig's house, Home Place, then at the Beacon, near Staplecross, a Victorian Gothic mansion the Brig bought in 1929 for the use of his children and their families. Jane remembers the Beacon as filled with cousins, often at least a dozen, as well as aunts, uncles, parents, brothers and friends. If Amis loved company and a house full of people because he had not had them when young, Jane loved them because she had. Throughout their seventeen years together they always lived with other people, not just Amis's children, for differing periods, but with Colin, Colin's friend Sargy Mann, Jane's mother and assorted friends.

Jane has thinly fictionalised her background in the novels of the Cazalet tetralogy – *The Light Years* (1990), *Marking Time* (1991), *Confusion* (1993) and *Casting Off* (1995). How thinly is made clear by her memoirs, which are startlingly frank and unblushing, beginning with their account of her relations with her father. David Howard, the model for Edward Cazalet in the novels, was a major before the age of twenty-one and a war hero. He won the Military Cross and Bar and was recommended for the Victoria Cross. After the war he entered the family firm and, though not much of a businessman, 'loved meeting people; he loved buying and selling wood'.³¹ Jane calls him 'one of the most gregarious people I have ever known, totally uncritical of any company he kept'; 'at the slightest encouragement' he behaved 'as though it was his birthday'.³² Women 'fell for him like rows of shingled ninepins'.³³ When Jane turned fifteen her father suddenly stopped treating her as a child.³⁴ After several assaults – kisses, fondlings – Jane learned to avoid being alone with him. She told no one about his behaviour, partly out of shame, and when she refused to reciprocate his ordinary affection 'incurred my mother's displeasure'.³⁵ The sense of shame her father's behaviour evoked in Jane partly derived from her mother, who looked with distaste on matters sexual. 'From her demeanour and attitude to it,' Jane writes of her mother, 'it was clear that she had never enjoyed sex.'³⁶ Between her father's advances and her mother's example, it is no wonder that Jane had problems in this area: from the time she was fifteen, 'the signals I received from my parents were that sex, or anything to do with the body, was disgusting and that sex in any explicit form was horrible. This was to influence the next thirty years of my life.'[37] Until, that is, the mid-1960s, when 'awoken' or 'rescued' by Amis. From this point, as we shall see, images of rescue and awakening appear prominently in Amis's poems and novels.

In 1962 Jane's life was as much in need of change as Amis's and had been for years. She had married for the first time in 1942, at nineteen, Peter Scott, aged thirty-three, the son of Captain Robert Falcon Scott, the Antarctic explorer. They had met in spring 1940 when Jane was about to enter drama school in London. Before joining the navy Scott had established a career as a successful painter, particularly of wildfowl, and he had also gained fame as a prize-winning yachtsman.[38] During the war he would prove himself a hero, fighting in destroyers throughout the Battle of the Atlantic, mentioned three times in dispatches, and winning the Distinguished Service Cross twice. His formidable mother, Kathleen Scott, Lady Kennet, had known Jane's mother since the First World War. In February 1943, Jane, still nineteen, gave birth to a daughter, Nicola. Scott loved Jane but her feelings for him were complicated, less certain.[39] In addition, the sex part of the marriage was unsatisfactory for her from the start: Scott 'never realised I had no idea about my own sexuality and that my continuing ignorance of it might prove a danger to us both'.[40] They had acrimonious rows 'about my dislike of bed', and when eventually these died down Jane suspected he was seeing another woman.[41] In her loneliness – Scott was often away on naval postings early in the marriage – and 'great hunger to be loved, to *be* in love',[42] she had several affairs, including one with Scott's stepbrother, Wayland Hilton-Young, later Lord Kennet. When Scott learned of this affair – the guilt-ridden couple confessed – 'he bedded me doggedly every single night, which I found more and more unbearable. I remember once . . . saying that he was digging his own grave'.[43] The marriage lasted four years. Jane left in 1946, aged twenty-three, determined to become a writer. Though her original ambition in life had been to be an actress, soon after her marriage it was supplanted by an ambition to write; like Amis, she had been writing since childhood. In both ambitions she had been encouraged by her unusual education. After the age of twelve[44] she was educated at home by a private tutor, Miss Cobham, who had been her mother's governess. She also had a music teacher, a series of French governesses, and separate drawing, riding and needlework lessons. Jane and her fellow pupils – the daughter of a neighbour up the road, the daughter of a doctor who lived and worked in Malaysia, the son of her piano teacher – spent many happy hours with Miss Cobham acting out plays, reading novels, writing stories, poems and short dramatic scenes, and memorising verse, though Miss Cobham also 'contrived to slip in some history (dates), geography (exports), arithemetic (we didn't get beyond fractions), plus a smattering of Latin and Greek'.[45] In some ways, it was an idyllic education; only later in life did Jane come to regret that she had not been more conventionally schooled or gone to university. She lacked discipline as a writer, she felt, a failing she partly attributed to her education: 'I'd never had to swot for exams, write essays to order, read books I'd found difficult.'[46]

Discipline was not Jane's problem in 1946, when she left Scott. 'I was selfishly determined to be a writer at any cost, to put it first, and I knew that I had to do it alone'[47] – that is, without three-year-old Nicola and her nanny, who remained behind in the family house at 8 Edwardes Square, Kensington. The decision to live alone Jane later saw as 'ill-judged and certainly selfish', but at the time 'I couldn't handle nursery life with what my own had become.' Eventually, after Scott gave up the Edwardes Square house, Nicola and the nanny moved in with a friend who had a child of similar age and Jane visited 'every week, miserably aware of how unsatisfactory this was and guilty'.[48] Nicola never again lived with her mother, though Jane was always in touch, took care of practicalities, overseeing her education, holidays and doctors' visits. As a friend put it: 'you do all the dull things that mothers have to do with their children, but you never have any fun with her'.[49] During the years Jane lived with Amis, guilt about Nicola, as well as inexperience as a full-time mother, doubtless complicated her inevitably tricky relations with Philip, Martin and Sally. That Nicola's name appears nowhere in Amis's correspondence during the years he and Jane lived together is worth remarking.

Once Jane moved out of Edwardes Square, it took her three years to finish *The Beautiful Visit*. She took no money from Scott, except for Nicola's expenses, supporting herself by work as a secretary, a continuity announcer at the BBC, a publisher's reader and copy-editor, notably for Chatto and Windus, a journalist, eventually as regular book reviewer for *Queen* magazine, and a model for *Vogue* (at three guineas a day). A year after she left Scott, her father released shares to her amounting to some £100 a year, the extent of the financial support she received from her family. The first publisher to whom she sent *The Beautiful Visit* was Jonathan Cape, and they accepted it within three weeks. After admiring notices from Antonia White and Francis Wyndham, among others, Jane was invited by Siriol Hugh-Jones, later Amis's early champion, to write for *Vogue*; other useful commissions followed. Her second novel, *The Long View*, took four years to write, and its success expanded what was already a glamorous circle of acquaintance. She was taken up by Stephen and Natasha Spender, met Cyril Connolly, Olivia Manning, Stevie Smith and Ivy Compton-Burnett. Her agent, A.D. Peters, perhaps the most respected literary agent in London, introduced her to the novelist Alec Waugh, Evelyn's brother, and the novelist and biographer Margaret Lane, whose husband, Jack Huntingdon, was a talented mural painter, Labour politician and earl. Other publishers courted her, including Hamish Hamilton, who introduced her to Princess Marina of Kent, Somerset Maugham and Cass Canfield, head of Harper & Row. While working at the BBC she became friends with Jill Balcon, the daughter of the film producer Michael Balcon, who gave her work at Ealing Studios. Through Jill she met Cecil Day-Lewis, with whom she had a brief affair in 1958 – 'one of the worst things I did in my life', as he and Jill had been married since 1951.[50] (One way to understand Jane's behaviour in this instance is to accept how romantic her ideas of love were: 'I wasn't able, then, to recognise that such things need not happen if they are resisted in the first place; I thought they simply struck one – like lightning – and that one had no choice.')[51] Jane also stayed in touch with people she had met through Peter Scott and the Kennet family, including Malcolm Sargent and Joyce Grenfell. It is typical of Jane's life that Paul Scofield was among the small number of her fellow pupils at drama school and later in student rep in Devon.

It was through Laurens and Ingrid Van der Post that Jane was introduced to her second husband, the Australian journalist and broadcaster James Douglas-Henry. They married in 1958, the year of the Day-Lewis affair. Douglas-Henry was charming, funny, attractive and had no visible means of support. When he discovered that Jane had less money than he thought she had, he turned against her. Jane wanted babies with Douglas-Henry, felt she was at last ready to be a proper mother, but after they were married he claimed she wasn't fit to have his children. From the first he was unfaithful: 'he was always going to bed with very rich middle-aged women'. Jane was certain that if anyone richer had turned up and wanted to marry him 'he'd have been off in a shot'. Yet he was wildly jealous, with a violent temper; in the early stages of her affair with Amis, Jane was terrified of what he would do if he found out. By 1962 Douglas-Henry was mostly living in Bristol, where he worked for Harlech Television, but would turn up in London, unannounced, and stay for days, sometimes weeks. Jane lived in a two-bedroom garden flat in Blomfield Road in Little Venice, with her younger brother Colin. Why she didn't throw Douglas-Henry out once she realised what he was like is, she admits, hard to explain. After the failure of her first marriage, she had spent twelve years on her own, through a succession of ultimately unsatisfactory love affairs. Determined to make her second marriage work, she somehow stuck with it for four and a half years before she met Amis.

Jane's brother, Colin, known as 'Monkey' to family and friends, got on well with Douglas-Henry, with whom he'd play tennis and poker. Douglas-Henry could be amusing and Colin, though devoted to Jane, found him 'a beguiling person, while recognising deep streaks of both cruelty and unreliability': 'He was opportunistic. He married Jane almost for a meal ticket. He thought she was a lot richer than she was, because of the way she lived . . . It might have been a disappointment to find that she wasn't and had to work quite hard to live in the way that she lived.' In the months before the Cheltenham Festival Jane was given expenses to hire a secretary. She chose Jackie Gomme (now Hume), previously secretary to John Moore, a novelist and Jane's predecessor as festival director. Jackie spent several weeks sleeping on a cot under the stairs in Blomfield Road, working during the day on festival correspondence. She was twenty-eight at the time, the same age as Colin, and immediately became a part of the household. In the evenings there was much entertaining: 'they had these dinner parties and they quite sparkled,' Jackie recalls. 'I was swept away by these very glamorous people.' As a boss, Jane 'knew exactly what she wanted. She told you what she wanted and you did it, and if you didn't get it right she told you.' Jane and Jackie became close friends and remain so to this day. Yet Jackie also got on with Douglas-Henry. When staying at Blomfield Road, she would often sit up all night with him and Colin playing poker, drinking whisky and cooking bacon and eggs for breakfast. 'He was a great charmer. I enjoyed his company. He was extremely nice to me.'[52] Jackie thought the marriage one of mutual convenience: Douglas-Henry was after Jane's money and connections; Jane hated living alone and often found it convenient 'to have a proper escort and a husband'. When Jane fell for Amis, Jackie remembers, Douglas-Henry 'wasn't exactly hurt but he was very scathing . . . He said: "I give it six months."'

Shortly before the festival began, Jane came up with the plan of renting a house in Cheltenham where speakers and panellists could stay. As she explained to the festival authorities, 'it would be far cheaper than putting writers up in the hotel . . . They could have a drink and sandwiches late at night after their show and talk to each other if they wanted to.'[53] A house was rented in George Street near the Town Hall and Jane hired her Irish daily to act as housekeeper. On Thursday, 4 October, the day of the 'Sex in Literature' panel, Joseph Heller was driven down to Cheltenham by Tom Maschler, his and Jane's editor at Cape. Carson McCullers, ill with cancer and in pain from a recent operation on the tendons of her left hand, had previously cabled that she would need a registered nurse to accompany her, a problem Jackie solved by co-opting her sister, Joanna, who was not only a qualified SRN but happened to be free; Colin was enlisted to drive them up from London. Romain Gary arrived alone, as did the Amises, who were the only ones to stay the night. The panel itself was held in the Town Hall in front of an audience of about a thousand people and by all accounts was a disappointment. McLachlan was a poor chairman, stilted, uncertain, unable to draw the speakers out.[54] All Jane remembered of the session was Amis saying that he disliked 'hairy-chested' sex in novels, though the *Daily Express* also reported that he declared it 'the novelist's duty not to be reticent about sex'.[55] Heller got a nod of approval from Amis when he declared of censorship: 'I think a line does have to be drawn, but I don't know anyone I'd trust to draw it.' When McCullers claimed that Jane Austen's novels were pornographic, Amis assented: 'Yes, I see what you mean – it's a sort of pecuniary pornography.' McCullers was also of the opinion that 'so long as a book is true and beautiful' it could not be pornographic, a view hard to refute.[56] Anthony Curtis, the literary editor of the *Sunday Telegraph* and the man who had invited Amis, thought him 'the only one on the panel to talk intelligently' about the topic; his contributions 'made me think he was a much better university lecturer than he'd made out'. Curtis was also impressed by Amis's treatment of McCullers, who was mostly incomprehensible, partly because of drink (or so Worsthorne thought); Amis was 'charming and courteous' and 'really tried to integrate her into the thing'.

The *Sunday Telegraph*, at the time in a ferocious circulation war with the *Sunday Times*, was anxious to make a splash at the festival. A dinner was laid on to follow the panel, at a country house hotel five or six miles outside Cheltenham. But the panel didn't begin until eight, followed by questions, it was a foggy night, the hotel was difficult to find, and it wasn't until 11.30 or 12 that everyone – the Amises, the Worsthornes, Jane, McLachlan, Pamela Berry, wife of the *Telegraph* proprietor, the Curtises, and Curtis's deputy, Rivers Scott – sat down to eat. Jane and Amis sat next to each other. When dinner ended and the party got back to Cheltenham, Hilly went to bed exhausted. Kingsley, however, wanted a nightcap and Jane 'didn't feel I could leave him to drink alone so I stayed up with him'. As she puts it in her memoirs: 'What had begun as a duty turned, during the ensuing hours, into something quite different.'

They talked all night, or what was left of it, 'about our work, our lives, our marriages and each other'. Amis made it clear that there were problems in his marriage, that both he and Hilly had been unfaithful, that Hilly had recently had an abortion, at his insistence, that he was bored with his teaching at Cambridge and disappointed with the place in general. He praised Jane's beauty. 'When he kissed me,' Jane recalls, 'I felt as though I could fly.'[57] On the drive back to London with Jackie that morning she was already acting like a woman in love: 'she felt it was pretty momentous. She felt it was a big deal.' Amis's recollections, as reported by Jacobs in his 1995 biography, are different: 'I sort of threw a pass at Jane which was sort of accepted.'[58] After 1980, when she left him, Amis almost always played down his feelings for Jane, but this account may well reflect his attitude at the time. He was then, he told Jacobs, 'what I always was, on the lookout for a good time'.[59] After the festival, Jane was going to the South of France for a week's holiday with friends. Amis asked her if she'd see him in London if he rang her on her return. She said yes. Jackie, meanwhile, stayed on at Blomfield Road for a few days to tidy up post-festival correspondence. Among the letters received was one from Hilly, addressed to 'Jane Howard's Secretary'. Hilly had lost a scarf and wondered if it had been found. She added: 'I don't think I've ever seen anybody as beautiful as Elizabeth Jane Howard.' 'Jane looked at this,' Jackie recalls, 'and made a sort of face.'

When Amis rang Jane upon her return from France they arranged to meet at a pub near Leicester Square. Amis made it clear in Cheltenham and over the phone that he wanted an affair, but said nothing about love. In the pub, he went straight to the point: '"Before we even have a drink I have to tell you something." He'd booked a room in a nearby hotel.[60] He knew it was presumptuous, but he'd done it anyway, and he needed to know at once how I felt about that. If I didn't want to spend the night with him he must cancel the room or it won't be fair on the hotel.' Jane admired Amis's straightforwardness: 'I preferred his coming out with it and being quite frank about it. It somehow simplified everything. I rather respected him for doing it.' She also thought he 'was genuinely worried about upsetting the hotel'. So she said yes. Amis's behaviour was not atypical. He was determinedly unromantic, almost in the manner of Roger Micheldene; that there may also have been a Roger-like bleakness about his behaviour is suggested by the poem 'A Point of Logic', submitted to Alan Ross at the *London Magazine* on 11 October, a week after Cheltenham. The poem's second stanza turns on the first, in the sense both of 'depends on' or 'follows from' and 'undermines':

> Love is a finding-out:
> Our walk to the bedroom
> (Hand in hand, eye to eye)
> Up a stair of marble
> Or decently scrubbed boards,
> As much as what we do
> In our abandonment,
> Teaches us who we are
> And what we are, and what
> Life itself is.
>
> Therefore put out the light,
> Lurch to the bare attic
> Over buckets of waste
> And labouring bodies;
> Leave the door wide open
> And fall on each other,
> Clothes barely wrenched aside;
> Stay only a minute,

Depart separately,
And use no names.

The speaker's pose of despair here is akin to that of the Byronic hero: there's glamour in facing and embracing stark realities, just as there's glamour in being the woman who rescues the hero from despair. In their correspondence, Jane often presents herself as timorous, in need of protection and reassurance, which allows Amis to assume the role of rescuer; but Amis, too, needs rescuing, from the dead end his life has become. In the manner of a heroine in a romantic novel, it is Jane, a species of damsel in distress, who will do the rescuing; they will rescue each other.

How Amis fell for Jane, more than simply wanting to sleep with her, was a puzzle to his friends. To some, she seemed mannered, actressy, posh; it was hard to imagine her at ease in a pub. Amis himself at times admitted that the class element was part of Jane's appeal. 'Kingsley once told me that he quite appreciated the hypergamy feeling,' Conquest wrote to Larkin on 29 June 1964, '(like Dr. Johnson, is it, and the duchess)[61] – I don't mean that Dr. J. screwed a duchess, but that he said sir a duchess makes a thrilling screw. But I wouldn't have thought that it'd last. Still, there are other thrills, doubtless; indeed K. speaks very highly of them.' Larkin's own suggestion was that Jane's appeal was partly that she was a novelist: 'He always had ideas about marrying, or what have you, a writer,' he wrote to Conquest on 24 November 1963, adding: 'Shall I get in touch with E. Jennings? Another Ted-Sylvia team?'[62] While Jane's physical attraction was obvious, her intelligence, humour and warmth were not always evident to Amis's friends, understandably, as they were also Hilly's friends. But the seductive power of these qualities is clear both from her letters and from her fiction. Consider the following episode from *After Julius*, the novel she was at work on when the affair began. Esmé Grace, the novel's middle-aged heroine, decides she wants a son. After ten years of marriage to Julius, a publisher, and the birth of their daughter, Cressida, 'she had begun to see the contrast between what she wanted and what she was expected to want, in a light which was both lurid and alarming'.[63] This realisation comes to Esmé on a night train to Inverness; Julius is in the adjoining sleeper, she calls out to him, but the communicating door is only just ajar and he doesn't hear her. What follows is a sex game in which Esmé seduces Julius by pretending to be an impressionable young actress. Julius enters into the game without prompting:

Suddenly, she leapt out of her bed, spilt some scent down her neck, took off her wedding ring and knocked on his door.

'I wonder if I might trouble you for a light?'

'But of course.' He had been hanging up his suit and was in his dressing-gown.

'You must think it funny of me, barging in like this, but I can't do without a last smoke before sleeping.'

'Not at all. Do take a seat – Miss –'

'Upjohn: Ruby Upjohn.'

'What a pretty name.' His face was impassive as he handed her his case.

'What a pretty case!'

'You think so?' He gave a modest laugh. 'As a matter of fact if that case could talk, it could tell us a thing or two.'

'Ooh – could it?'

'To cut a long story short, it was given by King Edward to my father in gratitude for some highly confidential service. Do you see?' And he showed her the ER (the case had been an engagement present to him in the days when she was Esmé Roland).

'You must be ever so proud, to own a valuable thing like that.'

'Naturally I wouldn't have told you if you hadn't seemed so interested.'

In a minute he would start asking her questions, so she crossed her legs, blew out her smoke in a manner which she hoped was beguilingly inexpert and said:

'Actually I'm running away!'

'Miss Upjohn!'

'Oh do call me Ruby –' and she launched into her tale about a cruel theatrical manager, at the end of which he exclaimed with glowing eyes:

'Ruby, what a splendid little girl you are! I think this calls for a drink.' He had unscrewed the clasp of his silver flask, and handed it to her: 'Let's drink to the brave new life opening out before you in Inverness.'

As she drank some, and choked prettily, he added: 'Don't ask me where the flask came from: it conjures up painful memories never far from my mind, which I should be happier to forget.'

'Ooh, I am sorry: I can't imagine a man like you having troubles.'

'Little Ruby! How touching that you should think that.' He gave a bitter laugh and stared moodily between her breasts.

By the time he had finished telling her about his wife whose whole nature was given to her rock garden, and who consequently had not a spare second over for beginning to understand him 'and I'm a funny, complicated sort of chap' the brandy was drunk, and she could say that it was funny they'd met wasn't it, both lonely, both in trouble. Well – she stood up – she thought that perhaps she had better be getting back to her bed now. Ruby – Ruby – he had seized her in a vice-like grip, wasn't there anything else she could do without before she went to sleep? 'Captain Fortesque!' 'Call me Valentine!' and she swooned neatly on to the bed, pulling him with her . . .

[. . .]

And that was when Emma was conceived.[64]

Esmé, like her creator, is posh, but also gently satirical about being posh; the seduction is clever, good-humoured, warm and funny; she and Julius, somewhat improbably inventive, play it well, and Jane gives him some of the best lines, including the marvellous 'and I'm a funny, complicated sort of chap'. The scene is romantic but unsentimental, like much of Howard's best fiction. This fiction is not to everyone's taste: some find its happy endings as improbable as Julius's inventive play-acting; the guying of class and other types, even here in Esmé's impersonation of little Ruby, is thought snobbish. But Amis – who was vigilant about romantic gush and class snobbery – admired Jane's novels. It is noteworthy that after she left Amis he never once disparaged her writing, either in private correspondence or in print. In *Experience*, Martin calls Jane 'with Iris Murdoch, the most interesting woman writer of her generation'.[65]

The qualities Martin identifies as making Jane so interesting a writer – 'elegance', 'a freakish and poetic eye', 'penetrating sanity' – are evident also in her love letters, along with humour, warmth and vulnerability. As for Amis's letters to Jane, they are unlike any other letters of his I have seen; but then I have seen no other love letters. That he wrote similar letters 'to all the girls', or even to some of them, is hard to imagine. What is clear is that he fell madly for Jane, almost as madly as she fell for him.[66] The emotional openness of the letters is striking, as is their happiness, optimism, gentleness, willingness to try new things and confidence. The correspondence was conducted in between weekly assignations in London, in hotel rooms and flats lent by friends; there were also frequent telephone calls to and from Peterhouse. 'What I value,' Jane wrote to Amis on 6 February 1963, in the earliest of her surviving letters, is 'the possibility of loving somebody who loved me'. Amis had 'touched something – through our mutual attraction . . . through gentleness, and general liking for my sex'. Though later in life Jane would conclude that Amis never really liked women, merely wanting to sleep with them, at the time she would not have been alone in thinking that he did. Two weeks after receiving her first letter, Amis appeared on the radio on *Woman's Hour* offering a 'Letter of Advice for Someone Else's Son', one of a series the programme was running. Amis's advice was that it was important to like women, by which he meant 'really liking them, not just pursuing them or being constantly in their company or talking about them all the time'.[67] The sort of men who really like women 'treat them with genuine and continuing affectionate interest'. Later in the talk he expands this description in a way that suggests he has Jane's history in mind: 'For all sorts of reasons (economic, social, biological, psychological) men have it in their power to damage women far more than women can damage men. A man who realizes he has this power and never uses it is a man who likes women.'[68] Later Amis changed his mind about the comparative damage men and women can inflict on each other.

Much of Jane's 6 February letter is about Amis's unhappiness and his anxieties. These anxieties are mostly generalised, though sometimes concern sex and loss of identity. From the start, Jane connects them with drink. 'If I were living with you we would stop drinking brandy and not drink spirits much at all, and we would try and design life around your writing more.' When Amis responds on 11 February he reassures her: 'My morale continues to be reasonably high. Being loved by you makes it harder for me to worry about myself. And I'm taking a lot more water with my whisky now. These two things are connected.' Amis had taken the lead in associating his unhappiness with drink, in the earliest surviving letter in the correspondence, written on 21 November 1962. He apologises for not writing earlier, 'but things kept coming up: mainly *feeling bloody awful*, not about us or you (on the contrary), but in the old undirected way I told you about. Last Wednesday and Thursday, for instance, I felt so alarmingly bloody that I decided to make a real anti-drink effort . . . Fell from grace on Saturday night – and thus held a public quarrel in a pub on the Sunday evening. But otherwise good: yesterday's score: 1 sherry, 2 beers, 3 gins, ½ bottle Beaujolais. Present state of health – moderate, though much upgraded at the moment by excitement and pleasure and tenderness about you.'

In addition to encouraging him to drink less, Jane sought to expand Amis's range of interests and tolerances. 'Perhaps you might enjoy *more* of your life through me,' she writes in an undated February letter: 'I mean collect aspects, add more bits to it. I know sometimes now when you're frightened: not of me of course, but of life generally and of your life in particular. I think I could change some of that, at least, for you.' Amis had declared his love for Jane several months earlier, on 6 December, in an ecstatic letter about 'that first time in room 238'. Sex was only part of the picture, though, a point he made on 8 January 1963: 'You get more beautiful all the time. I can't stop thinking about you. Every other woman I see reminds me of you – to her disadvantage. I love and enjoy everything about you. I love your clothes and the way you do your hair and I do feel awed by you as I said at lunch. I can't wait to see you. I do love you. Not just sexual friends any more – though that too. I admire and trust you.' Four days later, on the 12th, Amis confessed that he'd 'Never been so knocked over by love. In proof of which I send you the poem.[69] Never written a poem like this before, i.e. one that says I love you (any other attempts have been apologies for *not* loving, or wishing I had etc . . .).'

With love for Jane came a more general sense of well-being: 'sat up talking last night till 3 a.m., drinking whisky *in moderation* – woke up with *clear head* and greeted the day with *pleasurable anticipation* (rewarded by getting your letter)'.[70] Amis's behaviour changed in several ways, or so he reported to Jane: 'remembering you don't like people to be angry, and acting on remembering it, is as easy and natural and delightful to me as remembering the back of your neck is sensitive'; 'You make me feel a sort of complacent tolerance for people – "oh well, he is a bit of a bore, but we have to remember he hasn't got a bird like mine" and so on.' Only occasionally does the old Amis flicker to the surface in the correspondence: 'I like you to nag me,' he writes on 7 March, 'at least the amount you do it at present is all right.'[71] Otherwise the letters are pervaded by a sense of renewed strength. 'You make me feel like a man,' he writes in an undated letter of February 1963, '– not that I feel particularly feminine most of the time but I don't usually feel *confident*, non-harassable etc.'[72] On 13 March he reports that he is 'Shortly going to buy new typewriter as symbolic initiation of new, much more creative life'.[73] Even his sex drive, previously insatiable and pretty much indiscriminate, has been brought under control. 'My lack of interest in other women is beginning to get me down rather,' he reports, a confession immediately qualified: 'The *real* reason is, I think – leaving out those funny old ideas about being faithful etc – that I know it wouldn't be nearly as good. (Always go for the selfish motive first, as I told you.) When you've had champagne and orange juice a glass of South African red isn't so appealing.'[74]

As Jane's love makes Amis happier and more optimistic, his love makes her happier and more secure. Her letters often express self-doubt, to which he responds lovingly, patiently. When she accuses him of thinking her soft and sentimental, for example, he protests:

I *don't* mean you aren't tough: most people would have folded up under half of what you've had to put up with. I do mean you're tender and loving . . . When ill-treated you would hide yourself and cry rather than be unkind in return. The only bad part of it – from your point of view: there's no bad part of it from mine – is that it may make you emotionally gullible. If all I'd wanted from you – it was all I *did* want at the start – had been an exciting sensual affair I could have got it with no damage to myself but with quite a bit to you. But all this is the perennial man–woman situation. And the only nice women I have ever met would *always* risk being fooled rather than protect themselves by hardening their hearts.[75]

Elsewhere Amis tries to reassure Jane that he does not find her boring or annoying or demanding; that he is not thinking one thing about her and saying another. 'I want to repeat what I said about never rejecting you,' he writes on 7 March. 'That won't and couldn't happen. You must realise that I hold no view of you that's so to speak an alternative to the one you see me holding, not in any department. I always think about you in exactly the same way as the way I talk to you and treat you generally. Nothing you are or do is ever a nuisance – that's what you're afraid of, isn't it? Well, you needn't be. I know you need gentle handling but I *like* handling you gently.' Later in the same letter he says: 'I understand all the things you think of as your inadequacies and don't think of them as inadequacies at all. I love all of you, not just your beauty and brightness and tenderness and funniness.'

All this loving worked. Jane began to relax, to trust Amis, and in the process took a new pleasure in her body. In February she reported that a friend had bought Burton's translation of the *Kama Sutra*, 'and as I am now very interested in sex as well as love this is fascinating reading'. Douglas-Henry had been in London and was suspicious, trying to provoke her affections and touching her a lot 'because he knows I wd dislike it – not at all because he wants to'. Despite these unwelcome attentions, she remained physically quickened: 'My whole body feels different: breasts so sharp with feeling it hurts to put on a brassiere. Perhaps people in love shouldn't wear clothes.'[76] On 24 April, Amis wrote to tell her 'how utterly your pleasure transports me. Your joy is literally my joy.'[77] In *Experience*, Martin Amis tells a story about the incorrigible nature of adolescent male sexuality: when he and Philip were told by their father that 'the physical sensations of sex are hugely magnified by love', their first thought was, 'so *that's* why you went after love: for the sex'. An admission in Amis's letter of 24 April suggests that it took him quite some time to outgrow thinking like this: 'I always thought that was just a figure of speech,' he confesses wonderingly to Jane, '"it's great fun when you realise she's having a good time"', a good-hearted remark that does not convince.

The effect Jane had on Amis's creative health was clear from the start. 'Two new poems this year already,' he wrote to Conquest on 22 January 1963. 'It's the bird that does it.' The first of these poems, 'An Attempt at Time Travel', combines science fiction with romantic sentiment. The speaker imagines himself into a photograph showing his girlfriend at the age of nine (this is the 'attempt at time travel'); the self he imagines is ten, which corresponds to the real-life age difference between Amis and Jane. 'I doubt whether anyone else but you would understand it (10 & 9 years old and so on),' Amis wrote to her on 12 January, '– *but that's good. It's for you.*' January was also when Amis began signing his letters to Jane 'Hunter' (variously prefixed 'Lord', 'Maj.Gen.', 'Captain, Blue Howards', 'Admiral-of-the-Fleet', 'Grand Vizier', etc.), partly to conceal his identity in case the letter was found by Douglas-Henry, partly alluding to Max Hunter, a character in a new novel he was planning (while still at work on *One Fat Englishman*). This novel became *The Anti-Death League* (1966), which resembles 'An Attempt at Time Travel' in being both unambiguously romantic and formally generic or popular, drawing on ingredients from both science fiction and spy thrillers (incriminating documents, assumed identities, disguises, a pursuit, a happy ending, a hand-held atomic weapon). The novel is a departure from Amis's previous fiction in several ways: it contains relatively little comedy; its targets are meta-physical rather than social (God is the enemy, worshipped only by 'people with no sense of right or wrong',[78] a line of thought inspired in part by William Empson's *Milton's God* (1961), though implicit in Amis's earlier writings); the motives of its characters are for the most part treated generously, without satire or acerbity; and ideas, or at least conversations about weighty subjects, take precedence over characterisation, in the manner of a moral fable. *The Anti-Death League*, Amis told an interviewer, represented 'a big swing in the direction of seriousness, overt seriousness'.[79]

It is the central love interest that shows Jane's influence. The lovers are Catharine Casement, recovering from a nervous breakdown in a mental hospital in the English countryside, and James Churchill, a young officer at a nearby military establishment. This establishment is the site of a top-secret project, Operation Apollo, the aim of which is to inflict a particularly horrible death on randomly selected Communist Chinese soldiers. The camp resembles 'Special Welfare Research Station No. 4', the setting of Amis's science fiction story, 'Something Strange', from *My Enemy's Enemy*, as well as settings in James Bond novels. In each of Amis's previous novels, despite all sorts of differences, there is a single, identifiable Amis figure (Jim Dixon, John Lewis, Garnet Bowen, Patrick Standish, Roger Micheldene). Here the qualities of the Amis figure are more widely and thinly dispersed: Churchill is Amis-like in some respects but not others, which is true also of Max Hunter, his fellow officer. Hunter is alcoholic, wildly promiscuous, an implacable enemy of God, founder of the Anti-Death League and homosexual. Max uses alcohol to block out fears and horrors. His credo is the exact opposite of Amis's in the love letters: 'all emotional attachments are bad. Get what there is to be got out of somebody without undue effort and then pass on to the next. It's better for everybody that way.' While drying out in the hospital that is treating Catharine, Max is visited by Churchill. It is here that the lovers first see each other: 'when the girl turned and looked at the tall young man it was as if the sun went out for an instant. He flinched and drew in his breath almost with a cry.'

When Amis began work on *The Anti-Death League* he asked Jane if she'd like to name the heroine, who'd be partly based on her. It was Jane who chose the name Catharine Casement. The connections between Jane and Catharine are of several sorts. Like Jane, she was twice married, both times unhappily, the first time when only nineteen. Whether her second husband was Australian is unclear, though she met him in Australia. As she tells Churchill, 'I never see him. But I don't seem to be able to divorce him. He's in London. I live about fifteen miles away.'[80] In an interview at the time of its publication, Amis described *The Anti-Death League* as in part about 'a girl who had always been treated badly by men and how difficult it is for her to agree to be treated nicely by a man'.[81] When Churchill says he loves Catharine, she responds like Jane in the letters, openly, timidly, with a hint of play-acting: 'I'm going to love you too, probably by tomorrow. But I'll have to have just a little time. I thought I'd stopped, you see. Loving people. So it'll take me just a little time to start again. Is that all right?' Catharine's sexual history recalls Jane's. Her first husband married her because 'he wanted to be married. All his friends were, you see, the people he'd been in the Army with and so on. He never liked the idea of looking different.'[82] Catharine was sexually experienced at nineteen and 'thought I knew all about it. What I didn't know was what it was for.' As a consequence, 'I wasn't getting a great deal out of it at that stage, early on. That didn't worry me much, though. I thought that the people who said they got a lot out of it were natural exaggerators, or else that I was somebody it didn't happen to appeal to an awful lot.'[83] Her second husband had a violent temper, like Douglas-Henry, though unlike him he was physically as well as emotionally abusive: 'He was very careful not to bruise me where it showed. Then I'd cry, of course, and he'd cry too and start comforting me, and then he'd end up by fucking me. Then he'd be perfectly nice and cordial until the next time.'[84]

With such a background it is understandable that Catharine takes a while to trust Churchill. The scene in which she first allows him to make love to her calls to mind, in order to refute, Roger Micheldene's views on sex. As they walk in the countryside, Churchill takes her hand and 'girl, trees and stream formed a unity'. He feels 'his heart lift. This had never happened to him before, and he was surprised at how physical the sensation was. He was filled with joy.' Catharine, too, feels joy, a sense that 'everything's all right'.[85] When Churchill suggests that they sit down on a grassy bank, she asks him if what he really means is that they lie down on the bank. 'It's funny you should say that,' he answers, 'because it was lying down I had in mind.' 'In that case,' she answers, 'I think it would be easier for everybody if I took off my dress.' Their lovemaking is described from Churchill's point of view:

They kept their eyes on each other. He watched the steady change in her expression as it grew wilder and at the same time more serene, more longing and more contented. At first he thought she was becoming less human, less the person who was Catharine, but then he saw that she was really more human, more Catharine than ever.[86]

What Churchill expects, what he thinks at first he sees, is the way sex dehumanises (the Roger Micheldene view). As desire overcomes her, Catharine seems 'less human', though only for an instant. Churchill is no Micheldene and through love he recognises a human dimension in sexual desire, a mutuality in abandon. As Catharine's expression grows 'wilder', it still remains that of 'the person who was Catharine'; if anything, it is 'more human, more Catharine than ever', as well as 'more content', 'more serene'.

A moment later Churchill feels a lump in Catharine's breast. He is now at the centre of what the novel calls the 'node', a lethal grouping of malign events, a knot, a tumour, that has hovered at the edge of his life since the opening pages, knocking off peripheral figures (a dispatch rider, a corporal in his unit) and threatening the deaths of many more (through the murderous Operation Apollo). When Catharine's lump proves malignant, Churchill has a breakdown: 'it's as if he can't see anything but death anywhere'.[87] He becomes catatonic, unable or unwilling to respond to anyone, even when it is revealed that Operation Apollo will not go ahead. 'I think you're the only one he'll listen to,' Churchill's friend and fellow officer tells Catharine, 'because he loves you.' The scene in which this prediction proves right, in which Catharine rescues Churchill as he had rescued her, makes clear the nature of his fears. Catharine makes no attempt to deny the horrors God has inflicted on his creation, reassures Churchill that he is not mad and forces him to acknowledge the truth and goodness of their love.[88] 'Have you read *The Anti-Death League*,' Conquest asked Larkin in a letter of 16 April 1966, 'Very unkingsleyish, to my mind – on the whole.' Larkin's immediate response does not survive, but on 1 October 1969, he told Conquest: 'I can't agree with this stuff about The Anti-D L being his best book – his most *solemn*, most full of *bats from his belfry* unsalted by humour – oh yay, all that.' The critics were more respectful, whatever their verdict on its ultimate success. Even those who thought the novel sentimental or lacking in unity, too heterodox in its mixture of genre ingredients, applauded Amis's seriousness, ambition and willingness to try new things.[89] In his work as in his life, Jane helped to inspire this adventurousness.

Amis's poem 'Waking Beauty' shows Jane's effect, and the effect they had on each other, most directly. The second of the two poems alluded to in the letter to Conquest of 22 January 1963, it takes the form of a Gravesian allegory:

> Finding you was easy.
> At each machete-stroke
> The briers – neatly tagged
> By Freud the gardener –
> Fell apart like cut yarn.
> Your door was unfastened.
> You awoke instantly,
> Returning that first kiss
> As in no mere fable.
>
> But how should I get home
> Through far thornier tracts
> Of the wild rose-jungle,
> Dry, aching, encumbered
> By a still drowsy girl?
>
> Your eyes cleared and steadied.
> Side by side we advanced
> On those glossy giants
> And their lattice of barbs:
> But they had all withered.

Here are the main ingredients of the love letters versified. The brier-like neuroses and complexes 'neatly tagged by Freud' (equally, or indeterminately, his and hers) fall away like cut yarn as the rescuer hacks his way towards the sleeping girl. The kiss that wakes her wakes her fully, openly, unlike Porphyro's kiss of Madeline in Keats's 'Eve of St Agnes', the 'fable' Amis is alluding to at the end of the first stanza. When the speaker-rescuer pales at the prospect of the journey home, through 'far thornier tracts', his girl proves strong and resolute, no burden at all. Steady and clear of eye, she advances with him to face obstacles which prove no obstacle at all. In life, such obstacles were to prove more formidable. 'But how should I get home?' the speaker asks. What does 'home' mean here? What, moreover, did it mean for Amis when he wrote the poem? These questions are among the most puzzling in Amis's life. While he was declaring his passionate devotion to Jane, he was busy arranging a future for himself and his family in Majorca. He would only be able to visit her, he declared, perhaps 'two or three times a year'.[90]

20

Break-up

Hilly suspected from the start that something had gone on between Amis and Jane at Cheltenham. Jane was 'tossing her hair'[1] at him a lot, but then it was not unusual for Hilly to find Amis being flirted with, given his own flirtatiousness. When, in spring 1963, she discovered a love letter from Jane in Amis's jacket pocket, she was alarmed as well as angry. 'This was quite different,' she recalls. 'I didn't know Jane. She wasn't a friend. All the others had been sort of friends and we always remained friends afterwards somehow.' When in the past Hilly discovered Amis's affairs, he was contrite and promised to reform. Now he was defiant. Not only would he go on seeing Jane, but he planned to take her on holiday before the move to Majorca. Yet he claimed to have no wish to break up the marriage. Perhaps the closest we can come to Amis's thinking at this point (the letters to Jane mostly steer clear of the larger picture) is the account Jacobs gives of it in his biography, which Amis read and did not challenge. 'There was a sense,' Jacobs writes, 'in which a holiday with Jane could be seen as no great break with the past. Hilly knew about the affair, after all. What was so very different about making it semi-official for a few weeks on the understanding, which Amis willingly gave, that he would return to the fold when the weeks were over? This was an adjustment to previous behaviour, not a radical departure from old ways. Or so Amis persuaded himself. In this mood, he saw no reason why he should not go away with Jane and no reason why he should not come back to Hilly either.'[2]

Jane accepted Amis's plans. 'I thought I could settle for seeing Kingsley for two weeks a year for the rest of my life. I really believed that.'[3] That Amis would not leave his wife and family did not surprise her: 'I'd spent quite a lot of time in my life by then with married men with children.' Even when Amis told her that they'd 'have to be very discreet. "If it came out, I will blacken you – I want you to know that"', she did not protest.[4] Amis's letters, with their passionate praise and declarations of love, must have helped Jane to accept the terms he was offering; in addition, she recalls in the memoirs, 'three times a year was better than nothing, and I'd had nothing for a long time'.[5] Later, in interview, she explained her acquiescence more bluntly: 'my self-image was pretty fucking low by then'.

Hilly's self-image was not much better, but she was neither passive nor discreet in her protests, partly as a result of having lived some fifteen years with Amis. From the moment she discovered the affair and Amis refused to give Jane up, their rows grew more heated. For some time, Hilly had been drinking more heavily than usual ('I did get a bit irresponsible and drink too much').[6] She had also been taking pills. 'No, no, I don't drink,' her best friend Pat Gale once told Eve Thomas, 'I take drugs' (uppers mostly, Eve thought, which were easy to obtain and legal until 1964). According to Eve, Pat referred to Amis and her husband at this time as 'drunken louts'; she was not an emollient influence. That Amis and Gale sometimes *were* drunken louts is hard to deny. Partly this was a matter of *épater les bien pensants*. Maurice Cowling talks of 'a doctrine about being rude' shared by Amis, Gale and others (Henry Fairlie, John Raymond, Colin Welch, Paul Johnson). The idea was 'to upset a smooth liberal consensus', to show that one wasn't 'a higher liberal smoothie', something one could do from the left or the right or even if one called oneself a liberal.[7] Cowling thought Amis 'picked up, largely from George, probably, the manners of this doctrine'. When the two were together and drunk, the result was sometimes boorish, most memorably on the occasion of a formal drinks party Cowling gave in his rooms in Jesus College in the late spring of 1962. Amis and Gale, already well oiled, decided to go to the party in drag, dressed in Rona Williamson's maternity clothes. 'They thought it was a jolly funny joke,' Cowling explains, 'but there was also a desire to beard the bourgeois . . . They were giving me a dig.' Cowling remembers that the waiter couldn't stop laughing. He also remembers someone saying to Denis Brogan, 'Oh God, there's a third one over there', pointing to a woman who turned out to be Brogan's wife. Later that summer, Amis and Gale turned up drunk at Ted and Gwyneth Kenney's house, which Peterhouse owned and was planning to convert into rooms for Fellows for the coming academic year. Gwyneth Kenney was trying to get lunch when Amis and Gale rang the bell, announcing that they'd come to see Amis's new rooms. They were every inch Pat Gale's 'drunken louts'.

Hilly's unhappiness in the months leading to the break-up was not only with Amis's affair and the threat it posed to her marriage, but with the marriage itself, which at some level she may have been trying to escape. Hence her unrelenting vehemence. Yet as soon as they'd broken up, 'I felt very cross with myself for handling it so badly. I thought, how have I managed to get into this situation?' Similarly, some part of Amis must have wanted out of the marriage, or he would not have made it so difficult for Hilly to patch things up, rubbing her nose in the new affair, insisting openly on going on holiday with Jane. 'Most people like a fling,' Hilly has said, but Amis wanted more. You don't 'junk' (Hilly's word) or flirt with junking, 'a great lump of your life, unless it had become intolerable, which it might have done. I don't know.' If Jane's behaviour in this period was puzzlingly passive, Hilly's and Amis's was puzzlingly contradictory. Neither quite knew what they wanted, or were happy with what they wanted, or could face what they wanted. If what Amis wanted was simply to have his cake and eat it, he was unlikely to have admitted as much, to himself or others; at least this is what the passion of the love letters suggests. 'He was very much in love with Jane,' recalls Rukeyser, his closest confidant at the time. 'He would talk boyishly and sentimentally about her.' But he wouldn't – couldn't – break up the marriage. 'Never doubt that I love your mother,' he had told Martin and Philip late one night in Majorca. 'Never doubt that we will always be together.'[8] Rukeyser explains Amis's position by stressing his tendency to block out unpleasant or difficult thoughts, in the manner of Max Hunter in *The Anti-Death League*. 'I've never been particularly keen on having to think about things,' Hunter tells a superior officer, 'and on things that make you think about things.' 'To the extent that he thought it through at all,' conjectures Rukeyser, 'I guess Kingsley assumed that Hilly would never leave him . . . I don't think it ever occurred to him that he was going to have to choose.'

Amis's unsettled private life matched his unsettled public or professional life. Plans for the move to Majorca had been quickly set in motion after the return to Cambridge at the end of the summer. By 17 December 1962 Conquest was writing to Larkin that 'Kingsley now seems determined to leave Cantab at the end of the year.' Larkin, not yet aware of the Majorca plan, was amazed: 'Fancy Kingsley. What's he going to do? Go to Yankland? Ask if I can have his job. (Don't take this seriously.)'[9] When Amis told Butterfield of his intention to resign his fellowship, Butterfield was 'infinitely kind and decent', though shrewd in characterising his motives. Amis reproduces their exchange in the *Memoirs*:

'Sir, with great regret I want to resign my Fellowship at this college.'

'In heaven's name, why?' he asked in his unassuming way.

I gave a selective explanation, laying stress on a writer's need for solitude, being outside the hurly-burly, etc.

'Yes,' said Butterfield, having heard me out. 'Romanticism. That's what they used to call it in my day. The belief that you can help yourself to become an artist or be a better artist by going somewhere remote or in foreign parts.' But he raised no difficulties, indeed wished me well.[10]

By 21 December 1962, Amis's resignation was news. KINGSLEY AMIS TO QUIT 'STUFFY' CAMBRIDGE, read the headline in the *Daily Telegraph*. Though Amis was quoted as praising both the Fellows and students of Peterhouse, his misgivings about Cambridge customs and donnish malice put the noses of some Fellows out of joint. 'I dislike the formality of College life; too much dressing up and respectability. I don't like having to wait for a smoke after dinner until the port has gone round High Table twice. Dining out in other colleges as a guest seems to invite an excessive amount of protocol.' As for donnish backbiting, Amis called it 'positively indecent'. The most important reason for leaving Cambridge, however, was work. 'The academic time taken up at Peterhouse,' he declared, 'is substantially more than I had expected, and so much of my time and energy go into teaching that I have no chance to write in the evenings.' Cambridge, moreover, was too close to London, which he couldn't resist visiting weekly (for undisclosed reasons). Hence in part the decision to move to Majorca. 'I never travel by air,' he told the *Telegraph*, 'so it will be impossible for me to return to London for odd occasions from Majorca. I am rather pleased about that.' This remark came two weeks after Amis's letter of 6 December in which he declared his love for Jane.

In an interview of 8 March in the *Daily Mail* Amis offered further reasons for the decision to leave Cambridge.[11] Some concerned social class and custom. What the year in Princeton had taught him was 'that the whole class set-up isn't – like the weather – something you are stuck with. It was finding out you need not have a society ruled over by precedent and protocol.' Graves's example was evoked, the eight-foot bookshelf versus 'my own miserable output of seven books'. The glories of Majorca played a part: 'that year in America said "You must live somewhere other than England." Majorca said: "You must live here."' Amis also talked about wanting to write a new type of novel: 'I don't want to do documentary realism any more. In England one is supposed to be a writer about Britain in the '50s and '60s. I don't want to write that kind of book.' Amis's friends were sceptical about the move. Larkin was also censorious. For some time there had been a cooling in the friendship, mostly because Amis failed to keep in touch, though this failure may have been defensive. Amis never complained about Larkin or put him down to others in correspondence; Larkin, in contrast, often referred to Amis in this period in sarcastic terms. When Larkin suddenly collapsed at a Library Committee meeting in Hull on 6 March 1961 and was later hospitalised for tests in London, Amis and Hilly paid him a visit ('I envied them as they walked away into the evening sunshine')[12] but then Amis did not write to him. 'Glad to hear K. is all right,' Larkin wrote to Conquest on 5 August. 'His joy at learning I was discharged without any discoverable defect must have rendered his right hand useless: give him my sympathy. It must be hell not being able to toss off. Not that I really expect him to write now.' By the time Amis resigned from Peterhouse, Larkin was getting all his information about him from the newspapers and Conquest. His censorious comments about the resignation, from a letter to Conquest of 30 December, are prefaced by the admission that he hasn't heard from him in a year: 'I think it wd have been more graceful of K. to glide out of Cambridge without all this public posturing. If he made a mistake in thinking he could write there that's his fault, not anyone else's: no need to try to put them in the wrong. I can't imagine Majorca will be any better.' 'I agree about old K.,' Conquest responded on 4 January: 'He'll get screws from a dozen or so expatriate wives, and EVERYBODY WILL KNOW ALL ABOUT IT. And where will he do it? – In cactus groves, with a dozen sniffling local kids sniggering away behind covers.'

Two weeks after the appearance of the *Daily Mail* interview, Amis received a letter from his father, 'a cheerful letter in his customary neat and attractive hand'.[13] It was the last letter he would receive from his father, who would die of cancer within a month. At the end of the year in Princeton, William Amis had stayed on a while in the States, briefly contemplating living in Washington with Gladys and Virgil. When he returned to Swansea, he was lonely and bored. 'I stood by helplessly,' Amis recalls, 'as he tried to construct an independent morning for himself, walking or taking the bus into the centre, buying the *Daily Telegraph* and doing as much as he could of its crossword in a coffee-shop, going to a pub for a single and solitary glass of light ale, then back to the house for lunch, after which he was glaringly at a loose end.'[14] He had no friends his age in Swansea and nothing to do. Though adored by his grandchildren and treated well by Hilly, he must have sensed his son's boredom and irritation with his presence. According to Philip, his grandfather 'was just sad and lonely and frightened and my father was very rude to him, treated him very badly'. This was the way he'd always behaved towards his father, even as a boy. He acted this way, according to Philip, not because he'd been imposed upon and restricted when young, as the *Memoirs* and *You Can't Do Both* suggest, but because he'd been indulged, particularly by his mother. 'He was spoiled,' is Philip's explanation, 'he could do no wrong. I mean, imagine a baby called Kingsley. How can you call a baby Kingsley? He could boss his parents around, do whatever he wanted.' Martin explains his father's feelings about Daddy A, and his behaviour towards him, in the light of the closing lines of 'In Memoriam W.R.A.': 'I'm sorry you had to die / To make me sorry / You're not here now.' The 'delicate self-disgust' Martin senses in these lines hints at qualities that also help to explain Amis's puzzling behaviour over Jane and Hilly in the spring and summer of 1963: 'emotional indolence . . . resentment and obstinacy . . . the Amis paralysis'.[15]

In addition to being bored in Swansea, as well as rudely treated by his son, Daddy A was never fully comfortable with the family's bohemian ways. By June 1960 he moved to London,[16] where he worked for a period in a firm making 'domestic cleaning stuff like brushes and dusters, a come-down but better than idleness'.[17] In this period, he made several lady friends and was surprised to discover that even at his age, 'actually . . . well . . . yes!', a revelation he offered his son with 'diffident pride'. Amis found the revelation 'pleasing and touching',[18] though the ladies themselves were another matter (Hilly remembers them as 'desperate, awful'). The first Amis met seemed all right initially, which raised the question, as he wrote to the McAndrews on 2 May 1960, 'what was she doing with my father? Then it all came right: one evening when they were down here she talked to me about fifteen minutes straight off as I mixed a vodka fizz, alternating inquiries about what I was doing – "why are you putting ice in?" etc. – with a denunciation of the Jews.' The other lady friend Amis and Hilly remember was one William met after he moved from London to Burwash, location of Bateman's, Rudyard Kipling's home in Sussex. Sally Walker was an attractive woman in her late fifties (William was seventy-two or seventy-three at the time) on a visit to Burwash. They met in a pub, struck up a friendship, saw each other several times in London (she lived in Strawberry Hill, Twickenham) and at some point the idea arose of his lodging with her. Her background was mysterious. She had once sold antiques, had been a beautician at Harrods, had a grown-up daughter (who never knew the identity of her father) and her real name was Gladys May. She lived in an Edwardian terraced house with several paying guests, one a relative. According to her daughter, Coral Hughes, the source of my information about her, she may have led William Amis on a bit; he was keener on her than she was on him, though she thought him 'sweet', 'kindly', 'a perfect gentleman'. They went out together, often to social functions at the local cricket club. He was certainly happier and less lonely in Twickenham than he'd been in London, Burwash or Swansea. Some time early in 1963, however, after just over a year, he developed 'what he thought, or said he thought, was an ulcer but turned out to be an inoperable cancer'.[19]

This diagnosis Amis learned on a visit to his father's doctor in February, accompanied by Jane. The visit took place during the first weekend Amis and Jane spent alone together, in Tom Maschler's house in London. When Amis told Jane that he had to see his father's doctor and was dreading it, Jane agreed to go with him. They took a cab for miles into the suburbs, to Norbury or Norwood, she thinks. While Amis went in to see the doctor, she stayed in the cab. When he came out, he announced that his father had cancer: 'He's not

going to get better and I've got to figure out what to do about it.'
The letter William wrote to Amis on 23 March from Twickenham
came at the end of a day's visit from Hilly in which she explained
what she and Amis had planned for his future. On doctor's advice
the Amises decided not to tell him how ill he was, a not uncommon
decision made also by Robin Davies and his brother George when
faced with identical advice about their father's identical condition
in *You Can't Do Both*. Hilly had found a nursing home just outside
Cambridge where Daddy A could be cared for when his condition
worsened and where the family could visit easily. 'How can I thank
you enough for your great generosity,' he wrote in the first paragraph. 'It gave me a great kick and almost overpowered me, as Hilly
will tell you . . . Many thanks again for your anxiety about my
welfare.' Hilly had told him of the planned year in Majorca and the
preliminary trip she and Amis would make in two days' time to
scout out a house. He was 'heartened' by the arrangements they
proposed for him for the coming year and looked forward to
discussing them on their return. The letter ends: 'I hope you will
have a successful trip and find what you want without too much
difficulty. Hilly was kindness itself today and has put new heart into
me. She's a treasure. Love, Dad.'

On 2 April, Amis wrote to Rukeyser from Majorca to say that he
and Hilly had found a house in Soller, 'a real hidalgo's joint surrounded
by orange trees: we mustn't pick the fruit much, though. Reputedly
cold in winter, which oil heaters and such will lick – otherwise ideal.
3 miles from the beach and adequately flash hotels and bars.' The
rent was £9 per week; once they'd paid a deposit of £72 they were
free to move in any time after 1 October. Before they left, Juan Graves
took a photograph of a contemplative Amis picking an orange from
a tree in the surrounding groves. On 4 April, two days after settling
the house deal, Amis wrote to Jane that 'my father – must get this
over with – is evidently (H. said after our trip had begun) further
along the road than I'd thought and it seems he'll have to be put
into a nursing home near us when we get back. This will be handle-
able.' When Amis and Hilly returned and Daddy A was brought to
the nursing home, Martin and Philip were taken there 'for what was
clearly a final visit'. In *Experience* Martin recalls 'the awful rictus
of his attempted smile, the eyes bright against the kippering jaun-
dice, like a backlit pumpkin on Halloween. In private my brother
and I were nervously callous about the experience – about Gramps.

Or about death.'²⁰ Daddy A died on 18 April, less than a week after he'd entered the nursing home, and was buried next to his wife in the cemetery in Berkhamsted. 'He left all his possessions,' Amis records in the *Memoirs*, 'to one of the lady friends, who refused to let any of them go, even claiming back the watch and wallet Hilly had passed on to Philip and Martin. So I have nothing of his but that last letter, and nothing of my mother's at all.'²¹ If the lady friend in question was Sally Walker her daughter has never heard anything about the possessions, nor did any surface after her mother's death. Amis's only reference to his father's death in the correspondence is from a letter of 2 May to Mary Holland, at the time deputy editor of *Woman's Hour* (he says nothing about it in the several letters he wrote to Jane in the weeks immediately following): 'Since coming back from Majorca I've had several things to cope with, including my father's illness and death and the aftermath thereof, and am not straight yet.' It was shortly after William Amis's death that Hilly discovered Jane's love letter. Three months later Amis went on holiday with Jane, never to return to his family. 'I wouldn't want to venture any connection between the two events,' writes Martin, in the appropriately tentative context of a footnote, 'but the death of the father (and maybe particularly the death of that father) does embolden you, among other things.'²²

As relations between Amis and Hilly worsened, the house at Madingley Road was put up for sale. Amis was away in London a lot, often ferried by Bill Rukeyser, who was courting his future wife Lis at the time. Rukeyser seems to have been the only Amis friend the lovers saw socially, though they had several times run into other Amis friends or acquaintances in public. Once in a London restaurant they found themselves seated next to V.S. Pritchett and had to conduct what Jane remembers as a 'feverishly unreal' conversation for the rest of the meal; another time, very early in the morning, they encountered Violet Powell on a railway platform. As Rukeyser grew closer to Amis, Mark Rose grew closer to Hilly; the Amises' friends were beginning to take sides. 'Kingsley started not being there on the weekends,' Rose remembers, and Hilly would invite him over: 'my recollection is I was there most weekends.' Though the affair with Jane was now common knowledge, Hilly told Rose little about it. 'Kingsley's being fucking awful,' she would say; then she'd be 'ironic and funny, as Hilly always was'. Rose's friendship with Hilly and Pat Gale made it hard for him to remain close to

Bill Rukeyser, 'Kingsley's driver'. The Rukeysers remember going down to Swansea to stay with Stuart and Eve Thomas during this period. The Gales and Hilly were there as well and when Lis encountered George late the first night as she was heading back to her room, he growled: 'What the bloody hell are you doing here?' His hostility, the Rukeysers soon realised, was 'more than George just being drunk and rude'. 'They were very angry and they probably knew that we knew something.' Pat's influence over Hilly at this time was at its height. According to Peregrine Worsthorne, her 'atmosphere and way of life would have played a large part in determining Hilly's behaviour in that period and I think probably Kingsley could well be right in thinking what Hilly did was influenced by Pat'. Worsthorne, Pat's lifelong friend, could well imagine her saying something like 'Kingsley's a rotter and the sooner you get out of the marriage the better.'[23]

Well before Hilly learned of the affair with Jane, Amis had accepted an invitation for them both to attend the first Festival of Science Fiction Film in Trieste, in July 1963. The invitation came from the Italian Tourist Office, which would pay all expenses. Amis accepted because he knew that his SF friends Brian Aldiss and Harry Harrison would be there, along with their wives (in Aldiss's case, with his wife-to-be). Amis had known Aldiss since 1955, when they met at a talk Amis gave at Oxford; he first met Harrison, an American writer, at a SF conference in Gloucester in 1961. Other guests at the festival in Trieste included Umberto Eco, Ray Milland, there to promote his new film, *The Man with X-Ray Eyes*, and the French critic and filmmaker Pierre Kast. Like other festival invitees, the Amises were put up in Trieste's Grand Hôtel et de la Ville (in a letter to Jane, under the 'et' Amis drew an arrow and wrote 'yes, nonsense, but it says this outside, on stationery etc.'). When Aldiss arrived, he found Amis and Harrison sitting beneath an awning in front of the hotel, drinking Asti Spumante and whisky: 'The sun shone. The Spumanti sparkled. The talk bubbled.'[24] The films were shown at night in the courtyard of the Castle of San Guisto, overlooking the Bay of Trieste. Amis found a small bar at the back of the courtyard and the three friends watched from there, drinking and mocking the films. On one occasion, Harrison recalls, after barracking a particularly terrible low-budget American film, they were 'not at all put out when the lights came up and we discovered that the producer and the lead actor had been sitting just before us all the time'.[25] During the day the judges were free and Harrison suggested an excursion. He and his wife lived in Denmark and had driven to Trieste in a Volkswagen bus, once a Copenhagen taxi, now a converted camper. Harrison suggested that the three couples, plus the two small Harrison children, travel south in the camper into Yugoslavia. It would be Amis's first visit to a Communist country. After crossing the Istrian countryside to Koper, formerly Capodistria, the friends stopped at a country hotel with a tree-shaded garden, drank a 'pitcher' of slivovitz,[26] ate a good lunch, swam and slept in the sun. Amis and Hilly had been fighting for days about Jane. While he lay sleeping, she took out her lipstick and wrote on his back: 'I FAT ENGLISHMAN. I FUCK ANYTHING'. Both Aldiss and Harrison took photographs of their sleeping friend. In their published accounts of the festival this is the only episode in which Hilly figures.

Hilly almost didn't accompany Amis to Trieste. In the weeks leading up to the festival she was in a terrible state and relations between them were so bad that she moved out of the house for a period. On 11 June Amis wrote to Jane describing his return to Cambridge after a weekend they had spent together in London. Hilly was not at home when he arrived, but as soon as he walked in she was on the telephone, in 'denunciatory' mood:

. . . why was I neglecting kids etc. Reason was useless. This depressed me rather; and so did the 2 other times I rang her up and was hung up on, and so did the drunken-abusive-humorous-jeering call I got from her at 2 a.m. (aroused from sleep to take it). The next day I hear via Nickie, H. awoke with 2 sores on her face & bloodshot eyes and a hormone deficiency is suspected.

In the same letter Amis reported that rumours had begun to circulate that Hilly had left home for good. He wanted her back before the children heard them. When she returned, relations were still terrible. The night before they were scheduled to depart for Trieste was, Amis reported to Jane, the worst of his life (though an asterisk adds 'except when children ill etc.'). Writing from Trieste on 9 July, he described 'a scene that started as soon as I got home (12.10) and didn't end until 6.30 the next morning. The taxi to take us to Camb. Station (whence we departed for London, of course) was due at 6.40. Until then it was never certain whether we were going or not.

But things much, much better now.' Amis was shaken by Hilly's anger and unhappiness but also determined: 'I am not going to be bullied or blackmailed or coaxed into accepting any kind of future that doesn't include you – feature you prominently, I had better say.'[27] What Hilly remembers is that she wasn't prepared to accept what Amis seemed to be offering: 'My alternative was to sit it out until the big passion burnt out a bit and just have him as a visitor, have him call round and not break off relations. You know, so he had two homes. And I thought no, I don't want to do that, I'm not happy with that, that wouldn't make it any better.'

It was Amis's plan to take Jane on holiday to Spain, return to Cambridge, help with the move to Majorca and then spend the year there. Martin remembers the day Amis left for his holiday with Jane – the moment, even – in an image embarrassing or lowering for himself as well as his father, a proleptic allusion, perhaps, to his exit from his own marriage:

On the last page of his memoir about V.S. Naipaul, *Sir Vidia's Shadow*, Paul Theroux – rather tendentiously, some may feel – depicts the senior writer as 'scuttling' away from him down a London street. Well, I know a scuttle when I see one, and my father definitely scuttled down that gravel drive on the day he left the house in Madingley Road, Cambridge, in the summer of 1963. He was carrying a suitcase. A taxi waited . . . I am a good three or four inches shorter than my father, but our bodies are similarly disproportionate, with a low centre of gravity . . . Such legs are *made* for scuttling. He was en route from one reality to another; that taxi was part of a tunnel to a different world.[28]

Once he had gone, Eva Garcia came up alone from Swansea to help Hilly with the packing up of the house and with the children. It was she who, as Martin puts it in *Experience*, 'hoisted me out of my childhood'.[29] Martin was fourteen, a month away from fifteen, when Eva told him: 'You know your father's got this fancy woman up in London.' Martin didn't know. The next day, driving to school, his mother 'told me matter-of-factly that she and my father were going to separate (there was no mention of the fancy woman) . . . She asked me if I understood, and I think I said I did.'[30] Philip, only a year older but well out of childhood, was also told matter-of-factly about the separation, and about Jane as well. In addition, he was told that the decision to separate was final, though presumably this decision was Hilly's alone, one she came to only after Amis left (if he heard it, he didn't take it seriously). Philip claims not to have been bothered much by the news: 'Martin and I thought, oh, that's good, we get another present. It can't be all that bad because we're getting one more present.' Lis Rukeyser, though, remembers him as 'very very distraught about the whole thing', in contrast to Martin, whose attitude seemed to be 'this, too, shall pass'. As for nine-year-old Sally, she 'lived in her own little world . . . floated around doing her thing'.

The precise details of the break-up are opaque and contentious, beginning with the date of Amis's departure. In his biography Jacobs says Amis departed Cambridge on 21 July, Hilly's birthday, leaving a present behind on their bed, 'a black, baby-doll style nightie which, to make matters worse, Hilly suspected had been chosen for her by Jane'.[31] Jane denies knowing anything about the nightie and says in her memoirs that she and Amis spent the night of 20 July together in London, in a friend's flat in South Kensington, departing for the boat train to Dover and Barcelona the next morning. On 15 July (according to internal evidence, the letter is undated) Amis wrote to Jane from Cambridge to report 'All under control here – only just but under. Arrangements stand: at the moment am being *driven* up on Wednesday morning.' He also says that he'll phone Jane 'tomorrow (Tuesday)' and that she's not to worry 'about engagements, in evenings etc., that you feel you must keep: I will stay at home and feel very husbandly, or else have night out with the boys. Haven't seen them (Conquest etc.) for *3 months*, I now find.' Though the phrase 'at the moment' ought not to be forgotten, what the letter suggests is that Amis was to spend some days in London before the trip to Spain. It is also worth noting that among Amis's papers at the Harry Ransom Center in Texas are several letters dated 19 and 22 July and written by him on Jonathan Cape stationery, presumably from London. These letters solicited contributions to an anthology of science fiction stories Amis hoped to edit 'by prominent writers not associated with the field' (among them Somerset Maugham, C.P. Snow and Robert Graves, to whom Amis signed off, 'See you Sept.'). As the affair with Jane blossomed, Amis became friendly with Tom Maschler, her editor at Cape, a development which worried Victor Gollancz. The anthology never got off the ground but was the first of several signs that Amis had begun questioning yet another aspect of his life, his relationship with his publisher.

The discrepancy about the date of Amis's departure from Madingley Road serves as a reminder of the distortions surrounding this episode of his life. Leaving the nightie behind for Hilly on their bed was a tactless thing to do no matter what the date, but memorably tactless on her birthday. The length of the holiday also raises questions. According to Jacobs, Amis planned to go on holiday with Jane for three weeks;[32] according to Jane for two weeks.[33] In fact, Amis seems to have been away from home for at least seven weeks, from 21 July, at the latest, to 8 September, when the lovers returned to London (according to a letter Amis wrote to Rukeyser from Spain, advising him to reply c/o Gollancz 'on and after 8 Sept.'). Amis's version of what happened next, which is also Jacobs's version, is summarised by Martin in *Experience*: 'To the end of his life Kingsley maintained the following: "the idea was" that he would have his holiday with Jane, and then return to the family (and then go on seeing her as often as he could). Still, he knew he had crossed a line with my mother. He did come back to the house on Madingley Road. I imagine he must have been very frightened to find it empty, vacated by animals, children, wife. He didn't like empty houses anyway. There was nothing there, not even a note.'[34] In this version Amis returned to Cambridge with no idea that Hilly and the children had already left for Majorca, accompanied by Nickie and son, no idea even that the house would be empty of furniture. 'There was no note,' writes Jacobs, 'but he soon realised that Hilly had forced the issue. From friends he learned that she had gone off to Majorca, taking the children with her to the house Amis had rented at Soller.'[35]

No mention is made here of Amis having been away so long, at a time when there was so much to do at home – emptying the house for the new owners, putting things in storage, packing for a year's move, all with the children off school and Hilly distraught. Late in August a stringer from the *Daily Express* somehow discovered where Amis and Jane were staying in Spain, in Sitges, where the Amis family had gone on holiday two summers earlier, and the lovers only just escaped having their photograph taken together. They were in bed when he rang the bell and Jane, thinking it was a delivery of laundry, opened the door wearing Amis's dressing-gown.[36] The resulting diary squib, though snide, was less damaging or detailed than it might have been, in part because Amis had called George Gale, who worked at the *Express*, and asked him to try to suppress the story. What Jane calls 'our unofficial elopement'[37] was now common knowledge: Conquest had seen the squib and reported it to Larkin (who was 'glad the *Express* is on Kingsley's tail . . . they owe us a few bursts of honesty after all that family-man bull. About as much a f-m as Edw. VII');[38] Pat and Hilly were bound to have seen it, if still in Britain; it may even have been what precipitated the sudden departure to Majorca.[39] In her memoirs, Jane writes, 'We got back to England, and Kingsley got the news that Hilly had gone to Majorca' – that is, got the news in London, as soon as they returned. What Amis found when he went up to Cambridge on 10 September ('to pick up shirts or something,' Jane suggests, though also, Martin adds, to close up the house) may well have been desolating ('I felt terrible, full of sorrow,' he told an interviewer in 1996)[40] but is unlikely to have been a surprise. Only the absence of a note would have been a surprise. It is possible, also, that Hilly and the children moved earlier in August, and that Amis knew of the move, through either George Gale or Stuart Thomas. According to Jane, she and Amis had spent the night before their departure in Stuart's South Kensington flat (like George, though unlike Pat, Stuart seems not to have taken sides, at least not outwardly).[41] This possibility would help to explain how Amis felt able to stay away so long, as well as why Jane has no memory of their exceeding a return date. Neither Hilly nor the boys nor Pat can remember exactly when in the summer the move to Majorca took place. Nor do they identify the *Express* story as the precipitating factor in the move.

What Hilly remembers is feeling fed up. 'I couldn't believe he would leave me and never come back,' she told an interviewer. 'I hoped he would come back, because the children missed him so much, and I did, too. But in a way I was grateful because we had got into a rut of unfaithfulness.' The rumours that theirs had been an 'open marriage' were false, she told the interviewer: 'It was an unhappy unfaithfulness.'[42] Part of her, she told me, 'hoped he would follow. I thought, well, there's a chance, but I didn't hold out much hope'; part of her thought 'I don't want him back anyway. The same thing would happen again, the same sort of thing.' That she was not thinking straight at the time of the move, or when she arrived in Majorca, she freely acknowledges: 'I was in a terrible state.' Amis was also in turmoil when he returned to London from Cambridge. 'Perhaps I should have gone rushing off after them,' he once said, 'but I was very wrapped up with Jane and I didn't.'[43] Martin Amis throws scorn on 'the idea of Kingsley "rushing off" to Spain: If Mum had taken us off to Miggy's[44] (as Miggy, once, had come to her), then my father might have fought his way to Gretton. But Soller? To accomplish this he would have needed: someone to make all the bookings, someone to get him to Southampton, someone to share his cabin on the boat, and someone to lead him from Palma to Soller and right up to our front door. The only possible candidate for the task was Elizabeth Jane Howard.'[45] (Presumably it would have been too embarrassing to ask Stuart Thomas, George Gale or Bob Conquest.) Jacobs offers equally shaming reasons for the decision to stay in London: 'Amis took the line of least resistance. He had hoped to return to the bosom of his family but now he had another bosom to return to, Jane's. With her, he anticipated, there would be warmth and uncomplicated acceptance. There would be no rows to be gone through, no difficult reconciliations.'[46]

The time in Sitges must have played a part in Amis's decision. By Jane's account it was idyllic. Amis chose Sitges, he told Jane, because 'It'll be full of package tours . . . We'll be completely lost in the crowd',[47] though in the event they found themselves in a studio flat 'well away from the 50,000 English holidaymakers'.[48] This flat, on the first floor of a small apartment block on a quiet street, consisted of one large room with a double bed, a table and two chairs, a kitchenette, a small bathroom and a small balcony. Here Amis and Jane worked, made love, ate the meals Jane cooked and became increasingly infatuated with each other. They'd write in the mornings, go to the beach in the afternoons, where Jane bathed and Amis had a dip ('he never liked it, really'), have lunch 'at one of the many, but identical, restaurants where we got near-English food, with a few concessions to Spain like *gazpacho* or tiny fried fish', return to the flat for a siesta, work some more, have drinks, go out to dinner at another of the identical restaurants, and end the evening playing miniature golf (Jane calls it 'clock golf') by floodlight, 'which we both enormously enjoyed'.[49] The centrality of work to the holiday was an important factor in its success, as it was in the success of the relationship in general. Amis had promised Gollancz he would finish *One Fat Englishman* by mid-August. The novel had already been advertised and was on a tight production schedule; Gollancz was flying a man to Barcelona on the 14th to pick up the manuscript (at Amis's request this man would be bringing razor blades, pipe cleaners, filters for cigarette holders and Havana cigars, the latter to go with what Jane describes as the 'incredible' collection of drinks Amis had managed to acquire in Sitges, 'including frightful liqueurs such as *crème de bananes* or Parfait Amour').⁵⁰ The note Amis appended to the finished manuscript, dated 14 August and addressed to Victor Gollancz, began: 'Here it is, all of it, rather to my amazement. A fraction over 60,000 I compute.' He and Jane had already been away for three and a half weeks and judging by what he went on to say about arrangements for proofs, they had no intention of returning in the immediate future: 'I'll ring you on the 10th of next month (or soon after),' he wrote to Gollancz, which suggests that he wouldn't be back in England for another four weeks.

After the rows and upheavals of Madingley Road, the routine of the Sitges holiday must have been heaven for Amis, and the deadline was a vital distraction. In the final chapters of *One Fat Englishman*, Roger Micheldene becomes more vulnerable and human, declares his love for Helene, asks her to leave her husband and marry him and realises he's at a dead end and needs somehow to change. When Amis effected this softening is unclear, but even if he was working on a second draft at Sitges (as opposed to composing the ending for the first time), he would most likely have been working over the final chapters. In a letter of 26 August to Bill Rukeyser he claimed to have 'done about 22,500 words in 16 or so days, which still impresses me . . . After the last few weeks I feel I could work through a howitzer bombardment.' Meanwhile, Jane was making good progress on *After Julius*, thanks in part to Amis's discipline about the deadline. As Amis told Rukeyser in the same letter, 'J. has done some 6,000 in 28 or so, but conceivably these are better words than mine and she has made a lot of ratatouilles and piperades and that type of stuff.' Jane was also buoyed by Amis's reaction to the first of her novels he read, *The Sea Change*, which he had asked her to bring along to Spain ('It was the last book I'd written. I thought it was probably the best'). He began reading the novel in the afternoon of their first day in Sitges and finished it the following evening. During this period he gave Jane no clues as to his reaction and she hadn't the nerve to ask him. When he shut the book on the second day, as Jane remembers it, he told her with obvious pleasure that he thought it was very good.⁵¹ After his return from Spain, Amis confessed to Colin Howard that he'd not previously dared to read Jane's novels: 'He was infinitely relieved that he admired them.'⁵²

The Sea Change is one of Jane's strongest novels, with a complex multiple narrative, a wide range of characters, and touches of comic brilliance. There are dramatic surprises, the pacing is artful, as is the interweaving of points of view, and the settings – showbiz, upper-class, continental, transcontinental – are suitably alluring. The novel's content would also have appealed to Amis, especially at this moment in his life. Its larger theme, also prominent in the love letters and *One Fat Englishman*, is 'what people could change in themselves, and what was immutable'.[53] As in *The Anti-Death League*, everyone does the right thing at the end, for the best of reasons. The female lead, though somewhat improbably talented, possesses just the qualities Amis approved of in a heroine, being 'all in one piece – no acts, no exaggerations, no trying to make out she was different: she didn't get in the way of whatever she was talking about'.[54] The observations about people are tart and funny: the wife of Emmanuel Joyce, the famous playwright, spends her youth 'with fresh-faced young men . . . whose conversation would have read very like an engagement book with a narrow column for remarks';[55] good-looking Mr Westinghouse is said to have 'an appearance of nobility that had never got around to attaching itself to anything'.[56] The playwright's wife, a woman of imperious irrationality, has never got over the loss of her child. In her introduction to the Pan paperback version of the novel, Sybille Bedford describes her in terms very like those Amis would later apply to Jane herself: 'There she is, nursing her grief . . . with her chic, the care for her clothes and looks, the devouring self-regard, her need to be soothed and entertained or both at every minute. One could kick her; then one remembers. *Also* – she *is* beautiful (those large eyes . . .), and intelligent, and she can be nice, and is sensitive about at least some aspects of the outer world – landscapes, good food, flowers, paintings. She is articulate; nor is she devoid of self-knowledge. It is the application of it that falls short.'[57]

At the end of their day's work, over a drink, Amis and Jane got into the habit of reading aloud to each other what they'd written, commenting on it. These comments were local, practical, unwounding: 'that word doesn't seem quite right'; 'that needs cutting'; 'that doesn't feel right to me'. As Jane puts it, 'we learned to criticise each other's work', a habit she called 'the most enjoyable and enduring part of our relationship'. Sometimes they'd change what they'd written, sometimes not. 'The awfulness of Roger Micheldene really shocked me,' Jane recalls, 'apart from it being funny, it was so horrible.' This shock may have played some part in Roger's later softening. One morning they decided to write a scene each from the other's novel, which involved 'reading enough of each work to know what was going on, and then a careful briefing as to what each of us wanted to happen. In both cases they were party scenes.'[58] Jane remembers how their very different behaviours while writing simply reversed: 'Normally I'd sit groaning and biting my nails, staring into space, and Kingsley would sit for a moment, and then, suddenly charged up, would tap away at a steady rate, sometimes laughing aloud at his characters. So now while I was laughing and typing away, he was groaning and staring into space.'[59] The only person to recognise the changeover was Colin, though he can't remember how he did so. The impersonations are mostly seamless; if anything Amis's voice is easier to detect in Jane's novel than Jane's in Amis's: 'Cressy saw her grab Dick's hand – no mean feat considering her other manual commitments';[60] 'he wanted an excuse for getting out for a bit – away from the couple by the fireplace with their slowly but steadily increasing repulsiveness';[61] 'she stayed just as she was, down to mouth and eyes . . .' He also gets to describe a Daddy B figure, Major Hawkes, who takes a long time to grasp things and a longer time to arrange them, 'because he kept thinking of fresh things to explain to Esmé about the history of gunnery'.[62] Jane's contributions to *One Fat Englishman* are partly disguised by the prominence of Mollie Atkins in her pages. Amis, too, might have had Mollie say, as Jane does, 'He's quite patient and kind with people really'[63] or 'they could be a confounded nuisance'.[64] Jane's contribution ends with two perfectly Amisian sentences: 'Roger stood there a moment experiencing, unusually for him, a mixture of feelings. One of them resembled agitation.'[65]

In order to avoid the return of the *Daily Express* journalist, described by Amis as 'far too horrible to be rendered accurately in any work of realistic fiction',[66] the lovers immediately packed up and moved. With the help of the agent who had found them their original studio-flat, they moved across town to a second one, on the ground floor this time. Though Amis describes himself as 'trembling' during the encounter with the journalist and Jane as turning 'a curious olive-yellow colour, made up of tan and pallor', they seem also to have found the experience exhilarating. 'I did a quick move-plus-cover-up,' Amis reports to Rukeyser, on 26 August 'with a James Bond-type false trail laid to Barcelona. Rather to our chagrin as well as our relief, no packs of newshounds have been on our track and not a single photographer has broken cover. However, London may prove more exciting.' The naughty thrill of celebrity scandal sounds also in a later communication with Robert Conquest, dated 2 September. After advising Conquest that he'd be back 'in a week or so', Amis suggests that they have a drink and a chat: 'you can tell me what old Dame Rumour has been crediting me with since I've been away. Quite a lot, I'll warrant.' As for thoughts of Hilly and the children, these he avoided, or so the letter to Rukeyser suggests: 'My information about what's been happening at home, if "home" is an appropriate word to attach to it, is scanty and vague, but depressing. Don't you add to that information for the moment: I shall be (for your private information) in Cambridge on about the 10th and hope to see you if you're around.'

After returning to the empty house in Madingley Road, Amis got straight on a train to London and presented himself to Jane at 16 Blomfield Road. As Douglas-Henry was still intermittently on the scene, they soon decided to live elsewhere. Jane found a flat in Basil Mansions, in Basil Street, Knightsbridge, near Harrods, which they rented for three months (it was expensive, £15 per week). For some time, Douglas-Henry had been pressing Colin about Jane's love-life. He suspected she was having an affair with Amis but wasn't sure. 'I've worked it out,' Colin remembers him announcing, 'it's either John Wain[67] or Kingsley Amis.' Then, eyeing Colin narrowly, 'which do you think it is?' Douglas-Henry fancied himself a subtle poker player, but so did Colin: 'I said well I have no idea but my guess is of those people she'd be much more likely to go for someone like Kingsley Amis,' a double-bluff. By the time Jane went off to Spain, however, Douglas-Henry knew that Amis was her lover. As an aggrieved husband, Douglas-Henry left something to be desired: he himself was carrying on an affair with a wealthy woman at 32 Blomfield Road. Hence the frequency with which he was on the scene.

When Jane and Amis moved to Basil Mansions, Colin stayed on at Blomfield Road. He approved the affair with Amis: 'I'd seen how unhappy she'd been made by Douglas-Henry and how happy she was with Kingsley.' He also got on with Amis. They'd first met at Cheltenham: 'I remember Jane turning to me and saying give Mr. and Mrs. Amis a drink, Monkey. Kingsley and I got off to a very good start because the drink I poured was a very big one.' Several months into the affair, Colin met Amis and Jane in a London restaurant: 'They were dotty about each other as far as I could see. It was truly a happy time for them, for both of them.' Yet Colin continued to remain friends with Douglas-Henry ('I wanted peace and a quiet life') and eventually Jane and Amis told him they thought his behaviour 'inappropriate', possibly after he reported having breakfast down the road with Douglas-Henry and his mistress. Jane finally plucked up the courage to ask Douglas-Henry for a divorce, which he said he'd give her if she gave him 16 Blomfield Road, otherwise 'I'll divorce you and cite Kingsley.' She refused and it was the last time they saw each other. Amis, meanwhile, set about writing a television play, *A Question about Hell*, a modern version of *The Duchess of Malfi*, to be delivered to Granada Television on 1 October, another welcome deadline. Once he turned back to London from Cambridge, Amis's shock and sadness gave way partly to anger; his attitude to Hilly was, as Jane remembers it, 'the hell with her', though she does not remember his ever talking against her. 'He never disparaged her, never,' Colin told me, 'I think that was admirable.' On 3 October, Conquest reported to Larkin that he'd had lunch with Amis: 'Hilly seems to want him back – lucky for him, though Jane Howard is nice.' Jane felt no guilt about the break-up of Amis's marriage: 'when I met him Kingsley's marriage was in turmoil with mutual recriminations and infidelity'.[68] As Colin puts it, 'she didn't feel she was stealing somebody's husband. That didn't enter her mind. She felt that Amis and Hilly had made each other unhappy and that was that.' Jane also knew, again in Colin's words, that being with her 'had made Kingsley very much happier and he did ease up on the drinking a lot'. After the return from Spain Amis introduced Jane and Colin to Mavis and Geoff Nicholson and Mavis warned Jane that Amis's cutting back on drink was unlikely to last, 'that she was not to believe that Kingsley would not be a heavy drinker'. As Colin recalls, though, 'he certainly was very much more sober in those days than I remembered him since'. As Hilly's unhappiness deepened in Majorca, Amis's receded. In the autumn of 1963 he was full of plans and projects and very much in love.

21

Divisions

When in March 1963 Amis spoke of a desire to break free of documentary realism, to write a different kind of book, it was genre fiction as much as serious romantic fiction he had in mind. The break-up of his marriage coincided with what John Sutherland calls 'a ten-year-long experiment, a kind of late-life apprenticeship',[1] in which, in a manner reminiscent of Graham Greene, Amis alternated realistic works, or works predominantly realistic, with 'entertainments', in Amis's case reworkings, updatings and imitations of popular fictional types: a James Bond thriller (*Colonel Sun*, 1968), a ghost story (*The Green Man*, 1969), a classic detective novel (*The Riverside Villas Murder*, 1973) and two alternate world novels (*The Alteration*, 1976, *Russian Hide-and-Seek*, 1980). Even the realistic novels of this period are less realistic than their predecessors: *The Anti-Death League* folds a love story and study of character into a novel of ideas or moral fable, adding espionage and science fiction ingredients; *I Want It Now* (1968) combines social satire with fairy tale (like *The Anti-Death League* it is a 'Sleeping Beauty' novel); *Ending Up* (1974), the grimmest of farces, is Swiftian in form as well as content. Only *Girl, 20* (1971) and *Jake's Thing* (1978) are unmixed social satires, in the manner of such earlier novels as *That Uncertain Feeling* and *Take a Girl Like You*.

Amis's desire to move from the fiction of documentary realism to genre fiction has several sources. To begin with, there is his sense of writing as craft. What Amis admired about Graves was his versatility as well as his fluency, the variety as well as the number of the books ranged above his desk. 'I think of myself like a sort of mid- or late-Victorian person,' he told Dale Salwak in 1974, 'not in outlook but in the position of writing a bit of poetry (we forget that George Eliot also wrote verse), writing novels, being interested in questions of the day and occasionally writing about them, and being interested in the work of other writers and occasionally writing about that.'[2] In the same interview Amis quotes Graves's remark that 'the most dreadful thing in the world is that you're writing a book and you suddenly realize that you're writing a book that you've written before'.[3] Then there's Amis's habitual contrarianism: 'Oh, so I'm primarily a comic writer with some serious overtones and undertones? Try that with *The Anti-Death League* and see how that fits. So I'm a writer about society, twentieth-century man and our problems? Try that one on *The Green Man* . . . So you dislike the youth of today, Mr. Amis, as in *Girl, 20*? Try that on the one I'm writing now[4] where all the young people are sympathetic and all the old people are unsympathetic.'[5]

Over and above these motives is Amis's instinctive sense of the limitations of realism, at least as conventionally conceived, a sense that derives initially, as was suggested in Chapter 2, from the intense pleasures of childhood reading. These limitations Amis first voices when discussing science fiction, not only in *New Maps of Hell* but in the introductions he and Robert Conquest wrote for the five *Spectrum* anthologies (1961–66) and in the regular science fiction round-up reviews Amis wrote in the same period for the *Observer*.[6] What science fiction provides the reader, Amis and Conquest declare in the introduction to the first anthology, is a needed contrast to 'the admirable literature of personal, and of generalised, introspection', in which 'even external objects have tended to figure mainly as character-triggering stimuli. The best of the great novels of the past often derived much of their strength from a counter-balancing intrinsic interest in the outer world – Dickens is a prime example . . . We do not urge that people should read just [science fiction] and nothing else. We only feel that it is a natural and liberating complement to the novel of character.'[7] The same point is made in the quatrain Amis provides as an epigraph to the first anthology: 'Their light of pocket-torch, of signal flare, / Licks at the edge of unsuspected places, / While others scan, under an arc-lamp's glare, / Nursery, kitchen sink, or their own faces.' The gender division implicit here (nurseries, kitchen sinks and mirrors are associated with women) is like that alluded to by defenders of boys' or adventure stories as well as science fiction. 'If the critic is a woman,' wrote the novelist Walter Besant, in reference to Rider Haggard's *She* (1887), 'she will put down the book with the comment that it is impossible – almost all women have this feeling towards the marvellous.'[8] In the mid- to late Victorian period, the period Amis thought of as fostering his kind of writer, there was a revival of interest in fantasy and adventure fiction (as well as pointed debate about its merits, most notably between Besant, Henry James and Robert Louis Stevenson);[9] realistic fiction was associated with female novelists; adventure and fantasy with males. Amis and Conquest profess to want both: 'It is not, if we may say so, that we do not like or respect conventional fiction, but that we do not find that it gives us all we want. There are kinds of ingenuity, kinds of invention, kinds of question, ways of putting such questions, notions of possibility, effects of irony and wit, of wonder and terror that only science fiction offers and can offer.'[10]

Character is not the only aspect of the novel to take second place in genre fiction to qualities such as invention or ingenuity – so, too, does style. Amis and Conquest admit as much in the introduction to *Spectrum V* (1966). They quote Orwell on Jack London, whose stories 'are not well written, but are well told', extending Orwell's judgement not only to science fiction but to other sorts of popular fiction: 'The best thing, of course, is to have both virtues; but if we are to give up one or the other [in SF, that is], good telling without good writing seems indisputably preferable to good writing without good telling. In particular, it seems reasonable to decide that, while stylists like J.G. Ballard or Algis Budrys would be heartily welcome, stylistic distinction is neither a necessary nor a characteristic virtue of science fiction. Something humbler is more appropriate, the efficient prose of a Defoe . . . One might say the same of other kinds of genre fiction, the detective story, perhaps the espionage thriller.'[11]

The claims of genre fiction are extended in *The James Bond Dossier* (1965), which Amis originally intended as an article of 5,000 to 6,000 words and undertook on spec, 'for his own enjoyment'. The first surviving mention of the article is in an internal memo of 29 October 1963 from Dudley Barker, of the London office of Curtis Brown, to Emilie Jacobson, of the New York office: 'Kingsley intends to write a book in a year or two on the Spy novel in general. As a preliminary he wants to write a major article on the James Bond novels.' In a later memo, of 22 November, Barker says Amis is writing the article 'in the hope that the *New Yorker* will take it'. According to Eric Jacobs, Amis read through all twelve Bond novels and one volume of Bond stories on holiday,[12] presumably in Trieste or Sitges. On the dust jacket of each novel he carefully anatomised its contents, in notes such as 'B smiles 13 times by p.165' or 'descrip of nasties 107–8'.[13] The resulting study, like *New Maps of Hell*, partly guys academic procedures and pretensions by applying them to low-cultural objects, but is also informative, sensible, modestly admiring in its claims and often persuasive and funny. The impulse to provoke is clear from the start. 'As a recently retired university teacher,' Amis declares in the preface, 'I can't help being slightly drawn to any form of writing that (like science fiction) reaches no part of its audience through compulsion.'[14] There is much scholarly parading of instances and statistics. Though Bond is frequently denounced by critics as a womaniser, Amis's researches disclose that he 'collects almost exactly one girl per excursion abroad, which average he exceeds only once, by one', a score 'surely not at all in advance of what any reasonably personable, reasonably well-off bachelor would reckon to acquire on a foreign holiday or trip for his firm'.[15] As for the complaint that Bond's girls never reappear, 'the actual breakdown shows that between books he drops only five girls – and all five live abroad. How many other men with his advantages have such a record of moderation?'[16] In addition to such instancing, Amis tricks out the *Dossier* with footnotes, three appendices and a four-page 'Reference Guide', in chart form, characterising each novel in terms of 'places', 'girl', 'villain', 'villain's project', 'villain's employer', 'minor villains' and 'Bond's friends'.

The first of the appendices connects the Bond books and science fiction. In addition to sharing a fascination with global conspiracies and gadgets,[17] the two are united in their attitudes to fantasy and plausibility. 'Somewhere in all the Bond books,' Amis claims, 'there's a premise expressible as "This (perhaps) couldn't happen, but let's agree that it could and examine the logical consequences." This is the basic premise of science fiction.'[18] Hence, in both Bond and SF, the premium placed on technical detail and specialised knowledge, and the emphasis on logic and forethought. 'We know perfectly well,' writes Amis, 'that even if there are international criminal cartels like SPECTRE, they couldn't hijack a NATO bomber with a couple of nuclear bombs on board and wouldn't try. But *if* there were and they could and would, then they'd use someone exactly like Petacchi to do the job for them. We suspend our disbelief in SPECTRE and its designs while we're believing so heartily in Petacchi's earlier history, in his surrender to the Allies in World War II with his Focke-Wulf 200, one of the few of its type in the Italian air force (not just "with his plane"), and its load of the latest German pressure mines charged with the new Hexogen explosive (not just "a new type of mine").'[19] The other reason Amis adduces for loading the narratives of Bond and SF novels with detail recalls his childhood reading: 'the information itself is valuable, not simply *as* information, but in the relish and physical quality it lends to the narrative. A gunboat in a well-written boys' book can't just be a gunboat, it must be (say) of the *Zulu* class with five 4.7s arranged in two pairs for'ard and aft and a single one amidships – not, again, just to be believable or because we need to understand about the guns for later or because we like guns, but also so that the gunboat shall be fully *there*. To mention boys' books doesn't denigrate this interest; it merely helps to define it.'[20]

The most important way in which the *Dossier* extends Amis's defence of genre fiction is in its frank embrace of wish-fulfilment. Here, as elsewhere in the book, Amis is a near-orthodox Freudian. When *Thunderball* is disparaged as nothing more than a way of having 'adolescent inferiority feelings compensated for', Amis is unbothered: 'If it did manage to do this service, the book would be praiseworthy rather than blameworthy on that ground.' 'Compensation' is neither immature nor unhealthy: 'I think wish fulfilment is a common and normal human activity. I find self-advertised maturity, pride in maturity, at least equally suspect. No adult ought to feel an adult all the time.'[21] Again, what Amis is arguing for is variety: 'I like reading about you and me as much as the next man does, but not all the time.'[22] In making the case for wish-fulfilment, however, there are times when he seems to suggest, as does Freud, that it is at the heart of all writing and reading. Homer's works, he reminds us, provide 'a far more compendious compensation manual than those of Mr. Fleming. In Homer we can enjoy compensation for inferiority in bravery via Achilles, in fertility via Priam, in roughness via Ajax, in nobility via Hector, in cunning via Odysseus. And not only that. What about that episode where Odysseus, cast away *naked* on the shore, is awakened and *cared for* by the *beautiful young princess* Nausicaa and her attendant *maidens*? Blatant virility-impairment-refurbishment-substitution-syndrome.'²³

Even in works which set their face against escapist fantasy, distancing us from every character and insisting that we attend to reality at its bleakest, compensation is at work. However anti-escapist 'serious' literature may seem, 'one of the qualities that took us to it in the first place is its implicit assurance that life is coherent and meaningful, and I can think of no more escapist notion than that'.²⁴ This is a point Amis makes in his poem 'Fiction', published in the *Spectator* on 5 October 1962, the day after his appearance at the Cheltenham Festival. The poem's first two stanzas contrast realistic fiction with genre fiction: in the first, broad-shouldered, trustworthy Nurse Lee attends to her patients, then cycles home in anticipation of a pot of tea, 'Adcock's No. I Brew / (Now 2/8)'; in the second, a desperado named Eli Crumpacker rouses the local baddies to attack the sheriff, 'right there in the court-house'. Here is the poem's third and final stanza:

They – this chap and Nurse Lee –
Are pretty nicely off:
She not scratching gnat bites,
He with his rent paid up.
Lear just did what Lear did.
Fiction, where that is that
And will stay that, leaves me
Back here again, jealous
To see sorts of people
That feel their there and then,
That move from thing to thing.

The contrast the first two stanzas set up between types of fiction dissolves in the third stanza's contrast between all fiction, with its clear and determinate places, times and things, even in a work as complex as *King Lear* (*Othello* in the draft), and the implied indeterminacies and overdeterminations of real life.

It is no surprise that Amis clung to his desk and his deadlines throughout the fraught and messy dissolution of his marriage in the summer of 1963; he clung to his desk and his deadlines throughout his life, like the speakers of Larkin's 'Toads' and 'Toads Revisited'. Amis could 'work through a howitzer bombardment' in part because doing so allowed him to enter imaginatively into worlds where people 'feel their there and then', 'move from thing to thing' (in the draft, 'doing one thing at once'). As 'Fiction' implies, Amis shared the Jamesian or modernist view of reality as diffuse and various, without beginning or end, a process rather than a thing. For James, in 'Fiction as One of the Fine Arts' (1884), experience is like 'a kind of huge spider-web of the finest silken threads suspended in the chamber of consciousness, catching every air-borne particle in its tissue. It is the very atmosphere of the mind; and when the mind is imaginative – much more when it happens to be that of a man of genius – it takes to itself the faintest hints of life, it converts the very pulses of the air into revelations.'[25] Amis may have shared this view of experience, but he parts company with James over what the artist's or novelist's response or responsibility to it should be (he also had little time for James's way of explaining himself, as here). Amis's view was closer to that of Stevenson in 'A Humble Remonstrance' (also 1884), written in response to 'Fiction as One of the Fine Arts'. For Stevenson, 'life is monstrous, infinite, illogical, abrupt, and poignant; a work of art, in comparison, is neat, finite, self-contained, rational, flowing and emasculate'. The novel excels 'not by its resemblances to life, which are forced and material . . . but by its immeasurable difference from life, which is designed and significant, and is both the method and the meaning of the work'.[26] 'Monstrous' is the telling word here. It is striking that in this period of Amis's life, when he was most drawn to a Stevensonian view of the novel, his vision of the world was at its grimmest and most death obsessed. The more 'monstrous' the world seemed, in its meaninglessness and malignity, the more conventional the forms Amis chose in which to record and observe it.

Amis's attraction to Stevenson's view of the novel, his way of ordering experience, was partly a matter of temperament. Robert Conquest, with whom Amis was particularly close in the period from the mid-1960s to the mid-1970s, shared this temperament. Conquest's 'Reading Poetry after a Quarrel', from *Poems* (1955), succinctly makes the case for the Stevensonian view:

> Now the brain's tightnesses unclench
>   Into the timeless forms
> Where the golden leaf and the snow-bud
> Hang from the always-springtime branch.

> And that translucence of the best
>   Even among its storms
> Rebuilds the great impervious dream
> On which the world's foundations rest.[27]

The poem does not deny the existence of storms, including figurative ones such as quarrels, or that the timeless forms of art are a 'dream', hanging, as in one of Keats's Odes, from an 'always-springtime branch'. Such dreams, it asserts, are both necessary and honourable, no mere evasions, escapes or 'compensations'; upon them rest 'the world's foundations'.

It is the writer's job, according to this view, to shape life into stories, images, forms. Hence, in part, the string of anecdotes and portraits that make up Amis's *Memoirs*, in which no attempt at all is made to evoke experience as James understands it, or as Martin Amis attempts to evoke it in *Experience*. For Amis, experience in James's sense is ineffable, thus uninteresting as well as fearful, as little the artist's concern as the philosopher's (a view much in vogue in British philosophy departments at the time). Amis was in this respect, as in others, like Byron, James Bond's *fons et origo*. In Chapter 3 of *The Spy Who Loved Me* there is a sudden silence at the baccarat table: 'The table was becoming wary of this dark Englishman who played so quietly, wary of the half-smile of certitude on his rather cruel mouth. Who was he? Where did he come from? What did he do?' Amis's answer in *The James Bond Dossier* follows immediately from the quotation: 'Well, he started life about 1818 as Childe Harold in the later cantos of Byron's poem, reappeared in the novels of the Brontë sisters, and was around until fairly recently in such guises as that of Maxim de Winter in Miss Daphne du Maurier's *Rebecca*.'[28] As the previous chapter suggests, elements of his persona appear also in *The Anti-Death League* and 'Waking Beauty', as well as in the self-constructions in Amis's and Jane's love letters.

The connection between Amis and Byron that matters most, however, that tells us most about Amis, is epistemological. In Canto III of *Childe Harold* there is a telling moment. Under the influence of Shelley, Byron attempts a rare passage of Wordsworthian sublimity – that is, one which seeks to communicate a sense of ineffable oneness, as little his thing as Amis's.

I live not in myself, but I become
Portion of that around me; and to me,
High mountains are a feeling, but the hum
Of human cities torture. (III.72)

What is missing here is any sense of mystical striving, the sort found
in the passage's Wordsworthian or Shelleyan models. The poetical
voice is clear and distinct, even as it talks of merging; the sublimity
of nature ('high mountains') is matter-of-factly registered. Instead
of groping towards or circling around what Shelley calls 'the
vanishing apparitions which haunt the interlunations of life',[29] we
get the declarative solidity of 'to me / High mountains are a feeling.'
Byron was an acute and subtle psychologist, as alive to complexities of motive and tone as any poet, but he was also supremely a
poet of unclouded distinctions. These distinctions he made as a
person as well as a writer, as did Amis. Amis thought genre fiction
one type of thing and documentary realism another. He alternated
them for a period but also sought to combine elements from one
with elements from the other, making something new (though also
old, like the compendious novels of Dickens). He was clear and
untortured about what he was doing and about the differences
between one thing and another. So, too, with people and feelings,
even at times when he wavered or was guilty or desolate, as in the
break-up with Hilly. 'My information about what's been happening
at home,' Amis writes to Rukeyser from Spain (26 August), 'is scanty
and vague, but depressing. Don't you add to that information for
the moment.' One way to understand Amis's behaviour in the summer
of 1963 is to see it as a manifestation of a more general habit of
mind. He was the sort of person who could block out or compartmentalise thoughts, feelings, people and things (with the assistance
of work but also of alcohol and sex, dependencies he thought love
could help him to shake). In order to go on holiday with Jane, Hilly
recalls, 'he just cut us all out, like that, for that moment. It was the
only way he could do it.' This was how Amis functioned, keeping
fears and anxieties at bay.

By 26 August, the date of the Rukeyser letter, Hilly and the children had moved to Soller. Though they arrived when the Graveses
were away, Karl Gay, Graves's secretary, and Karl's wife, Irene, were
warm and welcoming. Among other kindnesses, they helped Hilly

to find a local school for Sally and to work out train times for the boys, who were to attend the International School in Palma. The house the Amises had rented, a newish and rather grand villa, was on the outskirts of Soller. To get to school the boys had to be driven into town, take the train to Palma, a thirty-minute journey, then catch a bus across the city. Hilly had no car when she arrived and spoke no Spanish. The battles with Amis over Jane and the solo move from Cambridge had left her physically and emotionally exhausted. 'I couldn't believe what had happened,' she remembers, 'I thought, how have I managed to get into this situation?' The boys were homesick for their father: 'After a few weeks in Soller my brother and I fell into a wordless routine,' Martin recalls in *Experience*. 'After breakfast we went through the orange grove to the iron gates and sat on the wall and waited. We were waiting for the postman. We were waiting for something from my father – something that his occasional notes and postcards weren't bringing us: they seemed paltry, tangential, wholly incommensurate.'[30] When school began, life was much better for the boys. Philip loved the International School: 'It was fantastic. Martin and I had the time of our lives.' Martin describes the school as 'casual and cosmopolitan and above all coeducational, featuring the daughters of businessmen and diplomats'.[31] In part because of a more tolerant attitude to the young in Spain, the boys enjoyed new freedoms: they could order a beer in a café, 'and once with a friend we had a brandy each *before* school';[32] Spain had no film ratings so they 'paid several visits to a perfunctorily dubbed *Psycho*'; Martin, aged fourteen, got a French kiss from a girl of sixteen, on the Soller–Palma train. Philip, meanwhile, was carrying on with Nickie, the au pair. Martin eventually discovered them in the shower, or Philip spilled the beans and then Martin discovered them in the shower, to Martin's horror (according to Philip). Guilty about subjecting the children to yet another relocation, Hilly 'appeased'[33] the boys with dirt-track motorbikes, which they drove into town and frequently crashed.

Philip remembers Hilly as 'very cut up' at Soller, often too depressed to get out of bed. As autumn arrived, the house grew cold. It had no heaters and the central fireplace 'took forever to warm up one room'.[34] By mid-November, as Philip puts it, 'it was all too much for her and she wanted a break'. The boys woke up to be told that they were going to London in two days, to visit their father. Though Philip remembers being told that Amis and Jane were living together,

Martin imagined him in a 'bachelor flat . . . in the unlikely role of a functioning, indeed rather houseproud single man'.³⁵ 'I was very excited,' Philip recalls, 'getting on a plane, going to see my father.' Neither he nor Martin remembers how they got from the airport to Basil Mansions. What they remember is their arrival. The plane had been delayed and they did not reach the flat until nearly midnight. The telegram Hilly sent announcing their visit never arrived; Jane doubts it existed. Here is Martin's description of Amis's reaction: 'I can see Kingsley now, in his striped pyjamas, rearing back from us in histrionic consternation . . . It wasn't just that he was surprised to see us. He was horrified to see us. We had busted him *in flagrante delicto*.' Amis's opening words to the boys were: 'You know I'm not alone.'³⁶ Philip remembers 'lots of talking and going on . . . We just walked in. They gave us something to eat. I didn't know we were unannounced.' It was Jane who provided the food. Martin describes her looming behind Amis 'in her white towel bathrobe, with her waist-long fair hair, tall, serious, worldly . . . – already busying herself, cooking eggs and bacon, finding sheets, blankets, for the beds in the spare room . . . It would have been an impossible heresy for me to admit that any woman was more beautiful than my mother. But I could tell at once that Jane, while also being beautiful, was certainly more *experienced* . . . I acknowledged the appeal of that with simple resignation and I did not feel disloyal to my mother.'³⁷ Philip's first impression of Jane was that she was 'obviously someone who didn't like children'. Jane watched the boys warily, while they watched her, she says, 'impassively, too weary even for the brink of hostility . . . We were all trying to conceal our shock – they hadn't known I'd be there, and we'd had no warning of their arrival.'³⁸

There then followed a week of what Jane calls 'grandiose treats' (mostly visits to the movies) and 'long and often tearful sessions spent by the boys alone with Kingsley'.³⁹ Martin remembers his father during these sessions as 'outwardly calm, unusually quiet-voiced', patiently taking 'whatever we threw at him', including, 'incredibly', Philip calling him 'a cunt'. Of the explanations Amis offered for why he left Hilly, Martin recalls only 'a derisory ramble about China tea – how Dad liked it, and Mum never remembered to buy it, and now here he was, awash with Earl Grey'.⁴⁰ This explanation is revealing, combining as it does an implicit complaint against Hilly about disorderliness and lack of due or respect – the sort

Graves received at Deya – with a desire to move upmarket, China tea being classier than Indian. Philip remembers Amis not so much explaining his decision as stating it as fact: 'I don't think he had to really say why. This was it. This was how it would be.' Jane's account of the emotional complexities of the visit is generous and perceptive. She begins with the boys:

Emotional protocol dictated that they should distrust and even dislike me. They were in their early teens: they'd lost their home in Cambridge and now, they feared, their father. In this situation everyone behaves in a younger manner than his or her age, reverts to an earlier period of childhood. The boys wanted scenes that would hopefully lead to Kingsley recanting, possibly returning with them when they went back to Majorca. Kingsley wanted them to love him, to forgive him – even to love me, whom they'd known for barely a week. And I wanted us all to be happy and understanding and kind to one another.[41]

Towards the end of the visit George Gale came to dinner. Early in the evening the journalist Quentin Crewe rang with the news that President Kennedy had been shot. Gale headed straight for his office in Fleet Street and after a day or so the boys returned to Majorca. Some months later, after she'd turned twelve, Sally came for a visit. Jane remembers her as 'very merry and self-possessed . . . more curious than hostile . . . but also keen on having as many treats as Philip and Martin had had'.[42] Hilly stayed in Soller during these visits and her depression deepened. When Martin and Philip returned in November, the au pair and her son were gone. The plan now was for Hilly and the children to return to England in the spring and live in London; Amis and Jane, now back in Blomfield Road, would then move into the vacant Soller house, which had been rented until October 1964. On 7 May Conquest wrote to Larkin in haste, 'as I have to give a reference for Mr. W. Kingsley Amis's ability to pay for a flat for Hilly'. This flat, in Ovington Gardens in Knightsbridge, had two bedrooms, one for Sally and Hilly, one for Martin and Philip. They stayed in it for only a month. Philip was re-enrolled in the Friends' School in Saffron Walden, returning to London at weekends; Martin was enrolled in a grammar school in Battersea, the Sir Walter St John's School; Sally went to a local private school. According to an interview Hilly gave in 1996, after Amis's death, Amis expected her to make all the arrangements for the children's education: 'He'd deny it if he were here now,' she told the interviewer, 'but he told me he wanted none of the responsibility. "I'll pay, but you do it all," he said. "I don't want to know anything about it."'[43] Hilly also remembers Amis coming round 'wherever I was living with the children in London' and saying '"I could live here again, I could live here." So he kept me dangling a bit.' Yet she remained ambivalent: 'I didn't know whether I'd want that again.' It was a horrible time for her, 'terribly hard and the boys were teenagers and being very difficult, understandably'. Nor did matters improve when Stuart Thomas, through whom money arrangements were handled, found them a bigger place to live, a slightly dilapidated house at 128 Fulham Road, opposite the Queen's Elm pub, rented for £12 a week.

This was in June 1964, Hilly's nadir. One night, after a drunken dinner with Sybil Burton, also recently left by her husband for a glamorous Elizabeth (the film star, Elizabeth Taylor), Hilly received a call from Mavis Nicholson. Mavis was alarmed by how Hilly sounded: despairing, slurred, repetitious. 'We're all disposable, darling,' she kept saying, an assertion of Sybil Burton's over dinner. Mavis tried to buck her up – she mustn't talk like that, it wasn't true – but Hilly hung up. When Mavis phoned back half an hour later, she got Sally, who was hysterical. She couldn't wake Hilly up. Mavis and Geoff lived in Highgate at the time, a long way across town from the Fulham Road, so she telephoned Amis immediately. It was late, Jane was asleep or away, and Amis and Colin had been up drinking. Half pissed, Amis was reluctant to make the journey from Blomfield Road. 'What do you mean I've got to go?' he kept saying. 'Why do I have to go?' Under the combined pressure of Mavis and Colin, he relented. When he and Colin arrived they discovered that Hilly had taken an overdose of sleeping pills, an accidental one, she later claimed, or a half-accidental one. The ambulance came, she was taken to hospital, and eventually, after several hours, was declared out of danger. When she came to, Amis stood over her bed and screamed at her for what she'd done.[44] Mavis, meanwhile, having borrowed taxi money from a neighbour, collected Sally and took her back to Highgate for the night. There Sally refused to let her sleep, afraid that she wouldn't open her eyes again, like her mother, or, nine years earlier, her grandmother. Martin was taken back to Blomfield Road by Colin. Martin's memory of this episode is of his mother's return from hospital: 'She lay in a curtained room.

I looked in and could see the bedside light and its pink lampshade. Someone, an adult, barred my entry. Her recovery was swift and total. When she talked to me about it afterwards she said she had been depressed because she was still in love with my father.'⁴⁵

Hilly's recovery may have been swift and total but it was not instantaneous. A day or two after her return from hospital, at nine in the morning, the phone rang at Blomfield Road. Jane answered it and Hilly said 'Jane? Well I'm off now, it's all up to you', and put the receiver down. She had gone off with Sally to Wivenhoe, in Essex, where the Gales now lived. At this time George Gale visited 128 Fulham Road. As Martin puts it: 'He went from room to room in solemn consternation. Every cupboard he opened had a fourteen-year-old girl in it.'⁴⁶ When Jane arrived at Fulham Road she discovered Martin alone in the house in bed, fully dressed, with a high fever. On previous meetings Martin had been mostly hostile, now he was also frightened. 'I said "You don't look very well, would you like some tea or an egg? And while you have them I'll make your bed." Well, of course, there wasn't any tea in the house, there wasn't an egg and there wasn't a single piece of clean linen.' Jane found the confusion and dirt of the house nauseating. She makes little allowance – nor did she then – for Hilly's state at the time. Immediately, at her insistence, she and Amis moved into the house to bring some order to it. They stayed for two weeks and though Amis mostly spent his days at Blomfield Road writing, she and Colin 'redecorated the house from top to bottom . . . We sanded the floors and polished them and painted the walls', carpets were laid, the fridge was cleaned and stocked with food.

During the renovation of 128 Fulham Road Hilly recovered her spirits. Towards the end of Jane and Amis's stay, Jane met an old friend on the Fulham Road, the film director Alexander Mackendrick, whose credits included *The Lady Killers*, *Whisky Galore* and *Sweet Smell of Success*. Mackendrick was going to the Caribbean to shoot a film adaptation of the Richard Hughes novel *A High Wind in Jamaica*. All parts had been cast except for one juvenile lead, a boy of about fourteen. Jane immediately thought of Martin and after an initial meeting at Fulham Road and a screen test, he got the part. Almost as soon as Hilly and Sally returned from Wivenhoe, they were on their way with Martin to the West Indies, 'first-class, BOAC – on a highly paid as well as a complimentary two-month holiday'.⁴⁷ Martin's fee for acting in the film was £50 per week, Hilly's, as chaperon, £20 per week, and even Sally earned money, as 'a busy extra'. Only Phil did not go, staying in school in Saffron Walden.[48] After filming finished in the Caribbean, then at Pinewood (where Nickie, the au pair, reappeared, her son serving as stand-in for Martin's younger brother in the film), Martin returned to Sir Walter St John's. He and Sally had missed most of the last two months of the previous school year, having left for the West Indies almost as soon as they had arrived. On the first day of the new academic year, resplendent in new blazer, Martin was 'instantly expelled (for chronic truancy)'.[49] By now Phil was living at home, having moved from the Friends' School to Davis, Laing and Dick, a well-known crammer in Notting Hill, where Martin joined him.

In the months before Hilly and the children returned to London from Soller, Jane decided to sell the flat in Blomfield Road. If she, Amis and Colin were to continue living together, as they were perfectly happy doing, they would need more room. Jane found a buyer for £8,000, who was to take possession early in August. Then she and Colin set about finding a house, the sort of task Amis hated but they adored. Some time in June they found what they were looking for: a five-bedroom Edwardian villa at 108 Maida Vale, with double drawing room, front study for Amis, basement with kitchen; and a dining room, bathroom, workroom and possible spare bedroom, octagonal conservatory and a large garden leading on to Hamilton Terrace. The house was a wreck and needed to be wholly rewired, replumbed and refurbished. Jane bought it for £2,000 on a ten-year lease,[50] using the remaining £6,000 from the sale of Blomfield Road for renovations, decoration and furniture. Colin, who earned his living making and reconditioning stereo systems, undertook the wiring; his friend Max Fordham, an engineer, volunteered to oversee the builders. When Jane and Amis set off for Soller in early August, Colin joined them for the first five weeks. Then he returned to London to begin work on the house, staying with Jackie Gomme who had a flat nearby at Greville Place. It would take almost six months to make 108 Maida Vale habitable.

Shortly before Amis finished *The James Bond Dossier* in May 1964, Granada Television broadcast *A Question about Hell* (27 April), his reworking and updating of *The Duchess of Malfi*. The drama is set in the Caribbean, the Duchess character comes from a socially prominent white family, and her lover is one of the family's black servants.

This was Amis's first writing for television, also the first of four plays linked by a loose series requirement that each touch on 'grim or ghastly matters'. Amis claims to have been unfazed by the restrictions of writing for television, including financial limitations ('not too many sets, not too many speaking parts, as little film as possible') and inevitable cuts in length (the screenplay was written 'to be pruned rather than padded'). He pronounced the experience 'a useful exercise in discipline, though not a very stringent one'.[51] The play itself was well received, praised for its daring (the inter-racial love scenes) and the heroine's grisly murder. T.C. Worsley, television critic for the *Financial Times*, doubted 'if anything so real, in the real sense, as that murder has been shown on television; and its reality is enhanced not diminished by being conceived in a non-realistic convention'.[52] Less real were the dialect clichés Amis gave the black characters: 'I done thought about you every minute', 'Them brothers is real crazy.'[53]

Amis took on such work not only because he was interested in diversifying as a writer, in writing as craft, but because he needed the money. The break-up with Hilly meant greater expenses and all three children were now at fee-paying schools. Jane's decision not to use any of Amis's money to buy, fix up and furnish Maida Vale was partly made to relieve him of financial pressures. In addition to taking on film and television work at this time, Amis sought out lucrative commissions from American magazines (not just the *New Yorker* and *Atlantic*, but *Holiday*, *Playboy* and *Mademoiselle*). A new toughness about money and fees entered his correspondence. In late May 1964 he resigned from the Society of Authors, declaring that 'I was just about prepared to go on paying £2–12–6 a year to an organisation that does nothing for me, but when the price goes up to £5–5–0 I jib.'[54] Several months later, Amis's agent, Graham Watson, wrote to Alan Collins of the New York office of Curtis Brown, warning that 'Kingsley has been restless for some time for no other reason excepting that it crucifies him to pay us a commission of 10%. Accordingly, he told me that his new book on Bond he is going to place himself with Cape' (Jonathan Cape was Ian Fleming's publisher).[55] In January 1965, Emilie Jacobson was shocked when Amis turned down a $1,500 offer from *Playboy* to write a long piece on detective fiction. 'For the last three years I have found it necessary to earn around 30,000 dollars a year,' Amis wrote to her on 6 January. To write and research the *Playboy* piece would take five weeks, a tenth of a year: 'one-tenth of that [$30,000] is 3,000 dollars'. Jacobson thought Amis's estimate of the market 'wildly inflated', but *Playboy* eventually came up with the fee and the piece appeared in the December 1966 issue, under the title 'My Favourite Sleuths: A Highly Personal Dossier on Fiction's Most Famous Detectives'.[56]

Amis wrote 'My Favourite Sleuths' for money, but not solely for money; he was genuinely interested in detective fiction. Some time after he submitted *The James Bond Dossier* to Cape in May 1964, he began a second Bond book, a quickie. Under the pseudonym 'Lt. Col. William ("Bill") Tanner', the name of M's Chief of Staff, he wrote a hundred-page, tongue-in-cheek how-to manual entitled *The Book of Bond, or, Every Man His Own 007*, which Cape published in 1965. An obvious pot-boiler, it has some good jokes, beginning with a reversible dust jacket ('for use in the field') bearing the title 'The Bible to Be Read as Literature'. A third Bond-related commission worked on by Amis at this time was for an outline for a film based on an original Ian Fleming idea. On 20 December 1965, five days after submitting the outline, Amis wrote to Theo Richmond, with whom he was collaborating on a screen adaptation of his short story 'Moral Fibre' (1958),[57] to say that he'd heard nothing back from the Fleming producer, who was, he guessed, 'too shocked and horrified and despairing to say a word since. However, he has already paid me. (Not much.)' Three years later, with money less tight, Amis seems to have provoked just this reaction in response to the screenplay he wrote for *I Want It Now*, or so Frederic Raphael suggests in a story published in *Punch* in 1996.[58] This story, 'Too Good to Be True', is about a famous novelist, 'Peter Ashman', who is asked to adapt his most recent novel for the screen. 'Ashman' is a thinly fictionalised Amis (a full-page cartoon of Amis, complete with Garrick Club tie and Macallan whisky bottle, accompanies the story): 'By the mid-Sixties his ascendancy over his peers had been confirmed: he not only published annual best-sellers, he also wrote thorny poems from which all rosy affectations had been pruned . . . He detested the so-called fine arts and stupid bloody unselfishness. He put the regular boot into writers who used French words,[59] even if they are French.' Ashman's novel, *Back in a Minute*, is optioned by an American producer/director named Victor England. England intends to produce the film, which he wants the story's narrator, 'Freddie', to direct. The screenplay Ashman turns in is no screenplay at all, being 'identical with the book, except that it had been broken into so-called scenes and the dialogue was centred instead of being at the left-hand margin'. England tells Freddie: 'I got Fox to pay him £25,000 to be a typist.' When Ashman is summoned to England's home in Chester Square to discuss the script, he arrives an hour and a half late, 'after an A-stream intellectual lunch at Bertorelli's'. The 'nervous disappointments' the producer expresses about the screenplay are met by Ashman 'with menacing tolerance'. He concedes that he has 'something to learn' about writing for the movies. 'After all,' he adds, 'he had never before done anything that *absolutely wasn't worth doing.*' When the producer asks for his money back Ashman refuses. As he gets up to leave he looks round the room and says: 'Forty-two shitty films you've made, and this is the best money can buy. Bloody hell.'

'Too Good to Be True', based on a real-life incident, was, in Raphael's phrase, 'truish' if not true.[60] *Back in a Minute* was *I Want It Now* and Ashman's behaviour was like Amis's. Though Raphael refused to name him, the real-life model for the horrified producer-director was Stanley Donen, who lived in London in 1968 and had taken out an option on *I Want It Now*. Among Amis's papers in the Huntington Library is a screen adaptation of the novel dated c. 1968. It is very close to the original. Amis/Ashman's rudeness in the Raphael story is brutal, but it is also funny: '*absolutely*' in '*absolutely wasn't worth doing*' is the master touch. *The Book of Bond* may not have been worth doing, but it wasn't *absolutely* not worth doing. And so, too, with other projects and commissions in this period. Amis's science fiction reviews in the *Observer*, for example, are for the most part perfunctory plot summary, but they helped to raise the genre's profile. For seven weeks in 1964, from 5 April to 24 May, Amis was guest film reviewer for the *Observer*, bringing the same appreciation and wit to the task that he brought to his accounts of popular literary culture. He praises *Children of the Damned*, for example, a sequel of sorts to *Village of the Damned*, an adaptation of John Wyndham's *The Midwich Cuckoos*, for its ending: 'as energetic a holocaust, with tanks and bazookas and flying masonry, as most of us could wish for. This is fun.' Even the scientists who seek to control the alien children, a staple of the genre, are 'handled intelligibly'.[61] As the film was directed by my father, I am partial to this example.

Soon after Amis arrived in Soller in early August, he set to work on a project initiated by Robert Conquest. In between poems and books on the Soviet Union, Conquest had written a rough draft of a comic novel. Amis agreed to collaborate with him by producing a second draft. The novel was *The Egyptologists* (1965), the basic premise of which Conquest had described to Amis as early as 1958.[62] This premise, borrowed by Conquest from an old friend, concerns a fake Egyptological Society established 'to give its members alibis for quiet non-domestic evenings and an occasional dirty-weekend'.[63] As Amis told Jacobs, his contribution consisted of inventing new scenes and characters ('one or two of whom we could have done without,' Conquest believes) and generally putting in the plot.[64] Among the novel's comic ingredients, or what are meant to be its comic ingredients (the book does its authors no favours, most readers agree), are several farcical set pieces and a number of jokes about wives. The main characters are the society's Secretary and Treasurer. 'Like most imaginative people,' the Treasurer 'had a rather literal mind. And so, as they knew, he was a keen reader of science fiction.' The Treasurer's wife thinks he is childish: 'Oh, they're a pack of great big schoolboys, every one of them,' she tells the other wives. 'Scratch a man and find a child.'[65] This view is shared by the wife of the Secretary, who sees through the society from the start. As her husband explains, her view was that 'I was the kind of person who enjoyed planning and plotting and people were nicer if they were allowed to do what they enjoyed doing, so I was given my head to plot and plan.'[66] After the novel came out, Larkin wrote to Conquest on 1 January 1966 to ask how it was getting on: 'I still see Kingsley as the Treasurer and you as the Secretary: wrong, perhaps, but it "helps me to imagine it."'[67] Larkin was not alone in these identifications. Conquest and Amis were fond of plotting and planning, no strangers to extra-marital deception and loyal members of the 'men's union', the phrase Conquest invoked to excuse his minor facilitating role in Amis's adulteries. In September, Conquest and his wife (a new one, Caroleen), came out to Soller, so that he and Amis could work on *The Egyptologists*. Jane describes the two friends as constantly laughing, 'egging each other on'. Neither man took much notice of the women. In addition to going over Amis's draft they devised literary jokes and schemes, among them an elaborate fantasy about 'little shags'. As Amis explained to Larkin, in a letter of 2 October 1964: 'Bob and I are working on a poem beginning: Up the airy mountain O'er the dizzy crags We seldom go out hunting. For fear of little shags: e.g. Wesker, Geo Hartley, Vicky, Leavis, Bronowski.' The poem, a parody of William Allingham's 'The Fairies', inspired a whole 'little shags' mythology, in which shortness of stature is explicitly linked to other undesirable qualities. The little shags, Conquest explained to me, are a primitive and unpleasant community living in fens and undergrowth in the north of England, much dependent on their inaccessible refuge, 'Boney's Rock' (named after Napoleon, the most famous of little shags). The fantasy survives only in memory, though the Huntington possesses a mock title-page, attributed to Conquest, reading '*FOR FEAR OF LITTLE SHAGS* By Alfred Huggins and Victor Gray,[68] Shatto and Windarse, London WC'. Shortly after he left Majorca, in a letter to Larkin of 22 October 1964, Conquest proclaimed their visit a success: after a fortnight 'with old K and J', he and Caroleen were 'fairly revelling in goat's milk cheese and flea salad'.[69]

The Egyptologists was published by Cape, a third bypassing of Gollancz (presumably Gollancz knew about *The Book of Bond* as well as the *The James Bond Dossier*, though I have found no reference to the former in Gollancz correspondence). When the original Bond article grew into the *Dossier*, Amis wrote to Gollancz on 1 May 1964 about his decision to offer it to Cape. The book's approach was 'that of a Fleming addict and its verdict largely a favourable one'. Amis felt 'pretty sure' that Gollancz had 'very little time for Fleming and the Fleming cult: at the very least your heart wouldn't be in it.' Cape, on the other hand, were Fleming's publishers and 'have an immense Fleming distribution and publicity machine already functioning. I have decided, after some not altogether comfortable pondering, that they shall publish this effort.' Amis took pains to reassure Gollancz that he remained his publisher for all future books and that he was not 'going over' to Cape. He said nothing about saved agent's fees or dissatisfaction with Gollancz, though his reference to Cape's 'immense' distribution and publicity machine may have been pointed.

On 27 September 1964, Amis again wrote to Gollancz with unwelcome news, this time about *The Egyptologists*. It was a tricky letter to write, since, as Conquest put it to Larkin on 13 February 1964, when news of the novel first appeared in the newspapers, 'KA has to deceive Gollancz into thinking this doesn't break his agreement with them, cheating sod.' Amis began innocently enough: 'Bob Conquest has written a light farcical novel – present title *The Egyptologists* – which he sent to Cape in the first place and which they have now agreed to publish. Bob, who as you know is an old pal of mine, asked me to go over it, which I've nearly finished doing. I've had a quick whiz through, generally livening it up, and though the result won't receive much in terms of critical acclaim, doing it has been a pleasant vacation job. I'm going to have my name put to it as well as Bob's.' An unfortunate side-effect of the collaboration had been a delay in getting down to *The Anti-Death League*, though Amis seeks to re-assure Gollancz by reminding him of a similar delay with *Take a Girl Like You* (interrupted by *I Like It Here*), which 'benefitted the result substantially'. He hoped to finish *The Anti-Death League* by May (a deadline he would miss, though only by a few months). There was one further worrying letter to Gollancz. While *The Anti-Death League* was in production, Amis wrote on 9 November about the proposed dust jacket. He was no longer content with the conventional Gollancz format, the instantly recognisable yellow cover: 'After some thought I've come to the conclusion that we ought to go the whole hog (and have a designed jacket with glossy paper). This will do more than anything else to show people that this is a new departure. It's the sort of book that could have a really arresting jacket picture (A bomb explosion etc.). I've tentatively spoken to a friend of mine called Raymond Hawkey, and he is willing. Ray is design editor of the *Observer* and also did the cover of Len Deighton's *Horse under Water*, which thereupon sold 80,000 in the first 2 days.'

Len Deighton's *Horse under Water* was published by Cape and it is likely that Amis learned of its sales figures from Tom Maschler, Cape's editorial director, though he may also have learned them from Hawkey. Maschler was Jane's editor and had been a friend and ally of the couple since Cheltenham; when they married in June 1965, he gave them a party at Cape. Though Maschler claims never to have wooed Amis as an author, to have had no strategy or campaign ('I don't do that kind of thing'), he encouraged the collaboration with Conquest and did an impressive job selling both *The Egyptologists* and the *Dossier*. Amis made a fair bit of money out of these early projects with Cape: the film rights to *The Egyptologists* were sold to Richard Attenborough for £25,000; the American paper-back rights to the *Dossier* were sold for $15,000. As Conquest wrote to Larkin on 16 May 1965, Amis liked Cape not only 'because they allow him to use words like prick, which Gollancz never would', but because it made him lots of money. 'Cash is pouring in, from film rights, paperback, US editions', Conquest enthused, 'we can live on it for the rest of our lives, very nearly. Peter Sellers starts filming it in September' (the film was never made). In addition to liking Maschler for the money he made him, Amis was amused by him. He was young, lively, absurdly self-assured and had lots of pretty girlfriends. He and Jane invited Maschler out to Soller when the Conquests were there and the visit went well.[70] Maschler brought with him the manuscript of the last Bond novel, *The Man with the Golden Gun*, only half of which Ian Fleming had corrected before his death on 18 August 1964. Cape wanted Amis, among others, to go through the manuscript to ready it for publication; they also wanted him to include comments on the novel in the *Dossier*, which meant revisions, though it also meant that the book's account of Fleming's *oeuvre* would now be complete. *The Man with the Golden Gun* was to be published on 1 April 1965, the *Dossier* on 1 June, more than a year after originally submitted. Amis agreed to undertake these tasks, and to accept the delay, buoyed by Fleming's reactions to the *Dossier*, which were relayed to him less than two months before Fleming's death. 'Intelligent, perceptive and of course to me highly entertaining,' was Fleming's verdict. 'The whole jape is quite spiffing and heaven knows what a smart reviewer will do about the book.'[71] It may have been on Soller that Maschler planted the idea of Amis writing his own Bond novel.

Literary discussion rarely figured in Maschler's relationship with Amis; not even of Amis's own books: 'I don't think I even discussed *Lucky Jim* with him.' Maschler read and commented on all Amis's novels for Cape but cannot remember a single instance in which Amis altered what he'd written 'as a result of what I said'. What Amis respected about Maschler was his skill as a salesman,[72] a skill he felt Gollancz had largely lost, despite the firm's reputation as a pioneer in marketing and publicity. Amis had other complaints about Gollancz: despite Victor Gollancz's moments of extreme generosity, there was something penny-pinching about the way the firm produced its books as well as publicised them (that it never gave him a book launch party also rankled). Then there was Victor Gollancz's domineering personality, which had driven several able colleagues (including Amis's original editor, Hilary Rubinstein, Gollancz's nephew) to seek work elsewhere. In comparison to Cape, Gollancz seemed dated, undynamic. Though he stuck with Gollancz through publication of *The Anti-Death League*, within weeks of Victor's death in February 1967 Amis wrote to Livia Gollancz, the publisher's daughter and successor, severing ties with the firm. 'This is a painful letter to write,' Amis began, but 'I had better just state the case bluntly. For some years I have been unhappy with Gollancz Ltd and would long ago have moved elsewhere but for my personal loyalty to Victor. Victor himself understood this perfectly well, and made no demur whatever about the get-out provision in the option clause of my last contract. Now, sadly, my loyalty is at an end, and I am off.' Maschler thinks that Amis delayed writing this letter because he lacked courage: 'Isn't this a parallel with the Majorca scene and the wife? He had enough guts to move but he didn't have enough guts to tell'; Amis himself, in the letter, describes the delay as 'cowardly'. He was marginally braver with Curtis Brown, his agents, whom he left in 1965, but here, too, there was a period of mixed signals and uncertainty. 'I really don't think we can any longer be said to be acting for KA,' Graham Watson wrote to Alan Collins on 11 May 1965, reporting on the sale of *The Egyptologists* to Lippincott. 'He is such an impossible man to deal with that I don't want to get involved further.' Watson's complaint here is in part about Amis cutting Curtis Brown out of the deal, in part about his not telling them what he was doing or what his intentions were. The agency Amis moved to was A.D. Peters, Jane's agency, whose founder, Peter Peters, Jane describes in her memoirs as 'the only professional associate who really believed in me'.[73]

When the year's rent was up on the house in Soller, in the first week of October 1964, Jane and Amis moved to Pollensa at the far north of the island, staying at a hotel described by her as 'a modern building that could have been anywhere'.[74] On 19 October Amis wrote to Maschler to say that he'd finished *The Egyptologists*. He'd also finished reading and making notes on *The Man with the Golden Gun* and added in a PS: 'Do I get 25 gns . . . ? Or more? Or less?' (Maschler paid him in wine). Jane, meanwhile, was 'bashing away' at *After Julius* with the end in sight. Their routine at Pollensa was similar to the routine at Sitges: work in the mornings in the small hotel bedroom, lunch in the huge hotel dining room, then reading or a walk or a nap (it was too cold to bathe), then work again until seven, then a drink while reading the day's work aloud to each other and commenting on it. Before dinner they often went out to a bar to play Beatles records on the jukebox, returning to the emptying hotel for a meal and more drinks. Amis was now 'deep into *The Anti-Death League*',[75] having completed his various pot-boiling tasks.

On 2 November Amis and Jane returned to London, not to 108

Maida Vale, which was still being worked on, but to a small, top-floor flat Colin had found for them in Keats Grove in Hampstead. In a letter to Conquest of 31 December, Amis describes this flat as 'very small and most of the time about a millimetre thick in coal-dust. To keep it warm (and thick in coal-dust) I have to go down and up 5 flights of stairs bearing first an empty, then a full, coal-bucket.' The smallness of the flat and the intensity and discipline of their writing life that autumn recalled Sitges and Pollensa. *After Julius* was finished 'on a dark grey evening in November';[76] while it was being typed Jane busied herself buying furniture and other items for Maida Vale. As she explains in her memoirs: 'Apart from clothes and books, Kingsley had nothing, and the contents of my four-roomed flat weren't going to go very far. Kingsley was totally uninterested in anything to do with the house, which left me in control, and I enjoyed it all.'[77] Russell Fraser, Amis's Princeton friend, recalls a visit to 4C Keats Grove: 'walking from the tube stop to their flat in Hampstead, you smelled coal smoke in the air in winter, mingled with the smell of Woodbines';[78] Jane remembers how 'squirrels came in and rummaged irritably through saucers of nuts or biscuits, slid down drainpipes if we approached them, then racketed off through the dead plane leaves below'.[79] It was a wonderful time for Jane: the novel was finished, she was in love, the new house would soon be ready and her days were spent scouring junk shops for bargains ('very rewarding in those days')[80] and deciding between wallpapers. Amis was also in fine spirits: 'I was cooking for us by now. Kingsley was eating more and drinking less and said he'd never felt so well: "It's my lovely life."'[81]

The decision to have Philip and Martin live at 108 Maida Vale originated in a conversation between Jane and Kingsley shortly after Hilly's overdose. Jane thought the chaotic life at 128 Fulham Road was harmful to the boys' education and said so. When she and Amis returned to London from Majorca in November 1964 they found the boys playing truant. As Philip describes it, the Notting Hill crammer was full of 'bad old teachers, retired teachers . . . so bad at teaching that you just got worse'. At Jane's urging, Hilly and Kingsley agreed to an arrangement in which the boys lived at 108 Maida Vale during the week and at 128 Fulham Road on week-ends. Philip was now, in early spring 1965, 'a deeply committed mod', with lamp-festooned scooter, anorak with 'The Who' written on the back, and a taste for hash, marijuana and speed. Both boys spent long afternoons bunking off school and trawling the King's Road for girls. Martin is very funny in *Experience* about these trawlings. At fifteen, 'after an aeon of petting and pleading',[82] he lost his virginity to a girl he met the same day in a Wimpy Bar; Philip, taller, good-looking and a year older, was more successful from the start. At Maida Vale the boys would lead an outwardly respectable life, pretending to go to school, even going sometimes, coming back to Maida Vale for dinner, pretending to do school prep, playing Scrabble or poker with Colin; at weekends they'd drive their scooters down the Fulham Road for what Phil (he was almost always Phil now) calls 'a real debauch'.

Life at Fulham Road was more orderly than it had been, but it was still thoroughly bohemian. Hilly's depression lifted, she took in lodgers and began finding work ('I always liked jobs, earning a bit of money on my own bat, a lovely feeling'). In a letter of 4 June 1965 to Philip Larkin, she brought him up to date: 'Things were *very nasty* for a couple of years for me but now things have got much better & I think everyone is better off. The boys are at K & J's place now & like it very much. Sally & I have a house filled to the brim with lodgers who all cause a good deal of merriment & you'd hate it because there are all sorts of shoes everywhere – never put away nicely. I had a lovely job at the zoo for 5 weeks – looking after all sorts of amazing animals (awful squirrels that mate your head when you go into their cages – you have to wear a crash helmet) but I had to leave because they liked you to work weekends & it was hard on Sally.'[83] Hilly's feelings about Amis and Jane were on the surface accepting: 'I think K is really much better off with some one like Jane – he can really be kingd she is really very Queenly. Anyway I'm really glad I had those years with K because I can't imagine anyone else teaching me so much and making me laugh as much & parts of it were wonderful.'

One of Hilly's lodgers at 128 Fulham Road was Penny Jones, an ex-art student from Swansea who had been engaged to Tim Houghton, Amis's Princeton student. Penny, now an air hostess, was twenty-five years old when she moved in with Hilly. There were two other young lodgers when she arrived, an actress fresh from drama school and a German boy. At first, as part of her rent, Penny helped out with the children. On weekends when Hilly and Sally were away, usually staying with the Gales in Wivenhoe, she was put in charge of the house. She remembers the boys as being impossible to control: 'they never went to school . . . were heavy on drugs . . . were bonking every female they could get their hands on'. There were wild parties and the neighbours complained of noise and discarded condoms ('their al fresco terrace was draped with used condoms'); there was LSD and pot in the fridge. Hilly, too, was 'partying all the time', with a succession of boyfriends. She saw a lot of the Nicholsons at this period, also the journalist Sally Vincent, who lived nearby, and old Swansea friends such as Davina Gammon. Pat Gale, a frequent visitor, remained her closest friend; Penny remembers the two of them as 'outrageous', 'naughty together'. 'We all went mad again, in a sense,' is how Hilly describes the Fulham Road period. 'We managed to keep the washing up under control, tried to make the surface look okay. But we were all reeling mad underneath and upset.' Yet Penny saw Hilly as 'a very loving mother . . . terrific to me, very motherly to me as well as the kids'.

When Phil and Martin arrived at Maida Vale in spring 1965 Jane quickly realised what she had let herself in for. The move had been her idea, undertaken out of a sense of duty; Amis himself would not have initiated it. Though he loved his children, he rarely exerted himself on their behalf, aside from earning the money to support them and buying them off with treats. Phil was the more overtly hostile of the boys, but Martin, at fifteen, was also difficult. Though easier with grown-ups than Phil, he had developed, as Penny Jones puts it, 'a very nasty tongue, a bit like his father actually . . . He'd make little observations that were nasty.' 'On the face of it they were both very cool,' Jane remembers: streetwise, cynical, overindulged 'from the money point of view'. Jane imagines their initial reaction to Maida Vale as something like: 'Well, Dad makes us laugh. Dad earns the money. We'll have more treats. We'll have more fun. There's bloody Jane, but we can freeze her out.' This account Phil pretty much corroborates. It didn't bother Phil that Jane was posh and that the set-up at Maida Vale was posh: 'Martin and I welcomed it because posh people equalled better presents, better rooms.' That this sort of comment masks pain is signalled, as in other moments in Phil's account of his childhood and adolescence, by a reference to the Garcias' house (where, as he saw it, the Amis children were often exiled): 'I thought: Good. Posh people. Anything better than that little house in Swansea. They were filthy.' 'I just couldn't bear Jane Howard and she couldn't bear me,' is how Phil describes the time at Maida Vale. What he says of his father is similarly harsh: 'In the end, all it boiled down to was I have my drink at a certain time and that's it, I don't care whatever else happens. As long as I'm fed and not alone, that's all I care about.'[84] Phil did not always feel this way about his father, nor was the time at Maida Vale wholly grim or unhappy, but, like Hilly, he was 'reeling mad underneath and upset'. 'I don't think anyone could have coped with me at that time,' he now says. 'I was just nuts.'

The figure who made relations between Jane and the boys bearable was Colin. To Philip, Colin was 'great fun, wonderful'; in *Experience*, Martin calls him 'sweet-natured'.[85] Though loyal to Jane, he could understand Martin and Phil: 'I felt very sorry for the boys . . . because I could identify with them. At the time when my father left my mother things were much more difficult.[86] I thought that's how I'd been. I could see Jane having an impossible job because I would have been totally unwilling to make any concessions towards my father's second choice and I couldn't see why they should. I think she had a most appalling battle over that and I'm sorry for everybody.' It was to the boys' 'great credit', Colin thinks, that he wasn't tarred with the same brush they used on Jane. He also thinks that it was 'necessary' for Jane to believe that she could do a better job of bringing the boys up than Hilly. Where she went wrong was in initially 'refusing to apportion any of the responsibility to Kingsley. She was prepared to load it all on Hilly, very unfairly.' Jane herself acknowledges a related misjudgement. Although she tried to bring order to the boys' lives, 'to feed them well, and regularly, and to be in every other practical way as reliable as I could manage', what she did not do 'was make any attempt to form any kind of relationship with Hilly. Our feelings then for each other were of mutual fear and dislike, but it might have been possible to lay these aside and put the boys first.'[87] She also acknowledges the acuteness of Martin's criticism in *Experience* – it comes after heartfelt thanks ('she salvaged my schooling . . . I owe her an unknowable debt') – that 'sometimes, early on, she would tell me things designed to make me think less of my mother, and I would wave her away, saying, Jane, this just makes me think less of *you*. And she worked on this little vice, and overcame it.'[88]

Martin eventually softened towards Jane. Phil never did. Matters came to a head early in 1966. Though 108 Maida Vale had five bedrooms it had only a single bath. Phil left his diary there, open, and Jane read it. It contained frequent references to drugs and a number of obscene drawings, some of Amis and Jane. Then Jane went through his clothing drawers and found his drug stash. 'It was no great feat of detection, finding Phil's drugs,' Martin has written, 'because they were kept in a box with PHIL'S DRUGS written on it in eyecatching multicoloured capitals.'[89] As Phil remembers it, Amis ran the ensuing interrogation, 'but under instructions from Jane Howard'. When Phil was grounded (or whatever not being allowed out in the evenings was called at the time), he rebelled: 'I just couldn't cope with it.' As Martin puts it, 'my brother, always more rebellious than me, more headlong than me, would *not* be grounded'.[90] At seventeen he stormed out of the house and, again in Martin's words, 'never came back. He came back in a different way, as an adult, but he never came back as a child of the house. He was gone.'[91] Glimpses of him – or, rather, of the way he moved in and out of Amis's life in subsequent years – can be seen in the shadowy appearances and disappearances of Harry Caldecote's son Piers in *The Folks that Live on the Hill*. Harry is never sure of what Piers is doing or where he's living or what he's living on. When Phil stormed out he was no longer at the Notting Hill crammer and had just that day, after a single session, walked out on the private tutor Jane found for him. He went straight into the arms of his girlfriend, with whom he lived, he says, 'until she put her head into a gas oven'. He then lived in a tiny room near Harrods, in a house divided into tiny rooms. His parents knew where he was, he stayed in contact and received a generous allowance from his father, but much of how he spent his days, before eventually, a year later, getting into art school, he kept to himself.

Martin's depiction of his father on the day of the confrontation with Phil focuses on his own interrogation:

It was seven o'clock in the evening when I crept home 'from school.' In fact I had spent the day in unstinting truancy ... When I came through that front door I was already wholly unmanned by hashish. My intention was to go down to the kitchen for a supersnack of starch and glucose. But then a deep-voiced summons drew me into the sitting-room, where my father, my step-mother and my step-uncle were unmistakably arrayed against my freedom ... Kingsley did have the power to make me frightened of him, though it was a card he played only when roused by a co-parent (anger was effortful: it was too much like work). Here he was doing his stuff, frowning and glowering; but I sensed

Howard knowhow in this triumvirate of adult unanimity. I was busted, in short. Not for drugged truancy: just for drugs. Busted, and grounded . . . 'We know you're on drugs,' Kingsley intoned. 'Phil claimed you weren't,' said Jane, 'and tried to defend you. But he's not very good at that kind of thing. And it came out.' Then we had a talk about the legal position and the possibility of 'calling the police'.[92]

Martin, 'far from clear-headed', immediately 'blabbed, feigned contrition, and gaped with paranoia', at which point the evening 'descended, or rose, into inconsequentiality and magical realism'.[93] He was taken out to dinner at the Italian restaurant, Biagi's, where his father launched into a lecture about the international trade in hashish and marijuana, 'a Communist plot'. As Martin afterwards realised, Amis was drunk when he delivered this lecture (though later Martin heard it delivered when Amis was sober). In *Experience*, the evening at Biagi's is likened to a scene in the White House: when Elvis Presley, stoned, volunteered to act as a figurehead in Richard Nixon's war on drugs. In the comparison, both Martin and his father are the Elvis figure, but his father is Nixon as well. After dinner, back home, Martin turned down the covers of his bed and found a note from Phil reading something like: '"They know *I* do but they don't know (*you* know)." I had been deceived.'[94]

Amis was a reluctant disciplinarian only in part because laying down the law seemed too much like work. Guilt played a part as well. Amis wanted his children to like and love him and was afraid that they wouldn't, because of what he'd done to the family. Jane is understandably bitter that he left her to take on the scold's role. 'It wasn't long before I found myself in the unenviable position of being the irritating killjoy, the tiresome prig.'[95] 'Jane Howard was the one who was Puritan,' Phil says, while also admitting that he provoked her, was 'just generally upset, behaved badly'. Colin and Amis were good friends in this period but Colin accuses Amis of opting out with the boys: 'He "arse-crept" – a nasty phrase, but he never minced words. What I mean is he sought his sons' approval, and when they didn't want to do something – homework or helping in the house – he would take their sides, which I thought was unforgivable. Jane could have said "Fine. They're not my children. They can turn into selfish little monsters." But she stuck at it, and that's when it started to go wrong.'[96] Both boys were excellent mimics, Phil in particular. He is as unsoftened towards Jane today as she is towards him. Jane's claim that looking after the Amis children held back her writing elicits nothing but scorn. 'Oh that's nonsense, absolute nonsense. She had her own study, a Mont Blanc study, with everything perfect. We never interrupted her writing.' It was true that Jane did all the cooking, 'but she wanted to do all the cooking. "Quite frankly I've been working all day, preparing the meal and I haven't had time to have a drink [plaintively, eyelids fluttering]. Do you think you could get me one?"' When asked what sparked the quarrels at Maida Vale, Colin mentioned messy rooms and meal-times, not coming when called, or coming with ill grace. When asked if this was not typical teenage behaviour, the sort familiar to most parents, his answer was: 'I'd be surprised if you'd seen anything in this league.' It was only after Phil left in March 1966 and Jane was able to interest Martin in reading and then in his studies that the atmosphere lightened. But the marriage had been damaged. In Colin's view, 'if the boys hadn't come to stay, then Kingsley and Jane would have got on better'. Yet he places no blame: 'They didn't want their family broken up. I can understand all that.'

Soon after their affair became public, Amis and Jane made several overtures to Larkin. On 31 December 1963, Larkin wrote to Conquest that 'I met Kingsley before Christmas through the good offices of EJH, whom we met at the Soc of As. Amiable relations were established, or re-established. She seemed nice – a bit given to likening things to Cocteau, though. Have to get her out of that.' On 27 March 1964, after reading newspaper articles about the happy couple, Larkin asked Conquest: 'How is Sultan Amis, the Rajah of Monogam?' Almost a year later, on 1 February 1965, Larkin informed Conquest: 'Had lunch with KWA & EJH a week or so ago – they seem to be settling down to a house in Edgware Road & to be happy as usual.' For Jane, sounding like a heroine in a romance novel, the early months at Maida Vale were 'a halcyon time for Kingsley and me. He was clearly happy – hardly anxious at all.' Though he sometimes drank too much, his mood was always benign.

'I have such a lovely life with you!' he would say repeatedly. He'd bring me presents when he'd been out to lunch with the Conquests and other luminaries – a bunch of flowers, two collages he bought at Heywood Hill, the bookseller, or a complete edition of George Eliot. He would take me out to lunch suddenly, to the Etoile, which he knew I loved. He quite liked going to dinner parties then, and having them. He hated boring dark socks, so I knitted him eight or nine pairs in brilliant colours. He was incredibly disciplined about his work and was a marvellous example for me, although I didn't have the same time to do it.[97]

Jane's divorce came through in May 1964[98] and Amis and Hilly's a year later, in June 1965. On 29 June, he and Jane were married at Marylebone Town Hall in the presence of Colin, Jane's daughter Nicola, Bill Rukeyser, Tom Maschler, and Jane's friend Cyril Frankel. That morning the boys brought them breakfast in bed, 'clearly a gesture of peace',[99] and after the ceremony, as Conquest put it in a letter to Larkin, there was a 'reception at the *bride's* publisher, as convention demands'.[100] The day ended with a small dinner in a private room at Prunier. The next morning the married couple took a train to Brighton for a two-day honeymoon at the Hotel Metropole. There were photographs and feature stories in the newspapers and when the newlyweds walked out on the pier at Brighton, the sideshow men 'offered us free turns at everything'.[101] 'We lashed out on the best,' Amis told a journalist. 'Front row seats at wrestling. All of five bob.' Jane's memory of the wrestling is of a losing combatant shouting to Amis '"Help me, Lord Jim." Kingsley said he'd never been confused with Conrad before.'[102]

The newspaper articles were hard for Hilly to take. 'They were always in the papers. You find yourself reading "I like to sleep on this side of the bed" and so on, and you think "aaarrrgh!" – rubbing your nose in it, you know. And I was still really in love with Kingsley, too. If I'd gone off him it would have been wonderful, but I hadn't.' In July 1965 Hilly gave up the Fulham Road house and moved to Wivenhoe with Sally. Wivenhoe, a pretty port village famous for its light, had long attracted artists and bohemian types, among them Francis Bacon. When the Gales moved there, they instantly became its social centre. There were wild parties every weekend at Ballast Quay, their house on the hill, described by Peregrine Worsthorne, who also had a house there, as 'part baronial hall and part gin palace'. To Worsthorne's French wife, Claudie, Ballast Quay was 'El Vino's-by-the-sea', so many were the journalists and politicians who showed up for weekends. It was Cambridge dons, however, who dominated what Worsthorne calls 'the guest (or cast) list, being drawn to Pat like bees to honey'.[103] Among them was Hilly's second-husband-to-be, David Roy Shackleton Bailey, Fellow in Classics and Bursar of Gonville and Caius,

University Lecturer in Tibetan and archetypal eccentric don, as improbable a successor to Amis as imaginable (among other reasons because Hilly may well have been the first woman he ever kissed).[104] It was Amis who bought Hilly the house in Wivenhoe (a 'mod-semi'), along with a car, before Shackleton Bailey was a serious suitor – if serious is the right word. He also sent her £15 a week spending money, in addition to money for Sally. On 12 May 1965, soon after the purchase had gone through, Hilly wrote to thank Amis, in a letter that suggests how strong her feelings for him still were:

First, I don't know how to thank you for the house – except a million XXXX & hugs & HUGE appreciation, the thing is I know lots of people at Wivenhoe & it's near Cambridge & 1 hour from London in the train . . . Sally will have a very good social life there (Frog Worsthorne) . . . has a smashing daughter (they live there too) of 14 & then there are lots of nice kids her age there – University Essex just up the road & boats & things on the estuary (like Lagharne was) and all in all a very good atmosphere. I hope to end up with goats or donkey at least – hens & things, which will be good for Sally & very good for me. As I've already said – it's very hard to find a husband after you, that doesn't irritate me barmy, quite apart from the shortage of free chaps – but I really am not – *not* getting married for spite – it's just there is no possibility *at ALL* they are so feeble & wet – & you were so amazing I don't suppose I'll ever get over it – BUT I WILL TRY HARDER – really . . . Anyway thanks my darling for all you do for me all the time.

In a series of postscripts Hilly then told Amis how kind George Gale had been to her ('a constant sweet Dad to me'), how she thought she'd seen Jane in London that morning ('& we smiled at each other – but most likely it wasn't her really'), how she appreciated 'what she & of course you are doing for the boys', how her parents were also appreciative ('and never say anything mean about you'). The final PS reads: 'I constantly thank my lucky stars you picked her', followed by the scrawled valediction 'XXX H' and an alarming cartoon self-portrait.

PPS — but I do appreciate what she & of course you are doing for the boys — I constantly thank my lucky stars you picked her.

In the face of the boys' continued hostility, holidays took on a greater importance for Amis and Jane. Soon after the publication of *The Egyptologists* and *The James Bond Dossier*, Amis decided to take seriously Tom Maschler's suggestion that he write his own Bond novel. 'Semi-thoughts drifted through my head over the weeks,' he recounted in the *Observer*, in an article of 31 March 1968, timed to coincide with the novel's publication. 'Where? Not Jamaica – Bond been there too often. Not the States – too expensive. Not France – too many Frenchmen about.'[105] In the end, the question of the novel's setting seems to have been solved by Amis's Princeton friends, Mike and Mary Keeley, who invited Amis and Jane to join them in Greece, where they spent every summer. The plot grew out of the setting, as Amis explains: 'Greece? Yes – Bond never been, I never been, sounds good, islands just right. Also, Eastern Mediterranean a sphere of Russian expansion, British interests there too. (This was September 1965.) But Russia versus Britain too old-hat. Then Red China versus Britain and also versus Russia. So Bond could team up with Russian agent. Female. Tough, like all Bond's girls. And Red China as villain is both new to Bond and obvious in the right kind of way. And Chinese master-villain would be fun . . .'[106] There were other advantages to Greece: Mike Keeley spoke Greek and was an authority on modern Greek literature; with Philip Sherrard he was translating the poems of George Seferis. Mary Keeley *was* Greek. If Amis set his novel in Greece, the Keeleys could provide him with the sort of specialist detail readers would expect to find in a Bond novel. Jane could swim and sightsee to her heart's content while Amis gathered material for the novel; their holiday would be work-related, a plus in Amis's eyes. As for Greece as cradle of Western Civilisation, this was a matter of indifference to Amis, for all his years studying classics at City of London School. When dragged to Delphi he found it 'massively, authentically unimpressive'.[107] 'I don't want to see yet another wall,' Mike Keeley remembers him complaining, 'or another piece of sculpture I don't understand. I don't want to see any more rubble.'

Amis and Jane set off for Athens on 2 September 1965, travelling first to Paris; then by night train to Venice, which neither had seen before (on their one day there, Jane writes, 'I parked Kingsley in a bar with newspapers and walked');[108] then by boat, a two-day trip, to Piraeus, the port of Athens. At Piraeus they were met by Mike and Mary Keeley, who drove them back to Mary's parents' apartment in Athens, where both couples would stay, the parents being away. At drinks and dinner on a terrace restaurant Jane took to the Keeleys right away. They were friendly, welcoming and careful not to refer too often to Princeton days. The Keeleys were impressed with Jane's beauty and intelligence, though Mike also missed Hilly ('just the way Kingsley did, because she was a lot of fun'). Jane's more literary conversation was part of her appeal: 'she was vivaciously involved in the writing business,' Mike remembers, 'and that was exciting'. As Jane grew more comfortable with the Keeleys, her warmth and humour emerged. She and Mary discovered that they both wanted children. 'Kingsley had said that if I wanted children he would be delighted. We even named them.'[109] On one occasion the two women lit candles in a church to ask that they might conceive. Neither did. When the doctor Jane consulted suggested that Amis, too, should be examined, he refused.[110]

After the barest minimum of sightseeing in Athens (Amis 'probably' saw the Parthenon, Mike Keeley imagines, 'from a distance'), the two couples visited several islands in southern Greece, including Hydra, Paros, Naxos and Spetses. They then returned to Athens briefly before setting off on a second excursion, a week's yachting trip on a friend's caique or skiff, the *Altair*, visiting the big island of Euboea, then Skopelos, then Skiros. It was in Athens that the Keeleys introduced Amis and Jane to Aleco Papadogonas, the owner of the *Altair*, and to his friend George Legakis. Amis planned to adhere to the Fleming formula by including at least one underwater diving scene in his Bond novel[111] and both Aleco and George were expert divers. Aleco, an ex-submarine commander, later a minister in the Greek government, was, according to Jane, 'devastatingly good-looking'; George, a Mobile Oil executive, was just good-looking. Aleco's girlfriend Sally was a Bluebell dancer, performing in Athens that summer; George's girlfriend, Metti, was from Denmark. In a letter of 1 November, written from Athens after the Amises had returned to London, Mike reported that Sally had departed for London and Metti for Copenhagen, 'or is it Lynn, or Greta, or Denise who has just gone back somewhere, while Nancy, Alice, Hilda, Marcia, Annette and Ingrid have just arrived'. Though Amis was now Larkin's 'Rajah of Monogam', he had no objection to meeting George and Aleco's pretty girlfriends.

The trip on Aleco's caique concluded with a visit to Skiros, where George Seferis and his wife were vacationing in a converted mill by the sea. The party from the *Altair* stayed in the oldest villa on the island, only yards from the sea. Here Jane started a new novel, *Odd Girl Out* (1972), the plot of which concerns the destructive effect a young girl has on a married couple (the girl is partly a figure out of the swinging Sixties, a world Amis himself would soon portray). There were other writers on the island, among them Natalie Sarraute and Alain Robbe-Grillet, whom Amis only narrowly escaped meeting. Though Seferis had been Greece's ambassador in London, spoke fluent English, and was an ardent jazz fan – enthusing to Henry Miller about Pee Wee Russell – he and Amis never quite hit it off. Seferis was unwell that summer and Jane remembers the dinners they had at his house as subdued, with little of the usual banter. Perhaps Seferis was not drinking, or not drinking enough. In any event, as Keeley remembers it, the two writers 'didn't have much to say to each other'. What Amis did on Skiros was what he did on any holiday: wrote, read, avoided the beach and the sights, napped (etc.) and had long boozy meals in restaurants. Writing to Conquest on 17 September, he pronounced himself pleased with the trip so far: 'The weather has been splendid all along, and Athens very appealing, also Paros, Hydra and Speze [Spetses].'[112] Throughout the holiday he peppered George and Aleco with questions about boats and diving, and Mike and Mary with questions about food, drink, customs, clothing, local lore. Amis: 'What's that fish I hate?' Keeley: 'Kalamari.' Amis: 'Octopus?' Keeley: 'No, squid.' Amis: 'I hate that, too.' Never a brave traveller, Amis was relieved to discover that a 'caique' was not a kayak.

For all his fears – in part the origin of the narrowness of his interests when abroad – Amis, like Jane, was 'fortified' (Martin's phrase)[113] by trips like these. The following summer, in July and August, he and Jane returned to Greece for a second holiday with the Keeleys. It began with a ten-day boat trip for Tom Maschler, a present to Maschler for all he'd done for them at Cape. After Maschler left, the two couples rented a house on Spetses for a month. Here Amis, Jane and Mike wrote novels (only Mary, herself a translator, steered clear of fiction). The house, a white cottage on the island's increasingly polluted harbour, was rented from a British expatriate named Matthews. It was an especially hot summer and Spetses was said to be the hottest island in Greece. Soon after the couples arrived, they discovered that their cottage was said to be the hottest on the island. Jane's method of coping with the heat was to 'stand under the cold shower until my long hair was soaked, then type until it was almost dry, and then I'd repeat the process'.[114] Heat, though, was only one of the cottage's drawbacks. In *Inventing Paradise* (1999), Mike Keeley recalls how Amis 'insisted that the cottage originally belonged to a family of malevolent midgets, since you couldn't move from one room to another without cracking your head on some picturesque lintel or beam ("I will just squat here and cry and never move again," poor Elizabeth Jane Howard once whimpered when a beam struck her for the second time that day in exactly the same place on her forehead).'[115] Outdoors was safer and cooler, especially in the evenings when, in Jane's words, 'we'd walk through the small town beset with rubble – the Greeks always seemed to be building – with the seductive scent of unseen jasmine filling the warm dark air, and then up a small hill on the crest of which was a restaurant much loved by us all . . . The smallest waiter in the world, the owner's heir, staggered from table to table in his nappy, laying glasses and plates.'[116] It was on Spetses that Amis encountered George Katsimbalis, bibliographer, translator, literary fixer, man of letters, Henry Miller's 'Colossus of Maroussi', precisely the sort of larger-than-life figure Amis could be counted on to dislike. 'I've never seen anything like it,'[117] Amis remarked to Keeley after first meeting the Colossus: 'the old man manages to transform a relentlessly boring story and a greasy fried onion into an epic experience simply by never giving up on it.' Amis's patience with Katsimbalis owed something to their shared passion for alcohol. Keeley quotes a Lawrence Durrell anecdote about Katsimbalis that begins 'after his thirtieth drink . . .'[118] But Dylan Thomas, another larger-than-life character, was also passionate about alcohol. It was Greece itself – and being on holiday – that softened Amis. Jane remembers these holidays 'as times of particular happiness . . . They were also, more importantly, times when we could be alone together, an ingredient vital for middle-aged marriages.'[119] What she means by 'alone together', of course, is without children or family.

Colonel Sun, Amis's Bond novel, was published under the pseudonym 'Robert Markham', a made-up name, unlike the borrowed 'Lt. Col. William "Bill" Tanner'. It draws playfully on people and experiences from the Greek trips but also from Amis's life back home. The Bond girl, Ariadne Alexandrou, invents two fictitious colleagues named 'Legakis and Papadogonas'; Chapter 9 is titled 'The Altair', the name given to a boat that figures in the concluding episodes; an ex-Nazi mass murderer appears, whose story Amis took from a real-life story told him by Philip Sherrard, Keeley's friend and co-translator; Bond's counterpart in Athens, '005', is named 'Stuart Thomas'; the doctor who treats Bond in Chapter 2 is named after Amis and Jane's doctor. The novel dutifully ticks off all the Fleming themes and tropes. When Ariadne orders ouzo she asks 'Have you Boutari?'[120] Bond cuts his Scotch with 'the excellent Nigrita mineral water'.[121] A nastie 'speaks a single word into his Hitachi solid-state receiver'.[122] Amis's Bond is suitably Byronic, though some critics thought him a trifle reflective.[123] The villain, Colonel Sun Liang-tan, of the Special Activities Committee, People's Liberation Army, is the best thing in the book, a Red Chinese Anglophile (the superiority of the English is a Fleming theme) and torturer of hideous ingenuity. When clichés appear – 'His mind was racing', 'A gasp of horror tore at Bond's throat' – they are intentional (as is the element of Fu-Manchuerie in Sun's depiction), though as Amis demonstrates in the *Dossier*, Fleming's writing also has moments of power and flair. To judge *Colonel Sun* as one would judge other Amis novels, as opposed to a James Bond novel, is to miss the point. It is an imitation, the application of a formula, a job of work. 'To be a ventriloquist is fun,' Amis told an American interviewer on 20 October 1967. 'The work cannot be completely copied. However, any respectable artist whether he is a writer or a composer should be able to strike a respectable though second rate copy of another artist.'[124] In a letter of 30 June 1968, Keeley pronounced the novel 'basically authentic . . . and this includes all the late local colour, my particular territory: nothing to worry about there, old man'. As a Bond novel, however, it is underpowered, low on action and menace, torture scenes excepted, as if the mechanical exercise of including every theme, trope and trait identified in the *Dossier* took up too much of Amis's energy. In later forays into genre fiction, as we shall see, Amis is looser and more innovative; craft and personal expression combine. Here they are mostly kept apart – one of many divisions in Amis's life at this time.

Lefties, Toffs and Bigots

Amis opened the *Observer* article about *Colonel Sun* (31 March 1968, timed to coincide with its publication) by discussing his reasons for writing the novel. He began with money: 'I do indeed expect to make quite a lot of money out of the venture, and jolly good luck to me.' Yet to write 'at any length *just* for money is a uniquely, odiously painful experience: not really worth the money, in fact'.[1] Then he turned to politics, relegating literary points – the undervalued pleasures of genre, admiration for Fleming's 'strong, simple feeling for the romantic and the strange',[2] the honour of having been selected to follow in his footsteps – to later paragraphs:

What at the outset was an unimportant motive, but has since developed into a major fringe benefit, is the thought of how cross with me the intellectual Left will get. A lot of the persons who will accuse me of having done it for the money will also, such is their nimbleness of mind, accuse me of having done it not for the money, but because I have embraced the *ideology* of Fleming and Bond, as was proved some time back when I declared my support for Allied resistance to Communist aggression in South-East Asia – not really enough, that, to constitute a whole ideology, you might think, but this now seems to be the official Lefty term for anything less than full approval of Russian imperialism.[3]

By 1968, the Lefty-baiting Amis of the later years was already at work. The evolution – if that is the word – of this Amis was slow and uneven in the post-Princeton period, but by 1965, the year of the move to 108 Maida Vale and of mass demonstrations in Britain and the United States against the Vietnam War, he was a prominent presence in newspaper and periodical debates. Initially, Amis's right-wing views were confined to debates over education, thus confirming Bob Conquest's 'Famous First Law, which runs, "Generally speaking, everybody is reactionary on subjects he knows about."'⁴ As early as Chapter 17 of *Lucky Jim*, Amis cast doubt on the wisdom of university expansion, a key objective of the Left (though it was a Conservative administration that accepted the Robbins Committee recommendation of 1963 to double university places over the next ten years). As Jim's English Department colleague Alfred Beesley puts it: 'If we institute an entrance exam to keep out the ones who can't read or write, the entry goes down by half, and half of us lose our jobs. And then the other demand: "We want two hundred teachers this year and we mean to have them." All right we'll lower the pass mark to twenty per cent and give you the quantity you want, but for God's sake don't start complaining in two years' time that your schools are full of teachers who couldn't pass the General Certificate themselves, let alone teach anyone else to pass it.' Dixon's politics, to the extent that they exist at all, are soft-left, but in this instance he 'agreed rather than disagreed with Beesley', without feeling 'interested enough to say so'.⁵

These were pretty much Amis's political attitudes in the mid-1950s. In March 1956 he wrote a letter to *Twentieth Century*, a monthly, recapitulating Beesley's arguments (though adding that greatly improved salaries for teachers would attract better graduates to the profession), then said nothing at all about the issue, at least in print, for four years. It was not until March 1960, in an article in *Encounter* entitled 'Lone Voices', ostensibly an attack on 'the sociologizing generalization'⁶ (also an example of it, as applied to the 1950s), that Amis returned to the debate: 'Nobody who has not seen it in all its majesty – I speak as a university lecturer – can imagine the pit of ignorance and incapacity into which British education has sunk since the war ... I am quite sure that a university admissions policy demanding even less than it now demands – for that is what a larger intake means – will wreck academic standards beyond repair.'⁷ At the very least, '*MORE* WILL MEAN *WORSE*', soon to become an Amis catch-phrase. 'I do not fancy teaching in something that is called a university but is really a rather less glamorous and authentic training college. And I do not fancy living in a society which has abandoned the notion of a university as a centre of learning . . . Not only will examination standards have to be lowered to enable worse and worse people to graduate – you cannot let them all in and then not allow most of them to pass – but the good people will be less good than they used to be: this has been steadily happening ever since I started watching in 1949.'[8] In the past, students of English could be expected to discuss 'the niceties of Pope's use of the caesura. What I explore with the chaps already tends to be the niceties of who Pope was.'[9] Such 'exploration' is obviously 'worse', certainly less fun, for Amis and his good students than more elevated or specialised discussion, though he says nothing of what it is for students who hadn't previously heard of Pope, some of whom might well be as intelligent as those who had. Larkin's joke (quoted in Chapter 5) about the only compliment paid to him as an undergraduate at Oxford ('Mr. Larkin can understand a point if it is explained to him') is relevant here. For Amis, university education is for students with points of their own. It is not enough merely to be capable of understanding a point when it is explained, though why this is not 'benefiting from university training' he does not say. Here and elsewhere in his political writings, Amis's approach is broad brush, axe grinding as well as axe wielding, with little interest in counter-argument or complication. When forced to acknowledge conflicting interests, he is blunt about priorities: 'I have in mind notions about safeguarding standards, safeguarding culture, that to me are more important than notions about egalitarianism.'[10]

On 26 February 1961, in what proved to be his last year at Swansea, Amis and four colleagues – Esmond Cleary, David Sims, R.F. Holland and Peter Winch – published an article in the *Observer* entitled 'The Threat of the Practical', a reply to an article of 8 January by A.D.C. Peterson, Director of the Department of Education at Oxford. Peterson argued both for the expansion of higher educa-tion and for the creation of new, less specialised degree courses, 'more in tune with the realities of the world outside'. Amis and his colleagues were alarmed by what they saw as Peterson's vocational and utilitarian outlook. New courses should be introduced for 'sound academic reasons, not as a piece of salesmanship'. If school-leavers weren't attracted to university courses, the solution was not to change the courses, but for the school-leavers to do something else. In addi-tion to 'requisite intellectual quality' (as measured by examination results), prospective university students needed 'a feeling of the importance of certain studies. If large numbers of those of under-graduate age do not have this feeling, as Mr. Peterson is in fact admitting, and as we should agree, then they are simply not suited for university work.' In subsequent correspondence in the *Observer* (5 March) and *New Statesman* (10 March) Amis reiterated this line with increasing vehemence, spurred on, no doubt, by the role played by the Principal of Swansea, John Fulton, in the expansionist camp. In 1960 Fulton, described by Amis as 'an Oxford–Balliol–Lindsay-sociological-philistine', made a speech proposing that the ratio of students to faculty in the modern university should be 8:1, that the number of lecturers and professors should be between 350 and 400, and that student numbers should therefore be around 3,000. He then left Swansea in the same year as Amis to become the first Vice-Chancellor of Sussex University.[11] As the 1960s progressed and men like Fulton rose to prominence, Amis's writing about education, like all his political writing, took on a wounding directness. On 18 April 1965 he wrote to the *Observer*: 'Perhaps only you could have published a whole article on university failures that laid no weight on the almost invariable cause of failure – *insufficient ability* or, alternatively, *excessive stupidity*.' In today's university classrooms, he wrote in a 1967 article in the *Sunday Telegraph*, 'while the thicks get what they need, the bright people doodle'.[12]

The *Sunday Telegraph* article, 'Why Lucky Jim Turned Right', explains how Amis's initial scorn for left-wing educational views spread to left-wing views in general. The article opens by recalling Amis's prediction in *Socialism and the Intellectuals* (1956) that 'unless something very nasty or very surprising happened' he would always vote Labour. In fact, 'in 1964 I voted Labour for the last time, chick-ened out the following year by voting for the Anti-Common Market character in my constituency and voted Conservative for the first time at the G.L.C. elections this spring',[13] though nothing especially nasty or surprising had happened since 1956 ('unless you place George Brown's appointment as Foreign Secretary in one category or another'). In addition to Labour's 'almost consciously destructive'[14] educational policies, left-wing attitudes to foreign policy helped to turn the tide. *Socialism and the Intellectuals* was written just after Russsia's invasion of Hungary. In ensuing years the 'speed and thor-oughness' with which the memory of the invasion 'has been revised or effaced' has been remarkable. 'That fabulously uninquisitive congeries, the young Left', now think of Hungary as 'something that happened to middle-aged people'.[15]

Whether over issues of education or foreign policy the irritant was the same: 'extremist people on the left-wing of the Labour party, or those following them'. As Amis told a gathering of the Conservative Political Centre at Christ Church, Oxford, in July 1967, 'I think that half an hour with a convinced Lefty is enough to make even the most progressive person wonder a bit whether Conservatism might not have a little more to offer.'[16] What Amis means by 'Lefty' he explains in more detail in 'Why Lucky Jim Turned Right', which was published in the *Sunday Telegraph* on 2 July 1967. 'My concern here is not with the professional Communist or open fellow traveller who just wants his side to win and makes no bones about, for instance, campaigning for the Viet Cong. I mean the kind of person who, over this conflict, professes neutralism while reciting Hanoi's line; who says the Eastern European satellites are really swinging places that have stopped bothering with politics; who used – when it was more newsy – to go on about Ian Smith's fascist regime; who thinks student freedom is impaired when a college applies its statutes; who buys unexamined the abortion-divorce-homosexuality-censorship-racialism-marijuana package.'[17] Such people oppose 'the system' or 'the way things are' either because they are young or youngish (seeing it 'as a product of authority, of parents and schoolmasters and vicars and employers') or because of what Amis calls 'the frustrations of trying to get on in a competitive society where most people, by definition, cannot get on very far'. For the older Lefty – 'mature' would be the wrong word here – the advantage of 'the system' is that it absolves one from blame: 'the reason we are failing to get on, or simply not having a good enough time, is not because we are lazy and stupid, but because of the system'. As for those who persist in Lefty views despite having 'got on pretty well by most standards', they do so either because 'political habit dies hard (as in my own case), success is always relative (the controversial poet gets bad reviews from the pundits, the popular actress finds an extra and even more appreciative audience at rallies), or an increasing bitterness develops as the system, having been repeatedly shouted at to pull itself together, chugs on much as before'.[18] In *Girl, 20* (1971) Amis offers one further motive for persisting in Lefty views: by 'arse-creeping' the young, as does the composer Sir Roy Vandervane in the novel, 'with a bit of luck they'll give you something you really start to want when you get to my time of life.[19] Shut up, I'm talking about uncritical admiration. A very rewarding thing to have, I can assure you' (the interjected 'Shut up' blocks a suggestion that his motive is to sleep with young girls). 'That's why I arse-creep youth,' Sir Roy concludes, by which he means, that's why I say Lefty things like 'You've got to look beyond these bloody categories we've all been brought up with. Under late capitalism, there's bound to be –.'[20] 'Mind you,' he adds, 'I go for their attitudes and the rest of it as well. Quite a bit, anyway.'[21] In the end, what draws Lefties of all stripes together for Amis is their inability or unwillingness to see 'how many of the evils of life – failure, loneliness, fear, boredom, inability to communicate – are ineradicable by political means, and that attempts so to eradicate them are disastrous'.[22] Though in 'Why Lucky Jim Turned Right' Amis describes himself as neither Tory nor right-wing but 'of the Centre, equally opposed to all forms of authoritarianism', to the extent that the Right acknowledges ineradicable evil and the Left does not, he is on the right.

How Amis came to this acknowledgement – unlike Sir Roy Vandervane – the article does not explain. Several sorts of answer suggest themselves. It is often said that people become more like their parents as they age. Mavis Nicholson, who fell out with Amis over politics in this period (as did her husband, Geoff, and other friends such as Mary Morgan, another ex-Swansea student, Al Alvarez and Karl Miller), thought this had happened to him. Then there was the continuing influence of George Gale and the circle of journalists connected with the *Spectator*, plus the anti-liberal bias of the Peterhouse historians, even those who called themselves liberals. Amis's gathering hostility to university life in general – where, as he puts it in 'A Tribute to the Founder,' published in the *Spectator* on 25 December 1959, 'Graft is refined among the tea and scones, / Bluster (new style) invokes the public good, / And doing-down gets done in pious tones' – also led him to the right, the academy being the Left's natural habitat. Finally, there was Amis's closeness to Robert Conquest. In 'Why Lucky Jim Turned Right', the single domestic issue Amis discusses is education. He never, for example, grouses about taxes or benefit fraud, despite his own increasing affluence.[23] On social issues, despite speeches to the boys about the marijuana trade being a Communist plot, he was permissive; even at sixty, he still passed what Julian Barnes called 'those three key liberal tests of the Sixties (abortion, hanging,

Above: KA and EJH at their wedding reception, the offices of Jonathan Cape, 29 June 1965.

Left: EJH, 1975.

Below: KA and EJH at 108 Maida Vale, c.1967.

Right: KA in the garden at Lemmons, 1970.

Below: Left to right, Sargy Mann, Colin Howard and EJH at Lemmons, 1969.

Right: KA and EJH at Lemmons, Sanderson advertisement.

Right: KA in Greece, summer 1969.

Below: KA and EJH with Mike and Mary Keeley, Greece, summer 1969.

Left: KA with Czech guide, Prague, 1966.

Below: EJH with Dolly Burns (far right), Jamaica, 1966.

Above: KA at Vanderbilt, 1967.

Left: Colin Howard, 1970.

Below left: Philip Amis, *c.* 1980.

Below centre: Martin Amis, author's photo, *The Rachel Papers*, 1973.

Below right: Sally Amis in Ronda, 1973.

Above left: Hilly and Jaime Boyd,
aged twelve, 1984.

Above right: Alastair Boyd,
Lord Kilmarnock, 1992.

Right: KA's 70th birthday party,
with Martin Amis, Paul Fussell and
Mavis Nicholson, 16 April 1992.

Below: Philip Larkin in the
Brynmor Jones Library, University
of Hull, 1981.

Above: KA, Virginia and Michael Rush and Stuart Thomas, Swansea, 1994.

Below: The Queen's, Regents Park Road: Back row, left to right: Richard Hough, Catharine Jaques, Hilly, KA, Judy Hough, Peter Quennell; front row, left to right: Tim Jaques, Ali (Lord Kilmarnock), Olivia Hill.

Right: KA at home, 194 Regents Park Road, 1990.

Below: The Coffee Room, Garrick Club, painting by Julian Barrow, 1989.

Above and left: KA after lunch, two steps before falling, Laugharne, 20 August 1995.

Below: KA, unwell, leaves the Rushes' house in Swansea, with Eric Jacobs, his biographer, in the background, 31 August 1995.

homosexuality) without a flutter'.[24] Increasingly, it was the refusal to acknowledge the evils of Communism that led Amis to anathematise the Left and no one in the West had done more to document these evils than Conquest. Though Conquest mostly steered clear of political conversation with Amis – not because he disapproved of Amis's opinions, but because opinions were all they were – his influence was considerable. It was Conquest who introduced Amis to Tibor Szamuely, a Hungarian refugee who had direct experience of Communism and whose name had begun to appear in various right-wing periodicals in the mid-1960s.[25] Szamuely had none of Conquest's reticence about talking politics with Amis. He also had 'a good knowledge of British and American literature, a predictable liking for Kipling (also popular in the USSR), a more unexpected one for the works of Anthony Powell'.[26]

Amis got to know Szamuely as a participant in the weekly 'fascist' lunches at Bertorelli's restaurant in Charlotte Street. These lunches, held first on Thursdays, then on Tuesdays, seem initially to have been an outgrowth of the lunching arrangements Amis made with London friends on his weekly visits from Cambridge. Bertorelli's was cheap, conveniently located near the *Spectator* offices, and large enough not to have to book ahead. It served unpretentious Anglo-Italian food unpretentiously. Martin Amis remembers the head waitress, Anna, saying things like 'Oh no. Don't have that. It's disgusting.'[27] The fascist label was coined by the lunchers themselves. As Martin explains in *Koba the Dread* (2002): 'Both Kingsley and Bob, in the 1960s, were frequently referred to as "fascists" in the general political debate. The accusation was only semi-serious (as indeed was the general political debate, it now seems. In my milieu, policemen and even traffic wardens were called fascists). Kingers and Conquers referred to their own weekly meetings, at Bertorelli's in Charlotte Street, as "the fascist lunch"; here they would chat and carouse with other fascists, among them the journalist Bernard Levin, the novelists Anthony Powell and John Braine (an infrequent and much-feared participant), and the defector historian Tibor Szamuely.'[28] Other regular participants included Anthony Hartley of the *Spectator*, D.C. Watt, the historian and political scientist, Russell Lewis, Director of the Conservative Political Centre (hence Amis's talk at Christ Church) and the American journalist Cy Friedin. Occasional invitees included Tory MPs (Nicholas Ridley, Tony Buck) and foreigners (Russell Fraser, Paul Fussell). Women were only very rarely invited. 'Contrary to rumour,' Amis declares, 'no plot or project was ever suggested at that table, but I learned quite a lot of history and politics now and then, before the rounds of grappa started'.[29]

Anthony Powell remembered the lunches as frivolous occasions. 'It was very gossipy. People would talk about who'd run away with somebody's wife, or something like that.' Alan Watkins, an occasional guest, 'went for the food, the drink and the wit, not the politics, which I found appalling'.[30] Paul Fussell also had difficulty with the politics: 'Sometimes I stared in wonder at the quasi-paranoid turn these conversations took, but the talk was so good, so passionate, inventive and energetic . . . that I demurred only once or twice, as when during Richard Nixon's period of killing North Vietnamese with relish Kingsley proposed a toast to Nixon and I had to decline, proposing instead "The Constitution of the United States"'.[31] According to Powell, the regular participants were mostly 'High Tory', though neither Amis nor Conquest would accept such a label. 'It's a pity that that power-crazed, pipe-smoking creep has got into No. 10,' wrote Amis to Conquest on 19 October 1964, after Harold Wilson's victory, 'but a substantially greater relief that that twitching upper-class buffoon [Alec Douglas-Home] is out of it.' When in a memoir Paul Johnson described the Bertorelli's regulars as 'all howling about the foul deeds of the Labour Government', Conquest reacted indignantly, in a letter to Amis of 29 November 1990: 'Absolute balls: at least I for one preferred Labour to Heathism – and would have preferred Labour to Heseltine, probably'[32] (as he later preferred Blair to Major). What the participants did share was an eye for solecisms and Lefty jargon. As Watkins puts it: 'It was mainly making fun of people who couldn't write.' What made John Braine a 'much-feared' participant was his tendency to preach to the converted: 'Nobody at those gatherings had much time for, say, the Soviet political system,' Amis recalls, 'but John made certain its demerits were never to be overlooked.'[33] To the occasional left-leaning guest, Braine would say things like: 'Why do you *love* despotism? Why do you *yearn* for tyranny?'[34] Amis's own technique with Lefty friends was only marginally less provoking. Martin Amis recalls being witness in the 1960s to 'hundreds of conversations like the following (the interlocutors here are my father and A.J. Ayer): "In the U.S.S.R., at least they're trying to forge something positive." "But it doesn't *matter* what they're trying to forge, because they've already killed five million people." "You keep going back to the five million." "If you're tired of that five million, then I'm sure I can find you another five million."' When the subject of such conversations was Vietnam as opposed to Soviet Russia, Martin recalls, 'people yelled, wept, fought, stalked out'.[35] The passion Vietnam generated exacerbated Amis's aggressive instincts. It also frightened him, which no doubt exacerbated them more. Philip Amis remembers his father genuinely fearing that anti-war demonstrators would march from Grosvenor Square to 108 Maida Vale, to storm the house and attack him bodily.

It is hard to believe that no plotting or planning took place at the Bertorelli's lunches. In the 1960s Amis was frequently in the letters pages of the broadsheet and periodical press, often as a signatory of group letters. 'KA has got very active politically,' Conquest wrote to Larkin on 15 January 1967, 'and just organised a letter to *The Times* saying balls to the Vietcong from all of us.' All of us, in this case, were the Bertorelli's fascists: Amis, Conquest, Braine, Levin, Worsthorne, Crispin [Bruce Montgomery, a regular when in town], Iain Hamilton [of the *Spectator*], Hartley, David Rees [another *Spectator* man, also an ex-pupil of Amis's from Swansea] and the novelist Simon Raven. The letter appeared on 21 January under the title 'Backing for U.S. Policies in Vietnam'. After admitting that the United States had made unspecified mistakes in Vietnam, it immediately attacked Lefty agit-prop. The criticism of the United States, it declared, is 'malicious and no more; much of it represents the impact of suspect information upon uncritical minds; and much of it, coming from conformist protesters, accords better with emotional habit than with any real concern for either truth or humanity'. These sweeping assertions about the war's opponents were matched by comparably sweeping self-assertions. The signatories described themselves as 'acquaintances without organisation or secretariat, but knowing that they speak for a much larger body of opinion' (despite overwhelming opposition to the war among fellow writers and intellectuals). In its final sentences the letter confronted readers with a stark choice: 'When all the lesser issues are cleared away, whose side are we on? Our answer must be that as in Korea and Berlin, and as under previous Presidents and Prime Ministers, we unequivocally support America and her allies from the Commonwealth and Asia.'

On 9 February Conquest wrote to Larkin about the stir the letter had caused: 'Reported on the news (BBC radio, and ITV, ie, though not the BBC Televietcong network, answered by scores of pompous cunts, attacked in Pravda and Private Eye, sensation in US etc. We just said, fuck the Commies in Vietnam, and stop boring us with their hysterical propaganda here. Good stuff. You should have joined in. – Old KA was the moving spirit, getting the signatures, taking them in, etc. etc. Committed, yet.' On 13 February, Amis organised a second letter, countering criticism that the first had simplified the nature and origins of the war. He did this by cleverly focusing on a question of definition: by 'unequivocally' in 'we unequivocally support America and her allies' the signatories meant 'unambiguously, clearly (O.E.D.), not, as Mr. Philip Toynbee and others seem to imagine, uncritically and abjectly'. As in the original letter, mistakes and complications were left unspecified; nothing at all was said about corruption and cronyism in the Diem and Ky regimes or about their inability to win popular support; nor was anything said about the nationalist aspirations and appeal of the North Vietnamese and Vietcong.

The most revealing of Amis's political writings of the 1960s is the poem 'After Goliath', first published in *A Look Round the Estate: Poems 1957–1967*, the volume he put together shortly after finishing *Colonel Sun* ('to show that I am full of integrity after all,' he wrote to Larkin on 21 May 1967). The poem begins by recounting the success achieved by David's deadly slingshot and the resulting 'howls of dismay' from Goliath's fans:

> From aldermen, adjutants, aunts,
> Administrators of grants,
> Assurance-men, auctioneers,
> Advisers about careers,
> And advertisers, of course,
> Plus the obvious b——s in force.

Here are all the targets of early Amis, political and cultural. Yet as soon as Goliath falls, David begins to feel uneasy: 'such an auspicious début / Was a little too good to be true.' What bothers David is the nature of the applause at his back. His supporters

> Sounded shrill and excessive now,
> And who were they, anyhow?
> Academics, actors who lecture,

> Apostles of architecture,
> Ancient-gods-of-the-abdomen men,
> Angst-pushers, adherents of Zen,
> Alastors, Austenites, A-test
> Abolishers –

Here are the targets of later Amis. Are they any better than Goliath's unlovely lot? The alphabetical parallel suggests not. And what of David himself? As he walks past the conquered Goliath he contemplates the tyrant's dropped sword:

> Trophy, or means of attack
> At the rapturous crowds at his back?
> He shrugged and left it, resigned
> To a new battle, fought in his mind,
> For faith that his quarrel was just,
> That the right man lay in the dust.

'My enemy's enemy is my friend,' the proverb from which Amis drew the title of one of his army stories (about 'adjutants', military 'b——s in force'), no longer applies. Such 'friends' now appal, leading David to half sympathise with Goliath, even briefly to contemplate using his sword (in the manner of the Soviets of 1917, against 'the rapturous crowds at his back'). This moment of contemplation is the opening skirmish in a new post-Goliath battle, that of keeping the faith. The odds against David winning this battle, the poem suggests, are long. Amis has said of the poem: 'It hits off to my own satisfaction something I had been trying to get said for a long time – that there is a disappointing lack of contrast between the enemies of progress (in any field: social, literary, political) and those theoretically on the side of progress.'[36]

What sets 'After Goliath' apart from Amis's other political writings in the 1960s is its detachment. The other writings are those of a new Goliath, the Goliath the poem's David threatens to become. Donald Davie makes a similar point about Amis's shift to the right in 'Hobbits and Intellectuals', an essay published in the October 1969 issue of *Encounter*. In this essay, Davie resurrects a distinction from his poem 'Creon's Mouse' (1953). In Amis's political writings, Davie argues, the 'Lefty' is an Antigone figure, while Amis, a lapsed Lefty, is now 'a Creon man'. As for Davie: 'I've always been pro-Ismene myself' – that is, a proponent of tolerance and moderation (in the poem, 'a self-induced and stubborn loss of nerve').[37] 'After Goliath' offers no such third way, no Ismene option. David must fight the good fight, against oppression from left or right; also from within. This fight Amis frequently lost, in polemic at least. As Christopher Ricks complains of the political essays in Amis's *What Became of Jane Austen?* (1970), 'there are two sides to every question, the right side and the wrong side. There is no time for qualifications'; 'the overriding impulse has become to dissociate oneself from David's fans. (Goliath's have suddenly and mysteriously become so harmless as to be invisible.)' In other words: 'the Lefty's unscrupulous selectivity is matched, not conquered'.[38]

One final factor in Amis's move to the right in the 1960s was Jane Howard, herself a lifelong Conservative. As Jacobs puts it, it was not so much that Jane 'preached her moderate Toryism at Amis. But living with someone who saw nothing wrong in being right-wing may have made it easier for him to give up the political habits of his adult life.'[39] At times, Amis's anti-Leftism, especially when arguing with the boys, was too much even for Jane, 'nearly turning me into a socialist'.[40] Like many people who knew him (though not his son Martin),[41] Jane mostly thought Amis's political activities a way of upsetting people or banding together with friends. For all his notoriety as a spokesman on the right, 'the truth was, I think, that he wasn't a political animal. It was more that he enjoyed the chappish company of people for whom politics was the social peg upon which they hung their conviviality. After the first few months in his company I never took his political views – of whatever party – seriously, although I never told him so.'[42]

The influence of Jane's Conservative friends on Amis's politics was complicated by questions of class – not a problem with the Bertorelli's Tories, even the posh ones like Powell and Worsthorne. Throughout his life Amis remained wry about and wary of the upper classes and the establishment. Conquest recalls him making arrangements before a party at Pamela Berry's: 'Meet you at the Club,[43] and we'll go on to Lady Pamela's afterwards. I never thought I'd be saying that.' Larkin was comparably amused (also bemused) at the idea of Amis as a toff, or a friend of toffs. 'Who would expect to meet the Fifties' mascot sporting a Moss Bros topper at Royal Ascot?' he wrote to Conquest on 23 July 1973. 'Kingsley treats his fans like God Almighty, Gives them first a lefty, then a righty. Heh-heh-heh.'

Though in later years, class antipathies and anxieties accompanied the deterioration of Amis's marriage to Jane, in the 1960s and early 1970s, as Worsthorne remembers it, Amis 'was curious about the life of luxury and country houses', showing 'every sign of enjoying that side of that life'. Very soon after the move to Maida Vale, Amis and Jane were invited to dine with the author and broadcaster Stephen Potter (Westminster, Coldstream Guards, Oxford). There they met Dolly and Bobby Burns. Dolly Burns was the only daughter of Lord Duveen, the art dealer, and Bobby Burns was a distinguished orthopaedic surgeon, now retired. Dolly was very rich, with houses in Mayfair and Jamaica, and was herself a collector (like one of her father's clients), though of people who were famous or good at something rather than works of art; her great ambition, according to Jane, was to preside over 'the most desirable salon in London'. At her dinner parties at Chesterfield Hill, usually for fourteen to sixteen, guests wore full evening dress. According to Brian Masters, in his book *Great Hostesses* (1983), 'a Burns dinner for sixteen might include the American Secretary of State for Defence, the writer Kingsley Amis, a member of the Hapsburg family, a duke or two, a reviewer on the *Times Literary Supplement*, a designer of shoes, a surgeon. It is more or less certain that none of them would have been offered the opportunity of meeting the others without the thought and foresight of Mrs. Burns. Hence the difference between a hostess and a lady who has dinner parties.'[44] Amis was amused by Dolly's flamboyant bossiness and got on well with Bobby, an amiable clubman and golfer. In early August 1965 Amis and Jane were invited to spend a few days with the Burnses in Cap d'Antibes, where they stayed, all expenses paid, at the Hôtel du Cap Eden Roc. 'The first evening,' Jane writes, 'we sat in the bar in extremely comfortable chairs drinking Paradis, a champagne cocktail laced with raspberry juice. After a short while Bobby said, "Well, what shall we talk about?" And Dolly immediately answered, "Sex is the most interesting subject in the world." Bobby sat urbanely smiling.'[45]

Dolly was in her early seventies in 1965, as was Bobby, and though she'd lost her figure, took great care over her appearance, especially her coiffure and 'operatic' make-up.[46] Although devoted to Bobby, she had a lover, a Russian composer named Sergei Barsakoff who 'happened' (Jane's quotation marks) to be living in Nice. Dolly would visit Sergei in the afternoons, driven over in her Rolls-Royce by a chauffeur who 'was only allowed to drive at fifteen miles an hour while she shouted at him to go slower'.[47] In addition to composing music, Sergei built models for ballet sets. Amis and Jane adored his accent. 'I made a muddle,' Jane remembers him saying: 'I made a very careful muddle and somebody said: "It is the most amazing muddle I have ever seen." I can think of nobody else who could have made this muddle but myself.' Amis enjoyed the stay in Antibes, partly because he always enjoyed grand hotel life, partly because Dolly's eccentricities fascinated him, in particular her need to have her way in everything. When she and Bobby extended a second invitation, to spend three weeks as their guests in Jamaica, staying at their house in Montego Bay and travelling at their expense, he and Jane accepted. Dolly might be 'uncontrollably rich' (Colin's phrase) but she was also good fun. In addition, she had what Jane called 'an endearing side: she was a romantic, vulnerable, naïve'.[48] They could escape the English winter, leaving in early January but returning in time for the publication of *The Anti-Death League* in March 1966. Colin was prepared to look after the boys and Bob Conquest even promised to help. 'I am acting as longstop to Jane's brother,' he wrote to Larkin on 6 January, 'in case the boys present him with a problem he can't handle (any brief moment of authority I get will be devoted to clipping the younger's long blonde locks; but I hope this won't arise).'

The stay in Jamaica was not a success, though the passage out was. Dolly had booked tickets for the Amises on a luxury banana boat, the SS *Golfito*. In the first of several letters addressed to 'Monkey, Philip and Martin' (Phil's 'bust' did not take place until after their return), a nervous Amis described the boat's captain, Bill Young, a large, likeable Ulsterman, as 'sober all the time' and with 'no signs of going mad. *Yet.*' Notable among the 120 passengers were the Bishop of Durham, 'a *fucking* old *fool*';[49] Princess Alice, Duchess of Gloucester, 'supposed to be George *V*'s sister; but on appearance could be George *IV*'s sister'; and 'a globular 16-stone female with cultural pretensions, who tried to obtrude herself on our group. I *drove her away* by being *studiedly rude.*' After a few days of rough weather the sun came out and flying fish appeared, described by Amis as 'quite fun, but small, and somehow verminous-looking'.[50] He and Jane had made '3 amiable chums', one of whom, he proudly announced, he had secured as a customer for Colin (for a stereo system), booze was cheap and the food 'the best I have ever had on a British ship'.[51] In the next day's addition to the letter, Amis described the tranquil scene of its composition: 'I sit now in the lounge awaiting Heidsieck-time: all silence but for the clack of scrabble-tiles, the yelling of small dusky children, the dash of spray and the tremendous gurgle and squelch as the water in the swimming-pool is shifted by the movement of the ship: sounds like the Thing from another world sucking King Kong's cock.'

The first port of call was Trinidad, where the passengers had six hours ashore. The first Trinidadian Amis encountered, 'a man of African descent', hurried up to him 'and assured me, in song, that this was his island in the sun, where his people had lived since time begun. Both these notions struck me as debatable at best.'[52] About an hour later, 'I was sitting half pissed in the Trinidad Hilton, eating Columbus Mangrove Root Oyster Cocktail – bloody good – and drinking Foreign Guinness, which as you know is to me the prince of beers' (Foreign Guinness will feature later in the trip). Eventually, Amis, Jane and chums 'lurched back on board and in due course bingo'd and champagned our way up to Kingston'. From Kingston, there was a five-hour train ride to Montego Bay, where Amis began not to like things. 'This is a rather lousy island,' is how he opens a letter of 3 February to Colin and the boys: 'beautiful and all that, good bathing, lots of – though by no means continuous – sun, but rather horrible rich white people and rather miserable resentful black people. My old left-wing, or just humanitarian, feelings came back with a rush. I wouldn't argue that they ought to have been given their independence, but they bloody well ought to have been given some means of livelihood.' The letter concludes: 'Flowers, humming-birds, planter's punch, and the Wog [Jane] are really the nicest things here. Apart from me, of course.'

Life at Fairlea, the Burnses' house, was excessively formal. 'I should think there were ten people staying in the house,' Jane remembers, 'and there were dinner parties every night and *all* of us were taken to dinner parties with other people who had ten people staying in their house. We all had to wear evening clothes, black tie and everything. I had a huge trunk of clothes for this purpose. Kingsley got amazingly bored with it, because they were on the whole very boring people – and he didn't like black tie.' Amis described Montego Bay in the letter of 3 February as 'filled with millionaires like Wm. Hill the bookie and aristocrats like the Prince and Princess Shomberg-Lippe . . . The rest of the white population appears to consist of deaf Americans.' In addition to formal dinner parties, Dolly insisted on the same routine each day: an excursion to Doctor's Cove in the morning, 'the smart place to swim',[53] then lunch and a sleep, to prepare for the rigours of the evening. Amis was not the only guest to chafe under these arrangements. As Jane wrote to the Keeleys on 27 January: 'The people here spend 3/4 energy on arguing about plans: nobody agrees and nobody gets what they want.'[54] Jane managed two short trips into the interior of the island, though Amis, never very adventurous or interested in sights, did not accompany her. 'After about ten days,' Jane writes in her memoirs, 'Kingsley grew restive.'[55] One afternoon he stormed into their room and insisted that they leave immediately: 'he couldn't stay after what had gone on between him and Dolly'.[56] What had gone on was that Amis had asked Dolly if he could have Foreign Guinness at lunch instead of Jamaican Red Stripe, the beer Dolly stocked, and she had said that he couldn't, since Foreign Guinness cost three cents more a can (or some such minuscule figure). Amis was incandescent. What difference could such a sum possibly mean to a millionaire like Dolly? Here was another example of her bossing her guests around and it was intolerable. Amis would not spend another night under her roof. As Jane pointed out, however, because he wouldn't fly they were stuck until the return of the banana boat. Then Dolly and Bobby appeared at the door. She was in tears, apologising profusely, and Amis was temporarily mollified. Back in London, though, he insisted that they send Dolly the cost of their passage and swore that he would never stay with the Burnses again. He then carica-tured Dolly as the odious Lady Baldock in *I Want It Now* (1968), which severed relations between the two couples temporarily.[57] Though Jane thought the caricature cruel, it was she who gave Amis the novel's premise. Dolly had no children of her own. What would it have been like to have had her as a mother?

Amis's eruption at Fairlea derived only in part from Dolly's behav-iour. The boring routines and conversation of the very rich contributed as well. As the letters home suggest, he was also uncom-fortable with the disparities of wealth on the island and the living conditions of black Jamaicans. When the Amises arrived, *four* black maids unpacked for them, 'so now', Jane reported to the Keeleys on 27 January, 'we can't find anything'. Later in the letter she added: 'I don't think the natives are very friendly', a view seconded by Amis in a postscript: 'on a first look, a negro would do better in Leopoldville, let alone Little Rock, than in Montego Bay. Wd perhaps break even in Johannesburg.' Before taking the boat back to London, Amis had a glimpse of a Jamaica that was more to his liking, more part of his world. He and Jane gave what she described as 'a kind of lecture together' at Kingston University, at the invitation of the West Indian novelist John Hearne, whom Amis had met in London. They then spent the night with Hearne and his wife Mary, in their house in the Blue Mountains outside Kingston. On 15 March, after their return to London, Conquest reported to Larkin that 'Kingers is back, unbronzed and bronzed off with the rich shags and cloudy skies of Jamaica'.

If the trip to Jamaica briefly revived Lefty feelings in Amis, a week's trip to Czechoslovakia in October 1966 hardened his feelings towards Communism and its apologists. In 1948 Amis had twice been interviewed for a lectureship in English Literature at Prague University and in later years he occasionally wondered what his life would have been like had he got it. His interest in Czechoslovakia was also spurred by the first tentative signs of liberalisation in the regime, as well as by admiration for Czech science fiction. For these reasons, when he and Jane were invited to a party at the new Czech Embassy in London, they accepted. After the party, the Embassy's cultural attaché wrote to Amis asking if he and Jane would like to visit Prague, partly under the auspices of the British Council. The visit would be for six days and Amis's only duties would be to deliver a lecture at the university and to meet some students and writers. The details of the trip were explained to Amis by an embassy official named Peter Pujman, described in the *Memoirs* as 'not only a nasty little man but one of a type almost immediately recognisable to anybody who has had to deal with that sort of person, not only so much of a faux bonhomme that you thought at first he might be trying to be funny, but also an exuder of equally false, and clearly false, decency, reliability, and just the right amount of sympathy for Western ways'. Amis was at first puzzled by the invitation, given his outspoken anti-Communism, until 'I realised, or was told, that of course to a Communist bureaucracy working at normal speed I was still an Angry Young Man.'[58] The six days proved more crowded than Pujman had suggested they would be: there were visits to the Ministry of Education and Culture, the Union of Writers, the Museum of Czech Literature, the Publishing House of Belles Lettres, the Club of Translators; there were lunches and dinners with various cultural bureaucrats, including a Rosa

Klebb–like Minister of Culture, 'as if selected by a Hollywood casting director . . . rather unimaginative in taste'.[59] They were taken to an international jazz festival, where they ran into Cleo Laine and Johnny Dankworth, friends of Amis from Victor Gollancz's anti-hanging rallies; they were also taken to a symphonic concert (Beethoven, Bartók, Brahms) and the opening of an exhibition of Penguin Books, which turned out to be sponsoring the visit in some way.

At the suggestion of an official of the British Council, both Amis and Jane wrote confidential reports on their trip for the Foreign Office, just the sort of no-risk espionage likely to appeal to a nervous Bond fanatic. Jane reported on the morale of the many Czech writers they had been introduced to, some of whom they were able to visit in their homes. 'Of all the Czechs we met,' she wrote, 'only one attempted to tell us how good everything was: the rest were pessimistic, despairing, many of them frightened in some degree or other: all took for granted the fact that our hotel room, our official car (driven by Party members of whom our interpreter was clearly terrified) was bugged, and therefore any frank talking was done in the open air or in their homes.' She also reported being told by a doctor that the suicide rate in Czechoslovakia was the highest in the world, except, he thought, for Russia; that she and Amis were careful never to quote one Czech to another; and that they left the country with mixed feelings, a combination of 'release from personal strain' and 'affection and sadness for people who even in six days had become our friends'. Chief among these friends were Josef Skvorecky, the novelist and jazz enthusiast, Josef Nesvadba, the science fiction writer, and Miroslav Holub, the poet. At the suggestion of another British Council representative in Prague, Jane also visited the studio of a Czech artist named Janacek who asked to draw her in the nude. Janacek spoke no English but made clear his desire to do more than draw her. She escaped his attentions by buying one of his drawings.

Amis's report for the Foreign Office, entitled 'Prague Visit: Confidential',[60] seconded Jane's remarks about morale, then concentrated on the prospects of reform under the Novotny regime (Dubcek and the Prague spring were some eighteen months away): 'The obvious question that interested me was the "liberalisation" of the regime and what lies behind this, particularly as it affects writers.' Amis's impression was that reform was both 'very incomplete, and also precarious'. In the *Memoirs*, he quotes one of the novelists he met in Prague: 'It is better here in Prague than anywhere else behind the Curtain; it is better now than at any time since the coup – and look at it!'⁶¹ In the *Memoirs*, Amis also provides concrete examples of the surveillance and intimidation mentioned in Jane's reports: '(In the car) "What building is that, Karel?" – "One of no historical interest," i.e. police barracks, etc. Subject at once dropped. (In the hotel, to a writer) "Come up to our room for a drink." – "Thank you no, but the bar is all right."'⁶² Amis's report concluded with a recommendation: 'We feel that as many of our writers as possible should be encouraged to visit Prague and other Czech cities.' Half a year later, in late spring or early summer 1967, Skvorecky, the writer they had come to know best in Prague, was given permission to visit London. Amis and Jane invited him to stay at 108 Maida Vale and hosted a party for him, to which they invited all the left-wing or left-leaning writers they knew, among them Arnold Wesker, David Storey, Iris Murdoch and Anthony Burgess. Czech embassy officials also attended the party, one of whom complimented Jane on her generosity in having Skvorecky to stay. 'He's no trouble at all,' Jane answered. 'This morning, for instance, he went off to the National Gallery by himself.' 'Oh, we know,' the official said.

In September 1966, the month before the trip to Prague, Amis and Jane returned to London from the second of their summers in Greece with the Keeleys to discover that both boys had done terribly in their exams. 'We are giving them one more chance to pass in January,' she wrote to the Keeleys on 26 October, 'and then sending them off to cramming boarding schools where they will be made to work and get through.' Phil resisted this plan but Martin was amenable, his interest in English having been sparked by Jane the year before. She had come across him 'lounging in a disaffected way, boredom seeping from every pore', and asked him what he wanted to do when he was older:

'Be a writer,' he said.

'You – a *writer*? But you never read anything. If you're so interested in writing why don't you read?'

He looked at me and said, 'Give me a book to read then.' I gave him *Pride and Prejudice*. A little later he came to me and said, 'Jane, you've got to tell me how it ends.'

'Of course I won't. You find out for yourself.' He argued with persuasive charm, but I felt on firm ground: he was obviously enjoying it. That was when he started to read properly – a very good moment for me.[63]

In the spring of 1967 Jane found what she thought would be a suitable boarding crammer for Martin, Sussex Tutors in Brighton (for all his talk of standards and incompetent teachers, Amis took little interest in his own children's education, until Martin began studying for Oxford entrance). As she explained to the master who would be teaching him, Mr Ardagh, 'Martin was almost totally uneducated but none the less extremely bright and, if decently taught, was scholarship material for university. I added that he wasn't my son and therefore he had to believe I wasn't saying this out of maternal blindness.'[64] Phil, meanwhile, was also the beneficiary of adult intervention. Colin's friend Sargy Mann encouraged him to apply to the Camberwell School of Art, which he got into and loved, studying first graphic design and then print-making. By 1967 both boys were launched on paths which would eventually lead them to their respective careers.

Sargy Mann became a significant presence in Amis's life in 1967. He and Colin met and quickly become close friends in the late 1950s, through a mutual interest in jazz. Sargy often visited Colin at Blomfield Road and then at 108 Maida Vale, joining in tennis and poker games with the boys. A kind and funny man, he was also a talented painter. He was born in 1937, three years after Colin, and educated at Dartington Hall, a progressive boarding-school near the family home in Devon. Instead of going to university he trained as an engineer, then studied at Camberwell art school and eventually ended up teaching painting and drawing there, for almost twenty years.[65] Amis liked Sargy from the start. Though Sargy's jazz tastes were wider than Amis's (deeper as well, for he was a musician, a jazz drummer), he 'had come up through the jazz that Kingsley liked' and often listened to records with him. Sargy could also hold his liquor, drinking and talking with Amis late into the night. It was another point in his favour that he was nimble and funny enough to take part in the verbal games and jokes Amis loved. When Amis was at work on *Girl, 20*, constructing Sir Roy Vandervane's slovenly speech ('sweep pickle', 'tim peaches', 'In thack case'), everyone in the household pitched in; Sargy's offering, 'vogka', arrived just too late for inclusion: 'he was furious that I hadn't come up with it earlier'.

Sargy ended up living in 108 Maida Vale as a consequence of

Amis and Jane's next and longest trip. This trip, to the US and Mexico, lasted just over half a year, from August 1967 to March 1968. Its instigator was Amis's old Princeton friend Russell Fraser, who had met Jane when he visited Keats Grove, either at the end of 1964 or early in 1965. In addition to teaching English at Princeton, Fraser had been an associate dean in the Graduate School, and in 1965 accepted the offer of chair of the English Department at Vanderbilt University, in Nashville, Tennessee. 'I was a young man and I wanted to see what I could do on my own,' is partly how he explains his decision to accept the offer. 'I had this sense that I could make the best English Department in America.' Fraser was a New Yorker but he had taught at Duke University in North Carolina and liked the South. That Vanderbilt was prepared to double his Princeton salary also figured in his decision, as did the opportunity to continue in administration, if only on a departmental level. Vanderbilt had a visiting professor programme and shortly after Fraser settled there he entered into correspondence with Amis with a view to bringing him to Nashville for a semester. Amis would be the third writer to come to the English Department under the programme, following Anthony Burgess and Allen Tate. If Fraser, the new chair, could bring Amis it would be an obvious feather in his cap.

Amis's first thought about Fraser's offer was that he wanted no part of it:

Then I noticed that the invitation was only for a semester or half-year, a period of something like four months from October to mid-January, and that the teaching load did not look heavy. Russ, a reliable fellow, affirmed too that the place in general was not like what they said and, more cunningly and tellingly, that no Englishman was ever seen in those parts. I was soon quite won round by the thought of a comparatively remote, still quite romantic-sounding part of America unpolluted by the kind of Brit they think you must be pining to see but actually loathe and dread.[66]

This passage from the *Memoirs* leaves out any mention of race, though when discussing his initial reluctance Amis lists 'lynchings and all that'[67] among disincentives (the others are country music and Southern writers). The South might seem remote, romantic-sounding and Brit-free, but the civil rights movement had put it very much in the news in the 1960s and Nashville was at the movement's centre, the site of the first student sit-ins (organised initially by James

Lawson, the second black student to be admitted to the Vanderbilt Divinity School, which immediately expelled him) and the training ground of freedom marchers and prominent civil rights leaders. Though Amis does not say so in the *Memoirs*, there is some evidence to suggest that one of his motives in choosing to accept Fraser's invitation was to irritate Lefties: first-hand observation was bound to refute knee-jerk assumptions about the South. 'You see,' Amis told an American interviewer at the end of his stay, 'the chief thing we wanted to find out about was this whole business of the Negro in the South. We came down here hoping and somehow expecting that in some rough-and-ready sort of way the South was well on the way to solving its own problems.'[68] One final motive for coming to Nashville was Amis's friendship with Fraser. When asked by people at Princeton why he wanted to go to Vanderbilt, he replied: 'My friend Russell makes me laugh and I like him and he asked me.' 'For Kingsley,' Jane believes, coming to Vanderbilt was partly a matter of showing 'solidarity with Russell'.[69]

When Amis and Jane accepted Fraser's invitation, Philip Amis was no longer living at 108 Maida Vale and Martin was boarding in Brighton.[70] Colin was prepared to look after the house and the boys, the latter in conjunction with Hilly in Wivenhoe, and up to the last minute it was assumed that Peregrine Worsthorne would act as resident 'longstop'. Worsthorne, Jane's cousin, had been living at 108 Maida Vale for several months, during a period of marital (also extra-marital) turbulence.[71] Though working all day at the *Sunday Telegraph* and out many evenings, he had become a quasi-member of the family, dining with Amis and Jane when at home, playing tennis with Sargy and Colin. As he remembers it, the Amises were kind, hospitable and 'enviably happy'; among the household's many enjoyable rituals, he singles out communal breakfasts round their 'enormous' double bed, 'at which all present would compete to read out the silliest lefty *bêtise* in the morning newspapers – a marvellous way, incidentally, to cure a hangover and get the adrenaline stirring for a good morning's work'.[72] Shortly before the Amises set sail for New York, however, Worsthorne decided to go back to his wife.[73] 'There is really no alternative but for me to return and do the best I can,' he wrote to Jane and Amis in an undated note. 'You will probably think me mad and a bloody nuisance for changing plans so soon before your departure for America. Please forgive me. You have all been amazingly kind.' It was at this point that Jane suggested to Colin that Sargy take Perry's place. Colin thought this an excellent idea, as did Sargy, who had very little money at the time and was living in a bed-sit off the Tottenham Court Road. From his standpoint, 108 Maida Vale was luxury. There was money for the upkeep of the house and for food, there was a cleaning lady and a gardener and there was lots to paint (as Iris Murdoch put it to Jane, in a thank-you note of 30 May 1975, 'How nice . . . to have a resident painter. To help you to keep seeing your charming places anew'). Sargy's duties consisted of keeping an eye on the garden, helping to look after the three cats, and occasionally cooking a meal ('We were very good at fish fingers'). The boys were frequent visitors, Martin on weekends and holidays, Phil for brief periods between moves, or just for a meal or a chat. 'They seemed to sort of whiz in and out on scooters,' Sargy remembers: 'There was quite a lot of games playing . . . bar billiards and quite a bit of poker.' At times Colin found it hard to act as intermediary between the boys and Amis and Jane. On 3 September 1967, he wrote to Nashville to ask whether it was true that Phil was meant to have an allowance of £55 10s. per month: 'If either of you *can* remember what was arranged financially *and* what it was supposed to include (rent, school fees, travelling, clothes etc.) I would feel better able to cope.' When Martin balked at taking a job Amis and Jane had helped to arrange, Colin negotiated an alternative. 'It would help,' he wrote to them on 23 January 1968, 'if when you write to him about the Latin or whatever, you could in a friendly way back up my plans.' What made Colin's position tolerable, in Sargy's view, was that the boys 'really did love and respect him'. For the most part, the six months Amis and Jane were away passed without incident. Martin, whose A-Level results had been good, continued to apply himself to his school work, keeping Amis and Jane posted with what in *Experience* he describes as Osric-like letters about books and why he should be allowed a flat of his own in Brighton (also why the job they'd arranged for him was a bad idea). After a rocky start, Phil found his feet at Camberwell. Nothing of note went wrong with the house, the cats or the garden.

Meanwhile, the news from Wivenhoe was also good, or at least not immediately alarming. Sally was getting on at Moira House, her boarding-school in Eastbourne, and Hilly and Shackleton Bailey, the don from Cambridge, had decided to marry. The wedding took place on 21 November in Wivenhoe, while Amis and Jane were in

Nashville, and whatever Amis's feelings about its suitability – Shackleton Bailey was gruff and eccentric, pathologically shy with women and notoriously mean about money – he understood Hilly's need for security. 'So glad about your news,' he wrote to her on 27 October 1966, almost a year before the wedding. 'It is good to know you are going to be settled (and you know I don't mean from the financial point of view, and I know you know). Funny to think you're going to wind up in Cambridge after all. How will you take to being a high-powered ACADEMIC HOSTESS?' At the end of the letter Amis told Hilly that he and Jane were happy to take Sally for the holidays, that she should apply to Stuart Thomas if she needed money (and to him when Stuart ran out), and that he was 'sorry to hear about your old dad' (Daddy B, aged eighty, had contracted pneumonia, from which he would not recover). The valediction to the letter was: 'Heaps of love, Binks.' In March 1967 Amis had a meeting with Hilly and Shackleton Bailey, presumably about the impending marriage and arrangements for Sally. 'Fine to see you the other day, and old Shack, who I thought was a very good bloke,' Amis wrote on 12 March, adding that 'J. and I were thinking it would be a good thing if *you* told Sally about the big decision.' The letter enclosed 'a bit of cig money!' and was signed 'Love X Binks.'

Amis and Jane set sail for New York on the *Queen Mary* on 30 August 1967. After a few days in the city, staying at the Algonquin Hotel and contacting old friends, they moved to Princeton for several days, staying with the Keeleys, who gave them a party. They then took a long zigzagging train journey from Trenton, New Jersey, to Nashville. As Jane remembers it, Russell Fraser's wife Phil was at the station in Nashville and took them to the house that had been rented for them, a two-mile drive from the Vanderbilt campus. The owners of the house, at 3627 Valley Vista Road, were Edgar and Ivar-Lou ('honestly', Amis wrote to Colin, 'pronounced Ahva-Leew')[74] Duncan. Both taught English, Edgar at Vanderbilt, Ivar-Lou at Belmont College, one of several small Christian colleges in Nashville. Edgar, a Chaucerian, had managed to wangle a two-year grant from the National Science Foundation to study obscure alchemical texts in Europe. As soon as Jane walked into the house, 'I knew it was going to be awful, but Kingsley didn't seem to notice. I was tired after the long train journey, and hadn't the guts to say I didn't want to live there.'[75]

Valley Vista Road is and was a quiet suburban street. The Duncan house, 'a drab and tasteless little place', was mostly on one floor, though there were two attics Amis and Jane were not to enter, crammed with the owners' possessions. The linen closet was also locked, perhaps, they conjectured, because the Duncans had read *Lucky Jim* and were worried about their sheets. Ivar-Lou was present for the handover and Jane took an instant dislike to her. The black maid was there, too, and Jane remembers Ivar-Lou saying in front of the maid: 'You'll have to give her something at Christmas . . . Just something cheap and gaudy – anything will do.' Jane, 'deeply ashamed',[76] noticed that the maid's face was impassive throughout. When Christmas came, with Ivar-Lou in mind, Jane thought, '"Fuck her," this horrible woman', and gave the maid a very expensive non-stick frying pan and a silk shirt. It was Ivar-Lou's parsimoniousness rather than her insensitivity that astonished Amis. 'She had tried to charge me for using her husband's typewriter,' Amis records in the *Memoirs*, 'a measure he vetoed.'[77] Amis's first impressions of the house, as relayed to Colin in a letter of 17 September, were more positive than Jane's. He was particularly struck by the many gadgets, though perhaps he just mentions them because he knew they were the sort of thing Colin liked: 'push button phones (to which I am a convert: each button makes a sweet little sort of piping noise when you push it), a TV remote control unit without any wires . . . a refrigerator thing whereby the ice-trays automatically drop their cubes into a container and then fill themselves up with water until freezing and so on until the container is full, at which point everything stops. Bloody good for you is what I say.' In Jane's memory, 'almost nothing worked – the fridge, the cooker, the deep-freeze, the television hardly waited for the sound of their owner's departing car to break down'.[78] The heating was no good and winter proved unusually cold and snowy. When a pipe broke and the cellar flooded, Ivar-Lou's jars of pickles and preserves (as Amis puts it, 'enough decaying provisions to have supported, once upon a time, a full platoon of Confederate troops for some days before they died of various toxins')[79] went floating through the room. The flood became an Amis party-piece.

Jane's unhappiness with the house was compounded by its distance from the Vanderbilt campus. The first thing she had to do after unpacking was to rent a car. As Amis could not drive, she would have to make the journey to campus twice a day, the second time stopping at the supermarket for groceries; there were no neighbourhood shops. Jane had been put forward to lecture at Fisk University, one of the premier black universities in America. In England she had almost no relations with black people and when she went to visit the Fisk campus, 'it was a revelation to see countless young, beautifully groomed black students'. When Fisk offered her the job she desperately wanted to accept it, 'but it proved impossible, as I couldn't combine it with driving Kingsley at arbitrary times of the day'.[80] There were other reasons for Jane's unhappiness. In England, she was a figure in her own right, used both to being made much of and to being out in the world. Though people in Nashville knew she was a writer, it was Amis they were interested in and whose novels they had read. Although she wrote, there was little to break up the day. One woman who claimed to have met the Amises nearly every weekend for two months at parties described Jane as 'tall, mod, really good looking, and very intense'.[81] 'At gatherings where Kingsley was lionised,' Richard Porter, a friend from that period, recalls, 'she was often shunted to the women. Jane was brilliant and urbane; many of the women were neither.'[82] Jane wore her long blonde hair straight down her back at this time and the shortest miniskirts in Nashville and she used four-letter words. Because she was bored and restless, she drank rather more than usual and was often contentious, in a society that sought harmony and consensus in conversation.

Nashville was hot and muggy when they arrived in September (it is on the same latitude as Tangier and Crete, Amis notes) and they were soaked with perspiration after a short walk; but then walking was frowned upon in the city's suburban neighbourhoods. 'People thought I was a tart,' Jane recalls; 'the police stopped me and said "What are you doing? Where are you going?"' This complaint is a cliché but to the Amises so was Nashville. To Jane, the centre of the city 'reminded me of the Edgware Road in London, and the rest was an endless suburb';[83] to Amis, it was 'a very lifelike version of what you see every time you put the TV on and are shown a main street in a standard US town put up or redone since I don't know when – 1950?'[84] 'Peckers up, both of you,' wrote Colin on 3 October; 'Your last letter was so depressing,' wrote Mike Keeley to Jane on 9 October, 'is Nashville really so awful?' Later in October, Jane was asked to address a local women's club. Among her papers at the Huntington is a thank-you note from its 'First Vice-President', addressed to 'Dear Mrs. Amis' (not 'Miss Howard'): 'None of those present will, I'm sure, ever forget the first meeting of the Adelicia Acklen Woman's Club this year. Your knowledgeable and illuminating observations on the modern novel made it the memorable occasion that it was. Thank you for this special favor to the club so charmingly bestowed. Best wishes to you and Dr. Amis as you pursue your interesting and successful careers. May your short sojourn in Nashville be a pleasant and profitable one. Sincerely yours, Doris B. Sloneckes, First Vice President.' Far from refuting Lefty prejudices about the South – or about America and Americans – Nashville seemed to be confirming them. 'The South is just what they say it is, only more so,' wrote Amis to Colin on 17 September; to which Colin replied, in a letter of 28 September, 'I quite see what with 26 yr. old negroes getting 90 years gaol for stealing £81 things aren't all they ought to be, but if *you*, K, come back all lefty I'll join the Temperance Society.'

Nashville might be provincial and stuffy, but Amis and Jane could hardly accuse it of being unsocial. Amis estimates that they were invited to some fifty social occasions during their four months in the city. As at Princeton and Swansea, Amis's social life was quickly stratified, though circles often overlapped. There was the department, there was a wider, wealthier set of acquaintances, to which they were introduced by the University's Chancellor, Alexander Heard, and there was a middling world of local writers. The people the Amises were closest to in Nashville were the Frasers and Richard and Brigitte Porter. Dick Porter, at the time a thirty-five-year-old assistant professor of Russian, had been raised and educated in Nashville. Handsome and reserved, Porter is described by Amis in the *Memoirs* as 'as civilised and unaffected a man as I have ever met'[85] and to Bob Conquest as a 'v. sound reactionary'.[86] His lively, pretty wife Brigitte is German. When the Porters met the Amises at a party in Smyrna, Tennessee, the two couples quickly took to each other and were soon having dinner at each other's houses at least once a week. The Porters endeared themselves to Jane by being one of only two 'self-catering' couples in Nashville (the other was the Frasers). Everyone else, it seemed to her, employed cooks and mostly served food she disliked. As she puts it in her memoirs, '*boeuf Stroganoff* with iced tea is refreshment I still can't face today'.[87]

The party at which the Amises met the Porters was given by Brainard ('Lon') Chaney, a writer associated with the Fugitives and Southern Agrarians, who had helped to make the Vanderbilt English

Department famous in the 1920s and 1930s. Among the writers associated with these groupings were John Crowe Ransom, Allen Tate, Donald Davidson, Cleanth Brooks and Robert Penn Warren, all of them at one time teachers or students at Vanderbilt. The fame of the Fugitives and Southern Agrarians rested in part on their role in originating and promoting the New Criticism, in part on a vision of the South as resisting the evils of urbanism, industrialism and materialism. The poetry magazine from which the Fugitives took their name (it ran for nineteen issues, from 1922 to 1925, and was published in Nashville) attracted a number of influential supporters, among them T.S. Eliot and Robert Graves. These supporters approved both the rigour of Fugitive poetry and criticism and the underlying conservatism of its social vision. After the demise of the magazine, the Fugitive writers came to be known as Southern Agrarians. Ransom, Tate, Davidson and Warren were among the 'Twelve Southerners' who contributed to *I'll Take My Stand: The South and the Agrarian Tradition* (1930), a sort of manifesto of the group. Though the book's contributors differed about the precise meaning of 'agrarian', over time the term came to signal a reaction against many aspects of the modern world. Southern Agrarians were generally thought of as traditionalist in culture, orthodox in religion and aristocratic or reactionary in politics. After the racial convulsions of the early 1960s, however, the 'stand' the Southern Agrarians and their followers were most closely associated with in Nashville was against integration. Donald Davidson, in particular, was an outspoken opponent of integration, both at Vanderbilt itself and in the South in general. Though Davidson had retired from the faculty in 1964, he still lived part of the year in Nashville and had influential friends in the English Department (Jane Howard thinks she and Amis may have met him once, but she isn't sure; he died shortly after they left). Davidson was gentle, soft-spoken, polite in conversation and a gifted teacher, but he was also a racist who believed in the innate inferiority of blacks. In the words of an historian of the university, Paul K. Conkin, the extremism of his views 'jeopardized his academic reputation, and eventually embarrassed Vanderbilt'.[88] When Amis arrived in Nashville, Davidson's main followers in the English Department were the novelist Walter Sullivan, on sabbatical in the fall semester, but living just six miles from campus, the eighteenth-century scholar Jack Aden, and Hal Weatherby, who spent much of his scholarly career working on Edmund Spenser. For some time the university had sought to distance itself from the views of men like Davidson, not just on race but on corporate America, the source of Vanderbilt's endowment, most of its trustees, and all the major funding foundations in American higher education (Ford, Rockefeller, etc.). By 1967 it was the announced goal of the university, according to Conkin, 'to break out of the provincial mould and become a truly national university'.[89] The hiring of Russell Fraser, an outsider and non-Southerner, was thought of as an important step in attaining this goal.

'Lon' and Fanny Chaney's party was held in a beautiful old house, Idler's Retreat (idleness or leisure was an important value in the writing of the Southern Agrarians, in defiance of urban bustle). At the party Amis and Jane met not only the Porters but also Walter and Jane Sullivan. Amis had heard of the Sullivans from both Anthony Burgess and Allen Tate. On 3 September Burgess wrote to say: 'Now do have a good time in dear Nashville, and eat good meals at Mario's, and give my fondest regards to Walter Sullivan and Jack Aden and their charming wives and tell them I think of them often . . . Also my regards to your friend Russell and the entire faculty when my hand is in.'[90] A week later, on the 14th, Tate wrote to Jane and Kingsley saying: 'You will enjoy the academic community. But town as well as gown will be fun. I am "alerting" town friends to your arrival. You will hear from them soon . . . P.S. You will find Walter and Jane Sullivan charming. Walter is one of the best Southern novelists.'[91] After the Chaney party the Amises began to meet some of the 'town' friends Tate had mentioned. At a party at the Chancellor's they met several wealthy Vanderbilt alumni and benefactors, including Jane and Guilford Dudley and Alan and Denmark Bell. Of the many oddly named people Amis encountered in Nashville (though someone named Kingsley is hardly one to talk), the Bells, along with Tupper Saucy (whose names Amis always wanted reversed), take the palm, since Alan was a woman, daughter of a wealthy Vanderbilt trustee, and Denmark, a lawyer and judge, a man.[92] The Porters remember giving a disastrous dinner party at their apartment to which they invited the Dudleys and another socially prominent couple.[93] Jane drank too much and was argumentative, Amis kept saying 'shit' and 'fuck', and the guests were aghast (though the Dudleys recovered and later entertained the Amises several times). Dick Porter describes Jane's behaviour at the dinner as uncharacteristic, but in her memoirs she makes clear that she was unhappy in Nashville and several times drank too much. The best nights with the Porters – the best times socially – were when just the two couples had dinner together. The Porters, who arrived on several occasions when Amis and Jane were reading their day's writing to each other, were thrilled to listen in on the readings and the comments afterwards. At such times Amis and Jane seemed to Dick Porter to be 'enormously fond of each other, wonderfully compatible'. Their comments were 'totally professional but tactful, they felt free to make suggestions'.

If Jane's miniskirts attracted notice in Nashville, so did Amis's socks. Under Jane's influence his clothes were now more colourful, stylish and expensive than they had been at Swansea and Cambridge; she was smartening him up. (On the rare occasions when he himself bought clothing, the results were deplorable, as when he emerged from a shoe shop with 'nine pairs of unspeakable shoes variously described by the boys as brothel-creepers, bovver boots, berk's footwear and one pair that they said was simply coming-out-into-the-open-about-being-a-shit'). Porter describes Amis in Nashville as 'dashing in his tweeds and the bright socks Jane had knitted for him',[94] and in an article in the Vanderbilt alumni magazine Amis is said to have 'amazed Nashvillians by wearing mauve shirts and purple ties, salmon socks and handkerchief to match'.[95] 'I suppose we do tend to be rather conservative here,' commented a faculty member, 'but we're just not used to seeing those canary shirts, lilac ties, and mauve hose all together at once.' Nor were Nashvillians used to Amis's frequent recourse to the snuffbox: 'it's the thumb in the nose that stops them every time'.[96] The student reaction to Amis was largely positive. Even in the 1960s Vanderbilt students were mostly conservative; fraternities and sororities ruled campus life and there was little sign of a counterculture. 'There are no hippies at Vanderbilt,' lamented an editorial in the student magazine on 6 October, shortly after Amis arrived: 'the value-orientation of the status-based materialistic Vanderbilt community is incapable of sustaining the Love Generation.' So no beads or groovy white boots to render Amis and Jane's appearance unremarkable. In a national newspaper profile of Amis published on 4 March 1968, one of his former students suggested that his 'considerable personal impact' on the undergraduates at Vanderbilt derived in part from a contrast with his immediate predecessor, Allen Tate. According to this student, Tate's manner was formal and aloof, quite unlike Amis's, and though

Tale was personally respected, his ideas were not: 'This sentimentalising of the Old South and its values doesn't go with students here.'[97]

Amis liked his students at Vanderbilt, describing those in his Modern British Novel class as 'about the best I have ever taught: punctual, polite, attentive, ready but not overready with questions and objections, containing that ingredient essential for a decent course of lectures, however much the lecturer may squirm at its presence: a couple of students of whom he is very slightly afraid'.[98] How many of these students could have told him anything about Alexander Pope he does not say; the authors he asked them to read were Len Deighton and Ian Fleming as well as Anthony Powell, William Golding, Iris Murdoch and Graham Greene.[99] Had Amis read the student newspaper for 17 November he would have liked what he learned about the politics of his students as well: according to a poll taken by the paper, 77 per cent favoured a complete American defeat of communist forces in Vietnam, a view shared by only 37 per cent of the faculty.[100] Yet even among the best of his students Amis found dismaying racial attitudes. In the *Memoirs* he describes how an exceptionally bright student named Julie Smith, who also happened to be 'one of the most beautiful girls I have ever seen', explained to Jane why today there was more trouble with coloured people in the North than the South: 'they didn't know how to keep 'em down', a remark delivered with 'a sort of chuckle and a wink'.[101]

Amis and Jane hated such remarks, Amis in part because they discredited conservatism in general. 'Actually Vanderbilt isn't too bad,' he wrote to Conquest on 1 November, presumably before the Julie Smith remark: 'it's Nashville that's the drag on the whole: *dinner parties* and the rest of it, and plenty racialism. The nigra gets talked about in terms that recall the most tedious lefty play. Buggers haven't learnt a bloody thing. One can forgive a lefty here, in that "conservative" opinion is so shitty. It would take some strength of mind not to say, in effect, "anybody who thinks like that about Negroes must be wrong about everything. Stop US murder in Vietnam."' Dick Porter and others in Nashville have suggested that it was precisely Amis's anti-Lefty attitudes that led him to be subjected to such talk. As Porter puts it, the Amises 'had been billed as staunch conservatives. People here wanted to be liked and did their best to talk conservative, not realising that race was an issue at which the Amises drew the line. I heard several people, wishing to please, make racial slurs around the Amises they would not have made other-wise.'[102] Porter is not denying that such people held racist views, only that they would express them in public, especially to a foreign visitor. Nashville conservatives may also have been misled by Amis's way of talking, which in Britain at least included the occasional racial epithet. 'Dearest Monk,' begins an undated letter to Colin of September 1967, 'The Wog [Jane, a case in point] erred splendidly when she said Fisk is the only nignog university in USA: there are quite a few.' A small handful of such epithets is scattered through Amis's correspondence, as, by all accounts, through his conversation; until the end of his life they had little bearing on his considered racial or religious attitudes or his friendships.

The liberals in the English Department – there were several – distrusted Amis on questions of race and ethnicity. Leonard Nathanson, a Renaissance scholar, was the first and only senior appointment Fraser was able to make at Vanderbilt. Though a scholar of 'national' calibre, with all the right qualifications, Nathanson suspects that 'one of the reasons that Russell was eager to hire me was that I was a Jew from New York'. The appointment was a way of sending signals of several sorts to the old guard, a way encouraged and licensed by Fraser's superiors. To this old guard, Nathanson thinks, 'I was the New York radical Jew' (at Nathanson's welcoming dinner, Ivar-Lou Duncan described him to Russell Fraser as 'rather . . . urban').[103] But not only to the old guard: 'Kingsley Amis saw me that way.' Nathanson liked Amis and enjoyed his company but had little doubt that he had 'a tendency to categorise people in a very stereotypical way'. Once he told Amis that he liked Hampstead: 'Well you would,' Amis answered, 'because you're a Lefty.' In Amis's world, such stereotypes were no big deal. Eve Thomas, Amis's great good friend from Swansea, had a son who lived on the Finchley Road in Swiss Cottage: 'Finkelstrasse in our family.' In Nashville or New York, such a remark would be taken as a sign of a more general orientation; in Amis's less embat-tled and sensitive world, it might not be (no doubt wrongly, in some cases). When, after they left Vanderbilt, Amis and Jane publicly denounced the racism they had encountered there, the liberals among the faculty reacted with mixed feelings. Vereen Bell, perhaps the closest the English Department had to a Lefty, resented what he called their 'sanctimoniousness', as if the outrage they expressed was unearned or illegitimate. Like those in Nashville whom the Amises quote so damagingly, he, too, found it difficult to square Amis's political conservatism ('drunken diatribes about saving the world from communism') with his anti-racism.

It was Jane who first publicly denounced the prejudices she encountered in Nashville, in an article published in the *Sunday Telegraph* on 7 April 1968, three days after the assassination of Martin Luther King. In this article, entitled 'The Real Tragedy of the South', Jane complained about the narrowness and parochialism of Nashville, which she related to its virulent racism, and cited a number of instances of bigotry both within and outside the university. The main thrust of the article was not that the people she met would have assassinated Martin Luther King but that men like James Earl Ray 'are very unlikely to stem from some social vacuum'. The article ends: 'Looking back on our time in Nashville, the most depressing conclusions are that this murder does not startle us, and that we can think of only three persons there whose reactions to it we would call honest, unhappy and sane.' Twenty-two years later, in the *Memoirs*, Amis seconded these wounding remarks in an account of his time at Nashville that raises several questions about memory and truthfulness. The most damning passage concerns Walter Sullivan:

From there I can cut straight to a dinner party at the house of a professor of English, the very man, in fact, Walter Sullivan by name, author of several novels, whose place I was in a sense taking during a period of his leave . . .

At first, as ever, all was well. Drink, conversation and cordiality, with one or two not ungraceful compliments to my homeland thrown in, the Old Country from which so many of those around me ultimately derived . . . The food was good and ample, but I have forgotten if there was any wine. Then, at about the stage of the second highball after dinner, as always, we got on to the staple subject. They, or some of them, started making remarks about the mental, moral, social qualities of black people that it would probably be illegal to print here and I would shrink away from putting on the page.

It is worth trying to get straight the kind of remarks that were made and the kind of tone they were made in. Individually they were often mild, no more than patronising, with points awarded for supposed black virtues of loyalty, obedience and so on and disapproval expressed of attempts to advance the black beyond his station. (The very familiarity of a lot of this made it the more disagreeable.) Some indeed were damned if they were going to see any more steps, or any steps, taken in that direction. With the couple of exceptions just mentioned, I never sensed, let alone heard, any disagreement from the consensus of irremediable and universal black inferiority, perhaps to be alleviated here and there but never altered, and the important thing was keeping 'em down. And Walter and his mates went on about it all the time . . .

Walter himself summed it up. (Remember he was a university teacher.) Whenever I tell this story, as I frequently do, I give him a Dixie chaw-bacon accent to make him sound even more horrible, but in fact he talked ordinary cultivated American-English, with a rather attractive Southern lilt. Anyway, his words were (verbatim), 'I can't find it in my heart to give a negro [pron. Nigra] or a Jew an A.'

There was a short and curious silence, which I almost broke by drop-ping in a sociable laugh and saying, 'You do it marvellously, Walter – for a moment there I thought you really . . .'

The others were not saying that. They were saying it was real good to hear that said, time people faced facts, they wouldn't stand for being pushed any further, *thank you* for saying that, Walter. The feeling in the air was reverential as well as tough, loyal, united, etc., rather as if an Englishman among friends had said he thought we hadn't made such a bad shot at running the jolly old Empire after all.[104]

Amis is very deliberate in this passage, making sure that there's no embroidery or evasion: 'Walter Sullivan by name'; 'It is worth trying to get straight the kind of remarks that were made and the kind of tone they were made in'; 'his words were (verbatim)'; 'in fact he talked ordinary cultivated American-English'. When the libel lawyers for Hutchinson got their hands on the manuscript of the *Memoirs* they wrote a lengthy report and warned against many passages, a number of them subsequently cut. In proof the book was substantially redrafted, after the deaths of several figures made possible the restoration of excised passages. The lawyers allowed the Sullivan anecdote to pass, though Sullivan was alive at the time, as he is today. When asked why he didn't sue, Sullivan replied: 'the damage had been done . . . it's more damned trouble than it's worth'. Jane was not present at the dinner described in the *Memoirs* and corroborating witnesses have not come forward. Neither Russell Fraser, Vereen Bell, Leonard Nathanson nor the Porters remember the occasion; from Amis's description, only the Porters are likely to have been invited. Walter Sullivan denies making the remark and has no memory of the dinner. What he remembers is something quite different: 'That famous remark that is attributed to me: I heard somebody report that such a remark had been made and that was at Russell's dinner party. Kingsley was there. I was there. Our wives were there . . . Somebody told a story that involved this line. Did I say it? No, I didn't say it. And should I have said it, would my colleagues have nodded and said well that's great? No. At that time we had a few black students at Vanderbilt and even fewer who had majored in English or taken advanced English courses. And as far as the Jews are concerned, I've got the record to prove that – I've given probably a disproportionate number of As to Jews.'

Though Sullivan himself admitted that in 1967 he opposed the integration of the university, that he was racist in his youth ('we all were then') and that changes in racial attitudes 'didn't happen in one night', he denies saying what Amis said he said. Fraser is reluctant to open old wounds: he has no more memory of the party Sullivan describes than he has of the one Amis describes; but he does not question Amis's integrity: 'I would never impute conscious dishonesty to him.' Vereen Bell 'never heard anyone say anything even close' to Sullivan's remark and doubts that he said it; but then Bell was known to disapprove of such talk and is unlikely to have been much exposed to it by colleagues and friends. Bell believes that the sort of people Amis describes at the Sullivan dinner 'would have more social sense than to say something like that'. Would Sullivan lie about having made the remark? 'I don't know,' Bell answered, which was Nathanson's answer as well. However, Bell also said: 'Well, you know, *I* would. And it's not hard for people to revise their personal histories.' Porter, a good friend of the Sullivans at the time, and an admirer and friend of Amis, 'never heard [Sullivan] say anything like that . . . It is a side of him I've never seen.' Also sceptical is John Seigenthaler, editor of the *Nashville Tennessean* in 1967, the more liberal of the city's newspapers (Jimmy Stahlman, the editor of its rival, the *Nashville Banner*, was an arch-segregationist and a powerful Vanderbilt trustee). Seigenthaler was a hero of the civil rights movement. During the Nashville sit-ins and the Montgomery Freedom Rides he was Robert Kennedy's point man and on one occasion was attacked by racists in Alabama and nearly killed, an episode which galvanised the Kennedys in the fight for civil rights. Seigenthaler remembers meeting Amis several times, once at a party at Chancellor Heard's house. He also knew Walter Sullivan. He does not doubt that Sullivan held racist views in 1967 and may even have thought something like what Amis says he said; but he doubts that he said it. He describes Sullivan as 'very astute, intuitive and in the Southern sense "proper"' (that is, cultivated, gentlemanly, like Donald Davidson). Sullivan says something similar: 'If I believed it, which I didn't, I wasn't a fool. By that time we were all on our guard about that sort of thing.'

Whether Amis's claim that he heard Sullivan utter the remark was a conscious falsehood, a drunken misapprehension or a trick of memory, Sullivan does not say. As I suggested at the beginning of this book, Amis is not always reliable in the *Memoirs*. In the Nashville chapter he makes several statements that are inaccurate. 'I asked somebody if there were any – I think I said "coloured" – students in the university. "Oh, certainly. He's called Mr. Moore." (This was and is not a joke.)' But there were at least fifty black students at Vanderbilt in 1967, as Amis must have known at the time. Jane remembers one of them, not Mr Moore, in Amis's Modern British Novel class. Amis also writes that Sullivan 'had like many of his neighbours thrown a party when Kennedy was shot'.[105] According to Vereen Bell, the party in question was to celebrate the award of a degree to one of Sullivan's graduate students. When Kennedy was shot, Sullivan called up Bell and told him that he had decided not to cancel the party and that, although he knew Bell would be upset about what had happened, he ought to come along, to be with friends. Sullivan was no fan of Kennedy, but the party was not thrown to celebrate Kennedy's death, as the *Memoirs* imply. In this case, of course, Amis was recounting a story he must have been told by others. In the case of the Sullivan remark, not only does he claim to have been present at the time but Jane remembers his telling her about it afterwards in Nashville. In the 1968 *Sunday Telegraph* article she quotes the remark: 'I met one of them who said (but not to me and not in my hearing) that he could not find it in his heart to give an A to either a Negro or a Jew.'

The episode is worth trying to unravel because it raises questions not only about Amis's veracity but about his treatment of people who thought they were his friends. What Bell especially disliked about Jane's and Amis's accounts of Nashville, in addition to what he called their 'sanctimoniousness', was that they 'misrepresented their relationship to the people they were quite close to on the ground here'. Sullivan claims to feel betrayed as well as slandered: 'I thought we were good friends. I sort of understood Jane's animosity towards us, because everybody made much of Kingsley as a novelist and nobody made anything of Jane as a novelist. It was pretty clear to me that this was getting to her. But she was so damned beautiful: this big voluptuous beauty that she had: I think it was hard for the men at any rate to get past that' (a comment with edge, like the claim that he'd given a 'disproportionate' number of A grades to Jews). The Porters were also shocked by Jane's article and Kingsley's account, though they come out well from them: 'I never once had the sense that they were appalled by what they saw here. It was completely unexpected.' In a memoir of Amis published in 1996 in the *Southern Review*, 'Lucky Jim as I Remember Him', Russell Fraser is ironic about the way the Amises ruffled the feathers of Nashvillians ('poor dears'); his only criticism, a slight one, is of Jane's *Sunday Telegraph* piece, which exempted one of his graduate students from blame: 'Naming this friend, she handed them a hostage. She was out of harm's way, far across the sea, but he lived around the corner, and they kicked him out of the program.'[106] Fraser was not alone in thinking there was something wrong in speaking out only from a distance. To do so was not only easy but involved an element of inconsiderateness, even ruthlessness, the sort often in evidence when novelists draw from life. Amis defends himself against such accusations in the *Memoirs*. He admits that he and Jane mostly kept quiet about their feelings in Nashville but asks what their alternatives were: 'What should I have done when Walter and his mates said things like the one quoted? Burst into real laughter? Tried to lead them along the road to reason? Had a fist-fight? Walked out? Every time, every night? Never gone out again? For four months? Resigned? For what I heard people say when I wasn't working? What I did was what almost everybody else would have done: kept my mouth shut, avoided assenting to what could not be assented to and made the most of the good bits, human and other. And, of course, had the notebook at the ready.'[107] The rejoinder here is that had the Amises made clear or clearer their feelings about race they might have escaped at least some of the remarks they quote in their accounts, as Vereen Bell seems to have done.

These issues play a part in *I Want It Now*, which is like a fairy tale not only in its Sleeping Beauty theme but in its choice of dragons slain, in particular Lady Baldock, who combines the qualities of toff or class snob and bigot, thus allowing the Amis-like hero, Ronnie Appleyard, to slay two tyrants with one stone. Amis was at work on the novel throughout his time in Nashville and clearly draws on his experiences there and at Montego Bay. Lady Baldock has firm views about the welfare of her daughter Simona (also called Simon or Mona), whom Ronnie wakens from sexual frigidity, falls for, and eventually rescues from her mother's clutches: 'what she needs – you've just said it: discipline. Somebody who will run her whole life and see that she does exactly as she's told.'[108] When Ronnie, who is on holiday with the Baldocks at their expense, has the temerity to question Lady Baldock's methods she replies with fury: 'I refuse to tolerate being told how to conduct myself towards my own child. For all I know that sort of behaviour may be perfectly acceptable wherever you come from, but it won't do in any household of mine. I bring you here and feed you and take you about in return for your services as Mona's . . . companion is, I suppose, the politest word, and you repay me by telling me my duty in public. And I won't have it.'[109] The 'it' here relates to the '*It*' of the novel's title, which Amis told Tom Maschler meant 'several things, but chiefly IT'.[110] One of the other things it meant is suggested when Lady Baldock is made to wait for her champagne: 'What's happened to my champagne? Why is there always this delay? I want it now.'[111] Lady Baldock comes originally from the American South, from Fort Charles, a fictional town in a state very like Tennessee. Fort Charles possesses several Nashville-like landmarks, including a courthouse based on a reconstruction of the temple of Ephesus (an obvious allusion to Nashville's full-scale model of the Parthenon, complete with roof and gold statue of Athena) and 'a synagogue built in ranch-house style'[112] (pointed out to me by Dick Porter in a ride round the city); it is also marked by endless suburbs and strip-mall clutter, so clichéd in its ugliness that Ronnie, who works in television, 'could have sworn he had seen it before as part of some unbiased documentary report on American civilization'.[113]

Here Ronnie encounters many of the sorts of remarks the Amises encountered in Nashville. Some are uttered by 'flaring Anglophile shags' (Amis's decription of Tupper Saucy):[114] 'I speak as somebody who loves and admires England,' declares a lean man dressed in black, perhaps a judge or a doctor. 'What I want is for England to preserve her traditions and her historical institutions and her culture. And here you-all go, letting them mix with you-all and work and live alongside you-all . . . In fifty years' time, less than that, they'll have dragged all of you-all down to their own level. We've lived with them all our lives and we know them.'[115] Ronnie's reaction to this speech recalls Amis's account in the *Memoirs* of his own silences; it may also reflect the thought processes beneath these silences:

Ronnie made some evasive and indeed quite wild reply. Now was not the moment for a stand on liberal principle, or on anything else. His feelings about coloured people, as about old people, hardly went further than a mild dislike, plus in this case an occasional twinge of discomfort on being momentarily outnumbered by a group of them in pub or street. Since nobody present, near or far, was going to report him to the *New Statesman* for backing down on race, he let the conversation take its course, rather savouring, in fact, the relief at not having to come back at this boring old fascist with pseudo-facts about how much the U.S. Negro's living and educational standards left to be desired, to say nothing of pseudo-concern.[116]

Though this account of Ronnie's silence is both realistic and plausible, *I Want It Now* is only in part a work of realism. In a later episode involving Ronnie and Southern bigotry, romance and wish-fulfilment take over completely and Ronnie at last speaks his mind. The episode is part of Ronnie's transformation from cynical smoothie and chancer, the hero as bastard or shit, to dragon-slaying knight in shining armour. That this transformation is forced and improbable is a frequent criticism of the novel, one Amis himself eventually acknowledged ('Obviously, there's something wrong with that book, because a lot of people say they find that Ronnie's sudden conversion is unconvincing').[117] Larkin admired *I Want It Now*, which he called 'good, very good', praising in particular its 'lean foul mouthed prose',[118] but he also thought it 'betrayed its hero', by making him sympathetic.[119]

The person Lady Baldock wants Simon to marry is a rich Fort Charles native with a name at least as good as Guilford Dudley or Brainard Chaney (Tupper Saucy's name is in a class of its own): Student Mansfield. Student has firm views about the Negro problem: 'We've solved the Negro problem. By realizing there is no problem, except keeping 'em down. That's what I said, keeping 'em down. They're inferior, they always will be inferior, and we in the South have the honest-to-God common sense to realize it. There's your so-called Negro problem solved.' By now Ronnie has given up all scheming and declared himself openly for Simon, regardless of Lady

Baldock's threat of disinheritance. During Student's speech, Ronnie's brain is in turmoil:

He was experiencing an emotion, a desire, a thought – whatever it was it was altogether new to him, remote, unpredictable by any intuition or technique, as if it had suddenly dawned upon him that what he had always most wanted to do was to induce a naked girl – or possibly a girl naked but for a transparent mackintosh – to stand before him while he pelted her with cream buns. All at once he knew what this sensation was. It was pure, authentic, violent sentiment of a liberal or progressive tendency.

'The only way to keep the Negro in his place is by *fear*. The only argument he understands is the *lash*.'

'Balls,' said Ronnie loudly.

'Pardon me?'

'Oh, come on. You heard. *Balls*. What you're saying is *balls*. Rubbish, nonsense, tosh, junk. And also extremely offensive, barbaric, inhumane, foolish, ignorant, outmoded and in the circumstances unforgivably rude.'

After an instant of silence, Lady Baldock said, 'I'll handle this, Student.'[120]

It takes a set-piece confrontation on television – the equivalent of the Merrie England speech in *Lucky Jim*, the Amis novel Larkin and others thought *I Want It Now* most resembled – for Ronnie finally to rout Lady Baldock. A dream of fulfilment and goodness ends the novel, perhaps a reflection of Amis's earliest happiness with Jane. With this dream goes a feeling Amis describes in the passage as a 'pure, authentic, violent sentiment of a liberal or progressive tendency'. It is liberal or progressive because it belongs to a realm in which evils are eradicable, a realm of romance. Real life is different. In real life, illusions from romance have dangerous as well as liberating consequences, as in the South's mythic sense of its past. This point Amis makes in his poem 'South', published in *Encounter* in September 1968. The first section of the poem describes a region out of pastoral or Romantic lyric: 'A sun as bright as noon in Sicily', 'A world of greenwood without end', 'the golden age', 'The noble savage', 'Wordsworth's peasants / In all innocence'. These are the underlying ingredients of the South's 'idea' of itself and of its 'history'. The poem's second section evokes the modern-day reality: 'ranch-style, eat-o-mat, drive-in / Headlight, tail-light, floodlight, neon'; '*You blind? Can't you see they're inferior? – / Our women's what they're really after.*' In the final section of the poem, the evils of the

South are denounced from what Amis sees as a Righty rather than a Lefty perspective – as ineradicable.

> III
> The history of thought is a side-issue
> When events begin, an idea
>   Is a lie.
>
> To north and west, hope, not yet in vain;
> Mexico too, not an illusion;
>   Africa even;
>
> But in the South, nothing now or ever.
> For black and white, no future.
>   None. Not here.[121]

23

Lemmons

In mid-January 1968 the Porters saw the Amises off on their last night in Nashville. 'We partied at our place until late,' Dick Porter remembers, 'then drove to our all-but-deserted railroad station, where they were to take the train to St. Louis. After hugs, we waved and waved as their train pulled out, and Brigitte and I watched a happy time come to an end'[1] – a happy time for them. For Amis and Jane, as Amis wrote to the Conquests on 5 February, Nashville in retrospect seemed 'like the days of the Captivity in the eyes of the children of Israel'. From St Louis the Amises were to catch a train to Mexico City, there to meet up with the Keeleys; they would then rent a car and go sightseeing. The plan was for the two couples to tour Mexico for two weeks and then, if a suitable place could be found, for Jane and Kingsley to stay on for a longer period, perhaps a month, to finish their novels (*Something in Disguise* and *I Want It Now*). Jane remembers the train journey from St Louis as 'splendid':[2] it took three days and two nights to reach Mexico City. Here Amis experienced his first earthquake, a forty-second tremor. 'No damage,' he reported to the Conquests on 5 February, 'but by Christ I thought the old coronary was upon me.' The touring began with a trip to Acapulco, which everyone hated and where Amis's suitcase was stolen from the car roof-rack within thirty seconds of arrival (the suitcase contained nothing important to him, only every item of expensive tailoring he possessed). The one good thing Amis had to say about Acapulco was that it supplied him with a possible opening sentence for a James Bond story: 'Bond had never liked Acapulco.' Among subsequent places visited were 'the pyramids at Teotihuacan was it, which impressed greatly', and Maximilian's palace in Cuernavaca, 'which was a fucking pain'.[3] The motoring was not without its tensions, mostly occasioned by the inflexible eating and drinking routines of the Amises. In addition to suitcases Amis carried with him what amounted to a cocktail cabinet: a large straw bag with handles in which he packed bottles of tequila, gin, vodka and Campari, as well as fruit juices, lemons, tomato juice, cucumber juice, Tabasco, knives, a stirring spoon and glasses. Amis insisted that wherever they were the car had to stop at 11.30 so that they all could have a drink: only one drink, though a big one, carefully prepared. Everyone had to get out of the car while Amis fetched his drinks basket and mixed elaborate cocktails. Mike Keeley remembers in particular a 'fake Negroni', made with gin, Campari and tonic. These drinks stops were more pleasurable for Amis than they were for Jane and the Keeleys. Mike Keeley was in charge of driving and the two couples usually didn't get on the road until 9.30 or 10. Jane was no less adamant about her own needs, which involved meals. By 1 p.m. she wanted lunch, but sometimes they found themselves in the Mexican hinterland at 1 p.m., with no restaurant in sight. 'She would get very touchy, very difficult,' Mike says. '"I've got to stop. I can't do it. I cannot go on any further,"' her irritation perhaps aggravated by Amis's general air of contentment, having had his drink.

These tensions were minor, though it was with some relief that the couples arrived at the final stop on their itinerary: San Miguel de Allende, a beautiful seventeenth-century Spanish colonial town, 200 miles north-west of Mexico City and 6,000 feet above sea level. The clear light of San Miguel, its dramatic hillside setting, cobbled streets and handsome buildings had long attracted artists and writers from North America, and the Amises and the Keeleys knew several current residents. There was David Dodge, whom Amis had met in 1958 at Princeton, a travel and mystery writer, author not only of *To Catch a Thief* (1952; film 1955) but of *Fly Down, Drive Mexico: A Practical Motorist's Handbook for Travel South of the Border* (1968), the party's guide for the previous two weeks. There was Dallas McCord Reynolds, known as 'Mack', an astonishingly prolific science fiction writer whom Amis had met at several science fiction conventions. Jane found Reynolds's wife Jeanette warm and maternal and forgave her not only for hating China tea, which she likened to Greek wine ('That was a left and a right, I thought,' Jane complained to the Keeleys), but for calling her 'Joanie'.

On 4 February the Keeleys headed back to Mexico City to catch their plane home; Mike had teaching duties at Princeton. The Amises stayed on in San Miguel, having found excellent rooms in the small and very cheap Hotel Posada de las Monjas run by an eccentric Spanish grandee named Don Jorge. Don Jorge's English was peppered with outdated slang ('I say, old boy, jolly good to see you') and his interest in the hotel seemed primarily social rather than financial. Jane described him to the Keeleys as doing 'absolutely *nothing* in a rather spirited way'.[4] The running of the hotel was left to 'innumerable' friendly servants, each, it seemed, with a single task: one to feed the parrots in the courtyard, another to water the geraniums, a third to lay wood fires in each bedroom, a fourth to fetch bread from the markets, a fifth to stock the self-serve drinks cabinet. This last item greatly appealed to Amis: guests simply took what they wanted from the cabinet and wrote down what they'd taken. 'I am on the terrace,' Amis wrote to the Conquests, 'bare to the waist and drinking a home-made tequila con sangrita, con, of course, limon y sal tambien . . . Very sustaining.' Amis and Jane had a two-room suite in the hotel and for most of each day stayed in and wrote. The weather turned cold and Jane never went bathing in the local hot springs, contenting herself with strolls in the market, with its stalls of orchids and other flowers, colourful parrots, in fact 'everything one could imagine wanting'.[5] The food at the hotel was no more than acceptable but Jane found marvellous snacks in town. As Amis wrote to Colin on 12 March, she soon became 'queen of the pension, with regular hand-kissing from the proprietor and universal acclamation when she did one of her curries for the whole household'. Evenings were spent talking with the Reynoldses or Don Jorge, whom they found 'amusing, cultivated, sad, funny, probably queer'.[6] Though they kept a distance from the arty types at the Instituto, Amis approved their influence. 'Old Mack Reynoldses is here and we're under his very solid wing,' he reported to the Conquests on 5 February. 'The town is full of American tourists and "artists," but that's fine because things like shops, bars and doctors always look up in such circumstances.' Among the guests at the hotel was an American woman who made papier mâché boxes and was spending the whole winter in San Miguel; in the market Jane bought

Amis 'a pair of mosaic opal cuff links from a Mexican/German/ Lesbian – rather a worrying combination'.

The writing went well for both Jane and Amis. Amis finished *I Want It Now* 'just before leaving Mexico. Hurrah for me!'[7] Jane wrote a great deal of *Something in Disguise* and what she wrote Amis pronounced 'as good as anything she's done and her funniest yet'.[8] San Miguel had been a tonic for them both, partly because it wasn't Nashville, partly because, as in Sitges in 1963 or Pollensa in 1964, work took centre stage, their routines were simple and enjoyable and there were few social distractions. In the house in Nashville neither had slept well; the bed in the main bedroom had been small and uncomfortable and Jane took to sleeping on a divan in the same room. In San Miguel sleeping arrangements were 'much friendlier . . . we got some of our life back'. 'We see the Reynolds[es],' Jane told the Keeleys, 'and otherwise, read, and write and have had a lovely time alone together which is making up for the winter nicely. I am even beginning to relax a bit and be able to sleep.' The homesickness both experienced in Nashville began to recede. They were buoyed by letters from Colin, Sargy and Martin. Colin recounted his battles with builders (there was a problem with the 'hot-water thing' at 108 Maida Vale) and said he thought Mexico sounded 'nearly as nice as Regent's Park'.[9] Sargy wrote of Phil's enthusiasm for his course at Camberwell. He also wrote of Martin's Oxford interviews. At Exeter College a trendy young don told Martin: '"You certainly know all the clichés, don't you?" "Well you can't be too careful," answered Mart and they all fell about laughing and thigh-slapping.'[10] Before this letter arrived, Martin rang up Amis and Jane to say that Exeter had awarded him an exhibition: 'Mr. Ardagh told me that Carey at St. John's[11] was embarrassed by the state of my languages,' Martin later wrote to Amis and Jane, on Boxing Day: 'but Wordsworth at Exeter[12] . . . doesn't care about that, and, I suspect, is rather proud of the fact that he doesn't care about that.'[13] In a letter of 9 January, Martin paid tribute to Jane: '*Very seriously*, though, thank you, O Wog, for quite literally getting me into Oxford . . . I have a huge debt to you which I shall work off by being an ever-dutiful stepson.'[14] Three days earlier Colin had written to Jane to say that both boys were pleased that Hilly, now married to Shackleton Bailey, seemed settled: 'and I think Phil may in time be less hostile to you'.[15] Martin's letters post-exhibition are warm, funny and marginally less Osric-like than those pre-exhibition. Having seen off the job threat, he had agreed to weekly tutoring in Latin, to prepare for language examinations in his first year at Oxford. His Latin tutor, he wrote to Amis and Jane, 'says things like "There are 140 first conjunction deponent verbs": I say "Well I never" and he says "They are Venor, Conor" and so on and on and on.'[16]

The train trip to Princeton, where Amis and Jane were to stay a few days with the Keeleys before sailing to England on 14 March, was as difficult as the trip to Mexico had been easy. 'BHQ [Bastards' Headquarters] struck fast and hard and twice over,' Amis wrote to Colin from Princeton: 'trying to prevent us from re-entering the US and then making us miss our connection at St. Louis: but in *both cases* we fought back and frustrated them.'[17] At Princeton the Keeleys gave the Amises a party and they saw the Fussells, Ed Cone, the composer and Professor of Music, a member of the Blackmur circle, and other friends. On 20 March, after almost seven months away, they arrived at Southampton on the *Queen Elizabeth* to be greeted by Colin and Martin in a hired car. That night, back at 108 Maida Vale, Sargy cooked the household 'a delicious meal', after which he said he thought he ought to be going: '"Don't go,"' Jane said, 'so he didn't. In fact he lived with us for about eight more years, until he married.'[18] The next day Amis went off to Bertorelli's for what Conquest described to Larkin as a 'Welcome Home Kingers (his wording) lunch'.[19] Colin thought the half-year away had been 'cementing' for Amis and Jane, though this impression owed more to the restorative month in San Miguel than it did to Nashville; both were delighted to be home. *Colonel Sun* was due out at the end of the month and Amis soon plunged into a round of interviews and profiles. He was also eager to return to political battles. As Amis discovered in San Miguel, Karl Miller had put a picture of Che Guevara on the cover of the *Listener*: 'We must plan a monster counter-offensive,' he wrote to Conquest on 5 February. He had also seen a piece by Peregrine Worsthorne in the *Sunday Telegraph* expressing doubts about the Vietnam War: 'J and I were both severely shaken,' he wrote to Conquest on 11 March, 'as if Tibor had started cataloguing the achievements of Bolshevism.' Within weeks of his return, Amis was back on the letters pages of the *New Statesman* and other periodicals, defending the war, excoriating communists. In the next few years he would orchestrate several high-profile political campaigns. In the letters pages of *The Times*, the *New Statesman* and the *Sunday Times*, he opposed the candidacy of Yevgeny

Yevtushenko for Professor of Poetry at Oxford, a post that eventually went to Roy Fuller. Amis had met Yevtushenko in 1962 in Cambridge and got on well with him, and at first thought his candidacy a good idea but, as he explains in the *Memoirs*, 'reflection and a little investigation changed my mind'.[20] A year after they'd met, Yevtushenko was rebuked by the Party 'and relapsed into what Robert Conquest has called "well-rewarded collaboration" with it'.[21] According to Amis, this collaboration involved attacks on genuinely liberal or dissident writers such as Sinyavsky and Daniel, a claim Yevtushenko and his supporters vehemently denied. A second campaign Amis helped to orchestrate took the form of a series of articles he and Conquest wrote in the 'Black Papers on Education' (1969–77), which were edited by Brian Cox and A.E. Dyson of the Critical Quarterly Society and appeared in *Critical Survey*, the society's periodical for teachers of English. It was Cox who approached Amis about the 'Black Papers' and asked him to write for them, in part because he agreed with Amis's widely reported prediction that 'More will mean worse' in higher education. Amis in turn recruited Conquest and put Cox and Dyson in touch with other participants, including Tibor Szamuely.[22] In addition to these campaigns Amis worked on several politically oriented television projects shortly after his return. In 1969 he wrote a synopsis for an anti-Soviet series entitled 'General Tomski's Army', concerning 'a small nucleus of freedom fighters' within the USSR whose aim 'is not to betray Russia to the west, but by their example to help their fellow countrymen to achieve freedom for themselves'. Among potential storylines for the series are 'sabotaging the Soviet space programme', 'helping priests, Jews, Tartars and members of other persecuted minority groups to evade the K.G.B.', 'attempting the assassination of Brezhnev or a satellite leader', and 'smuggling an imprisoned writer's manuscript to the west'. London Weekend Television was interested in the series and sought but failed to come up with American financing. Amis had better luck with 'The Importance of Being Hairy', a television play crudely and unfunnily satirising campus Lefties, perhaps the worst thing he ever wrote. It was broadcast on the BBC's Comedy Playhouse on 6 May 1971.

During the Nashville/Mexico period Amis and Larkin exchanged no letters. They had corresponded rarely throughout the 1960s. What they knew of each other was mostly gleaned from friends, in particular Bob Conquest and Bruce Montgomery. Conquest invited Larkin to the 'Welcome Home Kingers' lunch but Larkin did not attend. In mid-April, however, he wrote to Amis to say that he was coming to London for a meeting on 8 May and that they should have lunch beforehand. Amis readily agreed. The last time they'd had such a lunch, Larkin reminded him, in a letter of 22 April, he was far from sober when he turned up for his meeting, drawing 'many curious looks by my insane cackling and truculent conduct of business'.[23] All Larkin had to say of the 8 May lunch, in a letter to Conquest of 12 May, was that Amis 'babbled of £50,000 houses in Barnet – this must be the saying of Crazy Jane, mustn't it? Poor bugger.'[24] The house in question – this is its first mention in the correspondence – was to become Amis's residence for the next eight years. It was a late-Georgian mansion fifteen miles from the centre of London, with eight bedrooms, three reception rooms, two stair-cases, a large, high-ceilinged coach-house kitchen and offices; surrounding property included an ancient barn (a listed building), garages, a detached cottage, a conservatory, an enclosed courtyard at the side, a gravel drive and an enormous sloping garden at the back, including magnificent cedar woods and a meadow. Though within walking distance of the London underground's Northern Line – only just, and rarely for Amis – it faced directly on to Hadley Common; living there felt like living in the country. 'Oh heavenly city of Barnet beyond the spreading Cedar, oh light on the pond opposite,' begins an otherwise illegible verse thank-you from John Betjeman, a frequent visitor to the house.[25]

Jane's account in her memoirs of the decision to move to Barnet begins with practical considerations: the lease on 108 Maida Vale, in her name, was a short one and when she enquired about renewing it, the Eyre Estate, which owned it, demurred, having not yet decided whether to redevelop the property: 'In short, they'd guarantee us nothing.'[26] It was Amis, according to Jane, who originally suggested living outside London. As early as April 1966, in the course of a visit to Anthony and Violet Powell in Frome, near Somerset, they had enquired about a semi-derelict farmhouse in the valley just below the Powells' house. 'Controversy continues to rage about Manor Farm,' wrote Amis in his bread-and-butter letter to the Powells: 'I still talk about seeing if there's anything round Marlborough first, but I can foresee somebody else finding everything there subtly, or even blatantly, unsatisfactory.'[27] Like Larkin, Conquest could make no sense of the proposed move: 'Christ knows what old K is up to with this Barnet stuff,' he wrote to Larkin on 21 May. 'The theory of Barnet it seems, is that anyone going there for dinner stays the night. Worst of all sodding worlds, if you ask me.'

It was Jane who discovered the Barnet house, through an advertisement in *Country Life*. She and Colin went on a preliminary reconnaissance and then Amis, Martin and Sargy saw it as well. 'Everybody was mad about it,' remembers Jane, 'including me, but I realized we couldn't afford more than token help, and it would take a great deal of work to run'.[28] 'Jane gave us all quite a talking to,' Colin remembers. 'Were we prepared to take on all the chores? And we all said, "Yes, we are, we are," and then we demonstrably weren't.' Arranging the money for the house was difficult. At the suggestion of a friend, Jane had secured an accountant from a grand firm. The Barnet house was to be sold by auction and the accountant said that she and Amis could afford to bid up to £57,000. In the event, they obtained the house with a single bid of £48,000. 'Overjoyed, I rang our accountant,' Jane recalls in the memoirs. 'He replied that he was afraid the mortgage had fallen through, and he was off on holiday.'[29] An initial 10 percent of the purchase price had already been paid and the balance was due in three weeks. Jane rang Tom Maschler for advice and Maschler put her in touch with Anton Felton, an accountant who worked exclusively for writers. Felton managed to find them another mortgage within the three weeks. Amis's part in these manoeuvrings was predictably minor. On 17 May, less than a week before the auction, he wrote to Theo Richmond: 'frenetic activity about a possible new house . . . Huge tussles to win money out of publishers, agents, banks: Jane's done all the hard work, but it's been impossible to settle to anything. Auction next Thursday. All fingers crossed.' When finally the mortgage was secured and the remainder of the lease on Maida Vale sold for £10,000, Jane wrote to the Keeleys on 26 July, five days before she and Amis took possession of the house: 'We got it – for less money than we had been led to expect, but still fiendishly expensive. We have had to borrow all the money to buy it . . . a gang of us headed by Monkey are going to rewire the whole place thus saving fifteen hundred pounds.'

The house was in itself only part of the reason Amis and Jane found themselves in financial difficulties in the Barnet years; soon they discovered that the grand accountant had neglected to warn them of impending tax bills. As Colin remembers it: 'he didn't realise the size of his clients, how little they were'. At a time when Amis and Jane had no extra money, the accountant 'used to send letters saying: "We've had this communication from the Inland Revenue. It would help to keep matters quiet if you'd just enclose a cheque for £8,000."' Such tax bills nearly ruined Jane and Amis; they were rescued only by what Colin calls 'the skill and patience and guile' of Anton Felton, who soon took over their finances completely. In June 1970 Jane wrote to inform the Keeleys that they would not be coming to Greece that summer because 'we simply cannot afford to. We aren't having a good year earning-wise, and the tax situation has got even worse since last April. I am despairing about it: more so than K, I think, since I miss the lovely thought of sun and swimming and Greek food.' On 15 September 1972 Felton wrote to Michael Sissons of A.D. Peters seeking to bolster Jane and Amis's cash flow. Sissons in turn wrote to Harcourt Brace asking if Amis could receive the whole of the $12,000 advance for his next two books, *The Riverside Villas Murder* and *On Drink*, on signature, explaining that 'Kingsley is frankly very short of cash for the taxman at the moment.'³⁰ As Jane's letter to the Keeleys suggests, her reaction to money worries was to economise; Amis simply put his head down and wrote, which accounts in part for his astonishing productivity in the eight Barnet years, during which he produced ten books, five of them novels. As Jane puts it: 'Kingsley's attitude to any family or financial crisis was to go on writing and take no notice.'³¹ This attitude was facilitated by Amis's wholly traditional notions of the female domestic sphere, which included shopping, cleaning, cooking, budgeting household expenses and educating children. He expected Jane either to supervise these activities or to do them herself, though he did so less in the manner of a stern patriarch than an unconcerned or inconsiderate teenager. He also expected Jane to fulfil traditional male responsibilities: buy and drive the car, meet with accountants and bankers, mend fuses. His unspoken excuse for such behaviour, Colin thinks, was that he brought in the lion's share of the income, something he would have done even if Jane had been freer to write. The sole domestic responsibilities he assumed were laying the fire, mixing and serving drinks, entertaining guests and cooking enormous weekend fry-ups, blackening sausages (he liked blackened sausages) and filling the kitchen with smoke. When he and Jane left Barnet, he described his contribution to the move in a letter to Conquest of 5 July 1976: 'My main job so far has been drinking up the nearly-empty bottles, horrible stuff like cherry vodka, Mavrodaphne, raki etc.'

Because of the sometimes precarious state of their finances, Jane went without adequate help at Barnet. Sargy and Colin helped out in the garden and sometimes contributed towards the cost of their lodgings, though neither had much money in the early 1970s. In such circumstances, the house and the garden never reached their potential, a source of nagging regret to Jane, though a matter of indifference to Amis. 'Have *you* been to Barnet?' Bruce Montgomery wrote to Larkin on 24 November 1969. 'It's impressive, no doubt, but Jane's aim of gracious living seems to be being militated against by an almost total lack of servants. "Kingsley simply doesn't *realise*," Jane said to me rather despairingly when showing me around.'[32] Montgomery exaggerates: Jane had a housekeeper, Mrs Uniacke, who lived in the cottage on the property, also 'a very genteel person who ironed shirts twice a week' (the only person Jane's mother had ever seen who could mince and iron at the same time), an arthritic gardener named Mr Mayhew, who came three hours a week, and the occasional local girl who helped in the kitchen. This is hardly 'an almost total lack of servants', but neither is it adequate help for a house of over twenty rooms, a five-acre garden and a social schedule that included parties or house guests every weekend. What Jane needed was a full-time gardener and cook, but these, she decided, they could not afford. That she herself was a passionate gardener and cook may have played a part in this decision; had she not been, some have suggested, she might have found a way to economise elsewhere. In areas that mattered to Amis, in contrast, there was no stinting. Jane could risk 'really quite bad scenes if I tried to get him to spend less money on drink or cabs or whatever'. Hence Martin's impression that the Barnet house was 'a citadel of riotous solvency . . . There was a great sense of in-depth back-up, a cellar, a barrel of malt whisky, a walk-in larder: proof against snowstorm or shutdown.'[33] Though Amis's domestic duties were few, he carried them out with gusto and generosity. A common theme among the hundreds of thank-you notes from the Barnet years – they fill several boxes in Jane's archive in the Huntington Library – is the size and number of drinks Amis served his guests, often commented on ruefully; there are also many references to Amis's noises, impressions, jokes and comic turns.[34] At Barnet, Martin remembers, Amis was 'the hub of all humour and high-spirits, like an engine of comedy'. 'I felt so secure in that house,' Martin continues, 'that I always experienced a caress of apprehension as I climbed into the car on Sunday night, any Sunday night, and headed back to the motorway and Monday.'[35]

When the Amises bought the Barnet house it was called Gladsmuir, a name nobody liked. After looking through its early papers, Jane discovered that it had once been called Lemmons, presumably the name of a farmer who owned it. So Lemmons it again became. The ménage or commune – Sargy, Colin, Martin, Amis and Jane – moved in permanently on 28 November 1968 and by the following summer had settled into a routine. That summer the financial picture was rosy enough for Amis and Jane to join the Keeleys in Greece, this time in Rhodes and with another couple, Paul and Betty Fussell.[36] Paul Fussell describes the Rhodes holiday routine as divided 'into three invariable daily events'. The morning was spent sunning and swimming at the beach in front of the hotel, which Kingsley 'secretly' hated; he spent most of his time with the English newspapers, delivered a day late but filled with welcome foolishness. Lunch on the hotel terrace was the day's second communal event, preceded, of course, by a drink. According to Betty Fussell, Amis fretted over the opening hours of the hotel bar, which were later than he was used to, evidence of 'the feckless barbarism of the natives',[37] a joke complaint, but a complaint nonetheless. Once the bar opened, with lunch to follow, Amis was happy and expansive: 'by this time it was clear that his troubles for the day were over. Now he could dress up a bit, or at least shed the pink bathing trunks, his morning costume, and enjoy the first drink of the day.'[38] The meal to follow was also to his taste, being filling and un-fancy, with lots of wine. 'Hotel good,' Amis wrote to Conquest on 3 August, 'apart from roaring scooters at 6 a.m. and too many Krauts. And they serve you gnocci if you don't look out.' In a follow-up postcard of 8 August, he added that Rhodes was 'an important province of Little Shagland'. Though Fussell doesn't mention it, Amis, as usual, was working on holiday, and after a head-clearing nap there was a writing session. The third invariable event of the day was 'the quiet sunset stroll into town for dinner, usually seafood but always accompanied by copious amounts of local wine, with perhaps cognac and Turkish coffee after'.[39] Fussell remembers Amis on Rhodes as 'amiable, funny and forbearing in the face of all kinds of threats to decency, courtesy and good order';[40] Mike Keeley remembers him as 'hilarious'.

But the holiday had its stresses. After hearing of their summer plans, a friend of the Keeleys, the poet Caroline Kizer, decided to join them, taking a room in the same hotel. Amis didn't like Kizer and resented her presence. That she had written an unflattering review of *A Case of Samples* may have contributed to his dislike, but it was enough that she was an outsider.[41] 'He wanted his absolutely tight little club,' Betty Fussell explains, 'just the way he wanted his props' (drink, snuff, newspapers, routine). In addition, Kizer had brought her daughter, who was depressed over the recent death of a friend and, understandably, not much fun. Eventually Amis told the Keeleys and the Fussells that he didn't want Kizer and her daughter at their table. 'It was shocking,' Mike Keeley remembers, 'but she accepted it . . . because she had invited herself.' There was also a brief spat between Amis and Fussell, concerning 'trendy' Teddy Kennedy[42] and the drowning at Chappaquiddick, which had happened little more than a week earlier (on 18 July). 'Of all the people who adored Kingsley,' Betty Fussell claims, Paul 'adored him the most', yet at one point in argument he found himself saying to Amis, as Keeley remembers it, 'if you'd only use your judgement about Kennedy, as you do about other things, you'd know he was all right'. Amis was infuriated. There was also a misunderstanding about paying one's round, a crucial virtue and obligation in Amis's eyes. These spats and tensions had a wearing effect on the Keeleys, as did the rigidity of Amis's requirements and preferences.

The Keeleys were not alone among Amis's friends in finding his needs a burden. 'Just off to Aldeburgh,' Conquest reported to Larkin the following autumn, in a letter of 14 November (Caroleen's father had a flat there and the Conquests had invited the Amises for the weekend). 'The problem of getting enough and suitable food and drink for K is like one of those zoo crises (of how to make sure the newly captured Tibetan Shagger doesn't die for want of bamboo-shoots and yak-turds).' For Mary Keeley, two other factors made the Rhodes holiday difficult: the drinking, which seemed even more central and copious than in past holidays, and the general sense of being in a bubble of foreigners rather than in Greece. Though there was much fun and laughter on Rhodes, Mary remembers, 'I was crying, Betty Fussell was crying, Caroline Kizer was crying.'[43] Fussell's memory is that Amis and Jane got on well at Rhodes. Though she thought he drank too much and she sometimes talked of people 'he obviously had no interest in' (well-born people, Fussell thought), she could be smart and funny and 'was clearly a great sexual pal for him'. Betty Fussell has 'this wonderful visual image of Jane in a bikini with her back to us: this giantess, very striking'. Keeley also thought Amis and Jane got on well, but it was on Rhodes that Amis told him in confidence 'that there wasn't a day that went by that he didn't think of Hilly'. At this time, Hilly was living in America. In 1968 Shackleton Bailey had been offered and accepted a professorship in Latin at the University of Michigan and that summer Hilly and Sally accompanied him to Ann Arbor. Before plans for the move were finalised, Hilly suggested that she and Shack meet Amis and Jane to discuss the move, particularly as it affected Sally. A luncheon was arranged at the Savoy Hotel, with Mavis Nicholson acting as buffer or mediator. Amis had no objection to Sally going to Ann Arbor, provided he could see her in the holidays. Only Jane questioned the plan. Sally was thriving at her boarding-school in Eastbourne, the one Jane had found for her. Given how disrupted her education had been, was it really a good idea to uproot her again? Jane then said something that shocked everyone: 'Take her away if you wish, but don't send her back to me in two years' time if something goes wrong.' 'How could you think I'd do such a thing?' Jane remembers Hilly saying. 'What an extraordinary remark to make,' Amis later said to her. Shackleton Bailey, who was clearly infatuated with Hilly, remained silent. Jane's remark was wounding but she defends it on the grounds that it was based on experience: when Hilly was overwhelmed with depression in Majorca in 1963, the boys suddenly appeared at Basil Mansions; after her breakdown in 1964, she went off to Wivenhoe, leaving Jane to take care of Martin. Hilly thought the remark rich coming from Jane, given her history with her own daughter; more importantly, it was Sally's wish to follow her mother to America. Were Sally forced to stay in England, Jane might well be sending her the other way. That Sally was unstable or at risk was the unspoken assumption of them all.[44]

In the event, Jane was right about Hilly sending Sally back. The marriage to Shackleton Bailey was deeply unhappy, as we shall see, and Sally began to go off the rails; Hilly couldn't cope and one freezing morning in January 1970 Sally rang up Lemmons from Heathrow, having arrived alone and unannounced on a flight from Chicago. She had luggage but no coat and had just turned sixteen. At Lemmons empty vodka bottles began appearing in her room. 'She wasn't nasty,' Martin says, 'but she got into trouble and she drank.' She also smoked marijuana, took LSD and was wildly promiscuous. Jane remembers her at this time as pretty, with long blonde hair and beautiful, wide blue eyes; she also remembers her as evasive and untruthful. When Sally refused to go to school, it was difficult to figure out what she should do instead. 'That's when Jane had the bright idea of sending her to the Wrens,' Phil remembers, where she lasted less than a week. A series of jobs in London shops followed, including one at the Scotch House in Knightsbridge, where she told her boss she had terminal cancer and was believed. She lived at Lemmons for several years, off and on, then stayed with Phil for a while ('Phil, to be fair, tried very hard with her,' says Jane), visiting her mother for holidays. When attempting to explain the later calamities of Sally's life, family and close friends frequently refer to early traumas, the fall and fractured skull at two, the horrific experience a year later when her grandmother died and she was left alone with the body for hours. A story Jane tells is of the night before Sally went off to America in the summer of 1968. She was fourteen and at a farewell supper at Maida Vale Amis 'plied her with drink'. After supper she went upstairs and was terribly sick. Jane found her miserable and crying, cleaned up after her and tried to soothe her. She suspected that Sally was 'one of those people who couldn't handle alcohol' and she told her so. Sally replied: 'Don't worry, I'm never going to drink anything again in my life.'

In the summer of 1970 Hilly and Shackleton Bailey went touring in Europe, hiring a car in Rome and driving to Ronda in Andalusia, some fifty miles north of the Costa del Sol. Hilly had been having an affair in Ann Arbor with a recently retired academic named Milton Cohen. Though Cohen was now living in Crete, he had spent the previous Christmas touring southern Spain. Before he left for Spain Hilly asked him to try to find her a flat there for the summer: 'I had this idea of getting a place where the children could visit me.' Ideally she wanted somewhere near the beach, but what Cohen came up with was a five-bedroom flat in the old part of Ronda. It 'sounded lovely' and was reasonable, so she took it. At the end of the summer Hilly refused to return to Ann Arbor with Shackleton Bailey; the marriage had been a farce to begin with ('I don't know what got into me') and was now over. Cohen was expecting her to join him in Crete, having sent her a blank cheque for expenses, but before she could do so, Sally, who had been staying the summer, happened across a language school in the nearby Palacio de Mondragon, 'a rambling and incommodious town mansion', and suggested that Hilly come and see it. Sally thought the school looked interesting and might suit her.⁴⁵ 'There was a knock on the door at Mondragon,' remembers Alastair Boyd, the school's proprietor, soon to become Hilly's third husband, 'and the old concierge opened the door and there were Hilly and Sally on the doorstep . . . Hilly had a marvellous orange dress on which she'd been given by Gully [Martin's girlfriend] and her hair seemed to be more buttercup at that time and Sally was looking very blonde and voluptuous.' Ali and Hilly soon hit it off and she decided not to go to Crete. Instead she helped out at Ali's school, which had recently expanded its curriculum and was offering year-long courses, with winter and spring terms in Seville, an ambitious arrangement which eventually got it into financial difficulties. Sally stayed on in Spain as well, living in Seville with Ali and her mother and attending the school for several months; but she was unable to settle and returned to Lemmons.

In 1970, when Sally arrived at Lemmons, Martin was in his second year at Oxford. At the end of his third year, in 1971, he was awarded a formal First in English, the sort where you are called in for a viva and the examiners tell you how much they enjoyed reading your papers (in the past they stood up and applauded). He then worked as an editorial assistant at the *TLS* (1972–74) and as its fiction and poetry editor (1974–76). While at Oxford, he often visited Lemmons for weekends, bringing friends. It was at Lemmons, after returning from a summer in Spain with his mother and Alastair in 1971, that he began work on his first novel, *The Rachel Papers* (1973). He worked in the room directly above his father's study and was very private about the novel. As Martin remembers it, his father 'never expressed any desire that I should pursue the literary life, despite all the evidence that I had such a life in mind. I attributed this to sheer indolence on his part, but I now think he was obeying a parental instinct, and a good one.'⁴⁶ In their late teens, both boys had been asked by Amis what they wanted to be when they grew up. Phil said he wanted to be a painter and Martin a novelist. '"Good," said Kingsley, rubbing his hands together rapidly, even noisily, in that way he had. "That means the Amises are branching out into the other arts while keeping their stranglehold on fiction." He meant Jane, too.'⁴⁷ Martin can recall no instance in which his father offered him literary advice or counsel. *The Rachel Papers* was published by Tom Maschler at Cape, with Pat Kavanagh of A.D. Peters acting as Martin's agent. Both were frequent house guests at Lemmons. 'It was just sort of domestic,' Martin remembers, 'conversations I would have had in the kitchen with Pat and Tom. "Your reviews are very good. Are you working on anything long term?"' When the novel was finished Martin went on holiday, leaving a proof copy behind on his father's desk, along with a note. Amis wrote to him that summer, pronouncing the novel 'good and great fun, too'.

Martin lived at Lemmons until Christmas 1971, only moving to central London to share a flat with his friend Rob Henderson when he began work at the *TLS*. Whenever he could, he spent weekends at Lemmons: 'It was exciting to be there, the phone was always ringing, the film directors, Iris Murdoch coming for drinks.' ('What's Charlie Drake doing here?' Colin had asked one afternoon, as Murdoch approached the house.)[48] Among recurring names in the Lemmons Visitors' Book, in addition to Murdoch and John Bayley, were the Fussells, the Conquests, the Keeleys, the Szamuelys, the Powells, the Gales, Colin Welch, the journalist and his wife Sybil, Paul and Marigold Johnson, Bernard Levin, Tom Maschler, Pat Kavanagh (who originally handled Amis and Jane's journalism, short stories and serialisations for A.D. Peters), John Betjeman and Elizabeth Cavendish and Peter Yates, the film director. Martin brought several girlfriends: not just Gully Wells, stepdaughter of the philosopher A.J. Ayer, but Tamasin Day-Lewis, daughter of C. Day-Lewis and the actress Jill Balcon (also sister of Daniel Day-Lewis, as well as Jane's god-daughter) and Tina Brown. Colin tells a story about Tina Brown telephoning Lemmons after spending a weekend there. Colin had met and talked with her over the weekend and recognised her voice when she called. 'Is Martin there?' she asked. 'No,' Colin replied. 'Is Kingsley there?' 'No.' 'Is Jane there?' 'No.' 'Is *anybody* there?' Less determined girlfriends could find the atmosphere at Lemmons intimidating. Phil stayed there when between lodgings (in an entry in the Visitors' Book for 30 July 1972, he lists his address as '?'). A pretty girlfriend of his remembers being stiff with fright at dinner. As soon as she arrived, Martin made a pass at her. The banter at dinner, particularly among the Amis men, was clever, funny, fast and dismissive, sometimes of her. Phil was not dismissive of her but he was of others and he could be emotionally tricky, morose as well as nervy. When she first met him at a New Year's Eve party in 1974, she wished him 'Happy New Year.' 'The odds are against it,' he replied.

Pat Kavanagh was perhaps the most frequent of the Lemmons guests. She was first invited on her own soon after the Amises moved in, then frequently came for weekends with her boyfriend, James Durham, an Australian psychiatrist who was to become an important friend of Amis's. Jane liked having Pat as a house guest because, Pat explains, 'I was a good little sleeper and a good little eater. I had second helpings and I helped in the kitchen.' Amis liked her because 'I was a woman who could go to the pub, even though I didn't have much of a head for drink.' She, or she and Durham, would arrive late on Saturday morning, in time for a walk to the pub, which Amis liked to reach as soon as it opened at 11.30; then everyone would troop back to the house for lunch. At lunch, always in the kitchen, 'all the household would be there and people dropped in for different meals over the weekend or stayed'. 'It wasn't a great big empty house,' Pat remembers, 'it was thrumming.' Pat felt 'comfortable and cherished' at Lemmons. It was easy for her to see what attracted Amis both to Jane and to the life she had arranged for him there. In addition to being 'ravishingly beautiful', Jane made 'lovely spaces'; the household ran smoothly and there was always enough to eat and drink. Pat attributed Jane's ease and competence to her class background and always assumed there was money behind her: 'she had absolute class confidence and it went into all aspects of her life: into the space around her, what she chose to eat, the way she dressed, her familiarity with artists, painters, musicians, people with titles. She just seemed a completely confident character.' In minor but not negligent respects, the appeal of Lemmons to Amis was like Jane's appeal. When asked what his father got out of Lemmons, Martin replied: 'It was nice being grand. Go for a stroll with your drink on summer evenings, go once around the property. Come a long way.' Amis had no illusions about being grand himself or a country gentleman, but he liked it that the house was grand, just as he liked it that Jane was grand, when he liked Jane (when he didn't like Jane, or they fought, he held her grandness against her). Living in style or state – by literary-intellectual standards, at least – also suited Amis's provoking or contrarian nature. The element of play-acting in his defiance about having made it is nicely caught by Martin in *Experience*:

Kingsley said, one summer evening, in about 1975:
  —I'm going to get a gun.

—... What for, Dad? one or other of his sons responded.

And he said it deliberately, like a poem, heavily end-stopped:

—To fuck up

Anyone who comes here

Trying to take my stuff.

He was in the three-acre garden of the house on Hadley Common. Perhaps he was actually walking round its perimeter, in the late afternoon. This was a routine of his, a physical regime, for a short time, and only when the weather was good. It could well have been his only regular exercise since World War II.

—You're going to get a gun ...

—I'm going to get a gun ... to kill or otherwise *fuck up* ... anyone who comes here ... trying to take my stuff.[49]

The first of the novels Amis worked on at Lemmons was *The Green Man* (1969), an attempt to write a traditional ghost story that readers would treat seriously. Its starting point, Amis told Clive James in an interview of 1974, was a question: 'What happens when the man who sees ghosts is an alcoholic?'[50] From this question Amis created Maurice Allington, fifty-three-year-old proprietor of the Green Man, an upmarket inn forty or so miles north of London, with a history stretching back to the Middle Ages and an entry in the *Good Food Guide* (cleverly parodied on the novel's opening page, complete with endorsements from Denis Brogan, Bernard Levin, Johnny Dankworth and other Amis friends). Allington is 'on a bottle of Scotch a day, though this has been standard for twenty years', has 'the remains of a first-class constitution', but is showing alarming symptoms of deterioration.[51] His colour is bad, his large, florid face often wet with perspiration, and he suffers from jactitation, a neurological condition 'less disagreeable than it may sound' and exacerbated by drink. Jactitation, Allington explains, is the involuntary or convulsive jerking movement of the muscles, most commonly the leg muscles. In severe cases, such as his own, it is associated 'with hypnagogic (onset-of-sleep-accompanying) hallucinations. These antecede jactitation, taking place when the subject is more fully awake, or even wide awake, but with the eyes closed. They are not dreams. They might be described as visions of no obvious meaning seen under poor conditions.'[52] Usually the visions are of humans, or parts of humans, and loom out of the darkness with no sense of background or depth of frame.

Amis is having several types of fun here. As in science fiction or thrillers, ghost stories need a framing plausibility; when Allington's visions turn out to be actual ghosts, they are the more frightening for the rational, scientific-sounding explanations that precede their appearance. The second type of fun he is having is autobiographical and grimmer. It was on Rhodes that Mary Keeley began to be seriously upset by Amis's drinking. According to Jane Howard, by 1969 Amis was 'often' drinking the equivalent of a bottle of whisky a day and he, too, suffered from jactitation and something like hallucinations.[53] In addition to having what Conquest described to Larkin, in a letter of 15 January 1970, as 'an increasingly common experience of not remembering how he got home', Jane reports that several times he was unable to distinguish between real and imagined happenings and at one point argued with her for a whole day about the guest list of the previous evening's dinner party, an event which had never taken place. On 3 October 1970, Amis published a poem in the *Spectator* entitled 'Hours of Waking: An Insomniac's Bestiary' in which something like the sort of hypnagogic effects Allington talks of in connection with jactitation are described. The poem begins 'Midnight: no beast, no story', and then proceeds through eight numbered sections, each corresponding to a sleepless hour. Over the course of the poem – that is, over the course of the insomniac's sleepless night – the initial 'small shape / Back turned, in a light sleep' next to which he is lying grows progressively more monstrous, then less monstrous, shedding 'suckers and coils', 'nails by the hundred'. Here is what happens to it over the last four hours of the poem:

> 5: is almost real
> Almost an animal
> That prods with its muzzle,
> No more, while I lie still.

> 6: half human,
> or half woman
> To my half man.

> 7: a hundred faces,
> All known, and known voices.

> 8: wife, lover, child.

'Hours of Waking' is a companion piece to *The Green Man* in several respects, notably in the way its 'beasts' grow out of and resolve into 'wife, lover, child', which could also be said of Allington's ghosts, though they are real ghosts. In the immediate context, what is noteworthy is the way the visions appear and disappear, can't quite be grasped, metamorphose, and take place when the subject is awake but with eyes closed, like the pre-hypnagogic visions that antecede jactitation.

Several years after *The Green Man* was published, Amis admitted to similarities between himself and Allington. 'None of my heroes, not even old Lucky Jim, are me,' he wrote in 1972, 'but they can't help having pretty fair chunks of me in them, some more than others. And Allington in that book was one of the some. I'm more like him than I'm like most of the others.'[54] Though younger than Allington – forty-seven, not fifty-three, when *The Green Man* was published – Amis was thickening in the jowls and around the waist, his face growing more florid. What Martin, a loyal son, calls 'the other camp' may, he admits, have some basis when it claims that it was in the Lemmons years that alcohol began to take a significant toll on Amis's temper, though it seems not to have impeded his writing. Looking back in *Experience* on its account of the time at Barnet, Martin finds 'that a certain themelet in these pages – the Two Brewers, the cherry vodka, the Mavrodaphne, the raki – is doing its best to intrude'.[55] Maurice Allington is hardly the first Amis character to drink a lot – he is not even the first Amis character to be an alcoholic, a term notoriously difficult to define – but he is the first Amis *figure*, the first hero as bastard, to be an alcoholic (Max Hunter in *The Anti-Death League* has Amisian characteristics but is not an Amis figure; the novel doesn't have one). Amis was fully aware of the public's tendency to identify him with his heroes, and frequently played on it. He means us to note similarities between himself and Allington. But he also covers himself by making Allington's drunkenness an obvious plot device, a way of lending new life and seriousness to genre materials.

Amis's increasing tendency in the Lemmons years to treat drink as a hobby or interest, like jazz or science fiction, provides similar cover, while also being a genuine hobby or interest, as Allington's alcoholism is a genuine plot device. Like the preparation of elaborate cocktails in the middle of the Mexican countryside, being 'interested' in drink, and ostentatious about his interest, may have been a way of masking dependency, or outfacing those who suspected it. Tony Colwell, who worked at Jonathan Cape, remembered Amis's study at Lemmons: a large, wood-panelled room, furnished with desk and chair at one end and three rows of empty whisky and wine bottles ranged round the walls: 'Jane said he simply wouldn't allow her to throw them away.'[56] Sargy describes outings to the cinema in Barnet: 'We used to take more or less a drinks cabinet with us. We used to go and sit in the front row of the circle and then Kingsley would sort of say "What's yours, a gin and tonic?" and out of pockets would come bottles and glasses and then a thermos with some ice in it and somebody would cut up a lemon and it was such fun.' Less fun was an experience Phil recounts, in his last year at Camberwell in 1970: 'At the end of my stint there, everyone had a show of the stuff they'd been doing. And I asked my father to come have a look and he did, out of duty. And I remember him walking around where I had stuff on the wall and nodding and grunting: "Mm. Mm. Mm. Mm." Then he walked straight out. That sort of noise of his being: "Christ, what am I doing here? Mm. Mm. Mm. Mm. Let's go to the pub. What am I doing here? I just want to be in the pub." And then he walked right out. I'll always remember that. Complete disregard for anything I did.'

What is remarkable about *The Green Man* is that behaviour like this – wounding, egotistical, drink dependent – is coolly exposed. When Allington's wife announces she's leaving him, part of what she says is: 'You just have your own ideas about what to do and when and how, about everything, and they always stay the same, doesn't matter who you're dealing with or what they say to you . . . I don't know what you think about people, which is bad enough, but you certainly go on as if they're all in the way.'[57] Allington's deficiencies as a father begin with his thirteen-year-old daughter, Amy, who has suffered a terrible trauma, 'having her mother knocked down and killed in front of her eyes'.[58] The accident occurred eighteen months ago and Amy's withdrawn, untended air disturbs Allington's son, Nick, a don at a provincial university. Nick upbraids his father for not concerning himself enough with Amy, or talking with her about her mother, Allington's ex-wife at the time of the accident. When Allington says he feels somehow responsible for Amy's mother's death, Nick rounds on him: 'This is a load of crap, Dad. What's bothering you isn't that you were in any way responsible for her death, but that she died. Same with Gramps [whose death opens the novel]. Both those things remind you that you'll be going the same way yourself one of these days.'[59] Later Nick calls Allington 'just too lazy and arrogant and equal to everything (you think) to take the trouble to notice people like your son, and your wife, and deem them bloody well worthy of being let into the great secret of how you feel and what you think about everything, in fact, what you're like.'[60]

Allington drinks because it makes him feel good. 'I was drunk,' he tells us, after three quick double whiskies. 'In fact, drunk with that pristine freshness, that semi-mystical elevation of spirit which, every time, seems destined to last for ever. There was nothing worth knowing that I did not know, or rather would not turn out to know when I saw my way to turning my attention to it. Life and death were not problems, just points about which a certain rather limited type of misconception tended to agglutinate.'[61] What Allington says drink provides him with here is a moment of truth as well as pleasure. From the perspective of Dionysus, life and death are illusions ('not problems, just points', sites of 'misconception'), as is the self; it is liquid nature, the life force, that is the truth, and that drink allows one not just to celebrate but to experience pleasurably. According to this line, the truth of drink is allied to the truth of comedy and romance, in which youth and desire overpower age and restraint. In *Lucky Jim* drink frees Dixon to trust to his luck, liberating him from the Welches of this world and from his own captive self. Escaping to the pub and getting drunk on the night of the madrigals brings him in touch with Christine almost as a reward.[62] Just before the Merrie England speech, when it looks as if Jim has lost Christine and is bound, out of an obscure sense of duty, to return to Margaret, three sherries at the party before the lecture and 'a half dozen measures of Bill Atkinson's whisky' fail to elevate his spirits. Moments before the lecture, in the Gents, Dixon feels 'so low that he wanted to lie down and pant like a dog'.[63] Then Gore-Urquhart appears, gives him two more swigs of whisky (he has a flask), grips his arm and tells him: 'No need to worry: the hell with all this.'[64] Gore-Urquhart speaks for truth as well as pleasure: Dixon, now thoroughly drunk, lets rip in the lecture and ends up with Christine. In *The Green Man*, drink functions differently, notwithstanding Allington's moment of 'semi-mystical elevation': it anaesthetises and only 'seems' to liberate. 'Nodding my head confidentially to myself about the simple force of this perception,' continues

Allington in the 'I was drunk' passage, 'I left the pub and made for where there was a fair case for believing I had left the Volkswagen.'[65] So much for 'pristine freshness'.

'I'll teach you peace of mind,' the trendy Reverend Tom Rodney promises Allington at the end of the novel. 'Now there's an offer,' Allington thinks. 'I imagined myself not noticing myself for the rest of my life, losing myself, not vainly struggling to lose myself, in poetry and sculpture and my job and other people, not womanizing, not drinking.'[66] Darker even than this admission, in which losing oneself is hardly associated with pleasure or truth, is Allington's conviction that he *is* his true self and that 'any radical change, however unarguably for the better, is bound to seem a kind of self-destruction'.[67] A similarly pessimistic note is struck at the novel's conclusion, even after Allington has rescued his daughter from the malign spirits his own malignity seems to have awoken (these spirits consist principally of the ghost of a seventeenth-century necromancer and seducer of very young girls, Dr Thomas Underhill, and the *Waldteufel* or green man who serves him). In addition to ghosts, Allington also confronts God Himself, who appears as an affable young man 'about twenty-eight years old, with a squarish, clean-shaven humorous, not very trustworthy face, unabundant eyebrows and eyelashes, and good teeth'.[68] In the course of their conversation, God defends the presence of death in the world in terms Allington refers to at the novel's close:

I found I had begun to understand the meaning of the young man's prophecy that I would come to appreciate death and what it had to offer. Death was my only means of getting away for good from this body and all its pseudo-symptoms of disease and fear, from the constant awareness of this body, from this person, with his ruthlessness and sentimentality and ineffective, insincere, impracticable notions of behaving better, from attending to my own thoughts and from counting in thousands to smother them and from my face in the glass.[69]

Here Amis attains his ends: the pleasures of genre fiction, including those of wish-fulfilment, dragon-slaying (in this case, ghost-busting) and a good fright, combine with more 'serious' purposes: the realistic depiction of a man in despair, at a dead end very like that faced by Roger Micheldene.

In 1972 Amis revisited *The Green Man* in a short story entitled

'Who or What Was It?' which was broadcast on BBC Radio 3 on 27 May. Amis, who read the story, is its narrator. The tale he tells is of a hotel pub or inn he and Jane stayed in on their way back to Lemmons from a weekend with Jane's uncle and aunt in Westmorland, where Jane's real-life uncle and aunt lived (during the story Amis also refers to Bob Conquest, Monkey and Phil). The inn turns out to have uncanny similarities to the inn in *The Green Man*, though its name is different. To begin with, its proprietor is called Allington, though his first name is John, not Maurice; his deputy and barman also have similar names to their fictional counterparts. Among other coincidences, the proprietor has a fifteen-year-old daughter, Marilyn, who lives on the premises. Amis is unnerved by these coincidences. Jane is cautious and reasonable about them, 'very sensible, as usual'.[70] As in the novel, Amis has a confrontation with the Green Man, or so he thinks, while Jane is upstairs in their room. When Amis returns and tells Jane what has happened she says he must have been dreaming. They then have a discussion about whether the confrontation was real or imagined. This discussion, Jane has said, was 'based upon the actual exchange which took place after Amis had recollected the dinner party which had never happened'.[71] What is striking about the story is that not a word is said about the Amis narrator being 'a boozer, like my Allington'.[72] There is no indication that what he sees, or thinks he sees, in the night has anything to do with alcohol, which makes the story, for all its self-referentiality, more purely a genre exercise than the novel.

In 1972, the year 'Who or What Was It?' was broadcast, Amis published a book about alcohol. The germ of the book is found in a letter to Pat Kavanagh of 3 June 1969. Amis wants to publish a huge article or series of articles 'on Drink and Drinking':

The point is three-fold: we might make some money, I am interested in the subject, and, above all, if we can land a reasonably-sized commission to write such a piece or pieces, I could get something like six months' drink off tax, which would be a tremendous achievement.

The thing would cover quite a lot of ground: why and how wine is a pain, original cocktail, cup and punch recipes, hints on bartending, something of the sociology of alcohol . . . and a grand hangover manual, complete with a list of recommended classical records and an examination of Dostoievsky as the novelist of Hungover Man. As you see, a light-hearted romp round the scene, frightfully idiosyncratic and funny, but with plenty of serious information thrown in. Oh yes, and with the bonus of The Boozing Man's Diet: How to take off four pounds a week without stinting yourself a single drop.

This wizard idea eventually became *On Drink*, published in 1972. In the almost three years between its publication and the original idea, Amis immersed himself, with the hobbyist's ardour, in 'research'. Martin remembers him rushing around trying out new drinks, filling ice trays with milk, collecting obscure recipes, 'very busy with that, scampering around'. The importance of alcohol, to Amis and to everyone else, is briefly explained in the opening pages of *On Drink*, with the help of pop-anthropological assertions: that 'every present-day society uses alcohol, as have the majority of those of the past'; that wine and beer, in the countries that produce them, are 'drinks of the village and the poorer classes'; that an increase in the consumption of spirits coincides with 'the strains and stresses of urban living, to coin a phrase'.73 This last assertion Amis accepts only in part: 'I should single out one stress (or strain) as distinctly more burdensome, and also more widespread, than most: sudden confrontation with complete or comparative strangers in circumstances requiring a show of relaxation and amiability – an experience that I, for one, never look forward to without misgiving, even though I nearly always turn out to enjoy it in the event.' Such confrontations are more frequent in towns than villages, 'where strangers appeared seldom', and it is drink, 'simply and obviously', that makes them not only endurable but enjoyable: 'The human race has not evolved any way of dissolving barriers, getting to know the other chap fast, breaking the ice, that is one-tenth as handy and efficient as letting you and the other chap, or chaps, cease to be totally sober at about the same rate in agreeable surroundings.'

Amis's shyness with strangers and in public settings was noted earlier. Focusing on it here, giving it priority among the uses of drink, firmly establishes the book's register. The question of alcoholism, concomitantly, is given short shrift. Amis addresses it impatiently, rather as he admits to qualifying or complicating factors in political polemic; but what he says is revealing. 'What about those who drink not to cease to be totally sober, but to get drunk?' asks 'the serious student of the effects of drink'. 'What about the man who drinks *on his own*?' What these questions suggest is that for Amis the distinction between acceptable and unacceptable drinking, between drinker and alcoholic, is social. Amis craved company for all sorts of reasons, beginning, as was suggested in Chapter 1, with a sense of having been denied it in childhood. His attraction to pubs, parties and late-night company, even when merely watching television, his insistence that *everyone* get out of the car for a cocktail, had complex motivations; among these may have been a desire to avoid thinking of himself as an alcoholic, 'the man who drinks *on his own*'. As for why men become alcoholics, he refuses to speculate: 'there is very little we can safely add'.[74] What *On Drink* focuses on instead are 'different and more interesting' questions: 'Where and what and how [not the same as 'how much'] we drink, or should drink'.[75] Such questions are external rather than internal, about things, gear, expertise; the book is meant to be light.

Amis was less interested in and knowledgeable about wine than spirits; his tastes in alcohol were inclusive or democratic rather than exclusive or refined, and he is vigilant about drink snobbery. The book's first 'G.P.' (General Principle) is: 'Up to a point (i.e. short of offering your guests one of those Balkan plonks marketed as wine, Cyprus sherry, poteen and the like), go for quantity rather than quality. Most people would rather have two glasses of ordinary decent port than one of a rare vintage.'[76] In the chapter on 'Drinking Literature', a survey of guides, he claims that 'your true drink-man . . . reads everything on the subject that comes his way, from full-dress books to those tiny recipe-leaflets the makers tend to hang round the necks of their bottles'; the leaflets may be commercial, but the manufacturer 'knows more about his product than anybody else and, never mind what base motives, will have tested out his recommendations with the utmost care'. In a chapter on 'The Tools of the Trade', Amis often recommends the cheaper, more practical product, as in the vexed question of lemon squeezers: 'plastic is better than glass, because the flutes on the central dome are generally sharper'.[77] He is keen to avoid exaggeration, almost as common a failing of drinkers as of fishermen. In 'How Not to Get Drunk', he tells of having 'once shared a half-litre of Polish Plain Spirit (140° proof) with two chums. I only spoke twice, first to say "Cut out that laughing – it can't have got to you yet," and not all that much later to say, "I think I'll go to bed now."'[78] The funniest and best-known chapters are the 'Mean Sod's Guide', liberally borrowed from in *The Old Devils*, and 'The Hangover', with its distinction between physical and metaphysical varieties and appropriate remedies. The tone and purport of the book as a whole are caught by the opening suggestions for curing the metaphysical hangover: '1. Deal thoroughly with your P.H. [Physical Hangover] 2. When that ineffable compound of depression, sadness (these two are not the same), anxiety, self-hatred, sense of failure and fear for the future begins to steal over you, start telling yourself that what you have is a hangover. You are not sickening for anything, you have not suffered a minor brain lesion, you are not all that bad at your job, your family and friends are not leagued in a conspiracy of barely maintained silence about what a shit you are, you have not come to see life as it really is, and there is no use crying over spilt milk.'[79] The chapter concludes with 'Three Notable Breakfasts':

Sir Winston Churchill's
1 brace cold snipe
1 pint port

Horatio Bottomley's
1 pair kippers
1 tumbler brandy and water

Samuel Taylor Coleridge's (Sundays only)
6 fried eggs
1 glass laudanum and seltzer

On Drink landed Amis a lucrative column in *Penthouse* magazine, a post it is hard to see other major novelists of the period accepting (except, perhaps, Anthony Burgess). Conquest wrote with enthusiasm to Larkin on 4 June 1972 about attending a party at the magazine 'given in honour of their new Sherry Correspondent, K. Amis . . . full of glorious semi-nudes, ex-nudes, future nudes etc.'

Amis's writings about drink played a part in the renewal or recovery of his friendship with Larkin. Two years before *On Drink* was published, parts of it appeared, as envisioned in the initial letter to Pat Kavanagh, as a series of three articles in the *Daily Telegraph* magazine.[80] These articles were to be accompanied by mini-interviews between Amis and what he called, in a letter to Larkin on 11 August 1970, 'distinguished shags of my acquaintance'.[81] Would Larkin be willing to be such a shag? It would only involve having a drink with him, and a chat about drink, at a location of Larkin's choosing, and having his photograph taken. 'I could come to Hull, if need sodding be,' Amis adds, 'or it could be done in London. Anywhere you could notionally claim was a favourite drinking spot of yours.' The ensuing correspondence, though trivial on the surface, marks a turning point in the relationship between the two men, after the silences of the 1960s. Larkin agreed to Amis's original proposal and on 30 August Amis wrote again, to say that the *Telegraph* was pressing for completed copy by 11 September. Would Larkin be in London before then? 'If not, as I suspect, I will, if I may, despatch the photograph man up to see you in Hull, when he'll take perhaps ½ an hour of your time. He's a decent sort of shag, John Goldblatt by name – though he ate a couple of porkchops unhesitatingly enough.' As for Larkin's views on drink: 'it'll be easiest, on the assumption that you won't be in London, if you'd let me have some thoughts . . . which I could work up into about 250 jolly spontaneous-sounding words . . . the accent will be on drinking rather than drunkenness, and I promise you there won't be any Dylan's heirs stuff in the article.' On 4 September Amis wrote a third time: it turned out he'd only have room for 100 words and so 'I can make do with what you've already vouchsafed in your last letter, and needn't trouble you further or send you ten guineas, which would have had to come out of my pocket. But I can "offer you hospitality" when you're next this way, or buy you a meal in Oxford.'

At this point Larkin balks. He was, indeed, at Oxford at the time, as a two-term Visiting Fellow at All Souls College, working on *The Oxford Book of Twentieth Century English Verse* (1973). 'I'm afraid this idea is getting beyond me,' he replies.[82] 'The first suggestion was for an interview, and I agreed. Then this turned into a request for 250 words for nothing, which I wasn't so keen on. Now you suggest you make up a 100 words from about 50 of mine not chosen for publication at all. No, it might turn out all right, but chances are that I should feel I'd been misrepresented, and I should have only myself to blame. So let's scrub it. I don't suppose the British public will miss having my views.' By this point in his career, Larkin was not only long used to being deferred to by university and librarian colleagues at Hull, but was, as his current position at All Souls and assignment from Oxford University Press suggests, at least as eminent as Amis, if not as much of a celebrity. There had been a distance between the two friends for some years and his tone has a faint rattle to it. In his reply of 6 September, Amis continues to press Larkin, not out of will or necessity, but out of friendship, or so his good-humoured, firm and respectful manner suggests:

Nay, don't let's scrub it – whatever the nation may think, I want it to have your views on the topic and see your little flower-face.

My memory tells me, in faltering tones, perhaps, that I never asked you to write me a para for nothing. Not I, lad. I meant, if you jotted down a few cracks, I could work them up. Beer today is piss = He considers brewing standards have declined disastrously in the post-war period. Anyway, I enclose a draft for your vetting . . .

Do reconsider. The gallery of chaps (did I tell you old Betj is in on it?) would be the poorer for your absence. I will still buy you a large meal, *with drinks*, in Oxford quite soon. The pork-chop chap has no pork-chop chip, is easy to deal with, and will have no objection to being flung out when you have had enough of him. So don't let's scrub it.

In the end, Larkin agreed, making only a slight alteration to Amis's copy. Goldblatt came to Hull and took his photograph and then, as Amis put it to Larkin in a letter of 14 December, 'the posturing turd who helps to run the DT colour mag' cut the photo. Amis concludes the exchange with an apology: 'Anyway, sorry you had to endure the chop chap for fuck-all.' From this point onwards the friendship revived. Lunches and invitations followed; letters were more frequently exchanged and in them something of the old intimacy returned.

The death of C. Day-Lewis, then Poet Laureate, seems also to have played a part in the revival of the friendship. In the spring of 1972 Jane went to Greenwich to interview Day-Lewis for a profile in *Queen* magazine, after which Jill, his wife, joined them for lunch. Jane had known Day-Lewis and Jill for many years; her brief, guilt-ridden affair with him in 1958 had been forgiven and the three friends were fond of each other. That Day-Lewis had been seriously ill, Jane knew, but she was shocked to see how quickly his illness had progressed. He would soon, it was clear, be too weak to negotiate the stairs in the Greenwich house, with the bedroom two flights from the kitchen and a lavatory on a half-landing. The alternative was a hospital ward. Alarmed at this prospect, Jane that afternoon called Day-Lewis's doctor ('I knew his name because it had been mentioned several times that day'). She asked him what he thought of the idea of Day-Lewis and Jill moving to Lemmons, where there would be no problem with stairs. 'If you can manage it, it would be the best possible thing for them both,' he replied. Then Jane asked Amis what he thought of the idea. 'Kingsley had never been particularly fond of Cecil,' Jane remembers, 'but he was always generous about people in need of help, and he agreed readily.' The next day she rang Jill to thank her for lunch and to enquire about Day-Lewis. As Jane knew, Jill had a part in a television serial and was due to begin a week's filming at Elstree, an exhausting commute from Greenwich. They had no home help, so Jill felt that she could no longer leave Cecil alone all day. 'Luck was on my side,' writes Jane of this news: 'I asked her if she would like to come to Lemmons so conveniently near her job. She'd ask him. He was delighted.'[83] Whether Day-Lewis knew how ill he was – he had pancreatic cancer – Jill is uncertain; his doctor had forbidden her to tell him the truth about his condition and they never discussed it in any detail.[84] The idea of the move was presented to him as a solution to a practical problem; 'he probably thought of it as a sort of holiday'.

One other person needed to be consulted before Jane made this offer: her mother. Katharine ('Kit') Howard had moved to Lemmons to stay in 1970, no longer able to cope on her own in her small house in Tunbridge Wells, despite the proximity of her elder son, Robin, and his family ('Kingsley was very nice about this when I asked him, and even wrote her a letter saying how glad he was that she was coming, which pleased her enormously').[85] Kit broke her hip after she came to Lemmons and Jane fixed up a downstairs bedroom and adjoining bathroom for her as a separate suite, hiring Tessa Craig, the eldest daughter of her friend, Dosia Verney, to care for her (Tessa had been a nursing sister at the Middlesex Hospital). By spring 1972, Kit had recovered sufficiently to be moved to an upstairs bedroom, which meant that Tessa would be free to care for Day-Lewis. Kit agreed to this plan, her bedroom was prepared for Day-Lewis, Colin installing a record-player and Jane arranging flowers and books. On 6 April Cecil and Jill arrived; Cecil was settled downstairs, Jill was given a bedroom upstairs. Their daughter Tamasin, aged nineteen, also came to stay (she was working as a model for a year before going up to Cambridge); fifteen-year-old Daniel was at school at Bedales but came for weekends. The house was now full. In addition to Amis, Jane, Sargy and Colin, it contained

Jill, Cecil, Tamasin, Kit, Tessa and Sargy's painter pal Terry Raybould (temporarily estranged from his wife). After Jill's work at Elstree finished, Jane asked Cecil if he would like to stay longer: 'I should like to stay for months,' he replied. 'I'm very anxious to give Jill a rest.'[86] He stayed for five weeks, and died in his room at Lemmons on 22 May, surrounded by family and friends. Daniel had been summoned from school and was by his father's bedside when he died, holding his hand.

By all accounts Day-Lewis was remarkably brave at Lemmons. Martin, partly because he was 'a known lover of his daughter', at first steered clear of his room: 'But his equanimity, his stillness, drew me in closer. It was an extraordinary demonstration. He was showing you how you could keep your self-possession, right to the end.'[87] On reasonably sunny days Cecil would sit outside in the walled courtyard by the side of the house. Once he was able to make a tour of the garden, using Kit's wheelchair. The combined record collections of Colin, Sargy, Amis and Jane were put at his disposal; his bed was arranged so that he could watch the wind in the trees, the blossoming garden and the birds that visited the bird table outside his window. Amis soon came to like and admire Day-Lewis and made a point of visiting him each evening for a drink. It was in Day-Lewis's room that Amis's fiftieth birthday was celebrated, on 16 April, followed by Day-Lewis's own sixty-eighth birthday, on the 27th, and Daniel's fifteenth birthday, two days later. In his second week at Lemmons, Day-Lewis asked Jill to get him a notebook so that he could 'write a poem for the household'. When the poem was finished Amis received his copy the day after his birthday. According to Jane, 'he wept, but apart from what it seemed to tell him, he said objectively that it was a bloody good poem'.[88]

At Lemmons

Above my table three magnolia flowers
Utter their silent requiems.
Through the window I see your elms
In labour with the racking storm
Giving it shape in April's shifty airs.

Up there sky boils from a brew of cloud
To blue gleam, sunblast, then darkens again.

No respite is allowed
The watching eye, the natural agony.

Below is the calm a loved house breeds
Where four have come together to dwell
– Two write, one paints, the fourth invents –
Each pursuing a natural bent
But less through nature's formative travail
Than each in his own humour finding the self he needs.

Round me all is amenity, a bloom of
Magnolia uttering its requiems,
A climate of acceptance. Very well.
I accept my weakness with my friends'
Good natures sweetening every day my sick room.

C. Day-Lewis. For Jane, Kingsley, Colin and Sargy
With much love.

On 28 April, Amis wrote to Larkin, who had heard from Conquest of Day-Lewis's move to Lemmons and who had been a friend of Jill and Cecil for many years, several times staying at their house in Greenwich.[89] Day-Lewis 'would love to see you. If you're in London, you could pop up here without much difficulty, and we could easily, indeed would love to put you up for the night. He's very weak, but totally compos and cheerful (Christ).' If Larkin did decide to come, Amis added, he should come quickly: 'Nobody can really tell, of course, but somewhere between a week and a month seems probable.' On 3 May, Larkin came to visit; it was the first time he had been to Lemmons. As he reported to Conquest on 31 May, after Day-Lewis's death: 'Well, things moved quickly since I last wrote. I went to Lemmons: met Kingsley about 12.45 and drank steadily till midnight, being shelled in on poor C D-L about 5. He was obviously very ill, but maintained a cool and cheerful demeanour: all K said was true, from my hour with him. I took him a book of poems by one Joan Barton (pub-d in Hull) and he took the trouble to read it and to dictate a letter via Jill saying he liked it. Catch me doing that. I really think he was a nice man.' To Jane, in a thank-you note of 5 May, Larkin was full of praise for Lemmons: 'the view is tremendous', 'looks like miles from anywhere', 'my own hi-fi sounds like bloody nothing after Wednesday'. Amis was greatly buoyed by the visit: 'By the living God cully,' he wrote to Larkin on 7 May, 'that was a fine old time, as far as I remember. We did nothing else from about 7 on but play records, didn't we? Didn't we? I am inclined to the hopeful view that you were no less damaged than I because you left your record behind.'

Amis marked his fiftieth birthday by writing a poem, 'Ode to Me', and by beginning a diary of sorts. The poem appeared in the *Observer* on the birthday itself, with lines lamenting educational decline, apathy towards communism, the decay of the language. Its spirit is that of *On Drink* – matey, light, not probing too deeply. Here is how it opens:

> Fifty today, old lad?
> Well, that's not doing so bad:
> All those years without
> Being really buggered about.
> The next fifty won't be so good,
> True, but for now – touch wood –
> You can eat and booze and the rest of it,
> Still get a lot of the best of it,
> While the shags with fifty or so
> Actual years to go
> Will find most of them tougher,
> The going a good bit rougher
> Within the Soviet sphere –

The humour of the poem comes in part from Amis's willingness to play up to his public image, as when the first sentence rounds towards 'Within the Soviet sphere'. Amis is partly serious, partly having a laugh, off on a familiar hobby-horse. The ending too is amiable, projecting his sense of personal well-being and good fortune on to the world around him, which isn't really all that bad, at least for the present.

> So bloody good luck to you, mate,
> That you weren't born too late
> For at least a chance of happiness,
> Before unchangeable crappiness
> Spreads over all the land.

Be glad you're fifty –
And that you got there while things were nice,
In a world worth looking at twice.
So here's wishing you many more years,
But not all that many. Cheers!

The mood of 'Ode to Me' connects not only to the mood of *On Drink* but to that of the novel Amis was working on at the time, *The Riverside Villas Murder* (1973), with its warm evocation of childhood scenes and routines. Gratefulness pervades both works, perhaps influenced by Day-Lewis's capacity to take pleasure at Lemmons. Jill remembers his being given a teaspoon of ice-cream on the day he died. 'He sort of raised his eyes as if to say this is glorious.'

Amis's kindness during Day-Lewis's time at Lemmons is worth noting. Though the idea of moving Cecil to Lemmons had been Jane's and it was she who did most to make his stay comfortable, Amis's immediate agreement cannot have been easy. As Jill puts it, 'he was a very frightened man . . . to receive a dying man into his house', a man he was not particularly close to and did not much like, 'was monumentally generous'. Also generous was Amis's treatment of Day-Lewis once he arrived. It was Amis who organised the daily choice of records, in addition to looking in on him each day. In Day-Lewis's final week, the doorbell and the telephone rang constantly, as friends and relations came to say goodbye or to find out how he was. Amis was 'unfailingly polite' to them all. The Day-Lewis children loved him: 'he was sweet to them and funny'. He was also helpful and considerate to Jill. When the family was debating whether Cecil should be buried or cremated, Amis said nothing. Later, when alone with Jill, he reminded her that 'people will want to visit his grave'. 'He was absolutely right,' she realised. 'The Poet Laureate had to be buried somewhere where people could see the stone.' When told that Day-Lewis had died, Amis immediately went into his study and emerged some minutes later with a brief statement for the press, something Jill was in no fit state to produce herself. Jill had been Jane's friend and confidante for almost thirty years and knew full well the strains in her marriage. Before the stay at Lemmons, she had been both frightened of Amis ('I felt I couldn't come up to scratch on any level') and disapproving (of his drinking, his domineering personality, his politics, his treatment of Jane). After

Day-Lewis's death she saw him infrequently. Her memories of him at Lemmons, during a terrible time for her family, are of his sensitivity and tact.

The diary Amis began the day after his fiftieth birthday says very little about Day-Lewis's death. It was kept for almost three months and no entry is longer than two lines. For the first month only, each entry is followed by a number, never less than three, never more than eight. These numbers may signify drinks, presumably spirits, with wine and beer not counted. It is hard to think what else they could be, except pages written or marks out of ten for the day, though an entry like: 'F. Too hung to do anything exc abt 2 letters. 7. Read Arnold B's bk,' would seem to rule out all three possibilities, given the hangover. This entry (it is for 11 May) contains one other mysterious feature: 'F', which appears very infrequently in the diary. If it stands for what one thinks it does (as opposed to, say, 'fibrillation', never mentioned in the correspondence), what is it doing on a hangover day, unless it took place in the early hours of the morning, while drunk. One striking feature of the diary is how busy and social Amis was in this period. Here is a week's run, from Friday 21 April, two weeks after Jill and Cecil arrived, to Thursday 27 April:

21. Lot of ch 6 [of *The Riverside Villas Murder*]. P. Quennell & Marilyn [illegible] for dinner. V. pissed at end. 7.
22. Ch 6. Walked to Barnet midday. Sibyl Welch came. Terrifying TV, B. Stanwyck in Night Walker. W. [Wog, i.e. Jane] & Sib in our bed, me in Phil's. Nasty dream abt Mave. ?6.
23. Finished ch 6. Ralph H. [Harris, of the Institute of Economic Affairs, a neighbour] at pub. Univ. Chall. w Kit & Monk. W off w Sib to Alnwick for article. Jolly lunch: Monk, Sarg, Tess [Craig], Jill, Tam, Tam's boy-f Hugo. John Coleman jolly retort to my 50 ode in *Obs*. 7. 2 pals of Sarg's to din. All played monopoly, I records.
24. Hangover. Presumably typed. 4.
25. Tues. Lunch Time Life White Tower [presumably taken there by American journalists]: Prendergast & Ellison (US) Hofmanstahl, A[nthony] Sampson, Lord Goodman. Took AS to Berti's [Bertorelli's] for port. Bob [Conquest] back fr US. Chap & Vse [a radio programme] at Bush Ho. Melvyn Bragg won. Also saw J Gross, Clive James. 6.
26. Davis-Poynter [a small publishing firm, Amis was on the board]. Drink w Barb. Wootton before, Nigel L. [Lawson] after. Lunch at Wig & Pen w

Mart. V jolly v easy. BH [Bush House] 3.30. Geo MacB [Macbeth], recording for PAL's [Larkin's] 50th. 6.
27. Cecil's birthday. A few minutes' real fun. Up to start of ch 8. 5.

It was the next day, 28 April, that Amis wrote to Larkin about Day-Lewis's deteriorating condition, urging him to visit soon. The diary entry for the day of the visit, 3 May, reads: 'PAL. Lunch Braganza, records till 1 am. Lovely. 8.' On 13 May, four days before the mysterious numbers disappear, Amis writes: 'Letters. 5. Diet ceases.' The diary seems to have coincided with the turning over of a new leaf, a determination to drink less, eat less. Partly this may have been inspired by Jane, with whom he seems often to have been quarrelling. On 14 May Amis writes: 'I started big row last thing: break-up mentioned. 3 agn.' After Day-Lewis's death on 22 May and the funeral on the 26th, Stephen and Natasha Spender invited Jill and Jane to their house in Provence for two weeks, beginning at the end of June. It would be Jane's first holiday away from Amis. The entry for 31 May reads: 'Big Q with J, then big reconciliation.' The entry for 5 June reads: 'More novel. P150. Q late: why J going away w-out me?' The next day's entry begins: 'Tues. Reconc. a bit.' On 19 June he is 'V. low in a.m.' The next day, a Tuesday, 'J drove me up [to London] & said she disliked Phil, so v. low all day, exc. lunch.' On the 25th: 'J got tight, had bump & blamed me. V. low.' On the 29th: 'J said she cdn't come to IEA [Institute of Economic Affairs] & put me in wrong.' The next day, Jane left for France. The entry for 1 July begins: 'Crise in pub noon.'

The onset of difficulties between Jane and Amis can be variously tracked. Though Nashville drew them together, it also marked a cooling of sexual relations. In *Girl, 20* (1971), described by Martin as a 'sad and unautobiographical novel',[90] Roy Vandervane's wife, Kitty, is complexly drawn. While Roy is arse-creeping the young, in particular the horrible Sylvia, his 'girl, 20' (actually, 'girl, 17'), Kitty is at home weeping. 'There were tears in her eyes,' notes Douglas Yandell, Roy's friend and the novel's narrator, 'but then there so often were.'[91] Roy is bored with Kitty and irritated with her as well. To Douglas, while Kitty is 'still attractive in a plump, florid, not-my-cup-of-tea way, she had aged since I had seen her'.[92] What remains unchanged is her actressy self-consciousness, a quality associated, in later novels, not only with specifically Jane-like characters but with women in general. 'Kitty started back as if struck,' notes Douglas, 'or like somebody well-used to meeting the phrase in print.' When a disturbance breaks out in the upper floor of the Vandervanes' large house in Barnet, openly based on Lemmons, 'Kitty got up and behaved for a few seconds like somebody about to be machine-gunned from the air.'[93] As Roy and Douglas play a duet, Kitty enters the room:

Kitty was so good about not interrupting or distracting us, her mouth thinned and eyes narrowed with concentration as she fetched, opened, deployed and started on some sewing, that Roy and I had to work hard to prevent the closing pages degenerating into chaos. We finished approximately together. Kitty hurled down her sewing and clapped in the childish mode, hands pointing the same way instead of across each other at right angles.[94]

'It was sweet of you to come, Douglas dear,' she says later in the novel. 'Oh, it's good to get out for a bit,' he answers. 'How are you?' Both Kitty's answer and Douglas's reaction to the answer are subtly double: 'She gave me a brave, jerky smile that irritated me and made me feel sorry for her. "Oh . . . you know," she said with an affectation of affected lightness'[95] (earlier Douglas describes her as having 'challenged me challengingly').[96] Kitty knows precisely what effect her manner has on Douglas and Roy, without being able to do much about it. 'There's nothing left for me any more, Douglas, my dear. Nothing at all, anywhere . . . All I had was Roy and Roy's world. And now . . . that's all gone. I'm nothing. Nothing.'[97] When Kitty then asks Douglas if he believes her, the exchange that follows is also complex:

'Of course I do,' I said as stoutly as I could, with no idea whether or how much I meant it.

'Perhaps you do. Roy's the same. I think you both do in a way, but it's sort of how I say it you don't really believe. Or you don't like it, the way I say it. It's too much like how I say things when I'm only tired and cross or late for something. I know I go on an awful lot. I ought to have always said just I feel bloody fed up and bugger it and what a bastard, and then I'd have been all right now with this when it came along, and you'd both have believed me. But it's too late for that . . .'[98]

Only a few pages later, this moment of self-awareness on Kitty's part is matched by a similar moment on Douglas's, where he acknowledges the prejudice lurking in his view not only of Kitty but, by extension, of all women, and the meanness of spirit it involves. Before going out, Kitty issues household instructions:

She did so briskly and without self-consciousness, or with only as much as was appropriate, and inevitable, in a woman being efficient to a male audience. Neither then, nor during our walk to the pub . . . nor on the taxi journey through Hendon, Swiss Cottage and farther did she lapse into paraded bravery. She came out with sound, forgettable stuff about Christopher's tribulations at his university, the Common Market, whether she ought to take up Ouspenskyism again and when was I going to bring this new girl of mine along for her to meet. I was tempted to regard the impeccable smoothness of this part as further evidence of earlier insincerity, until I saw that what I really was doing was refusing to give her credit or sympathy however she might behave: not a very nice response from a supposed friend. So I started trying harder, but had hardly done more than start when she started acting like somebody summoning up courage for something.[99]

Kitty resembles Jane in some ways. Jane had been an actress. She was and is a firm and outspoken opponent of the Common Market. Throughout the 1960s and early 1970s she dabbled in Ouspenskyism and allied spiritualist movements (about which she writes wittily and bitingly in *Something in Disguise*, published in autumn 1969). In addition to gardening, cooking and decorating, she is expert at needlework. While Amis was at work on *Girl, 20* her morale was at rock bottom. She was worried about money, worn out with running the house, in the midst of the menopause and not writing. 'The situation was masked in a way by drugs,' she writes in her memoirs. 'Our doctor discovered me crying one Sunday morning when everybody else had gone to the pub and I was peeling innumerable potatoes. He prescribed Tryptosil and Valium in what today would be regarded as over-generous quantities. I stopped crying and slept heavily at night.'[100]

There were also, only partly as a consequence, problems with sex, principally that Amis had begun to go off it, not only with Jane but in general. Jane thinks he had two brief flings during their marriage, a far cry from the rampant promiscuity of the Hilly years. Though drink did not impede Amis's capacity to work, by the age of fifty it seems to have put a damper on his libido, as well as making him less patient with and considerate of others. In the fiction of the period, boredom with straight or married sex is seen as inevitable and those who seek sex outside marriage, or non-straight sex, are depicted as aberrant, deluded and dangerous. When Douglas asks Roy what's special about Sylvia he says that what's special about her is that he met her and started going to bed with her. 'Oh, the being young thing and knowing things is important, sure, but a lot of other kids have got that. Only I haven't met and gone to bed with them. Another point about her is that she isn't my wife.' Roy continues: 'As you get older you'll find that absolutely straight-down-the-middle sex doesn't strike you in quite the same way as it did when you started off. It *is* the same when you get to it, in fact it may be rather better, because you'll probably have picked up a few tips over the years, got better control and so on, but it doesn't strike you as the same. And there's no whacking fucking as a side of life where how things strike you matters at least as much as what the things are really like.'[101] Roy's point of view is shared by Maurice Allington, who has gone off straight-down-the-middle sex not only with his wife but with his mistress. Hence his attempts to manoeuvre them into a threesome, a scheme his wife, improbably, is willing to consider, though with wifely matter-of-factness. Here, in one of the novel's few comic passages, is how she pictures the threesome working:

you'd, well, do her, for instance, and then she and I would work each other over for a bit, until you were ready again, and then you'd do me from behind, I don't mean, you know, just *from* behind while she sort of did the front of me, and then she and I would go on together again until perhaps you could do the same thing again only the other way round, or else you and I could divide her up and take different bits of her, and then you and she could take different bits of me, and so on. Is that the kind of thing?

'Roughly, yes.' Listening to Joyce's outline had been not altogether unlike having the plot of *Romeo and Juliet* summarized by a plasterer's mate.[102]

In sexual terms Maurice is like Roger Micheldene, greedy, selfish and manipulative. In *One Fat Englishman* we are encouraged to see Roger's behaviour as growing out of despair; in *The Green Man* Allington's similar behaviour calls forth the ghost of Underhill, who threatens his daughter. In *Girl, 20* Roy's desires also have a corrupting

effect. He considers the topic of sexual maniacs: 'You know, I sometimes wonder if I might not end up one of those, when Girl, 20 and
going down and all the rest of it are as if they'd never been. You
could easily find yourself flashing what was left of your hampton
at Girl, 8. Or I suppose by that stage it might even be Boy, 8.'[103]
Though only seventeen, Sylvia is too horrible to be considered a
victim of Roy's needs. When his daughter Penny ends up on heroin,
though, Roy's selfishness, masquerading as permissiveness, is singled
out for blame. 'He's always let us do exactly as we like,' Penny's
brother Christopher says, in words very like Nick Allington's about
his own father, 'and we liked that until we realized that it was all
just less trouble for him.'[104] In *The Riverside Villas Murder*, the
innocence of fourteen-year-old Peter Furneaux is threatened by adult
desire. Mrs Trevelyan, his neighbour, likes to be the dominant partner
in sex, which her husband doesn't like. After seducing Peter, she
explains her problems with her husband:

'He wants to be the one, like most men, I suppose. Now and then I can
get him to let me be it for a little while, but only as a kind of game. And
it isn't a game. I always have to be careful not to let him see it isn't a
game as far as I'm concerned.'

'What if he did?'

'He wouldn't like it. He'd think I was abnormal. I probably am. I don't
know. It's only wanting to be the one.'

'But a boy doesn't mind, because it's all strange to him anyway, and he's
so terrifically keen on everything to do with it, and he isn't like a customer
in a shop who can complain or go to another one.'

'I expect so.' She looked at him carefully out of her very dark-brown
eyes. 'I've been with . . . a couple of other boys, you know. But you're nicer
than any of them. You're – please don't mind me saying it – you're the
most beautiful of the lot.'[105]

Like *The Green Man*, *The Riverside Villas Murder* mostly conforms
to genre expectations: Peter's innocence is as undamaged by the
seduction as it is by his mutual masturbation sessions with Reg.[106]
Desire in youth is pure, but in adults it is dangerous, as in the case
both of Mrs Trevelyan, who is evil, and Colonel Manton, the homosexual detective, who is not. 'How sound your instincts are,' Manton
tells Peter at the novel's conclusion. 'I now know you know what
I am', by which he means, not only that he is homosexual but that

he is not a threat. Yet his sexuality links him to Mrs Trevelyan. 'That – thing in me enabled me to understand her and to predict how she would behave, with a result I expect could be called socially useful. But friendship between us has become impossible, I'm afraid. It's the sort of penalty one pays for – well, for existing really. Still, there's always youth.' What Manton means here by 'existing' is not merely existing as a homosexual, but as an adult, one who accepts limitations. The attempt to recapture the intensity of youthful desire is unnatural, a rebellion against ageing and death, and produces unnatural results, attempts to seduce fourteen-year-old boys or eight-year-old girls. Those characters who cannot accept natural loss damage others or themselves. *Girl, 20* ends with Penny, blissed out on heroin, rejecting Douglas. 'Does your father know about this?' Douglas asks:

'I don't think so. I suppose he'll find out eventually. He won't do anything about it either. Why should he? He's got his own life to lead. You know, Douglas, going off with that girl is going to be the best thing he'll ever have done. For everybody, not just him. We're all free now.'[107]

This bleakest of endings recalls the social dimension of Roy's selfishness, the way it feeds off and into the permissiveness of the 1960s, the equivalent of 1930s and 1940s permissiveness, the sort Amis questions in *You Can't Do Both* and associates with Lawrence, Layard, Homer Lane and early Auden. To Frank Kermode, the tone of *Girl, 20* 'is extremely difficult to describe; one laughs a lot, but the sourness builds up, and then turns to something resembling tragedy. Like *The Anti-Death League* it's much more serious than it sounds, and Amis is not only an accomplished comedian but an original poet.'[108] To Christopher Hitchens, *Girl, 20* is not only Amis's 'neglected masterpiece' but a work that had a profound effect on the intellectual Left, 'which at that time had more wit than the right, as well as more conviction, and was more subversive'. 'I had the feeling reading *Girl, 20*,' he recalls, 'that he managed to inflict a satirical wound on the consensus that meant it could never present itself in the same way.' Hitchens thinks A.J. Ayer 'the obvious model' for Roy and that Amis gets his tone 'exactly right and he makes you realise the implications'.

Jane read *Girl, 20* in draft, writing suggestions in the margins. She wanted another sentence at the close, after 'We're all free now':

'I still think there shd be some – v. short – reflection of Douglas's at end – Something to the effect that so they all were, and perhaps he most of all & what does one *do* with that?' She thought Roy's face 'cd do with a bit of repeated description. You know – one feature at a time (after initial description in Chap 1).' She also asks: 'Why did Roy marry Kitty?' a query Amis ponders in a following note: ''cos good music pupil? Or line of most resistance?' Douglas's long-time girlfriend Viv doesn't much excite him, for all her enthusiasm in bed; languid Penny is sexier. Jane's note reads: 'I think there shd be more of Penny in bed. Better than Viv?' to which Amis replies in the margin: 'body excites him (see p.24) old style'. These exchanges are workmanlike, impersonal, with no suggestion of hidden tensions. Both novelists focus on the larger artistic purposes served by autobiographical elements. Though Jane recognised and was dismayed by the use to which Amis put these elements, she made no objection; her fiction was comparably bold in its use of real-life materials. That she and Amis still discussed each other's work was a sign of the continuing life of the marriage ('we relied on each other in our work'), which, for all its stresses, neither wanted to fail. It was not the only sign. When Day-Lewis came to Lemmons, he had to switch from his Greenwich doctor to a local doctor. Jill remembers asking the new doctor: 'How can I ever thank these people for what they're doing for us?' He replied: 'it might be doing something for them'. What Jill thought it did, temporarily, was to bring them together: 'they were united in wanting to make Cecil's end a good end, and that was very moving'.

24

Dissolution

Amis worked hard at Lemmons. In addition to producing ten books in eight years, he was a frequent contributor to newspapers, magazines, and radio and television programmes. In 1973 he appeared in the media over fifty times, in 1972, 1974 and 1975 over forty times, in 1971 over thirty times.[1] Among these appearances were stints as a political columnist for the *Daily Express* and drinks columnist for the *Daily Telegraph*, *Penthouse* and *High Life* (the in-flight magazine of British Airways); he was also for brief periods a regular panellist on the radio programmes *Chapter and Verse* and *Whatever You Think*. In 1973 Pat Kavanagh negotiated deals with the *Telegraph* and the *Observer*, each of which agreed to pay Amis £1,000 for periodic reviewing, and with the *Sunday Times*, which offered him £3,000 in advance for 'work and advice in connection with features'.[2] These deals were a response to pressure from his accountant Anton Felton. On 13 June 1973, Felton wrote again to Michael Sissons of A.D. Peters, as he had done in September 1972, complaining that Amis and Jane were short of cash. 'I keep a fairly clear budgeting control over their affairs,' he announced; 'there is no feasible way of reducing their expenditure.' In addition to arranging journalism deals, Amis's agents at A.D. Peters suggested that he appear in print and television advertisements, 'providing the product was absolutely right'. On 4 July 1973, he was sent a list of possible products: Martini, Dubonnet, Cockburn's Port, Cinzano, Campari, Justerini Wines, Vladimir Vodka, Smirnoff, Kossak, Gilbey's Gin.[3] It was a non-alcoholic product, however, that made the first offer. On 25 July Amis was approached by Sanderson Fabrics to appear in a print advertisement. Sanderson would come to Lemmons, decorate one of its rooms, a photograph of Jane and Amis would be taken sitting in the room, and they would receive a generous fee. The photograph would appear under the tag-line: 'Very Kingsley Amis, Very Sanderson', a formula used previously in ads with Diana Rigg, Joan Bakewell and Hammond Innes. Other offers quickly followed, including from drinks companies and W.H. Smith's, the booksellers. On 25 June 1976, *Private Eye*, which Smith's refused to stock, mocked both it and Amis's advertisement. Beneath a photo of 'the famous writer' Kingsley Amis and a strap-line quotation ('W.H. Smug is the most wonderful bookshop in the entire world'), the copy reads: 'but then they offered me this wonderful cheque for £10,000, so then I said "you get your advertising people to write anything they like old boy and I'll put my name to it."' Later the copy alludes to Smith's cutting back on its book stock, something a writer might be expected to deplore: 'It's not all just pop records, porn mags and filing cabinets, you know. They still keep books at some W.H. Smug's.' If Amis saw these money-spinning activities as a threat to his authorial dignity he never said so.

The non-fiction books Amis produced at Lemmons were also undertaken for money, though hardly with an eye to the bestseller lists. The first of these books, *What Became of Jane Austen? And Other Questions* (1970), a collection of essays and reviews, was carefully constructed to display the breadth and diversity of his interests. Though all its pieces are reprints, many were revised. Amis made stylistic corrections, cut some pieces 'so as not to cover the same ground twice' and lengthened others in several ways: 'by restoring editorial cuts, incorporating material contributed elsewhere, adding remarks that happened not to have occurred to me the first time round, or (in the case of my note on John le Carré) taking subsequent developments into account'.[4] Amis had to fight for the book's mix of high culture and low. Maschler at Cape wanted him to include only literary criticism, omitting 'more journalistic and ephemeral pieces'.[5] In resisting this pressure, Amis made clear the sort of critic he admired. The book is a 'miscellany', he wrote to Maschler in a letter of 27 March 1970:

So it is a positive strength to have a piece about horror movies rubbing shoulders with one on Jane Austen and another on God. Some of these subjects are admittedly more ephemeral than others, though not in any straightforward way: Austen is more important and lasting than horror movies, but horror movies are more important, etc., than Richard Hoggart. I think that *you* are in danger of assuming that lit. crit. is by definition more important than, say, political polemics. Maybe so, in the end, but my contributions to each can be of equal merit, and I have as interesting things to say about Dracula as about D.H. Lawrence. And dammit, if people want to read Orwell on comic postcards, and they do, they might want to read me on detectives.

As an essayist Amis refused to be confined to literary or highbrow subjects; as an editor and anthologist he had high or scholarly standards. In 1971 Penguin invited him to edit a selection of Tennyson in its *Poet to Poet* series. Amis undertook the job conscientiously, consulting Christopher Ricks, editor of the 'splendid' Longmans edition,[6] over annotations, insisting that *In Memoriam* be published in its entirety, a decision praised by Betjeman ('*In Memoriam* is the best of the old boy and you were right to include the whole of it').[7] When proofs of the edition arrived in May 1972, Amis was appalled to discover the omission of line numbers and wrote in protest to his editor at Penguin: 'If you want to sell the volume in schools and colleges, which I hopefully suppose you do, it is quite essential to number every 10th if not every 5th line, so that people can find the place without delay; I have taught, and I know. Also, if you are going through the Notes checking your knowledge, imagine the fun of finding line 259 of Morte d'Arthur. So you must really put those numbers in: every 10 will do . . . The alternative, of course, is to insert on p.22: "The decision to leave the lines unnumbered was the publishers', not mine."'[8] Penguin put them in. Even when Amis had only to select and introduce works, as in his edition of Chesterton's *Selected Stories* (1972) or *Harold's Years: Impressions from the New Statesman and Spectator* (1977), he took the job seriously. 'There is, at the moment,' wrote V.S. Pritchett in a review of the Chesterton selection, 'a very decent attempt to dig out the best of Chesterton from the mountain of witty debris under which he has lain for thirty years or more. W.H. Auden, with his eye for aphorism, has done a selection of his prose and now Kingsley Amis has gone through his stories, to which he has written a frank and perceptive introduction.'[9] This introduction defends the selection, which concentrates on the period 1904–10 and includes a number of previously undervalued Father Brown stories, making the edition a revaluation or rereading, no mere reprinting. In the case of *Harold's Years*, begun just before the move from Lemmons, the 'mountain of debris' drawn from is even larger. 'No joke, boiling 60 million words down into 60,000,' Amis wrote to Conquest on 7 April 1977. The purpose of the selection is only in part to give an account of the 'grubby eleven-odd years' of the Wilson era.[10] It is also to illustrate the virtues of the periodicals themselves. 'What may help me and others, if not to make sense of that period, then at least to play over its characteristic themes,' Amis writes in the Introduction, 'is the continued existence throughout it of the *New Statesman* and the *Spectator*', which 'have no parallel that I know of in the English-speaking world' and draw on 'most of the leading writers of our day'.[11] By viewing the period through the pages of these journals, including pages devoted to social and personal comment, the arts and entertainment, the reader recaptures its 'nuances and overtones, as well as the major currents'. Though in 1977 Amis was a firm and combative right-winger, in this context at least he approved the articulate expression of contrary views. The respective positions of the two journals 'to left and right of centre – though each has always been remarkably hospitable to views it opposes editorially – make them usefully complementary, as do their respective styles, the *Statesman* being by tradition the brighter and sillier of the two'.[12]

Amis's tolerant attitude to the *New Statesman* may owe something to Martin's presence there. In 1974, the year he won the Somerset Maugham Award for *The Rachel Papers*, Martin left the *TLS* to become the *Statesman*'s assistant literary editor, under Claire Tomalin. In early 1977, when Tomalin resigned, he took over as literary editor, a post he held until 1979. In 1975 Martin's second novel, *Dead Babies*, a satire of drug-taking, communal living and other 1970s excesses, was published to admiring, if sometimes queasy, reviews; soon he would occupy a position in literary and journalistic circles similar to the one his father occupied twenty years earlier. Anthony Howard, a friend of Amis's, was editor of the *New Statesman* at the time and Amis would occasionally drop by his office at the end of the day, usually on a Monday or a Tuesday. James Fenton, who worked on the political half of the paper, as did Christopher Hitchens, remembers how, as with other visiting celebrities, when Amis appeared in the building, everyone, Martin included, would end up in Howard's office, drinking and chatting. What Fenton sensed about Amis was his enormous pleasure at being in company. 'There was a particular atmosphere about these occasions,' he recalls, 'at the end of a day's writing, released from home, out on the town, with lots of things stored up to say, almost as if he had an agenda in his mind.' Often what Amis wanted to discuss was what he'd been reading, usually rereading, or some foolishness in the papers or on television. He was full of fun but 'if you took issue with him then you were in trouble'. On one occasion Amis launched into a discussion of Public Lending Right and Fenton found himself saying, 'Oh we aren't going to talk about that are we, it's such a boring topic.' At the time, Amis barely knew Fenton, who was still in his twenties. 'That's what you would think because you're not a successful author,' he replied, a remark Fenton thought doubly unjust, since he made no pretence of being a successful author and yet he *was* one, having recently published a well-received first book of poems. 'He wouldn't scruple over your feelings,' Fenton recalls, certainly not when challenged impertinently. Amis soon came to like and admire Fenton, both for his poetry and for his political reportage. Though Fenton was a Lefty, his alarmed and alarming early reports on the Khmer Rouge were 'absolutely noted'. The line Amis and Conquest took was: 'There. You see? Now you're beginning to see.'

In addition to his visits to Anthony Howard's office, Amis began to join the Friday lunches attended by Martin and other *New Statesman* employees, including Fenton, Hitchens, and Martin's deputy, Julian Barnes. These lunches were an outgrowth of the Friday lunches initiated by Clive James and Terry Kilmartin, respectively television critic and literary editor of the *Observer*. The *Observer* lunches were held at a restaurant called Mother Bunch's Wine House, near the paper's offices in Blackfriars. James liked to refer to its lunchers as the 'Modish London Literary World' (a Leavisite slur, adopted in the same spirit as 'fascist' was adopted by the Bertorelli's crowd) or 'the Scum' ('because a woman I knew, a high-stepping socialite, called us scum'). Martin, who had written reviews for Kilmartin, was a frequent attender, as were the poet Peter Porter and the cartoonist Mark Boxer. By late 1976, the location of the lunches had shifted to the Bursa Kebab House, off Theobald's Road, nearer the *New Statesman* offices. At both locations, great quantities of lager and red wine were consumed, along with steak, chips, kebabs and all manner of fried dishes (according to Julian Barnes, the tiny kitchen at the Bursa was so close to the Gents that the chef 'could fry your steak and have a piss at the same time'). Most of those who attended the lunches were of Martin's generation and left of centre politically, but Amis was always treated, as Barnes puts it, 'as an honourable addition'. 'He was very much a favoured figure to have around,' Fenton recalls. 'Kingsley and Robert Conquest loved joining us,' James remembers: 'it was a nice example of how the London literary world in general has got quite a large tolerance for ideological differences.' When Amis first started attending the Friday lunches is unclear. They are not mentioned in his diaries or correspondence until an entry of 4 January 1974: 'To Blackfriars & Mother Bunch's w. J:[13] M [Martin], Tina [Brown], Clive, Dai [Russell Davies], Terry [Kilmartin], Val Jenkins [later Grove], Peter [Porter] & chum. Denunciatns of Steiner (general) & Ian Hamilton (me). Talked to Peter abt music: v. nice man.'

According to Fenton, Martin was the presiding spirit of the Friday lunches, certainly after the move to the Bursa: 'people wanted to talk like him, picked up his language, his verbal mannerisms, his attitudes and so on. All the people who came to the lunches were best described in some kind of relation to Martin.' For a while Hitchens and Martin had 'a sort of double act', full of in-jokes and hip coinages ('rug' for hair, 'rug-rethink' for haircut, 'sock' for flat, all of which found their way into Martin's fiction), but everybody chipped in. According to James, the talk mostly consisted of quick, gossipy repartee, all reaction and improvisation; set pieces or extended anecdotes were frowned upon. James credits Mark Boxer's 'hair-trigger yawn' with helping to establish the tone; James especially valued 'hearing people like Hitchens and Kingsley and Conquest trading quotations and imitations and so on with no reference to their political positions'. Among the people Amis records having met at the Friday lunches at the Bursa, in addition to those named so far, are John Fuller, the denounced Ian Hamilton (a great friend of Martin's), Lorna Sage, Claire Tomalin and Martin's girlfriend, Mary Furness (others invited included Craig Raine, Christopher Reid, Jonathan Keates and Christopher Ward, assistant editor of the *Sunday Mirror*). Women came infrequently; the atmosphere was masculine and competitive ('it was considered a thing to be invited to the table,' James remembers, 'and a worse thing if you weren't invited back'); even the most accomplished writers could find the lunches intimidating. Ian McEwan, part of the inner circle, records a humiliating moment from the early 1980s, after the venue had shifted a second time, to Bertorelli's. McEwan had recently been slighted in the *Spectator* and before setting off for the Friday lunch typed a quick, indignant reply, which he brought along:

At some point in the conversation, as the main course was being served, the *Spectator* article about me came up. I produced my stinging reply, and it was passed around the table, from Clive James to Mark Boxer, Martin Amis to Karl Miller, from Christopher Hitchens to Terry Kilmartin to Peter Porter to Julian Barnes. Gratifying that, having the writers and critics whose opinions I valued most read my letter. There was a general silence, then some throat clearing, and a move to change the subject as Jeremy Treglown, who had seen the carbon last, cupped his hand and murmured kindly in my ear, 'There's a dangler in the first sentence.' Dah! – as Amis and Hitchens liked to say. In the first *word*. That indignantly detached participle. 'Sir,' would have been the sort of thing. 'Having destroyed my meaning with dishonestly juxtaposed quotation, I find myself perplexed by your reviewer's sudden concession to probity when . . .' Osso bucco never tasted so vile.[14]

Father and son delighted in each other's company at the Friday lunches. On meeting they would kiss and embrace, which startled Martin's friends; it seemed very un-Amisy. Fenton thought Amis more like a favourite uncle to Martin than a father. Hitchens thought Martin 'had a relation to his father like nobody I've ever met', one of total frankness. When Martin revealed that he'd been to bed with a female friend of Amis and Jane's, Amis gave him a look and replied, 'Like father like son.' That Martin was, in Fenton's phrase, 'completely apolitical' in the mid-1970s, was important to good relations. Also important was the fact that Martin's celebrity was only just beginning to rival Amis's. As for Amis's non-political hobby-horses, especially those concerning language (what Fenton calls 'his endless thing about whether you say "uninterested" or "disinterested"'), Martin was wholly sympathetic. It was Martin who initiated the 'This English' column in the *New Statesman* to go with the 'This England' column. 'They clearly loved one another's company,' Julian Barnes recalls, 'perhaps the most in those circumstances; it wasn't like Martin having to look after his dad.' On the contrary, Amis seemed to Barnes to be 'at his most relaxed, most in his element' at the Friday lunches, buoyed by fast talk and the admiration of younger writers, most of whom could quote chunks of *Lucky Jim* by heart. 'Martin was very proud of him,' James remembers, 'and I think Kingsley was proud of Martin's intelligence. There's no question that he respected Martin's speed of mind. There was a real "that's my boy" look when Martin scored a point.'

In addition to the Friday Bursa lunches and the Tuesday Bertorelli's lunches, after May 1973 there were also Garrick Club lunches. Amis had been a member of the Travellers Club, but when he was elected to the Garrick he became a much more active clubman.[15] By the mid-1970s he was making the hour-long commute to London at least three times a week after the morning's stint writing. The presence of Jane's mother, Kit, during the day, and the absence of Sargy and Colin at work, may have been extra incentives to lunch in town. Kit Howard was an unhappy woman with a sharp tongue, not an easy presence in the household for anyone. Jane, who bore the brunt of her unhappiness, felt duty bound to take her in when it was clear that she could no longer manage on her own. 'I particularly admire Jane for doing this,' Colin says, 'because she was a bad mother where Jane was concerned. She was a good mother where I was concerned . . . She was always devoted to Robin and me and really quite acerbic in her references to Jane. She never gave her credit for what she achieved. I think she might have been jealous of Jane.' Kit went in for cutting remarks, as when, after reading Jane's second novel, *The Long View* (1956), she pronounced her 'quite a good writer. What a pity she hasn't got anything to write about.' She also took exception to any mention of sex in Jane's fiction. As her mother's health declined, Jane found it almost impossible to communicate with her. 'When I went into her room, she'd turn off the radio and smile – a rictus – displaying a pleasure that she, poor thing, evidently didn't feel in the least.'[16] Colin's relation to his mother at Lemmons was only marginally easier. In his youth, after his father abandoned the family, Colin was his mother's sole emotional support. As Jane puts it, 'our mother had leaned on him to an unbearable degree'.[17] As an adult, however, Colin felt unable to tell his mother about his life, principally about his homosexuality, something he was uncomfortable and inhibited about expressing to others as well. (That Amis encouraged Colin to be more open about his sexuality, to go to clubs and so forth, was 'very much a plus' in Martin and Phil's view.)[18] 'On the occasions I got near to telling her things about myself,' Colin remembers, 'she would say something that so completely put me off that I was back to square one and so we became estranged and I know it upset her very much.' Amis was not the only member of the household for whom passing Kit's downstairs room was a difficult business ('like shooting the rapids,' he would say).[19] Colin's inability to level with her about his life led to feelings of guilt and pity: 'I remember to my great shame sort of creeping past her room hoping she wouldn't hear me because she'd call me in. So it wasn't an easy time.'

Kit's intelligence, wit and sharpness of tongue are clear from her correspondence, as is her tendency to sudden violent outbursts, a trait Colin has inherited, along with a tendency to pessimism. When Jane and Amis were in Nashville, Kit wrote several times. 'This is just a blether,' begins a letter of 17 November 1967, 'so that you get something from home in what sounds to be a wilderness of uncongeniality.' She has a new gardener: 'a dynamic little man with an unbelievable quantity of "equipment" with which he could raze (and poison) my garden to a bare desert'. Martin reports that though his father never liked Kit, he was dutiful about her. 'With much sighing and making that trumpeting noise Phil is so good at imitating, he would prepare to go and have his half hour or twenty minutes with Kit . . . in a good sort of Protestant work ethic way.'[20] Amis's diary entries corroborate Martin's view, both of dutifulness and dislike: 17 January 1974: 'Found it was Kit's birthday so had drink w. her'; 18 May 1974: 'Made Cool Moon w white wine, pernod, crème de menthe. Gt. Success . . . Lunch adorned w Kit.' Entries like these make one feel sorry for Kit, but she was not easy to like. Here is how she closes the 1967 letter to Jane and Amis: 'I'm told by Robin that rats are increasing in this country faster than humans and that they are immune to all pesticides – so by the time the blacks take over they'll have quite a problem. Perhaps they'll eat each other – Much love, M.'

Kit's moments of verbal violence, like Amis's sighing and snide diary entries, Colin's creeping past the room and Jane's inability to please, find their way into *Ending Up* (1974), a feast of malice and ill humour, one of the best and most artfully constructed of Amis's novels. The book was long-incubated, a product of all five adult inhabitants of Lemmons – Amis, Jane, Colin, Sargy and Kit – living under the same roof since 1970. Though their average age was much younger than that of the dramatis personae of *Ending Up*, when

Jane one day wondered what would happen 'if we all went on living together and grew old together',[21] a seed was planted. Some three years later,[22] Amis began writing, on 29 January 1973,[23] though the egotism and unattractiveness of old people had long been a favourite theme, both in the correspondence and in the fiction, from 'The Legacy' onwards.[24] The carefully crafted nature of the novel is clear from the eight pages of elaborate notes Amis made for it, beginning with a list of forty-five 'ways of being annoying'. Next to each item in the list Amis put one of five letters, indicating categories: X for Shit, Z for Bore, B for Egotist, Y for Fool, A for Perverse shag. Here are the first ten items in the list:

X Being deaf – the which? – contemptuous when told
Z Talking quietly, then v. loudly
Y Repeating the wrong bit
A Telling people to do what they'll do anyway & what they know
A Wrong end of stick through eye of needle
X Anger at simple questions
B Whining – I'm old, on scrap-heap
Y Punning[,] dud spoonerisms
Y Polysyllabic facetiousness
B Lying about what's happened, whose side was on in argt

After the first thirty-three ways of being annoying, Amis counted up the number in each category, as if making sure they balanced, then added the remaining twelve. They all appear in the novel. At some point while working on the list he attached each category to a named character, to whom he gave a year of birth:

1901 A Adela Bastable
1899 B Marigold Pyke
1897 X Bernard Bastable
1899 Y Derrick Shortell
1902 Z George Hayek ['Zeyer' in the finished novel]

Then he wrote out potted biographies for each of the characters. Here are the first three:

A [Adela] (72) – X's sister. Never married (too ugly, but really too boring or annoying). Ex-matron. Runs house. Wrong end of stick. A bit deaf?

Likes X. Admirable industry. Cat. Unknown bad heart, or has stroke, but seems v. fit. Pension.

B [Marigold] (74) – A's oldest friend. Widow. Ex-'actress.' Has children. Hates X & Y. Laxative (for Y). Rt wing. Hates homos, lefties, nig nogs, EEC. Loves children. In pain. Writes letters. Goes out & sees friends. Money fr dead husband. Can't drive. Makes convenience of A, enjoys showing herself superior to her. Upper class. Amnesia just starting.

X [Bernard] (76) – Old queer but has child. Deaf. Malicious. Amnesiac. Hates everyone. Telephone wire for B. Heated wine for Y. Funny. 'Bad leg.' Dying & knows it. Waterpistols cats. India (for laxative). Can't drink. Small pension. Reads. Not enough to do.

By the end of the description of the fifth character, George or 'Z', plot points emerge: 'His arrival, by making X worse, precipitates the climax.' There are diagrams of both floors of Tuppenny-hapenny Cottage, the novel's sole setting, and a rudimentary timeline explaining when each inhabitant arrived:

X & Y joined by A cos of X's leg, then B, then Z.
1946   1963   1969   1972

There are also notes about furnishings and food and the petty mean-nesses and plots of the oldsters, in particular those of Bernard, the novel's central character, whose malice extends to his ex-lover and military servant, 'Shorty' (Derrick Shortell), with whom he has lived since 1946, his sister Adela, who wants only affection and never gets any, and the cat and the dog (as well as water-pistolling the cat, he tries to get the dog evicted). Bernard has terminal cancer and three months to live: 'his only relief, and that a mild, transient one, had turned out to lie in malicious schemes, acts and remarks'. When the sound of his sister's car is heard, 'he limp[s] quickly off towards the kitchen in confident hope of an opportunity to ridicule and distress her'.[25] Marigold, the ex-'actress', is terrified of losing her memory, so he fabricates examples of her forgetfulness. Shorty is alcoholic and sometimes incontinent, so he pours warm piss over him as he sleeps. George, a stroke victim, is stuck upstairs in bed and lonely for company, so he devises objections to bringing him downstairs. None of Bernard's victims is as bad as he is – Amis called him 'the most unpleasant of my characters since Roger Micheldene'[26] – but none is especially likeable, or at least unannoying. At the novel's close, Amis gleefully kills them off one by one, in the spirit of Bernard himself. Bernard is the first to go, falling from a ladder he has used to cut the telephone wires to the cottage and prevent Marigold from hearing from her family. Then Marigold tumbles down the stairs, having slipped on the dog's tennis ball, which she left where it lay earlier in the day, hoping Bernard or Shorty would slip on it, then forgot. Shorty, drunk and loose of bowels, swallows a fatal dose of laxative, mistaking it for a binding potion. Adela returns home in the car, 'her headlights just missing Bernard's corpse by the wall', discovers Shorty's body in the lavatory, 'lying in a considerable pool of brownish water with long streaks of dark blood in it', rushes into the hall to discover Marigold's body at the base of the stairs, and has a heart attack: '"Oh, my dearest, whatever have you done to yourself?" she said in a thicker voice than usual. She was aware of something like a huge weight against her chest, and then of nothing at all.' George, having heard Marigold's fall, drops out of bed in an attempt to help her, has a second stroke, one that renders him speechless as well as motionless, and presumably starves to death, since 'nobody except the postman, who noticed nothing out of the ordinary, came to Tuppenny-hapenny Cottage for several days'.[27] All five deaths occur in the space of two pages, in keeping with the economy of the narrative as a whole, which is divided into forty brief chapters, none longer than 1,500 words.

Ending Up was named Book of the Year by the *Yorkshire Post* and was shortlisted for the Booker McConnell Prize. In addition to its black humour and the machine-like efficiency of its plot, it was much praised for its linguistic invention and economical character drawing. George, the stroke victim, suffers from nominal aphasia, which he seeks to overcome through periphrasis. 'Did you watch, you know, the thing on the switching it on last night?' (he means the television).[28] When George is cured, his speech and thought are all nouns: 'Adela was bound to arrive eventually in her car. Yes, her car, with its wheels, tyres, axles, windows, gear-lever, dashboard . . .'[29] Then there is Marigold, who refers to children as 'kiddie-widdles' and drinks as 'drinkle-pinkles'. Marigold had a real-life prototype, a woman Amis and Jane had been told about who actually said, "Would you like a piece of fishy-wishy-dishy?" Amis was decided:

Marigold could talk like that for the whole of the book.[30] Marigold's cat reclines on 'a coverlet divided into six sections, each bearing an incompetently appliquéd slogan. In order these ran: *milkie-pilkies, sardeenies, mousie, bunnie-wunnie, collar-waller with bellsie-wellsies,* and *creamie.*'[31] Adela's ways of being annoying are less exclusively linguistic. In addition to telling people to do what they do anyway and what they know, and getting the wrong end of the stick, they include apologising for what doesn't matter, and not for what does, getting physically in the way, being unable to be on time or do what was promised, not distinguishing between whats ('I tell you what' – 'What?' – 'I TELL YOU WHAT') and answering the question 'When are we leaving?' by saying 'As soon as I've done x, y, z' ('*Yes*, but *when*?'). Because Adela is gentle, tolerant and selflessly devoted to the comfort of others, principally Bernard and Marigold, the cruelty with which she is depicted contributes to the book's bite. Hearing the arrival of Marigold's relations, she runs out to greet them 'like a rugby forward following up a kick'.[32] Trevor, Marigold's grandson, grips her by the upper arms 'to forestall any attempt at a hug'; Tracy, his wife, 'coached in advance, did the same when it came to her turn. She would have done more if Adela hadn't smelt so old.'[33]

Shortly after *Ending Up* was published in late May 1974, Amis went on holiday abroad, something he hadn't done in almost three years. Not going abroad had been a conscious decision on Amis's part, one he came to in August 1971, while on holiday with Jane in the beach resort of Albufeira in Portugal. Amis, of course, disliked the beach and only set foot on it in Albufeira after several days' resistance, doing so 'not as prelude or postlude to bathing, which I had given up years before that, nor please God to sunbathe, but merely to be of the party. I was trying with little good-humour to find a comfortable posture in which to read my paperback when Jane said helpfully that there was a bar of sorts further along where surely there would be chairs as well as beer. So it proved. Five minutes later I was sitting quite contentedly in the shade when it hit me. I realised in a blinding flash that I could have had all that in a superior version at home and stayed in pocket, not to mention not had to stroll a couple of thousand miles.'[34] This account comes from a *Sunday Times* article entitled 'Amis Abroad', written in September 1980 in France, on what turned out to be Amis's last trip outside

Britain. Earlier in the same article, Amis mentions nervousness or anxiety as another reason for his reluctance to travel, though he discusses it only in general terms, in the relaxed manner he used to discuss alcoholism in the Introduction to *On Drink*: 'I brooded, then and later, on travel-angst, a topic worth some study. I get it a lot, but I suspect that everybody gets it at least a bit, gets, that is, more discomfort than the situation warrants . . . One factor might be that to make a complete voluntary departure from home and group is a very recent piece of behaviour and when it goes wrong the poor old naked ape is likely to feel naked indeed.'[35]

Amis's refusal to go on holiday for the next three years played a part in the continuing dissolution of relations with Jane, as well as reflecting that dissolution. Jane loved Lemmons but found it exhausting to run, especially with the added burden of Kit's declining health. Jane needed holidays; the sun and the sea refreshed and energised her and helped her to relax. If Amis wouldn't go abroad, she'd go by herself, or with friends. In the summer of 1972, after Day-Lewis's death, she and Jill took up the Spenders' invitation to spend two weeks recuperating in Provence. The next summer Jane also went away for two weeks, first to France, to stay with Sybil and Colin Welch, then to Tuscany, to stay with Woodrow and Verushka Wyatt. During her absence she arranged for people to stay with Amis at Lemmons, in addition, that is, to Kit, Sargy and Colin. Amis kept no diary that summer but the letters he and Jane exchanged during her absence are warm and hopeful. 'I have been missing you very much,' Jane writes in a postcard on 7 August, *en route* from France to Italy. 'I do hope there will be a letter from you at the Wyatts . . . I really do miss you, so when I come back you'll have to talk to me a lot. Give Rosie [Jane's dog] a kiss on her forehead from me. I wish we were having a drink together. I do feel *much* better and less depressed. *LOVE* from W.' Amis replied on 13 August, both to this postcard and to an earlier letter, now lost: 'Got your dear letter, little one, also ridiculous card.[36] V. heartening letter. We'll both have to work at things. I'll certainly try . . . Hope you get this. I'll see you in a week. All well here. Still missing you and wondering how you are. Love from old Bun.'

Though Jane remembers Amis as resentful when she got back,[37] efforts seem to have been made on both sides to 'work at things'. On 3 October 1973, Conquest wrote to Larkin to say that the Amises were 'just back from, evidently, a weekend *together* at Tony Powell's. But there you get separate rooms. All the same, perhaps a sign of one more shot at the problem.'[38] Three weeks later, on 22 October, Conquest reports seeing the Amises together again, at a party celebrating the twentieth birthday of *Encounter*: 'It's rumoured that they're trying to make a go at it.'[39] The 'it' in question is their marriage, of course, but also Amis's 'problem' or loss of libido. When in mid-January 1974 Jane went to Washington to interview Rose Kennedy for the *Radio Times*, Phil and Martin came to stay for the first weekend, Amis spent a few days in town with the Conquests, then the newly married Jim Durham, his Australian psychiatrist friend, and Jim's wife, Nita, a radiologist, came for the following weekend. Jane was due back the next day, on Monday, 21 January. In his diary Amis records: 'Tiny bkfst & lunch (salami). Walked to Barnet – bank, daffs for J's return . . . off to airport 8pm & met J at once.' In the entries that follow, good moments and bad interweave. 'V. depressed,' reads the entry for 28 January, 'Pat G[ale] invited us for w/e, J not keen.' The next day, however, they are of one mind, over writing, characteristically: 'Talked w J abt PLR [Public Lending Right] . . . Talked of descrip in writg: agreed it can never be pure.' Two months later, after lunch in town and drinks at several locations, Amis concludes the entry for 26 March curtly: 'Din at B'ellis' w J for birthday. Row.' Writing, though, always brought them together. In an entry of 4 May, after weeks of worried entries about 'The Crime of the Century', a serial Amis was writing for the *Sunday Times*,[40] he records a breakthrough: 'Elated at cracking *CC* . . . Finished episode V of *CC* and decided to leave it there. J approved.' Two days later, for reasons the diary does not specify, Jane goes to Norwich for the night, which upsets Amis, especially as Kit has been temporarily removed to the housekeeper's cottage: 'Nobody here . . . Kit gone to cottage because Mrs. U can't cross stained floor, still drying. M *phoned* w news he has WSM award. J phoned in evg fr Norwich. Lonely dinner. Watched TV w Rosie. Face the Music. V. uneasy.'

When made uneasy or frightened Amis lashed out, accusing Jane of selfishness and inconsiderateness. Here and elsewhere in the 1974 diary he presents himself as victim. Amidst the notes for *Ending Up* is a half-page that has nothing to do with the novel. It begins with what sounds like the transcription of a row with Jane:

I haven't got my key. Where's your key?
I've never had a key.

No, you've never done anything, taken any responsibility.
You won't get away with blaming this on me.
Try doing something about us, about Portugal.
But you – you (whatever it was) bitch (probably 'egotistical')
You're 'a spoilt, drunken child.' Verbatim.

Here the Jane voice is being unreasonable and defensive about the keys, whatever the truth of her accusations; their truth is not the point, not why the snatch of dialogue is being recalled. Beneath the dialogue Amis appends a list of accusations against Jane, like the list of oldsters' 'ways of being annoying':

If I were to have a heart attack, it would be my fault.
I mean, actually, that that would be *her* version.
Pissing on me for being selfish about forcing the Fussells to come in with
    me on my train. 'You only think about yourself.'
Not reminding me about Liz and Betj dinner.
Not apologising after not picking me up in Meadway because the car
    wouldn't start, no keys or whatever.
Mart and Phil – I love you *both*.

These, presumably, are the sorts of grievances and resentments Amis brought to his rows with Jane. Again, the fairness of Jane's accusation of selfishness is not addressed; in a mood such as the one prompting this list, the accusation is seen as part of a pattern of inconsiderateness, egotism and spite. The last line is moving. Who has accused Amis of loving only one of his sons? Jane? Phil? It is impossible to say. That he writes of loving 'you' not 'them' signals genuine feeling, for the boys but also for himself, as misunderstood and in need of allies.

It was Jim Durham who caused Amis to reconsider his refusal to travel abroad. Although Durham had been a Freudian when very young, by the time he met Amis in the 1960s he thought of psychoanalysis as 'a great waste of time'. After training in Adelaide and Melbourne he moved to Britain in 1964, aged thirty-seven, and worked for a dozen years as a consulting psychiatrist in London hospitals and clinics, including the Priory Clinic in Roehampton, in south-west London. Though Amis on occasion discussed his anxieties with Durham, 'he didn't talk about these things any more than was necessary to indicate his wishes, when it came to a question of flying or going abroad on a holiday, so to speak. He didn't invite psychological advice or anything like that.' Durham, however, remembers explaining to Amis 'a few times' the mechanism of panic disorder, the aetiology of which he sees as partly chemical, and about which he speaks with a level, reassuring practicality. In his *Memoirs* Amis calls Durham 'the only sane and sensible psychiatrist I have ever met'.[41] That Durham was no Lefty, liked a drink, and had an easy, unflappable manner ('I am by nature not very combative') also played a part in their friendship. As Amis's diaries make clear, he sometimes turned to Durham for medical as well as psychological advice. On 19 January 1974 he records being 'up in time for Jim & Nita to take blood samples'; on 24 March he experiences 'nasty pains in L arm like fibrositis. Jim said virus.' In the winter and spring of 1974, the Durhams were frequent visitors to Lemmons and at some point a plan was devised for both couples to visit Rome together, shortly after the publication of *Ending Up*. Russell Fraser and his family were in Rome for the year and Phil Fraser had written to the Amises in November 1973 saying that they should visit; in April she wrote again, enclosing a brochure for a nearby hotel.

Jane had mixed feelings about the trip to Rome. On the one hand, she was delighted that Amis was again willing to travel abroad; on the other hand, it irked her that he only considered doing so when Jim Durham was involved. It also irked Jane that he was suddenly happy to tour museums, galleries and churches. 'Kingsley had always said he had no interest in buildings or pictures,' writes Jane in her memoirs; 'with Jim his attitude to these pleasures changed and he became enthusiastic. Jim was only too pleased to take him round to everything he was to see.'[42] Buildings and pictures had always been pleasures to Jane, but she disliked being told about or discussing them before forming her own impressions. 'So, in galleries I left them to it, and went round on my own. I'm sure this was taken as me being contrary and sulking, but the situation was such – Kingsley spent all his time talking to Jim, and Nita was wrapped up in the new-found happiness of marriage – that to be on my own was a relief.' Amis, of course, still depended on Jane; though he would not have gone to Rome with her alone, he would not have gone with the Durhams alone either: 'he needed, however grumpily, to take me for granted'.[43] The Durhams were aware of Jane's discontent, but they had been aware of it from the start. 'By the time I

knew them it was quite clear that their interests were divergent,'
Jim Durham recalls. 'Jane I like . . . but she did get on Kingsley's
nerves in a thousand little ways . . . He didn't pick quarrels with her
but he didn't go to any elaborate pretence of warmth and affection.
He showed her the conventional signs of his affection, but he wouldn't
mask his irritation.'

As Amis's diary of the Rome trip shows, he made a serious effort
to engage with the visual culture of the Renaissance, principally its
sculpture and painting. He had less to say about architecture, which
in the *Memoirs*, as we have seen, he declares 'ought to be comprehensively done away with'.[44] The diary also documents Amis's struggles to keep travel angst at bay and the shifting nature of his
relations with Jane. The party travelled to Rome by rail and ferry,
stopping in Milan to change trains. The first building Amis
comments on in the diary is the Cathedral in Milan, which Jane
thought 'ungodly' and he calls 'underfurnished, too tall', with 'dark,
bad, stained glass'. In subsequent entries, Jane's point about ungod-
liness is applied by Amis to other buildings and works of art. When
the two couples arrived in Rome they discovered that their hotel
had 'tried to give us rooms without baths'; they refused to accept
them. In the ensuing argument, which they won, Jane figured prominently, or as Amis puts it in his diary, was 'v. gd.'[45] That night a fast
taxi took them to an open-air restaurant in Trastevere which played
'yelling' music but had very good food. Amis particularly liked this
restaurant, Durham remembers, because as soon as you sat down
two half-litres or litres of opened wine were placed on your table:
'he thought that was bloody marvellous'. When one or the other
of the wine bottles ran low, it would be replaced immediately, which
he also liked: 'He didn't like to see the prospect of the bottle on
the table emptying and there being an interval of time when there'd
be nothing on the table. He liked to see where the next drink was
coming from.' The two couples went back to the restaurant
frequently.

Over the next three weeks Amis was a dutiful, mostly uncom-
plaining tourist. 'He must have said to himself I better be on my
best behaviour,' Durham conjectures, 'because these other two want
to look at things and so I should show some interest in them.'
Among the sights Amis comments on are the Victor Emmanuel
Monument, praised for its 'wonderfully unashamed vulgarity'; the
Forum, 'a bit of a junk yard'; and the Etruscan Museum, which did

not impress: 'endless black on red at start then a gd deal of red on black. I hate pottery anyway.' Amis's opinion of the Etruscans was not high: 'Keen on death unendearing lot, well worth wiping out. Only gave arch.' He thought no better of the Egyptians, examples of whose art he encountered in the Vatican Museum: 'glad I didn't live then Same death-thing as Etruscan.' The rooms devoted to medieval painting surprised him. The pictures were 'better than expected . . . not thinking how gd y are all the time like Renaiss.' After the morning in the Vatican Museum, then lunch, it was off to St Peter's. Amis's comment on St Peter's echoes Jane's on the Cathedral in Milan: 'pro-Pope>pro-God', a theme he would develop in *The Alteration* (1976), his next novel. Though he calls the statues in St Peter's 'theatrically violent, gesturing', mostly his remarks about sculpture and painting concern content or character rather than form or style. Hence comments such as 'Apostles all looking v fed up', 'berkish "Defeated Boxer"', 'Boring yg man', 'Filippo Lippi jolly gd drapery but terrifying chubby child' (Andrea del Sarto wins the award for 'heftiest bambino'), 'Susanna I wdn't have bothered to spy on her' and 'Commodus real shit' (elsewhere: '*yg* Commodus incipient *older* C just contemptible/shit rampage any Sat a.m. in London'). On 9 June the party visited the Appian Way and the Garden of the Villa Chigi: 'No more to do in it than in any other garden,' he records in the diary, 'short of gardening. I only like v formal, artificl gdns w fountains parterres etc v boring ruins of nothg in partic . . . Tk Xt [Christ] nobody thought to bring filthy picnic.' He approved, though, of the new apartment blocks along the way: 'better than England: bright plain colours, good serious balconies, no knobs on facades, not aggressively different w architect showing off'.

When the possibility arose of a three-day side trip to Sardinia with the Frasers, one that involved a flight, Jane decided that she wanted to go. On 10 June Amis records: 'J announced she was going to Sardinia early tmrw and wd have to leave the hotel tonight to doss w the Frasers and be off to catch plane at 9am. Shd she return Fri or Sat? I said Sat. She said Fri because she wanted to be back then. A little later, she wd be back Fri because she thought she *ought* to be back for my sake. I behaved like a shit by pretending not to be dashed by her absence.' The Durhams would be with Amis while Jane was away, but they were returning to London on Sunday (the Amises were staying another week); if there was any delay or problem with the flight back from Sardinia, Amis would be on his own. 'Her last words to me: I'll try to be back on Fri . . . Also left me with sleeping reservations to check at station.' The entry for 10 June ends with a rare ironic remark about Durham: 'Jim helped greatly by saying he had no sedatives at all, tho "I might care to try N's anti-histamines wch *perh* had some soporific effect."' As it turned out, Jane made it back on Friday. The night before the Durhams left, on 15 June, the two couples had a farewell dinner in Trastevere: 'Big argt abt the foundations of morality. J & I agst Wog, who was rather dashed.' After the Durhams left, the Amises saw the Frasers daily and visited more churches and museums. On their last day in Rome, the Frasers came to their hotel and they all walked to the Museo Borghese. Amis drank his last Negroni and his last dodgy grappa and after dinner the Frasers accompanied them to the station. There Amis insisted that the Frasers not leave until the train pulled out of the station: 'He was seated, he peered from the window, gesticulating frantically like a stage Italian. Stay put, his hands were telling us, and we had to.'[46] On 28 June Conquest wrote to Larkin announcing that 'Old KA is just back; he loved Rome, oddly enough. It'll be in his next book, apparently.'[47]

The Alteration, the last of the novels Amis wrote at Lemmons, is the most ingenious of his reworkings of genre material. He began the first draft on 11 April 1975 and finished it on 18 November. Two months into the writing, Amis and Jane and the Durhams made a second trip to Rome, this time by car. 'Off to Wopland at the end of the week – not for long,' wrote Amis to Larkin on 23 June: 'Just the feeling you want to do what you won't be able to do again, ever, in a year or two' (he was fifty-three at the time of this letter). As on the holiday with the Keeleys in Mexico, there were tensions over driving.[48] The point of driving to Rome, so Durham thought, was to see the Alps, crossing into Italy via the Grossglockner, a scenic Alpine pass. Once they were in the Alps, according to Durham, Jane declared that mountains depressed her. Lunch was another source of tension, this time involving Amis rather than Jane. The Durhams were perfectly prepared to stop for lunch, but not for what Amis, in Durham's words, called 'a proper lunch, which meant lunch with drink'. Once the party reached Rome, however, 'we never had a cross word' and Amis included a brief, vivid description of the

Alps in Chapter 4 of *The Alteration*, when the hero makes a similar journey to Rome.

This hero, Hubert Anvil, is ten years old and has been summoned to Rome by Pope John XXIV, a bluff Yorkshireman modelled in speech and manner on John Braine. The time is the present, 1976, and Stephen III, King of England and her Empire, has just died and been succeeded by King William V. These and other puzzling details derive from the novel's counterfactual premise: that the Reformation never happened. *The Alteration* is an alternate world novel, a species of SF, or, in its own terminology, TR, for 'Time Romance', the favourite reading matter of Hubert and his friends. In the novel's alternate past, Martin Luther moderated his views and reconciled with Rome, becoming Pope Germanius I in 1535; Henry VII's son, Arthur, not only married Catherine of Aragon, as in real life, but produced an heir, Stephen II; Arthur's younger brother, 'Henry the Abominable', never, therefore, became Henry VIII and Sir Thomas More was never martyred (he became Pope Hadrian VII instead). The uninterrupted reign of the Catholic Church in Europe meant no democracy, no nationalism, no socialism, no national socialism. In the novel's present, Muscovy and Almaigne are ruled by emperors subject to the Pope. The key functionaries in the Holy Office are Monsignori Henricus and Lavrentius, that is, Heinrich Himmler and Lavrenti Beria; among their underlings are Foot, Redgrave and the Lord Stansgate; the Pope is attended by Cardinal Berlinguer, named after Enrico Berlinguer, the real-world leader of the 1970s Italian Communist Party; Church doctrine is the province of the Jesuit theologian Monsignor Jean-Paul Sartre, author of *De existentiae natura*, and A.J. Ayer, Professor of Dogmatic Theology at New College. The totalitarian society these figures buttress, like the one their real-world models would lead us towards, Amis is suggesting, is corrupt, cowed and credulous.

But it is not without culture. In imagining alternate world art works Amis drew heavily on the Rome trips. His notes for the novel begin with a list of terms from ecclesiastical architecture, the sort one finds in the fronts of guidebooks. These terms Amis uses in describing the Cathedral Basilica of St George at Coverley (Cowley, home of British Leyland), with its Turner ceiling in commemoration of the 'Holy Victory' in the 'War of the English Succession',[49] frescoes of St Augustine by Blake, William Morris spandrels, spires by Brunel, western windows by Gainsborough, and 'Ecce Homo' mosaic by David Hockney (a joke Amis should have resisted). It is here that Hubert, who has a divine voice, sings Mozart's Second Requiem (K878), 'the crown of his middle age'. If Amis's alternate world is good to Mozart, giving him a long life, it is bad to Shakespeare, who is excommunicated for heresy, has his plays destroyed, and dies in exile in the Republic of New England, a distant and oddly un-threatening haven from Catholic Europe. As there has been no Enlightenment or French Revolution, there has been no Romantic movement (Shelley, an 'excommunicate English runaway and minor versifier', is said to have committed suicide in 1853, after setting fire to Castel Gandolfo, a Papal property);[50] even more gratifyingly, there has been no modernist movement. The consciously off or antique language of the novel, a matter of subtle shifts in meaning ('contingency' for 'emergency', 'detension' for 'détente', 'concurrence' for 'coincidence'), reinforces the peculiarity and backwardness of the society depicted, a consequence of the Church's disapproval of science. This is a modern England in which most people travel by horse and wear hessian or moleskin.

The exceptions to the backwardness of Amis's alternate world England are jokey and allusive. There is diesel transport for eccle-siastical officials and a train, the Eternal City Rapid, with a top speed of 195 m.p.h. The anomaly of a transport system combining horse and high-speed rail is a genre convention, like the improba-bilities in Chesterton, whose alternate world novel, *The Napoleon of Notting Hill* (1904), Amis called 'an important source book' for *The Alteration*.[51] The Eternal City Rapid runs along 'continuously-welded rails on their cushioned sleepers' and is said to be 'the work of the great Harrison',[52] an allusion to Harry Harrison, Amis's friend and the author of an alternate world novel entitled *A Transatlantic Tunnel, Hurrah!* (1972). It belongs with the coal-fired, fourteen-engined, steam-turbine-driven flying battleship in Harrison's novel, or the motorised 'minibiles' of Ward Moore's *Bring the Jubilee* (1953), an alternate world novel in which the South won the American Civil War (minibiles are guided not by steering wheels or joysticks but by reins, like horses). A more recent equivalent of such vehicles is the DeLorean time machine in *Back to the Future*, an alternate world film. When *The Alteration* won the John W. Campbell Memorial Award for the best science fiction novel of 1976, T.A. Shippey, now Professor Tom Shippey, of Washington University in St Louis, the awards secretary, claimed that it contained references to almost every major work of the 'alternate world' sub-genre.[53] Prominent among its models, he and others claimed, is Philip K. Dick's *The Man in the High Castle* (1962), in which the Axis powers win the Second World War and occupy the United States. Hubert and his friends have heard of Philip K. Dick; one of their number has even read *The Man in the High Castle*, which is 'alternate' to him in ways the real-life author never intended. The real-life Philip K. Dick was a fan of *The Alteration*. On 10 September 1979 he wrote to Amis calling it 'one of the best – possibly *the* best – alternate world novels in existence'.

Almost as artful as Amis's flattering allusions to SF predecessors is the gradual and indirect manner in which the novel's counter-factual premise is revealed, a manner which worried its American publisher at Viking (Sissons had encouraged Amis to leave Harcourt Brace for better money at Viking). This publisher was Amis's Princeton friend Alan Williams, who thought readers would find the book's opening chapters bewildering. 'I have been giving your plea for altering The Alteration some study,' wrote Amis in response. 'Let me try to put the case for leaving it unaltered.'

The reader soon knows he is in England, but almost as soon realises that it's not the England he is acquainted with, nor is the world the same. Even if he is an American (no sneer intended) he will have been able to pick up plenty of clues by the foot of MS p.1: King William V? Where is Queen Elizabeth? Surely Portugal has no king? Naples? Crown Prince of Muscovy? Dauphin? Where's New Spain? Candia? What's all this Catholic shit . . . Towards the end of section 1 he will have found well enough where he is, except for the date, which is supplied in the last sentence.

Consider the alternative. To *tell* the reader where he is to start with turns every clue into a tedious piece of decoration, slowing things up. If you are asked to construct a picture by joining up a number of points, what leads you on is not knowing what the picture will be (and, with luck, wanting to). If you know already what the picture is, why bother to join up the points? Or in thriller terms: if the reader knows that the corpse is that of the Russian Ambassador, he will be impatient at the efforts of the other characters to discover what he knows already, despise them for their slowness and unawareness of what is (to him) obvious. One *direct* and *complete* tip-off instead of hundreds of indirect and partial tip-offs would impose a disastrously simplistic strategy on the book.[54]

Williams seems to have accepted Amis's case for leaving the novel unaltered. He also seems to have accepted his appearance in it as a character. Pastor Alan Williams, chaplain to the Archpresbyter of Arnoldstown, is one of several New Englanders who seek to rescue Hubert. It is Pastor Williams who explains to Hubert why so many of the native inhabitants of New England are servants. The mind of the Indian 'is less capable to be developed than yours or mine, because his brain is smaller, as our scientists have proved. To mingle with him truly is impossible, and no good can come of trying to. That's why, under God's guidance, we in New England have a design we call separateness.'[55]

The 'serious' component of *The Alteration*, its thematic engine, grew out of an incident Amis recounted to Clive James in a 1974 interview.[56] The previous year Amis heard on the radio a scratchy 1909 recording of Alessandro Moreschi, the last known castrato, singing the Bach-Gounod 'Ave Maria'. Moreschi was forty-four at the time of the recording but his voice was that of a child. Amis thought his singing 'very fine' but found the hint of a whine in his voice so 'intolerable' that it left him in a state of 'jittery depression' for days. As he brooded over Moreschi's voice, Amis began to fixate on the moment when 'someone – he or his father – must have *consented* to this operation. And that decision brings out everything of importance in human life. Your arguments for and against your duties to God, to sing his music. Your duty to art. Sex. Love. Marriage. Children. Fame. Money. Security.' Here was an excellent topic for a novel, though it would probably have to be an historical novel, involving much tedious research. Eventually a less laborious solution presented itself, one he was working out at the time of the James interview: 'I've always wanted to write an SF book, but as with the ghost story, you couldn't do it on purpose. You have to have a reason. And here was the reason . . . [B]y using Alternate World, I could have the castrato living here and now. All you have to do is go back and change history.'

The Green Man combines a ghost story with the depiction of a hero with a serious drinking problem; *The Alteration* combines science fiction with the depiction of a hero in danger of losing his sexual capacity. Shortly before *The Alteration* was published in October 1976, Amis agreed to consult the first of several sex therapists in an attempt to revive his libido and his marriage ('various difficulties had arisen between us which I will not go into,' is how he describes relations with Jane at this period in the *Memoirs*).[57] The preoccupations of Amis's personal life find disguised expression in the novel. A key question the novel examines, as young Hubert seeks to understand what exactly his 'alteration' will deny him, is the nature and value of sex. Related questions are the comparative values of art and sex and the connections between sexual and artistic potency. Behind these questions lie fears that may have contributed to the 'jittery depression' occasioned by the Moreschi recording. They may also animate the depiction of the adult castrati Viaventosa and Mirabilis, the Papal envoys who confirm Hubert's potential as a singer of genius. Amis describes the envoys as 'plump, dandified and unhealthy-looking'; Viaventosa, the more epicene of the two, has 'moist eyes and an absurd moustache that might almost have been painted or pencilled'.[58] The fate to which he and Mirabilis consign Hubert troubles Viaventosa: 'His youth is to vanish, with his manhood, and his humanity. He'll be what we are, a gelding, an ox, a wether, a capon.'[59] In *The Green Man*, *Girl, 20* and *The Riverside Villas Murder*, adult sexuality is seen as dangerous and corrupting; in *The Alteration* so is its absence. As Richard Bradford puts it, 'the ideology that permeates every part of the novel's social, political and cultural landscape is sanctioned and enforced by men who have chosen to live without sex'.[60]

Amis's willingness to consult sex therapists in the mid-1970s grew in part out of a prior willingness to consult therapists over other matters, principally travel angst, which had begun to trouble him on journeys to London as well as abroad. As he explains in the *Memoirs*, one afternoon, probably shortly after he returned from the second trip to Rome, 'I found myself stuck in an otherwise seemingly empty tube train for ten minutes or so outside Barnet station, above ground but effectively in solitary confinement. Thereafter I had to manage my travelling back and forth so that there were always people about for certain, which in practice meant going for rush-hours.' The alternatives to this strategy were to get Jane or someone else to accompany him (hence Jane's jibe about 'forcing the Fussells to come in with me') or to drive him or paying a ten-mile taxi fare or consulting a shrink, all of which he tried. One shrink who practised in Windsor took Amis out on overground train journeys, asked him innumerable questions and then told him 'with admirable promptitude and honesty' that there was nothing he could do for him. A second was 'a young and amiable South African',[61] Dr Julian Hafner, who had written a book, or most of a book, on agoraphobia, which he claimed was closer to what Amis was suffering from than claustrophobia. Amis read the book in manuscript and saw the therapist for a number of sessions; not many, is the impression given in the *Memoirs*. The treatment Dr Hafner advocated had two stages: the first consisted of taking the patient with him into just the place – bus, supermarket – he or she found frightening; the second consisted of making the patient go alone. When Hafner described as 'remarkable' the number of patients who 'relapsed, often totally' at stage two, Amis lost patience: 'Surely what would have been remarkable would have been their *not* relapsing. There you were with your syringe of intravenous Valium, enough to calm a runaway horse, and you were *there*, a doctor, ready to help, to explain they weren't mad, just upset, and then next time there you weren't.' When a third psychiatrist, Dr Gerald Wooster, offered a crude Freudian explanation for Amis's fear of being stuck in the underground, his response was 'to get up and walk out of Dr. Wooster's consulting-room, ignoring his protestations that we were on the verge of uncovering the mystery, and never return'. Dr. Wooster's explanation was that 'being afraid of nothing arriving in his Underground[62] was the result of his mother's fear of something arriving in her Underground', a theory Amis put in the mouth of one of the therapists in *Jake's Thing* (1978), his next novel.

Amis's fear of tube travel and love of company eventually led him to agitate for a move closer to town. One morning at the end of the summer of 1975, as Jane recalls it, he turned to her and said: 'I don't want to live here any more. It's too bloody cut off. I want to go back to London.' Jane's reaction was dismayed but accepting: 'I didn't in the least want to leave the house or, even more, the garden, but I thought it wasn't fair for two people to live where one of them didn't want to. I thought also that if we *did* move, Kingsley would be happier and therefore so should I.' When asked where he wanted to live, Amis's answer was 'uncharacteristically clear. He wanted to be within five minutes' walk of Hampstead tube station – otherwise he didn't care what the place was like'[63] (presumably he thought he would overcome his fear of the underground, though he never did). With the help of Colin, Jane eventually found exactly what Amis ordered: a house no more than five minutes from Hampsted tube station, in Flask Walk, reached via a pretty paved passage leading on to the High Street. Gardnor House was named after the man who built it in the eighteenth century and also managed the springs in nearby Well Walk; it is the largest and grandest house in Flask Walk, although nowhere near as large and grand as Lemmons. What Jane liked about it was that the top floor could be made into a comfortable flat for the housekeeper, Mrs Uniacke, and that it contained, among others, three especially large, attractive rooms: a ground-floor dining room looking out through a magnificent bow window on to a walled back garden, a drawing room right above it, and a handsome master bedroom above that. Colin had a bedroom on the first floor, also overlooking the garden, and there was a study for Jane next to the master bedroom. Amis's study was on the ground floor. The house had a front garden as well as a back one, but both were heavily overlooked. As Colin puts it, 'they didn't get any sun in the right places and Jane couldn't really garden there properly, so she was fairly miserable'.

The Lemmons ménage or commune had largely disbanded by the time of the move to Gardnor House in July 1976. Kit had died in March 1975, shortly after her eightieth birthday, on a weekend when both Mrs Uniacke and Tessa Craig were away and the house was full of guests. When Kit complained of feeling unwell, her doctor was summoned, pooh-poohed her symptoms, gave her Valium, and she died that night of a heart attack. Amis was good to Jane and Colin over Kit's death, as over arrangements for the funeral. 'He had a great sense of conventional propriety.' A little less than a year after Kit's death, Sargy moved out of Lemmons. On 31 January 1976 he married his girlfriend and ex-pupil, the painter Frances Carey. Before a pre-wedding lunch for the groom attended by Amis, Jane, Martin, Colin, Mrs Uniacke, the painter Terry Raybould, the journalist Christopher Ward, and his wife, Fanny, a model, Sargy signed the Lemmons Visitors' Book, dating it '3 August 1968 to 31 Jan 1976.' Franny had been a great household favourite at Lemmons, as charming as Sargy and very pretty. She remembers her first encounter with Amis as terrifying, with everyone grouped around him at the far end of the kitchen table and Jane sitting at the near end, anxious that there wasn't enough food. Franny was young and only vaguely knew who Amis was ('I half thought he'd written *The Water Babies*'). 'I kept jolly quiet,' she says. 'I just jolly well knew I had to keep quiet.' On later visits she relaxed, but she always found Amis slightly alarming, 'on the verge of being irascible'. Also, he had 'this laser pick-up for anything pretentious', though she and Sargy never saw him be hurtful to anyone except Jane. 'He wasn't unkind,' Sargy remembers, but 'I don't think there'd be many people who'd stop him from saying something he wanted to say.' Like many an art student, Franny went in for a stylish disorder in dress and appearance. 'Why have you got a crooked parting?' Amis once asked her, not in front of others. 'It's very crappy and so affected.' Though Franny was taken aback, she thought: 'He's right'.

At Lemmons, Martin, Phil, Sally and their friends came to stay at weekends and holidays; with the move to Hampstead, their visits were confined to meals or drinks. Martin was living in a two-room flat in Kensington Gardens Square in Bayswater, 'a cold-water walk-up sock', according to Hitchens, working on the back pages of the *New Statesman* and writing his third novel, *Success* (1978). After its publication, the critic Neil Powell described him as 'the most praised and the most publicised new writer of full-length fiction in England in the past decade'.[64] He was also making a lot of money. 'Did I tell you Martin is spending a year abroad as a TAX EXILE?' Amis wrote to Larkin on 9 July 1979: 'Last year he earned £38,000. Little shit. 29, he is. Little shit.' As for Larkin's godson, Philip, by the time of the move to Gardnor House he had steady work as a graphic artist (he designed the label for Rebel Yell bourbon, among other products) and a serious girlfriend, Jane Galsworthy, of whom Amis initially approved. 'She impressed more than ever as likely to be good for him, he for her, too, no doubt,' Amis wrote to Jane on 15 September 1976 (Jane was in France, recuperating from the move to Gardnor House). On 11 October Amis wrote to Larkin informing him of Phil's marriage: 'I told him not to expect anything like a pipe of port, something more like your undertaking to guarantee the education of his no Christ leggo my.' Phil continued to paint and in March 1978 had an exhibition in a gallery near Gardnor House. On 18 March Amis wrote to Conquest to say that Phil had sold nine paintings, 'including one of, oddly, Franco, that went for £400, which seems quite a lot to me'. Phil's marriage, however, was soon shaky, partly because of drink. 'We were both pretty damaged people,' he recalls, 'and sometimes they attract each other.' As for Sally, on 16 January 1974, the day before her twentieth birthday, Amis wrote in his diary of visiting her at the wine bar where she worked, on the Edgware Road, near 108 Maida Vale. Working in a wine bar, of course, was a terrible idea for an alcoholic. Sally became romantically involved with the wine bar's owner, Nigel Service, whom she would marry early in 1976, when she was twenty-two and he forty-one. Amis paid for the wedding and at some point during it Martin turned to him and asked how he thought it was going. 'Complete fucking disaster' was his answer, a remark not unlike one made on a later occasion, when Sally arrived at Gardnor House drunk and passed out on the stairs. According to Martin, Amis took one look at her, muttered 'You fucking wreck', stepped over her body to go upstairs, then came back, stepping over her body again, and asked: 'What are we going to do about Sal?' On 16 September 1976, Amis wrote to Jane to say that the couple 'came to sups last night and I must say seemed fonder of each other in a comfy marital way than I've ever seen them before'. But the marriage did not last a year. Service was 'quite posh', a wine merchant as well as a wine bar owner; at some point, not long after sups with Amis, Sally went off the rails: she drank up everything in Service's wine cellar at home, then, according to Martin, 'she fucked all the builders'. By 1978 her life was a string of calamities, as recorded in Amis's diary: 20 March: 'Sal panic allayed – but on and off all week'; 21 March: 'Wog & Mart to Sal Mrs. Reynolds at Colby';[65] 22 March: 'Wog & Mart to Colby re Sal'; 25 March: 'Sal in rehabilitation centre'; 3 April: '5.15 Sally thrown out of re-h centre 9.45 off w Dr Banner'; 20 May: 'Sal says Irish Martin beating her up . . . Irish Martin arrested for theft'; 3 June: 'Sal rang. Will have baby' (on 3 July Amis wrote to Robert Conquest: 'Sally is pregnant by some Irish berk: funny how you take it for granted that the arrival of your first grandchild will be a joyful occasion, sod it'); 19 August: 'finished W [a piece on Waugh] w Sal and Irish Martin phoning all the time'; 2 September: 'Sal at police station / Martin Irish in gaol'; 4 September: 'XII met Sal at St. Pancras and took her to Ch army hostel in Cosway St'; 23 December: 'Sal in Hospital in Isleworth I go to hospital 1 a.m. Sal gives birth 7:45 Heidi.' On 6 February 1979 Amis wrote to Conquest: 'Sally's baby got taken away for adoption yesterday, the least bad thing that can happen in the circumstances.'

Despite the gloom and anxiety occasioned by such entries and his gathering disaffection with Jane, Amis had not given up on the marriage. During the Gardnor House years he also made an heroic effort to deal with his loss of interest in sex. At the suggestion of Jim Durham he went to see Dr Patricia Gillan, a Harley Street psychotherapist and psychologist. Dr Gillan ran a sex therapy clinic at the Maudsley Hospital, where Durham worked as a consultant, and she and her husband, Richard, a psychiatrist, had written *Sex Therapy Today* (1976), a copy of which is to be found in Amis's library in the Huntington, inscribed by the authors to Amis and Jane. After Amis had three or four sessions with Dr Gillan, she asked to see Jane as well. 'From all I've heard about you,' Jane remembers her saying, 'I thought you were going to be simply *awful*, and you're not, are you?'[66] Jane went to one or two more sessions with Amis and then to a final session with Gillan alone. 'She asked me what I wanted, and I heard myself saying I wanted to stop smoking. "I know just the person for that," she said.' This person, a therapist named Kate Hopkinson, Jane went to see weekly, and soon smoking was no longer the main issue in their sessions. As Amis became bored and disillusioned with therapy – first with Dr Gillan, then with Dr John Cobb, a psychologist and sex therapist described in the *Memoirs* as 'a sort of highbrow marriage coun-sellor' – Jane grew more interested and involved, a source of fric-tion between them. Amis's complaints about his therapists, aside from the fact that their therapies didn't seem to be working, was that what they had to say, what Dr Cobb in particular had to say, was so obvious: 'So we were having trouble with our marriage, were we? Well being nicer to each other would help, of course. Finding out what the other one liked to eat, where he or she liked going for the evening, etc., and acting on it could not fail to be useful.' In the *Memoirs*, Amis depicts himself as impatient with Dr Cobb: 'My growing boredom with the whole enterprise, which I suppose I could have tried harder to conceal, he mistook for surly defensiveness – perhaps it *was* surly defensiveness. If so he failed to break it down.'[67]

Amis's account in the *Memoirs* of his experiences with therapy in the period 1977–80 does not square with the entries in the engagement diaries. Amis began seeing Dr Hafner about his travel anxieties and phobias some time in 1976 and was still seeing him until the summer of 1977. Dr Wooster (who had the theory about Amis's mother's 'Underground') he saw only twice, in September 1977. He began seeing Dr Cobb about the 'various difficulties' in his marriage in August 1977 (unusually, the sessions were held at Gardnor House) and continued to see him regularly until March 1980, a period of two and a half years. *Simultaneously*, he was seeing Dr Gillan, who treated him both for travel anxieties and as a sex therapist, from spring 1977 to winter 1979. In addition, there are several entries for 'workshops' in 1977 (not the same as Jane's workshops, which are also noted). Although Amis disparages Dr Cobb in the *Memoirs*, he not only stuck with him longer than the other therapists but seems to have made efforts to follow his therapeutic regimen. On 30 August 1978 a note in the diary reads: 'Aim at what targets with John Cobb? Make list of fears & intensities links between fears count blessings when pub speaking going to sleep, glow etc. going on TV Booze record & dreams etc.' Though the diaries don't record how many drinks Amis had each day, as the diary he began in April 1972 seems to do, they do contain brief notes about his dreams. In 1977 he also began entering coded symbols in the diary: ten small triangles appear during the period 1 January to 15 February; the entry for 2 May reads: 'Dr. H [triangle symbol] detoured me.' What the triangles represent – assignations? orgasms? fucks? – is unclear. What *is* clear is the role therapy played in Amis's life in the years leading up to the dissolution of his second marriage.

This role was not solely therapeutic. It had a literary dimension as well. On 25 April 1977, while he was seeing Dr Hafner and Dr Gillan, Amis began writing *Jake's Thing*, which contains a mocking account of sex therapy and therapists. The diary entries record his progress on the novel as well as the therapy sessions he attended, as in 'p.141 Horror dreams early am Dr. G' (16 November 1977). It was only after their sessions ended that Dr Gillan discovered the kind of book Amis was writing, about a man who loses his libido and goes to a sex therapist. Amis told her about *Jake's Thing* because he needed her help; he asked her to act as a consultant or adviser on the book. As she was writing another book at the time, also about sex therapy, and Amis's questions helped her to clarify her ideas, she agreed. In addition, she enjoyed Amis's company, as in the therapy sessions: 'we built up a great rapport'. Amis struck Gillan as sincere in his attitude towards therapy: 'he was genuinely trying to solve his problems with Jane'. She remembers no truculence or defensiveness: 'he was straightforward, honest and charming'. The same was true of Jane. The therapy didn't work, she thinks, because 'they didn't go together . . . they wanted different things', an odd remark for a therapist to make (though also representative in its obviousness, Amis might say, like Dr Cobb's 'try being nicer'). Amis, though, liked Gillan, and he and Jane began to see her and her husband socially. The two couples went out to dinner together several times and the Amises even suggested that they go on holiday together, on a boat trip on the canals.

It was Gillan's understanding that Amis would show her the manuscript of *Jake's Thing* when it was finished. He never did. When it was published he sent her a copy inscribed: 'Love to Patricia who helped me to think of some of this.' When Gillan read it she was 'very disappointed. I felt let down.' Amis had told her from the start that she was in it, disguised as Jake's Irish sex therapist, Dr Proinsias Rosenberg, MD, MA (Dip. Psych.). Making her a man was a way of protecting Gillan, Amis said. Dr Rosenberg is shrewd and well intentioned but ignorant: 'Rosenberg didn't know where Freud functioned, what had happened in 1848 or who James Bond was . . . had never heard of the *Titanic*, haggis, T.S. Eliot, plutonium, Lent, Vancouver (city, let alone island or chap), Herodotus, Sauternes, the Trooping of the Colour, the *Times Literary Supplement*, the battle of Gettysburg, Van Gogh, Sibelius, *Ulysses* – (a) good going for an Irishman (b) and no doubt Ulysses too – chlorophyll, Florence Nighingale, the Taj Mahal, pelota, lemurs, Gary Cooper and Hadrian's Wall.'[68] Gillan was naturally upset by the portrayal, particularly as she thinks of herself as possessing wide cultural as well as scientific interests; her husband was a painter, she told me, as well as a psychiatrist. In contrast, the therapy sessions depicted in the novel she thought 'pretty close' to Amis's real-life sessions: 'he describes them very well. They would be of help to other people.' In all but one particular, the laboratory tests Jake undergoes were identical to those Amis underwent at the Maudsley. Amis, too, was given 'pictorial pornographic materials' for stimulation (in the novel these provoke Jake's comparison of the female genitalia to 'the inside of a giraffe's ear, or a tropical fruit not much prized by the natives')[69] and had his erections measured by a machine called a plethysmograph. What upset Gillan was that in the novel the testing was conducted in front of an audience, whereas at the Maudsley it took place in a small laboratory with only herself and one other person in attendance. Amis made the session 'into a display, an exhibitionist set-up, a farce.' She had no complaint, however, about Amis's account of what in the novel is called a 'nocturnal mensurator', another device for measuring 'penile tumescence'. Jake puts the device on before going to sleep, as did Amis in real life. As for the procedures Jake and Brenda are asked to employ to reawaken their sex life, these are exactly as described in the Gillans' book: first, 'non-genital sensate focusing', which means touching and stroking of faces, shoulders, backs, all the non-genital bits; second, 'genital sensate focusing'; third, intercourse. Amis found stage one awkward and embarrassing, Gillan remembers, as does Jake. It is astonishing that he went through any of these procedures, a mark of how serious he was about keeping the relationship going or recovering his potency (or of how beaten down he felt, like Jake, though he didn't strike Gillan as beaten down). That he would at the same time write a damning novel about them can be variously explained, as the novelist's habitual treachery (keep your mouth shut, avoid assenting to what cannot be assented to, have notebook at the ready), defensiveness, a tendency to compartmentalise aspects of his life. When Martin asked his father if he'd really gone through the procedures described in *Jake's Thing*, Amis answered: 'Yes, some of it', adding that 'in a case like this you have to show willing'; to which Martin replied: 'the *novel* didn't show willing, did it?'[70]

When *Jake's Thing* was published Amis and Jane were photographed walking arm in arm in Hampstead, as if to forestall or defy biographical readings.[71] But the novel upset Jane, not only because people would identify her with cake-eating Brenda ('I didn't like the way he depicted Brenda,' Dr Gillan recalls. 'Jane is a beautiful woman'), but because of the depiction of Geoffrey Mabbott, a friend of the Richardsons for whom Brenda leaves Jake at the novel's end. Geoffrey shares what Amis came to think of as Colin's irritatingly interrogative manner, wilful eccentricity of dress and desire to be singular or outlandish in opinion ('so as to seem to be someone').[72] 'He wasn't his old self to me,' Colin remembers of the Hampstead years. 'It took the form of ribbing me for never understanding what was said to me, to such an extent that he'd fixated on it . . . I did mind that a bit, particularly as I don't think it's fair or accurate.' As Jane puts it, Amis 'had turned against him, was endlessly sniping at him, putting him down, and grumbling about him when he wasn't there'.[73] At Lemmons, Colin recalls, Amis had once called him his closest friend, but as relations with Jane deteriorated, anyone associated with her became a target; Colin and Sargy were vulnerable (though Sargy was never grumbled about or sniped at to his face) because neither had much money, which meant that Amis invariably treated at pubs and restaurants. He began to feel that his generosity was being taken a bit for granted. In addition to the personal digs in *Jake's Thing*, Jane was dismayed not only by the hostile things Jake says about women and therapy in general, but by the novel's overriding pessimism.

Though Jane had published a well-received volume of stories in 1975 entitled *Mr Wrong*, she hadn't published a novel since *Odd Girl Out* (1972). The only regular writing she managed in the later years at Lemmons and at Gardnor House was journalism, in particular a monthly column for *Bride* magazine, though she also had occasional commissions for television (episodes of *Upstairs, Downstairs*, one-off plays for London Weekend Television, an adaptation of *After Julius* for Yorkshire Television). In the *Bride* column Jane offered advice on a range of topics: how to buy a house, how to give a party, how to write a thank-you note, how to give presents (luxury, utility or romantic), how to avoid and manage conflict in marriage, how to be a step-parent, how to travel with a loved one, how to feed your man and how to hang on to your personality in marriage. The columns were assured and full of good sense, with no indication at all that they were written by a woman whose marriage was falling apart. Yet this was the period in which Jane came to realise not only that Amis didn't love her but that he didn't like her, though at moments he seemed to want to love and like her. In her memoirs she recalls a successful long weekend in Oxfordshire, a trip suggested by one of Amis's therapists. 'This was my last most truly happy time with Kingsley,' Jane writes. 'He was relaxed, affectionate, funny, communicative, said how much he was enjoying being alone with me, and that we should do this sort of thing regularly. It was like old times – not the breathless beginning but something that held the promise of endurance, of an honest and companionable future.'[74] At a later moment, in Gardnor House, Jane was standing by the window of their bedroom looking out at the garden and feeling sad, like a heroine in one of her novels. 'He came to me, put his arms round me and gave me a long, gentle kiss, and said "I used to be so much in love with you." Before I could say anything, he turned and walked out of the room.'[75] In the Gardnor House years, she remembers, Amis went to sleep drunk most nights, was quarrelsome, stopped sharing a room at night because he claimed that when she turned over in bed it woke him and he couldn't get back to sleep. 'I couldn't spend the night completely still without being awake,' Jane protests. 'He was angry about this as well.'[76]

Only then did Jane begin fully to understand the depth and intensity of Amis's anxieties. She remembers one incident in particular, at a weekend party given by the philanthropist Drue Heinz at her country house in Ascot in Berkshire. Amis drank an enormous amount the first night and Jane had to help him upstairs (at Gardnor House, Colin remembers, Amis often went upstairs to bed on all fours, too unsteady to walk, though he never missed a morning at the typewriter). The house was very large and the Amises' room was at the end of a wing. When they finally found it, Amis had a sudden attack of depersonalisation, a condition that made him 'cease to seem real' to himself.[77] 'He howled and howled and howled,' Jane remembers, 'and I got a cushion and I said I'll hold your hands and you howl into the cushion. I didn't know what else to do.' These howls 'weren't a sound I'd ever heard anybody make before in my life and I didn't know where they came from. Nothing like that had ever happened before . . . It went on for what seemed like half an hour but was probably five or ten minutes and I was absolutely desperate. I didn't know where Drue lived in the house. I didn't know what was going to happen next. I didn't know whether to get a doctor. It was night and everybody'd gone to bed. I was holding him all the time. I had my arms around him. I said do you feel better now? He was very very drunk and he said let's just go to bed. And we went to bed and he went to sleep and I didn't. The next morning he said nothing about it at all. By then he'd become extremely difficult to talk to for me, because he'd always say you're getting at me about drink.'

Jane believes she knows what brought on Amis's fit. She was on the council of the Writers' Guild and had to go to the Annual General Meeting that Sunday in London (apparently the AGM was always held on a Sunday); a lift back home had been arranged for Amis on the Monday. 'And, of course, that meant he was going to have to spend the night in his bedroom alone.' Amis never said he didn't want Jane to go or was frightened of being alone in the room: 'he was cross that I was doing this but he didn't seem particularly perturbed. But I think now that that might have been what set it off.' A similar fright was witnessed by Jane in the summer of 1980, at the start of what turned out to be the last of the holidays she and Amis would have together, also Amis's last trip abroad. Anthony and Violet Powell had asked the Amises to join them on a fortnight's Swan cruise from Southampton down the north-west coast of France, Spain, Portugal and Spain again, finishing up in Nice. With the Powells' permission Amis invited the Fussells to join the party. The trip got off to an inauspicious start when Jane misunderstood the time of departure. After a hair-raising taxi ride round the Southampton docks – the taxi driver had no idea how to find the ship – they arrived at the correct dock just as the gangway was being raised. It was lowered to allow Amis and Jane to scramble on board. 'Kingsley was absolutely white with rage at me,' Jane remembers. 'He was so frightened it was a relief to be angry at me.' She imagines what must have been going through his mind: 'it's her fault that I'm feeling so awful, because she's so bloody awful an organiser and she makes all the mistakes and says she doesn't make them'. Such thinking 'was a good way out of being bloody terrified'. In the *Sunday Times* article Amis wrote about the trip he only hints at the fear he experienced. It was 'a hot afternoon at the end of July when, just about understandably misled by a passage in the travel documents, Jane and I began the urgent task of discovering where, in the whole of Southampton docks, our ship, M.T.S. *Orpheus*, might be. I kept a good deal to myself for the next half-hour, at the end of which we proceeded on board under the eyes, it seemed, of all passengers and crew.'[78] Once on board Amis was somewhat buoyed not only by how old his fellow passengers were ('in this company I was a relative youngster') but by 'relief at not after all having to be winched down to the sun-deck of the *Orpheus* from a helicopter and self-approval for not ballocking Jane – she it was who had screwed the time-table.'[79]

Amis enjoyed the cruise itself, even the sightseeing. Though it was 'a dark moment, as charged with significance as seeing the lights of Scilly fade, when I quaffed the last drops of The Macallan 10-year-old from my travelling flask', he made do with large ouzos and plenty of Greek wine (*Orpheus* was a Greek ship). Once Amis had worked out 'the question of timing and achieving one's shit',[80] the almost-daily sightseeing tours, involving early disembarkation, coaches and tour guides who, leaving nothing to chance, explained that the cows they were passing 'produced milk and butter',[81] not only proved enjoyable but gave Amis and his fellow passengers the impression of having 'earned' their off-time and meals, 'a very British arrangement'.[82] In the diary he kept of the trip, Amis quotes Anthony Powell as saying he 'even likes or likes best sitting in a halted bus'. As Amis writes at the end of his article, 'I had grown into the routine; I was going to miss waking up to a completely new sight through the porthole, the bustle of getting off and into the bus, the sightsee, the lunch, however shitty the food, the final sense of duty done and of course the plunge back into the grateful bosom of the ship. Altogether it was as pleasant a way of dealing with abroad – by not really leaving England – as I can imagine.'[83]

This sense of security and familiarity is reflected in the comparatively good-humoured nature of Amis's observations about churches, museums, landscapes and works of art. Of the Museu Calouste Gulbenkian: 'I enjoyed it very much and advise anyone who gets within a hundred miles of it not to miss it on any account.' Of Turner's 'Shipwreck of the *Minotaur* on the sandbanks of Haar': 'the artist at his most vertiginous, evoking a sympathetic groan for the wretched mariners'. Even disparaging remarks are comparatively mild. One reason Amis liked the Gulbenkian museum was that it contains 'virtually nothing of the twentieth century at all', an absence explained by the fact that, as Gulbenkian says in a note, 'in assembling his collection he was always and exclusively guided by his personal taste'. Amis asks the reader: 'Which pictures would *you* take to a desert island if you had a completely free choice and nobody was ever going to see or hear from you again? Faced with (say) a Raeburn or a Braque, which would you take? Really?' Only Amis's settled hostility to gardens and tapestries can explain his description of the Alcazar in Seville, a place of spectacular beauty, as 'rather boring'. Of tapestries he writes: 'How could anybody ever have thought that they were a good idea when there were paintings about, and have they all got to be lifeless or was that put in on purpose, and why are they always the same two dull colours.' Of the park of Maria Luisa he says only that 'one lemon tree or orange tree is much like another',[84] a judgement derived in part, as are all Amis's negative comments about gardens, from the fact that seeing them can require a good deal of walking. The Alhambra in Granada suffered from a similar drawback. Amis describes it as 'a must for people who like climbing a lot of steps not very slowly in the sun with the humidity chasing a record'.[85] It was on this trip that Amis thought he'd discovered 'a straightforward inverse correlation between nations and their food-and-drink. Spanish, like English, nice people, nasty food; French, nasty people, nice food. Oh yes, and Greeks, nice people, *terrifying* food. But then, Italians, nice people, nice food. Danes too. Surely there must be . . . Got it: Germans, nasty people, nasty food (drink better, but beer overrated, wine no good with food, schnappses often delicious but not enough on their own). Also Belgians – Walloons anyway.'[86]

These words Amis wrote in the week or so after the cruise, while staying in the Dordogne, at the home of his and Jane's friends Richard and Joy Law. In addition to underplaying his fury at Southampton, Amis's account of the cruise edits out much of his rigidity, about routines and preferences, and his rudeness towards outsiders, especially those who threatened to intrude. Betty Fussell, at this point something of a Jane person rather than a Kingsley person (a distinction difficult to avoid in the Hampstead years, in part because of Jane's obvious unhappiness, in part because of Amis's reluctance to see her friends), described Amis's behaviour on the cruise as 'impossible'. In a letter of 31 August 1980, written shortly after returning from the holiday, she praised Jane and deplored Amis: 'it's ironic you should be linked to a writer who has continuously narrowed and limited his range of interest and emotion to the point where he seems to be drying up as you are re-blossoming'. Powell, a Kingsley person, took the Kingsley view, describing Jane as 'almost as little "natural" as any woman could be'.[87] What Powell seems not to have realised, or taken into consideration, was how tense Jane was on the cruise, a state unlikely to encourage natural behaviour. 'We stopped at a number of places – Mont Saint-Michel, Oporto and Lisbon,' Jane writes in her memoirs, 'but I can't remember much because, the moment we were alone, Kingsley's irritation with me was like the atmosphere before an impending thunderstorm, and this dominated the cruise for me. I dreaded being alone with him.'[88] When the cruise ended, the Powells flew back to London from Nice but the Fussells stayed on a night, to see Amis and Jane off to the Dordogne the next afternoon, 14 August. Amis dreaded the train journey and so did Jane, already on edge from his behaviour towards her on the cruise and from their hair-raising arrival at Southampton. To deaden his fear Amis drank steadily all afternoon and was 'surly drunk' by the time the Fussells saw them off at the station: 'I felt their relief at parting from us.'[89] On the journey itself he continued to drink until he fell asleep. When they arrived at midnight at the railway station at Souillac in the Dordogne, 'I could hardly get him off the train.'

The division between Jane people and Kingsley people, often a matter of gender, did not apply to all their friends, but it applied to the Laws. Joy Law had known Jane since the 1950s; when the two couples got together, it was her husband, Richard, a city trader and Garrick Club member, also a passionate fan of music, with whom Amis mostly talked. When, therefore, Joy Law alone met the Amises at the railway station, Amis immediately asked where Richard was. Joy replied that he was in London and would be unable to get away until the last two days of the visit. The Amises' stay was for ten days and each morning Amis worked on his article, was briefly communicative at lunch, then spent the rest of the day making it clear, in Jane's words, 'that he wasn't enjoying himself'.[90] Alone in their room, Amis repeatedly told Jane that he wouldn't have come to the Dordogne had he known Richard wasn't going to be there. There was another couple staying for the week, a painter and his wife, who also painted, old friends of the Laws with no prior connection to Amis or Jane. In the mornings, Amis wrote, the painter painted, his wife read, sewed or sunbathed and Joy and Jane usually went off to the village to shop for lunch. 'Jane would sit in the car in the village square in tears,' Joy remembers, 'telling me how awful her life was.' In the afternoons Amis sometimes went on excursions with the painter and his wife, while Jane and Joy went on separate outings or busied themselves around the house. Joy remembers the couple as mesmerised by the speed and hostility of the sniping between Jane and Kingsley: 'it was really like watching table tennis, it was worrying because of the animosity but wonderful to listen to'. Amis was always polite to the couple and to Joy and when Jane was not present, according to the painter's wife, 'was perfectly civilised and pleasant to be with'.[91] At moments he was even considerate to Jane. One afternoon he returned from an outing to the local village having bought Jane a box of wild strawberries, which he knew she loved. 'It was touching,' Joy Law recalls, 'considering the state they were in.' Though Joy knew that the visit from the Amises would be 'very difficult', and had arranged outings and restaurant lunches to enliven it, for the most part, in Jane's words, 'Kingsley remained obdurately determined *not* to enjoy it.'[92] In a letter of 10 September to Robert Conquest, he corroborates this view: 'All in all the cruise was quite fun. More so than the stay in the Dordogne that followed. Pretty enough, but filthy French food – you know, elaborate sauces to persuade you to swallow stuff you would otherwise have hesitated to give the dog – sod-all to do and no host, just a hostess.' Amis told Jacobs a single anecdote about the Dordogne stay, about rowing with Jane over Scrabble: '"If you go on like this," he told her, "we won't be able to play Scrabble." To which he recollects her replying, "I think I'd better see my solicitor." Jane, however, denies any talk of lawyers.'[93]

Amis, in turn, denied Jane's account of what happened after the stay in the Dordogne. Almost as soon as they got back to Gardnor House the Amises were invited to visit the Edinburgh Festival by their friends Dickie and Patricia Temple-Muir. Dickie Temple-Muir owned a restaurant in Walton Street in London called La Popotte and co-owned the Roxburghe Hotel in Edinburgh. The Amises had met the Temple-Muirs at a party near Wivenhoe, to which they'd been brought by the Gales. They were invited to stay for a week or so as Dickie's guests at the hotel. When they arrived, Amis found a welcoming bottle of whisky in the room 'and Dickie got full marks for that'. The festival itself did not appeal. 'Leftiness and trendiness have invaded it,' Amis wrote to Conquest in the letter of 10 September: 'There was a German shag whose art-form was chatting to you while he drew things on a blackboard. I didn't go to him. Nor to any of the concerts, all of which contained either a Mahler symphony or some jerk's first performance. Did let myself be taken to Lilian Hellman's play, *Watch on the Rhine*. Frightful piss, of course, but different from contemporary piss. She wasn't *trying* to write piss, like Beckett or Stoppard, she was just totally failing to be good.' According to Jane, Amis not only refused to go to any festival events, 'he also refused to let me go'.[94] In addition, he refused to go out to dinner, even in the hotel, wanting instead to have sandwiches and drinks in their room. They were invited, with the Temple-Muirs, to have lunch with Willy and Gaia Mostyn-Owen, 'who had a charming little castle outside Edinburgh'.[95] Claudio Abbado was there – he was performing at the festival – and Amis was rude to him. In the midst of a disagreement about Mozart, he told Abbado 'that he didn't know what he was talking about. It was a large lunch party, and conversation virtually stopped at this. Abbado looked at Kingsley with some curiosity, then turned to our hostess and changed the subject.'[96] Patricia Temple-Muir (now Woods) remembers this incident as taking place at the end of lunch, after Amis had had a lot to drink. It was embarrassing and Jane was visibly upset. Later at the hotel Amis denied that he had been rude to Abbado and turned on Jane. When Jacobs was working on his biography he asked Amis about the incident. Amis claimed to have no recollection of it.[97] He also denied Jane's account of a bizarre episode concerning the manuscript of his *Sunday Times* article. When they returned to London from France, Amis unpacked and couldn't find the manuscript. Jane claims that he then accused her of destroying it. 'He was serious. This shocked me probably more than anything else that had happened between us.' After calling Joy Law in France to see whether the article might have been left behind in their room, and learning that Joy couldn't find it, Jane took out Amis's suitcase and found it in a zipped compartment. 'When I gave it to him, he said simply, "Oh. You've found it."'[98] Jacobs repeats this story in his biography, adding that Amis denies having made the accusation. In Amis's copy of the manuscript of the biography, next to the sentence, 'According to Jane, he then accused her of destroying it,' he wrote simply: 'No.' People remember things differently, but Jane's account of the Abbado exchange is corroborated by Patricia Woods and it seems unlikely that Jane would have made up Amis's accusation that she'd destroyed his article. As early as 10 January 1976, Conquest was reporting to Larkin both on Amis's rudeness when drunk and on the difficulties he had defending himself afterwards: 'Old KA was telling me his problem about these missing hours – denying Jane's charges that he behaved badly at such-and-such a party, while at the same time trying to elicit what it was he did, without admitting that he didn't know. "Of *course* the shagbags weren't offended"; "Oh, I suppose they like people who pee in the soup?" etc etc.'

Amis and Jane returned to Hampstead on 7 September. *Russian Hide-and-Seek*, perhaps the weakest of his novels, had been published two months before the Swan cruise. He was deeply unhappy, drinking hard and having so much trouble with his next novel that he decided to abandon it and start a different one. Meanwhile, he resumed his lunches at the Garrick and he and Jane continued to entertain in the evenings at Gardnor House. On 1 November Jane began a ten-day visit to Shrublands, a health farm in Suffolk she had been to twice before. Patricia Temple-Muir accompanied her. On the morning of her departure Amis was in the kitchen at Gardnor House and when Jane said she was going he simply said 'I see' and didn't look up from his newspaper. Amis's diary for 1 November reads: 'J to Shrublands Nig & Mandy [friends of Colin] up.' Ten days later, on the morning Jane was due back, a letter was hand-delivered to Amis by Jane's solicitors. It read:

This is to tell you that I'm leaving. You know that I have been – we've both been – unhappy for years. I've thought about this for a long time and have come to the conclusion that there isn't the slightest hope of things getting any better. They don't, they simply get quietly worse. You are not going to stop drinking and I cannot live with the consequences – I tried to tell you in Edinburgh that it was not the *rows* that were the worst things – it was the awful sterile desert in between them that I can't take any more. I'd rather live alone than the way we've been living for the last few years. I've tried to talk to you about our parting amicably, but you simply accused me of blackmailing so the only thing to do is just to go, before we make each other even more miserable.

This has been the most agonising decision and I've taken all the trouble I know to be sure that it is the right one, but I have made it, and it is final.

25

Nadir

Amis's emotional state when he received Jane's letter had been brewing throughout the Hampstead years. His unhappiness at Gardnor House may have been less overt than Jane's but his friends commented upon it and it was everywhere apparent in his writings. 'Funny you should say he's glum,' Conquest wrote to Larkin on 25 November 1979. 'Tony Powell was just remarking that he'd sounded so on a radio programme they'd listened to.' Conquest had not seen Amis for several weeks but had spoken to him on the telephone. Perhaps, Conquest suggested, he was suffering from post-partum depression, having recently finished *Russian Hide-and-Seek* (on 5 October, according to his diary). Perhaps the problem was longer term: 'Do you think that Jake's Thing reflects, as most of his books do, a personal problem, even if in an exaggerated way? (I have some reason to believe this to be so.) If so, does he mind? Does he feel he's aging? Or rather, *slowing* up in some way?'[1]

The answer was yes. On 23 September 1979 Larkin had written Amis a very funny letter full of gloomy complaints.[2] On 29 September Amis countered with his own complaints, beginning with 'hideous memories':

Mine include behaving like a shit, pissing on harmless people, etc . . . On my self-pity themes, don't tempt me son. They include year-round hay-fever, high blood-pressure so that I stream with sweat at the slightest exertion or upset, permanently-itching places on my scalp (side-effect of anti-blood-p pills) from which descend flakes of scurf the size of 1p pieces, increasing phobias that stop me travelling almost anywhere (that one's not so bad) and make me dread and hate being alone, this along with a wife who puts herself first and the rest nowhere and constantly goes out to GROUPS and WORKSHOPS and crappy 'new friends' and total loss of sex-drive. I haven't had a fuck for more than a year and a wank for over a month. Don't tell anyone. Your thing about not reading anything new struck a chord. Nearly all my reading is comfort-reading now, done while I wait for whisky and sleeping-pills to get me torpid enough to go to bed – alone, of course. Still, I've got my work oh I say thanks most awfully.

The work was not going well. In this period Amis abandoned several book projects, including two novels. In March 1978 he agreed to compile a Faber 'Book of Limericks', then backed out, on the grounds that he wouldn't find enough good ones and that those that he liked would be impossible to illustrate.[3] In January 1979 he was in enthusiastic correspondence with Oxford University Press about a projected 'Little Book of Booze', which never materialised. In the summer of 1980, after several months' planning, he gave up on the idea of compiling a 'Science Fiction Companion' for Hutchinson (though in 1981 he edited an anthology of favourite stories, *The Golden Age of Science Fiction* for Hutchinson, with an introduction lamenting the genre's decline). On 14 October 1980, he complained to Conquest about 'not getting down to a rewrite of New Maps which would be (a) a pest to do (b) not at all well paid. Now I find if I repay a bit of the advance I've had, I can get out of it.' Only the publication of his *Collected Short Stories*, late in the autumn, to generally warm reviews, lightened the gloom. His uncertainties and false starts with novels were also worrying. Amis submitted *Jake's Thing* in February 1978 and began drafting *Russian Hide-and Seek* about a year later, finishing it in October 1979. This was a normal gestation period for the middle or Lemmons years. Almost as soon as he began *Russian Hide-and-Seek*, he was complaining to Larkin about it, in a letter of 19 January 1979: 'It's not so much thinking up things for the people to say and do, *though there is that*; it's more the putting into words of difficult, intractable concepts like a man leaving a house by the front door. Testing stuff liek priek like that.'[4] When the novel was published in May 1980, it was poorly received. Even Anthony Burgess, normally an admirer, was disappointed: 'Naturally, I hate to say this,' he wrote in the *Observer* on 12 May: 'Mr. Amis, even at his less than best, is the most entertaining novelist alive . . . I wonder if the overall dullness and, may I say, futility of the book, represent a deliberate aesthetic, rather like the willed torpors of Kubrick's "Space Odyssey".' By the time Amis read these words he was planning the novel that would become *Stanley and the Women*. At some point, though (the diaries offer no help with dates), he put the new novel aside and began work on a different one, with a homosexual narrator. This new new novel, referred to in correspondence as 'Difficulties with Girls', he began drafting in October 1980, a month before Jane left him. Nine months later he had written only 130 draft pages. He then abandoned the novel and returned to the 'Stanley' novel, which took another two years to finish. The four-year period between *Russian Hide-and-Seek* and *Stanley and the Women*, published in May 1984, was roughly twice that of previous intervals. The abandoned 'Difficulties' remained abandoned, though he recycled the title for the 1988 sequel to *Take a Girl Like You*. If Amis felt that he was 'slowing up in some way', as Conquest suspected, his writing life as well as his love-life may have prompted the feeling.

It is difficult not to bring in *Jake's Thing* at this point. Jake Richardson's 'problem' extends beyond sex. His sense of lost potency is partly a product of age – his own, or his own and Brenda's – but also of the age, which he finds everywhere alien and alienating. Professionally, Jake is at a standstill, condemned by what he thinks of as his 'integrity' ('with some assistance from laziness') to a readership at Oxford as opposed to a professorial chair.[5] He is as unengaged with his work as he is with his wife, rarely publishes anything or revises his lectures and seminar materials. Nor has he sustaining hobbies or outside interests; even gardening has 'begun to be too much for him, not physically but mentally or morally' (which is exactly how he views lovemaking, with Brenda or anyone else). Several critics have compared Jake to Jim Dixon (Richardson is 'Dick's son', that is, Dixon, thirty years on, Amis told the novelist, Joseph Connolly):[6] both are inhibited professionally by intellectual honesty, have lowbrow tastes, are pursued by a neurotic woman who fakes a suicide attempt, at last speak their minds in set-piece public outbursts (the Merrie England speech for Jim, Jake's denunciation of women at the College Meeting and of therapy at a workshop run by the sadistic American 'facilitator', Ed). The difference between the two heroes is that Jim's gathering irritation leads to freedom and pleasurable release, Jake's to exhaustion and stasis.

When Jake contemplates sex with Brenda what he feels is hard for him to identify: 'Reluctance? Yes. Revulsion? No. Fear? No. Embarrassment? No. Boredom? Er, no. Dejection? Yes, but still not the right section of the thesaurus. Disfavour? Yes, but not much further forward. *Dismay* – of a peculiar kind, one not encountered before in any of his admittedly unhabitual attempts to analyse his emotions: it was profound . . . and . . . unalloyed . . . and . . . absorbing . . . and . . . (Christ) . . . very very mild, like so much else.'[7]

It was also pervasive. In Chapter 1, Jake's consultation with a Harley Street doctor is rushed so that an Arab sheikh can be ushered into the office. He finds hailing a taxi all but impossible since 'no sooner had one black, brown or yellow person, or group of such, been set down on the pavement than Americans, Germans, Spaniards were taken up and vice versa'.[8] At the off-licence, Jake decides to splurge on a single bottle of Château Talbot 1967 at £4.09, while the cigar-smoking customer ahead of him, in 'very very dirty whitish overalls', pays for his purchases by peeling off at least five notes from a roll of twenties, while chatting familiarly to the shopman about the virtues of 'twelve-year-old' over 'eight-year-old' and 'the '61 over 'the '62'. At the till, Jake queries his bill:

'Er, the . . . You've charged the full price for the chocolates.'
'Right.'
'But your notice says 10p in the pound off everything.'
'Everything bar chocolates and smokes.'
'But it says everything.'
'It means everything bar chocolates and smokes.'
'But . . .'
'You want them, do you, squire?'
'. . . Yes.'
'Right.'[9]

Chapter 1 ends with Jake's return to his London home, in a long brick terrace 'put up a hundred years before to house the workers at some vanished local industry and these days much in demand among recently married couples, pairs of homosexuals and older persons whose children had left or never existed. Jake had bought no. 47 in 1969; he couldn't have afforded to now.'[10]

Jake is like Amis's father at a similar age (closer to sixty than fifty, Amis's age at the time of writing), which is to say, like one of

Warwick Deeping's 'ideal' readers, as described by Amis in his essay 'Pater and Old Chap' (discussed in Chapter 2). Jake, too, feels 'menaced by a falling real income, a decline in status and the emergence into power and affluence of uncouth persons who sneer at what he feels and stands for'.[11] These feelings were shared by Amis himself, for all his success and celebrity; hence, in part, his enthusiasm for Margaret Thatcher. Amis, of course, was hardly alone in his sense that something was wrong with Britain in 1978, the year of the 'winter of discontent'. A year later Margaret Thatcher and the Tories would be voted into office partly on the strength of Jake-like sentiments in the population. Even non-Thatcherites expressed dismay at the state of the country. A year before *Jake's Thing* was published, Margaret Drabble's *The Ice Age*, an overt 'condition of England' novel, described the nation as 'sliding, sinking, shabby, dirty, lazy, inefficient, dangerous, in its death throes, worn out, clapped out, occasionally lashing out'. Keith Miller, in an excellent account of *Jake's Thing*, accompanies this quotation with comparable quotations from John Fowles's *Daniel Martin* (1977) and William Golding's *Darkness Visible* (1979).[12]

Amis's poems from the Gardnor House years reinforce the impression of world-weariness and dismay expressed in *Jake's Thing*. While he was having difficulty with both fiction and non-fiction, Amis was experiencing a small revival as a poet. Larkin was blocked as a poet at this time, or dried up, and even more depressed than Amis; their correspondence was dominated by very funny laments about physical and mental deterioration, with occasional moments of advice and encouragement. 'I wouldn't be too sure about po[etry] defecting if I were you,' wrote Amis to Larkin on 28 August 1977. 'If may compare unworthy self, I wrote not a line between July '74 and November '76, then turned out 200 of the buggers and one or two shorts have followed. Try an extended one. It's great not having to have finishing it in mind all the sodding time.' The 200-line poem Amis mentions here was 'A Reunion', about a gathering of signals officers from his unit (discussed in Chapter 6). Amis's longest poem, it is suffused with a sense of loss. Like all but one of the eight poems he published in this period, it first appeared in the books pages of the *New Statesman*.[13] Thirty years ago, he writes in its final section,

> . . . what we had to do
> Showed us off perfectly, when

We were not so much young as new,
With some shine still on us, unmarked
(At least only mildly frayed),
When everything in us worked,
And no allowances made.

Amis was fifty-four when he wrote the poem, which ends:

Disbandment has come to us
As it comes to all who grow old;
Demobilized now, we face
What we faced when we first enrolled.
Stand still in the middle rank!
See you show them a touch of pride! –
Left-right, left-right, bags of swank –
On the one-man pass-out parade.

Here is the manly alternative to therapy: discipline, humour, self-pride, male camaraderie, precisely the qualities Amis approves in another of the poems he wrote in this period, 'Drinking Song', in praise of the Garrick Club, published in the *New Statesman* on 7 April 1978. In 'A Reunion', none of the old comrades at the gathering get drunk; in 'Drinking Song', thoughts of the 'one-man pass-out parade' delay the speaker's move downstairs from the club bar:

Look at old Morrison!
Isn't he wonderful?
Fit as a fiddle
    And tight as a tick;
Seventy-seven
And spouting his stories –
Just listen a minute
    And laugh yourself sick.

Same with the other chaps:
Bloody good company,
Never let anyone
    Drink on his own;
Out of your parish
Or widowed or derelict –

Once you're in here
   You're no longer alone.

Different for Weatherby,
Stuck with incontinence,
Mute in his wheelchair
   And ready to go;
Different for Hooper,
Put back on the oxygen,
Breathing, but breathing
   Uncommonly slow.

Did what we could, of course,
While there was anything;
Best to remember 'em
   Not as they are,
But as they used to be,
Chattering, chaffing and . . .
You go and eat
   And I'll stay in the bar.

Such poems are verse equivalents of the 'swank' called for at the end of 'A Reunion', also of the social face Amis presented at club and pub. The same is true of 'Delivery Guaranteed' and 'Equal Made', the 'Two Impromptus' Amis published in the *Statesman* on 13 November 1978, both, again, about death and ageing, both briskly sardonic. Even 'Senex', published a year before *Jake's Thing*, on 20 May 1977, swanks, in that the speaker's loss of libido is lamented with perfect self-control.[14] In classical comedy, as in Amis's earlier novels, the plot involves the overcoming or pushing aside of an older blocking figure, a 'Senex'. Now the Senex takes centre stage, pondering his ills in dignified quatrains:

To find his sexual drives had ceased
   For Sophocles was no disaster;
He said he felt like one released
   From service with a cruel master.

I envy him – I miss the lash
   At which I used to snort and snivel;

Oh that its unremitted slash
    Were still what makes me drone and drivel!

The poem's old-fashioned orderliness and Latin title are character-istic. The two quatrain-long 'Impromptus' also have an antique feel, like classical epigrams, while 'Advice to a Story-Teller', published in the *Statesman* on 10 March 1978, is sub-headed 'after Martial'. What helps to make the composure of the poetic voices in these poems possible is their sense of the unappealing character of the contemporary world. 'Look thy last on all things shitty,' begins 'Shitty', originally published with 'Senex' in the *Statesman*. This is a 'Senex' poem not only in what it deplores ('German tourists, plastic roses, / Face of Mao and face of Che') but in its closeness to 'Crisis Song', published in the *Statesman* on 22 March 1974, which envi-sions an England of Soviet-style scarcities (except for 'stacks of bloody salt / – Mined by you and me'). Here was Amis again lamenting decline, a trait of the old he himself elsewhere mines for comic effect (think of Jenny Bunn's dad in *Take a Girl Like You*). 'Farewell Blues', written by Amis in July 1978, just in time for inclu-sion in the *Collected Poems*, is modelled on Betjeman's 'Dorset', itself modelled on Hardy's 'Friends Beyond'. The poem laments the death of jazz in 'Senex' syntax: 'Dead's the note we loved that swelled within us.' It is intricately worked and indebted to advice from Larkin. On 27 July 1978, after an uncharacteristic period of silence from Larkin, Amis sent him a draft of the poem: 'Apart from hoping to resume touch I write to ask if you can improve the enclosed out of your greater knowledge. I mean in a sense disimprove by suggesting even crappier examples in lines 1–3 and 5–6. You might also help me with the churchyards.[15] Brunswick sounds all right but the others less so.' Here is the draft:

FAREWELL BLUES

Bongo, sitar, 'cello, flute, electric piano, bass guitar,
Training Orchestra, Research Team, Workshop, Group, Conservatoire,
Seascape, Nexus, Barbaraesque, Distortions, Voltage – bloody row,
For Louis Armstrong, Benny Goodman, Walter Page and Sidney Catlett
    lie in Brunswick churchyard now.

Trumpets berserk, drums contingent, saxophones that bleat or bawl,
Keyless, barless, poor-man's Boulez, improvising on fuck-all,

Far beyond what feeling, reason, even decency allow,
While Teddy Wilson, Floyd O'Brien, Sterling Bose and Henry Allen lie
   in Gennett churchyard now.

Dead's the note we loved that swelled within us, made us gasp and
   stare,
Simple joy and simple sadness thrashing the indignant air;
What replaced them no one asked for, but it turned up anyhow,
And Coleman Hawkins, Johnny Hodges, Bessie Smith and Pee Wee
   Russell lie in
Victor churchyard now.

By Larkin's 'greater knowledge' Amis meant of jazz labels, artists
and bands or combos, crappy and contemporary as well as good
and bygone. Larkin's suggested improvements, in a letter of 1 August
1978, a number adopted by Amis, show how exacting a craftsman
he was; they also warn Amis against Senex-like tendencies:

I think you should stick to chaps who are dead: Goodman, Wilson aren't.
Floyd O'Brien? Labels: ideally you . . . should line up the chaps with the
labels they chiefly recorded on, but this is virtually impossible. Gennett is
pretty hopeless: only Oliver and the Wolverines. I should substitute Decca –
but of course they did all sorts of things in later years. I 2 [stanza one, line
two]: 'Art Ensemble,' 'Globe Unity,' 'Spontaneous Music Ensemble' are all
real names. I 3: 'Seascape' doesn't sound quite right. How about 'Square
Root' – horrible mathematical, and they think they're being jazz-rockly funny?
II 1: this sounds a bit like your father on Lester Young et al. Wants improving.
Trumpets that don't sound like trumpets, fast as clarinets: 'castrato trum-
pets'? 'Bagpipe saxophones that fart'? Get the boot in. Think of Coltrane.
II 2: excellent. II 3: decency sounds like yr. dad. III 1: why gasp and stare?
Gurgle yeah wd be more like it. III 2: why *indignant* air? III 3: fine. For
names, how about Bubber Miley, Muggsy Spanier, Eddie Condon? Mildred
Bailey? Sidney Bechet?[16]

When Larkin suggests that Amis is echoing his father, Amis takes
the criticism to heart: 'decency' is replaced by 'mother-wit' in the
line 'Far beyond what feeling, reason, even decency allow' and
'Trumpets berserk' becomes 'Trumpets gelded'. Sounding like his
father was a vice in poetry and fiction; in social contexts, interviews
and newspaper polemic, Amis was less bothered. In 'Their Oxford',

published first in the *Collected Poems*, where it appears between 'A Reunion' and 'Senex', Amis acutely anatomises the pull of nostalgia and oldster grumbling. Like Larkin's 'Dockery and Son', written much earlier, present-day Oxford is contrasted with the Oxford of 'my day'. Though the present is worse, Amis is careful not to gild the past; his Oxford, wartime Oxford, was low on 'Brideshead' glamour. Here are the poem's last three stanzas:

> Where once a line of college barges lay,
> Haunt of the rich (comparatively) few,
> A single hulk welters and rots away;
> So goes the Oxford that I hardly knew.
>
> With mildly coveting what I could see
> Went disapproval, but at this remove,
> When no one here cares how it used to be
> Except the old, can I still disapprove?
>
> What seemed to be so various is all one,
> A block of time, which like its likenesses
> Looks better now the next such has begun;
> Looks, and in this case maybe really is.

It is partly loss of energy, the energy needed to discriminate and recall, that makes a once-various past now seem 'all one / A block of time'. The last line is qualified but there is also an acceptance or letting go about it, like the acceptance or letting go which mostly characterised Amis's response to his ageing body in the Hampstead years, a source of appalled amusement and dismay in correspondence.[17] It was at Gardnor House, according to Mavis Nicholson, that Amis began to look as well as to sound like his father.

Russian Hide-and-Seek reinforces the impression of Amis as disillusioned, despairing, deteriorating. To begin with, it retreads old ground, being a dystopian alternate world novel like *The Alteration*, published four years earlier. Its counterfactual premise, that of a Russian takeover of Britain in 1980, the year of the book's publication, probably underlies 'Crisis Song' as well; it came to Amis, he told Dale Salwak, at Lemmons: 'One summer afternoon he stood looking out into the garden, and heard himself say, with satisfaction, "You're not here yet, Ivan, or Boris, or whoever." He had the same feeling while staying at a much grander home in Northamptonshire, and thinking, "Ah, yes, this is where the Russian Regional Controller would live."[18] Amis imagines the Russian takeover happening in stages, which he lays out in notes for the novel in the 1969 notebook: '1. commie coup and call for assistance. 2. Russn troops go in, restore order, hand over Eng commies & mostly leave. 3. Eng behave with gt ferocity.[19] 4. Pop uprising. Many killed incl. lots of govt. 5. Russns return & stay for direct rule.' The novel's setting is the English Democratic Republic in 2030, fifty years after 'the Pacification'. Many of the Republic's Russian residents, soldiers and bureaucrats, no longer believe in Marxism – that went out ten years earlier – and in its place cultivate aristocratic or feudal values, those of the 'great predecessors of Petrograd'. These predecessors are shadowy and romanticised figures to the Russians of the Republic, who know them only through biased and imperfect official histories. A plot evolves, spearheaded by a bored cavalry officer, twenty-one-year-old Alexander Petrovsky, to return England to the natives. The plot is hopelessly inept and fails and the novel ends with the authorities still firmly in control.

The novel's political purposes are overt and simple. What made the Soviet takeover possible is explained in familiar terms: 'There had been disorders here, runaway inflation, mass unemployment, strikes, strike-breaking, rioting, then much fiercer rioting when a leftist faction seized power.' The result of fifty years of Soviet rule is a society as materially impoverished as that of *The Alteration*, though less inventively imagined. Here, too, in 2030, transport is by horse and mule and the English spoken is strangely off ('Fine to see you, old customer'; 'How are you making, old chap?').[20] Richard Bradford sees the disastrous attempts of the authorities to reintroduce Shakespeare and other elements of the old national culture to the populace as a direct satire on government arts subsidies. The state's 'New Cultural Programme' recalls Labour's 'National Programme for the Arts and Entertainment', much derided in Amis's 1979 pamphlet *An Arts Policy?* The general apathy and brutishness of upper as well as lower levels of society (the novel's title refers to a game in which officers hunt each other at night with pistols) is merely an extension or playing out of the tendencies deplored in *Jake's Thing* and poems like 'Shitty'. 'I'd hate it to be thought of as a novel about the Russian menace,' Amis told Salwak. 'It's more about the destruction of beliefs. It is a warning not about what the Russians may do to us; it is a warning about what we may do to ourselves.'[21]

The novel's satire is underpowered as well as familiar. As Burgess puts it: '"The Alteration" was a brilliant grim joke, what with its Cardinal Sartre and its John Braine Pope. There one had the genuine image of an entire world Catholic and unreformed: it bustled, was consistent in its mad logic, and its characters were compelling. In this new book we are presented with a twenty-first-century world limited to a British rural province and a group of idle, not very convincing Russians.' What has been happening outside Britain? Burgess asks. What has brought about the death of Marxism? What is the native population doing and thinking? All we are shown of this population are three minor characters, a doctor, a blind rector and the rector's daughter, Petrovsky's mistress. Amis invents the title of a newspaper, *Angliskaya Pravda*, but 'we don't get any news'. What we do get is seen from a single perspective. No character speaks with passion or interest on behalf of the controlling authorities, as several characters do in *The Alteration*, nor are the plotters any more articulate or principled. The failed coup and Petrovsky's part in it are unengaging, partly because they are matters of gesture rather than conviction. John McDermott, among the most ardent and persuasive of Amis's academic champions, describes Petrovsky as 'without any redeeming charm, wit or talent. It is this unrelieved quality that accounts for [the novel's] comparative lack of success.'[22] When Amis's purposes are literary rather than political they are no more appealingly realised. From *New Maps of Hell* onwards Amis had remarked on the absence of sex in science fiction. Here he sets out to break new ground, in the form of Petrovsky's affair with the wife of the Deputy Director of the Republic, which is rendered with uncharacteristic explicitness. Presumably the sex scenes were meant to arouse and shock, in the manner of the seduction and masturbation scenes in *The Riverside Villas Murder*, as unexpected in a classic detective novel as they would be in a work of science fiction. Presumably they were also meant to show how debased feeling had become in this society. Their extremity, however, is embarrassing. At one point Petrovsky and the Deputy's wife, naked and elaborately harnessed, copulate in mid-air, while the Deputy's nubile daughter looks on, waiting her turn. Though Amis was often glad to see the back of novels he had finished and anxious about their reception, they didn't usually leave him exhausted. When he finished *Russian Hide-and-Seek* he wrote to Larkin on 4 December 1979, explaining a recent silence: 'Actually I was finishing a novel. Don't know that I'll ever start another. Too much like hard work what? And anxiety-promoting. Like walking to Antarctica *and* being afraid *all the time* you're going to fall over and break your hip.' The letter also announces: 'Had a wank this morning, which makes it a light-grey-letter day.'

The grace notes in the Hampstead years were mostly public or official. *Russian Hide-and-Seek* was published on 12 May 1980, the day of a drinks party given at 10 Downing Street by Margaret Thatcher. Amis had met Mrs Thatcher several years earlier, when she was in opposition, through Robert Conquest. When Conquest was staying at Gardnor House on a visit to London, Mrs Thatcher invited him to dinner at 19 Flood Street in Chelsea, and when he explained that he was staying with Amis she 'very decently invited me to join the party' (Jane was unwell at the time). The date of the dinner was 27 October 1977 and the only other guest was Professor Julius Gould, 'sometimes described as the only right-wing sociologist in captivity'[23] (Amis had met him in Swansea thirty years earlier). Both Denis Thatcher and Mark Thatcher were present. Amis enjoyed himself and was impressed with his hostess. 'I thought her bright and tough and nice,' he wrote to Larkin the next day, 'and by God she doesn't half hate lefties. All in all a tonic.' Amis also enjoyed the party at Downing Street: 'No 10 was quite fun,' he wrote to Larkin three weeks later, on 4 June 1980, adding in the margin: 'Plenty to drink, for instance.' He brought an inscribed copy of *Russian Hide-and-Seek* for Mrs Thatcher. 'Asked what it was about I said a future Russian takeover, to which she said reprovingly, "Get another crystal ball," a good example of four words requiring about 444 to get right.' It was during this period that Amis first met the Queen. On 26 March 1975 he was invited to Buckingham Palace, for one of a number of small luncheon parties the Queen and the Duke of Edinburgh held 'to meet distinguished people from all professions, trades and callings'.[24] Amis found himself one of eight guests, none of the others literary; the only one with a background in the arts was the Secretary-General of the Arts Council, Roy Shaw, berated by Prince Philip, much to Amis's delight, for wasting money on provincial theatre. Amis was placed next to the Queen, who asked him what he liked to read, confessing that she didn't read much herself ('So much of my work is reading'). When Amis answered 'Anthony Powell, Ian Fleming, Dick Francis', the Queen replied: 'Oh, yes, Mummy's jockey.'[25] 'She was fine,' he told Jack Gohn, an American graduate student writing a dissertation about him (Gohn would later become Amis's bibliographer), 'I *enjoyed* it.'[26] Philip Amis was staying at Lemmons at the time of the Buckingham Palace invitation and remembers coming downstairs around eleven on the morning of the lunch. It was a lovely day and Amis was standing outside in the garden drinking a whisky. When Jane appeared, she said: 'Bunny, do you have to have a drink?' As Phil remembers it, Amis's 'pissy' response was: '"Look, I'm Kingsley Amis, you see, and I can drink whenever I want." And then he went off . . . and came home drunk' (Amis had been anxious about the lunch and needed fortifying: 'he had been terrified for days about the unpremeditated fart or belch,' Conquest wrote to Larkin on 27 March, 'and was on a strict non-bean-and-onion diet'). The next time Amis went to Buckingham Palace was to receive his CBE, awarded to him in the 1981 New Year's Honours List.

Honours came from the academic world as well. St John's College, Oxford awarded him an honorary fellowship. Amis was 'much tickled' by the award, which put him, he wrote to Larkin on 23 October 1976, 'alongside (or shortly behind) Graves and you'. Earlier, in 1974, Oxford University Press had invited him to edit *The New Oxford Book of Light Verse* (1978). 'I was quite bowled over by your suggestion,' he responded on 26 March to Jon Stallworthy of OUP: 'an honour to be asked.' Larkin was also excited by the invitation. He thought of his *Oxford Book of Twentieth-Century English Verse* (1973), the successor to Yeats's *Oxford Book of Modern Verse* (1936), partly as a challenge to modernism and expected Amis's volume to be so as well. 'We shall have stamped our taste on the age between us in the end,' he predicted to a colleague at Hull.[27]

That Amis shared something of Larkin's sense of mission as an editor is clear from the care he took with the anthology, both with the compilation and with the Introduction. As he explained in a 1980 talk entitled 'Anthologies', reprinted in *The Amis Collection* (1990), he began by reading 'a great many anthologies', then he read 'the complete works of all the poets who in their different ways seemed to me to be light-verse poets, like Praed and Gilbert', then he read through 'poets who had written some light verse, like Chesterton and Auden', then poets who might be considered to have written some light verse 'if you looked at them in a certain way, like Betjeman and Larkin', then 'poets who might have turned out to have written the odd bit of light verse if you read their complete works, like Hardy and Hopkins'.[28] What was especially enjoyable about these researches, which took Amis about a year, was finding 'a single light poem by some monolith of sobriety, like Southey or Masefield'; less enjoyable was then reading through their complete works in search of another, 'and finding just that one and no more'.[29]

In the end, Amis compiled enough material for an anthology twice the length demanded. The selection process that followed, completed while still at Lemmons, was shaped by three pressures: to print only poems that satisfied his taste, to honour 'the tradition', and to differ from Auden. 'Reconciling those three pressures made the task of preparing a text quite good fun in its way.'[30] The Auden pressure was the easiest of the three to negotiate. Amis's concept of light verse was almost the exact opposite of Auden's. Auden's principles of selection, Amis writes in his Introduction, 'have to do with the kind of poet who unselfconsciously shares the common life and language of ordinary men and writes of the one in the other, in something close to the speaking voice: what he then produces will be light';[31] hence Auden's inclusion of folk songs, ballads and blues lyrics, even those about murder and betrayal. For Amis, on the contrary, the key feature of light verse is its self-consciousness: 'light verse is unimaginable in the absence of high verse . . . It is altogether literary, artifical and impure' (that is, the opposite of untutored).[32] In determining the parameters of the anthology, where it began and ended in particular, personal taste triumphed over tradition. Old and medieval verse was out because it was unfunny: 'Light verse need not be funny, but what no verse can afford to be is unfunny, a proposition that disposes with amazing speed of most of the earlier material commonly proffered as light or comic by anthologists.'[33] Most contemporary poetry was also out, for reasons Larkin might be thought to approve: 'when what is presumably aspiring to be high verse abandons form, a mortal blow is dealt to light verse, to which form has always been of the essence'.[34] Light verse may be a lesser thing than high verse, but the light versifier must be a master technician. Early in the Introduction Amis makes an illuminating comparison: 'A concert pianist is allowed a wrong note here and there; a juggler is not allowed to drop a plate.'[35]

It was only after Amis had made his selection that he set about the task of defining light verse. This definition, as William H. Pritchard has suggested, neatly fits much of Amis's poetry: 'a kind of realistic verse that is close to some of the interests of the novel: men and women among their fellows, seen as members of a group or class in a way that emphasizes manners, social forms, amusements, fashion (from millinery to philosophy), topicality, even gossip, all these treated in a bright, perspicuous style'.[36] The definition is found in Amis's Introduction to the anthology, written in February 1977, in his first year at Gardnor House. Almost twice the length of Auden's Introduction, it is among Amis's finest and most considered pieces of critical writing, a product of the same care he lavished not only on the selection but on texts, notes and proofs.[37] This care paid off, as did Amis's determination to exclude what was unfunny or failed to appeal, however well known. The book received excellent reviews and sold well. On 3 July 1978, Amis wrote to Conquest to say that it was number two on the bestseller list for the third week in a row. Inevitably, though, there were complaints about omissions. Germaine Greer attacked Amis for including only a single female poet. In the 1980 'Anthologies' lecture he answered cleverly if also a trifle evasively: 'Why only one woman poet? Because I only found one.[38] Ms. Greer sadly failed to mention the names of the other sixty-two who would have supplied sexual parity and rescued me from what was presumably tokenism as well as sexism.'[39] In 1980, the year Jane would leave him, Amis was in no mood to view the discoveries of recent feminist literary scholars, including Germaine Greer, with much sympathy, though light verse in Amis's sense was precisely the genre in which women poets from past periods were most likely to flourish, because least likely to feel threatened or presumptuous. Four years later, when favourably reviewing Roger Lonsdale's *New Oxford Book of Eighteenth-Century Verse*, an anthology packed with newly discovered women poets, Amis awarded the palm to Mary Leapor: 'The daughter of a Northamptonshire gardener, dead at twenty-four, she writes here with rare skill, reason and imagination on woman in society . . . in the general manner of Pope, with whom she has no need to fear comparison.'[40]

Behind Amis's praise for the Lonsdale anthology and his championing of light verse, lies a view of poetry and its audience analagous to his view of fiction and its audience. Just as the serious novel needs to find a way to widen its appeal – to recapture the range of pleasures, including childish pleasures, offered by, say, Dickens – so high poetry needs to reconnect with or revive a once large and enthusiastic audience for verse, the audience that existed a century or so ago for what Amis calls 'public poetry'. Amis defines public poetry as the sort that had once been 'tremendously well known to people who don't think of themselves as readers of poetry at all'.[41] The examples he gives are 'Gray's *Elegy*, "Ye Mariners of England," "Lead, Kindly Light," "Horatius," "Say Not the Struggle Naught Availeth," and Kipling'.[42] While working on the fiddly last stages of the light verse anthology, the texts and notes stages, Amis embarked on a second anthology, *The Faber Popular Reciter* (described to Conquest as 'The Faber Book of Non-Trendy Verse'),[43] 'a much less anxious affair'.[44] 'No problems of unfamiliarity and discovery here,' Amis explained: 'Ninety-five per cent of the contents of the *Reciter* was in my notebook after a couple of evenings with *The Oxford Dictionary of Quotations*.' Again, what his work on the *Reciter* revealed was what everything seemed to be revealing to him in the late 1970s: that what he admired was in decline or disappearing. 'I discovered incidentally, and not surprisingly,' he reveals in the 'Anthologies' lecture, 'that the kind of popular verse in question stopped being written soon after 1914. It wasn't just that the Great War made it difficult to go on being patriotic and devout in the old way; to write a poem like "Horatius" you need confidence in your civilisation and its values, and the battle of the Somme put paid to that.'[45] The poems in the *Reciter*, we learn from its Introduction, are distinguished by 'clarity, heavy rhythms, strong rhymes . . . the vehicles of confidence, of a kind of innocence of shared faiths and other long-extinct states of mind'.[46] The values they celebrate and exemplify are the sort implicitly commended in 'A Reunion' and the other poems of the Gardnor House years: courage, community, self-respect, magnanimity and the stoical acceptance of loss.

* * *

These are the values Amis sought to draw on in the immediate aftermath of Jane's departure. Jane's decision to leave Amis had been
long pondered and was carefully planned. For some weeks, whenever Amis went out to lunch at the Garrick, she would remove suitcases of her clothes to the Camden house of her friend Ursula Vaughan
Williams, widow of the composer Ralph Vaughan Williams. It was
at Vaughan Williams's house that Jane would live after her return
from Shrublands. Jane arranged for the note announcing her decision to leave to be hand-delivered to Amis on the day she was due
back, so that he would already have had a period without her. In
addition to her solicitors, to Patricia Temple-Muir and to Ursula
Vaughan Williams, she gave advance warning of her plan to Anton
Felton, the accountant, who said 'I'm amazed you hadn't done it
before'; Mrs Uniacke, the housekeeper, who agreed to stay on and
look after Amis; Helen Benckendorf, a friend and part-time secretary for both Amis and Jane, who agreed to smuggle Rosie, Jane's
dog, out of Gardnor House ('I was afraid that if I left her Kingsley
wouldn't let me have her later');[47] Jonathan Clowes, Jane and Amis's
agent since 1976; Phil, who was living at Gardnor House at the
time, after the disintegration of his marriage; and Colin, who by
1980 was spending most of the week in Huntingdon, Cambridgeshire,
where he had a job with an electronics firm, returning to Gardnor
House on weekends only. Colin had previously been self-employed;
when he joined the Huntingdon firm he was at last eligible for a
mortgage and shortly before Jane left had begun looking for a place
of his own in London (he would find one in February 1981). Colin
remembers Jane as very worried that Amis would have a panic attack
if left alone in the house. When Colin returned to London, several
days after Jane's note had been delivered, Amis was reserved but
not hostile: 'there was no self-pity, there were no heart-to-hearts'.
Colin was worried that Amis would press him about when he had
known of Jane's decision to leave, 'rather like [her second husband]
Jim Douglas-Henry', but he didn't. Amis's appointment diary for 12
November, the day he received Jane's letter, reads: '11.30 Dr. K 12:30
Mirror then Bertis' Chr [Christopher] Ward Martin Jane off.' The
casual final note – 'Jane off' – was like the face Amis presented to
the public. Privately, to Philip, he was 'visibly shaken, it shook him
to the ground. He was absolutely petrified of being alone at that
point.' The next day, the 13th, Amis had lunch with Mavis, later
meeting with BBC people at Gardnor House. Within the week George

Gale came to see him. He also had lunch with Susie Allison, the widow of his doctor, John Allison, and part-time secretary to John Betjeman. It took him a week to face the Garrick. Phil remembers his father needing to be reassured each day: 'Will you be back this evening?' 'Yes, Dad, I'll be there.' 'Thank God. You don't know what it means to me.' Phil lost his job shortly after Jane left; it was a bad time for father and son. But it was also an important time in relations between them. As Phil puts it: 'I was just grateful that he needed me. I thought, at last I'm useful to him in some sort of way, and we got very close and then I was the one who did the supporting.' 'Your godson is providentially around,' Amis wrote to Larkin on 5 December, 'having left his intolerable wife and been sacked from his job. I think he's the nicest fellow I've ever met.'

Phil called Martin as soon as Amis received Jane's letter. In Martin's reconstruction of the call Phil said 'It's happened' and Martin knew right away what he meant: 'that was just the way the whole thing was *tending*'.[48] The ensuing discussion between the brothers concerned immediate arrangements:

It wasn't a question of two sons planning to console a father who had lost a wife. It was much more elementary. One or other of us had to be there all the time. Not round the clock but every evening, every night, every morning. He still had his housekeeper there, loyal Mrs. Uniacke, and her presence would help him get through the day; but only family or thoroughly trusted friends were any good to him through the hours of darkness . . .

My memory of that night has Kingsley perched on the brink of the low armchair (this was his characteristic back-favouring posture: in Philip's imitation of it, he is attached to his seat by about a millimetre of outer coccyx), blinking more rapidly than usual, and fiercely worrying his thumb cuticles with the nails of his forefingers. And saying almost nothing. He would answer questions about the logistical end of it (Jane's failure to return from the health farm; the note delivered by her solicitor's office) but nothing was ventured about his feelings, about love, about broken hearts, broken vows. His needs at that moment seemed basic, almost animal: shelter, warmth, the heat of known beasts. My brother and I repeated what was most immediately necessary for him to hear:

 —Dad, you won't spend a night alone. One of us will always be here.
 —Thank you both for that.[49]

Now began the days of serious Dadsitting, a practice that had begun a year or so earlier, when Jane was 'constantly' out with what Amis called 'her GROUPS and WORKSHOPS and crappy "new friends"'.[50] Among Martin's friends, James Fenton, Julian Barnes, newly married to Pat Kavanagh, and Christopher Hitchens were enlisted to help. Though Hitchens would soon be off to live in the United States, he figures on several occasions in Amis's diary in the month immediately following the break-up and more frequently in entries for previous months. Hitchens describes a typical Dadsitting evening as 'like an absolute blue-collar fiesta'. When they didn't take Amis out to the movies, Martin and friends would arrive with clinking bags of booze and bulging sacks of curry; videos would be lined up; there'd be much drinking, 'talking piss', and watching films or junk televison. Sometimes Fenton would come over by himself and he and Amis would discuss poetry. Richard and Joy Law also looked out for Amis at this time. In the first three months after Jane left, according to Richard Law, Amis 'was a constant visitor for lunch and dinner, especially on weekends'. In that initial period, Law remembers, 'I never heard Kingsley utter a single criticism of Jane.'

Amis, in Martin's phrase, was 'heartsick: romantically mortified' by Jane's departure. On the night of 12 November, 'he was writing to her and about her in his head – a pleading letter, and also a poem',[51] though only the letter was finished (Conquest remembers Amis saying he'd written 'two or three' heart-broken poems about Jane, but none survives). In addition to the fear of being left alone and the humiliation of being left, Amis was overcome by a sense of waste, one Martin connects with 'Wasted', a poem published by the Poem of the Month Club in August 1973, a time of seeming contentment:

> That cold winter evening
> The fire would not draw,
> And the whole family hung
> Over the dismal grate
> Where rain-soaked logs
> Bubbled, hissed and steamed.
> Then, when the others had gone
> Up to their chilly beds,
> And I was ready to go,
> The wood began to flame

> In clear rose and violet,
> Heating the small hearth.
>
> Why should that memory cling
> Now the children are all grown up,
> And the house – a different house –
> Is warm at any season.

Martin's reading of 'Wasted' is biographical: 'What is, what has been "wasted"? Not just the surge of warmth from the fire, clearly enough. "A different house": there is something dismissive, something warding-off in the dashes that gird these three words. The poem is about the recurrent grief, endemic to the male divorcee – grief for the lost family. More than that, though, the sadness here is defeatist. It is saying that it wasn't worth it. The aggregate of familial pain, of familial disconnection: *that* is what has been wasted.'[52] With Jane gone, this feeling redoubled. On 24 June 1981 Amis wrote to Larkin about meeting an old friend at a party: 'She said how miserable I had made Hilly, thus (unnecessarily) reminding me that Jane's departure has stopped me pretending to myself that my treatment of H was at least sort of worth while somehow a bit.'

'Wasted' was published with another poem by Amis, 'Kipling at Bateman's'. This poem grew out of a visit to Kipling's house in Burwash, Sussex, where Amis's father had lived briefly in the 1960s. Amis and a BBC television crew went there to make a short film in a series of films about writers and their houses. Bateman's made a strong negative impression on the whole crew and Amis decided that he would dislike spending even twenty-four hours there. The visit is recounted in *Rudyard Kipling and His World* (1975), a short study of Kipling's life and writings. Amis's view of Kipling's career is like his view of Chesterton's: the writing that mattered was early, in Kipling's case from the period 1885–1902. After 1902, the year of the move to Bateman's, not only did the work decline but Kipling found himself increasingly at odds with the world, changes Amis attributes in part to the depressing atmosphere of the house. Here is the poem:

> He came here when he was thirty-seven
> And left, feet first, thirty-four years later.
> She organised his life, dealt with all his

Correspondence, set out his engagements,
Filtered his visitors, so that nothing
Could ever come between him and his work.

There's a portrait of her in the study:
Not bad, by Philip Burne-Jones, his cousin;
Less than full length, cut off near the ankles,
Supposedly to conceal her smallness;
Her look one of calm or satisfaction,
And, hanging from her waist, some sort of key.

Two years after the publication of 'Kipling at Bateman's' Amis told Jane that he wanted to leave Lemmons and move back to London. Jane was unlike Caroline Kipling in any number of ways, starting with the fact that she was tall, but Amis may have begun to see her as similarly controlling, in part because he felt imprisoned or cut off in Barnet. According to Jane, it was at Lemmons that Amis began turning her into his mother, a restricting figure on whom he depended, and whom he therefore resented. For some months after Jane's departure Amis tried to persuade her to return; when he gave up, in early 1981, she became increasingly monstrous in his eyes, in ways that recall the final lines of 'Kipling at Bateman's'. Eventually the process of what Martin calls 'unpersoning' or 'unloving' Jane produced the monstrous wives of *Stanley and the Women*.

The letters Amis and Jane wrote to each other in the weeks after Jane left have not survived. Martin remembers them as 'a fruitless exchange of conditions and ultimatums'.[53] The day Jane returned to London, Amis sent her a letter: 'It said that although life with me hadn't been much fun, it would be worse without me, and if I'd return he would try to drink less and be a better husband. I was tempted, but I knew from perceived experience that people who drink as much as he did can't cut it down for more than a week or two: they then simply revert.'[54] Jane's all-or-nothing terms were described by Amis in a letter to Larkin of 14 January 1981. 'Glad to hear you're not entirely off the drink for ever. Looks as if I shall be just that before long. Jane mentions that as her first condition for coming back to me, the second being presumably that I saw off my head and serve it up to her with a little hollandaise sauce.' Jane's demand that Amis give up drink entirely made him, as Phil puts it, 'absolutely furious', in part because it was presented as an ultimatum. 'He would never stop drinking,' Phil explains, imagining his father's reaction as childishly defiant: 'He was Kingsley Amis and he could drink whenever he wanted to because he bought it with his money, because he was Kingsley Amis and he was so famous.' In the letter of 5 December, Amis explained to Larkin why he thought Jane had left him and why, despite her faults, he wanted her back:

She did it partly to punish me for stopping wanting to fuck her and partly because she realised I didn't like her much. Well, I liked her as much as you could like anyone totally wrapped up in themselves and unable to tolerate the slightest competition or anything a raving lunatic could see as opposition and having to have their own way in everything all the time. Well, I expect reading between the lines there you can sense that we hadn't been getting on too well of late. Yeah, but not having her around and trying to take in the fact that she never will be around is immeasurably more crappy than having her around. I've had a wife for 32 years.

Larkin first heard of Jane's leaving Amis in a letter of 1 December 1980 from Conquest, who had gone through an acrimonious split with his own wife, Caroleen, in 1975. 'Naturally I was able to say "when I was your age," and how he'd get over it and have a nice young woman. But I figure he was far more settled than I was . . . Poor sod, wish there was anything one could do – we offered refuge here[55] but he doesn't want to – Also would risk returning to find his house carried by a coup de main . . . One sure thing is that the scarcely noticeable restraint in his prose works when being hard on womanhood will now be removed – we should look forward to something on the lines of one of the more misogynist Early Fathers.' This letter was perceptive in several respects: not only in its predictions about the character of Amis's next novel and the likelihood of disputes over property, but in its sense of how dependent he was on his marriage. As Amis admitted to Brian Aldiss on 15 December: 'By God she was hard to live with but living without her seems absolutely pointless. I had no idea she meant so much to me.'

It was at or around this moment that Amis probably wrote his bleakest poem. Undated, untitled, unpublished and, perhaps, unfinished, it was deposited in 1987 in the Huntington Library, which purchased Amis's papers in 1984. The poem lay unnoticed until early 2004, when I published it in the *TLS*. It is Amis's *ne plus ultra*:

> Things tell less and less:
> The news impersonal
> And from afar; no book
> Worth wrenching off the shelf.
> Liquor brings dizziness
> And food discomfort; all
> Music sounds thin and tired,
> And what picture could earn a look?
> The self drowses in the self
> Beyond hope of a visitor.
> Desire and those desired
> Fade, and no matter:
> Memories in decay
> Annihilate the day.
>
> There once was an answer:
> Up at the stroke of seven,
> A turn round the garden
> (Breathing deep and slow),
> Then work, never mind what,
> How small, provided that
> It serves another's good.
>
> But once is long ago
> And, tell me, how could
> Such an answer be less than wrong,
> Be right all along?
>
> Vain echoes, desist

When these lines were published in the *TLS* on 14 May 2004, I suggested that they were written in the late 1970s or early 1980s. Two weeks later Christopher Hitchens wrote to the paper to support the dating, citing a passage from *Jake's Thing* (1978): 'In that moment he saw the world in its true light, as a place where nothing had ever been any good and nothing of significance done: no art worth a second look, no philosophy of the slightest appositeness, no law but served the state, no history that gave an inkling of how it had been and what had happened. And no love, only egotism, infatuation and lust.' To this passage I would add a passage from a Larkin letter to Amis of 31 July 1983: 'Have reached the point where *all* my records are too boring to take *down* even . . . I get progressively gloomy – if I could write poems I'd write a few gloomy ones, not the cheerful stuff I've done up to now.' An earlier and more general influence may have been Larkin's 'Aubade', published in the *TLS* on 23 December 1977. As for whether the poem is finished, Jonathan Clowes thinks not: Amis always showed him finished poems and never showed him these lines, nor does he recall being sent an Amis poem without a title (Robert Conquest also remembers Amis as 'a great titles man'). Nowhere in Amis's correspondence is the poem mentioned, nor was it seen by Conquest, Martin Amis or Jane Howard before 2004. It resembles the *New Statesman* poems of the Gardnor House years in its darkness and disillusion, but differs from them in its extremity, the unadorned quality of its distress, beyond humour or swank. Amis may have left it unfinished and withheld it from publication for personal rather than aesthetic reasons, thinking it too confessional to appear while he was alive or even to have been circulated among friends. Powerful even when least finished (as in the absence of punctuation at its close) it also benefited from revision: 'tell' in the first line, with its double sense of 'count' and 'explain', is one of several improvements from earlier partial drafts.

As negotiations between Amis and Jane faltered and positions hardened, Philip, who bore the main burden of looking after his father, began to seek a more permanent solution to the question of who should take care of him. The alternatives he and Martin faced are laid out in *Experience*: 'Either he [Amis] had to go somewhere (club, set of rooms, hotel?) or someone had to come to him. Whoever came to him would have to be . . . How to define it? It would have to be someone who understood, and so forgave, his frailty. And it would have to be someone he liked very much indeed. I was thirty-one, Philip thirty-two: a bit early, we felt, to commit our lives to Dadsitting – but we couldn't rule it out.'[56] Amis himself was at a loss. On 9 March 1981 he wrote to Conquest thanking him again for the invitation to come to Washington, though again declining (on the grounds of a 'deep-seated and incurable' phobia about flying). 'Where the hell am I going to get the sort of companion/housekeeper

I need?'[57] It was Philip who came up with the answer: in the village of Thornburgh in Buckinghamshire, in a tiny three-room cottage ('two up and one-and-a-half down')[58] bequeathed in 1978 to the seventh Baron Kilmarnock, Chief of Clan Boyd, by his nanny. The seventh Baron Kilmarnock was Alastair Boyd, who inherited the title in 1975, making Hilly, who married him two years later, Lady Kilmarnock. Ali and Hilly had wanted to marry as early as 1971 but Shackleton Bailey had refused to grant Hilly a divorce. On 27 January 1972 Hilly had given birth to Ali's son, Jaime, also called James. Because of Shackleton Bailey's intransigence ('vindictiveness,' in Hilly's eyes), Jaime was born out of wedlock and thus barred from inheriting his father's title. A year later, a second son, Romulus, was born who died within hours of birth.

In the Gardnor House years, as Amis's marriage deteriorated, his finances prospered, aided in part by the shrewd dealings of his agent, Jonathan Clowes. In the same period, Hilly's situation was exactly the reverse: her relationship with Ali was stable, their finances insecure. In Ali she met a man who was charming, considerate and had perfect manners ('I wasn't used to that,' she says, with Shackleton Bailey as well as Amis in mind). What Ali didn't have was money or, it seemed, much of a knack for making any. The expansion of the language school to Seville in 1970 had not worked out and after he and Hilly returned to Ronda, in 1971, they took in paying guests and ran art classes to make ends meet. Then they opened a bar in the cavernous garage and stable area of their house.[59] The bar was a success, quickly becoming a popular hangout for Rondenos as well as tourists. In his memoir, *Sierras of the South: Travels in the Mountains of Andalusia* (1992), Ali writes of the large quantities of Hilly's *sangria* and delicious *tapas* consumed there, the latter 'advertised on an old school blackboard and sent down in little oval saucers from the kitchen above'.[60] After a while, however, the bar began to attract local rowdies, there was an incident with a female language student, and in a fit of zeal the city's chief of police, a Franco supporter, closed it down, deaf to appeals. Partly to make money and partly because Hilly had always wanted to live in the country, she and Ali then decided to sell their house in Ronda – a substantial town house, subsequently the home of one of the city's mayors – and move to the countryside or *campo*, a twenty-minute drive away. Here, in the plains below Ronda, Hilly could keep animals and Jaime could grow up in rural freedom.

Ali's title came without property or income.[61] Though as Baron Kilmarnock his line stretched back only to 1831, the Boyd clan, of which he became head in 1975, can be traced to the thirteenth century. Ali started out in the City, a career for which he soon realised he 'displayed a singular lack of talent'.[62] In 1957 he and his first wife, Diana, moved to Ronda, where he lived for the next twenty years. When he inherited his title, he felt that he ought to return to England 'to get my feet into that pond'. He had a number of friends and contacts in London, among them Amis's friend Simon Raven, and could count on their hospitality. Bringing the family with him while he scouted out prospects, however, would be difficult. Until he found a place 'where we felt we could jointly live in the UK', Hilly and Jaime would stay behind in Spain. These were hard times for Hilly. Their house in the *campo* had beautiful vistas but was small and primitive, difficult of access, and on a polluted river. Hilly felt cut off from her friends in Ronda. It would be two years before she and Jaime could join Ali, who was only able to return for visits twice a year, at Easter and Christmas. The two winters Ali was away were exceptionally harsh, the river flooded and the dirt track to the house was difficult to manoeuvre. During this period Jaime often spent weekends with the family of Ali's long-time housekeeper, Ana, whom he describes as cook, maid, nanny and 'second mother'. Jaime's first language was Spanish, which Ali spoke fluently but Hilly hardly at all, though as Hilly puts it, 'we read each other pretty well; I knew what he wanted all right.'

In London Ali took up his seat in the House of Lords and attended regularly. From 1976 to 1981 he sat on the cross-benches, though when the Social Democratic Party was founded in 1981 he realised that 'this was more or less my bit of the [political] spectrum'. By 1977 he had still not found employment that would enable him to buy or rent somewhere for the family to live, but Hilly and Jaime came over anyway. The reunited family stayed at friends' houses 'in exchange for looking after their kids while they went off somewhere'.[63] When Ali inherited the Buckinghamshire cottage in 1978 they decided to move in, despite its distance from London. In order to sit in the Lords and collect his stipend, Ali would have to board with friends during the week, an inconvenience Hilly was prepared to put up with in exchange for a bit of privacy and independence. Soon, however, she felt as isolated in Thornburgh as she had in the *campo*: she knew no one in the village, the car broke down, money was scarce and six-year-old Jaime was unhappy (before he learned English and made friends at school). Hilly found small jobs at Jaime's school and was briefly employed as 'a semi-manageress of quite a posh tea-rooms' in Winslow, the nearest town. She also made a friend in the village, Marie Greenall, with whom she decided to set up in business: running a hot-dog van on a motorway lay-by. 'Lugging butanes was the plague of my life,' she recalls. 'It was also quite frightening, on those lay-bys, you know, with weird drivers coming along.' In Ann Arbor, Hilly and a friend had opened a fish and chips shop called Lucky Jim's; in Ronda there was the *tapas* bar; the hot-dog van was in the same line, though as Hilly puts it, 'you couldn't have called it a career'.

Running the van proved difficult and dangerous and Hilly and her partner soon packed it in. It was at this point that Hilly received a call from Phil. She was desperate: 'I was more and more marooned again and there was only one bus a day into the very charming town of Buckingham. I felt thoroughly hemmed in . . . I missed the sun. It was freezing, always raining. We couldn't do anything. We had no money.' After chatting a bit, Phil asked: 'How about looking after Dad?' to which Hilly's immediate reply, as she recalls it today, was 'Oh, God.' Though she had only weeks before bought a copy of *The Lady* in search of 'jobs that offered a bungalow or something in exchange for looking after a couple of old people', she did not at first take Phil's proposal seriously. Later, when she talked to Ali about it, she began to recognise its advantages, chiefly that it would enable the family to live together in London, that they wouldn't have to pay for an ad or answer one or be interviewed by strangers. Then Phil called a second time, 'mentioning the magic word of £50 a week. I was lucky if I made £20 a week normally. Fifty pounds! And our keep and board. I thought, bloody marvellous.' She decided to tell Phil that they were interested.

A weekend was fixed for Hilly, Ali and Jaime to come up to London and stay at Gardnor House. This was not the first contact Hilly and Ali had had with Amis since their return from Spain; they had met Amis and Jane to discuss Sally's future, though the meeting had taken place at a friend's house. Sally had decided that she wanted to become an actor and the meeting was about whether Amis should pay for her to go to drama school. The two couples went off to a bedroom to discuss the idea. Jane thought it absurd. As Hilly recalls, she said: 'She can't even walk properly.' Hilly took a different view: 'In fact, I think it would have been rather good for her. She would have been a comic actress, not a big, glamorous actress. She was good at all that sort of thing' (though Hilly also admits that 'she wouldn't probably have stuck it'). The meeting ended amicably, 'but I was left with the job of telling Sally she couldn't go to drama school unless she fixed it up herself'.

The Gardnor House weekend began with a dinner which included Martin and Phil. All went swimmingly – as Martin puts it, 'my brother and I were exchanging complacent smiles. Everyone present was coming across as a model of flexibility and discretion'[64] – until dessert:

When the dessert course began, Jaime, eight years old and unimprovable throughout, reached for the fruitbowl. It contained oranges, apples, grapes – and a single peach. As Jaime's fingers met its surface, Kingsley, like a man hailing a cab across the length of Oxford Circus during a downpour on Christmas Eve, shouted:

—*HEY!!!*

. . . It was an extraordinary manifestation, hideously harsh, hideously sudden. The sound Kingsley had uttered would have been just about appropriate if Jaime had reached, not for a peach, but for the pin of a hand grenade. There was no silence: everyone reeled back, groaning, swearing. Even Jaime whispered 'Jesus Christ' as he shrivelled up in his chair. I can't remember – I can't even imagine – how we survived the rest of the evening.[65]

As Hilly remembers it, as soon as Amis shouted about the peach, 'Jaime dropped it like a burning coal. He was terrified and I thought, well, I have to leave; I can't have James jumping out of his skin every ten minutes. I always made bloody sure I had my own fruit bowl in the bedroom after that.' The adult Jaime remembers the scene clearly: 'The second I picked up the peach I heard this incredible: "That's *my* peach," which totally freaked me out. It's the last thing you expect. I'd never been in a situation where picking up a peach was so drastic.' Philip explains Amis's behaviour as a sign of how needy and vulnerable he was at this time: 'Kingsley was jealous of Jaime because Hilly was very protective of him and so was Ali. And he was having more attention paid to him than Kingsley was.' Martin offers a similar explanation when he asks: 'If you're a grown man who is frightened of the dark – what happens when someone leaves you? . . . It is rudimentary, it is zero-rudimentary. Part of you becomes a child that wants its mother.'[66]

Somehow the episode was smoothed over and, eventually, Amis himself, as Jaime remembers it, took to telling the story of the peach.[67] The trial weekend was on 24–27 July 1981 and a month later Hilly, Ali and Jaime moved in to Gardnor House. Ali's view of the arrangement was that he was willing to give it a try. Hilly had made it clear to Amis that she 'was an employee. I was always very firm about that. I'm not your wife again, or anything like that, I'm employed here to look after you', though she also realised that it would be 'a far closer looking after than most people would have tolerated'. Amis told Larkin about the arrangement in a letter of 27 August: 'my morale is much improved, in fact today I felt *all right* for about 20 mins, because I've found, and yesterday installed here, the couple who'll look after me. They are Hilly and her 3rd husband, Lord Kilmarnock. Nay, stare not so. Well, you'd be justified in staring a bit, but it was their suggestion, the boys are much in favour, it's the only way for me to have a bit of family, all that. Anyhow, the day this was decided on I started a new novel, and the day they came, yesterday as I said, I got the plot of same sorted out. They have a little boy of 9. Yes, but he's very nice. No, but there it is. Oh well.' That the arrangement would be harder on Hilly and Ali than on Amis, he fully acknowledged. 'It did take great courage – on her part more than on mine,' he recalled in a 1989 interview.[68] What Amis hoped for – and felt he had found, according to the interview – 'was someone to share things with. Now I can say to Hilly: "Guess who was at the club today?" or "Do you know that Denise has gone off with Roger after all." And she'll understand . . . Hilly is not a third wife for me or a companion but someone whom I was with for 17 years, with a lot of shared experience.' In 1981, however, it was by no means clear that the arrangement would succeed. As Martin puts it in *Experience*, 'Philip and I thought it might work for a good six months, maybe even a year';[69] Ali and Hilly also had their doubts, which is why, despite their need for money, they kept the Buckinghamshire cottage, as they'd kept the place in Spain.

Gardnor House had been put on the market in February, the month Jane filed for divorce on the grounds of 'unreasonable behaviour' (as Amis put it to Anthony Powell, in a letter of 12 February 1981, 'things like trying to stop her getting away with murder and bestial stuff like that'). On 6 June, after 'droves' of prospective buyers trooped through the house, at what Amis described to Larkin as 'enormous length or for insultingly short periods, standing outside my study talking loudly in Arabic etc.',[70] an offer was made and accepted, at a price of £265,000. Nothing was then heard from the prospective buyers for weeks: 'their surveyors have come and gone and a great silence reigns,' Amis wrote to Larkin in the letter of 27 August. 'I think they've found some terrible defect that'll cost £249,999 to put right, and are about to offer me the odd £5 for the place . . . That will make ole Jane jolly sick, means she won't be able to afford her delightful little William and Mary house with its tiny unexpected patch of vivid green.'

In addition to delays there were wranglings over money. On 30 July Conquest wrote to Larkin to say that Amis was 'v pissed off with Jane's financial manoeuvres'. On 20 October Amis wrote to Brian Aldiss about the continued delay in the sale of the house, a product of the surveyors' findings: 'The delay is reported to have greatly incensed Jane, who is putting it about that I am selfishly luxuriating here and putting the price up to deter all possible buyers.' On 4 November Conquest reported to Larkin that Jane was infuriated by the idea of Hilly living in 'her' house. Later that month Jane gave an interview to the *Evening Standard* laying out her complaints about life with Amis, in particular her conviction that looking after his children and running the house had stopped her from writing. In December she gave a second interview to the *Sunday Express*, making similar complaints. Conquest's reaction to the two interviews, in a letter to Larkin of 27 January 1982, was to imagine what Jane's next novel would be like: 'perhaps we'll figure in it too, as minor villains. "Never has Miss Howard's touch been so sure as with Rex's revolting coterie of friends with their intellectual pretensions and drunken coarseness of speech and action. Larry Perkins and Robin Langouste in particular . . ."'

The wrangling over money centred on Jane's initial purchase of 108 Maida Vale. 'Jane is trying to see that I get *much less than half* of the money for the sale of G Ho,' Amis wrote to Larkin in late December 1981.[71] 'She wants the cash back she got from the sale of her flat in 1964 which she put into the house we had in Maida Vale, or rather she wants the 1981 equivalent of that sum. Odd woman.' This equivalent, Amis told Conquest in a letter of

21 December, amounted to £40,000. In her memoir Jane says, 'I'd been advised to ask for my half of the house plus the original fourteen thousand pounds with which I'd bought Maida Vale. It was suggested I should claim the interest on it, but this seemed wrong to me. Kingsley's lawyers refused at first to believe that I'd bought the house, and Anton had to produce the papers to prove that I had.'[72] When Jane later disputed Amis's £40,000 figure (it appeared in the Jacobs biography), Amis did not defend it, complaining instead, in Jacobs's paraphrase, that she 'took all the suitcases so that when he needed one to go away he had to borrow it from Mrs. Uniacke'.

While the lawyers argued over who was owed what, Amis and the Kilmarnocks moved into a temporary flat at 25C Gayton Road, just around the corner from and within sight of Gardnor House. The flat was temporary because Amis had made an offer on a small house in Kentish Town, at 186 Leighton Road, NW5, into which he and the Kilmarnocks were due to move on 8 January 1982. Amis worried that the delay in sorting out the money from Gardnor House might lose him the house in Kentish Town. Jane was also upset about the delay. She had found Amis's initial inactivity – the length of time it took him to sell Gardnor House and to find somewhere else to live – infuriating; without her share of the money from its sale she could not buy a place of her own.[73]

The house Amis bought at 186 Leighton Road was comfortable but small. Conquest described it as 'a bit cramped after Hampstead and Barnet';[74] to Phil it was 'like going back to his [Amis's] parents' house'; to Michael Davie, a visiting journalist, it was 'in no sense grand', in a 'nondescript' neighbourhood.[75] Amis's quarters were on the top floor and consisted of a bedsitting-room and a fair-sized study. In neither room was there space for a wardrobe so he hung his clothes behind the study door. The Kilmarnocks were quartered on the floor below and everybody shared a bathroom on the landing and a basement kitchen, an arrangement not without awkwardness. Initially, Amis thought the house 'just right for us', a view he would soon revise.[76] As for the neighbourhood, in a letter to Larkin of 15 February he described it as 'not a bad area, no violent thick blacks to speak of' (there are several such comments in his and Larkin's late correspondence); the pubs, however, all played music and the local shopping centre had neither China tea nor any malt whisky but Glenfiddich.

When the sale of Gardnor House finally went through, Jane began removing furniture and possessions. Amis had moved into Jane's Blomfield Road flat in September 1963 with nothing but his clothes and some books. Everything in 108 Maida Vale was either already Jane's or purchased by Jane with money from the sale of the flat. Subsequent furniture, fittings, paintings and decorative objects – for Maida Vale, for Lemmons, for Gardnor House – were, however, purchased from a joint bank account, one Amis was right to regard as containing mostly his money. Jane explains: 'As Kingsley and I became better off, I suggested to him that all our earnings should go into a joint account and that from it we should each have £1,500 in separate accounts to spend exactly as we individually pleased, on clothes or presents. This meant that the mortgage, the house bills, the money for the boys, the car and holidays were paid for from the main account, and I had some idea of what we could afford. By the time I left, Kingsley was earning about eighty thousand a year and I was earning between three and four thousand.'[77] Some of the household goods and furnishings Jane purchased from the time this arrangement was made may have come from her separate £1,500 account, though most would have come from the joint account, as did purchases made before the arrangement. Everything in the house, regardless of who paid for it, would have been picked out by Jane. To Amis, Phil and Hilly it looked as if Jane was taking it all. As Phil puts it: 'Jane came back and took all the best furniture. I remember her taking everything, quickly grabbing everything she could. I got this sense that you're just taking my Dad to the cleaners. That's all my father's money. My poor Dad.' Amis's account, in a letter to Conquest of 21 December, was only marginally less aggrieved: 'When she came to the house in my pre-arranged absence for her to collect her "share" of the contents she rifled the place, taking all the best crockery, glassware, etc., including the remains of a case of decent claret a club-mate had given me for doing him a favour.' Accusations like these are obviously one-sided (and hotly denied not only by Jane, who points out that if she was after money she would have asked for and received alimony, but by Colin), hardly unusual in cases of divorce and rehearsed here only because they help to explain the venom of *Stanley and the Women*, the novel Amis had just at this moment embarked on, or re-embarked on.[78] The venom was shared by Hilly. Theo Richmond remembers 'the joint fury projected at Jane during the acrimony after she and Kingsley finally parted company'.[79] Hilly's 'bitterness and rage' derived not only from the fact that she thought of Jane as having broken up her family, but from what she thought of Jane's behaviour subsequently. In Hilly's view, as Richmond remembers it, Jane had behaved 'unnecessarily badly'.

Amis began work on *Stanley and the Women* in August 1981, a month or so after abandoning 'Difficulties with Girls'. The decision to abandon 'Difficulties', after almost a year's writing, was unique in his career and deserves a moment's attention. 'Usually my novels obey the course that I set them,' he explained in a 1984 interview. 'I may change my mind a bit as I go, but not much. This time the whole plan got entirely out of hand and I wasn't going to finish the thing.'[80] Amis explained the novel's 'plan' in a letter to Conquest of 14 October 1980, beginning with the decision to have a homosexual protagonist: 'I can say lots of crappy things about women (and men) *as well as* about queers. If anything on these lines occurs to you, let me have it. The point is that the queer is narrator, so he can just muse to himself from time to time.' As Amis subsequently explained in a letter of 17 December 1982 to Larkin, the narrator's musings were meant only in part to be about gays and gayness; their more direct focus was marriage and the behaviour of women. 'The Lie [*Private Eye*] got it wrong as always. I did 130 pp v. slowly and unenjoyably, then shelved it. Thing was, it was supposed to be going to be an account of a couple of marriages, i.e. the hetero world, seen by a 1st-person queer – for distancing, unexpectedness etc., plus him being talked in front of and confided in in a way not open to a hetero. But it turned out, as you'd expect from a queer, to be all about him and being queer, which doesn't sort of appeal to me enough. And of course since only about 17 people in the country know what a novel is, the rest will think I must be one of the boys myself.'

The queer protagonist is a twenty-year-old student of French at a university in an industrial town north of Manchester, 'a society implacably hostile to homosexuality'.[81] His name is Robert and pretty much all we learn of his past is that he comes from Scotland, where his father runs a garage. Robert knows a lot about flowers and gardens, has impeccable taste, and is living for the summer with Adrian and Ann Marriott, for whom he drives and does informal babysitting in exchange for room and board (ten-year-old Jason, Adrian's son from his first marriage, is the child he sits for). The novel is set in the early 1960s and Amis's notes for it list period details ('Daily Herald still, Macmillan, no miniskirts yet, "Smoking and Health" Royal Coll of Physians').[82] Adrian's younger brother Reggie, 'a fashionable (well-known) writer',[83] and his wife Paula, have come from London to visit, on their way to Scotland. With them is Tom Vaccarro, twenty-two, an American student of the sort Amis attracted to England after his year in Princeton. Unlike Amis's Princeton students, however, Tom is exceptionally naïve, not only about British customs and habits but about his sexuality: he thinks he's gay, though Robert knows he isn't. Amis seems to have meant the plot's main strands to involve Adrian, a cross between George Gale and Amis himself (he is described as 'bulky, short-legged',[84] 'devoted to pubs, almost dependent on them'),[85] who is having an affair with Paula, and Adrian's monstrous wife, Ann, who succeeds in seducing Robert and will, eventually, as Amis told Jacobs,[86] accuse Robert of molesting Jason, out of spite. 'Her great thing is cracking her bloody whip and watching you jump,' Adrian tells Robert, 'bending people to her will, especially men . . . De-queering you is just the sort of pissy challenge she'd find irresistible.' According to Jacobs (presumably repeating what he'd heard from Amis), Adrian, 'for reasons of marital harmony',[87] was meant to end up supporting Ann's accusations, though he knew they were untrue. In the 130 pages Amis completed, these plot strands are only hinted at. What we get instead are many passages about Robert and what it is like to be gay in Britain in the years before homosexuality was decriminalised (with the 1967 Sexual Offences Act), also about Tom, a tediously obtuse and implausible figure who will emerge in altered form, though no less obtuse and implausible, as Tim Valentine in the published *Difficulties with Girls*. Tim, too, thinks he's gay when he isn't, a conclusion he, like Tom, has been led to by a shrink.[88] The unpublished 'Difficulties' also contains a malicious gay classics don and several older male suitors of Robert, one a hopeless schoolteacher named Bill Carpenter.

Amis's interest in men who are uncertain about their sexuality may have been sparked by Colin Howard. In an interview in 1988 Amis said of Tim Valentine that he 'knew somebody like that. "After all I must be something,' he used to say. "I can't be nothing,"' a sentiment that recalls not only Tom in 'Difficulties', but Geoffrey, the Colin-like character in *Jake's Thing*.[89] For the most part, certainly before the Gardnor House years, Amis was unprejudiced in his attitude to Colin's sexual ambivalence or reticence, encouraging him, as he'd encouraged Larkin, to be bolder in pursuit of pleasure, to seek out partners (in Colin's case, in gay pubs and clubs). But he was hardly without intolerant moments, especially in the later years of his life. Martin remembers an episode at Lemmons almost as harsh, sudden and envy-inspired as the peach episode at Gardnor House. Philip was having a party in town and Colin and Martin were loading the car with booze. Amis came out of the house and asked where they were going. When told about Philip's party he asked why he hadn't been invited, all the time worrying his thumb cuticles with the nails of his forefingers. Colin was embarrassed and mumbled something about 'probably having more in common with the people there than you have'. 'You mean they're all *queers*, do you?' Amis answered, in a fury.[90] There is little of this sort of animus in either the abandoned 'Difficulties with Girls' or the quite different published novel, but both give Amis scope for wounding generalisations. Amis believed that deceit, disguise and dissimulation were inevitable byproducts of the laws against homosexuality still in operation in Britain in the early 1960s. Hence Robert's description of Tom's truthfulness as 'a serious disqualification for the mode of life he had recently chosen to embrace'[91] (a remark that recalls Amis on the 'queer' origins of Auden's and James Fenton's poetical obscurity, their sense that 'you must never give yourself away about anything').[92] There are also hurtful comparisons of women and gays, as in their shared propensity to treat all topics of conversation as occasions for self-projection. 'It's like talking to one of them [i.e., a woman],' Adrian complains of Robert's way of arguing: 'they think you're getting at them for something, so they go on saying the opposite of what they think you're saying until it's time to go home.'[93] When Tom claims that he doesn't like women because they talk about themselves all the time, something he doesn't do, Robert agrees, both about women and about Tom, thus confirming his sense that Tom is straight. These 'insights' serve only to underline the most noteworthy feature of Amis's treatment of gay life in the abandoned 'Difficulties': how thinly textured it is, as thinly textured as the life of the native English in *Russian Hide-and-Seek*. Amis worried that readers would wonder how he knew so much about gay life; in fact, as he admitted to Dale Salwak in 1982, a year after giving the novel up, he 'knew too little' about it.

During the period between Jane's leaving and the abandonment of 'Difficulties', Amis reached a low point. As he told an interviewer in 1986, 'I was a tiny bit mad. For the first time in my life I had no sense of direction and I felt very lonely and frightened.'[94] This was the time when Martin feared his father 'might be finished' as a writer. In addition to his problems with fiction – not just the abandoning of 'Difficulties' but the weakness of *Russian Hide-and-Seek*[95] – Amis seemed to have dried up as a poet. For almost six years, from November 1978 to April 1984, he published no verse at all. As 1982 and the first half of 1983 passed, still without a new novel, worried queries began appearing in Robert Conquest's letters. 'How are you doing on SAY YOU LORDS?' he asked on 25 July 1983 (*Stanley* did not yet have its title). 'How's *A Ministering Angel Thou*, or whatever your new book is called, coming along?' he asked on 8 August. Two weeks later, on the 22nd, he again voiced friendly concern: 'And how is your own book getting on? – A chap was writing somewhere that writer's block was a good thing, stopping you writing piss.' 'How's your roman going?' he asked in a letter of 9 November.[96]

Now Amis got seriously fat. 'When your personal life takes a down turn, you resort to comfort eating,' he explained in a 1995 interview. 'Chocolate biscuits, cake. It began when Jane left me. Carbohydrates evidently have a tranquillising effect. People who are depressed like curling up with a bar of chocolate.'[97] In a letter of 11 November 1982, Amis told Larkin that he was 'enormously fat, but feel slimmer as a result of buying trousers MEASURING FORTY TWO INCHES ROUND THE WAIST instead of wearing my old 38"s I think about an inch and a half above my cock. Too scared to weigh myself.' Larkin wrote back ten days later with reassuring news: 'forty-two inches is nothing. I'm forty-six.' By November 1982 other factors aside from fear and depression were contributing to Amis's weight gain. On 10 March 1982, he stumbled coming out of the bathroom at Leighton Road, braced himself awkwardly to avoid a fall, and broke his leg standing up. The stumble occurred at night, under the combined influence of a day's drinking and a sleeping-pill, and resulted in an operation followed by three weeks' recuperation in the Royal Free Hospital in Hampstead. After hospital,

Amis spent nine weeks immobile in Leighton Road, a difficult period for Hilly, especially as he had been ordered by his doctors to cut out drinking completely until the leg healed. Amis managed to abstain from alcohol for almost six months, without much trouble, he claimed. It was his first extended period of sobriety in something like forty years.[98] The only withdrawal symptoms he seems to have suffered were mild hallucinations in the first ten days ('just a few voices and non-existent cats,' he told Conquest), which may have been a reaction to the anaesthetic. An account of these hallucinations, entitled 'A Peep Round the Twist', appeared in 1991 in the *Memoirs*, though Amis wrote it, or a version of it, much earlier, in June 1982.[99] Otherwise, as Amis wrote to Conquest on 20 March, giving up drink proved 'no strain at all – jolly good, no chemical dependence at least', though 'the testing time – 12.30 in the Garrick bar – has yet to come'. After twenty-one weeks without a drink, he wrote to Larkin on 3 August minimising the effects of sobriety: 'the differences are really negligible, apart from so far not falling over and breaking my neck. Not pouring with sweat at the least exertion or room warmer than 65°F, true. Not – not what? Can't think of any other nots. Remembering what I've been reading last thing, yes. Confidently signing my name at any hour, yes. And that's it. Not getting hangovers – at least not feeling shitty on waking? No. Remembering better in general? *No.*' In this period, Amis grew what Conquest described as an 'ill-advised moustache',[100] one he told Dale Salwak he would shave off once he could drink again (he seems never to have considered staying on the wagon or winning Jane back). He also gave up smoking permanently. For six months, then, from March to September, starch and glucose were his only crutches.

The resulting 'late-night carbo-fests' and 'two-hour super-snacks' (Martin's phrases) were more than merely calming for Amis: 'his nocturnal gorging was a complex symptom, regressive, self-isolating. It cancelled him out sexually. It seemed to say that it was over: the quest for love, and the belief in its privacy.'[101] A comparable self-isolating impulse began to affect Amis's relations with friends and admirers at this time. Now began the period of testing rudeness, of the radical winnowing of friendships. On 28 October 1982, as a belated sixtieth birthday tribute, Donald Trelford, editor of the *Observer*, arranged a dinner in Amis's honour at a private room in the Garrick. Those invited were Martin Amis, Anthony Howard, the paper's deputy editor, Terence Kilmartin, its literary editor, Blake

Morrison, his deputy, and Amis's friends, the *Observer* writers and columnists Clive James, Julian Barnes, Alan Watkins, Geoff Nicholson and Hugh McIlvanney. In Alan Watkins's reconstruction, after Trelford's fulsome toast, Amis stood up and said: 'I just want to make a few remarks. The first thing I've got to say to you is the *Observer* is a bloody awful paper.'[102] He then proceeded to take strenuous exception, among other things, to a recent *Observer* story which attributed the massacre of Palestinians in Beirut to the Israelis and quoted Yasser Arafat and the PLO representative in New York as sources. Watkins was surprised as well as embarrassed by what Trelford was to describe as Amis's 'rather graceless response',[103] having 'never before heard him demonstrate the slightest interest in the troubled politics of the Middle East'.[104] An uncomfortable silence ensued, with much staring up at the ceiling or down at the table. Then Martin suggested to Trelford and others that they 'leave the old bugger to stew in his port and go and play snooker'. Individual friends, including several at this dinner, as we shall see, were treated with comparable aggression on private occasions.

By the time of the *Observer* dinner, Amis was well into *Stanley and the Women*, the most hate-filled of his novels, a work of great power and feeling. In *Experience* Martin dates what he thought of as his father's recovery as a writer not from *Stanley* but from the novel which succeeded it, *The Old Devils*, 'the book he will be remembered for'.[105] *Stanley* dismayed Martin: 'It seemed to me that his strategy was to shed sentiment as he moved closer to death. The indispensable value, romantic love, would therefore have to be exposed as an illusion.' Amis the habitual 'contrarian' and 'un-popularity courter', the public Amis, had, it seemed, taken over the novelist, exiling half the human race. 'If his soul was unhappy (and it was), then it couldn't be *his* fault. The world did it.[106] Women did it.' *Stanley* was the precipitate of this unhappiness and Hilly, as Martin saw it, was the figure who rescued him from it: 'He got *Stanley* out of the way and then he wrote *The Old Devils* and *Difficulties with Girls* and *The Folks that Live on the Hill* and the *Memoirs* and "A Twitch on the Thread" and *The Russian Girl* and *You Can't Do Both* and *The Biographer's Moustache* and *The King's English* and a few more poems.' In a loving apostrophe, Martin concludes: 'He could never have written them without you, because you reminded him of love. Mum: You were the peach.'[107]

This tribute undervalues both *Stanley* and the creative power of anger. In its darkness and pessimism, *Stanley* belongs with *Jake's Thing* and *Russian Hide-and-Seek*, novels of debility in several senses. But it differs from them in drive and energy. In *Stanley*, despair gives way to an invigorating rage. As Martin himself admits, the novel is 'viciously well-organised'. He calls it 'mean', 'sour', 'spare', 'closed up and walled off'. These adjectives apply to the depiction of Stanley's wives and the therapists who treat his schizophrenic son Steve, but they hardly apply to Stanley's feelings about Steve himself, which carry not only Amis's fears for his own sanity but his fears for Sally, seemingly beyond cure in this period. Steve's isolation and unhappiness foreshadow Fiona's isolation and unhappiness in *The Folks That Live on the Hill*. The monstrousness of most of the women in the novel is Amis's way of getting back at Jane and feminism and what he saw as the failure and fatuity of the therapy culture, but it is also a response to the mystery and cruelty of Steve's illness, of the world's sudden and inexplicable malignities. 'Disasters happen to people,' reads an early note for the novel: 'No use trying to make sense of them.'[108] What Stanley remembers of the dissolution of his first marriage is that 'after thirteen years and at no particular point that I could see she had gone and set up with this Bert Hutchinson';[109] which is to say, trying to make sense of the behaviour of women is as impossible as trying to explain the world's disasters (that is, their inevitability, in one form or another). Amis's attack on women in *Stanley* is an attack on the world. For Martin, love returns his father to health as a novelist, opening him to the emotions of forgiveness and regret; but anger could be said to have got him back on track as well.

'The new one is about a chap with a nasty wife,' Amis wrote to Larkin on 3 August 1982. 'At the beginning he thinks she's a nice wife, but then he finds out she's really a nasty wife all the time. She's a writer, but *he's not* you see. Ha ha ha ha ha ha.' Soon after Jane left him, Amis began turning her into a comic character in his correspondence, as he had done with Daddy B. While he was in hospital Jane sent Amis a proof of her new novel, *Getting It Right*. 'It must be meant to fuck me up in some way,' he wrote to Larkin on 22 March 1982, 'but I haven't yet divined what.' The letter goes on to imagine a scene between Jane and a 'girl-chum':

'But why?' says g-c. 'Oh . . . he saw quite a lot of the early chapters before we . . .' 'You mean he took an interest in them?' 'Oh yes,' – a lot of work with eyes and hands here, 'things could be . . . quite good even . . . late on.

He isn't the most . . . outgoing of men but he . . . really cares about . . . art. That's one of the things I've always respected about him,' – eyelids batting fast here – 'and I hope he knows it. Because if he doesn't it's . . . too late to . . .' 'You know, darling,' says g-c to husband later, 'poor old Jane has taken that Kingsley business really hard. It's such a pity in a way that she had to leave him.' 'Had to?' says the husband. 'Darling, don't be silly, of course she had to.' 'How do we know that?' 'Darling she *did*, didn't she? That shows she had to.' 'Oh, I see,' says husband, and goes off to drink and laugh with male friends.

When Amis began reading *Getting It Right* its creative effect on him was like a visit from Daddy B or Larkin: 'All agog to get down to my novel,' he wrote to Conquest on 20 March, on the eve of leaving hospital, 'the more so since, oddly I thought and still think, Jane sent me a proof of her latest a couple of, well, about a week ago . . . I thought it was quite good, but at the same time not-much-good enough to encourage me a good deal to get on with mine. (The cynical Martin said in answer to this that reading *any* contemporary novel was an encouragement of that sort).' In the same letter of 20 March, Amis makes an early connection between women and the Soviet Union. Pat Kavanagh had seen an interview in which Jane expressed doubts about having left Amis and about whether she was suited to living alone. Jane also said that she wanted to be friends with Amis. Amis's reaction, as relayed in the letter to Conquest, was '*Christ!!* Sorry about that, Kingers; let's have a nice chat and forget it, or perhaps I could move in with you and Hilly. Talk about women = the USSR. We regret the damage done to your homeland and the infliction of numerous casualties. We are now satisfied that the decision to rectify our common frontier was taken in error. Those responsible for it have been punished. There being no longer any friction between our two peoples, we look forward to an era of common understanding and increased prosperity on a co-operative basis.' Once out of hospital and at work on *Stanley*, Amis was in no mood to soften. The arrangement with the Kilmarnocks had worked out. His leg had mended and he was able to drink again. He discovered ancillary benefits to living without Jane. At Christmas he went to stay with George Gale, who had left Pat and was living with his new wife, Mary, also a journalist (as Gale wonderingly told Conquest, she was 'no trouble at all'), in an enormous flat in a baronial mansion in Sawbridgeworth near Harlow. On 17 December, shortly after his divorce came through, Amis wrote to Larkin about his movements over the holiday: 'I'll be in Herts getting drunk with old George Gale. It's at this time of year that my thoughts turn inevitably to Jane and bring many a sigh *of heartfelt relief*, in particular at not having to spend a day or two in the effing Wess Tend going round classy jewellers' etc. shops looking for presents for her, like a very nice pair of Georgian bush-brushes with enamel-inlaid backs and filigreed crab-louse remover attached, only £6,844.95 the set.'

As *Stanley and the Women* suggests, Amis's hatred of Jane was of a piece with his hatred of therapy and the Women's Movement, both of which Jane was influenced by in the Gardnor House years. For Jane, therapy worked. It had helped to make her a better and a happier person, as had the Women's Movement. In the late spring of 1978 she began attending a women's group run by an American colleague of Kate Hopkinson, Jane's first therapist. The previous groups Jane had attended were mostly one-day affairs but they had proved useful to her: 'When I watched other people working on their own problems, the solutions often seemed easy to me. If this was so, others must think the same of me, so if I could understand my own nature, there *was* a way forward.' In her American therapist, Jane found a person 'who could say anything to the people with whom she worked without bruising their personality'.[110] Jane began working with the therapist in individual sessions but also in sessions in the women's group, which she has now been a member of for almost thirty years. In her memoir, Jane describes these sessions as having given her 'a steadier view of myself',[111] taught her 'to feel more responsible for myself' and 'enormously helped the old bugbear, self-pity'. Though perfectly aware that 'some people will dub all this indulgent self-absorption', she argues that 'feeling good, or at least better, about yourself enables you to be of more use to other people'. That she has become a nicer person as she has become more certain of herself is a comment voiced by several old friends. As she herself concludes: 'I am openly and deeply grateful for the opportunity therapy has given me to grow up.'[112]

Amis had moments, some of them, as we've seen, inspired by Jane, in which he admired such openness, though not without qualification, associating it specifically with women. Perhaps the best-known of these moments is the passage about love poetry in 'A Bookshop Idyll', with its quotation from Byron's *Don Juan*:

> Should poets bicycle-pump the human heart
>   Or squash it flat?
> Man's love is of man's life a thing apart;
>   Girls aren't like that.
>
> We men have got love well weighed up; our stuff
>   Can get by without it.
> Women don't seem to think that's good enough;
>   They write about it.
>
> And the awful way their poems lay them open
>   Just doesn't strike them.
> Women are really much nicer than men.
>   No wonder we like them.

Such praise is often drowned out in the fiction by a more jaundiced or jeering view. When women go on about love or their emotions in Amis's novels, men frequently find their openness irritating or embarrassing. 'How close we seem to be tonight, James,' says Margaret in *Lucky Jim*, 'all the barriers are down at last, aren't they' – an expression of feeling that makes Jim, as we have seen, want to 'give an inarticulate shout and run out of the bar'. For Jim, as for Amis, feeling was usually cheapened or rendered suspect by open or direct expression. At the time of *Stanley and the Women*, Amis's distrust of such expression was exacerbated by feminism, or at least that strain of feminism that embraced gender division (as opposed to the strain that sought gender equality and equality of opportunity). 'Sharing' of feelings was identified as a specifically female as well as therapeutic virtue, one unlikely to flourish in male company. The early 1980s saw a proliferation of women's classes, collectives, gyms, health centres, bookstores, sentences (like Virginia Woolf's or Dorothy Richardson's sentences, loose, capacious, supposedly subversive of existing or 'patriarchal' systems). As her fiction shows, Jane was neither uncritical, doctrinaire nor man-hating in her allegiance to feminism, nor did she go in for women's sentences, but she was open and unembarrassed about the allegiance. When Amis complained of her constantly going out 'to GROUPS and WORK-SHOPS and crappy "new friends"', it was women friends he had in mind. Personal animus underlay *Stanley*, as it had *Jake's Thing*, but both novels were seen by Amis as attacking large social trends. When the paperback version of *Jake's Thing* was published, Amis gave readings from the novel, prefaced by comments about its genesis and aims. In these comments (several pages of handwritten notes, now in the Huntington) he admits to hating 'all those people who irresponsibly manipulate our minds and emotions in the name of ? science? personal curiosity? power? . . . my book is a slight assault on them'. This admission is then followed by a reading of the scene in which Jake brings home a girlie magazine 'on psychological advice', for the purposes of 'self-administered sexual therapy'. After reading the scene, Amis comments: 'There's more to it than that, I hope.'[113] When I talked to the Hutchinson reps, I said rather *rashly*, old Lucky Jim turned out to be something new and helped to determine how things were going to run in the '50s. I added, even more rashly, that the same thing might happen with *Jake's Thing* in the late 1970s. The reception of the hardback leads me to believe, reasonably seriously, that I might have been right.' Though the starting point for *Stanley* was personal, the personal was political, in the jargon of the age. To Anthony Burgess, who welcomed *Stanley* as a return to form, those likely to be offended by it had only themselves to blame: 'Lady reviewers will express whimsical wonder that the great lessons of the new feminism have not sunk into yet another obdu-rately piggish male brain. They've sunk in all right. Women wanted the big division, and by God they've got it.'[114] The hostile John Carey, who has described Amis's writing career as 'downhill all the way',[115] summarised Stanley's attitude to women as a mixture of hatred, contempt, fear, 'largely ineffectual' lust and paranoia: 'Women, [Stanley] is convinced, are bonded together in a conspiracy to degrade and destroy men. Formerly they did it only when provoked, but Women's Lib has given them an excuse for doing it as a matter of principle.'[116] In Stanley's own words, in conversation with his GP friend, Cliff Wainwright: 'they seem to feel they can get on with the job of fucking you up any time they feel like it. That's what Women's Lib is for.' To which Cliff answers: 'It's getting worse now they're competing on equal terms in so many places and find they still finish behind men. They can't even produce a few decent fucking *jugglers*.'[117] These remarks are Stanley's and Cliff's, of course, but Amis was less emphatic than his defenders in distancing himself from them. As he told Blake Morrison in the *Observer*, in a profile on the eve of publication: 'I wouldn't like it to be thought that Stanley's thoughts [on women] are the author's last word on the subject. But they're certainly my thoughts up to a point, enough for me to be able to present a man thinking them.'[118]

Amis's intemperance about women was partly a product of depression, divorce, debility, but it was also a response to feminist intemperance. Among Jane Howard's papers in the Huntington is a handwritten transcription of a group therapy session held on 16 June 1984, shortly after the publication of *Stanley and the Women*. The session was conducted not by Jane's regular therapist but by another American facilitator, also a woman, and the transcription was made by one of the group members. In these sessions, the group focused on a single individual, in this case Jane. At the end of the transcription the person who did the transcribing wrote: 'Dear Jane, Thank you for sharing your session and feelings – and the example of your courage.' The session begins with Jane's admission that she finds it hard to ask people for things and the facilitator encourages her to be open in requesting favours from the group: 'Look at each person – slowly – and see if there's anything you want.' One of the group members is also a writer and eventually Jane says to her: 'I'd like to spend some time talking about writing. I've no one to do that. I'd like to try . . . We may find we can't do it, but for me it would be of great value.' The woman agrees and when the facilitator speculates to Jane that 'writing is a lonely business and you'd like to connect with someone to share', Jane replies: 'I've had this twice in my life (Tears) I'm looking for it wherever I might find it.' Jane is referring here to Cecil Day-Lewis and Amis, and the facilitator initiates the following exchange:

J. I feel sad about the people I haven't got.
F. Put them here.
J. I'm sad you're dead and I can't talk to you.
F. You can. Give a name.
J. Cecil. I wish you – I'd like to talk to you about this large new work.

F. I *am* going to talk to you.

J. I don't know if I can do that.

F. Put Cecil here who is alive and experiment . . . Express how you feel.

Jane then proceeds to do so, first taking on the part of herself asking things of Cecil, then replying in Cecil's voice. As it turns out, what she particularly wants to ask Cecil about is a planned trilogy of novels 'which begins in 1937 and goes through to 1947' (it would become the Cazalet Chronicle). The advice Cecil then gives Jane, as imagined by Jane, is practical and sensible and makes her feel better. When Jane says she still misses him, the facilitator says: 'You'll miss him, yes, [but] when you let him come alive for you again . . . that Cecil is still available for you.'

Then the facilitator asks Jane to address Amis, the second writer whose advice she misses. Jane admits that she 'misses not being able to talk about writing with you all the time' and begins to cry again. At this point the facilitator enters into an imagined dialogue with Jane, taking Jane's place (though at times she forgets herself, speaking *in propria persona*), while Jane pretends to be Amis:

F. Switch.

K. [J. as K.] I don't want to have anything more to do with you. I'm finished with you.

F. Why?

K. For leaving me. She thought of nothing but herself all the time.

F. An alcoholic baby is no good to have around.

K. You are not going to have what you want. I'm glad there's something I can still do.

F. You certainly are revengeful and self-destructive. I just saw your new book. Who do you have to talk about writing now?

K. Nobody. And she's done that too.

At this point the facilitator pulls out of the dialogue and asks Jane how she feels. When Jane says she thinks it might still be possible to talk about writing with Amis ('I know 90% it's not going to happen but a little bit hopes') the facilitator gets tough. 'He's a toxic poisonous person for anyone near him, Jane. Breathe and look. Is there anything remaining to express?' Jane then says: 'I wish we'd had more time to ourselves at the beginning. I don't think we stood a chance as things were. I don't know if it would have made a difference.' The facilitator dismisses such talk as fantasy, Jane's longing for 'a dream Kingsley'. Her hostility to Amis is clear throughout, a product of what she feels for Jane and of her sense of what Jane needs. But its intensity may also derive from 'that book', as if confronting Amis's continuing importance to Jane involved confronting an enemy to the therapeutic culture and to women in general, to 'sharing' and tears and the admirable openness of the group. She was not wrong, not for the Amis of this period.

26

Return

When Amis finished *Stanley and the Women* he wrote to Larkin on 3 December 1983 to apologise for having been out of touch. In the push to finish the novel he had written no letters, gone out to no lunches, though 'getting pissed was allowed'. If previously he had 'seriously feared' the novel would never be finished, now 'I quite seriously fear it will get me murdered by feminists.' Larkin took his time writing back, not having heard from Amis in three months. In a reply of 29 January, he commented on the new novel's theme: 'I thought you'd given women a pretty good going-over in JT; still got some more to say, eh?'[1] On 8 February, Amis answered that *Stanley* was 'not another JT by any means. None of the sentimental mollycoddling that women get in that. This has moments of definite hostility.' When the novel came out in May 1984 Amis was surprised by the mildness of the response it received from 'females' (now a term of abuse, or mock abuse):[2] 'Ones I have never met write to me,' he reported to Conquest on 2 July. 'Others I know only say as wives of acquaintances seek me out, all saying too bloody true and about time someone said it. Suggests perhaps that the pendulum has started to swing back.' The most remarkable notice the novel received appeared in the *London Review of Books*, where Marilyn Butler, an English don at Oxford, later King Edward VII Professor of English at Cambridge, pronounced it pro-women: 'It would have to be a superficial reading that perceived this novel as an anti-feminist tract . . . tougher-minded women readers are going to feel gratified rather than insulted by Stanley's witness, because he is delightfully demoralised.'[3]

'That's balls, isn't it,' Martin asked his father. 'Oh, absolutely,' he replied.[4]

American women reviewers were less tolerant, or less wrong-headed, in their reactions to *Stanley*, deploring the novel only in part on feminist grounds. To Mary Mackey, writing in the *San Francisco Chronicle*, Amis was 'one of those rare writers about whom it is almost impossible to be objective. Or to put it another way, much of Kingsley Amis is like an ethnic joke: If you think that sort of thing funny, then you'll love him, but if you get offended by prejudice and stereotypes, you may wonder why anyone could laugh at his work, much less think it light entertainment.'[5] Rhoda Koenig, in *New York* magazine, objected to the novel on grounds very much like those of Martin: 'There is no love in thought or deed in this book – a fact more appalling than any outrage against politeness.'[6] Resistance to the novel had been voiced by American women well before it appeared in print in the United States. Several major publishing houses turned it down, according to an article written in January 1985 by John Gross in the *New York Times Book Review*, 'because of feminist pressures . . . over its unflattering depiction of women'. Earlier, in November 1984, Christopher Hitchens reported in the *Times Literary Supplement* that three potential publishers had 'candidly excused the rescinding of offers by reference to feminists on the editorial board',[7] a story picked up by *Newsweek*, *Time*, *Publishers Weekly* and *Saturday Review*. Among the houses that passed on *Stanley* were Viking, Amis's current American publisher, and Harcourt Brace, his publisher from 1955 to 1976. When Summit Books, a division of Simon and Schuster, finally bought it, the editor who made the deal, Ileene Smith, received indignant phone calls from several women colleagues. The novel had been recommended to Smith by Penny Perrick, literary editor of the *Sunday Times* and a self-described 'ardent feminist'. 'She told me that she was prepared to hate the book,' Smith recalled, 'but absolutely adored it.' Ben Sonnenberg, editor of *Grand Street*, the New York literary period-ical, also recommended the novel to Smith. When the controversy broke after Gross's piece appeared in the *New York Times Book Review*, Smith had only just received the novel from Clowes, whose office had unaccountably sent it by sea. Once she'd read it, she pronounced it 'very, very mischievous', 'not evil at all', 'a fascinating book about alienation, insanity and madness'.[8] Yet she remained uncertain about publication, wondering 'why were all my colleagues passing?' Only when James H. Silberman, president of Summit, read *Stanley* and found it 'wildly funny', not so much 'anti-woman' as 'anti-human', did Smith OK the deal. 'I had to take a little bit of heat,' she said, 'but nothing I can't defend.'⁹ This heat derived from the novel's perceived anti-Semitism as well as its perceived misogyny. 'It wasn't the women the publishers were afraid of offending,' Amis later told James Atlas, in a profile in the March 1987 issue of *Vanity Fair*, 'it was the Jews.'¹⁰ Stanley refers casually to 'Jewboys' in the novel and says things like 'I don't think it's egotistical or funny or like a Jew or like a gangster of me to fancy the idea of my wife getting herself up in a bit of style.'¹¹ 'You can't have Stanley say the kinds of things he does, apparently,' Amis told Atlas, despite the fact that these are the kinds of things a character like Stanley would say ('mildly anti-semitic remarks came naturally to someone like me born where and when I was'). Stanley, Amis insisted, 'hasn't got anything against Jews', like his creator. 'My own father had a nice big nose,' he told Atlas, in a manner like that of the novel. 'He could have been mistaken for a Jew.'¹²

Jonathan Clowes had helped to set in motion the campaign to get *Stanley* an American publisher. It was he who passed news of its rejection, 'a form of censorship', to the *New York Times*.¹³ The resulting furore helped to increase sales when the novel was finally published in the United States in September 1985, but Amis never sold well there. In Britain, sales were also disappointing, despite good reviews and controversy. According to Richard Cohen, Amis's editor at Hutchinson, writing to Clowes on 26 February 1986, the novel's sales remained 'disappointingly around the 10,000 mark'. What Cohen hoped for in succeeding books was 'a minimum sale of 15,000 and ideally something nearer 25,000'. Clowes was equally concerned with sales. He had first met Amis in the mid-1970s, when their mutual accountant, Anton Felton, introduced them. Clowes had been an agent since 1960 and had an interesting background. He was born in 1930, left school at fifteen, became a Communist and was thrice imprisoned for refusing to do compulsory military service (with spells in Wormwood Scrubs, Wandsworth and Brixton prisons, where he read avidly, as he'd done in school). Clowes was wholly self-taught as an agent, which he became by accident, while working as a painter and decorator. A man on his crew, Henry Chapman, had written a play and Clowes managed to get it to Joan Littlewood, whom he admired but had never met. Littlewood loved it and agreed to put it on, after which Clowes got another friend's first novel published by Faber and Faber. He then found a third client, a graphic artist named Len Deighton, whose first novel, *The Ipcress File*, made them both a fortune. It was with *The Ipcress File* that Clowes negotiated his first film deal. The producer Harry Saltzman sent him an enormous, largely incomprehensible contract. Clowes sent it back three times, each time with the message: 'this is totally unacceptable'. By taking careful note of how the contract improved with each rejection, a process which took a year, Clowes learned how to negotiate a film deal.

By the mid-1970s Clowes represented not only novelists, including Doris Lessing as well as Deighton, and literary estates, notably the Conan Doyle Estate, but television writers, producers and personalities, among them Carla Lane, Desmond Wilcox and David Bellamy. In the mid-1970s Jane was keen to write television scripts and felt she wasn't getting enough encouragement from the Peters agency to do so. When Felton arranged for Clowes to meet Jane and Amis, Clowes convinced her that he would have no trouble finding her lucrative television work. He also claimed that he could increase Amis's income from screen adaptations of his novels. Both then agreed to go over to Clowes for television and film, staying with A.D. Peters for books and journalism. Jane soon received several remunerative commissions, which she enjoyed writing and which helped her to regain confidence as a writer, and Amis's income from options and adaptations increased. Then Felton approached Clowes a second time. Amis and Jane's overdraft was still too high; Jane remained blocked as a novelist; and Michael Sissons of A.D. Peters was not encouraging about increased sales or advances for Amis's fiction. As Clowes remembers it: 'Anton said: "Can you do better?" and I said I could.' A second meeting was arranged at Lemmons, at which 'Jane did most of the talking.' Jane had had an extremely close relation with Peter Peters, who founded the A.D. Peters agency, and a more formal one with Michael Sissons, his successor as agent both to Amis and herself. When she met Clowes, she recalls in her memoirs, 'there were two things about him that reminded me of Peter Peters: he had a very quiet voice and he gave the impression of being shy'.[14] Amis listened to Clowes make his case and expressed some worry about reactions from the Peters agency, 'especially from Pat'. In the end, however, both Amis and Jane agreed to make the move, writing to inform Sissons of their decision in a joint letter of 13 April 1977.

Clowes's first task was to visit Tom Maschler at Cape, to persuade him to increase the advertising budget for *Jake's Thing* and to pay Amis a larger advance. Maschler refused both requests, arguing that Amis's audience was fixed, that he was already a celebrated novelist, and that advertising his fiction was therefore a waste of money. So Clowes moved Amis to Hutchinson, in a deal that, to Maschler's annoyance, more than doubled Amis's advance and included a guaranteed £15,000 promotional budget. What had persuaded Amis to make the move was Clowes's conviction that it was not his audience that was fixed but his literary reputation. The move to Hutchinson, a slightly more commercial house than Cape, was an attempt to 'break through the sales barrier . . . to crack through to the next level'. This move Amis approved for financial reasons but perhaps also because widening the audience – ignoring the boundary between popular and literary fiction – was a matter of principle for him. 'He wasn't worried about his literary reputation,' Clowes says. 'He was disappointed with his sales.' When *Jake's Thing* proved a huge success, Clowes attributed its sales not only to its being 'a good book to move', but to the more aggressive or commercial manner in which it was promoted.

Both Amis and Jane stayed with Clowes after their break-up, a tribute partly to the money he'd made them, partly to his shrewd sense of their different needs. Relations with Amis were smoothed by their parallel political trajectories ('he knew that I greatly admired Mrs Thatcher') and shared reticence about personal matters. Amis never once mentioned Jane to Clowes after she left Gardnor House, though it was clear both to Clowes and to Ann Evans, who worked in the agency and would soon marry Clowes, that he was rocked by her departure. When Clowes and Evans married, they gave a huge party for their clients. They knew that Amis would not come if Jane was there, so they tossed a coin to decide who would be invited. Amis won and, in compensation, Jane, already a friend of Ann Evans, was invited to spend the weekend at their house in Sussex.

With the exception of these instances, Amis's twenty-year relationship with the Clowes agency was without tension. When Clowes advised changing publishers or renegotiating deals, Amis 'would always say: "I rely on you to do what you think best"'. Clowes in turn 'never advised Amis about what he should write', even in the four-year nadir between *Russian Hide-and-Seek* and *Stanley and the Women*. Clowes can remember only a single instance of authorial uncertainty on Amis's part, over the draft of the unfinished 'Difficulties': 'he was quite upset about it . . . felt it wasn't as good as it should have been . . . was in a bad way'. Clowes read the draft, listened sympathetically and was relieved when, having abandoned 'Difficulties', Amis's confidence gradually returned, a recovery Clowes attributes partly to the influence of Hilly and the Kilmarnocks, partly to the decision to turn back to the novel that would become *Stanley and the Women*. 'He was getting better, slowly,' Clowes remembers; on visits to the agency, located on Prince Albert Road, not far from Primrose Hill, Amis again comfortably discussed future writing plans, expecting Clowes 'to say "that's a good idea" or "that's interesting"', answers that Clowes was happy to supply, since 'usually his ideas were quite interesting'. Amis regularly sent Clowes drafts, partly because he wanted his opinion but partly out of a neurotic fear that 'the house might burn down' and the work be lost. Clowes mostly queried 'very minor things . . . I might say is it right that so and so should do something or other and Kingsley would either defend it or he'd modify it.'

These pro forma consultations suited Clowes, who was happy to concentrate on maximising income for his authors rather than shaping their works (though some authors, Doris Lessing for example, welcomed editorial suggestions). He earned his commission by negotiating higher advances ('I have always taken the view that it is better that money should be in the writer's hands rather than the publisher's, and, therefore, I try to pitch advances so that publishers have to work very hard to earn them out');[15] charging a fee to renew rights to a book (as opposed to allowing the publisher to hold them for as long as the book is in print), an innovation; challenging the traditional 50/50 split on paperback rights ('I'd always felt that was pretty outrageous'), another innovation; requiring that contracts specify promotional budgets; and moving authors at the slightest hint that a publishing house 'had started to run out of energy'. Amis's last contract with Cape and A.D. Peters had been for *The Alteration* (1976), for which he received an advance of £7,500; in 1977 Clowes moved him to Hutchinson on a two-book deal worth £35,000 (£17,500 per book for *Jake's Thing* and *Russian Hide-and-Seek*). In 1980 Clowes again almost doubled Amis's advance, with a second two-book contract, worth £60,000 (for what would become *Stanley and the Women* and *The Old Devils*). After the success of *The Old Devils*, which won the Booker Prize, Clowes procured a third two-book contract from Hutchinson, worth £200,000, more than three times the advance of the previous contract (the new contract was for what turned out to be *Difficulties with Girls* and *The Folks That Live on the Hill*). These advances were supplemented by advances for non-fiction, licence fees, paperback deals, radio and television fees and royalties, permissions fees, journalism fees and serial rights. Clowes's aim was to get Amis as close as possible to an annual income of £200,000. According to figures for the last five years of his life, after winning the Booker, in 1991 Amis grossed £160,000, in 1992 £192,000, in 1993 £218,489, in 1994 £172,854. The figure for 1995, the year he died, was £79,995, a falling off partly attributable to illness and debility.[16]

Amis needed such an income and spent virtually all of it. In the mid-1980s, after selling his papers and correspondence to the Huntington Library, a deal arranged by Clowes (through Bernard Quaritch, the London book dealer, and George Robert Minkoff, a dealer in the United States), Amis and the Kilmarnocks moved from the Leighton Road house to a larger house in Primrose Hill, at 194 Regents Park Road.[17] A new place was needed, Amis explained to Larkin in a letter written on 18 June 1984, while still in Kentish Town, because 'there isn't any hall or dining room in this one, and it's getting a bit common round here'. Regents Park Road, he explained in a later letter, of 18 December, was 'v. near (btwi ftwi betwixt ourselves) where I used to give it to ole-Janey girl in the long-ago' (i.e., in Tom Maschler's house in Chalcot Crescent). The house needed work, as well as fixtures and fittings; it also needed furniture, which Eve Thomas came up from Swansea to help Hilly purchase. Amis paid for everything, while continuing to concern himself as little as possible with his finances. When Jane left Amis, Anton Felton went with her, recommending Martin Cohen, another accountant who worked for writers, as a replacement. Cohen quickly realised that Amis expected him to make all financial decisions: he would sign papers but wasn't interested in details. Cohen was surprised at how little money Amis had, especially given the Rolls-Royce divorce he and Jane had embarked on. He remembers counting six lawyers and accountants assembled for lengthy meetings about the sale of Gardnor House: 'the costs must have been astronomical'.

Household expenses were Hilly's province and Amis gave her the money she needed to pay bills and buy provisions, in addition, initially, to a £50 weekly salary. Ali Kilmarnock was busy in the House of Lords, where he played a key role in the newly formed Social Democratic Party, eventually serving as SDP Whip, Deputy Leader, health and social services spokesman, then chairman of the All-Party Parliamentary Group on AIDS. None of these activities earned him much money.[18] When in 1983 it was decided that Jaime, aged eleven, should go to Wolverstone Hall, an ILEA boarding-school which he attended for five years, Amis paid the fees. Amis also supported Sally, including paying for treatment at private medical and rehabilitation centres. When Philip needed money, during times of unemployment or to buy a flat, Amis provided it, either directly or through Hilly. As for Amis's own expenses, these ought to have been modest: he owned no car, took no holidays abroad, had little interest in possessions. Yet the bills he ran up for drink, taxis, restaurants and the Garrick Club were large. Here are some figures compiled by Janet Hart, the accountant who succeeded Martin Cohen in 1985. In the month of February 1993, while still active and ambulatory, if not exactly fit, Amis spent £315 on radio taxis, £432 on the Garrick Club (not including annual subscription) and £1,038 on drink (the highest such monthly figure Hart recorded, though other months were close). As for yearly earnings and expenses, in 1994, as we have seen, he grossed £172,854 (£155,256, less commissions), while his expenses, including taxes, came to £133,000. 'Wish I could feel secure about cash,' he lamented to Larkin on 1 October 1985. 'My accountant tells me I can retire on my 75th birthday.' When asked, in an interview of 27 October 1986, what he spent his money on, Amis answered: 'Oh, mortgages. Horrible things like that.' After the divorce, 'all of a sudden the bit of fat you've accumulated over the years is gone and you have to start again. Which is not easy when you're nearly sixty as I was then. I didn't bother about it until my second marriage broke up. That brought with it all sorts of insecurities, not just those directly related to it, but when something like that happens you lose your confidence completely, even your confidence in being able to earn your own living.'[19]

Amis and the Kilmarnocks moved to Primrose Hill in July 1985. It was now clear that their unconventional ménage, though not without its tensions, worked. The success of *Stanley and the Women* had helped to dispel Amis's fears of blockage and writerly deterioration. Though Sally and Philip were still worries, Martin was a successful and celebrated writer. On 27 September 1984, the day his novel, *Money*, was published, to admiring reviews (though Amis himself 'hated its way of constantly reminding me of Nabokov'),[20] Martin married Antonia Phillips, a lecturer in philosophy at the University of London, also a part-time editor at the *Times Literary Supplement*, described by her new father-in-law as 'nice girl (also rich)', to which he adds 'we are not quite grand enough for her'.[21] 'I love looking at her,' Amis told Martin at the wedding party. On 15 November, Antonia gave birth to their first child, Louis Nathaniel Amis; a second son, Jacob Augustus Amis, was born two years later, on 24 May 1986.

At the time of the move to Regents Park Road, Amis was well advanced on *The Old Devils*, a work that reflects his improved circumstances. Though darkly comic in its treatment of age and loss, the note it ends on is one of rescue, release, renewal. The idea for the novel grew out of what became a yearly ritual for Amis. When the Garrick Club closed for three weeks in August and September for its summer holiday, Amis would return to Wales to stay with Stuart and Eve Thomas. The first of these stays occurred in 1979, when Amis refused to travel abroad and Jane went without him. There was then a hiatus of several years; the pattern of annual visits seems not to have begun until 1982. Amis felt safe with the Thomases, who lived in a comfortable bungalow at 4 Mary Twill Lane, on a hill above Swansea Bay in Mumbles. He was able to establish a daily routine with them not unlike the one he followed in London: work in the morning at home, while Stuart went off to his office; drinks at noon in the Bristol Channel Yacht Club (until Stuart's expulsion in 1993); lunch at a pub or local restaurant, perhaps La Gondola or the Bee's Knees, described by Jacobs as providing 'an acceptable lunch at however unconventionally late an hour Amis and party reached it';[22] nap in the afternoon, sometimes followed by a second work session; more drinks at the Yacht Club or a pub; supper at home, prepared by Eve; television; whisky. Stuart went to bed early, so Eve stayed up with Amis each night ('I might as well have got one of those blow-up dolls to sit with him'). While Amis was in Swansea the Kilmarnocks took their own holiday, usually in Spain.

Both Stuart and Eve Thomas were big drinkers and so were many of their friends, a number of whom Amis had known from his time at Swansea. It was in Swansea that Amis resumed drinking, six months after having broken his leg in March 1982, in part because the leg had healed, in part because it was impossible to abstain in such company.[23] The Thomases' friends were mostly *crachach* rather than university types, retired, in their sixties and seventies. According to Jacobs, it was 'while Amis was putting on his shoes to go to the Yacht Club that he got the idea for . . . *The Old Devils*, about a bunch of oldsters retired from most serious activities apart from that of drinking their heads off'.[24] In an interview at the time *The Old Devils* was published, Amis described the novel as growing out of a question he posed himself: 'What would happen were I to retire to Wales?' Alun Weaver, the character whose return, with his wife Rhiannon, sets the plot in motion, was 'me coming back to Wales, or me as I used to be, or perhaps as I wanted to be, but anyway treating women in a cynical and uncaring way'.[25] Alun is an Amis shit in the line of Patrick Standish, Roger Micheldene, Sir Roy Vandervane and Bernard Bastable. A professional Welshman, he has made his living on television in part as an acolyte of the poet Brydan, a Dylan Thomas figure. Upon his return, he sets about seducing the wives of his friends, several of whom he has seduced in the past. One of these wives, Gwen Cellan-Davies, describes him as a 'selfish monster and windbag and hypocrite and broken-down Don Juan and phony Welshman'.[26] What she leaves out is Alun's energy: he's livelier than the other old devils and more aggressive, quick-witted, rude, a master of abuse:

'What is the vintage port?' asked Alun.

   'Port is a fortified wine from Portugal,' said the waiter, having perhaps misheard slightly, 'and vintage port is made from –'

   'I didn't ask for a bloody lecture on vinification, you horrible little man.' Alun laughed a certain amount as he spoke. 'Tell me the shipper and the year and then go back to your hole and pull the lid over it.'[27]

When at a party another of the old devils, Garth Pumphrey, a retired veterinarian, boring, self-satisfied and mean with money, teases Alun about his expensive suit and the wattles under his chin, Alun goes for him, again with a *faux-bonhomme* laugh:

'I can't do anything about your terrible mind, Garth,' said Alun, grinning harder than before. 'I can't help your inability to notice anything that doesn't directly involve your pathetic self,' he continued, starting to shake with mirth, 'but when you start vaunting your supposed moral superiority, you bloody little cowshed mountebank', and here he started laughing as he spoke, 'then at least I can tell you to shut your blathering trap before I slam your doubtless irreproachable dentures down your fucking throat.'

By now he and Garth had their arms round one another's shoulders, both of them bent in the middle and red in the face, roaring fit to burst.[28]

Alun is one of several old devils to be given Amisian traits, a cause of confusion to reviewers. In a typical complaint, P.J. Kavanagh, in the *Spectator*, confessed that he could never remember 'who was speaking, or who was married to whom'. He admired the novel but thought it 'almost Russian in its confusing welter of Christian names'.[29] Anthony Powell also admired the novel, enough to read it three times. On the second reading he made 'a list of Welsh names of characters, with wives, necessary to steer through the narrative, with brief notes on behaviour'.[30] That Amis partly cultivated this confusion is suggested by the first line of an undated sheaf of notes he made for the novel: 'Keep the reader guessing – wch the Amis char?'[31] Peter Thomas and Charlie Norris, who watch Alun rip into Garth, are cases in point. Forty years ago, Peter, a retired chemical engineer, previously an academic, loved and abandoned Rhiannon. He was slim and handsome then, now he's enormously fat, stuffing himself with 'cakes mostly. Profiteroles. Brandy-snaps. Anything with cream or jam or chocolate. Also cake, Genoa cake, Dundee cake with almonds. Seed cake with a glass of Malmsey.' As Peter explains to his son, William, who will marry Alun and Rhiannon's clever daughter, Rosemary, 'it's partly giving up smoking . . . But it's also partly, partly I don't know what to call it. Scared as much as anything I mean.' To which William replies: 'Yes, I was reading the other day where the fellow said, Welshman too by God, he said carbohydrates, which is what we're talking about, they're tranquillizing, just mildly.'[32] Charlie Norris, who co-owns a restaurant, the Glendower, with his brother, Victor, shares Peter's and Amis's anxious disposition, suffering from nightmares, panic attacks, unable to be alone, especially in the dark. When Alun, in revenge at Charlie's damning verdict on his novel-in-progress, leaves him to make his own way home at night over unfamiliar territory (they are in the Laugharne-like village of Birdarthur, where the poet Brydan lived and is buried, and where the Weavers have taken a cottage), the resulting panic attack recalls Jane's description of Amis's howling in Drue Heinz's house in Ascot: 'Charlie had turned a curious colour, that of a red-faced man gone very pale. His eyes were tightly screwed up and he was pressing hard with both hands on a grubby handkerchief that covered his mouth, in spite of which the wailing noise was quite loud at its loudest . . . Now and then Charlie took the handkerchief away from his mouth and got out a word or two in a brief squeal before stuffing it back again.'[33] Charlie calms down when given a syringe full of Largactil, a powerful tranquillizer. His wife, Sophie, explains what has happened: 'He's not mad, if that's what you're thinking. An attack of depersonalization. Panic by being cut off from the possibility of immediate help and then self-renewing, as it were.'[34]

Sophie, another of Alun's conquests, or reconquests, 'quite likes' Charlie, who guesses that she's been to bed with Alun but makes no fuss. 'As always, he and Sophie had not exchanged so much as a glance about it. Let it be. Something like half-way through the twenty-two years he had in any case given up a large part of the right to a say in that area of Sophie's life.'[35] Peter Thomas has also forgone a say in such matters. He and his wife Muriel 'had not touched each other for nearly ten years'.[36] However, Peter's lot is happier than Charlie's. Rhiannon's goodness wakens him at the novel's end, after Muriel leaves him and Alun expires in a fit of rage and revulsion (in a brilliant comic scene). Rhiannon forgives Peter ('After everything I've done? After the way I treated you?')[37] and Peter at last finds words to express his feelings, an activity he usually avoids, 'like talking about Wales' (which can't be talked about, according to Rhiannon, 'unless you're making a collection of dishonesty and self-deception and sentimental bullshit'). Here is Peter's declaration of love: '"Though you might not think so," he said with care, "and there was certainly a time when I forgot it myself, I've always loved you and I do to this day. I'm sorry it sounds ridiculous because I'm so fat and horrible, and not at all nice or even any fun, but I mean it. I only wish it was worth more."'[38] This declaration is made at the end of the book, at the wedding of William and Rosemary. The wedding party is in full swing and Rhiannon is unable to respond properly, telling Peter to ring her later that night. Rhiannon is like Jenny Bunn or Barbara Bowen, the wife of Garnet Bowen in *I Like It Here*, or the Hilly of 'Instead of an Epilogue', from Amis's *Memoirs*, 'who spoke to say something, laughed when amused'. As Rhiannon runs off, we are told that 'one of her distinctions from other females had always been that she only ran to catch buses and such, not to let the world know about her wild free spirit or alternately the coruscating wave of emotion that for the moment enfolded her'.[39] Rhiannon met Peter when he was in his twenties. Like Hilly, she got pregnant, but unlike Hilly she went through with the abortion; then Peter 'set about looking further', as Amis says of himself in 'Instead of an Epilogue'. At the end of the novel, Peter moves in with Rhiannon. It was Muriel, his wife, who had the money, owned the family house and put it on the market when she decided to leave Wales. Muriel is English and William was her 'last reason or excuse for hanging on any longer round here'. Whether Peter moves to England with her, she tells him, is 'entirely up to you'.[40] The remaining old devils are fascinated by Peter and Rhiannon's cohabitation, which in some respects resembles that of Amis and the Kilmarnocks. 'Has he ever said if he hands over any cash for his bed and board?' Gwen Cellan-Davies asks her husband, Malcolm. 'Makes any contribution to the household?' As for the 'scandalous' aspects of the new arrangement, these are greeted with amusement. 'Nay, stare not so,' Amis wrote to Larkin, as we've seen, just after announcing that the Kilmarnocks were moving in: 'Well, You'd be justified in staring a bit.' The old devils react to Peter and Rhiannon's living arrangements as Amis imagines his friends reacted to his and the Kilmarnocks'. 'Fascinating,' declares Gwen. 'In Wales. Under the same roof as an unprotected female in Wales. And her a widow too. You'd think you were in the twentieth century.' To which Malcolm replies: 'Good luck to them is what I say.'[41]

Malcolm's reply is generous. He, too, has always loved Rhiannon. Though fussy and pedantic, Malcolm is the most romantic of the old devils, the one most likely to put intimate feelings into words. It is no accident that he also writes poems about Wales. Shortly after Rhiannon returns he arranges an outing with her along the Gower peninsula, one she is rightly apprehensive about, given his feelings for her. As they walk by the water's edge, she recalls the agonies and awkwardnesses of beach outings in their youth ('hoping you looked wonderful with wet hair', 'smiling and trying to feel if half your bottom was out of your bathing-costume').[42] Rhiannon's purpose in recalling these minor embarrassments 'was to show him that she was not the curious creature, something between Snow White and a wild animal, that he had seemed to take her for, but an actual friend of his, and by now quite an old one'.[43] Malcolm has been leading her towards a tiny church on the promontory of Pwll Glan bay, 'a wonderful spot. Peaceful. Solitary'[44] (according to Amis's notes for the novel, it is based on Oxwich Bay, just beyond Swansea and Carswell Bays, which makes St Mary's, the church they visit, St Illtyd's, accurately described by Amis). It was here that Malcolm first declared his love for Rhiannon, many years ago: 'I said, I know I'll never mean as much to you as you mean to me, anywhere near, and I'm not complaining, I said, but I want to tell you nobody will ever mean as much to me as you do, and I want you to remember that, I said. And you said you would, and I think perhaps you have, haven't you, Rhiannon?'[45] To her great distress, Rhiannon hasn't remembered, which she tries valiantly to hide. 'You don't remember any of it, do you?' Malcolm eventually realises: 'Not having lunch or walking up to St. Mary's or what I said or anything.' Rhiannon begins to cry: 'I'm so stupid, so hopeless, no good to anybody, I just think of myself all the time, don't notice other people. It's not much to ask, remembering a lovely day out, but I can't even do that.'[46] This reaction again recalls the Hilly of 'Instead of an Epilogue', who 'if things went wrong, feared she might be at fault'.

Malcolm is an inept lover, an inept doting swain as well, but he's a decent man. His excursion with Rhiannon resembles Jenny Bunn's date with Graham McClintoch in *Take a Girl Like You*. Rhiannon's tears elicit an immediate gesture of sympathy: 'I can't have you apologizing to me, my dear Rhiannon. Honestly now.' At which point, the two old friends busy themselves with face-saving bustle, wonderfully observed: 'She got to work with her tissues and comb and he wandered about making suitable points like the church being *probably* twelfth century and having effigies of a member of the de Courcey family and his lady in the south wall of the chancel'.[47] The chapter ends with Malcolm lamenting the disappearance of a village along the bay and Rhiannon at last remembering something, the garden of a grand house nearby ('Didn't we go there once before, one summer, not a very nice day?').[48] As Malcolm seems on the point of drifting back on to dangerously sentimental territory, Rhiannon decides she must 'let him say what he likes now':

She reached out and took and squeezed his hand as they walked down to the churchyard gate and took it again on the far side, in comfort or apology or what she hoped would pass as understanding, or perhaps like one person letting another know that whatever it was they were facing they would face it together. He squeezed back but kept quiet after all until they were on their way inland through the marshes, and then for once in his life he talked about nothing in particular.[49]

Throughout this scene sound deeply felt echoes of the poems of Philip Larkin, in particular 'To the Sea', 'Church Going' and 'An Arundel Tomb'. As Malcolm and Rhiannon approach the beach they glimpse half-naked people 'all loaded with food and drink containers, tents, boats, sports kits, games, anything and everything for children'; then they see 'the groups of young men straggling down from the car park with no shirts on, satisfied with that being all right and not bothering about looking horrible, being it too for not bothering.'[50] Once out of the car park, Malcolm leads Rhiannon 'down crosswise towards the sea'. As in Larkin's 'To the Sea', 'To step over the low wall that divides / Road from concrete walk above the shore / Brings sharply back something known long before', not just 'the miniature gaiety of seasides', but the way innocent pleasures and care for loved ones overcome awkwardnesses and inadequacies:

> . . . If the worst
> Of flawless weather is our falling short,
> It may be that through habit these do best,
> Coming to water clumsily undressed
> Yearly; teaching their children by a sort
> Of clowning; helping the old, too, as they ought.[51]

The church Malcolm leads Rhiannon towards is locked and there hasn't been a service there since 1959, 'longer than half the people on the beach can remember'.[52] As they speculate on the disappearance of churches, their conversation recalls Larkin's 'Church Going'. Unlike Malcolm, 'one of the crew / That tap and jot and know what rood-lofts were', the speaker of Larkin's poem hasn't much idea of what he's looking at when he enters the church. When Rhiannon asks Malcolm if he believes, he answers: 'in a way I suppose I do. I certainly hate to see it all disappearing . . . I like to come here occasionally. It helps me.' The banality of Rhiannon's response – 'It certainly has an atmosphere' – suggests how far the sea of faith has receded. When Rhiannon holds Malcolm's hand at the end of the scene, the meaning of the gesture is complex, like the handclasp of the stone figures in Larkin's 'An Arundel Tomb'.[53] Larkin's account of the meaning of these clasped hands is as undeceived and poignant as Amis's account of the meaning of Rhiannon and Malcolm's hand-clasp. What does it matter if the earl and countess's 'faithfulness in effigy' was an artistic convention or convenience, a sculptor's flourish 'Thrown off in helping to prolong / The Latin names around the base'?

> . . . The stone fidelity
> They hardly meant has come to be
> Their final blazon, and to prove
> Our almost-instinct almost true:
> What will survive of us is love.[54]

These are not the only Larkin echoes in *The Old Devils*. Rhiannon's difficulty with Malcolm is 'to find / Words at once true and kind / Or not untrue and not unkind' ('Talking in Bed'); when Charlie declares 'Life was first boredom, then more boredom', he rewrites Larkin's 'Life is first boredom, then fear' ('Dockery and Son'); the title of the novel nods to Larkin's 'The Old Fools'. A more general debt underlies the novel's conclusion, which lifts the reader out of the realm of satire and documentary realism into a higher realm, as do the endings of so many Larkin poems: not the literal realm of air and sky, as in the endings of 'High Windows', 'The Whitsun Weddings', 'Here', and 'Vers de Société', but a figurative realm, that of myth or romance. The marriage of William and Rosemary, who are admired and respected, is revivifying and full of promise; it has what William H. Pritchard, in the *New York Times Book Review*, calls a 'mythy' feel.[55] From the moment early in the year when it is announced, 'Peter had been given a new lease of life. Every time he thought of it he felt as if he had been reading a communiqué announcing a catastrophic defeat of the shits.'[56] What drew Amis towards this more positive outlook, what made it available to him, was partly the reunion with Hilly. But it was partly also the feelings released in him by a darker turn of events: the dying and death of Philip Larkin.

It was while Amis was at work on *The Old Devils* that Larkin's comic complaints about his health took on a worrying seriousness. In the letters of 1984 and the first half of 1985, these complaints inspired friendly competition and may have spurred Amis's accounts of the old devils' illnesses and bodily indignities. 'We must exchange more paunch talk,' Larkin wrote to Amis on 22 October 1984. 'Do you get breathless, dear? Of course, you don't have shoes to lace' (not having a proper job to dress up for, Larkin is implying).[57] But Amis had toenails to clip. Peter's toenails, the subject of a bravura passage in *The Old Devils*, are sharp, jagged and too long. After numerous failed experiments, Peter ends up cutting them outdoors, where 'at least he could let the parings fly free, and fly they bloody well did, especially the ones that came crunching off his big toes, which were massive enough and moved fast enough to have brought down a sparrow on the wing, though so far this had not occurred.'[58]

Paunch talk led to drink talk. 'Glad to hear you are all right again,' Amis wrote to Larkin on 28 November. 'When I drink for 2/3 days now I follow with ½ nights of waking at 3.30, lying awake till 5.0 and then extreme drowsiness plus nightmares as long as I care to go on. You too? No? I am such an anxious cunt that by the time I've drunk enough to slow me down I've also drunk enough to make me very anxious.' On 20 March 1985 Larkin reported to Amis that he had 'been going through about six weeks' panic about my health, involving blood tests, x-rays, liver scans, barium enemas (grand lads, those) and the like'. His doctors had advised him to drink less, 'though as usual no one ever says what "drinking less" means'.[59] Amis wrote back on 2 April: 'Oh shit: what can I say? V. sorry to hear of your ordeals. Barium enemas, Christ.' Amis himself had recently cut down on booze, limiting himself 'to 4–5 drinks a day'.[60] If Larkin cut down, 'my exp. says you will feel a hell of a lot better, like being quite prepared to start the day . . . Get your appetite back, too. You're probably there already by the time you get this.' On 7 May Larkin wrote to Conquest: 'My own drama is winding slowly to its close; Act I: The Colon, Act II: The Liver. The curtain goes up next week on Act III: The Stomach . . . Everybody has written to me recently, except of course Kingsley, though come to that it's my turn to write to him.' When Larkin did write to Amis, three days later, he reported having cut down on drink and lost a stone, 'but am still very much a daily drinker and my mutinous liver may not think I've done enough'. He felt generally debilitated, 'sodding OLD, like someone pushing 63',[61] the age his father died.

On 11 June Larkin's oesophagus was removed in an operation at the Hull Royal Infirmary ('The Building' in *High Windows*). It was cancerous and another cancerous tumour was discovered in his throat, too advanced to be removed. On 19 June, while still in hospital, Larkin vomited after drinking most of a bottle of whisky, went into a coma and nearly died. It took him a month to recover from the episode and to leave hospital. Amis wrote to Larkin on 20 July to commiserate: 'Needless to say I've been thinking of you a great deal over the last weeks. Let me know if I can do anything. One thing I can do is write to you. So I will again "before very long." I suppose you have some time to go there still after that crise? Hilly sends her love (it's her bithrayd today: 57, Xt), also Allie. Now GTE WLLE SNOO.' Four days later, having spoken to Larkin on the telephone, Amis reported to Conquest: 'He sounded very back-to-form on the blower . . . as regards tone, that is. Content pretty gloomy, though no dread words were dropped. Doesn't expect to work (at lib.) again. Not much one can say, but I intend to keep up a barrage of letters.' Towards the end of the letter Amis reported his progress on *The Old Devils*: he was 'coming up to 200 book-pages', more than half the finished novel.

As so often in Amis's career, novel-writing took precedence over correspondence, shockingly so in this instance. On 27 August Larkin wrote Amis a very gloomy letter: he had lost his appetite, was in terrible spirits, 'whereas in the past I used to think about death three quarters of the time, I now think about it *all* the time'.[62] It took Amis a month to reply. 'I can do better than this, this rate of writing I mean,' began his letter of 24 September. 'It sounds ridiculous to say I'm sorry you feel so rotten, though I am, *and* to say I often think of you, though I do.' Tentatively, he offered Larkin advice: 'for low spirits I don't know. I'd get a lot of magazines sent, so there was always something fresh to read in the mornings. And if it's not too silly have you thought of getting yourself a kitten? As you will have noticed yourself, they are uncommonly engaging, also funny.' Towards the end of the letter, after passages on jazz, literary gossip and the first American reviews of *Stanley*, Amis introduced the idea of a visit: 'Hey: H. and I are on our own for a bit and ready for trips. Would you like us to come up and see you? Just that: we will appear at stated time, stay, depart when prearranged. You needn't do anything. If it's not a good idea for any reason, you can say so without giving the reason. *I won't refer to it again.*' Larkin, in a letter of 4 October, scotched the idea, though gently: 'It's very nice of you to offer to visit; having pondered, I think we had better leave it for a bit. I shd love to see you both, but am in no state for a visit of more than an hour or two, and that wd be hell for you (no *through* King's X- Hull trains any more . . . Moreover, it wd be bound to centre on LUNCH, and I can't fuckin eat fuck all).' The doctors had assured him that he would slowly get better: 'To my mind I am slowly getting worse. The GP listens to this sympathetically, but rather as if he were the next door neighbour – without suggesting, that is, that it has any special relevance to his own knowledge or responsibilities.' The letter is in part valedictory: 'Thirty years in print – well, what with your *Lord Jim* thing (celebrated in Penguins I'm pleased to see) I think we can say we've done *something* of what we hoped when unknown lads.'

Larkin's letter of 4 October upset Amis, who wrote to Conquest about it three days later. Larkin had complained about not having anything to do; Amis wanted him to put together an edition of unpublished early poems. The problem with broaching this idea was that it was 'impossible not to imply "while you're still around," and he wouldn't anyway, the silly old perfectionist'. Conquest liked Amis's idea and tried to work out ways to suggest it, in a letter of 7 November: 'V. sound that Philip should do a book. What about an Odd Pieces, prose and verse . . . Having prose would indicate that the verse wasn't to be taken too seriously etc. I'll suggest it, though the idea that it is therapy for invalids must be left out. "I've always wanted to see . . . now that you are half time . . ." maybe.' Larkin did not hear from Amis for another month. On 17 November a letter arrived beginning: 'No, I don't, do I, seem to have stuck to my intention of writing more often. Though I hope things will improve when novel is done, now entering its climacteric (sense li in COD).'[63] Amis now had a different idea for Larkin, one that recalled earlier jokey literary collaborations: 'I have as I may have said a Dylan-like character in [*The Old Devils*], safely long dead but some of the others bother about him. I wish you'd take your finger out and run me up half a dozen lines of sub-Thomas to come swimming back into someone's head. I think I could do it myself, though not as well, and there's no actual need for it anyway but it would be fun to have it there for a chap to wonder whether it was genius or piss. What about having a shot?'

On 21 November Larkin wrote what would turn out to be his last letter to Amis, dictating into a tape-recorder, 'almost the only way I can communicate these days'. He had undergone more tests and had a big one to come; his morale was 'about as low as I can remember'. Though the doctors remained cheerful and optimistic, 'I don't really trust them any more. Only Monica's reiterated "You look all right" brings me encouragement.' He apologised for being unable to run up the sub-Thomas lines, suggesting instead that 'you use your wonderful stuff from *That Uncertain Feeling*' (meaning from Gareth Probert, an earlier sub-Thomas): '"Crewe junction down the sleepers of the breath" – well, if I can remember that after thirty years it must be pretty good, or pretty funny, and it's perfectly clear whose behind you are kicking.' This compliment, an obvious friendship-assertion, is followed by a passage about Sally and Hilly:

I must mention Sally's letter and photograph which arrived this morning. Of course they deserve a separate acknowledgement, and *may* one day get one. I am so glad to see strong resemblances in her to Hilly, who is the most beautiful woman I have ever seen without being in the least pretty (I am sure you know what I mean, and I hope she will too).

Well, the tape draws to an end; think of me packing up my pyjamas and shaving things for today's ordeal, and hope all goes well. I really feel this year has been more than I deserve; I suppose it's all come at once, instead of being spread out as with most people.

You will excuse the absence of the usual valediction,

Yours ever,

Phillip

The ending of this letter, with its omitted 'bum', is as memorable as Keats's 'I always made an awkward bow.' Eleven days later, on 2 December, Larkin was dead.

Amis and Hilly attended the funeral, travelling up to Hull by train on 9 December with Andrew Motion, once a colleague of Larkin's at Hull, Motion's wife, the literary journalist Jan Dalley, Charles Monteith, Larkin's editor at Faber, and Blake Morrison, who had commissioned reviews from Larkin for the *Observer*. Larkin had lived in Hull for thirty years and this was the first time Amis had come to visit, though he had previously visited Larkin in Leicester and Belfast and Larkin had visited Amis in Swansea, Cambridge and London.[64] He never made it to the city itself, nor to Larkin's home. As Amis explained to Conquest in a letter of 1 January, Terence Whelden, Larkin's solicitor, met the train at a suburban stop, gave Amis and the others lunch at his house, 'which commanded wonderful mysterious view of the tops of the bridge above the mist' (the Humber bridge), then drove them to the university church in Cottingham, where the service was held. The church was packed, 'perhaps 500 strong'. Amis gave the address and he and Hilly were also among a handful of mourners to go on to the graveside. Monica, who lived with Larkin, had been too ill to attend either the service or the burial and there was no invitation back to the house. As Amis reported to Conquest: 'we buggered off rather miserably, in our case without ever having seen it. Back on the train with junk food and Scotch.' Both before and after the funeral, Amis wrote to Conquest about how he missed Larkin: 'not just for his poetry and friendship, but in some broader, more general way' (24 December); 'as you say, one thinks of the old lad a lot, and even when not thinking of him feels him around in the background' (23 February 1996). In the weeks after Larkin's death, while at work on *The Old Devils*, Amis felt haunted by what, in a New Year's Day letter to Conquest, he called Larkin's 'presence'.[65] The qualities he singled out for praise in the funeral address were Larkin's humour and honesty and the consoling power of his poetry. His poems 'offer comfort, and not cold comfort either. They are not dismal or pessimistic, but invigorating; they know that for all its shortcomings life must be got on with.' Just such knowledge underlies *The Old Devils*, a work almost as indebted to Larkin as *Lucky Jim* and for many its main rival, or one of its main rivals, for pre-eminence among Amis's novels.

This judgement was shared by a majority of the Booker Prize panel. The judges for 1986 were the novelists Bernice Rubens and Isabel Quigly, the radio critic Gillian Reynolds, Edna Healey, the writer, filmmaker and wife of Denis Healey (she was the panel's 'general reader'), and Anthony Thwaite, the sole male judge, also the panel's chair (and an old Amis fan). According to Amis's diary, the novel was submitted to the panel on 3 August, a month before publication; it was one of 127 entries, a record at the time. The other short-listed novels, in what was generally thought a strong list, were Robertson Davies's *What's Bred in the Bone*, Margaret Atwood's *The Handmaid's Tale*, Timothy Mo's *An Insular Possession*, Kazuo Ishiguro's *An Artist of the Floating World* and Paul Bailey's *Gabriel's Lament*. On the day the shortlist was announced Ladbroke's made *The Old Devils* 2–1 favourite; as the two previous winners had been women,[66] there was some talk, in the press and on arts programmes, of its being time for a man to win; the predominantly female panel may also have been influenced by Amis's perceived softening towards women. Bernice Rubens told me that she fought hard for the Robertson Davies novel, 'which should have won'. Edna Healey also supported the Davies novel. Amis's firm supporters were Thwaite and Gillian Reynolds, with Isabel Quigley on the fence. Until five minutes before the announcement the panel was deadlocked; then Quigly came down on Amis's side. In chairmanly fashion, Thwaite described the judges' deliberations as 'without dissent'.

Amis brought Mavis Nicholson with him on the night the prize was announced, first making sure she dressed up properly (when she and Geoff accompanied him to Buckingham Palace in 1981, for his CBE, he was very anxious that she wear hat *and* gloves: 'a real little boy from Norbury, this is,' she told him). As Thwaite declared to the assembled Booker shareholders and literati in the London Guildhall that *The Old Devils* had won, Amis made what Mavis recognised as his 'amazed' face and leaned across the table to give her a big, exaggerated hug. He had been uncomfortable at the dinner, seated between strangers and anxious about making a fool of himself in public. He only relaxed a bit when he'd thought up a couple of football clichés to use after the announcement: 'How do I feel? Sick as a parrot, Brian'; 'Oh, over the moon, Keith.' Then he said what he'd buy with the prize money: 'booze, of course', 'new curtains' ('though I bought nothing specific with that money,' he later wrote, 'which merely slimmed down my overdraft'); 'I also said, grinning from ear to ear to show I was joking, that until just now I had thought the Booker Prize a rather trivial, showbizzy caper, but now I considered it a very serious, reliable indication of literary merit.'[67] Back home at Regents Park Road, before the decision was broadcast, Hilly scrubbed the kitchen floor 'for the first time in my life', trying to keep busy and avoid getting drunk. 'I was so excited. We had champagne ready. Some awful person rang us up in the middle of the programme and said "He's got it." I said I don't want to know, I want to see it on the telly. We were all excited, Philip and Sally were here . . . When his name was announced, we roared like teenagers.'[68]

The high spirits continued throughout the week. When Theo Richmond and his wife Lee Langley were invited to lunch at Regents Park Road the following Sunday they were greeted at the door by

Hilly and Amis who had stuck yellow 'Booker Nominee' labels on their noses, the sort you find in large bookstores, and were bobbing their heads up and down 'like those nodding dolls'. Ali was there and Martin and 'there was such a celebratory mood'. When the party sat down to lunch, a cheese platter with an enormous Victorian dome over it was pushed towards Lee: 'Dig in,' Amis said. When she lifted the lid there was a live hamster twitching its whiskers at her. 'After that, we moved on to the pork pies.' The good mood was sustained in succeeding months by money news in particular. In addition to the £15,000 prize money, winning the Booker meant increased sales: within a week of the announcement, Hutchinson received orders for a further 30,000 copies. Sales of the subsequent paperback were also remarkable. On 2 February 1988 Peter Carson of Penguin wrote to Clowes to say that 180,000 copies had been sold to date, three times the figure for *Stanley and the Women* (1984) and twice that of *Russian Hide-and-Seek* (1980).[69] Ancillary benefits were of several sorts. On 9 December, Macmillan made a large bid to woo Amis from Hutchinson; Clowes made sure Hutchinson got wind of the bid and within days Amis was offered a new two-book deal, the one for £100,000 a title. Dent had a deal to publish *The Crime of the Century*, Amis's 1975 *Sunday Times* serial, in book form, in the spring of 1987; after Amis won the prize, both its projected print run and his advance were doubled. In April, Amis's *Collected Short Stories* (1980) was reissued by Hutchinson, with the addition of only two new stories ('Investing in Futures' and 'Affairs of Death'). 'It is doubtful that the appearance of just two more would have merited a new edition if it had not been for the Booker Prize,' commented the reviewer in the *Independent*.[70] There was also good news from America. When *The Old Devils* was published there in February, it received excellent reviews in both the daily and the Sunday *New York Times*. The Pritchard review, on Sunday, 22 February 1988, was accompanied by a long front-page article by Malcolm Bradbury entitled 'Of English Letters'. In the article, Bradbury compared Waugh and Amis, calling them 'major writers of extraordinary dimensions and decided influence'. Amis was Waugh's heir, a dominant force in English letters: 'few contemporary comic writers can get free of the comic intonations of Kingsley Amis'.[71]

By the date of the American reviews Amis was well into his next novel, *Difficulties with Girls*, another return, as we shall see. The

excitement of the Booker had energised him. On 23 April he reported
to Conquest that the 'new novel has been coming in a bloody flood,
well, p.68 today, and have been arse-creeping the Muse'.[72] He also
began doing more journalism. After Jane left him in November 1980,
Amis's journalistic output declined markedly. In the three-year period
from January 1981 to January 1984, he wrote fewer than twenty
articles for newspapers and periodicals.[73] Early in 1984, however,
Amis's friend Mike Molloy, editor of the *Daily Mirror*, offered him
a job as the paper's 'Poetry Editor', an improbable commission from
a tabloid. Amis took the job seriously, selecting and introducing a
poem every weekday for a year, unpatronisingly tailoring the column
to what he saw as the interests and capacities of its mass audience.
The column began on 19 March 1984 and lasted until 15 March
1985, when it was discontinued by Robert Maxwell, who purchased
the paper six months into Amis's one-year contract. On 18 July
1984, Amis wrote to Conquest about his selections: 'there I am
feeding them (I quote from the last few weeks) Browning, Tennyson,
Housman, Kipling, Edward Thomas and Isaac Watts when I could
be giving them Adrian Mitchell, Tony Harrison and John Ashbery'.
In fact he did eventually select an Ashbery poem, 'Fear of Death',
on 14 February 1985, two days after printing Sylvia Plath's 'The
Moon and the Yew Tree'. The introduction to the Ashbery poem is
typical in length and tone: 'Ashbery has a great following in his
native America, where he has been more than once called the greatest
poet now writing in the English language. British readers have been
more cautious. His meaning is usually implied rather than stated
and it is sometimes hard to gain more than a general impression.'
In an introduction to *The Pleasure of Poetry* (1990), which reprints
Amis's selections and introductions, he calls the *Mirror* column 'the
most enjoyable job I ever had'.[74]

Other regular journalistic work followed. From 1985 onwards
Amis published several dozen pieces a year, in addition to contri-
butions to radio programmes and appearances on television.
Apologies for not writing letters once again mentioned not only
novels but 'deadlined crap like doing the links for Poetry Please on
Radio 4'.[75] At the end of 1985 Amis began writing regular restau-
rant reviews, something he continued to do until a year before his
death, first for the *Illustrated London News* (October 1985 to
January 1988), then for *Harper's and Queen* (September 1990 to
December 1993), then, very briefly, for *The Oldie* (April to June

1994). These reviews were mostly of grand and very expensive establishments, often of hotel restaurants, and the bills Amis ran up were impressive, partly because of what and how much he drank. On 18 September 1988, on the eve of publication of *Difficulties with Girls*, the restaurant columnist for the *Sunday Express* took Amis to lunch at the Berkeley Hotel in Knightsbridge. The amounts Amis ate and drank were typical of such occasions (though he ordered less expensive wine when his own employers picked up the tab). He began with a couple of martinis ('a proper drink') while deciding to eat dressed crab and steak tartare. After he 'boasted modestly' that he knew nothing of wine, Amis ordered a Chablis grand cru (£44) and a Chatêau Lafite-Rothschild 1970 (£160). He then drank a glass of Sauternes with his raspberries, a port with his cheese and a large Calvados to follow.

Amis's restaurant columns manage to combine extravagance with blokey straightforwardness. Little attempt is made to disguise the limitations of his palate or his dislike of fine or fancy food, which sometimes seems the point of going to fine or fancy restaurants. At *Harper's and Queen* he was paid £400 a column plus expenses (i.e., the cost of one meal per restaurant for himself and a guest); representative claims from 1990 and 1991 include £130 (The Connaught), £127 (The Berkeley), £140 (The Ritz). Paul Fussell writes well about Amis's restaurant criticism, which he admires and sees as animated by the same impulse as all his criticism: 'the quest for enjoyment, unmarred by anxiety about fashionableness and alert to the slightest hint of phoniness or fraud'.[76] For Amis, Fussell continues, the restaurant manager's job is to simplify and delete: 'cut out the music, canned or strolling; restrict cooking and preparation to the kitchen, avoiding showy salad constructions and silly flames at the table; prevent waiters from reciting "specials"; repress the designer-chef's urge to make his products look like paintings (long ago Amis learned to "distrust any dish that appeals to the eye"); and eliminate the hype and fakery from the wine list and all needless French from the menu. All these are analogous to "moral seriousness" in writing and good workmanship there.'[77] In his fiction Amis offers several scenes of rudeness to waiters. The restaurant columns contain examples of waiterly rudeness. In an account of Green's Restaurant and Oyster Bar in St James these examples are categorised by nationality. The waiter who served him 'imparted an international flavour, being very much the Frenchman in his obvious surprise, even disapproval, on hearing what I proposed to eat, British in bringing the wrong things and in not apologizing when this was pointed out, and French again in implying that differences at such a low level were pretty un-important.'[78]

Fussell's explanation of why Amis chose to review so many expensive hotel restaurants, twenty-six altogether, is that he was a contrarian: 'Is it a commonplace among the sophisticated that hotel restaurants are usually disappointing? Then he will review a lot of them and delight in finding them admirable.'[79] This explanation seems to me partial in several senses. Eating in expensive hotel restaurants had a complex signification for Amis. In addition to allowing him to ridicule pretension and pomposity and champion simplicity and honesty (of ingredients, workmanship, presentation), it was a sign of how far he'd come ('a real little boy from Norbury, this is') as well as of what he thought was his due. Part of the fun of ordering £160 bottles of wine at someone else's expense was the knowledge that he was allowed to do so because he was Kingsley Amis. In personal as well as professional relations, especially towards the end of his life, receiving his due became increasingly important to Amis. After behaving badly with Julian Barnes and Pat Kavanagh at a dinner at the Garrick – we shall return to this scene – Amis's defence to Martin was that Julian had not shown him proper respect 'as a senior writer'. Barnes admired Amis and for a time seriously contemplated writing his biography, but his reaction to this remark was that the senior writers he respected 'didn't refer to themselves as senior writers'. When in 1987 Amis's copy was cut and altered by a junior editor at the *Sunday Times*, his letter of protest began: 'It's a bit galling for someone of my generation to have written to a given length and find himself subsequently cut and also corrected here and there, and without being consulted, even with a UK number for you and a couple of weeks to do it in.'[80] In December 1987 the Director of the National Portrait Gallery, John Hayes, made the mistake of inviting Amis to sit for a joint portrait with Martin. 'This is one of the most amazingly inept and tactless suggestions that has ever been made to me,' he wrote in reply. 'If this refusal leaves your artist with time on his hands, you might get him to knock up a picture of the Two Ronnies.'[81] One other factor underlies Amis's attraction to grand hotel restaurants: the greedy character of his pursuit of pleasure, as in 'I want more than my fair share before anyone else has had any at all.' Picking the Ritz to review, then the

Connaught, then the Savoy, then Claridge's, is a form of gobbling, like celebrating your birthday every week.

Amis's editor at *Harper's and Queen* was Rosie Boycott, who quickly became a steady lunching companion and friend. On the surface theirs was the least likely of friendships. Boycott had worked in the underground press in the 1960s, was a founding editor of the feminist magazine *Spare Rib* and a founding board member of the feminist publishing house Virago. Her move from *Spare Rib* to *Harper's and Queen*, via the *Daily Mail* and the *Daily Telegraph*, was driven by finances rather than ideology ('I had a kid and I needed to make money'); politically, she remained on the left. In addition, or as Amis might say, as against that, she didn't drink. Yet she was lively, good-looking and tough. She came to the magazine as deputy editor in the spring of 1990, some months before Amis began his column and some months after the dissolution of her marriage to the journalist David Leitch. It was decided that as deputy editor she was senior enough to look after Amis, a task she approached with weariness rather than trepidation (not being much given to trepidation): 'this will be a chore,' she thought, 'but he'll be an interesting person to have as a restaurant columnist.' Initially, Amis tried to bait her: 'he'd make jokes about "nightmare-tough women" and then he'd look at me; he'd smile that sort of loony, funny, rather irresistible Kingsley smile and I'd just laugh'. In fact, 'Kingsley really liked tough women.' He liked Mrs Thatcher, after all, about whom they'd have 'these nice arguments, the kind I like, about whether Mrs Thatcher was good for women or not'. Boycott found that she could tease Amis in turn: about why he was so right-wing or what made him think he could turn up for lunch in an egg-spattered tie.

It was the topic of drink that moved the friendship to a deeper level. Amis asked Boycott why she didn't drink and she said because she was an alcoholic.[82] He was fascinated by her sobriety and began asking questions: 'how I managed not to drink, how one lived a life without drink, what drink did to me'. He also talked about himself and his family, in particular about Sally's drinking, how much it worried him and what he could do about it. 'He'd say things like: "How come you're so happy for someone who used to drink? How come you've done it? What did you do?" And I would tell everything I could think of that might be remotely helpful.' During their lunches, which took place perhaps three times a month, sometimes at a restaurant Amis was reviewing, sometimes not, Amis drank as usual, about as much as with the restaurant columnist of the *Sunday Express*. Boycott felt unthreatened and unpressured by his drinking and only once or twice early on told him she thought he drank too much or asked him if he thought he was an alcoholic. 'I didn't think Kingsley *was* an alcoholic,' she says, partly because of his age (sixty-eight in 1990, to her thirty-nine): 'There's something about people who get to be that age and can drink. That they've survived and they're still tottering along probably means that the alcohol is not quite as destructive to them as it is to younger people.' In Boycott's view, real alcoholics die before they reach sixty-eight: 'David[83] died, Sally died, people die; something like only 5 per cent of alcoholics get to die natural deaths.[84] The figures are incredibly dreary and Kingsley and I would kind of go through the figures. He was very very sad about it. He did think it [Sally's alcoholism] was his fault; like any father he felt a fantastic sense of responsibility.'

Boycott used to invite Amis around to her house for supper, in addition to having lunches with him. On several occasions he went upstairs to read her seven-year-old daughter Daisy bedtime stories. After the surprise of discovering how much fun it was being with Amis, Boycott was flattered by his company, finding him 'fantastically interesting'. At their lunches, usually lasting until four in the afternoon ('one of the joys of working for the glossies'), Amis would tell her about the novel he was working on and ask her the sorts of questions he used to ask Hilly, Mavis and Jane: 'He'd say: "She's got to do this, she's got to do that, any suggestions?"' What struck Boycott most about Amis was how open he was about his feelings: 'He talked about his family, he talked about his wives, he talked about not being able to sleep or turn the light out at night, he talked about how he had screwed things up . . . He talked a lot about being afraid and I thought that very touching.' That few people knew of their friendship ('it could have ended up in all sorts of diary items') made it special, and may partly account for Amis's openness; 'it was something separate'. After lunch, 'we'd shuffle off to find Kingsley a taxi, arm in arm'.

In 1992 Boycott was appointed editor of *Esquire* (later she would edit the *Independent*, *Independent on Sunday* and *Daily Express*). In her new job there was little time for three-hour lunches and 'I drifted away from Kingsley.' 'You've got to make more effort if this relationship is going to work,' was the first thing he said to her when they met for lunch some months after she'd begun the job. The remark made her wonder: 'Have I really not got something right here?' That she hadn't, or hadn't completely, was suggested by a letter she received from Martin Amis after his father's death, describing her as 'the last person [i.e., woman] Kingsley felt something for'. This something was not sexual, or not seriously sexual, though for a while Amis thought that it might have been. When he suggested as much to Martin, Martin told him that he'd made a pass at Boycott years ago and hadn't got anywhere: 'Maybe you'll have better luck.' As Boycott remembers it, though the lunches were flirty, it was 'in the way an older man is flirty with a younger woman, there was nothing predatory ever about Kingsley'. What Amis wanted from her, she believes, 'was for me to sort of be there more, like I had been'. Amis clearly looked forward to their lunches: 'he'd send me postcards in advance, postcards afterwards, letters, he'd phone quite often'. Boycott looked forward to them as well, but her new job absorbed most of her energy and she saw Amis infrequently in the very last years of his life. In 1995, on a flight back to London from Johannesburg, she picked up a newspaper and read that he had died. She burst into tears, full of remorse at having neglected the friendship.

Boycott was not the only person with whom Amis developed an emotional intimacy in the last years of his life. When he stayed with George and Mary Gale in Northumberland or Virginia and Michael Rush in Swansea (friends he had made through Eve and Stuart Thomas), he came to confide in his hostesses, who found his vulnerability and gratitude for their kindnesses affecting. Antonia Phillips, Martin's wife, also found Amis affecting and was 'enormously fond of him', despite the sometimes tense nature of his visits for Sunday lunch or early supper. In 1992 Cyril Metliss, Amis's close friend from the City of London School, re-established contact. According to Amis's diaries, he and Metliss began lunching together regularly in November, around the time Boycott became unavailable. They would talk about music and old times but also about more personal worries and concerns: their families, the choices they had made in their lives. At the Garrick Club, though it was mostly the public Amis who was on display, a formidable and forbidding not a vulnerable man, there were moments of softening. When Timothy Odhams, a long-standing member, was terminally ill in hospital and not up to visitors, Amis wrote to him 'instead of turning up in person'. 'As you will have heard,' he wrote on 23 January 1992, 'everybody at the old club shows concern for you and is constantly asking questions about how you are . . . I would say myself that I have been missing you and your shy affectionate smile in the same way as I miss the brother I never had. Everybody who has ever had anything to do with you has been cheered and warmed by the experience. I hope you'll let me know if there's anything I can do, and if you ever feel like being dropped in on, I'll be there. Yours ever, Kingsley.'

Difficulties with Girls, the novel Amis published in 1988, two years after *The Old Devils*, shows his feeling side only in respect to its heroine. This heroine is Jenny Bunn, now Jenny Standish; the novel is a sequel to *Take a Girl Like You*. Jenny and Patrick have been married for six years and live in a flat in a modern block near Waterloo (based on the Cut, where the Nicholsons once lived). The unpublished 'Difficulties' was set in the early 1960s, the published one is set in 1967, the year homosexuality was decriminalised in Britain. The Standishes have no children: Jenny miscarried the pregnancy that brought Patrick to the altar and they've been unable to conceive again. Patrick is in publishing (classics teachers having become 'decreasingly relevant', in the words of his old headmaster)[85] and is still fooling around; Jenny describes herself as 'just Patrick's wife' and remains true to 'those old Bible-class ideas'. She gave up work as a primary school teacher because 'in her opinion no wife could have a full-time job and expect to look after her husband properly'.[86] Jenny turns a blind eye to Patrick's infidelities; confronting them is 'just painful without doing any good'.[87] When finally Patrick forces a confession upon her, she is as irritated at his doing so as at his unfaithfulness. Patrick is intensely fond of Jenny, even loves her, and 'provided his trousers were where they should have been . . . was always glad when [she] appeared'.[88] He takes pleasure in the way she has furnished and decorated their sunny flat, with its 'pale blue distemper' walls and table with 'pretty cotton cloth', 'bowl of fruit' and 'glass vase of fresh flowers',[89] the design equivalents of having hair that smelt 'of freshly-brushed hair' (like Christine's in *Lucky Jim*). The change in Jenny in the sequel is that she's shrewder, instantly spotting the exculpatory function of Patrick's apologies: 'So that's all right, isn't it, Patrick?' (from the scene discussed in Chapter 14, in which she likens Patrick to Tom Jones, opposing Maugham to Fielding). Some critics find Jenny's Griselda-like patience provoking.

To Gabriele Annan, writing in the *New York Review of Books*, she's 'just too much: devastatingly attractive (everyone tries to pick her up) . . . monogamous and forbearing beyond belief . . . the male chauvinist pig's dream girl, forever making cups of milky coffee for her circle of male admirers, tormentors and lame ducks'.[90]

This circle is made up largely of the Standishes' neighbours, including the obtuse and implausible Tim Valentine, discussed in the previous chapter, and a middle-aged homosexual couple, Eric Davidson and Stevie Barstow, whose existence may owe something to the homosexual couple in Jane Howard's *Getting It Right*, or to the real-life couple on whom they were based (friends of Colin's who came to Lemmons to help paint the house, described by Jane as 'funny, interesting, devoted to each other and wildly unfaithful: they got on, or off with everybody').[91] Eric and Stevie function in the novel the way Robert, the gay protagonist in the unfinished 'Difficulties', was meant to function: they allow Amis to 'say crappy things about women (and men) *as well as* about queers'. Perhaps the crappiest of these things is said by Eric, the 'top' or 'male' in the couple. 'You and I are by nature, by our respective natures,' he tells Patrick, 'males who are irresistibly attracted by a non-male principle. In your case, straightforward women; in my case not straightforward, not women – *but*, non-male, except anatomically. And it's the clash between male and non-male that causes all the trouble. They're different from us. More like children. Crying when things go wrong. Making difficulties just so as to be a person.'[92]

Eric's remarks echo a poem Amis was at work on in this period, one calculated to cause maximum offence. It is found in its fullest though still unfinished form in a letter to Conquest of 23 April 1987:

Women and queers and children
Cry when things go wrong:
Not fair! – why me? – can't take it!
[So] drones/sounds their dismal [eternal] song.

The usual sort of men
Who hold the world together
Manage to face their front
In any sort of weather.

> With rueful grins and curses
> They push the world along;
> But women and queers and children
> Cry when things go wrong.[93]

According to Jacobs, Amis subsequently polished the last two lines of the first stanza to read: 'Why me? – not him! You're horrid / Always the same old song.'[94] In both the poem and the novel, tears stand for emoting in general. Among Patrick's conquests is his next-door neighbour, Wendy Porter-King, a direct descendant of Margaret Peel in *Lucky Jim*. At the moment of seduction, Wendy asks Patrick what they should drink to:

With a sense of the ghosts of millions of men shaking their heads at him and droning in unison, 'You poor son of a bitch,' he told her in vivacious tones that of course she must be the one to settle what they should drink to.

'Then let it be to the moment,' she cried. 'The one and only unrepeatable moment.'

'To the moment,' he said, feeling that with any luck he could safely leave the rest of it.

'They're so few, aren't they? So pitifully few.'

'What are?'

'Oh, the moments in our sad little lives that make us real. Frighteningly few, those golden moments. I expect you think that's a silly word.'

'Which one?' He spoke before he could stop himself.

'Golden,' she said, her eager, wide-eyed look dimming slightly.

'No, never. Thank you for not being afraid to use it. That's where men so often fail. When the occasion comes it scares them into silence. Women are braver.'

'Then, Patrick, you do feel it too? You do feel . . . something? It would be so bleak if you felt nothing. That's what scares women, you know.'

'I do know, and you needn't be scared. I feel something all right.'

'Promise me you'll always treat me as a person.'

'I promise.'

'Promises are so easily given.'

'I'll fulfil this one. Let me show you.'[95]

Patrick calls having to put up with such talk 'cock-tax'. Later, after Wendy's 'outstanding' performance in bed, the sun shines down on them through half-drawn curtains. Wendy clasps her arms round her drawn-up knees and says: 'The sky is blue and I feel gay.' The next paragraph reads: 'She never knew how close she came to losing her front teeth for that. Taken off guard again, Patrick again spoke too quickly. "Are you an American?"'[96] (this was a favourite insult, though 'he always said he had nothing against real Americans, most of them anyway').[97]

That Jenny sounds nothing like Wendy and disapproves of 'openness' even more than Patrick are signs of her uniqueness, in Patrick's eyes certainly. Here is Patrick comparing Jenny to one of his firm's authors: 'He could not afford to undervalue the fact that Deirdre was not merely an Irishwoman and an old Irishwoman but a bloody woman as well; only with Jenny had it ever been safe to disregard that for more than a couple of minutes on end and even possible to forget it.'[98] But Jenny is not the only woman in the novel to speak out against openness. Tim's sister does as well, attributing his confused sexuality to the therapy culture. A friend once advised Tim 'to bring the whole business out in the open . . . or words to that effect. Isn't that the most half-witted, irresponsible advice you can imagine? In my experience if a thing's been hidden away for a long time and kept quiet about, then there's a jolly good cause for leaving it there. Of course, I realise people think they know better these days.'[99] The blimpish touch at the end here only partly succeeds in distancing the views expressed from Amis, which is also true of the blimpish attitudes other characters in the novel express – towards gays, or the openness about gays brought by, or resulting in, decriminalisation (Jenny, for example, is uncomfortable being around gay men and appalled to discover what they do together), as well as blacks ('No to all immigrant restrictions, eh?' says Patrick: 'They haven't got to live with 'em').[100] Part of the temptation to associate these views with Amis rather than his characters is the way the characters speak. To Jeremy Treglown, writing in the journal *Grand Street*, 'Jenny's Priestleyesque homespun wisdom sometimes reads awry, but so does Patrick's often unreconstructed late-Amis idiolect. There's too much old-chapping, to my ear, for a young 1960s publisher, and generally it's hard to hear Patrick as a person distinct from Amis.'[101] There are also problems with the novel's setting. Period features appear like bits of decoration, more talked about than dramatised; nor are there very many of them (virtually no references to 1960s clothing, despite lists of such clothing in the notes, or to drugs). Instead we get what Annan calls 'bullet-ridden old targets: the London literary scene with special reference to publishers and their ghastly parties, psychiatry and modern education'.[102] The familiarity of these targets diminishes the novel's more compelling ingredients, those involving Patrick and Jenny's marriage, as does the thin or unrealistic setting.

Difficulties with Girls was treated respectfully by most critics, a result Amis had predicted. 'When you're old enough you can get away with piss,' he wrote to Conquest on 17 September 1988, on the eve of publication: 'cf G. Greene.'[103] In a journal entry of 26 September, after characterising the novel's coverage as 'extensive, on the whole good', Anthony Powell noted that 'Kingsley brought off a notable double by having an obsequious piece written about him by John Mortimer in one Colour Supplement, and Kingsley himself being egregiously rude to Mortimer in another on the same day.' Two years later, in the Honours List of June 1990, Amis's grand old man status was confirmed by a knighthood. His appointment diary for 25 July reads: '10–10.30 Buckingham Palace.' The day before, he wrote a note to Julian Barnes worrying that he was bound to fall over the Queen's foot, fart or say fuck: 'Oh Xt. Think of it.' Mavis and Geoff Nicholson, properly dressed, took him to the Palace. By this stage in his life Amis had become what Martin calls 'a martyr to IBS or Irritable Bowel Syndrome', a condition aggravated 'by mild but undeniable paranoia'.[104] Before the great day, 'KA had his doctor lay down a firewall of Imodium, and there was some doubt, afterwards, whether he would ever again go to the toilet. When the crisis was over I told him that he would have been remembered as the prick who died for a Sir. He laughed at this, to my surprise, because he was as sensitive about IBS as he was about HRH.' On the morning of the 25th, Amis and the Nicholsons inched towards Buckingham Palace in a long queue of cars. When they arrived at the gate, the guard asked for their invitations: Amis had left his behind. It was Mavis who saved the day, a palace official having recognised her from her appearances on television. The party was let through and the ceremony itself proved disaster free. It was the government of Amis's beloved Margaret Thatcher which was responsible for the honour. As Martin says, 'I suppose Kingsley got it partly for being audibly and visibly right-wing, or conservative/monarchist.'[105] Once he'd become Sir Kingsley, Amis never again mentioned it in his correspondence. 'He never talked about the knighthood,' Martin writes in *Experience*, just as he 'never talked about prizes or advances or sales'.[106]

27

Ending Up

The characters of Jenny Standish and Rhiannon Weaver were tributes to Hilly, and apologies of sorts.[1] Though the Kilmarnocks lived
in comfort at 194 Regents Park Road, in a self-contained flat in
the basement, with kitchen, bath, bedroom, living room, study and
patio garden, and all expenses paid, Hilly's lot was not an easy one,
mostly because Amis was not easy. Amis had a bedroom and study
on the ground floor and a kitchen and sitting room/dining room
on the first floor. Jaime's bedroom was on the second floor, where
there was also a spare bedroom, used for periods by Phil. While
Jaime or Phil had to pass by Amis's floors on their way to their
rooms, Ali and Hilly could stay in the basement except when doing
chores for Amis or joining in on social occasions. The joining in
was infrequent, certainly on Ali's part. The photographs that show
Amis and the Kilmarnocks together in Amis's sitting room record
what Hilly calls 'very rare occasions'. Hilly found such occasions
'uncomfortable', 'I was so on tenterhooks.' Ali was always formal
and correct – Jaime and Philip called him 'the Alien' because 'he
never batted an eyelid' – but Amis could express impatience, irritation, disdain. 'I think he thought I was a dangerous Lefty,' Ali says.
Ali got the *Guardian*, for its coverage of health issues and the social
services, his brief in the House of Lords. He remembers Amis referring to the newspaper as 'the traitors' gazette'. In the diary he began
in 1992, as a sort of *aide-mémoire* for his biography, Eric Jacobs
describes driving Amis home from the pub and stopping outside the
house at Regents Park Road. Ali was standing at the door, having

forgotten his key. 'Who's that?' Amis said. 'Is it Ali? In his ridiculous beret. Upper-class fool.' They sat in the car and watched as Ali walked away. Amis 'made no effort to call him back and let him in'.² 'Separating Kingsley and Ali used to give me the jumps,' Hilly remembers. 'I was so conscious that they were completely different animals. On the surface you managed very well but I knew all the mutterings that Kingsley did when Ali wasn't there. I was very angry and protective of Ali.' Ali saw the relationship as amiable but distant, 'arm's length': 'There wasn't any other sort of relationship that one could have. And I was out practically all the time. Sitting in the Lords until late. I often didn't come back until ten, eleven, twelve. The physical contact, apart from stairs and things, was really fairly minimal.' In the early days the three tried to entertain together: there was a lunch with Simon Raven, drinks with neighbours. But as Ali puts it, such occasions 'were always a failure, because Kingsley was determined to monopolise the conversation . . . It worked in the household, but as a threesome socially, we certainly didn't work.'

Hilly's duties were to run the house, prepare Amis's suppers and weekend meals, clean (though Amis never took much notice of cleaning), make his bed, sort out his medicines, of which there were many, and sit with him in the evenings in front of the television, at least until nine. This last duty she found onerous. 'We weren't allowed to watch anything on telly that he didn't want to watch,' Hilly remembers, 'and I was more or less trapped there . . . He wanted me to stay till he went to bed, which could be any time, because he used to drop off to sleep the whole time in his chair and wake up every now and then. I'd always say good-night at nine. I had to put my foot down. I need my rest and I also needed to see Ali and Jaime. They led a very solitary sort of life down there, down in the bottom.' It was at home that Amis was most demanding. In order to earn money (to pay off the mortgage and the overdraft and to support his extended family), to write the books he wanted to write, to face down his fears and to drink as much as he wanted, Amis needed someone to do everything else, in the last ten years of his life in particular. 'He does nothing for himself,' his biographer, Eric Jacobs, recorded in a diary entry of 28–30 August 1992, while Amis was in Swansea staying with the Thomases:

I'm pretty sure he doesn't lift a finger to help around the Thomases' house. There is something childish, too, in his appetites. I don't say he would cry if he didn't get his drink or food when he wanted them but you can't help feeling he might. He guzzles, like a child sucking a tit. And he is not happy with strangers or with anything that threatens to take him out of his normal routines. You have to win his acceptance and you have to play things his way, eg, drink and eat according to his schedule, or he will get bored, petulant. And he has to be entertained constantly – by books, people, television . . . None of this is meant to detract from his great qualities: wit, intelligence and a lot more. And perhaps it's got something to do with success and age: why, after all, should he not have what he wants at the end of a long and distinguished career? And why should he waste a moment of his diminishing number of years doing things he doesn't want to?[3]

Even when Amis sought to please the people he lived with it was, as Ali puts it, 'on his terms, what he'd like to do'. 'He'd take James and me out for meals the whole time,' Hilly remembers, 'he'd take Sally and me out. Terrific treats the whole time. But again we had to sit through *hours* of him having his two stiff drinks before the meal. We weren't interested, really. Sally wasn't supposed to drink . . . We went out to very expensive places, terribly expensive places. I was exhausted and we'd get back at about four and then liqueurs after that. The treats became rather ordeals.' Amis's 'great thing', Hilly explains, was 'let's get drunk', but it's 'no good having a drink if you're not in the mood'. Amis, however, 'was always in the mood'. At first, at Gardnor House and Leighton Road, 'I thought it was great fun because I'd been starved of alcohol – maybe a bottle of red at weekends. I thought, oh boy, how lovely, back to Princeton days almost. But I couldn't take it.'

The suppers Hilly provided for Amis at home were simple, like the food his mother prepared in Norbury: fishcakes, cold cuts, sausage and mash, 'no fancy muck', as Hilly put it.[4] She would bring the meal into Amis's sitting room on a tray, then sit with him while he ate it, often in front of the television. Sally sometimes took over this job from Hilly, though 'if she wasn't feeling so hot (in other words, she'd been on the bottle) I'd have to have everything practically done, like the fishcakes, the mashed bananas, but she'd take the tray to him. She was the only one who could really sit in the house and look after him.' On occasion, Philip also helped out, especially 'when I had my hospital incidents. I broke a hip in the house and then I had shingles.' The shingles developed in October 1991; the hip was broken in June 1992. 'Hilly Kilmarnock has broken her hip,' reads Anthony Powell's journal entry for 11 June: 'no doubt worked to death.' One of the most problematic of Hilly's tasks was sorting out Amis's medication. There were pills for everything and he could not always remember which ones to take and in what dosages. Once when he thought Hilly had given him the wrong pills he yelled at her so fiercely that she burst into tears and ran down to the basement. Jaime was nineteen or twenty at the time. When he came home from art college to discover Hilly in tears he raced upstairs to confront Amis: 'We met on the stairs because Kingsley was on his way down, I think to apologise to Mum. And I caught him and I was white with anger and I remember shouting at him: "Don't you *ever* make my mother cry again or we'll be out of here so quickly . . ."' It was a well-judged threat. 'For me this was a weapon,' Jaime explains, 'because I knew that Kingsley couldn't bear the thought of being without Mum and us and this whole arrangement that we had.' As Jaime remembers it, Amis 'was totally shocked. His first reaction was a sort of "How dare you talk to me like this", but when he realised that this wasn't going to work and I carried on at him he sort of shrank back. A while later he came down and apologised to Mum.' After that, Amis was always a little nervous with Jaime, though he also had affection for him and respected him. Hilly likens Amis's attitude to Jaime to his attitude to Martin, 'also someone Kingsley didn't like to cross. Could stand up for himself, very much so.' Amis's quarrels with Martin were quick flashes. 'I was present at a few arguments,' Jaime remembers. 'Kingsley would get sort of angry, but not outrageously . . . You know – "You've got to be crazy", "You fucking fool" – and Martin would never swear at Kingsley.' With Philip, the arguments were more volatile. 'There was more shouting with Philip than with Martin. Sometimes Kingsley would be outright rude . . . Philip would storm out of the room.'

Sally's closeness to Amis in the Regents Park Road years was important to them both. 'She loved him to death,' is how Hilly puts it, 'she was the priestess.' But she could only be the priestess when sober. 'She was in the wrong so often about stealing drink,' Hilly recalls, 'that she also had a difficult time juggling when she was the boss cat and when she was in disgrace.' Sally was rarely aggressive when drinking, but she was sloppy, maudlin and a cause for anxiety, particularly for Hilly. On a visit to 194 Regents Park Road in July 1985, Dale Salwak's wife Patti had a chat with Sally before supper.

The Salwaks had just been to see Philip Larkin in Hull and when Patti Salwak praised Larkin's 'sweetness and sensitivity', Sally told her about 'Born Yesterday', the poem he had written on the occasion of her birth. Then she told Patti about her marriage and divorce ('we all make mistakes'), about how she'd had no education, about Michigan, where she'd been made fun of because of her accent and miniskirts. She said she was devoted to her father and liked 'to sit around and talk with him, be creative'. This didn't happen too much, 'because of his drinking'. She told Patti many things, including something 'she hadn't told anyone': that she'd begun writing, at her father's suggestion. Her writing was 'very sensitive, like her father's', not like her brother's, which is 'quite crude'. She was 'not in good shape', she admitted, because her best friend had just died. The friend was 'twenty-one or twenty-two', seven months pregnant, and 'just started to haemorrhage and she died holding Sally's hand'. Towards the end of the chat, Sally returned to the subject of her failed marriage. 'Sally left her husband because she got very bored with him,' according to Patti. 'Similar with her father. He gets bored very fast. Very emotional. Started to cry a couple of times when talking. Fighting back tears. Drinking lots of red wine. Smoking.'

In *The Folks That Live on the Hill* (1990) Amis offers a thinly disguised portrait of Sally (discussed in Chapter 12). Though the domestic circumstances of the novel's main character, Harry Caldecote, are different from those of Amis (Harry lives with his sister, not his ex-wife, and her third husband, and with a dog not a cat), his circle of friends and their manner of meeting up – at the local post office, the pub, each other's houses (for drinks, meals and parties) – was much like that of Amis's Primrose Hill circle. It was through Peter and Marilyn Quennell, the only members of the circle to be fictionalised in the novel (so thinly as to shock Anthony Powell) that Amis and the Kilmarnocks met Tim and Catharine Jaques. The Jaqueses lived on the same tiny street as the Quennells, just off Regents Park Road. Marilyn Quennell gave small drinks parties two or three times a week and at one of these Catharine Jaques, a pretty New Zealand woman in her late forties, who had worked as a secretary for the publisher Leo Cooper, spent most of the party chatting to Hilly. Hilly liked her and her husband and the next day rang them up to invite them over for drinks. Tim Jaques is a painter and illustrator who started his career as a graphic designer, mostly in educational publishing. He served as a commissioned officer in the

Cavalry, then went on to art school. Old-fashioned in his opinions and outspoken, he 'adored' Amis and shared a number of his views. Like others of Amis's friends, Sargy Mann for example, another artist, he thought Amis a marvellous teacher and felt privileged to listen to his talk. When they differed, 'I used to shut up.' A ritual developed in which the Jaqueses would come over to 194 Regents Park Road every Saturday evening at 6.30 for drinks. 'I would always be first,' Tim remembers, 'and Catharine would go downstairs and stay with Hilly.' After a few minutes – a delay which made Amis impatient – the women would come up and join the men. By 8 or 8.30 the Jaqueses were back home. When Hilly and Ali were busy or out with friends, the Jaqueses would give Amis supper or lunch. 'We were geographical friends. There was the convenience of it,' Tim Jaques explains. 'We knew him as a domestic man, not as a public man and actually there's a big difference.' At the Garrick, Jaques suggests, Amis was 'rather more magisterial than he was at home'.

The Jaqueses never stayed on for supper on Saturday nights because on Saturday nights Amis and Hilly, never Ali, had supper with Richard and Judy Hough, one week at the Houghs' flat, a short walk up the hill, the next at home. Richard Hough was a friend of Amis's from the Garrick, where he was a much-admired member. He had a glamorous past, having flown fighter-bombers during the war and had an affair with Joan Fontaine. Hough worked in publishing before becoming an astonishingly prolific writer, the author of some 111 books, including naval histories, biographies and novels, some for children. Like nearly all Amis's Primrose Hill friends, he was a good drinker, and he shared Amis's right-wing views. His wife Judy was a Labour supporter, however, and the two men enjoyed baiting her. Judy's maiden and professional name was Taylor; she was Dick Hough's second wife, a publisher of children's books and the author of a biography of Beatrix Potter (Hough's daughter, the novelist Deborah Moggach, was from his previous marriage). It was Judy Hough who persuaded Amis to turn his 1975 television screenplay, 'We Are All Guilty', an episode in the series *Against the Crowd*, into a short 'teenage' novel, published in 1991; she also got him to write the words for a picture-book for children, 'The Cat-astrophe: A Likely Story', though this was never published.[5] The main human characters in the picture-book, like the main characters in *The Folks That Live on the Hill*, are an adult brother and sister who live together; 'Teeks', the feline protagonist, is jet black, the exact opposite of Amis's cat, Sarah, a Hertfordshire white, whom he admitted to neglecting ('every cat has one person, and I am her person,' he told a journalist, and 'I don't give her enough attention').[6] *We Are All Guilty*, the teenage novel, is about seventeen-year-old Clive Rayner, 'a Cockney lad' arrested for breaking and entering. Though guilty of the crime, and willing to admit his guilt, everyone he meets – local vicar, social worker, judge – sees him as a victim of society. In the Foreword, Amis likens his decision to turn the screenplay into a novel to his decision to write a sequel to *Take a Girl Like You*: in both cases it was a central character he wanted to return to: Jenny Bunn in *Difficulties*, Clive in *We Are All Guilty*. 'I found as I wrote that I cared more about him,' writes Amis of Clive, 'than about any of my previous male characters that I could remember.'[7] The novel got very poor reviews, though Judy Hough, to whom it is dedicated, thought it had 'quite a lot to say'. Before Amis agreed to write it, he'd had little time for children's and teenage fiction, describing them to Judy as lesser genres; what are lesser about *We Are All Guilty* are the obvious political designs it has on its readers (also Clive's voice, which does not convince). In the words of one reviewer, 'it all smells of the establishment believing that the lower classes would be all right if they'd just shape up'.[8]

The Saturday night dinners were more comfortable for Amis and Dick Hough than they were for the women. Judy explains Ali's absence, and Hilly's willingness to be there without him, as dictated by Amis's needs: 'Kingsley couldn't do without her, couldn't bear to be without her' and was never quite at ease in Ali's presence, which put everyone else, especially Hilly, on edge. When Amis and Hough said intolerant things – about Lefties and blacks and Jews – it was partly a game, Judy felt. 'He and Kingsley had a lovely time talking outrageously.' These are almost the exact words Amis uses in describing the political pronouncements of the old devils in the Bible and Crown:

they got on to politics and had a lovely time seeing who could say the most outrageous thing about the national Labour Party, the local Labour Party, the Labour-controlled county council, the trade unions, the education system, the penal system, the Health Service, the BBC, black people and youth. (Not homosexuals today.) They varied this with eulogies of

President Reagan, Enoch Powell, the South African government, the Israeli hawks and whatever his name was who ran Singapore.[9]

Such talk sometimes upset Judy: 'I had a very difficult time because there's no point in arguing and you either accept it or you get up and leave.' Hilly, too, kept quiet. 'Only afterwards would she say "Oh wasn't Kingsley dreadful last night?"' or make him call the next morning to apologise for having upset his hostess. These apologies – Catharine Jaques received them as well – were anxious and heartfelt; Amis was very fond of Judy, as he was of Catharine. Tim Jaques explains the outrageous remarks as an expression of 'male bonding or commonality, of each understanding what the other means . . . If one's talking about blacks one will go back a generation and talk like one's parents. One doesn't really mean it.' This is not quite Judy Hough's view. She believes that at the end of his life Amis believed a number of the outrageous things he said, 'though you don't find them in the writing'. As Amis himself put it, in his poem 'Coming of Age', from *A Look Round the Estate*, he 'played his part so well / that he started living it . . . / His trick of camouflage no longer a trick'. A similar process, she believes, underlay his exceptional rudeness in later years: 'He got into the habit of behaving badly. He knew it was expected of him quite often, I'm sure of that . . . So he thought, well, I'll jolly well do it. He didn't pretend about anything, during the years I knew him. If he didn't like something he'd say so and probably say so very forcefully.' Judy sees Amis's behaviour towards Ali as a case in point: 'If [Ali] would come in for some reason or other, to deliver a message or something, Kingsley would almost say "What do you want?"' When Hilly was unwell or exhausted, Ali would take over her chores, including making Amis's bed; Amis would then mock him as 'the butler', though never to his face. Julian Barnes remembers being invited over for 'a bite of supper' at Leighton Road. He and Amis were in the sitting room when Ali walked in carrying a tray for two. 'Ali was barely out of the room when Kingsley said: "Not bad for a boy from Norbury, eh? Get your dinner from a peer of the realm."' Many found Ali's forbearance in such circumstances surprising. I once asked Ali if he hated Amis: 'I'm not the hating type,' he said, before going on to insist that Amis 'was nicer underneath than he allowed himself to be on top . . . that there were probably nicer impulses lying down below', a view seconded by Hilly, also by Judy, Jaime and Tim and Catharine Jaques.[10]

This view of Amis is unlikely to have been shared by strangers or fans who approached him when he was with his circle at the Queen's public house. Amis's life in his last years was increasingly regimented, as the lively opening chapter of Eric Jacobs's biography, 'Portrait of the Artist in Age', makes clear. Every Saturday, to take a day Jacobs only partly documents, after a morning's writing and before Hilly's sandwiches at lunch (always the same, containing cheese, onion, Branston pickle and 'much more besides', and so tasty that Amis began looking forward to eating them 'soon after breakfast on Fridays'),[11] there were drinks at the Queen's. Amis would arrive at noon, to meet a little weekend club of neighbourhood friends: the Quennells, the Houghs, the Jaqueses, Richard Law, whose house in France Amis and Jane had visited in the summer of 1980. The first arrival bought the first round (regulars knew who drank what). The group would stay until 1 or 1.30, drink perhaps four rounds of doubles and seldom eat anything more than a packet of crisps. Amis insisted upon vetting guests. If the Gales or Fussells or Mavis Nicholson were in town and available, they came. Amis tried to recruit new members (Catherine Freeman, a neighbour whom he had known since the 1950s *Spectator* days, Selina Hastings, another neighbour); 'he would round people up. It was his do,' Judy explains, and 'he didn't like people coming without his invitation; he couldn't be free, relaxed, rude about people, he couldn't do his act.' Judy felt that the Saturday pub sessions were really 'a boys' time'; the men would tell their stories about work or what they'd read in the papers; the women tended to listen and to leave early, to run errands and prepare meals. Judy herself felt inhibited by the public nature of the gatherings. Amis was a celebrity and his presence with his chums was common knowledge in the neighbourhood. The circle always sat in the same end nook of the pub (as the old devils always sat in a back room of the Bible and Crown) and outsiders often eavesdropped or stared. Judy disliked the idea of being on show, but the men 'didn't care at all and they would talk loudly and tell their stories. A lot of people went to the pub just to sit and listen.' One of the several examples Jacobs provides of Amis freezing out strangers or flustering the uninvited, even uninvited acquaintances, involves a young man seeking help with a book he was writing. The young man approached Amis timidly: "'I know it would be a frightful bore . . ." "Ye-e-e-ah," interrupted Amis at the word "bore," loudly and pointedly. The young man stuttered out the rest of his sentence somehow and disappeared, seen off for good with a bit of luck.'[12]

Once Amis got into the habit of behaving badly, even old friends were fair game, especially friends who challenged or patronised him. When Pat Kavanagh and Julian Barnes married, Amis and Jane gave them a wedding party at Gardnor House. In the years after Jane left Amis, Pat and Julian were particularly attentive to him. In 1983 they gave him a belated sixtieth birthday dinner, over which much trouble was taken. As Barnes recounts it, Amis was invited to pick the guest list and was consulted about the menu, a tricky business. For example, he agreed to lamb, 'but it mustn't be pink' and 'there shouldn't be anything like garlic near it'; after vetoing every vegetable Barnes and Kavanagh could think of, he finally said, grudgingly, 'braised onions would be nice'; fruit salad was OK for dessert, as long as it wasn't 'too authentic'. The dinner took place a few days after the disastrous *Observer* dinner at the Garrick. At the meal itself someone mentioned the previous dinner and Martin said, in front of everyone and in a manner Barnes thought rehearsed: 'If you go on like that you'll just be left with the dregs of the Garrick to see your life out with.' Barnes recalls that 'Kingsley looked pretty shocked and said: "Well, that's enough about that, old boy, let's not spoil the evening." And they didn't and the time was jolly.' Amis was on form that night, by which Barnes meant 'wonderfully entertaining and usefully provocative'.

The friendship with Amis came to an end in 1986, though it had been under strain for several years. 'The price you had to pay for his company got higher,' Barnes explains. 'Every meeting would involve at least one remark, aside, riff at which you thought, well, I'm just not going to rise to that. It would be nignogs, it would be Jews, it would be women, it would be Irish, it would be gays . . . You would think, we'll let that pass, but increasingly . . . it seemed that the price to pay was swallowing what you believed about things.' Barnes had become a successful novelist over the course of the friendship and grown in confidence. When *Flaubert's Parrot* was published in 1984, it was as well received as *Stanley and the Women* and *Money*.[13] He began to feel 'too old' to keep quiet in the face of Amis's goading; it felt like 'toadying', 'there was a power thing involved'. One evening in 1986 Amis invited Barnes and Kavanagh to dinner at the Garrick. When they came to pick him up, Barnes parked in the forecourt of Bibendum, the wine store opposite Amis's house. Barnes was a frequent customer at Bibendum and as he and Amis got into the car, the shop's owner strolled over for a chat. When Barnes drove off, Amis said, impatiently and sarcastically: '*Very* good of that chap to *assume* we didn't have enough to say to one another.' Barnes thought: 'Right, that's the starting point.' At the Garrick they had drinks, ordered some wine and tasted it. The wine seemed fine to Barnes, who knows about wine, but Amis sent it back: 'It was clear that he was spoiling for a fight.' Amis then spent 'about an hour' complaining of 'people in his publishing house wanting to change his prose and his agent having views on his books'. When he'd finished he turned to Barnes and said: 'Well, I suppose you're writing a book.' On the previous occasion Amis had asked Barnes about his writing, the book Barnes was at work on was *Flaubert's Parrot* 'and after about thirty seconds of fervently explaining *Flaubert's Parrot* to Kingsley, out of the corner of my eye I caught him with a look which meant "If you'd only hand me a machete I'd have this man's head off in an instant"'. So this time Barnes said something like: 'It's all right Kingsley, I'll let you off.' Kavanagh then leaned forward, patted Amis on the forearm, and said: 'There, there, Kingsley, well done' (for asking about the book). Both Pat's words and her gesture were meant 'in the spirit of pure affection'. When she got up to go to the loo, Amis turned to Barnes and said: 'By the way, none of this "character" stuff' – that is, none of this trying to turn me into a character.

Now Amis was up for 'a big rumble'. He got on to South Africa, his position being, in Barnes's paraphrase, that 'white civilisation was under threat and the only solution was to shoot all black agitators, all of whom were Communists. That way white civilisation would be restored.' Barnes had been to South Africa, 'unlike Amis', and Kavanagh had spent the first twenty years of her life there and had more facts at her disposal than either man. She joined in the discussion and it soon became rancorous. 'When Kingsley was arguing,' Barnes explains, 'he didn't just despise your opinions, he despised you personally.' Barnes had asked him: 'So what's, actually, your scenario for what's going to happen?' To Amis, the use of the word 'scenario' 'proved that I was a fucking fool'. 'Well, I'll tell you my *scenario* and you can tell me your *scenario*,' Amis replied. Then he said again 'You should shoot as many blacks as possible.'

Kavanagh burst into tears and got up and left the table. Amis turned to Barnes and said: 'What's the matter with *her*?' Barnes felt in an impossible position: 'If you stood up and argued with him you were a fucking fool. If you nodded while he said insulting things about blacks or Jews you were a sycophant or an arse-crawler, as I think he refers to me in the *Letters*.' When Kavanagh came back to the table they drove Amis home and Barnes decided that 'I didn't really want to go out to dinner with him again.' The next day Martin relayed Amis's account of the evening to Barnes: not a word about the argument, only the complaint about not showing respect to a senior writer.

How to account for such behaviour? Barnes discussed Amis's racist remarks with several mutual friends. Peter Porter thought it had to do with a fear of death: 'He's getting rid of everything that attaches him to life except drink and sycophants', a view Barnes thought 'over-elaborate'. Karl Miller said: 'You have to understand that Kingsley has a sadistic side to him and that he will look for your weak spot and then he will press it.' Barnes's own conclusion was like that of Judy Hough, or of Amis himself: 'I can't improve, unfortunately, on the old image of the mask sticking to the face and his coming not to see any distance between "shoot the nignogs" as a sort of thing to say to your chums and really believing it.' Kavanagh stressed Amis's age, believing that over time 'we all become hardened in our least acceptable characteristics'. In Amis's case, this process was exacerbated by drink, fame, a dominating personality and a life, as Barnes puts it, 'run absolutely on your terms'. When challenged by a young, successful novelist and a desirable younger woman, and condescended to, or so he thought, Amis set out to wound. The things he said were shameful, as is the possibility that he said them mostly to get back at Kavanagh and Barnes.

In a tape-recorded conversation of 18 May 1995 with Eric Jacobs, Amis tried to explain such remarks. '"One should shoot the lot" just means "I think this quite wrong." He didn't hate anyone,' even John Pilger or Tony Benn, and certainly not blacks: 'You should never be nasty, legally or socially, to any such person. I wouldn't want to be an active member of any society that would be hard on black people, legally or socially, or cheated women in that kind of way.' Though his personal contacts with black people were limited, he was always anxious to stop those he met 'from thinking "he's another of them," another oppressive, sneering anti-black person'.

At the same time, he disapproved of reverse discrimination and thought some races or peoples more 'talented in culture and science' than others. 'Any nation with a lot of Jews has a reason to congratulate itself,' he told Jacobs. But he would not say the same thing about a nation with 'a lot of blacks': 'An intelligent and capable black person is as intelligent and capable as any white person, but I don't think there are as many of them as white people.'

When Amis made this tape he was on page 38 of a new novel, one he would never finish. The title of the novel, which exists in a typescript of 106 pages, was 'Black and White' and its subject was prejudice in several forms. The novel's heroine is Helen Soames, a tall, good-looking twenty-year-old black woman who wants to be an actor.[14] The hero is a thirty-four-year-old gay man named Christopher MacAndrew, also an actor, as well as a part-time drama lecturer.[15] Amis told Jacobs that the plot of the novel would involve Helen's being offered a part and then worrying that she only got it because she was black, which makes it sound like *We Are All Guilty* (Clive, too, worries that his good fortune at escaping prison is unearned).[16] Though Amis had written twelve pages of the novel by 29 April, these were eventually replaced by a new opening (the original pages have not survived). It was only on 12 May that he decided to put Helen together with Christopher, who meets her at the very beginning of the surviving manuscript. At some point after 12 May, Amis must also have decided that Helen and Christopher would be attracted to each other sexually.[17]

Christopher 'had never had to decide what he felt about black people in general', because he'd had so little contact with them.[18] Once, to himself, he refers to Helen's father as a 'jig', the only racial slur in the manuscript. When he actually meets the father, in the family's neat 'red-brick villa' in Enfield, he realises immediately 'that virtually all the time he had spent being afraid of Mr. Soames because he was black should by rights have been spent being afraid of him because he was a grown-up person's father and therefore boring'.[19] In describing his depiction of this meeting to Jacobs, Amis spoke of Christopher 'having his nose rubbed in the family's Britishness'.[20] Helen's father is a master carpenter, there's an SDP poster in the window of the house, and his formal manners are mocked by his younger son, the angrier of Helen's two brothers: 'Very lifelike, I congratulate you. We'll make an Englishman of you yet, poppa.'[21] Like other sympathetic Amis heroines, Helen has an easy and open manner. The closest she comes to stridency is when she explains to Christopher why she has invited him to meet her parents:

'If they were white I wouldn't try to insist upon your meeting them.'

'Oh, you're fighting the good old fight on behalf of your black brothers and sisters, are you?'

'Don't talk in that silly sneering way,' she said, starting to blink fast. 'Wasn't every Jew in Nazi Germany fighting the Hitlerites whether he or she knew it or not?'

'That's enough,' he said, starting to get up. 'Nice to have known you.'

'You just stay right where you are, whitey. Of course I'm not such a bloody fool as to say or even let it cross my mind that this place is remotely like the other. Why do you think we all come and settle here? – and don't start talking to me about unemployment benefit. But if you're going to try and tell me every black person here *isn't* some sort of non-citizen then it's on your way, mate.'[22]

Though Helen's manner is meant to be self-consciously jokey ('You just stay right where you are, whitey' matches Christopher's 'Nice to have known you'), the exchange is unconvincing, partly because, like many late Amis characters, Helen sounds like Amis ('then it's on your way, mate'). Her views, however, like Christopher's, are unpredictable; it is not clear from the surviving manuscript what's going to happen between them or where Amis stands on the issues raised in the exchange, even on Helen's remark at the end about being a non-citizen. This remark is matched by a later one from Christopher about being gay, which he likens to being 'surrounded by enemies many or most of whom are too thick individually to recognise that that's what they are'.[23] Christopher's remark occurs four pages before the manuscript breaks off. In *Experience*, Martin calls 'Black and White' 'rather slow, and perhaps rather weakly focused',[24] but what we have of it is more promising than the unfinished 'Difficulties with Girls'. There are fewer false notes and clichés in the depiction of gays than in 'Difficulties' and the passages dealing with race are intriguing, as if Amis were determined to put his casual prejudices to the test or under the microscope.

One final instance of these prejudices is worth considering. Among Amis's rituals after the move to Primrose Hill was a weekly meal with Martin and his family in their house in Ladbroke Grove, usually on a weekday night, though occasionally on a Sunday for lunch. In

1992 he arrived one Sunday in a mood. He had recently been in low spirits and was 'expected without great enthusiasm'. As Martin explains, 'his low spirits took aggressive form: having cast me as a dutiful plaything of multicultural correctness, he would then attempt to scandalise me with the ruggedness of his heresies'.[25] Shortly after the publication of *Stanley and the Women* Martin had asked his father what it felt like to be 'mildly anti-Semitic'. 'What's it feel like?' Amis answered. 'Well. Very mild, as you say. If I'm watching the end of some new arts programme I might notice the Jewish names in the credits and think, Ah there's another one. Or: Oh I see. There's another one . . . You just notice them. You wouldn't want anyone to *do* anything about it. You'd be horrified by that.'[26] On this occasion, when Amis walked downstairs to the kitchen he noticed a book on the table: 'What's that you're reading? Some *Jew*?' What Martin was reading was Primo Levi's *If This Is a Man*, an account of Levi's experiences in Auschwitz. As Martin prepared Amis's drink (gin and white onions, a vermouthless Gibson), he recounted a scene from the book in which Levi and other Jews rounded up by the Fascist Militia readied themselves for deportation to Auschwitz: 'the men all spent that last night drinking and fucking and fighting. The women all spent it washing their children and their children's clothes and preparing meals. And he writes, something like – when the sun came up, like an ally of our enemy, the barbed wire round the camp was full of children's washing hung out in the wind to dry.' When Martin turned round to hand his father his drink,

my first thought was to reach for a kitchen towel. How had he had *time* to cry so much? His motionless face was a mask of unattended tears. He said steadily,

— That's one thing I feel more and more as I get older. Let's *not* round up the women and the children. Let's *not* go over the hill and fuck up the people in the next town along. Let's not do any of that ever again.[27]

Amis's tears hardly excuse his slurs, but they put them in perspective. Saying mildly anti-Semitic things to wind people up, or to test them, or to bend them to your will, or to assert male commonality, or because you're in a mood, is not the same thing as saying them because you hate Jews and want to exterminate them. But it's not all right, not given what has happened to the Jews. Similar objections can be made to slurs against blacks.

Amis's bigoted remarks in his last years had a wilful, childish quality about them, like his rudeness. Nowhere is the rudeness clearer than in the *Memoirs* (1991), which offended a number of people, including Robert Conquest. 'Have been drenched under flood of publicity for my memoirs,' wrote Amis to Conquest on 18 March 1991, 'also great volumes of piss thrown on me from most quarters . . . Of course attacks from Guardian etc. sting for ten minutes or so and then fade, but the volume does mount up.' On 24 March Amis wrote to Anthony Thwaite to thank him for writing to him praising the *Memoirs*, which Thwaite had enjoyed, apart from one or two 'attacks on people who really shouldn't have been attacked'.[28] 'I was delighted as always to hear from you, perhaps a shade more than usual this time as a contrast to the variously sized bits of shit that have come my way since the memoirs appeared. I never expected them. I thought I was trying to be a) honest b) funny but not a bit of it, it appears.' Amis then mentions Thwaite's invented comment on 'Thwaite' in the style of the *Memoirs*, in which the supposed meanness of Yorkshiremen (Thwaite is a Yorkshireman) is likened to that of 'Hebrews'. 'I roared with laughter at your evocation of a Thwaite para in them, but went a bit quiet at the Hebrew bit; not really my style, I hope.' Not his style in print, certainly, not in the *Memoirs*, not even in *Stanley and the Women*. Moreover, it is in the *Memoirs* that he denounces the bigotry encountered in Nashville and pays tribute to the tolerance of the City of London School, 'where differences of class, upbringing, income group and religion counted for so little'.

In an interview in the *Daily Telegraph* Amis claimed that he had four motives for writing the *Memoirs*: 'he was writing a new novel in the autumn[29] but needed something to do in the meantime; it was "more fun" to look back than forward; he had not tried fact rather than fiction before and he had picked up so many good anecdotes during his life that they were "too good to be lost"'. In the same interview Amis also admitted that he had 'deliberately set out to settle some scores, particularly about "my revolting grandparents – at least three out of four anyway – and what they had done to one of my uncles and to an aunt whom they had locked up"'.[30] That the book was funny was admitted by all: John Carey thought it Amis's 'funniest book since *Lucky Jim*';[31] Blake Morrison called it 'horrible but also horribly enjoyable', adding that 'the chief feeling is shame at laughing *quite* so much'.[32] That it was honest was less clear. When

Enoch Powell was asked about the chapter in which he is described as treating Amis rudely, in an argument over the Latin derivation of the verb *impinge*, he replied: 'I have no recognition of the man. We have never met. I have not set eyes on him.'[33] Anthony Powell thought Amis's account of his dancing with the black psychiatrist Marie Singer, wife of the Cambridge poet Burns Singer, 'totally imaginary': 'True, I did dance with her, kissed her at the end, because the party was closing down, although she was not in the least attractive and, so far from being flirtatious or bawdy, spent all her time talking about how hard it was to be black . . . This disregard for the truth on Kingsley's part I find rather shocking.'[34] James Michie had 'no memory' of scrounging a free lunch off Amis, as he is shown doing in the chapter on him, adding that 'it seems a small matter to remember after a lifetime'.[35] As Michie's complaint suggests, the pettiness of some of Amis's attacks dismayed critics of the book almost as much as their inaccuracy. 'Among chapters devoted to Americans is one on a character named Rosen, man of utter obscurity, who offended Kingsley by making too small Bloody Marys, in general entertained inadequately.' This is Anthony Powell, referring to a chapter on Leo Rosten (not Rosen), author of *The Education of H*y*m*a*n K*a*p*l*a*n* (1937) and *The Return of H*y*m*a*n K*a*p*l*a*n* (1959), best-selling collections of comic tales, most first published in the *New Yorker*, about a fictional East-European immigrant to America (Amis thought Rosten's books 'genuinely funny in a closely observed verbal way'). Powell's larger point about the depiction of Rosten is a fair one and applies to other depictions; in brief chapters meant to sum up a friend, acquaintance or notable figure, the *Memoirs* frequently dwell on minor instances of bad or unappealing behaviour, such as slowness to pay a round or refill a glass. 'All this shows Kingsley's extreme sensitivity to the way people treat himself,' Powell writes in his Journal, 'attitude so characteristic of those (e.g. the Sitwells) peculiarly insensitive about the way they treat other people.'[36] In a letter to Conquest of 7 March 1991, Powell relays a theory his wife has about the *Memoirs*: 'Violet says that spoilt people (which Kingsley obviously has been from the word go, and then phenomenal success) always take against everyone else.'[37]

The most unexpected of the 'bits of shit' the *Memoirs* brought Amis came from Robert Conquest. Amis had taken care to involve Conquest in the chapter he was writing about him. 'Remember,' he says in a letter of 31 January 1990, 'the more you give me, the longer the chapter in my mems about you will be, if that's any inducement. Anecdotal stuff is best, serious ones as well as frivolous.' It is in this letter that Amis first recounts the drainpipe story (discussed in the Introduction). 'I would swear on the book that that was what you told me,' he adds, concluding, though, that 'of course you shall view my finished text'. On 3 November 1990 George Gale died. Amis, Hilly and Sally took the train up to Northumberland for the funeral and some time after they got back Amis wrote an uncharacteristic letter to Conquest: uncharacteristic not only because it is undated but because of the way it spells out what he feels for his friend:

I'm afraid my infrequent responses may have made you think otherwise, but when in the past you wrote to me every week or so, I appreciated your letters very much, and used to wish, as I still do, that I were more of a natural correspondent myself, and certainly that I could come up with limericks and such as often as you, or at least more often than once every half-dozen years . . . Though I didn't come to it first, G's [George Gale's] death is really what got me going into writing this now. With Tibor [Szamuely] and Philip gone already, only four of my seven great chums survive, and only one of them in GB. (Stuart T in Swansea, and he's 76 and hardly 100% fit. Actually Paul Fussell is over here for the year, but he's so odd that I can hardly talk to him much any more.) That leaves Jim Durham in Sydney, and you. I say this to you now partly because I never said anything like it to Tibor, Philip and George while there was time, and partly in the course of saying I hope nothing is wrong between the two of us. Please forgive me if I've offended you, and let me know if you will that you've received this safely, and send me another limerick. And give my love to Liddie. Hope to see you over here soon. Cheers, K.[38]

When Amis sent Conquest a draft of his chapter about him, with the drainpipe story excised (as we've seen, it was transferred to the chapter on Philip Toynbee), Conquest wrote back objecting to a passage involving his second wife, Tatiana. 'Of course at your request I'll withdraw the offending passage,' Amis replied on 2 June 1990, 'under a slight whimper of protest, viz. I remember the incident clearly enough, much more so than the drainpipe adventure, and I think it *was* typical of *one bit* of your marriage to T., and so does Hilly. *But* of course under the no-need-to-make-you-look-a-shit rule it goes . . . I enclose a revised page, with Julian S[ymons] rather dragged in to fill it up.' When the book appeared in March 1991 the Tatiana passage was still there. Conquest was incensed, leading Powell to ponder in his Journal 'as to curious manner in which people will go out of their way to wreck a friendship, Bob being far closer friend of Kingsley than I have ever been'.[39] Conquest did not communicate his reaction to Amis until 6 May. He had been 'fearfully busy', as Amis had guessed, 'but, yes, I have also been pretty pissed off with you. First and most obvious, you have restored that nasty, pointless and misleading bit you told me you'd remove . . . There are a number of smaller things too, of course. No verisimilitude in your story about me and the US publisher; what possessed you to rewrite the Hearst thing while still attributing it to me; etc etc etc etc. But all in all a bad taste in the mouth. And at that I am lucky compared with what you say about poor old Bruce and others. Even Philip.'[40] The Philip reference is to an anecdote Amis includes in the Larkin chapter in which Larkin, caught short on a visit to a school literary society (Bruce Montgomery was teaching at the school), wets himself. 'You asked me if you should remove the pissing his pants story, and I said you should. But I didn't know he'd actually told it to you in confidence!' Conquest would not write again for four months. He only forgave Amis in late August or early September 1991, an 'amnesty' occasioned by the collapse of the Soviet Union. As soon as he received Conquest's letter, after returning to London from his annual summer visit to Swansea on 10 September, Amis wrote back 'to signal my delight and relief. I had been on the verge of saying something similar. Bless you for getting in first. But I still apologise for my offences.'

In public, Amis was unrepentant about the *Memoirs*. 'The people who challenge my facts are suffering from diplomatic lapses of memory,' he told the *Daily Telegraph*: 'They just don't want to remember embarrassing things.' Then he made a revealing comparison: 'It's like the end of Henry IV when Falstaff is rejected with "I know thee not, old man . . . How ill white hairs become a fool and jester." I *am* Falstaff.'[41] At a literary lunch at Foyles on 5 March, according to the *Daily Telegraph* arts correspondent, Amis was 'in splenetic and unforgiving mood', claiming in his speech to have 'witnesses who would back him up for all the occasions where he had been accused of fiction', laying into the book's targets – Enoch Powell, Tony Benn, Arnold Wesker, Dylan Thomas, Malcolm Muggeridge, among others – with renewed vigour, to murmurings of 'shame!' and 'how boring!'[42] Earlier, in an interview with the journalist John Walsh, Amis said of the book's harsh portraits: 'it's a question of whether they made me *cross* ... John Wain, for instance – his allegations against my wife, Hilly[43] made me very cross ... He deserves what I said about him.' Wain had apparently told a friend that the reason he declined invitations to visit *chez* Amis was his fear that Hilly 'would break down his bedroom door' to seduce him. Amis continued: 'A lot of the other stuff isn't very serious; the spirit in which I am writing is to say, "Oh pull yourself together, what absurd behaviour."' Amis's defence against the charge that all his portraits are cruel or critical is that goodness writes white: 'I've had several marvellous friends in my life of whom there's nothing to be said except that I've enjoyed many amusing hours in their company, getting drunk, learning things – you can't make an interesting chapter out of that.'[44]

The relative claims of honesty and tact figure prominently in Amis's life and writing in this period, especially in reference to literary judgement. In *The Old Devils* Charlie tells Alun exactly what he thinks of 'Coming Home', Alan's novel-in-progress. According to Alun, 'Coming Home' is meant to be 'a serious novel, a proper one, you know, with no ham or balls or flannel about it'. Charlie is asked to give it 'a free-from-bullshit certificate'.[45] In the bar at White's Hotel in Birdarthur (an allusion to Brown's Hotel in Laugharne) Alun presses Charlie for his verdict. 'You did ask for my honest opinion,' Charlie begins, which makes Alun's face fall. 'How much did you manage to struggle through?' Alun asks. Charlie's answer is 'the first twenty pages carefully, then skipped to the end'.[46] On the bullshit question, Charlie is emphatic: 'The whole tone of voice, the whole attitude is one that compels bullshit ... Now I'm sure that you've tried your hardest not to put in anything you didn't mean or you thought was playing to the gallery, but it all gets swallowed up and turned into the same thing.' When Alun asks if there's anything to be salvaged from the novel Charlie answers: 'Nothing I saw. I'm sorry.' That Charlie's verdict on the novel is accurate, the reader has no reason to doubt. But is it a disinterested verdict? Alun, after all, has been to bed with Sophie, Charlie's wife. It is a great strength of Amis's fiction that it admits such complications. The personal consequences of Charlie's truthfulness are painful: Alun exacts a terrible revenge (leaving Charlie in the dark to make his way home alone, with resulting panic attack). The public consequences are negligible: the tide of bullshit rises inexorably.

In August 1989 the American academic Dale Salwak sent Amis the complete typescript of *Kingsley Amis: Modern Novelist*, his third book on Amis's life and writing. A year later, not having heard from Amis, he asked him if he would be willing to read at least the first three chapters of a revised version of the book, these being the chapters with the most biographical material. Amis was at work on his *Memoirs* at the time and agreed to read the chapters. In addition to books on Amis, Salwak had published studies of John Braine (1979), John Wain (1981), A.J. Cronin (1983), Carl Sandburg (1988) and Philip Larkin (1989). He first corresponded with and met Amis in 1973 while at work on a doctoral dissertation on Amis's fiction. The current book was a much reworked, expanded and updated version of the dissertation. Amis was helpful and encouraging to Salwak in the 1970s and 1980s, granting him several long and illuminating interviews, but his letters from 1990 flicker with irritation and impatience. When finally he commented on Salwak's chapters, on 10 October 1990, he was brutally dismissive. Having read them 'with the attention they deserve', he was very sorry to have to tell him 'that I consider them altogether unsatisfactory'. Nothing that Salwak had written was 'offensive in any way, or improper to its subject', but the level of his performance was 'so low as not to earn a place on any serious publisher's list'. As for whether anything was salvageable from the manuscript, Amis was as blunt as Charlie had been with Alun: 'no imaginable rewriting would rectify the situation'. The letter ends: 'I think it would be best if the book were to be withdrawn.' Amis then enlisted the help of his agent, Jonathan Clowes, to persuade Harvester Wheatsheaf, a division of Simon and Schuster, not to publish the book. As Clowes was later to write to the book's editor – when neither she nor Salwak was prepared to withdraw it – Amis's criticisms were 'purely professional . . . Sir Kingsley found Professor Salwak personally very pleasant and amiable.'[47]

Salwak was baffled as well as cast down by Amis's letter. 'It contradicts everything he communicated to me in person and in letters over the previous seventeen years.'[48] The book had been accepted for publication on the basis of independent readers' reports, notably one by Barbara Everett of Somerville College, Oxford, who called it 'a splendidly spacious, relaxed yet shrewd study of Amis's work . . . ideally suited to the general reader' (a judgement corroborated after publication by several reviewers). Salwak's queries may have irritated Amis, as did the errors of fact, emphasis and interpetation he found in the draft, but Salwak's intentions were wholly honourable and he was a devoted admirer of Amis's writings. Intentions, however, were not Amis's concern; he would not sugar-coat his assessment of Salwak's performance. It is not clear whether he understood how brutal he was being in this assessment or if so whether he cared. Similar questions are raised by slighting or defamatory remarks and anecdotes in the *Memoirs*.

Amis had already begun work on *The Russian Girl* (1992) when he wrote the Salwak letter. At the heart of the novel is a dilemma faced by Dr Richard Vaisey, Lecturer in Slavonic Studies at the 'London Institute of Slavonic Studies'. Vaisey is a Russian expert, middle-aged, elitist, a defender of tradition and much exercised by falling standards. His own standards are thoroughly Amisian. In matters of literary judgement, 'it's not a question of taste or how people feel, it's to do with truth'.[49] For Vaisey, as T.J. Binyon puts it in a review of the novel in the *Times Literary Supplement*, 'honesty of intention has no relation to artistic merit'.[50] Nor does sympathy with the artist's views, political or otherwise. This last point is made forcefully by Andrei Kotolynov, a prominent Russian dissident Vaisey meets. According to Kotolynov, 'You don't crush literature from outside by killing writers or intimidating them or not letting them publish ... You do better to induce them to destroy it themselves by inducing them to subordinate it to political purposes.'[51] Something like this has happened in the Soviet Union, where 'it is agreed to be irrelevant or unseemly or even actually dangerous to ask *Is it any good?*'[52] Vaisey's new head of department takes a more flexible view on matters of literary principle. Among other things, she wants him to teach *Crime and Punishment* in English, knowing that his students aren't up to the Russian. Richard refuses, for reasons explained to her predecessor: 'You know as well as I do that every word Dostoyevsky writes is written in a way only he can write it. A translation, even the best imaginable, has got to leave all that out.'[53] Eventually, he resigns from his job over this issue.

Richard's dilemma arrives in the form of a visiting Russian poet, Anna Danilova, with whom he falls in love. Anna asks him to help her to organise and publicise a petition to free her brother from a Soviet prison. As he soon discovers, her poetry is terrible: sincere, loving, but terrible. For Richard to support her petition, lending his authority to a campaign based on the implicit assumption that she's a poet of consequence, is to compromise his professional integrity, subordinating the claims of art and truth to those of politics and love; if he doesn't support the petition, he'll almost certainly lose her. Strictly speaking, as Richard would remind us, we have to take the terribleness of Anna's poems on trust, because the few specimens Amis offers us are in translation. In *The Old Devils* Charlie's description of the terribleness of Alun's novel is easy to accept, even though Amis offers no specimen passages; it sounds terrible in ways wholly typical of its author. Anna's poems, in contrast, are partly terrible in ways that endear, like those of the women poets in 'A Bookshop Idyll' ('the awful way their poems lay them open / Just doesn't strike them'); Anna's sincerity, in life and on paper, distinguishes her from the artificiality and self-consciousness of Richard's monstrous wife, Cordelia, who is like a character from *Stanley and the Women*. Of the two specimens of her poetry we are given, one is so obviously bad no translator could redeem it. Its title is 'me in lingerie' and it ends 'if you wanna make fuckish / get your ass into some lingerie & smell good'.[54]

The second Anna poem has been expertly translated. In the Huntington, there's a half-page of notes on *The Russian Girl* written by Amis on an incomplete and crossed draft of a typewritten letter to Robert Conquest. The letter is undated but seems to have been written after Conquest's 'amnesty' in late August 1991. After thanking Conquest for sending him his Stalin book, Amis asks a favour: 'Could you possibly run up a very bad poem for use in my current novel? In English though translated from Russian (very well, the text says). 10–15 lines, young Russn girl's sincere tribute to her English bloke who's in his 40s. Any suggestns welcome.' It was Amis himself who ended up writing these lines.

> man of all men in Shakespeare's island,
> eyes that shine through the rain in my heart,
>   where I came as a stranger,
> finding a hand grasping as firmly as time,
>   knowledge that burns like fire
> and makes my heart round and red again,
> music in unity in my snowflake veins,
> thanks, all thanks be in my eyes for seeing,
> and I
>   can face
>   the dawn mounted on our love

which is you and my love and I and your love,
quickcatchitbeforeitdisappearslikethenight
over the river   never let go,
spreading through the world like a boy's tear,
to turn all the blackest dogs away,
and you
              have spoken
                            and I have listened,
until like a spring the world runs down,
and never fear the dark.

Before Richard can pronounce on the poem, or evade doing so with 'professional bullshit about further study needed for definitive judgement', Anna turns away from him and gently points out that 'it goes on over the page'.[55] To save him embarrassment she also tells him that she's always known that he thought her poems without merit; his willingness to suggest otherwise she took as a sign of 'how much you loved me'. When she says of the present poem, 'I hope you can tell that at least I mean what I say in it',[56] they both dissolve into tears.

Amis's decision to have his hero respond to the claims of love and loyalty can be interpreted in several ways: as characteristically contrary (So you think I'm an unfeeling brute, do you?) or wish-fulfilling (Anna says she knew he was lying 'within a few seconds', so he gets to have his cake and eat it, too, dissembling for love but too full of integrity to do so properly). Richard's uncertainty and agonising are in marked contrast to the settled face Amis presented to critics of the *Memoirs* or to Salwak. Here is how Vaisey imagines and judges the sort of person who would have sacrificed Anna for the sake of art or truth: 'Richard made up his mind that a man who could have done that, would have been a much more unselfish man than he was, but that he would not have been able to get very friendly with such a man, assuming he wanted to.'[57] That it takes some moments to work out what this sentence is saying suggests irresolution, internal conflict on Richard's part, understandable reactions given the views of his creator. Amis is both like Richard and like the man Richard imagines: the sort of man who would have sent Salwak the letter Amis sent him.

There is another explanation for the difficulty or convolution of Richard's sentence. From *Stanley and the Women* onwards critics began to notice and comment on Amis's 'late' style. Difficulty and convolution were hallmarks of this style, which Blake Morrison anatomises in a review of the successor to *The Russian Girl*, *You Can't Do Both* (1994), a novel much drawn on in the opening chapters of this book:[58] 'liberal use of double negatives (as in "that not very narrow stretch of road"), double qualifiers ("in wartime such arrangements, or non-arrangements, were common, or not uncommon") or sardonic negative qualifiers ("his father, being dead, was no longer in a position to formulate even the mildest satisfaction with his son"); reversal of a word's connotations, from positive to pejorative ("strictly dishonourable") or vice versa ("docile enough, even perhaps verging on the well-behaved"); obsessively cautious avoidance of ambiguous pronouns, even by people who are in casual conversation ("He, my old Dad, he's always been afraid of sinking into the working class"); boldly abrupt sentence endings ("This mood deepened when George, having got up spontaneously to announce he would walk him to the station, did so") or, more commonly, boldly protracted ones.'[59] Sometimes late Amis can be as orotund and impenetrable as late James, a comparison Amis would not have welcomed. Here are some examples from *The Old Devils*, concerning Alun's feelings about the opening chapters of his manuscript: 'As they stood, or with some minor surgery, they were supposed to be, he had striven to make them, his devoutest hope was that they were, the opening section of the only really serious piece of prose he had written since his schooldays'[60] (a sentence whose complications mirror Alun's thought processes); 'Having unrestively waited rather longer than strict equity would have entailed'[61] (rather harder to justify on character-drawing grounds); 'Up to something was what he could reckon being charged with having been'[62] (a joke?). Here is a more extended example, from *The Russian Girl*: 'They [Richard's students] suspected with good reason that he despised them just a little, which was harder on them than inordinately, for being rather in favour of looking through this old foreign book or that from time to time, provided of course some geezer had done it up into proper TV English, and for thinking they ought to be paid for it.'[63] Such sentences can be variously explained: as a product of laziness, lordliness, lack of control, even experimentation (when asked if what he was attempting in the later novels was *style indirect libre*, Amis replied: 'Yeh, mmn, yeh, people's thoughts are rather, I suppose, like the way they might utter those thoughts').[64] When

Martin asked about the new style, Amis simply said: 'It's the way I want to write now, the way it's come out.'[65] In a journal entry on *The Folks That Live on the Hill*, Anthony Powell called the writing in the later novels 'dreadfully slipshod, determination not to be pretentious developing into a form of pretentiousness'.[66] In his review of the *Memoirs*, John Carey likened a typical late Amis sentence to 'an articulated lorry trying to back down a narrow passageway. The aim, apparently, is colloquial informality, but the effect is quite other. Far from easing communication, the laborious casual medium sets strict limits to what can be said in it. Tenderness or sensitivity of any kind would be out of the question.' 'His prose style,' Carey continues, 'seems to exert masculinity at the expense of feeling.'[67]

This line was taken earlier by Lorna Sage in a review of *The Folks That Live on the Hill* in the *Times Literacy Supplement*. Her starting point was a sentence about Harry and his son Piers: 'Harry was no great one for suddenly realising things or even realising them at all, but given the leisure and the inclination he might have been able to set down how his son was looking at him just then, without the sort of peering of muscles round the eyes, half squint, half gaze, that unless hostility was present always had the hint of a smile – seriously, in fact.'[68] After describing the sentence as the work of 'an avatar of Henry James', Sage attributes its convolution to 'the difficulty he [Harry, but also Amis, implictly] has in arriving at the word "seriously": the rules of the game say that serious things are almost unsayable, to be avoided not just because they mean trouble (this is just Harry's easy-going cover-story) but because you spoil and desecrate and falsify them by naming. It's a moral reticence and Harry is its latest mouthpiece.' Harry's reticence is contrasted with the fashionable frankness of the horrible Désirée, his sister-in-law, who talks to everyone in detail about her husband's prostatectomy. 'The power of language to distort people's lives – and particularly to confuse them about sex – is awesome, and women's wordiness is its most subversive manifestation (in this Uncle Harry agrees unwittingly with the radical feminists). Hence the deliberate chums-and-chaps slang that leaves all *that* outside.'[69]

Hence also the Garrick Club, the ethos of which perfectly suited Amis, fostering the sorts of male friendships he enjoyed, ones some members think the presence of women inhibits. The nature of these friendships is evoked by Amis's queries about what Bill Rukeyser's brother was like, which boiled down to 'Does he drink? Is he jolly?' Rukeyser explains: 'You were not going to unburden yourself of your innermost feelings, that wasn't the way it went. Once you accepted this rather heavy price, he gave excellent value.' By the mid-1990s there were other prices to pay. Though Richard Hough could tick Amis off when he was rude to fellow members of the Garrick or domineering, few others at the club would challenge him. Most Garrick members were pleased and flattered to have Sir Kingsley as a fellow member, happy to be entertained and informed by him. 'He was a curmudgeon but we all knew it was an act,' Keith Waterhouse told an interviewer. 'It was very enjoyable.'[70] Not everyone at the Club shared Waterhouse's certainty that it was an act. 'I never quite know how seriously to take his anti-women stuff, whether he is just being mischievous,' Jacobs records in his diary on 1 April 1993, 'but on the whole I think the answer is pretty seriously.' Another Garrick friend recalls a rare instance of a fellow member upbraiding Amis for selfishness. When the man persisted, Amis told him to 'Fuck off. No, fuck off *a lot.*' Within Amis's circle, according to this friend, the phrase 'a lot' quickly became a sort of code, a way of responding to a dig or a tease. Amis didn't bother with codes. 'Z, over here,' he would summon Ronald Zeegen, his friend and doctor, from across the bar, seeking rescue from a club bore, a gesture the club bore was meant to spot. That Amis could be 'very dictatorial' at lunch or in the bar, Richard Law openly admits. 'Oh Christ, you're not going to talk about that!' Amis would complain, when Richard Hough asked Law a question about the stock market. So the subject was dropped.

Amis's rudeness was mostly directed at those outside his circle, behaviour that led some members to consider him a bad clubman. Although he clearly loved the Garrick and called it the best place in the world, he made a thing of not being able to abide bores, defined for Jacobs as 'someone with nothing interesting, intelligent or amusing to say'. 'No harm in the chap,' Amis used to say to Jacobs, 'just happens to be a bore.'[71] The Garrick, however, encourages friendliness to all members, frowning upon those who eat or drink alone. Amis hated eating and drinking alone but was shy of strangers as well as hyper-alert to bores; he needed a more exclusive club than the Garrick. Hence his circle of regular chums (Richard Hough, Dominick Harrod, who worked at the BBC, Eric

Shorter, the theatre critic, and Eric Jacobs); hence also his attraction to the 1400 Club, a more formal club within the club, which came into existence in 1980, at the instigation of Roger Morgan, Librarian to the House of Lords and son of the novelist Charles Morgan.[72] It was Morgan who organised the first scheduled lunch, on 7 March 1980. The members of the 1400 Club, which is still active, meet in the bar on the first Friday of each month; adjourn to a small private dining room at the titular hour, after ample time for drinks (the point of the club and an obvious attraction to Amis). A member is designated beforehand to choose the wine and the food, though the bill is shared; if there's a vacancy at the table, an acceptable straggler from the bar is invited along; seating is arranged by lot, though Morgan often 'found it was worthwhile juggling the names a little', particularly in Amis's case. For a while, John Osborne attended regularly, travelling up to London from Herefordshire. He and Amis had little to say to each other and it was best to keep them apart. 'Kingsley wasn't nice to Osborne,' Morgan remembers. 'It was a bit of arrogance. Kingsley did like having *his* audience and we [mostly] were listeners.'

At lunch in the coffee room, when seated at a communal table, Amis was not always able to talk only to chums or vetted guests. Here he met actors, publishers, civil servants, advertising men, lawyers, judges, doctors, architects and politicians, as well as writers and journalists. He took pleasure in the variety and distinction of the club's members, many of whom were surprised to discover that he could be amiable. In principle, Amis thought it an obligation to be good-humoured in company, and not only at one's club. 'More than once, in general chat, he and I had reached a modest conclusion about social and familial behaviour,' writes Martin. 'There is a moral duty to be cheerful. There is a solemn duty to be cheerful.'[73] The Rukeyser questions – 'Does he drink? Is he jolly?' – are relevant here: when it came to drink, Amis had no trouble discharging his duty (though even with drink he could be dictatorial, immediately ordering Gewürztraminer for those he sat with, though deferring on the choice of red); being jolly was not always so easy. Once in the Queen's in Primrose Hill Amis complained that he'd recently sat in the bar at the Garrick for something like twenty minutes 'and nobody came near me'. Richard Hough's reply was: 'Kingsley, doesn't it strike you that it could be because you can be so *fucking curmudgeonly*.' 'Kingsley took that one absolutely on the chin,' Richard

Law remembers. 'It didn't alter his behaviour. He heard it and harrumphed.'

Morgan remembers seeing Amis once sitting alone under the stairs, a place reserved for members only, though visible to guests (in *The Folks That Live on the Hill*, when Harry is at last eligible to sit in the Irving's Senior Parlour, he does so 'in the first place to sneer at those not yet "senior" enough to do so').[74] The date was early December 1980 and Amis, unusually, had not been seen at the Garrick for a week. His first words to Morgan were: 'My wife's left me.' 'He was furious,' Morgan remembers. 'He felt absolutely that she'd done something that she shouldn't have done, for no reason *he* could think of.' Given what Amis wanted from the Garrick and how he wished to present himself there, Morgan's reply was perfectly judged: 'Oh, bad luck, Kingsley. Have a drink?' And up they went to the bar. Some might find this exchange suspect. In a hostile review of *The Folks that Live on the Hill*, Craig Brown welcomed the introduction of a new territory, the Gentleman's Club, to Amis's fiction. But he deplored the tameness of Amis's treatment of this territory, invoked 'only to ignore its mammoth pretensions and to genuflect at its, to my mind, largely bogus otherworldliness'. The element of play-acting in the exchange – a way of avoiding embarrassing feeling, rather than a sign of its absence – is obvious.

To Larkin, Amis explained his attraction to the Garrick straightforwardly. 'If nothing else kept me in London that place would,' he wrote on 18 December 1984. 'Somewhere to get pissed in jovial not very literary bright *all-male* company.' After Larkin's death, as Amis settled into his persona as curmudgeonly grand old man – part Evelyn Waugh, part Samuel Johnson – the Garrick provided a handsome setting. That Amis was aware that there was something antique, if not 'otherworldly' or 'bogus' about this persona, is suggested by the form he chose for 'In Praise of the Garrick', the second of the two poems he wrote about the club.[75] Whereas the idiom of 'Drinking Song', its predecessor, was largely contemporary, the second poem is pure eighteenth century:

> When pressures of the world become intense
> And humankind seems destitute of sense,
> With none but fools and madmen everywhere,
> Come to the Garrick for relief from care.

The Popean or Johnsonian manner is sustained throughout, nowhere more clearly than in lines about club dullards:

> When bores and pedants drive you up the wall,
> Come to the Garrick and forget 'em all.
> Or nearly all: some haunt the coffee room,
> Assiduous to spread a little gloom,
> And some the bar; yet such beneficence,
> Such solace, lies in this bright ambience,
> Even the dullards hold a certain charm,
> As ghosts in sunlight lose their power to harm
> . . .
> Should dullness try to turn the world to ash,
> Here is one place it may find hard to smash;
> The last of its opponents to submit,
> The citadel of kindness, sense and wit.

This is what Amis wished the Garrick to be and what many of his fellow members wished it to be, still wish it to be. The ideal aspired to might be what Brown, in his review, calls a 'mammoth pretension' but Amis and his circle took it seriously, without, of course, going on about it. The circle also colluded with Amis in creating and sustaining his persona as great man. But then, as Ronald Zeegen puts it, 'there *was* something great about him.' And the persona was amusing, for Amis as well as his chums. In a diary entry of 19 May 1995, Jacobs records having a conversation with Amis about politics: 'The essence of what he said seemed to be that he kept up his red-faced clubman, shoot-the-lot reactionary's stance because it was fun more than that he cared all that much.'

It was at the Garrick that Amis first met Jacobs, who was to become his Boswell. Jacobs was born in Glasgow in 1936, the son of a prominent Jewish doctor and a non-Jewish nurse. He was educated at a Scottish public school, Loretto, read English at Pembroke College, Oxford, and did National Service with the Queen's Own Royal Glasgow Yeomanry, where he served for a while in Iraq, as a tank instructor to the Iraqi army. He then embarked on a career in journalism, working on the *Glasgow Herald*, the *Guardian*, the *Sunday Times* and Eddie Shah's short-lived *Today* newspaper. For some years he was an industrial correspondent. He also served briefly as press officer to the Prices and Incomes Board. His experiences covering the 1978 'winter of discontent' and other industrial crises led him to the right politically; as a reporter on trade union affairs, he was likened by one union leader to 'a vet who hates cats'.[76] According to his friend Alan Watkins, who would know, Jacobs was 'a link to old Fleet Street', a hard-drinking, long-lunching professional. His last staff job was writing leaders for *Today*, a post he almost didn't get. As Watkins explains, when *Today* was launched, its executives declared that if there was one sort of journalist they didn't want, 'it was an overweight, lazy, middle-aged hack who got by on the minimum amount of work'. In other words, a link to old Fleet Street. A competition for the post of leader-writer was held, with applicants given forty-five minutes to produce an anonymous opinion piece on the subject of the Grunwick dispute. There was one outstanding piece, which, of course, turned out to be by Jacobs. Only after what Watkins calls 'a very solemn dispute' did the dismayed executives give Jacobs the job.

In the early 1990s, when Jacobs first met Amis, he was in his mid-fifties and out of work, for what Watkins calls 'reasons which weren't entirely his own fault'. Watkins thinks Jacobs was lonely. He had recently separated from his wife 'and didn't seem to have any lady friend in tow'. Amis 'fulfilled a function in his life', the two men 'just hit it off', 'had similar tastes', 'both drank a lot'. It was Jacobs who broached the idea of a biography, writing to Amis with a formal proposal on 25 July 1992: 'If you felt well-disposed then I'm sure we could come to some arrangement about how to proceed. I would not, of course, want to go ahead without your consent and approval.'[77] What Jacobs called his 'slim claims' as a biographer were twofold: admiration for Amis's fiction and 'a genuine enthusiasm . . . for having a go'. 'I have always been a fan – well I must be because you are the only twentieth-century British novelist apart from Waugh and Greene whose whole output I have read.' In the biography itself, Jacobs calls Amis 'the only writer whose latest novel I still customarily bought on publication at the full hardback price'.[78] Amis wrote back on the 27th with a response Jacobs fairly characterises, in a letter to Clowes of 19 December 1996, as 'reluctant but perhaps open to persuasion': 'If the answer must be No, please be assured that, far from thinking your suggestion in any way inappropriate, I take it as a great compliment. You seem to me to be ideally suited for the project in general. I simply feel that to say yes would involve me in an immeasurable amount of work that I would sooner avoid. I did a bit of digging for my Memoirs and would much prefer not to face a second and deeper dig.' Jacobs then asked Amis what he could do to persuade him: 'He said, what about lunch? I said, Where? He said, Simpson's-in-the-Strand. So we had lunch there, about which I can remember only that we drank a lot, it cost a lot and we were somehow in business at the end of it.'[79]

For the rest of Amis's life, some three years and three months, Jacobs was his constant 'companion and gofer' (a phrase from *The Times* obituary of Jacobs).[80] In an article entitled 'The Authorised Biographer', Jacobs describes these meetings as sometimes lasting 'up to ten hours', though only one or two hours were devoted to formal questions. 'During these sessions we might eat,' Jacobs writes, 'but invariably drank, quite often getting quite drunk by the finish.'[81] Amis was given a draft of the biography to read – it is among his papers in the Huntington – and wrote comments in the margins, some of them impatient or intemperate. Next to an anecdote about scaring off bores, Amis wrote 'Rubbish'; next to a remark about being rude to a woman at the pub, he wrote 'COCK!!'; he denied ordering Gewürztraminer at the club 'as an acceptable way to get the drinks side of the meal going'; next to a sentence beginning 'There was Peggy's hatred of Dora', he wrote 'Was there?'; next to a passage about school essays, he wrote 'Lazy' (presumably because all the material in the passage comes from the *Memoirs*). Some corrections are precise and thought-provoking: 'nowadays women don't interest him' was altered by Amis to 'nowadays women as "birds" don't interest him'; 'what he dislikes about this story is not his racism, which he despises' became '. . . which he does not like'; 'in fury', a description of how Amis exploded at Victor Gollancz, became 'in synthetic fury'; it was not true that Amis's dislike of games, both indoors and outdoors, was 'because he hated losing'. At the end of a description of the way the port was circulated at Peterhouse, Jacobs wrote: 'It is not difficult to imagine Amis keeping an anxious eye on this procedure.' Amis added: 'Thanks to the likes of you.'

Most of Amis's suggested corrections were factual or stylistic, the sort any biographer would be glad to have. The only significant objections he made to the biography's methodology concerned Jacobs's readings of the novels. After a list of obvious similarities between Harry Caldecote's routines and Amis's, Amis wrote: 'Any *differences*?' When Jacobs noted that both Robin Davies's mother, in *You Can't Do Both*, and Amis's, are called Peggy, Amis wrote: 'Oh God!' Jacobs made no alterations in these instances. In the Preface to the biography, Jacobs admits that he and Amis argued a good deal about the autobiographical content of his novels, but 'we agreed when Amis summed up our differences by saying that I probably saw more of him in his fiction, and he probably saw less of himself, than was there'.[82] It is in the Preface that Jacobs also declares, accurately, given the evidence of the draft, that Amis made no attempt 'to remove anything at all that might seem to show him in a less than shining light'.[83] Whether Amis skipped pages or chapters, or read some less attentively than others, is hard to tell. One passage in the biography, however, a passage that particularly upset Ali, he had clearly read in draft (correcting a spelling mistake and a small error of fact). The passage concerns a drunken dinner Amis attended at the Savile Club at which he heard rumours of Ali's 'dishonesty and general crappiness'. These false rumours, Jacobs immediately adds, 'turned out not to be reliable'.[84] Ali was so upset by the passage that he demanded a written apology from both Jacobs and Amis. On 16 June 1995 Amis wrote to Ali, heading his letter 'Private and Confidential'. Amis accepted that there was a difference between legal defamation and defamation in a non-legal context: 'I am qualified to judge of what is bad behaviour in a non-legal context and here I feel I have been and am at fault. I understand and have taken to heart your disappointed remarks about my having done something to spoil the happy private atmosphere between us three, meaning the two of us and Hilly. I apologise for having done so and wish very much that I had put things differently in what Jacobs quoted.' The letter ends: 'all things considered I beg your pardon and ask your forgiveness'.

Hilly's feelings had also been hurt by the biography, particularly by passages quoting Amis's insulting remarks about Daddy B. Amis bore the brunt of her complaints, which were communicated to friends as well as family, but the biographer felt them too. When Jacobs and the family quarrelled after Amis's death, over Jacobs's attempts, within three days of the death, to serialise his account of Amis's last days, including indelicate details of his debility and failing health, the earlier upset played a part. As Jacobs's diary also makes clear, the relation between biographer and subject was not without tensions. On 26 May 1995 he records the following entry:

Kingsley was difficult last night, over having lunch with a journalist from The Australian. They want to do an excerpt from my biography, plus an interview with Kingsley to go with it. What was in it for him? Why should he have lunch alone with an unknown journalist, which might turn out to be two hours of utter boredom and do nothing useful for him? We watched The Two Ronnies at which he laughed more than I did. Then I left him with Sally and his jellied eels supper, feeling that I had seen his selfish side more clearly than before.

Amis was aware of this selfish side, and of the effect it might have on Jacobs – or so *The Biographer's Moustache* (1995), the last of his published novels, suggests. Also suggested by *The Biographer's Moustache* is the self-interested character of relations between biographers and their living subjects, however friendly. Gordon Scott-Thompson, the biographer, is a struggling hack and deracinated Scot, but he's no Jacobs; Jimmy Fane, his subject, is a novelist, but he's no Amis (among other things, his novels are not very good, and he's a stupendous social snob).[85] Jacobs reviewed *The Biographer's Moustache* in the *Spectator* and could find only a single resemblance between his dealings with Amis and those of Scott-Thompson with Fane: the inaugurating or exploratory lunch. In the fictional one, Fane orders the most expensive items on the menu, knowing that the hard-up Scott-Thompson is paying. As his wife later explains: 'I don't think he was just enjoying the simple pleasure of getting somebody else to spend money on him, though perhaps one shouldn't put that past him in general. No, I think what he was doing was showing you who was master, coming out on top in a battle of wills.'[86] That Fane is a shit is admitted by all, Fane included. When pressed, he agrees to read a very few pages of what Scott-Thompson has written. After doing so, he addresses the question of bad behaviour: 'It doesn't matter that some of my actions have been, how to put it, offensive to conventional morality, in fact it's a great advantage . . . These days the public *like* to think of an artist as a, as a *shit*, known to behave in ways they would shrink from.'[87] As for his biographer's obvious interest in making money out of him, as Scott-Thompson himself admits: 'Scotsmen are notorious for being on the make, don't forget. Newspaper editors are prepared to pay quite a lot for a scandalous story about an upper-crust figure like Jimmy Fane.'[88] In the end, Scott-Thompson can't take Fane's rudeness, declaring that 'there are limits to how much of a shit one can face writing about.'[89] As he explains in their final conversation: 'You're not a reluctant shit and certainly not an unconscious shit, you're a self-congratulatory shit.'[90] Even sleeping with Fane's wife is inadequate compensation.

Amis received an advance of £135,000 for *The Biographer's Moustache*, half of a two-book contract negotiated by Clowes with HarperCollins. It was Hutchinson that forced the move to Harper-Collins, by offering only £40,000 for the novel; Clowes immediately turned to other publishers. On the eve of signing the contract, a lunch was arranged for Amis and Eddie Bell, the new chief executive of HarperCollins (previously Jacobs's employer at *Today*). Clowes made it clear to Amis that he wanted the deal done, and Amis 'behaved impeccably and was very funny'. The lunch got off to a good start when Bell, described by Clowes as 'a likeable character', presented Amis with a bottle of his favourite whisky, the ten-year-old Macallan.[91] That *The Biographer's Moustache* is one of Amis's weaker novels was, doubtless, a disappointment to his new publishers, but no cause for panic; its immediate predecessor, *You Can't Do Both*, published just a year before, is especially strong; moreover, the deficiencies of *The Biographer's Moustache* – thin plot, dated social *aperçus*, the 'patrician condescension' of its style[92] – are as plausibly explained by haste (the book was written and published within a year) as by failing powers; the haste might even be a sign of creative health. Still, the novel was harshly reviewed. Martin Amis, himself recently roughed up in the press – for assorted dental and marital difficulties and for changing agents – described the book's notices as 'eagerly unfavourable' and the accompanying interviews and profiles as 'more onerous than anything that had been written about me that year.'[93] Though Amis was not the sort to obsess about bad reviews, famously claiming that they might ruin his breakfast but not his lunch, Martin hoped that he was past caring.

He was past caring, though in a way that was worrying. By the time the reviews came out, in late August and early September, Amis was in bad shape, physically and mentally. He had had a fall in Wales, during his annual summer visit, and had been forced to return to London early, while Hilly and Ali were still in Spain. Amis had gone to Swansea earlier than usual because his friend Stuart

Thomas was dying. Thomas had bladder cancer and had been seriously ill for some years. The visit of Amis and Hilly the previous Christmas was also cut short, when Stuart was rushed to hospital on Christmas Eve. On 13 August, a Friday, Amis arrived at the Rushes' and immediately wanted to visit the Thomases.[94] Eve put him off (as Virginia Rush remembers it, she told him it was 'not really convenient'). He was 'mortally upset'. The next evening Stuart died. Michael Rush recalls Amis as very quiet, depressed not only about Stuart's death but about not having been able to say goodbye: 'He kept on saying: "All I wanted was to say 'Cheerio, chum.'"'[95] On 16 August, Amis and the Rushes went round to Mary Twill Lane to see Eve. The next day, at the funeral, Amis delivered a eulogy, calling Thomas 'somebody I never got to the end of', praising his 'inexhaustible vivacity, entertainingness, whatever you call it, a quality you only had to spend a couple of minutes with him to recognise and start to enjoy'.

When Amis arrived in Swansea from London, he was flustered and unhealthy looking. He had been driven down by Jack Prince, who often drove for the Rushes. Prince, who had a military background, acted as tour guide, fixer and driver when Amis, the Rushes, Stuart Thomas and other Swansea friends went on excursions to nearby villages and pubs, either in minivan or flexibus. Amis much enjoyed these motorised pub crawls, known to the Rushes as 'Kingsley's Rural Rides', and he liked and trusted Prince. For the past few summers, Amis had hired Prince to drive up to London from Swansea, collect him at Primrose Hill, then drive back to Swansea. The journey from Primrose Hill to the Rushes' took about five hours and had by now become routine: 'I always arrived at eleven. Sir Kingsley was always ready: there was his raincoat, his typewriter, a sheaf of paper, a case of Macallan ten-year-old Scotch and a plastic bag.' The plastic bag, easily carried in one hand, contained all Amis's kit and clothing for the visit ('Sir Kingsley always travelled light'). Once on the road, Amis insisted on stopping every thirty minutes, for a drink or to have a pee. On this occasion, Prince filled a hip flask with Macallan and water and gave it to Amis as soon as they set off; that way they could get out of London without a stop. On the motorway, meals and breaks were carefully planned. Lunch was at 12.30 or 1, depending on traffic, always 'at the approved hostelry' (off Junction 13 on the M4, at an inn where there was no music, no children, and Macallan on the optic). Amis drank his usual amount: two large whiskies, red wine with sandwiches, pudding wine with dessert. After several further stops they arrived at the Rushes', some time between four and five. The sun was brutal that day, especially in the front passenger seat, where Amis always sat. Prince's minivan was air-conditioned but Amis arrived hot, disoriented and complaining that 'I couldn't get the sun out of my eyes.' Understandably, given the events of the next few days, his spirits did not improve. Michael Rush's 'very clear impression' was that Stuart's death and funeral 'triggered something in Kingsley's own condition'.

That condition was as one would expect of a seventy-three-year-old man of Amis's habits, even one with an iron constitution. Amis had been drinking at least a bottle of whisky a day for many years. He took no exercise, was obese, chronically anxious and chaotic about his medication. On 18 June 1993, partly because he had no clear idea of the pills Amis had been prescribed by other doctors, Zeegen asked him to write out a list of what he was meant to take each day. Here is the list:

2 x Frumil [a diuretic, for swollen legs]
3 x Verapamil 80 mg [for cardiac irregularity]
1 x Disprin [to thin the blood]
3 x Brufen 200 mg [an analgesic, for pain]
1 x Allopurinol 100 mg [for gout]
3 x Senokot 25 mg. [for constipation]
4 teaspoons Lactulose [also for constipation][96]

Missing from this list is benzodiazepine, which Amis took to sleep or when anxious, and medication for hypertension (mentioned in a letter to Larkin of 23 September 1979). Amis had originally been referred to Zeegen in 1989 by Ali's brother, Dr Robin Boyd, known to the family as 'Tiger'. Boyd reported that Amis was suffering from constipation and was anxious that he might have bowel cancer. Zeegen, a consultant physician and gastroenterologist, ordered tests, all of which proved negative. At their first meeting, Amis told Zeegen that he'd also had several episodes in which he 'spoke nonsense'. These episodes lasted approximately thirty seconds and he was aware he was talking nonsense when they happened. On 23 June 1989, therefore, Amis had a brain scan, which produced no evidence of stroke, though it is still possible that the nonsense episodes were 'ischaemic' in nature, a product of lack of blood to the brain.

Zeegen urged Amis to cut down on his drinking. In October 1989, he arranged for him to see a clinical psychologist with an interest in alcohol-related problems. Amis saw him twice. Three years later, after episodes of atrial fibrillation or heart flutter, Zeegen sent Amis back to his cardiologist, who reported no angina, moderate exercise intolerance and pain from swollen legs, a consequence, Zeegen believed, of excessive drinking. Amis made it clear to the cardiologist, as he had to Zeegen and the clinical psychologist, that he was unlikely to cut down his consumption of alcohol, at least in the absence of a medical emergency. The doctors were left, as one of them put it, to 'lurch from one crisis to another'. Zeegen could do little more than monitor Amis's liver, which, surprisingly, showed only slight signs of enlargement, and attempt to ameliorate his symptoms. Perhaps the most noticeable of these symptoms, along with increasing immobility, was Amis's unsteadiness on his feet. As Martin puts it in *Experience*: 'Kingsley fell over all the time . . . To hear my mother tell it, some of these collapses sounded like a chest of drawers jettisoned from an aeroplane. "Absolutely deafening. But you're not supposed to mention it. It happens so often that we don't even go up. Unless he's wedged. Then he bangs on the floor and I send Ali."'97

The fall in Wales occurred on 20 August, three days after Stuart Thomas's funeral. Amis and the Rushes had been invited to Sunday lunch in Laugharne by Roger Morgan and his wife. The Morgans had a cottage overlooking the estuary, along the narrow lane leading to Dylan Thomas's boathouse. Amis had stayed there six years previously, partly to gather impressions for *The Old Devils*. Before the lunch, according to Morgan, Amis drank between a half and a quarter bottle of whisky, Gewürztraminer with the meal itself and a Cointreau as *digestif*. Morgan remembers him as 'completely articulate' at the end of the meal. 'He wasn't drunk or anything like that,' Virginia Rush remembers. When Michael Rush brought the car round to the front of the Morgans' cottage, Amis said his goodbyes and successfully negotiated the walk to the front gate and the first two steps down to the lane. The third step, to street level, he misjudged, perhaps because the lane is on a slight incline. He lost his balance, fell backwards and hit his head. A young off-duty policewoman happened to be walking by and ran to assist Amis, who never lost consciousness. He was helped to his feet and into the car; aside from a slight graze on the back of his head, he said he was all right. On the ride back to Swansea he was very quiet, though he answered normally when addressed. The Morgans called that evening to see how Amis was, and the Rushes said he was fine. The next morning, however, he complained of pain in his back and asked to see a doctor. Virginia's GP came round, examined him, said there wasn't really anything she could do except to give him painkillers, and suggested that if the pain persisted, perhaps he should return to London to see his own doctors.

Zeegen was away, Ali and Hilly were still in Spain, but would be back soon, and Amis, in a state, kept complaining that his 'loins' were aching. Virginia's doctor was again summoned and again said there wasn't much she could do, unless he wanted to go to hospital, something it was thought best to do in London. This unsatisfactory state of affairs continued for several days, with Amis in increasing pain and reluctant to move, even to go to the lavatory. It was at this point that Amis was interviewed by Glenys Roberts for the *Daily Telegraph* and Joanna Coles for the *Guardian*. Roberts arrived on the day Virginia Rush's GP had been summoned a second time. Amis refused her invitation to lunch, subjected her to long silences and kept interrupting the interview to find out what was happening in the Test Match. When the GP arrived, Roberts was summarily dismissed. 'It isn't often that one comes from London to Swansea to meet a famous figurehead, and encounters such a lack of civility for one's pains,' she later wrote, in a profile entitled 'Angrier by the Minute'.[98] To Coles, who saw Amis several days earlier, he was less rude: 'I've pulled a muscle in my loins,' he announced loudly, by way of a greeting: 'It must be all that romping about, what? I'm staying here with my new friends because the friend I normally stay with died on Sunday.'[99] Then Eric Jacobs arrived, summoned by Amis (who made Virginia promise she wouldn't tell Jacobs how badly he felt). Jacobs was staying in a bed and breakfast and because Amis was unable to leave the house, 'kept coming round every five minutes';[100] he, too, like Amis, had to be fed and watered. By the time he arrived, Zeegen had been contacted. His advice was that Amis be brought back to London immediately; a room would be found for him at the Chelsea and Westminster Hospital in the Fulham Road, where Zeegen worked. The Rushes had also been able to contact Martin, who'd been away as well. On 31 August, unsteadily, Amis signed the Rushes' visitors' book:

DATE	NAME	ADDRESS	DATE
Dec 27-29th	Chickie Hoss	2358 Barnabas Street 8.01 Nov 4	
		Thank you for a wonderful time	
		a truly wonderful Christmas au si sana	
"	Robert Carl.	Paraiso Mar, Calpe, Alicante.	25.02.96
		Muchas gracias!	
July 8-10	Gw & Joyce Kego		
July 15-22	Carol, Emily and Serge	Wonderful company, wonderful hospitality, food, "le hérisson", le jeu, the luxrious and loustead — what more do we want! It was super; thank you very much!	25/04/1996
11-31 August	Kingsley Amis		29/5/1996
8-12 Sept	Chickie Hoss	I am here again and had a wonderful time as always -	29-8-96. 7-8-96

'Kingsley Amiss'. After an assurance from Virginia's doctor that Amis was well enough to travel, the Rushes and Jacobs got him into the back seat of Jacobs's car. With Virginia also in the back seat, Jacobs set off for London. It was a 'ghastly journey', according to Virginia, involving much tension and embarrassment, especially when Amis had to stop to pee. At the hospital that evening, Martin called and Amis told him not to come round till the morning: 'I'd rather save you up for tomorrow, if you know what I mean.'[101] Jacobs went to an off-licence and bought Amis more whisky, then he, Amis and Virginia had a drink in Amis's room, at about seven. Outside the room, Jacobs met Zeegen, who had Amis's X-rays: Amis had two crushed or wedged lower vertebrae, one a recent fracture, one an old one. Hence the pain. Other tests revealed no significant neurological disease. As far as Zeegen could tell, Amis had not suffered a stroke. When asked by a nurse if it was all right for Amis to drink, Zeegen said yes, 'with a look which asked, what was the point of denying it to him?'[102] Later that evening, Zeegen and his houseman, a woman doctor, came to see Amis. Amis was drinking whisky and Zeegen told the houseman not to stop him. 'It's about a bottle, is it?' he asked Amis. 'No, two,' Amis answered, though Zeegen thinks this may have been bravado, to impress the female houseman.

Amis stayed at the Chelsea and Westminster Hospital from 31 August to 5 September, when, against Zeegen's advice, he persuaded the senior nurse and consultant orthopaedic surgeon to discharge him. His treatment in hospital had been bed rest and painkillers, DF 118 (Dihydrocodeine). This treatment, Amis argued, could be continued at home. Despite grogginess and confusion, a side-effect of the painkillers, especially when mixed with alcohol, he felt better.[103] Though Zeegen warned him that he was by no means cured, Amis was determined to get back to writing. Also, Zeegen suspected, he wanted to drink more than he'd been able to drink in hospital. Hilly and the Kilmarnocks were now back from Spain, which meant, as Amis told Jacobs: 'Regents Park is there.'[104] Amis even talked of going for lunch at the Garrick (which he did eventually, returning, as Hilly put it, 'paralytic' with drink).[105] Though still unsteady on his feet and in considerable pain, he could manage at home by confining himself to the ground floor, where his bedroom and study were. Once a television set was installed he'd have everything he needed. On his first night back, a little party assembled in his bedroom, consisting of Martin, Sally, Hilly and Jacobs. As Jacobs records in his diary, the party was cheerful, with Martin in good form. Hilly had not spoken to Jacobs since the biography was published, but at the party 'announced that she had "buried the hatchet" with me'.[106]

The next day Amis was able to walk by himself to the bath-room and back, though not without pain. Getting out of bed in the morning was agony. Because of the painkillers and alcohol, his speech was slurred and often hard to make out. He also seemed slower mentally, both to Jacobs and to Martin. Though Amis had his desk and typewriter moved into the bedroom, and was heard typing away, his new novel remained stuck on page 106. Among the papers left in his room after his death were thirteen sheets headed 'p.106' or mis-headed 'p.109'. None gets much past the same few sentences or phrases; all contain alarming spelling mistakes and typos. Hilly told Martin that she sometimes heard Amis at work at five in the morning. When she later checked to see what he had typed, she found only '*i*'s and *e*'s' and the repeated word '*seagulls*'. Meanwhile, because Ali was away in Luxembourg when Amis returned from hospital, Hilly had to do most of the fetching and carrying, especially at night, when Sally was not around to help. Hilly's knees were not good and she was on a waiting list for operations on both of them. Jacobs records seeing her haul herself up the stairs on her hands and knees. Amis got into a routine of shouting for painkillers before dawn. When she had fetched them for him, she often didn't return to bed, fearing she would wake Ali. Sally didn't arrive until 8 a.m. Hilly made it clear to Philip, Martin and Jacobs that caring for Amis was wearing her out, and they urged her to hire a nurse. But Hilly thought a nurse would frighten and upset Amis. What was also clear was that neither she nor Amis was able to manage his pills: there were so many of them and he was often unable to remember how many he'd taken or should take. On 15 September, ten days after leaving hospital, Hilly called Zeegen to say that she thought Amis was deranged. He didn't know what day it was; he thought he was writing a book about his health; he claimed he had to go to see the British consul about the book.[107] The next day he said he wanted a party. Then, as Martin puts it, 'he told everybody – Mum, Ali, Connie[108] – to fuck off. Everybody went downstairs. He followed everybody into the basement flat and told everybody to fuck off. Then he went upstairs. Everybody followed, with caution. Then he told everybody to fuck off.'[109] The next day he asked Hilly if he'd missed his funeral. 'He's poisoning himself,' Philip told Martin. It was the pills, he believed, jumbled up in a shoebox, washed down with whisky.

Zeegen was away at a conference in Warwickshire. When he returned, Hilly asked him to come to see Amis at Regents Park Road. Zeegen did not make house calls: it was not what he did, he did not even own a doctor's black bag. But he was happy to see Amis at the Chelsea and Westminster and to readmit him directly. Then Robin Boyd was summoned to straighten out Amis's pills and to look into finding a full-time nurse. For a day, Amis recovered his senses. Jacobs asked how he felt and he replied: 'like a spider trying to get around his web on two legs'. Then he got worse. The Jaqueses came over and neither they nor Jacobs could make sense of what he was saying. He tried to sit down on a non-existent chair. He suddenly headed upstairs, then downstairs. Hilly was terrified that he'd do the same thing at night, when only she and Ali were there; if he fell, they'd have to call 999. On 20 September, in the middle of the night, Amis woke up, dressed himself, undressed himself, took a shower and when Hilly awoke mumbled something about catching a train. Hilly got him back into bed and the next morning he walked out of the front door into Regents Park Road and tried to flag down passing cars. He thought they were taxis and wanted one to take him to the Garrick. Hilly then called the local GP practice and two doctors came round to see Amis. After examining him and talking with Hilly, they decided he should go to hospital. That same day an ambulance arrived and Amis was taken to University College Hospital in Gower Street. Jacobs accompanied him. In the ambulance, Amis was 'meek and manageable'; in the hospital, 'he became piteous, fearful', partly, Jacobs suspects, because it took so long for the hospital to find him a room. A doctor came to ask permission to give Amis a brain scan. He refused, terrified. When a room was found for him in a private wing (a mistake, since he feared and hated being alone), it took a porter and two nurses to get him into it. He kept trying to escape from the wheelchair, which the porter tilted back as they headed towards the room. He grabbed at anything that passed. Once in the room he begged Jacobs not to leave him.

The doctor who treated Amis at University College Hospital, a consultant geriatrician, took a different line from Zeegen over the question of drink, partly because circumstances had clearly changed by now. Amis was brought to hospital in a state of acute confusion and paranoia. The cause of this confusion and paranoia was overmedication with DF 118, a product of bad pill management, combined with alcohol. Routine blood tests and X-rays were normal. When the brain scan was finally taken, it showed no evidence of stroke. The consultant prescribed alcohol withdrawal, accompanied by a standard anti-DT drug called Heminevrin. Cold turkey. All other medications were discontinued. When Jacobs came to see Amis the next day, 21 September, he asked him if there was anything he wanted: 'Liberty,' Amis answered. When Philip and Martin came to see him, he told them: 'I'm in Hell.'[110] He spent the first night at UCH incessantly phoning Hilly, who was forced to change her number. The next day he resumed pleading with Jacobs and other visitors to take him back to Regents Park Road. He phoned Richard Hough so frequently that Hough was forced to turn off his answering machine. On 22 September, Philip came to visit and Amis told him to fuck off. He could no longer read, let alone write, and wanted no visitors (though he said to Sally that people shouldn't mind when he told them to bugger off). On 25 September the consultant told Hilly that Amis would recover once he got through alcohol withdrawal and that he would be able to come home. By 29 September he began to show signs of improvement. When Jaime came to visit, he seemed delighted to see him. 'I *used* to be important,' he told Jaime, 'apparently quite cheerfully.'[111] Then he tried to get Jacobs to sneak him out of the hospital.

On 7 October Amis's condition suddenly deteriorated. The nurses found him lying on the floor. He gave all the appearance of having suffered a stroke or 'cerebrovascular accident' (as the death certificate puts it): increased apathy, intellectual deterioration, incontinence, a tendency to fall to the right. He now faced a period of extended rehabilitation and the doctors decided to move him to an open geriatric ward in St Pancras Hospital, the Phoenix Ward, home to what doctors refer to as 'crumble'. Before the move, Philip went to see Amis, who said two things to him: 'For God's sake, you bloody fool, kill me' and 'For God's sake, you bloody fool, give me a drink.' Philip put a drop of whisky on his tongue, from a miniature he was carrying, and Amis fell asleep. When Hilly came to visit he was awake and restive. She dabbed his face with 4711 and said: 'You can go to sleep now, darling. You've done everything you needed to do.' As Martin puts it: 'you could feel his anxiety submit to a trusted ritual'.[112] On 12 October, Amis was moved to the Phoenix Ward of St Pancras Hospital.

The Phoenix Ward was administered by nurses who astonished the Amises with their kindness.[113] Many of the patients in the ward were frail or seemed gaga, but 'no one cries or moans'.[114] Amis was mostly unresponsive or incoherent when he arrived, but when Jacobs came to see him and said 'Hullo, Kingsley,' he said 'Hullo, old chap.' Later, Eric Shorter, his Garrick friend, asked Amis how he was feeling. Martin, to whom Amis had hardly spoken a word for days, was stunned to hear his father respond in a clear voice: 'Absolutely fucking awful, mate!' Two days later, Amis contracted pneumonia and was given antibiotics and morphine. Now he was running a fever, sweating, with a fan by the side of his bed and a single sheet covering him. He kept pushing the sheet down, exposing his naked body, oblivious to visitors and to the other patients in the ward. A nurse came and used a syringe to 'inject' food into his mouth. On 21 October, the antibiotics that would cure his pneumonia were stopped; the quantities needed would kill him anyway. Feeding was also stopped. Family and friends were alerted to say their last good-byes. Sally had been by his side for ten hours, 'smoothing him, lulling him'.[115] On the morning of 22 October, at 11.10 a.m., while Sally held his hand, Amis died in his sleep. After weeks of struggle and the loss of everything he needed to live – the ability to write, to drink, to joke, to laugh – he simply stopped breathing.

28

Afterlife

Amis's death was a front-page story in all the broadsheet papers and a lead item on radio and television news broadcasts. Obituaries ran to half a page, a length once reserved for heads of state. *The Times* printed three separate articles about him, in addition to an obituary and a diary piece, with tributes from John Bayley, John Mortimer, Keith Waterhouse and Auberon Waugh. The *Sunday Times* gave his death comparable prominence. In an article titled 'A Modern Master', John Sutherland dispensed with qualifiers: Amis was 'a great novelist', whose greatness was 'corrective' in nature, moving a literary form 'in a necessary direction': 'Just as Philip Larkin resolved that the future of English poetry lay not with complex Pound and Eliot but with simple Hardy and Betjeman, so Amis decided that the English novel must regenerate itself not by alliance with modernist "crap," but by reconnection with "genre" – that reservoir of popular fiction from which, as if in some uneasy middle-class family, the "quality novel" constantly labours to raise itself.'[1] Sutherland's tribute ended by invoking Amis's criterion of 'readability': 'the raw stuff of readability is to be found in what the common reader consumes for pleasure. The practical demonstration of this proof is Amis's chief bequest to the English novel.' In the *Independent*, John Walsh, the literary editor, concentrated on Amis as controversialist: 'just watching (or reading) him in action was a terrific sideshow to the business of literature'.[2] In the obituary in the *Independent*, David Lodge called Amis 'the most gifted of the British novelists who began publishing in the 1950s', 'scrupulously exact, honest and undeceived' and as 'fundamentally sceptical' as Samuel Beckett (not a comparison Amis would have liked), though 'cushioned or concealed by the conventions of the well-made novel'.[3] In the *Guardian*, Karl Miller, never extravagant in praise, called Amis 'a good poet, a good critic, and a comic artist of genius with lots of staying power. He did more to lift the spirits than any other writer in this country since the war.' The *Guardian* ran a full-page obituary by Jacobs and tributes from, among others, Penelope Fitzgerald, A.S. Byatt, who described Amis as the writer she 'loved to hate', and David Lodge, for whom early Amis in particular was 'one of those novelists who open up a whole new vista of possibility for fellow practitioners'.[4] Malcolm Bradbury, writing in the *Daily Mail*, seconded Lodge's point about early Amis: 'We felt people like us were now in literature – and his kind of person (novelist and poet, writer and academic) was what we'd all like to be.' As Amis's career progressed, 'with book after book, poem after poem, [he] captured what post-war Britain felt like and stood for'. Bradbury ended his piece by calling Amis 'one of our greatest and most English writers'.[5] American tributes were equally glowing. 'He has been so prominent, funny and nettlesome for so long,' wrote Paul Gray, in a full-page obituary in *Time* magazine, 'that his passing inspires valedictory thoughts that go beyond the stilling of a single voice . . . [T]he British decades between 1955 and 1995 should in fairness be called "the Amis era."'[6]

Amis's funeral was held on Tuesday, 31 October, at St Mark's Church, near Regents Park Road. After a brief ceremony, his body was cremated at Golders Green Cemetery. Amis had told Sally that he wanted his ashes scattered over Swansea Bay, but they were divided up among the children and Sally's portion rested in an urn on her mantelpiece. 'I kiss him "Good Morning!" and I kiss him "Good night!"' she told Clive Gammon. 'And when "The Bill" comes on TV, I sit him down to watch it with me.'[7] The service at St Mark's was attended by friends, family and neighbours, including the woman who owned Odette's, Amis's favourite local restaurant, and the man who owned the local delicatessen. There was no address or eulogy, for a proper memorial service was planned. In *Experience*, Martin describes the senior Amises – Hilly, Sally, Philip and Martin himself – riding back in a Daimler from the cemetery to the wake at 194

Regents Park Road, 'all smoking, all coughing'.[8] At the funeral, they'd all been crying.

Eric Jacobs was conspicuous by his absence on the day. He was Amis's friend as well as his authorised biographer and in his last days attended him as faithfully as anyone in the family, except perhaps Sally. But within two days of his friend's death Jacobs had offered his diary entries about Amis to the *Daily Mail* and the *Sunday Times*, expecting a large serialisation fee. Amis had died on a Sunday and by Wednesday negotiations to sell extracts from the diaries were well advanced. On Wednesday, three days after his father's death, Martin got a call from Jacobs: 'He said he had kept some "jottings" on Kingsley – notes for a second book he was intending to write about him' and that the *Sunday Times* thought them publishable. Martin remembers saying: 'Well that probably sounds okay', and Jacobs replying: 'It seemed right you should see it first.' Martin felt unperturbed by the exchange: he was grateful to Jacobs for the help he had given his father and the family in the last months of Amis's life. In addition, 'I expected these jottings to be affectionate and anodyne' and 'liked the idea of the hard-up biographer making some money as he added to the general glow of the obituaries'.[9] When Martin read the jottings, however, he was horrified: 'Agonising violation was inflicted on the immediate family (and on peripheral figures too: my sons, for example), and the central event, the rite of passage, was unbearably demeaned. It was quite something, like a visit to a world without affect, to see my father, at his most helpless, and literally naked, described without a particle of decorum. He had been dead for seventy-two hours.'[10] Martin began making telephone calls – to his agent, Andrew Wylie (partner of Jacobs's agent, Gillon Aitken), to the *Sunday Times*, where Martin was chief book reviewer, to his mother and brother. When the *Sunday Times* argued for publication, Martin threatened the paper with an injunction. 'This wasn't what I wanted to be doing, with my father not yet in his coffin and the funeral only days away.'[11] As soon as Jacobs realised how upset the family was, he asked that the diaries be withdrawn, writing letters of apology to Martin and Hilly. But the family was unforgiving: word was passed to him that he would not be welcome at the funeral.

Jacobs's public account of the incident came out several months later, after Martin had informed him that he would not be editing Amis's correspondence. Privately, in a letter to Hilly of 27 October, which he copied to Martin, he was contrite and apologetic.[12] He began by explaining the origin and nature of the diaries. In April Amis had proposed to him that he write a sort of Postscript to the biography, based on tape-recorded conversations. This Postscript, Amis suggested, would most likely appear round about the time of his death, either as a separate book or as an addendum to a second edition of the biography. Jacobs would do all the work: recording and transcribing conversations, deciding which topics to discuss, editing the transcripts, though Amis expected to have 'powers of amendment if he were still alive when I finished it'. Jacobs thinks Amis's main motive in proposing this second book was a desire to 'renew the Thursday night sessions we had when I was working on his biography, which he had come to enjoy'. Once the recordings began, however, they 'did not seem to be yielding much that would be worth publication'. The recordings, which Jacobs deposited in the Huntington, are uneven in interest, some tapes showing impatience or peevishness on Amis's part, or fatigue on Jacobs's part, others containing unexpected opinions and moments of insight, as in the remarks about race quoted in the previous chapter. The tapes would not by themselves make a book, however, even much of an addendum to the biography, which is why Jacobs continued to keep the diary. As he wrote to Hilly: 'I had no clear aim in mind other than to keep a record in the vague hope that it might throw up material about Kingsley worth publishing in some form at some time.' Amis knew about the diary and had made no objection to its existence.

When Jacobs was summoned to Swansea after Amis's fall, he simply 'continued to jot things down as they happened, as I had been doing on and off for months'. The first of his mistakes was in making the diary available for publication so soon after Amis's death: 'I realise now that it was a very serious error of judgement on my part.' The jottings were 'an affectionate, if grim, portrait of a great man's last days'. Though they contained potentially hurtful details, about the family in particular, he had no intention of publishing anything without the family's consent. This was why he had the extracts sent to Martin. What he now also realised was that 'letting journalists on the Mail and Sunday Times read the whole thing made it possible that some of those hurtful details might, as it were, enter the journalistic bloodstream and emerge in print one day'. He had therefore instructed his agent to 'take all possible steps' to see that the diaries were returned immediately and to ensure that none of their contents would be revealed by those who had seen them. 'Strangely enough', he had confidence that the details would remain unrevealed. The last paragraph of the letter begins: 'Dear Hilly, I do apologise most deeply and sincerely for creating all this fuss. Please believe me when I say that I had no intention of cashing in on the sensational minutiae of Kingsley's death or the family gossip.' His errors were a product of grief rather than greed: 'I think, since Kingsley died, I have been going through a most peculiar phase of what I suppose must be called grieving, in which my normal judgement must have been suspended in a kind of limbo.'

But Jacobs also wanted and needed the money. 'Eric behaved like a complete gutter journalist,' says Alan Watkins. In private, Jacobs admitted as much. 'I suppose you think I've been a bit of a shit,' he said to Christopher Hitchens. 'Yes, I do,' Hitchens replied: 'What could possibly have come over you? And how did you imagine you'd get away with it?' To which Jacobs replied: 'All right. I know I've been a bit of a shit.'[13] That Jacobs was unhappy about what had happened is not in doubt. That Martin, too, was unhappy, not just about what Jacobs had done but about banning him from the funeral, is also clear. 'I felt sorry for him,' he writes in *Experience*, 'and gratitude lingered.' What Martin did not make clear, either over the telephone or in a subsequent letter to Jacobs, was that 'the family, of course, wanted no further dealings with Eric', which meant, as Martin puts it, 'firing him from the job, not yet begun, of editing Kingsley's *Letters*'.[14] Amis had agreed to give this job to Jacobs when they discussed the Postscript and though the contract had been drawn up, it had not been signed. For some weeks, Jacobs was allowed to continue in the mistaken assumption or hope that the job would still be his.[15]

At this point I enter the story. Martin and I had been friends for a decade and sometimes discussed our work together. We also talked about his father's novels, which he knew I admired. He had read some of my books and reviews and was aware that I'd recently begun work on the Oxford Authors Shelley. The main reason he asked me to edit his father's letters was that he thought I would do the job thoroughly. He also trusted me; and whoever took the job on would have to spend time with the family, which mostly meant with him. My inevitable queries about dates, names and places could fit into established patterns of friendship. There would be problems of tact and decorum, but we could work these out.

I persuaded Oxford University Press to extend my deadline and to hire a co-editor, Michael O'Neill, of Durham University, then I accepted Martin's offer. I would return to the Shelley, which I'd been at work on for a year, once I'd finished the Amis. *The Letters of Kingsley Amis* came out in 2000, four years after I'd begun work on it, and the Oxford Authors *Shelley*, now renamed *Percy Bysshe Shelley: The Major Works*, was published in 2003. Editing Amis's letters has been the most enjoyable job of my scholarly career.

In March 1996, word of my appointment as Jacobs's replacement came out in a newspaper interview with Martin. Jacobs was furious. When, some months earlier, he had learned that his contract to edit the letters had been cancelled, he had written to Martin for an explanation. Martin never replied. 'That's bad manners,' Jacobs was quoted as saying in the *Sunday Times*, in an article of 10 March 1996: 'I feel very disappointed and upset and badly used. I thought executors were supposed to follow the wishes of the person they represent, but this is the exact opposite of what Kingsley wanted.'[16] He now felt no compunction about publishing the diary. 'I feel I should be guided by what I think Kingsley would have approved of, rather than anyone else. If I do publish it, would he say "What a shit you are," or that it was okay? I think, on the whole, he wouldn't mind at all.' In the same article, Martin was quoted as claiming that he was sure his father would concur with the family: 'I know he would have agreed. Eric should disabuse himself of the counter-argument.' But Jacobs was in no mood to be disabused. Instead, he set in motion a campaign in the weeks prior to the diary's serialisation: there were articles in the *Daily Telegraph*, the *Guardian*, the *Independent* and several other papers.[17]

The diary was serialised in the *Sunday Times* on 17 and 24 March. Martin was sent proofs prior to publication. In an added entry for 31 October, according to Martin, Jacobs described the funeral as a 'perfunctory affair' at which 'only Sally cried'. When Martin read the entry he called Jacobs up and told him he should cut the description of the funeral. It wasn't accurate. Everybody cried at the funeral, as many people present could confirm. 'You weren't there, were you, Eric,' Martin said. 'Who told you only Sally cried?' 'Someone who was . . . who was there.' 'Whoever it was was mistaken.'[18] The phrase 'only Sally cried' was cut in the published version. Some months later, after I'd begun work on the *Letters*, I wrote to Jacobs, asking if he'd be willing to let me see the hundred or so Amis letters Robert Conquest had photocopied for him. I wrote at Conquest's request, to spare him a second round of photocopying. In my letter I told Jacobs I'd had nothing to do with his firing. He never replied. When the project was nearing completion, however, Jacobs passed along copies of several letters Amis had sent him. These concerned his appointment as authorised biographer and the protracted and public row he conducted with the Bodleian Library at Oxford over Amis's letters to Larkin (to which the Library had denied Jacobs access, despite Amis writing on his behalf).[19] When my edition of the *Letters* came out, Jacobs reviewed it in *The Times*, twice. Unsurprisingly, he had nothing nice to say about the editing, though he effusively praised the letters themselves.[20]

The memorial service in St Martin-in-the-Fields was held on 22 October 1996, exactly a year after Amis's death. The church was packed with admirers. Jacobs was pointed out to me, two rows away, his face bathed in tears. The service was secular – no readings from scripture or hymns or sermons – and Martin opened it by recalling an exchange between his father and Yevgeny Yevtushenko, about God. The exchange has already been quoted, but I repeat it here: 'You atheist?' asked Yevtushenko. 'Well yes,' Amis replied, 'but it's more that I hate him.' Martin later spoke about Amis's posthumous reputation: 'Now we would begin to see him differently, and not just as the old devil; we would begin to see the whole man.'[21] Karl Miller, the first of the speakers, talked about Amis as novelist and critic, Tim Jaques about Amis's Primrose Hill rituals, Blake Morrison about Amis as poet, Mavis Nicholson reminisced about Amis in Swansea, Christopher Hitchens talked about Amis in all his guises, but particularly as a social being, and Dominick Harrod talked about Amis at the Garrick. After the last speech, Martin played a recording of a posthumously broadcast radio interview in which Amis performed one of his imitations: of FDR addressing his British Allies across the North Atlantic on a faulty short-wave radio in the dark days of World War II. The tears now were of uncontrollable laughter.

Like other speakers, Christopher Hitchens, described by Martin as his father's 'ideal reader', did not shy away from Amis's flaws. At times, Hitchens admitted, 'his imitation of the old fogy or even the old brute was a touch too persuasive'. What Hitchens chiefly remembered about Amis, 'paradoxical and pious though it might sound', was 'the sweetness of his manners'. On the occasion of Hitchens's first engagement dinner, it was Amis who recognised at the beginning of the gathering 'that tiny undercurrent of unease lest things not be perfectly swell'. With no initial prompting, he 'told all his jokes, did all his imitations, spurred by requests, some of them highly specialised, made all his noises, and by all I don't just mean the Metropolitan Line train approaching the station at Edgware Road, and I don't just mean the brass band approaching on a foggy day . . . or even the one described by Philip Larkin as unusually demanding and very seldom performed, of four British soldiers attempting to start a lorry on a freezing morning in Bavaria. There were moments that night when his lobster-like flush was truly alarming.'[22] The performance struck Hitchens as characteristic in its generosity. Amis was lavish in all respects: 'with himself and his wit and his opinions and his hospitality and with his wrath and his booze and his prejudices'. As Martin introduced the FDR imitation at the end of the speeches, he alerted listeners to the incredulous laughter of the interviewer and to the tone of Amis's answer to a final question: 'Is that how you'd like to be remembered, as Kingsley Amis the critic, the poet, the serious writer, or as Kingsley Amis the man who wrote books that made people laugh?' 'Oh, I'd like to be remembered as somebody who made people laugh,' Amis answered, though one could sense his irritation at the question. Finally, to the strains of 'Spider Crawl' and other jazz favourites, the assembly filed slowly out on to the porch of St Martin-in-the-Fields, which overlooks Trafalgar Square. There Hilly and Jane greeted each other with a peck on the cheek and Paul Johnson stalked off, furious that neither he nor any other friend from the Right had been invited to speak. Hilly, Ali, Philip, Sally and Jaime said their goodbyes at the church; the reception afterwards at the Garrick was not for them. Among the novelists at the reception were Iris Murdoch, V.S. Naipaul, David Lodge, Ian McEwan and Salman Rushdie, whom Amis had publicly supported during the early days of the *fatwa*.

Five months after the memorial service, in March 1997, HarperCollins published *The King's English: A Guide to Modern Usage*, a book Amis had all but finished by the time of his death. Amis originally intended the book as an updating of Henry Fowler's *Dictionary of Modern English Usage* (1926). When he learned that R.W. Burchfield, the lexicographer, was already at work on an updating (for Oxford University Press, to be published in 1996), he was undiscouraged, continuing to record his observations and opinions about language on odd sheets of paper, in breaks between novel-writing. After his death, Amis's editors at HarperCollins were presented with an unordered pile of these sheets. It was they who decided that the material was best ordered alphabetically, as in *Modern English Usage*, and that the book's title should be borrowed from an earlier book by Fowler, co-written with his brother Frank, *The King's English* (1906). Amis's book is less formal and pedagogic than its celebrated model, though Fowler, too, as Amis puts it in the 'Editor's Preface' (a title also bestowed by HarperCollins), sought 'to settle scores, to shake things up, to make people think about what they said and wrote, to be provocative without being unjust'.[23]

The book received excellent notices, with admiring attention paid to what reviewers saw as its surprising flexibility and tolerance. In *The Biographer's Moustache*, Jimmy Fane's snobbery is linguistic as well as social; his word-pedantry, wrongly identified as Amisian, marks him as ultimately second rate: 'These days I'm told the creatures have the impertinence to call themselves *gay*, thereby rendering unusable, thereby destroying, a fine old English word with its roots deep in the language.' Compare this with the entry under *gay* in *The King's English*:

The use of this word as an adjective or noun applied to a homosexual has attracted unusually prolonged execration. The 'new' meaning has been generally current for years. *Gay lib* had made the revised Roget by 1987 and the word itself was listed in the 1988 *COD* under sense 5 as a homosexual. There, however, the noun was entered in the slang category, i.e. current among a restricted group, and anybody who can read must have long known what *gay* means. And yet in this very spring of 1995 some old curmudgeon is still frothing on about it in the public print and demanding the word 'back' for proper heterosexual use.[24]

The tone of this entry is representative, as is its brisk learning and good sense. Throughout the book, change *per se* is not lamented, what is lamented is loss of precision and force, or bite. Consider Amis on the expression 'Honesty is the best policy', rendered toothless by the disappearance of the original meaning of 'policy' as devious calculation: 'When a piece of accurate cynicism or well-directed spite passes out of currency, something is lost.' Though old hobby-horses get a good ride in *The King's English*, there are plenty of surprises, as in Amis's defence of 'not-un' constructions, mocked by Orwell as typically 'English' in their caution. A phrase like 'not unpromising' may be 'waffle', but it has its uses. Those who scorn it undervalue 'the possible virtues as well as the more selfish advantages of an unwillingness to commit oneself'.[25] Elsewhere, frankly subjective judgements are robustly championed. Here is how Amis defends his preference for 'all right' over 'alright': 'No doubt as fully aware as most people that language is nothing but a series of signs to convey meaning, and that in this sense no damage seems to be threatening any part of our existing arrangements, I still feel that to inscribe *alright* is gross, coarse and to be avoided, and I now say so.' *The King's English* makes one regret the books Amis did not live to write. The unfinished 'Black and White', he told Jacobs, was to be followed by a novel entitled 'The Last Old Devil'.

Three months after Amis's death the terms of his will were made public. For over forty years he had been a prolific and successful writer, but he left a relatively modest estate. It was valued at £615,503 to be divided between Hilly and the children. The will also stipulated that Mrs Uniacke, his and Jane's housekeeper at Lemmons and Gardnor House, be left £1,000. The family would, in addition, benefit in years to come from the proceeds of Amis's literary estate, including royalties and the rights to his published and unpublished manuscripts and correspondence. Within six months of his death, the Kilmarnocks sold 194 Regents Park Road and bought a flat in Mornington Crescent. Two years later they let the flat and moved back to Ronda, to their little house in the *campo*. Jaime was already there and helped them to settle in. Some years later, Philip also moved to Ronda, though to the city proper. Philip's relations with his father were often stormy, but his feelings for him are generous and forgiving: 'Deep down he was very vulnerable, incredibly vulnerable, and soft. I *knew* that he loved me and he knew that I loved him, and that was good.' Since moving to Ronda, Philip has remarried and continues to paint and to exhibit his work. Jaime, who has inherited Ali's love of travel in Spain, takes parties of tourists and students all over the country and into Morocco. As for Martin, in the decade since his father's death, in addition to *Experience* and *Koba the Dread*, he has published a novel, a novella, a book of short stories and a volume of essays. He and Antonia Phillips separated in the summer of 1993, divorced in 1996, and in 1998 he married the writer Isabel Fonseca,[26] with whom he has two daughters, Fernanda (b. 1996) and Clio (b. 1999). Martin's third daughter, Delilah Seale, born in 1976, he came to know early in the summer of 1995, shortly before his father's death. Amis would never meet her (she was touring South America in the summer and autumn of 1995, having just finished at Oxford), though he had been told of her existence.

Sally's fate was not happy. In the last years of his life, Amis told Martin, he was haunted by the thought of what would happen to her after his death.[27] While the Kilmarnocks remained in London, she seemed all right. When they returned to Ronda, she chose not to join them; she did not want to leave her flat in Kentish Town, not far from where Martin now lived, at the opposite end of Regents Park Road from his parents' house. A corner of Sally's flat, Martin writes, 'was given over to what the newspapers would call a "shrine." A shrine to Kingsley: signed copies of his books, photographs, memorabilia.'[28] Four years after Amis's death, Sally would still call Martin in tears when 'having "a bad Dad day"'.[29] By now she was drinking again and in a long depression. In November 2000, she was suddenly taken ill, lost consciousness in hospital, and died after five days in intensive care. She was forty-six. Present at her funeral, anonymously, was the daughter she had given up for adoption in 1979. Soon after the funeral, this daughter, Catherine, aged twenty-two, established contact with Martin, and met her cousins, Jacob, Louis, Fernanda and Clio. In spring 2001, with the encouragement of her foster-parents, she joined her uncle and cousins in a trip to Ronda, where she met her grandmother and step-grandfather for the first time, along with Philip and Jaime. She and Delilah Seale met later and quickly hit it off.

Amis's posthumous reputation has been dependent on changes in fashion and in the nature of the book business and the reading public. The immediate afterlife of writers with long and successful careers is often marked by a falling off in interest and standing. In Amis's case, this falling off was slowed in 2000, a half-decade after his death, by the near-simultaneous publication of the *Letters* and *Experience*. All Amis's novels will soon be in print, either in Penguin or Vintage paperbacks. *Take a Girl Like You* and *Lucky Jim* have recently been adapted for television, though to uneven effect. There are plans to televise several other novels and Amis is frequently quoted and referred to in newspapers and periodicals. Now that the second half of the twentieth century has become a 'period', as opposed to the day before yesterday, academics as well as literary journalists are beginning to acknowledge his centrality, without ever much approving of it (partly because modernist prejudices remain strong in English departments, partly because he's funny, so not serious, partly because of his politics). His work matters not only for its influence, but for the pleasure it affords, and the breadth and depth of its achievement. As for the man, he was in life as he was on the page: commanding, abrasive, invigorating, full of fear, full of fun.

Acknowledgements

My first debt is to Martin Amis, who gave me the job of writing his father's authorised biography and then went off to Uruguay and let me get on with it, never once interfering. He and Jonathan Clowes, co-executors of the Kingsley Amis Literary Estate, have been supportive throughout. For patiently submitting to innumerable queries I am much indebted to the Amis family, including Lady Kilmarnock (Hilly Amis), Philip Amis, Jaime Boyd and Lord Kilmarnock (Alastair Boyd); to Elizabeth Jane Howard, Colin Howard and Sargy Mann; and to Robert Conquest. Thanks also are due to all those who agreed to formal interviews for the book (a full list is provided at the head of the Notes section), many of whom provided help in subsequent letters and telephone calls. For advice and assistance I am grateful to the administration and staff of the Huntington Library in San Marino, California, in particular to Jill Coogan, Sara S. Hodson, Alan Jutzie, Suzi Krasnoo, Gayle Richardson and Roy Ritchie; to Judith Priestman of the Department of Western Manuscripts, Bodleian Library, Oxford; to Philip Moss of the Oxford University Archives; to Bryan Dyson and Helen Roberts of the Brynmor Jones Library, University of Hull; to Andrew Motion, Anthony Thwaite and Jeremy Crow of the Philip Larkin Literary Estate; to Jenny Watt, Linda Thomas, Lyndie Brimstone and Neil Taylor of Roehampton University; to Vivien Green, of Sheil Land; to my publishers, Jonathan Cape, especially to Dan Franklin, who commissioned the book, Ellah Allfrey, its exemplary editor, and Natalie Boyd, Beth Humphries, Miles Potter, Charles Taylor and

Julia Silk, who assisted in its production; and to Douglas Matthews, who prepared the index.

For careful reading of the entire manuscript I am grateful to Martin Amis, Lindsay Duguid, John Gross and Anthony Thwaite. Lindsay Duguid improved the book at every stage of its composition. For reading portions of the book in manuscript, correcting mistakes and offering advice I am grateful also to Robert Conquest, Elizabeth Jane Howard, David Papineau, Elaine Showalter and Erik Tarloff.

I must thank the following institutions for permissions and for providing information: Bodleian Library, Oxford; Boston University Library; Written Archive Centre, British Broadcasting Company, Caversham Park, Reading, Berkshire; Carcanet Press Ltd. for permission to quote 'Down, Wanton, Down!' from *Robert Graves, The Complete Poems*; City of London School; Department of Manuscripts, British Library; Rare Book and Manuscript Library, Butler Library, Columbia University; Curtis Brown Ltd, New York; Brynmor Jones Library, University of Hull; Henry E. Huntington Library, San Marino, California; Marlborough College; the Marvell Press; Oxford University Archives; the Secretary to the Delegates of the Oxford University Press; Harry Ransom Humanities Research Center, University of Texas at Austin; Department of Rare Books and Special Collections, Firestone Library, Princeton University; Seeley G. Mudd Manuscript Library, Princeton University Library; Random House Group Ltd. for permission to quote 'At Lemmons', by C. Day-Lewis, from *The Complete Poems* by Cecil Day-Lewis published by Sinclair-Stevenson 1992, Copyright © 1992 in this edition, The Estate of C. Day-Lewis; Library, University of Reading; Royal Society of Literature; St John's College, Oxford; Society of Authors; Jean and Alexander Heard Library, Vanderbilt University; Modern Records Centre, University of Warwick Library.

Other institutions I must thank for help with enquiries include: Army Records Centre, Hayes, Middlesex; Newspaper Library (British Library); *Daily Express*; *Daily Mail*; *Daily Mirror*; *Daily Telegraph*; Faber and Faber; Granada Television; *Guardian*; HarperCollins; Hutchinson; *Illustrated London News*; King Henry VIII School Coventry; London Library; *London Review of Books*; *New Statesman*; *New York Review of Books*; *New York Times*; Penguin Books; Peterhouse, Cambridge; Peters Fraser and Dunlop Group Ltd; Public Records Office, National Archives, Kew, Surrey; *Spectator*; *Sunday Telegraph*; *Sunday Times*; *Times Literary*

Supplement; Library, Personnel Office and Registry, University of Wales, Swansea.

In addition to the people who provided me with interviews, thanks are due to the following individuals for permitting me to quote from or consult letters and for supplying information or help with enquiries: Gillon Aitken; Brian Aldiss; John Amis; John Bayley; John Beer; Sir George Blunden; David Bradbury; Maeve Brennan; Stephen Brook; Sally Brown; Katherine Bucknell; Chris Calladine; Tony Colwell; Mrs Maurice Cowling (Pat Gale); Barry Darling; Peter Davison; Roger Deakin; Richard Eyre; D.J. Enright; Paul Ferris; Isabel Fonseca; Roy Foster; D.A. Frampton; Michael Frohnsdorff; Selina Hastings; Emma Jacobs; Rhoda Koenig; Roger Lewis; R.W. Lovatt; Jean McAndrew; Kevin McCarron; Robert MacDowell; W.Y. McNeil; Douglas Matthews; Edward Mendelson; Michael Mewshaw; Tom Miller; Jan Montefiori; Antonia Phillips; Anthony Powell and Lady Violet Powell; William H. Pritchard; T.E. Rogers; Janice Rossen; Dale Salwak; Thomas Shippey; Ruth (Bowman) Siverns; Richard Skaer; John Sutherland; Jeremy Taylor; Sir John Meurig Thomas; Ann Thwaite; Tom Treadwell; Malcolm Vale; Ursula Vaughan Williams; Graham Watson; David Whittle; James Willcox; Lois Wilson; Brian Wormald; Tony Wrigley.

For financial assistance I must thank the Leverhulme Foundation for a Research Fellowship; the Huntington Library for the award of a Fletcher Jones Foundation Distinguished Fellowship; Roehampton University for Research Leave; and the Arts and Humanities Research Board for a Research Grant to supervise the creation of the *Kingsley Amis Journalism Archive*. The AHRB grant enabled me to employ Ann Totterdell to compile the Archive and its accompanying *Alphabetical and Chronological Catalogue*, a vital resource for students of Amis's life and writing. The *Catalogue* is available on-line at www.roehampton.ac.uk/KingsleyAmisJournalismArchive and photocopies of most of the over 1,300 uncollected items it lists have been deposited in the Bodleian Library, the British Library, the Huntington Library and the Learning Resources Centre at Roehampton University.

Finally, I am thankful for the encouragement and patience of friends, colleagues and students, and for the love and support of my wife, Alice Leader, and our sons, Nick and Max Leader.

Notes

Unless specified, all unpublished or manuscript material by Kingsley Amis is to be found in the Henry E. Huntington Library, San Marino, California, the principal repository of Amis's papers. The Amis Collection in the Huntington consists of 1,211 catalogued items, plus ephemera (Call numbers: AMS 1–1165; FAC 1094–1104, 1326–1335, 1338).

The location of unpublished Amis letters is provided in the notes. Published letters by Kingsley Amis are from Zachary Leader, ed., *The Letters of Kingsley Amis* (London: HarperCollins, 2000) where locations are provided. When dates of published letters are supplied in the text, notes are omitted. Five hundred and thirty-one Amis letters to Larkin are located in the Bodleian Library, Oxford (MSC.Eng.c.6044–54).

The papers of Eric Jacobs, author of *Kingsley Amis: A Biography* (1995), are located in the Huntington Library. Among these papers (there are eight boxes in all) is a typescript of the 'Amis Diaries', portions of which were published in the *Sunday Times* on 17 and 24 March 1995. This typescript, from which I quote, is expurgated; an unexpurgated version of the 'Amis Diaries' is restricted from view until 2040. For an account of the nature and origin of the diaries see Chapters 27 and 28.

Published letters by Philip Larkin are from Anthony Thwaite, ed., *Selected Letters of Philip Larkin 1940–1985* (London: Faber and Faber, 1992). The location of unpublished Larkin letters to Amis is provided in the notes.

All letters to and from Elizabeth Jane Howard, except those to Edmund and Mary Keeley, are located among the Elizabeth Jane Howard papers in the Huntington Library. Letters jointly addressed to Elizabeth Jane Howard and Kingsley Amis are also found among the Elizabeth Jane Howard papers. All letters to the Keeleys are located among the Edmund Keeley papers in the Department of Rare Books and Special Collections, Firestone Library, Princeton University. Letters to employees of the A.D. Peters Agency are located in the Boston University Library. Letters to employees of the Curtis Brown Agency, in both London and New York, are located in the Rare Book and Manuscript Library, Butler Library, Columbia University. Most letters to J.H. McCallum, Amis's editor at Harcourt, are located at Harcourt Brace and Company, Orlando, Florida.

Texts cited in the notes refer to the editions used by the author. Full publication details for these editions, along with details of original publication, can be found in the bibliography.

All unattributed quotations come from the following interviews with Zachary Leader:

Susan Allison, 6 May 2003, London; Al Alvarez, 23 July 2002, London; John Amis, 5 April 2002, London; Martin Amis, 6 June, 6 October 2005, London; Philip Amis, 9, 10, 11 April 2002, Ronda; Jill Balcon (Day-Lewis), 13 June 2002, London; Sir Peter Baldwin, 24 May 2002, London; Julian Barnes, 11 September, 2002, London; Vereen Bell, 26 February 2003, Nashville; Rosie Boycott, 6 April 2006, London; Jaime Boyd, 9, 10 April 2002, Ronda; Sir Merwyn Brown, 29 March, 17 May 2002, London; Esmond and Jean Cleary, 2, 3 July 2002, Swansea; Jonathan Clowes (with Ann Evans), 14 September 2002, Charras, France; Martin Cohen, 13 May 2003, London; Edward Cone, 8 December 2002, Princeton; Liddie Conquest, 20, 21 April 2001, Stanford, CA; Robert Conquest, 20, 21 April 2002, Stanford, CA; Megan (McAndrew) Cooper, 5 December 2002, Durham, NH; Maurice Cowling (with Pat Gale), 2 July 2002, Swansea; Anthony Curtis, 2 June 2002, London; Sam Dawson, 2 July 2002, Swansea; Frank Deford, 27 April 2002, Los Angeles; James Durham, 4 June 2002, London; James Fenton, 11 May 2004, London; Robert Foster, 25 April 2002, Newport Beach, CA; Russell Fraser, 5 March 2003, Honolulu (telephone interview); Catherine Freeman, 6 June 2002, London; Betty Fussell, 11 December 2002, New York; Harriette

Fussell, 13 December 2002, Philadelphia; Paul Fussell, 13 December 2002, Philadelphia; Clive Gammon, 30 June 2002, Swansea; Michael Garcia, 5 July 2002, Swansea; Lord Gavron, 22 July 2002, London; Patricia Gillan, 18 December 2005 (telephone interview); Juan Graves, 19 July 2004, Deya, Majorca; Tomas Graves, 18 July 2004, Deya, Majorca; William Graves, 18 July 2004, Deya, Majorca; John Gross, 12 June 2002, London; Valerie Grove, 13 September 2002, London; Janet Hart, 23 September 2002, Berkhamsted; Christopher Hitchens, 2 March 2003, Beverly Hills, CA; Judy Hough, 13 June 2002, London; Colin Howard, 10 June 2002, London; Elizabeth Jane Howard, 26 September 2002, 15, 16 May 2003, Bungay, Suffolk; Coral Hughes, 15 April 2002, Lewes, Sussex; Jackie Hulme, 18 July 2002, London; Clive James, 24 June 2002, London; Tim and Catharine Jaques, 26 June 2002, London; Paul and Marigold Johnson, 14 July 2002, London; Pat Kavanagh, 11 September 2002, London; Edmund and Mary Keeley, 27, 29 July 2002, Athens; Mina Kempton, 8 December 2002, Princeton; E.J. Kenney, 19 June 2002, Cambridge; Lady Kilmarnock (formerly Hilly Amis), 17, 18 August 2001, 30 June 2004, Ronda; Lord Kilmarnock (Alastair Boyd), 18 August 2002, Ronda; Penny King, 5 July 2002, Swansea; Joy Law, 20 December 2005, London (telephone interview); Richard Law, 24 July 2002, London; Gene Lichtenstein, 4 June 2003, Los Angeles; Sargy Mann (with Frances Mann), 9, 10 March 2002, Bungay, Suffolk; Tom Maschler, 29 May 2002, London; Cyril Metliss, 5 April 2002, London; Karl Miller, 15 June 2002, London; Roger Morgan, 26 June 2002, London; Blake Morrison, 24 July 2002, London; Leonard Nathanson, 26 February 2003, Nashville; Mavis Nicholson, 18 June 2002, London; Denis Norden, 27 March 2002, London; Tom Pocock, 10 January 2005, London; Richard and Brigitte Porter, 24 February 2003, Nashville; John and Mary Postgate (with Jim Silvester), 15 April 2002, Lewes, Sussex; Tristram Powell, 19 May 2003, London; Jack Prince, 2 July 2002, Swansea; Theo Richmond (with Lee Langley), 22 July 2002, London; Margaret (Bardwell) Righton, 26 June 2002, Gretton, Glos.; Mark Rose, 28 June 2003, Montecito, CA; William and Elisabeth Rukeyser, 24, 25 February 2003, Knoxville, TN; 25 November 2003, Beverly Hills; Michael and Virginia Rush, 30 June, 2 July 2002, Swansea; John Seigenthaler, 27 February 2003, Nashville, TN; Ann Smith, 1 July 2002, Whitland, Wales; Walter Sullivan, 26 February 2003,

Nashville; Helen Szamuely, 19 May 2003, London; Eve Thomas, 4, 5 July 2002, Swansea; John Veale, 25 March 2004, Woodeaton, Oxfordshire; Alan Watkins, 5 May 2005, London; Anthony Whittom, 27 September 2002, London; Sir Glanmor Williams, 1 July 2002, Swansea; John and Rona Williamson, 11 June 2002, Abbots Langley, Herts.; Tony Wrigley, 19 June 2002, Cambridge; Patricia Woods (Temple-Muir), 20 December 2005 (telephone interview); Sir Peregrine Worsthorne, 6 September 2002, Hedgerley, Bucks.; Dr Ronald Zeegen, 18 May 2006, London

The following abbreviations are used in the notes:

KA	Kingsley Amis
RC	Robert Conquest
EJH	Elizabeth Jane Howard
PL	Philip Larkin

AC	Kingsley Amis, *The Amis Collection: Selected Non-Fiction 1954–1990*, intro. John McDermott (London: Hutchinson, 1990); Penguin, 1991.
LKA	*The Letters of Kingsley Amis*, ed. Zachary Leader (London: HarperCollins, 2000; New York: Talk Miramax, 2001); HarperCollins edition cited.
WBJA	Kingsley Amis, *What Became of Jane Austen? And Other Questions* (London: Jonathan Cape, 1970; New York: Harcourt Brace, 1971); Penguin, 1981.

Brynmor Jones	Brynmor Jones Library, University of Hull
Columbia	Rare Book and Manuscript Library, Butler Library, Columbia University, New York
Huntington	Henry E. Huntington Library, San Marino, California
Ransom Center	Harry Ransom Humanities Research Center, The University of Texas at Austin

INTRODUCTION

1 Twenty-five novels including the 'teenage' novel *We Are All Guilty*, Reinhardt Books, 1991. See Bibliography for a complete list of Amis's novels and editions used.

2 'Against the Current', a review of Martin Seymour Smith, *Robert Graves: His Life and Work*, and Paul O'Prey, ed., *In Broken Images: Selected Letters of Robert Graves 1914–1946*, *Observer*, 16 June 1982, reprinted in *The Amis Collection: Selected Non-Fiction 1954–1990*, Penguin, 1991, p. 201.

3 'Real and Made-up People', *Times Literary Supplement*, 27 July 1973, reprinted in *AC*, p. 201.

4 Kingsley Amis, *Memoirs*, Penguin, 1992, p. xv.

5 'Real and Made-Up People', *AC*, pp. 4, 5.

6 Andrew Davies, 'How I Adapted to That Old Devil Amis', *Evening Standard*, 5 March 1982.

7 *AC*, p. 5.

8 This story is told in an article entitled 'The Lobster's Claw – Narrative of an Author's Revenge', *National Review*, 2 June 1989.

9 *Girl, 20*, Panther, 1975 p. 154.

10 Martin Amis, *Experience*, Jonathan Cape, 2000, p. 299.

11 Eric Jacobs, 'Amis Diaries', 1 April 1993. The Diaries are deposited among the Eric Jacobs papers in the Huntington. Extracts were published in the *Sunday Times* on 17 and 24 March 1995. See Chapters 27 and 28 for accounts of the nature and origin of the Diaries.

12 KA to RC, *c*. November 1990.

13 See, for example, Anthony Powell, *Journals 1990–1992*, Heinemann, 1998, p. 103. In the entry for 24 March 1991, Powell writes of Amis's deliberate 'disregard for the truth' in the *Memoirs*, though he was relatively kindly treated in them. For similar complaints about the *Memoirs* see Chapter 27.

14 Eric Jacobs, *Guardian* obituary, 23 October 1995.

15 This claim was forwarded in a letter of 9 July 1995 to the *Sunday Times*, in response to John Carey's charge, in a review of the biography, that it was 'under-researched'. 'One cannot do homework on material that doesn't exist . . . If I am right, future biographers of Amis will be able to do little more than rearrange the same pieces of information. But they will lack the priceless chance to check their speculations against Amis in person.'

16 Jacobs, 'Amis Diaries', 21 July 1995.

17 RC to KA, 7 October 1980 (Huntington); quoted in *LKA*, p. xvii.

18 For this harsh reference to Amis see PL to RC, 25 September 1983 (recipient).

19 Anthony Powell, *Journals 1987–1989*, Heinemann, 1996, p. 27.

20 Henry James, *Roderick Hudson* (1875), Penguin, 1969, p. 11 (Preface).

21 *You Can't Do Both*, Flamingo, 1996, p. 34.
22 *Take a Girl Like You*, Penguin, 1962, p. 257.
23 Ibid., p. 66.
24 *You Can't Do Both*, p. 27.
25 Ibid., p. 305.
26 *Memoirs*, p. 15.

CHAPTER I

Family

1 According to Martin Amis and Mavis Nicholson, a friend of the Amis family since 1950.
2 *Memoirs*, Penguin, 1992, pp. 11–12.
3 Ibid., p. 12.
4 Martin Amis, *Experience*, Jonathan Cape, 2000, p. 168.
5 *One Fat Englishman*, Penguin, 1966, p. 110.
6 Valerie Jenkins, *When I Was Young: Memories of London Child-hoods*, Hart-Davis, MacGibbon, 1976, p. 82.
7 *Stanley and the Women*, Penguin, 1985, p. 147.
8 Jenkins, *When I Was Young*, p. 82.
9 *Memoirs*, p. 17.
10 In the visual arts it appears only in Camille Pissarro's *Beech Trees at Norbury Park, Surrey*.
11 'The Yellow Face', in Arthur Conan Doyle, *The Memoirs of Sherlock Holmes* (1894), Jonathan Cape, 1974, pp. 57, 46.
12 *The Riverside Villas Murder*, Penguin, 1984, p. 220. According to *Norbury: The Story of a London Suburb. Its Geography and History*, a booklet compiled in 1977 by Barbara Mullen and Graham Harker for Norbury Manor High School for Boys (and deposited among the Jacobs papers in the Huntington), the population of Norbury was 9,413 in 1921 and 15,538 in 1931 (p. 12).
13 *The Riverside Villas Murder*, p. 11.
14 Philip Larkin, 'I Remember, I Remember', from *The Less Deceived*, 1955; reprinted in Anthony Thwaite, ed., *Philip Larkin: Collected Poems*, Marvell Press/Faber and Faber, 1988, p. 81.
15 Jenkins, *When I Was Young*, p. 86.
16 In Jacobs, 'Amis Diaries', 17 August 1993, there is some dispute about the third address; on a visit to Norbury with Jacobs, Amis says the address is 53 Stanford Road not 53 Gilpin Road, which he had previously always said was the address. Jacobs refers to Gilpin Road in the 'Diaries'. The two roads are similar in appearance, as are the houses at number 53, and Jacobs thinks Amis 'simply confused them.'

17 'Why?' asks Robin Davies of a comparable paternal insistence in *You Can't Do Both*, Flamingo, 1996, p. 5. After all, 'his father had very little to say to him at these times, almost nothing to justify lifting his eyes from the columns of the *Morning Post*'.

18 Ray Connolly, 'A Childhood: Kingsley Amis', *The Times*, 24 March 1990. In an interview with Graham Turner in the *Sunday Telegraph*, 28 September 1986, 'Kingsley Amis and Those Uncertain Feelings', Amis declared, 'my parents were hanging on by their teeth to the middle class'. This is certainly the impression given by Peter's and Robin's parents in *The Riverside Villas Murder* and *You Can't Do Both*. When Peter's father takes exception to fifteen-year-old Daphne Hodgson, who lives next door, it is not just to the provocative trousers she wears, but to her lower-class accent. When Robin's mother promises to 'make it all right' with his father if ever Robin wants to invite a friend to tea, she adds: 'Mind you, I'll expect you to pick someone reasonable, not some awful common creature' (p. 18).

19 *Memoirs*, Penguin, 1992, p. 16.

20 *You Can't Do Both*, p. 19.

21 *The Riverside Villas Murder*, p. 122.

22 Ibid., p. 145.

23 *You Can't Do Both*, p. 47.

24 *Memoirs*, p. 14.

25 Ibid., p. 18.

26 'From Aspidistra to Jukebox', a review of Richard Hoggart, *The Uses of Literacy*, *Spectator*, 1 March 1957; reprinted in *What Became of Jane Austen? And Other Questions*, Penguin, 1981, p. 84.

27 See John Amis, *Amiscellany: My Life, My Music*, Faber and Faber, 1985, p. 138.

28 *Carrow Works Magazine* 14: 2 (January 1921), pp. 51–52.

29 Jenkins, *When I Was Young*, p. 83

30 *Memoirs*, p. 18.

31 The woman was Nancy Lewis, wife of the Princeton professor and Edith Wharton scholar R.W.B. Lewis (letter to the author, 19 February 2003).

32 *Memoirs*, pp. 18–19.

33 A profile in James Atlas, 'Out to Lunch with Kingsley Amis', *Vanity Fair*, March 1987, p. 156.

34 *Memoirs*, p. 17.

35 Interview with Lynda Lee-Potter, 'I've Been Lucky Considering the Outrageous Way I've Behaved', *Daily Mail*, 13 May 1995.

36 John Amis's memory of 'Uncle Bill' was recounted to me in interview; his sister Joan's memory is from a letter to Kingsley Amis, 15 April 1991 (Huntington).

37 *Memoirs*, pp. 18, 19, 2, 1.

38 *You Can't Do Both*, p. 115.

39 Ibid.

40 See, for example, Patrick Swinden, 'Kingsley Amis', in Robert H. Bell, ed., *Critical Essays on Kingsley Amis*, G. K. Hall, 1998, p. 206 (an excerpt from Swinden's *The English Novel in History and Society, 1940–1980*, Macmillan, 1984).

41 For the Pritchett quote about his father and the way Pritchett's characters turn life 'into performance and spectacle' see James Wood, 'V.S. Pritchett and English Comedy', in Zachary Leader, ed., *On Modern British Fiction*, Oxford University Press, 2003, pp. 11–19. Wood connects Pritchett's characters to those of Dickens, about whom Pritchett writes penetratingly. For Pritchett, Dickens's characters 'take on the dramatic role of solitary pronouncers. All Dickens's characters, comic or not, issue personal pronouncements that magnify their inner life . . . what we find in this comedy is people's projections of their self-esteem . . . They live by some private idea or fiction . . . Our comedy, Dickens seems to say, is not in our relations with each other but in our relations with ourselves' (p. 11).

42 Quoted in Eric Jacobs, *Kingsley Amis: A Biography*, Hodder and Stoughton, 1995, p. 32.

43 *You Can't Do Both*, p. 115.

44 Similarly, in *The Riverside Villas Murder*, the insecurity of Peter's father, and his consequent self-inflation, lead to external as well as internal deceptions. In order to sustain a false image of his status and character, he lies to family, friends and police, with near-disastrous consequences: 'I'm a conceited man, Peter,' he confesses at the end of the novel: 'Or vain, I don't know the right word. And it's made me dishonest' (p. 221). Growing up for Peter partly means learning this truth about his father.

45 *Experience*, p. 166.

46 Amis invariably acknowledges typos like 'agreee' in this way.

47 Dale Salwak, 'An Interview with Kingsley Amis', *Contemporary Literature* 16: 1 (Winter 1975); reprinted in Bell, ed., *Critical Essays*, p. 270.

48 *Memoirs*, p. 10.

49 Interview with John Morrish, 'A Joke Shared with Jesus Is Never Wasted', *Sunday Telegraph*, 20 October 1994.

50 Dale Salwak, 'An Interview with Kingsley Amis', in Bell, ed., *Critical Essays*, p. 270.

51 *Memoirs*, p. 14.

52 Martin Amis, *Experience*, pp. 165–166.

53 Similarly, when Robin's father is about to banish Nancy in *You Can't Do Both*, 'anybody, even someone who was used to him, would have said he was deeply troubled' (p. 134).

54 *Memoirs*, p. 15.
55 'Pater and Old Chap', *Observer*, 13 November 1957; reprinted in *WBJA*, pp. 38, 39.
56 *You Can't Do Both*, p. 196.
57 'Pater and Old Chap', *WBJA*, pp. 37–38.
58 *Memoirs*, p. 17.
59 'Pater and Old Chap', *WBJA*, p. 39.
60 Ibid., p. 40.
61 In 'A Memoir of My Father', in *WBJA*, p. 188; I have been unable to trace the publication in which this article, dated 1967, originally appears.
62 A copy of William Amis, 'A Journey – There and Back', can be found among the Eric Jacobs papers in the Huntington. This quotation is from p. 7; preceding quotations from pp. 1–2.
63 Ibid., p. 7.
64 'From Aspidistra to Jukebox', in *WBJA*, p. 85.
65 William Amis, 'A Journey – There and Back', p. 12.
66 Ibid., p. 21. A similar vision of paradise is provided by Amis Senior's account of the American South, which arises out of his determination 'to get to the bottom' of the race question. What he has learned is that 'it all started with the importation of black slaves by the Northern States, but that the climate was most unsuited to them so they began to die off like flies. Thus they migrated to the Southern states where the climate agreed with them and they became as happy as slaves can be. They would still be happy to-day especially after their emancipation if they had stayed South, but they have gradually infiltrated into the North, where the lure of the dollar was so strong, and their numbers have become so embarrassing as to create a problem' (p. 7). This crackpot history partly draws on familiar Southern myth (picked up from sister Gladys, perhaps, or her second husband, Virgil A. Case, a native Southerner, or other Amis relatives in the United States, including 'a very Dixie-style Uncle Tom, probably a cousin of my grandfather's' [*Memoirs*, p. 3]): that the South was mannerly, hierarchical, pastoral (that is, both agrarian and virtuous), while the North was pushy, mobile, urban (and thus materialistic), and that blacks were better off as slaves than as free citizens. This myth has obvious connections with an imperial vision of the white man's burden, in which officers and men such as those Amis Senior encounters on the voyage home secure the interests of otherwise chaotic and uncivilised native populations.
67 *Memoirs*, p. 16.
68 There are six slices in *You Can't Do Both*.
69 Interview with Graham Turner, 'Kingsley Amis and Those Uncertain Feelings', *Sunday Telegraph*, 23 September 1986.
70 According to Mavis Nicholson, in an interview with the author.
71 'Kingsley Amis and Those Uncertain Feelings'.

72 *You Can't Do Both*, p. 4.

73 *Memoirs*, p. 20.

74 *You Can't Do Both*, p. 26.

75 *The Riverside Villas Murder*, pp. 118, 192, 113.

76 *Lucky Jim*, Penguin, 1976, p. 144.

77 *The Riverside Villas Murder*, p. 154.

78 *Memoirs*, p. 20.

79 *Lucky Jim*, pp. 70, 167, 178.

80 *Take a Girl Like You*, Penguin, 1962, p. 17.

81 *Experience*, p. 164.

82 KA to PL, 28 October 1977; *You Can't Do Both*, p. 279.

83 *Memoirs*, p. 21.

84 Ibid., p. 19.

85 John Amis, 'Remembering Kingsley Amis', *The Author* (Summer 2001), p. 66.

86 *You Can't Do Both*, p. 39; on the same page the parlour's occasional table (a name Robin finds 'mysterious') is said to be made up of 'some dark polished wood', unspecified either because Amis, or young Robin, couldn't care less about wood furniture or because it is itself unmemorable.

87 *The Riverside Villas Murder*, p. 44.

88 *Memoirs*, p. 22.

89 'Remembering Kingsley Amis', p. 66.

90 *Memoirs*, p. 21.

91 *You Can't Do Both*, pp. 22, 24.

92 Interview with Cynthia Kee, 'Flavour of the Month', in *London Portrait Magazine*, December 1986.

93 *Bookmark* television profile, broadcast on BBC2, 6 March 1991. The neighbour at 9 Ena Road recalls the father of Peter's friend Reg in *The Riverside Villas Murder*, a buyer for Jay's department store in Oxford Circus.

94 Jenkins, *When I Was Young*, p. 84.

95 Jacobs, 'Amis Diaries', 22 April 1993.

96 Larkin's comment about Amis's parents is recounted by Amis in 'Kingsley Amis and Those Uncertain Feelings'.

97 Jacobs, 'Amis Diaries', 4 March 1993.

98 *The Folks That Live on the Hill*, Penguin, 1991, p. 203.

99 *Memoirs*, p. 6.

100 Ibid., p. 7.

101 Ibid., p. 11.

102 Ibid., p. 10.

103 Ibid., pp. 9, 10.

104 Ibid., p. 4.

105 Ibid., pp. 4–5.

106 Ibid., p. 14.

CHAPTER 2
Reading and Writing

1 This information, plus the preceding quotations, including the initial quotation from Larkin, come from an interview with Ray Connolly, 'A Childhood: Kingsley Amis', *The Times*, 24 March 1990.
2 Eric Jacobs, 'Amis Diaries', 11 June 1993.
3 'Louis Armstrong and Tea at Grandma's', in Frederic Raphael, ed., *Bookmarks: Writers on Their Reading*, Quartet Books, 1975, p. 3; the essay is dated 1974, though it was written for the volume.
4 Kingsley Amis, *Memoirs*, Penguin, 1992, p. 21.
5 Interview with Ray Connolly, 'A Childhood: Kingsley Amis'.
6 *Memoirs*, p. 21. For an account of 'good trash' for women readers see Nicola Humble, *The Feminine Middlebrow Novel 1920s to 1950s*, Oxford University Press, 2001.
7 Boots ran a lending library at the time.
8 George Orwell, 'Good Bad Books', *Tribune*, 2 November 1945, reprinted in Volume 4 of *Collected Essays, Journalism and Letters of George Orwell*, ed. Sonia Orwell and Ian Angus, Secker and Warburg, 1968, p. 37.
9 Ibid., p. 275.
10 *Memoirs*, p. 15.
11 Ibid., p. 15. The reference to masturbation aside, these are almost exactly the words that open *The Riverside Villas Murder*. Captain Furneaux is speaking: 'For goodness' sake, Peter, stop ruining your eyes and get out into the fresh air. The first spot of sun we've had for weeks, and you have to sit there poring over that tripe' (Penguin, 1984, p. 9).
12 *Memoirs*, p. 17.
13 Ibid., p. 5.
14 Ibid., p. 21.
15 Ibid., p. 25.
16 Quoted in 'Croydon Schools: Their History and Work', an anonymous article in the *Croydon Times*, 24 September 1932.
17 From 'Kingsley Amis Writes on Biggles', the first in a series of articles on 'Childhood Heroes', *Observer* magazine, 27 June 1965. For Amis's fond memories of Norbury College see 'City Ways', *Spectator*, 2 May 1958, reprinted in *What Became of Jane Austen? And Other Questions*, Penguin, 1981, p. 136.
18 'City Ways', in *WBJA*, p. 135.
19 This notebook is the first item in the Kingsley Amis Collection in the Harry Ransom Humanities Research Center in Austin, Texas.
20 *Memoirs*, p. 26.
21 *The Amis Anthology: A Personal Choice of English Verse*, Arena, 1989, p. 337.
22 'Poets in Mothballs', a review of J. R. Watson, ed., *Everyman's*

Book of Victorian Verse, in *Observer*, 25 April 1982, reprinted in *The Amis Collection: Selected Non-Fiction 1954–1990*, Penguin, 1991, p. 158.

23 'Old Chestnuts', a review of Charles Causley, *Poetry Please!*, in *Observer*, 14 July 1985; reprinted in *AC*, p. 165.

24 Ibid.

25 *Memoirs*, p. 26.

26 From the Ray Connolly interview, 'A Childhood: Kingsley Amis', in *The Times*, 24 March 1990.

27 *The Riverside Villas Murder*, p. 68.

28 George Orwell, 'Boy's Weeklies', *Horizon*, March 1940, reprinted in Volume 1 of *Collected Essays, Journalism and Letters of George Orwell*, ed. Sonia Orwell and Ian Angus, p. 467.

29 'Kingsley Amis Writes on Biggles', *Observer* magazine, 27 June 1965.

30 *You Can't Do Both*, p. 9.

31 Orwell, 'Boy's Weeklies', p. 483.

32 See KA, 'The Man Who Gave Us Billy Bunter', review of Frank Richards, *The Chap behind the Chums*, in *Sunday Telegraph*, 30 October 1988, reprinted in *AC*, p. 54.

33 Orwell, 'Boys' Weeklies', p. 483.

34 'The Man Who Gave Us Billy Bunter', *AC*, p. 54.

35 Ibid., p. 56.

36 *The Riverside Villas Murder*, p. 81.

37 'Louis Armstrong and Tea at Grandma's', in Raphael, ed., *Bookmarks*, p. 3.

38 Ibid., p. 4.

39 Ibid., p. 5.

40 Earlier in his career, in 'Lit Hist', *Spectator*, 20 January 1956, a review of the third volume of A. C. Ward, ed., *An Illustrated History of English Literature*, Amis took a somewhat different line. When Ward describes his book as 'addressed to those who read for enjoyment', Amis sensibly objects that 'most literature of the past needs study before it can be much enjoyed'.

41 KA to RC, 9 November 1982.

42 'Brandy to Brown Ale', a review of Philip Henderson, *Swinburne*, in *Observer*, 24 May 1974, reprinted in *AC*, p. 194.

43 F. R. Leavis, *The Common Pursuit*, Chatto and Windus, 1962, p. v.

44 'The Poet and the Lunatics', a review of G. K. Chesterton, *The Man Who Was Thursday*, in *New Statesman*, 26 February 1971, reprinted in *AC*, p. 43. A shorter version of this essay serves as the Introduction to the 1984 Penguin edition of the novel.

45 Ibid.

46 G. K. Chesterton, *The Man Who Was Thursday*, Penguin, 1986, p. 10.

47 In 'Heroic Absurdities', a review of Ian Boyd, *The Novels of G. K. Chesterton*, and G. K. Chesterton, *The Apostle and the Wild Ducks and Other Essays*, ed. Dorothy E. Collins, *Observer*, 29 June 1975.

48 'The Poet and the Lunatics', in *AC*, p. 46.

49 Ibid.

50 Ibid., p. 45.

51 'Kingsley Amis', in Peter Firchow, *The Writer's Place: Interviews on the Literary Situation in Contemporary Britain*, University of Minnesota Press, 1974, p. 30.

52 John Amis, 'Remembering Kingsley Amis', *The Author*, Summer 2001, p. 66.

53 'The Unfading Genius of Rudyard Kipling', *The Kipling Journal* 45: 205 (March 1978), p. 10.

54 Ibid., p. 11.

55 *You Can't Do Both*, p. 32.

56 Ibid., p. 36.

57 Ibid., p. 67.

CHAPTER 3

City of London

1 Quoted in Thomas Hinde, *Carpenter's Children: The Story of the City of London School,* James and James, 1995, p. 12.

2 A.E. Douglas Smith, *The City of London School*, Basil Blackwell, 1965, p. 69.

3 Ibid., p. 98.

4 Hinde, *Carpenter's Children*, pp. 93–94.

5 John Gross, *A Double Thread: A Childhood in Mile End and Beyond*, Vintage, 2002, p. 145.

6 *Memoirs*, Penguin, 1992, p. 26.

7 Ibid.

8 See Hinde, *Carpenter's Children*, pp. 57, 119.

9 *You Can't Do Both*, Flamingo, 1996, p. 7.

10 *Memoirs*, p. 29.

11 As is Peter at the beginning of Chapter 5 of *The Riverside Villas Murder* (p. 68).

12 *Memoirs*, p. 18.

13 Interview with Lynda-Lee Potter, 'I've Been Lucky Considering the Outrageous Way I've Behaved', *Daily Mail*, 13 May 1995.

14 Douglas Smith, *The City of London School*, p. 390.

15 Gross, *A Double Thread*, pp. 144–145.

16 Quoted in Frank W. Helyar, ed., *The City of London School at Marlborough*, 2000, p. 109 (the book is self-published, and can be consulted in the CLS library).

17 Quoted ibid., pp. 106–107.

18 Gross, *A Double Thread*, p. 144.

19 *Memoirs*, p. 26.

20 Ibid., p. 27.

21 Gross, *A Double Thread*, p. 144.
22 As recalled by a fellow student, Adrian Vale, in Helyar, ed., *The City of London School at Marlborough*, p. 141.
23 *You Can't Do Both*, p. 6.
24 Ibid., p. 44.
25 Hinde, *Carpenter's Children*, p. 92.
26 *You Can't Do Both*, p. 10.
27 Ibid., p. 11.
28 Ibid., p. 29.
29 Ibid., p. 43.
30 'City Ways', *WBJA*, p. 137.
31 KA, 'Lessons for Life', *Sunday Telegraph* magazine, 9 November 1986.
32 This quotation is from Eric Jacobs's notes to an interview with Richenberg on 6 January 1993 (among the Jacobs papers in the Huntington).
33 'Lessons for Life'.
34 Ibid.
35 Quoted in Helyar, ed., *The City of London School at Marlborough*, p. 127; 'CVA' in the quote stands for the 'A' stream of 'CV' or fifth-form classics.
36 Quoted in ibid., p. 129.
37 C. N. Vokins's undated handwritten memories of Amis are to be found among Eric Jacobs's papers in the Huntington.
38 'Lessons for Life'.
39 Quoted in Helyar, ed., *The City of London School at Marlborough*, p. 127.
40 Quoted in ibid., p. 125.
41 'Lessons for Life'.
42 *Memoirs*, p. 31.
43 Quoted in Helyar, ed., *The City of London School at Marlborough*, p. 129.
44 Ibid., p. 106.
45 Martin Amis, *Experience*, Jonathan Cape, 2000, p. 335.
46 Quoted in Helyar, ed., *The City of London School at Marlborough*, p. 108.
47 *Memoirs*, p. 29.
48 Ibid., p. 27. This was also the year that Robin Davies was similarly puzzled by Auden's 'Get there if you can'.
49 *The City of London School Magazine* 60: 267 (March 1937), p. 47.
50 *The City of London School Magazine* 59: 266 (December 1936), p. 168.
51 Ibid., p. 28.
52 *Memoirs*, p. 31. The tribute to Ellingham as 'the man who actually taught me most' occurs on p. 28.
53 Quoted in *The City of London School Magazine* 63: 276 (March 1940), p. 28.

54 *The Amis Anthology: A Personal Choice of English Verse*, Arena, 1989, p. 338.
55 *Memoirs*, p. 28.
56 See *The City of London School Magazine* 63: 277 (July 1940), p. 71.
57 *Memoirs*, p. 28.
58 Ibid.
59 *The Anti-Death League*, Harcourt Brace, 1966, p. 228.
60 *Memoirs*, p. 237.
61 'Godforsaken', *Spectator*, 18 April 1987, reprinted in *The Amis Collection: Selected Non-Fiction 1954–1990*. Penguin, 1991, p. 226.
62 'Lessons for Life'.
63 Ibid.
64 C. J. Ellingham, *Essay Writing: Bad and Good*, A. Wheaton, 1935, p. 12.
65 Ibid., p. 13.
66 Ibid., pp. 14–15.
67 Ibid., p. 16.
68 Ibid., p. 45.
69 Ibid., p. 47.
70 Ibid., p. 81.
71 Ibid., p. 83.
72 Ibid.
73 Ibid., pp. 85–86.
74 Ibid., p. 92.
75 *Memoirs*, p. 29.
76 Ibid., p. 30.
77 Puttees are strips of cloth bound round each leg from ankle to knee; they frequently came undone during marches, were never worn in battle by real soldiers and were hated by the boys.
78 *Memoirs*, p. 30.
79 Eric Jacobs, *Kingsley Amis: A Biography*, Hodder and Stoughton, 1995, p. 59.
80 This quotation is Metliss's reconstruction in interview.
81 Jacobs, *Biography*, pp. 58–59.
82 *You Can't Do Both*, p. 15.

CHAPTER 4

CLS at Marlborough

1 *The City of London School Magazine* 61: 272 (December 1938), p. 225.
2 Eric Jacobs, *Kingsley Amis: A Biography*, Hodder and Stoughton, 1995, p. 56.

3 Quoted in Frank W. Helyar, ed., *The City of London School at Marlborough*, 2000, p. 206 (the book is self-published, and can be consulted in the CLS library).

4 Quoted in A.E. Douglas Smith, *The City of London School*, Basil Blackwell, 1965, p. 441.

5 Quoted in Thomas Hinde, *Carpenter's Children: The Story of the City of London School,* James and James, 1995, p. 97.

6 For four days in late August 1939, well before the start of the new school year, masters and boys arrived each morning at CLS, suitcases in hand, to await evacuation orders from County Hall. In addition to clothing, the suitcases were meant to contain a pillowslip, knife, fork, dessert spoon and teaspoon. Each boy carried a stamped postcard in his pocket (to send home upon arrival in Wiltshire), some money (Dale advised ten shillings) and a day's worth of food, with a 'reserve' of chocolate. Labels were issued and hung round the necks of the younger boys. Those who travelled to school by train, like Amis, bought single not return tickets, in case evacuation orders came that day. Each morning the school rehearsed marching in columns to Blackfriars underground station. Older boys were instructed not to outmarch younger ones. There were gas-mask drills, described in the school magazine as 'a rabble of snouts and flapping gills, with eyepieces steamed from dogged endeavour' (December 1939). Concerned parents peppered masters with questions the masters could not answer – about travel routes, billeting arrangements, the precise date and time of the move.

On Friday, 1 September, two days before war was declared, CLS was evacuated to Wiltshire. Some 400 boys (roughly two-thirds of the school, the other third being still on holiday or having arranged separate transport to Marlborough) assembled by the school's front entrance. At 12.15, carrying suitcases, gas masks and a bag each of emergency rations, boys and masters set off for Blackfriars underground station, where normal District Line services alternated with special fast trains for evacuees. At 12.30 the school boarded an empty train direct to Ealing, where it was to catch another special train to Marlborough. At Ealing, though, anxious evacuation officials ushered boys and masters on to a non-stop Taunton Express, a mistake only rectified after heated negotiations and, according to one account, a *Boy's Own* episode involving the Economics master, Charles Wilmot, marshal and organiser of the evacuation. As the train passed through Reading, Wilmot was said to have flung a message on to the station platform, wrapped in a towel. It was picked up by a Great Western Railway official, orders were put through to the train's driver and the express was allowed to make an unscheduled stop at Savernake, the station for Marlborough (see Helyar, ed., *The City of London School at Marlborough*, p. 209, and Hinde, *Carpenter's Children*, p. 96). How much of this drama was true, or known to Amis, who was on the train, Amis does not say. His sole memory of the trip was of the 'delicious' haversack rations issued for the journey. These consisted of tinned corned beef, condensed milk, evaporated milk, cream crackers and a quarter of a bar of Cadbury's chocolate. Over the next two days Amis drank something like twenty tins of the sweetened condensed milk, 'the discarded residue of my companions' train rations' (*Memoirs*, Penguin, 1992, p. 32).

7 Quoted in Helyar, ed., *The City of London School at Marlborough*, p. 127.

8 *Memoirs*, p. 34.

9 CLS boys attended early classes while the Marlborough boys and masters ate breakfast and attended morning prayers and assembly. Breakfast for CLS was at nine. The two schools boxed and coxed for the rest of the day, alternately occupying classrooms, playing fields, dining hall and Chapel. On Tuesdays and Thursdays CLS had its tea at 6.30, on Mondays, Wednesdays and Fridays at 5.15.

10 Helyar, ed., *The City of London School at Marlborough*, p. 207. See also pp. 202 and 250.

11 See 'Lessons for Life', *Sunday Telegraph* magazine, 9 November 1986.

12 *Memoirs*, p. 34.

13 From notes to an interview with Eric Jacobs, 23 October 1992, among the Jacobs papers in the Huntington.

14 *Memoirs*, p. 30.

15 *You Can't Do Both*, Flamingo, 1996, p. 20.

16 Ibid., pp. 97–98.

17 This quotation is from Eric Jacobs's notes to an interview with Richenberg on 6 January 1992 (among the Jacobs papers in the Huntington).

18 *Memoirs*, p. 29.

19 In C.N. Vokins's undated handwritten notes in the Jacobs archive in the Huntington Library.

20 Interview with Cynthia Kee, 'Flavour of the Month', *London Portrait Magazine*, December 1986.

21 *Memoirs*, p. 26.

22 See Jacobs, *Biography*, p. 52.

23 Sir George Blunden to the author, 18 September 1996.

24 Jacobs, *Biography*, p. 57.

25 *Memoirs*, p. 29.

26 Ibid., p. 33.

27 Ibid., p. 29.

28 Len Dowsett, quoted in an obituary notice of Amis in *The John Carpenter Club Gazette* 256 (January 1996), p. 10 (this is the journal of the CLS Old Boys' Association).

29 Dowsett thinks Dale decided to treat Amis as he treated another boy, Rommie Pignatelli. According to Pignatelli, Dale called him

into his office and told him he was being made a sub-prefect: 'You are the most disruptive boy in the school, but I believe this will give you a proper sense of discipline so you can make something of yourself' (which he did, becoming a financial adviser to the Vatican, later a Vatican count). Amis was nowhere near as disruptive as Pignatelli, was barely disruptive at all, but as Richenberg remembers, 'all the boys who were prefects were inclined to be prigs – to take themselves too seriously. Amis might have seemed to them not the sort of chap to keep boys in order' (ibid.).

30 *The Riverside Villas Murder*, Penguin, 1984, pp. 12–13.
31 For Peter's feelings for Reg see ibid., p. 108.
32 *You Can't Do Both*, p. 70.
33 Andrew Davies, 'How I Adapted to That Old Devil Amis', *Evening Standard*, 5 March 1982.
34 *You Can't Do Both*, p. 69.
35 Ibid., p. 70.
36 For the pass Jeremy makes at Robin see ibid., pp. 71–72.
37 *The Riverside Villas Murder*, p. 12.
38 *Memoirs*, p. 33.
39 Ibid., p. 31. This description appears first in a letter to Harry Ritchie, 24 July 1986, where Amis also calls 'Prelude' 'modernist in the sense of being self-indulgently obscure and pointless'.
40 'Prelude', in contrast, starts 'Thus I set out' and ends 'Thus I return'. It is also wildly uneven in tone, like the singing of a boy whose voice keeps breaking:

> And now we gaze about the white-walled room,
> Looking towards the tall grey houses, where
> The sunlight gleams, and one of us remarks:
> 'A ripping day'.

At which point the anonymous William Amis makes an appearance:

> Soon summer will be here
> And the remarks will be not only about the day,
> But 'Leave this stupid noise, and get outside;
> Get some fresh air.' This is not what I want.

Later the speaker asks: 'As for happiness / What is happiness? I am too young to know'.

41 Philip Larkin, *Jill*, Faber and Faber, 1975, p. 15.
42 *The City of London School Magazine* 63: 274 (March 1940), p. 1.
43 Hinde, *Carpenter's Children*, p. 97.
44 Jacobs, *Biography*, p. 53; the reports themselves are unsigned.
45 *Memoirs*, p. 29.

46 Quotations from the School Parliament debate come from *The City of London School Magazine* 64: 279 (Easter 1941), pp. 17–18.

47 Ibid., p. 18.

48 The 'black is white' motion, the final in an impromptu debating competition held on 4 February 1940 and attended by 100 boys, was proposed by a boy named Partridge, who declared that the senses were deceptive 'as Kant had proved', that colours didn't really exist, and that black was only another shade of white. Amis in reply, in an account he again probably wrote, 'said the motion was manifestly absurd. He appealed to experience and conviction. The damnable heresy that black is as good as white had led the white man to make the black his brother, and this had resulted in a pollution of the air by Duke Ellington. Colours were different because they produced different emotions. In conclusion he appealed to the common sense of the audience. Amis was the victor' (see *The City of London School Magazine* 63: 276 (March 1940), pp. 27–28, not only for these quotations but for reports on all the debates mentioned here).

49 *The City of London School Magazine* 63: 276 (March 1940), p. 29.

50 See 'Rondo for My Funeral', *Sunday Times*, 1 July 1973; reprinted in *AC*, p. 384.

51 'City Ways', *Spectator*, 2 May 1958, reprinted in *WBJA*, p. 140.

52 Jacobs, *Biography*, p. 42.

53 'Rondo for My Funeral', *AC*, p. 388.

54 Ibid.

55 Ibid., p. 389.

56 Ibid., p. 388.

57 Ibid., p. 385.

58 *The City of London School Magazine* 62: 275 (December 1939), p. 178.

59 *Memoirs*, p. 33.

60 For Marsh's comments see C.N. Vokins's notes among the Jacobs papers in the Huntington.

61 According to C. N. Vokins's handwritten notes in the Huntington.

62 *Memoirs*, p. 36.

63 Ibid., p. 34.

64 Ibid.

CHAPTER 5

Wartime Oxford

1 Kingsley Amis, *Memoirs*, Penguin, 1992, p. 36.

2 Roy Jenkins, *A Life at the Centre*, Macmillan, 1992, p. 29.

3 Philip Larkin, *Jill*, Faber and Faber, 1975, p. 53.

4 Alan Ross, *Blindfold Games*, Harvill, 1986, p. 143.

5 Brian Harrison, ed., *The History of the University of Oxford* (Volume VIII: The Twentieth Century), Clarendon Press, 1994, p. 174.

6 Quoted in Andrew Motion, *Philip Larkin: A Writer's Life*, Faber and Faber, 1993, p. 38.

7 PL, *Jill*, p. 12.

8 *Memoirs*, p. 36.

9 PL, *Jill*, p. 11.

10 Undated entry in St John's College Kitchen Book for Michaelmas Term 1945 – Hilary Term 1947.

11 Ibid.

12 PL, *Michaelmas Term at St Bride's*, in *Trouble at Willow Gables and Other Fictions*, ed. James Booth, Faber and Faber, 2002, p. 178.

13 *Memoirs*, p. 36.

14 Larkin, *Jill*, pp. 14–15.

15 *Memoirs*, p. 38.

16 Noel Hughes to Eric Jacobs, 17 November 1992, among the Jacobs papers in the Huntington.

17 *Memoirs*, p. 60.

18 PL to J. B. Sutton, 10 November 1941, in *Selected Letters of Philip Larkin 1940–1985*, ed. Anthony Thwaite, Faber and Faber, 1992, p. 26.

19 *Memoirs*, p. 38.

20 Ibid.

21 Motion, *Philip Larkin: A Writer's Life*, p. 40.

22 *Memoirs*, p. 38.

23 Ibid., p. 53.

24 At Iles's suggestion, Amis told Andrew Motion, Larkin cut most of the 'group stuff' (seminars, study sessions) and 'didn't go to lectures much . . . not even [C.S.] Lewis's' (Motion, *Philip Larkin: A Writer's Life*, p. 41). To Amis, Lewis was 'the best lecturer I ever heard' (*Memoirs*, p. 102). Edward du Cann, a St John's contemporary (later Sir Edward, Conservative MP and Minister), remembers Larkin as 'monstrously flippant and disrespectful' and having 'no contact with the dons' (Motion, *Philip Larkin: A Writer's Life*, p. 46).

25 *Memoirs*, p. 38.

26 Norman Iles, 'Our Group', *London Magazine* 39: 9–10 (December 1999/January 2000), p. 30.

27 In a letter of 10 November 1941 to his friend James Sutton, Larkin complains of one such borrowing. What, he fantasises, would happen if he tried to live more naturally or self-reliantly?

> If I had my little shack, little axe & knife & bowls and saucepans &c., along would come Norman and live in the

shack, lose the axe in the brook, forget to give me back the knife, and smash & sell most of the rest of the things. This he would excuse by perfectly good arguments against meanness and parsimony, and it would probably end by my silently clearing out and starting alone again somewhere. For instance, we have just had a smouldering quarrel about a pencil. I keep 2 pencils in my right-hand jacket pocket, always. Norman has no pencils, wants one, so borrows one of mine. I gladly pay up to avoid being robbed of both, congratulating myself on still having one even when the needs of Norman have been met. Then Norman mislays the pencil – not loses, but is just too lazy to remember where he put it – and, needing a pencil, borrows mine. While he can see nothing wrong in this proceeding, I am sent into boiling fury at it.

28 When Anthony Thwaite was editing Larkin's *Selected Letters* Amis told him that he had lost most of Larkin's letters; the forty-two letters that turned up from the period 1941–47, with a gap in 1944, were, Thwaite guessed, borrowed by Larkin when he was working on the reissue of *Jill* or *The North Ship*, and never returned. As Thwaite warns, they 'aren't necessarily a *full* record' (personal communication to the author, 14 February 2006).

29 PL, *Jill*, p. 13.

30 *Memoirs*, p. 38.

31 'Our Group', p. 31.

32 PL, *Jill*, p. 13.

33 John Wain, *Hurry On Down*, Penguin, 1961, pp. 12–13.

34 In KA, *Collected Short Stories*, Penguin 1984, p. 184.

35 Larkin, *Jill*, pp. 13–14.

36 According to testimony in Motion, *Philip Larkin: A Writer's Life*, pp. 17–18.

37 Ibid., p. 18.

38 Ibid., p. 24; Larkin's career at King Henry VIII Grammar School was much like Amis's at CLS in that he, too, only came into his own in the sixth form, gaining a reputation with the masters as 'innocently mischievous' (p. 19) as well as able.

39 Ibid., p. 20.

40 Ibid., p. 19.

41 *Memoirs*, p. 51.

42 Motion, *Philip Larkin: A Writer's Life*, p. 27.

43 Like Iles, Gunner was openly mocking of authority. Though he 'had no literary ambitions' and was to fail his School Certificate, Gunner, according to Larkin, 'was a natural writer. His English essays came back with "Vigorous" written at the bottom' (Foreword to Gunner's *Adventures with the Irish Brigade*, 1981, reprinted in *Further*

Requirements: Interviews, Broadcasts, Statements and Book Reviews, ed. Anthony Thwaite, Faber and Faber, 2001, p. 121). After war service Gunner worked, until 1972, in mines and oil fields in Britain, Africa and the Middle East; from 1972 to 1985 he was a postmaster and newsagent in Coventry, during which time he wrote the privately printed *Adventures*.

44 Motion, *Philip Larkin: A Writer's Life*, pp. 23–24.

45 Sutton was also intense and confiding, and there may have been an erotic or romantic component to the friendship, on Larkin's part at least. According to Frank Smith, a fellow King Henry VIII and Oxford student, Sutton 'had qualities Philip would have liked to have. He looked nice, you know, in that wiry sort of way [Gunner and Iles were stocky], and Philip was very conscious of his own plain damn ugliness – galumphing was a favourite word of his. I think he was half in love with Jim' (ibid., p. 22).

46 See Ibid., p. 21.

47 Ibid., p. 22.

48 Quoted in ibid., pp. 28–29.

49 Ibid., p. 29.

50 *Memoirs*, p. 55.

51 Ibid., p. 52.

52 Larkin told his friend the historian John Kenyon that his father 'had a statue of Hitler on the mantelpiece which at the touch of a button leapt into a Nazi salute' (Motion, *Philip Larkin: A Writer's Life*, p. 12).

53 That Larkin feared and sometimes hated his father had much to do with the effect the father had on Larkin's mother and older sister. 'I think the situation was technically his fault,' he wrote in the 1950s, in an autobiographical fragment unpublished in his lifetime. 'His personality had imposed that taut ungenerous defeated pattern of life on the family, and it was only to be expected that it would make them miserable and that their misery would react on him. And despite the fact that my mother grew to be such an obsessive snivelling pest, I think if my father had handled her properly she would have done much better' (Motion, *Philip Larkin: A Writer's Life*, p. 14). This sounds like something out of a Lawrence novel. That Lawrence also helped Larkin to understand and come to terms with his father's politics is suggested by the letter to Sutton of 6 July 1942: 'If there is any new life in the world today, it is in Germany. True, it is a vicious and blood-brutal kind of affair – the new shoots are rather like bayonets. It won't suit me. By "new" life I don't mean better life, but a change, a new direction. Germany has revolted back too far, into the other extremes. But I think they have many valuable new habits. Otherwise how could D.H.L. be called fascist?' Amis's left politics, his open membership of the student branch of the Oxford Communist Party,

may have made Larkin wary, helping to explain his initial reluctance to reveal himself fully to his new friend. As their friendship grew, especially in the letters written just after Amis left Oxford in 1942, politics remained a tricky area. 'Whether a fascist or not,' Larkin writes to Amis on 19 September 1942 (Huntington), shortly after the German attack on Stalingrad, 'I object to [Dryden's] reactionary tendencies . . . Incidentally, also, I don't like to mention it, but things don't look too good, do they, old boy? No, old boy, they don't, old boy.'

54 Quoted in Motion, *Philip Larkin: A Writer's Life*, p. 60.
55 Quoted in ibid., p. 61.
56 Ibid., p. 60.
57 *Michaelmas Term at St Bride's*, in *Trouble at Willow Gables*, ed. Booth, p. 179.
58 Ibid., p. 181.
59 *You Can't Do Both*, Flamingo, 1996, pp. 74–75.
60 Ibid., p. 159.
61 Ibid.
62 Ibid., p. 304.
63 Ibid., p. 81.
64 Ibid., p. 80.
65 Ibid., p. 86.
66 Ibid., p. 89.
67 Ibid., p. 90.
68 Ibid., p. 92.
69 One sign of the good health of fourteen-year-old Peter Furneaux in *The Riverside Villas Murder* is the dogged determination and unembarrassability with which he pursues sexy Daphne Hodgson, who is haughty, older and uninterested.
70 Jacobs, *Biography*, p. 74; the book was *Ideal Marriage* (1926) by H. Van de Velde, a reference I owe to Elaine Showalter.
71 *You Can't Do Both*, p. 92.
72 Peter J. Conradi, *Iris Murdoch: A Life – The Authorized Biography*, Harper Collins, 2001, p. 84.
73 Jenkins, *A Life at the Centre*, pp. 36–37.
74 Denis Healey, *The Time of My Life*, Michael Joseph, 1989, p. 34.
75 Ibid.
76 Philip Toynbee, *Friends Apart: A Memoir of Esmond Romilly and Jasper Ridley in the Thirties*, MacGibbon and Kee, 1954, pp. 62–63.
77 Conradi, *Iris Murdoch*, p. 130.
78 Toynbee, *Friends Apart*, p. 61.
79 Martin Amis, *Koba the Dread: Laughter and the Twenty Million*, Jonathan Cape, 2002, p. 6.
80 John Lloyd to the author, 10 April 1997.
81 Martin Amis, *Koba the Dread*, pp. 7–8.

82 This admission was made to Mavis Nicholson in *Mavis Catches up with Sir Kingsley*, broadcast on ITV on 21 January 1991.

83 *Memoirs*, p. 37.

84 Interview with Graham Turner, 'Kingsley Amis and Those Uncertain Feelings,' *Sunday Telegraph* magazine, 28 November 1986.

85 Conradi, *Iris Murdoch*, p. 30.

86 *The City of London School Magazine* 64: 281 (December 1941), p. 133.

87 Peter Jones, 'Amis's Trousers', *John Carpenter's Gazette* 256 (January 1996), p. 11.

88 'Kingsley Amis and Those Uncertain Feelings'.

89 *The City of London School Magazine* 65: 283 (July 1942), p. 58.

90 Motion, *Philip Larkin: A Writer's Life*, p. 79. Larkin got to know Rudingerova, or got to know her better, because he himself had joined the Labour Club, in February 1942. As there is little evidence from his letters or elsewhere of political conversion he probably did so for social reasons: at Amis's urging, or because Amis published two of his poems in the Labour Club *Bulletin*, or because of Amis's success with girls from the club. It was unlikely to have been a secret that Amis lost his virginity to a Labour Club girl; George Blunden certainly knew. Such non-political factors ought not to be underestimated when discussing political affiliations. Iris Murdoch's friend Lilian Eldridge joined the Communist Party 'mainly to go to Saturday-night "hops" at Ruskin' (Conradi, *Iris Murdoch*, p. 131). In his memoirs, Denis Healey explains his refusal to join the breakaway Oxford University Democratic Socialist Club as having little to do with political ideology. In the autumn of 1939 he was chairman of the Labour Club and extremely active in the affairs of the student branch of the Communist Party. When Chamberlain announced that he would introduce conscription, Healey organised a mass meeting against it, one that involved much planning, including consultation with the non-student branch of the Communist Party headquartered at Hythe Bridge Street. When the Democratic Socialist Club was formed in the Trinity term, Healey's last at Oxford, he opposed it, he admits, 'more from inertia and indifference than from conviction. I was too busy making up for my lost term to take much notice of University politics' (Healey, *The Time of My Life*, p. 46). In other words, he was facing final examinations.

91 PL, *Jill*, p. 15.

92 Ibid., p. 16.

93 Interview with Michael Parkinson on *Desert Island Discs*, BBC Radio 4, 9 November 1986.

94 PL, *Jill*, p. 16.

95 Quoted in Jacobs, *Biography*, p. 73.

96 PL, *Jill*, p. 16.

97 Quoted in Jacobs, *Biography*, pp. 73–74, from an unpublished talk, 'Brave Causes', on the BBC Home Service, 6 June 1961.

98 'Lucky Jim as I Remember Him', *The Southern Review* 32: 4 (Autumn 1996), p. 784.

99 *Memoirs*, p. 66.

100 PL, *Jill*, p. 15.

101 Ibid., p. 16.

102 *The Riverside Villas Murder*, Penguin, 1984, p. 49.

103 Ibid., p. 106.

104 'Take Five: Kingsley Amis', Interview with James Hogg, *Jazz Express*, July 1989, pp. 9, 23.

105 Quoted in Motion, *Philip Larkin: A Writer's Life*, p. 57.

106 *Memoirs*, p. 65.

107 Interview with Michael Parkinson on *Desert Island Discs*, BBC Radio 4, 9 November 1986.

108 *Memoirs*, p. 66.

109 PL, *All What Jazz: A Record Diary 1961–1971*, Faber and Faber, 1970, p. 16.

110 *Memoirs*, p. 52.

111 Motion, *Philip Larkin: A Writer's Life*, p. 47.

112 Quoted in Philip Larkin, *Larkin's Jazz: Essays and Reviews 1940–1948*, ed. Richard Palmer and John White, Continuum, 2001, p. 7.

113 PL, *All What Jazz*, p. 16.

114 Motion, *Philip Larkin: A Writer's Life*, p. 57.

115 PL, 'Jazz as a Way of Life', *Daily Telegraph*, 11 August 1962; reprinted in Larkin, *All What Jazz*, p. 68.

116 PL, *Jill*, p. 17.

117 PL to KA, 7 January 1946 (Huntington).

118 James Willcox to the author, 30 May 2002.

119 *Memoirs*, p. 53.

120 This story is undated but Motion, in *Philip Larkin: A Writer's Life*, p. 64, conjectures a date of late 1941. It exists in a thirty-page handwritten manuscript among the Larkin papers in the Brynmor Jones Library.

121 Motion, *Philip Larkin: A Writer's Life*, p. 69.

122 In Motion, ibid., and Jacobs, *Biography*, p. 70, Willcox rather than Morris is listed among the Seven, but Willcox has no memory of 'The Seven'; Norman Iles, 'Our Group', lists Morris instead of Willcox.

123 Edward Mendelson, *Early Auden*, Faber and Faber, 1981, p. 13n.

124 Gerald Heard, 'The Group Movement and the Middle Classes', in R. H. S. Crossman, ed., *Oxford and the Groups*, Basil Blackwell, 1934, p. 98.

125 Gerald Heard, *Social Substance of Religion*, Harcourt Brace, 1931, p. 307, quoted in Mendelson, *Early Auden*, p. 26.

126 Quoted in Mendelson, *Early Auden*, p. 26.

127 'Our Group', p. 26.

128 The letter is unfinished, unpublished, undated and found in the Brynmor Jones Library; in a subsequent letter, written on 19 October, Larkin declares that he 'rejoices' that Amis has purchased, read and likes the book.

129 Motion, *Philip Larkin: A Writer's Life*, p. 64.

130 This, at least, is the impression given by extracts from, and an account of, Larkin's still-unpublished correspondence with Monica Jones in Anthony Gardner, 'What Will Survive of Us Is Love', *Sunday Times* magazine, 21 November 2004, pp. 30–38. According to Gardner, Larkin wrote over 1,400 letters and 500 cards and telegrams to Monica Jones (p. 32).The extracts Gardner prints contain several disparaging remarks about Amis.

131 This essay, entitled 'Biographical Details: OXFORD', is dated October 1943 and deposited among the Larkin papers in the Brynmor Jones Library. The reference to Amis occurs on p. 3.

132 Amis makes this suggestion in 'What's Cooking' a section (not really a chapter) of Amis's unfinished wartime novel, 'Who Else Is Rank'. Archer, the Amis character, reassures Stephen, that they'll be welcome on a visit to Oxford: 'If all else fails we can go and see my moral tutor. He'll be delighted to see me; he always is; he wants to sleep with me.' For the tutor's propensities see also KA to Anthony Thwaite, 5 May 1991 (recipient).

133 For Amis on the dangers of sticking to real-life characters and situations see 'Real and Made-up People', *Times Literary Supplement*, 27 July 1973, reprinted in *The Amis Collection: Selected Non-Fiction 1954–1990*, Penguin, 1991, p. 4.

134 *Memoirs*, p. 52.

135 This quotation is from a letter to Andrew Motion, quoted in *Philip Larkin: A Writer's Life*, p. 24.

136 Ibid., p. 42.

137 PL, *Jill*, p. 14.

138 *Anglo-Saxon Poetry* is a work of some seventy-nine pages; the essay itself is only sixteen pages.

139 The draft manuscript of Jacobs's *Biography*, with Amis's handwritten comments, can be found among the Jacobs papers in the Huntington.

140 Quoted in *Memoirs*, p. 53.

141 PL to KA, 18 October 1942 (Huntington).

142 *Memoirs*, p. 54.

143 Jacobs, 'Amis Diaries', 1 April 1993.

144 PL to KA, 19 September 1942 (Huntington).

145 Quoted in Motion, *Philip Larkin: A Writer's Life*, p. 86.

146 See KA to PL, 15 December 1959.

147 Motion, *Philip Larkin: A Writer's Life*, p. 56.

148 Amis suggests Larkin's leadership through a mock 'Personnel' in a letter to him of 29 September 1948 (Bodleian). The band is 'NORMAN ILES AND THE GILER HAMFATS':

> Iles (vocal) *directing* Phil Larkin (tpt), Bill Amis (alto), Dave Williams (tmb), Dennis Groves (pno), Phil Brown (xyl), Nick Russel (gtr), H. Morris (bass), Jimmy Willcox (ds). Oxford 1942

The first of the 'records' listed after the personnel is 'Do what Norman say / Revolutionary blues (featuring Bill Amis)'. After the records Amis offers sample 'reviews': 'Iles . . . loud and uncouth vocal noises . . . Larkin . . . unobtrusive but definite lead . . . Amis . . . uncertain of the effects he wants . . .'

149 *Memoirs*, pp. 54–55.
150 Quoted in Motion, *Philip Larkin: A Writer's Life*, p. 54.
151 Quoted ibid.
152 Quoted ibid., p. 24.
153 Ross, *Blindfold Games*, p. 150.
154 Larkin, *Jill*, p. 16.
155 This is the October 1943 essay titled 'Biographical Details: OXFORD' in the Brynmor Jones Library. Motion quotes this passage in *Philip Larkin: A Writer's Life*, p. 70.
156 Quoted in Jacobs, *Biography*, p. 68.
157 Healey, *The Time of My Life*, p. 32.

CHAPTER 6

The War

1 Kingsley Amis, *Memoirs*, Penguin, 1992, p. 72.
2 Ibid., pp. 37–38.
3 Ibid., p. 79.
4 Ibid., p. 80.
5 Interview with Graham Turner, 'Kingsley Amis and Those Uncertain Feelings', *Sunday Telegraph*, 28 September 1986, p. 10.
6 Quoted in Eric Jacobs, *Kingsley Amis: A Biography*, Hodder and Stoughton, 1995, p. 67.
7 'I Spy Strangers' was first published by Gollancz in the 1962 collection, *My Enemy's Enemy* (my quotation is from the 1965 Penguin edition, p. 53). In *Memoirs*, p. 80, Amis also quotes the passage, introducing it as follows: 'In this training period I also did a great deal of what the army had desperately longed for Signals to do, "learning to fight as infantry". I once described this in a short story of 1962 in words that fit my present situation'.

8 Jacobs, *Biography*, p. 88.

9 Interview with Ray Connolly, 'A Childhood: Kingsley Amis', *The Times*, 24 March 1990.

10 *Memoirs*, pp. 85–86.

11 Quoted by Jacobs in a note on Amis's army experiences. This note, not part of the 'Amis Diaries', is dated 14 July 1993 and can also be found with the Jacobs papers in the Huntington; in addition, see Jacobs, *Biography*, p. 89.

12 *Memoirs*, p. 85.

13 The towns and villages Amis's company advanced through were Cruelly, Tracy Bocage, La Trinité-des-Laitiers, Menantissart, Holsbeck, Lindel, Helmond, Geldrop, Sonnis, Aarle, Horst, Dingden, Borghorst, Ohlendorf, Riepe, Lüneburg and Bunde.

14 *Memoirs*, p. 85.

15 Coles probably met Amis in OCTU at Catterick (this is suggested in the chapter entitled 'Schemes', where Francis Archer writes to Stephen Lewis about an officer 'you will remember I'm afraid from the line transmission lecs at the octu', though in the opening chapter the two friends clearly meet for the first time at Headington in Oxford).

16 *Memoirs*, p. 78.

17 Quoted in Andrew Motion, *Philip Larkin: A Writer's Life*, Faber and Faber, p. 77.

18 Philip Larkin, *Jill*, Faber and Faber, 1975, p. 18.

19 *Memoirs*, p. 40

20 'Court of Inquiry', *Spectator*, 23 November 1956; reprinted in *My Enemy's Enemy*, Penguin, 1965, p. 42.

21 Ibid., p. 41.

22 Ibid., p. 51.

23 Ibid., p. 92. In an unfinished, undated and untitled short story Amis wrote at the very end of his time with the Second Army, while stationed at a Reinforcement Holding Unit or RHU in Bruges, Archer is confronted in the mess by an elderly eccentric major, perhaps mad. 'F began to shake with fright . . . "What's your name?" – "Archer, sir." He felt slightly faint and his cheeks burned.' The story is only partly compatible with the material in 'Who Else Is Rank', with which it is grouped at the Huntington. See, also, a chapter of 'Who Else Is Rank' entitled 'Le Lac des Cygnes', in which Archer sits with a pretty French woman: 'It was surprisingly easy to talk to her and very soon my hands stopped shaking.'

24 Interview with Michael Barber, 'The Art of Fiction LIX', *Paris Review* 16: 64 (Winter 1975), p. 76.

25 'Court of Inquiry', *My Enemy's Enemy*, p. 44.

26 Ibid., p. 38.

27 Ibid., p. 42.

28 Jacobs's description, *Biography*, p. 94.

29 'Court of Inquiry', *My Enemy's Enemy*, p. 40.

30 Ibid.

31 *Memoirs*, p. 80.

32 KA to PL, *c.*1943 (Bodleian).

33 I have been unable to trace the earlier letter.

34 These passages are from the section of 'Who Else Is Rank' entitled 'Jeeps'.

35 'My Enemy's Enemy' was first published in the June 1955 issue of *Encounter*.

36 'Court of Inquiry', *My Enemy's Enemy*, pp. 42–43.

37 Ibid., p. 45.

38 Interview with John Walsh, 'An Old Devil in Telling Form', *Sunday Times*, 17 February 1991.

39 'Court of Inquiry', *My Enemy's Enemy*, p. 45.

40 In 'What's Cooking', in 'Who Else Is Rank', Coles suggests that Francis's 'lack of assurance could not all be traced to the Colonel's reception' (which had been curt and menacing, making Francis too nervous to eat). In 'Stephen in Purple', a companion character sketch to 'Francis in Sackcloth', Archer describes himself as 'always easily deflated' and needing 'someone wiser than myself to lean on'.

41 Like Embleton in *You Can't Do Both*.

42 'My Enemy's Enemy', *My Enemy's Enemy*, p. 23.

43 *Memoirs*, p. 85.

44 Ibid., p. 88.

45 'My Enemy's Enemy', *My Enemy's Enemy*, p. 24.

46 Ibid., p. 25. Later in the story, Dalessio's bad opinion of Thurston is corroborated. The Adjutant, a figure like Major Raleigh, has taken against Dalessio and sets out to punish him, with the eventual aim of removing him from the unit entirely. Dalessio may be a technical wizard but his unsoldierly appearance and demeanour offend the Adjutant, who plans a spot inspection to catch him out. Though Dalessio has never been very friendly to Thurston, Thurston defends him (partly because he rightly thinks him a victim of anti-Italian prejudice, though 'if anyone in the mess admired Mussolini . . . it was the Adjutant', p. 17); so when the Adjutant tells Thurston of the spot check he does so with a threat: '"You wouldn't think of tipping your friend Dally the wink about this little treat we've got lined up for him, would you? If you do, I'll have your guts for garters." Laughing heartily, he dug Thurston in the ribs and added: "Your leave's due at the end of the month, isn't it? Better watch out you don't make yourself indispensable here. We might not be able to let you go, do you see?"' (p. 29). Thurston has been dreaming of visiting his several married girlfriends on his leave and doesn't alert Dalessio. Another captain, a forty-year-old non-commissioned officer named Bentham, does instead. It is Bentham who denounces Thurston at the story's conclusion, in terms that recall Amis's lesser timidities or conformities at school and Oxford:

'I've no doubt you've got your excuses for not letting on. In spite of the fact that I've always understood you were the great one for pouring scorn on the Adj. and Rowney and Cleaver and the rest of the crowd. Yes, you could talk about them till you were black in the face, but when it came to doing something, talking where it would do some good, you kept your mouth shut . . . You don't care beyond talking, any road. I think you're really quite sold on the Adj.'s crowd, never mind what you say about them' (p. 39).

What Bentham stands for is a code of honour and loyalty independent of political or career interests. Bentham has come up from the ranks and has no time for Dalessio's slovenliness and insubordination. In political terms, Dalessio is his enemy and the Adjutant his friend.

47 'I Spy Strangers', *My Enemy's Enemy*, p. 88.
48 Ibid., p. 49.
49 Ibid., p. 56.
50 *Memoirs*, p. 80.
51 Ibid., p. 81.
52 'My Enemy's Enemy', *My Enemy's Enemy*, p. 16.
53 'Court of Inquiry', *My Enemy's Enemy*, pp. 40–41. These accessories Amis lends to Sergeant Doll six years later, in 'I Spy Strangers' (p. 73).
54 Both quotations are from Chapter 11 of 'Who Else is Rank'.
55 'Court of Inquiry', *My Enemy's Enemy*, p. 41.
56 Ibid., p. 31.
57 'I Spy Strangers', *My Enemy's Enemy*, p. 74.
58 Ibid., p. 65.
59 Ibid., p. 66.
60 *Memoirs*, pp. 81–82.
61 'I Spy Strangers', *My Enemy's Enemy*, p. 76.
62 Ibid., p. 96.
63 Ibid., p. 85.
64 Ibid., p. 70.
65 Interview with Clive James, 'Kingsley Amis: A Profile', *New Review*, July 1974, p. 27.
66 In his biography of Amis, Jacobs writes that 'in 1943 Kingsley spent the first part of a leave with Elisabeth and the second part at home in Berkhamsted' (p. 87). Amis had met Elisabeth in August, so the leave in question must have taken place after his course ended in October. This is the date of the only leave referred to in 1943 in the Amis–Larkin correspondence, one which ended on 19 November, when Amis was posted to Headington. By December he had been posted to High Wycombe. In the 'Schemes' chapter of 'Who Else Is Rank', Archer writes to Lewis from Headington,

which explains the phrase 'when I go up to see her'. It is possible, I suppose, that the 1943 leave Jacobs is referring to was not the leave Amis took immediately after his course ended but a second leave some time in late November or, more likely, in December, perhaps for the Christmas holidays. But neither he nor Amis in the *Memoirs* nor Archer in 'Schemes' makes any mention of the Christmas holidays and if the leave took place earlier it would have been within weeks of the first leave, which strikes me as unlikely.

67 *Memoirs*, p. 13.
68 Jacobs, *Biography*, p. 87.
69 *Memoirs*, p. 13.
70 Ibid.
71 Tom Thurston's leave in *My Enemy's Enemy* is also scheduled for March 1945. It is to include 'four days with Denise in Oxford, and then a nice little run up to Town for five days with Margot' (p. 26).
72 KA to PL, 8 July 1946 (Bodleian).
73 See also PL to KA, 12 October 1943 (Huntington).
74 Jacobs, *Biography*, p. 85.
75 See PL to KA, 16 September 1943 (Huntington).
76 PL to KA, 12 October 1943.
77 Jacobs, *Biography*, p. 86.
78 *Memoirs*, p. 91.
79 The Huntington possesses Amis's copies of each of these books, having purchased his library as well as his papers.
80 Stephen Spender, 'W. H. Auden and His Poetry' (1953), reprinted in Monroe K. Spears, ed., *Auden: A Collection of Critical Essays*, Prentice-Hall, 1964, p. 28.
81 Ibid., p. 30.
82 'I Spy Strangers', *My Enemy's Enemy*, p. 85.
83 *Socialism and the Intellectuals*, Fabian Society, 1957, p. 1.
84 Jacobs, *Biography*, p. 101.
85 *Socialism and the Intellectuals*, p. 4.
86 'I Spy Strangers', *My Enemy's Enemy*, p. 62.
87 Ibid., p. 70.
88 Clive James, 'The Examined Life of Kingsley Amis', in James's collection of essays and reviews, *From the Land of Shadows*, Jonathan Cape, 1982, p. 141.
89 Paul Fussell, *The Anti-Egotist: Kingsley Amis, Man of Letters*, Oxford University Press, 1994, p. 170.
90 Ibid.
91 James, 'The Examined Life of Kingsley Amis', *From the Land of Shadows*, pp. 141–142.
92 *Memoirs*, p. 81.
93 'My Enemy's Enemy', *My Enemy's Enemy*, p. 14.
94 Radar detects the direction and range of ships and aircraft by the

reflection of radio waves (the word itself is an acronym of 'radio', 'detection', 'and', 'ranging'). In the poem, its powers are conceived of as active. The valve will 'bind forever the sense of the plunging wave'.

95 As opposed to the Far East.
96 *Memoirs*, p. 99.
97 Jacobs, *Biography*, p. 101.
98 'What's Cooking', from 'Who Else Is Rank'.
99 Interview with Michael Barber, 'The Art of Fiction LIX', *Paris Review* 16: 64 (Winter 1975), p. 176.

CHAPTER 7

Post-war Oxford

1 Kingsley Amis, *Memoirs*, Penguin, 1992, p. 40.
2 KA, 'I Spy Strangers', *My Enemy's Enemy*, Penguin, 1965, pp. 95–96.
3 The frequency of the correspondence during wartime is difficult to gauge, since only three of Amis's wartime letters to Larkin survive and only two dozen or so from Larkin to Amis. Larkin wrote Amis ten long letters in September and October 1943 but whether he and Amis wrote at this rate throughout the war is unclear.
4 KA to PL, 22 April 1947 (Bodleian).
5 PL to KA, 14 December 1945 (Huntington).
6 KA to PL, 25 May 1947 (Bodleian); quoted in the introduction to Zachary Leader, ed., *The Letters of Kingsley Amis*, HarperCollins, 2000, p. xvii.
7 In my edition of Amis's *Letters*, p.xvii, I mistakenly attribute this remark to Amis. It comes from PL to KA, 17 July 1946 (Brynmor Jones Library), in a passage omitted from Anthony Thwaite, ed., *Selected Letters of Philip Larkin 1940–1985*, Faber and Faber, 1992, p. 119.
8 KA to PL, 11 August 1945 (Bodleian).
9 KA to PL, 28 December 1945 (Huntington); quoted in the introduction to Leader, ed., *LKA*, p. xvii.
10 KA to PL, 11 December 1945 (Bodleian).
11 PL to KA, 10 December 1945 (Huntington).
12 KA to PL, 11 December 1945 (Bodleian).
13 KA to PL, 31 January 1946 (Bodleian).
14 Margaret Bardwell, Hilly's sister, claims that brother Bill loaned Amis many records which he never returned.
15 Hilly in interview with Deborah Ross, 'The Old Devil Upstairs', *Daily Mail*, 16 March 1992.
16 KA to PL, 25 February 1946.
17 KA to PL, 7 March 1946 (Bodleian).
18 Ibid.

19 Hilly Amis in interview with Deborah Ross, 'The Old Devil Upstairs', *Daily Mail*, 16 March 1992.

20 Ibid.

21 *The Map of Love* (1939), a collection of prose and verse by Dylan Thomas.

22 *You Can't Do Both*, Flamingo, 1996, pp. 127–128.

23 PL to KA, 8 January 1946 (Huntington).

24 Philip Larkin, 'The Girls', in *Required Writing: Miscellaneous Pieces 1955–1982*, Faber and Faber, 1983, p. 260.

25 Ibid., p. 262.

26 Ibid.

27 Martin Amis, *Experience*, Jonathan Cape, 2000, p. 130.

28 Margery Bardwell, 'In My Young Days', is 226 typed pages long. She began writing it in 1960 and finished it in 1962. The manuscript belongs to Hilly, Lady Kilmarnock. This quotation is from p. 119.

29 Ibid., pp. 119–120.

30 Ibid., p. 193.

31 Ibid., p. 194.

32 Martin Amis, *Experience*, p. 130.

33 KA to PL, 19 May 1952.

34 She had three brothers, as Amis would discover.

35 KA to PL, 15 July 1946 (Bodleian).

36 PL to KA, 17 July 1946 (Huntington).

37 Martin Amis, *Experience*, p. 131.

38 Interview with Ray Connolly, 'A Childhood: Kingsley Amis', *The Times*, 24 March 1990.

39 Not nineteen, as in Eric Jacobs, *Kingsley Amis: A Biography*, Hodder and Stoughton, 1995, p. 126, and elsewhere.

40 'The Legacy', p. 211.

41 Ibid., p. 100.

42 In KA to PL, 7 July 1947 (Bodleian), though not in 'The Legacy' itself, this Caton-like figure is referred to as 'Mr Seton of the Horoscope Press'.

43 'The Legacy', p. 2.

44 Ibid., p. 14.

45 Ibid., p. 46.

46 Ibid., p. 71.

47 For Doreen Marston's report see Leader, ed., *LKA*, p. 252n.

48 'The Legacy', p. 126.

49 Ibid., p. 127.

50 Ibid., p. 126.

51 Ibid., p. 128.

52 An old girlfriend, the daughter also of the president of the local Conservative Association.

53 'The Legacy', pp. 128–129.

54 *Memoirs*, p. 13.
55 KA to PL, 20 July 1946 (Bodleian).
56 KA to PL, 30 July 1946.
57 KA to PL, 21 September 1946 (Bodleian).
58 PL to KA, 24 September 1947, in *Selected Letters of Philip Larkin 1940–1985*, ed. Anthony Thwaite, Faber and Faber, 1992, p. 124.
59 'A Childhood: Kingsley Amis'.
60 'The Legacy', pp. 207–208.
61 Ibid., p. 75.
62 KA to PL, 29 September 1948 (Bodleian).
63 *The Legacy*, p. 252.
64 KA to PL, 3 September 1948 (Bodleian).
65 KA to PL, 11 December 1945 (Bodleian).
66 I have not been able to trace this radio broadcast. The manuscript of 'The Comic Muse' is in the Huntington, dated pre-1987. The quotation is from p. 28.
67 'The Legacy', p. 20.
68 Ibid., p. 24.
69 Ibid., p. 27.
70 Ibid., p. 25.
71 Ibid., p. 149.
72 *Memoirs*, p. 55.
73 'A Conversation with Neil Powell', in PL, *Further Requirements: Interviews, Broadcasts, Statements and Book Reviews*, ed. Anthony Thwaite, Faber and Faber, 2001, p. 33; see also 'The Traffic in the Distance', in PL, *Required Writing*, pp. 274–277.
74 According to a passage from a letter from KA to PL, 9 May 1949, omitted in Leader, ed., *LKA*.
75 Letter to an otherwise unidentified Mr Heppner, 14 July 1967.
76 'A Childhood: Kingsley Amis'.
77 PL to KA, 12 December 1945 (Huntington).
78 KA to PL, 25 May 1947 (Bodleian).
79 KA to PL, 5 May 1948 (Bodleian).
80 See letters of 2 and 15 March 1948 (Bodleian), in the second of which Amis admits that he finds Larkin's puff 'a little deep wreck o' Tory'.
81 KA to PL, 29 September 1948 (Bodleian).
82 KA to PL 19 October 1948 (Bodleian)
83 KA, 'Publishers Be Damned', *Sunday Telegraph* magazine, August 1988.
84 'Elisabeth's Intermesso', in *Bright November*, Fortune Press, 1947.
85 See Clive James, 'Kingsley Amis: A Profile', *New Review*, July 1974, p. 27.
86 In 'Bare Choirs', a review of William Empson, *Argufying*, *Sunday Telegraph*, 29 November 1987; reprinted in *The Amis Collection: Selected Non-Fiction 1954–1990*, Penguin, 1991, p. 53.

87 Ibid.

88 Ibid.

89 Al Alvarez, *Where Did It All Go Right?* Bloomsbury, 2002, p. 132.

90 Ibid., p. 128.

91 Ibid., p. 132.

92 John Sutherland, *Stephen Spender: The Authorised Biography*, Penguin, 2004, pp. 232–233.

93 *Memoirs*, p. 49.

94 From a tape-recorded interview with Jacobs, 11 May 1995 (Huntington).

95 A fragment of 'ape's bumfodder' written about the year 1000.

96 *Memoirs*, p. 46.

97 This letter does not square with the *Memoirs*, p. 46, where Amis says he got his highest marks on the Old English paper; the university itself has no record of marks for individual papers.

98 KA to PL, 22 June 1947 (Bodleian).

99 KA to PL, 25 July 1947 (Bodleian).

100 Interview with Graham Turner, 'Kingsley Amis and Those Uncertain Feelings', *Sunday Telegraph*, 28 September 1986; in *Memoirs*, p. 114, he says of the date of this visit: 'I suppose I was twenty-four at the time'.

101 *Memoirs*, p. 114.

102 Ibid., p. 48.

103 As reported to PL in a letter of 19 December 1946.

104 KA to PL, 13 January 1947 (Bodleian).

105 KA to PL, 5 June 1947 (Bodleian).

106 KA to PL, 1 September 1947 (Bodleian).

107 KA to PL, 6 November 1947 (Bodleian).

108 Actually, only until she was twenty-one, though other monies would come to her later.

109 As KA reported to PL in a letter of 6 February 1947.

110 KA to PL, 19 December 1946 (Bodleian).

111 KA to PL, 22 August 1947 (Bodleian).

112 *Memoirs*, p. 22.

CHAPTER 8

Newly Married: Oxford and Eynsham

1 See KA to PL, 25 January 1948.

2 Kingsley Amis, *Memoirs*, Penguin, 1992, p. 48.

3 Ibid.

4 Ibid., p. 46.

5 Ibid., p. 103.

6 Ibid., p. 46.

7 KA to PL, 24 April 1948 (Bodleian).

8 KA to PL, 11 May 1948 (Bodleian); this letter appears in an abridged form, with this passage omitted, in Zachary Leader, ed., *The Letters of Kingsley Amis*, HarperCollins, 2000, p. 171.

9 Monica Jones, a friend of Larkin's from Leicester, where she taught English at the university.

10 KA to PL, 21 May 1948 (Bodleian).

11 *Memoirs*, p. 103.

12 Ibid.

13 KA to PL, 11 May 1948 (Bodleian).

14 *Memoirs*, p. 103.

15 Ibid., p. 101.

16 Al Alvarez, *Where Did It All Go Right?* Bloomsbury 2002, p. 126.

17 *Memoirs*, p. 103.

18 Ibid., p. 101.

19 Ibid., p. 103.

20 This title appears in a letter by Amis to the Faculty Board, 19 October 1948 (Oxford University Archives). The letter, forwarded to Lord David Cecil to relay to the Board, requests permission to switch supervisors.

21 Oxford English Faculty Board to KA, 17 March 1948; quoted in Leader, ed., *LKA*, p. 199n.

22 Alvarez, *Where Did It All Go Right?* p. 127.

23 Quoted in Francis Mulhern, *The Moment of 'Scrutiny'*, Verso, 1979, p. 300.

24 Ibid., p. 298.

25 Alvarez, *Where Did It All Go Right?* p. 127.

26 Quoted in Mulhern, *The Moment of 'Scrutiny'*, p. 301.

27 *Memoirs*, p. 103.

28 Ibid., p. 101.

29 Ibid., p. 104.

30 Interview with Graham Turner, 'Kingsley Amis and Those Uncertain Feelings', *Sunday Telegraph* magazine, 28 September 1986.

31 *Memoirs*, p. 71.

32 Alan Ross, *Blindfold Games*, Harvill, 1986, p. 144.

33 Philip Larkin, *Jill*, Faber and Faber, 1975, p. 18.

34 Ibid., p. 19.

35 Quoted in Andrew Motion, *Philip Larkin: A Writer's Life*, Faber and Faber, 1993, p. 88.

36 *Memoirs*, p. 74.

37 PL, *Jill*, p. 18.

38 I owe this comment to David Whittle, at work on a biography of Montgomery. Armstrong communicated it to Whittle in a letter of 10 January 1990.

39 *Memoirs*, p. 72.

40 KA to PL, 6 December 1947 (Bodleian); this letter appears in an

abridged form, with this passage omitted, in Leader, ed., *LKA*, p. 147. The description in the *Memoirs*, p. 73, is different, involving composers not dramatists, the older one decent and the younger one pushy.

41 *Memoirs*, p. 76.
42 KA to PL, 9 January 1950; this letter appears in an abridged form, with this passage omitted, in Leader, ed., *LKA*, p. 226.
43 The draft can be found in the Huntington, dated June 1949.
44 *Memoirs*, p. 73.
45 Ibid.
46 See KA to PL, 22 June 1948 (Bodleian).
47 KA to PL, 23 July 1948 (Bodleian).
48 KA to PL, 27 October 1948 (Bodleian).
49 KA to PL, 18 November 1948 (Bodleian).
50 KA to PL, 23 January 1949 (Bodleian).
51 Neither the money nor the book ever materialised.
52 *Lucky Jim*, Penguin 1976, p. 14.
53 Ibid., p. 229.
54 Not lungs, as *Memoirs* and Jacobs's *Biography* suggest; the problem with lungs happens later in Wain's life.
55 John Wain, *Sprightly Running: Part of an Autobiography*, Papermac, 1965, p. 138.
56 Ibid., p. 188.
57 KA to PL, 15 October 1946 (Bodleian).
58 *Memoirs*, p. 42.
59 Ibid.
60 KA to PL, 4 April 1948 (Bodleian).
61 KA to PL, 23 April 1949 (Bodleian).
62 KA to PL, 27 February 1952 (Bodleian).
63 KA to PL, 23 October 1952 (Bodleian).
64 Ibid.
65 KA to PL, 3 March 1953 (Bodleian).
66 *Memoirs*, p. 108.
67 Michie was reading Classics.
68 KA to PL, 18 November 1948 (Bodleian).
69 *Memoirs*, p. 108.
70 Ibid., p. 109.
71 Obituary, *London Review of Books*, 16 November 1995.
72 KA and James Michie, eds., *Oxford Poetry 1949*, Basil Blackwell, 1949, p. 3.
73 Ibid., p. 4.
74 *Memoirs*, p. 46.
75 KA to PL, 27 October 1948 (Bodleian).
76 See KA to PL, 9 November 1948 (Bodleian).
77 KA to PL, 27 October 1948 (Bodleian).
78 KA to PL, 2 November 1948 (Bodleian).
79 KA to PL, 11 May 1948.

80 KA to PL, undated (Bodleian); a date of June 1948 in square brackets and in Amis's hand has been added subsequently.
81 See Hilly Amis to Larkin, undated letter (Bodleian), also written some time in June 1948.
82 *Memoirs*, p. 48.
83 KA to PL, 23 July 1948 (Bodleian).
84 KA to PL, 22 March 1948 (Bodleian).
85 KA to PL, 29 March 1948 (Bodleian).
86 He had been plagued with cysts and boils.
87 KA to PL, 23 July 1948 (Bodleian).
88 KA to PL, 20 May 1948 (Bodleian).
89 KA to PL, 29 July 1948 (Bodleian).
90 KA to PL, 20 August 1948 (Bodleian).
91 KA to PL, 14 September 1948 (Bodleian).
92 This quote and the ones to follow are from a letter to the author, 26 January 1999.
93 KA to PL, 28 May 1948 (Bodleian).
94 KA to PL, 29 September 1948 (Bodleian).
95 KA to PL, 15 October 1948 (Bodleian).
96 *Memoirs*, p. 56.
97 Monica's colleagues in the English Department at Leicester.
98 KA to PL, 20 August 1948 (Bodleian).
99 PL to KA, 2 November 1948 (Bodleian).
100 *Memoirs*, p. 57.
101 Ibid., p. 50.
102 Ibid., p. 49.
103 KA to PL, 5 December 1948 (Bodleian).
104 These recollections derive from interviews with Hilly and Mavis Nicholson.
105 KA to PL, 9 May 1949.
106 Hilary Amis to PL, 30 December 1949 (Bodleian).
107 KA to PL, 4 April 1949 (Bodleian).
108 KA to PL, 22 June 1949 (Bodleian).
109 KA to PL, 20 March 1949 (Bodleian)
110 KA to PL, 25 May 1949 (Bodleian).
111 Presumably not Bedford College.
112 KA to PL, 6 September 1949 (Bodleian).
113 Ibid.
114 KA to PL, 6 October 1949 (Bodleian).
115 Ibid.
116 *Memoirs*, p. 120.
117 KA to Marguerite Cutforth, 7 January 1957 (BBC Written Archives Centre, Caversham Park, Reading).
118 KA to PL, 17 October 1949 (Bodleian).
119 *Lucky Jim*, p. 245.
120 Hilly burned them.

121 See, for example, KA to PL, 17 October 1949 (Bodleian).
122 KA to PL, 29 October 1949 (Bodleian).
123 KA to PL, 22 November 1949 (Bodleian).
124 KA to PL, 23 December 1949 (Bodleian).

CHAPTER 9

Swansea

1 Kingsley Amis, *Memoirs*, Penguin, 1992, p. 127. Measuring relative currency values is tricky, partly because the choice of commod-
   ities, public goods and services available at different historical
   periods is so different. The EH.Net website (http://eh.net/hmit),
   supported by the Economic History Association, allows one to
   compare relative values of the £ from 1830 to 2004 ('hmit' stands
   for 'how much is that?'). Very roughly, using average earnings as
   a measure for computing the relative value of wages, salaries or
   other income, Amis's 1949 salary of £300 plus child benefit would
   be the equivalent of £24,000 in 2004, the closest the website comes
   to the present. This confirms Amis's estimate in the *Memoirs* and
   seems a plausible figure. Using the same measure, Hilly's £3 a
   week from her mother's inheritance would equal £177 a week in
   2004.
2 KA to PL, 27 January 1950 (Bodleian).
3 Margaret's recollections are from a letter to Dale Salwak, 28
   December 1987 (recipient).
4 Hilly in interview with Deborah Ross, 'The Old Devil Upstairs',
   Daily Mail, 16 March 1992.
5 If this essay has been published, I have not been able to trace it. It
   exists in manuscript in the Huntington (AMS545).
6 Interview with Cynthia Kee, 'Flavour of the Month', *London Portrait
   Magazine*, December 1986.
7 *Memoirs*, p. 126.
8 Ibid., p. 123.
9 KA to PL, 22 November 1949 (Bodleian).
10 These figures are from the published 'Twenty-ninth Annual Report'
   of the Council of the University College of Swansea. The report was
   presented to the Court of Governors at the Annual General Meeting
   of the Council, held on 18 November 1949.
11 According to his colleague Sam Dawson.
12 *Memoirs*, p. 123.
13 According to Esmond Cleary, another colleague, a lecturer in
   economics.
14 According to an untitled and unpublished essay by Clive Gammon,
   written in November 1995, shortly after Amis's death. Gammon intended
   the article to be published in the *Mail on Sunday* magazine (*You*), which

had previously published his article 'The Old Devil as a Young Man', in the 5 April 1992 issue. I possess a copy of the unpublished article.

15 Ibid.

16 John Morgan, 'The Amis Industry', in the *Western Mail*, 25 November 1986.

17 *Memoirs*, p. 125.

18 Quoted in Eric Jacobs, *Kingsley Amis: A Biography*, Hodder and Stoughton, 1995, p. 127.

19 Thomas got his job as Professor of English in 1921, at thirty-one, after a stint at the University of Saskatchewan. Fulton, who would never have hired him (they did not get on, according to Dawson: Fulton was 'too energetic' for Thomas, Thomas too laid-back for Fulton), was appointed only two years before Amis, in 1947, from Balliol College, Oxford, where he had been Fellow in Politics. Though Fulton had published scholarly articles on political philosophy, he made his name as an administrator rather than an academic.

20 According to Esmond Cleary.

21 KA to PL, 6 February 1950 (Bodleian).

22 *Memoirs*, p. 123.

23 Ibid., p. 122.

24 Ibid.

25 Clive Gammon, 'The Old Devil as a Young Man', *You* magazine, *Mail on Sunday*, 5 April 1992.

26 *That Uncertain Feeling*, Penguin, 1985, p. 143.

27 KA to PL, 11 October 1950 (Bodleian).

28 *That Uncertain Feeling*, p. 162.

29 KA to PL, 29 October 1949 (Bodleian).

30 According to Esmond Cleary.

31 *Memoirs*, p. 121.

32 Ibid., p. 122.

33 KA to PL, 29 October 1949.

34 Ibid.

35 Ibid.; this letter, located in the Bodleian, appears in an abridged form, with this passage excised, in Zachary Leader, ed., *The Letters of Kingsley Amis*, HarperCollins, 2000, pp. 218–222.

36 KA to PL, 27 January 1950 (Bodleian).

37 Ibid.

38 KA to PL, 18 February 1950 (Bodleian).

39 KA to PL, 9 April 1950 (Bodleian).

40 Ibid.

41 See Philip Larkin, *Trouble at Willow Gables and Other Fictions*, ed. James Booth, Faber and Faber, 2002, pp. 469–482.

42 KA to PL, 12 May 1950 (Bodleian).

43 Ibid.

44 'Dixon and Christine', the first version of *Lucky Jim*.

45 KA to PL, 12 May 1950 (Bodleian).

46 KA to PL, 11 October 1950 (Bodleian).

47 Ibid.

48 KA, 'The Curious Elf: A Note on Rhyme in Keats', *Essays in Criticism* 1: 2 (April 1951), pp. 189–192.

49 KA to PL, 28 October 1950 (Bodleian).

50 KA to PL, 12 November 1950 (Bodleian).

51 KA to PL, 8 January 1951 (Bodleian).

52 Its revised title was 'English Non-dramatic Poetry 1850–1900 and the Victorian Reading Public'.

53 *Memoirs*, p. 106.

54 Ibid., pp. 105–106.

55 KA, 'English Non-dramatic Poetry 1850–1900 and the Victorian Reading Public', p. 1 (a copy of the thesis is deposited in the Kingsley Amis Collection, Ransom Center).

56 Ibid., pp. 1–2.

57 Here are some instances from the first two chapters, though diffident touches occur throughout: Dante Gabriel Rossetti 'exemplifies best of all such value as there may be in my hypothesis' (p. 7); 'this argument, since response to it will depend on personal conviction, cannot be stressed' (p. 24); 'Without the self-infliction of technicalities, it may be suggested that' (p. 26); 'It seems best to conclude that the data from the two anthologies do not directly contradict the existence of an outer audience for Rossetti' (p. 31); 'to my mind it [the chapter on Rossetti] illustrates best both the weaknesses and the possible strength of my main hypothesis' (p. 36); 'negatives are hard to prove, but a deduction, even at this stage, that Meredith did not much bother with his friends' opinions of his verse seems hard to avoid' (p. 41); 'a few other facts about Meredith, not easily placed under any main heading, may yet be relevant' (p. 56).

58 Sometimes Amis goes out of his way to point up weaknesses. 'Although a number of facts have been presented,' he writes in the conclusion to the chapter on Swinburne, 'there have also been some attempts to make deductions from them, of which several are precarious' (p. 113). At other times he concedes exceptions so freely that it is unclear what he's arguing, especially as the concessions are invariably sensible and intelligent.

59 Ibid., p. 1.

60 Ibid., p. 144.

61 Claude K. Hyder, *Swinburne's Literary Career and Fame*, Duke University Press, 1933.

62 *Memoirs*, p. 105. In the thesis, Amis writes: 'This subject is very fully documented by an excellent piece of research by the American scholar Claude K. Hyder, and by Thomas J. Wise's bibliography, which might have been written with the present purpose in view' (p. 104).

63 *Memoirs*, p. 105.

64 KA, 'English Non-dramatic Poetry', p. 35.

65 J. B. Bamborough to the author, 18 July 2004.
66 Jacobs, *Biography*, p. 143.
67 Hilly Amis to PL, 12 January 1951 (Bodleian).
68 KA to PL, 26 January 1951 (Bodleian).
69 Martin Amis, *Experience*, Jonathan Cape, 2000, p. 132.
70 According to Mavis Nicholson.
71 KA to PL, 8 January 1951 (Bodleian).

CHAPTER 10

Making *Lucky Jim*

1   KA to PL, 26 January 1951 (Bodleian).
2   KA to PL, 12 March 1951 (Bodleian).
3   'What Became of Jane Austen?', *Spectator*, 4 October 1957; reprinted in *What Became of Jane Austen? And Other Questions*, Penguin, 1981, p. 14.
4   'Dark Fears in Wimpole Street', review of Donald Thomas, *Robert Browning: A Life Within Life*, *Observer*, 29 August 1982, reprinted in *The Amis Collection: Selected Non-Fiction 1954–1990*, Penguin, 1991, p. 183.
5   'The Cockney's Homer', *Spectator*, 1 January 1956; reprinted in *WBJA*, p. 31.
6   'What Became of Jane Austen?', *WBJA*, p. 12.
7   'Dark Fears in Wimpole Street', *AC*, p. 183.
8   'The Cockney's Homer', *WBJA*, p. 31.
9   *The North Ship* was Larkin's first volume of poems, published in 1945 by Fortune Press, London.
10 John Betjeman, *Old Lights for New Chancels*, John Murray, 1940.
11 Henry Green, *Living*, J.M. Dent and Sons, London and Toronto, 1929.
12 KA to PL, 8 January 1951; on 12 March Amis wrote to Larkin that the Arts Council now wanted to turn the opera into a ballad opera, which meant spoken dialogue. This change Amis approved, since his libretto would 'be audible instead of drowned by a lot of filthy music' (Bodleian).
13 Money is an important theme in the libretto: Sir Thomas loves the house but is too poor to keep it; if only his wife would ask her wealthy father for a loan, 'a mere particle of your father's vast fortune would solve my difficulty overnight' (p. 6).
14 KA to PL, 26 January 1951 (Bodleian).
15 'Amberley Hall', p. 10.
16 That the Town is rejected may owe something to Amis's recent disappointments in Oxford (just as the prospect of a saving loan from Phyllis's father may owe something to Hilly's recent windfall):

ALL: Farewell to Town, the gimcrack paradise
Of shoddy pleasure, yawn-provoking vice;
Our witty friends would say we mean
That competition's keen.
The pikes of little streams we'd rather be
Than exiled minnows struggling in the sea;

THOMAS: On food,
FREDERICK: on books,
PHYLLIS: on wifely arts.
ALL: Henceforth we set our hearts.

This message to your notice we would bring,
That love, like marriage, is a splendid thing;
Sweet pair, but money, don't forget,
Can make them sweeter yet.

(p. 13)

17 The fate of 'Amberley Hall' was complicated. On 12 June 1951, Amis wrote to Larkin that Montgomery had still not set all the words: 'BECAUSE HE WAS WRITING FLITHY FILM SCORES AND STING-KING STORIES FOR THE POPULAR PRESS'. In addition, Montgomery told Amis that the Arts Council didn't like the libretto: by ballad opera they had meant 'song then six lines of conventional dialogue then duet of eight lines of c.d. then song, do you see. Our idea was the same, except that we read "150" for "six" and "200" for "eight".' The whole sorry business 'ground me greatly, and made me think I was a fail, yer'.

18 See D. L. Ross of the BBC to KA, 28 March 1952; KA OKs the fee on 4 April; in his letter Ross says of their programme: 'we would like to include in this [*Apollo in the West*] the ballad opera AMBERLEY HALL (4'25")' (BBC Written Archives Centre, Caversham Park, Reading). If this means four minutes and twenty-five seconds then clearly they've used only some of 'Amberley Hall', but the letter doesn't say they'll be using only some of it. In *Memoirs*, Penguin, 1992, Amis says 'it was never performed that I heard of' (p. 74).

19 John Morgan, 'The Amis Industry', *Western Mail*, 25 November 1986.

20 KA to PL, 12 March 1951 (Bodleian).

21 Ibid.

22 KA to PL, 12 June 1951.

23 Martin Amis, *Experience*, Jonathan Cape, 2000, p. 104.

24 Ibid., pp. 104–105.

25 KA to PL, 6 April 1951 (Bodleian).

26 KA to PL, 8 April 1951 (Bodleian).

27 KA to PL, 3 November 1951 (Bodleian).

28 See PL to Winifred Arnott, 27 December 1951.

29 There were rumours of a job in the English Department at Queen's University, Belfast.

30 See KA to PL, 7 January 1952 (Bodleian).

31 'The Legacy'.

32 *Jill* and *A Girl in Winter*.

33 An utterance peculiar to Bertrand in *Lucky Jim*, a version of 'you see'.

34 KA to PL, 18 January 1952 (Bodleian).

35 KA to PL, 7 February 1952 (Bodleian).

36 KA to PL, 10 March 1952 (Bodleian).

37 KA to PL, 27 February 1952.

38 Ibid.

39 See *Lucky Jim*, Penguin, 1976, p. 87.

40 KA to PL, 18 June 1952; for the second rejection see KA to PL, 23 June 1952 (Bodleian).

41 Belfast itself and/or its English Department, neither of which impressed him much, may also figure here. See KA to PL, 29 April 1951.

42 See KA to PL, 24 July 1952.

43 'Real and Made-up People', *Times Literary Supplement*, 27 July 1973, reprinted in *AC*, p. 5; Dixon, of course, is the fellow who doesn't fit in; Welch the boring boss; Margaret Peel ('Veronica Beale' in 'Dixon and Christine') the boring girl; Christine Callaghan ('Christine Reardon' in 'Dixon and Christine') the nice girl; and Bertrand Welch the someone else whose property she is. So far, so similar. The manuscript of 'Dixon and Christine' is located in the Kingsley Amis Collection in the Ransom Center.

44 In *Lucky Jim*, Michie's Christian name is simply omitted, as are the names of the Principal of the college ('W. Bardwell Sharrock', whose surname was borrowed from Larkin's tutorial partner at St John's, Roger Sharrock), the town where the college is located ('Hamberton' in Yorkshire, used previously in 'The Legacy' and 'Who Else Is Rank'), the small town outside it where the Welches live (Pusebridge) and its pub (The Fish).

45 'Dixon and Christine', p. 8.

46 The business magnate is Sir George Wettling, MP, the richest man in Hamberton, chairman of the college Senate, patron of the arts and owner of the local art gallery. Another character who makes no actual appearance in 'Dixon and Christine' is the sinister Charles Catchpole, who is said to have precipitated Veronica/Margaret's suicide attempt. It is Teddy Wilson, a young economist on a year's visit from Princeton (Esmond Cleary had recently been on exchange to Princeton), who reports Catchpole's revelations.

47 Either they sleep together, Dixon has decided, or 'agree to abandon all sexual interest in each other' ('Dixon and Christine', p. 19).

48 Ibid., p. 136.

49 Ibid., p. 146.

50 For KA on PL's contribution to *Lucky Jim*, see *Memoirs*, p. 57.

51 PL's comment is from 'An Interview with *Paris Review*' (1982), reprinted in *Required Writing: Miscellaneous Pieces 1955–1982*, Faber and Faber, 1983, p. 59.

52 KA to PL, 24 July 1951 (Bodleian); this letter appears in an abridged form, with this passage excised, in Zachary Leader, ed., *The Letters of Kingsley Amis*, HarperCollins, 2000, p. 228.

53 KA to PL, 23 October 1952.

54 KA to PL, 9 June 1949.

55 KA to PL, 5 August 1952 (Bodleian). Other proposed additions included Dixon's decision to offer his students a 'special subject' in History (which to his horror only Michie ends up taking) and making L.S. ('Lazy Sod') Caton 'the editor of a phoney learned journal'.

56 KA to PL, 21 August 1952 (Bodleian).

57 Christopher Hitchens, 'The Man of Feeling', *Atlantic Monthly*, May 2002, p. 107.

58 Larkin's handwritten comments on this revised draft of 'Dixon and Christine' (not yet *Lucky Jim*) come from the manuscript in the Ransom Center. The manuscript is incomplete, missing twenty-four pages (among them the first page, which might have contained a title). The quoted comments come from pp. 87, 74, 14.

59 KA to PL, 4 October 1952 (Bodleian); this letter appears in an abridged form, with this passage excised, in Leader, ed., *LKA*, p. 293.

60 'Dixon and Christine', pp. 169, 64, 77, 81.

61 Ibid., p. 16.

62 Previously he had considered calling it 'The Man of Feeling', since 'Dixon has more to feel about than he had before', KA to PL, 11 August 1952.

63 See Harry Ritchie, *Success Stories: Literature and the Media in England, 1950–1959*, Faber and Faber, 1988, p. 8.

64 Quoted in Blake Morrison, *The Movement: English Poetry and Fiction of the 1950s*, Oxford University Press, 1980, p. 43.

65 Ibid., p. 44.

66 Quoted in Ritchie, *Success Stories*, p. 100.

67 'An Interview with *Paris Review*', reprinted in PL, *Required Writing*, p. 59.

68 PL to Judy Egerton, 20 February 1957; see also Andrew Motion, *Philip Larkin: A Writer's Life*, Faber and Faber, 1993, p. 165.

69 That is, the glasses were large and black-rimmed.

70 Motion, *Philip Larkin: A Writer's Life*, p. 167.

71 *Lucky Jim*, p. 38.
72 Ibid., p. 76.
73 Ibid., p. 11.
74 Ibid., p. 23.
75 Ibid., p. 25.
76 See Jacobs, *Biography*, p. 146.
77 Motion, *Philip Larkin: A Writer's Life*, p. 169.
78 *Lucky Jim*, p. 10.
79 Anthony Powell, *Journals 1982–1986*, Heinemann, 1995, pp. 268–269.
80 Dale Salwak, 'An Interview with Kingsley Amis', *Contemporary Literature*, Winter 1975, reprinted in Robert H. Bell, ed., *Critical Essays on Kingsley Amis*, G. K. Hall, 1998, p. 271.
81 *Lucky Jim*, p. 201.
82 Ibid., p. 202.
83 Motion, *Philip Larkin: A Writer's Life*, p. 169.
84 KA to PL, 4 October 1952 (Bodleian), in the passage omitted from Leader, ed., *LKA*, p. 293.
85 See Anthony Gardner's account of Larkin's unpublished correspondence with Monica Jones, in 'What Will Survive of Us Is Love', *Sunday Times* magazine, 21 November 2004.
86 KA to PL, 12 May 1951; this letter appears in an abridged form, with this passage excised, in Leader, ed., *LKA*, p. 260.
87 Winifred's initials.
88 KA to PL, 23 October 1952; this letter appears in an abridged form, with this passage excised, in Leader, ed., *LKA*, p. 296.
89 KA to PL, 12 December 1951 (Bodleian).
90 KA to PL, 6 November 1952; this letter appears in an abridged form, with this passage excised, in Leader, ed., *LKA*, p. 297.
91 KA to PL, 8 September 1952. 'You tell Monica that I'm cutting at some frightful Welsh girl, and I'll tell Margaret [Vakil] that I'm cutting at some frightful Leicester girl.'
92 Motion, *Philip Larkin: A Writer's Life*, p. 239.
93 'Dixon and Christine', p. 55.
94 *Lucky Jim*, p. 51.
95 Motion, *Philip Larkin: A Writer's Life*, p. 165; Motion has Larkin meeting Monica Jones early in 1947, but according to Anthony Thwaite, in a personal communication (24 January 2006), Jones told him she first met Larkin in their first term at Oxford, hence in autumn 1946.
96 PL to Patsy Strang, 6 July 1953.
97 See PL, *Trouble at Willow Gables and Other Fictions*, ed. James Booth, Faber and Faber, 2002, p. 373n; for the earlier notebook reference about Augusta's development see p. 450; for Booth's discussion of the novel's relation to *Lucky Jim* see pp. xli–xliii.
98 Ibid., p. 451.
99 Ibid., p. 423.
100 For both the charge and the claim that Larkin meant it seriously

see Janice Rossen, 'Philip Larkin and *Lucky Jim*', *Journal of Modern Literature* 22: 1 (Fall 1998), pp. 147–164.

101 KA to PL, 13 January 1953.

102 Larkin's provisional title for 'the Leicester one' was 'A New World Symphony', which is the title James Booth adopts in *Trouble at Willow Gables and Other Stories*. Booth's edition prints both the novel's incomplete manuscript and Larkin's Workbook Outlines for it.

CHAPTER 11

Fame and Friendship

1 He thought it 'vulgar and anti-cultural', Eric Jacobs, *Kingsley Amis: A Biography*, Hodder and Stoughton, 1995, p. 155; see also KA to Harry Ritchie, 28 January 1987: 'Hilary Rubinstein told me the other day that Gollancz didn't read Lucky Jim until the attention it had attracted made him think perhaps he better had.'

2 Interview with Pearson Phillips, 'How the Angry Brigade Got Lucky', *Observer*, 17 September 1978.

3 KA to PL, 23 January 1954.

4 KA to Hilary Rubinstein, 2 September 1955.

5 KA to Hilary Rubinstein, 20 July 1953.

6 KA to PL, 17 September 1953: '*Jim* may not come out until *January* now. They are waiting for His cock to make his next couple of choices. I suppose I can't really call them sods for this though I'd like to.'

7 Hilary Rubinstein to KA, 14 August 53 (Gollancz).

8 KA to PL, 17 September 1953.

9 Andrew Motion, *Philip Larkin: A Writer's Life*, Faber and Faber 1993, p. 242.

10 See KA to PL, 26 May 1953.

11 KA to PL, 3 August 1953 (Bodleian).

12 KA to PL, 14 March 1954.

13 KA to Hilary Rubinstein, 17 July 1953. The two sentences Massingham objected to were: 'In spite of the ravages brought by his headache, Dixon felt happier as he wondered what foods would this morning afford concrete proofs of the Welches' prosperity', and 'He remembered his father, who until the war had always worn stiff white collars, being reproved by the objurgatory jeweller as excessively "dignant" in demeanour'.

14 Blake Morrison, *The Movement: English Poetry and Fiction of the 1950s*, Oxford University Press, 1980, p. 42.

15 Ibid., p. 46.

16 This letter by Fraser appeared in the *New Statesman* on 1 August 1953.

17 'A Conversation with Ian Hamilton', in PL, *Further Requirements:*

Interviews, Broadcasts, Statements and Book Reviews, ed. Anthony Thwaite, Faber and Faber, 2001, p. 20.

18 Pritchett's summation was entitled 'First Stop Reading!'

19 A Larkin poem, reprinted in *Collected Poems*, ed. Anthony Thwaite, Faber and Faber, 1988, p. 134.

20 Davie's 'thing' was a poem entitled '"Surprised by Joy": Dr. Johnson at Ranelagh'.

21 W. R. Rodgers, like Kathleen Raine, a poet disapproved of by 'Empsonian' types.

22 KA to PL, 27 November 1953 (Bodleian).

23 'Wild Ones' was the Gunn parody.

24 KA to PL, 24 September 1956; this letter appears in an abridged form, with this passage excised, in Zachary Leader, ed., *The Letters of Kingsley Amis*, HarperCollins, 2000, p. 480.

25 See KA to PL, 27 December 1956.

26 KA to PL, 28 September 1956 (Bodleian).

27 The parody was 'At the Poetry Reading', by the pseudonymous Dr Aloysius C. Pepper, *Spectator*, 30 December 1955; Wain was suspected of writing it, which he denied; see Morrison, *The Movement*, p. 302.

28 For the parodies themselves, see appendix B in Leader, ed., *LKA*, pp. 1141–1145; for a more extended account of them see Zachary Leader, 'Raising Ron Cain: How Amis and Larkin Mocked Their Own Movement', *Times Literary Supplement*, 5 May 2000, pp. 13–14, which also prints the parodies.

29 Quoted from an email to the author, 26 February 2006.

30 See, for example, the suspicions of Denis Healey and Christopher Hitchens, in a profile of Robert Conquest by Andrew Brown, 'Scourge and Poet', *Guardian*, 15 February 2003.

31 Ibid.

32 *Memoirs*, Penguin, 1992, p. 140.

33 Ibid., p. 146.

34 Ibid., p. 141.

35 See Robert Conquest, 'Profile', in Dale Salwak, ed., *Kingsley Amis: In Life and Letters*, Macmillan, 1990, p. 11.

36 *Memoirs*, p. 142.

37 'Profile', in Salwak, ed., *Life and Letters*, p. 12.

38 *Memoirs*, p. 143.

39 'Profile', in Salwak, ed., *Life and Letters*, p. 12.

40 *Memoirs*, p. 144.

41 Ibid.

42 Ibid., p. 145; the dates of the fictitious cases, in KA's account in the *Memoirs*, are 1959 and 1962, which are impossible, since the joke took place in 1958. I've changed them so as not to distract the reader.

43 Letter from KA to the editor of the *Listener*, 6 November 1952.

44 Quoted in Morrison, *The Movement*, p. 52.

45 A description from an email to the author, 26 February 2006. Tatiana was to live on until 1982, when she committed suicide; see Leader, ed., *LKA*, p. 936n.

46 Quoted in Leader, ed., *LKA*, p. 1165.

47 This old guard was mostly unspecified, but was understood to include, *inter alia*, Dylan Thomas and his followers, Raine and the neo-Symbolists, Sitwell, Rodgers, George Barker, and the so-called 'New Apocalypse' poets of the 1941 anthology *The White Horseman*, edited by J. F. Hendry and Henry Treece.

48 Phillip Oakes, *At the Jazz Band Ball*, André Deutsch, 1983, p. 223 (I owe this reference to Harry Ritchie, *Success Stories: Literature and the Media in England, 1950–1959*, Faber and Faber, 1988, p. 17); Hartley's review appeared on the same day, 10 July, as a *TLS* review of *Springtime*, in which the anonymous reviewer repeated Fraser's and Fletcher's line in the introduction about the new 'academic' poets, singling out Amis, Wain, Alvarez and Davie as examples. Hartley, then, was hardly alone in his campaign.

49 KA to PL, 19 February 1954.

50 John Pope-Hennessy (1913–94) was an art historian and museum curator, at the time Keeper at the Department of Architecture and Sculpture, Victoria and Albert Museum; James Pope-Hennessy (1916–74), a writer, had been literary editor of the *Spectator* from 1947 to 1949.

51 Hilary Rubinstein to KA, 17 February 1954 (Gollancz).

52 Anthony Powell, 'Booking Office', *Punch*, 3 February 1954.

53 John Betjeman, 'Amusing Story of Life at a Provincial University', *Daily Telegraph*, 5 February 1954.

54 Anonymous review, 'New Fiction: Standing Alone', *The Times*, 27 January 1954; John Metcalf, 'New Novels', *Spectator*, 29 January 1954.

55 Julian Maclaren-Ross, 'High Jinks and Dirty Work', *Sunday Times*, 24 January 1954.

56 KA to PL, 19 February 1954.

57 John Wain to KA, undated but probably written just after publication (Huntington).

58 Quoted in a profile by Godfrey Smith, 'The Golden, Gifted Mimic inside a Lucky Jim Jacket', *Sunday Times*, 28 September 1986.

59 KA to Hilary Rubinstein, 1 February 1954.

60 As reported to Hilary Rubinstein, 15 February 1954.

61 KA to PL, 19 February 1954.

62 KA to PL, 29 March 1954 (Bodleian).

63 KA to PL, 9 December 1953 (Bodleian).

64 KA to PL, 8 January 1954 (Bodleian).

CHAPTER 12
Uncertain Feelings

1 Interview with Eric Jacobs, 'A Knight of Many Pleasures', *Independent on Sunday*, 30 January 1994.
2 KA to Hilary Rubinstein, 8 May 1955.
3 KA to PL, 7 October 1953 (Bodleian).
4 KA to PL, 15 December 1953.
5 KA to PL, 27 February 1952.
6 Eric Jacobs, *Kingsley Amis, A Biography*, Hodder and Stoughton, 1995, p. 349.
7 Anthony Powell thought the novel only a 'slight improvement' on its immediate predecessor, *Difficulties with Girls*, 'tho' nothing like as good as *The Old Devils*' (*Journals 1990–1992*, Heinemann, 1998, p. 24).
8 4 March 1990, ibid., p. 17.
9 26 July 1991, ibid, p. 133.
10 *The Folks that Live on the Hill*, Penguin, 1991, p. 116.
11 Ibid., p. 61.
12 Ibid., p. 118.
13 Ibid., p. 122.
14 Ibid., p. 208.
15 Ibid., p. 233.
16 'The Lobster's Claw', *National Review*, 2 June 1989; a typewritten draft of this article can be found among the Amis papers in the Huntington.
17 Martin Amis, *Koba the Dread: Laughter and the Twenty Million*, Jonathan Cape, 2002, p. 268.
18 Robert H. Bell, 'Introduction: Kingsley Amis in the Great Tradition in Our Times', in Robert H. Bell, ed., *Critical Essays on Kingsley Amis*, G. K. Hall, 1998, p. 14.
19 *The Folks that Live on the Hill*, p. 69.
20 KA to PL, 3 August 1953 (Bodleian).
21 KA to Hilary Rubinstein, 17 August 1953.
22 KA to PL, 22 September 1953; this letter appears in an abridged form, with this passage excised, in Zachary Leader, ed., *The Letters of Kingsley Amis*, HarperCollins, 2000.
23 KA to PL, 29 December 1953 (Bodleian).
24 KA is referring here to *Lucky Jim*.
25 Anthony Powell, 'Amis Country', in Salwak, ed., *Kingsley Amis: In Life and Letters*, Macmillan, 1990, p. 6.
26 Paul Fussell, *The Anti-Egotist: Kingsley Amis, Man of Letters*, Oxford University Press, 1994, p. 66.
27 Karl Miller, *Dark Horses: An Experience of Literary Journalism*, Picador, 1998, p. 32.
28 Ibid., p. 34. Apropos the older literati, see Russell Fraser, 'Lucky Jim as I Remember Him', *The Southern Review* 32: 4 (Autumn

1996), p. 187: 'Cyril Connolly, an establishment figure in Kingsley's youth, heard at a party that these faces [Edith Sitwell, Evelyn Waugh, Sex Life in Ancient Rome] were worth seeing. "Would you mind just . . . ?" He asked in that elliptical way of theirs, leaving the rest of the question to you. Not wanting to show off but wanting to oblige, Kingsley performed as requested. "I don't think that's funny," Connolly said.'

29 In an untitled omnibus fiction review in *Spectator*, 21 May 1954.

30 *Spectator*, 8 October 1954.

31 Quoted in Harry Ritchie, *Success Stories: Literature and the Media in England, 1950–1959*, Faber and Faber, 1988, p. 67.

32 In addition to Amis, they were Wain, Elizabeth Jennings, Thom Gunn, John Holloway, Donald Davie, D. J. Enright and Iris Murdoch.

33 Anthony Powell, 'Amis Country', in Salwak, ed., *Life and Letters*, p. 9.

34 KA to PL, 14 March 1954.

35 KA to Victor Gollancz, 7 September 1955.

36 PL to Monica Jones, January 1955, quoted in Anthony Gardner's account of Larkin's unpublished correspondence with Monica Jones, in 'What Will Survive of Us Is Love', *Sunday Times* magazine, 21 November 2004.

37 Monica's dislike of Amis was kept under the surface, though doubtless sensed: when Amis saw her in Leicester on a visit in February 1954 he found her 'very amiable' (see KA to PL, 28 March 1954 (Bodleian)).

38 KA to PL, 15 September 1955 (Bodleian).

39 The plot of *That Uncertain Feeling* anticipates and may have influenced the plot of John Braine's *Room at the Top* (1957). Amis did not meet Braine until the summer of 1958, at a *Spectator* party on 30 July.

CHAPTER 13

'Fun'

1 KA to PL, 3 August 1953 (Bodleian).

2 KA to PL, 28 September 1953 (Bodleian).

3 *That Uncertain Feeling*, Penguin, 1985, pp. 228–229.

4 See 'Simple Truth His Utmost Skill', KA's review of Andrew Motion, *Philip Larkin: A Writer's Life*, in *Spectator*, 3 April 1993.

5 See James Booth's introduction to PL, *Trouble at Willow Gables and Other Fictions*, Faber and Faber, 2002, pp. vii–xlvii; also John Carey, 'The Two Philip Larkins', in Booth, ed., *New Larkins for Old: Critical Essays*, Macmillan, 2000, pp. 51–65.

6 'Revue Bar Strip', in Robert Conquest, *New and Collected Poems*, Century Hutchinson, 1988, pp. 83–84.

7 See KA to PL, 3 March 1953.

8 RC, *New and Collected Poems*, pp. 122–129.

9 *Take a Girl Like You*, Penguin, 1962, pp. 210–211.

10 Ibid., p. 212.

11 *That Uncertain Feeling*, p. 99.

12 *Take a Girl Like You*, pp. 211–212.

13 *That Uncertain Feeling*, p. 60.

14 Ibid., p. 93.

15 *Take a Girl Like You*, p. 244.

16 *That Uncertain Feeling*, pp. 160–161.

17 See KA to PL, 9 November 1957.

18 Al Alvarez, *Where Did It All Go Right?* Bloomsbury, 2002, p. 210.

19 KA to PL, 20 October 1954.

20 KA to PL, 27 December 1957 (Bodleian).

21 Alvarez, *Where Did It All Go Right?* p. 210.

22 *That Uncertain Feeling*, pp. 231–233.

23 Hence my dating of the poem as late 1950s or early 1960s, in what Conquest called his 'periods of bachelordom-in-practice in the UK', or 'c. August–December 1956, and c. March 1964' (see Zachary Leader, ed., *The Letters of Kingsley Amis*, HarperCollins, 2000, p. 1155).

24 *That Uncertain Feeling*, p. 60.

25 *Take a Girl Like You*, p. 69.

CHAPTER 14
Abroad

1 KA to Hilary Rubinstein, 28 March 1955 (Bodleian); for KA to PL, on the same day, see Zachary Leader, ed., *The Letters of Kingsley Amis*, HarperCollins, 2000, p. 425, which quotes only part of the letter.

2 KA to PL, 5 June 1955 (Bodleian).

3 KA to PL, 10 July 1955.

4 KA to PL, 28 July 1955.

5 KA to PL, 10 July 1955.

6 KA to PL, 28 July 1955.

7 Ibid.

8 KA to Esmond and Jean Cleary, undated (recipients). In place of a date, Amis heads the letter to the Clearys: 'This HQ closes Monchique 220800 Reopens Swansea 272000 approx'.

9 KA to PL, 10 July 1955.

10 See Eric Jacobs, *Kingsley Amis: A Biography*, Hodder and Stoughton, 1995, p. 211.

11 KA to PL, 28 July 1955.

12 'People thought I was attacking Europe. But I was attacking the people who like it,' Amis declared in an interview with Pat Williams,

'My Kind of Comedy', *Twentieth Century*, July 1961; 'I'm not grumpy about furrin parts, only about people being silly about them' (letter to the *Spectator*, 8 July 1955).

13 *Lucky Jim*, Penguin, 1976, p. 44.

14 KA to PL, 5 June 1955 (Bodleian).

15 *I Like It Here*, Penguin, 1968, p. 23.

16 KA to PL, 10 July 1955.

17 Ibid.

18 *I Like It Here*, p. 23.

19 Anthony Hartley, *A State of England*, Heinemann, 1963, p. 48, quoted in Blake Morrison, *The Movement: English Poetry and Fiction of the 1950s*, Oxford University Press, 1980, p. 60.

20 KA to RC, 31 July 1955 (recipient).

21 'Via Portello', quoted in Morrison, *The Movement*, p. 61.

22 According to D. J. Enright, letter to the author, 26 May 2002.

23 'Real and Made-up People', *Times Literary Supplement*, 27 July 1973, reprinted in *The Amis Collection: Selected Non-Fiction 1954–1990*, Penguin, 1991, p. 201.

24 Samuel Hynes, 'Random Events and Random Characters', *Commonweal*, 21 March 1958; G. S. Fraser, 'New Novels', *New Statesman*, 18 January 1958.

25 *I Like It Here*, p. 59.

26 Ibid., p. 13.

27 Ibid., p. 7.

28 Ibid., p. 16.

29 Ibid., p. 18.

30 Ibid., p. 20.

31 Ibid., p. 76.

32 Ibid., p. 80.

33 Ibid., pp. 101–102.

34 *Memoirs*, Penguin, 1992, p. 197.

35 As Amis told Eric Jacobs, *Biography*, p. 210.

36 *I Like It Here*, p. 76.

37 Ibid., p. 102.

38 Ibid., p. 15.

39 Ibid., p. 167.

40 Ibid., p. 168.

41 Ibid., p. 167.

42 Ibid., p. 173.

43 Dale Salwak, 'An Interview with Kingsley Amis', *Contemporary Literature* 16: 1 (Winter 1975), reprinted in Robert H. Bell, ed., *Critical Essays on Kingsley Amis*, G. K. Hall, 1998, p. 271.

44 *I Like It Here*, p. 187.

45 John McDermott, *Kingsley Amis: An English Moralist*, Macmillan, 1989, pp. 89–90.

46 F. R. Leavis, *The Great Tradition, George Eliot, Henry James, Joseph*

Conrad, Chatto and Windus, 1979, p. 3. For KA on Leavis's view of Fielding see 'The Necessity of Mr Murray', *Spectator*, 11 May 1956, a review of John Middleton Murry's *Unprofessional Essays*. For Amis, Fielding's moral preoccupation is different from Leavis's, and 'probably all the better for that, considering how readily [Leavis's] confuses itself . . . with intense moral fuss' (quoted in McDermott, *Kingsley Amis: An English Moralist*, p. 259).

47 *I Like It Here*, p. 132. That Amis admired Maugham, as Bowen seems to do here, is clear from his thank-you letter to him (for funding the prize). Amis wrote on 28 November 1955: 'You taught me that what mattered first was narrative, and that if one wanted to do anything extra one must first see to it that the story stood up on its own. Further, I learnt that subtlety is only valuable in the presence of recognisable outlines firmly and clearly drawn.'

48 See Bell, 'Introduction: Kingsley Amis in the Great Tradition in Our Times', in Bell, ed., *Critical Essays*, p. 2.

49 Ibid., pp. 2–3.

50 *Difficulties with Girls*, Penguin, 1999, p. 239.

51 Ibid., p. 238.

52 Ibid., p. 263.

53 *I Like It Here*, p. 180.

54 Somerset Maugham, *Ten Novels and Their Authors*, Vintage, 2001, pp. 34–35.

55 Ibid., p. 34.

56 Ibid., p. 39.

57 *I Like It Here*, p. 28.

58 Ibid., p. 162.

59 Ibid.

60 Ibid., p. 29.

61 This book would be *A Case of Samples: Poems 1946–1956* (1956).

62 KA to PL, 19 July 1956 (Bodleian).

63 See Gollancz to KA, 23 December 1957 (Gollancz) : 'I'm dreadfully sorry about your upset over the postponement of *I Like It Here*. Graham [Watson of Curtis Brown, Amis's agent] and I discussed it at great length, in relation to (a) the crowded Christmas season, (b) the "Punch" serialisation, (c) the difficulty of reprinting quickly enough in December; and we eventually agreed that it would be better to put it off till the first publication day in January.'

64 Alan Watkins, *A Short Walk Down Fleet Street: From Beaverbrook to Boycott*, Duckworth, 2001, p. 66.

65 Ibid., p. 40.

66 Ibid., p. 66.

67 Peregrine Worsthorne, *Tricks of Memory: An Autobiography*, Weidenfeld and Nicolson, 1993, p. 158.

68 KA to RC, 17 April 1956 (recipient).

69 KA to RC, 28 September 1956.

70 Bruce Montgomery to PL, 19 June 1956 (Bodleian).

71 Fairlie once arranged a cricket match between his London team and Cleary's local Swansea team, then completely forgot about it; the Swansea team had made an elaborate tea and arrangements for lodgings.

72 In *I Like It Here* the wait for the boat to Portugal is long enough 'for Sandra to fall off a bench on to her face' (p. 36).

73 The date of the obituary was 27 February 1990.

74 KA to PL, 4 November 1956.

75 For KA's reaction to the finished film see 27 December 1956 to PL: 'Have I told you about my film at all? In public I am all smiles about this, but in private, ah ha sir, a very different kettle of fish, I assure you ... They play for laughs all the time, you see. This wouldn't matter so much if they were certain to get them. Atkinson is a major, 4-star disaster, Bertrand is Terry-Thomas, Margaret is a minor, dimly-glimpsed irritation, about as important to Dixon as a touch of indigestion. There is an awful DOG they have brought in from nowhere, he's BERTRAND'S DOG, you see and he DOESN'T LIKE Bertrand, no, he LIKES DIXON, and he GETS IN THE WAY A LOT, and helps to MUCK UP THE LECTURE, and when Dixon gets pissed HE GETS PISSED TOO.'

76 KA to PL, 27 January 1957.

77 KA to PL, 8 March 1957 (Bodleian).

78 KA to PL, 9 September 1956.

79 Amis alludes to this trip to France in a postcard to Anthony Powell, 26 June 1957 (recipient).

CHAPTER 15

Widening Horizons

1 Stuart Thomas lived all his life in Swansea, excluding military service. For some years, though, he and his wife also kept a flat in Onslow Square in South Kensington, which helped them to stay in touch with Amis.

2 The friend was Michael Rush; the anecdote from Ralph Maud was told to me in a telephone conversation (not a formal interview) of February 1999.

3 She was born and spent the first eighteen years of her life in the Far East, where her Welsh father worked as a docks engineer in Shanghai. She then travelled by herself to Swansea to attend university, transferring after a year to Aberystwyth, where she read law. In 1938 she married Richard Edwards, an Anglicised Welshman, and they spent three years living in Hong Kong. Edwards was killed in the war, and after his death she and their two young children were evacuated to Australia, where she had maternal relations. It was while reading law at Aberystwyth that she became acquainted

with Stuart Thomas and he kept in touch with her during the war. When she returned to Wales he came to see her, they renewed their friendship, he proposed to her, she accepted and ten months later gave birth to a son, their only child together.

4 Rona Thomas eventually married the novelist John Williamson, just down from Oxford (where he'd read English at St John's, three years after Amis). Before going out with her, John Williamson had a dalliance with the Amises' friend Maggie Ashbury Vakil, later Aeron-Thomas. Like Elizabeth Gruffyd Williams, Maggie 'made what people in this part of the world still call a good marriage' (*That Uncertain Feeling*, Penguin, 1985, p. 24). John Aeron-Thomas was described by Eve Thomas as 'very nice, very formal, extremely Anglicised and rich; I have no picture of him drinking a pint of beer in a pub', unlike everyone else in her circle in the early years, women included.

5 *That Uncertain Feeling*, p. 41.

6 Ibid., p. 14.

7 Ibid., p. 56.

8 Ibid., p. 13.

9 Ibid., p. 194.

10 Dale Salwak, 'An Interview with Kingsley Amis,' *Contemporary Literature* 16: 1 (Winter 1975), reprinted in Robert H. Bell, ed., *Critical Essays on Kingsley Amis*, G. K. Hall, 1998, pp. 272–273.

11 KA to PL, 15 September 1955 (Bodleian).

12 Quoted in Harry Ritchie, *Success Stories: Literature and the Media in England, 1950–1959*, Faber and Faber, 1988, p. 70; see also Blake Morrison, *The Movement: English Poetry and Fiction of the 1950s* (Oxford University Press, 1980), pp. 58–59, for a discussion of class bias in early attitudes to Amis and the writers with whom he was grouped in the mid-1950s.

13 Ritchie, *Success Stories*, p. 69.

14 *That Uncertain Feeling*, p. 171.

15 John McDermott, *Kingsley Amis: An English Moralist*, Macmillan, 1989, p. 97.

16 For quotations from reviews of *Look Back in Anger* see: Kenneth Tynan, *Observer*, 3 May 1956; T. C. Worsley, *New Statesman*, 19 May 1956; Derek Grainger, *Financial Times*, 9 May 1956; John Bevan, *Time and Tide*, July 1956.

17 Quoted in Humphrey Carpenter, *The Angry Young Men: A Literary Comedy of the 1950s*, Allen Lane, 2002, p. 130.

18 See ibid., p. 137; 'surprised and unflattered' are Carpenter's words.

19 The one reference I have found to Hastings occurs in Amis's *Memoirs*, in a description of a lecture Amis gave in Prague in 1967 which poured 'brief doses of contempt on a David Storey or a Michael Hastings or two' (*Memoirs*, Penguin, 1992, p. 271).

20 KA's review of *The Outsider*, from which these quotations are taken, appeared under the title 'The Legion of the Lost', *Spectator*, 15 June

1956. The review is reprinted in *What Became of Jane Austen? And Other Questions*, Penguin, 1981, pp. 88–92.

21 Amis's draft is handwritten at the foot of Wilson's letter of 15 July 1956. The letter is among Amis's papers in the Huntington.

22 As Wilson points out, this interest did not surface in print until much later. See Carpenter, *The Angry Young Men*, p. x. As a matter of fact, Wilson claims that it was Amis who was the potential murderer. As he told Jasper Gerard in 'Still an Angry Man, Always an Outsider', an interview in the *Sunday Times*, 20 June 2004: 'Even though I tried very hard and thought we were friends, he always had this terrific resentment against me, so he actually tried to push me off this flat roof overlooking London once at Anthony Blond's.' 'Was he serious?' 'Perfectly serious. He was drunk and said, "Look, there's that bugger Wilson, I'm going to push him off," and John Wain . . . grabbed him. I was totally unaware this was going on behind me. He would probably have broken my neck because it was quite high.' The story is recounted in Colin Wilson's autobiography, *Dreaming to Some Purpose: The Autobiography of Colin Wilson*, New York, Random House/Century, 2004, p. 188, where it is dated 1968–69. Blond was not present when it is meant to have happened – the party was wild and drunken and he was taking another guest to hospital – but he heard about it (according to an interview Blond had with Richard Bradford in the summer of 2005). Wilson's three letters to Amis (of 15, 21 and 29 June 1956) are among Amis's papers in the Huntington.

23 See KA to Harry Ritchie, 28 January 1987. James Durham is the most likely 'psychiatrist pal', though Amis was not introduced to him until the late 1960s or early 1970s.

24 Tom Maschler, ed., *Declaration*, MacGibbon and Kee, 1957, pp. 8–9.

25 Al Alvarez, *Where Did It All Go Right?*, Bloomsbury, 2002, p. 153.

26 Ibid., p. 154.

27 *Memoirs*, p. 43. Amis later told Larkin that his combined English and American advances for *Lucky Jim* came 'to nearly twice John's' (KA to PL, 17 September 1953), which suggests he had an opportunity to get back at Wain.

28 *Memoirs*, p. 43. Not much later, Amis recounts, there was a third exchange:

> John said, 'You're always going on about what nice people the Welsh are. I'm afraid I didn't take much notice at first, but then just recently I've run into some of them and I rather agree with you. You ought to write a novel about them one of these days.'
>
> 'My second novel [published a couple of years earlier] is set in Wales,' I said, telling him nothing he had not known already.
>
> He gave me another sly wink. 'M'm, but, well, a proper one – you know' (ibid., p. 43).

29 KA to Hilary Rubinstein, 6 November 1953.

30 Salwak, 'An Interview with Kingsley Amis' (1975), reprinted in Bell, ed., *Critical Essays*, p. 268.

31 Ibid., p. 267.

32 'The Legion of the Lost', *WBJA*, p. 90.

33 Dixon is only brave in fantasy or for the purposes of plot (knocking Bertrand down towards the end of the novel is a comic contrivance, as realistic as Gore-Urquhart's job offer).

34 J. D. Scott, 'Britain's Angry Young Men', *Saturday Review*, 27 July 1957, p. 9.

35 *Lucky Jim*, Penguin, 1976, p. 136.

36 Ibid., p. 73.

37 KA to Harry Ritchie, 24 July 1986 (recipient).

38 In his introduction to *Declaration*, Maschler professed surprise at Amis's refusal to participate, 'in the light of the able Fabian pamphlet [he] penned' (p. 9).

39 KA, *Socialism and the Intellectuals*, Fabian Society, 1957, p. 1.

40 David Quinn to Dale Salwak, 31 March 1988 (recipient).

41 KA, *Socialism and the Intellectuals*, p. 1.

42 Ibid., p. 3.

43 Ibid.

44 Ibid., p. 6.

45 Ibid., p. 8.

46 Ibid., p. 6.

47 Ibid., p. 7.

48 Ibid., p. 11.

49 Ibid.

50 Eric Jacobs to Paul Wilkinson, 7 October 1993 (among the Jacobs papers in the Huntington); Wilkinson helped to organise the march.

51 KA, *Socialism and the Intellectuals*, p. 11.

52 Ibid., p. 12.

53 Ibid., p. 7.

54 See, for example, KA to PL, 24 September 1956 (Bodleian).

55 KA, *Socialism and the Intellectuals*, p. 12.

56 Ibid., p. 13.

57 Ibid.

58 Ibid., p. 1.

59 Ibid.

60 When Lambert, in his 6 January 1957 review of *Socialism and the Intellectuals*, criticises Amis for only 'reluctantly' or 'at last' admitting his identity as intellectual, he means as Thirties-style intellectual. In a letter of 13 January 1957 to the *Sunday Times*, Amis protested against Lambert's criticism: he 'explicitly' identifies himself as an intellectual three times in the pamphlet, 'the first time in the opening paragraph'. But these admissions are obscured by the exemption of academics and the focus on those who are self-employed.

Lambert has a point: where exactly Amis places himself among middle-class intellectuals is not always clear in the pamphlet.

61 David Quinn to Dale Salwak, 31 March 1988 (recipient).

62 Elizabeth Jane Howard, *Slipstream: A Memoir*, Macmillan, 2002, p. 412.

63 Peregrine Worsthorne, *Tricks of Memory: An Autobiography*, Weidenfeld and Nicolson, 1993, p. 168.

64 Nor were its contributors, as Karl Miller, its literary editor at the time, suggests, of a type: 'the journal had its snobs and its prigs, its party politicians, belletrists, university wits and Fleet Street show-offs' (*Dark Horses: An Experience of Literary Journalism*, Picador, 1998, p. 25).

65 Worsthorne, *Tricks of Memory*, p. 154.

66 *Memoirs*, p. 172.

67 Interview with Blake Morrison, 'Kingsley and the Women', *Observer*, 13 May 1984.

68 Worsthorne, *Tricks of Memory*, p. 153.

69 Ibid.

70 Bruce Montgomery to PL, 19 June 1956 (Bodleian).

71 The neighbour was Paul du Feu, three doors down, who was later married to Germaine Greer and then to Maya Angelou.

72 *Memoirs*, p. 74.

73 'Why You Won't Sell Me the Bright Lights: No – Not Even Now I've Hit the Jackpot', *Daily Express*, 14 September 1957.

74 KA to PL, 21 June 1953 (Bodleian).

75 KA to Hilary Rubinstein, 25 June 1953 (Gollancz). Even the pro-Swansea *Daily Express* article elicited a 'ballocking' from the Principal when it appeared, 'for allowing room for misinterpretation – by maniacs presumably' (KA to PL, 15 October 1957).

76 Glanmor Williams remembers asking him how he was getting on after a year or so as professor. 'I like being a professor,' he said, 'gives you a taste of blood, and there's no substitute for it.' Though he left the day-to-day running of the department to Isabel Westcott, otherwise he ruled 'with an iron hand' (Sam Dawson's phrase).

77 See Eric Jacobs, *Kingsley Amis: A Biography*, Hodder and Stoughton 1995, p. 139.

78 These figures are from ibid.; but see also KA to PL, 28 March 1955 (Bodleian): 'I look like staying here indefinitely, which I don't really mind especially not now I pull in £1100, including kids' allowances.'

79 According to Esmond Cleary.

80 'The Curious Elf: A Note on Rhyme in Keats', *Essays in Criticism* 1: 2 (April 1951), pp. 189–192; 'Emily-Coloured Primulas', a contribution to the 'Critical Forum' pages of *Essays in Criticism* 2:3 (July 1952), pp. 342–345; 'Communication and the Victorian Poets', *Essays in Criticism* 4:4 (October 1954), pp. 386–399.

81 KA to RC, 2 March 1955 (recipient).

82 KA to PL, 28 March 1955 (Bodleian).
83 Paul Fussell, *The Anti-Egotist: Kingsley Amis, Man of Letters*, Oxford University Press, 1994, p. 69.
84 Quoted in ibid., pp. 68, 67. For Amis's attacks on modernism see, for example, 'Phoenix Too Frequent', a review of D. H. Lawrence, *Selected Literary Criticism, Spectator*, 3 February 1956, reprinted in *WBJA*, pp. 48–51; 'Art and Craft', 13 July 1956, a review of John Lehmann, ed., *The Craft of Letters in England*, reprinted in *The Amis Collection: Selected Non-Fiction 1954–1990*, Penguin, 1991, pp. 19–22.
85 Richard Bradford, *Lucky Him: The Life of Kingsley Amis*, Peter Owen, 2001, p. 13.
86 For the dispute with Kinsley see also KA to PL, 19 April 1956.
87 KA to PL, 19 April 1956.
88 Quoted in Graham Turner, 'Kingsley Amis and Those Uncertain Feelings', *Sunday Telegraph*, 28 September 1986.
89 Martin Amis, *Experience*, Jonathan Cape, 2000, p. 221.
90 Ibid.
91 Ibid., p. 137.
92 Ibid., p. 156.
93 Ibid.
94 Ibid., p. 135.
95 Ibid., p. 148.
96 Bruce Montgomery to PL, 17 January 1956 (Bodleian).
97 KA to PL, 28 October 1977.
98 Jacobs, *Biography*, p. 235.
99 KA to Derek Gardner, 27 March 1957 (Rare Book Room, Pennsylvania State University).
100 *Memoirs*, p. 22.

CHAPTER 16

Princeton

1 KA to PL, 17 September 1953.
2 KA to PL, 24 February 1954 (Bodleian).
3 Elizabeth Jane Howard, *Slipstream: A Memoir*, London, Macmillan, 2002, p. 350.
4 KA to Elsa Wolfram, 15 January 1956.
5 According to Edward Cone, a composer and Professor of Music at Princeton, who served on the Gauss Committee and saw how Blackmur operated. 'Richard Blackmur would say: "These are the people that I have in mind for next year. Shall we get them?" And everybody would say yes' (from an interview with the author).
6 According to Edward Cone.
7 Whether McCallum lobbied for Amis over Princeton, or Blackmur asked him to sound Amis out is unclear, though they do seem to

have worked together on other occasions. 'I have heard privately but authoritatively that C. S. Lewis would like to spend a semester in America,' McCallum wrote to Blackmur on 30 September 1959, shortly after the Amises returned to Swansea. 'I will get in touch with Golding, through you if you prefer,' Blackmur wrote to McCallum on 19 June 1962, 'I agree that he would be awfully good, and would make a good follow-up to Amis and [Sean] O'Faolain' (these letters, as all subsequent letters written by or to R. P. Blackmur, can be found among the Blackmur papers, or the papers of Edmund Keeley, in the Department of Rare Books and Special Collections, Firestone Library, Princeton University). These writers were being offered what Amis was offered: a year teaching creative writing to selected Princeton undergraduates and in some cases an invitation to deliver Gauss Seminars.

8 Eric Jacobs, *Kingsley Amis: A Biography*, Hodder and Stoughton, 1995, p. 217.

9 *Jake's Thing*, Hutchinson, 1978, p. 153.

10 *Memoirs*, Penguin, 1992, pp. 193–194.

11 Ibid., p. 22.

12 KA to Roy P. Basler, 5 May 1958.

13 Cleanth Brooks to R. P. Blackmur, 6 August 1958 (Manuscript Division, Department of Rare Books and Special Collections, Princeton University Library).

14 *Memoirs*, p. 205.

15 This anecdote was told to me by Robert Conquest.

16 He seems to have got it in the end; how, though, is unclear and impossible to check, as Fulbright keeps no records pre-1964 and neither Hilly nor anyone from Princeton can remember.

17 KA to Violet and Anthony Powell, 29 July 1958.

18 KA to PL, 24 May 1958.

19 KA to PL, 30 July 1958.

20 *Memoirs*, p. 193.

21 Not 235, as Amis gives it in ibid., p. 194; 235 was the McAndrews' address.

22 PL to RC, 18 October 1958 (recipient).

23 *Memoirs*, p. 194.

24 Ibid.

25 This anecdote is from Mina Kempton.

26 The poem is published in Berryman's collection, *Love and Fame*, Farrar, Straus & Giroux, 1970.

27 'Oblique' is Al Alvarez, *Where Did It All Go Right?*, Bloomsbury, 2002, p. 165; 'gnomic' is Joseph Frank and 'cramped and literal' is Conrad Aiken, both quoted in Russell Fraser, *A Mingled Yarn, The Life of R.P. Blackmur*, Harcourt Brace Jovanovich, 1981, pp. 274 and 271 respectively. In an interview with the author, Paul Fussell called Blackmur 'a prose Wallace Stevens'.

28 Joseph Frank, 'Blackmur's Texts: An Introduction', in *The Legacy of R.P. Blackmur: Essays, Memoirs, Texts*, ed. Edward T. Cone, Joseph Frank and Edmund Keeley, Eccho Press, 1987, p. 188.

29 Edward Cone's phrase.

30 Edmund Keeley, 'Richard Palmer Blackmur', in Patricia H. Marks, ed., *Luminaries: Princeton Faculty Remembered*, Princeton University Press, 1996, p. 32.

31 Alvarez, *Where Did It All Go Right?*, p. 167; Alvarez's phrase 'moved out' is misleading, since she and Blackmur never lived together.

32 E. D. H. Johnson's word, in an admiring account of Blackmur, 'Seminars under R. P. Blackmur', in Cone *et al.*, eds., *The Legacy of R. P. Blackmur*, p. 152.

33 *Memoirs*, p. 210.

34 Keeley, 'Richard Palmer Blackmur,' in Marks, ed., *Luminaries*, p. 35.

35 Alvarez, *Where Did It All Go Right?*, p. 167.

36 *Memoirs*, p. 210.

37 Ibid. The rumour about Amis having 'one of the finest collections of science fiction' was untrue.

38 Ibid.

39 Ibid., p. 197.

40 This article was reprinted in the *Daily Princetonian*, 6 January 1959.

41 *Memoirs*, p. 197. For Amis's recommendation of Deford see KA to Mrs Edith Sewell (of Curtis Brown, New York), 21 May 1959; for the recommendation of Hirsch, see KA to Edith Haggard, 19 February 1959. Cindy Degner of Curtis Brown, to whom Haggard passed Deford's play, 'Mr First', tried to get it produced and almost succeeded. Degner's fiancé at the time was the agent Sterling Lord, Deford's agent for over forty years.

42 Julian Moynahan to Dale Salwak, 9 September 1986 (recipient); Amis had been sold to Princeton in part as a teacher. On 13 May 1958, in a Report to the Dean of the Faculty for Transmission to the President (now in the Seelye Mudd Library in Princeton), Blackmur described Amis as follows, under the heading 'Evaluation as a teacher': 'In answer to every enquiry made, Mr Amis is reported as an excellent and highly effective teacher in England. We know that he has a long training in public lecturing as well . . . Reports also indicate that he is a man of great charm and humour, and in our past experience with men teaching Creative Writing we have every reason to believe that he would add one more to our record of distinguished success.' Under the heading 'Evaluation as a scholar' Blackmur wrote: 'Mr Amis is not, so far as is known, what is usually called a scholar and for the teaching we have in mind for him this is perhaps not necessary. It is his novels and his poetry and his very high standing among younger English writers that led us to request

his appointment. If critical opinion about him is various, it varies around a norm of high praise.'

43 *Memoirs*, p. 197.
44 Ibid., p. 196.
45 Wick Dufford, 'Amis Joins Faculty Next Fall', *Daily Princetonian*, 23 May 1958 (the article was sub-headed 'Angry Young Man').
46 *Memoirs*, p. 201.
47 Ibid., p. 202.
48 Ibid., pp. 199–200.
49 Ibid., p. 69.
50 Ibid.
51 Ibid., p. 197.
52 This was William Jovanovich, president of Harcourt Brace.
53 KA to Violet and Anthony Powell, 29 October 1958.
54 *Memoirs*, p. 198.
55 Lichtenstein adds: 'Auden's apartment had six rooms and at least one extra bedroom and he stayed over.'
56 *Memoirs*, p. 210. Amis had met Macdonald in London 'and liked him sufficiently well as a drinking companion, but I came to realise that he really was a bit of an old ass, a New York ex-Trotskyist and just the chap to fall for the kind of popular social anthropology that was starting to become all the rage in the States just then' (p. 209).
57 KA to RC, 26 October 1958.
58 *Memoirs*, p. 199.
59 Ibid., p. 203.
60 Ibid.
61 Ibid., pp. 203–204.
62 KA to Roy P. Basler, 25 September 1958.
63 'Breakfast at the Welches' from Chapter 6 of *Lucky Jim*; 'The Dangers of Disguise' from Chapter 10 of *That Uncertain Feeling*, and 'An Anecdote' from Chapter 12 of *I Like It Here*.
64 In D. J. Enright, ed., *Poets of the 1950s*, Kenyusha Press, 1955, pp. 17–18.
65 See Report to the Dean of the Faculty for Transmission to the President, 13 May 1958, signed by Blackmur, Willard Thorpe, of Princeton's English Department, and Whitney J. Oates (in Princeton's Seelye Mudd Library).
66 W. S. Merwin, 'He Can Be Funny, Too', review of *A Case of Samples: Poems 1946–1956*, *New York Times*, 17 March 1957.
67 KA to Jan Montefiore, 12 August 1986.
68 Quoted in Ian Hamilton, *A Poetry Chronicle: Essays and Reviews*, Faber and Faber, 1973, p. 141.
69 It is also the last poem in *A Case of Samples: Poems 1946–1956*.
70 Megan McAndrew remembers Hilly as 'probably slightly out of control' but also as 'very hands-on' as a mother: 'she met the kids at the school bus and walked them home and made them tea'.

71 Hilly Amis, diary entry of 1 November 1958. This diary, written in what looks like a school excercise book, contains entries for October and November 1958, plus snapshots (several of which are reproduced in this book). It is in the possession of Lady Kilmarnock.

72 Ibid., 8 November 1958.

73 Ibid., 13 November 1958.

74 Ibid., 9 November 1958.

75 Ibid., 14 November 1958.

76 The answered questionnaires can be found in the Gauss files at Princeton.

77 All quotations from the 'seminars' are from the book they became, *New Maps of Hell: A Survey of Science Fiction*, Gollancz, 1961; this particular quotation is from p. 118; there are no manuscripts for the seminars, either in the Huntington or the Ransom Center or at Princeton.

78 See Keeley, 'Robert Fitzgerald: Blackmur, Princeton, and the Early Gauss Seminars', in Cone et al., eds., *The Legacy of R. P. Blackmur*, p. 133.

79 The essay in *Harper's* is reprinted (and retitled, 'Who Needs No Introduction') in *What Became of Jane Austen? And Other Questions*, Penguin, 1981, p. 151.

80 *New Maps of Hell*, pp. 16–17.

81 Ibid., p. 18.

82 Ibid., p. 21.

83 Ibid., p. 23.

84 KA, *The New Oxford Book of Light Verse*, Oxford University Press, 1978, p. xvii.

85 See KA to Brian Aldiss, 24 December 1958.

86 *New Maps of Hell*, p. 48.

87 'Another and much more unlikely reason for Ray Bradbury's fame,' he declared in the fourth seminar, 'is that, despite his regrettable tendency to dime-a-dozen sensitivity, he is a good writer' (ibid., p. 106).

88 Ibid., p. 48.

89 Ibid., p. 49.

90 Ibid., p. 66. Much of the second seminar was taken up with statistics and gleanings from the questionnaires, about audience size, magazine circulation, the average SF reader, the average SF writer, and obstacles to successful translation into other media. This last topic leads to some surprisingly gloomy conclusions: that the boom in SF movies had passed; that such movies were never very inventive ('most of the animal kingdom has been successively blown up to giantism and launched against the world: we have had king-sized wasps, ants, spiders, squids, sea-snails, lizards, beetles, birds, and pterodactyls'); that the situation is no less dire on television: 'my own survey, which took a long time

and was very horrible to do, shows that of five hundred programme hours studied, only six and one-half, or one and three-tenths per cent, could possibly be classed as science fiction' (p. 62).

91 Ibid., p. 63.

92 For example, stories in which the human race 'will be ousted by another form of terrestrial life, an enlightened kind of rat in one case, more often an unenlightened and formidable strain of ants, an obvious symbol, I suppose, for the society that may in fact compete successfully with our own, being highly organised, unindividualistic, ruthless, unemotional, inexhaustible in numbers, and whatever else it may be or seem to be' (ibid., p. 70).

93 For example, that scientists are usually heroes and administrators fools or worse (ibid., p. 80); that religion is treated 'with casual disrespect', as if it were 'tacitly agreed to have an earthly, or Terrene, limitation when the scale of human activity has become galactic' (ibid., p. 83); that democracy is a good thing (it is only in fantasy that one finds 'approval of authoritarianism, of any regime built on gross inequality or the suppression of freedom, of any state of society that licenses cruelty or irresponsible whim', (ibid., p. 101)); and that the hero's aim 'is always to resist or undo harmful change, not to promote useful change', making the genre 'radical in attitude and temper, but strongly conservative in alignment' (ibid., p. 110).

94 Ibid., p. 86.

95 Ibid., p. 44.

96 'The right of the explorers – naturally they will be British or American explorers – to go round setting up their trading stations wherever they please is . . . taken for granted in science fiction as in many other circles. However: the concept of dealing kindly with the intelligent, while setting off a good deal of naïve speculation about the difficulty of measuring the IQ of a Procyonian, is reassuringly widespread' (ibid., p. 93).

97 'Gradations of sexual privilege, compulsory chastity plus artificial insemination, demolition for adulterers – I look in vain even for such simplicities as these, all of which strike me as a good deal more plausible than the average alien invasion' (ibid., p. 115).

98 Ibid., p. 127.

99 Ibid., p. 133.

100 Ibid., p. 124.

101 Ibid., p. 133.

102 Ibid., p. 150.

103 Ibid., p. 156.

104 Rose's interest in science fiction was a point of connection with Amis, as was William Rukeyser's interest in jazz. Rose remembers driving to Manhattan with the Amises. He and Rukeyser were in the back seat and Amis turned around to Rose to ask

him something about jazz. Rose said: 'No, he's jazz, I'm science fiction.'

105 Quoted in John McDermott, *Kingsley Amis: An English Moralist*, Macmillan, 1989, p. 40.

106 *Memoirs*, p. 207.

107 Betty Fussell, *My Kitchen Wars*, North Point Press, 2000, p. 121.

108 Ibid., p. 122.

109 Ibid., p. 123.

110 Ibid., p. 124.

111 Ibid.

112 *One Fat Englishman*, Penguin, 1966, p. 74.

113 Ibid.

114 Ibid., p. 110.

115 Betty Fussell, *My Kitchen Wars*, p. 125. Paul Fussell taught English at Rutgers not Princeton and the Fussells were only introduced to the Blackmur–Princeton crowd in 1958, through R. W. B. Lewis, whom they had met in Germany. Both Lewis and Fussell spent the academic year 1957–58 in Germany on Fulbrights.

116 Betty Fussell writes of another party, on a barge on the Delaware River by New Hope, in which drunken revellers 'who'd been screwing in dark corners . . . kept falling off and having to be fished out of the water half naked' (ibid.).

117 Martin Amis, *Experience*, Jonathan Cape, 2000, p. 139.

118 *Memoirs*, p. 211.

119 This was the car Hilly used for a special treat for the children: during thunderstorms she'd drive round the neighbourhood while the children stood on the back seat with their heads sticking through the roof.

120 *Take a Girl Like You*, Penguin, 1962, p. 81.

121 The only close friends of the Amises from the Princeton year who would not be interviewed were Liz and Julian Moynahan.

CHAPTER 17

Patrick and Dai

1 *Take a Girl Like You*, Penguin, 1962.

2 Ibid., p. 160.

3 Mark Rose, 'Harold Be Thy Name', *Nassau Literary Magazine* 119: 2 (Winter 1961), pp. 3–24.

4 The *Spectrum* anthologies printed between eight to ten stories per volume, by British as well as American writers, including previously unpublished stories by J. G. Ballard, John Wyndham, Arthur C. Clarke, Brian Aldiss, Isaac Asimov, Frederik Pohl, Robert Sheckley and Robert Heinlein (the story by John Berryman is by an SF writer, not the poet). Each volume was prefaced by a short introduction,

though in the case of Volume 4 this took the form of a conversation about the genre between Amis, Aldiss and C. S. Lewis.

5 Mark Rose to the author, 7 March 2003.

6 Rose, 'Harold Be Thy Name', p. 16.

7 Ibid., p. 18. Amis had put on weight since Princeton. 'I'm dieting,'
Amis wrote to the Powells on 4 June 1960, 'i.e. more or less not
eating. It's now two hours since I didn't have lunch and another
hour and a half or so till I don't have tea.' Ibid., p. 7.

8 The letter is in the possession of the Clearys.

9 Andrew Brown is the Swansea colleague who introduced the Amises
to the Tyrells in Portugal.

10 'You That Love England; or, Limey Stay Home', *New World Writing*
16 (1960), pp. 139–40. Gene Lichtenstein remembers a disastrous
meeting he engineered towards the end of Amis's stay in Princeton
between Amis and the English writer Anthony Bailey. Bailey's parents
were not wealthy, but he'd gone to Oxford and to Lichtenstein 'spoke
like somebody who'd gone to Winchester and Oxford'. He worked
for the *New Yorker* and wrote fiction in the tradition of Wodehouse
and Powell. The Baileys lived below Lichtenstein and were invited up
to have a drink with Amis. 'Amis in those days was more radical or
anti-establishment and Tony was not anti-establishment,' Lichtenstein
remembers. 'Whatever Tony said, Kingsley Amis stepped on . . . it was
a disastrous encounter.'

11 'You That Love England', p. 141.

12 KA to McCallum, 4 September 1959.

13 'You That Love England', p. 143.

14 Ibid., pp. 142–143.

15 'She Was a Child and I Was a Child', reprinted in *What Became of
Jane Austen? And Other Questions*, Penguin, 1981, pp. 77–83.

16 Ibid., p. 79. The sort of people who love 'style' in this sense also
disapprove of genre fiction.

17 Ibid.

18 Ibid., p. 80.

19 Ibid.

20 Ibid., p. 83.

21 'Sacred Cows', in *The Amis Collection: Selected Non-Fiction
1954–1990*, Penguin, 1991, p. 17. This article is undated in *AC* but
is a reworking of an article entitled 'The Great American Disaster',
Sunday Times magazine, 17 April 1977, in a series entitled 'Sacred
Cows'.

22 Ibid., p. 19.

23 At a conference in April 2000 at the Huntington Library on 'The
Novel in Britain, 1950–2000'.

24 See 'The Curious Elf: A Note on Rhyme in Keats', *Essays in Criticism*
1:2 (April 1951), pp. 189–192.

25 *Take a Girl Like You*, p. 177.

26 Christopher Ricks, 'Cant Trap', review of *One Fat Englishman*, *New Statesman*, 29 November 1966.

27 Dale Salwak, 'An Interview with Kingsley Amis', Robert H. Bell, ed., *Critical Essays on Kingsley Amis*, G. K. Hall, 1998, p. 270.

28 *Take a Girl Like You*, p. 134.

29 Anonymous review, 'The Uses of Comic Vision', *Times Literary Supplement*, 9 September 1960; John Coleman, 'King of Shaft', *Spectator*, 23 September 1960.

30 David Lodge, in Bell, ed., *Critical Essays*, p. 52, excerpted from David Lodge, *Language of Fiction* (1960).

31 John McDermott, *Kingsley Amis: An English Moralist*, p. 110; see also Bernard Bergonzi, for whom the fantasies of aggression in early Amis are also 'less controlled' ('Kingsley Amis and the Situation of the Novel', in Bell, ed., *Critical Essays*, p. 29).

32 See Karl Miller, *Dark Horses: An Experience of Literary Journalism*, Picador, 1998, p. 49; for a contrasting view see Russell Fraser, 'Lucky Jim as I Remember Him', *The Southern Review* 32: 4 (Autumn 1996), p. 788, for whom 'the brutality of [Amis's] critical prose makes one blink. Dismissing Keats or Jane Austen, he wasn't downright, only coarse. Skewering convention was his fatal chimera: "rotten Italy", "filthy French food". After a while, it gets old.'

33 *Take a Girl Like You*, p. 279.

34 Ibid., p. 137.

35 Ibid., p. 109.

36 Ibid., p. 153.

37 Ibid., p. 155.

38 Ibid., p. 231.

39 Ibid., p. 30.

40 Ibid., p. 109.

41 *The Evans Country* was first published in 1962 in pamphlet form by the Fantasy Press. It consisted of only six poems and was 'Dedicated to the Patrons and Staff of the Newton Inn, Mumbles, Swansea'. It was expanded to eleven poems, plus dedicatory quatrain, in *A Look Round the Estate: Poems 1957–1967*.

42 McDermott, *Kingsley Amis: An English Moralist*, p. 199.

43 Salwak, 'An Interview with Kingsley Amis', Bell, ed., *Critical Essays*, p. 270.

44 PL to RC, 7 October 1960 (recipient).

45 Anthony Powell, *Journals 1987–1989*, Heinemann, 1996, p. 141.

46 *Take a Girl Like You*, p. 23.

47 Ibid., p. 55.

48 Ibid., p. 32.

49 Evelyn Waugh, *Scoop*, Penguin, 1943, p. 36.

50 *Take a Girl Like You*, p. 53.

51 Martin Amis, *Experience*, Jonathan Cape, 2000, p. 374.

52 *Take a Girl Like You*, p. 92.

53 Ibid., pp. 49–50.

54 Ibid., p. 178.

55 Salwak, 'An Interview with Kingsley Amis', Bell, ed., *Critical Essays*, p. 270.

56 PL to RC, 7 October 1960 (recipient); see also PL to Judy Egerton, 21 October 1960.

57 *Take a Girl Like You*, pp. 216–217.

58 See Bernard Bergonzi, *Wartime and Aftermath: English Literature and its Background 1939–1960*, Oxford University Press, 1993, p. 207, and Malcolm Bradbury, *The Modern British Novel 1878–2001*, Penguin, 2001, pp. 342–343.

59 Salwak, 'An Interview with Kingsley Amis', Bell, ed., *Critical Essays*, p. 275.

60 The Portugal notebook, now located in the Ransom Center, is not large, measuring 6 1/2 inches by 5 inches, though Amis writes in an unusually small hand and skips few lines.

61 Salwak, 'An Interview with Kingsley Amis', Bell, ed., *Critical Essays*, p. 273.

62 Some of the name changes are noteworthy: Jenny Bunn was originally Jenny Baker, Anna's last name was 'de Jong', as in Max de Jong in 'The Legacy'.

63 Portugal Notebook, p. 1.

64 Ibid., p. 20.

65 Ibid., p. 19.

66 Ibid., p. 9.

67 Ibid., p. 31.

68 *Take a Girl Like You*, p. 155.

69 Portugal Notebook, p. 11.

70 *Take a Girl Like You*, p. 84.

71 KA to Hilary Rubinstein, 11 July 1960 (Gollancz).

72 The serialisation was over five weeks, beginning on 21 January 1961.

73 KA to Violet and Anthony Powell, 27 September 1960 (recipient).

74 The science fiction columns for the *Observer* began on 10 April 1960 and the fiction round-ups on 5 June 1960.

75 The only SF stories Amis published in this period were 'Something Strange', in the *Spectator*, 25 November 1960, and 'Hemingway in Space', in *Punch*, 21 December 1960. The former appeared in Amis's first collection of stories, *My Enemy's Enemy* (1962).

76 RC to PL, 2 November 1960 (Bodleian).

77 KA to Michael Rubinstein, 23 November 1960.

78 See RC to PL, 13 September 1960 (Bodleian): 'Kingkongsley seemed in fine fettle, and I have to go down to Swansea in a week or two, for a collaborative conference [about *Spectrum*, presumably] and so on. Hillie still regrets USA'; also KA to the McAndrews, 4 October 1960: 'I give England (and Wales) about another couple of years before we finally walk out on them . . . Actually v. depressed about

the old place. Only a more or less continuous diet of Americans keeps us going.'

79 *One Fat Englishman.*
80 See KA to Alan Collins, 18 May 1961.
81 KA to J. H. McCallum, 17 April 1961.
82 KA to Alan Collins, 18 May 1961.

CHAPTER 18
Cambridge

1 Peregrine Worsthorne, *Tricks of Memory: An Autobiography*, Weidenfeld and Nicolson, 1993, p. 49.
2 See *Independent* obituary by Nicholas Vincent, 8 April 2005.
3 Obituary in *The Times*, 6 May 2005.
4 Vincent, obituary, *Independent*, 8 April 2005.
5 Eric Jacobs, *Kingsley Amis: A Biography*, Hodder and Stoughton, 1995, p. 233.
6 This comment was related by John Beer, Amis's successor as Fellow in English at Peterhouse, in a letter to the author, 10 July 2002.
7 Chris Calladine, Fellow in Engineering at Peterhouse, in a letter to the author, 20 August 2002.
8 Richard Skaer, in a letter to the author, 24 July 2002.
9 John Beer to the author, 10 July 2002.
10 Jacobs, *Biography*, p. 231.
11 *Memoirs*, Penguin, 1992, p. 217.
12 Ibid., pp. 216–217.
13 'No More Parades', *Encounter*, February 1964, reprinted in *What Became of Jane Austen? And Other Questions*, Penguin, 1981, p. 177.
14 Ibid., p. 178.
15 Donald Davie, *These the Companions: Recollections*, Cambridge University Press, 1982, p. 136.
16 'No More Parades', *WBJA*, p. 181.
17 Calladine to the author, 20 August 2002.
18 At the time a Fellow in English at Queen's College, Cambridge, Holloway was the man Amis had wanted as head of department at Swansea. See Davie, *These the Companions*, p. 136.
19 For F. R. Leavis on Amis see *English Literature in Our Time and the University*, Chatto and Windus, 1969, p. 56, where Leavis declares interest in Amis to be a sign of decadence: 'the spectacle of an academic critic going out of his way to pronounce a Kingsley Amis novel a "serious study in amorality" would have been possible only in a period marked by a collapse of standards'.
20 The source of this anecdote is Al Alvarez, to whom it was told in 1962, when he came up to Cambridge to address the Doughty Club

and stayed with the Amises. A possible date for Amis's lecture is suggested by a comment in a letter Robert Conquest wrote to Larkin on 1 February 1961: 'KA . . . departed to tell the Cambridge audience about the moral motivations of literature' (Bodleian).

21 *Memoirs*, p. 217.

22 Davie, *These the Companions*, p. 136.

23 *Memoirs*, p. 221; Davie, though, was hardly immune from Cambridge careerist gossip. In later years, Larkin sent Amis a 'song' he had written about Davie, to the tune of 'Daisy, Daisy': 'Davie, Davie, / Give me a bad review; / That's your gravy, / Telling chaps what to do. / Forget about style and passion, / As long as it's in fashion: – / But let's be fair, it's got you a chair, / Which was all it was meant to do.' Amis suggested an improvement on the last lines, in a letter of 6 December 1976: 'But it's got you a chair, which, let's be fair, / Was the most that you had in view.'

24 George Watson, 'I Was Kingsley Amis', *Hudson Review*, Winter 1997, p. 617.

25 Ibid., p. 610.

26 Ibid., p. 612.

27 *Memoirs*, p. 221.

28 Amis, 'No More Parades', *WBJA*, p. 181.

29 Ibid., p. 179.

30 *Memoirs*, p. 222.

31 Chris Calladine to the author, 20 August 2002.

32 Richard Skaer to the author, 29 June 2002.

33 Amis remembered at least one item discussed by the Fellows and put it, 'thinly disguised', according to Calladine, into Chapter 12 of *Jake's Thing*. This item concerned the Peterhouse burial plot in Cherry Hinton Churchyard and came up in December 1961, after the funeral of the College Dean, Joseph Sanders. At the funeral someone noticed that an interloper had been buried in the Peterhouse plot. Butterfield wrote a letter to the local vicar protesting sharply. The vicar wrote back an abject apology explaining that he'd been away when the interloper died and had left the parish in the hands of a locum. There was a lengthy and vigorous debate among the Fellows about what to do. Someone suggested altering the hedge that bordered the plot to exclude the interloper. Someone else suggested electing him a Fellow retrospectively. Exhumation was considered. Much of the debate appears in *Jake's Thing*, Hutchinson, 1978, pp. 204–206; the Master of Comyns College, where Jake Richardson is a Fellow, is, according to Calladine, very like Butterfield.

34 *Memoirs*, p. 216.

35 It was only when Cowling came in 1964 that the college's association with the Conservative Party began to be remarked upon. Among Cowling's pupils at Peterhouse were Michael Portillo and Peter Lillie.

36 Roger Deakin to the author, 15 August 2002; all subsequent Deakin quotations are from this letter.

37 *Memoirs*, p. 224.

38 Amis, 'No More Parades', *WBJA*, p. 184.

39 Now a fish restaurant.

40 Richard Eyre, email to the author, 16 July 2002.

41 Jeremy Taylor to the author, 4 July 2002; all subsequent Taylor quotations are from this letter.

42 Michael Frohnsdorff was one of the students Amis inherited when he arrived. Like others in his situation, Frohnsdorff had not liked being farmed out for supervisions and thought of Amis's arrival as 'providential'. He remembers Amis as 'very kind and considerate, always ready to give encouragement and to bring out the best in us' (Michael Frohnsdorff to the author, 5 July 2002; all subsequent Frohnsdorff quotations in the text are from this letter). It was Frohnsdorff who Amis enthusiastically encouraged to study for and sit a forbidden combination of papers. Calladine remembers meeting another student who had been taught by Amis and 'almost had a nervous breakdown when he discovered that Kingsley had entered him for a wrong paper'. Robert MacDowell, who came to Peterhouse in Amis's second year there, was set an essay on *Othello* for his first supervision, though *Othello* was not one of the set texts for Prelims. After dutifully completing the essay he asked Amis why he'd suggested it. 'The play's set for Prelims, isn't it?' Amis replied. When informed that it wasn't, Amis apologised profusely, and though MacDowell describes him as a 'very pleasant, bright, lively and entertaining supervisor', as well as 'efficient and helpful' in setting up specialist supervisions, he learned not to trust him about university regulations (MacDowell to the author, 17 July 2002).

43 Derek Frampton to the author, 22 October 2002; all subsequent Frampton quotations are from this letter.

44 *Memoirs*, p. 226.

45 This description is from Tony Wrigley, a Fellow in Geography, in an interview with the author at Peterhouse, 19 June 2002.

46 *Memoirs*, p. 224.

47 Ibid., p. 226.

48 *Experience*, p. 102.

49 *Memoirs*, p. 226.

50 Ibid.

51 Ibid.

52 Ibid., p. 172.

53 Rukeyser tells the story of a young woman who was staying at the house and encountered Amis in the early hours of the morning. She was wearing a bathrobe and as Amis passed her in the hall he said: 'Open it up, let's see what you have.' According to Rukeyser, the girl thought: 'Well, what the hell.' Lis Rukeyser tells a related story.

She first met Amis in Swansea, when he was teaching her older brother. She was sixteen at the time and Amis made a pass at her. When her brother upbraided him, she remembers being indignant that he thought she needed protecting. The pass was friendly and hadn't frightened her: 'It was just an offer: "If you're game, let's do it."' Of the incident with Amis and the girl in the bathrobe, she says: 'The mindset in that house was that people did that.'

54 Now a student residence.

55 *Experience*, 2000, p. 102.

56 This story has several sources, among them Worsthorne, Rukeyser, Rose and Martin Amis.

57 Louis Rukeyser was later to become presenter of the American television programme *Wall $treet Week with Louis Rukeyser*.

58 *Memoirs*, p. 222.

59 Ibid.

60 Ibid., p. 227.

61 See KA to Victor Gollancz, 1 March 1962, and Graham Watson to Perry Knowlton, 6 March 1962 (Columbia).

62 In a letter of 19 May 1967, Mike Keeley wrote to Amis and Jane about an exhibition at the Princeton University Library in which *One Fat Englishman* was said not to be 'in any way ad hominem, personal, scandalous, or the like'. Keeley refrained from displaying 'in the same case a little map I made up of the relevant territory around Princeton . . . Collins' estate and the like'.

63 *One Fat Englishman*, Penguin, 1966, p. 10.

64 Ibid., p. 89.

65 Russell Fraser, 'Kingsley Amis as I Remember Him', *Southern Review* 32: 4 (Autumn 1996), p. 791.

66 *One Fat Englishman*, p. 51.

67 Ibid., p. 140.

68 Ibid., p. 75.

69 Salwak, 'An Interview with Kingsley Amis', in Robert H. Bell, ed., *Critical Essays on Kingsley Amis*, G. K. Hall, 1998, p. 276.

70 *One Fat Englishman*, p. 6.

71 Ibid., p. 48.

72 Ibid., p. 110.

73 Ibid., pp. 110–112.

74 Ibid., p. 110.

75 Ibid., pp. 111–112.

76 Ibid., p. 112.

77 Ricks, 'Cant Trap', review of *One Fat Englishman*, in *New Statesman*, 29 November 1966.

78 John McDermott, *Kingsley Amis: An English Moralist*, Macmillan, 1989, p. 123.

79 *One Fat Englishman*, p. 90.

80 Ibid.

81 Ibid., p. 109.

82 Ibid., p. 111.

83 This view is hinted at jokingly in earlier novels, as in Patrick's references to 'Bastards' H.Q.' in *Take a Girl Like You*, the place where things are made to go wrong. See Bergonzi, 'Kingsley Amis and the Situation of the Novel', in Bell, ed., *Critical Essays*, pp. 33–34, on *That Uncertain Feeling*: '"Life, that resourceful technician, had administered a typical rebuke", is what John Lewis thinks after swallowing a mouthful of tea leaves – just after entertaining adulterous thoughts; this is what Patrick Standish calls "Bastards' H.Q."' These instances are connected to 'the natural oppugnancy between man and objects' also on display in the early novels, as in Roger's friend Joe Derlanger's violent struggles with deckchairs in *One Fat Englishman*.

CHAPTER 19

Waking Beauty

1 Martin Amis, *Experience*, Jonathan Cape, 2000, p. 41.

2 Ian Hamilton, 'Four Conversations: Philip Larkin', *London Magazine*, November 1964, p. 77.

3 Blake Morrison, *The Movement: English Poetry and Fiction of the 1950s*, Oxford University Press, 1980, p. 220.

4 *Memoirs*, p. 212.

5 Ibid.

6 Ibid.

7 Philip Larkin, 'Keeping Up with the Graveses', *Manchester Guardian*, 15 May 1959, an omnibus poetry review, beginning with Graves's *Collected Poems*; see PL, *Further Requirements: Interviews, Broadcasts, Statements and Book Reviews*, ed. Anthony Thwaite, Faber and Faber, 2001, pp. 203–204.

8 Quoted in Miranda Seymour, *Robert Graves: Life on the Edge*, Scribner 2003, p. 70.

9 See James Jensen, 'The Construction of *Seven Types of Ambiguity*', *Modern Language Quarterly* 27:3 (September 1966), pp. 243–249 especially. Jensen quotes the following note by Empson in the first edition of *Seven Types of Ambiguity*: 'I derive the method I am using from Mr. Robert Graves' analysis of a Shakespeare Sonnet, "The expense of spirit is a waste of shame", in *A Survey of Modernist Poetry*' (p. 244).

10 Seymour, *Robert Graves*, p. 351.

11 *Memoirs*, Penguin, 1992, p. 212.

12 Eric Jacobs, *Kingsley Amis: A Biography*, Hodder and Stoughton, 1995, p. 251.

13 Seymour, *Robert Graves*, p. 231.

14 This is a reference to the shore of Deya's beach.

15 Martin Amis, *Experience*, p. 40.

16 *Memoirs*, p. 213.

17 This car, rented in London, was jinxed. Amis wrote a brief account of its breakdowns on the drive back in 'Something Does Not Work with My Car', *Spectator*, 23 November 1962, reprinted in *The Amis Collection: Selected Non-Fiction 1954–1990*, Penguin, 1991, pp. 347–349.

18 *Memoirs*, p. 213.

19 'Robert Graves: A Great Poet in an Island Paradise,' *Show*, December 1962, p. 128.

20 Ibid., p. 78.

21 *Memoirs*, p. 214.

22 Ibid.

23 When Amis's friends got wind of the planned move they were incredulous. Larkin's reaction, in a letter to Robert Conquest of 30 December 1962, suggests something of the distance that had grown up between the two friends at the time: 'Whose flat will he borrow there? Who'll he screw?' (recipient).

24 Elizabeth Jane Howard, *Slipstream: A Memoir*, Macmillan, 2002, p. 334.

25 Ibid., p. 164.

26 Ibid., p. 216.

27 Ibid., p. 164.

28 Ibid., p. 60.

29 Ibid., p. 5.

30 Ibid, p. 16: 'My mother's family was pretty hard up,' Jane writes in partial explanation of why her mother did not resist the Brig's insistence, and she 'wasn't conventionally good-looking'.

31 Ibid., p. 14.

32 Ibid., p. 15.

33 Ibid., p. 14.

34 'One moment he was remarking on how fast I was growing up and the next minute I was caught in his arms, one hand hurting my breast, and stifled by what I afterwards learned was a French kiss' (ibid., p. 68).

35 Ibid.

36 Ibid., p. 16.

37 Ibid., p. 69.

38 For a sympathetic treatment of Scott's remarkable life see Elspeth Huxley, *Peter Scott*, Faber and Faber, 1993.

39 As Jane explains in *Slipstream*, p. 94: 'I was secretly amazed that someone so old and glamorous should notice me – more than amazed, fascinated'. As Scott kept saying he loved her, 'I began to feel that I must be in love with him'. He kissed her a lot, the idea of which she enjoyed 'more than the practice', and she responded with 'what I hoped was appropriate ardour'.

40 Ibid., p. 122.

41 Ibid., p. 174.

42 Ibid., p. 178.

43 Ibid., p. 151.

44 At eleven and a half Jane was removed from the Frances Holland School near Sloane Square, because of ill health, in part brought on by bullying.

45 Ibid., p. 51.

46 Ibid., p. 216.

47 Ibid., p. 198.

48 Ibid., p. 197.

49 Ibid., p. 229.

50 Ibid., p. 291.

51 Ibid.

52 As Jackie points out, though, until the advent of Amis neither Jane nor Douglas-Henry discussed with her the tensions in their marriage ('I was very much a junior').

53 EJH, *Slipstream*, pp. 333–334.

54 According to Anthony Curtis, McClaughlan had a bee in his bonnet about explicit sex scenes in fiction and, because he was looking for an argument, was disappointed when Amis said that he, too, disapproved of such scenes, though on literary rather than moral grounds.

55 Jacobs, *Biography*, p. 254.

56 Quotes from the session are from Nicola Bennett, *Speaking Volumes*, Sutton Publishing, 1999, pp. 45–46; Jacobs, *Biography*, p. 254, attributes Heller's censorship line to Romain Gary.

57 EJH, *Slipstream*, p. 338.

58 Jacobs, *Biography*, p. 255.

59 Ibid.

60 EJH, *Slipstream*, pp. 339–340.

61 Conquest is thinking of a quotation from Boswell's *Life*: 'Were it not for imagination, Sir, a man would be as happy in the arms of a chambermaid as of a Duchess' (see entry of 9 May 1778 in volume 3 of *Boswell's Life of Johnson*, ed. George Birkbeck Hill, rev. L.F. Powell, Clarendon Press, 1934, p. 341).

62 PL to RC, 24 November 1963 (recipient).

63 EJH, *After Julius*, Pan Books, 1995, p. 18.

64 Ibid., pp. 19–20.

65 Martin Amis, *Experience*, p. 215.

66 See also interview with Valerie Grove, 'Soft Centre Shows Behind the Old Devil's Brimstone', *Sunday Times*, 25 March 1990: 'I must not pretend that I did not fall in love with my second wife.'

67 From *For Someone Else's Son: Extracts and Talks from a Series Broadcast on BBC Woman's Hour, Spring 1963*, a BBC publication, 1963, p. 29; among other speakers in the series were Christopher Fry, Frederic Warburg, the publisher, Kenneth Horne, the radio

commentator, a policeman, a Borstal governor and a London magistrate.

68 Ibid., p. 30.

69 'An Attempt at Time-Travel', first published in *A Look Round the Estate: Poems 1957–1967* (1967), reprinted in *Collected Poems 1944–1979*, Penguin, 1980, p. 102.

70 KA to EJH, 6 December 1962.

71 KA to EJH, 7 March 1963.

72 KA to EJH, February 1963.

73 KA to EJH, 13 March 1963.

74 KA to EJH, 29 April 1963.

75 KA to EJH, 11 February 1963.

76 The letter from which this quote and the one that precedes it are taken is undated, but Amis responds to it on 25 February 1963.

77 KA to EJH, 24 April 1963.

78 *The Anti-Death League*, Harcourt Brace, 1966, p. 228.

79 From an interview with Dale Salwak, 23 January 1973, quoted in Dale Salwak, *Kingsley Amis: Modern Novelist*, Harvester, 1992, p. 146.

80 *The Anti-Death League*, p. 71.

81 Arthur Pottersman, 'Books', *Sun*, 17 December 1966.

82 *The Anti-Death League*, p. 163.

83 Ibid. The sexual component of Catharine's marriage did not improve in this regard and 'it's no good if one of you just has no particular objection. I reckon that sort of thing undermines at least as many women as sex not being all right' (p. 165).

84 Ibid., p. 165.

85 Ibid., p. 170.

86 Ibid., p. 171.

87 Ibid., p. 298.

88 Ibid., pp. 302–303.

89 See Bernard Bergonzi, 'Anything Goes', an omnibus review of three novels, including *The Anti-Death League*, *New York Review of Books*, 6 October 1966: 'I don't think the moral concerns mix very well with the thriller elements; as a novel of ideas *The Anti-Death League* is interesting, but it is a feeble and unconvincing novel . . . At the same time, his seriousness deserves respect, and so too does his determination to write a different book each time, and avoid self-imitation'; Christopher Ricks, 'Operation Malvolio', a review of *The Anti-Death League*, *New Statesman*, 18 March 1966 praises the novel's seriousness about death and generosity towards 'many people whom it could very easily despise', but he also complains that when L.S. Caton enters the novel, 'the claustrophobic world of omens and top-security is ripped open to the winds of early Amis. Or – more damagingly – to the world of that unfunny romp, *The Egyptologists* . . . Caton is a figure from a quite different world'; A. S. Byatt in 'Mess and Mystery', a review of *The Anti-Death League*, in *Encounter*, 27 July 1966,

writes: 'if none of the characters is complicated enough to involve us, a surprisingly large number of them . . . arouse that automatic pure affection we feel for the heroes of fairy tales and for Tom Jones. But the novel is, in the last resort, too timid to engage the problems it raises. It is neither real enough nor allegorical enough.'
90 EJH, *Slipstream*, p. 340.

CHAPTER 20

Break-up

1   Eric Jacobs, *Kingsley Amis: A Biography*, Hodder and Stoughton, 1995, p. 255.
2   Elizabeth Jane Howard, *Slipstream: A Memoir*, Macmillan, 2002, p. 259.
3   Ibid., p. 340.
4   All he meant, she decided, was that 'if he wanted to keep his family together, he would have to side with them. I could see that that was very nasty for me, but again he was being honest about it and a lot of men would have said nothing but would have turned out nasty.' A part of her also thought: 'it's quite difficult to blacken me. I'm pretty black already.'
5   EJH, *Slipstream*, p. 340.
6   Mary Riddell, 'For the Love of an Old Devil', interview in *You* magazine, *Mail on Sunday*, 14 July 1996.
7   As Gale invariably did, though his views were mostly right wing. Cowling describes Gale as 'a Denis Brogan liberal – that is, without all the rubbishy illusions'.
8   Martin Amis, *Experience*, Jonathan Cape, 2000, p. 103.
9   PL to RC, 18 December 1962 (recipient).
10 *Memoirs*, Penguin, 1992, p. 227.
11 Interview with Tom Baistow, 'Lucky Jim Is Leaving', *Daily Mail*, 8 March 1963.
12 PL to Maeve Brennan, 18 April 1961, quoted in Maeve Brennan, *The Philip Larkin I Knew*, University of Manchester Press, 2002, p. 157.
13 *Memoirs*, p. 23.
14 Ibid., p. 22.
15 Martin Amis, *Experience*, pp. 166–167.
16 See KA to Violet and Anthony Powell, 4 June 1960.
17 *Memoirs*, p. 22.
18 Ibid., p. 23.
19 Ibid.
20 Martin Amis, *Experience*, pp. 165–166.
21 *Memoirs*, p. 23.
22 Martin Amis, *Experience*, p. 165.
23 Pat herself would not be interviewed formally for this book, having

'nothing nice to say about Kingsley'. Informally, she was generous in corroborating stories.

24 Brian Aldiss, '"im', in Dale Salwak, ed., *Kingsley Amis: In Life and Letters*, Macmillan, 1990, p. 47.

25 Harry Harrison, 'Amis vs SF', ibid., p. 54.

26 Ibid.

27 KA to EJH, 11 June 1963.

28 Martin Amis, *Experience*, pp. 100–101.

29 Ibid., p. 129.

30 Ibid., pp. 105–106.

31 Jacobs, *Biography*, p. 259.

32 Ibid., p. 258.

33 EJH, *Slipstream*, p. 344.

34 Martin Amis, *Experience*, pp. 142–143.

35 Jacobs, *Biography*, p. 260.

36 Or so he wrote to Bill Rukeyser on 26 August, ten days after it happened; Jane, in *Slipstream*, p. 437, says she was wrapped in a sheet.

37 EJH, *Slipstream*, p. 348.

38 RC to PL, 2 September 1963 (Bodleian); Larkin to Conquest, 8 September 1963 (recipient).

39 EJH, *Slipstream*, p. 348.

40 Interview with Graham Turner, 'Kingsley Amis and Those Uncertain Feelings', *Sunday Telegraph*, 28 September 1986.

41 See KA to Rukeyser, 26 August 1963: 'you may have heard [George Gale] and I had a far from hostile lunch together my last day in London.'

42 Andrew Alderson, 'Death of an Old Devil Unites His Women', *Sunday Times*, 13 October 1996.

43 'Kingsley Amis and Those Uncertain Feelings'.

44 Aunt Margaret (Bardwell) Partington.

45 Martin Amis, *Experience*, p. 143.

46 Jacobs, *Biography*, p. 260.

47 EJH, *Slipstream*, p. 345.

48 KA to Victor Gollancz, 1 August 1963.

49 EJH, *Slipstream*, p. 346.

50 Ibid.

51 Ibid.

52 Later in life, Amis would write a novel about a man in a similar situation. In *The Russian Girl* (1992), Richard Vaisey, a lecturer in Slavonic Studies, falls in love with Anna Danilova, a visiting Russian poet. At her first public reading he is moved to tears: by the content of her poetry, so obviously serious and sincere, and by the crudity and self-indulgence of its style.

53 EJH, *Slipstream*, p. 294.

54 EJH, *The Sea Change*, Pan Books, 1995, p. 180.

55 Ibid., pp. 223–224.
56 Ibid., p. 151.
57 Sybille Bedford, in the introduction to *The Sea Change*, p. xii.
58 EJH, *Slipstream*, p. 347.
59 Ibid.
60 EJH, *After Julius*, Pan Books, 1995, p. 181.
61 Ibid., pp. 181–182.
62 Ibid., p. 181.
63 *One Fat Englishman*, Penguin, 1966, p. 136.
64 Ibid.
65 Ibid., p. 138.
66 KA to Rukeyser, 26 August 1963.
67 He may have said John Braine, Colin Howard cannot remember.
68 EJH, *Slipstream*, p. 341.

CHAPTER 21

Divisions

1 John Sutherland, 'A Modern Master', *Sunday Times*, 29 October 1995.
2 Dale Salwak, 'An Interview with Kingsley Amis', reprinted in Robert H. Bell, ed., *Criticial Essays on Kingsley Amis*, G. K. Hall, 1998, p. 280.
3 Ibid., p. 275.
4 *Ending Up* (1974).
5 Salwak, 'An Interview with Kingsley Amis', Bell, ed., *Critical Essays*, p. 275.
6 There were thirty-three of these round-up reviews, written between 13 December 1959 and 30 May 1965.
7 Kingsley Amis and Robert Conquest, eds., *Spectrum: A Science Fiction Anthology. Volume One*, Victor Gollancz, 1961, pp. 10–11.
8 The Besant comment is from a letter to Haggard of 2 January 1887, quoted in volume 1 of H. Rider Haggard, *The Day of My Life: An Autobiography*, Longman's, Green and Co., 1926, p. 249.
9 In 'The Art of Fiction', an essay published in the September 1884 issue of *Longman's Magazine* and provoked in part by Walter Besant's lecture 'Fiction as One of the Fine Arts' (delivered at the Royal Institution, 25 April 1884), Henry James made a plea for 'the illusion of life' and 'the air of reality' in fiction, in the process alluding to *Treasure Island*. Stevenson answered him in the December issue of *Longman's Magazine*, in an essay entitled 'A Humble Remonstrance', arguing that the secret of fiction was that it did not attempt to 'compete with life', as James had claimed: 'Man's one method, whether he reasons or creates, is to half-shut his eyes against the dazzle and confusion of reality'. For a discussion of the exchange between Besant, James and Stevenson see Janet

Adam Smith, *Henry James and Robert Louis Stevenson*, Rupert Hart-Davis, 1948, pp. 62–67, 91–92 (from which I have taken the preceding quotations).

10 Amis and Conquest, eds., *Spectrum, Volume One*, p. 10.

11 Ibid., pp. 10–11.

12 Eric Jacobs, *Kingsley Amis: A Biography*, Hodder and Stoughton, 1995, p. 268.

13 Both from the dust jacket to *The Spy Who Loved Me*, in Amis's copy in the Huntington.

14 KA, *The James Bond Dossier*, Jonathan Cape, 1965, p. x.

15 Ibid., p. 36.

16 Ibid., p. 41n.

17 Ibid., p. 133.

18 Ibid., p. 135.

19 Ibid., p. 99.

20 Ibid., p. 100.

21 Ibid., pp. 34–35.

22 Ibid., p. 9.

23 Ibid., p. 35.

24 Ibid., p. 138.

25 Henry James, 'The Art of Fiction' (1884), quoted in Janet Adam Smith, *Henry James and Robert Louis Stevenson*, pp. 65–66.

26 Robert Louis Stevenson, 'A Humble Remonstrance' (1884), quoted in ibid. pp. 91–92.

27 'Reading Poetry after a Quarrel' is reprinted in Robert Conquest, *New and Collected Poems*, Century Hutchinson, 1988, p. 14.

28 *The James Bond Dossier*, p. 26.

29 'A Defence of Poetry' (1821), *Percy Bysshe Shelley: The Major Works*, ed. Zachary Leader and Michael O'Neill, Oxford University Press, p. 698.

30 Martin Amis, *Experience*, Jonathan Cape, 2000, p. 144.

31 Ibid., p. 146.

32 Ibid.

33 Ibid.

34 According to Hilly.

35 Martin Amis, *Experience*, p. 144.

36 Ibid.

37 Ibid., pp. 144–145.

38 Elizabeth Jane Howard, *Slipstream: A Memoir*, Macmillan, 2002, p. 349.

39 Ibid., p. 349.

40 Martin Amis, *Experience*, p. 145.

41 EJH, *Slipstream*, pp. 349–350.

42 Ibid., p. 350.

43 Hilly in interview with Mary Riddell, 'For the Love of an Old Devil', *You* magazine, *Mail on Sunday*, 14 July 1996.

44 According to Penny King.

45 Martin Amis, *Experience*, p. 295.

46 Ibid., p. 292.

47 Ibid.

48 When Martin generously gave Philip £50 from his film money, 'he told me what he was going to do with it. He was going to hail a taxi (we only used taxis in emergencies) and say, "*Carnaby* Street"' (ibid.).

49 Ibid., p. 294.

50 According to Jacobs, *Biography*, p. 264; in *Slipstream*, Jane calls the lease 'of about fourteen years' (p. 350).

51 'Writing for a TV Series', *Listener*, 19 and 26 December 1974, reprinted in *The Amis Collection: Selected Non-Fiction 1954–1990*, Penguin, 1991, p. 28.

52 T. C. Worsley', 'The Alternative', *The Financial Times*, 29 April 1964.

53 This flaw Amis wittily avoids in *I Want It Now*, partly set in the American South, by offering a single extreme instance, 'Armegeddon Pierstaff' ('I'm getting pissed off') (p. 61), then reverting to normal speech. As Russell Fraser, Amis's Princeton and Vanderbilt friend, puts it, 'After that, spooning in the grits and hominy was the reader's business' ('Lucky Jim as I Remember Him', *The Southern Review* 32: 4 (Autumn 1996), p. 785).

54 KA to Elizabeth Barber, 27 May 1964 (Society of Authors).

55 Graham Watson to Alan Collins, 11 August 1964 (Columbia).

56 Reprinted in *What Became of Jane Austen? And Other Questions*, Penguin, 1981, under the title 'Unreal Policemen', pp. 109–124.

57 The story was reprinted in *My Enemy's Enemy*, Penguin, 1965. Richmond produced a detailed outline, or treatment, of the film (a sixty-two-page typed copy of which, entitled 'The More We Are Together' and dated 28 January 1963, can be found in the Huntington), but no screenplay was ever written.

58 Frederic Raphael, 'Too Good to Be True', *Punch*, September 1996, pp. 14–20.

59 Such as Frederic Raphael.

60 Personal communication to the author, 3 July 2006.

61 'Smiling Through', review of 'The Anatolian Smile', 'Children of the Damned' and 'Johnny Cool', *Observer*, 12 April 1964.

62 See KA to PL, 30 July 1958, in which the novel's basic premiss is described as 'quite good'.

63 Kingsley Amis and Robert Conquest, *The Egyptologists*, Penguin, 1968, p. 125.

64 Jacobs, *Biography*, p. 267.

65 KA and RC, *The Egyptologists*, p. 75.

66 Ibid., p. 202.

67 Conquest had denied any such identification in an earlier letter to Larkin (16 May 1965, in the Bodleian): 'No, of course I'm not the Sec, nor K the Treasurer – these are mere figments of my imagina-

tion, characterised a bit by old K later.' He goes on to add that 'the women are pretty well entirely his' and that 'My view is that if we'd stuck to highspeed farce, when what happens is more to the point than who it happens to, we could have fucked the characterisation.'

68 One of Conquest's pseudonyms as a limerick-writer. Conquest also possesses a single half-page, part of an undated letter to Amis, with a possible opening for 'Little Shags; Chap I': '"The Prof" huddled in a roughly hewed tree-stump. The others had gone off somewhere into the gathering dusk, and left me with the wisest of them, apparently charged with instructing me. He droned on, ". . . then yer see they comes after us with ferrets – I got to tell you about what ter do when ferret bell rings." . . . His attention seemed to wander, as he looked round vaguely at the various noises of the evening. An owl hooted. He made some movement under his cloak which seemed to be different from the routine scratching. He looked at me, chuckling. "When screech-owl calls Count your balls . . . ar he was a wise one was Boney . . . one of his Sayings, that."' On 12 November 1976 (Huntington), Conquest wrote to Amis about 'a new character for *Spring Interior*, the French Ambassador, small chap, called de L'ile-Chague'.

69 RC to PL, 22 October 1964 (Bodleian).

70 See KA to Tom Maschler, 5 October 1964.

71 These comments were passed on to Amis in a letter of 24 June 1964 by Michael Howard of Cape; according to Jacobs, *Biography*, p. 271, Fleming also conveyed his impressions personally, over lunch at L'Etoile restaurant in Charlotte Street: 'Amis went with some misgivings. Although his book was more pro than anti, Amis had pulled Fleming up where he thought he had gone wrong, complaining, for instance, when the Bond books slipped into "the idiom of the novelette". But Fleming wasn't worried about any of that. He had only two complaints to make. Oddjob had been sucked, not blown, out of the pressure-cabin of an aircraft. And there was no St Andrews Golf Club; the club in question was the Royal and Ancient Golf Club. Apart from these, Fleming had no objections or corrections and no quarrel with Amis's critical judgements' (p. 271).

72 This was Conquest's view as well. In a letter to Larkin of 2–3 August 1965 (Bodleian), Conquest described Maschler as 'one of those raving pissers old K gets pally with from time to time. But a great seller'.

73 EJH, *Slipstream*, p. 376; she means the only such associate up to that point in her life who believed in her.

74 Ibid., p. 254.

75 Ibid., p. 354.

76 Ibid., p. 355.

77 Ibid.

78 'Lucky Jim as I Remember Him', p. 784.

79 EJH, *Slipstream*, pp. 354–355.

80 Ibid., p. 355.

81 Ibid.

82 Martin Amis, *Experience*, p. 294.

83 Hilly Amis to PL, 4 June 1965 (Bodleian).

84 Jane's view in *Slipstream* is not much different: 'He simply wanted everybody to settle down so that he could write his books in peace and enjoy himself when he wasn't working' (p. 357).

85 Martin Amis, *Experience*, p. 189.

86 At home, that is, where Colin, the youngest, was now the only child.

87 EJH, *Slipstream*, p. 356.

88 Martin Amis, *Experience*, p. 215.

89 Ibid., p. 97.

90 Ibid.

91 Ibid., p. 98.

92 Ibid., pp. 96–97.

93 Ibid., p. 97.

94 Ibid., p. 98.

95 EJH, *Slipstream*, p. 357.

96 In a 'Relative Values' interview, *Sunday Times*, 29 November 1998.

97 EJH, *Slipstream*, p. 359.

98 Douglas-Henry, as threatened, cited Amis as co-respondent, and, as the *Daily Telegraph* put it on 7 May 1964, was granted a decree nisi 'because of misconduct by his wife'.

99 Jane's verdict in *Slipstream*, p. 364.

100 RC to PL, 2–3 August 1965 (Bodleian).

101 EJH, *Slipstream*, p. 364.

102 Ibid.

103 Peregrine Worsthorne, *Tricks of Memory: An Autobiography*, Weidenfeld and Nicolson, 1993, p. 240.

104 Or so she has told me in interview.

105 'A New James Bond', *Observer*, 31 March 1968, reprinted in *WBJA*, p. 69.

106 Ibid.

107 KA to Colin Howard, 31 July 1966.

108 EJH, *Slipstream*, p. 360.

109 Ibid., p. 362.

110 Ibid.

111 As Amis notes in *The James Bond Dossier*, p. 101, Fleming invests such scenes 'with an energy that shows he's dealing with something personally important to him'.

112 KA to RC, 17 September 1965 (recipient).

113 Quoted in Jacobs, *Biography*, p. 264.

114 EJH, *Slipstream*, p. 361.

115 Edmund Keeley, *Inventing Paradise: The Greek Journey 1937–47*, Farrar, Straus and Giroux, 1999, p. 96.

116 EJH, *Slipstream*, p. 361.
117 KA (as Robert Markham), *Colonel Sun*, Jonathan Cape, 1968, p. 96.
118 Keeley, *Inventing Paradise,* p. 172.
119 EJH, *Slipstream*, p. 362.
120 *Colonel Sun*, p. 69.
121 Ibid., p. 94.
122 Ibid., p. 17.
123 See D. J. Enright, 'A Cloud that's Dragonish', review of *Colonel Sun, Listener*, 28 March 1968: 'The new Bond, I would say, is beset by distinctly more scruples, and by scruples rather more acute, than was the old Bond.'
124 Dianne Hershey, 'Visiting Professor Amis Enjoys Writing and Teaching', *The Vanderbilt Hustler*, 20 October 1967.

CHAPTER 22

Lefties, Toffs and Bigots

 1 'A New James Bond', *Observer*, 31 March 1968, reprinted in *What Became of Jane Austen? And Other Questions*, Penguin, 1981, p. 65.
 2 Ibid., p. 67.
 3 Ibid., pp. 65–66.
 4 *Memoirs*, Penguin, 1992, p. 146.
 5 *Lucky Jim*, Penguin, 1976, p. 170.
 6 'Lone Voices', *Encounter*, March 1960; reprinted in *WBJA*, p. 155.
 7 Ibid., pp. 158–159.
 8 Ibid., p. 159.
 9 Ibid.
10 KA to *New Statesman*, 21 July 1967.
11 Eric Jacobs, *Kingsley Amis: A Biography*, Hodder and Stoughton, 1995, p. 187.
12 'Why Lucky Jim Turned Right', *Sunday Telegraph*, 2 July 1967; reprinted in *WBJA*, p. 198.
13 Ibid., p. 196; his first Tory vote in a national election was in 1970.
14 Ibid., p. 198.
15 Ibid., p. 197.
16 Both quotes are from page 16 of 'Lucky Jim's Politics', a Conservative Policy Centre pamphlet, published in July 1968. This pamphlet consists of a five-page transcript of the July 1967 talk, itself little more than a synopsis of 'Why Lucky Jim Turned Right', bulked out with a transcript of the question-and-answer session that followed.
17 'Why Lucky Jim Turned Right'; reprinted in *WBJA*, p. 199. In an anonymous review of 'Lucky Jim's Politics' in *Encounter* in September 1968, 'R' (Goronwy Rees) queried Amis's use of the term 'Lefty'. In reply, in a letter in the following issue, Amis provided further

details about the Lefty's nature and natural habitat: 'The Lefty is an intellectually disreputable and morally desensitised person whom the Labour Party tolerates within itself – and who, incidentally, flourishes more or less unchecked, not only in the *New Statesman* (where 'R' locates him), but in *The Times*, the *Guardian*, the *Daily Mirror*, the *Sun*, the *Observer*, the *Sunday Times*, The *Times Literary Supplement*, *Tribune*, and – most of all and most trendily – the *Listener* [edited at the time by Karl Miller], not to speak of *Panorama* and *24 Hours*.'

18 Ibid., p. 200.

19 Amis was fifty-three at the time.

20 *Girl, 20*, Panther, 1975, p. 112.

21 Ibid., p. 113; something like Roy's motives for persisting with left-wing views had been identified by Amis as early as November 1968, in the *Encounter* letter about Lefties: 'Has R taken account of the number of people who stay on the Left, or even move perceptibly Leftwards, in the hope of seeming to remain active, or with it, or in touch with youth, or young?'

22 'Why Lucky Jim Turned Right', reprinted in *WBJA*, p. 201.

23 'I am no economist,' he admits, 'and, if I strain myself, can nearly imagine that the unchecked rise in the cost of living is part of some frightfully subtle plan to send it rocketing down again. I would say more, if I knew more and had thought more, about those governmental decisions which reflect, if they are not actually designed to promote, the increasing power of the State over the individual' (ibid., p. 198).

24 From 'Barnestorming', an interview with Olinda Adeane, *Harpers and Queen*, April 1982.

25 Szamuely was born in 1925 in Moscow into a politically well-connected émigré family. Despite his father's disappearance during Stalin's Great Purges, he rose to prominence as an academic in Moscow and was 'outwardly an active servant of the regime' (*Memoirs*, p. 253), eventually becoming Vice-Chancellor of Budapest University in 1958, a progress that was not without its hiccups. He had been in the Gulag, but was freed because he had very strong Stalinist roots (through Matyas Rakosi, secretary of the Hungarian Workers' Party, also, briefly, Prime Minister). After returning to Hungary, he was allowed to move with his family to Kwame Nkrumah's Sovietised Ghana. Eventually, through a series of remarkable and ingenious manoeuvrings, Szamuely managed to get not only himself, his wife and his children to Britain, but his library as well. Amis met him a year or so after he arrived in Britain in 1964, by which time he was a lecturer at Reading University and on his way to becoming 'one of the world's most authoritative historians of modern Russia and commentators on the contemporary scene' (*Memoirs*, p. 257).

26 Ibid., p. 259.
27 Martin Amis quoted in 'Capital Letter', *Sunday Telegraph*, 17 September 1995.
28 Martin Amis, *Koba the Dread: Laughter and the Twenty Million*, Jonathan Cape, 2002, p. 10.
29 *Memoirs*, p. 147.
30 Both Watkins and Powell are quoted by Catherine Bennett in 'My Life and Silly Old Sods', *Guardian*, 25 February 1991.
31 Paul Fussell, 'Kingsley, As I Know Him', in Dale Salwak, ed., *Kingsley Amis: In Life and Letters*, Macmillan 1990, p. 19.
32 RC to KA, 29 November 1990 (Huntington).
33 *Memoirs*, p. 156.
34 Martin Amis, *Koba the Dread*, p. 23.
35 Ibid., pp. 10–11.
36 Quoted by Christopher Ricks, in 'I Was Like That Myself Once', a review of *WBJA*, *Listener*, 26 November 1970.
37 For Amis's response to Davie's article see KA to the editor, *Encounter*, December 1969.
38 Christopher Ricks, 'I Was Like That Myself Once', *Listener*, 26 November 1970.
39 Jacobs, *Biography*, p. 280.
40 Elizabeth Jane Howard, *Slipstream: A Memoir*, Macmillan, 2002, p. 380.
41 See Martin Amis, *Koba the Dread*, p. 272, the passage beginning: 'You were ideological and I am not'.
42 EJH, *Slipstream*, p. 412.
43 The Travellers, to which Conquest had helped to get Amis elected.
44 Brian Masters, *Great Hostesses*, Constable, 1983, pp. 3–4.
45 EJH, *Slipstream*, p. 364.
46 Ibid., p. 365.
47 Ibid.
48 Ibid.
49 'Fucking fools' were, or became, a distinct category for Amis: as Jacobs puts it, they were 'not necessarily stupid, just wrong. Lord Longford, the prison-visiting, Catholic former Labour Minister is for Amis a particularly splendid specimen of this breed on any number of grounds' (*Biography*, p. 12). David Jenkins, a successor Bishop of Durham to the one mentioned here, might well have qualified as a 'fucking fool' in this specialised sense, given his radical political and theological views. The quotations about Princess Alice and the Bishop of Durham come from the 18 January instalment of KA to Colin Howard, Philip and Martin Amis, 18, 19 January 1966.
50 KA to Colin Howard, Philip and Martin Amis, 19 January 1966.
51 Ibid., 18 January 1966.
52 KA to Colin Howard, Philip and Martin Amis, 3 February 1966.

53 EJH, *Slipstream*, p. 366.

54 All EJH's letters to the Keeleys are to be found among the Keeley papers in Princeton; in subsequent quotations from them, where dates are supplied in the main text, they will not be included in the notes.

55 EJH, *Slipstream*, p. 367.

56 Ibid.

57 Janet Morgan (Lady Balfour), a trustee of Dolly Burns's estate, was a frequent visitor to Fairlea. She agrees that Dolly could be bossy but points out in mitigation how difficult and complex a business it was organising grand house parties in Jamaica, where provisions, particularly of luxury goods, were hard to obtain, and much thought needed to be given to logistics.

58 *Memoirs*, p. 267.

59 Ibid., p. 269.

60 Both Amis's report and Jane's, entitled 'Private and Confidential Report on a Visit to Prague', are among the EJH papers in the Huntington.

61 Quoted in *Memoirs*, p. 272.

62 Ibid., p. 270.

63 EJH, *Slipstream*, p. 358; Martin may have had this moment in mind in *Money*, Penguin, 2000, p. 203, when John Self is given *Animal Farm* by Martina Twain.

64 EJH, *Slipstream*, p. 371.

65 Sargy's road to painting was long and winding. He was apprenticed at sixteen to Morris Motors in Oxford. After five years as an apprentice, he decided to read maths at university. Partly in defiance of the apprenticeship milieu, Sargy became 'arty' while in Oxford, drawing and buying postcards of paintings. In 1960 an art school friend saw his drawings and encouraged him to apply to Camberwell, an idea that instantly appealed. After finishing his degree there in 1964, he spent several years teaching art in a secondary school and on extra-mural courses, painting all the while. In 1966, aged twenty-nine, he enrolled in a postgraduate course in Camberwell.

66 *Memoirs*, p. 279.

67 Ibid.

68 Bruce Cook, 'Amis on a Southern Campus Taught – and Learned – a Lot', *National Observer*, 4 March 1968.

69 The exchange between Princeton friends and Amis was recollected by Jane in interview.

70 Martin would return to Brighton the following year to prepare for Oxford entrance examinations, A-Level results permitting.

71 For Worsthorne's account of this turbulence see *Tricks of Memory: An Autobiography*, Weidenfeld and Nicolson, 1993, pp. 221–222.

72 Ibid., p. 222.

73 Claudie Worsthorne's long illness, the result of a brain tumour (see

Hilly's letter to Amis of 12 May 1965, cited in Chapter 21), had taken a turn for the worse.

74 KA to Colin Howard, 17 September 1967.

75 EJH, *Slipstream*, p. 367.

76 Ibid., p. 368.

77 *Memoirs*, p. 289.

78 EJH, *Slipstream*, p. 368.

79 *Memoirs*, p. 289.

80 EJH, *Slipstream*, p. 368.

81 Quoted in Bruce Cook, 'Amis on a Southern Campus Taught – and Learned – a Lot.'

82 Richard Porter, 'Kingsley in Nashville', in Salwak, ed., *Kingsley Amis: In Life and Letters*, p. 39.

83 EJH, *Slipstream*, pp. 368–369.

84 *Memoirs*, p. 280.

85 Ibid., p. 284.

86 KA to RC, 1 November 1967. Porter had attended the Montgomery Bell Academy, a private boys' school in Nashville, and then gone on to Vanderbilt, where he excelled in English and Russian. After Vanderbilt he spent his military service partly in California, in an army language school, partly in Berlin, in intelligence work. He then went to Freiburg for a year on a Fulbright and to Indiana for two years of graduate study in Russian before returning to Vanderbilt to teach German and Russian (instead of English, which had also offered him a job). It was in Freiburg that Porter met his German wife, Brigitte, who was astonished to discover that he was an American, so impeccable was his German.

87 EJH, *Slipstream*, p. 369.

88 Paul K. Conkin, *Gone with the Ivy: A Biography of Vanderbilt University*, University of Tennessee Press, 2002, p. 345. According to David Halberstam, in *The Children*, Ballantine, 1999, an account of the start of the civil rights movement in the early 1960s, the organised segregationist forces in Tennessee were exceptionally weak: 'The fact that the Vanderbilt English department harboured some of the segregationist leadership seemed to reflect both the weakness and the eccentricity of that leadership' (p. 24).

89 Conkin, *Gone with the Ivy*, p. 346.

90 Anthony Burgess to EJH and KA, 3 September 1967 (among the EJH papers in the Huntington).

91 Allen Tate to EJH and KA, 14 September 1967.

92 Jane remembers the Chancellor's house as like something out of *Gone with the Wind*, but then many of the houses in Nashville struck her as 'like stage sets . . . they didn't seem like real houses'; she also remembers the Chancellor's wife serving lethal drinks called 'Salty Dogs', which Amis loved.

93 Porter's colleague John Cheek and his wife. Cheek was a scion of the Maxwell House coffee family. He and his wife had helped to introduce the Porters to Belle Meade society (Belle Meade is a wealthy suburb in Nashville). The Dudleys were even richer than the Cheeks: Guilford Dudley was the president of the largest insurance company in Nashville, a centre of the insurance industry.

94 'Kingsley in Nashville', in Salwak, ed., *Kingsley Amis: In Life and Letters*, p. 36.

95 Elizabeth Chase, 'Classes and Conversations with Kingsley Amis', *Vanderbilt Alumnus* 53: 3 (January–February 1968), pp. 10–13.

96 'Amis on a Southern Campus Taught – and Learned – a Lot'.

97 Ibid.

98 *Memoirs*, p. 288.

99 Amis also took over Walter Sullivan's creative writing class, which he seems to have found less enjoyable and harder to teach, at least according to Sullivan himself, perhaps not the best witness (at Princeton creative writing had been taught one-on-one, in tutorial).

100 *Hustler* (the Vanderbilt Student newspaper), 17 November 1967.

101 *Memoirs*, p. 290.

102 Porter, 'Kingsley in Nashville', in Salwak, ed., *Kingsley Amis: In Life and Letters*, pp. 38–39.

103 Russell Fraser, 'Lucky Jim as I Remember Him', *The Southern Review* 32: 4 (Autumn 1996), p. 785.

104 *Memoirs*, pp. 282–284.

105 Ibid., p. 291.

106 'Lucky Jim as I Remember Him', p. 785. One of the reasons the department was able to let the graduate student go was that Fraser himself had left Vanderbilt. Only weeks after the Amises arrived, he accepted a job as chair of the English Department at the University of Michigan, a bigger and more prestigious university than Vanderbilt. Dick Porter thinks that the Amises' attitudes to Nashville may have been coloured by Fraser's difficulties with the department; at one point it seemed as if the old guard were about to run him out of town. As Fraser himself admits in his memoir: 'I was dying with my boots on as chairman of Vanderbilt's English department' (p. 783). But Jane has no memory of Fraser's complaining about colleagues and Amis's only references to divisions in the department are slight and passing.

107 *Memoirs*, p. 284.

108 *I Want It Now*, Penguin, 1988, p. 131.

109 Ibid., p. 134.

110 KA to Tom Maschler, 28 September 1967.

111 Ibid. *I Want It Now*, pp. 182–183.

112 Ibid., p. 146.

113 Ibid.

114 KA to RC, 1 November 1968.

115 *I Want It Now*, p. 160.

116 Ibid., pp. 160–161.

117 Salwak, 'An Interview with Kingsley Amis', reprinted in Robert H. Bell, ed., *Critical Essays on Kingsley Amis*, G.K. Hall, 1998, p. 277.

118 PA to RC, 2 November 1968 (recipient).

119 Ronnie's conversion was also a problem for Michael Sissons, Amis's agent at A. D. Peters. In an undated note to Sissons (Boston University Library), Amis half accepted the criticism: 'As regards the sudden emergence of Ronnie's golden heart: something in that perhaps, but I hope a second reading (ahem) would show him getting slightly and tentatively golden at a comparatively early stage.'

120 *I Want It Now*, p. 184.

121 In 2006, Richard Porter informs me, James Lawson, leader of the student sit-in movement in Nashville, was voted Vanderbilt alumnus of the year, despite having been expelled by the Divinity School in 1963 for refusing to abandon the movement. Lawson had been in Memphis to visit Martin Luther King when King was assassinated. When James Earl Ray was imprisoned for shooting King, Lawson forced himself, as Porter puts it, 'to offer his ministry to Ray, and Ray accepted. They saw each other regularly. In time, Ray entered into a prison marriage and asked Lawson to perform the ceremony' (email to the author, 12 February 2006). Perhaps, Porter seems to be suggesting, Amis was overly pessimistic about the South's future.

CHAPTER 23

Lemmons

1 Richard Porter, 'Kingsley in Nashville', in Dale Salwak, ed., *Kingsley Amis: In Life and Letters*, Macmillan, 1990, p. 38.

2 Elizabeth Jane Howard, *Slipstream: A Memoir*, Macmillan, 2002, p. 370.

3 KA to Robert and Caroleen Conquest, 5 February 1968.

4 EJH to the Keeleys, 18 February 1968.

5 EJH, *Slipstream*, p. 371.

6 EJH to the Keeleys, 18 February 1968.

7 KA to Tom Maschler, 9 March 1968 (University of Reading Library).

8 KA to Colin Howard, 11 March 1968.

9 Colin Howard to KA and EJH, 6 February 1968.

10 Sargy Mann to EJH, 19 December 1967.

11 The critic John Carey.

12 Jonathan Wordsworth, a Wordsworthian as well as a Wordsworth.

13 Martin Amis to KA and EJH, undated but c. 26 December 1967.

14 Martin Amis to KA and EJH, 9 January, 1968; Jane seems to have had a similar positive effect on a second promising young man,

Daniel Day-Lewis, according to a bread-and-butter note he wrote to her in January 1975: 'Just a note to say thank you for a brief but lovely stay. It was so nice to see everyone at Lemmons again. You went to so much trouble to find the books, and paper and everything, and there was exactly the right pressure on me to make me work. I am just about to send the essay off having found the man's address. I thought going home would be difficult, but as it turned out, the reception I got was far from the icy one expected, the atmosphere was probably relieved of a fair amount of tension, by the changed attitude having got some work done . . . I am being [illegible] as you suggested, and coolly getting everything done without fuss, and my efficiency has been noticed.'

15 There were also reports on the cats, from both Sargy and Martin. Katsika's kneading left Sargy 'soaked with drool and with torn and bleeding chest, stomach and thighs – I do love her'; 'Princely Hugo' is described batting a cream lid off the kitchen table, then transferring his attention to the cereal bowl, 'with his well known "what cream lid?" expression' (19 December 1967). Martin also writes of Hugo, 'spinning away the hours in his habitual placid wonderment' (c. 26 December 1967). Both Sargy's and Martin's letters are among EJH's paper in the Huntington.

16 Martin Amis to KA and EJH, 12 February 1968.

17 KA to Colin Howard, 12 March 1968.

18 EJH, *Slipstream*, p. 371.

19 RC to PL, 18 March 1968 (Bodleian); this was a special lunch, not the regular Tuesday gathering.

20 *Memoirs*, Penguin, 1992, p. 240.

21 Ibid.

22 KA's eventual contributions to the 'Black Papers' (several with RC) are reproduced in *The Amis Collection: Selected Non-Fiction 1954–1990*, Penguin, 1991, pp. 265–283.

23 PL to KA, 22 April 1968 (Huntington).

24 PL to RC, 12 May 1968 (recipient).

25 John Betjeman to KA and EJH, 3 August 1970.

26 EJH, *Slipstream*, p. 372.

27 KA to Violet and Anthony Powell, 19 April 1966.

28 EJH, *Slipstream*, p. 372.

29 Ibid.

30 Anton Felton to Michael Sissons, 15 September 1972, and Michael Sissons to J. H. McCallum, c. September 1972 (the letter is undated). Both letters in the Peters Fraser and Dunlop archive in Boston University Library.

31 EJH, *Slipstream,* pp. 372–373.

32 This letter is to be found among the Larkin papers in the Bodleian.

33 Martin Amis, *Experience*, Jonathan Cape, 2000, p. 53.

34 'You have a very engaging household there, to put it mildly,' begins

a not atypical thank-you of 14 October 1970, from Jacqueline Wheldon, wife of the broadcaster Huw Wheldon: 'Lovely memories of Hadley Common include that marvellous misty air and a view from a most comfortable room, a house full of companionable people, lots of books and a log fire. A kind of classical image of the perfect weekend slightly softened at the edges by Lucky Jims, Bloody Marys, and brandy milk drinks – all unsurpassable I would think.'

35 Martin Amis, *Experience*, p. 53.

36 In late July, Amis received a cheque for £3,000 from Stanley Donen for the 'first phase' of his screen adaptation of *I Want It Now*, and the hotel the Keeleys had found in Rhodes, the Mediterranean, was inexpensive, like almost everything else in Greece in 1969.

37 Betty Fussell, 'Kingsley's Rituals', in Salwak, ed., *Kingsley Amis: In Life and Letters*, p. 33.

38 Paul Fussell, 'Kingsley, As I Knew Him', in Salwak, ed., *Kingsley Amis: In Life and Letters*, pp. 19–20.

39 Ibid., p. 20.

40 Ibid.

41 See RC to PL, 10 September 1958 (Bodleian), which mentions the review. For the review itself see Caroline Kizer, 'Four English Poets', *Poetry* 91 (October 1957). That Conquest had seen the review suggests that Amis had.

42 See 'Kingsley, As I Knew Him', p. 19, where the incident is mentioned and 'trendy' is attributed to Amis.

43 To get away from the Kizers – or, in the case of the Fussells and Keeleys, to get Amis away from the Kizers – a boat was hired for several nights to take the three couples and the two Fussell children (Tucky and Sam) to the island of Kos and then to the small Turkish village of Bodrum, ancient Halicarnassus. Landing on Kos the party discovered that there were no available hotels or *pensions*, at which point, as Jane puts it in *Slipstream*, 'a smiling man appeared and said "come with me," and we all stayed in his house. He and his wife slept in their double bed in the garden. I slept on a wooden chest. We weren't allowed to pay' (p. 361). At Bodrum there weren't any hotels either, but a farmer put them up and that night Fussell dropped his expensive leather wallet, containing all his credit cards and money, down the farm's primitive lavatory, a hole in the ground described by Jane as 'inexpressibly deep and murky' (p. 361). Through a supreme effort of will, Fussell fished the wallet out with his hand. In *Abroad: British Literary Travelling between the Wars*, Oxford University Press, 1980, p. 40, a study, among other things, of the differences between tourists and travellers, Fussell uses this incident to explain the distinction: 'it was the arm of a traveller that reached deep, deep into that cloaca'.

44 According to Mavis Nicholson.

45 Alastair Boyd, *The Sierras of the South: Travels in the Mountains*

of *Andalusia*, HarperCollins, 1992, p. 9n. Sally lured Hilly to the Casa by what Boyd calls her 'insistence that I harboured Arabian princelings under my roof'.

46 Martin Amis, *Experience*, p. 23.

47 Ibid., p. 25.

48 A joke first used at Maida Vale.

49 Martin Amis, *Experience*, p. 183.

50 Clive James, 'Kingsley Amis: A Profile', *New Review*, July 1974, pp. 21–28.

51 *The Green Man*, Penguin, 1998, p. 16.

52 Ibid.

53 See Richard Bradford, *Lucky Him: The Life of Kingsley Amis*, Peter Owen, 2001, p. 253.

54 'Who or What Was It?', in *Collected Short Stories*, Penguin, 1984, p. 220.

55 Martin Amis, *Experience*, p. 220.

56 Tony Colwell, letter to the author, 7 May 1999.

57 *The Green Man*, p. 169.

58 Ibid., p. 83.

59 Ibid., p. 82.

60 Ibid., p. 113.

61 Ibid., p. 41.

62 This line of interpretation is advanced by Thomas B. Gilmore, *Equivocal Spirits: Alcoholism and Drinking in Twentieth-Century Literature*, University of North Carolina Press, 1987, p. 151.

63 *Lucky Jim*, Penguin, 1976, pp. 219–220.

64 Ibid., p. 221.

65 *The Green Man*, p. 41.

66 Ibid., p. 168.

67 Ibid.

68 Ibid., p. 138.

69 Ibid., p. 175.

70 'Who or What Was It?', in *Collected Short Stories*, p. 217.

71 Quoted in Bradford, *Lucky Him: The Life of Kingsley Amis*, p. 262.

72 'Who or What Was It?', in *Collected Short Stories*, p. 219.

73 *On Drink*, Jonathan Cape, 1972, p. 11.

74 Ibid., p. 12.

75 Ibid., p. 13.

76 Ibid., p. 15.

77 Ibid., p. 47.

78 Ibid., p. 108.

79 Ibid., pp. 94–95.

80 'The Amis Drinker's Companion', *Daily Telegraph* magazine, 20 November 1970; 'De-Canting Wine', *Daily Telegraph* magazine, 27 November 1970; 'Rude Awakening' and 'Drinking Man's Diet', *Daily Telegraph* magazine, 4 December 1970.

81 The other distinguished shags were Brian Aldiss, John Betjeman, John Arlott, Robert Conquest and the newscaster Reginald Bosanquet.

82 This letter is also dated 4 September 1970, like the letter to which it replies; perhaps Amis had also talked to him that day on the telephone. The Larkin letter is among the Amis papers in the Huntington.

83 EJH, *Slipstream*, p. 384.

84 It was Amis's strong feeling, as he put it in 'Death of a Poet', *Observer*, 28 May 1972, that Day-Lewis 'came to draw his own conclusions from his physical decline and increasingly severe – though happily intermittent – bouts of pain, but out of kindness and abnegation of self, chose not to discuss the matter'.

85 EJH, *Slipstream*, p. 375.

86 Ibid., p. 385.

87 Martin Amis, *Experience*, p. 190.

88 EJH, *Slipstream*, p. 385.

89 Larkin got to know Day-Lewis well when he was Compton Lecturer in Poetry, a visiting post at Hull.

90 Martin Amis, *Experience*, p. 119.

91 *Girl, 20*, Panther, 1975, p. 19.

92 Ibid., p. 17.

93 Ibid., p. 20.

94 Ibid., p. 37.

95 Ibid., p. 124.

96 Ibid., p. 17.

97 Ibid., p. 127.

98 Ibid., pp. 128–129.

99 Ibid., p. 135.

100 EJH, *Slipstream*, p. 383. See EJH to the Keeleys, 9 June 1970: 'My mama jolly nearly died this winter after I got back from America, and what with hospital and long convalescence with nurses *living in and* all three children for what felt like months I nearly broke down. I have three lovely tranquillizers a day now . . . K. is about a third of the way through very funny novel about musicians: he is having fun with it in the most enviable way.'

101 *Girl, 20*, pp. 57–58.

102 *The Green Man*, p. 115.

103 *Girl, 20*, p. 174.

104 Ibid., p. 157. Penny has some talent for music, which Roy does nothing to encourage, out of laziness masquerading as principle. As KA told Clive James in 'Kingsley Amis: A Profile', *New Review*, July 1974: Roy 'should have fostered Penny's talent. He should have said, "Here is a violin and a piano. Get through these exercises by the end of the week." "Why, Dad?" "Never mind why. That's what you do."'

105 *The Riverside Villas Murder*, Penguin, 1984, p. 140.

106 These sessions have much to commend them when compared to the trouble and expense of going out with girls: 'the only snag was that girls were attractive and boys were not' (ibid., p. 131).

107 *Girl,* 20, p. 204.

108 Frank Kermode, 'The British Novel Lives', *Atlantic Monthly,* July 1972.

CHAPTER 24

Dissolution

1 For more precise numbers and individual publications see the Chronological *Catalogue to the Kingsley Amis Journalism Archive.*

2 See Pat Kavanagh to KA, 22 August 1973, and Pat Kavanagh to Harold Evans, 27 November 1973 (Boston University Library).

3 See Anthony Jones to KA, 4 July 1973. Jones was the source not only of the list but of the quote about the product needing to be 'absolutely right' (Boston University Library).

4 'What Became of Jane Austen?', in *What Became of Jane Austen? And Other Questions,* Penguin 1981, p. 9.

5 Tom Maschler to KA, 18 February 1970 (University of Reading Library).

6 'Splendid' comes from KA to Christopher Ricks, 21 June 1971; see also KA to Ricks, 16 July 1971.

7 John Betjeman to KA, 27 May 1973 (Huntington).

8 KA to Alex MacCormick, Penguin Books, 13 May 1972 (a copy of this letter is deposited among the Peters Fraser and Dunlop papers, Boston University Library).

9 V. S. Pritchett, 'Pugnacious Paradoxes', review of G. K. Chesterton, *Selected Stories,* ed. Kingsley Amis, in *New Statesman,* 19 January 1973.

10 Kingsley Amis, ed., *Harold's Years: Impressions from the 'New Statesman' and the 'Spectator',* Quartet, 1977, p. 7.

11 Ibid., p. 9.

12 Ibid.

13 Presumably Jane, a rare wifely appearance.

14 Ian McEwan, 'Mother Tongue', in Zachary Leader, ed., *On Modern British Fiction,* Oxford University Press, 2003, pp. 42–43.

15 Eric Jacobs, *Kingsley Amis: A Biography,* Hodder and Stoughton, 1995, p. 7.

16 Elizabeth Jane Howard, *Slipstream: A Memoir,* Macmillan, 2002, p. 390.

17 Ibid., p. 394.

18 This is Martin's comment, in interview.

19 According to Jill Balcon.

20 This quotation is from an interview with the author, but see also Martin Amis, *Experience,* Jonathan Cape, 2000, pp. 189–190.

21 According to EJH, in interview.

22 Again, according to EJH, in interview.

23 The date at the top of the notebook page on which the notes for *Ending Up* begin.

24 See the depiction of old Cecil Masters, a fellow boarder of 'Kingsley' in 'The Legacy'.

25 *Ending Up*, Penguin, 1987, p. 164.

26 For this quotation, from an interview with Dale Salwak of 14 July 1980, see Dale Salwak, *Kingsley Amis: Modern Novelist*, Harvester Press, 1992, p. 190.

27 *Ending Up*, p. 175.

28 Ibid., p. 24.

29 Ibid., pp. 29, 51.

30 As recalled by EJH in interview.

31 *Ending Up*, p. 76.

32 Ibid., p. 37.

33 Ibid., p. 38.

34 Though written in September 1980, 'Amis Abroad' was not published in the *Sunday Times* until 26 July 1981, reprinted in *The Amis Collection: Selected Non-Fiction 1954–1990*, Penguin, 1991, p. 341.

35 Ibid., p. 328.

36 'A bientot mon petit lapin' it reads on the front, below a picture of a rabbit.

37 See EJH, *Slipstream*, p. 412.

38 RC to PL, 3 October 1973 (Bodleian).

39 RC to PL, 22 October 1973 (Bodleian).

40 The serial ran in six instalments from 13 July 1975 to 28 September 1975. There was a six-week gap between the fifth and sixth instalments to allow readers to enter a competition to solve the murder and write their own version of the final episode. *The Crime of the Century* was published in book form in 1987. One of its characters is a detective novelist whose hero is named James Fenton.

41 *Memoirs*, Penguin, 1992, p. 309.

42 EJH, *Slipstream*, p. 400.

43 Ibid., pp. 400–401.

44 *Memoirs*, p. 31.

45 The room they ended up with had a bath and toilet, as promised, but the bathroom had no lock and the flush was weak, just the sorts of details to make Amis regret agreeing to come abroad.

46 Russell Fraser, 'Lucky Jim as I Remember Him', *Southern Review* 32: 4 (Autumn 1996), p. 791.

47 RC to PL, 28 June 1975 (Bodleian).

48 'I thought she wanted to drive actually some of the way,' Durham remembers, 'and I didn't want her to drive; and so there was a bit of tension all through the whole holiday between me and Jane.' 'When I offered to take my turn at the considerable driving involved,'

Jane writes in *Slipstream*, 'he turned me down. He and Nita did that. I felt like an anonymous outsider' (p. 400).

49 *The Alteration*, Penguin, 1988, p. 27.

50 Ibid., p. 199.

51 Quoted in Tom Miller, 'Kingsley Amis: A Novelist of Our Times', *Illustrated London News*, September 1978, cited in Salwak, *Kingsley Amis: Modern Novelist*, p. 198.

52 *The Alteration*, p. 105.

53 A copy of Shippey's speech at the awards ceremony can be found among Amis's papers in the Huntington. I have drawn on it for some of the novel's allusions to alternate world novels, as well as for examples of the novel's off or antique language.

54 This draft letter is contained in the Peters Fraser and Dunlop files at Boston University.

55 *The Alteration*, p. 179.

56 Clive James, 'Kingsley Amis: A Profile', *New Review*, July 1974.

57 *Memoirs*, pp. 117–118.

58 *The Alteration*, p. 33.

59 Ibid., p. 34.

60 Richard Bradford, *Lucky Him: The Life of Kingsley Amis*, Peter Owen, 2001, p. 297.

61 *Memoirs*, p. 115.

62 Ibid., pp. 116–117.

63 EJH, *Slipstream*, pp. 405–406.

64 Neil Powell, 'What Life Is: The Novels of Martin Amis', *PN Review* 20, 7: 6 (1981), pp. 42–45.

65 Corby, in the Midlands, where Sal was living with 'Mrs Reynolds', who had some connection with a disreputable boyfriend of Sal's.

66 EJH, *Slipstream*, p. 401.

67 *Memoirs*, p. 118.

68 *Jake's Thing*, Hutchinson, 1978, pp. 155–156.

69 Ibid., pp. 55–56.

70 Martin Amis, *Experience*, p. 310.

71 See Auberon Waugh, 'Amis: A Singular Man', *Sunday Telegraph* magazine, 17 September 1978.

72 *Jake's Thing*, p. 171.

73 EJH, *Slipstream*, p. 416.

74 Ibid., p. 402.

75 Ibid., p. 417.

76 Ibid.

77 Jacobs, *Biography*, p. 112.

78 'Amis Abroad', *Sunday Times*, 26 July 1981, reprinted in *AC*, p. 328.

79 Ibid., p. 329.

80 Ibid.

81 Ibid., p. 334.

82 Ibid., p. 335.

83 Ibid., p. 345.
84 Ibid., p. 341.
85 Ibid., p. 342.
86 Ibid.
87 Anthony Powell to RC, 7 July 1981 (recipient).
88 EJH, *Slipstream*, p. 423.
89 Ibid., p. 424.
90 Ibid.
91 This comment from the wife of a painter friend of Joy and Richard Law, who wishes to remain anonymous, comes from a letter of 28 June 2002 to Joy Law, a response in part to a disobliging remark Amis made about Joy in a letter of 10 September to Robert Conquest. 'Both of us recall very clearly that time with you for several reasons,' the painter continues, 'not least the incapability of K.A. to use his hands properly, apart from lifting a glass; and the astonishingly low level of scrabble playing, plus the added fact that neither E Jane nor K.A. had any visual sense whatsoever. Strangely, we know other writers just like that last.'
92 EJH, *Slipstream*, p. 424.
93 Jacobs, *Biography*, p. 323.
94 EJH, *Slipstream*, p. 424.
95 Ibid., p. 425.
96 Ibid., p. 426.
97 Jacobs, *Biography*, p. 324.
98 EJH, *Slipstream*, p. 424.

CHAPTER 25

Nadir

1 RC to PL, 25 November 1979 (Bodleian).
2 PL to KA, 23 September 1979 (Bodleian).
3 According to correspondence in the archives of Jonathan Clowes Ltd., Amis's agent.
4 KA to PL, 19 January 1979 (Bodleian).
5 *Jake's Thing*, Hutchinson, 1978, p. 136.
6 Joseph Connolly, 'I Wish I'd Written', *Guardian*, 20 March 1997.
7 *Jake's Thing*, p. 139.
8 Ibid., p. 12.
9 Ibid., p. 14.
10 Ibid.
11 'Pater and Old Chap,' *Observer*, 13 November 1957, reprinted in *What Became of Jane Austen? And Other Questions*, Penguin, 1981, p. 139.
12 Keith Miller, 'Jim, Jake and the Years Between: Stasis in the Contemporary British Novel', *Ariel* 13 (January 1982), pp. 55–69,

reprinted in Robert H. Bell, ed., *Critical Essays on Kingsley Amis*, G. K. Hall, 1998, pp. 197–198.

13 'A Reunion', *New Statesman*, 24–31 December 1976.

14 John Betjeman's 'Senex' from *Old Lights for New Chancels* (1940), is an obvious model. Betjeman's poem begins: 'Oh would I could subdue the flesh / Which sadly troubles me!'

15 In place of 'Mellstock churchyard', used in the refrains in Hardy's and Betjeman's poems, Amis substitutes the trade labels of old 78s.

16 PL to KA, 1 August 1978 (Huntington).

17 'I am getting ugly now because I am getting old,' Amis wrote to Larkin on 14 January 1980, aged fifty-seven. 'Being fat doesn't matter eh, and people can't see your teeth properly, in any case I have one in each jaw still working. What I am doing is getting huge jowls under my chin like Mr Heath and Chuck Snow. They show when I do television, and no doubt all the rest of the time come to that. They make me feel humiliated in some way. No use slimming because the flaps of the skin will still be waving to and fro after you've taken the fat out if you ever do.'

18 From an interview of 14 July 1980, quoted in Dale Salwak, *Kingsley Amis: Modern Novelist*, Harvester, 1992, p. 214.

19 An arrow here points to a prior note: 'The Eng did all the dreadful things to England – "but couldn't have done them without our support"'.

20 *Russian Hide-and-Seek*, Hutchinson, 1980, p. 16.

21 Salwak, *Kingsley Amis: Modern Novelist*, p. 215.

22 John McDermott, *Kingsley Amis: An English Moralist*, Macmillan, 1989, p. 151.

23 *Memoirs*, Penguin, 1992, p. 315.

24 Ronald Allison and Sarah Liddell, eds., *The Royal Encyclopedia*, Macmillan, 1991, p. 32.

25 Eric Jacobs, 'Amis Diaries', 14 January 1993.

26 KA to Jack Gohn, 27 March 1975.

27 PL to J. Norton Smith, 14 April 1974, quoted in Andrew Motion, *Philip Larkin: A Writer's Life*, Faber and Faber, 1993, p. 434.

28 'Anthologies', The *Amis Collection: Selected Non-Fiction 1954–1990*, Penguin, 1991, p. 141, where it is identified as 'Lecture, given in 1980' (p. 145).

29 Ibid., p. 142.

30 Ibid., p. 143.

31 *The New Oxford Book of Light Verse*, Oxford University Press, 1978, p. v.

32 Ibid.

33 Ibid., p. x.

34 Ibid., p. xxi.

35 Ibid., p. viii.

36 Ibid., p. xviii.

37 For Amis's conscientiousness as an editor and Auden's lack of consci-

entiousness, see Paul Fussell, *The Anti-Egotist: Kingsley Amis, Man of Letters*, Oxford University Press, 1994, pp. 135–145.

38 Phyllis McGinley.

39 'Anthologies', in *AC*, p. 145.

40 The review, 'Eighteenth Century Verse', originally appeared in the *Listener*, 6 December 1984, reprinted in *AC*, p. 156.

41 'Anthologies', in *AC*, p. 145.

42 Ibid.

43 See KA to RC, 12 August 1977.

44 'Anthologies', in *AC*, p. 145.

45 Ibid.

46 KA, *The Faber Popular Reciter*, Faber and Faber, 1978, p. 16.

47 EJH, *Slipstream: A Memoir*, Macmillan, 2002, p. 427.

48 Martin Amis, *Experience*, Jonathan Cape, 2000, p. 307.

49 Ibid., pp. 307–308.

50 Jane denies this characterisation. As she remembers it, during the Gardnor House years she saw her therapist an hour a week and attended only four one-day workshops and one two-day workshop. Though in *Slipstream*, p. 421, she suggests that the meetings of her women's group did not begin until spring 1978, her therapist, she later told me, thinks they didn't begin until late 1979 or early 1980. These meetings were fortnightly.

51 Martin Amis, *Experience*, p. 308.

52 Ibid., p. 219.

53 Ibid., p. 309.

54 EJH, *Slipstream*, p. 428.

55 In Washington, DC, where Conquest and his new American wife (he had split with Caroleen in 1975), Elizabeth, known as Liddie, lived, and where he worked as a Research Fellow at the Heritage Foundation.

56 Martin Amis, *Experience*, p. 311.

57 According to Eric Jacobs, *Kingsley Amis: A Biography*, Hodder and Stoughton, 1995, p. 331, Susie Allison, recently widowed, was briefly considered, but never asked.

58 Ali's description.

59 Alistair Boyd, *The Sierras of the South: Travels in the Mountains of Andalusia*, HarperCollins, 1992, p. 25.

60 Ibid., p. 26.

61 The family shipping business had not prospered.

62 Quoted in Jacobs, *Biography*, p. 333.

63 These are Hilly's words, from an interview with the author.

64 Martin Amis, *Experience*, p. 310.

65 Ibid., p. 312.

66 Ibid.

67 According to Jacobs, *Biography*, p. 332, the dinner at Gardnor House was preceded by a preliminary dinner at Bertorelli, with just Amis, Hilly, Philip and Martin. On 14 January 1981, in an entry

in his engagement diary, Amis writes 'Drinks H', and on 15 January he writes 'Hill here', but the hand is unclear and this could be 'Jill here'.

68 'The Agony of Mr Amis', interview with David Lewin, *Daily Mail*, 30 December 1989.

69 Martin Amis, *Experience*, p. 311.

70 KA to PL, 9 June 1981.

71 This is a rare undated letter.

72 Jane's figure of £14,000 is puzzling, not only because it differs from Amis's £40,000, but because Jane also claims in *Slipstream*, p. 350, that she bought the Maida Vale house in 1964 for £2,000, spending another £6,000 on its renovation (£8,000 being what she received from the sale of Blomfield Road). The discrepancy comes from a misremembering on Jane's part. The £14,000 figure was what she received for the sale of 108 Maida Vale, not what she paid for it. The £40,000 figure may have been floated by Jane's lawyers before she heard it and decided it was unfair; presumably it was the £14,000 figure adjusted for inflation and/or with interest added. When Jacobs published the £40,000 figure in his biography, Jane wrote to him on 21 September 1994 disputing it: 'I did not ask for £40,000 as well as half of the sale price of Gardnor House. I asked for the £14,000 which did not "help us to buy Maida Vale", I bought the lease, paid for the extensive building repairs and also the furnishings.'

73 As a consequence of what Jane saw as Amis's inactivity, she was forced to lodge with Ursula Vaughan Williams, whom in *Slipstream* she calls 'utterly staunch' (p. 430), for almost two and a half years, though she also stayed for some weeks with her daughter, Nicola, and Nicola's second husband, in Gloucestershire, and with Jonathan Clowes and his wife, Ann Evans, in Sussex. Ann Evans worked at the Clowes agency.

74 See RC to PL, 24 August 1982 (Bodleian).

75 Michael Davie, 'Lucky Jim Discovers There's Life after Sixty', *Observer*, 23 April 1982.

76 KA to RC, quoted in Jacobs, *Biography*, p. 334, where it is dated 'mid-February'.

77 EJH, *Slipstream*, p. 429.

78 KA to PL, 3 August 1982, makes the chronology clear: 'Restart my new novel tomorrow. Did I tell you I've junked my old new novel?' That this new new novel, *Stanley and the Women*, developed out of the one he was planning before 'Difficulties with Girls' is suggested by a page of undated notes in one of Amis's notebooks in the Huntington (AMS651).

79 Theo Richmond to the author, 6 August 2002.

80 Michael Barber, 'Misogyny and Madness: Michael Barber Talks with Kingsley Amis', *Books and Bookmen*, May 1984.

81 'Difficulties with Girls', unfinished manuscript (Huntington), p. 46.

82 The commas in this list are my addition.
83 'Difficulties with Girls', unfinished manuscript (Huntington), p. 11.
84 Ibid., p. 45.
85 Ibid., p. 109.
86 Jacobs, *Biography*, pp. 335–336.
87 Ibid., p. 336. The preceding quotation, about monstrous Ann, comes from 'Difficulties with Girls', unfinished manuscript (Huntington), p. 41.
88 Dr Best in *The Anti-Death League* is another shrink who tries to convince his patients they are gay.
89 Amis may also have been thinking of Paul Fussell, who at this time, the time of the break-up of his own marriage, went through a homosexual phase. See Betty Fussell, *My Kitchen Wars*, North Point Press, 2000, pp. 207–215.
90 This exchange, recounted by Martin Amis in interview, was corroborated by Colin.
91 'Difficulties with Girls', unfinished manuscript (Huntington), p. 34.
92 KA to RC, 9 November 1982.
93 'Difficulties with Girls', unfinished manuscript (Huntington), p. 33.
94 Interview with Graham Turner, 'Kingsley Amis and Those Uncertain Feelings', *Sunday Telegraph*, 28 September 1986.
95 To Martin, *Russian Hide-and-Seek* was 'KA's worst, or least good, novel' (*Experience*, p. 229).
96 All three Conquest letters are among Amis's papers in the Huntington.
97 Interview with Lynda-Lee Potter, 'I've Been Lucky Considering the Outrageous Way I've Behaved', *Daily Mail*, 13 May 1995.
98 See KA to RC, 30 March 1982.
99 On 22 June 1982 Amis wrote to Jonathan Clowes enclosing 'the article on my mini-madness' and asking Clowes for comments. As far as I know the article was not published before it became the last chapter of the *Memoirs*.
100 RC to PL, 11 May 1982 (Bodleian).
101 Martin Amis, *Experience*, p. 93.
102 According to Alan Watkins, recollected in an interview with the author.
103 Donald Trelford to Eric Jacobs, 5 December 1992, among the Jacobs papers (Huntington).
104 Alan Watkins, 'The Lucky, Uncertain Old Devil', review of Eric Jacobs, *Kingsley Amis: A Biography*, in the *Spectator*, 10 June 1995.
105 Martin Amis, *Experience*, p. 257, though in a footnote Martin adds: 'Along with *Lucky Jim* of course, and, I would hope, pre-eminently, *The Green Man*, *The Alteration*, *Girl, 20*, *Ending Up*, the stories "Dear Illusion", "All the Blood Within Me" and "A Twitch on the Thread", the *Collected Poems*, *The King's English* and perhaps the *Letters*.'
106 Ibid., pp. 178–179.
107 Ibid., pp. 312–313.

108 For the note see AMS 122 (Huntington).

109 *Stanley and the Women*, Penguin, 1985, p. 45.

110 EJH, *Slipstream*, p. 421.

111 Ibid., p. 438.

112 Ibid., p. 439.

113 Referring to the description, which contains the 'giraffe's ear' and 'tropical fruit' passage, of the girlie magazine (*Jake's Thing*, pp. 55–56).

114 Anthony Burgess, review of *Stanley and the Women*, 'Woman Trouble', *Observer*, 20 May 1984.

115 John Carey, 'At Home with the Old Devil', review of Zachary Leader, ed., *The Letters of Kingsley Amis*, *Sunday Times*, 27 May 2000.

116 John Carey, 'Kingsley among the Amazons', *Sunday Times*, 20 May 1984.

117 *Stanley and the Women*, p. 315.

118 Blake Morrison, 'Kingsley and the Women', *Observer*, 13 May 1984.

CHAPTER 26

Return

1 PL to KA, 29 January 1984 (Huntington).

2 See Martin Amis, *Experience*, Jonathan Cape, 2000, p. 310: 'Around now, too, he started referring to the opposite sex as "females". "Dad, don't *say* that word!" I used to tell him; and he partly moderated this habit when I was present.'

3 Marilyn Butler, 'Women and the Novel', *London Review of Books*, 7–20 June 1984, pp. 7–8. Butler's argument turns on Amis's supposed distance from Stanley's views and on Stanley's imperfections: 'Amis maintains his distance from the petty chauvinist Stanley more unmistakably than he did from the separatist Jake, so that what Stanley says and what the book says must be two very different things'; '[Stanley] is eventually revealed as Mr Doublebind, passive and spineless as a father, rigid in his mental processes, and, confronted by a "mad" Steve, instantly ready to gang up – first with Nowell, afterwards with Susan – to have him admitted to hospital.' Butler also denies that the novel is an attack on the therapeutic culture: 'Although it may look at the outset as though Amis means to satirise the trendy anti-psychiatrists of the Sixties and Seventies, this is not . . . the case.' The horrible psychiatrist, Dr Trish Collings, who treats Stanley's son Steve, 'seems justified in her criticisms of Stanley, which means that she is also broadly right about the hidebound and limited insights of Nash and of Wainwright, Stanley's double inside the medical profession.'

4 Martin Amis, *Experience*, p. 318.

5 Mary Mackey, 'A Hate-Novel against Women', *San Francisco Chronicle*, 8 September 1985.

6 Rhoda Koenig, 'Mad Dames and Englishmen', *New York*, 7 October 1985.

7 Christopher Hitchens, 'American Notes', *Times Literary Supplement*, 16 November 1984.

8 As reported by Edwin McDowell in 'Publish: Calm Reaction to Disputed Book', *New York Times*, 8 October 1985, an article that appeared at the time of the American publication.

9 See *Inside Bookselling* 1: 20 (30 September 1985).

10 James Atlas, 'Out to Lunch with Kingsley Amis', *Vanity Fair*, March 1987.

11 *Stanley and the Women*, Penguin, 1985, p. 14.

12 James Atlas, 'Out to Lunch with Kingsley Amis', *Vanity Fair*, March 1987. For Stanley's remark about 'where and when' he was born, see *Stanley and the Women*, pp. 54–55. One other factor may have played a part in the difficulties Clowes had in finding an American publisher for *Stanley*: it was initially offered in tandem with *Russian Hide-and-Seek*, not only anti-Lefty but a critical and commercial flop in Britain, a point made much of by Virgil Nemoianu in an untitled review of both novels in the *American Spectator*, January 1986. *Russian Hide-and-Seek* never did find an American publisher.

13 See Blake Morrison, 'Kingsley and the Women', *Saturday Review*, May/June 1985, a reprinting of his *Observer* article of the same name (13 May 1984).

14 EJH, *Slipstream: A Memoir*, Macmillan, 2002, p. 419.

15 Jonathan Clowes to KA, 3 August 1989 (Jonathan Clowes has a copy of the letter).

16 These figures come from author accounts compiled by Harts, Chartered Accountants, 3 Churchgates, Church Lane, Berkhamsted.

17 In a letter to Quaritch of 5 April 1984, Minkoff explained his difficulties in selling the archive in the United States. Though a dozen institutions were interested, only one, the Huntington, was prepared to make an offer. The 'major problem' was that the archive lacked '*Lucky Jim* and several early manuscripts' (these had been purchased previously by the Ransom Center in Texas, which was short of money now because of the recent Pforzheimer purchase). The Huntington did not quibble about the missing manuscripts: 'all they want is to buy the letters [that is, to Amis, from Betjeman, Conquest, et al.] and the manuscripts at the same time.' In the end, the sale was made for $90,000.

18 In 1992 Ali's memoir, *The Sierras of the South: Travels in the Mountains of Andalusia*, HarperCollins, 1992, with drawings by Philip Amis, was published by HarperCollins, but this, too, brought in little income.

19 Interview with Margarette Driscoll, 'The Old Devil Himself', *Today*, 27 October 1986.

20 KA to PL, 18 December 1984.

21 KA to PL, 18 June 1984. The phrase 'also rich' in this quotation is a handwritten, asterisked interpolation.

22 Eric Jacobs, *Kingsley Amis: A Biography*, Hodder and Stoughton, 1995, p. 351.

23 Ibid., p. 326.

24 Ibid., p. 351.

25 Andrew Dixon, 'Time Mellows an Old Devil', *News of the World*, 14 September 1986.

26 *The Old Devils*, Penguin, 1987, p. 179.

27 Ibid., p. 92.

28 Ibid., pp. 174–175.

29 P. J. Kavanagh, 'The Cracks Fill Up' (one of his 'Life and Letters' columns), *Spectator*, 27 September 1986. Kavanagh's remarks about *The Old Devils* are quoted in Robert H. Bell, ed., *Critical Essays on Kingsley Amis*, G. K. Hall, 1998, p. 324.

30 Anthony Powell, *Journals 1990–1992*, Heinemann, 1998, p. 116.

31 These notes are to be found in AMS 80 in the Huntington.

32 *The Old Devils*, pp. 170–171.

33 Ibid., p. 316.

34 Ibid., p. 319.

35 Ibid., p. 110.

36 Ibid., p. 163.

37 Ibid., p. 374.

38 Ibid., p. 375.

39 Ibid.

40 Ibid., p. 354.

41 Ibid., p. 382.

42 Ibid., p. 207.

43 Ibid., p. 208.

44 Ibid., p. 221.

45 Ibid., p. 222.

46 Ibid., p. 224.

47 Ibid. p. 225.

48 Ibid., p. 226.

49 Ibid.

50 Ibid., p. 206.

51 From Philip Larkin, *Collected Poems*, ed. Anthony Thwaite, Faber and Faber, 1988, pp. 173–174.

52 *The Old Devils*, p. 226.

53 In the Larkin poem, the stone effigies on the tomb, those of 'earl and countess' (like the effigies of 'a member of the de Courcey family and his lady' in the chancel of St Mary's) lie 'side by side, their faces blurred', their 'proper habits' only 'vaguely shown'. The speaker, as little a 'ruin-bibber' as the speaker of 'Church Going', thinks the figures barely worth a glance, until his eye is caught by the earl's ungloved hand: 'One sees, with a sharp tender shock, / His hand

withdrawn, holding her hand.' So much has disappeared since the deaths of the earl and countess: 'the old tenantry', the meaning of Latin inscriptions ('How soon succeeding eyes begin / To look, not read'). Only the clasped hands 'involve the eye'.

54 Larkin, *Collected Poems*, ed. Thwaite, pp. 110–111.

55 William H. Pritchard, 'Amis Behavin', review of *The Old Devils*, *New York Times Book Review*, 22 March 1987.

56 *The Old Devils*, p. 348. Amis celebrates the marriage as Larkin celebrates the marriages in 'The Whitsun Weddings'. In both novel and poem, various examples of 'our falling short' are documented, humorously, unflinchingly; then what is best about us, what we 'do best', takes centre stage.

57 PL to KA, 22 October 1984 (Huntington).

58 *The Old Devils*, pp. 157–158.

59 PL to KA, 20 March 1985 (Huntington).

60 KA to PL, 2 April 1985.

61 PL to KA, 10 May 1985 (Huntington).

62 PL to KA, 27 August 1985 (Huntington).

63 COD refers to the *Concise Oxford Dictionary*; the letter of RC to KA, 7 November 1985, is in the Huntington.

64 In an entry of 22 June 1995 in the 'Amis Diaries', Jacobs recounts a conversation with Amis in which Amis said that at first he was to blame for not visiting Hull, because he was reluctant to sleep in a strange bed, but that after about 1970 he'd got over this fear and it was Larkin who resisted his coming to visit: 'He could only speculate about whether Larkin was ashamed of the work he did, or the low-grade people he lived and worked among.'

65 The question of whether Amis was still at work on *The Old Devils* at the time of Larkin's death is complicated. In a letter to Paul Fussell of 10 February 1993, in response to a Fussell query, Amis says his publisher has told him that he 'delivered the first ten chapters on 26.11.85, i.e. well before Philip's death in the December [six days before it].' As for the novel's ending, 'I cannot prove that I didn't think of ending the book with a wedding without any reference to Larkin at all . . . I "conceived" the novel in September, 1984, before I knew Larkin was even ill. I personally think that a possible connection between the two is the sort of idea you academic types come up with.' There are several problems here. To begin with, it is not clear what 'the first ten chapters' means; the finished novel only has ten chapters and in a diary entry of c. 28 November 1985, two days after Hutchinson is supposed to have received 'the first ten', Amis writes: 'love scene Alun/Sophie', as if he had just written it or was about to write it. The novel was published early in September 1986, exactly two years after it was conceived. It was Amis's second-longest novel, after *Take a Girl Like You*, and he claimed to have taken more trouble with it than with any book since *Lucky Jim*. If he submitted a whole

draft to Hutchinson on 26 November 1985, that means he wrote c. 180 pages in four months, given the letter of 20 July to Robert Conquest in which he reports 'coming up to 200 book-pages'.

66 Keri Hulme, an unknown New Zealander, won for *The Bone People* in 1985; Anita Brookner won for *Hotel du Lac* in 1984.

67 *Memoirs*, Penguin, 1992, pp. 325–326.

68 These quotations come from unpublished notes taken by Dale Salwak, 27 September 1989.

69 Peter Carson to Jonathan Clowes, 2 February 1988 (recipient).

70 Susannah Murray, 'Chips from a Master's Workbench', *Independent*, 30 April 1987.

71 The review in the daily *New York Times* followed on the 25th. It was by Michiko Kakutani, who had reviewed *Stanley and the Women* unfavourably. Kakutani had nothing but praise for the 'depth and emotional chiaroscuro' of *The Old Devils*: 'Instead of making fun of his characters' dilemmas, Mr Amis has chosen this time to write each of them – men *and* women – from the inside.'

72 KA to RC, 23 April 1987 (recipient).

73 According to the *Chronological Catalogue* in Ann Totterdell's *Kingsley Amis Journalism Archive*, in 1981 Amis wrote six articles, in 1982 he wrote eight, in 1983 only three.

74 *The Pleasure of Poetry*, Cassell, 1990, p. xvi. Amis's other journalistic contributions for 1984 consisted of three short book reviews, one book recommendation, a poem ('Everyone Knows', in the *Times Literary Supplement*, 27 April) and a tribute to John Betjeman, who died on 21 May.

75 KA to RC, 7 June 1986. Among other broadcasting assignments, in early February 1986 (round about the time word got out that Stuart Thomas had appointed him a trustee of the Dylan Thomas Estate, with ensuing controversy) Amis travelled to Swansea for Radio Wales to make a programme entitled 'Amis on Wales'. A year later, in February and March 1987, he broadcast six BBC radio programmes on jazz, *Blues with a Difference*; one each devoted to Bix Beiderbecke, Henry 'Red' Allen, Bessie Smith, Pee Wee Russell, Bill Davison and Sidney Bechet.

76 Paul Fussell, *The Anti-Egotist: Kingsley Amis, Man of Letters*, Oxford University Press, 1994, p. 105.

77 Ibid., p. 106.

78 I have taken this quotation from ibid., p. 107. It does not come from the one review of Green's Restaurant by Amis I have seen, 'Bangers and Cash', *Harper's and Queen*, June 1992.

79 Fussell, *The Anti-Egotist*, p. 109.

80 KA to Rebecca Thynne, 31 August 1987.

81 KA to John Hayes, December 1987; see Zachary Leader, ed., *The Letters of Kingsley Amis*, HarperCollins, 2000, p. 1066 n. for dating and controversy surrounding the letter.

82 She had written a memoir about being an alcoholic, *A Nice Girl Like Me: A Story of the Seventies*, Chatto and Windus, 1984.

83 Her husband, whom she describes as 'outrageously alcoholic'.

84 Sally Amis died at forty-six, David Leitch at sixty-seven, though by then he could not be thought of as 'still tottering along' (i.e. functioning).

85 *Difficulties with Girls*, Penguin, 1999, p. 41.

86 Ibid., p. 61.

87 Ibid., p. 204.

88 Ibid., p. 41.

89 Ibid., p. 26.

90 Gabriele Annan, 'The Old Devil', *New York Review of Books*, 15 June 1995, pp. 12–14, reprinted in Bell, ed., *Critical Essays*, p. 298.

91 EJH, *Slipstream*, p. 432.

92 *Difficulties with Girls*, p. 256.

93 KA to RC, 23 April 1987 (Huntington); Conquest sent Amis a fourth stanza, now lost.

94 Jacobs, *Biography*, p. 348.

95 *Difficulties with Girls*, pp. 118–119.

96 Ibid., p. 120.

97 Ibid., p. 158.

98 Ibid., p. 168.

99 Ibid., p. 150.

100 Ibid., p. 85.

101 Jeremy Treglown, 'What Are Little Girls Made Of?', *Grand Street* 9 (Autumn 1989), reprinted in Bell, ed., *Critical Essays*, p. 172.

102 Gabriele Annan, 'The Old Devil', reprinted in Bell, ed., *Critical Essays*, p. 298.

103 KA to RC, 17 September 1988 (recipient).

104 Martin Amis, *Experience*, p. 302n.

105 Ibid., p. 90 n.

106 Ibid.

CHAPTER 27

Ending Up

1 According to Martin Amis, Amis had originally wanted the dedication to *Difficulties with Girls* to read, 'To Hilly, a shining exception'.

2 This episode from Jacobs's 'Amis Diaries' is dated 12 December 1992 and was published in the first instalment of extracts in the *Sunday Times*, 17 March 1996.

3 From Jacobs, 'Amis Diaries', also excerpted in the *Sunday Times*, 17 March 1996.

4 Deborah Ross, interview with Hilly, 'The Old Devil Upstairs', *Daily Mail*, 16 March 1992.

5 It was never published as a separate picture-book but it did appear in the autumn 1995 issue of the *Duncan Lawrie Journal*, a publication of Duncan Lawrie Ltd., the private bank used by Amis at the end of his life. The *Journal* was distributed free to the bank's customers.

6 Alison Nadel, 'Kingsley Amis's Cat', in 'Animal Passions', *Daily Telegraph* magazine, 14 April 1990.

7 *We Are All Guilty*, Reinhardt Books, 1991. The book's one-page Foreword has no page number.

8 From an anonymous review in the American periodical *Kirkus Reviews*, 15 February 1992.

9 *The Old Devils*, Penguin, 1987, p. 87.

10 There were even moments when Amis was prepared to acknowledge Ali's virtues. In an entry of 4 March 1993 in the 'Amis Diaries', Jacobs records Amis describing Ali as 'very good' to him when he was in a panic about his health, waiting for the results of X-rays, for example: 'Ali "made a very good speech – things will be all right here, etc." He is "a very good man". He "had his shortcomings" but "reliability and decency he has"'.

11 Eric Jacobs, *Kingsley Amis: A Biography*, Hodder and Stoughton, 1995, p. 10.

12 Ibid., pp. 8–9.

13 Amis is disparaging about it in the correspondence, as he was about *Money*. See KA to PL, 28 November 1984: 'I stopped reading F's P as soon as it was clear that the fellow wasn't going to find in F's works concealed instructions for finding a hidden treasure in a sleepy little village in the Vosges. Compulsive reading – have you ever tried a chap called Sapper?'

14 Helen spent the first few years of her life 'on some lesser known Caribbean island' ('Black and White', unfinished manuscript, p. 6) but now lives in Enfield with her parents and two younger brothers. She wants to act on stage but also auditions for television. The manuscript of 'Black and White' is among the Amis Papers in the Huntington (AMS 480).

15 Christopher, too, is good-looking, but 'short-arsed' (ibid., p. 3).

16 Amis also told Jacobs that he planned to consult his Garrick friend, the playwright Ronald Harwood, over stage lore (see 'Amis Diaries', 21 April). Harwood remembers Amis telling him that he had some questions for him 'about theatre' and 'about being Jewish', but before Amis could pose them, he was taken ill; Harwood never saw him again (personal communication to the author, 1 August 2006).

17 Like Robert in the unpublished 'Difficulties with Girls', Christopher is clearly gay (as opposed to merely thinking he might be, like Robert's friend Tom Vaccarro or Tim Valentine in the published *Difficulties*), but he, too, sleeps with a woman, which opens the possibility that he might go on to sleep with Helen.

18 'Black and White', p. 10.
19 Ibid., p. 72.
20 Jacobs, 'Amis Diaries', 27 May 1995.
21 'Black and White', p. 76.
22 Ibid., pp. 42–43.
23 Ibid., p. 102.
24 Martin Amis, *Experience*, Jonathan Cape, 2000, p. 305n.
25 Ibid., p. 95.
26 Ibid., p. 93.
27 Ibid., p. 95.
28 Anthony Thwaite's account of his reactions comes from a letter to the author, 16 November 1988.
29 *The Russian Girl* (1992).
30 Interview with Nigel Reynolds, 'Kingsley Lashes Out at Literary Lunch', *Daily Telegraph*, 6 March 1991.
31 John Carey, review of *Memoirs*, 'With Malice Towards All', *Sunday Times*, 3 March 1991.
32 Blake Morrison, 'My Friends and Other Enemies', *Independent on Sunday*, 10 March 1991.
33 See Mark Palmer, 'Something Amiss with Amis', *Sunday Telegraph*, 3 March 1991.
34 Anthony Powell, *Journals 1990–1992*, Heinemann, 1998, p. 103 (entry of 24 March 1991).
35 Quoted by Catherine Bennett in 'My Life and Silly Old Sods', *Guardian*, 25 February 1991.
36 Anthony Powell, *Journals 1990–1992*, p. 102 (entry of 24 March 1991).
37 Anthony Powell to RC, 7 March 1992 (recipient).
38 KA to RC, *c.* November 1990.
39 Anthony Powell, *Journals 1990–1992*, p. 107 (entry of 10 April 1991).
40 RC to KA, 6 May 1990 (Huntington).
41 From an unsigned Diary piece in the *Daily Telegraph* entitled 'Old Men Forget', 6 March 1991.
42 'Kingsley Lashes Out at Literary Lunch'.
43 As John Walsh reports in 'An Old Devil in Telling Form', *Sunday Times*, 17 February 1991, Wain apparently told a friend that the reason he declined invitations to visit *chez* Amis was his fear that Hilly 'would break down his bedroom door' to seduce him (or so Amis told Walsh).
44 Ibid.
45 *The Old Devils*, p. 294.
46 Ibid., p. 296.
47 Jonathan Clowes to Jackie Jones, 18 September 1991 (Jonathan Clowes has a copy of the letter).

48 Dale Salwak to the author, 27 July 1999.

49 *The Russian Girl*, p. 147.

50 T. J. Binyon, 'Haranguing the Muse', *Times Literary Supplement*, 10 April 1992. Christopher Hitchens describes Vaisey's dilemma in a review in the *London Review of Books* ('Liber Amoris', 28 May 1992): 'life and judgement can be tricky if something, or somebody, turns out to be jolly nice but no bloody good'.

51 *The Russian Girl*, p. 167.

52 Ibid., p. 243.

53 Ibid., p. 4.

54 Ibid., p. 53.

55 Ibid., p. 292.

56 Ibid., p. 293.

57 Ibid., p. 112.

58 Amis began work on the new novel almost as soon as he'd finished its predecessor. By 1 February 1993 his engagement diary records '203 days of novel (p. 142)', which means he'd begun writing in July 1992.

59 Blake Morrison, 'Have It Any Way You Can', review of *You Can't Do Both*, *Independent on Sunday*, 18 September 1994.

60 *The Old Devils*, p. 277.

61 Ibid., p. 150.

62 Ibid., p. 101.

63 *The Russian Girl*, pp. 52–53.

64 It is David Sexton, in 'The Writer That Lives on the Hill', an interview with Amis in the *Sunday Correspondent*, 25 March 1990, who likens late Amis's prose to *style indirect libre*.

65 Martin Amis's recollection, recounted to the author in interview.

66 Powell, *Journals 1990–1992*, p. 26 (entry of 10 April 1990).

67 'With Malice Toward All', review of *Memoirs*, in *Sunday Times*, 3 March 1991.

68 *The Folks that Live on the Hill*, Penguin, 1991, p. 148.

69 Lorna Sage, review of *The Folks that Live on the Hill*, 'The Anti-Language League', *Times Literary Supplement*, 30 March 1990.

70 Quoted in Caroline Davies, 'Literary World Loses its "great bright light"', *Daily Telegraph*, 23 October 1995.

71 Jacobs, *Biography*, p. 9.

72 Because the House of Lords never sat on Friday evenings, Morgan felt free to put in only a morning's work on Fridays, though a full morning's work. This meant that he wouldn't arrive at the Garrick for drinks until after 1.00. One Friday, by the time Morgan and the friends he'd been drinking with at the bar were prepared to go down to lunch in the club's main dining room (known as the coffee room) it was full. They were then invited into the smaller of the club's private dining rooms, which contained a single table seating as many as fifteen. As Morgan remembers it: 'We thought, this is rather nice. We can

take our jackets off. Let's do this again, regularly.' It was Morgan who thought up the '1400' name, 'from my days in the military'.

73 Martin Amis, *Experience*, p. 94.

74 *The Folks that Live on the Hill*, p. 173.

75 The date of this unpublished poem is unknown. The manuscript (AMS 62) is among the Amis papers in the Huntington, where it was deposited in 1987.

76 This quote and the preceding biographical information come from an anonymous obituary in *The Times*, 4 March 2003.

77 Jacobs sent this letter plus Amis's reply to Jonathan Clowes in December 1996, for use in my edition of Amis's *Letters*, Harper Collins, 2000.

78 Jacobs, *Biography*, p. xiii.

79 Eric Jacobs to Jonathan Clowes, 19 December 1996 (recipient).

80 He and Amis met three or four times a week, 'in the Garrick Club and the Queen's public house or at his home in Primrose Hill' (Jacobs, *Biography*, p. xi).

81 Jacobs, 'The Authorized Biographer' in Dale Salwak, ed., *The Literary Biography: Problems and Solutions*, Macmillan, 1996, p. 136.

82 Jacobs, *Biography*, p. xii.

83 Ibid., p. xi.

84 Ibid., p. 332.

85 In the entry of 4 August 1995 in the 'Amis Diaries', Jacobs writes that Amis had given him permission to reveal in his *Spectator* review of *The Biographer's Moustache* not only that Jimmy bore certain resemblances to Peter Quennell, but that in the manuscript, which Jacobs read for Amis, Quennell's name was twice absentmindedly used for Fane's.

86 *The Biographer's Moustache*, Flamingo, 1996, p. 47.

87 Ibid., p. 250.

88 Ibid., p. 125.

89 Ibid., p. 254.

90 Ibid., p. 267.

91 The Amis contract baffled rival publishers, unlike other recent high-cost signings by HarperCollins, including million-pound deals for Jeffrey Archer, James Herbert and Len Deighton, another of Clowes's clients. 'We can't understand what Eddie Bell is up to,' a bemused executive, not from Hutchinson, was quoted as saying in an anonymous news squib in the *Bookseller*, 4 November 1994: 'Does he think he's got Martin?' (He would get Martin soon enough, in another controversial deal.)

92 David Nokes, review of *The Biographer's Moustache*, 'Boring for Britain', *Sunday Times*, 20 August 1995.

93 Martin Amis, *Experience*, p. 299.

94 The Rushes believe the date was the 13th, though their Guest Book mistakenly lists his visit as from 11 to 31 August.

95 According to Virginia Rush.
96 KA to Ronald Zeegen, 18 June 1993 (recipient).
97 Martin Amis, *Experience*, p. 283.
98 The profile appeared in the *Daily Telegraph* on 28 August 1995.
99 Interview with Joanna Coles, 'Curmudgeons Never Say Die', *Guardian*, 26 August 1995.
100 This quotation is from Virginia Rush.
101 Martin Amis, *Experience*, p. 286.
102 Jacobs, 'Amis Diaries', 2–4 September 1995.
103 Another side-effect of DF 118 was constipation.
104 Jacobs, 'Amis Diaries', 2–4 September 1995.
105 Martin Amis, *Experience*, p. 297.
106 Jacobs, 'Amis Diaries', 6 September 1995.
107 Martin Amis, *Experience*, p. 299.
108 An old friend of Hilly's visiting from Ann Arbor, co-proprietress of Lucky Jim's fish-and-chip shop.
109 Martin Amis, *Experience*, pp. 302–303.
110 Ibid., p. 314.
111 Ibid., p. 330.
112 Ibid., p. 326.
113 See ibid., p. 341.
114 Ibid., p. 351.
115 Ibid.

CHAPTER 28

Afterlife

1 John Sutherland, 'A Modern Master', *Sunday Times*, 29 October 1995.
2 John Walsh, 'The Pragmatic Entertainer Who Said the Unsayable', *Independent*, 23 October 1995.
3 David Lodge, obituary, *Independent*, 23 October 1995.
4 Quoted in Sally Weale, 'Kingsley Amis, Comic Master, Dies at 73', *Guardian*, 23 October 1995.
5 Malcolm Bradbury, 'The Angry Young Man Who Became a Raging Old Devil', *Daily Mail*, 23 October 1995.
6 Paul Gray, 'The Irritable Young Man: Kingsley Amis 1922–1995', *Time*, 6 November 1995.
7 From an unpublished article for the *Mail on Sunday* review section. The article was written shortly after Amis's death and titled simply 'Kingsley Amis piece'. Gammon gave me a copy of it.
8 Martin Amis, *Experience*, Jonathan Cape, 2000, p. 378.
9 Ibid., p. 373.
10 Ibid., p. 374.
11 Ibid.

12 Eric Jacobs to Lady Kilmarnock, 27 October 1995 (recipient).

13 Recounted, in Martin Amis, *Experience*, p. 377.

14 Ibid., p. 374.

15 He was encouraged, perhaps, by Martin's having told him, as Jacobs puts it in the final entry in the 'Amis Diaries', dated 31 October 1995, that though family feeling was running high at the moment, 'things would have calmed down by the time of the memorial service'.

16 What Jacobs meant by 'this' was not only his firing, but his replacement by the 'curiously named' Zachary Leader, Martin's 'tennis partner'. The phrase 'curiously named' comes from a letter of 27 April 1997 that Jacobs wrote to Roger Lewis, the biographer of Peter Sellers and Anthony Burgess. Peter Sellers played the part of John Lewis in *Only Two Can Play*, the film version of *That Uncertain Feeling*, and I had written to Lewis to ask if he knew of any Amis letters to Sellers. He replied that he'd sent Jacobs photocopies of several Amis letters and would write to him about my request. Jacobs's reply to Lewis, which Lewis forwarded to me on 7 May, was that he was disinclined to help 'the curiously named Zachary Leader', but that if Leader was interested he could consult the photocopies in the Huntington, where Jacobs had deposited them.

17 I received a phone call from a journalist at the *Sunday Times* asking if I'd be willing to have my picture taken for the newspaper. I said that I'd rather not, since the quarrel between Martin and Jacobs had nothing to do with me and I'd had nothing to do with Jacobs's firing. Ten minutes later the same journalist called back. He thought I should know that his editor was threatening to doorstep me if I wouldn't agree to be photographed, and that photographs taken in such circumstances always made their subjects look furtive and guilty. I thanked him for his concern but said that I'd take my chances. As far as I know, no photographer was sent.

18 Martin Amis, *Experience*, pp. 375–376.

19 The position of the Bodleian, as Jacobs explains it in *Kingsley Amis: A Biography*, Hodder and Stoughton, 1995, was 'not to open up for inspection or use the letters of someone still alive, on the grounds that other living people might be hurt by what was said in them' (p. xv). As Jacobs argued, though, the letters of dead people (of Larkin, for example, which the Bodleian allowed to be published) could be just as hurtful to the living. The library was unmoved, even after pro-Jacobs queries from Lord Jenkins, the Chancellor of Oxford University, and John Patten, the Secretary of State for Education. When, after prolonged pressure, it finally agreed to release the letters to Amis himself, it might have guessed that they would quickly find their way to Jacobs; as they did, 'days after my first version of this book reached the publisher' (p. xv).

20 A year or so before Jacobs's death, at the suggestion of his agent, Gillon Aitken, I met Jacobs at a pub in Highgate, near where he

lived. At the meeting he was correct though hardly warm. But he agreed to meet me for a formal, tape-recorded interview. He died on 23 February 2003, before the interview could be arranged.

21 These words are Martin Amis's paraphrase of what he said (*Experience*, p. 379).

22 From a transcript of Hitchens's speech at the memorial service.

23 *The King's English: A Guide to Modern Usage*, HarperCollins, 1997, p. vii. In *Experience*, Martin approves the book's title, both as a nod to Fowler and as a reflection of its personal nature: '"the King", along with Kingers, was a diminutive, one seldom used in Kingsley's presence although he knew about it and vaguely approved of it . . . So the title is apt: the book is about *his* English – the King's English – as well as everybody else's' (p. 203n). In 'Kingsley's Corrections', a review of 9 March 1997 in the *Sunday Telegraph*, Ian Hamilton makes a similar point when arguing that a better title would have been 'Kingsley's English', given Amis's championing of precision and 'instantly clear meanings'.

24 Ibid., p. 83.

25 Ibid., p. 136.

26 Fonseca's memories of Amis, whom she met four or five times in the two years prior to his death, are wholly positive. He 'energetically' put her at her ease, was generous with his whisky (though he forbade her from having it with ice) and was attentive to what she said. She was surprised to discover herself 'in the presence of a man who enjoyed the company of women'. The last time she saw him was in the Phoenix Ward at St Pancras. She and Martin had stopped in on their way home after dinner. The ward was dim and he was unconscious. She was struck by how handsome he looked in sleep, though changed: 'you realised how central the beam of his intelligent gaze was'. From an email to the author, 18 May 2006.

27 See Martin Amis, *Koba the Dread: Laughter and the Twenty Million*, Jonathan Cape, 2002, p. 268.

28 Ibid., p. 352.

29 Martin Amis, *Experience*, p. 366.

Bibliography

NOVELS
(First publication details and editions cited)

Lucky Jim (London: Victor Gollancz, 1954; New York: Doubleday, 1954); Penguin, 1976.

That Uncertain Feeling (London: Victor Gollancz, 1955; New York: Harcourt Brace, 1955); Penguin, 1985.

I Like It Here (London: Victor Gollancz, 1958; New York: Harcourt Brace, 1958); Penguin, 1968.

Take a Girl Like You (London: Victor Gollancz, 1960; New York: Harcourt Brace, 1961); Penguin, 1962.

One Fat Englishman (London: Victor Gollancz, 1963; New York: Harcourt Brace, 1964); Penguin, 1966.

The Egyptologists (with Robert Conquest) (London: Jonathan Cape, 1965; New York: Random House, 1966); Penguin, 1968.

The Anti-Death League (London: Victor Gollancz, 1966; New York: Harcourt Brace, 1966); Harcourt Brace edition cited.

Colonel Sun (as Robert Markham) (London: Jonathan Cape, 1968; New York: Harper and Row, 1968); Cape edition cited.

I Want It Now (London: Jonathan Cape, 1968; New York: Harcourt Brace, 1969); Penguin, 1988.

The Green Man (London: Jonathan Cape, 1969; New York: Harcourt Brace, 1970); Penguin, 1988.

Girl, 20 (London: Jonathan Cape, 1971; New York: Harcourt Brace, 1972); Panther, 1975.

The Riverside Villas Murder (London: Jonathan Cape, 1973; New York: Harcourt Brace, 1973); Penguin, 1984.

Ending Up (London: Jonathan Cape, 1974; New York: Harcourt Brace Jovanovich, 1974); Penguin, 1987.

The Alteration (London: Jonathan Cape, 1976; New York: Viking Press, 1977); Penguin, 1988.

Jake's Thing (London: Hutchinson, 1978; New York: Viking Press, 1978); Hutchinson edition cited.

Russian Hide-and-Seek (London: Hutchinson, 1980).

Stanley and the Women (London: Hutchinson, 1984; New York: Summit, 1985); Penguin, 1985.

The Old Devils (London: Hutchinson, 1986; New York: Summit, 1987); Penguin, 1987.

The Crime of the Century (London: J. M. Dent, 1987; London: Century Hutchinson, 1987; New York: Mysterious Press, 1989); Orion, 1993.

Difficulties with Girls (London: Hutchinson, 1988; New York: Summit, 1989); Penguin, 1999.

The Folks that Live on the Hill (London: Hutchinson, 1990; New York: Summit, 1990); Penguin, 1991.

We Are All Guilty (London and New York: Viking/Reinhardt Books, 1991).

The Russian Girl (London: Hutchinson, 1992; New York: Viking Penguin, 1994); Penguin, 1993.

You Can't Do Both (London: Hutchinson, 1994); Flamingo, 1996.

The Biographer's Moustache (London: HarperCollins, 1995); Flamingo, 1996.

POETRY
(Books and pamphlets)

Bright November (London: Fortune Press, 1947).

A Frame of Mind (Reading: School of Art, University of Reading, 1953).

Kingsley Amis: No. 22. The Fantasy Poets (Oxford: Fantasy Press, 1954).

A Case of Samples: Poems 1946–1956 (London: Victor Gollancz, 1956; New York: Harcourt Brace, 1957).
The Evans Country (Oxford: Fantasy Press, 1962).
Penguin Modern Poets 2 (with Dom Moraes and Peter Porter) (Harmondsworth: Penguin, 1962).
A Look Round the Estate: Poems 1957–1967 (London: Jonathan Cape, 1967; New York: Harcourt Brace, 1968).
Wasted, Kipling at Bateman's (London: Poem-of-the-Month Club, 1973).
Collected Poems 1944–1979 (London: Hutchinson, 1979; New York: Viking Press, 1980); Penguin, 1980.

SHORT STORIES
(Collected or as separate publications)

My Enemy's Enemy (London: Victor Gollancz, 1962; New York: Harcourt Brace, 1962); Penguin, 1965.
Penguin Modern Stories II (with others) (Harmondsworth: Penguin, 1972).
Dear Illusion (London: Covent Garden Press, 1972).
The Darkwater Hall Mystery (Edinburgh: Tragara Press, 1978).
Collected Short Stories (London: Hutchinson, 1980; 2nd edn, 1987, adds 'Investing in Futures' and 'Affairs of Death'); Penguin, 1984.
Mr Barrett's Secret and Other Stories (London: Hutchinson, 1993); Penguin, 1994.

RADIO PLAYS

Touch and Go (BBC, 1957).
I Want It Now (BBC, 1978).
Captain Nolan's Chance (BBC, 1994).

TELEVISION PLAYS

A Question about Hell (Granada, 1964).
One Fat Englishman (Granada, 1967).
The Importance of Being Hairy (BBC, 1970).

'See What You've Done', episode of *Softly, Softly* (BBC, 1974).
Dr Watson and the Darkwater Hall Mystery (BBC, 1974).
'We Are All Guilty', episode of *Against the Crowd* (ITV, 1975).

NON-FICTION
(Including criticism, polemical pamphlets and
miscellaneous writings)

Socialism and the Intellectuals (London: Fabian Society,
1957).
New Maps of Hell: A Survey of Science Fiction (New York:
Harcourt Brace, 1960; London: Victor Gollancz, 1961);
Gollancz edition cited.
The James Bond Dossier (London: Jonathan Cape, 1965;
New York: New American Library, 1965); Cape edition
cited.
The Book of Bond, or Every Man His Own 007 (as Lt-Col
William ('Bill') Tanner) (London: Jonathan Cape, 1965;
New York: Viking, 1965); Cape edition cited.
Lucky Jim's Politics (London: Conservative Policy Centre,
1968).
Black Papers on Education (Manchester: Critical Quarterly
Society, 1968–75).
What Became of Jane Austen? And Other Questions (London:
Jonathan Cape, 1970; New York: Harcourt Brace, 1971);
Penguin, 1981.
On Drink (London: Jonathan Cape, 1972; New York:
Harcourt Brace, 1973); Cape edition cited.
Rudyard Kipling and His World (London: Thames and
Hudson, 1975; New York: Charles Scribner's Sons, 1976).
An Arts Policy? (London: Centre for Policy Studies, 1979).
Every Day Drinking (London: Hutchinson, 1983).
How's Your Glass? (London: Weidenfeld and Nicolson, 1984).
The Amis Collection: Selected Non-Fiction 1954–1990, intro.
John McDermott (London: Hutchinson, 1990); Penguin,
1991.
Memoirs (London: Century Hutchinson, 1991; New York:
Summit, 1991); Penguin, 1992.
The King's English: A Guide to Modern Usage (London:

HarperCollins, 1997; New York: St Martin's/Griffin, 1999);
HarperCollins edition cited.

The Letters of Kingsley Amis, ed. Zachary Leader (London:
HarperCollins, 2000; New York: Talk Miramax, 2001);
HarperCollins edition cited.

EDITED BOOKS

Oxford Poetry 1949 (co-edited with James Michie) (Oxford:
Basil Blackwell, 1949).

Oscar Wilde: Poems and Essays (London: Collins, 1956).

Spectrum: A Science Fiction Anthology, 5 vols (co-edited and
introduced with Robert Conquest) (London: Victor
Gollancz, 1961–65; New York: Harcourt Brace, 1962–67);
Gollancz edition cited.

G. K. Chesterton: Selected Stories (London and Boston: Faber
and Faber, 1972).

Tennyson (in *Poet to Poet* series) (Harmondsworth: Penguin,
1973).

Harold's Years: Impressions from the New Statesman *and the*
Spectator (London: Quartet, 1977).

The Faber Popular Reciter (London and Boston: Faber and
Faber, 1978).

The New Oxford Book of Light Verse (London and New
York: Oxford University Press, 1978).

The Golden Age of Science Fiction (London: Hutchinson,
1981; New York: Penguin, 1983).

The Great British Songbook (co-edited with James Cochrane)
(London: Pavillion/Michael Joseph, 1986).

The Amis Anthology: A Personal Choice of English Verse
(London: Hutchinson, 1988); Arena, 1989.

The Pleasure of Poetry (London: Cassell, 1990).

The Amis Story Anthology: A Personal Choice of Short Stories
(London: Hutchinson, 1992).

BOOKS WITH CONTRIBUTIONS BY KINGSLEY AMIS

'Foreword', in Barry Ulanov, *A Handbook of Jazz* (London:
Hutchinson, 1958).

'Afterword', in Samuel Butler, *Erewhon* (New York: New American Library/Signet, 1960).

'Foreword', in H.G. Wells, *The War of the Worlds* (New York; Platt and Monk, 1963).

'Foreword', in Sarban (John W. Wall), *The Sound of His Horn* (London: Sphere, 1970).

'Foreword', in Peter Haining, ed., *The Lucifer Society* (London: W.H. Allen, 1972).

'Four Fluent Fellows: An Essay on Chesterton's Fiction', in *G.K. Chesterton: A Centenary Appraisal*, ed. John Sullivan (London: Paul Elek, 1973).

'Foreword', in Arthur Conan Doyle, *The Memoirs of Sherlock Holmes* (1894; London: Jonathan Cape, 1974).

'Foreword', in Ward Moore, *Bring the Jubilee* (London: Nelson, 1976).

'Speaking Up for Excellence', in Patrick McCormack, ed., *Right Turn: Eight Men Who Changed Their Minds* (London: Cooper, 1978).

'Foreword', in Michael Wharton, ed., *The Stretchford Chronicles* (London: Daily Telegraph, 1980).

'Ten to Make and Match to Win', in Michael Meyer, ed., *Summer Days: Writers on Cricket* (London: Eyre Methuen, 1981).

'Introduction', in G.K. Chesterton, *The Man Who Was Thursday* (London: Hutchinson, 1986).

'Foreword', in Cyril Ray, ed., *The Complete Imbiber No. 14* (London: Beaumont Books, 1989).

'Foreword', in Alan Lomax, *Mr Jelly Roll* (London: Virgin Books, 1991).

REFERENCE GUIDES

Clare D. Kinsman and Mary Ann Tennenhouse, eds., *Contemporary Authors: A Bio-Bibliographical Guide to Current Authors and Their Works* (Detroit: Gale, 1974).

J.B. Gohn, *Kingsley Amis: A Checklist* (Kent, Ohio: Kent State University Press, 1976).

Dale Salwak, *Kingsley Amis: A Reference Guide* (Boston: G.K. Hall, 1978).

Ann Totterdell, *An Alphabetical and Chronological Catalogue*

of the Short Writings of Kingsley Amis (2004) (copies of
the Catalogue, funded by the Arts and Humanities
Research Board, together with photocopies of all
uncollected items listed in it, have been deposited in the
Bodleian Library, the British Library, the Huntington
Library and the Learning Resources Centre at Roehampton
University; the Catalogue can be consulted online at
www.roehampton.ac.uk/KingsleyAmisJournalismArchive.

SELECTED INTERVIEWS

Daniel Farson, 'Look! There are Llamas in the Mountains',
 Evening Standard, 4 May 1956.
Robert Muller, 'Oh, Lucky Jim, Do I Envy Him', Sunday
 Dispatch, 12 January 1958.
Diane Norman, 'Does Mr. Amis Write About Himself?',
 Women's Mirror, 14 January 1961.
Pat Williams, 'My Kind of Comedy', Twentieth Century, July
 1961.
Quentin Crewe, 'Pride and Prejudice and Your Sons and
 Daughters', Daily Mail, 23 January 1962.
'Mandrake' (In the 'Sunday Morning with Mandrake' column),
 'Anti-Death League', Sunday Telegraph, 14 February 1965.
Anon., 'It Was Just Like Lucky Jim', Daily Sketch, 30 June 1965.
John Silverlight, 'Profile: Kingsley Amis', Observer, 14 January
 1968.
Dick Adler, 'Portrait of a Man Reading', Book World, 2
 October 1968.
Ann Jefferson, 'I Like it Here', Isis, 18 October 1969.
Harry Fieldhouse, 'Penthouse Interview: Kingsley Amis',
 Penthouse, October 1970.
Dennis Chambers, 'Kingsley Amis Interview', Writer, February
 1973.
Pauline Peters, 'Two on an Island', interview with Kingsley
 Amis and Elizabeth Jane Howard, Sunday Times, 3
 February 1974.
Clive James, 'Kingsley Amis: A Profile', New Review, July
 1974.
Kevin Byrne, 'The Two Amises', interview with Kingsley Amis
 and Martin Amis, Listener, 15 August 1974.

Malcolm Oram, 'Publishers Weekly Interview: Kingsley Amis', *Publishers Weekly*, 28 October 1974.

Peter Firchow, 'Kingsley Amis', in Peter Firchow, *The Writer's Place: Interviews on the Literary Situation in Contemporary Britain* (Minneapolis: University of Minnesota Press, 1974).

Melvyn Bragg, 'Kingsley Amis Looks Back', *Listener*, 25 February 1975.

Michael Barber, 'The Art of Fiction LIX', *Paris Review* 16: 64 (Winter 1975).

Dale Salwak, 'An Interview with Kingsley Amis', *Contemporary Literature* 16: 1 (Winter 1975).

Auberon Waugh, 'Kingsley Amis: A Singular Man', *Sunday Telegraph* magazine, 17 September 1978.

Tom Miller, 'Kingsley Amis: A Novelist of Our Times', *Illustrated London News*, September 1978.

Pearson Phillips, 'How the Angry Brigade Got Lucky', *Observer*, 17 September 1978.

Michael Billington, 'Writing and Warning – An Interview with Kingsley Amis', *Listener*, 15 February 1979.

Anon., 'Looking Back . . . ?', *Eton College Chronicle*, 22 June 1979.

Blake Morrison, 'Kingsley and the Women', *Observer*, 13 May 1984.

Lynn Barber, 'Things I Wish I'd Known at Eighteen: Kingsley Amis', *Sunday Express*, 3 June 1984.

Hugh David, 'Our Time Is Coming', *Times Educational Supplement*, 22 June 1984.

Graham Turner, 'Kingsley Amis and Those Uncertain Feelings', *Sunday Telegraph*, 28 September 1986.

Margarette Driscoll, 'The Old Devil Himself', *Today*, 27 October 1986.

Cynthia Kee, 'Flavour of the Month', *London Portrait Magazine*, December 1986.

Byron Rogers, 'The Old Devil at Peace', *Standard*, 16 April 1987.

John Mortimer, 'Would You Take a Man Like Him?', *Sunday Times*, 18 September 1988.

Michael Barber, 'Lucky Old Shag', *Standard*, 22 September 1988.

Chris Peachment, 'Rhymes with Reasons', *The Times*, 15 November 1988.

James Hogg, 'Take Fire: Kingsley Amis', *Jazz Express*, July 1989.

Joe Steeples, 'Relative Values', with Martin Amis, *Sunday Times*, 3 December 1989.

Philip Purser, 'Lucky Him', *Sunday Telegraph*, 24 December 1989.

David Lewin, 'The Agony of Mr Amis', *Daily Mail*, 30 December 1989.

Ray Connolly, 'A Childhood: Kingsley Amis', *The Times*, 24 March 1990.

Angela Levin, 'At Home with Kingsley Amis', *Mail on Sunday*, 25 March 1990.

Valerie Grove, 'Soft Centre Shows behind the Old Devil's Brimstone', *Sunday Times*, 25 March 1990.

Alison Nadel, 'Animal Passions', *Daily Telegraph*, 14 April 1990.

John Walsh, 'An Old Devil in Telling Form', *Sunday Times*, 17 February 1991.

Catherine Bennett, 'My Life and Silly Old Sods', *Guardian*, 25 February 1991.

David Holloway, 'Loose Talk of the Old Devil', *Daily Telegraph*, 2 March 1991.

Peter Grosvenor, 'Out to Lunch with the Defiant Knight', *Daily Express*, 7 March 1991.

Kate Muir, 'What's Amiss with Amis', *The Times*, 8 March 1991.

Anthony Quinn, 'Lucky Him: From Underdog to Fat Cat', *Independent*, 9 March 1991.

Anon., 'I'm a Great Man for Tyrannies,' *Economist*, 9 March 1991.

Jane Gordon, 'Kingsley and the Wimmin', *Today*, 29 November 1991.

Clive Gammon, 'The Old Devil as Young Man', *Mail on Sunday*, 5 April 1992, in *You* magazine.

Valerie Grove, 'The Impatience of Being Kingsley Amis', *The Times*, 10 April 1992.

Serena Allott, 'What Else Is There to Do', *Daily Telegraph*, 18 April 1992.

Ginny Dougary, 'Old Devil's Advocate', *The Times*, 10 September 1994.

John Morrish, 'A Joke Shared with Jesus Is Never Wasted', *Sunday Telegraph*, 30 October 1994.

Lynda Lee-Potter, 'I've Been Lucky Considering the Outrageous Way I've Behaved', *Daily Mail*, 13 May 1995.
Joanna Coles, 'Curmudgeons Never Say Die', *Guardian*, 26 August 1995.
Glenys Roberts, 'Angrier by the Minute', *Daily Telegraph*, 28 August 1995.

BOOKS ON AMIS

Martin Amis, *Experience* (London: Jonathan Cape, 2000).
Robert H. Bell, ed., *Critical Essays on Kingsley Amis* (New York: G.K. Hall, 1998).
Richard Bradford, *Kingsley Amis* (London: Edward Arnold, 1989).
Richard Bradford, *Lucky Him: The Life of Kingsley Amis* (London: Peter Owen, 2001).
Paul Fussell, *The Anti-Egotist: Kingsley Amis, Man of Letters* (New York and Oxford: Oxford University Press, 1994).
Philip Gardner, *Kingsley Amis* (Boston: Twayne Publishers, 1981).
Eric Jacobs, *Kingsley Amis: A Biography* (London: Hodder and Stoughton, 1995).
Gavin Keulks, *Father and Son: Kingsley Amis, Martin Amis, and the British Novel since 1950* (Madison: University of Wisconsin Press, 2003).
William E. Laskowski, *Kingsley Amis* (New York: Twayne Publishers, 1998).
John McDermott, *Kingsley Amis: An English Moralist* (London: Macmillan, 1989).
Merritt Mosely, *Understanding Kingsley Amis* (Charleston: South Carolina Press, 1993).
Dale Salwak, ed., *Kingsley Amis: In Life and Letters* (London: Macmillan, 1990).
Dale Salwak, *Kingsley Amis: Modern Novelist* (Hemel Hempstead: Harvester Wheatsheaf, 1992).

OTHER WORKS CONSULTED (SELECTED)

Kenneth Allsop, *The Angry Decade: A Survey of the Cultural Revolt of the Nineteen-fifties* (1958; London: John Goodchild, 1985).

Al Alvarez, *Where Did It All Go Right?* (1999; London: Bloomsbury, 2002).

John Amis, *Amiscellany: My Life, My Music* (London: Faber and Faber, 1985).

Martin Amis, *Experience* (London: Jonathan Cape, 2000).

Martin Amis, *Koba the Dread: Laughter and the Twenty Million* (London: Jonathan Cape, 2002).

M.P. Ashley and C.T. Saunders, *Red Oxford: A History of the Growth of Socialism in the University of Oxford* (Oxford: Oxford University Labour Club, 1933).

Calvin Bedient, *Eight Contemporary Poets* (London and New York: Oxford University Press, 1971).

Bernard Bergonzi, *The Situation of the Novel* (1970; Harmondsworth: Penguin, 1972).

Bernard Bergonzi, *Wartime and Aftermath: English Literature and its Background 1939–1960* (Oxford: Oxford University Press, 1993).

John Betjeman, *Collected Poems* (London: John Murray, 1970).

Gavin Bone, *Anglo-Saxon Poetry: An Essay with Specimen Translations in Verse* (Oxford: The Clarendon Press, 1943).

James Booth, ed., *New Larkins for Old: Critical Essays* (London: Macmillan, 2000).

Alastair Boyd, *The Sierras of the South: Travels in the Mountains of Andalusia* (London: HarperCollins, 1992).

Malcolm Bradbury, *Possibilities: Essays on the State of the Novel* (London: Edward Arnold, 1973).

Malcolm Bradbury, ed., *The Novel Today: Contemporary Writers on Modern Fiction* (1977; London: Fontana, 1990).

Malcolm Bradbury, *The Modern British Novel 1878–2001* (Harmondsworth: Penguin, 1993; revised 2001).

Malcolm Bradbury and David Palmer, eds., *The Contemporary English Novel* (London: Edward Arnold, 1979).

John Braine, *Room at the Top* (1957; Harmondsworth: Penguin, 1959).

Humphrey Carpenter, *The Angry Young Men: A Literary Comedy of the 1950s* (London: Allen Lane/Penguin, 2002).

Peter Clarke, *Hope and Glory: Britain 1900–1990* (1996; Harmondsworth: Penguin, 1997).

Edward T. Cone, Joseph Frank and Edmund Keeley eds., *The*

Legacy of R.P. Blackmur: Essays, Memoirs, Texts (New York: Eccho Press, 1987).

Paul K. Conkin, *Gone with the Ivy: A Biography of Vanderbilt University* (Knoxville: University of Tennessee Press, 2002).

Steven Connor, *The English Novel in History, 1950–1995* (London: Routledge, 1996).

Robert Conquest, *The Abomination of Moab* (London: Maurice Temple-Smith, 1979).

Robert Conquest, *New and Collected Poems* (London: Century Hutchinson, 1988).

Robert Conquest, *Reflections on a Ravaged Century* (1999; New York: W.W. Norton, 2001).

Peter J. Conradi, *Iris Murdoch: A Life – The Authorized Biography* (London: HarperCollins, 2001).

Chris Cook and John Stevenson, *The Longman Companion to Britain since 1945* (London: Longman, 1996).

William Cooper, *Scenes from Provincial Life* (1950; Harmondsworth: Penguin, 1959).

R.H.S. Crossman, ed., *Oxford and the Groups* (Oxford: Basil Blackwell, 1934).

Donald Davie, *Thomas Hardy and British Poetry* (London: Routledge, 1973).

A.E. Douglas Smith, *The City of London School* (1937; Oxford: Basil Blackwell, 1965).

C.J. Ellingham, *Essay Writing: Bad and Good* (London: A. Wheaton, 1935).

D.J. Enright, ed., *Poets of the 1950s* (Tokyo: Kenyusha Press, 1955).

G.S. Fraser, *The Modern Writer and His World* (1953; Harmondsworth: Penguin, 1964).

Russell Fraser, *A Mingled Yarn: The Life of R.P. Blackmur* (New York: Harcourt Brace Jovanovich, 1981).

Betty Fussell, *My Kitchen Wars* (New York: North Point Press, 2000).

Paul Fussell, *Abroad: British Literary Travelling between the Wars* (Oxford: Oxford University Press, 1980).

Andrzej Gasiorek, *Post-War British Fiction: Realism and After* (London: Routledge, 1995).

Thomas B. Gilmore, *Equivocal Spirits: Alcoholism and Drinking in Twentieth-Century Literature* (Chapel Hill and London: University of North Carolina Press, 1987).

James Gindin, *Postwar British Fiction: New Accents and Attitudes* (Berkeley: University of California Press, 1962).

John Gross, *The Rise and Fall of the Man of Letters: Aspects of English Literary Life since 1800* (1969; London: Penguin, 1991).

John Gross, *A Double Thread: A Childhood in Mile End and Beyond* (2001; London: Vintage, 2002).

John Haffenden, *Viewpoints: Poets in Conversation with John Haffenden* (London: Faber and Faber, 1981).

John Haffenden, *Novelists in Interview* (London: Methuen, 1985).

David Halberstam, *The Children* (1998; New York: Fawcett Books/Ballantine, 1999).

Ian Hamilton, *A Poetry Chronicle: Essays and Reviews* (London: Faber and Faber, 1973).

Brian Harrison, ed., *The History of the University of Oxford* (Volume VIII: *The Twentieth Century*) (Oxford: Clarendon Press, 1994).

Elizabeth Hatziolou, *John Wain: A Man of Letters* (London: Pisces Press, 1997).

Dominic Head, *The Cambridge Introduction to Modern British Fiction, 1950–2000* (Cambridge: Cambridge University Press, 2002).

Denis Healey, *The Time of My Life* (London: Michael Joseph, 1989).

Frank W. Helyar, ed., *The City of London School at Marlborough* (2000) (the book is self-published, and can be consulted in the CLS library).

Robert Hewison, *In Anger: Culture in the Cold War 1945–60* (London: Weidenfeld and Nicolson, 1981).

Thomas Hinde, *Carpenter's Children: The Story of The City of London School* (London: James and James, 1995).

Richard Hoggart, *The Uses of Literacy* (1957; Harmondsworth: Penguin, 1992).

Elizabeth Jane Howard, *The Sea Change* (1959; Pan Books, 1995).

Elizabeth Jane Howard, *After Julius* (1965; Pan Books, 1995).

Elizabeth Jane Howard, *Odd Girl Out* (1972; Pan Books, 1994).

Elizabeth Jane Howard, *Getting It Right* (1982; Pan Books, 1996).

Elizabeth Jane Howard, *Slipstream: A Memoir* (Macmillan, 2002).

Nicola Humble, *The Feminine Middlebrow Novel 1920s to 1950s* (Oxford: Oxford University Press, 2001).

Christopher Isherwood, *Lions and Shadows* (1938; New York: Four Square Books, 1963).

Clive James, *From the Land of Shadows* (London: Jonathan Cape, 1982).

Clive James, *Other Passports: Poems 1958–1985* (London: Jonathan Cape, 1986).

Roy Jenkins, *A Life at the Centre* (London: Macmillan, 1992).

Valerie Jenkins, *When I Was Young: Memories of London Childhoods* (London: Hart-Davis, MacGibbon, 1976).

Edmund Keeley, *Inventing Paradise: The Greek Journey 1937–47* (New York: Farrar Straus and Giroux, 1999).

Philip Larkin, *Jill* (1946; London: Faber and Faber, 1975).

Philip Larkin, *Collected Poems*, ed. Anthony Thwaite, (1955; London: Marvell Press/Faber and Faber, 1988).

Philip Larkin, *All What Jazz: A Record Diary 1961–1971* (Faber and Faber, 1970).

Philip Larkin, *Required Writing: Miscellaneous Pieces 1955–1982* (London: Faber and Faber, 1983).

Philip Larkin, *Selected Letters of Philip Larkin 1940–1985*, ed. Anthony Thwaite (London: Faber and Faber, 1992).

Philip Larkin, *Further Requirements: Interviews, Broadcasts, Statements and Book Reviews*, ed. Anthony Thwaite (London: Faber and Faber, 2001).

Philip Larkin, *Larkin's Jazz: Essays and Reviews 1940–1948*, ed. Richard Palmer and John White (London: Continuum, 2001).

Philip Larkin, *Trouble at Willow Gables and Other Fictions*, ed. James Booth (London: Faber and Faber, 2002).

Zachary Leader, ed., *On Modern British Fiction* (Oxford: Oxford University Press, 2003).

F.R. Leavis, *The Common Pursuit* (London: Chatto and Windus, 1962).

F.R. Leavis, *The Great Tradition, George Eliot, Henry James, Joseph Conrad* (London: Chatto and Windus, 1979).

David Lodge, *Language of Fiction* (1966; London: Routledge, 1984).

David Lodge, *The Novelist at the Crossroads* (London: Routledge, 1971).

David Lodge, *The Modes of Modern Writing. Metaphor and*

Metonymy and the Typology of Modern Literature
(London: Edward Arnold, 1977).

Arthur Marwick, *British Society since 1945* (1982;
Harmondsworth: Penguin, 1996).

Tom Maschler, ed., *Declaration* (London: MacGibbon and Kee,
1957).

Alan Massie, *The Novel Today* (London: Longman, 1990).

Brian Masters, *Great Hostesses* (London: Constable, 1983).

Somerset Maugham, *Ten Novels and Their Authors* (1954;
London: Vintage 2001).

Edward Mendelson, *Early Auden* (London: Faber and Faber,
1981).

Rod Mengham, ed., *An Introduction to Contemporary Fiction*
(Cambridge: Polity Press, 1999).

Karl Miller, *Dark Horses: An Experience of Literary
Journalism* (London: Picador, 1998).

Blake Morrison, *The Movement: English Poetry and Fiction of
the 1950s* (Oxford: Oxford University Press, 1980).

Andrew Motion, *Philip Larkin: A Writer's Life* (London: Faber
and Faber, 1993).

Francis Mulhern, *The Moment of 'Scrutiny'* (London: Verso,
1979).

William Van O'Connor, *The New University Wits and the End
of Modernism* (Carbondale: University of Illinois Press, 1963).

George Orwell, *The Collected Essays, Journalism and Letters
of George Orwell*, ed. Sonia Orwell and Ian Angus (Secker
and Warburg, 1968).

Anthony Powell, *Journals 1982–1986* (London: William
Heinemann, 1995).

Anthony Powell, *Journals 1987–1989* (London: William
Heinemann, 1996).

Anthony Powell, *Journals 1990–1992* (London: William
Heinemann, 1998).

Rubin Rabinovitz, *The Reaction against Experiment in the
English Novel, 1950–1960* (New York: Columbia
University Press, 1967).

Frederic Raphael, ed., *Bookmarks: Writers on Their Reading*
(London: Quartet Books, 1975).

Harry Ritchie, *Success Stories: Literature and the Media in
England, 1950–1959* (London and Boston: Faber and
Faber, 1988).

Lorna Sage, *Women in the House of Fiction: Post-war Women Novelists* (Basingstoke: Macmillan, 1992).

Dale Salwak, *Interviews with Britain's Angry Young Men* (San Bernadino: Borgo Press, 1984).

Dale Salwak, ed., *Philip Larkin: The Man and His Work* (Basingstoke: Macmillan, 1989).

Margaret Scanlan, *Traces of Another Time: History and Politics in Postwar British Fiction* (Princeton: Princeton University Press, 1990).

Miranda Seymour, *Robert Graves: Life on the Edge* (1995; New York: Scribner, 2003).

Elaine Showalter, *Faculty Towers: The Academic Novel and its Discontents* (Oxford: Oxford University Press, 2005).

Monroe K. Spears, ed., *Auden: A Collection of Critical Essays* (Englewood Cliffs, N.J.: Prentice-Hall, 1964).

Randall Stevenson, *The British Novel since the Thirties* (London: Batsford, 1986).

Randall Stevenson, *The Oxford English Literary History Volume 12: The Last of England* (Oxford: Oxford University Press, 2004).

John Sutherland, *Stephen Spender: The Authorised Biography* (London: Penguin, 2004).

Patrick Swinden, *The English Novel of History and Society, 1940–80* (London: Macmillan, 1984).

D.J. Taylor, *A Vain Conceit: British Fiction in the 1980s* (London: Bloomsbury, 1989).

D.J. Taylor, *After the War: The Novel and England since 1945* (London: HarperCollins, 1993).

Anthony Thwaite, ed., *Larkin at Sixty* (London: Faber and Faber, 1982).

Philip Toynbee, *Friends Apart: A Memoir of Esmond Romilly and Jasper Ridley in the Thirties* (London: MacGibbon and Kee, 1954).

John Wain, *Hurry on Down* (1953; Harmondsworth: Penguin, 1961).

John Wain, *Sprightly Running: Part of an Autobiography* (1962; London: Papermac, 1965).

Philip Waller, *Chronology of the Twentieth Century* (Oxford: Helicon, 1995).

George Watson, *British Literature since 1945* (New York: St Martin's Press, 1991).

Patricia Waugh, *Harvest of the Sixties: English Literature and Its Background 1960–1990* (Oxford: Oxford University Press, 1990).

Colin Wilson, *Dreaming to Some Purpose: The Autobiography of Colin Wilson* (New York: Random House/Century, 2004).

Peregrine Worsthorne, *Tricks of Memory: An Autobiography* (London: Weidenfeld and Nicolson, 1993).

Index

132, 139–40, 148, 156–7; Auden's influence on poetry, 144–5, 152–6, 404; first novel ('The Legacy') rejected, 187–8; poems published by Caton at Fortune Press, 188–9; Empson's influence on, 190–1, 404; collaborates on musical works with Montgomery, 196, 210, 213–14, 249, 259–60; commissioned to write on Graham Greene, 214–15; aims and qualities of poetry, 218, 404–10; co-edits *Oxford Poetry*, 218–19; argument of thesis on Victorian poets and their audiences, 252–5; Larkin's influence on, 277; contributes to *Spectator*, 281–2, 308–10, 357, 359, 432, 526, 618; and controversy over Movement poets, 284; involvement in literary scene, 285; light verse and limericks, 291; replies to Edith Sitwell in *Spectator*, 295–6; journalism and reviewing, 308–10, 357, 359–60, 376–7, 432, 446, 536, 642, 754–5; blocked as writer of poetry, 325–6; wins Somerset Maugham Award (1955), 330; cast with Angry Young Men, 358–9; publications while at Swansea, 376; US reputation and publication, 383–4; lectures on science fiction at Princeton, 394, 412–18; reviews films for *Esquire*, 401–2; poetry reading at Library of Congress, 403–6; opposition to Romanticism, 409–10; suspicion of American writing, 433; on importance of homeland to writers, 434–5; prepared to sell manuscripts to highest bidder, 446; Graves's influence on poetry, 472–3; attends 1962 Cheltenham Festival, 478, 485–6; influence of EJH on, 494–5, 498; interest in science fiction, 509–10, 521–2, 524, 538, 695; discusses writing with EJH, 517, 588, 729; writes for television, 520, 535–6, 605; breaks free of documentary realism, 521; and genre fiction, 523–6, 537, 557–8, 622, 811; earnings, 536–7, 541,

608, 735–7, 753, 800; published by Cape, 536–7, 540, 542–3; resigns from Society of Authors, 536; satirised in Frederic Raphael story, 537–8; film reviewing for *Observer*, 538; moves from Curtis Brown to A.D. Peters (literary agency), 543; sets Bond novel in Greece, 553; contributes to 'Black Papers on Education', 605; productivity, 608, 642; writes on drink, 623–6; keeps diary, 634–5, 656, 659, 661, 670, 672, 682; essays, 643–4; editing, 644–5; attends *New Statesman* lunches, 646–9; unproductive period (1978–80), 685–6; revival as poet, 688–91; edits anthologies, 697–700; defines light verse, 699; reads EJH's *Getting It Right*, 723–4; takes Clowes as agent, 734–7; wins Booker Prize, 737, 751–4; self-portrayal in *The Old Devils*, 741–3; as Poetry Editor of *Daily Mirror*, 754; restaurant criticisms, 755–8; late style, 789–91; editing and publication of *Letters*, 815–16; diary serialised, 816; posthumous reputation, 821–2

PERSONAL: birth, 10; junior schooling, 13, 37–42; on mother, 27; home life with parents, 29–31; flying experience, 31, 44; at City of London School, 52–5, 57–9, 61–3, 67; in Officer Training Corps at school, 67–8; wartime evacuation to Marlborough, 72–4, 76, 78–9, 84; adolescent romantic impulses, 82; passes School and Higher School Certificates, 89–90; prepares for university scholarship, 89–90; wins Exhibition to St John's College, Oxford, 90; at Oxford University (St John's College), 92–6; loses virginity at Oxford, 105, 107; subversive attitude to Oxford English studies, 123–4; driving, 136, 298; appearance and dress, 166–7, 174, 219, 237, 588; visits Hilly's family, 176; consults psychiatrists and therapists, 196, 223, 665–7, 670–3; and Hilly's